FRENCH·ENGLISH
ENGLISH·FRENCH
DICTIONARY

DICTIONNAIRE
FRANÇAIS·ANGLAIS
ANGLAIS·FRANÇAIS

COLLINS
GEM
DICTIONARY

FRENCH·ENGLISH
ENGLISH·FRENCH

FRANÇAIS·ANGLAIS
ANGLAIS·FRANÇAIS

Pierre-Henri Cousin

new edition
nouvelle édition

HarperCollinsPublishers

first published in this edition 1979
revised edition 1988

© William Collins Sons & Co. Ltd. 1988

Latest reprint 1991

ISBN 0 00 458539 9

---

contributors/avec la collaboration de
Claude Nimmo, Lorna Sinclair,
Philippe Patry, Hélène Lewis,
Elisabeth Campbell, Renée Birks,
Jean-François Allain

editorial staff/secrétariat de rédaction
Catherine Love, Lesley Robertson,
Angela Campbell, Vivian Marr

Printed and bound by
Collins Manufacturing, Glasgow

INTRODUCTION

L'usager qui désire comprendre l'anglais – qui déchiffre – trouvera dans ce dictionnaire un vocabulaire moderne et très complet, comprenant de nombreux composés et locutions appartenant à la langue contemporaine. Il trouvera aussi dans l'ordre alphabétique les principales formes irrégulières, avec un renvoi à la forme de base où figure la traduction, ainsi qu'abréviations, sigles et noms géographiques choisis parmi les plus courants.

The user whose aim is to read and understand French will find a comprehensive and up-to-date wordlist including numerous phrases in current use. He will also find listed alphabetically the main irregular forms with a cross-reference to the basic form where a translation is given, as well as some of the most common abbreviations, acronyms and geographical names.

L'usager qui veut s'exprimer – communiquer – dans la langue étrangère trouvera un traitement détaillé du vocabulaire fondamental, avec de nombreuses indications le guidant vers la traduction juste, et lui montrant comment l'utiliser correctement.

The user who wishes to communicate and to express himself in the foreign language will find clear and detailed treatment of all the basic words, with numerous indications pointing to the appropriate translation, and helping him to use it correctly.

ABRÉVIATIONS

ABBREVIATIONS

adjectif, locution adjective	a	adjective, adjectival phrase
abréviation	ab(b)r	abbreviation
adverbe, locution adverbiale	ad	adverb, adverbial phrase
administration	ADMIN	administration
agriculture	AGR	agriculture
anatomie	ANAT	anatomy
architecture	ARCHIT	architecture
l'automobile	AUT(O)	the motor car and motoring
aviation, voyages aériens	AVIAT	flying, air travel
biologie	BIO(L)	biology
botanique	BOT	botany
anglais de Grande-Bretagne	Brit	British English
conjonction	cj	conjunction
langue familière (! emploi vulgaire)	col (!)	colloquial usage (! particularly offensive)
commerce, finance, banque	COMM	commerce, finance, banking
informatique	COMPUT	computing
construction	CONSTR	building
nom utilisé comme adjectif, ne peut s'employer ni comme attribut, ni après le nom qualifié	cpd	compound element: noun used as an adjective and which cannot follow the noun it qualifies
cuisine, art culinaire	CULIN	cookery
déterminant: article, adjectif démonstratif ou indéfini etc	dét, det	determiner: article, demonstrative etc.
économie	ECON	economics
électricité, électronique	ELEC	electricity, electronics
exclamation, interjection	excl	exclamation, interjection
féminin	f	feminine
langue familière (! emploi vulgaire)	fam (!)	colloquial usage (! particularly offensive)
emploi figuré	fig	figurative use
(verbe anglais) dont la particule est inséparable du verbe	fus	(phrasal verb) where the particle cannot be separated from main verb
dans la plupart des sens; généralement	gén, gen	in most or all senses; generally
géographie, géologie	GEO	geography, geology
géométrie	GEOM	geometry
informatique	INFORM	computing
invariable	inv	invariable
irrégulier	irg	irregular
domaine juridique	JUR	law
grammaire, linguistique	LING	grammar, linguistics
masculin	m	masculine
mathématiques, algèbre	MATH	mathematics, calculus

ABRÉVIATIONS

ABBREVIATIONS

médecine	MED	medical term, medicine
masculin ou féminin, suivant le sexe	m/f	either masculine or feminine depending on sex
domaine militaire, armée	MIL	military matters
musique	MUS	music
nom	n	noun
navigation, nautisme	NAVIG, NAUT	sailing, navigation
adjectif ou nom numérique	num	numeral adjective or noun
	o.s.	oneself
péjoratif	péj, pej	derogatory, pejorative
photographie	PHOT(O)	photography
physiologie	PHYSIOL	physiology
pluriel	pl	plural
politique	POL	politics
participe passé	pp	past participle
préposition	prép, prep	preposition
psychologie, psychiatrie	PSYCH	psychology, psychiatry
temps du passé	pt	past tense
nom non comptable: ne peut s'utiliser au pluriel	q	collective (uncountable) noun: is not used in the plural
quelque chose	qch	
quelqu'un	qn	
religions, domaine ecclésiastique	REL	religions, church service
	sb	somebody
enseignement, système scolaire et universitaire	SCOL	schooling, schools and universities
singulier	sg	singular
	sth	something
subjonctif	sub	subjunctive
sujet (grammatical)	su(b)j	(grammatical) subject
techniques, technologie	TECH	technical term, technology
télécommunications	TEL	telecommunications
télévision	TV	television
typographie	TYP(O)	typography, printing
anglais des USA	US	American English
verbe	vb	verb
verbe ou groupe verbal à fonction intransitive	vi	verb or phrasal verb used intransitively
verbe ou groupe verbal à fonction transitive	vt	verb or phrasal verb used transitively
zoologie	ZOOL	zoology
marque déposée	®	registered trademark
indique une équivalence culturelle	≈	introduces a cultural equivalent

TRANSCRIPTION PHONÉTIQUE

CONSONNES

NB. p, b, t, d, k, g sont suivis.
d'une aspiration en anglais.

CONSONANTS

NB. p, b, t, d, k, g are not
aspirated in French.

poupée	p	puppy
bombe	b	baby
tente thermal	t	tent
dinde	d	daddy
coq qui képi	k	cork kiss chord
gag bague	g	gag guess
sale ce nation	s	so rice kiss
zéro rose	z	cousin buzz
tache chat	ʃ	sheep sugar
gilet juge	ʒ	pleasure beige
	tʃ	church
	dʒ	judge general
fer phare	f	farm raffle
valve	v	very rev
	θ	thin maths
	ð	that other
lent salle	l	little ball
rare rentrer	ʀ	
	r	rat rare
maman femme	m	mummy comb
non nonne	n	no ran
agneau vigne	ɲ	
	ŋ	singing bank
hop!	h	hat reheat
yeux paille pied	j	yet
nouer oui	w	wall bewail
huile lui	ɥ	
	x	loch

DIVERS

pour l'anglais: précède la
syllabe accentuée

pour l'anglais: le r final se
prononce en liaison devant
une voyelle

MISCELLANEOUS

'   in French wordlist and
transcription: no liaison

*

PHONETIC TRANSCRIPTION

VOYELLES

NB. La mise en équivalence de certains sons n'indique qu'une ressemblance approximative.

VOWELS

NB. The pairing of some vowel sounds only indicates approximate equivalence.

ici vie lyre	i i:	heel bead
	ɪ	hit pity
jouer été	e	
lait jouet merci	ɛ	set tent
plat amour	a æ	bat apple
bas pâte	ɑ ɑ:	after car calm
	ʌ	fun cousin
le premier	ə	over above
beurre peur	œ	
peu deux	ø ə:	urn fern work
or homme	ɔ	wash pot
mot eau gauche	o ɔ:	born cork
genou roue	u	full soot
	u:	boon lewd
rue urne	y	

DIPHTONGUES

DIPHTHONGS

ɪə	beer tier
ɛə	tear fair there
eɪ	date plaice day
aɪ	life buy cry
aʊ	owl foul now
əʊ	low no
ɔɪ	boil boy oily
ʊə	poor tour

NASALES

NASAL VOWELS

matin plein	ɛ̃
brun	œ̃
sang an dans	ɑ̃
non pont	ɔ̃

FRANÇAIS - ANGLAIS
FRENCH - ENGLISH

A

A *abr de* **autoroute**.
a *vb voir* **avoir**.

MOT-CLÉ

à (à + le = **au**, à + **les** = **aux**) [a, o] *prép* **1** (*endroit, situation*) at, in; **être à Paris/ au Portugal** to be in Paris/Portugal; **être à la maison/à l'école** to be at home/at school; **à la campagne** in the country; **c'est à 10 km/à 20 minutes (d'ici)** it's 10 km/20 minutes away
2 (*direction*) to; **aller à Paris/au Portugal** to go to Paris/Portugal; **aller à la maison/à l'école** to go home/to school; **à la campagne** to the country
3 (*temps*): **à 3 heures/minuit** at 3 o'clock/midnight; **au printemps/mois de juin** in the spring/the month of June
4 (*attribution, appartenance*) to; **le livre est à Paul/à lui/à nous** this book is Paul's/his/ours; **donner qch à qn** to give sth to sb
5 (*moyen*) with; **se chauffer au gaz** to have gas heating; **à bicyclette** on a *ou* by bicycle; **à la main/machine** by hand/machine
6 (*provenance*) from; **boire à la bouteille** to drink from the bottle
7 (*caractérisation, manière*): **l'homme aux yeux bleus** the man with the blue eyes; **à la russe** the Russian way
8 (*but, destination*): **tasse à café** coffee cup; **maison à vendre** house for sale
9 (*rapport, évaluation, distribution*): **100 km/unités à l'heure** 100 km/units per *ou* an hour; **payé à l'heure** paid by the hour; **cinq à six** five to six.

---

abaisser [abese] *vt* to lower, bring down; (*manette*) to pull down; (*fig*) to debase; to humiliate; **s'~** *vi* to go down; (*fig*) to demean o.s.

abandon [abãdɔ̃] *nm* abandoning; giving up; withdrawal; **être à l'~** to be in a state of neglect.

abandonner [abãdɔne] *vt* (*personne*) to abandon; (*projet, activité*) to abandon, give up; (*SPORT*) to retire *ou* withdraw from; (*céder*) to surrender; **s'~** *vi* to let o.s. go; **s'~ à** (*paresse, plaisirs*) to give o.s. up to.

abasourdir [abazurdir] *vt* to stun, stagger.

abat-jour [abaʒur] *nm inv* lampshade.

abats [aba] *nmpl* (*de bœuf, porc*) offal *sg*; (*de volaille*) giblets.

abattement [abatmã] *nm* (*déduction*) reduction; **~ fiscal** = tax allowance.

abattis [abati] *nmpl* giblets.

abattoir [abatwar] *nm* slaughterhouse.

abattre [abatr(ə)] *vt* (*arbre*) to cut down, fell; (*mur, maison*) to pull down; (*avion, personne*) to shoot down; (*animal*) to shoot, kill; (*fig*) to wear out, tire out; to demoralize; **s'~** *vi* to crash down; **s'~ sur** to beat down on; to rain down on.

abbaye [abei] *nf* abbey.

abbé [abe] *nm* priest; (*d'une abbaye*) abbot.

abcès [apsɛ] *nm* abscess.

abdiquer [abdike] *vi* to abdicate // *vt* to renounce, give up.

abeille [abej] *nf* bee.

aberrant, e [aberã, -ãt] *a* absurd.

abêtir [abetir] *vt* to make morons of (*ou* a moron of).

abîme [abim] *nm* abyss, gulf.

abîmer [abime] *vt* to spoil, damage; **s'~** *vi* to get spoilt *ou* damaged.

ablation [ablɑsjɔ̃] *nf* removal.

aboiement [abwamɑ̃] *nm* bark, barking *q*.

abois [abwa] *nmpl*: **aux ~** at bay.

abolir [abɔlir] *vt* to abolish.

abondance [abɔ̃dɑ̃s] *nf* abundance; *(richesse)* affluence.

abondant, e [abɔ̃dɑ̃, -ɑ̃t] *a* plentiful, abundant, copious.

abonder [abɔ̃de] *vi* to abound, be plentiful; **~ dans le sens de qn** to concur with sb.

abonné, e [abɔne] *nm/f* subscriber; season ticket holder.

abonnement [abɔnmɑ̃] *nm* subscription; *(transports, concerts)* season ticket.

abonner [abɔne] *vt*: **s'~ à** to subscribe to, take out a subscription to.

abord [abɔr] *nm*: **être d'un ~ facile** to be approachable; **~s** *nmpl* surroundings; **au premier ~** at first sight, initially; **d'~** *ad* first.

abordable [abɔrdabl(ə)] *a* approachable; reasonably priced.

aborder [abɔrde] *vi* to land // *vt (sujet, difficulté)* to tackle; *(personne)* to approach; *(rivage etc)* to reach; *(NAVIG: attaquer)* to board.

aboutir [abutir] *vi (négociations etc)* to succeed; **~ à/dans/sur** to end up at/in/on.

aboyer [abwaje] *vi* to bark.

abrégé [abreʒe] *nm* summary.

abréger [abreʒe] *vt* to shorten.

abreuver [abrœve] *vt (fig)*: **~ qn de** to shower *ou* swamp sb with; **s'~** *vi* to drink; **abreuvoir** *nm* watering place.

abréviation [abrevjɑsjɔ̃] *nf* abbreviation.

abri [abri] *nm* shelter; **à l'~** under cover; **à l'~ de** sheltered from; *(fig)* safe from.

abricot [abriko] *nm* apricot; **abricotier** *nm* apricot tree.

abriter [abrite] *vt* to shelter; *(loger)* to accommodate; **s'~** to shelter, take cover.

abroger [abrɔʒe] *vt* to repeal.

abrupt, e [abrypt] *a* sheer, steep; *(ton)* abrupt.

abrutir [abrytir] *vt* to daze; to exhaust; to stupefy.

absence [apsɑ̃s] *nf* absence; *(MÉD)* blackout; mental blank.

absent, e [apsɑ̃, -ɑ̃t] *a* absent; *(distrait: air)* vacant, faraway // *nm/f* absentee; **s'absenter** *vi* to take time off work; *(sortir)* to leave, go out.

absolu, e [apsɔly] *a* absolute; *(caractère)* rigid, uncompromising; **~ment** *ad* absolutely.

absolve *etc vb voir* **absoudre**

absorber [apsɔrbe] *vt* to absorb; *(gén MÉD: manger, boire)* to take.

absoudre [apsudr(ə)] *vt* to absolve.

abstenir [apstənir]: **s'~** *vi (POL)* to abstain; **s'~ de qch/de faire** to refrain from sth/from doing.

abstraction [apstraksjɔ̃] *nf* abstraction; **faire ~ de** to set *ou* leave aside.

abstrait, e [apstrɛ, -ɛt] *a* abstract.

absurde [apsyrd(ə)] *a* absurd.

abus [aby] *nm* abuse; **~ de confiance** breach of trust.

abuser [abyze] *vi* to go too far, overstep the mark // *vt* to deceive, mislead; **~ de** *vt* to misuse; *(violer, duper)* to take advantage of; **s'~** *vi* to be mistaken; **abusif, ive** *a* exorbitant; excessive; improper.

acabit [akabi] *nm*: **de cet ~** of that type.

académie [akademi] *nf* academy; *(ART: nu)* nude; *(SCOL: circonscription)* = regional education authority.

acajou [akaʒu] *nm* mahogany.

acariâtre [akarjɑtr(ə)] *a* cantankerous.

accablement [akɑbləmɑ̃] *nm* despondency.

accabler [akɑble] *vt* to overwhelm, overcome; *(suj: témoignage)* to condemn, damn; **~ qn d'injures** to heap *ou* shower abuse on sb.

accalmie [akalmi] *nf* lull.

accaparer [akapaʀe] vt to monopolize; (suj: travail etc) to take up (all) the time ou attention of.

accéder [aksede]: ~ à vt (lieu) to reach; (fig) to accede to, attain; (accorder: requête) to grant, accede to.

accélérateur [akseleʀatœʀ] nm accelerator.

accélération [akseleʀɑsjɔ̃] nf acceleration.

accélérer [akseleʀe] vt to speed up // vi to accelerate.

accent [aksɑ̃] nm accent; (inflexions expressives) tone (of voice); (PHONÉTIQUE, fig) stress; mettre l'~ sur (fig) to stress; ~ aigu/grave acute/grave accent.

accentuer [aksɑ̃tɥe] vt (LING) to accent; (fig) to accentuate, emphasize; s'~ vi to become more marked ou pronounced.

acceptation [aksɛptɑsjɔ̃] nf acceptance.

accepter [aksɛpte] vt to accept; (tolérer) : ~ que qn fasse to agree to sb doing; ~ de faire to agree to do.

acception [aksɛpsjɔ̃] nf meaning, sense.

accès [aksɛ] nm (à un lieu) access; (MÉD) attack; fit, bout; outburst // nmpl (routes etc) means of access, approaches; d'~ facile easily accessible; ~ de colère fit of anger.

accessible [aksesibl(ə)] a accessible; (livre, sujet) : ~ à qn within the reach of sb; (sensible) : ~ à open to.

accessoire [akseswaʀ] a secondary; incidental // nm accessory; (THÉÂTRE) prop.

accident [aksidɑ̃] nm accident; par ~ by chance; ~ de la route road accident; ~ du travail industrial injury ou accident; **accidenté, e** a damaged; injured; (relief, terrain) uneven; hilly.

acclamer [aklame] vt to cheer, acclaim.

accointances [akwɛ̃tɑ̃s] nfpl: avoir des ~ avec to have contacts with.

accolade [akɔlad] nf (amicale) embrace; (signe) brace.

accoler [akɔle] vt to place side by side.

accommodant, e [akɔmɔdɑ̃, -ɑ̃t] a accommodating; easy-going.

accommoder [akɔmɔde] vt (CULIN) to prepare; (points de vue) to reconcile; ~ à to put up with; to make do with.

accompagnateur, trice [akɔ̃paɲatœʀ, -tʀis] nm/f (MUS) accompanist; (de voyage: guide) guide; (: d'enfants) accompanying adult; (: de voyage organisé) courier.

accompagner [akɔ̃paɲe] vt to accompany, be ou go ou come with; (MUS) to accompany.

accompli, e [akɔ̃pli] a accomplished.

accomplir [akɔ̃pliʀ] vt (tâche, projet) to carry out; (souhait) to fulfil; s'~ vi to be fulfilled.

accord [akɔʀ] nm agreement; (entre des styles, tons etc) harmony; (MUS) chord; d'~! OK!; se mettre d'~ to come to an agreement; être d'~ to agree.

accordéon [akɔʀdeɔ̃] nm (MUS) accordion.

accorder [akɔʀde] vt (faveur, délai) to grant; (harmoniser) to match; (MUS) to tune; s'~ to get on together; to agree.

accoster [akɔste] vt (NAVIG) to draw alongside // vi to berth.

accotement [akɔtmɑ̃] nm verge (Brit), shoulder.

accouchement [akuʃmɑ̃] nm delivery, (child)birth; labour.

accoucher [akuʃe] vi to give birth, have a baby; (être en travail) to be in labour // vt to deliver; ~ d'un garçon to give birth to a boy.

accouder [akude]: s'~ vi: s'~ à/contre to rest one's elbows on/against; **accoudoir** nm armrest.

accoupler [akuple] vt to couple; (pour la reproduction) to mate; s'~

to mate.

accourir [akuʀiʀ] *vi* to rush *ou* run up.

accoutrement [akutʀəmɑ̃] *nm* (*péj: tenue*) outfit.

accoutumance [akutymɑ̃s] *nf* (*gén*) adaptation; (*MÉD*) addiction.

accoutumé, e [akutyme] *a* (*habituel*) customary, usual.

accoutumer [akutyme] *vt*: **s'~ à** to get accustomed *ou* used to.

accréditer [akʀedite] *vt* (*nouvelle*) to substantiate.

accroc [akʀo] *nm* (*déchirure*) tear; (*fig*) hitch, snag.

accrochage [akʀɔʃaʒ] *nm* (*AUTO*) collision.

accrocher [akʀɔʃe] *vt* (*suspendre*): ~ **qch à** to hang sth up on; (*attacher: remorque*): ~ **qch à** to hitch sth (up) to; (*heurter*) to catch; to catch on; to hit; (*déchirer*): ~ **qch (à**) to catch sth (on); (*MIL*) to engage; (*fig*) to catch, attract; **s'~** (*se disputer*) to have a clash *ou* brush; **s'~ à** (*rester pris à*) to catch on; (*agripper, fig*) to hang on *ou* cling to.

accroître [akʀwatʀ(ə)] *vt* to increase; **s'~** *vi* to increase.

accroupir [akʀupiʀ]: **s'~** *vi* to squat, crouch (down).

accru, e [akʀy] *pp de* **accroître.**

accueil [akœj] *nm* welcome; **comité d'~** reception committee.

accueillir [akœjiʀ] *vt* to welcome; (*loger*) to accommodate.

acculer [akyle] *vt*: ~ **qn à** *ou* **contre** to drive sb back against.

accumuler [akymyle] *vt* to accumulate, amass; **s'~** *vi* to accumulate; to pile up.

accusation [akyzasjɔ̃] *nf* (*gén*) accusation; (*JUR*) charge; (*partie*): **l'~** the prosecution; **mettre en ~** to indict.

accusé, e [akyze] *nm/f* accused; defendant; ~ **de réception** acknowledgement of receipt.

accuser [akyze] *vt* to accuse; (*fig*) to

emphasize, bring out; to show; ~ **qn de** to accuse sb of; (*JUR*) to charge sb with; ~ **qch de** (*rendre responsable*) to blame sth for; ~ **réception de** to acknowledge receipt of.

acerbe [asɛʀb(ə)] *a* caustic, acid.

acéré, e [aseʀe] *a* sharp.

achalandé, e [aʃalɑ̃de] *a*: **bien ~** well-stocked; well-patronized.

acharné, e [aʃaʀne] *a* (*lutte, adversaire*) fierce, bitter; (*travail*) relentless, unremitting.

acharner [aʃaʀne]: **s'~** *vi*: **s'~ sur** to go at fiercely; **s'~ contre** to set o.s. against; to dog; **s'~ à** faire to try doggedly to do; to persist in doing.

achat [aʃa] *nm* buying *q*; purchase; **faire des ~s** to do some shopping.

acheminer [aʃmine] *vt* (*courrier*) to forward, dispatch; (*troupes*) to convey, transport; (*train*) to route; **s'~ vers** to head for.

acheter [aʃte] *vt* to buy, purchase; (*soudoyer*) to buy; ~ **qch à** (*marchand*) to buy *ou* purchase sth from; (*ami etc: offrir*) to buy sth for; **acheteur, euse** *nm/f* buyer; shopper; (*COMM*) buyer.

achever [aʃve] *vt* to complete, finish; (*blessé*) to finish off; **s'~** *vi* to end.

achoppement [aʃɔpmɑ̃] *nm*: **pierre d'~** stumbling block.

acide [asid] *a* sour, sharp; (*CHIMIE*) acid(ic) *// nm* (*CHIMIE*) acid.

acier [asje] *nm* steel; **aciérie** *nf* steelworks *sg.*

acné [akne] *nf* acne.

acolyte [akɔlit] *nm* (*péj*) associate.

acompte [akɔ̃t] *nm* deposit; (*versement régulier*) instalment; (*sur somme due*) payment on account.

à-côté [akote] *nm* side-issue; (*argent*) extra.

à-coup [aku] *nm* (*du moteur*) (hic)cough; (*fig*) jolt; **par ~s** by fits and starts.

acoustique [akustik] *nf* (*d'une salle*) acoustics *pl.*

acquéreur [akeʀœʀ] *nm* buyer.

purchaser.

acquérir [akerir] *vt* to acquire.

acquis, e [aki, -iz] *pp de* **acquérir** // *nm* (accumulated) experience; **être ~ à** (*plan, idée*) to fully agree with; **son aide nous ~e** we can count on her help.

acquit [aki] *vb voir* **acquérir** // *nm* (*quittance*) receipt; **par ~ de conscience** to set one's mind at rest.

acquitter [akite] *vt* (*JUR*) to acquit; (*facture*) to pay, settle; **s'~ de** (*promesse*) to discharge, fulfil.

âcre [ɑkr(ə)] *a* acrid, pungent.

acrobate [akrɔbat] *nm/f* acrobat.

acte [akt(ə)] *nm* act, action; (*THÉÂTRE*) act; **~s** *nmpl* (*compte-rendu*) proceedings; **prendre ~ de** to note, take note of; **faire ~ de candidature** to apply; **faire ~ de présence** to put in an appearance; **~ de naissance** birth certificate.

acteur [aktœr] *nm* actor.

actif, ive [aktif, -iv] *a* active // *nm* (*COMM*) assets *pl*; (*fig*): **avoir à son ~** to have to one's credit; **population active** working population.

action [aksjɔ̃] *nf* (*gén*) action; (*COMM*) share; **une bonne ~** a good deed; **actionnaire** *nm/f* shareholder; **actionner** *vt* to work; to activate; to operate.

activer [aktive] *vt* to speed up; **s'~** *vi* to bustle about; to hurry up.

activité [aktivite] *nf* activity.

actrice [aktris] *nf* actress.

actualiser [aktɥalize] *vt* to actualize; to bring up to date.

actualité [aktɥalite] *nf* (*d'un problème*) topicality; (*événements*): **l'~** current events; **les ~s** (*CINÉMA, TV*) the news.

actuel, le [aktɥɛl] *a* (*présent*) present; (*d'actualité*) topical; **~lement** *ad* at present; at the present time.

acuité [akɥite] *nf* acuteness.

adaptateur [adaptatœr] *nm* (*ÉLEC*) adapter.

adapter [adapte] *vt* to adapt; **~ qch à** (*approprier*) to adapt sth to (fit);

~ qch sur/dans/à (*fixer*) to fit sth on/into/to; **s'~** (**à**) (*suj: personne*) to adapt to.

addition [adisjɔ̃] *nf* addition; (*au café*) bill.

additionner [adisjɔne] *vt* to add (up).

adepte [adɛpt(ə)] *nm/f* follower.

adéquat, e [adekwa, -at] *a* appropriate, suitable.

adhérent, e [aderɑ̃, -ɑ̃t] *nm/f* (*de club*) member.

adhérer [adere]: **~ à** *vi* (*coller*) to adhere to or stick to; (*se rallier à*) to join; to support; **adhésif, ive** *a* adhesive, sticky // *nm* adhesive; **adhésion** *nf* joining; membership; support.

adieu, x [adjø] *excl* goodbye // *nm* farewell; **dire ~ à qn** to say goodbye ou farewell to sb.

adjectif [adʒɛktif] *nm* adjective.

adjoindre [adʒwɛ̃dr(ə)] *vt*: **~ qch à** to attach sth to; to add sth to; **s'~** (*collaborateur etc*) to take on, appoint; **adjoint, e** *nm/f* assistant; **adjoint au maire** deputy mayor; **directeur adjoint** assistant manager.

adjudant [adʒydɑ̃] *nm* (*MIL*) warrant officer.

adjudication [adʒydikasjɔ̃] *nf* sale by auction; (*pour travaux*) invitation to tender (*Brit*) ou bid (*US*).

adjuger [adʒyʒe] *vt* (*prix, récompense*) to award; (*lors d'une vente*) to auction (off); **s'~** *vt* to take for o.s.

adjurer [adʒyre] *vt*: **~ qn de** to implore ou beg sb to do.

admettre [admɛtr(ə)] *vt* (*laisser entrer*) to admit; (*candidat: SCOL*) to pass; (*tolérer*) to allow, accept; (*reconnaître*) to admit, acknowledge.

administrateur, trice [administratœr, -tris] *nm/f* (*COMM*) director; (*ADMIN*) administrator; **~ judiciaire** receiver; **~ délégué** managing director.

administration [administrasjɔ̃] *nf* administration; **l'A~** ≈ the Civil Service.

administrer [administʀe] *vt* (*firme*) to manage, run; (*biens, remède, sacrement etc*) to administer.

admirable [admiʀabl(ə)] *a* admirable, wonderful.

admirateur, trice [admiʀatœʀ, -tʀis] *nm/f* admirer.

admiration [admiʀɑsjɔ̃] *nf* admiration.

admirer [admiʀe] *vt* to admire.

admis, e *pp de* **admettre**.

admissible [admisibl(ə)] *a* (*candidat*) eligible; (*comportement*) admissible, acceptable.

admission [admisjɔ̃] *nf* admission; acknowledgement; **demande d'~** application for membership.

adolescence [adɔlesɑ̃s] *nf* adolescence.

adolescent, e [adɔlesɑ̃, -ɑ̃t] *nm/f* adolescent, teenager.

adonner [adɔne]: **s'~ à** *vt* (*sport*) to devote o.s. to; (*boisson*) to give o.s. over to.

adopter [adɔpte] *vt* to adopt; (*projet de loi etc*) to pass; **adoptif, ive** *a* (*parents*) adoptive; (*fils, patrie*) adopted.

adorer [adɔʀe] *vt* to adore; (*REL*) to worship.

adosser [adɔse] *vt*: **~ qch à ou contre** to stand sth against; **s'~ à ou contre** to lean with one's back against.

adoucir [adusiʀ] *vt* (*goût, température*) to make milder; (*avec du sucre*) to sweeten; (*peau, voix*) to soften; (*caractère*) to mellow.

adresse [adʀɛs] *nf* (*voir droit*) skill, dexterity; (*domicile*) address; **à l'~ de** (*pour*) for the benefit of.

adresser [adʀɛse] *vt* (*lettre: expédier*) to send; (: *écrire l'adresse sur*) to address; (*injure, compliments*) to address; **~ la parole à** to speak to, address; **s'~ à** (*parler à*) to speak to, address; (*s'informer auprès de*) to go and see; (: *bureau*) to enquire at; (*suj: livre, conseil*) to be aimed at.

adroit, e [adʀwa, -wat] *a* skilful, skilled.

adulte [adylt(ə)] *nm/f* adult, grown-up // *a* (*chien, arbre*) fully-grown, mature; (*attitude*) adult, grown-up.

adultère [adylteʀ] *nm* (*acte*) adultery.

advenir [advəniʀ] *vi* to happen.

adverbe [advεʀb(ə)] *nm* adverb.

adversaire [advεʀsεʀ] *nm/f* (*SPORT, gén*) opponent, adversary; (*MIL*) adversary, enemy.

adverse [advεʀs(ə)] *a* opposing.

aération [aeʀɑsjɔ̃] *nf* airing; ventilation.

aérer [aeʀe] *vt* to air; (*fig*) to lighten; **s'~** *vi* to get some (fresh) air.

aérien, ne [aeʀjɛ̃, -jεn] *a* (*AVIAT*) air *cpd*, aerial; (*câble, métro*) overhead; (*fig*) light.

aéro... [aeʀɔ] *préfixe*: **~bic** *nm* aerobics *sg*; (*~gare** *nf* airport (buildings); (*en ville*) air terminal; **~glisseur** *nm* hovercraft; **~naval, e** *a* air and sea *cpd*; **~port** *nm* airport; **~porté, e** *a* airborne, airlifted; **~sol** *nm* aerosol.

affaiblir [afeblîʀ] *vt*, **s'~** *vi* to weaken.

affaire [afεʀ] *nf* (*problème, question*) matter; (*criminelle, judiciaire*) case; (*scandaleuse etc*) affair; (*entreprise*) business; (*marché, transaction*) deal; business *q*; (*occasion intéressante*) bargain; **~s** *nfpl* affairs; (*activité commerciale*) business *sg*; (*effets personnels*) things, belongings; **ce sont mes ~s** (*cela me concerne*) that's my business; **ceci fera l'~** this will do (nicely); **avoir ~ à** to be faced with; to be dealing with; **les A~s étrangères** Foreign Affairs; **s'affairer** *vi* to busy o.s., bustle about.

affaisser [afese]: **s'~** *vi* (*terrain, immeuble*) to subside, sink; (*personne*) to collapse.

affaler [afale]: **s'~** *vi*: **s'~ dans/sur** to collapse *ou* slump into/onto.

affamé, e [afame] a starving.

affecter [afɛkte] vt to affect; (telle ou telle forme etc) to take on; ~ **qch à** to allocate ou allot sth to; ~ **qn à** to appoint sb to; (diplomate) to post sb to.

affectif, ive [afɛktif, -iv] a emotional.

affection [afɛksjɔ̃] nf affection; (mal) ailment; **affectionner** vt to be fond of.

affectueux, euse [afɛktɥø, -øz] a affectionate.

afférent, e [aferɑ̃, -ɑ̃t] a: ~ **à** pertaining ou relating to.

affermir [afɛrmir] vt to consolidate, strengthen.

affichage [afiʃaʒ] nm billposting; (électronique) display.

affiche [afiʃ] nf poster; (officielle) notice; (THÉÂTRE) bill; **tenir l'~** to run.

afficher [afiʃe] vt (affiche) to put up; (réunion) to put up a notice about; (électroniquement) to display; (fig) to exhibit, display.

affilée [afile]: **d'~** ad at a stretch.

affiler [afile] vt to sharpen.

affiner [afine] vt to refine.

affirmatif, ive [afirmatif, -iv] a affirmative.

affirmation [afirmasjɔ̃] nf assertion.

affirmer [afirme] vt (prétendre) to maintain, assert; (autorité etc) to assert.

affligé, e [afliʒe] a distressed, grieved; ~ **de** (maladie, tare) afflicted with.

affliger [afliʒe] vt (peiner) to distress, grieve.

affluence [aflyɑ̃s] nf crowds pl; **heures d'~** rush hours; **jours d'~** busiest days.

affluent [aflyɑ̃] nm tributary.

affluer [aflye] vi (secours, biens) to flood in, pour in; (sang) to rush, flow.

affolement [afɔlmɑ̃] nm panic.

affoler [afɔle] vt to throw into a panic; **s'~** vi to panic.

affranchir [afrɑ̃ʃir] vt to put a

stamp ou stamps on; (à la machine) to frank (Brit), meter (US); (fig) to free, liberate; **affranchissement** nm postage.

affréter [afrete] vt to charter.

affreux, euse [afrø, -øz] a dreadful, awful.

affrontement [afrɔ̃tmɑ̃] nm clash, confrontation.

affronter [afrɔ̃te] vt to confront, face.

affubler [afyble] vt (péj): ~ **qn de** to rig ou deck sb out in; (surnom) to attach to sb.

affût [afy] nm: **à l'~ (de)** (gibier) lying in wait (for); (fig) on the lookout (for).

affûter [afyte] vt to sharpen, grind.

afin [afɛ̃]: ~ **que** cj so that, in order that; ~ **de faire** in order to do, so as to do.

africain, e [afrikɛ̃, -ɛn] a, nm/f African.

Afrique [afrik] nf: **l'~** Africa; **l'~ du Sud** South Africa.

agacer [agase] vt to pester, tease; (involontairement) to irritate.

âge [aʒ] nm age; **quel ~ as-tu?** how old are you?; **prendre de l'~** to be getting on (in years); **l'~ ingrat** the awkward age; **l'~ mûr** maturity.

âgé, e a old, elderly; **âgé de 10 ans** 10 years old.

agence [aʒɑ̃s] nf agency, office; (succursale) branch; ~ **immobilière** estate (Brit) ou real estate (US) agent's (office); ~ **matrimoniale** marriage bureau; ~ **de voyages** travel agency.

agencer [aʒɑ̃se] vt to put together; to arrange, lay out.

agenda [aʒɛ̃da] nm diary.

agenouiller [aʒnuje]: **s'~** vi to kneel (down).

agent [aʒɑ̃] nm (aussi: ~ **de police**) policeman; (ADMIN) official, officer; (fig: élément, facteur) agent; ~ **d'assurances** insurance broker; ~ **de change** stockbroker; ~ **(secret)** (secret) agent.

agglomération [aglɔmeʀɑsjɔ̃] nf town; built-up area; l'~ parisienne the urban area of Paris.

aggloméré [aglɔmeʀe] nm (bois) chipboard; (pierre) conglomerate.

agglomérer [aglɔmeʀe] vt to pile up; (TECH: bois, pierre) to compress.

aggraver [agʀave] vt to worsen, aggravate; (JUR: peine) to increase; s'~ vi to worsen.

agile [aʒil] a agile, nimble.

agir [aʒiʀ] vi to act; **il s'agit de** it's a matter ou question of; it is about; (il importe que): **il s'agit de faire** we (ou you etc) must do.

agitation [aʒitɑsjɔ̃] nf (hustle and) bustle; agitation, excitement; (politique) unrest, agitation.

agité, e [aʒite] a fidgety, restless; agitated, perturbed; (mer) rough.

agiter [aʒite] vt (bouteille, chiffon) to shake; (bras, mains) to wave; (préoccuper, exciter) to perturb.

agneau, x [aɲo] nm lamb.

agonie [agɔni] nf mortal agony, death pangs pl; (fig) death throes pl.

agrafe [agʀaf] nf (de vêtement) hook, fastener; (de bureau) staple; **agrafer** vt to fasten; to staple; **agrafeuse** nf stapler.

agraire [agʀɛʀ] a land cpd.

agrandir [agʀɑ̃diʀ] vt to enlarge; (magasin, domaine) to extend, enlarge; s'~ vi to be extended; to be enlarged; **agrandissement** nm (PHOTO) enlargement.

agréable [agʀeabl(ə)] a pleasant, nice.

agréé, e [agʀee] a: **concessionnaire ~** registered dealer.

agréer [agʀee] vt (requête) to accept; ~ à vt to please, suit; **veuillez ~ ...** (formule épistolaire) yours faithfully.

agrégation [agʀegɑsjɔ̃] nf highest teaching diploma in France; **agrégé, e** nm/f holder of the agrégation.

agrément [agʀemɑ̃] nm (accord) consent, approval; (attraits) charm,

attractiveness; (plaisir) pleasure.

agrémenter [agʀemɑ̃te] vt to embellish, adorn.

agresser [agʀese] vt to attack.

agresseur [agʀesœʀ] nm aggressor, attacker; (POL, MIL) aggressor.

agressif, ive [agʀesif, -iv] a aggressive.

agricole [agʀikɔl] a agricultural.

agriculteur [agʀikyltœʀ] nm farmer.

agriculture [agʀikyltyʀ] nf agriculture; farming.

agripper [agʀipe] vt to grab, clutch; (pour arracher) to snatch, grab; s'~ à to cling (on) to, clutch, grip.

agrumes [agʀym] nmpl citrus fruit(s).

aguerrir [ageʀiʀ] vt to harden.

aguets [agɛ]: **aux ~** ad: **être aux ~** to be on the look-out.

aguicher [agiʃe] vt to entice.

ahuri, e [ayʀi] a (stupéfait) flabbergasted; (idiot) dim-witted.

ai vb voir **avoir**.

aide [ɛd] nm/f assistant // nf assistance, help; (secours financier) aid; à l'~ de (avec) with the help ou aid of; **appeler (qn) à l'~** to call for help (from sb); ~ **judiciaire** nf legal aid; ~ **sociale** nf (assistance) state aid; ~ **soignant, e** nm/f auxiliary nurse; ~-**mémoire** nm inv memoranda pages pl; (key facts) handbook.

aider [ɛde] vt to help; ~ à qch (faciliter) to help (towards) sth; s'~ de (se servir de) to use, make use of.

aie etc vb voir **avoir**.

aïe [aj] excl ouch.

aïeul, e [ajœl] nm/f grandparent, grandfather/grandmother; forebear.

aïeux [ajø] nmpl grandparents; forebears, forefathers.

aigle [ɛgl(ə)] nm eagle.

aigre [ɛgʀ(ə)] a sour, sharp; (fig) sharp, cutting; **aigreur** nf sourness; sharpness; **aigreurs d'estomac** heartburn sg; **aigrir** vt (personne) to embitter; (caractère) to sour.

aigu, ë [egy] a (objet, arête, douleur, intelligence) sharp; (son, voix) high-pitched, shrill; (note) high(-pitched).

aiguille [eguij] nf needle; (de montre) hand; ~ à tricoter knitting needle.

aiguiller [eguije] vt (orienter) to direct.

aiguillon [eguijɔ̃] nm (d'abeille) sting; **aiguillonner** vt to spur ou goad on.

aiguiser [egize] vt to sharpen; (fig) to stimulate; to excite.

ail [aj] nm garlic.

aile [ɛl] nf wing; **aileron** nm (de requin) fin; **ailier** nm winger.

aille etc vb voir **aller**.

ailleurs [ajœʀ] ad elsewhere, somewhere else; **partout/nulle part ~** everywhere/nowhere else; **d'~** ad (du reste) moreover, besides; **par ~** ad (d'autre part) moreover, furthermore.

ailloli [ajɔli] nm garlic mayonnaise.

aimable [ɛmabl(ə)] a kind, nice.

aimant [ɛmɑ̃] nm magnet.

aimer [eme] vt to love; (d'amitié, affection, par goût) to like; (souhait): **j'aimerais...** I should like; **bien ~ qn/qch** to like sb/sth; **j'aime mieux ou autant vous dire que** I may as well tell you that; **j'aimerais autant y aller maintenant** I'd rather go now; **j'aimerais mieux faire** I'd much rather do.

aine [ɛn] nf groin.

aîné, e [ene] a elder, older; (le plus âgé) eldest, oldest // nm/f oldest child ou one, oldest boy ou son/girl ou daughter; **aînesse** nf: **droit d'aînesse** birthright.

ainsi [ɛ̃si] ad (de cette façon) like this, in this way, thus; (ce faisant) thus // cj thus, so; **~ que** (comme) (just) as; (et aussi) as well as; **pour ~ dire** so to speak; **et ~ de suite** and so on.

air [ɛʀ] nm air; (mélodie) tune; (expression) look, air; **prendre l'~** to get some (fresh) air; (avion) to take

off; **avoir l'~** (sembler) to look, appear; **avoir l'~ de** to look like; **avoir l'~ de faire** to look as though one is doing, appear to be doing.

aire [ɛʀ] nf (zone, fig, MATH) area.

aisance [ɛzɑ̃s] nf ease; (richesse) affluence.

aise [ɛz] nf comfort // a: **être bien ~ que** to be delighted that; **être à l'~ ou à son ~** to be comfortable; (pas embarrassé) to be at ease; (financièrement) to be comfortably off; **se mettre à l'~** to make o.s. comfortable; **être mal à l'~ ou à son ~** to be uncomfortable; to be at ease; **en faire à son ~** to do as one likes; **aisé, e** a easy; (assez riche) well-to-do, well-off.

aisselle [ɛsɛl] nf armpit.

ait vb voir **avoir**.

ajonc [aʒɔ̃] nm gorse q.

ajourner [aʒuʀne] vt (réunion) to adjourn; (décision) to defer, postpone.

ajouter [aʒute] vt to add; **~ foi à** to lend ou give credence to.

ajusté, e [aʒyste] a: **bien ~** (robe etc) close-fitting.

ajuster [aʒyste] vt (régler) to adjust; (vêtement) to alter; (coup de feu) to aim; (cible) to aim at; (TECH, gén: adapter): **~ qch à** to fit sth to.

alambic [alɑ̃bik] nm still.

alarme [alaʀm(ə)] nf alarm; **donner l'~** to give ou raise the alarm; **alarmer** vt to alarm; **s'alarmer** vi to become alarmed.

album [albɔm] nm album.

albumine [albymin] nf albumin; **avoir ou faire de l'~** to suffer from albuminuria.

alcool [alkɔl] nm: **l'~** alcohol; **un ~** a spirit, a brandy; **~ à brûler** methylated spirits (Brit), wood alcohol (US); **~ à 90°** surgical spirit; **~ique** a, nm/f alcoholic; **~isé, e** a alcoholic; **~isme** nm alcoholism; **alco(o)test** ® nm Breathalyser ®; (test) breath-test.

aléas [alea] nmpl hazards; **aléatoire** a uncertain; (INFORM) random.

alentour [alɑ̃tuʀ] *ad* around (about); **~s** *nmpl* surroundings; **aux ~s de** in the vicinity ou neighbourhood of, around about; *(temps)* around about.

alerte [alɛʀt(ə)] *a* agile, nimble; brisk, lively // *nf* alert; warning; **alerter** *vt* to alert.

algèbre [alʒɛbʀ(ə)] *nf* algebra.

Alger [alʒe] *n* Algiers.

Algérie [alʒeʀi] *nf*: **l'~** Algeria; **algérien, ne** *a, nm/f* Algerian.

algue [alg(ə)] *nf* *(gén)* seaweed *q*; *(BOT)* alga *(pl* algae).

alibi [alibi] *nm* alibi.

aliéné, e [aljene] *nm/f* insane person, lunatic *(péj)*.

aligner [aliɲe] *vt* to align, line up; *(idées, chiffres)* to string together; *(adapter)*: **~ qch sur** to bring sth into alignment with; **s'~** *(soldats etc)* to line up; **s'~ sur** *(POL)* to align o.s. on.

aliment [alimɑ̃] *nm* food.

alimentation [alimɑ̃tɑsjɔ̃] *nf* feeding; supplying; *(commerce)* food trade; *(produits)* groceries *pl*; *(régime)* diet; *(INFORM)* feed.

alimenter [alimɑ̃te] *vt* to feed; *(TECH)*: **~ (en)** to supply (with); to feed (with); *(fig)* to sustain, keep going.

alinéa [alinea] *nm* paragraph.

aliter [alite]: **s'~** *vi* to take to one's bed.

allaiter [alete] *vt* to (breast-)feed, nurse; *(suj: animal)* to suckle.

allant [alɑ̃] *nm* drive, go.

allécher [aleʃe] *vt*: **~ qn** to make sb's mouth water; to tempt ou entice sb.

allée [ale] *nf* *(de jardin)* path; *(en ville)* avenue, drive; **~s et venues** *nfpl* comings and goings.

alléger [aleʒe] *vt* *(voiture)* to make lighter; *(chargement)* to lighten; *(souffrance)* to alleviate, soothe.

allègre [alɛgʀ(ə)] *a* lively, cheerful.

alléguer [alege] *vt* to put forward (as proof ou an excuse).

Allemagne [aləmaɲ] *nf*: **l'~** Germa-

ny; **l'~ de l'Est/Ouest** East/West Germany; **allemand, e** *a, nm, nf* German.

aller [ale] *nm* *(trajet)* outward journey; *(billet: aussi:* **~ simple)** single *(Brit)* ou one-way *(US)* ticket // *vi* *(gén)* to go; **~ à** *(convenir)* to suit; *(suj: forme, pointure etc)* to fit; **~ avec** *(couleurs, style etc)* to go (well) with; **je vais y aller/me fâcher** I'm going to go/to get angry; **~ voir** to go and see, go to see; allez! come on!; allons! come now!; **comment allez-vous?** how are you?; **comment ça va?** how are you?; *(affaires etc)* how are things?; **il va bien/mal** he's well/not well, he's fine/ill; **ça va bien/mal** *(affaires etc)* it's going well/not going well; **~ mieux** to be better; **cela va sans dire** that goes without saying; **il y va de leur vie** their lives are at stake; **s'en ~** *vi* *(partir)* to be off, go, leave; *(disparaître)* to go away; **~ (et) retour** *nm* *(trajet)* return journey *(Brit)*, round trip; *(billet)* return ticket *(Brit)*, round trip ticket *(US)*.

allergique [alɛʀʒik] *a*: **~ à** allergic to.

alliage [aljaʒ] *nm* alloy.

alliance [aljɑ̃s] *nf* *(MIL, POL)* alliance; *(mariage)* marriage; *(bague)* wedding ring.

allier [alje] *vt* *(métaux)* to alloy; *(POL, gén)* to ally; *(fig)* to combine; **s'~** to become allies; to combine.

allô [alo] *excl* hullo, hallo.

allocation [alɔkɑsjɔ̃] *nf* allowance; **~ (de) chômage** unemployment benefit; **~ (de) logement** rent allowance; **~s familiales** = child benefit.

allocution [alɔkysjɔ̃] *nf* short speech.

allonger [alɔ̃ʒe] *vt* to lengthen, make longer; *(étendre: bras, jambe)* to stretch (out); **s'~** *vi* to get longer; *(se coucher)* to lie down, stretch out; **~ le pas** to hasten one's step(s).

allouer [alwe] *vt* to allocate, allot.

allumage [alymaʒ] nm (AUTO) ignition.

allume... [alym] préfixe: ~**cigare** nm inv cigar lighter; ~**gaz** nm inv gas lighter.

allumer [alyme] vt (lampe, phare, radio) to put ou switch on; (pièce) to put ou switch the light(s) on in; (feu) to light; s'~ vi (lumière, lampe) to come ou go on.

allumette [alymet] nf match.

allure [alyr] nf (vitesse) speed, pace; (démarche) walk; (maintien) bearing; (aspect, air) look; **avoir de l'~** to have style; **à toute ~** at top speed.

allusion [alyzjɔ̃] nf allusion; (sous-entendu) hint; **faire ~ à** to allude ou refer to; to hint at.

aloi [alwa] nm: **de bon ~** of genuine worth ou quality.

MOT-CLÉ

alors [alɔr] ad 1 (à ce moment-là) then, at that time; **il habitait ~ à Paris** he lived in Paris at that time 2 (par conséquent) then; **tu as fini? ~ je m'en vais** have you finished? I'm going then; **et ~?** so what?
alors que cj 1 (au moment où) when, as; **il est arrivé ~ que je partais** he arrived as I was leaving 2 (pendant que) while, when; **~ qu'il était à Paris, il a visité ...** while ou when he was in Paris, he visited ...
3 (tandis que) whereas, while; **~ que son frère travaillait dur, lui se reposait** whereas ou while his brother was working hard, HE would rest.

---

alouette [alwɛt] nf (sky)lark.

alourdir [alurdir] vt to weigh down, make heavy.

aloyau [alwajo] nm sirloin.

alpage [alpaʒ] nm pasture.

Alpes [alp(ə)] nfpl: **les ~** the Alps.

alphabet [alfabɛ] nm alphabet; (livre) ABC (book); **alphabétiser** vt

to teach to read and write; to eliminate illiteracy in.

alpinisme [alpinism(ə)] nm mountaineering, climbing; **alpiniste** nmf mountaineer, climber.

Alsace [alzas] nf Alsace; **alsacien, ne** a, nm/f Alsatian.

altérer [altere] vt to falsify; to distort; to debase; to impair.

alternateur [alternatœr] nm alternator.

alternatif, ive [alternatif, -iv] a alternating // nf (choix) alternative; **alternativement** ad alternately.

Altesse [altɛs] nf Highness.

altitude [altityd] nf altitude, height.

alto [alto] nm (instrument) viola.

altruisme [altruism(ə)] nm altruism.

aluminium [alyminjɔm] nm aluminium (Brit), aluminum (US).

alunir [alynir] vi to land on the moon.

amabilité [amabilite] nf kindness, amiability.

amadouer [amadwe] vt to coax, cajole; to mollify, soothe.

amaigrir [amegrir] vt to make thin(ner).

amande [amɑ̃d] nf (de l'amandier) almond; (de noyau de fruit) kernel; **amandier** nm almond (tree).

amant [amɑ̃] nm lover.

amarrer [amare] vt (NAVIG) to moor; (gén) to make fast.

amas [amɑ] nm heap, pile.

amasser [amase] vt to amass.

amateur [amatœr] nm amateur; **en ~** (péj) amateurishly; **~ de musique/sport** etc music/sport etc lover.

amazone [amazon] nf: **en ~** side-saddle.

ambages [ɑ̃baʒ] sans ~ ad plainly.

ambassade [ɑ̃basad] nf embassy; (mission): **en ~ on a mission; ambassadeur, drice** nm/f ambassador/ambassadress.

ambiance [ɑ̃bjɑ̃s] nf atmosphere.

ambiant, e [ɑ̃bjɑ̃, -ɑ̃t] a (air, milieu) surrounding; (température) ambient.

ambigu, ë [ãbigy] *a* ambiguous.

ambitieux, euse [ãbisjø, -øz] *a* ambitious.

ambition [ãbisjɔ̃] *nf* ambition.

ambulance [ãbylɑ̃s] *nf* ambulance; **ambulancier, ière** *nm/f* ambulance man/woman (*Brit*), paramedic (*US*).

ambulant, e [ãbylɑ̃, -ãt] *a* a travelling, itinerant.

âme [ɑm] *nf* soul; ~ **sœur** kindred spirit.

améliorer [ameljɔʀe] *vt* to improve; **s'~** *vi* to improve, get better.

aménagements [amenaʒmɑ̃] *nmpl* developments; ~ **fiscaux** tax adjustments.

aménager [amenaʒe] *vt* (*agencer, transformer*) to fit out; to lay out; (: *quartier, territoire*) to develop; (*installer*) to fix up, put in; **ferme aménagée** converted farmhouse.

amende [amɑ̃d] *nf* fine; **mettre à l'~** to penalize; **faire ~ honorable** to make amends.

amender [amɑ̃de] *vt* (*loi*) to amend; **s'~** *vi* to mend one's ways.

amène [amɛn] *a* affable; **peu** ~ unkind.

amener [amne] *vt* to bring; (*causer*) to bring about; (*baisser: drapeau, voiles*) to strike; **s'~** *vi* (*fam*) to show up, turn up.

amenuiser [amənɥize]: **s'~** *vi* to grow slimmer, lessen; to dwindle.

amer, amère [amɛʀ] *a* bitter.

américain, e [ameʀikɛ̃, -ɛn] *a, nm/f* American.

Amérique [ameʀik] *nf* America; **l'~ centrale/latine** Central/Latin America; **l'~ du Nord/du Sud** North/South America.

amerrir [ameʀiʀ] *vi* to land (on the sea).

amertume [amɛʀtym] *nf* bitterness.

ameublement [amœbləmɑ̃] *nm* furnishing; (*meubles*) furniture.

ameuter [amøte] *vt* (*badauds*) to draw a crowd of; (*peuple*) to rouse.

ami, e [ami] *nm/f* friend; (*amant/maîtresse*) boyfriend/girlfriend *nf* a:

pays/groupe ~ friendly country/group; **être** ~ **de l'ordre** to be a lover of order; **un** ~ **des arts** a patron of the arts.

amiable [amjabl(ə)]: **à l'**~ *ad* (*JUR*) out of court; (*gén*) amicably.

amiante [amjɑ̃t] *nm* asbestos.

amical, e, aux [amikal, -o] *a* friendly // *nf* (*club*) association; **amicalement** *ad* in a friendly way; (*formule épistolaire*) regards.

amidon [amidɔ̃] *nm* starch.

amincir [amɛ̃siʀ] *vt* (*objet*) to thin (down); ~ **qn** to make sb thinner *ou* slimmer; **s'~** *vi* to get thinner *ou* slimmer.

amiral, aux [amiʀal, -o] *nm* admiral.

amitié [amitje] *nf* friendship; **prendre en** ~ to befriend; **faire** *ou* **présenter ses** ~**s à qn** to send sb one's best wishes.

ammoniac [amɔnjak] *nm*: (**gaz**) ~ ammonia.

ammoniaque [amɔnjak] *nf* ammonia (water).

amoindrir [amwɛ̃dʀiʀ] *vt* to reduce.

amollir [amɔliʀ] *vt* to soften.

amonceler [amɔ̃sle] *vt*, **s'~** *vi* to pile *ou* heap up; (*fig*) to accumulate.

amont [amɔ̃]: **en** ~ *ad* upstream; (*sur une pente*) uphill.

amorce [amɔʀs(ə)] *nf* (*sur un hameçon*) bait; (*explosif*) cap; primer; priming; (*fig: début*) beginning(s), start.

amorphe [amɔʀf(ə)] *a* passive, lifeless.

amortir [amɔʀtiʀ] *vt* (*atténuer: choc*) to absorb, cushion; (*bruit, douleur*) to deaden; (*COMM: dette*) to pay off; (: *mise de fonds, matériel*) to write off; ~ **un abonnement** to make a season ticket pay (for itself); **amortisseur** *nm* shock absorber.

amour [amuʀ] *nm* love; (*liaison*) love affair, love; **faire l'**~ to make love; **s'~acher de** (*péj*) to become infatuated with; ~**eux, euse** *a* (*regard, tempérament*) amorous; (*vie,*

problèmes) love *cpd*; (*personne*): **~eux (de qn)** in love (with sb) // *nmpl* courting couple(s); **~-propre** *nm* self-esteem, pride.

amovible [amɔvibl(ə)] *a* removable, detachable.

ampère [ɑpɛʀ] *nm* amp(ere).

amphithéâtre [ɑfiteatʀ(ə)] *nm* amphitheatre; (*d'université*) lecture hall *ou* theatre.

ample [ɑpl(ə)] *a* (*vêtement*) roomy, ample; (*gestes, mouvement*) broad; (*ressources*) ample; **ampleur** *nf* (*importance*) scale, size; extent.

amplificateur [ɑplifikatœʀ] *nm* amplifier.

amplifier [ɑplifje] *vt* (*son, oscillation*) to amplify; (*fig*) to expand, increase.

ampoule [ɑpul] *nf* (*électrique*) bulb; (*de médicament*) phial; (*aux mains, pieds*) blister.

ampoulé, e [ɑpule] *a* (*péj*) pompous, bombastic.

amputer [ɑpyte] *vt* (*MÉD*) to amputate; (*fig*) to cut *ou* reduce drastically.

amusant, e [amyzɑ, -ɑt] *a* (*divertissant, spirituel*) entertaining, amusing; (*comique*) funny, amusing.

amuse-gueule [amyzgœl] *nm inv* appetizer, snack.

amusement [amyzmɑ] *nm* amusement; (*jeu etc*) pastime, diversion.

amuser [amyze] *vt* (*divertir*) to entertain, amuse; (*égayer, faire rire*) to amuse; (*détourner l'attention de*) to distract; **s'~** *vi* (*jouer*) to amuse o.s., play; (*se divertir*) to enjoy o.s., have fun; (*fig*) to mess around.

amygdale [amidal] *nf* tonsil.

amygdalite [amidalit] *nf* tonsillitis.

an [ɑ] *nm* year; **le jour de l'~, le premier de l'~, le nouvel ~** New Year's Day.

analogique [analɔʒik] *a* analogical; (*INFORM, montre*) analog.

analogue [analɔg] *a*: **~ (à)** analogous (to), similar (to).

analphabète [analfabɛt] *nm/f* illiterate.

analyse [analiz] *nf* analysis; (*MÉD*) test; **analyser** *vt* to analyse; to test.

ananas [anana] *nm* pineapple.

anarchie [anaʀʃi] *nf* anarchy.

anathème [anatɛm] *nm*: **jeter l'~ sur** to curse.

anatomie [anatɔmi] *nf* anatomy.

ancêtre [ɑsɛtʀ(ə)] *nm/f* ancestor.

anchois [ɑʃwa] *nm* anchovy.

ancien, ne [ɑsjɛ, -jɛn] *a* old; (*de jadis, de l'antiquité*) ancient; (*précédent, ex-*) former, old // *nm/f* (*dans une tribu*) elder; **anciennement** *ad* formerly; **ancienneté** *nf* oldness; antiquity; (*ADMIN*) (length of) service; seniority.

ancre [ɑkʀ(ə)] *nf* anchor; **jeter/lever l'~** to cast/weigh anchor; **à l'~** at anchor.

ancrer [ɑkʀe] *vt* (*CONSTR*: *câble etc*) to anchor; (*fig*) to fix firmly; **s'~** *vi* (*NAVIG*) to (cast) anchor.

Andorre [ɑdɔʀ] *nf* Andorra.

andouille [ɑduj] *nf* (*CULIN*) sausage made of chitterlings; (*fam*) clot, nit.

âne [ɑn] *nm* donkey, ass; (*péj*) dunce.

anéantir [aneɑtiʀ] *vt* to annihilate, wipe out; (*fig*) to obliterate, destroy; to overwhelm.

anémie [anemi] *nf* anaemia; **anémique** *a* anaemic.

ânerie [ɑnʀi] *nf* stupidity; stupid *ou* idiotic comment *etc*.

anesthésie [anɛstezi] *nf* anaesthesia; **faire une ~ locale/générale à qn** to give sb a local/general anaesthetic.

ange [ɑʒ] *nm* angel; **être aux ~s** to be over the moon.

angélus [ɑʒelys] *nm* angelus; evening bells *pl*.

angine [ɑʒin] *nf* throat infection; **~ de poitrine** angina.

anglais, e [ɑglɛ, -ɛz] *a* English // *nm/f*: **A~, e** Englishman/woman // *nm* (*LING*) English; **les A~** the English; **filer à l'~e** to take French leave.

angle [ãgl(ə)] nm angle; (coin) corner; ~ **droit** right angle.

Angleterre [ãglətɛʀ] nf: l'~ England.

anglo... [ãglɔ] préfixe Anglo-, anglo(-); ~**phone** a English-speaking.

angoissé, e [ãgwase] a (personne) full of anxieties ou hang-ups (fam).

angoisser [ãgwase] vt to harrow, cause anguish to // vi to worry, fret.

anguille [ãgij] nf eel.

anicroche [anikʀɔʃ] nf hitch, snag.

animal, e, aux [animal, -o] a, nm animal.

animateur, trice [animatœʀ, -tʀis] nm/f (de télévision) host; (de groupe) leader, organizer.

animation [animasjɔ̃] nf (voir animé) business ['bɪznɪs]; liveliness; (CINÉMA: technique) animation.

animé, e [anime] a (lieu) busy, lively; (conversation, réunion) lively, animated; (opposé à inanimé) animate.

animer [anime] vt (ville, soirée) to liven up; (mettre en mouvement) to drive.

anis [ani] nm (CULIN) aniseed; (BOT) anise.

ankyloser [ãkiloze]: s'~ vi to get stiff.

anneau, x [ano] nm (de rideau, bague) ring; (de chaîne) link.

année [ane] nf year.

annexe [anɛks(ə)] a (problème) related; (document) appended; (salle) adjoining // nf (bâtiment) annex(e); (de document, ouvrage) annex, appendix; (jointe à une lettre) enclosure.

anniversaire [anivɛʀsɛʀ] nm birthday; (d'un événement, bâtiment) anniversary.

annonce [anɔ̃s] nf announcement; (signe, indice) sign; (aussi: ~ publicitaire) advertisement; **les petites** ~**s** the classified advertisements, small ads.

annoncer [anɔ̃se] vt to announce;

(être le signe de) to herald; **s'~ bien/difficile** to look promising/difficult; **annonceur, euse** nm/f (TV, RADIO: speaker) announcer; (publicitaire) advertiser.

annuaire [anɥɛʀ] nm yearbook, annual; ~ **téléphonique** (telephone) directory, phone book.

annuel, le [anɥɛl] a annual, yearly.

annuité [anɥite] nf annual instalment.

annulaire [anɥlɛʀ] nm third finger.

annuler [anɥle] vt (rendez-vous, voyage) to cancel, call off; (mariage) to annul; (jugement) to quash (Brit), repeal (US); (résultats) to declare void; (MATH, PHYSIQUE) to cancel out.

anodin, e [anɔdɛ̃, -in] a harmless; insignificant, trivial.

anonyme [anɔnim] a anonymous; (fig) impersonal.

anorak [anɔʀak] nm anorak.

ANPE sigle f (= Agence nationale pour l'emploi) national employment agency.

anse [ãs] nf (de panier, tasse) handle; (GÉO) cove.

antan [ãtã]: **d'~** a of long ago.

antarctique [ãtaʀktik] a Antarctic // nm: l'A~ the Antarctic.

antécédents [ãtesedã] nmpl (MÉD etc) past history sg.

antenne [ãtɛn] nf (de radio) aerial; (d'insecte) antenna (pl **ae**); (poste avancé) outpost; (petite succursale) sub-branch; **passer à l'~** to go on the air; **prendre l'~** to tune in; **2 heures d'~** 2 hours' broadcasting time.

antérieur, e [ãteʀjœʀ] a (d'avant) previous, earlier; (de devant) front.

anti... [ãti] préfixe anti-.; ~**aérien, ne** a anti-aircraft; **abri** ~ air-raid shelter; ~**alcoolique** a anti-alcohol; ~**atomique** a: **abri** ~**atomique** fallout shelter; ~**biotique** nm antibiotic; ~**brouillard** a: **phare** ~**brouillard** fog lamp.

anticipation [ãtisipasjɔ̃] nf: **livre/**

film d'~ science fiction book/film.

anticipé, e [ɑ̃tisipe] *a*: avec mes remerciements ~s thanking you in advance *ou* anticipation.

anticiper [ɑ̃tisipe] *vt* (*événement, coup*) to anticipate, foresee.

anticonceptionnel, le [ɑ̃tikɔ̃sɛpsjɔnɛl] *a* contraceptive.

antidote [ɑ̃tidɔt] *nm* antidote.

antienne [ɑ̃tjɛn] *nf* (*fig*) chant, refrain.

antigel [ɑ̃tiʒɛl] *nm* antifreeze.

antihistaminique [ɑ̃tiistaminik] *nm* antihistamine.

Antilles [ɑ̃tij] *nfpl*: les ~ the West Indies.

antilope [ɑ̃tilɔp] *nf* antelope.

antimite(s) [ɑ̃timit] *a, nm*: (produit) ~ mothproofer; moth repellent.

antiparasite [ɑ̃tiparazit] *a* (*RADIO, TV*): dispositif ~ suppressor.

antipathique [ɑ̃tipatik] *a* unpleasant, disagreeable.

antiphrase [ɑ̃tifʁaz] *nf*: par ~ ironically.

antipodes [ɑ̃tipɔd] *nmpl* (*GÉO*): les ~ the antipodes; (*fig*): être aux ~ de to be the opposite extreme of.

antiquaire [ɑ̃tikɛʁ] *nm/f* antique dealer.

antique [ɑ̃tik] *a* antique; (*très vieux*) ancient, antiquated.

antiquité [ɑ̃tikite] *nf* (*objet*) antique; l'A~ Antiquity; magasin d'~s antique shop.

antirabique [ɑ̃tiʁabik] *a* rabies *cpd*.

antirouille [ɑ̃tiʁuj] *a inv* anti-rust *cpd*; traitement ~ rustproofing.

antisémite [ɑ̃tisemit] *a* anti-semitic.

antiseptique [ɑ̃tisɛptik] *a, nm* antiseptic.

antivol [ɑ̃tivɔl] *a, nm*: (dispositif) ~ anti-theft device.

antre [ɑ̃tʁ(ə)] *nm* den, lair.

anxieux, euse [ɑ̃ksjø, -øz] *a* anxious, worried.

AOC *sigle f* (= *appellation d'origine contrôlée*) label guaranteeing the quality of wine.

août [u] *nm* August.

apaiser [apeze] *vt* (*colère, douleur*) to soothe; (*faim*) to appease; (*personne*) to calm (down), pacify; s'~ *vi* (*tempête, bruit*) to die down, subside.

apanage [apanaʒ] *nm*: être l'~ de to be the privilege *ou* prerogative of.

aparté [aparte] *nm* (*THÉÂTRE*) aside; (*entretien*) private conversation.

apatride [apatrid] *nm/f* stateless person.

apercevoir [apɛʁsəvwaʁ] *vt* to see; s'~ de *vt* to notice; s'~ que to notice that.

aperçu [apɛʁsy] *nm* (*vue d'ensemble*) general survey; (*intuition*) insight.

apéritif [apeʁitif] *nm* (*boisson*) aperitif; (*réunion*) drinks *pl*.

à-peu-près [apøpʁɛ] *nm inv* (*péj*) vague approximation.

apeuré [apœʁe] *a* frightened, scared.

aphone [afɔn] *a* voiceless.

aphte [aft(ə)] *nm* mouth ulcer.

aphteuse [aftøz] *af*: fièvre ~ foot-and-mouth disease.

apiculture [apikyltyʁ] *nf* beekeeping, apiculture.

apitoyer [apitwaje] *vt* to move to pity; s'~ (sur) to feel pity (for).

aplanir [aplaniʁ] *vt* to level; (*fig*) to smooth away, iron out.

aplatir [aplatiʁ] *vt* to flatten; s'~ *vi* to become flatter; to be flattened; (*fig*) to lie flat on the ground.

aplomb [aplɔ̃] *nm* (*équilibre*) balance, equilibrium; (*fig*) self-assurance; nerve; d'~ *ad* steady; (*CONSTR*) plumb.

apogée [apɔʒe] *nm* (*fig*) peak, apogee.

apologie [apɔlɔʒi] *nf* vindication, praise.

apostolat [apɔstɔla] *nm* (*REL*) apostolate; (*gén*) evangelism.

apostrophe [apɔstʁɔf] *nf* (*signe*) apostrophe.

apostropher [apɔstʀɔfe] vt (interpeller) to shout at, address sharply.

apothéose [apɔteoz] nf (pinnacle (of achievement); (MUS) grand finale.

apôtre [apotʀ(ə)] nm apostle.

apparaître [apaʀɛtʀ(ə)] vi to appear // il va aussi attribut to appear, seem.

apparat [apaʀa] nm: **tenue/dîner d'~** ceremonial dress/dinner.

appareil [apaʀɛj] nm (outil, machine) piece of apparatus, device; appliance; (politique, syndical) machinery; (avion) (aero)plane, aircraft inv; (téléphonique) phone; (dentier) brace (Brit), braces (US); **qui est à l'~?** who's speaking?; **dans le plus simple ~** in one's birthday suit; **~ photographique, ~(-photo)** nm camera; **~ 24 x 36 ou petit format** 35mm camera.

appareiller [apaʀeje] vi (NAVIG) to cast off, get under way // vt (assortir) to match up.

apparemment [apaʀamɑ̃] ad apparently.

apparence [apaʀɑ̃s] nf appearance.

apparent, e [apaʀɑ̃, -ɑ̃t] a visible; obvious; (superficiel) apparent.

apparenté, e [apaʀɑ̃te] a: **~ à** related to; (fig) similar to.

appariteur [apaʀitœʀ] nm attendant, porter (in French universities).

apparition [apaʀisjɔ̃] nf appearance; (surnaturelle) apparition.

appartement [apaʀtəmɑ̃] nm flat (Brit), apartment (US).

appartenir [apaʀtəniʀ]: **~ à** vt to belong to; **il lui appartient de** it is up to him to, it is his duty to.

apparu, e pp de **apparaître**.

appât [apɑ] nm (PÊCHE) bait; (fig) lure, bait.

appauvrir [apovʀiʀ] vt to impoverish.

appel [apɛl] nm call; (nominal) roll call; (: SCOL) register; (MIL: recrutement) call-up; **faire ~ à** (invoquer) to appeal to; (avoir recours à) to call on; (nécessiter) to call for, require; **faire ~** (JUR) to appeal;

faire l'~ to call the roll; to call the register; **sans ~** (fig) final, irrevocable; **~ d'offres** (COMM) invitation to tender; **faire un ~ de phares** to flash one's headlights; **~ (téléphonique)** (tele)phone call.

appelé [aple] nm (MIL) conscript.

appeler [aple] vt to call; (faire venir: médecin etc) to call, send for; (fig: nécessiter) to call for, demand; **être appelé à** (fig) to be destined to; **~ qn à comparaître** (JUR) to summon sb to appear; **en ~ à** to appeal to; **s'~: elle s'appelle Gabrielle** her name is Gabrielle, she's called Gabrielle; **comment ça s'appelle?** what is it called?

appendice [apẽdis] nm appendix; **appendicite** nf appendicitis.

appentis [apɑ̃ti] nm lean-to.

appesantir [apzɑ̃tiʀ]: **s'~** vi to grow heavier; **s'~ sur** (fig) to dwell on.

appétissant, e [apetisɑ̃, -ɑ̃t] a appetizing, mouth-watering.

appétit [apeti] nm appetite; **bon ~!** enjoy your meal!

applaudir [aplodiʀ] vt to applaud // vi to applaud, clap; **applaudissements** nmpl applause sg, clapping sg.

application [aplikɑsjɔ̃] nf application.

applique [aplik] nf wall lamp.

appliquer [aplike] vt to apply; (loi) to enforce; **s'~** vi (élève etc) to apply o.s.

appoint [apwɛ̃] nm (extra) contribution ou help; **avoir/faire l'~** (en payant) to have/give the right change ou money; **chauffage d'~** extra heating.

appointements [apwɛ̃tmɑ̃] nmpl salary sg.

appontement [apɔ̃tmɑ̃] nm landing stage, wharf.

apport [apɔʀ] nm supply; contribution.

apporter [apɔʀte] vt to bring.

apposer [apoze] vt to append; to affix.

apprécier [apresje] *vt* to appreciate; (*évaluer*) to estimate, assess.

appréhender [apreɑ̃de] *vt* (*craindre*) to dread; (*arrêter*) to apprehend.

apprendre [aprɑ̃dr(ə)] *vt* to learn; (*événement, résultats*) to learn of, hear of; ~ **qch à qn** (*informer*) to tell sb (of) sth; (*enseigner*) to teach sb sth; ~ **à faire qch** to learn to do sth; ~ **à qn à faire qch** to teach sb to do sth; **apprenti, e** *nm/f* apprentice; (*fig*) novice, beginner; **apprentissage** *nm* learning; (*COMM, SCOL: période*) apprenticeship.

apprêté, e [aprete] *a* (*fig*) affected.

apprêter [aprete] *vt* to dress, finish.

appris, e *pp* de **apprendre**.

apprivoiser [aprivwaze] *vt* to tame.

approbation [aprɔbasjɔ̃] *nf* approval.

approche [aprɔʃ] *nf* approaching; approach.

approcher [aprɔʃe] *vi* to approach, come near // *vt* to approach; (*rapprocher*): ~ **qch (de qch)** to bring ou put sth near (to sth); ~ **de** *vt* to draw near to; (*quantité, moment*) to approach; **s'~ de** *vt* to approach, go ou come near to.

approfondir [aprɔfɔ̃dir] *vt* to deepen; (*question*) to go further into.

approprié, e [aprɔprije] *a*: ~ **(à)** appropriate (to), suited to.

approprier [aprɔprije]: **s'~** *vt* to appropriate, take over.

approuver [apruve] *vt* to agree with; (*autoriser: loi, projet*) to approve, pass; (*trouver louable*) to approve of.

approvisionner [aprɔvizjɔne] *vt* to supply; (*compte bancaire*) to pay funds into; **s'~ en** to stock up with.

approximatif, ive [aprɔksimatif, -iv] *a* approximate, rough; vague.

appt *abr* de **appartement**.

appui [apɥi] *nm* support; **prendre** ~ **sur** to lean on; to rest on; **l'~ de la fenêtre** the windowsill, the window ledge; **appui-tête, appuie-tête** *nm*

inv headrest.

appuyer [apɥije] *vt* (*poser*): ~ **qch sur/contre** to lean ou rest sth on ou against; (*soutenir: personne, demande*) to support, back (up) // *vi*: ~ **sur** (*bouton, frein*) to press, push; (*mot, détail*) to stress, emphasize; (*suj: chose: peser sur*) to rest (heavily) on, press against; **s'~ sur** *vt* to lean on; to rely on; ~ **à droite** to bear (to the) right.

âpre [ɑpr(ə)] *a* acrid, pungent; (*fig*) harsh; bitter; ~ **au gain** grasping.

après [aprɛ] *prép* after // *ad* afterwards; **2 heures** ~ **2 hours later;** ~ **qu'il est ou soit parti/avoir fait** after he left/having done; **d'~** *prép* (*selon*) according to; ~ **coup** *ad* after the event, afterwards; ~ **tout** *ad* (*au fond*) after all; **et (puis)** ~? so what?; ~-**demain** *ad* the day after tomorrow; ~-**guerre** *nm* postwar years *pl*; ~-**midi** *nm ou nf inv* afternoon.

à-propos [aprɔpo] *nm* (*d'une remarque*) aptness; **faire preuve d'~** to show presence of mind.

apte [apt(ə)] *a* capable; (*MIL*) fit.

aquarelle [akwaʀɛl] *nf* (*tableau*) watercolour; (*genre*) watercolours *pl*.

aquarium [akwaʀjɔm] *nm* aquarium.

arabe [aʀab] *a* Arabic; (*désert, cheval*) Arabian; (*nation, peuple*) Arab // *nm/f*: **A~** Arab // *nm* (*LING*) Arabic.

Arabie [aʀabi] *nf*: **l'~ (Saoudite)** Saudi Arabia.

arachide [aʀaʃid] *nf* (*plante*) groundnut (plant); (*graine*) peanut, groundnut.

araignée [aʀeɲe] *nf* spider.

arbitraire [aʀbitʀɛʀ] *a* arbitrary.

arbitre [aʀbitʀ(ə)] *nm* (*SPORT*) referee; (*TENNIS, CRICKET*) umpire; (*fig*) arbiter, judge; (*JUR*) arbitrator; **arbitrer** *vt* to referee; to umpire; to arbitrate.

arborer [aʀbɔʀe] *vt* to bear, display.

arbre [aʀbʀ(ə)] *nm* tree; (*TECH*) shaft; ~ **généalogique** family tree; ~ **de transmission** (*AUTO*) driveshaft.

arbuste [aʀbyst(ə)] *nm* small shrub.

arc [aʀk] *nm* (*arme*) bow; (*GÉOM*) arc; (*ARCHIT*) arch; **en ~ de cercle** *a* semi-circular.

arcade [aʀkad] *nf* arch(way); **~s** arcade *sg*, arches.

arcanes [aʀkan] *nmpl* mysteries.

arc-boutant [aʀkbutɑ̃] *nm* flying buttress.

arc-bouter [aʀkbute]: **s'~** *vi*: **s'~ contre** to lean *ou* press against.

arceau, x [aʀso] *nm* (*métallique etc*) hoop.

arc-en-ciel [aʀkɑ̃sjɛl] *nm* rainbow.

arche [aʀʃ(ə)] *nf* arch; **~ de Noé** Noah's Ark.

archéologie [aʀkeɔlɔʒi] *nf* archeology; **archéologue** *nm/f* archeologist.

archet [aʀʃɛ] *nm* bow.

archevêque [aʀʃəvɛk] *nm* archbishop.

archipel [aʀʃipɛl] *nm* archipelago.

architecte [aʀʃitɛkt(ə)] *nm* architect.

architecture [aʀʃitɛktyʀ] *nf* architecture.

archive [aʀʃiv] *nf* file; **~s** *nfpl* archives.

arctique [aʀktik] *a* Arctic // *nm*: **l'A~** the Arctic.

ardemment [aʀdamɑ̃] *ad* ardently, fervently.

ardent, e [aʀdɑ̃, -ɑ̃t] *a* (*soleil*) blazing; (*fièvre*) raging; (*amour*) ardent, passionate; (*prière*) fervent.

ardoise [aʀdwaz] *nf* slate.

ardt *abr de* **arrondissement**.

arène [aʀɛn] *nf* arena; **~s** *nfpl* bullring *sg*.

arête [aʀɛt] *nf* (*de poisson*) bone; (*d'une montagne*) ridge; (*GÉOM etc*) edge.

argent [aʀʒɑ̃] *nm* (*métal*) silver; (*monnaie*) money; **~ liquide** ready money, (ready) cash; **~ de poche** pocket money; **argenterie** *nf* silverware; silver plate.

argentin, e [aʀʒɑ̃tɛ̃, -in] *a* (*son*)

silvery; (*d'Argentine*) Argentinian, Argentine.

Argentine [aʀʒɑ̃tin] *nf*: **l'~** Argentina, the Argentine.

argile [aʀʒil] *nf* clay.

argot [aʀgo] *nm* slang; **argotique** *a* slang *cpd*; slangy.

arguer [aʀgɥe]: **~ de** *vt* to put forward as a pretext *ou* reason.

argument [aʀgymɑ̃] *nm* argument.

argumentaire [aʀgymɑ̃tɛʀ] *nm* sales leaflet.

argumenter [aʀgymɑ̃te] *vi* to argue.

argus [aʀgys] *nm* guide to second-hand car etc prices.

arguties [aʀgysi] *nfpl* quibbles.

aristocratique [aʀistɔkʀatik] *a* aristocratic.

arithmétique [aʀitmetik] *a* arithmetic(al) // *nf* arithmetic.

armateur [aʀmatœʀ] *nm* shipowner.

armature [aʀmatyʀ] *nf* framework; (*de tente etc*) frame.

arme [aʀm(ə)] *nf* weapon; (*section de l'armée*) arm; **~s** *nfpl* weapons, arms; (*blason*) (coat of) arms; **~ à feu** firearm.

armée [aʀme] *nf* army; **~ de l'air** Air Force; **l'~ du Salut** the Salvation Army; **~ de terre** Army.

armement [aʀmamɑ̃] *nm* (*matériel*) arms *pl*, weapons *pl*; (: *d'un pays*) arms *pl*, armament.

armer [aʀme] *vt* to arm; (*arme à feu*) to cock; (*appareil-photo*) to wind on; **~ qch de** to fit sth with; to reinforce sth with.

armistice [aʀmistis] *nm* armistice; **l'A~** = Remembrance (*Brit*) *ou* Veterans (*US*) Day.

armoire [aʀmwaʀ] *nf* (tall) cupboard; (*penderie*) wardrobe (*Brit*), closet (*US*).

armoiries [aʀmwaʀi] *nfpl* coat *sg* of arms.

armure [aʀmyʀ] *nf* armour *q*, suit of armour.

armurier [aʀmyʀje] *nm* gunsmith; armourer.

arnaquer [aʀnake] *vt* to swindle.

aromates [aʀɔmat] *nmpl* seasoning *sg*, herbs (and spices).

aromatisé, e [aʀɔmatize] *a* flavoured.

arôme [aʀom] *nm* aroma; fragrance.

arpenter [aʀpɑ̃te] *vt* (*salle, couloir*) to pace up and down.

arpenteur [aʀpɑ̃tœʀ] *nm* surveyor.

arqué, e [aʀke] *a* bandy; arched.

arrache-pied [aʀaʃpje]: **d'~** *ad* relentlessly.

arracher [aʀaʃe] *vt* to pull out; (*page etc*) to tear out, tear out; (*légumes, herbe*) to pull up; (*bras etc*) to tear off; **~ qch à qn** to snatch sth from sb; (*fig*) to wring sth out of sb; **s'~** *vt* (*article recherché*) to fight over.

arraisonner [aʀɛzɔne] *vt* (*bateau*) to board and search.

arrangeant, e [aʀɑ̃ʒɑ̃, -ɑ̃t] *a* accommodating, obliging.

arranger [aʀɑ̃ʒe] *vt* (*gén*) to arrange; (*réparer*) to fix, put right; (*régler*) to settle, sort out; (*convenir à*) to suit, be convenient for; **s'~** (*se mettre d'accord*) to come to an agreement; **je vais m'~** I'll manage; **ça va s'~** it'll sort itself out.

arrestation [aʀɛstɑsjɔ̃] *nf* arrest.

arrêt [aʀɛ] *nm* stopping; (*de bus etc*) stop; (*JUR*) judgment, decision; **rester ou tomber en ~ devant** to stop short in front of; **sans ~** non-stop; continually; **~ de mort** capital sentence; **~ de travail** stoppage (of work).

arrêté [aʀete] *nm* order, decree.

arrêter [aʀete] *vt* to stop; (*chauffage etc*) to turn off, switch off; (*fixer: date etc*) to appoint, decide on; (*criminel, suspect*) to arrest; **~ de faire** to stop doing; **s'~** *vi* to stop.

arrhes [aʀ] *nfpl* deposit *sg*.

arrière [aʀjɛʀ] *nm* back; (*SPORT*) fullback // *a inv* siège/roue **arrière** back *ou* rear seat/wheel; **à l'~** *ad* behind, at the back; **en ~** *ad* behind; (*regarder*) back, behind; (*tomber, aller*) backwards; **arriéré, e** *a* (*péj*) backward // *nm* (*d'argent*) arrears *pl*;

~-goût *nm* aftertaste; **~-grand-mère** *nf* great-grandmother; **~-grand-père** *nm* great-grandfather; **~-pays** *nm inv* hinterland; **~-pensée** *nf* ulterior motive; mental reservation; **~-plan** *nm* background; **~-saison** *nf* late autumn; **~-train** *nm* hindquarters *pl*.

arrimer [aʀime] *vt* to stow; to secure.

arrivage [aʀivaʒ] *nm* arrival.

arrivée [aʀive] *nf* arrival; (*ligne d'arrivée*) finish; **~ d'air/de gaz** air/gas inlet.

arriver [aʀive] *vi* to arrive; (*survenir*) to happen, occur; **il arrive à Paris à 8h** he gets to *ou* arrives in Paris at 8; **~ à** (*atteindre*) to reach; **~ à faire qch** to succeed in doing sth; **il arrive que** it happens that; **il lui arrive de faire** he sometimes does; **arriviste** *nm/f* go-getter.

arrogant, e [aʀɔgɑ̃, -ɑ̃t] *a* arrogant.

arroger [aʀɔʒe]: **s'~** *vt* to assume (without right).

arrondir [aʀɔ̃diʀ] *vt* (*forme, objet*) to round; (*somme*) to round off; **s'~** *vi* to become round(ed).

arrondissement [aʀɔ̃dismɑ̃] *nm* (*ADMIN*) ≈ district.

arroser [aʀoze] *vt* to water; (*victoire*) to celebrate (over a drink); (*CULIN*) to baste; **arrosoir** *nm* watering can.

arsenal, aux [aʀsənal, -o] *nm* (*NAVIG*) naval dockyard; (*MIL*) arsenal; (*fig*) gear, paraphernalia.

art [aʀ] *nm* art; **~s ménagers** home economics *sg*.

artère [aʀtɛʀ] *nf* (*ANAT*) artery; (*rue*) main road.

arthrite [aʀtʀit] *nf* arthritis.

artichaut [aʀtiʃo] *nm* artichoke.

article [aʀtikl(ə)] *nm* article; (*COMM*) item, article; **à l'~ de la mort** at the point of death; **~ de fond** (*PRESSE*) feature article.

articulation [aʀtikylɑsjɔ̃] *nf* articulation; (*ANAT*) joint.

articuler [aʀtikyle] *vt* to articulate.

artifice [aʀtifis] *nm* device, trick.

artificiel, le [aʀtifisjɛl] *a* artificial.

artificieux, euse [aʀtifisjø, -øz] *a* guileful, deceitful.

artisan [aʀtizɑ̃] *nm* artisan, (self-employed) craftsman; **artisanal, e, aux** *a* of *ou* made by craftsmen; (*péj*) cottage industry *cpd*, unsophisticated; **artisanat** *nm* arts and crafts *pl*.

artiste [aʀtist(ə)] *nm/f* artist; (*de variétés*) entertainer; performer; **artistique** *a* artistic.

as [a] *vb voir* **avoir** // *nm* [ɑs] ace.

ascendance [asɑ̃dɑ̃s] *nf* (*origine*) ancestry.

ascendant, e [asɑ̃dɑ̃, -ɑ̃t] *a* upward // *nm* influence.

ascenseur [asɑ̃sœʀ] *nm* lift (*Brit*), elevator (*US*).

ascension [asɑ̃sjɔ̃] *nf* ascent; climb; **l'A~** (*REL*) the Ascension.

aseptiser [asɛptize] *vt* to sterilize; to disinfect.

asiatique [azjatik] *a, nm/f* Asiatic, Asian.

Asie [azi] *nf*: **l'~** Asia.

asile [azil] *nm* (*refuge*) refuge, sanctuary; (*POL*): **droit d'~** (political) asylum; (*pour malades etc*) home.

aspect [aspɛ] *nm* appearance, look; (*fig*) aspect, side; **à l'~ de** at the sight of.

asperge [aspɛʀʒ(ə)] *nf* asparagus *q*.

asperger [aspɛʀʒe] *vt* to spray, sprinkle.

aspérité [aspeʀite] *nf* excrescence, protruding bit (of rock *etc*).

asphalte [asfalt(ə)] *nm* asphalt.

asphyxier [asfiksje] *vt* to suffocate, asphyxiate; (*fig*) to stifle.

aspirateur [aspiʀatœʀ] *nm* vacuum cleaner.

aspirer [aspiʀe] *vt* (*air*) to inhale; (*liquide*) to suck up; (*suj: appareil*) to suck up; **~ à** *vt* to aspire to.

aspirine [aspiʀin] *nf* aspirin.

assagir [asaʒiʀ] *vt*, **s'~** *vi* to quieten down, sober down.

assaillir [asajiʀ] *vt* to assail, attack.

assainir [aseniʀ] *vt* to clean up; to purify.

assaisonner [asɛzɔne] *vt* to season.

assassin [asasɛ̃] *nm* murderer; assassin.

assassiner [asasine] *vt* to murder; (*esp POL*) to assassinate.

assaut [aso] *nm* assault, attack; **prendre d'~** to storm, assault; **donner l'~ à** to attack; **faire ~ de** (*rivaliser*) to vie with each other in.

assécher [aseʃe] *vt* to drain.

assemblée [asɑ̃ble] *nf* (*réunion*) meeting; (*public, assistance*) gathering; assembled people; (*POL*) assembly.

assembler [asɑ̃ble] *vt* (*joindre, monter*) to assemble, put together; (*amasser*) to gather (together), collect (together); **s'~** *vi* to gather.

assener, asséner [asene] *vt*: **~ un coup à qn** to deal sb a blow.

assentiment [asɑ̃timɑ̃] *nm* assent, consent; approval.

asseoir [aswaʀ] *vt* (*malade, bébé*) to sit up; to sit down; (*autorité, réputation*) to establish; **s'~** *vi* to sit (o.s.) down.

assermenté, e [asɛʀmɑ̃te] *a* sworn, on oath.

asservir [asɛʀviʀ] *vt* to subjugate, enslave.

asseye *etc vb voir* **asseoir**.

assez [ase] *ad* (*suffisamment*) enough, sufficiently; (*passablement*) rather, quite, fairly; **~ de pain/ livres** enough *ou* sufficient bread/ books; **vous en avez ~?** have you got enough?

assidu, e [asidy] *a* assiduous, painstaking; regular; **assiduités** *nfpl* assiduous attentions.

assied *etc vb voir* **asseoir**.

assiéger [asjeʒe] *vt* to besiege.

assiérai *etc vb voir* **asseoir**.

assiette [asjɛt] *nf* plate; (*contenu*) plate(ful); **~ anglaise** assorted cold meats; **~ creuse** (soup) dish, soup plate; **~ à dessert** dessert plate; **~ de l'impôt** basis of (tax) assessment; ~ **plate** (dinner) plate.

assigner [asiɲe] vt: ~ **qch à** (poste, part, travail) to assign sth to; (limites) to set sth to; (cause, effet) to ascribe sth to; ~ **qn** à to assign sth to.

assimiler [asimile] vt to assimilate, absorb; (comparer): ~ **qch/qn à** to liken ou compare sth/sb to; s'~ vi (s'intégrer) to be assimilated ou absorbed.

assis, e [asi, -iz] pp de **asseoir** // a sitting (down), seated // nf (fig) basis (pl bases), foundation; ~es nfpl (JUR) assizes; (congrès) (annual) conference.

assistance [asistɑ̃s] nf (public) audience; (aide) assistance.

assistant, e [asistɑ̃, -ɑ̃t] nm/f assistant; (d'université) probationary lecturer; **les** ~**s** nmpl (auditeurs etc) those present; ~**e sociale** social worker.

assisté, e [asiste] a (AUTO) power assisted.

assister [asiste] vt to assist; ~ **à** vt (scène, événement) to witness; (conférence, séminaire) to attend, be at; (spectacle, match) to be at, see.

association [asosjasjɔ̃] nf association.

associé, e [asosje] nm/f associate; partner.

associer [asosje] vt to associate; ~ **qn à** (profits) to give sb a share of; (affaire) to make sb a partner in; (joie, triomphe) to include sb in; ~ **qch à** (joindre, allier) to combine sth with; s'~ (suj pl) to join together; (COMM) to form a partnership: s'~ vt (collaborateur) to take on (as a partner); s'~ **à qn pour faire** to join (forces) with sb to do; s'~ **à** to be combined with; (opinions, joie de qn) to share in.

assoiffé, e [aswafe] a thirsty.

assombrir [asɔ̃bʀiʀ] vt to darken; (fig) to fill with gloom.

assommer [asɔme] vt to batter to death; (étourdir, abrutir) to knock

out; to stun.

Assomption [asɔ̃psjɔ̃] nf: l'~ the Assumption.

assorti, e [asɔʀti] a matched, matching; (varié) assorted; ~ **à** matching.

assortiment [asɔʀtimɑ̃] nm assortment, selection.

assortir [asɔʀtiʀ] vt to match; ~ **qch à** to match sth with; ~ **qch de** to accompany sth with; s'~ **de** to be accompanied by.

assoupi, e [asupi] a dozing, sleeping; (fig) (be)numbed; dulled; stilled.

assouplir [asupliʀ] vt to make supple; (fig) to relax.

assourdir [asuʀdiʀ] vt (bruit) to deaden, muffle; (suj: bruit) to deafen.

assouvir [asuviʀ] vt to satisfy, appease.

assujettir [asyʒetiʀ] vt to subject.

assumer [asyme] vt (fonction, emploi) to assume, take on.

assurance [asyʀɑ̃s] nf (certitude) assurance; (confiance en soi) (self-) confidence; (contrat) insurance (policy); (secteur commercial) insurance; ~ **maladie** health insurance; ~ **tous risques** (AUTO) comprehensive insurance; ~**s sociales** ≈ National Insurance (Brit), ≈ Social Security (US); ~**-vie** nf life assurance ou insurance.

assuré, e [asyʀe] a (certain): ~ **de** confident of // nm/f insured (person); ~**ment** ad assuredly, most certainly.

assurer [asyʀe] vt to insure; (stabiliser) to steady; (victoire etc) to ensure; (frontières, pouvoir) to make secure; (service, garde) to provide; to operate; ~ **qch à qn** (garantir) to secure sth for sb; (procurer) to assure sb of sth; ~ **à qn que** to assure sb that; ~ **qn de** to assure sb of; s'~ (contre) (COMM) to insure o.s. (against); (vérifier) to make sure of/that; s'~ (de) (aide de qn) to secure.

asthme [asm(ə)] nm asthma.

asticot [astiko] nm maggot.

astiquer [astike] vt to polish, shine.

astre [astr(ə)] nm star.

astreignant, e [astrɛɲɑ̃, -ɑ̃t] a demanding.

astreindre [astrɛ̃dr(ə)] vt: ~ qn à qch to force sth upon sb; ~ qn à faire to compel ou force sb to do.

astrologie [astrɔlɔʒi] nf astrology.

astronaute [astronot] nm/f astronaut.

astronomie [astronɔmi] nf astronomy.

astuce [astys] nf shrewdness, astuteness; (truc) trick, clever way; (plaisanterie) wisecrack; **astucieux, euse** a clever.

atelier [atəlje] nm workshop; (de peintre) studio.

athée [ate] a atheistic // nm/f atheist.

Athènes [atɛn] n Athens.

athlète [atlɛt] nm/f (SPORT) athlete; **athlétisme** nm athletics sg.

atlantique [atlɑ̃tik] a Atlantic // nm: l'(océan) A~ the Atlantic (Ocean).

atlas [atlɑs] nm atlas.

atmosphère [atmɔsfɛr] nf atmosphere.

atome [atom] nm atom; **atomique** a atomic, nuclear; (nombre, masse) atomic.

atomiseur [atɔmizœr] nm atomizer.

atone [atɔn] a lifeless.

atours [atur] nmpl attire sg, finery sg.

atout [atu] nm trump; (fig) asset; trump card.

âtre [ɑtr(ə)] nm hearth.

atroce [atrɔs] a atrocious.

attabler [atable]: s'~ vi to sit down at (the) table.

attachant, e [ataʃɑ̃, -ɑ̃t] a engaging, lovable, likeable.

attache [ataʃ] nf clip, fastener; (fig) tie.

attacher [ataʃe] vt to tie up; (étiquette) to attach, tie on; (souliers) to do up // vi (poêle, riz) to stick; s'~ à (par affection) to become attached

to; s'~ à faire to endeavour to do; ~ qch à to tie ou attach sth to.

attaque [atak] nf attack; (cérébrale) stroke; (d'épilepsie) fit.

attaquer [atake] vt to attack; (en justice) to bring an action against, sue; (travail) to tackle, set about // vi to attack.

attardé, e [atarde] a (passants) late; (enfant) backward; (conceptions) old-fashioned.

attarder [atarde]: s'~ vi to linger; to stay on.

atteindre [atɛ̃dr(ə)] vt to reach; (blesser) to hit; (émouvoir) to affect.

atteint, e [atɛ̃, -ɛ̃t] a (MÉD): être ~ de to be suffering from // nf attack; hors d'~e out of reach; porter ~e à to strike a blow at; to undermine.

atteler [atle] vt (cheval, bœufs) to hitch up; (wagons) to couple; s'~ à (travail) to buckle down to.

attelle [atɛl] nf splint.

attenant, e [atnɑ̃, -ɑ̃t] a: ~ (à) adjoining.

attendre [atɑ̃dr(ə)] vt (gén) to wait for; (être destiné ou réservé à) to await, be in store for // vi to wait; s'~ à (ce que) to expect (that); ~ un enfant to be expecting a baby; ~ de faire/d'être to wait until one does/is; ~ que to wait until; ~ qch de to expect sth of; en attendant ad meanwhile, in the meantime; be that as it may.

attendrir [atɑ̃drir] vt to move (to pity); (viande) to tenderize.

attendu, e [atɑ̃dy] a (visiteur) expected; ~ que considering that, since.

attentat [atɑ̃ta] nm assassination attempt; ~ à la bombe bomb attack; ~ à la pudeur indecent exposure q; indecent assault q.

attente [atɑ̃t] nf wait; (espérance) expectation.

attenter [atɑ̃te]: ~ à vt (liberté) to violate; ~ à la vie de qn to make an attempt on sb's life.

attentif, ive [atɑtif, -iv] *a* (*auditeur*) attentive; (*travail*) scrupulous; careful: ~ à mindful of; careful to.

attention [atɑsjɔ̃] *nf* attention; (*prévenance*) attention, thoughtfulness *q*; à l'~ de for the attention of; faire ~ (à) to be careful (of); faire ~ (à ce) que to be *ou* make sure that; ~! careful!, watch out!; **attentionné, e** *a* thoughtful, considerate.

atténuer [atenɥe] *vt* to alleviate, ease; to lessen.

atterrer [atεʀe] *vt* to dismay, appal.

atterrir [atεʀiʀ] *vi* to land; **atterrissage** *nm* landing.

attestation [atεstɑsjɔ̃] *nf* certificate.

attester [atεste] *vt* to testify to.

attirail [atiʀaj] *nm* (*péj*) paraphernalia.

attirant, e [atiʀɑ̃, -ɑ̃t] *a* attractive, appealing.

attirer [atiʀe] *vt* to attract; (*appâter*) to lure, entice; ~ qn dans un coin/vers soi to draw sb into a corner/towards one; ~ l'attention de qn (sur) to attract sb's attention (to); to draw sb's attention (to); s'~ des ennuis to bring trouble upon o.s., get into trouble.

attiser [atize] *vt* (*feu*) to poke (up).

attitré, e [atitʀe] *a* qualified; accredited; appointed.

attitude [atityd] *nf* attitude; (*position du corps*) bearing.

attouchements [atuʃmɑ̃] *nmpl* touching *sg*; (*sexuels*) fondling *sg*.

attraction [atʀaksjɔ̃] *nf* (*gén*) attraction; (*de cabaret, cirque*) number.

attrait [atʀε] *nm* appeal, attraction; lure.

attrape-nigaud [atʀapnigo] *nm* con.

attraper [atʀape] *vt* (*gén*) to catch; (*habitude, amende*) to get, pick up; (*fam: duper*) to con.

attrayant, e [atʀεjɑ̃, -ɑ̃t] *a* attractive.

attribuer [atʀibɥe] *vt* (*prix*) to award; (*rôle, tâche*) to allocate, assign; (*imputer*): ~ qch à to attribute sth to; s'~ *vt* (*s'approprier*)

to claim for o.s.

attribut [atʀiby] *nm* attribute; (*LING*) complement.

attrister [atʀiste] *vt* to sadden.

attroupement [atʀupmɑ̃] *nm* crowd, mob.

attrouper [atʀupe]: s'~ *vi* to gather.

au [o] *prép* + *dét voir* à.

aubade [obad] *nf* dawn serenade.

aubaine [obεn] *nf* godsend; (*financière*) windfall.

aube [ob] *nf* dawn, daybreak; à l'~ at dawn *ou* daybreak.

aubépine [obepin] *nf* hawthorn.

auberge [obεʀʒ(ə)] *nf* inn; ~ de jeunesse youth hostel.

aubergine [obεʀʒin] *nf* aubergine.

aubergiste [obεʀʒist(ə)] *nm/f* innkeeper, hotel-keeper.

aucun, e [okœ̃, -yn] *dét* no, *tournure négative* + any; (*positif*) any // *pronom* none, *tournure négative* + any; none, *tournure négative* + any; sans ~ doute without any doubt; plus qu'~ autre more than any other; ~ des deux neither of the two; ~ d'entre eux none of them; d'~s (*certains*) some; **aucunement** *ad* in no way, not in the least.

audace [odas] *nf* daring, boldness; (*péj*) audacity; **audacieux, euse** *a* daring, bold.

au-delà [odla] *ad* beyond // *nm*: l'~ the hereafter; ~ de *prép* beyond.

au-dessous [odsu] *ad* underneath; below; ~ de *prép* under(neath), below; (*limite, somme etc*) below, under; (*dignité, condition*) below.

au-dessus [odsy] *ad* above; ~ de *prép* above.

au-devant [odvɑ̃]: ~ de *prép*: aller ~ de (*personne, danger*) to go (out) and meet; (*souhaits de qn*) to anticipate.

audience [odjɑs] *nf* audience; (*JUR: séance*) hearing.

audio-visuel, le [odjovizɥεl] *a* audio-visual.

auditeur, trice [oditœʀ, -tʀis] *nm/f* listener.

audition [odisjɔ̃] *nf* (*ouïe, écoute*) hearing; (*JUR: de témoins*) examination; (*MUS, THÉÂTRE: épreuve*) audition.

auditoire [oditwaʀ] *nm* audience.

auge [oʒ] *nf* trough.

augmentation [ɔgmɑ̃tasjɔ̃] *nf*: ~ (**de salaire**) rise (in salary) (*Brit*), (pay) raise (*US*).

augmenter [ɔgmɑ̃te] *vt* (*gén*) to increase; (*salaire, prix*) to increase, raise, put up; (*employé*) to increase the salary // *vi* to increase.

augure [ɔgyʀ] *nm* soothsayer, oracle; **de bon/mauvais** ~ of good/ill omen.

augurer [ɔgyʀe] *vt*: ~ **bien de** to augur well for.

aujourd'hui [oʒuʀdɥi] *ad* today.

aumône [omon] *nf* alms *sg* (*pl inv*); **faire l'~ (à qn)** to give alms (to sb).

aumônier [omonje] *nm* chaplain.

auparavant [opaʀavɑ̃] *ad* before(hand).

auprès [opʀɛ]: ~ **de** *prép* next to, close to; (*recourir, s'adresser*) to; (*en comparaison de*) compared with.

auquel [okɛl] *prép* + *pronom voir* **lequel**.

aurai etc *vb voir* **avoir**.

auréole [oʀeɔl] *nf* halo; (*tache*) ring.

auriculaire [oʀikylɛʀ] *nm* little finger.

aurons etc *vb voir* **avoir**.

aurore [oʀɔʀ] *nf* dawn, daybreak.

ausculter [oskylte] *vt* to sound.

aussi [osi] *ad* (*également*) also, too; (*de comparaison*) as // *cj* therefore, consequently; ~ **fort que** as strong as; **moi** ~ me too; ~ **bien que** as well as.

aussitôt [osito] *ad* straight away, immediately; ~ **que** as soon as.

austère [ostɛʀ] *a* austere; stern.

austral, e [ostʀal] *a* southern.

Australie [ostʀali] *nf*: **l'~** Australia; **australien, ne** *a, nm/f* Australian.

autant [otɑ̃] *ad* so much; (*comparatif*): ~ **(que)** as much (as);

(*nombre*) as many (as); ~ **(de)** so much (*ou* many), as much (*ou* many); ~ **partir** we (*ou* you *etc*) may as well leave; ~ **dire que...** one might as well say that...; **pour** ~ for all that; **pour** ~ **que** *cj* assuming, as long as; **d'~ plus/mieux (que)** all the more/the better (since).

autel [otɛl] *nm* altar.

auteur [otœʀ] *nm* author.

authentique [otɑ̃tik] *a* authentic, genuine.

auto [oto] *nf* car.

auto... [oto] *préfixe* auto..., self-; **~biographie** *nf* autobiography.

autobus [otobys] *nm* bus.

autocar [otokaʀ] *nm* coach.

autochtone [otɔktɔn] *nm/f* native.

auto-collant, e [otokɔlɑ̃, -ɑ̃t] *a* self-adhesive; (*enveloppe*) self-seal // *nm* sticker.

auto-couchettes [otokuʃɛt] *a*: **train** ~ car sleeper train.

autocuiseur [otokɥizœʀ] *nm* pressure cooker.

autodéfense [otodefɑ̃s] *nf* self-defence; **groupe d'~** vigilante committee.

autodidacte [otodidakt(ə)] *nm/f* self-taught person.

auto-école [otoekɔl] *nf* driving school.

autogestion [otoʒɛstjɔ̃] *nf* self-management.

autographe [otogʀaf] *nm* autograph.

automate [otomat] *nm* (*machine*) (automatic) machine.

automatique [otomatik] *a* automatic // *nm*: **l'~** direct dialling; **~ment** *ad* automatically; **automatiser** *vt* to automate.

automne [otɔn] *nm* autumn (*Brit*), fall (*US*).

automobile [otomobil] *a* motor *cpd* // *nf* (motor) car; **l'~** motoring; the car industry; **automobiliste** *nm/f* motorist.

autonome [otonɔm] *a* autonomous; **autonomie** *nf* autonomy; (*POL*) self-government, autonomy.

autopsie [ɔtɔpsi] *nf* post-mortem (examination), autopsy.

autoradio [ɔtɔradjo] *nm* car radio.

autorisation [ɔtɔrizasjɔ̃] *nf* permission, authorization; (*papiers*) permit.

autorisé, e [ɔtɔrize] *a* (*opinion, sources*) authoritative.

autoriser [ɔtɔrize] *vt* to give permission for, authorize; (*fig*) to allow (of), sanction.

autoritaire [ɔtɔritɛr] *a* authoritarian.

autorité [ɔtɔrite] *nf* authority; faire ~ to be authoritative.

autoroute [ɔtɔrut] *nf* motorway (*Brit*), highway (*US*).

auto-stop [ɔtɔstɔp] *nm*: faire de l'~ to hitch-hike; ~**peur, euse** *nm/f* hitch-hiker.

autour [ɔtur] *ad* around; ~ **de** *prép* around; **tout** ~ **ad** all around.

MOT-CLÉ

autre [otr(ə)] ♦ **a 1** (*différent*) other, different; **je préférerais un** ~ **verre** I'd prefer another *ou* a different glass

2 (*supplémentaire*) other; **je voudrais un** ~ **verre d'eau** I'd like another glass of water

3: ~ **chose** something else; ~ **part** *ad* somewhere else; **d'**~ **part** *ad* on the other hand

♦ *pronom*: **un** ~ another (one); **nous/ vous** ~**s** us/you; **d'**~**s** others; **l'**~ the other (one); **les** ~ **s** the others; (*autrui*) others; **l'un et l'**~ both of them; **se détester l'un l'**~/ **les uns les** ~**s** to hate each other *ou* one another; **d'une semaine à l'**~ from one week to the next; (*incessamment*) any week now; **entre** ~**s** among other things.

---

autrefois [otrəfwa] *ad* in the past.

autrement [otrəmɑ̃] *ad* differently; in another way; (*sinon*) otherwise; ~ **dit** in other words.

Autriche [otriʃ] *nf*: l'~ Austria; **autrichien, ne** *a, nm/f* Austrian.

autruche [otryʃ] *nf* ostrich.

autrui [otrɥi] *pronom* others.

auvent [ovɑ̃] *nm* canopy.

aux [o] *prép* + *dét voir* à.

auxiliaire [ɔksiljɛr] *a, nm/f* auxiliary.

auxquels, auxquelles [okɛl] *prép* + *pronom voir* **lequel**.

av. *abr de* avenue.

avachi, e [avaʃi] *a* limp, flabby.

aval [aval] *nm* (*accord*) endorsement, backing; (*GÉO*): **en** ~ downstream, downriver; (*sur une pente*) downhill.

avalanche [avalɑ̃ʃ] *nf* avalanche.

avaler [avale] *vt* to swallow.

avance [avɑ̃s] *nf* (*de troupes etc*) advance; progress; (*d'argent*) advance; (*opposé à retard*) lead; being ahead of schedule; ~**s** *nfpl* overtures; (*amoureuses*) advances; (**être**) **en** ~ (to be) early; (*sur un programme*) (to be) ahead of schedule; **à l'**~, **d'**~ in advance.

avancé, e [avɑ̃se] *a* advanced; well on *ou* under way.

avancement [avɑ̃smɑ̃] *nm* (*professionnel*) promotion.

avancer [avɑ̃se] *vi* to move forward, advance; (*projet, travail*) to make progress; (*être en saillie*) to overhang; to jut out; (*montre, réveil*) to be fast; to gain // *vt* to move forward, advance; (*argent*) to advance; (*montre, pendule*) to put forward; **s'**~ *vi* to move forward, advance; (*fig*) to commit o.s.; to overhang; to jut out.

avant [avɑ̃] *prép* before // *ad*: **trop/ plus** ~ too far/further forward // *a inv*: **siège/roue** ~ front seat/wheel // *nm* (*d'un véhicule, bâtiment*) front; (*SPORT: joueur*) forward; ~ **qu'il parte/de faire** before he leaves/ doing; ~ **tout** (*surtout*) above all; **à l'**~ (*dans un véhicule*) in the front; **en** ~ forward(s); **en** ~ **de** *prép* in front of.

avantage [avɑ̃taʒ] *nm* advantage; ~**s sociaux** fringe benefits; **avantager** *vt* (*favoriser*) to favour; (*embellir*) to flatter; **avantageux, euse** *a* attractive; attractively priced.

avant-bras [avɑ̃bʀa] *nm inv* forearm.

avant-dernier, ère [avɑ̃dɛʀnje, -ɛʀ] *a, nm/f* next to last, last but one.

avant-goût [avɑ̃gu] *nm* foretaste.

avant-hier [avɑ̃tjɛʀ] *ad* the day before yesterday.

avant-première [avɑ̃pʀəmjɛʀ] *nf (de film)* preview.

avant-projet [avɑ̃pʀɔʒɛ] *nm* (preliminary) draft.

avant-propos [avɑ̃pʀɔpo] *nm* foreword.

avant-veille [avɑ̃vɛj] *nf*: **l'~** two days before.

avare [avaʀ] *a* miserly, avaricious // *nm/f* miser; **~ de** *(compliments etc)* sparing of.

avarié, e [avaʀje] *a* rotting.

avaries [avaʀi] *nfpl (NAVIG)* damage *sg*.

avatar [avataʀ] *nm* misadventure.

avec [avɛk] *prép* with; *(à l'égard de)* to(wards), with.

avenant, e [avnɑ̃, -ɑ̃t] *a* pleasant; **à l'~** *ad* in keeping.

avènement [avɛnmɑ̃] *nm (d'un roi)* accession, succession; *(d'un changement)* advent, coming.

avenir [avniʀ] *nm* future; **à l'~** in future; **politicien d'~** politician with prospects *ou* a future.

Avent [avɑ̃] *nm*: **l'~** Advent.

aventure [avɑ̃tyʀ] *nf* adventure; *(amoureuse)* affair; **s'aventurer** *vi* to venture; **aventureux, euse** *a* adventurous, venturesome; *(projet)* risky, chancy.

avenue [avny] *nf* avenue.

avérer [aveʀe]: **s'~** *vb avec attribut* to prove (to be).

averse [avɛʀs(ə)] *nf* shower.

averti, e [avɛʀti] *a* (well-)informed.

avertir [avɛʀtiʀ] *vt*: **~ qn (de qch/que)** to warn sb (of sth/that); *(renseigner)* to inform sb (of sth/that); **avertissement** *nm* warning; **avertisseur** *nm* horn, siren.

aveu, x [avø] *nm* confession.

aveugle [avœgl(ə)] *a* blind; **aveu-**

glément *ad* blindly; **aveugler** *vt* to blind.

aviateur, trice [avjatœʀ, -tʀis] *nm/f* aviator, pilot.

aviation [avjasjɔ̃] *nf* aviation; *(sport)* flying; *(MIL)* air force.

avide [avid] *a* eager; *(péj)* greedy, grasping.

avilir [aviliʀ] *vt* to debase.

avion [avjɔ̃] *nm* (aero)plane *(Brit)*, (air)plane *(US)*; **aller (quelque part) en ~** to go (somewhere) by plane, fly (somewhere); **par ~** by airmail; **~ à réaction** jet (plane).

aviron [aviʀɔ̃] *nm* oar; *(sport)*: **l'~** rowing.

avis [avi] *nm* opinion; *(notification)* notice; **changer d'~** to change one's mind; **jusqu'à nouvel ~** until further notice.

avisé, e [avize] *a* sensible, wise.

aviser [avize] *vt (voir)* to notice, catch sight of; *(informer)*: **~ qn de/que** to advise *ou* inform sb of/that // *vi* to think about things, assess the situation; **s'~ de qch/que** to become suddenly aware of sth/that; **s'~ de faire** to take it into one's head to do.

avocat, e [avɔka, -at] *nm (JUR)* barrister *(Brit)*, lawyer // *nm (CULIN)* avocado (pear); **~ général** assistant public prosecutor.

avoine [avwan] *nf* oats *pl*.

MOT-CLÉ

avoir [avwaʀ] ♦ *nm* assets *pl*, resources *pl*; *(COMM)* credit
♦ *vt* **1** *(posséder)* to have; **elle a 2 enfants/une belle maison** she has (got) 2 children/a lovely house; **il a les yeux bleus** he has (got) blue eyes

2 *(âge, dimensions)* to be; **il a 3 ans** he is 3 (years old); **le mur a 3 mètres de haut** the wall is 3 metres high; *voir* **faim, peur** *etc*

3 *(fam: duper)* to do; **on vous a eu!** you've been done *ou* had!

4: **en ~ contre qn** to have a grudge against sb; **en ~ assez** to be fed up with j'en ai pour une demi-heure it'll take me half an hour

♦ **auxiliaire 1** to have; **~ mangé/ dormi** to have eaten/slept
2 (*avoir* + à + *inf*): **~ à faire qch** to have to do sth; **vous n'avez qu'à lui demander** you only have to ask him

♦ *vb impersonnel* **1**: **il y a** (+ *sing*) there is; (+ *pl*) there are; **qu'y-a-t-il?, qu'est-ce qu'il y a?** what's the matter?, what is it?; **il doit y ~ une explication** there must be an explanation; **il n'y a qu'à ... we** (*ou* **you** *etc*) will just have to ...
2 (*temporel*): **il y a 10 ans** 10 years ago; **il y a 10 ans/longtemps que je le sais** I've known it for 10 years/ a long time; **il y a 10 ans qu'il est arrivé** it's 10 years since he arrived.

avoisiner [avwazine] *vt* to be near *ou* close to; (*fig*) to border *ou* verge on.

avortement [avɔʀtəmɑ̃] *nm* abortion.

avorter [avɔʀte] *vi* (*MÉD*) to have an abortion; (*fig*) to fail.

avoué, e [avwe] *a* avowed // *nm* (*JUR*) ≈ solicitor.

avouer [avwe] *vt* (*crime, défaut*) to confess (to); **~ avoir fait/que** to admit *ou* confess to having done/that.

avril [avʀil] *nm* April.

axe [aks(ə)] *nm* axis (*pl* axes); (*de roue etc*) axle; (*fig*) main line; **~ routier** trunk road, main road; **axer** *vt*: **axer qch sur** to centre sth on.

ayons *etc vb voir* **avoir**.

azote [azɔt] *nm* nitrogen.

B

babines [babin] *nfpl* chops.

babiole [babjɔl] *nf* (*bibelot*) trinket; (*vétille*) trifle.

bâbord [babɔʀ] *nm*: **à ou par ~** to port, on the port side.

baby-foot [babifut] *nm* table football.

bac [bak] *abr m de* **baccalauréat** // *nm* (*bateau*) ferry; (*récipient*) tub; tray; tank.

baccalauréat [bakalɔʀea] *nm* high school diploma.

bachelier, ière [baʃəlje, -jɛʀ] *nm/f* holder of the baccalauréat.

bâcher [baʃe] *vt* to cover (with a canvas sheet *ou* a tarpaulin).

bachot [baʃo] *abr m de* **baccalauréat**.

bachoter [baʃɔte] *vi* (*fam*) to cram (for an exam).

bâcler [bakle] *vt* to botch (up).

badaud, e [bado, -od] *nm/f* idle onlooker, stroller.

badigeonner [badiʒɔne] *vt* to distemper; to colourwash; (*barbouiller*) to daub.

badin, e [badɛ̃, -in] *a* playful.

badiner [badine] *vi*: **~ avec qch** to treat sth lightly.

badminton [badminton] *nm* badminton.

baffe [baf] *nf* (*fam*) slap, clout.

bafouer [bafwe] *vt* to deride, ridicule.

bafouiller [bafuje] *vi, vt* to stammer.

bagage [bagaʒ] *nm*: **~s** luggage *sg*; **~s à main** hand-luggage.

bagarre [bagaʀ] *nf* fight, brawl; **se bagarrer** *vi* to have a fight *ou* scuffle, fight.

bagatelle [bagatɛl] *nf* trifle.

bagne [baɲ] *nm* penal colony.

bagnole [baɲɔl] *nf* (*fam*) car.

bagout [bagu] *nm*: **avoir du ~** to have the gift of the gab.

bague [bag] *nf* ring; **~ de fiançailles** engagement ring; **~ de serrage** clip.

baguette [bagɛt] *nf* stick; (*cuisine chinoise*) chopstick; (*de chef d'orchestre*) baton; (*pain*) stick of (French) bread; **~ magique** magic wand.

bahut [bay] *nm* chest.

baie [bɛ] *nf* (*GÉO*) bay; (*fruit*) berry; **~ (vitrée)** picture window.

baignade [bɛɲad] *nf* bathing.

baigner [beɲe] vt (bébé) to bath; se ~ vi to have a swim, go swimming ou bathing; (dans un bain) to bath(tub).

bail, baux [baj, bo] nm lease.

bâiller [baje] vi to yawn; (être ouvert) to gape.

bailleur [bajœʀ] nm: ~ de fonds sponsor, backer.

bâillon [bajɔ̃] nm gag; **bâillonner** vt to gag.

bain [bɛ̃] nm bath; **prendre un** ~ to have a bath; **se mettre dans le** ~ (fig) to get into it ou things; **~ de foule** walkabout; **prendre un** ~ **de soleil** to sunbathe; **~s de mer** sea bathing sg; **faire chauffer au** ~-**marie** (boîte etc) to immerse in boiling water.

baiser [beze] nm kiss // vt (main, front) to kiss; (fam!) to screw (!).

baisse [bɛs] nf fall, drop; '~ **sur la viande**' 'meat prices down'.

baisser [bese] vt lower; (radio, chauffage) to turn down; (AUTO: phares) to dip (Brit), to lower (US) // vi to fall, drop, go down; se ~ vi to bend down.

bal [bal] nm dance; (grande soirée) ball; ~ **costumé** fancy-dress ball.

balader [balade] vt (traîner) to trail round; se ~ vi to go for a walk ou stroll; to go for a drive.

balafre [balafʀ(ə)] nf gash, slash; (cicatrice) scar.

balai [balɛ] nm broom, brush; ~-**brosse** nm (long-handled) scrubbing brush.

balance [balɑ̃s] nf scales pl; (de précision) balance; (signe): la B~ Libra.

balancer [balɑ̃se] vt to swing; (lancer) to fling, chuck; (renvoyer, jeter) to chuck out // vi to swing; se ~ vi to swing; to rock; to sway; se ~ de (fam) not to care about; **balancier** nm (de pendule) pendulum; (perche) (balancing) pole; **balançoire** nf swing; (sur pivot) seesaw.

balayer [baleje] vt (feuilles etc) to sweep up, brush up; (pièce) to sweep; (chasser) to sweep away; to sweep aside; (suj: radar) to scan; **balayeur, euse** nm/f, nf roadsweeper.

balbutier [balbysje] vi, vt to stammer.

balcon [balkɔ̃] nm balcony; (THÉÂTRE) dress circle.

baleine [balɛn] nf whale; (de parapluie, corset) rib; **baleinière** nf whaleboat.

balise [baliz] nf (NAVIG) beacon; (marker) buoy; (AVIAT) runway light, beacon; (AUTO, SKI) sign, marker; **baliser** vt to mark out (with lights etc).

balivernes [balivɛʀn(ə)] nfpl nonsense sg.

ballant, e [balɑ̃, -ɑ̃t] a dangling.

balle [bal] nf (de fusil) bullet; (de sport) ball; (paquet) bale; (fam: franc) franc; ~ **perdue** stray bullet.

ballerine [balʀin] nf ballet dancer.

ballet [balɛ] nm ballet.

ballon [balɔ̃] nm (de sport) ball; (jouet, AVIAT) balloon; (de vin) glass; ~ **de football** football.

ballot [balo] nm bundle; (péj) nitwit.

ballottage [balɔtaʒ] nm (POL) second ballot.

ballotter [balɔte] vi to roll around; to toss // vt to shake about; to toss.

balnéaire [balneɛʀ] a seaside cpd.

balourd, e [baluʀ, -uʀd(ə)] a clumsy // nm/f clodhopper.

balustrade [balystʀad] nf railings pl, handrail.

bambin [bɑ̃bɛ̃] nm little child.

ban [bɑ̃] nm round of applause, cheer; ~s nmpl (de mariage) banns; **mettre au** ~ **de** to outlaw from.

banal, e [banal] a banal, commonplace; (péj) trite.

banane [banan] nf banana.

banc [bɑ̃] nm seat, bench; (de poissons) shoal; ~ **d'essai** (fig) testing ground; ~ **de sable** sandbank.

bancaire [bɑ̃kɛʀ] a banking, bank cpd.

bancal, e [bɑ̃kal] a wobbly; bow-legged.

bandage [bɑ̃daʒ] nm bandage.

bande [bɑ̃d] nf (de tissu etc) strip; (MÉD) bandage; (motif) stripe; (magnétique etc) tape; (groupe) band; (: péj) bunch; **par la ~** in a roundabout way; **donner de la ~** to list; **faire ~ à part** to keep to o.s.; **~ dessinée** comic strip; **~ sonore** sound track.

bandeau, x [bɑ̃do] nm headband; (sur les yeux) blindfold; (MÉD) head bandage.

bander [bɑ̃de] vt (blessure) to bandage; (muscle) to tense; **~ les yeux à qn** to blindfold sb.

banderole [bɑ̃drɔl] nf banner, streamer.

bandit [bɑ̃di] nm bandit; **banditisme** nm violent crime, armed robberies pl.

bandoulière [bɑ̃duljɛr] nf: **en ~** (slung ou worn) across the shoulder.

banlieue [bɑ̃ljø] nf suburbs pl; **lignes/ quartiers de ~** suburban lines/areas; **trains de ~** commuter trains.

bannière [banjɛr] nf banner.

bannir [banir] vt to banish.

banque [bɑ̃k] nf bank; (activités) banking; **~ d'affaires** merchant bank.

banqueroute [bɑ̃krut] nf bankruptcy.

banquet [bɑ̃kɛ] nm dinner; (d'apparat) banquet.

banquette [bɑ̃kɛt] nf seat.

banquier [bɑ̃kje] nm banker.

banquise [bɑ̃kiz] nf ice field.

baptême [batɛm] nm christening; baptism; **~ de l'air** first flight.

baquet [bakɛ] nm tub, bucket.

bar [bar] nm bar.

baraque [barak] nf shed; (fam) house; **~ foraine** fairground stand.

baraqué, e [barake] a well-built, hefty.

baraquements [barakmɑ̃] nmpl huts (for refugees, workers etc).

baratin [baratɛ̃] nm (fam) smooth

talk, patter; **baratiner** vt to chat up.

barbare [barbar] a barbaric.

barbe [barb(ə)] nf beard; **quelle ~!** (fam) what a drag ou bore!; **à la ~ de qn** under sb's nose; **~ à papa** candy-floss (Brit), cotton candy (US).

barbelé [barbəle] nm barbed wire q.

barboter [barbɔte] vi to paddle, dabble.

barboteuse [barbɔtøz] nf rompers pl.

barbouiller [barbuje] vt to daub; **avoir l'estomac barbouillé** to feel queasy.

barbu, e [barby] a bearded.

barda [barda] nm (fam) kit, gear.

barde [bard(ə)] nf piece of fat bacon.

barder [barde] vi (fam): **ça va ~** sparks will fly, things are going to get hot.

barème [barɛm] nm scale; table.

baril [baril] nm barrel; keg.

baromètre [barɔmɛtr(ə)] nm barometer.

baron [barɔ̃] nm baron; **baronne** nf baroness.

baroque [barɔk] a (ART) baroque; (fig) weird.

barque [bark(ə)] nf small boat.

barrage [baraʒ] nm dam; (sur route) roadblock, barricade.

barre [bar] nf bar; (NAVIG) helm; (écrite) line, stroke.

barreau, x [baro] nm bar; (JUR): **le ~** the Bar.

barrer [bare] vt (route etc) to block; (mot) to cross out; (chèque) to cross (Brit); (NAVIG) to steer; **se ~** vi (fam) to clear off.

barrette [barɛt] nf (pour cheveux) (hair) slide (Brit) ou clip (US).

barricader [barikade] vt to barricade.

barrière [barjɛr] nf fence; (obstacle) barrier; (porte) gate.

barrique [barik] nf barrel, cask.

bas, basse [bɑ, bɑs] a low // nm bottom, lower part; (vêtement) stocking // nf (MUS) bass // ad low; (parler) softly; **avoir la vue basse**

to be short-sighted; **au ~ mot** at the lowest estimate; **en ~** down below; **at** (ou **to**) **the bottom**; (*dans une maison*) downstairs; **en ~ de** at the bottom of; **mettre ~ à** to give birth; **à ~...!** 'down with ...!'; **~ morceaux** *nmpl* cheap cuts.

basané, e [bazane] *a* tanned, bronzed.

bas-côté [bakote] *nm* (*de route*) verge (*Brit*), shoulder (*US*).

bascule [baskyl] *nf*: (**jeu de**) **~** seesaw; (**balance à**) **~** scales *pl*; fauteuil **à ~** rocking chair.

basculer [baskyle] *vi* to fall over, topple (over); (*benne*) to tip up ◊ *vt* to topple over; to tip out, tip up.

base [baz] *nf* base; (*POL*) rank and file; (*fondement, principe*) basis (*pl* bases); **de ~** basic; **à ~ de café** *etc* coffee *etc* (*based*); **~ de données** database; **baser** *vt* to base; **se baser sur** (*preuves*) to base one's argument on.

bas-fond [baf5] *nm* (*NAVIG*) shallow; **~s** (*fig*) dregs.

basilic [bazilik] *nm* (*CULIN*) basil.

basket [basket] *nm* trainer (*Brit*), sneaker (*US*); (*aussi*: **~-ball**) basketball.

basque [bask(ə)] *a, nf* Basque.

basse [bas] *a, nf voir* bas; **~-cour** *nf* farmyard.

bassin [basɛ̃] *nm* (*cuvette*) bowl; (*pièce d'eau*) pond, pool; (*de fontaine, GÉO*) basin; (*ANAT*) pelvis; (*portuaire*) dock.

basson [bas5] *nm* bassoon.

bastingage [bastɛ̃gaʒ] *nm* (ship's) rail.

bas-ventre [bavɑ̃tʀ(ə)] *nm* (lower part of the) stomach.

bat *vb voir* **battre**.

bât [ba] *nm* packsaddle.

bataille [bataj] *nf* battle; fight.

bâtard, e [bataʀ, -aʀd(ə)] *nm/f* illegitimate child, bastard (*péj*).

bateau, x [bato] *nm* boat, ship; **~-mouche** *nm* (*passenger*) pleasure boat (*on the Seine*).

bateleur, euse [batlœʀ, -øz] *nm/f* street performer.

batelier, ière [batəlje, -jɛʀ] *nm/f* (*de bac*) ferryman/woman.

bâti, e [bati] *a*: **bien ~** well-built.

batifoler [batifɔle] *vi* to frolic about.

bâtiment [batimɑ̃] *nm* building; (*NAVIG*) ship, vessel; (*industrie*) building trade.

bâtir [batiʀ] *vt* to build.

bâtisse [batis] *nf* building.

bâton [bat5] *nm* stick; **à ~s rompus** informally.

bâtonnier [batɔnje] *nm* ≈ president of the Bar.

bats *vb voir* **battre**.

battage [bataʒ] *nm* (*publicité*) (hard) plugging.

battant [batɑ̃] *nm* (*de cloche*) clapper; (*de volets*) shutter, flap; (*de porte*) side; (*fig: personne*) fighter; **porte à double ~** double door.

battement [batmɑ̃] *nm* (*de cœur*) beat; (*intervalle*) interval (*between classes, trains etc*); **~ de paupières** blinking *q* (*of eyelids*); **10 minutes de ~** 10 minutes to spare.

batterie [batʀi] *nf* (*MIL, ÉLEC*) battery; (*MUS*) drums *pl*, drum kit; **~ de cuisine** pots and pans *pl*; kitchen utensils *pl*.

batteur [batœʀ] *nm* (*MUS*) drummer; (*appareil*) whisk.

battre [batʀ(ə)] *vt* to beat; (*suj: pluie, vagues*) to beat ou lash against; (*blé*) to thresh; (*passer au peigne fin*) to scour ◊ *vi* (*cœur*) to beat; (*volets etc*) to bang, rattle; **se ~ vi** to fight; **la mesure** to beat time; **~ en brèche** to demolish; **~ son plein** to be at its height, be going full swing; **~ des mains** to clap one's hands.

battue [baty] *nf* (*chasse*) beat; (*policière etc*) search, hunt.

baume [bom] *nm* balm.

bavard, e [bavaʀ, -aʀd(ə)] *a* (very) talkative; gossipy; **bavarder** *vi* to chatter; (*indiscrètement*) to gossip; to blab.

bave [bav] *nf* dribble; *(de chien etc)* slobber; *(d'escargot)* slime; **baver** *vi* to dribble; to slobber; *(en* *fam)* to have a hard time (of it); **bavette** *nf* bib; **baveux, euse** *a (omelette)* runny.

bavure [bavyʀ] *nf* smudge; *(fig)* hitch; blunder.

bayer [baje] *vi*: ~ **aux corneilles** to stand gaping.

bazar [bazaʀ] *nm* general store; *(fam)* jumble; **bazarder** *vt (fam)* to chuck out.

B.C.B.G. *sigle a* (= *bon chic bon genre*) preppy, smart and trendy.

B.C.G. *sigle m* (= *bacille Calmette-Guérin*) BCG.

bd. *abr de* boulevard.

B.D. *sigle f de* bande dessinée.

béant, e [beã, -ãt] *a* gaping.

béat, e [bea, -at] *a* showing open-eyed wonder; blissful; **béatitude** *nf* bliss.

beau(bel), belle, beaux [bo, bɛl] *a* beautiful, lovely; *(homme)* handsome // *nf (SPORT)* decider // *ad*: **il fait** ~ the weather's fine; **un** ~ **jour** one (fine) day; **de plus belle** more than ever, even more; **on a** ~ **essayer** however hard we try; **bel et bien** well and truly; **faire le** ~ *(chien)* to sit up and beg.

MOT-CLÉ

---

beaucoup [boku] *ad* **1** a lot; **il boit** ~ he drinks a lot; **il ne boit pas** ~ he doesn't drink much ou a lot
2 *(suivi de plus, trop etc)* much, a lot, far; **il est** ~ **plus grand** he is much ou a lot ou far taller
3: ~ **de** *(nombre)* many, a lot of; *(quantité)* a lot of; ~ **d'étudiants/de touristes** a lot of ou many students/tourists; ~ **de courage** a lot of courage; **il n'a pas** ~ **d'argent** he hasn't got much ou a lot of money
4: **de** ~ *ad* by far.

beau-fils [bofis] *nm* son-in-law; *(remariage)* stepson.

beau-frère [bofʀɛʀ] *nm* brother-in-law.

beau-père [bopɛʀ] *nm* father-in-law; *(remariage)* stepfather.

beauté [bote] *nf* beauty; **de toute** ~ beautiful; **en** ~ *ad* brilliantly.

beaux-arts [bozaʀ] *nmpl* fine arts.

beaux-parents [boparã] *nmpl* wife's/husband's family *sg ou pl*, in-laws.

bébé [bebe] *nm* baby.

bec [bɛk] *nm* beak, bill; *(de récipient)* spout; lip; *(fam)* mouth; ~ **de gaz** (street) gaslamp; ~ **verseur** pouring lip.

bécane [bekan] *nf (fam: vélo)* bike.

bec-de-lièvre [bɛkdəljɛvʀ(ə)] *nm* harelip.

bêche [bɛʃ] *nf* spade; **bêcher** *vt* to dig.

bécoter [bekɔte]: **se** ~ *vi* to smooch.

becqueter [bɛkte] *vt (fam)* to eat.

bedaine [bədɛn] *nf* paunch.

bedonnant, e [bədɔnã, -ãt] *a* pot-bellied.

bée [be] *a*: **bouche** ~ gaping.

beffroi [befʀwa] *nm* belfry.

bégayer [begeje] *vt, vi* to stammer.

bègue [bɛg] *nm/f*: **être** ~ to have a stammer.

béguin [begɛ̃] *nm*: **avoir le** ~ **de** ou **pour** to have a crush on.

beige [bɛʒ] *a* beige.

beignet [bɛɲɛ] *nm* fritter.

bel [bɛl] *a voir* beau.

bêler [bele] *vi* to bleat.

belette [bəlɛt] *nf* weasel.

belge [bɛlʒ] *a, nm/f* Belgian.

Belgique [bɛlʒik] *nf*: **la** ~ Belgium.

bélier [belje] *nm* ram; *(signe)*: **le** B~ Aries.

belle [bɛl] *af, nf voir* beau; ~-**fille** *nf* daughter-in-law; *(remariage)* step-daughter; ~-**mère** *nf* mother-in-law; stepmother; ~-**sœur** *nf* sister-in-law.

belliqueux, euse [belikø, -øz] *a* aggressive, warlike.

belvédère [belvedɛʀ] *nm* panoramic viewpoint *(or small building there)*.

bémol [bemɔl] nm (MUS) flat.

bénédiction [benediksjɔ̃] nf blessing.

bénéfice [benefis] nm (COMM) profit; (avantage) benefit; **bénéficier de** vt to enjoy; to benefit by ou from; to get, be given; **bénéfique** a beneficial.

benêt [bənɛ] nm simpleton.

bénévole [benevɔl] a voluntary, unpaid.

bénin, igne [benɛ̃, -iɲ] a minor, mild; (tumeur) benign.

bénir [benir] vt to bless; **bénit, e** a consecrated; **eau bénite** holy water; **bénitier** nm font.

benjamin, e [bɛ̃ʒamɛ̃, -in] nm/f youngest child.

benne [bɛn] nf skip; (de téléphérique) (cable) car; **~ basculante** tipper (Brit), dump truck (US).

béotien, ne [beɔsjɛ̃, -jɛn] nm/f philistine.

B.E.P.C. sigle m voir **brevet**.

béquille [bekij] nf crutch; (de bicyclette) stand.

bercail [bɛrkaj] nm fold.

berceau, x [bɛrso] nm cradle, crib.

bercer [bɛrse] vt to rock, cradle; (suj: musique etc) to lull; **~ qn de** (promesses etc) to delude sb with; **berceuse** nf lullaby.

béret (basque) [bere(bask(ə))] nm beret.

berge [bɛrʒ(ə)] nf bank.

berger, ère [bɛrʒe, -ɛr] nm/f shepherd/shepherdess.

berlingot [bɛrlɛ̃go] nm (emballage) carton (pyramid shaped).

berlue [bɛrly] nf: **j'ai la ~** I must be seeing things.

berne [bɛrn(ə)] nf: **en ~** at half-mast.

berner [bɛrne] vt to fool.

besogne [bəzɔɲ] nf work q, job; **besogneux, euse** a hard-working.

besoin [bəzwɛ̃] nm need; (pauvreté): **le ~** need, want; **faire ses ~s** to relieve o.s.; **avoir ~ de qch/faire qch** to need sth/to do sth; **au ~** if need be.

bestiaux [bestjo] nmpl cattle.

bestiole [bestjɔl] nf (tiny) creature.

bétail [betaj] nm livestock, cattle pl.

bête [bɛt] nf animal; (bestiole) insect, creature // a stupid, silly; **il cherche la petite ~** he's being pernickety ou overfussy; **~ noire** pet hate.

bêtise [betiz] nf stupidity; stupid thing (to say ou do).

béton [betɔ̃] nm concrete; **(en) ~** (alibi, argument) cast iron; **~ armé** reinforced concrete; **bétonnière** nf cement mixer.

betterave [bɛtrav] nf beetroot (Brit), beet (US); **~ sucrière** sugar beet.

beugler [bøgle] vi to low; (radio etc) to blare // vt (chanson) to bawl out.

beurre [bœr] nm butter; **beurrer** vt to butter; **beurrier** nm butter dish.

beuverie [bɛvri] nf drinking session.

bévue [bevy] nf blunder.

Beyrouth [berut] n Beirut.

bi... [bi] préfixe bi..., two-.

biais [bjɛ] nm (moyen) device, expedient; (aspect) angle; **en ~, de ~** (obliquement) at an angle; (fig) indirectly; **biaiser** vi (fig) to sidestep the issue.

bibelot [biblo] nm trinket, curio.

biberon [bibrɔ̃] nm (feeding) bottle; **nourrir au ~** to bottle-feed.

bible [bibl(ə)] nf bible.

biblio... [biblijo] préfixe: **~bus** nm mobile library van; **~phile** nm/f booklover; **~thécaire** nm/f librarian; **~thèque** nf library; (meuble) bookcase.

bicarbonate [bikarbɔnat] nm: **~ (de soude)** bicarbonate of soda.

biceps [bisɛps] nm biceps.

biche [biʃ] nf doe.

bichonner [biʃɔne] vt to groom.

bicolore [bikɔlɔr] a two-coloured.

bicoque [bikɔk] nf (péj) shack.

bicyclette [bisiklɛt] nf bicycle.

bide [bid] nm (fam: ventre) belly; (THÉÂTRE) flop.

bidet [bidɛ] nm bidet.

bidon [bidɔ̃] nm can // a inv (fam) phoney.

bidonville [bidɔ̃vil] nf shanty town.

bidule [bidyl] nm (fam) thingumajig.

bielle [bjɛl] nf connecting rod.

MOT-CLÉ

bien [bjɛ̃] ♦ nm 1 (avantage, profit): faire du ~ à qn to do sb good; dire du ~ de to speak well of; c'est pour son ~ it's for his own good
2 (possession, patrimoine) possession, property; son ~ le plus précieux his most treasured possession; avoir du ~ to have property; ~s (de consommation etc) (consumer etc) goods
3 (moral): le ~ good; distinguer le ~ du mal to tell good from evil
♦ ad 1 (de façon satisfaisante) well; elle travaille/mange ~ she works/eats well; croyant ~ faire, je/il ... thinking I/he was doing the right thing, I/he ...; c'est ~ fait! it serves him (ou her etc) right!
2 (valeur intensive) quite; ~ jeune quite young; ~ assez quite enough; ~ mieux (very) much better; j'espère ~ y aller I do hope to go; je veux ~ le faire (concession) I'm quite willing to do it; il faut ~ le faire it has to be done
3: ~ du temps/des gens quite a time/a number of people
♦ a inv 1 (en bonne forme, à l'aise): je me sens ~ I feel fine; je ne me sens pas ~ I don't feel well; on est ~ dans ce fauteuil this chair is very comfortable
2 (joli, beau) good-looking; tu es ~ dans cette robe you look good in that dress
3 (satisfaisant) good; elle est ~, cette maison/secrétaire it's a good house/she's a good secretary
4 (moralement) right; (: personne) nice; (respectable) respectable; ce n'est pas ~ de ... it's not

right to ...; elle est ~, cette femme she's a nice woman, she's a good sort; des gens ~ respectable people
5 (en bons termes): être ~ avec qn to be on good terms with sb
♦ préfixe: ~-aimé, e a, nm/f beloved; ~-être nm well-being; ~faisance nf charity; ~faisant, e a (chose) beneficial; ~fait nm act of generosity, benefaction; (de la science etc) benefit; ~faiteur, trice nm/f benefactor/benefactress; ~fondé nm soundness; ~-fonds nm property; ~heureux, euse a happy; (REL) blessed, blest
bien que cj (al)though
bien sûr ad certainly.

---

bienséant, e [bjɛ̃seã, -ãt] a seemly.

bientôt [bjɛ̃to] ad soon; à ~ see you soon.

bienveillant, e [bjɛ̃vɛjã, -ãt] a kindly.

bienvenu, e [bjɛ̃vny] a welcome // nf: souhaiter la ~ à to welcome; ~e à welcome to.

bière [bjɛʀ] nf (boisson) beer; (cercueil) bier; ~ blonde lager; ~ brune brown ale; ~ (à la) pression draught beer.

biffer [bife] vt to cross out.

bifteck [biftɛk] nm steak.

bifurquer [bifyʀke] vi (route) to fork; (véhicule) to turn off.

bigarré, e [bigaʀe] a multicoloured; (disparate) motley.

bigarreau, x [bigaʀo] nm type of cherry.

bigorneau, x [bigɔʀno] nm winkle.

bigot, e [bigo, -ɔt] (péj) a bigoted.

bigoudi [bigudi] nm curler.

bijou, x [biʒu] nm jewel; ~terie nf jeweller's (shop); jewellery; ~tier, ière nm/f jeweller.

bikini [bikini] nm bikini.

bilan [bilã] nm (COMM) balance sheet; end of year statement; (fig) (net) outcome; (: de victimes) toll; faire le ~ de to assess; to review;

déposer son ~ to file a bankruptcy statement.

bile [bil] *nf* bile; **se faire de la ~** (*fam*) to worry o.s. sick.

bilieux, euse [biljø, -jøz] *a* bilious; (*fig:* colérique) testy.

bilingue [bilɛ̃g] *a* bilingual.

billard [bijaʀ] *nm* billiards *sg*; billiard table; **c'est du ~** (*fam*) it's a cinch.

bille [bij] *nf* (*gén*) ball; (*du jeu de billes*) marble; (*de bois*) log.

billet [bijɛ] *nm* (*aussi:* ~ **de banque**) (bank)note; (*de cinéma, de bus etc*) ticket; (*courte lettre*) note; ~ **circulaire** round-trip ticket; ~ **de faveur** complimentary ticket.

billion [biljɔ̃] *nm* billion (Brit), trillion (US).

billot [bijo] *nm* block.

bimensuel, le [bimɑ̃sɥɛl] *a* bimonthly.

binette [binɛt] *nf* hoe.

binocle [binɔkl(ə)] *nm* pince-nez.

bio... [bjo] *préfixe* bio-...; ~**graphie** *nf* biography; ~**logie** *nf* biology; ~**logique** *a* biological.

Birmanie [biʀmani] *nf* Burma.

bis, e [bi, biz] *a* (*couleur*) greyish brown // *ad* [bis]: **12 ~ 12a** *ou* A // *excl, nm* [bis] encore // *nf* (*baiser*) kiss; (*vent*) North wind.

bisannuel, le [bizanɥɛl] *a* biennial.

biscornu, e [biskɔʀny] *a* twisted.

biscotte [biskɔt] *nf* (*breakfast*) rusk.

biscuit [biskɥi] *nm* biscuit; sponge cake.

bise [biz] *a, nf voir* **bis**.

bissextile [bisɛkstil] *a*: **année ~** leap year.

bistouri [bisturi] *nm* lancet.

bistro(t) [bistʀo] *nm* bistro, café.

bitume [bitym] *nm* asphalt.

bizarre [bizaʀ] *a* strange, odd.

blafard, e [blafaʀ, -aʀd(ə)] *a* wan.

blague [blag] *nf* (*propos*) joke; (*farce*) trick; **sans ~!** no kidding!; ~ **à tabac** tobacco pouch.

blaguer [blage] *vi* to joke // *vt* to tease.

blaireau, x [blɛʀo] *nm* (ZOOL) badger; (*brosse*) shaving brush.

blairer [blɛʀe] *vt* (*fam*): **je ne peux pas le ~** I can't bear *ou* stand him.

blâme [blɑm] *nm* blame; (*sanction*) reprimand.

blâmer [blɑme] *vt* to blame.

blanc, blanche [blɑ̃, blɑ̃ʃ] *a* white; (*non imprimé*) blank; (*innocent*) pure // *nm/f* white, white man/woman // *nm* (*couleur*) white; (*espace non écrit*) blank; (*aussi:* ~ **d'œuf**) (egg-)white; (*aussi:* ~ **de poulet**) white meat; (*aussi:* **vin ~**) white wine // *nf* (MUS) minim (Brit), half-note (US); ~ **cassé** off-white; **chèque en ~** blank cheque; **à ~** *ad* (*chauffer*) white-hot; (*tirer, charger*) with blanks; ~**-bec** *nm* greenhorn.

blancheur [blɑ̃ʃœʀ] *nf* whiteness.

blanchir [blɑ̃ʃiʀ] *vt* (*gén*) to whiten; (*linge*) to launder; (CULIN) to blanch; (*fig: disculper*) to clear // *vi* to grow white; (*cheveux*) to go white; **blanchisserie** *nf* laundry.

blaser [blaze] *vt* to make blasé.

blason [blazɔ̃] *nm* coat of arms.

blatte [blat] *nf* cockroach.

blazer [blazɛʀ] *nm* blazer.

blé [ble] *nm* wheat.

bled [blɛd] *nm* (*péj*) hole.

blême [blɛm] *a* pale.

blessé, e [blese] *a* injured *nm/f* injured person; casualty.

blesser [blese] *vt* to injure; (*délibérément:* MIL *etc*) to wound; (*suj:* souliers *etc, offenser*) to hurt; **se ~** to injure o.s.; **se ~ au pied** *etc* to injure one's foot *etc*.

blessure [blesyʀ] *nf* injury; wound.

bleu, e [blø] *a* (*bifteck*) very rare // *nm* (*couleur*) blue; (*novice*) greenhorn; (*contusion*) bruise; (*vêtement: aussi:* ~**s**) overalls *pl*; ~ **marine** navy blue.

bleuet [bløɛ] *nm* cornflower.

bleuté, e [bløte] *a* blue-shaded.

blinder [blɛ̃de] *vt* to armour; (*fig*) to harden.

bloc [blɔk] *nm* (*de pierre etc*) block;

(de papier à lettres) pad; (ensemble) group, block; **serré à ~** tightened right down; **en ~** in a block; wholesale; **~ opératoire** operating ou theatre block; **~ sanitaire** toilet block.

blocage [blɔkaʒ] nm blocking; jamming; freezing; (PSYCH) hang-up.

bloc-notes [blɔknɔt] nm note pad.

blocus [blɔkys] nm blockade.

blond, e [blɔ̃, -ɔ̃d] a fair; blond; (sable, blés) golden; **~ cendré** ash blond.

bloquer [blɔke] vt (passage) to block; (pièce mobile) to jam; (crédits, compte) to freeze.

blottir [blɔtiʀ]: **se ~** vi to huddle up.

blouse [bluz] nf overall.

blouson [bluzɔ̃] nm blouson jacket; **~ noir** (fig) ≈ rocker.

bluffer [blœfe] vi to bluff.

bobard [bɔbaʀ] nm (fam) tall story.

bobine [bɔbin] nf reel; (ÉLEC) coil.

bocage [bɔkaʒ] nm grove.

bocal, aux [bɔkal, -o] nm jar.

bock [bɔk] nm glass of beer.

bœuf [bœf, pl bø] nm ox (pl oxen), steer; (CULIN) beef.

bof! [bɔf] excl (fam) don't care!; (: pas terrible) nothing special.

bohème [bɔɛm] a happy-go-lucky, unconventional.

bohémien, ne [bɔemjɛ̃, -jɛn] nm/f gipsy.

boire [bwaʀ] vt to drink; (s'imprégner de) to soak up; **~ un coup** to have a drink.

bois [bwa] nm wood; **de ~, en ~** wooden.

boisé, e [bwaze] a woody, wooded.

boisson [bwasɔ̃] nf drink; **pris de ~** drunk, intoxicated.

boîte [bwat] nf box; (entreprise) place, firm; **aliments en ~** canned ou tinned (Brit) food; **~ d'allumettes** box of matches; (vide) matchbox; **~ (de conserves)** can ou tin (Brit) (of food); **~ à gants** glove compartment; **~ aux lettres** letter box; **~ de nuit** night club; **~ pos-**

tale (B.P.) PO Box; **~ de vitesses** gear box.

boiter [bwate] vi to limp; (fig) to wobble; to be shaky.

boîtier [bwatje] nm case.

boive etc vb voir **boire**.

bol [bɔl] nm bowl; **un ~ d'air** a breath of fresh air.

bolide [bɔlid] nm racing car; **comme un ~** at top speed, like a rocket.

bombance [bɔ̃bɑ̃s] nf: **faire ~** to have a feast, revel.

bombarder [bɔ̃baʀde] vt to bomb; **~ qn de** (cailloux, lettres) to bombard sb with; **bombardier** nm bomber.

bombe [bɔ̃b] nf bomb; (atomiseur) (aerosol) spray.

bomber [bɔ̃be] vi to bulge; to camber // vt: **le torse** to swell out one's chest.

MOT-CLÉ

bon, bonne [bɔ̃, bɔn] ♦ a **1** (agréable, satisfaisant) good; **un ~ repas/ restaurant** a good meal/restaurant; **être ~ en maths** to be good at maths

2 (charitable): **être ~ (envers)** to be good (to)

3 (correct) right; **le ~ numéro/ moment** the right number/moment

4 (souhaits): **~ anniversaire** happy birthday; **~ voyage** have a good trip; **bonne chance** good luck; **bonne année** happy New Year; **bonne nuit** good night

5 (approprié, apte): **~ à/pour** fit to/for

6: ~ enfant a inv accommodating, easy-going; **bonne femme** nf (péj) woman; **de bonne heure** early; **~ marché** a inv, ad cheap; **~ mot** nm witticism; **~ sens** nm common sense; **~ vivant** nm jovial chap; **bonnes œuvres** nfpl charitable works, charities

♦ nm **1** (billet) voucher; (aussi: **~ cadeau**) gift voucher; **~ d'essence** petrol coupon; ~ du Trésor Treasury bond 2: avoir du ~ to have its good points; pour de ~ for good ♦ nf (domestique) maid; bonne d'enfant nanny; bonne à tout faire general help ♦ ad: il fait ~ it's *ou* the weather is fine; sentir ~ to smell good; tenir ~ to stand firm ♦ excl good!; ah ~? really?

bonbon [bɔ̃bɔ̃] nm (boiled) sweet.

bonbonne [bɔ̃bɔn] nf demijohn.

bond [bɔ̃] nm leap; faire un ~ to leap in the air.

bonde [bɔ̃d] nf (d'évier etc) plug; (: trou) plughole; (de tonneau) bung; bunghole.

bondé, e [bɔ̃de] a packed (full).

bondir [bɔ̃diʀ] vi to leap.

bonheur [bɔnœʀ] nm happiness; porter ~ (à qn) to bring (sb) luck; au petit ~ haphazardly; par ~ fortunately.

bonhomie [bɔnɔmi] nf goodnaturedness.

bonhomme [bɔnɔm] nm (pl bonshommes [bɔ̃zɔm]) fellow; ~ de neige snowman.

bonification [bɔnifikasjɔ̃] nf bonus.

bonifier [bɔnifje] vt to improve.

boniment [bɔnimɑ̃] nm patter q.

bonjour [bɔ̃ʒuʀ] excl, nm hello; good morning (ou afternoon).

bonne [bɔn] a, cf voir bon; ~ment ad: tout ~ment quite simply.

bonnet [bɔnɛ] nm bonnet, hat; (de soutien-gorge) cup; ~ d'âne dunce's cap; ~ de bain bathing cap.

bonneterie [bɔnɛtʀi] nf hosiery.

bonsoir [bɔ̃swaʀ] excl good evening.

bonté [bɔ̃te] nf kindness q.

bonus [bɔnys] nm no-claims bonus.

bord [bɔʀ] nm (de table, verre, falaise) edge; (de rivière, lac) bank; (de route) side; (dimensions) à ~ (to go) on board; jeter par-dessus ~ to throw overboard; le commandant/ les hommes du ~ the ship's master/crew; au ~ de la mer at the seaside; être au ~ des larmes to be on the verge of tears.

bordeaux [bɔʀdo] nm Bordeaux (wine) // a inv maroon.

bordel [bɔʀdɛl] nm brothel; (fam!) bloody mess (!).

border [bɔʀde] vt (être le long de) to border; to line (garnir); border sth with; to trim sth with; (qn dans son lit) to tuck up.

bordereau, x [bɔʀdəʀo] nm slip; statement.

bordure [bɔʀdyʀ] nf border; en ~ de on the edge of.

borgne [bɔʀɲ(ə)] a one-eyed.

borne [bɔʀn(ə)] nf boundary stone; (aussi: ~ kilométrique) kilometre-marker; ~ milestone; ~s nfpl (fig) limits; dépasser les ~s to go too far.

borné, e [bɔʀne] a narrow; narrow-minded.

borner [bɔʀne] vt to limit; to confine; se ~ à faire to content o.s. with doing; to limit o.s. to doing.

bosquet [bɔskɛ] nm grove.

bosse [bɔs] nf (de terrain etc) bump; (enflure) lump; (du bossu, du chameau) hump; avoir la ~ des maths etc to have a gift for maths etc; il a roulé sa ~ (fam) he's been around.

bosser [bɔse] vi (fam) to work; to slave (away).

bossu, e [bɔsy] nm/f hunchback.

bot [bo] am: pied ~ club foot.

botanique [bɔtanik] nf botany // a botanic(al).

botte [bɔt] nf (soulier) (high) boot; (gerbe): ~ de paille bundle of straw; ~ de radis bunch of radishes; ~s de caoutchouc wellington boots.

botter [bɔte] vt to put boots on; to kick; (fam!): ça me botte I fancy that.

bottin [bɔtɛ̃] nm directory.

bottine [bɔtin] nf ankle boot.

bouc [buk] nm goat; (barbe) goatee; ~ émissaire scapegoat.

boucan [bukɑ̃] nm din, racket.

bouche [buʃ] *nf* mouth; le ~ à ~ the kiss of life; ~ **d'égout** manhole; ~ **d'incendie** fire hydrant; ~ **de métro** métro entrance.

bouché, e [buʃe] *a* (*temps, ciel*) overcast; (*péj: personne*) thick.

bouchée [buʃe] *nf* mouthful; ~**s à la reine** chicken vol-au-vents.

boucher, ère [buʃe, -ɛʀ] *nm/f* butcher // *vt* (*pour colmater*) to stop up; to fill up; (*obstruer*) to block (up); se ~ **le nez** to hold one's nose; se ~ *vi* (*tuyau etc*) to block up, get blocked up.

boucherie [buʃʀi] *nf* butcher's (shop); (*fig*) slaughter.

bouche-trou [buʃtʀu] *nm* (*fig*) stop-gap.

bouchon [buʃɔ̃] *nm* stopper; (*en liège*) cork; (*fig: embouteillage*) holdup; (*PÊCHE*) float; ~ **doseur** measuring cap.

boucle [bukl(ə)] *nf* (*forme, figure*) loop; (*objet*) buckle; ~ (**de cheveux**) curl; ~ **d'oreilles** earring.

bouclé, e [bukle] *a* curly.

boucler [bukle] *vt* (*fermer: ceinture etc*) to fasten; (: *magasin*) to shut; (*terminer*) to finish off; (: *budget*) to balance; (*enfermer*) to shut away; (: *quartier*) to seal off // *vi* to curl.

bouclier [buklije] *nm* shield.

bouddhiste [budist(ə)] *nm/f* Buddhist.

bouder [bude] *vi* to sulk // *vt* to turn one's nose up at; to refuse to have anything to do with.

boudin [budɛ̃] *nm* (*CULIN*) black pudding.

boue [bu] *nf* mud.

bouée [bwe] *nf* buoy; ~ (**de sauvetage**) lifebuoy.

boueux, euse [bwø, -øz] *a* muddy // *nm* refuse collector.

bouffe [buf] *nf* (*fam*) grub, food.

bouffée [bufe] *nf* puff; ~ **de fièvre/ de honte** flush of fever/shame.

bouffer [bufe] *vi* (*fam*) to eat.

bouffi, e [bufi] *a* swollen.

bouge [buʒ] *nm* (*low*) dive; hovel.

bougeoir [buʒwaʀ] *nm* candlestick.

bougeotte [buʒɔt] *nf*: **avoir la** ~ to have the fidgets.

bouger [buʒe] *vi* to move; (*dent etc*) to be loose; (*changer*) to alter; (*agir*) to stir // *vt* to move.

bougie [buʒi] *nf* candle; (*AUTO*) sparking plug.

bougonner [bugɔne] *vi, vt* to grumble.

bouillabaisse [bujabɛs] *nf* type of fish soup.

bouillant, e [bujɑ̃, -ɑ̃t] *a* (*qui bout*) boiling; (*très chaud*) boiling (hot).

bouillie [buji] *nf* gruel; (*de bébé*) cereal; **en** ~ (*fig*) crushed.

bouillir [bujiʀ] *vi, vt* to boil.

bouilloire [bujwaʀ] *nf* kettle.

bouillon [bujɔ̃] *nm* (*CULIN*) stock q.

bouillonner [bujɔne] *vi* to bubble; (*fig*) to bubble up; to foam.

bouillotte [bujɔt] *nf* hot-water bottle.

boulanger, ère [bulɑ̃ʒe, -ɛʀ] *nm/f* baker.

boulangerie [bulɑ̃ʒʀi] *nf* bakery.

boule [bul] *nf* (*gén*) ball; (*pour jouer*) bowl; (*de machine à écrire*) golf-ball; ~ **de neige** snowball.

bouleau, x [bulo] *nm* (*silver*) birch.

boulet [bulɛ] *nm* (*aussi*: ~ **de canon**) cannonball.

boulette [bulɛt] *nf* ball.

boulevard [bulvaʀ] *nm* boulevard.

bouleversement [bulvɛʀsəmɑ̃] *nm* upheaval.

bouleverser [bulvɛʀse] *vt* (*émouvoir*) to overwhelm; (*causer du chagrin*) to distress; (*pays, vie*) to disrupt; (*papiers, objets*) to turn upside down.

boulier [bulje] *nm* abacus.

boulon [bulɔ̃] *nm* bolt.

boulot [bulo] *nm* (*fam: travail*) work.

boulot, te [bulo, -ɔt] *a* plump, tubby.

boum [bum] *nm* bang // *nf* party.

bouquet [bukɛ] *nm* (*de fleurs*) bunch (of flowers), bouquet; (*de persil etc*) bunch; (*parfum*) bouquet.

bouquin [bukɛ̃] *nm* (*fam*) book; **bouquiner** *vi* to read; to browse around (in a bookshop); **bouquiniste** *nm/f* bookseller.

bourbeux, euse [buʀbø, -øz] *a* muddy.

bourbier [buʀbje] *nm* (quag)mire.

bourde [buʀd(ə)] *nf* (*erreur*) howler; (*gaffe*) blunder.

bourdon [buʀdɔ̃] *nm* bumblebee.

bourdonner [buʀdɔne] *vi* to buzz.

bourg [buʀ] *nm* small market town.

bourgeois, e [buʀʒwa, -waz] *a* (*péj*) ≈ (upper) middle class; bourgeois.

bourgeoisie [buʀʒwazi] *nf* ≈ upper middle classes *pl*; bourgeoisie.

bourgeon [buʀʒɔ̃] *nm* bud.

Bourgogne [buʀɡɔɲ] *nf*: **la** ~ Burgundy // *nm*: **b~** Burgundy (wine).

bourguignon, ne [buʀɡiɲɔ̃, -ɔn] *a* of *ou* from Burgundy, Burgundian.

bourlinguer [buʀlɛ̃ɡe] *vi* to knock about a lot, get around a lot.

bourrade [buʀad] *nf* shove, thump.

bourrage [buʀaʒ] *nm*: ~ **de crâne** brainwashing; (*SCOL*) cramming.

bourrasque [buʀask(ə)] *nf* squall.

bourreau, x [buʀo] *nm* executioner; (*fig*) torturer; ~ **de travail** workaholic.

bourrelet [buʀlɛ] *nm* draught excluder; (*de peau*) fold *ou* roll (of flesh).

bourrer [buʀe] *vt* (*pipe*) to fill; (*poêle*) to pack; (*valise*) to cram (full); ~ **de coups** to hammer blows on, pummel.

bourrique [buʀik] *nf* (*âne*) ass.

bourru, e [buʀy] *a* surly, gruff.

bourse [buʀs(ə)] *nf* (*subvention*) grant; (*porte-monnaie*) purse; **la B~** the Stock Exchange.

boursoufler [buʀsufle] *vt* to puff up, bloat.

bous *vb voir* **bouillir**.

bousculade [buskylad] *nf* rush; crush.

bousculer [buskyle] *vt* to knock over; to knock into; (*fig*) to push, rush.

bouse [buz] *nf* dung *q*.

boussole [busɔl] *nf* compass.

bout [bu] *vb voir* **bouillir** // *nm* bit; (*extrémité: d'un bâton etc*) tip; (: *d'une ficelle, table, rue, période*) end; **au** ~ **de** at the end of, after; **pousser qn à** ~ to push sb to the limit; **venir à** ~ **de** to manage to finish; **à** ~ **portant** at point-blank range; ~ **filtre** filter tip.

boutade [butad] *nf* quip, sally.

boute-en-train [butɑ̃tʀɛ̃] *nm inv* live wire (*fig*).

bouteille [butɛj] *nf* bottle; (*de gaz butane*) cylinder.

boutique [butik] *nf* shop; **boutiquier, ière** *nm/f* shopkeeper.

bouton [butɔ̃] *nm* button; (*BOT*) bud; (*sur la peau*) spot; (*de porte*) knob; ~ **de manchette** cuff-link; ~ **d'or** buttercup; **boutonner** *vt* to button up; **boutonnière** *nf* buttonhole; ~-**pression** *nm* press stud.

bouture [butyʀ] *nf* cutting.

bovins [bɔvɛ̃] *nmpl* cattle.

bowling [bɔliŋ] *nm* (tenpin) bowling; (*salle*) bowling alley.

box [bɔks] *nm* lock-up (garage); (*d'écurie*) loose-box.

boxe [bɔks(ə)] *nf* boxing.

boyau, x [bwajo] *nm* (*galerie*) passage(way); (narrow) gallery // *nmpl* (*viscères*) entrails, guts.

B.P. *abr de* **boîte postale**.

bracelet [bʀaslɛ] *nm* bracelet; ~-**montre** *nf* wristwatch.

braconnier [bʀakɔnje] *nm* poacher.

brader [bʀade] *vt* to sell off; **braderie** [bʀadʀi] *nf* cut-price shop *ou* stall.

braguette [bʀaɡɛt] *nf* fly *ou* flies *pl* (*Brit*), zipper (*US*).

brailler [bʀaje] *vi* to bawl, yell.

braire [bʀɛʀ] *vi* to bray.

braise [bʀɛz] *nf* embers *pl*.

brancard [bʀɑ̃kaʀ] *nm* (*civière*) stretcher; (*bras, perche*) shaft; **brancardier** *nm* stretcher-bearer.

branchages [bʀɑ̃ʃaʒ] *nmpl* boughs.

branche [bʀɑ̃ʃ] *nf* branch.

branché, e [brɑ̃ʃe] *a* (*fam*) trendy.

brancher [brɑ̃ʃe] *vt* to connect (up); (*en mettant la prise*) to plug in.

branle [brɑ̃l] *nm*: **donner le ~ à**, **mettre en ~** to set in motion.

branle-bas [brɑ̃lba] *nm inv* commotion.

branler [brɑ̃le] *vi* to be shaky // *vt*: **~ la tête** to shake one's head.

braquer [brake] *vi* (*AUTO*) to turn (the wheel) // *vt* (*revolver etc*): **~ qch sur** to aim sth at, point sth at; (*mettre en colère*): **~ qn** to put sb's back up.

bras [bra] *nm ans* // *nmpl* (*fig: travailleurs*) labour *sg*, hands; **saisir qn à ~-le-corps** to take hold of sb (a)round the waist; **à ~ raccourcis** with fists flying; **~ droit** (*fig*) right hand man.

brasier [brazje] *nm* blaze, inferno.

brassard [brasar] *nm* armband.

brasse [bras] *nf* (*nage*) breaststroke; **~ papillon** butterfly.

brassée [brase] *nf* armful.

brasser [brase] *vt* to mix; **~ l'argent/les affaires** to handle a lot of money/business.

brasserie [brasri] *nf* (*restaurant*) café-restaurant; (*usine*) brewery.

bravache [bravaʃ] *nm* blusterer, braggart.

brave [brav] *a* (*courageux*) brave; (*bon, gentil*) good, kind.

braver [brave] *vt* to defy.

bravo [bravo] *excl* bravo // *nm* cheer.

bravoure [bravur] *nf* bravery.

break [brɛk] *nm* (*AUTO*) estate car.

brebis [brəbi] *nf* ewe; **~ galeuse** black sheep.

brèche [brɛʃ] *nf* breach, gap; **être sur la ~** (*fig*) to be on the go.

bredouille [brəduj] *a* empty-handed.

bredouiller [brəduje] *vi, vt* to mumble, stammer.

bref, brève [brɛf, brɛv] *a* short, brief // *ad* in short; **d'un ton ~** sharply, curtly; **en ~** in short, in brief.

Brésil [brezil] *nm* Brazil.

Bretagne [brətaɲ] *nf* Brittany.

bretelle [brətɛl] *nf* (*de fusil etc*) sling; (*de vêtement*) strap; (*d'autoroute*) slip road (*Brit*), entrance/exit ramp (*US*); **~s** *nfpl* (*pour pantalon*) braces (*Brit*), suspenders (*US*).

breton, ne [brətɔ̃, -ɔn] *a, nm/f* Breton.

breuvage [brœvaʒ] *nm* beverage, drink.

brève [brɛv] *a, nf voir* **bref**.

brevet [brəvɛ] *nm* diploma, certificate; **~ (d'invention)** patent; **~ d'études du premier cycle** (*B.E.P.C.*) *school certificate* (*taken at age 16*); **breveté, e** *a* patented; (*diplômé*) qualified.

bribes [brib] *nfpl* bits, scraps; snatches; **par ~** piecemeal.

bricolage [brikɔlaʒ] *nm*: **le ~** do-it-yourself.

bricole [brikɔl] *nf* trifle; small job.

bricoler [brikɔle] *vi* to do DIY jobs; to potter about // *vt* to fix up; to tinker with; **bricoleur, euse** *nm/f* handyman/woman, DIY enthusiast.

bride [brid] *nf* bridle; (*d'un bonnet*) string, tie; **à ~ abattue** flat out, hell for leather; **laisser la ~ sur le cou à** to give free rein to.

bridé, e [bride] *a*: **yeux ~s** slit eyes.

brider [bride] *vt* (*réprimer*) to keep in check; (*cheval*) to bridle; (*CULIN: volaille*) to truss.

bridge [bridʒ(ə)] *nm* bridge.

brièvement [brijɛvmɑ̃] *ad* briefly.

brigade [brigad] *nf* (*POLICE*) squad; (*MIL*) brigade; (*gén*) team.

brigadier [brigadje] *nm* sergeant.

brigandage [brigɑ̃daʒ] *nm* robbery.

briguer [brige] *vt* to aspire to.

brillamment [brijamɑ̃] *ad* brilliantly.

brillant, e [brijɑ̃, -ɑ̃t] *a* brilliant; bright; (*luisant*) shiny, shining // *nm* (*diamant*) brilliant.

briller [brije] *vi* to shine.

brimer [brime] *vt* to harass; to bully.

brin [brɛ̃] nm (de laine, ficelle etc) strand; (fig): **un ~ de** a bit of; **~ d'herbe** blade of grass; **~ de muguet** sprig of lily of the valley.

brindille [brɛ̃dij] nf twig.

brio [brijo] nm: **avec ~** with panache.

brioche [brijɔʃ] nf brioche (bun); (fam: ventre) paunch.

brique [brik] nf brick // a inv brick red.

briquer [brike] vt to polish up.

briquet [brikɛ] nm (cigarette) lighter.

brise [briz] nf breeze.

briser [brize] vt, **se ~** vi to break.

britannique [britanik] a British // nm/f British person, Briton; **les B~s** the British.

broc [brɔ] nm pitcher.

brocante [brɔkɑ̃t] nf junk, secondhand goods pl.

brocanteur, euse [brɔkɑ̃tœr, -øz] nm/f junkshop owner; junk dealer.

broche [brɔʃ] nf brooch; (CULIN) spit; (MÉD) pin; **à la ~** spit-roasted.

broché, e [brɔʃe] a (livre) paperbacked.

brochet [brɔʃɛ] nm pike inv.

brochette [brɔʃɛt] nf skewer.

brochure [brɔʃyr] nf pamphlet, brochure, booklet.

broder [brɔde] vt to embroider // vi to embroider the facts; **broderie** [brɔdri] nf embroidery.

broncher [brɔ̃ʃe] vi: **sans ~** without flinching; without turning a hair.

bronches [brɔ̃ʃ] nfpl bronchial tubes; **bronchite** [brɔ̃ʃit] nf bronchitis.

bronze [brɔ̃z] nm bronze.

bronzer [brɔ̃ze] vt to tan // vi to get a tan; **se ~** to sunbathe.

brosse [brɔs] nf brush; **coiffé en ~** with a crewcut; **~ à cheveux** hairbrush; **~ à dents** toothbrush; **~ à habits** clothesbrush; **brosser** vt (nettoyer) to brush; (fig: tableau etc) to paint; to draw; **se brosser les dents** to brush one's teeth.

brouette [bruɛt] nf wheelbarrow.

brouhaha [bruaa] nm hubbub.

brouillard [brujar] nm fog.

brouille [bruj] nf quarrel.

brouiller [bruje] vt to mix up; to confuse; (rendre trouble) to cloud; (désunir: amis) to set at odds; **se ~** vi (vue) to cloud over; (détails) to become confused; (gens) to fall out.

brouillon, ne [brujɔ̃, -ɔn] a disorganised; unmethodical // nm draft.

broussailles [brusɑj] nfpl undergrowth sg; **broussailleux, euse** a bushy.

brousse [brus] nf: **la ~** the bush.

brouter [brute] vt to graze.

broutille [brutij] nf trifle.

broyer [brwaje] vt to crush; **~ du noir** to be down in the dumps.

bru [bry] nf daughter-in-law.

bruiner [brɥine] vb impersonnel: **il bruine** it's drizzling, there's a drizzle.

bruire [brɥir] vi to murmur; to rustle.

bruit [brɥi] nm: **un ~** a noise, a sound; (fig: rumeur) a rumour; **le ~** noise; **sans ~** without a sound, noiselessly; **~ de fond** background noise.

bruitage [brɥitaʒ] nm sound effects pl.

brûlant, e [brylɑ̃, -ɑ̃t] a burning; (liquide) boiling (hot); (regard) fiery.

brûlé, e [bryle] a (fig: démasqué) blown // nm: **odeur de ~** smell of burning.

brûle-pourpoint [brylpurpwɛ̃]: **à ~ ad** point-blank.

brûler [bryle] vt to burn; (suj: eau bouillante) to scald; (consommer: électricité, essence) to use; (feu rouge, signal) to go through // vi to burn; (jeu) to be warm; **se ~** to burn o.s.; to scald o.s.; **se ~ la cervelle** to blow one's brains out.

brûlure [brylyr] nf (lésion) burn; (sensation) burning (sensation); **~s d'estomac** heartburn sg.

brume [brym] nf mist.

brun, e [brœ̃, -yn] a (brown); (che-

veux, personne) dark; **brunir** *vi* to
get a tan.

brusque [bʀysk(ə)] *a* abrupt;
~ment *ad* abruptly; **brusquer** *vt*
to rush.

brut, e [bʀyt] *a* raw, crude, rough;
(COMM) gross; *(données)* raw // *nf*
brute; **(pétrole)** ~ crude (oil).

brutal, e, aux [bʀytal, -o] *a* brutal;
~iser *vt* to handle roughly, manhandle.

brute [bʀyt] *a, nf voir* **brut.**

Bruxelles [bʀysɛl] *n* Brussels.

bruyamment [bʀɥijamɑ̃] *ad* noisily.

bruyant, e [bʀɥijɑ̃, -ɑ̃t] *a* noisy.

bruyère [bʀyjɛʀ] *nf* heather.

bu, e *pp de* **boire.**

buccal, e, aux [bykal, -o] *a*: **par
voie ~e** orally.

bûche [byʃ] *nf* log; **prendre une ~**
(fig) to come a cropper; **~ de Noël**
Yule log.

bûcher [byʃe] *nm* pyre; bonfire // *vb*
(fam) vi to swot *(Brit)*, slave (away)
// *vt* to swot up *(Brit)*, slave away at.

bûcheron [byʃʀɔ̃] *nm* woodcutter.

budget [bydʒɛ] *nm* budget.

buée [bɥe] *nf* *(sur une vitre)* mist;
(de l'haleine) steam.

buffet [byfɛ] *nm* *(meuble)* sideboard;
(de réception) buffet; **~ (de gare)**
(station) buffet, snack bar.

buffle [byfl(ə)] *nm* buffalo.

buis [bɥi] *nm* box tree; *(bois)*
box(wood).

buisson [bɥisɔ̃] *nm* bush.

buissonnière [bɥisɔnjɛʀ] *af*: **faire
l'école ~** to skip school.

bulbe [bylb(ə)] *nm* *(BOT, ANAT)*
bulb; *(coupole)* onion-shaped dome.

Bulgarie [bylgaʀi] *nf* Bulgaria.

bulle [byl] *nf* bubble; *(papale)* bull.

bulletin [byltɛ̃] *nm* *(communiqué,
journal)* bulletin; *(papier)* form;
(SCOL) report; **~ d'informations**
news bulletin; **~ météorologique**
weather report; **~ de salaire** pay-
slip; **~ de santé** medical bulletin; **~
(de vote)** ballot paper.

bureau, x [byʀo] *nm* *(meuble)* desk;

(pièce, service) office; **~ de change**
(foreign) exchange office *ou* bureau;
~ d'embauche employment office;
~ de location box office; **~ de
poste** post office; **~ de tabac** tobacconist's (shop); **~ de vote** polling
station; **~cratie** [-kʀasi] *nf* bureaucracy.

burin [byʀɛ̃] *nm* cold chisel; *(ART)*
burin.

burlesque [byʀlɛsk(ə)] *a* ridiculous;
(LITTÉRATURE) burlesque.

bus *vb* [by] *voir* **boire** // *nm* [bys]
bus.

busqué, e [byske] *a (nez)* hook(ed).

buste [byst(ə)] *nm* *(ANAT)* chest;
bust.

but [by] *vb voir* **boire** // *nm* *(cible)*
target; *(fig)* goal; aim; *(FOOTBALL
etc)* goal; **de ~ en blanc** point-
blank; **avoir pour ~ de faire** to
aim to do; **dans le ~ de** with the intention of.

butane [bytan] *nm* butane; Calor gas
®.

buter [byte] *vi*: **~ contre/sur** to
bump into; to stumble against // *vt* to
antagonize; **se ~** *vi* to get obstinate;
to dig in one's heels.

butin [bytɛ̃] *nm* booty, spoils *pl*;
(d'un vol) loot.

butte [byt] *nf* mound, hillock; **être
en ~ à** to be exposed to.

buvais *etc vb voir* **boire.**

buvard [byvaʀ] *nm* blotter.

buvette [byvɛt] *nf* bar.

buveur, euse [byvœʀ, -øz] *nm/f*
drinker.

C

c' [s] *dét voir* **ce.**

CA *sigle m de* **chiffre d'affaires.**

ça [sa] *pronom (pour désigner)* this;
(: plus loin) that; *(comme sujet indéfini)* it; **~ va?** how are you?; how
are things?; *(d'accord?)* OK?, all
right?; **~ alors!** well really!; **~ fait
10 ans (que)** it's 10 years (since);

c'est ~ that's right.

çà [sa] *ad:* ~ **et là** here and there.

cabane [kaban] *nf* hut, shack.

cabaret [kabaʀɛ] *nm* night club.

cabas [kabɑ] *nm* shopping bag.

cabillaud [kabijo] *nm* cod *inv.*

cabine [kabin] *nf (de bateau)* cabin; *(de plage)* beach hut; *(de piscine etc)* cubicle; *(de camion, train)* cab; *(d'avion)* cockpit; ~ **d'essayage** fitting room; ~ **spatiale** space capsule; ~ **(téléphonique)** call *ou* (tele)phone box.

cabinet [kabinɛ] *nm (petite pièce)* closet; *(de médecin)* surgery *(Brit)*, office *(US)*; *(de notaire etc)* office; *(: clientèle)* practice; *(POL)* Cabinet; ~**s** *nmpl (w.-c.)* toilet *sg*; ~ **d'affaires** business consultants' *(bureau)*, business partnership; ~ **de toilette** toilet; ~ **de travail** study.

câble [kɑbl(ə)] *nm* cable.

cabrer [kɑbʀe]: **se** ~ *vi (cheval)* to rear up; *(avion)* to nose up; *(fig)* to revolt, rebel.

cabriole [kabʀijɔl] *nf* caper; somersault.

cacahuète [kakaɥɛt] *nf* peanut.

cacao [kakao] *nm* cocoa (powder); *(boisson)* cocoa.

cache [kaʃ] *nm* mask, card (for masking) // *nf* hiding place.

cache-cache [kaʃkaʃ] *nm:* **jouer à** ~ to play hide-and-seek.

cachemire [kaʃmiʀ] *nm* cashmere.

cache-nez [kaʃne] *nm inv* scarf, muffler.

cacher [kaʃe] *vt* to hide, conceal; ~ **qch à qn** to hide *ou* conceal sth from sb; **se** ~ *vi* to hide; to be hidden *ou* concealed; **il ne s'en cache pas** he makes no secret of it.

cachet [kaʃɛ] *nm (comprimé)* tablet; *(sceau: du roi)* seal; *(: de la poste)* postmark; *(rétribution)* fee; *(fig)* style, character; **cacheter** *vt* to seal.

cachette [kaʃɛt] *nf* hiding place; **en** ~ on the sly, secretly.

cachot [kaʃo] *nm* dungeon.

cactus [kaktys] *nm* cactus.

cadavre [kadavʀ(ə)] *nm* corpse, (dead) body.

caddie [kadi] *nm* (supermarket) trolley.

cadeau, x [kado] *nm* present, gift; **faire un** ~ **à qn** to give sb a present *ou* gift; **faire** ~ **de qch à qn** to make a present of sth to sb, give sb sth as a present.

cadenas [kadna] *nm* padlock.

cadence [kadɑ̃s] *nf (MUS)* cadence; *(: tempo)* rhythm; *(de travail etc)* rate; **en** ~ rhythmically; in time.

cadet, te [kadɛ, -ɛt] *a* younger; *(le plus jeune)* youngest // *nm/f* youngest child *ou* one, youngest boy *ou* son/girl *ou* daughter.

cadran [kadʀɑ̃] *nm* dial; ~ **solaire** sundial.

cadre [kɑdʀ(ə)] *nm* frame; *(environnement)* surroundings *pl*; *(limites)* scope // *nm/f (ADMIN)* managerial employee, executive; **rayer qn des** ~**s** to dismiss sb; **dans le** ~ **de** *(fig)* within the framework *ou* context of.

cadrer [kɑdʀe] *vi:* ~ **avec** to tally *ou* correspond with // *vt* to centre.

caduc, uque [kadyk] *a* obsolete; *(BOT)* deciduous.

cafard [kafaʀ] *nm* cockroach; **avoir le** ~ to be down in the dumps.

café [kafe] *nm* coffee; *(bistro)* café // *a inv* coffee(-coloured); ~ **au lait** white coffee; ~ **noir** black coffee; ~ **tabac** tobacconist's *ou* newsagent's also serving coffee and spirits; **cafetier, ière** *nm* café-owner // *nf (pot)* coffee-pot.

cafouillage [kafuja3] *nm* shambles *sg.*

cage [ka3] *nf* cage; ~ **(des buts)** goal; ~ **d'escalier** (stair)well; ~ **thoracique** rib cage.

cageot [ka3o] *nm* crate.

cagibi [ka3ibi] *nm* shed.

cagneux, euse [kaɲø, -øz] *a* knock-kneed.

cagnotte [kaɲɔt] *nf* kitty.

cagoule [kagul] *nf* cowl; hood; *(SKI*

etc) cagoule.

cahier [kaje] *nm* notebook; ~ de brouillons roughbook, jotter; ~ d'exercices exercise book.

cahot [kao] *nm* jolt, bump.

caïd [kaid] *nm* big chief, boss.

caille [kaj] *nf* quail.

cailler [kaje] *vi (lait)* to curdle; *(sang)* to clot.

caillot [kajo] *nm* (blood) clot.

caillou, x [kaju] *nm* (little) stone; ~teux, euse *a* stony; pebbly.

Caire [kɛʀ] *nm*: le ~ Cairo.

caisse [kɛs] *nf* box; *(où l'on met la recette)* cashbox; till; *(où l'on paye)* cash desk *(Brit)*, check-out; *(de banque)* cashier's desk; *(TECH)* case, casing; ~ enregistreuse cash register; ~ d'épargne savings bank; ~ de retraite pension fund; **caissier, ière** *nm/f* cashier.

cajoler [kaʒɔle] *vt* to wheedle, coax; to surround with love.

cake [kɛk] *nm* fruit cake.

calandre [kalɑ̃dʀ(ə)] *nf* radiator grill.

calanque [kalɑ̃k] *nf* rocky inlet.

calcaire [kalkɛʀ] *nm* limestone // *a (eau)* hard; *(GEO)* limestone *cpd*.

calciné, e [kalsine] *a* burnt to ashes.

calcul [kalkyl] *nm* calculation; le ~ *(SCOL)* arithmetic; ~ *(biliaire)* (gall)stone; ~ *(rénal)* (kidney) stone; ~ateur *nm*, ~atrice *nf* calculator.

calculer [kalkyle] *vt* to calculate, work out; *(combiner)* to calculate.

calculette [kalkylɛt] *nf* pocket calculator.

cale [kal] *nf (de bateau)* hold; *(en bois)* wedge; ~ sèche dry dock.

calé, e [kale] *a (fam)* clever, bright.

caleçon [kalsɔ̃] *nm* pair of underpants, trunks *pl*; ~ de bain bathing trunks *pl*.

calembour [kalɑ̃buʀ] *nm* pun.

calendes [kalɑ̃d] *nfpl*: renvoyer aux ~ grecques to postpone indefinitely.

calendrier [kalɑ̃dʀije] *nm* calendar;

(fig) timetable.

calepin [kalpɛ̃] *nm* notebook.

caler [kale] *vt* to wedge; ~ *(son moteur/véhicule)* to stall (one's engine/vehicle).

calfeutrer [kalføtʀe] *vt* to (make) draughtproof; se ~ *vi* to make o.s. snug and comfortable.

calibre [kalibʀ(ə)] *nm (d'un fruit)* grade; *(d'une arme)* bore, calibre; *(fig)* calibre.

califourchon [kalifuʀʃɔ̃]: à ~ *ad* astride.

câlin, e [kalɛ̃, -in] *a* a cuddly, cuddlesome; tender.

câliner [kaline] *vt* to fondle, cuddle.

calmant [kalmɑ̃] *nm* tranquillizer, sedative; *(pour la douleur)* painkiller.

calme [kalm(ə)] *a* calm, quiet // *nm* calm(ness), quietness.

calmer [kalme] *vt* to calm (down); *(douleur, inquiétude)* to ease, soothe; se ~ *vi* to calm down.

calomnie [kalɔmni] *nf* slander; *(écrite)* libel; **calomnier** *vt* to slander; to libel.

calorie [kalɔʀi] *nf* calorie.

calorifuge [kalɔʀify3] *a* (heat-) insulating, heat-retaining.

calotte [kalɔt] *nf (coiffure)* skullcap; *(gifle)* slap.

calquer [kalke] *vt* to trace; *(fig)* to copy exactly.

calvaire [kalvɛʀ] *nm (croix)* wayside cross, calvary; *(souffrances)* suffering.

calvitie [kalvisi] *nf* baldness.

camarade [kamaʀad] *nm/f* friend, pal; *(POL)* comrade; ~rie *nf* friendship.

cambiste [kɑ̃bist(ə)] *nm (COMM)* foreign exchange dealer, exchange agent.

cambouis [kɑ̃bwi] *nm* dirty oil ou grease.

cambrer [kɑ̃bʀe] *vt* to arch.

cambriolage [kɑ̃bʀijɔlaʒ] *nm* burglary.

cambrioler [kɑ̃bʀijɔle] *vt* to burgle

(*Brit*), burglarize (*US*); **cambrioleur, euse** *nm/f* burglar.

came [kam] *nf*: **arbre à ~s** camshaft.

camelot [kamlo] *nm* street pedlar.

camelote [kamlɔt] *nf* rubbish, trash, junk.

caméra [kameʀa] *nf* (*CINÉMA*, *TV*) camera; (*d'amateur*) cine-camera.

camion [kamjɔ̃] *nm* lorry (*Brit*), truck; (*plus petit, pour lait*) ~ **de dépannage** breakdown (*Brit*) ou tow (*US*) truck; ~**-citerne** *nm* tanker; **camionnage** *nm* haulage (*Brit*), trucking (*US*); **camionnette** *nf* (small) van; **camionneur** *nm* (*entrepreneur*) haulage contractor (*Brit*), trucker (*US*); (*chauffeur*) lorry (*Brit*) ou truck driver; van driver.

camisole [kamizɔl] *nf*: ~ (**de force**) straitjacket.

camomille [kamɔmij] *nf* camomile; (*boisson*) camomile tea.

camoufler [kamufle] *vt* to camouflage; (*fig*) to conceal, cover up.

camp [kɑ̃] *nm* camp; (*fig*) side.

campagnard, e [kɑ̃paɲaʀ, -aʀd(ə)] a country *cpd*.

campagne [kɑ̃paɲ] *nf* country, countryside; (*MIL*, *POL*, *COMM*) campaign; **à la** ~ in the country.

camper [kɑ̃pe] *vi* to camp // *vt* to sketch; **se** ~ **devant** to plant o.s. in front of; **campeur, euse** *nm/f* camper.

camphre [kɑ̃fʀ(ə)] *nm* camphor.

camping [kɑ̃piŋ] *nm* camping; (**terrain de**) ~ campsite, camping site; **faire du** ~ to go camping.

Canada [kanada] *nm*: **le** ~ **Canada**; **canadien, ne** a, *nm/f* Canadian // (*veste*) fur-lined jacket.

canaille [kanaj] *nf* (*péj*) scoundrel.

canal, aux [kanal, -o] *nm* canal; (*naturel*) channel.

canalisation [kanalizasjɔ̃] *nf* (*tuyau*) pipe.

canaliser [kanalize] *vt* to canalize; (*fig*) to channel.

canapé [kanape] *nm* settee, sofa.

canard [kanaʀ] *nm* duck.

canari [kanaʀi] *nm* canary.

cancans [kɑ̃kɑ̃] *nmpl* (malicious) gossip *sg*.

cancer [kɑ̃seʀ] *nm* cancer; (*signe*): **le C~** Cancer.

cancre [kɑ̃kʀ(ə)] *nm* dunce.

candeur [kɑ̃dœʀ] *nf* ingenuousness, guilelessness.

candi [kɑ̃di] a inv: **sucre** ~ (sugar-) candy.

candidat, e [kɑ̃dida, -at] *nm/f* candidate; (*à un poste*) applicant, candidate; **candidature** *nf* candidature; application; **poser sa candidature** to submit an application, apply.

candide [kɑ̃did] a ingenuous, guileless.

cane [kan] *nf* (female) duck.

caneton [kantɔ̃] *nm* duckling.

canette [kanet] *nf* (*de bière*) (fliptop) bottle.

canevas [kanva] *nm* (*COUTURE*) canvas.

caniche [kaniʃ] *nm* poodle.

canicule [kanikyl] *nf* scorching heat.

canif [kanif] *nm* penknife, pocket knife.

canine [kanin] *nf* canine (tooth).

caniveau, x [kanivo] *nm* gutter.

canne [kan] *nf* (walking) stick; ~ **à pêche** fishing rod; ~ **à sucre** sugar cane.

cannelle [kanel] *nf* cinnamon.

canoë [kanɔe] *nm* canoe; (*sport*) canoeing.

canon [kanɔ̃] *nm* (*arme*) gun; (*HISTOIRE*) cannon; (*d'une arme: tube*) barrel; (*fig*) model; (*MUS*) canon; ~ **rayé** rifled barrel.

canot [kano] *nm* ding(h)y; ~ **pneumatique** inflatable ding(h)y; ~ **de sauvetage** lifeboat; **canotage** *nm* rowing.

canotier [kanɔtje] *nm* boater.

cantatrice [kɑ̃tatʀis] *nf* (opera) singer.

cantine [kɑ̃tin] *nf* canteen.

cantique [kɑ̃tik] *nm* hymn.

canton [kɑ̃tɔ̃] *nm* district consisting

of several communes; **(en Suisse)** canton.

cantonade [kɑ̃tɔnad]: **à la ~** ad to everyone in general; from the roof-tops.

cantonner [kɑ̃tɔne] vt (MIL) to quarter, station; **se ~ dans** to confine o.s. to.

cantonnier [kɑ̃tɔnje] nm roadmender.

canular [kanylar] nm hoax.

caoutchouc [kautʃu] nm rubber; **~ mousse** foam rubber.

cap [kap] nm (GÉO) cape; headland; (fig) hurdle; watershed; (NAVIG): **changer de ~** to change course; **mettre le ~ sur** to head ou steer for.

C.A.P. sigle m (= Certificat d'aptitude professionnelle) vocational training certificate taken at secondary school.

capable [kapabl(ə)] a able, capable; **~ de qch/faire** capable of sth/doing.

capacité [kapasite] nf (compétence) ability; (JUR, contenance) capacity; **~ (en droit)** basic legal qualification.

cape [kap] nf cape, cloak; **rire sous ~** to laugh up one's sleeve.

C.A.P.E.S. [kapεs] sigle m (= Certificat d'aptitude pédagogique à l'enseignement secondaire) teaching diploma.

capillaire [kapilεr] a (soins, lotion) hair cpd; (vaisseau etc) capillary.

capitaine [kapiten] nm captain; **~ des pompiers** fire chief, firemaster.

capital, e, aux [kapital, -o] a major; of paramount importance; fundamental // nm capital; (fig) stock; asset // nf (ville) capital; (lettre) capital (letter); **~ (social)** authorized capital // nmpl (fonds) capital sg; **~ (social)** authorized capital; **~iser** vt to amass, build up; **~isme** nm capitalism; **~iste** a, nm/f capitalist.

capiteux, euse [kapitø, -øz] a heady.

capitonné, e [kapitɔne] a padded.

caporal, aux [kapɔral, -o] nm lance corporal.

capot [kapo] nm (AUTO) bonnet (Brit), hood (US).

capote [kapɔt] nf (de voiture) hood (Brit), top (US); (fam) condom.

capoter [kapɔte] vi to overturn.

câpre [kɑpr(ə)] nf caper.

caprice [kapris] nm whim, caprice; passing fancy; **capricieux, euse** a capricious; whimsical; temperamental.

Capricorne [kaprikɔrn] nm: **le ~** Capricorn.

capsule [kapsyl] nf (de bouteille) cap; (BOT etc, spatiale) capsule.

capter [kapte] vt (ondes radio) to pick up; (eau) to harness; (fig) to win, capture.

captieux, euse [kapsjø, -øz] a specious.

captivité [kaptivite] nf captivity.

capturer [kaptyre] vt to capture.

capuche [kapyʃ] nf hood.

capuchon [kapyʃɔ̃] nm hood; (de stylo) cap, top.

capucine [kapysin] nf (BOT) nasturtium.

caquet [kake] nm: **rabattre le ~ à qn** to bring sb down a peg or two.

caqueter [kakte] vi to cackle.

car [kar] nm coach // cj because, for.

carabine [karabin] nf carbine, rifle.

caractère [karaktεr] nm (gén) character; en **~s gras** in bold type; en petits **~s** in small print; en **~s d'imprimerie** (block) capitals; avoir bon/mauvais **~** to be good-ill-natured; **caractériel, le** a (of) character // nm/f emotionally disturbed child.

caractérisé, e [karakterize] a: **c'est une grippe ~e** it is a clear(-cut) case of flu.

caractéristique [karakteristik] a, nf characteristic.

carafe [karaf] nf decanter; carafe.

caraïbe [karaib] a Caribbean // n: **les C~s** the Caribbean (Islands); **la mer des C~s** the Caribbean Sea.

carambolage [kaʀɑ̃bɔlaʒ] *nm* multiple crash, pileup.

caramel [kaʀamɛl] *nm* (*bonbon*) caramel, toffee; (*substance*) caramel.

carapace [kaʀapas] *nf* shell.

caravane [kaʀavan] *nf* caravan; **caravaning** *nm* caravanning; (*emplacement*) caravan site.

carbone [kaʀbɔn] *nm* carbon; (*feuille*) carbon, sheet of carbon paper; (*double*) carbon (copy).

carbonique [kaʀbɔnik] *a:* neige ~ dry ice.

carbonisé, e [kaʀbɔnize] *a* charred.

carboniser [kaʀbɔnize] *vt* to carbonize; to burn down, reduce to ashes.

carburant [kaʀbyʀɑ̃] *nm* (motor) fuel.

carburateur [kaʀbyʀatœʀ] *nm* carburettor.

carcan [kaʀkɑ̃] *nm* (*fig*) yoke, shackles *pl*.

carcasse [kaʀkas] *nf* carcass; (*de véhicule etc*) shell.

cardiaque [kaʀdjak] *a* cardiac, heart *cpd* // *nm/f* heart patient.

cardigan [kaʀdigɑ̃] *nm* cardigan.

cardiologue [kaʀdjɔlɔg] *nm/f* cardiologist, heart specialist.

carême [kaʀɛm] *nm:* le C~ Lent.

carence [kaʀɑ̃s] *nf* incompetence, inadequacy; (*manque*) deficiency.

caresse [kaʀɛs] *nf* caress.

caresser [kaʀese] *vt* to caress, fondle; (*fig: projet*) to toy with.

cargaison [kaʀgɛzɔ̃] *nf* cargo, freight.

cargo [kaʀgo] *nm* cargo boat, freighter.

carie [kaʀi] *nf:* la ~ (*dentaire*) tooth decay; une ~ a bad tooth.

carillon [kaʀijɔ̃] *nm* (*d'église*) bells *pl*; (*de pendule*) chimes *pl*; (*de porte*) door chime ou bell.

carlingue [kaʀlɛ̃g] *nf* cabin.

carnassier, ière [kaʀnasje, -jɛʀ] *a* carnivorous.

carnaval [kaʀnaval] *nm* carnival.

carnet [kaʀnɛ] *nm* (*calepin*) notebook; (*de tickets, timbres etc*) book; (*d'école*) school report; (*journal intime*) diary; ~ de chèques cheque book.

carotte [kaʀɔt] *nf* carrot.

carpette [kaʀpɛt] *nf* rug.

carré, e [kaʀe] *a* square; (*fig: franc*) straightforward // *nm* (*de terrain, jardin*) patch, plot; (*MATH*) square; mètre/ kilomètre ~ square metre/kilometre.

carreau, x [kaʀo] *nm* (*en faïence etc*) (floor) tile; (*wall*) tile; (*de fenêtre*) (window) pane; (*motif*) check, square; (*CARTES: couleur*) diamonds *pl*; (*: carte*) diamond; tissu à ~x checked fabric.

carrefour [kaʀfuʀ] *nm* crossroads *sg*.

carrelage [kaʀlaʒ] *nm* tiling; (tiled) floor.

carrelet [kaʀlɛ] *nm* (*poisson*) plaice.

carrément [kaʀemɑ̃] *ad* straight out, bluntly; completely, altogether.

carrer [kaʀe]: **se ~** *vi*: se ~ dans to settle o.s. comfortably in.

carrière [kaʀjɛʀ] *nf* (*de roches*) quarry; (*métier*) career; militaire de ~ professional soldier.

carriole [kaʀjɔl] *nf* (*péj*) old cart.

carrossable [kaʀɔsabl(ə)] *a* suitable for (motor) vehicles.

carrosse [kaʀɔs] *nm* (horse-drawn) coach.

carrosserie [kaʀɔsʀi] *nf* body, coachwork *q*; (*activité, commerce*) coachbuilding.

carrousel [kaʀuzɛl] *nm* (*ÉQUITATION*) carousel; (*fig*) merry-go-round.

carrure [kaʀyʀ] *nf* build; (*fig*) stature, calibre.

cartable [kaʀtabl(ə)] *nm* (*d'écolier*) satchel, (school)bag.

carte [kaʀt(ə)] *nf* (*de géographie*) map; (*marine, du ciel*) chart; (*de fichier, d'abonnement etc, à jouer*) card; (*au restaurant*) menu; (*aussi:* ~ postale) (post)card; (*aussi:* ~ de visite) (visiting) card; à la ~ (au *restaurant*) à la carte; ~ **bancaire** cash card; ~ **de crédit** credit card; **la** ~ **grise** (AUTO) ≈ the (car) registration book, the logbook; ~ **d'identité** identity card; ~ **routière** road map; ~ **de séjour** residence permit.

carter [kaʀtɛʀ] nm sump.

carton [kaʀtɔ̃] nm (matériau) cardboard; (boîte) (cardboard) box; (d'invitation) invitation card; **faire un** ~ (au tir) to have a go at the rifle range; to score a hit; ~ (à dessin) portfolio; **cartonné, e** a (livre) hardback, cased; ~-**pâte** nm pasteboard.

cartouche [kaʀtuʃ] nf cartridge; (de cigarettes) carton.

cas [kɑ] nm case; **faire peu de / grand** ~ **de** to attach little/great importance to; **en aucun** ~ on no account; **au** ~ **où** in case; **en** ~ **de** in case of, in the event of; **en** ~ **de besoin** if need be; **en tout** ~ in any case, at any rate; ~ **de conscience** matter of conscience.

casanier, ière [kazanje, -jɛʀ] a/nm/f stay-at-home.

casaque [kazak] nf (de jockey) blouse.

cascade [kaskad] nf waterfall, cascade; (fig) stream, torrent.

cascadeur, euse [kaskadœʀ, -øz] nm/f stuntman/girl.

case [kɑz] nf (hutte) hut; (compartiment) compartment; (pour le courrier) pigeonhole; (sur un formulaire, de mots croisés, d'échiquier) box.

caser [kɑze] vt (trouver de la place pour) to put in ou away; to put up; (fig) to find a job for; to marry off.

caserne [kazɛʀn(ə)] nf barracks pl.

cash [kaʃ] ad: **payer** ~ to pay cash down.

casier [kazje] nm (à journaux etc) rack; (de bureau) filing cabinet; (: à cases) set of pigeonholes; (compartiment) compartment; (: à clef) locker; ~ **judiciaire** police record.

casino [kazino] nm casino.

casque [kask(ə)] nm helmet; (chez le coiffeur) (hair-)drier; (pour audition) (head-)phones pl, headset(s).

casquette [kaskɛt] nf cap.

cassant, e [kɑsɑ̃, -ɑ̃t] a brittle; (fig) brusque, abrupt.

cassation [kɑsɑsjɔ̃] nf: **cour de** ~ final court of appeal.

casse [kɑs] nf (pour voitures): **mettre à la** ~ to scrap; (dégâts): **il y a eu de la** ~ there were a lot of breakages.

casse... [kɑs] préfixe: ~-**cou** a inv daredevil, reckless; ~-**croûte** nm inv snack; ~-**noisette(s)**, ~-**noix** nm inv nutcrackers pl; ~-**pieds** (fam): **il est** ~-**pieds** he's a pain (in the neck).

casser [kɑse] vt to break; (ADMIN: gradé) to demote; (JUR) to quash; **se** ~ vi to break.

casserole [kɑsʀɔl] nf saucepan.

casse-tête [kɑstɛt] nm inv (jeu) brain teaser; (difficultés) headache (fig).

cassette [kɑsɛt] nf (bande magnétique) cassette; (coffret) casket.

casseur [kɑsœʀ] nm hooligan.

cassis [kɑsis] nm blackcurrant; (de la route) dip, bump.

cassoulet [kasulɛ] nm bean and sausage hot-pot.

cassure [kɑsyʀ] nf break, crack.

castor [kastɔʀ] nm beaver.

castrer [kastʀe] vt (mâle) to castrate; (: cheval) to geld; (femelle) to spay.

catalogue [katalɔg] nm catalogue.

cataloguer [katalɔge] vt to catalogue, to list; (péj) to put a label on.

catalyseur [katalizœʀ] nm catalyst.

cataplasme [kataplasm(ə)] nm poultice.

cataracte [kataʀakt(ə)] nf cataract.

catastrophe [katastʀɔf] nf catastrophe, disaster.

catastrophé [katastʀɔfe] a (fam) deeply saddened.

catch [katʃ] nm (all-in) wrestling; ~**eur, euse** nm/f (all-in) wrestler.

catéchisme [kateʃism(ə)] nm catechism.

catégorie [kategɔʀi] nf category.

cathédrale [katedʀal] nf cathedral.

catholique [katɔlik] a, nmf (Roman) Catholic; **pas très ~** a bit shady ou fishy.

catimini [katimini]: **en ~** ad on the sly.

cauchemar [koʃmaʀ] nm nightmare.

cause [koz] nf cause; (JUR) lawsuit, case; **à ~ de** because of, owing to; **pour ~ de** on account of, owing to; **(et) pour ~** and for (a very) good reason; **être en ~** to be at stake; to be involved; to be in question; **mettre en ~** to implicate; to call into question; **remettre en ~** to challenge.

causer [koze] vt to cause // vi to chat, talk.

causerie [kozʀi] nf talk.

caution [kosjɔ̃] nf guarantee, security; deposit; (JUR) bail (bond); (fig) backing, support; **payer la ~ de qn** to stand bail for sb; **libéré sous ~** released on bail.

cautionner [kosjone] vt to guarantee; (soutenir) to support.

cavalcade [kavalkad] nf (fig) stampede.

cavalier, ière [kavalje, -jɛʀ] a (désinvolte) offhand // nm/f rider; (au bal) partner // nm (ÉCHECS) knight; **faire ~ seul** to go it alone.

cave [kav] nf cellar // a: **yeux ~s** sunken eyes.

caveau, x [kavo] nm vault.

caverne [kavɛʀn] nf cave.

caviar [kavjaʀ] nm caviar(e).

C.C.P. sigle m voir **compte**.

CD sigle m = compact disc.

MOT-CLÉ
---

ce(c'), cet, cette, ces [sə, sɛt, se] dét (proximité) this; these pl; (nonproximité) that; those pl; **cette maison-ci/-là** this/that house; **cette nuit** (qui vient) tonight; (passée) last night

♦ pronom 1: **c'est** it's ou it is; **c'est un peintre** he's ou he is a painter; **ce sont des peintres** they're ou they are painters; **c'est le facteur** etc (à la porte) it's the postman; **qui est-ce?** who is it?; (en désignant) who is he/she?; **qu'est-ce?** what is it?

2: **~ qui, ~ que** what; (chose qui): **il est bête, ~ qui me chagrine** he's stupid, which saddens me; **tout ~ qui bouge** everything that ou which moves; **tout ~ que je sais** all I know; **~ dont j'ai parlé** what I talked about; **~ que c'est grand!** it's so big!; voir aussi **-ci**, **est-ce que**, **n'est-ce pas**, **c'est-à-dire**.

---

ceci [səsi] pronom this.

cécité [sesite] nf blindness.

céder [sede] vt to give up // vi (pont, barrage) to give way; (personne) to give in; **~ à** to yield to, give in to.

CEDEX [sedɛks] sigle m (= courrier d'entreprise à distribution exceptionnelle) postal service for bulk users.

cédille [sedij] nf cedilla.

cèdre [sɛdʀ(ə)] nm cedar.

C.E.E. sigle f (= Communauté économique européenne) EEC.

ceinture [sɛ̃tyʀ] nf belt; (taille) waist; (fig) ring; belt; circle; **~ de sécurité** safety ou seat belt; **ceinturer** vt (saisir) to grasp (round the waist).

cela [s(ə)la] pronom that; (comme sujet indéfini): **quand/où ~?** when/where (was that)?

célèbre [selɛbʀ(ə)] a famous.

célébrer [selebʀe] vt to celebrate; (louer) to extol.

céleri [sɛlʀi] nm: **~-(rave)** celeriac; **~ en branche** celery.

célérité [seleʀite] nf speed, swiftness.

célibat [seliba] nm celibacy; bachelor/spinsterhood.

célibataire [selibatɛʀ] a single, unmarried.

celle, celles [sɛl] pronom voir **celui**.

cellier [selje] nm storeroom.

cellulaire [selylɛʀ] a: **voiture** ou **fourgon** ~ prison ou police van.

cellule [selyl] nf (gén) cell.

cellulite [selylit] nf excess fat, cellulite.

celui, celle, ceux, celles [səlɥi, sɛl, sø] pronom
1: ~-ci/-là, celle-ci/-là this one/that one; ceux-ci, celles-ci these (ones); ceux-là, celles-là those (ones); ~ de mon frère my brother's; ~ du salon/du dessous the one in (ou from) the lounge/below
2: ~ qui bouge the one which ou that moves; (personne) the one who moves; ~ que je vois the one (which ou that) I see; ~ dont je parle the one I'm talking about
3 (valeur indéfinie): ~ qui veut whoever wants.

cendre [sɑ̃dʀ(ə)] nf ash; ~s (d'un foyer) ash(es), cinders; (volcaniques) ash sg; (d'un défunt) ashes; **sous la** ~ (CULIN) in (the) embers; **cendrier** nm ashtray.

cène [sɛn] nf: **la** ~ (Holy) Communion.

censé, e [sɑ̃se] a: **être** ~ **faire** to be supposed to do.

censeur [sɑ̃sœʀ] nm (SCOL) deputy-head (Brit), vice-principal (US); (CINÉMA, POL) censor.

censure [sɑ̃syʀ] nf censorship.

censurer [sɑ̃syʀe] vt (CINÉMA, PRESSE) to censor; (POL) to censure.

cent [sɑ̃] num a hundred, one hundred; **centaine** nf: **une centaine (de)** about a hundred, a hundred or so; **plusieurs centaines (de)** several hundred; **des centaines (de)** hundreds (of); **centenaire** a hundred-year-old // nm (anniversaire) centenary; **centième** num hundredth; **centigrade** nm centigrade; **centilitre** nm centilitre; **centime**

nm centime; **centimètre** nm centimetre; (ruban) tape measure, measuring tape.

central, e, aux [sɑ̃tʀal, -o] a central // nm: ~ (**téléphonique**) (telephone) exchange // nf power station.

centre [sɑ̃tʀ(ə)] nm centre; ~ **d'apprentissage** training college; ~ **commercial** shopping centre; **le** ~-**ville** the town centre, downtown (area) (US).

centuple [sɑ̃typl(ə)] nm: **le** ~ **de qch** a hundred times sth; **au** ~ **a** hundredfold.

cep [sɛp] nm (vine) stock.

cèpe [sɛp] nm (edible) boletus.

cependant [səpɑ̃dɑ̃] ad however.

céramique [seʀamik] nf ceramics sg.

cerceau, x [sɛʀso] nm hoop.

cercle [sɛʀkl(ə)] nm circle; (objet) band, hoop; ~ **vicieux** vicious circle.

cercueil [sɛʀkœj] nm coffin.

céréale [seʀeal] nf cereal.

cérémonie [seʀemɔni] nf ceremony; ~s (péj) fuss sg, to-do sg.

cerf [sɛʀ] nm stag.

cerfeuil [sɛʀfœj] nm chervil.

cerf-volant [sɛʀvɔlɑ̃] nm kite.

cerise [s(ə)ʀiz] nf cherry; **cerisier** nm cherry (tree).

cerné, e [sɛʀne] a: **les yeux** ~s with dark rings ou shadows under the eyes.

cerner [sɛʀne] vt (MIL etc) to surround; (fig: problème) to delimit, define.

certain, e [sɛʀtɛ̃, -ɛn] a certain // dét certain; **d'un** ~ **âge** past one's prime, not so young; **un** ~ **temps** (quite) some time; ~ **s** pronom some; **certainement** ad (probablement) most probably ou likely; (bien sûr) certainly.

certes [sɛʀt(ə)] ad admittedly; of course; indeed (yes).

certificat [sɛʀtifika] nm certificate.

certitude [sɛʀtityd] nf certainty.

cerveau, x [sɛʀvo] nm brain.

cervelas [sɛʀvəla] nm saveloy.

cervelle [sɛʀvɛl] nf (ANAT) brain.

ces [se] *dét voir* **ce**.

C.E.S. *sigle m* (= *Collège d'Enseignement Secondaire*) = (junior) secondary school (*Brit*), = junior high school (*US*).

cesse [sɛs]: **sans ~** *ad* continually, constantly; continuously); **il n'avait de ~ que** he would not rest until.

cesser [sese] *vt* to stop // *vi* to stop, cease; **~ de faire** to stop doing.

cessez-le-feu [seselfø] *nm inv* ceasefire.

c'est-à-dire [sɛtadir] *ad* that is (to say).

cet [sɛt] *dét voir* **ce**.

cette [sɛt] *dét voir* **ce**.

ceux [sø] *pronom voir* **celui**.

C.F.D.T. *sigle f* = *Confédération française et démocratique du travail*.

C.G.C. *sigle f* = *Confédération générale des cadres*.

C.G.T. *sigle f* = *Confédération générale du travail*.

chacun, e [ʃakœ̃, -yn] *pronom* each; (*indéfini*) everyone, everybody.

chagrin [ʃagrɛ̃] *nm* grief, sorrow; **chagriner** *vt* to grieve; to bother.

chahut [ʃay] *nm* uproar; **chahuter** *vt* to rag, bait // *vi* to make an uproar.

chai [ʃɛ] *nm* wine store.

chaîne [ʃɛn] *nf* chain; (*RADIO, TV: stations*) channel; **travail à la ~** production line work; (*haute-fidélité ou hi-fi*) hi-fi system; **~ de montage** *ou* **de fabrication** production *ou* assembly line; **~ (de montagnes)** (mountain) range; **~ (stéréo)** stereo (system).

chair [ʃɛr] *nf* flesh // *a*: (**couleur**) ~ flesh-coloured; **avoir la ~ de poule** to have goosepimples *ou* gooseflesh; **bien en ~** plump, well-padded; **en ~ et en os** in the flesh.

chaire [ʃɛr] *nf* (*d'église*) pulpit; (*d'université*) chair.

chaise [ʃɛz] *nf* chair; **~ longue** deckchair.

chaland [ʃalɑ̃] *nm* (*bateau*) barge.

châle [ʃal] *nm* shawl.

chaleur [ʃalœr] *nf* heat; (*fig*) warmth; fire, fervour; heat.

chaleureux, euse [ʃalœrø, -øz] *a* warm.

chaloupe [ʃalup] *nf* launch; (*de sauvetage*) lifeboat.

chalumeau, x [ʃalymo] *nm* blowlamp, blowtorch.

chalutier [ʃalytje] *nm* trawler.

chamailler [ʃamaje]: **se ~** *vi* to squabble, bicker.

chambard [ʃɑ̃bar] *nm* rumpus.

chambouler [ʃɑ̃bule] *vt* to disrupt, turn upside down.

chambranle [ʃɑ̃brɑ̃l] *nm* (door) frame.

chambre [ʃɑ̃br(ə)] *nf* bedroom; (*TECH*) chamber; (*POL*) chamber, house; (*JUR*) court; (*COMM*) chamber; federation; **faire ~ à part** to sleep in separate rooms; **~ à un lit/deux lits** (*à l'hôtel*) single-/twin-bedded room; **~ à air** (*de pneu*) (inner) tube; **~ d'amis** spare *ou* guest room; **~ à coucher** bedroom; **~ noire** (*PHOTO*) dark room.

chambrer [ʃɑ̃bre] *vt* (*vin*) to bring to room temperature.

chameau, x [ʃamo] *nm* camel.

champ [ʃɑ̃] *nm* field; **prendre du ~** to draw back; **~ de bataille** battlefield; **~ de courses** racecourse; **~ de tir** rifle range.

champagne [ʃɑ̃paɲ] *nm* champagne.

champêtre [ʃɑ̃pɛtr(ə)] *a* country *cpd*, rural.

champignon [ʃɑ̃piɲɔ̃] *nm* mushroom; (*terme générique*) fungus (*pl* i); **~ de Paris** button mushroom.

champion, ne [ʃɑ̃pjɔ̃, -jɔn] *a, nm/f* champion; **championnat** *nm* championship.

chance [ʃɑ̃s] *nf*: **la ~** luck; **une ~** a stroke *ou* piece of luck *ou* good fortune; (*occasion*) a lucky break; **~s** *nfpl* (*probabilités*) chances; **avoir de la ~** to be lucky.

chanceler [ʃɑ̃sle] *vi* to totter.

chancelier [ʃɑ̃səlje] *nm* (*allemand*)

chancellor.

chanceux, euse [ʃɑ̃sø, -øz] *a* lucky.

chandail [ʃɑ̃daj] *nm* (thick) sweater.

chandelier [ʃɑ̃dəlje] *nm* candlestick.

chandelle [ʃɑ̃del] *nf* (tallow) candle; dîner aux ~s candlelight dinner.

change [ʃɑ̃ʒ] *nm* (COMM) exchange.

changement [ʃɑ̃ʒmɑ̃] *nm* change; ~ de vitesses gears; gear change.

changer [ʃɑ̃ʒe] *vt* (*modifier*) to change, alter; (*remplacer, COMM, rhabiller*) to change // *vi* to change, alter; se ~ *vi* to change (o.s.); ~ de (*remplacer: adresse, nom, voiture etc*) to change one's; (*échanger, alterner: côté, place, train etc*) to change + *npl:* ~ de couleur/ direction to change colour/direction; ~ d'idée to change one's mind; ~ de vitesse to change gear.

chanson [ʃɑ̃sɔ̃] *nf* song.

chant [ʃɑ̃] *nm* song; (*art vocal*) singing; (*d'église*) hymn.

chantage [ʃɑ̃taʒ] *nm* blackmail; faire du ~ to use blackmail.

chanter [ʃɑ̃te] *vt, vi* to sing; si cela lui chante (*fam*) if he feels like it.

chanteur, euse [ʃɑ̃tœʀ, -øz] *nm/f* singer.

chantier [ʃɑ̃tje] *nm* (building) site; (*sur une route*) roadworks *pl;* mettre en ~ to put in hand; ~ naval shipyard.

chantilly [ʃɑ̃tiji] *nf voir* **crème**.

chantonner [ʃɑ̃tɔne] *vi, vt* to sing to oneself, hum.

chanvre [ʃɑ̃vʀ(ə)] *nm* hemp.

chaparder [ʃapaʀde] *vt* to pinch.

chapeau, x [ʃapo] *nm* hat; ~ mou trilby.

chapelet [ʃaplɛ] *nm* (REL) rosary.

chapelle [ʃapɛl] *nf* chapel; ~ ardente chapel of rest.

chapelure [ʃaplyʀ] *nf* (dried) breadcrumbs *pl.*

chapiteau, x [ʃapito] *nm* (de cirque) marquee, big top.

chapitre [ʃapitʀ(ə)] *nm* chapter; (*fig*) subject, matter.

chapitrer [ʃapitʀe] *vt* to lecture.

chaque [ʃak] *dét* each, every; (*indéfini*) every.

char [ʃaʀ] *nm* (à foin etc) cart, waggon; (de carnaval) float; ~ (d'assaut) tank.

charabia [ʃaʀabja] *nm* (*péj*) gibberish.

charade [ʃaʀad] *nf* riddle; (*mimée*) charade.

charbon [ʃaʀbɔ̃] *nm* coal; ~ de bois charcoal.

charcuterie [ʃaʀkytʀi] *nf* (*magasin*) pork butcher's shop and delicatessen; (*produits*) cooked pork meats *pl;* **charcutier, ère** *nm/f* pork butcher.

chardon [ʃaʀdɔ̃] *nm* thistle.

charge [ʃaʀʒ(ə)] *nf* (*fardeau*) load, burden; (*explosif, ÉLEC, MIL, JUR*) charge; (*rôle, mission*) responsibility; ~s *nfpl* (*du loyer*) service charges; à la ~ de (*dépendant de*) dependent upon; (*aux frais de*) chargeable to; j'accepte, à ~ de revanche I accept, provided I can do the same for you one day; prendre en ~ to take charge of; (*suj: véhicule*) to take on; (*dépenses*) to take care of; ~s sociales social security contributions.

chargement [ʃaʀʒəmɑ̃] *nm* (*objets*) load.

charger [ʃaʀʒe] *vt* (*voiture, fusil, caméra*) to load; (*batterie*) to charge // *vi* (MIL *etc*) to charge; se ~ de to see to; ~ qn de (*faire*) qch to put sb in charge of (doing) sth.

chariot [ʃaʀjo] *nm* trolley; (*charrette*) waggon; (de machine à écrire) carriage.

charité [ʃaʀite] *nf* charity; faire la ~ à to give (something) to.

charmant, e [ʃaʀmɑ̃, -ɑ̃t] *a* charming.

charme [ʃaʀm(ə)] *nm* charm; **charmer** *vt* to charm.

charnel, le [ʃaʀnɛl] *a* carnal.

charnière [ʃaʀnjɛʀ] *nf* hinge; (*fig*) turning-point.

charnu, e [ʃaʀny] *a* fleshy.

charpente [ʃaʀpɑ̃t] *nf* frame(work);

charpentier *nm* carpenter.

charpie [ʃaʀpi] *nf*: **en ~** (*fig*) in shreds *ou* ribbons.

charrette [ʃaʀɛt] *nf* cart.

charrier [ʃaʀje] *vt* to carry (along); to cart, carry.

charrue [ʃaʀy] *nf* plough (*Brit*), plow (*US*).

chasse [ʃas] *nf* hunting; (*au fusil*) shooting; (*poursuite*) chase; (*aussi*: **~ d'eau**) flush; **la ~ est ouverte** the hunting season is open; **~ gardée** private hunting grounds *pl*; **prendre en ~** to give chase to; **tirer la ~ (d'eau)** to flush the toilet, pull the chain; **~ à courre** hunting.

chassé-croisé [ʃasekʀwaze] *nm* (*fig*) mix-up where people miss each other in turn.

chasse-neige [ʃasnɛʒ] *nm inv* snow-plough.

chasser [ʃase] *vt* to hunt; (*expulser*) to chase away *ou* out, drive away *ou* out; **chasseur, euse** *nm/f* hunter // *nm* (*avion*) fighter.

châssis [ʃasi] *nm* (*AUTO*) chassis; (*cadre*) frame; (*de jardin*) cold frame.

chat [ʃa] *nm* cat; **~ sauvage** wild-cat.

châtaigne [ʃatɛɲ] *nf* chestnut; **châtaignier** *nm* chestnut (tree).

châtain [ʃatɛ̃] *a inv* chestnut (brown); chestnut-haired.

château, x [ʃato] *nm* castle; **~ d'eau** water tower; **~ fort** strong-hold, fortified castle.

châtier [ʃatje] *vt* to punish; (*fig*: *style*) to polish; **châtiment** *nm* punishment.

chaton [ʃatɔ̃] *nm* (*ZOOL*) kitten.

chatouiller [ʃatuje] *vt* to tickle; (*l'odorat, le palais*) to titillate; **chatouilleux, euse** *a* ticklish; (*fig*) touchy, over-sensitive.

chatoyer [ʃatwaje] *vi* to shimmer.

châtrer [ʃatʀe] *vt* (*mâle*) to castrate; (*: cheval*) to geld; (*femelle*) to spay.

chatte [ʃat] *nf* (she-)cat.

chaud, e [ʃo, -od] *a* (*gén*) warm; (*très chaud*) hot; (*fig*) hearty; heated; **il fait ~** it's warm; it's hot; **avoir ~** to be warm; to be hot; **ça me tient ~** it keeps me warm; **rester au ~** to stay in the warm.

chaudière [ʃodjɛʀ] *nf* boiler.

chaudron [ʃodʀɔ̃] *nm* cauldron.

chauffage [ʃofaʒ] *nm* heating; **~ central** central heating.

chauffard [ʃofaʀ] *nm* (*péj*) reckless driver; hit-and-run driver.

chauffe-eau [ʃofo] *nm inv* water-heater.

chauffer [ʃofe] *vt* to heat // *vi* to heat up, warm up; (*trop chauffer: moteur*) to overheat; **se ~** *vi* (*se mettre en train*) to warm up; (*au soleil*) to warm o.s.

chauffeur [ʃofœʀ] *nm* driver; (*privé*) chauffeur.

chaume [ʃom] *nm* (*du toit*) thatch.

chaumière [ʃomjɛʀ] *nf* (thatched) cottage.

chaussée [ʃose] *nf* road(way).

chausse-pied [ʃospje] *nm* shoe-horn.

chausser [ʃose] *vt* (*bottes, skis*) to put on; (*enfant*) to put shoes on; **~ du 38/42** to take size 38/42.

chaussette [ʃosɛt] *nf* sock.

chausson [ʃosɔ̃] *nm* slipper; (*de bébé*) bootee; **~ (aux pommes)** (apple) turnover.

chaussure [ʃosyʀ] *nf* shoe; **~s basses** flat shoes; **~s de ski** ski boots.

chauve [ʃov] *a* bald.

chauve-souris [ʃovsuʀi] *nf* bat.

chauvin, e [ʃovɛ̃, -in] *a* chauvinistic.

chaux [ʃo] *nf* lime; **blanchi à la ~** whitewashed.

chavirer [ʃaviʀe] *vi* to capsize.

chef [ʃɛf] *nm* head, leader; (*de cuisine*) chef; **en ~** (*MIL etc*) in chief; **~ d'accusation** charge; **~ d'entreprise** company head; **~ d'état** head of state; **~ de** (*de parti etc*) leader; **~ de gare** station master; **~ d'orchestre** conductor.

chef-d'œuvre [ʃɛdœvʀ(ə)] *nm*

masterpiece.

chef-lieu [ʃɛfljø] nm county town.

chemin [ʃəmɛ̃] nm path; (itinéraire, direction, trajet) way; **en ~** on the way; **~ de fer** railway (Brit), railroad (US); **par ~ de fer** by rail.

cheminée [ʃəmine] nf chimney; (à l'intérieur) chimney piece, fireplace; (de bateau) funnel.

cheminement [ʃəminmɑ̃] nm progress; course.

cheminer [ʃəmine] vi to walk (along).

cheminot [ʃəmino] nm railwayman.

chemise [ʃəmiz] nf shirt; (dossier) folder; **~ de nuit** nightdress.

chemisier [ʃəmizje] nm blouse.

chenal, aux [ʃənal, -o] nm channel.

chêne [ʃɛn] nm oak (tree); (bois) oak.

chenil [ʃənil] nm kennels pl.

chenille [ʃənij] nf (ZOOL) caterpillar; (AUTO) caterpillar track.

chèque [ʃɛk] nm cheque (Brit), check (US); **~ sans provision** bad cheque; **~ de voyage** traveller's cheque; **chéquier** nm cheque book.

cher, ère [ʃɛʀ] a (aimé) dear; (coûteux) expensive, dear // ad: cela coûte **~** it's expensive // nf: la bonne chère good food.

chercher [ʃɛʀʃe] vt to look for; (gloire etc) to seek; **aller ~** to go for, go and fetch; **~ à faire** to try to do.

chercheur, euse [ʃɛʀʃœʀ, -øz] nm/f researcher, research worker.

chère [ʃɛʀ] a, nf voir cher.

chéri, e [ʃeʀi] a beloved, dear; (mon) ~ darling.

chérir [ʃeʀiʀ] vt to cherish.

cherté [ʃɛʀte] nf: la **~** de la vie the high cost of living.

chétif, ive [ʃetif, -iv] a puny, stunted.

cheval, aux [ʃəval, -o] nm horse; (AUTO) **~ (vapeur)** (C.V.) horsepower q; **faire du ~** to ride; **à ~** on horseback; **à ~ sur** astride; (fig) overlapping; **~ de course** race

horse.

chevalet [ʃəvalɛ] nm easel.

chevalier [ʃəvalje] nm knight.

chevalière [ʃəvaljɛʀ] nf signet ring.

chevalin, e [ʃəvalɛ̃, -in] a: **boucherie ~e** horse-meat butcher's.

chevaucher [ʃəvoʃe] vi (aussi: se **~**) to overlap (each other) // vt to be astride, straddle.

chevaux [ʃəvo] nmpl voir cheval.

chevelu, e [ʃəvly] a with a good head of hair, hairy (péj).

chevelure [ʃəvlyʀ] nf hair q.

chevet [ʃəvɛ] nm: **au ~ de qn** at sb's bedside; **lampe de ~** bedside lamp.

cheveu, x [ʃəvø] nm hair // nmpl (chevelure) hair; **avoir les ~x courts** to have short hair.

cheville [ʃəvij] nf (ANAT) ankle; (de bois) peg; (pour une vis) plug.

chèvre [ʃɛvʀ(ə)] nf (she-)goat.

chevreau, x [ʃəvʀo] nm kid.

chèvrefeuille [ʃɛvʀəfœj] nm honeysuckle.

chevreuil [ʃəvʀœj] nm roe deer inv; (CULIN) venison.

chevronné, e [ʃəvʀɔne] a seasoned.

chevrotant, e [ʃəvʀɔtɑ̃, -ɑ̃t] a quavering.

MOT-CLÉ

chez [ʃe] prép **1** (à la demeure de) (: direction) to; **~ qn** at/to sb's house ou place; **~ moi** at home; (direction) home

2 (+ profession) at; (: direction) to; **le boulanger/dentiste** at the baker's/dentist's; to the baker's/dentist's

3 (dans le caractère, l'œuvre de) in; **~ les renards/Racine** in foxes/Racine.

---

chez-soi [ʃeswa] nm inv home.

chic [ʃik] a inv chic, smart; (généreux) nice, decent nm stylishness; **avoir le ~ de** to have the knack of; **~!** great!

chicane [ʃikan] nf (obstacle) zigzag;

(querelle) squabble.

chiche [ʃiʃ] *a* niggardly, mean // *excl* (à un défi) you're on!

chichi [ʃiʃi] *nm* fuss.

chicorée [ʃikɔʀe] *nf (café)* chicory; *(salade)* endive.

chien [ʃjɛ̃] *nm* dog; **en ~ de fusil** curled up; **~ de garde** guard dog.

chiendent [ʃjɛ̃dɑ̃] *nm* couch grass.

chienne [ʃjɛn] *nf* dog, bitch.

chier [ʃje] *vi (fam!)* to crap (!).

chiffon [ʃifɔ̃] *nm (piece of)* rag.

chiffonner [ʃifɔne] *vt* to crumple; *(tracasser)* to concern.

chiffonnier [ʃifɔnje] *nm* rag-and-bone man.

chiffre [ʃifʀ(ə)] *nm (représentant un nombre)* figure; numeral; *(montant, total)* total, sum; **en ~s ronds** in round figures; **~ d'affaires** turnover; **chiffrer** *vt (dépense)* to put a figure to, assess; *(message)* to (en)code, cipher.

chignon [ʃiɲɔ̃] *nm* chignon, bun.

Chili [ʃili] *nm*: **le ~** Chile.

chimie [ʃimi] *nf* chemistry; **chimique** *a* chemical; **produits chimiques** chemicals.

Chine [ʃin] *nf*: **la ~** China.

chinois, e [ʃinwa, -waz] *a* Chinese // *nm/f* Chinese.

chiot [ʃjo] *nm* pup(py).

chips [ʃips] *nfpl* crisps.

chiquenaude [ʃiknod] *nf* flick, flip.

chiromancien, ne [kiʀɔmɑ̃sjɛ̃, -ɛn] *nm/f* palmist.

chirurgical, e, aux [ʃiʀyʀʒikal, -o] *a* surgical.

chirurgie [ʃiʀyʀʒi] *nf* surgery; **~ esthétique** plastic surgery; **chirurgien, ne** *nm/f* surgeon.

choc [ʃɔk] *nm* impact; shock; crash; *(moral)* shock; *(affrontement)* clash.

chocolat [ʃɔkɔla] *nm* chocolate; *(boisson)* (hot) chocolate; **~ au lait** milk chocolate.

chœur [kœʀ] *nm (chorale)* choir; *(OPÉRA, THÉÂTRE)* chorus; **en ~** in chorus.

choisir [ʃwaziʀ] *vt* to choose, select.

choix [ʃwa] *nm* choice, selection; **avoir le ~** to have the choice; **premier ~** *(COMM)* class one; **de ~** choice, selected; **au ~** as you wish.

chômage [ʃomaʒ] *nm* unemployment; **mettre au ~** to make redundant, put out of work; **être au ~** to be unemployed ou out of work; **chômeur, euse** *nm/f* unemployed person.

chope [ʃɔp] *nf* tankard.

choquer [ʃɔke] *vt (offenser)* to shock; *(commotionner)* to shake (up).

choriste [kɔʀist(ə)] *nm/f* choir member; *(OPÉRA)* chorus member.

chorus [kɔʀys] *nm*: **faire ~ (avec)** to voice one's agreement (with).

chose [ʃoz] *nf* thing; **c'est peu de ~** it's nothing (really); it's not much.

chou, x [ʃu] *nm* cabbage; **mon petit ~** (my) sweetheart; **~ à la crème** cream bun *(made of choux pastry)*.

chouchou, te [ʃuʃu, -ut] *nm/f (SCOL)* teacher's pet.

choucroute [ʃukʀut] *nf* sauerkraut.

chouette [ʃwɛt] *nf* owl // *a (fam)* great, smashing.

chou-fleur [ʃuflœʀ] *nm* cauliflower.

choyer [ʃwaje] *vt* to cherish; to pamper.

chrétien, ne [kʀetjɛ̃, -ɛn] *a, nm/f* Christian.

Christ [kʀist] *nm*: **le ~** Christ; **christianisme** *nm* Christianity.

chrome [kʀom] *nm* chromium; **chromé, e** *a* a chromium-plated.

chronique [kʀɔnik] *a* chronic // *nf (de journal)* column, page; *(historique)* chronicle; *(RADIO, TV)*: **la ~ sportive/théâtrale** the sports/theatre review; **la ~ locale** local news and gossip.

chronologique [kʀɔnɔlɔʒik] *a* chronological.

chronomètre [kʀɔnɔmɛtʀ(ə)] *nm* stopwatch; **chronométrer** *vt* to time.

chrysanthème [kʀizɑ̃tɛm] *nm* chrysanthemum.

C.H.U. sigle m (= centre hospitalier universitaire) ≈ (teaching) hospital.

chuchoter [ʃyʃɔte] vt, vi to whisper.

chuinter [ʃɥɛ̃te] vi to hiss.

chut [ʃyt] excl sh!

chute [ʃyt] nf fall; (de bois, papier: déchet) scrap; (de ~ des cheveux hair loss; **faire une ~** (de 10 m) to fall (10 m); **~s de pluie/neige rain/snowfalls**; **~ (d'eau) waterfall**; **~ libre** free fall.

Chypre [ʃipʀ] Cyprus.

-ci, ci- [si] ad voir par, ci-contre, ci-joint etc // dét: **ce garçon-ci/-là** this/that boy; **ces femmes-ci/-là** these/those women.

ci-après [siapʀɛ] ad hereafter.

cible [sibl(ə)] nf target.

ciboulette [sibulɛt] nf (smaller) chive.

cicatrice [sikatʀis] nf scar.

cicatriser [sikatʀize] vt to heal.

ci-contre [sikɔ̃tʀ(ə)] ad opposite.

ci-dessous [sidəsu] ad below.

ci-dessus [sidəsy] ad above.

cidre [sidʀ(ə)] nm cider.

Cie abr (= compagnie) Co.

ciel [sjɛl] nm sky; (REL) heaven; **cieux** nmpl sky sg. skies; **à ~ ouvert** open-air; (mine) opencast.

cierge [sjɛʀʒ(ə)] nm candle.

cieux [sjø] nmpl voir ciel.

cigale [sigal] nf cicada.

cigare [sigaʀ] nm cigar.

cigarette [sigaʀɛt] nf cigarette.

ci-gît [siʒi] ad + vb here lies.

cigogne [sigɔɲ] nf stork.

ci-inclus, e [siɛ̃kly, -yz] a, ad enclosed.

ci-joint, e [siʒwɛ̃, -ɛt] a, ad enclosed.

cil [sil] nm (eye)lash.

ciller [sije] vi to blink.

cime [sim] nf top; (montagne) peak.

ciment [simɑ̃] nm cement; **~ armé** reinforced concrete.

cimetière [simtjɛʀ] nm cemetery; (d'église) churchyard.

cinéaste [sineast(ə)] nm/f filmmaker.

cinéma [sinema] nm cinema; **~tographique** a film cpd, cinema cpd.

cinéphile [sinefil] nm/f cinema-goer.

cinglant, e [sɛ̃glɑ̃, -ɑ̃t] a (échec) crushing.

cinglé, e [sɛ̃gle] a (fam) crazy.

cingler [sɛ̃gle] vt to lash; (fig) to sting.

cinq [sɛ̃k] num five.

cinquantaine [sɛ̃kɑ̃tɛn] nf: **une ~ (de)** about fifty; **avoir la ~** (âge) to be around fifty.

cinquante [sɛ̃kɑ̃t] num fifty; **~naire** a, nm/f fifty-year-old.

cinquième [sɛ̃kjɛm] num fifth.

cintre [sɛ̃tʀ(ə)] nm coat-hanger.

cintré, e [sɛ̃tʀe] a (chemise) fitted.

cirage [siʀaʒ] nm (shoe) polish.

circonflexe [siʀkɔ̃flɛks(ə)] a: **accent ~** circumflex accent.

circonscription [siʀkɔ̃skʀipsjɔ̃] nf district; **~ électorale** (d'un député) constituency.

circonscrire [siʀkɔ̃skʀiʀ] vt to define, delimit; (incendie) to contain.

circonstance [siʀkɔ̃stɑ̃s] nf circumstance; (occasion) occasion.

circonstancié, e [siʀkɔ̃stɑ̃sje] a detailed.

circonvenir [siʀkɔ̃vniʀ] vt to circumvent.

circuit [siʀkɥi] nm (trajet) tour, (round) trip; (ÉLEC, TECH) circuit.

circulaire [siʀkylɛʀ] a, nf circular.

circulation [siʀkylasjɔ̃] nf circulation; (AUTO): **la ~** (the) traffic.

circuler [siʀkyle] vi to drive (along); to walk along; (train etc) to run; (sang, devises) to circulate; **faire ~** (nouvelle) to spread (about), circulate; (badauds) to move on.

cire [siʀ] nf wax.

ciré [siʀe] nm oilskin.

cirer [siʀe] vt to wax, polish.

cirque [siʀk(ə)] nm circus; (GÉO) cirque; (fig) chaos, bedlam; carry-on.

cisaille(s) [sizaj] nf(pl) (gardening) shears pl.

ciseau, x [sizo] nm: **~** (à bois) chisel // nmpl (pair of) scissors.

ciseler [sizle] vt to chisel, carve.

citadin, e [sitadɛ̃, -in] nm/f city dweller.

citation [sitasjɔ̃] nf (d'auteur) quotation; (JUR) summons sg.

cité [site] nf town; (plus grande) city; ~ **universitaire** students' residences pl.

citer [site] vt (un auteur) to quote (from); (nommer) to name; (JUR) to summon.

citerne [sitɛrn(ə)] nf tank.

citoyen, ne [sitwajɛ̃, -ɛn] nm/f citizen.

citron [sitrɔ̃] nm lemon; ~ **vert** lime; **citronnade** nf lemonade; **citronnier** nm lemon tree.

citrouille [sitruj] nf pumpkin.

civet [sive] nm stew.

civière [sivjɛr] nf stretcher.

civil, e [sivil] a (JUR, ADMIN, poli) civil; (non militaire) civilian; **en** ~ in civilian clothes; **dans le** ~ in civilian life.

civilisation [sivilizasjɔ̃] nf civilization.

civisme [sivism(ə)] nm public-spiritedness.

clair, e [klɛr] a light; (chambre) light, bright; (eau, son, fig) clear // ad: **voir** ~ to see clearly; **tirer qch au** ~ to clear sth up, clarify sth; **mettre au** ~ (notes etc) to tidy up; **le plus** ~ **de son temps** the better part of his time; ~ **de lune** moonlight; ~**ement** ad clearly.

clairière [klɛrjɛr] nf clearing.

clairon [klɛrɔ̃] nm bugle.

clairsemé, e [klɛrsəme] a sparse.

clairvoyant, e [klɛrvwajɑ̃, -ɑ̃t] a perceptive, clear-sighted.

clandestin, e [klɑ̃dɛstɛ̃, -in] a clandestine, covert; **passager** ~ stowaway.

clapier [klapje] nm (rabbit) hutch.

clapoter [klapɔte] vi to lap.

claque [klak] nf (gifle) slap.

claquer [klake] vi (drapeau) to flap; (porte) to bang, slam; (coup de feu) to ring out // vt (porte) to slam,

bang; (doigts) to snap; **se** ~ **un muscle** to pull ou strain a muscle.

claquettes [klakɛt] nfpl tap-dancing sg.

clarinette [klarinɛt] nf clarinet.

clarté [klarte] nf lightness; brightness; (d'un son, de l'eau) clearness; (d'une explication) clarity.

classe [klɑs] nf class; (SCOL: local) class(room); (: leçon, élèves) class; **faire la** ~ (SCOL) to be a ou the teacher; to teach.

classement [klɑsmɑ̃] nm (rang: SCOL) place; (: SPORT) placing; (liste: SCOL) class list (in order of merit); (: SPORT) placings pl.

classer [klɑse] vt (idées, livres) to classify; (papiers) to file; (candidat, concurrent) to grade; (JUR: affaire) to close; **se** ~ **premier/dernier** to come first/last; (SPORT) to finish first/last.

classeur [klɑsœr] nm (cahier) file; (meuble) filing cabinet.

classique [klasik] a classical; (sobre: coupe etc) classic(al); (habituel) standard, classic.

claudication [klodikasjɔ̃] nf limp.

clause [kloz] nf clause.

claustrer [klostre] vt to confine.

clavecin [klavsɛ̃] nm harpsichord.

clavicule [klavikyl] nf collarbone.

clavier [klavje] nm keyboard.

clé ou **clef** [kle] nf key; (MUS) clef; (de mécanicien) spanner (Brit), wrench (US); **prix** ~s **en main** (d'une voiture) on-the-road price; ~ **anglaise** (monkey) wrench; ~ **de contact** ignition key.

clément, e [klemɑ̃, -ɑ̃t] a (temps) mild; (indulgent) lenient.

clerc [klɛr] nm: ~ **de notaire** solicitor's clerk.

clergé [klɛrʒe] nm clergy.

cliché [kliʃe] nm (PHOTO) negative; print; (LING) cliché.

client, e [klijɑ̃, -ɑ̃t] nm/f (acheteur) customer, client; (d'hôtel) guest, patron; (du docteur) patient; (de l'avocat) client; **clientèle** nf (du *magasin)* customers *pl,* clientèle; *(du docteur, de l'avocat)* practice.

cligner [kliɲe] *vi:* ~ **des yeux** to blink (one's eyes); ~ **de l'œil** to wink.

clignotant [kliɲɔtɑ̃] *nm (AUTO)* indicator.

clignoter [kliɲɔte] *vi (étoiles etc)* to twinkle; *(lumière)* to flash; *(: vaciller)* to flicker.

climat [klima] *nm* climate.

climatisation [klimatizasjɔ̃] *nf* air conditioning; **climatisé, e** *a* air-conditioned.

clin d'œil [klɛ̃dœj] *nm* wink; **en un** ~ in a flash.

clinique [klinik] *nf* nursing home.

clinquant, e [klɛ̃kɑ̃, -ɑ̃t] *a* flashy.

cliqueter [klikte] *vi* to clash; to jangle, jingle; to chink.

clochard, e [klɔʃaʀ, -aʀd(ə)] *nm/f* tramp.

cloche [klɔʃ] *nf (d'église)* bell; *(fam)* clot; ~ **à fromage** cheese-cover.

cloche-pied [klɔʃpje]: **à** ~ *ad* on one leg, hopping (along).

clocher [klɔʃe] *nm* church tower; *(en pointe)* steeple // *vi (fam)* to be ou go wrong; **de** ~ *(péj)* parochial.

cloison [klwazɔ̃] *nf* partition (wall).

cloître [klwatʀ(ə)] *nm* cloister.

cloîtrer [klwatʀe] *vt:* **se** ~ to shut o.s. up ou away.

cloque [klɔk] *nf* blister.

clore [klɔʀ] *vt* to close; **clos, e** *a voir* **maison, huis** // *nm* (enclosed) field.

clôture [klotyʀ] *nf* closure; *(barrière)* enclosure; **clôturer** *vt (terrain)* to enclose; *(débats)* to close.

clou [klu] *nm* nail; *(MÉD)* boil; ~**s** *nmpl* = passage clouté; **pneus à** ~**s** studded tyres; **le** ~ **du spectacle** the highlight of the show; ~ **de girofle** clove; ~**er** *vt* to nail down ou up.

clown [klun] *nm* clown.

club [klœb] *nm* club.

C.N.R.S. *sigle m* = **centre national de la recherche scientifique**.

coasser [kɔase] *vi* to croak.

cobaye [kɔbaj] *nm* guinea-pig.

coca [kɔka] *nm* Coke ®.

cocagne [kɔkaɲ] *nf:* **pays de** ~ land of plenty.

cocaïne [kɔkain] *nf* cocaine.

cocasse [kɔkas] *a* comical, funny.

coccinelle [kɔksinɛl] *nf* ladybird *(Brit)*, ladybug *(US)*.

cocher [kɔʃe] *nm* coachman // *vt* to tick off; *(entailler)* to notch.

cochère [kɔʃɛʀ] *af:* **porte** ~ carriage entrance.

cochon, ne [kɔʃɔ̃, -ɔn] *nm* pig // *a (fam)* dirty, smutty; **cochonnerie** *nf (fam)* filth; rubbish, trash.

cocktail [kɔktɛl] *nm* cocktail; *(réception)* cocktail party.

coco [kɔko] *nm voir* **noix**; *(fam)* bloke.

cocorico [kɔkɔriko] *excl, nm* cock-a-doodle-do.

cocotier [kɔkɔtje] *nm* coconut palm.

cocotte [kɔkɔt] *nf (en fonte)* casserole; ~ **(minute)** pressure cooker; **ma** ~ *(fam)* sweetie (pie).

cocu [kɔky] *nm* cuckold.

code [kɔd] *nm* code // *a:* **phares** ~**s** dipped lights; **se mettre en** ~**(s)** to dip one's (head)lights; ~ **à barres** bar code; ~ **civil** Common Law; ~ **pénal** penal code; ~ **postal** *(numéro)* post *(Brit)* ou zip *(US)* code; ~ **de la route** highway code.

cœur [kœʀ] *nm* heart; *(CARTES: couleur)* hearts *pl;* *(: carte)* heart; **avoir bon** ~ to be kind-hearted; **avoir mal au** ~ to feel sick; **en avoir le** ~ **net** to be clear in one's own mind (about it); **par** ~ by heart; **de bon** ~ willingly; **cela lui tient à** ~ that's (very) close to his heart.

coffre [kɔfʀ(ə)] *nm (meuble)* chest; *(d'auto)* boot *(Brit)*, trunk *(US)*; ~**(-fort)** *nm* safe.

coffret [kɔfʀe] *nm* casket.

cognac [kɔɲak] *nm* brandy, cognac.

cogner [kɔɲe] *vi* to knock.

cohérent, e [kɔeʀɑ̃, -ɑ̃t] *a* coherent,

consistent.

cohorte [kɔɔrt(ə)] nf troop.

cohue [kɔy] nf crowd.

coi, coite [kwa, kwat] a: **rester ~** to remain silent.

coiffe [kwaf] nf headdress.

coiffé, e [kwafe] a: **bien/mal ~** with tidy/untidy hair; **~ en arrière** with one's hair brushed ou combed back.

coiffer [kwafe] vt (fig) to cover, top; **~ qn** to do sb's hair; **se ~** vi to do one's hair; to put on one's hat.

coiffeur, euse [kwafœr, -øz] nm/f hairdresser // nf (table) dressing table.

coiffure [kwafyr] nf (cheveux) hairstyle, hairdo; (chapeau) hat, headgear q; (art): **la ~** hairdressing.

coin [kwɛ̃] nm corner; (pour coincer) wedge; (pour graver) die; **l'épicerie du ~** the local grocer; **dans le ~** (aux alentours) in the area, around about; locally; **au ~ du feu** by the fireside; **regard en ~** sideways glance.

coincer [kwɛ̃se] vt to jam.

coïncidence [kɔɛ̃sidɑ̃s] nf coincidence.

coïncider [kɔɛ̃side] vi to coincide.

coïte [kwat] nf voir **coi**.

col [kɔl] nm (de chemise) collar; (encolure, cou) neck; (de montagne) pass; **~ roulé** polo-neck; **~ de l'utérus** cervix.

colère [kɔlɛr] nf anger; **une ~** a fit of anger; (se mettre) **en ~** (to get) angry; **coléreux, euse** a, **colérique** a quick-tempered, irascible.

colifichet [kɔlifiʃɛ] nm trinket.

colimaçon [kɔlimasɔ̃] nm: **escalier en ~** spiral staircase.

colin [kɔlɛ̃] nm hake.

colique [kɔlik] nf diarrhoea; colic (pains).

colis [kɔli] nm parcel.

collaborateur, trice [kɔlabɔratœr, -tris] nm/f (aussi POL) collaborator; (d'une revue) contributor.

collaborer [kɔlabɔre] vi to collaborate; **~ à** to collaborate on; (revue) to contribute to.

collant, e [kɔlɑ̃, -ɑ̃t] a sticky; (robe etc) clinging, skintight; (péj) clinging // nm (bas) tights pl.

collation [kɔlasjɔ̃] nf light meal.

colle [kɔl] nf glue; (à papiers peints) (wallpaper) paste; (devinette) teaser, riddle; (SCOL fam) detention.

collecte [kɔlɛkt(ə)] nf collection.

collectif, ive [kɔlɛktif, -iv] a collective; (visite, billet) group cpd.

collection [kɔlɛksjɔ̃] nf collection; (ÉDITION) series; **collectionner** vt (tableaux, timbres) to collect; **collectionneur, euse** nm/f collector.

collectivité [kɔlɛktivite] nf group.

collège [kɔlɛʒ] nm (école) (secondary) school; (assemblée) body; **collégien, ne** nm/f schoolboy/girl.

collègue [kɔlɛg] nm/f colleague.

coller [kɔle] vt (papier, timbre) to stick (on); (affiche) to stick up; (enveloppe) to stick down; (morceaux) to stick ou glue together; (fam: mettre, fourrer) to stick, shove; (SCOL fam) to keep in // vi (être collant) to be sticky; (adhérer) to stick; **~ à** to stick to.

collet [kɔlɛ] nm (piège) snare, noose; (cou): **prendre qn au ~** to grab sb by the throat; **~ monté** a inv straight-laced.

collier [kɔlje] nm (bijou) necklace; (de chien, TECH) collar; **~ de barbe** narrow beard along the line of the jaw.

collimateur [kɔlimatœr] nm: **avoir qn/qch dans le ~** (fig) to have sb/ sth in one's sights.

colline [kɔlin] nf hill.

collision [kɔlizjɔ̃] nf collision, crash; **entrer en ~** (avec) to collide (with).

colmater [kɔlmate] vt (fuite) to seal off; (brèche) to plug, fill in.

colombe [kɔlɔ̃b] nf dove.

colon [kɔlɔ̃] nm settler.

colonel [kɔlɔnɛl] nm colonel.

colonie [kɔlɔni] nf colony; **~ (de vacances)** holiday camp (for children).

colonne [kɔlɔn] nf column; se mettre en ~ par deux to get into twos; ~ de secours rescue party; ~ (vertébrale) spine, spinal column.

colorant [kɔlɔrɑ̃] nm colouring.

colorer [kɔlɔre] vt to colour.

colorier [kɔlɔrje] vt to colour (in).

coloris [kɔlɔri] nm colour, shade.

colporter [kɔlpɔrte] vt to hawk, peddle.

colza [kɔlza] nm rape.

coma [kɔma] nm coma.

combat [kɔ̃ba] nm fight; fighting q; ~ de boxe boxing match.

combattant [kɔ̃batɑ̃] nm: ancien ~ war veteran.

combattre [kɔ̃batr(ə)] vt to fight; (épidémie, ignorance) to combat, fight against.

combien [kɔ̃bjɛ̃] ad (quantité) how much; (nombre) how many; (exclamatif) how; ~ de how much; how many; ~ de temps how long; ~ coûte/pèse ceci? how much does this cost/weigh?

combinaison [kɔ̃binɛzɔ̃] nf combination; (astuce) device, scheme; (de femme) slip; (d'aviateur) flying suit; (d'homme-grenouille) wetsuit; (bleu de travail) boiler suit (Brit), coveralls pl (US).

combine [kɔ̃bin] nf trick; (péj) scheme, fiddle (Brit).

combiné [kɔ̃bine] nm (aussi: ~ téléphonique) receiver.

combiner [kɔ̃bine] vt to combine; (plan, horaire) to work out, devise.

comble [kɔ̃bl(ə)] a (salle) packed (full); (du bonheur, plaisir) height; ~s nmpl (CONSTR) attic sg, loft sg; c'est le ~! that beats everything!

combler [kɔ̃ble] vt (trou) to fill in; (besoin, lacune) to fill; (déficit) to make good; (satisfaire) to fulfil.

combustible [kɔ̃bystibl(ə)] nm fuel.

comédie [kɔmedi] nf comedy; (fig) playacting q; ~ musicale musical; **comédien, ne** nm/f actor/actress.

comestible [kɔmɛstibl(ə)] a edible.

comique [kɔmik] a (drôle) comical; (THÉÂTRE) comic // nm (artiste) comic, comedian.

comité [kɔmite] nm committee; ~ d'entreprise works council.

commandant [kɔmɑ̃dɑ̃] nm (gén) commander, commandant; (NAVIG, AVIAT) captain.

commande [kɔmɑ̃d] nf order; (COMM) order; ~s nfpl (AVIAT etc) controls; sur ~ to order; ~ à distance remote control.

commandement [kɔmɑ̃dmɑ̃] nm command; (REL) commandment.

commander [kɔmɑ̃de] vt (COMM) to order; (diriger, ordonner) to command; ~ à qn de faire to command ou order sb to do.

commando [kɔmɑ̃do] nm commando (squad).

MOT-CLÉ

comme [kɔm] ♦ prép 1 (comparaison) like; tout ~ son père just like his father; fort ~ un bœuf as strong as an ox; joli ~ tout ever so pretty
2 (manière) like; faites-le ~ ça do it like this, do it this way; ~ ci, ~ ça so-so, middling
3 (en tant que) as a; donner ~ prix to give as a prize; travailler ~ secrétaire to work as a secretary

♦ cj 1 (ainsi que) as; elle écrit ~ elle parle she writes as she talks; si as if
2 (au moment où, alors que) as; il est parti ~ j'arrivais he left as I arrived
3 (puisque, parce que) as; ~ il était en retard, il ... as he was late, he

♦ ad: ~ il est fort/c'est bon! he's so strong/it's so good!

---

commémorer [kɔmemɔre] vt to commemorate.

commencement [kɔmɑ̃smɑ̃] nm beginning, start, commencement.

commencer [kɔmɑ̃se] vt, vi to begin, start, commence; ~ à ou faire to begin *ou* start doing.

comment [kɔmɑ̃] *ad* how; **~?** *(que dites-vous)* pardon? // *nm*: **le ~ et le pourquoi** the whys and wherefores.

commentaire [kɔmɑ̃tɛr] *nm* comment; remark.

commenter [kɔmɑ̃te] *vt (jugement, événement)* to comment (up)on; *(RADIO, TV: match, manifestation)* to cover.

commérages [kɔmeraʒ] *nmpl* gossip *sg.*

commerçant, e [kɔmɛrsɑ̃, -ɑ̃t] *nm/ f* shopkeeper, trader.

commerce [kɔmɛrs(ə)] *nm (activité)* trade, commerce; *(boutique)* business; **vendu dans le ~** sold in the shops; **commercial, e, aux** *a* commercial, trading; *(péj)* commercial; **commercialiser** *vt* to market.

commère [kɔmɛr] *nf* gossip.

commettre [kɔmɛtr(ə)] *vt* to commit.

commis [kɔmi] *nm (de magasin)* (shop) assistant; *(de banque)* clerk; **~ voyageur** commercial traveller.

commissaire [kɔmisɛr] *nm (de police)* ≈ (police) superintendent; **~-priseur** *nm* auctioneer.

commissariat [kɔmisarja] *nm* police station.

commission [kɔmisjɔ̃] *nf (comité, pourcentage)* commission; *(message)* message; *(course)* errand; **~s** *nfpl (achats)* shopping *sg.*

commissure [kɔmisyr] *nf*: **les ~s des lèvres** the corners of the mouth.

commode [kɔmɔd] *a (pratique)* convenient, handy; *(facile)* easy; *(air, personne)* easy-going; *(personne)*: **pas ~** awkward (to deal with) // *nf (meuble)* chest of drawers; **commodité** *nf* convenience.

commotion [kɔmosjɔ̃] *nf*: **~ (cérébrale)** concussion; **commotionné, e** *a* shocked, shaken.

commun, e [kɔmœ̃, -yn] *a* common; *(pièce)* communal, shared; *(réunion, effort)* joint // *nf (ADMIN)* commune, ≈ district; *(: urbaine)* ≈ borough;

~s *nmpl (bâtiments)* outbuildings; **cela sort du ~** it's out of the ordinary; **le ~ des mortels** the common run of people; **en ~** *(faire)* jointly; **mettre en ~** to pool, share.

communauté [kɔmynote] *nf* community; *(JUR)*: **régime de la ~** communal estate settlement.

communication [kɔmynikasjɔ̃] *nf* communication; **~ (téléphonique)** (telephone) call; **~ interurbaine** long distance call.

communier [kɔmynje] *vi (REL)* to receive communion; *(fig)* to be united.

communion [kɔmynjɔ̃] *nf* communion.

communiquer [kɔmynike] *vt (nouvelle, dossier)* to pass on, convey; *(maladie)* to pass on; *(peur etc)* to communicate; *(chaleur, mouvement)* to transmit // *vi* to communicate; **se ~ à** *(se propager)* to spread to.

communisme [kɔmynism(ə)] *nm* communism; **communiste** *a, nm/f* communist.

commutateur [kɔmytatœr] *nm (ELEC)* (change-over) switch, commutator.

compact, e [kɔ̃pakt] *a* dense; compact.

compagne [kɔ̃paɲ] *nf* companion.

compagnie [kɔ̃paɲi] *nf (firme, MIL)* company; *(groupe)* gathering; **tenir ~ à qn** to keep sb company; **fausser ~ à qn** to give sb the slip, slip *ou* sneak away from sb; **~ aérienne** airline (company).

compagnon [kɔ̃paɲɔ̃] *nm* companion.

comparable [kɔ̃parabl(ə)] *a*: **~ (à)** comparable (to).

comparaison [kɔ̃parɛzɔ̃] *nf* comparison.

comparaître [kɔ̃parɛtr(ə)] *vi*: **~ (devant)** to appear (before).

comparer [kɔ̃pare] *vt* to compare; **~ qch/qn à** *ou* **et** *(pour choisir)* to compare sth/sb with *ou* and; *(pour établir une similitude)* to sth/sb to.

comparse [kɔ̃pars(ə)] nm/f (péj) associate, stooge.

compartiment [kɔ̃partimɑ̃] nm compartment.

comparution [kɔ̃parysjɔ̃] nf appearance.

compas [kɔ̃pa] nm (GÉOM) (pair of) compasses pl; (NAVIG) compass.

compassé, e [kɔ̃pase] a starchy.

compatible [kɔ̃patibl(ə)] a compatible.

compatir [kɔ̃patir] vi: ~ (à) to sympathize (with).

compatriote [kɔ̃patrijɔt] nm/f compatriot.

compenser [kɔ̃pɑ̃se] vt to compensate for, make up for.

compère [kɔ̃pɛr] nm accomplice.

compétence [kɔ̃petɑ̃s] nf competence.

compétent, e [kɔ̃petɑ̃, -ɑ̃t] a (apte) competent, capable.

compétition [kɔ̃petisjɔ̃] nf (gén) competition; (SPORT: épreuve) event; la ~ competitive sport; la ~ automobile motor racing.

complainte [kɔ̃plɛ̃t] nf lament.

complaire [kɔ̃plɛr]: se ~ vi: se ~ dans/ parmi to take pleasure in/in being among.

complaisance [kɔ̃plɛzɑ̃s] nf kindness; pavillon de ~ flag of convenience.

complaisant, e [kɔ̃plɛzɑ̃, -ɑ̃t] a (aimable) kind, obliging.

complément [kɔ̃plemɑ̃] nm complement; remainder; ~ d'information (ADMIN) supplementary ou further information; **complémentaire** a complementary; (additionnel) supplementary.

complet, ète [kɔ̃plɛ, -ɛt] a complete; (plein: hôtel etc) full // nm (aussi: ~-veston) suit; **complètement** ad completely; **compléter** vt (porter à la quantité voulue) to complete; (augmenter) to complement, supplement; to add to.

complexe [kɔ̃plɛks(ə)] nm com-

plex; **complexé, e** a mixed-up, hung-up.

complication [kɔ̃plikɑsjɔ̃] nf complexity, intricacy; (difficulté, ennui) complication.

complice [kɔ̃plis] nm accomplice.

compliment [kɔ̃plimɑ̃] nm (louange) compliment; ~s nmpl (félicitations) congratulations.

compliqué, e [kɔ̃plike] a complicated, complex; (personne) complicated.

complot [kɔ̃plo] nm plot.

comportement [kɔ̃pɔrtəmɑ̃] nm behaviour.

comporter [kɔ̃pɔrte] vt to consist of, comprise; (être équipé de) to have; (impliquer) to entail; se ~ vi to behave.

composante [kɔ̃pozɑ̃t] nf component.

composé [kɔ̃poze] nm compound.

composer [kɔ̃poze] vt (musique, texte) to compose; (mélange, équipe) to make up; (faire partie de) to make up, form // vi (transiger) to come to terms; se ~ de to be composed of, be made up of; ~ un numéro to dial a number.

compositeur, trice [kɔ̃pozitœr, -tris] nm/f (MUS) composer.

composition [kɔ̃pozisjɔ̃] nf composition; (SCOL) test; de bonne ~ (accommodant) easy to deal with.

composter [kɔ̃pɔste] vt to date stamp; to punch.

compote [kɔ̃pɔt] nf stewed fruit q; ~ de pommes stewed apples; **compotier** nm fruit dish ou bowl.

compréhensible [kɔ̃preɑ̃sibl(ə)] a comprehensible; (attitude) understandable.

compréhensif, ive [kɔ̃preɑ̃sif, -iv] a understanding.

comprendre [kɔ̃prɑ̃dr(ə)] vt to understand; (se composer de) to comprise, consist of.

compresse [kɔ̃prɛs] nf compress.

compression [kɔ̃presjɔ̃] nf compression; reduction.

comprimé [kɔ̃prime] nm tablet.

comprimer [kɔ̃prime] vt to compress; (fig: crédit etc) to reduce, cut down.

compris, e [kɔ̃pri, -iz] pp de **comprendre** // a (inclus) included; ~ entre (situé) contained between; la maison ~e/non ~e, y/non ~ la maison including/excluding the house; 100 F tout ~ 100 F all inclusive ou all-in.

compromettre [kɔ̃prɔmɛtr(ə)] vt to compromise.

compromis [kɔ̃prɔmi] nm compromise.

comptabilité [kɔ̃tabilite] nf (activité, technique) accounting, accountancy; (d'une société: comptes) accounts pl, books pl; (: service) accounts office.

comptable [kɔ̃tabl(ə)] nm/f accountant.

comptant [kɔ̃tɑ̃] ad: payer ~ to pay cash; acheter ~ to buy for cash.

compte [kɔ̃t] nm count, counting; (total, montant) count, (right) number; (bancaire, facture) account; ~s nmpl accounts, books; (fig) explanation sg; en fin de ~ (fig) all things considered; à bon ~ at a favourable price; (fig) lightly; avoir son ~ (fig: fam) to have had it; pour le ~ de on behalf of; pour son propre ~ for one's own benefit; tenir ~ de to take account of; travailler à son ~ to work for oneself; rendre ~ (à qn) de qch to give (sb) an account of sth; ~ chèques postaux (C.C.P.) Post Office account; ~ courant current account; à rebours countdown; voir aussi rendre.

compte-gouttes [kɔ̃tgut] nm inv dropper.

compter [kɔ̃te] vt (facturer) to charge for; (avoir à son actif, comporter) to have; (prévoir) to allow, reckon; (penser, espérer) ~ réussir to expect to succeed // vi to count; (être économe) to economize;

(figurer): ~ parmi to be ou rank among; ~ sur to count (up)on; ~ avec qch/qn to reckon with ou take account of sth/sb; sans ~ que besides which.

compte rendu [kɔ̃trɑ̃dy] nm account, report; (de film, livre) review.

compte-tours [kɔ̃ttur] nm inv rev(olution) counter.

compteur [kɔ̃tœr] nm meter; ~ de vitesse speedometer.

comptine [kɔ̃tin] nf nursery rhyme.

comptoir [kɔ̃twar] nm (de magasin) counter.

compulser [kɔ̃pylse] vt to consult.

comte, comtesse [kɔ̃t, kɔ̃tɛs] nm/f count/countess.

con, ne [kɔ̃, kɔn] a (fam!) damned ou bloody (Brit) stupid (!).

concéder [kɔ̃sede] vt to grant; (défaite, point) to concede.

concentrer [kɔ̃sɑ̃tre] vt to concentrate; se ~ vi to concentrate.

concept [kɔ̃sɛpt] nm concept.

conception [kɔ̃sɛpsjɔ̃] nf conception; (d'une machine etc) design.

concerner [kɔ̃sɛrne] vt to concern; en ce qui me concerne as far as I am concerned.

concert [kɔ̃sɛr] nm concert; de ~ ad in unison; together.

concerter [kɔ̃sɛrte] vt to devise; se ~ vi (collaborateurs etc) to put our ou their etc heads together.

concessionnaire [kɔ̃sesjɔnɛr] nm/f agent, dealer.

concevoir [kɔ̃svwar] vt (idée, projet) to conceive (of); (méthode, plan d'appartement, décoration etc) to plan, design; (enfant) to conceive; bien/mal conçu well-/badly-designed.

concierge [kɔ̃sjɛrʒ(ə)] nm/f caretaker; (d'hôtel) head porter.

concile [kɔ̃sil] nm council.

conciliabules [kɔ̃siljabyl] nmpl (private) discussions, confabulations.

concilier [kɔ̃silje] vt to reconcile; se ~ qn to win sb over.

concitoyen, ne [kɔ̃sitwajɛ̃, -jɛn]

nm/f fellow citizen.

concluant, e [kɔ̃klyɑ̃, -ɑ̃t] *a* conclusive.

conclure [kɔ̃klyʀ] *vt* to conclude.

conclusion [kɔ̃klyzjɔ̃] *nf* conclusion.

conçois *etc vb voir* **concevoir**.

concombre [kɔ̃kɔ̃bʀ(ə)] *nm* cucumber.

concorder [kɔ̃kɔʀde] *vi* to tally, agree.

concourir [kɔ̃kuʀiʀ] *vi* (SPORT) to compete; ~ **à** *vt* (effet etc) to work towards.

concours [kɔ̃kuʀ] *nm* competition; (SCOL) competitive examination; (assistance) aid, help; ~ **de circonstances** combination of circumstances; ~ **hippique** horse show.

concret, ète [kɔ̃kʀɛ, -ɛt] *a* concrete.

concrétiser [kɔ̃kʀetize] *vt* (plan, projet) to put in concrete form; se ~ *vi* to materialize.

conçu, e [kɔ̃sy] *pp de* **concevoir**.

concubinage [kɔ̃kybinaʒ] *nm* (JUR) cohabitation.

concurrence [kɔ̃kyʀɑ̃s] *nf* competition; **jusqu'à** ~ **de** up to.

concurrent, e [kɔ̃kyʀɑ̃, -ɑ̃t] *nm/f* (SPORT, ÉCON etc) competitor; (SCOL) candidate.

condamner [kɔ̃dane] *vt* (blâmer) to condemn; (JUR) to sentence; (porte, ouverture) to fill in, block up; (malade) to give up (hope for); ~ **qn à 2 ans de prison** to sentence sb to 2 years' imprisonment.

condensation [kɔ̃dɑ̃sɑsjɔ̃] *nf* condensation.

condenser [kɔ̃dɑ̃se] *vt*, se ~ *vi* to condense.

condisciple [kɔ̃disipl(ə)] *nm/f* school fellow, fellow student.

condition [kɔ̃disjɔ̃] *nf* condition; ~**s** *nfpl* (tarif, prix) terms; (circonstances) conditions; **sans** ~ *a* unconditional // *ad* unconditionally; **à** ~ **de/que** provided that; **conditionnel, le** *a* conditional // *nm* conditional (tense); **conditionner** *vt* (déterminer) to determine; (COMM: produit)

to package; (fig: personne) to condition; **air conditionné** air conditioning.

condoléances [kɔ̃dɔleɑ̃s] *nfpl* condolences.

conducteur, trice [kɔ̃dyktœʀ, -tʀis] *nm/f* driver // *nm* (ÉLEC etc) conductor.

conduire [kɔ̃dyiʀ] *vt* to drive; (délégation, troupeau) to lead; se ~ *vi* to behave; ~ **vers/à** to lead towards/to; ~ **qn quelque part** to take sb somewhere; to drive sb somewhere.

conduite [kɔ̃dyit] *nf* (comportement) behaviour; (d'eau, de gaz) pipe; **sous la** ~ **de** led by; ~ **à gauche** left-hand drive; ~ **intérieure** saloon (car).

cône [kon] *nm* cone.

confection [kɔ̃fɛksjɔ̃] *nf* (fabrication) making; (COUTURE) dressmaking; **la** ~ the clothing industry; **vêtement de** ~ ready-to-wear ou off-the-peg garment.

confectionner [kɔ̃fɛksjɔne] *vt* to make.

conférence [kɔ̃feʀɑ̃s] *nf* (exposé) lecture; (pourparlers) conference; ~ **de presse** press conference.

confesser [kɔ̃fese] *vt* to confess; se ~ *vi* (REL) to go to confession.

confession [kɔ̃fesjɔ̃] *nf* confession; (culte: catholique etc) denomination.

confetti [kɔ̃feti] *nm* confetti ou **s**.

confiance [kɔ̃fjɑ̃s] *nf* confidence, trust; faith; **avoir** ~ **en** to have confidence ou faith in, trust; **mettre qn en** ~ to win sb's trust; ~ **en soi** self-confidence.

confiant, e [kɔ̃fjɑ̃, -ɑ̃t] *a* confident; trusting.

confidence [kɔ̃fidɑ̃s] *nf* confidence.

confidentiel, le [kɔ̃fidɑ̃sjɛl] *a* confidential.

confier [kɔ̃fje] *vt*: ~ **à qn** (objet en dépôt, travail etc) to entrust to sb; (secret, pensée) to confide to sb; se ~ **à qn** to confide in sb.

confiné, e [kɔ̃fine] *a* enclosed; stale.

confins [kɔ̃fɛ̃] *nmpl*: **aux** ~ **de** on the borders of.

confirmation [kɔ̃firmasjɔ̃] *nf* confirmation.

confirmer [kɔ̃firme] *vt* to confirm.

confiserie [kɔ̃fizʀi] *nf* (*magasin*) confectioner's ou sweet shop; ~s *nfpl* (*bonbons*) confectionery *sg*; **confiseur, euse** *nm/f* confectioner.

confisquer [kɔ̃fiske] *vt* to confiscate.

confit, e [kɔ̃fi, -it] *a*: **fruits ~s** crystallized fruits // *nm*: ~ **d'oie** conserve of goose.

confiture [kɔ̃fityʀ] *nf* jam; ~ **d'oranges** (orange) marmalade.

conflit [kɔ̃fli] *nm* conflict.

confondre [kɔ̃fɔ̃dʀ(ə)] *vt* (*jumeaux, faits*) to confuse, mix up; (*témoin, menteur*) to confound; **se** ~ *vi* to merge; **se** ~ **en excuses** to apologize profusely.

confondu, e [kɔ̃fɔ̃dy] *a* (*stupéfait*) speechless, overcome.

conforme [kɔ̃fɔʀm(ə)] *a*: ~ **à** in accordance with; in keeping with; true to.

conformément [kɔ̃fɔʀmemã] *ad*: ~ **à** in accordance with.

conformer [kɔ̃fɔʀme] *vt*: **se** ~ **à** to conform to.

conformité [kɔ̃fɔʀmite] *nf*: **en** ~ **avec** in accordance with, in keeping with.

confort [kɔ̃fɔʀ] *nm* comfort; **tout** ~ (*COMM*) with all modern conveniences; **confortable** *a* comfortable.

confrère [kɔ̃fʀɛʀ] *nm* colleague; fellow member; **confrérie** *nf* brotherhood.

confronter [kɔ̃fʀɔ̃te] *vt* to confront; (*textes*) to compare, collate.

confus, e [kɔ̃fy, -yz] *a* (*vague*) confused; (*embarrassé*) embarrassed.

confusion [kɔ̃fyzjɔ̃] *nf* (*voir confus*) confusion; embarrassment; (*voir confondre*) confusion, mixing up.

congé [kɔ̃ʒe] *nm* (*vacances*) holiday; **en** ~ on holiday; off (work); **semaine de** ~ week off; **prendre** ~ **de qn** to take one's leave of sb; **donner son** ~ **à** to give in one's notice to; ~ **de maladie** sick leave; ~s

payés paid holiday.

congédier [kɔ̃ʒedje] *vt* to dismiss.

congélateur [kɔ̃ʒelatœʀ] *nm* freezer, deep freeze.

congeler [kɔ̃ʒle] *vt* to freeze.

congère [kɔ̃ʒɛʀ] *nf* snowdrift.

congestion [kɔ̃ʒɛstjɔ̃] *nf* congestion; ~ **cérébrale** stroke.

congestionner [kɔ̃ʒɛstjɔne] *vt* to congest; (*MÉD*) to flush.

congrès [kɔ̃gʀɛ] *nm* congress.

congru, e [kɔ̃gʀy] *a*: **la portion** ~**e** the smallest ou meanest share.

conifère [kɔnifɛʀ] *nm* conifer.

conjoint, e [kɔ̃ʒwɛ̃, -wɛt] *a* joint // *nm/f* spouse.

conjonction [kɔ̃ʒɔ̃ksjɔ̃] *nf* (*LING*) conjunction.

conjonctivite [kɔ̃ʒɔ̃ktivit] *nf* conjunctivitis.

conjoncture [kɔ̃ʒɔ̃ktyʀ] *nf* circumstances *pl*; climate.

conjugaison [kɔ̃ʒygɛzɔ̃] *nf* (*LING*) conjugation.

conjuguer [kɔ̃ʒyge] *vt* (*LING*) to conjugate; (*efforts etc*) to combine.

conjuration [kɔ̃ʒyʀasjɔ̃] *nf* conspiracy.

conjurer [kɔ̃ʒyʀe] *vt* (*sort, maladie*) to avert; (*implorer*) to beseech, entreat.

connaissance [kɔnɛsɑ̃s] *nf* (*savoir*) knowledge *q*; (*personne connue*) acquaintance; **être sans** ~ to be unconscious; **perdre/reprendre** ~ to lose/regain consciousness; **à ma/sa** ~ to (the best of) my/his knowledge; **avoir** ~ **de** to be aware of; **prendre** ~ **de** (*document etc*) to peruse; **en** ~ **de cause** with full knowledge of the facts.

connaître [kɔnɛtʀ(ə)] *vt* to know; (*éprouver*) to experience; (*avoir*) to have; to enjoy; ~ **de nom/vue** to know by name/sight; **ils se sont connus à Genève** they (first) met in Geneva.

connecté, e [kɔnɛkte] *a* on line.

connecter [kɔnɛkte] *vt* to connect.

connerie [kɔnʀi] *nf* (*fam!*) stupid

thing (to do *ou* say).

connu, e [kɔny] *a* (*célèbre*) well-known.

conquérir [kɔkerir] *vt* to conquer, win; **conquête** *nf* conquest.

consacrer [kɔsakre] *vt* (*REL*) to consecrate; (*fig: usage etc*) to sanction, establish; (*employer*) to devote, dedicate.

conscience [kɔsjɑs] *nf* conscience; **avoir/prendre ~ de** to be/become aware of; **perdre ~** to lose consciousness; **avoir bonne/mauvaise ~** to have a clear/guilty conscience; **consciencieux, euse** *a* conscientious; **conscient, e** *a* conscious.

conscrit [kɔskri] *nm* conscript.

consécutif, ive [kɔsekytif, -iv] *a* consecutive; **~ à** following upon.

conseil [kɔsɛj] *nm* (*avis*) piece of advice, advice *q*; (*assemblée*) council; **prendre ~** (**auprès de qn**) to take advice (from sb); **~ d'administration** board (of directors); **le ~ des ministres** ≈ the Cabinet.

conseiller [kɔseje] *vt* (*personne*) to advise; (*méthode, action*) to recommend, advise; **~ à qn de** to advise sb to.

conseiller, ère [kɔseje, kɔsɛjɛr] *nm/f* adviser.

consentement [kɔsɑtmɑ] *nm* consent.

consentir [kɔsɑtir] *vt* to agree, consent.

conséquence [kɔsekɑs] *nf* consequence; **en ~** (*donc*) consequently; (*de façon appropriée*) accordingly; **ne pas tirer à ~** to be unlikely to have any repercussions.

conséquent, e [kɔsekɑ, -ɑt] *a* logical, rational; (*fam: important*) substantial; **par ~** consequently.

conservateur, trice [kɔsɛrvatœr, -tris] *nm/f* (*POL*) conservative; (*de musée*) curator.

conservatoire [kɔsɛrvatwar] *nm* academy; (*ÉCOLOGIE*) conservation area.

conserve [kɔsɛrv(ə)] *nf* (*gén pl*)

canned *ou* tinned (*Brit*) food; **en ~** canned, tinned (*Brit*).

conserver [kɔsɛrve] *vt* (*faculté*) to retain, keep; (*amis, livres*) to keep; (*préserver, aussi CULIN*) to preserve.

considérable [kɔsiderabl(ə)] *a* considerable, significant, extensive.

considération [kɔsiderasjɔ] *nf* consideration; (*estime*) esteem.

considérer [kɔsidere] *vt* to consider; **~ qch comme** to regard sth as.

consigne [kɔsiɲ] *nf* (*de gare*) left luggage (office) (*Brit*), checkroom (*US*); (*ordre, instruction*) instructions *pl*; **~** (*automatique*) left-luggage locker.

consigner [kɔsiɲe] *vt* (*note, pensée*) to record; (*punir*) to confine to barracks; to put in detention; (*COMM*) to put a deposit on.

consistant, e [kɔsistɑ, -ɑt] *a* thick; solid.

consister [kɔsiste] *vi*: **~ en/dans/à faire** to consist of/in/in doing.

consœur [kɔsœr] *nf* (*lady*) colleague; fellow member.

consoler [kɔsɔle] *vt* to console.

consolider [kɔsɔlide] *vt* to strengthen; (*fig*) to consolidate.

consommateur, trice [kɔsɔmatœr, -tris] *nm/f* (*ÉCON*) consumer; (*dans un café*) customer.

consommation [kɔsɔmasjɔ] *nf* (*boisson*) drink; **~ aux 100 km** (*AUTO*) (fuel) consumption per 100 km.

consommer [kɔsɔme] *vt* (*suj: personne*) to eat *ou* drink, consume; (*suj: voiture, usine, poêle*) to use, consume // *vi* (*dans un café*) to (have a) drink.

consonne [kɔsɔn] *nf* consonant.

conspirer [kɔspire] *vi* to conspire.

conspuer [kɔspɥe] *vt* to boo, shout down.

constamment [kɔstamɑ] *ad* constantly.

constant, e [kɔstɑ, -ɑt] *a* constant; (*personne*) steadfast.

constat [kɔ̃sta] nm (d'huissier) certified report; (de police) report; (affirmation) statement.

constatation [kɔ̃statɑsjɔ̃] nf (observation) (observed) fact, observation; (affirmation) statement.

constater [kɔ̃state] vt (remarquer) to note; (ADMIN, JUR: attester) to certify; (dire) to state.

consterner [kɔ̃stɛrne] vt to dismay.

constipé, e [kɔ̃stipe] a constipated.

constitué, e [kɔ̃stitɥe] a: ~ de made up ou composed of.

constituer [kɔ̃stitɥe] vt (comité, équipe) to set up; (dossier, collection) to put together; (suj: éléments: composer) to make up, constitute; (représenter, être) to constitute; se ~ prisonnier to give o.s. up.

constitution [kɔ̃stitysjɔ̃] nf (composition) composition, make-up; (santé, POL) constitution.

constructeur [kɔ̃stryktœr] nm manufacturer, builder.

construction [kɔ̃stryksjɔ̃] nf construction, building.

construire [kɔ̃stryir] vt to build, construct.

consul [kɔ̃syl] nm consul; **~at** nm consulate.

consultation [kɔ̃syltɑsjɔ̃] nf consultation; ~s nfpl (POL) talks; **heures de ~** (MÉD) surgery (Brit) ou office (US) hours.

consulter [kɔ̃sylte] vt to consult // vi (médecin) to hold surgery (Brit), to be in the office (US).

consumer [kɔ̃syme] vt to consume; se ~ vi to burn.

contact [kɔ̃takt] nm contact; au ~ de (air, peau) on contact with; (gens) through contact with; **mettre/couper le ~** (AUTO) to switch on/off the ignition; **entrer en** ou **prendre ~ avec** to get in touch ou contact with; **~er** vt to contact, get in touch with.

contagieux, euse [kɔ̃taʒjø, -øz] a contagious; infectious.

contaminer [kɔ̃tamine] vt to contaminate.

conte [kɔ̃t] nm tale; **~ de fées** fairy tale.

contempler [kɔ̃tɑ̃ple] vt to contemplate, gaze at.

contemporain, e [kɔ̃tɑ̃pɔrɛ̃, -ɛn] a, nm/f contemporary.

contenance [kɔ̃tnɑ̃s] nf (d'un récipient) capacity; (attitude) bearing, attitude; **perdre ~** to lose one's composure.

conteneur [kɔ̃tnœr] nm container.

contenir [kɔ̃tnir] vt to contain; (avoir une capacité de) to hold.

content, e [kɔ̃tɑ̃, -ɑ̃t] a pleased, glad; **~ de** pleased with; **contenter** vt to satisfy, please; se **contenter de** to content o.s. with.

contentieux [kɔ̃tɑ̃sjø] nm (COMM) litigation; litigation department.

contenu [kɔ̃tny] nm (d'un bol) contents pl; (d'un texte) content.

conter [kɔ̃te] vt to recount, relate.

contestable [kɔ̃testabl(ə)] a questionable.

contestation [kɔ̃testɑsjɔ̃] nf (POL) protest.

conteste [kɔ̃test(ə)]: **sans ~** ad unquestionably, indisputably.

contester [kɔ̃teste] vt to question, contest // vi (POL, gén) to protest, rebel (against established authority).

contexte [kɔ̃tɛkst] nm context.

contigu, ë [kɔ̃tigy] a: ~ (à) adjacent (to).

continent [kɔ̃tinɑ̃] nm continent.

continu, e [kɔ̃tiny] a continuous; (courant) ~ direct current, DC.

continuel, le [kɔ̃tinɥɛl] a (qui se répète) constant, continual; (continu) continuous.

continuer [kɔ̃tinɥe] vt (travail, voyage etc) to continue (with), carry on (with), go on (with); (prolonger: alignement, rue) to continue // vi (pluie, vie, bruit) to continue, go on; (voyageur) to go on; **~ à** ou **de faire** to go on ou continue doing.

contorsionner [kɔ̃tɔrsjɔne]: se ~ vi to contort o.s., writhe about.

contour [kɔ̃tuʀ] *nm* outline, contour.

contourner [kɔ̃tuʀne] *vt* to go round.

contraceptif, ive [kɔ̃tʀaseptif, -iv] *a, nm* contraceptive.

contraception [kɔ̃tʀasεpsjɔ̃] *nf* contraception.

contracté, e [kɔ̃tʀakte] *a* tense.

contracter [kɔ̃tʀakte] *vt* (*muscle etc*) to tense, contract; (*maladie, dette, obligation*) to contract; (*assurance*) to take out; **se ~** *vi* (*métal, muscles*) to contract.

contractuel, le [kɔ̃tʀaktɥεl] *nm/f* (*agent*) traffic warden.

contradiction [kɔ̃tʀadiksjɔ̃] *nf* contradiction; **contradictoire** *a* contradictory, conflicting.

contraindre [kɔ̃tʀɛ̃dʀ(ə)] *vt:* **~ qn à faire** to compel sb to do.

contraint, e [kɔ̃tʀɛ̃, -ɛ̃t] *a* (*mine, air*) constrained, forced *// nf* constraint.

contraire [kɔ̃tʀεʀ] *a, nm* opposite; **~ à** contrary to; **au ~** *ad* on the contrary.

contrarier [kɔ̃tʀaʀje] *vt* (*personne*) to annoy, bother; (*fig*) to impede; to thwart, frustrate.

contraste [kɔ̃tʀast(ə)] *nm* contrast.

contrat [kɔ̃tʀa] *nm* contract; **~ de travail** employment contract.

contravention [kɔ̃tʀavɑ̃sjɔ̃] *nf* (*amende*) fine; (*P.V. pour stationnement interdit*) parking ticket.

contre [kɔ̃tʀ(ə)] *prép* against; (*en échange*) (in exchange) for; **par ~** on the other hand.

contrebande [kɔ̃tʀəbɑ̃d] *nf* (*trafic*) contraband, smuggling; (*marchandise*) contraband, smuggled goods *pl*; **faire la ~ de** to smuggle.

contrebas [kɔ̃tʀəba]: **en ~** *ad* (down) below.

contrebasse [kɔ̃tʀəbas] *nf* (double) bass.

contrecarrer [kɔ̃tʀəkaʀe] *vt* to thwart.

contrecœur [kɔ̃tʀəkœʀ]: **à ~** *ad* (be)grudgingly, reluctantly.

contrecoup [kɔ̃tʀəku] *nm* repercussions *pl*; **par ~** as an indirect consequence.

contredire [kɔ̃tʀədiʀ] *vt* (*personne*) to contradict; (*témoignage, assertion, faits*) to refute.

contrée [kɔ̃tʀe] *nf* region; land.

contrefaçon [kɔ̃tʀəfasɔ̃] *nf* forgery.

contrefaire [kɔ̃tʀəfεʀ] *vt* (*document, signature*) to forge, counterfeit; (*personne, démarche*) to mimic; (*dénaturer: sa voix etc*) to disguise.

contre-jour [kɔ̃tʀəʒuʀ]: **à ~** *ad* against the sunlight.

contremaître [kɔ̃tʀəmεtʀ(ə)] *nm* foreman.

contrepartie [kɔ̃tʀəpaʀti] *nf* compensation; **en ~** in return.

contre-performance [kɔ̃tʀəpεʀfɔʀmɑ̃s] *nf* below-average performance.

contre-pied [kɔ̃tʀəpje] *nm:* **prendre le ~ de** to take the opposing view of; to take the opposite course to.

contre-plaqué [kɔ̃tʀəplake] *nm* plywood.

contrepoids [kɔ̃tʀəpwa] *nm* counterweight, counterbalance.

contrer [kɔ̃tʀe] *vt* to counter.

contresens [kɔ̃tʀəsɑ̃s] *nm* misinterpretation; mistranslation; nonsense *q*; **à ~** *ad* the wrong way.

contretemps [kɔ̃tʀətɑ̃] *nm* hitch; **à ~** *ad* (*MUS*) out of time; (*fig*) at an inopportune moment.

contrevenir [kɔ̃tʀəvniʀ]: **~ à** *vt* to contravene.

contribuable [kɔ̃tʀibɥabl(ə)] *nm/f* taxpayer.

contribuer [kɔ̃tʀibɥe]: **~ à** *vt* to contribute towards; **contribution** *nf* contribution; **contributions directes/ indirectes** direct/indirect taxation; **mettre à contribution** to call upon.

contrôle [kɔ̃tʀol] *nm* checking *q*, check; supervision; monitoring; (*test*) test, examination; **perdre le ~ de** (*véhicule*) to lose control of; **~ continu** (*SCOL*) continuous assessment; ~ **d'identité** identity check; ~ **des naissances** birth control.

contrôler [kɔ̃trole] *vt* (*vérifier*) to check; (*surveiller*) to supervise; to monitor, control; (*maîtriser*, COMM: *firme*) to control; **contrôleur, euse** *nm/f* (*de train*) (ticket) inspector; (*de bus*) (bus) conductor/tress.

contrordre [kɔ̃trɔrd(ə)] *nm*: **sauf** ~ unless otherwise directed.

controversé, e [kɔ̃trɔvɛrse] *a* (*personnage, question*) controversial.

contusion [kɔ̃tyzjɔ̃] *nf* bruise, contusion.

convaincre [kɔ̃vɛ̃kr(ə)] *vt*: ~ **qn** (**de qch**) to convince sb (of sth); (*pousser à*): ~ **qn de faire** to persuade sb (to do); ~ **qn de** (JUR: *délit*) to convict sb of.

convalescence [kɔ̃valesɑ̃s] *nf* convalescence.

convenable [kɔ̃vnabl(ə)] *a* suitable; (*assez bon, respectable*) decent.

convenance [kɔ̃vnɑ̃s] *nf*: **à ma/votre** ~ to my/your liking; ~s *nfpl* proprieties.

convenir [kɔ̃vnir] *vi* to be suitable; ~ **à** to suit; **il convient de** it is advisable to; (*bienséant*) it is right *ou* proper to; ~ **de** (*bien-fondé de qch*) to admit (to), acknowledge; (*date, somme etc*) to agree upon; (*que* (*admettre*) to admit that; ~ **de faire** to agree to do.

convention [kɔ̃vɑ̃sjɔ̃] *nf* convention; ~**s** *nfpl* (*convenances*) convention *sg*; ~ **collective** (ÉCON) collective agreement; **conventionnel, e** *a* (ADMIN) applying charges laid down by the state.

convenu, e [kɔ̃vny] *pp de* **convenir** // *a* agreed.

conversation [kɔ̃vɛrsasjɔ̃] *nf* conversation.

convertir [kɔ̃vɛrtir] *vt*: ~ **qn** (**à**) to convert sb (to); ~ **qch en** to convert sth into; **se** ~ (**à**) to be converted (to).

conviction [kɔ̃viksjɔ̃] *nf* conviction.

convienne *etc vb voir* **convenir**.

convier [kɔ̃vje] *vt*: ~ **qn à** (*dîner etc*) to (cordially) invite sb to.

convive [kɔ̃viv] *nm/f* guest (*at table*).

convivial, e [kɔ̃vivjal] *a* (INFORM) user-friendly.

convocation [kɔ̃vɔkasjɔ̃] *nf* (*document*) notification to attend; summons *sg*.

convoi [kɔ̃vwa] *nm* (*de voitures, prisonniers*) convoy; (*train*) train; ~ (**funèbre**) funeral procession.

convoiter [kɔ̃vwate] *vt* to covet.

convoquer [kɔ̃vɔke] *vt* (*assemblée*) to convene; (*subordonné*) to summon; (*candidat*) to ask to attend; ~ **qn** (**à**) (*réunion*) to invite sb (to attend).

convoyeur [kɔ̃vwajɔ̃r] *nm* (NAVIG) escort ship; ~ **de fonds** security guard.

coopération [kɔɔperasjɔ̃] *nf* cooperation; (ADMIN): **la C~** ≈ Voluntary Service Overseas (*Brit*), ≈ Peace Corps (*US alternative to military service*).

coopérer [kɔɔpere] *vi*: ~ (**à**) to co-operate (in).

coordonner [kɔɔrdɔne] *vt* to coordinate.

copain, copine [kɔpɛ̃, kɔpin] *nm/f* mate, pal.

copeau, x [kɔpo] *nm* shaving.

copie [kɔpi] *nf* copy; (SCOL) script, paper; exercise.

copier [kɔpje] *vt, vi* to copy; ~ **sur** to copy from.

copieur [kɔpjœr] *nm* (*photo*)copier.

copieux, euse [kɔpjø, -øz] *a* copious.

copine [kɔpin] *nf voir* **copain**.

copropriété [kɔprɔprijete] *nf* co-ownership, joint ownership.

coq [kɔk] *nm* cock, rooster.

coq-à-l'âne [kɔkalan] *nm inv* abrupt change of subject.

coque [kɔk] *nf* (*de noix, mollusque*) shell; (*de bateau*) hull; **à la** ~ (CULIN) (soft-)boiled.

coquelicot [kɔkliko] *nm* poppy.

coqueluche [kɔklyʃ] *nf* whooping-cough.

coquet, te [kɔkɛ, -ɛt] *a* flirtatious; appearance-conscious; pretty.

coquetier [kɔktje] *nm* egg-cup.

coquillage [kɔkijaʒ] *nm* (*mollusque*) shellfish *inv*; (*coquille*) shell.

coquille [kɔkij] *nf* shell; (*TYPO*) misprint; ~ St Jacques scallop.

coquin, e [kɔkɛ̃, -in] *a* mischievous, roguish; (*polisson*) naughty.

cor [kɔr] *nm* (*MUS*) horn; (*MÉD*): (au pied) corn; réclamer à ~ et à cri to clamour for.

corail, aux [kɔraj, -o] *nm* coral q.

Coran [kɔrɑ̃] *nm*: le ~ the Koran.

corbeau, x [kɔrbo] *nm* crow.

corbeille [kɔrbɛj] *nf* basket; ~ à papier waste paper basket *ou* bin.

corbillard [kɔrbijar] *nm* hearse.

corde [kɔrd(ə)] *nf* rope; (de violon, raquette, d'arc) string; (*ATHLÉTISME, AUTO*): la ~ the rails *pl*; ~ à linge washing *ou* clothes line; ~ raide tight-rope; ~ à sauter skipping rope; ~s vocales vocal cords; usé jusqu'à la ~ threadbare.

cordée [kɔrde] *nf* (d'alpinistes) rope, roped party.

cordialement [kɔrdjalmɑ̃] *ad* (formule épistolaire) (kind) regards.

cordon [kɔrdɔ̃] *nm* cord, string; ~ sanitaire/de police sanitary/police cordon; ~ ombilical umbilical cord.

cordonnerie [kɔrdɔnri] *nf* shoe repairer's (shop).

cordonnier [kɔrdɔnje] *nm* shoe repairer.

coriace [kɔrjas] *a* tough.

corne [kɔrn(ə)] *nf* horn; (de cerf) antler.

corneille [kɔrnɛj] *nf* crow.

cornemuse [kɔrnəmyz] *nf* bagpipes *pl*.

corner [kɔrnɛr] *nm* (*FOOTBALL*) corner (kick).

cornet [kɔrnɛ] *nm* (paper) cone; (de glace) cornet, cone; ~ à piston cornet.

corniaud [kɔrnjo] *nm* (chien) mongrel; (péj) twit, clot.

corniche [kɔrniʃ] *nf* (de meuble, neigeuse) cornice; (route) coast road.

cornichon [kɔrniʃɔ̃] *nm* gherkin.

Cornouailles [kɔrnwaj] *nf* Cornwall.

corporation [kɔrpɔrasjɔ̃] *nf* corporate body.

corporel, le [kɔrpɔrɛl] *a* bodily; (punition) corporal.

corps [kɔr] *nm* body; à son ~ défendant against one's will; à ~ perdu headlong; perdu ~ et biens lost with all hands; prendre ~ to take shape; ~ à ~ *ad* hand-to-hand // *nm* clinch; le ~ électoral the electorate; le ~ enseignant the teaching profession; ~ de garde guardroom.

corpulent, e [kɔrpylɑ̃, -ɑ̃t] *a* stout.

correct, e [kɔrɛkt] *a* correct; (passable) adequate.

correction [kɔrɛksjɔ̃] *nf* (voir corriger) correction; (voir correct) correctness; (rature, surcharge) correction, emendation; (coups) thrashing.

correctionnel, le [kɔrɛksjɔnɛl] *a* (*JUR*): tribunal ~ ≈ criminal court.

correspondance [kɔrɛspɔ̃dɑ̃s] *nf* correspondence; (de train, d'avion) connection; cours par ~ correspondence course; vente par ~ mail-order business.

correspondant, e [kɔrɛspɔ̃dɑ̃, -ɑ̃t] *nm/f* correspondent; (*TÉL*) person phoning (ou being phoned).

correspondre [kɔrɛspɔ̃dr(ə)] *vi* to correspond, tally; ~ à to correspond to; ~ avec qn to correspond with sb.

corrida [kɔrida] *nf* bullfight.

corridor [kɔridɔr] *nm* corridor.

corriger [kɔriʒe] *vt* (devoir) to correct; (punir) to thrash; ~ qn de (défaut) to cure sb of.

corrompre [kɔrɔ̃pr(ə)] *vt* to corrupt; (acheter: témoin etc) to bribe.

corruption [kɔrypsjɔ̃] *nf* corruption; bribery.

corsage [kɔrsaʒ] *nm* bodice; blouse.

corse [kɔrs(ə)] *a, nm/f* Corsican // *nf*: la C~ Corsica.

corsé, e [kɔrse] *a* vigorous; (vin,

goût full-flavoured; *(fig)* spicy; tricky.

corset [kɔʀsɛ] *nm* corset; bodice.

cortège [kɔʀtɛʒ] *nm* procession.

corvée [kɔʀve] *nf* chore, drudgery *q*.

cosmétique [kɔsmetik] *nm* beauty care product.

cossu, e [kɔsy] *a* well-to-do.

costaud, e [kɔsto, -od] *a* a strong, sturdy.

costume [kɔstym] *nm* (*d'homme*) suit; (*de théâtre*) costume; **costumé, e** a dressed up.

cote [kɔt] *nf* (*en Bourse etc*) quotation; quoted value; (*d'un cheval*): la ~ **de** the odds *pl* on; (*d'un candidat etc*) rating; (*sur un croquis*) dimension; ~ **d'alerte** danger *ou* flood level.

côte [kot] *nf* (*rivage*) coast(line); (*pente*) slope; (: *sur une route*) hill; (*ANAT*) rib; (*d'un tricot, tissu*) rib, ribbing *q*; ~ **à** ~ side by side; la **C~** (**d'Azur**) the French Riviera.

côté [kote] *nm* (*gén*) side; (*direction*) way, direction; **de chaque** ~ (**de**) on each side (of); **de tous les** ~**s** from all directions; **de quel est-il parti?** which way did he go?; **de ce/de l'autre** ~ this/the other way; **du** ~ **de** (*provenance*) from; (*direction*) towards; (*proximité*) near; **de** ~ *ad* sideways; on one side; to one side; aside; **laisser/mettre de** ~ to leave/put to one side; **à** ~ *ad* (*right*) nearby; beside; next door; (*d'autre part*) besides; **à** ~ **de** beside; next to; être **aux** ~**s de** to be by the side of.

coteau, x [kɔto] *nm* hill.

côtelette [kotlɛt] *nf* chop.

coter [kɔte] *vt* (*en Bourse*) to quote.

côtier, ière [kotje, -jɛʀ] a coastal.

cotisation [kɔtizasjɔ̃] *nf* subscription, dues *pl*; (*pour une pension*) contributions *pl*.

cotiser [kɔtize] *vi*: ~ (**à**) to pay contributions (to); se ~ *vi* to club together.

coton [kɔtɔ̃] *nm* cotton; ~ **hydro-**

phile cotton wool *(Brit)*, absorbent cotton *(US)*.

côtoyer [kotwaje] *vt* to be close to; to rub shoulders with; to run alongside.

cou [ku] *nm* neck.

couchant [kuʃɑ̃] a: **soleil** ~ setting sun.

couche [kuʃ] *nf* (*strate: gén, GÉO*) layer; (*de peinture, vernis*) coat; (*de bébé*) nappy *(Brit)*, diaper *(US)*; ~**s** *nfpl* (*MÉD*) confinement *sg*; ~**s sociales** social levels *ou* strata; **culotte** ~ disposable nappy *(Brit)* ou diaper *(US)* and waterproof pants in one.

couché, e [kuʃe] a lying down; (*au lit*) in bed.

coucher [kuʃe] *nm* (*du soleil*) setting // *vt* (*personne*) to put to bed; (: *loger*) to put up; (*objet*) to lay on its side // *vi* to sleep; se ~ *vi* (*pour dormir*) to go to bed; (*pour se reposer*) to lie down; (*soleil*) to set; ~ **de soleil** sunset.

couchette [kuʃɛt] *nf* couchette; (*de marin*) bunk.

coucou [kuku] *nm* cuckoo.

coude [kud] *nm* (*ANAT*) elbow; (*de tuyau, de la route*) bend; ~ **à** ~ *ad* shoulder to shoulder, side by side.

coudre [kudʀ(ə)] *vt* (*bouton*) to sew on; (*robe*) to sew (up) // *vi* to sew.

couenne [kwan] *nf* (*de lard*) rind.

couette [kwɛt] *nf* duvet, quilt.

couffin [kufɛ̃] *nm* Moses basket.

couiner [kwine] *vi* to squeal.

couler [kule] *vi* to flow, run; (*fuir: stylo, récipient*) to leak; (*sombrer: bateau*) to sink // *vt* (*cloche, sculpture*) to cast; (*bateau*) to sink; (*fig*) to ruin, bring down.

couleur [kulœʀ] *nf* colour; (*CARTES*) suit; **film/télévision en** ~ colour film/television.

couleuvre [kulœvʀ(ə)] *nf* grass snake.

coulisse [kulis] *nf*: ~**s** *nfpl* (*THÉÂTRE*) wings; (*fig*): **dans les** ~**s** behind the scenes; **coulisser** *vi* to slide, run.

couloir [kulwar] nm corridor, passage; (de bus) gangway; (de la route) bus lane; (SPORT: de piste) lane; (GÉO) gully; ~ aérien/de navigation air/shipping lane.

coup [ku] nm (heurt, choc) knock; (affectif) blow, shock; (aggressif) blow; (avec arme à feu) shot; (de l'horloge) chime; stroke; (SPORT) stroke; shot; (fam: fois) time; ~ de coude nudge (with the elbow); ~ de tonnerre clap of thunder; ~ de sonnette ring of the bell; ~ de crayon stroke of the pencil; donner un ~ de balai to give the floor a sweep; avoir le ~ (fig) to have the knack; boire un ~ to have a drink; être dans le ~ to be in on it; du ~... so (you see)...; d'un seul ~ (subitement) suddenly; (à la fois) at one go; in one blow; du premier ~ first time; du même ~ at the same time; à ~ sûr definitely, without fail; ~ sur ~ in quick succession; sur le ~ outright; sous le ~ de (surprise etc) under the influence of; ~ de chance stroke of luck; ~ de couteau stab (of a knife); ~ d'envoi kick-off; ~ d'essai first attempt; ~ de feu shot; ~ de filet (POLICE) haul; ~ franc free kick; ~ de frein (sharp) braking (q); ~ de main: donner un ~ de main à qn to give sb a (helping) hand; ~ d'œil glance; ~ de pied kick; ~ de poing punch; ~ de soleil sunburn q; ~ de téléphone phone call; ~ de tête (sudden) impulse; ~ de théâtre (fig) dramatic turn of events; ~ de vent gust of wind; en ~ de vent in a tearing hurry.

coupable [kupabl(ə)] a guilty // nm/f (gén) culprit; (JUR) guilty party.

coupe [kup] nf (verre) goblet; (à fruits) dish; (SPORT) cup; (de cheveux, de vêtement) cut; (graphique, plan) (cross) section; être sous la ~ de to be under the control of.

coupe-papier [kuppapje] nm inv paper knife.

couper [kupe] vt to cut; (retrancher) to cut (out); (route, courant) to cut off; (appétit) to take away; (vin, cidre) to blend; (: à table) to dilute // vi to cut; (prendre un raccourci) to take a short-cut; se ~ vi (se blesser) to cut o.s.; ~ la parole à qn to cut sb short.

couperosé, e [kuproze] a blotchy.

couple [kupl(ə)] nm couple.

couplet [kuplɛ] nm verse.

coupole [kupɔl] nf dome; cupola.

coupon [kupɔ̃] nm (ticket) coupon; (de tissu) remnant; roll; ~-réponse nm reply coupon.

coupure [kupyr] nf cut; (billet de banque) note; (de journal) cutting; ~ de courant power cut.

cour [kur] nf (de ferme, jardin) (court)yard; (d'immeuble) back yard; (JUR, royale) court; faire la ~ à qn to court sb; ~ d'assises court of assizes; ~ martiale court-martial.

courage [kuraʒ] nm courage, bravery; **courageux, euse** a brave, courageous.

couramment [kuramɑ̃] ad commonly; (parler) fluently.

courant, e [kurɑ̃, -ɑ̃t] a (fréquent) common; (COMM, gén: normal) standard; (en cours) current // nm current; (fig) movement; trend; être au ~ (de) (fait, nouvelle) to know (about); mettre qn au ~ (de) (fait, nouvelle) to tell sb (about); (nouveau travail etc) to teach sb the basics (of); se tenir au ~ (de) (techniques etc) to keep o.s. up-to-date (on); dans le ~ de (pendant) in the course of; le 10 ~ (COMM) the 10th inst; ~ d'air draught; ~ électrique (electric) current, power.

courbature [kurbatyr] nf ache.

courbe [kurb(ə)] a curved // nf curve.

courber [kurbe] vt to bend.

coureur, euse [kurœr, -øz] nm/f (SPORT) runner (ou driver); (péj) womanizer/manhunter; ~ **automobile** racing driver.

courge [kuʀʒ(ə)] nf (CULIN.) marrow.

courgette [kuʀʒɛt] nf courgette (Brit), zucchini (US).

courir [kuʀiʀ] vi to run // vt (SPORT: épreuve) to compete in; (risque) to run; (danger) to face; **les magasins** to go round the shops; **le bruit court que** the rumour is going round that.

couronne [kuʀɔn] nf crown; (de fleurs) wreath, circlet.

couronnerons etc vb voir **courir**.

courrier [kuʀje] nm mail, post; (lettres à écrire) letters pl; long/moyen ~ a (AVIAT) long/medium-haul.

courroie [kuʀwa] nf strap; (TECH) belt.

courrons etc vb voir **courir**.

cours [kuʀ] nm (leçon) lesson; class; (série de leçons) course; (cheminement) course; (écoulement) flow; (COMM) rate; price; **donner libre** ~ à to give free expression to; **avoir** ~ (monnaie) to be legal tender; (fig) to be current; (SCOL) to have a class **ou lecture; en** ~ (année) current; (travaux) in progress; **en** ~ **de** route on the way; **au** ~ **de** in the course of, during; **d'eau** waterway; ~ **du soir** night school.

course [kuʀs(ə)] nf running; (SPORT: épreuve) race; (d'un taxi, autocar) journey, trip; (petite mission) errand; ~**s** nfpl (achats) shopping sg; **faire des** ~**s** to go some shopping.

court, e [kuʀ, kuʀt(ə)] a short // ad short // nm: ~ (**de tennis**) (tennis) court; **tourner à** ~ to come to a sudden end; **ça fait** ~ that's not very long; **à** ~ **de** short of; **prendre qn de** ~ to catch sb unawares; **tirer à la** ~ **e paille** to draw lots; ~**-circuit** nm short-circuit.

courtier, ère [kuʀtje, -jɛʀ] nm/f broker.

courtiser [kuʀtize] vt to court, woo.

courtois, e [kuʀtwa, -waz] a courteous.

couru, e pp de **courir** // a: **c'est** ~ it's a safe bet.

cousais etc vb voir **coudre**.

couscous [kuskus] nm couscous.

cousin, e [kuzɛ̃, -in] nm/f cousin.

coussin [kusɛ̃] nm cushion.

cousu, e [kuzy] pp de **coudre**.

coût [ku] nm cost; **le** ~ **de la vie** the cost of living.

coûtant [kutɑ̃] am: **au prix** ~ at cost price.

couteau, x [kuto] nm knife; ~ **à cran d'arrêt** flick-knife.

coûter [kute] vt, vi to cost; **combien ça coûte?** how much is it?, what does it cost?; **coûte que coûte** at all costs; **coûteux, euse** a costly, expensive.

coutume [kutym] nf custom.

couture [kutyʀ] nf sewing; dressmaking; (points) seam.

couturier [kutyʀje] nm fashion designer.

couturière [kutyʀjɛʀ] nf dressmaker.

couvée [kuve] nf brood, clutch.

couvent [kuvɑ̃] nm (de sœurs) convent; (de frères) monastery.

couver [kuve] vt to hatch; (maladie) to be sickening for // vi (feu) to smoulder; (révolte) to be brewing.

couvercle [kuvɛʀkl(ə)] nm lid; (de bombe aérosol etc, qui se visse) cap, top.

couvert, e [kuvɛʀ, -ɛʀt(ə)] pp de **couvrir** // a (ciel) overcast // nm place setting; (place à table) place; (au restaurant) cover charge; ~**s** nmpl cutlery sg; ~ **de** covered with **ou** in; **mettre le** ~ to lay the table.

couverture [kuvɛʀtyʀ] nf blanket; (de bâtiment) roofing; (de livre, assurance, fig) cover; (presse) coverage; ~ **chauffante** electric blanket.

couveuse [kuvøz] nf (de maternité) incubator.

couvre... [kuvʀ(ə)] préfixe: ~**-chef**

nm hat; ~-**feu** *nm* curfew; ~-**lit** *nm* bedspread.

couvrir [kuvʀiʀ] *vt* to cover; **se** ~ *vi* (*ciel*) to cloud over; (*s'habiller*) to cover up; (*se coiffer*) to put on one's hat.

crabe [kʀab] *nm* crab.

cracher [kʀaʃe] *vi, vt* to spit.

crachin [kʀaʃɛ̃] *nm* drizzle.

craie [kʀɛ] *nf* chalk.

craindre [kʀɛ̃dʀ(ə)] *vt* to fear; to be afraid of; (*être sensible à: chaleur, froid*) to be easily damaged by.

crainte [kʀɛ̃t] *nf* fear; **de** ~ **de/que** for fear of/that; **craintif, ive** *a* timid.

cramoisi, e [kʀamwazi] *a* crimson.

crampe [kʀɑ̃p] *nf* cramp.

cramponner [kʀɑ̃pɔne]: **se** ~ *vi*: **se** ~ (**à**) to hang *ou* cling on (to).

cran [kʀɑ̃] *nm* (*entaille*) notch; (*de courroie*) hole; (*courage*) guts *pl*; ~ **d'arrêt** safety catch.

crâne [kʀɑn] *nm* skull.

crâner [kʀɑne] *vi* (*fam*) show off.

crapaud [kʀapo] *nm* toad.

crapule [kʀapyl] *nf* villain.

craquement [kʀakmɑ̃] *nm* crack, snap; (*du plancher*) creak, creaking q.

craquer [kʀake] *vi* (*bois, plancher*) to creak; (*fil, branche*) to snap; (*couture*) to come apart; (*fig*) to break down // *vt* (*allumette*) to strike.

crasse [kʀas] *nf* grime, filth.

cravache [kʀavaʃ] *nf* (riding) crop.

cravate [kʀavat] *nf* tie.

crawl [kʀol] *nm* crawl; **dos crawlé** backstroke.

crayeux, euse [kʀɛjø, -øz] *a* chalky.

crayon [kʀɛjɔ̃] *nm* pencil; ~ **à bille** ball-point pen; ~ **de couleur** crayon, colouring pencil; ~ **optique** light pen.

créancier, ière [kʀeɑ̃sje, -jɛʀ] *nm/f* creditor.

création [kʀeasjɔ̃] *nf* creation.

créature [kʀeatyʀ] *nf* creature.

crécelle [kʀesɛl] *nf* rattle.

crèche [kʀɛʃ] *nf* (*de Noël*) crib; (*garderie*) crèche, day nursery.

crédit [kʀedi] *nm* (*gén*) credit; ~s *nmpl* funds; **payer/acheter à** ~ to pay/buy on credit *ou* on easy terms; **faire** ~ **à qn** to give sb credit; **créditer** *vt*: **créditer un compte** (**de**) to credit an account (with).

crédule [kʀedyl] *a* credulous, gullible.

créer [kʀee] *vt* to create; (*THÉÂTRE*) to produce (for the first time).

crémaillère [kʀemɑjɛʀ] *nf* (*RAIL*) rack; **pendre la** ~ to have a house-warming party.

crématoire [kʀematwaʀ] *a*: **four** ~ crematorium.

crème [kʀɛm] *nf* cream; (*entremets*) cream dessert // *a inv* cream(-coloured); **un** (*café*) ~ **a** white coffee; ~ **chantilly** ~ **fouettée** whipped cream; ~ **à raser** shaving cream; **crémerie** *nf* dairy; **crémeux, euse** *a* creamy.

créneau, x [kʀeno] *nm* (*de fortification*) crenel(le); (*fig*) gap, slot; (*AUTO*): **faire un** ~ to reverse into a parking space (between cars alongside the kerb).

crêpe [kʀɛp] *nf* (*galette*) pancake // *nm* (*tissu*) crêpe; **crêpé, e** *a* (*cheveux*) backcombed; ~**rie** *nf* pancake shop *ou* restaurant.

crépir [kʀepiʀ] *vt* to roughcast.

crépiter [kʀepite] *vi* to sputter, splutter; to crackle.

crépon [kʀepɔ̃] *nm* seersucker.

crépu, e [kʀepy] *a* frizzy, fuzzy.

crépuscule [kʀepyskyl] *nm* twilight, dusk.

cresson [kʀesɔ̃] *nm* watercress.

crête [kʀɛt] *nf* (*de coq*) comb; (*de vague, montagne*) crest.

creuser [kʀøze] *vt* (*trou, tunnel*) to dig; (*sol*) to dig a hole in; (*bois*) to hollow out; (*fig*) to go (deeply) into; **ça creuse** that gives you a real appetite; **se** ~ (**la cervelle**) to rack one's brains.

creux, euse [krø, -øz] a hollow // nm hollow; (fig: sur graphique etc) trough; **heures creuses** slack periods; off-peak periods.

crevaison [krəvɛzɔ̃] nf puncture.

crevasse [krəvas] nf (dans le sol) crack, fissure; (de glacier) crevasse.

crevé, e [krəve] a (fatigué) all in, exhausted.

crever [krəve] vt (papier) to tear, break; (tambour, ballon) to burst // vi (pneu) to burst; (automobiliste) to have a puncture (Brit) ou a flat tire (US); (fam) to die; **cela lui a crevé un œil** it blinded him in one eye.

crevette [krəvɛt] nf: ~ **(rose)** prawn; ~ **grise** shrimp.

cri [kri] nm cry, shout; (d'animal: spécifique) cry, call; **c'est le dernier ~** (fig) it's the latest fashion.

criant, e [krijɑ̃, -ɑ̃t] a (injustice) glaring.

criard, e [krijar, -ard(ə)] a (couleur) garish, loud; (voix) yelling.

crible [kribl(ə)] nm riddle; **passer qch au ~** (fig) to go over sth with a fine-tooth comb.

cric [krik] nm (AUTO) jack.

crier [krije] vi (pour appeler) to shout, cry (out); (de peur, de douleur etc) to scream, yell // vt (ordre, injure) to shout (out), yell (out).

crime [krim] nm crime; (meurtre) murder; **criminel, le** nm/f criminal; murderer.

crin [krɛ̃] nm hair q; (fibre) horsehair.

crinière [krinjɛr] nf mane.

crique [krik] nf creek, inlet.

criquet [krikɛ] nm locust; grasshopper.

crise [kriz] nf crisis (pl crises); (MÉD) attack; fit; ~ **cardiaque** heart attack; ~ **de foie** bilious attack; ~ **de nerfs** attack of nerves.

crisper [krispe] vt to tense; (poings) to clench; **se ~ vi** to tense; to clench; (personne) to get tense.

crisser [krise] vi (neige) to crunch; (pneu) to screech.

cristal, aux [kristal, -o] nm crystal.

cristallin, e [kristalɛ̃, -in] a crystal-clear.

critère [kritɛr] nm criterion (pl ia).

critiquable [kritikabl(ə)] a open to criticism.

critique [kritik] a critical // nm/f (de théâtre, musique) critic // nf criticism; (THÉÂTRE etc: article) review.

critiquer [kritike] vt (dénigrer) to criticize; (évaluer, juger) to assess, examine (critically).

croasser [krɔase] vi to caw.

croc [kro] nm (dent) fang; (de boucher) hook.

croc-en-jambe [krɔkɑ̃ʒɑ̃b] nm: **faire un ~ à qn** to trip sb up.

croche [krɔʃ] nf (MUS) quaver (Brit), eighth note (US).

croche-pied [krɔʃpje] nm = **croc-en-jambe.**

crochet [krɔʃɛ] nm hook; (détour) detour; (TRICOT: aiguille) crochet hook; (: technique) crochet; ~**s** nmpl (TYPO) square brackets; **vivre aux ~s de qn** to live ou sponge off sb; **crocheter** vt (serrure) to pick.

crochu, e [krɔʃy] a hooked; claw-like.

crocodile [krɔkɔdil] nm crocodile.

crocus [krɔkys] nm crocus.

croire [krwar] vt to believe; **se fort** to think one is strong; ~ **que** to believe ou think that; ~ **à, ~ en** to believe in.

crois vb voir **croître.**

croisade [krwazad] nf crusade.

croisé, e [krwaze] a (veston) double-breasted.

croisement [krwazmɑ̃] nm (carrefour) crossroads sg; (BIO) crossing; crossbreed.

croiser [krwaze] vt (personne, voiture) to pass; (route) to cross, cut across; (BIO) to cross // vi (NAVIG) to cruise; **se ~** (personnes, véhicules) to pass each other; (routes, lettres) to *(regards)* to meet.

croiseur [krwazœr] *nm* cruiser *(warship)*.

croisière [krwazjɛr] *nf* cruise; **vitesse de ~** *(AUTO etc)* cruising speed.

croisillon [krwazijɔ̃] *nm* lattice.

croissance [krwasɑ̃s] *nf* growth.

croissant [krwasɑ̃] *nm* (*à manger*) croissant; *(motif)* crescent.

croître [krwatr(ə)] *vi* to grow.

croix [krwa] *nf* cross; **en ~**, ad in the form of a cross; **la C~ Rouge** the Red Cross.

croque... [krɔk] *préfixe:* **~-monsieur** *nm inv* toasted ham and cheese sandwich.

croquer [krɔke] *vt* (*manger*) to crunch; to munch; *(dessiner)* to sketch // *vi* to be crisp *ou* crunchy; **chocolat à ~** plain dessert chocolate.

croquis [krɔki] *nm* sketch.

crosse [krɔs] *nf* (*de fusil*) butt; *(de revolver)* grip.

crotte [krɔt] *nf* droppings *pl*.

crotté, e [krɔte] *a* muddy, mucky.

crottin [krɔtɛ̃] *nm* dung, manure.

crouler [krule] *vi* (*s'effondrer*) to collapse; *(être délabré)* to be crumbling.

croupe [krup] *nf* rump; **en ~** pillion.

croupir [krupir] *vi* to stagnate.

croustillant, e [krustijɑ̃, -ɑ̃t] *a* crisp; *(fig)* spicy.

croûte [krut] *nf* crust; (*du fromage*) rind; *(MÉD)* scab; **en ~** *(CULIN)* in pastry.

croûton [krutɔ̃] *nm* *(CULIN)* crouton; *(bout du pain)* crust, heel.

croyable [krwajabl(ə)] *a* credible.

croyant, e [krwajɑ̃, -ɑ̃t] *nm/f* believer.

C.R.S. *sigle fpl* (= *Compagnies républicaines de sécurité*) *a* state security police force // *sigle m* member of the C.R.S.

cru, e [kry] *pp de* **croire** // *a* *(non cuit)* raw; *(lumière, couleur)* harsh;

(paroles, description) crude // *nm* *(vignoble)* vineyard; *(vin)* wine.

crû *pp de* **croître**.

cruauté [kryote] *nf* cruelty.

cruche [kryʃ] *nf* pitcher, jug.

crucifix [krysifi] *nm* crucifix.

crucifixion [krysifiksjɔ̃] *nf* crucifixion.

crudités [krydite] *nfpl* *(CULIN)* salads.

crue [kry] *nf* *voir* **cru**.

cruel, le [kryɛl] *a* cruel.

crus *etc* **crûs** *etc*, *vb voir* **croire**, **croître**.

crustacés [krystase] *nmpl* shellfish.

Cuba [kyba] *nf* Cuba.

cube [kyb] *nm* cube; *(jouet)* brick; **mètre ~** cubic metre; **2 au ~ 2** cubed.

cueillir [kœjir] *vt* *(fruits, fleurs)* to pick, gather; *(fig)* to catch.

cuiller *ou* **cuillère** [kɥijɛr] *nf* spoon; **~ à café** coffee spoon; *(CULIN)* ≈ teaspoonful; **~ à soupe** soup-spoon; *(CULIN)* ≈ tablespoonful; **cuillerée** *nf* spoonful.

cuir [kɥir] *nm* leather; **~ chevelu** scalp.

cuirassé [kɥirase] *nm* *(NAVIG)* battleship.

cuire [kɥir] *vt* (*aliments*) to cook; *(au four)* to bake; *(poterie)* to fire // *vi* to cook; **bien cuit** *(viande)* well done; **trop cuit** overdone.

cuisant, e [kɥizɑ̃, -ɑ̃t] *a* (*douleur*) stinging; *(fig: souvenir, échec)* bitter.

cuisine [kɥizin] *nf* (*pièce*) kitchen; *(art culinaire)* cookery, cooking; *(nourriture)* cooking, food; **faire la ~** to cook; **cuisiner** *vt* to cook; *(fam)* to grill // *vi* to cook; **cuisinier, ière** *nm/f* cook // *nf* (*poêle*) cooker.

cuisse [kɥis] *nf* thigh; *(CULIN)* leg.

cuisson [kɥisɔ̃] *nf* cooking; firing.

cuit, e *pp de* **cuire**.

cuivre [kɥivr(ə)] *nm* copper; **les ~s** *(MUS)* the brass.

cul [ky] *nm* *(fam!)* arse *(!)*.

culasse [kylas] *nf* *(AUTO)* cylinder-head; *(de fusil)* breech.

culbute [kylbyt] *nf* somersault; (*accidentelle*) tumble, fall.

culminant, e [kylminɑ̃, -ɑ̃t] *a*: **point ~** highest point.

culminer [kylmine] *vi* to reach its highest point; to tower.

culot [kylo] *nm* (*effronterie*) cheek.

culotte [kylɔt] *nf* (*pantalon*) trousers *pl* (*Brit*), pants *pl* (*US*); (*de femme*) knickers *pl* (*Brit*), panties *pl*; **~ de cheval** riding breeches *pl*.

culpabilité [kylpabilite] *nf* guilt.

culte [kylt(ə)] *nm* (*religion*) religion; (*hommage, vénération*) worship; (*protestant*) service.

cultivateur, trice [kyltivatœr, -tris] *nm/f* farmer.

cultivé, e [kyltive] *a* (*personne*) cultured, cultivated.

cultiver [kyltive] *vt* to cultivate; (*légumes*) to grow, cultivate.

culture [kyltyʀ] *nf* cultivation; growing; (*connaissances etc*) culture; **~ physique** physical training; **culturisme** *nm* body-building.

cumin [kymɛ̃] *nm* (*CULIN*) caraway seeds *pl*; cumin.

cumuler [kymyle] *vt* (*emplois, honneurs*) to hold concurrently; (*salaires*) to draw concurrently; (*JUR: droits*) to accumulate.

cupide [kypid] *a* greedy, grasping.

cure [kyʀ] *nf* (*MÉD*) course of treatment; **n'avoir ~ de** to pay no attention to.

curé [kyʀe] *nm* parish priest.

cure-dent [kyʀdɑ̃] *nm* toothpick.

cure-pipe [kyʀpip] *nm* pipe cleaner.

curer [kyʀe] *vt* to clean out.

curieux, euse [kyʀjø, -øz] *a* (*étrange*) strange, curious; (*indiscret*) curious, inquisitive // *nmpl* (*badauds*) onlookers; **curiosité** *nf* curiosity; (*site*) unusual feature.

curriculum vitae [kyʀikylɔmvite] *nm inv* (*abr* **C.V.**) curriculum vitae (C.V.).

curseur [kyʀsœʀ] *nm* (*INFORM*) cursor.

cuti-réaction [kytiʀeaksjɔ̃] *nf* (*MÉD*) skin-test.

cuve [kyv] *nf* vat; (*à mazout etc*) tank.

cuvée [kyve] *nf* vintage.

cuvette [kyvɛt] *nf* (*récipient*) bowl, basin; (*GÉO*) basin.

C.V. *sigle m* (*AUTO*) *voir* **cheval**; (*COMM*) = **curriculum vitae**.

cyanure [sjanyʀ] *nm* cyanide.

cyclable [siklabl(ə)] *a*: **piste ~** cycle track.

cycle [sikl(ə)] *nm* cycle.

cyclisme [siklism(ə)] *nm* cycling.

cycliste [siklist(ə)] *nm/f* cyclist // *a* cycle *cpd*; **coureur ~** racing cyclist.

cyclomoteur [siklomɔtœʀ] *nm* moped.

cyclone [siklon] *nm* hurricane.

cygne [siɲ] *nm* swan.

cylindre [silɛ̃dʀ(ə)] *nm* cylinder; **cylindrée** *nf* (*AUTO*) (cubic) capacity.

cymbale [sɛ̃bal] *nf* cymbal.

cynique [sinik] *a* cynical.

cystite [sistit] *nf* cystitis.

D

d' *prép de* **de**.

dactylo [daktilo] *nf* (*aussi:* **~graphe**) typist; (*aussi:* **~graphie**) typing; **~graphier** *vt* to type (out).

dada [dada] *nm* hobby-horse.

daigner [deɲe] *vt* to deign.

daim [dɛ̃] *nm* (*fallow*) deer *inv*; (*peau*) buckskin; (*imitation*) suede.

dalle [dal] *nf* paving stone; slab.

daltonien, ne [daltɔnjɛ̃, -jɛn] *a* colour-blind.

dam [dam] *nm*: **au grand ~ de** much to the detriment (*ou* annoyance) of.

dame [dam] *nf* lady; (*CARTES, ÉCHECS*) queen; **~s** *nfpl* (*jeu*) draughts *sg* (*Brit*), checkers (*US*).

damner [dɑne] *vt* to damn.

dancing [dɑ̃siŋ] *nm* dance hall.

Danemark [danmaʀk] *nm* Denmark.

danger [dɑ̃ʒe] *nm* danger; **dangereux, euse** *a* dangerous.

danois, e [danwa, -waz] *a* Danish //
nm/f: D~, e Dane // *nm* (LING) Danish.

MOT-CLÉ

dans [dɑ̃] *prép*
1 (*position*) in; (*à l'intérieur de*) inside; c'est ~ le tiroir/le salon it's
in the drawer/lounge; ~ la boîte in
ou inside the box; **marcher** ~ **la
ville** to walk about the town
2 (*direction*) into; elle a couru ~ le
salon she ran into the lounge
3 (*provenance*) out of, from; je l'ai
pris ~ le tiroir/salon I took it out of
ou from the drawer/lounge; **boire** ~
un verre to drink out of ou from a
glass
4 (*temps*) in; ~ **2 mois** in 2 months,
in 2 months' time
5 (*approximation*) about; ~ **les 20 F**
about 20 F.

---

danse [dɑ̃s] *nf:* la ~ dancing; une ~
a dance; **danser** *vi, vt* to dance;
danseur, euse *nm/f* ballet dancer/
ballerina; (*au bal etc*) dancer; partner.

dard [daʁ] *nm* sting (*organ*).

date [dat] *nf* date; de longue ~ a
longstanding; ~ de naissance date
of birth; **dater** *vt, vi* to date; **dater
de** to date from; à dater de (as)
from.

datte [dat] *nf* date; **dattier** *nm* date
palm.

dauphin [dofɛ̃] *nm* (ZOOL) dolphin.

davantage [davɑ̃taʒ] *ad* more; (*plus
longtemps*) longer; ~ de more.

MOT-CLÉ

de (*de + le* = du, *de + les* = des)
[də, dy, de] ◆ *prép* **1** (*appartenance*) of; le toit de la maison the
roof of the house; la voiture
d'Élisabeth/de mes parents
Elizabeth's/my parents' car
2 (*provenance*) from; il vient de
Londres he comes from London;
elle est sortie du cinéma she came

out of the cinema
3 (*caractérisation, mesure*): un mur
de brique/bureau d'acajou a brick
wall/mahogany desk; un billet de 50
F a 50 franc note; une pièce de 2m
de large ou large de 2m a room
2m wide, a 2m-wide room; un bébé
de 10 mois a 10-month-old baby; 12
mois de crédit/travail 12 months'
credit/work; augmenter de 10 F to
increase by 10 F; de 14 à 18 from 14
to 18

◆ *dét* **1** (*phrases affirmatives*)
(*souvent omis*): du vin, de l'eau,
des pommes (some) wine, (some)
water, (some) apples; des enfants
sont venus some children came;
pendant des mois for months
2 (*phrases interrogatives et néga-
tives*) any; a-t-il du vin? has he got
any wine?; il n'a pas de pommes/
d'enfants he hasn't (got) any
apples/children, he has no apples/
children.

---

dé [de] *nm* (*à jouer*) die ou dice (*pl
dice*); (*aussi*: ~ à coudre) thimble.

déambuler [deɑ̃byle] *vi* to stroll
about.

débâcle [debakl(ə)] *nf* rout.

déballer [debale] *vt* to unpack.

débandade [debɑ̃dad] *nf* rout; scat-
tering.

débarbouiller [debaʁbuje] *vt* to
wash; se ~ *vi* to wash (one's face).

débarcadère [debaʁkadɛʁ] *nm*
wharf.

débardeur [debaʁdœʁ] *nm* docker,
stevedore; (*maillot*) tank top.

débarquer [debaʁke] *vt* to unload,
land // *vi* to disembark; (*fig*) to turn
up.

débarras [debaʁa] *nm* lumber room;
junk cupboard; **bon** ~! good rid-
dance!

débarrasser [debaʁase] *vt* to clear;
~ qn de (*vêtements, paquet*) to relieve sb of; se ~ de *vt* to get rid of.

débat [deba] *nm* discussion, debate.

débattre [debatʁ(ə)] *vt* to discuss,

debate; se ~ *vi* to struggle.

débaucher [debo∫e] *vt* (*licencier*) to lay off, dismiss; (*entraîner*) to lead astray, debauch.

débile [debil] *a* weak, feeble; (*fam: idiot*) dim-witted; ~ **mental, e** *nm/f* mental defective.

débit [debi] *nm* (*d'un liquide, fleuve*) flow; (*d'un magasin*) turnover (of goods); (*élocution*) delivery; (*bancaire*) debit; ~ **de boissons** drinking establishment; ~ **de tabac** tobacconist's; **débiter** *vt* (*compte*) to debit; (*liquide, gaz*) to give out; (*couper: bois, viande*) to cut up; (*péj: paroles etc*) to churn out; **débiteur, trice** *nm/f* debtor // *a* in debit; (*compte*) debit *cpd*.

déblayer [debleje] *vt* to clear.

débloquer [debloke] *vt* (*frein*) to release; (*prix, crédits*) to free.

déboires [debwaʀ] *nmpl* setbacks.

déboiser [debwaze] *vt* to deforest.

déboîter [debwate] *vt* (*AUTO*) to pull out; **se ~ le genou** *etc* to dislocate one's knee *etc*.

débonnaire [deboneʀ] *a* easy-going, good-natured.

débordé, e [debɔʀde] *a*: **être ~ (de)** (*travail, demandes*) to be snowed under (with).

déborder [debɔʀde] *vi* to overflow; (*lait etc*) to boil over; ~ **qch** (*dépasser*) to extend beyond sth.

débouché [debu∫e] *nm* (*pour vendre*) outlet; (*perspective d'emploi*) opening.

déboucher [debu∫e] *vt* (*évier, tuyau etc*) to unblock; (*bouteille*) to uncork // *vi*: ~ **de** to emerge from; ~ **sur** to come out onto; to open out onto.

débourser [debuʀse] *vt* to pay out.

debout [dəbu] *ad*: **être ~** (*personne*) to be standing, stand; (: *levé, éveillé*) to be up; (*chose*) to be upright; **être encore ~** (*fig: en état*) to be still going; **se mettre ~** to stand up; **se tenir ~** to stand; ~! stand up!; (*du lit*) get up!; **cette histoire ne tient pas ~** this story

doesn't hold water.

déboutonner [debutɔne] *vt* to undo, unbutton.

débraillé, e [debʀaje] *a* slovenly, untidy.

débrancher [debʀã∫e] *vt* to disconnect; (*appareil électrique*) to unplug.

débrayage [debʀɛjaʒ] *nm* (*AUTO*) clutch.

débrayer [debʀeje] *vi* (*AUTO*) to declutch; (*cesser le travail*) to stop work.

débris [debʀi] *nm* (*fragment*) fragment // *nmpl* rubbish *sg*; debris *sg*.

débrouillard, e [debʀujaʀ, -aʀd(ə)] *a* smart, resourceful.

débrouiller [debʀuje] *vt* to disentangle, untangle; **se ~** *vi* to manage.

débusquer [debyske] *vt* to drive out (from cover).

début [deby] *nm* beginning, start; ~**s** beginnings; **début** *sg*.

débutant, e [debytã, -ãt] *nm/f* beginner, novice.

débuter [debyte] *vi* to begin, start; (*faire ses débuts*) to start out.

deçà [dəsa]: **en ~ de** *prép* this side of.

décacheter [deka∫te] *vt* to unseal.

décadence [dekadãs] *nf* decadence; decline.

décaféiné, e [dekafeine] *a* decaffeinated.

décalage [dekalaʒ] *nm* gap; discrepancy; ~ **horaire** time difference (between time zones); time-lag.

décaler [dekale] *vt* (*dans le temps: avancer*) to bring forward; (: *retarder*) to put back; (*changer de position*) to shift forward *ou* back.

décalquer [dekalke] *vt* to trace; (*par pression*) to transfer.

décamper [dekãpe] *vi* to clear out *ou* off.

décanter [dekãte] *vt* to allow to settle (and decant).

décaper [dekape] *vt* to strip; (*avec abrasif*) to scour; (*avec papier de verre*) to sand.

décapiter [dekapite] *vt* to behead.

(par accident) to decapitate.

décapotable [dekapɔtabl(ə)] *a* convertible.

décapsuler [dekapsyle] *vt* to take the cap *ou* top off; **décapsuleur** *nm* bottle-opener.

décédé, e [desede] *a* deceased.

décéder [desede] *vi* to die.

déceler [desle] *vt* to discover, detect; to indicate, reveal.

décembre [desɑ̃bʀ(ə)] *nm* December.

décemment [desamɑ̃] *ad* decently.

décennie [deseni] *nf* decade.

décent, e [desɑ̃, -ɑ̃t] *a* decent.

déception [desɛpsjɔ̃] *nf* disappointment.

décerner [desɛʀne] *vt* to award.

décès [desɛ] *nm* death, decease.

décevoir [desvwaʀ] *vt* to disappoint.

déchaîner [deʃene] *vt* to unleash, arouse; se ~ to be unleashed.

déchanter [deʃɑ̃te] *vi* to become disillusioned.

décharge [deʃaʀʒ(ə)] *nf* *(d'ordures)* rubbish tip *ou* dump; *(électrique)* electrical discharge; à la ~ de in defence of.

décharger [deʃaʀʒe] *vt* *(marchandise, véhicule)* to unload; *(ÉLEC, faire feu)* to discharge; ~ qn de *(responsabilité)* to release sb from.

décharné, e [deʃaʀne] *a* emaciated.

déchausser [deʃose] *vt* *(skis)* to take off; se ~ *vi* to take off one's shoes; *(dent)* to come *ou* work loose.

déchéance [deʃeɑ̃s] *nf* degeneration; decay, decline; fall.

déchet [deʃɛ] *nm* *(de bois, étoffe etc)* scrap; *(perte: gén COMM)* wastage, waste; ~s *nmpl* *(ordures)* refuse *sg*, rubbish *sg*.

déchiffrer [deʃifʀe] *vt* to decipher.

déchiqueter [deʃikte] *vt* to tear *ou* pull to pieces.

déchirement [deʃiʀmɑ̃] *nm* *(chagrin)* wrench, heartbreak; *(gén pl: conflit)* rift, split.

déchirer [deʃiʀe] *vt* to tear; *(en morceaux)* to tear up; *(pour ouvrir)*

to tear off; *(arracher)* to tear out; *(fig)* to rack; to tear (apart); se ~ *vi* to tear, rip; se ~ **un muscle** to tear a muscle.

déchirure [deʃiʀyʀ] *nf* *(accroc)* tear, rip; ~ **musculaire** torn muscle.

déchoir [deʃwaʀ] *vi* *(personne)* to lower o.s., demean o.s.

déchu, e [deʃy] *a* fallen; deposed.

décidé, e [deside] *a* *(personne, air)* determined; c'est ~ it's decided.

décidément [desidemɑ̃] *ad* undoubtedly; really.

décider [deside] *vt*: ~ **qch** to decide on sth; ~ **de faire/que** to decide to do/that; ~ **qn (à faire qch)** to persuade sb (to do sth); ~ **de qch** to decide upon sth; *(suj: chose)* to determine sth; se ~ **(à faire)** to decide (to do); se ~ **pour** to decide on *ou* in favour of.

décilitre [desilitʀ(ə)] *nm* decilitre.

décimal, e, aux [desimal, -o] *a, nf* decimal.

décimètre [desimɛtʀ(ə)] *nm* decimetre; **double** ~ (20 cm) ruler.

décisif, ive [desizif, -iv] *a* decisive.

décision [desizjɔ̃] *nf* decision; *(fermeté)* decisiveness, decision.

déclaration [deklaʀasjɔ̃] *nf* declaration; registration; *(discours: POL etc)* statement; ~ **(d'impôts)** ≈ tax return; ~ **(de sinistre)** *(insurance)* claim.

déclarer [deklaʀe] *vt* to declare; *(décès, naissance)* to register; se ~ *vi* *(feu, maladie)* to break out.

déclasser [deklase] *vt* to relegate; to downgrade; to lower in status.

déclencher [deklɑ̃ʃe] *vt* *(mécanisme etc)* to release; *(provoquer)* to trigger off; se ~ *vi* to release itself; to go off.

déclic [deklik] *nm* trigger mechanism; *(bruit)* click.

décliner [dekline] *vi* to decline // *vt* *(invitation)* to decline; *(responsabilité)* to refuse to accept; *(nom,* *adresse*) to state.

déclivité [deklivite] *nf* slope, incline.

décocher [dekɔʃe] *vt* to throw; *qn* to shoot.

décoiffer [dekwafe] *vt*: ~ qn to mess up sb's hair; to take sb's hat off; se ~ *vi* to take off one's hat.

décois *etc vb voir* **décevoir**.

décollage [dekɔlaʒ] *nm* (*AVIAT*) takeoff.

décoller [dekɔle] *vt* to unstick // *vi* (*avion*) to take off; se ~ *vi* to come unstuck.

décolleté, e [dekɔlte] *a* low-cut; wearing a low-cut dress // *nm* low neck(line); (*bare*) neck and shoulders; (*plongeant*) cleavage.

décolorer [dekɔlɔre] *vt* (*tissu*) to fade; (*cheveux*) to bleach, lighten; se ~ *vi* to fade.

décombres [dekɔ̃br(ə)] *nmpl* rubble *sg*, debris *sg*.

décommander [dekɔmɑ̃de] *vt* to cancel; (*invités*) to put off; se ~ *vi* to cancel one's appointment *etc*, cry off.

décomposé, e [dekɔ̃poze] *a* (*pourri*) decomposed; (*visage*) haggard, distorted.

décompte [dekɔ̃t] *nm* deduction; (*facture*) detailed account.

déconcerter [dekɔ̃sɛrte] *vt* to disconcert, confound.

déconfit, e [dekɔ̃fi, -it] *a* crestfallen.

déconfiture [dekɔ̃fityr] *nf* failure, defeat; collapse, ruin.

décongeler [dekɔ̃ʒle] *vt* to thaw.

déconner [dekɔne] *vi* (*fam*) to talk rubbish.

déconseiller [dekɔ̃seje] *vt*: ~ qch (à qn) to advise (sb) against sth.

déconsidérer [dekɔ̃sidere] *vt* to discredit.

décontracter [dekɔ̃trakte] *vt*, se ~ *vi* to relax.

déconvenue [dekɔ̃vny] *nf* disappointment.

décor [dekɔr] *nm* décor; (*paysage*) scenery; ~s *nmpl* (*THÉÂTRE*) scenery *sg*, décor *sg*; (*CINÉMA*) set *sg*.

décorateur [dekɔratœr] *nm* (interior) decorator; (*CINÉMA*) set designer.

décoration [dekɔrasjɔ̃] *nf* decoration.

décorer [dekɔre] *vt* to decorate.

décortiquer [dekɔrtike] *vt* to shell; (*riz*) to hull; (*fig*) to dissect.

découcher [dekuʃe] *vi* to spend the night away from home.

découdre [dekudr(ə)] *vt* to unpick; se ~ *vi* to come unstitched; en ~ (*fig*) to fight, do battle.

découler [dekule] *vi*: ~ de to ensue ou follow from.

découper [dekupe] *vt* (*papier, tissu etc*) to cut up; (*volaille, viande*) to carve; (*détacher: manche, article*) to cut out; se ~ sur (*ciel, fond*) to stand out against.

décourager [dekuraʒe] *vt* to discourage; se ~ *vi* to lose heart, become discouraged.

décousu, e [dekuzy] *a* unstitched; (*fig*) disjointed, disconnected.

découvert, e [dekuvɛr, -ɛrt(ə)] *a* (*tête*) bare, uncovered; (*lieu*) open, exposed // *nm* (*bancaire*) overdraft // *nf* discovery.

découvrir [dekuvrir] *vt* to discover; (*apercevoir*) to see; (*enlever ce qui couvre ou protège*) to uncover; (*montrer, dévoiler*) to reveal; se ~ *vi* to take off one's hat; to take something off; (*au lit*) to uncover o.s.; (*ciel*) to clear.

décret [dekrɛ] *nm* decree; **décréter** *vt* to decree; to order; to declare.

décrire [dekrir] *vt* to describe.

décrocher [dekrɔʃe] *vt* (*dépendre*) to take down; (*téléphone*) to take off the hook; (: *pour répondre*) ~ (le téléphone) to lift the receiver; (*fig: contrat etc*) to get, land // *vi* to drop out; to switch off.

décroître [dekrwatr(ə)] *vi* to decrease, decline.

décrypter [dekripte] *vt* to decipher.

déçu, e [desy] *pp de* **décevoir**.

décupler [dekyple] *vt, vi* to increase tenfold.

dédaigner [dedɛɲe] *vt* to despise, scorn; (*négliger*) to disregard, spurn.

dédain [dedɛ̃] *nm* scorn, disdain.

dédale [dedal] *nm* maze.

dedans [dədɑ̃] *ad* inside; (*pas en plein air*) indoors, inside // *nm* inside; au ~ on the inside; inside; en ~ (*vers l'intérieur*) inwards; *voir aussi* là.

dédicacer [dedikase] *vt*: ~ à (qn) to sign (for sb), autograph (for sb).

dédier [dedje] *vt* to dedicate.

dédire [dediʀ]: se ~ *vi* to go back on one's word; to retract, recant.

dédommager [dedɔmaʒe] *vt*: ~ qn (de) to compensate sb (for); (*fig*) to repay sb (for).

dédouaner [dedwane] *vt* to clear through customs.

dédoubler [deduble] *vt* (*classe, effectifs*) to split (into two); ~ les trains to run additional trains.

déduire [dedɥiʀ] *vt*: ~ qch (de) (*ôter*) to deduct sth (from); (*conclure*) to deduce *ou* infer sth (from).

déesse [deɛs] *nf* goddess.

défaillance [defajɑ̃s] *nf* (*syncope*) blackout; (*fatigue*) (sudden) weakness q; (*technique*) fault, failure; (*morale etc*) weakness; ~ cardiaque heart failure.

défaillir [defajiʀ] *vi* to faint, to feel faint; (*mémoire etc*) to fail.

défaire [defɛʀ] *vt* (*installation*) to take down, dismantle; (*paquet etc, nœud, vêtement*) to undo; se ~ *vi* to come undone; se ~ de *vt* (*se débarrasser de*) to get rid of; (*se séparer de*) to part with.

défait, e [defɛ, -ɛt] *a* (*visage*) haggard, ravaged // *nf* defeat.

défalquer [defalke] *vt* to deduct.

défaut [defo] *nm* (*moral*) fault, failing, defect; (*d'étoffe, métal*) fault, flaw, defect; (*manque, carence*) ~ de lack of; shortage of; en ~ at fault; in the wrong; faire ~ (*manquer*) to be lacking; à ~ *ad* failing that; à ~ de for lack *ou* want of; par ~ (*JUR*) in his (*ou* her *etc*) absence.

défavoriser [defavɔʀize] *vt* to put at a disadvantage.

défection [defɛksjɔ̃] *nf* defection, failure to give support *ou* assistance; failure to appear; faire ~ (*d'un parti etc*) to withdraw one's support, leave.

défectueux, euse [defɛktɥø, -øz] *a* faulty, defective.

défendre [defɑ̃dʀ(ə)] *vt* to defend; (*interdire*) to forbid; ~ à qn qch/de faire to forbid sb sth/to do; se ~ *vi* to defend o.s.; il se défend (*fig*) he can hold his own; se ~ de/contre (*se protéger*) to protect o.s. from/ against; se ~ de (*se garder de*) to refrain from; (*nier*): se ~ de vouloir to deny wanting.

défense [defɑ̃s] *nf* defence; (*d'éléphant etc*) tusk; '~ de fumer/cracher' 'no smoking/spitting'.

déférer [defeʀe] *vt* (*JUR*) to refer; ~ à *vt* (*requête, décision*) to defer to.

déferler [defɛʀle] *vi* (*vagues*) to break; (*fig*) to surge.

défi [defi] *nm* (*provocation*) challenge; (*bravade*) defiance.

défiance [defjɑ̃s] *nf* mistrust, distrust.

déficit [defisit] *nm* (*COMM*) deficit.

défier [defje] *vt* (*provoquer*) to challenge; (*fig*) to defy, brave; se ~ de *vi* (*se méfier de*) to distrust.

défigurer [defigyʀe] *vt* to disfigure.

défilé [defile] *nm* (*GÉO*) (narrow) gorge *ou* pass; (*soldats*) parade; (*manifestants*) procession, march.

défiler [defile] *vi* (*troupes*) to march past; (*sportifs*) to parade; (*manifestants*) to march; (*visiteurs*) to pour, stream; se ~ *vi* (*se dérober*) to slip away, sneak off.

définir [definiʀ] *vt* to define.

définitif, ive [definitif, -iv] *a* (*final*) final, definitive; (*pour longtemps*) permanent, definitive; (*sans appel*) final, definite // *nf*: en définitive eventually; (*somme toute*) when all is said and done.

définitivement [definitivmã] *ad* definitively; permanently; definitely.

déflagration [deflagrasjõ] *nf* explosion.

défoncer [defõse] *vt* (*caisse*) to stave in; (*porte*) to smash in ou down; (*lit, fauteuil*) to burst (the springs of); (*terrain, route*) to rip ou plough up.

déformation [defɔʀmasjõ] *nf:* ~ **professionnelle** conditioning by one's job.

déformer [defɔʀme] *vt* to put out of shape; (*corps*) to deform; (*pensée, fait*) to distort; **se** ~ *vi* to lose its shape.

défouler [defule]: **se** ~ *vi* to unwind, let off steam.

défraîchir [defʀeʃiʀ]: **se** ~ *vi* to fade; to become worn.

défrayer [defʀeje] *vt:* ~ **qn** to pay sb's expenses; ~ **la chronique** to be in the news.

défricher [defʀiʃe] *vt* to clear (for cultivation).

défroquer [defʀɔke] *vi* (*aussi:* **se** ~) to give up the cloth.

défunt, e [defœ̃, -œ̃t] *a:* **son** ~ **père** his late father // *nm/f* deceased.

dégagé, e [degaʒe] *a* clear; (*ton, air*) casual, jaunty.

dégagement [degaʒmã] *nm:* **voie de** ~ slip road; **itinéraire de** ~ alternative route (*to relieve traffic congestion*).

dégager [degaʒe] *vt* (*exhaler*) to give off; (*délivrer*) to free, extricate; (*désencombrer*) to clear; (*isoler: idée, aspect*) to bring out; **se** ~ *vi* (*odeur*) to be given off; (*passage, ciel*) to clear.

dégainer [degene] *vt* to draw.

dégarnir [degaʀniʀ] *vt* (*vider*) to empty, clear; **se** ~ *vi* (*tempes, crâne*) to go bald.

dégâts [dega] *nmpl* damage *sg*.

dégel [deʒɛl] *nm* thaw.

dégeler [deʒle] *vt* to thaw (out);

(*fig*) to unfreeze // *vi* to thaw (out).

dégénérer [deʒeneʀe] *vi* to degenerate; (*empirer*) to go from bad to worse.

dégingandé, e [deʒɛ̃gãde] *a* gangling.

dégivrer [deʒivʀe] *vt* (*frigo*) to defrost; (*vitres*) to de-ice.

déglutir [deglytiʀ] *vt, vi* to swallow.

dégonflé, e [degõfle] *a* (*pneu*) flat.

dégonfler [degõfle] *vt* (*pneu, ballon*) to let down, deflate; **se** ~ *vi* (*fam*) to chicken out.

dégouliner [deguline] *vi* to trickle, drip.

dégourdi, e [deguʀdi] *a* smart, resourceful.

dégourdir [deguʀdiʀ] *vt:* **se** ~ (**les jambes**) to stretch one's legs (*fig*).

dégoût [degu] *nm* disgust, distaste.

dégoûtant, e [degutã, -ãt] *a* disgusting.

dégoûté, e [degute] *a* disgusted; ~ **de** sick of.

dégoûter [degute] *vt* to disgust; ~ **qn de qch** to put sb off sth.

dégoutter [degute] *vi* to drip.

dégradé [degʀade] *nm* (*PEINTURE*) gradation.

dégrader [degʀade] *vt* (*MIL: officier*) to degrade; (*abîmer*) to damage, deface; **se** ~ *vi* (*relations, situation*) to deteriorate.

dégrafer [degʀafe] *vt* to unclip, unhook.

degré [dəgʀe] *nm* degree; (*d'escalier*) step; **alcool à 90** ~**s** surgical spirit.

dégressif, ive [degʀesif, -iv] *a* on a decreasing scale.

dégrèvement [degʀɛvmã] *nm* tax relief.

dégringoler [degʀɛ̃gɔle] *vi* to tumble (down).

dégrossir [degʀosiʀ] *vt* (*fig*) to work out roughly; to knock the rough edges off.

déguenillé, e [degnije] *a* ragged, tattered.

déguerpir [degɛʀpiʀ] *vi* to clear off.

dégueulasse [degølas] a (fam) disgusting.

déguisement [degizmã] nm disguise.

déguiser [degize] vt to disguise; se ~ vi (se costumer) to dress up; (pour tromper) to disguise o.s.

déguster [degyste] vt (vins) to taste; (fromages etc) to sample; (savourer) to enjoy, savour.

dehors [dəɔʀ] ad outside; (en plein air) outdoors // nm outside // nmpl (apparences) appearances; mettre ou jeter ~ (expulser) to throw out; au ~ outside; outwardly; au ~ de outside; en ~ (vers l'extérieur) outside; outwards; en ~ de (hormis) apart from.

déjà [deʒa] ad already; (auparavant) before, already.

déjeuner [deʒœne] vi to (have) lunch; (le matin) to have breakfast // nm lunch; breakfast.

déjouer [deʒwe] vt to elude; to foil.

delà [dəla] ad: par ~, en ~ (de), au ~ (de) beyond.

délabrer [delabʀe]: se ~ vi to fall into decay, become dilapidated.

délacer [delase] vt to unlace.

délai [dele] nm (attente) waiting period; (sursis) extension of time; (temps accordé) time limit; à bref ~ shortly, very soon; at short notice; dans les ~s within the time limit.

délaisser [delese] vt to abandon, desert.

délasser [delase] vt (reposer) to relax; (divertir) to divert, entertain; se ~ vi to relax.

délateur, trice [delatœʀ, -tʀis] nm/f informer.

délavé, e [delave] a faded.

délayer [deleje] vt (CULIN) to mix (with water etc); (peinture) to thin down.

delco [dɛlko] nm (AUTO) distributor.

délecter [delɛkte]: se ~ vi: se ~ de to revel ou delight in.

délégué, e [delege] nm/f delegate; representative.

déléguer [delege] vt to delegate.

délibéré, e [delibeʀe] a (conscient) deliberate; (déterminé) determined.

délibérer [delibeʀe] vi to deliberate.

délicat, e [delika, -at] a delicate; (plein de tact) tactful; (attentionné) thoughtful; (exigeant) fussy, particular; **procédés peu ~s** unscrupulous methods; **délicatement** ad delicately; (avec douceur) gently.

délice [delis] nm delight.

délicieux, euse [delisjø, -jøz] a (au goût) delicious; (sensation, impression) delightful.

délier [delje] vt to untie; ~ qn de (serment etc) to release sb from.

délimiter [delimite] vt to delimit, demarcate; to determine; to define.

délinquance [delɛ̃kɑ̃s] nf criminality.

délinquant, e [delɛ̃kɑ̃, -ɑ̃t] a, nm/f delinquent.

délirer [deliʀe] vi to be delirious; (fig) to be raving, be going wild.

délit [deli] nm (criminal) offence.

délivrer [delivʀe] vt (prisonnier) to (set) free, release; (passeport, certificat) to issue; ~ qn de (ennemis) to deliver ou free sb from; (fig) to relieve sb of; to rid sb of.

déloger [deloʒe] vt (locataire) to turn out; (objet coincé, ennemi) to dislodge.

deltaplane [dɛltaplan] nm hang-glider.

déluge [delyʒ] nm (biblique) Flood.

déluré, e [delyʀe] a smart, resourceful; (péj) forward, pert.

demain [dəmɛ̃] ad tomorrow.

demande [dəmɑ̃d] nf (requête) request; (revendication) demand; (ADMIN, formulaire) application; (ÉCON): la ~ demand; ' ~s d'emploi ' 'situations wanted'; ~ en mariage (marriage) proposal; ~ de poste job application.

demandé, e [dəmɑ̃de] a (article etc): **très ~** (very) much in demand.

demander [dəmɑ̃de] vt to ask for;

(date, heure etc) to ask; *(nécessiter)* to require, demand; ~ **qch à qn** to ask sb for sth; **to ask sb sth;** ~ **à qn de faire** to ask sb to do; **se** ~ **si/ pourquoi** *etc* to wonder if/why *etc*; *(sens purement réfléchi)* to ask o.s. if/why *etc*; **on vous demande au téléphone** you're wanted on the phone.

demandeur, euse [dəmãdœʀ, -øz] *nm/f*: ~ **d'emploi** job-seeker; *(job)* applicant.

démangeaison [demãʒɛzɔ̃] *nf* itching.

démanger [demãʒe] *vi* to itch.

démanteler [demãtle] *vt* to break up; to demolish.

démaquillant [demakijã] *nm* make-up remover.

démaquiller [demakije] *vt*: **se** ~ to remove one's make-up.

démarche [demaʀʃ(ə)] *nf (allure)* gait, walk; *(intervention)* step; approach; *(fig: intellectuelle)* thought processes *pl*; approach; **faire des** ~**s auprès de qn** to approach sb.

démarcheur, euse [demaʀʃœʀ, -øz] *nm/f (COMM)* door-to-door salesman/woman.

démarquer [demaʀke] *vt (prix)* to mark down; *(joueur)* to stop marking.

démarrage [demaʀaʒ] *nm* start.

démarrer [demaʀe] *vi (conducteur)* to start (up); *(véhicule)* to move off; *(travaux)* to get moving; **démarreur** *nm (AUTO)* starter.

démêler [demele] *vt* to untangle.

démêlés [demele] *nmpl* problems.

déménagement [demenaʒmã] *nm* move, removal; **camion de** ~ removal van.

déménager [demenaʒe] *vt (meubles)* to (re)move // *vi* to move (house); **déménageur** *nm* removal man; *(entrepreneur)* furniture remover.

démener [demne] *vt*: **se** ~ *vi* to thrash about; *(fig)* to exert o.s.

dément, e [demã, -ãt] *a (fou)* mad, crazy; *(fam)* brilliant, fantastic.

démentiel, le [demãsjɛl] *a* insane.

démentir [demãtiʀ] *vt* to refute; ~ **que** to deny that.

démerder [demɛʀde] *(fam)*: **se** ~ *vi* to sort things out for o.s.

démesuré, e [demezyʀe] *a* immoderate.

démettre [demɛtʀ(ə)] *vt*: ~ **qn de** *(fonction, poste)* to dismiss sb from; **se** ~ *(de ses fonctions)* to resign (from) one's duties; **se** ~ **l'épaule** *etc* to dislocate one's shoulder *etc*.

demeurant [dəmœʀã]: **au** ~ *ad* for all that.

demeure [dəmœʀ] *nf* residence; **mettre qn en** ~ **de faire** to enjoin ou order sb to do; **à** ~ *ad* permanently.

demeurer [dəmœʀe] *vi (habiter)* to live; *(séjourner)* to stay; *(rester)* to remain.

demi, e [dəmi] *a*: **et** ~: **trois heures/ bouteilles et** ~**es** three and a half hours/bottles, three hours/ bottles and a half; **il est 2 heures/ midi et** ~**e** it's half past 2/12 // *nm (bière)* ≈ half-pint *(.25 litre)*; **à** ~ *ad* half-; **à la** ~ *(heure)* on the half-hour.

demi... [dəmi] *préfixe* half-, semi-, demi-; ~**cercle** *nm* semicircle; **en** ~**cercle** a semicircular // *ad* in a half circle; ~**douzaine** *nf* half-dozen, half a dozen; ~**finale** *nf* semifinal; ~**frère** *nm* half-brother; ~**heure** *nf* half-hour, half an hour; ~**jour** *nm* half-light; ~**journée** *nf* half-day, half a day; ~**litre** *nm* half-litre, half a litre; ~**livre** *nf* half-pound, half a pound; ~**mot**: **à** ~**mot** *ad* without having to spell things out; ~**pension** *nf (à l'hôtel)* half-board; ~**place** *nf* half-fare.

démis, e [demi, -iz] *a (épaule etc)* dislocated.

demi-saison [dəmisɛzɔ̃] *nf*: **vêtements de** ~ spring ou autumn clothing.

demi-sel [dəmisɛl] *a inv (beurre, fromage)* slightly salted.

demi-sœur [dəmisœʀ] nf half-sister.

démission [demisjɔ̃] nf resignation; **donner sa ~** to give ou hand in one's notice; **démissionner** vi (de son poste) to resign.

demi-tarif [dəmitaʀif] nm half-price; (TRANSPORTS) half-fare.

demi-tour [dəmituʀ] nm about-turn; **faire ~** to turn (and go) back; (AUTO) to do a U-turn.

démocratie [demɔkʀasi] nf democracy.

démocratique [demɔkʀatik] a democratic.

démodé, e [demɔde] a old-fashioned.

démographique [demɔgʀafik] a demographic, population cpd.

demoiselle [dəmwazɛl] nf (jeune fille) young lady; (célibataire) single lady, maiden lady; **~ d'honneur** bridesmaid.

démolir [demɔliʀ] vt to demolish.

démon [demɔ̃] nm (enfant turbulent) devil, demon; **le D~** the Devil.

démonstration [demɔ̃stʀasjɔ̃] nf demonstration; (aérienne, navale) display.

démonté, e [demɔ̃te] a (fig) raging, wild.

démonter [demɔ̃te] vt (machine etc) to take down, dismantle; (personne) to put out of countenance.

démontrer [demɔ̃tʀe] vt to demonstrate.

démordre [demɔʀdʀ(ə)] vi: **ne pas ~ de** to refuse to give up, stick to.

démouler [demule] vt (gâteau) to turn out.

démuni, e [demyni] a (sans argent) impoverished.

démunir [demyniʀ] vt: **~ qn de** to deprive sb of; **se ~ de** to part with, give up.

dénatalité [denatalite] nf fall in the birth rate.

dénaturer [denatyʀe] vt (goût) to alter; (pensée, fait) to distort.

dénégations [denegasjɔ̃] nfpl denials.

déniaiser [denjeze] vt: **~ qn** to teach sb about life.

dénicher [deniʃe] vt to unearth; to track ou hunt down.

dénier [denje] vt to deny.

dénigrer [denigʀe] vt to denigrate, run down.

dénivellation [denivelasjɔ̃] nf, **dénivellement** [denivɛlmɑ̃] nm ramp; dip; difference in level.

dénombrer [denɔ̃bʀe] vt (compter) to count; (énumérer) to enumerate, list.

dénomination [denɔminasjɔ̃] nf designation, appellation.

dénommer [denɔme] vt to name.

dénoncer [denɔ̃se] vt to denounce; **se ~** vi to give o.s. up, come forward.

dénouement [denumɑ̃] nm outcome.

dénouer [denwe] vt to unknot, undo.

dénoyauter [denwajote] vt to stone.

denrée [dɑ̃ʀe] nf: **~s (alimentaires)** foodstuffs.

dense [dɑ̃s] a dense.

densité [dɑ̃site] nf density.

dent [dɑ̃] nf tooth (pl teeth); **en ~s de scie** serrated; jagged; **~ de lait/sagesse** milk/wisdom tooth; **dentaire** a dental.

dentelé, e [dɑ̃tle] a jagged, indented.

dentelle [dɑ̃tɛl] nf lace q.

dentier [dɑ̃tje] nm denture.

dentifrice [dɑ̃tifʀis] nm toothpaste.

dentiste [dɑ̃tist(ə)] nm/f dentist.

dénuder [denyde] vt to bare.

dénué, e [denɥe] a: **~ de** devoid of; lacking in.

dénuement [denymɑ̃] nm destitution.

déodorant [deɔdɔʀɑ̃] nm deodorant.

dépannage [depanaʒ] nm: **service de ~** (AUTO) breakdown service.

dépanner [depane] vt (voiture, télévision) to fix, repair; (fig) to bail out, help out; **dépanneuse** nf breakdown lorry (Brit), tow truck (US).

dépareillé, e [depaʀeje] a (collec-

tion, service) incomplete; (*objet*) odd.

déparer [depare] *vt* to spoil, mar.

départ [depar] *nm* leaving *q*, departure; (*SPORT*) start; (*sur un horaire*) departure; **au ~** at the start; **à son ~** when he left.

départager [departaʒe] *vt* to decide between.

département [departəmã] *nm* department.

départir [departir]: **se ~ de** *vt* to abandon, depart from.

dépassé, e [depase] *a* superseded, outmoded; (*affolé*) panic-stricken.

dépasser [depase] *vt* (*véhicule, concurrent*) to overtake; (*endroit*) to pass, go past; (*somme, limite*) to exceed; (*fig: en beauté etc*) to surpass, outshine; (*être en saillie sur*) to jut out above (*ou* in front of) // *vi* (*jupon*) to show.

dépaysé, e [depeize] *a* disoriented.

dépecer [depəse] *vt* to joint, cut up.

dépêche [depeʃ] *nf* dispatch.

dépêcher [depeʃe] *vt* to dispatch; **se ~ vi** to hurry.

dépeindre [depɛ̃dr(ə)] *vt* to depict.

dépendre [depɑ̃dr(ə)]: **~ de** *vt* to depend on; (*financièrement etc*) to be dependent on.

dépens [depɑ̃] *nmpl*: **aux ~ de** at the expense of.

dépense [depɑ̃s] *nf* spending *q*, expense, expenditure *q*; (*fig*) consumption; expenditure.

dépenser [depɑ̃se] *vt* to spend; (*gaz, eau*) to use; (*fig*) to expend, use up; **se ~ vi** (*se fatiguer*) to exert o.s.

dépensier, ière [depɑ̃sje, -jɛr] *a*: **il est ~** he's a spendthrift.

déperdition [deperdisjɔ̃] *nf* loss.

dépérir [deperir] *vi* to waste away; to wither.

dépêtrer [depɛtre] *vt*: **se ~ de** to extricate o.s. from.

dépeupler [depœple] *vt* to depopulate; **se ~ vi** to be depopulated.

déphasé, e [defaze] *a* (*fig*) out of touch.

dépilatoire [depilatwar] *a* depilatory, hair removing.

dépister [depiste] *vt* to detect; (*voleur*) to track down; (*poursuivants*) to throw off the scent.

dépit [depi] *nm* vexation, frustration; **en ~ de** *prép* in spite of; **en ~ du bon sens** contrary to all good sense; **dépité, e** *a* vexed, frustrated.

déplacé, e [deplase] *a* (*propos*) out of place, uncalled-for.

déplacement [deplasmã] *nm* (*voyage*) trip, travelling *q*.

déplacer [deplase] *vt* (*table, voiture*) to move, shift; (*employé*) to transfer, move; **se ~ vi** to move; (*voyager*) to travel // *vt* (*vertèbre etc*) to displace.

déplaire [deplɛr] *vi*: **ceci me déplaît** I don't like this, I dislike this; **déplaisant, e** *a* disagreeable.

dépliant [deplijã] *nm* leaflet.

déplier [deplije] *vt* to unfold.

déployer [deplwaje] *vt* to open out, spread; to deploy; to display, exhibit.

dépoli, e [depoli] *a*: **verre ~** frosted glass.

déporter [deporte] *vt* (*POL*) to deport; (*dévier*) to carry off course.

déposer [depoze] *vt* (*gén: mettre, poser*) to lay *ou* put down; (*à la banque, à la consigne*) to deposit; (*passager*) to drop (off), set down; (*roi*) to depose; (*ADMIN: faire enregistrer*) to file; to register; (*JUR*): **~ (contre)** to testify *ou* give evidence (against); **se ~ vi** to settle; **dépositaire** *nm/f* (*COMM*) agent.

dépôt [depo] *nm* (*à la banque, sédiment*) deposit; (*entrepôt, réserve*) warehouse, store; (*gare*) depot; (*prison*) cells *pl*.

dépotoir [depotwar] *nm* dumping ground, rubbish dump.

dépouille [depuj] *nf* (*d'animal*) skin, hide; (*humaine*): **~ (mortelle)** mortal remains *pl*.

dépouillé, e [depuje] *a* (*fig*) bare, bald.

dépouiller [depuje] *vt* (*animal*) to skin; (*spolier*) to deprive of one's possessions; (*documents*) to go through, peruse; ~ qn/qch de to strip sb/sth of; ~ le scrutin to count the votes.

dépourvu, e [depurvy] *a:* ~ de lacking in, without; au ~ ad unprepared.

déprécier [depresje] *vt*, se ~ *vi* to depreciate.

déprédations [depredasjɔ̃] *nfpl* damage *sg*.

dépression [depresjɔ̃] *nf* depression; ~ (**nerveuse**) (nervous) breakdown.

déprimer [deprime] *vt* to depress.

─────────────
MOT-CLÉ
─────────────

depuis [dəpɥi] ◆ *prép* **1** (*point de départ dans le temps*) since; **il habite Paris** ~ **1983/l'an dernier** he has been living in Paris since 1983/ last year; ~ **quand le connaissez-vous?** how long have you known him?
2 (*temps écoulé*) for; **il habite Paris** ~ **5 ans** he has been living in Paris for 5 years; **je le connais** ~ **3 ans** I've known him for 3 years
3 (*lieu*): **il a plu** ~ **Metz** it's been raining since Metz; **elle a téléphoné** ~ **Valence** she rang from Valence
4 (*quantité, rang*) from; ~ **les plus petits jusqu'aux plus grands** from the youngest to the oldest
◆ *ad* (*temps*) since (then); **je ne lui ai pas parlé** ~ I haven't spoken to him since (then)
depuis que *cj* (ever) since; ~ **qu'il m'a dit ça** (ever) since he said that to me.

─────────────

député, e [depyte] *nm/f* (POL) ≈ Member of Parliament (*Brit*), ≈ Member of Congress (*US*).

députer [depyte] *vt* to delegate.

déraciner [derasine] *vt* to uproot.

dérailler [deroje] *vi* (*train*) to be derailed; **faire** ~ to derail.

déraisonner [derɛzɔne] *vi* to talk nonsense, rave.

dérangement [derɑ̃ʒmɑ̃] *nm* (*gêne*) trouble; (*gastrique etc*) disorder; (*mécanique*) breakdown; **en** ~ (*téléphone*) out of order.

déranger [derɑ̃ʒe] *vt* (*personne*) to trouble, bother; to disturb; (*projets*) to disrupt, upset; (*objets, vêtements*) to disarrange; **se** ~ *vi* to put o.s. out; to (take the trouble to) come *ou* go out; **est-ce que cela vous dérange si...?** do you mind if...?

déraper [derape] *vi* (*voiture*) to skid; (*personne, semelles, couteau*) to slip.

dérégler [deregle] *vt* (*mécanisme*) to put out of order; (*estomac*) to upset.

dérider [deride] *vt*, **se** ~ *vi* to brighten up.

dérision [derizjɔ̃] *nf*: **tourner en** ~ to deride.

dérivatif [derivatif] *nm* distraction.

dérive [deriv] *nf* (*de bateau*) centre-board; **aller à la** ~ (NAVIG, *fig*) to drift.

dérivé, e [derive] *nm* (TECH) by-product // *nf* (MATH) derivative.

dériver [derive] *vt* (MATH) to derive; (*cours d'eau etc*) to divert // *vi* (*bateau*) to drift; ~ **de** to derive from.

dermatologue [dermatɔlɔg] *nm/f* dermatologist.

dernier, ière [dernje, -jɛr] *a* last; (*le plus récent*) latest, last; **lundi/le mois** ~ last Monday/month; **du** ~ **chic** extremely smart; **les** ~**s honneurs** the last tribute; **en** ~ *ad* last; **ce** ~ the latter; **dernièrement** *ad* recently.

dérobé, e [derɔbe] *a* (*porte*) secret, hidden; **à la** ~**e** surreptitiously.

dérober [derɔbe] *vt* to steal; ~ **qch à** (**la vue de**) **qn** to conceal *ou* hide sth from sb('s view); **se** ~ *vi* (*s'esquiver*) to slip away; to shy away; **se** ~ **sous** (*s'effondrer*) to give way beneath; **se** ~ **à** (*justice,*

dérangement [derɑ̃ʒmɑ̃] *nm* (*gêne*)

regards) to hide from; (obligation) to shirk.

dérogation [derɔgasjɔ̃] nf (special) dispensation.

déroger [derɔʒe]: ~ à vt to go against, depart from.

dérouiller [deruje] vt: se ~ les jambes to stretch one's legs (fig).

déroulement [derulmɑ̃] nm (d'une opération etc) progress.

dérouler [derule] vt (ficelle) to unwind; (papier) to unroll; se ~ vi (avoir lieu) to take place; (se passer) to go on; to go (off); to unfold.

déroute [derut] nf rout; total collapse.

dérouter [derute] vt (avion, train) to reroute, divert; (étonner) to disconcert, throw (out).

derrière [dɛrjɛr] ad, prép behind // nm (d'une maison) back; (postérieur) behind, bottom; les pattes de ~ the back ou hind legs; par ~ from behind; (fig) behind one's back.

des [de] dét, prép + dét voir de.

dès [de] prép from; ~ que cj as soon as; ~ son retour as soon as he was (ou is) back; ~ lors ad from then on; ~ lors que cj from the moment that (that).

désabusé, e [dezabyze] a disillusioned.

désaccord [dezakɔr] nm disagreement.

désaccordé, e [dezakɔrde] a (MUS) out of tune.

désaffecté, e [dezafɛkte] a disused.

désaffection [dezafɛksjɔ̃] nf: ~ pour estrangement from.

désagréable [dezagreablə] a unpleasant.

désagréger [dezagreʒe]: se ~ vi to disintegrate, break up.

désagrément [dezagremɑ̃] nm annoyance, trouble q.

désaltérer [dezaltere] vt: se ~ to quench one's thirst.

désamorcer [dezamɔrse] vt to defuse; to forestall.

désapprouver [dezapruve] vt to disapprove of.

désarçonner [dezarsɔne] vt to unseat, throw; (fig) to throw, puzzle.

désarroi [dezarwa] nm disarray.

désarticulé, e [dezartikyle] a (pantin, corps) dislocated.

désastre [dezastr(ə)] nm disaster.

désavantage [dezavɑ̃taʒ] nm disadvantage; (inconvénient) drawback, disadvantage; **désavantager** vt to put at a disadvantage.

désavouer [dezavwe] vt to disown.

désaxé, e [dezakse] a (fig) unbalanced.

descendre [desɑ̃dr(ə)] vt (escalier, montagne) to go (ou come) down; (valise, paquet) to take ou get down; (étagère etc) to lower; (fam: abattre) to shoot down // vi to go (ou come) down; (passager: s'arrêter) to get out, alight; ~ à pied/en voiture to walk/drive down; ~ de (famille) to be descended from; ~ du train to get out of ou get off the train; ~ d'un arbre to climb down from a tree; ~ de cheval to dismount; ~ à l'hôtel to stay at a hotel.

descente [desɑ̃t] nf descent, going down; (chemin) way down; (SKI) downhill (race); au milieu de la ~ halfway down; ~ de lit bedside rug; ~ (de police) (police) raid.

description [dɛskripsjɔ̃] nf description.

désemparé, e [dezɑ̃pare] a bewildered, distraught.

désemparer [dezɑ̃pare] vi: sans ~ without stopping.

désemplir [dezɑ̃plir] vi: ne pas ~ to be always full.

déséquilibre [dezekilibr(ə)] nm (position): en ~ unsteady; (fig: des forces, du budget) imbalance.

déséquilibré, e [dezekilibre] nm/f (PSYCH) unbalanced person.

déséquilibrer [dezekilibre] vt to throw off balance.

désert, e [dezɛr, -ɛrt(ə)] a deserted // nm desert.

déserter [dezɛrte] vi, vt to desert.

désertique [dezɛʀtik] a desert cpd; barren, empty.

désespéré, e [dezɛspeʀe] a desperate.

désespérer [dezɛspeʀe] vt to drive to despair // vi: ~ **de** to despair of.

désespoir [dezɛspwaʀ] nm despair; **en ~ de cause** in desperation.

déshabillé [dezabije] nm négligée.

déshabiller [dezabije] vt to undress; **se ~** vi to undress (o.s.).

désherbant [dezɛʀbɑ̃] nm weed-killer.

déshériter [dezeʀite] vt to disinherit.

déshérités [dezeʀite] nmpl: **les ~** the underprivileged.

déshonneur [dezɔnœʀ] nm dishonour.

déshydraté, e [dezidʀate] a dehydrated.

desiderata [deziderata] nmpl requirements.

désigner [dezine] vt (montrer) to point out, indicate; (dénommer) to denote; (candidat etc) to name.

désinfectant, e [dezɛ̃fɛktɑ̃, -ɑ̃t] a, nm disinfectant.

désinfecter [dezɛ̃fɛkte] vt to disinfect.

désintégrer [dezɛ̃tegʀe] vt, **se ~** vi to disintegrate.

désintéressé, e [dezɛ̃teʀese] a disinterested, unselfish.

désintéresser [dezɛ̃teʀese] vt: **se ~ (de)** to lose interest (in).

désintoxication [dezɛ̃tɔksikasjɔ̃] nf: **faire une cure de ~** to undergo treatment for alcoholism (ou drug addiction).

désinvolte [dezɛ̃vɔlt(ə)] a casual, off-hand; **désinvolture** nf casualness.

désir [deziʀ] nm wish (fort, sensuel) desire.

désirer [deziʀe] vt to want, wish for; (sexuellement) to desire; **je désire ... (formule de politesse)** I would like ...

désister [deziste]: **se ~** vi to stand down, withdraw.

désobéir [dezɔbeiʀ] vi: **~ (à qn/qch)** to disobey (sb/sth); **désobéissant, e** a disobedient.

désobligeant, e [dezɔbliʒɑ̃, -ɑ̃t] a disagreeable.

désodorisant [dezɔdɔʀizɑ̃] nm air freshener, deodorizer.

désœuvré, e [dezœvʀe] a idle.

désolé, e [dezɔle] a (paysage) desolate; **je suis ~** I'm sorry.

désoler [dezɔle] vt to distress, grieve.

désolidariser [desɔlidaʀize] vt: **se ~ de ou d'avec** to dissociate o.s. from.

désopilant, e [dezɔpilɑ̃, -ɑ̃t] a hilarious.

désordonné, e [dezɔʀdɔne] a untidy.

désordre [dezɔʀdʀ(ə)] nm disorder(liness), untidiness; (anarchie) disorder; **~s** nmpl (POL) disturbances, disorder sg; **en ~** in a mess, untidy.

désorienté, e [dezɔʀjɑ̃te] a disorientated.

désormais [dezɔʀmɛ] ad from now on.

désosser [dezose] vt to bone.

desquels, desquelles [dekɛl] prép + pronom voir **lequel**.

dessaisir [desɛziʀ]: **se ~ de** vt to give up, part with.

dessaler [desale] vt (eau de mer) to desalinate; (CULIN) to soak.

desséché, e [desefe] a dried up.

dessécher [desefe] vt to dry out, parch; **se ~** vi to dry out.

dessein [desɛ̃] nm design; **à ~** intentionally, deliberately.

desserrer [deseʀe] vt to loosen; (frein) to release.

dessert [desɛʀ] nm dessert, pudding.

desserte [desɛʀt(ə)] nf (table) side table; (transport): **la ~ du village est assurée par autocar** there is a coach service to the village.

desservir [desɛʀviʀ] vt (ville, quartier) to serve; (nuire à) to go against, put at a disadvantage; (débarrasser): ~ **(la table)** to clear the table.

dessin [desɛ̃] nm drawing; (œuvre, art) drawing; (motif) pattern, design; (contour) (out)line; ~ **animé** cartoon (film); ~ **humoristique** cartoon.

dessinateur, trice [desinatœʀ, -tʀis] nm/f drawer; (de bandes dessinées) cartoonist; (industriel) draughtsman (Brit), draftsman (US).

dessiner [desine] vt to draw; (concevoir) to design.

dessoûler [desule] vt, vi to sober up.

dessous [dəsu] ad underneath, beneath // nm underside // nmpl (sous-vêtements) underwear sg; en ~, par ~ underneath; below; au~ (de) below; (peu digne de) beneath; avoir le ~ to get the worst of it; ~**-de-plat** nm inv tablemat.

dessus [dəsy] ad on top; (collé, écrit) on it // nm top; en ~ above; par ~ ad over it // prép over; au~ (de) above; avoir le ~ to get the upper hand; ~**-de-lit** nm inv bedspread.

destin [destɛ̃] nm fate; (avenir) destiny.

destinataire [destinatɛʀ] nm/f (POSTES) addressee; (d'un colis) consignee.

destination [destinasjɔ̃] nf (lieu) destination; (usage) purpose; à ~ de bound for, travelling to.

destinée [destine] nf fate; (existence, avenir) destiny.

destiner [destine] vt: ~ **qn à** (poste, sort) to destine sb for; ~ **qn/qch à** (prédestiner) to destine sb/sth to + verbe; ~ **qch à qn** (envisager de donner) to intend sb to have sth; (adresser) to intend sth for sb; **être destiné à** (sort) to be destined to + verbe; (usage) to be meant for; (suj: sort) to be in store for.

destituer [destitɥe] vt to depose.

désuet, ète [desɥɛ, -ɛt] a outdated, outmoded; **désuétude** nf: **tomber en désuétude** to fall into disuse.

détachant [detaʃɑ̃] nm stain remover.

détacher [detaʃe] vt (enlever) to detach, remove; (délier) to untie; (ADMIN: ~ qn auprès de/à) to post sb (to); **se** ~ vi (tomber) to come off; to come out; (se défaire) to come undone; **se** ~ **sur** to stand out against; **se** ~ **de** (se désintéresser) to grow away from.

détail [detaj] nm detail; (COMM): **le** ~ retail; **au** ~ ad (COMM) retail; separately; **en** ~ in detail.

détaillant [detajɑ̃] nm retailer.

détailler [detaje] vt (expliquer) to explain in detail; to detail; (examiner) to look over, examine.

détartrant [detaʀtʀɑ̃] nm scale remover.

détecter [detɛkte] vt to detect.

détective [detɛktiv] nm (Brit: policier) detective; (privé) private detective.

déteindre [detɛ̃dʀ(ə)] vi (tissu) to fade; (fig): ~ **sur** to rub off on.

dételer [detle] vt to unharness.

détendre [detɑ̃dʀ(ə)] vt: **se** ~ to lose its tension; to relax.

détenir [detniʀ] vt (fortune, objet, secret) to be in possession of; (prisonnier) to detain, hold; (record, pouvoir) to hold.

détente [detɑ̃t] nf relaxation; (d'une arme) trigger.

détention [detɑ̃sjɔ̃] nf possession; detention; holding; ~ **préventive** (pre-trial) custody.

détenu, e [detny] nm/f prisoner.

détergent [detɛʀʒɑ̃] nm detergent.

détériorer [deteʀjɔʀe] vt to damage; **se** ~ vi to deteriorate.

déterminé, e [detɛʀmine] a (résolu) determined; (précis) specific, definite.

déterminer [detɛʀmine] vt (fixer) to determine; (décider): ~ **qn à faire** to decide sb to do.

déterrer [deteʀe] vt to dig up.

détersif [detɛʀsif] nm detergent.

détestable [detɛstabl(ə)] a foul,

ghastly; detestable, odious.

détester [deteste] vt to hate, detest.

détonation [detɔnɑsjɔ̃] nf detonation, bang, report (of a gun).

détonner [detɔne] vi (MUS) to go out of tune; (fig) to clash.

détour [detuʀ] nm detour; (tournant) bend, curve; sans ~ (fig) plainly.

détourné, e [detuʀne] a (moyen) roundabout.

détournement [detuʀnəmɑ̃] nm: ~ d'avion hijacking; ~ de mineur corruption of a minor.

détourner [detuʀne] vt to divert; (par la force) to hijack; (yeux, tête) to turn away; (de l'argent) to embezzle; se ~ vi to turn away.

détracteur, trice [detʀaktœʀ, -tʀis] nm/f disparager, critic.

détraquer [detʀake] vt to put out of order; (estomac) to upset; se ~ vi to go wrong.

détrempé, e [detʀɑ̃pe] a (sol) sodden, waterlogged.

détresse [detʀɛs] nf distress.

détriment [detʀimɑ̃] nm: au ~ de to the detriment of.

détritus [detʀitys] nmpl rubbish sg, refuse sg.

détroit [detʀwa] nm strait.

détromper [detʀɔ̃pe] vt to disabuse.

détrôner [detʀone] vt to dethrone.

détrousser [detʀuse] vt to rob.

détruire [detʀɥiʀ] vt to destroy.

dette [dɛt] nf debt.

D.E.U.G. [døg] sigle m = diplôme d'études universitaires générales.

deuil [dœj] nm (perte) bereavement; (période) mourning; (chagrin) grief; être en ~ to be in mourning.

deux [dø] num two; les ~ both; ses ~ mains both his hands, his two hands; ~ points colon sg;

deuxième num second;

deuxièmement ad secondly, in the second place; ~-pièces nm inv (tailleur) two-piece suit; (de bain) two-piece (swimsuit); (appartement) two-roomed flat (Brit) ou apartment

(US); ~-roues nm inv two-wheeled vehicle.

devais etc vb voir **devoir**.

dévaler [devale] vt to hurtle down.

dévaliser [devalize] vt to rob, burgle.

dévaloriser [devalɔʀize] vt, se ~ vi to depreciate.

dévaluation [devaluɑsjɔ̃] nf depreciation; (ÉCON: mesure) devaluation.

devancer [dəvɑ̃se] vt to be ahead of; to get ahead of; to arrive before; (prévenir) to anticipate.

devant [dəvɑ̃] ad in front; (à distance: en avant) ahead // prép in front; ahead of; (avec mouvement: passer) past; (fig) before, in front of; faced with; in view of // nm front; prendre les ~s to make the first move; les pattes de ~ the front legs, the forelegs; par ~ (boutonner) at the front; (entrer) the front way; aller au-~ de to go out to meet sb; aller au-~ de (désirs de qn) to anticipate.

devanture [dəvɑ̃tyʀ] nf (façade) (shop) front; (étalage) display; (shop) window.

déveine [devɛn] nf rotten luck q.

développement [devlɔpmɑ̃] nm development.

développer [devlɔpe] vt to develop; se ~ vi to develop.

devenir [dəvniʀ] vb avec attribut to become; ~ instituteur to become a teacher; que sont-ils devenus? what has become of them?

dévergondé, e [devɛʀgɔ̃de] a wild, shameless.

déverser [devɛʀse] vt (liquide) to pour (out); (ordures) to tip (out); se ~ dans (fleuve, mer) to flow into.

dévêtir [devetiʀ] vt, se ~ to undress.

devez etc vb voir **devoir**.

déviation [devjɑsjɔ̃] nf deviation; (AUTO) diversion (Brit), detour (US).

dévider [devide] vt to unwind.

devienne etc vb voir **devenir**.

dévier [devje] vt (fleuve, circulation)

to divert; (*coup*) to deflect // *vi* to veer (off course).

devin [dəvɛ̃] *nm* soothsayer, seer.

deviner [dəvine] *vt* to guess; (*prévoir*) to foresee; (*apercevoir*) to distinguish.

devinette [dəvinɛt] *nf* riddle.

devins *etc vb voir* **devenir**.

devis [dəvi] *nm* estimate, quotation.

dévisager [devizaʒe] *vt* to stare at.

devise [dəviz] *nf* (*formule*) motto, watchword; (*ECON: monnaie*) currency; ~s *nfpl* (*argent*) currency *sg*.

deviser [dəvize] *vi* to converse.

dévisser [devise] *vt* to unscrew, undo; se ~ *vi* to come unscrewed.

dévoiler [devwale] *vt* to unveil.

devoir [dəvwaʀ] *nm* duty; (*SCOL*) homework *q*; (: *en classe*) exercise // *vt* (*argent, respect*): ~ qch (à qn) to owe (sb) sth; (*suivi de l'infinitif: obligation*): **il doit le faire** he has to do it, he must do it; (: *intention*): **il doit partir demain** he is (due) to leave tomorrow; (: *probabilité*): **il doit être tard** it must be late.

dévolu, e [devɔly] *a*: ~ à allotted to // *nm*: **jeter son ~ sur** to fix one's choice on.

dévorer [devɔʀe] *vt* to devour; (*suj: feu, soucis*) to consume.

dévot, e [devo, -ɔt] *a* devout, pious.

dévotion [devosjɔ̃] *nf* devoutness; **être à la ~ de qn** to be totally devoted to sb.

dévoué, e [devwe] *a* devoted.

dévouer [devwe]: se ~ *vi* (*se sacrifier*): se ~ (**pour**) to sacrifice o.s. (for); (*se consacrer*): se ~ **à** to devote o.s. to.

dévoyé, e [devwaje] *a* delinquent.

devrai *etc vb voir* **devoir**.

diabète [djabɛt] *nm* diabetes *sg*; **diabétique** *nm/f* diabetic.

diable [djɑbl(ə)] *nm* devil.

diacre [djakʀ(ə)] *nm* deacon.

diagnostic [djagnɔstik] *nm* diagnosis *sg*.

diagonal, e, aux [djagɔnal, -o] *a*, *nf* diagonal; **en ~e** diagonally; **lire**

en ~e to skim through.

diagramme [djagʀam] *nm* chart, graph.

dialecte [djalɛkt(ə)] *nm* dialect.

dialogue [djalɔg] *nm* dialogue.

diamant [djamɑ̃] *nm* diamond; **distmantaire** *nm* diamond cutter.

diamètre [djamɛtʀ(ə)] *nm* diameter.

diapason [djapazɔ̃] *nm* tuning fork.

diaphragme [djafʀagm] *nm* diaphragm.

diaporama [djapɔʀama] *nm* slide show.

diapositive [djapozitiv] *nf* transparency, slide.

diarrhée [djaʀe] *nf* diarrhoea.

dictateur [diktatœʀ] *nm* dictator; **dictature** *nf* dictatorship.

dictée [dikte] *nf* dictation.

dicter [dikte] *vt* to dictate.

dictionnaire [diksjɔnɛʀ] *nm* dictionary.

dicton [diktɔ̃] *nm* saying, dictum.

dièse [djɛz] *nm* sharp.

diesel [djezɛl] *nm, a inv* diesel.

diète [djɛt] *nf* (*jeûne*) starvation diet; (*régime*) diet.

diététique [djetetik] *a*: **magasin ~** health food shop.

dieu, x [djø] *nm* god; **D~** God; **mon D~!** good heavens!

diffamation [difamasjɔ̃] *nf* slander; (*écrite*) libel.

différé [difeʀe] *nm* (*TV*): **en ~** (pre-)recorded.

différence [difeʀɑ̃s] *nf* difference; **à la ~ de** unlike.

différencier [difeʀɑ̃sje] *vt* to differentiate.

différend [difeʀɑ̃] *nm* difference (of opinion), disagreement.

différent, e [difeʀɑ̃, -ɑ̃t] *a*: ~ (**de**) different (from); ~s **objets** different *ou* various objects.

différer [difeʀe] *vt* to postpone, put off // *vi*: ~ (**de**) to differ (from).

difficile [difisil] *a* difficult; (*exigeant*) hard to please; **~ment** *ad* with difficulty.

difficulté [difikylte] *nf* difficulty; **en**

~ (bateau, alpiniste) in difficulties.

difforme [difɔrm(ə)] a deformed, misshapen.

diffuser [difyze] vt (chaleur, bruit) to diffuse; (émission, musique) to broadcast; (nouvelle, idée) to circulate; (COMM) to distribute.

digérer [diʒere] vt to digest; (fig: accepter) to stomach, put up with; **digestif** nm (after-dinner) liqueur.

digne [diɲ] a dignified; ~ de worthy of; ~ de foi trustworthy.

dignité [diɲite] nf dignity.

digression [digresjɔ̃] nf digression.

digue [dig] nf dike, dyke.

dilapider [dilapide] vt to squander.

dilemme [dilɛm] nm dilemma.

diligence [diliʒɑ̃s] nf stagecoach; (empressement) despatch.

diluer [dilɥe] vt to dilute.

diluvien, ne [dilyvjɛ̃, -jɛn] a: **pluie ~ne** torrential rain.

dimanche [dimɑ̃ʃ] nm Sunday.

dimension [dimɑ̃sjɔ̃] nf (grandeur) size; (cote, de l'espace) dimension.

diminuer [diminɥe] vt to reduce, decrease; (ardeur etc) to lessen; (personne: physiquement) to undermine; (dénigrer) to belittle // vi to decrease, diminish; **diminutif** nm (surnom) pet name; **diminution** nf decreasing, diminishing.

dinde [dɛ̃d] nf turkey.

dindon [dɛ̃dɔ̃] nm turkey.

dîner [dine] nm dinner // vi to have dinner.

dingue [dɛ̃g] a (fam) crazy.

diplomate [diplɔmat] a diplomatic // nm diplomat; (fig) diplomatist.

diplomatie [diplɔmasi] nf diplomacy.

diplôme [diplom] nm diploma; **diplômé, e** a qualified.

dire [dir] nm: **au ~ de** according to; **leur ~s** what they say // vt to say; (secret, mensonge) to tell; ~ **l'heure/la vérité** to tell the time/the truth; ~ **qch à qn** to tell sb sth; ~ **à qn qu'il fasse** ou **de faire** to tell sb to do; **on dit que** they say that;

ceci dit that being said; (à ces mots) whereupon; **si cela lui dit** (plaire) if he fancies it; **que dites-vous de** (penser) what do you think of; **on dirait que** it looks (ou sounds etc) as if; **dis/dites (donc)** I say; (à propos) by the way.

direct, e [dirɛkt] a direct // nm (TV): **en** ~ live; ~**ement** ad directly.

directeur, trice [dirɛktœr, -tris] nm/f (d'entreprise) director; (de service) manager/eress; (d'école) head(teacher) (Brit), principal (US).

direction [dirɛksjɔ̃] nf management; conducting; supervision; (AUTO) steering; (sens) direction; **'toutes ~s'** 'all routes'.

dirent vb voir **dire**.

dirigeant, e [diriʒɑ̃, -ɑ̃t] a managerial; ruling // nm/f (d'un parti etc) leader; (d'entreprise) manager.

diriger [diriʒe] vt (entreprise) to manage, run; (véhicule) to steer; (orchestre) to conduct; (recherches, travaux) to supervise; (braquer: regard, arme): ~ **sur** to point ou aim at; **se** ~ (s'orienter) to find one's way; **se** ~ **vers** ou **sur** to make ou head for.

dirigisme [diriʒism(ə)] nm (ÉCON) state intervention, interventionism.

dis etc vb voir **dire**.

discerner [disɛrne] vt to discern, make out.

discipline [disiplin] nf discipline; **discipliner** vt to discipline; to control.

discontinu, e [diskɔ̃tiny] a intermittent.

discontinuer [diskɔ̃tinɥe] vi: **sans** ~ without stopping, without a break.

disconvenir [diskɔ̃vnir] vi: **ne pas** ~ **de qch/que** not to deny sth/that.

discordant, e [diskɔrdɑ̃, -ɑ̃t] a discordant; conflicting.

discothèque [diskɔtɛk] nf (disques) record collection; (: dans une bibliothèque) record library; (boîte de nuit) disco(thèque).

discourir [diskuʀiʀ] *vi* to discourse, hold forth.

discours [diskuʀ] *nm* speech.

discret, ète [diskʀɛ, -ɛt] *a* discreet; *(fig)* unobtrusive; quiet.

discrétion [diskʀesjɔ̃] *nf* discretion; **être à la ~ de** qn to be in sb's hands; **à ~** unlimited; as much as one wants.

discrimination [diskʀiminasjɔ̃] *nf* discrimination; **sans ~** indiscriminately.

disculper [diskylpe] *vt* to exonerate.

discussion [diskysjɔ̃] *nf* discussion.

discutable [diskytabl(ə)] *a* debatable.

discuté, e [diskyte] *a* controversial.

discuter [diskyte] *vt (contester)* to question, dispute; *(débattre: prix)* to discuss // *vi* to talk; *(ergoter)* to argue; **~ de** to discuss.

dise *etc vb voir* **dire.**

disette [dizɛt] *nf* food shortage.

diseuse [dizøz] *nf*: **~ de bonne aventure** fortuneteller.

disgracieux, euse [disgʀasjø, -jøz] *a* ungainly, awkward.

disjoindre [disʒwɛ̃dʀ(ə)] *vt* to take apart; **se ~** *vi* to come apart.

disjoncteur [disʒɔ̃ktœʀ] *nm (ÉLEC)* circuit breaker.

disloquer [disləke] *vt (chaise)* to dismantle; **se ~** *vi (parti, empire)* to break up; **se ~ l'épaule** to dislocate one's shoulder.

disons *vb voir* **dire.**

disparaître [dispaʀɛtʀ(ə)] *vi* to disappear; *(à la vue)* to vanish, disappear; to be hidden ou concealed; *(se perdre: traditions etc)* to die out; **faire ~** to remove; to get rid of.

disparition [dispaʀisjɔ̃] *nf* disappearance.

disparu, e [dispaʀy] *nm/f* missing person; *(défunt)* departed.

dispensaire [dispãsɛʀ] *nm* community clinic.

dispenser [dispãse] *vt (donner)* to lavish, bestow; *(exempter)*: **~ qn de** to exempt sb from; **se ~ de** *vt* to avoid; to get out of.

disperser [dispɛʀse] *vt* to scatter; *(fig: son attention)* to dissipate.

disponibilité [disponibilite] *nf (ADMIN)*: **être en ~** to be on leave of absence.

disponible [disponibl(ə)] *a* available.

dispos [dispo] *am*: **(frais et) ~** fresh (as a daisy).

disposé, e [dispoze] *a*: **bien/mal ~** *(humeur)* in a good/bad mood; **~ à** *(prêt à)* willing ou prepared to.

disposer [dispoze] *vt (arranger, placer)* to arrange // *vi*: **vous pouvez ~** you may leave; **~ de** vt to have (at one's disposal); to use; **se ~ à faire** to prepare to do, be about to do.

dispositif [dispozitif] *nm* device; *(fig)* system, plan of action; set-up.

disposition [dispozisjɔ̃] *nf (arrangement)* arrangement, layout; *(humeur)* mood; *(tendance)* tendency; **~s** *nfpl (mesures)* steps, measures; *(préparatifs)* arrangements; *(loi, testament)* provisions; *(aptitudes)* bent *sg*, aptitude *sg*; **à la ~ de** qn at sb's disposal.

disproportionné, e [dispʀɔpɔʀsjɔne] *a* disproportionate, out of all proportion.

dispute [dispyt] *nf* quarrel, argument.

disputer [dispyte] *vt (match)* to play; *(combat)* to fight; *(course)* to run, fight; **se ~** *vi* to quarrel; **~ qch à** qn to fight with sb over sth.

disquaire [diskɛʀ] *nm/f* record dealer.

disqualifier [diskalifje] *vt* to disqualify.

disque [disk(ə)] *nm (MUS)* record; *(forme, pièce)* disc; *(SPORT)* discus; **~ compact** compact disc; **~ d'embrayage** *(AUTO)* clutch plate.

disquette [diskɛt] *nf* floppy disk, diskette.

disséminer [disemine] *vt* to scatter.

disséquer [diseke] *vt* to dissect.

dissertation [disɛʀtasjɔ̃] *nf (SCOL)* essay.

disserter [diserte] vi: ~ **sur** to discourse upon.

dissimuler [disimyle] vt to conceal.

dissiper [disipe] vt to dissipate; (fortune) to squander; se ~ vi (brouillard) to clear, disperse; (doutes) to melt away; (élève) to become unruly.

dissolu, e [disɔly] a dissolute.

dissolvant, e [disɔlvɑ̃, -ɑ̃t] nm solvent; ~ (gras) nail polish remover.

dissonant, e [disɔnɑ̃, -ɑ̃t] a discordant.

dissoudre [disudʀ(ə)] vt to dissolve; se ~ vi to dissolve.

dissuader [disɥade] vt: ~ **qn de faire/ de qch** to dissuade sb from doing/from sth.

dissuasion [disɥazjɔ̃] nf: **force de** ~ deterrent power.

distance [distɑ̃s] nf distance; (fig: écart) gap; **à** ~ at ou from a distance; **distancer** vt to outdistance.

distant, e [distɑ̃, -ɑ̃t] a (réservé) distant; ~ **de** (lieu) far away from.

distendre [distɑ̃dʀ(ə)] vt, se ~ vi to distend.

distiller [distile] vt to distil; **distillerie** nf distillery.

distinct, e [distɛ̃(kt), distɛ̃kt(ə)] a distinct; **distinctif, ive** a distinctive.

distingué, e [distɛ̃ge] a distinguished.

distinguer [distɛ̃ge] vt to distinguish.

distraction [distʀaksjɔ̃] nf (manque d'attention) absent-mindedness; (oubli) lapse (in concentration); (détente) diversion, recreation; (passetemps) distraction, entertainment.

distraire [distʀɛʀ] vt (déranger) to distract; (divertir) to entertain, divert; se ~ vi to amuse ou enjoy o.s.

distrait, e [distʀɛ, -ɛt] a absentminded.

distribuer [distʀibɥe] vt to distribute; to hand out; (CARTES) to deal (out); (courrier) to deliver; **distributeur** nm (COMM) distributor; (automatique) (vending) machine; (: de billets) (cash) dispenser; **distri-**

bution nf distribution; (postale) delivery; (choix d'acteurs) casting, cast.

dit, e [di, dit] pp de **dire** // a (fixé): **le jour** ~ the arranged day; (surnommé): **X, ~ Pierrot** X, known as Pierrot.

dites vb voir **dire**.

divaguer [divage] vi to ramble; to rave.

divan [divɑ̃] nm divan.

divers, e [divɛʀ, -ɛʀs(ə)] a (varié) diverse, varied; (différent) different, various // dét (plusieurs) various, several; (frais) ~ sundries, miscellaneous (expenses).

divertir [divɛʀtiʀ] vt to amuse, entertain; se ~ vi to amuse ou enjoy o.s.

divin, e [divɛ̃, -in] a divine.

diviser [divize] vt (gén, MATH) to divide; (morceler, subdiviser) to divide (up), split (up); **division** nf division.

divorce [divɔʀs(ə)] nm divorce; **divorcé, e** nm/f divorcee; **divorcer** vi to get a divorce, get divorced; **divorcer de ou d'avec qn** to divorce sb.

divulguer [divylge] vt to divulge, disclose.

dix [dis] num ten; **dixième** num tenth.

dizaine [dizɛn] nf (10) ten; (environ 10): **une** ~ **(de)** about ten, ten or so.

do [do] nm (note) C; (en chantant la gamme) do(h).

dock [dɔk] nm dock.

docker [dɔkɛʀ] nm docker.

docte [dɔkt(ə)] a learned.

docteur [dɔktœʀ] nm doctor.

doctorat [dɔktɔʀa] nm: ~ (d'Université) doctorate; ~ **d'état** = Ph.D.

doctrine [dɔktʀin] nf doctrine.

document [dɔkymɑ̃] nm document.

documentaire [dɔkymɑ̃tɛʀ] a, nm documentary.

documentaliste [dɔkymɑ̃talist(ə)] nm/f archivist; researcher.

documentation [dɔkymɑ̃tasjɔ̃] nf documentation, literature; (PRESSE, TV: service) research.

documenter [dɔkymɑ̃te] vt: se ~ (sur) to gather information (on).

dodeliner [dɔdline] vi: ~ de la tête to nod one's head gently.

dodo [dɔdo] nm: aller faire ~ to go to beddy-byes.

dodu, e [dɔdy] a plump.

dogue [dɔg] nm mastiff.

doigt [dwa] nm finger; à deux ~s de within an inch of; un ~ de lait a drop of milk; ~ de pied toe.

doigté [dwate] nm (MUS) fingering; (fig: habileté) diplomacy, tact.

doit etc vb voir **devoir**.

doléances [dɔleɑ̃s] nfpl complaints; grievances.

dolent, e [dɔlɑ̃, -ɑ̃t] a doleful.

dollar [dɔlar] nm dollar.

D.O.M. [deɔɛm, dɔm] sigle m ou mpl = département(s) d'outre-mer.

domaine [dɔmɛn] nm estate, property; (fig) domain, field.

domanial, e, aux [dɔmanjal, -o] a (forêt, biens) national, state cpd.

domestique [dɔmɛstik] a domestic // nm/f servant, domestic.

domicile [dɔmisil] nm home, place of residence; à ~ at home; **domicilié, e** a: être domicilié à to have one's home in ou at.

dominant, e [dɔminɑ̃, -ɑ̃t] a dominant; predominant.

dominateur, trice [dɔminatœr, -tris] a dominating; domineering.

dominer [dɔmine] vt to dominate; (passions etc) to control, master; (surpasser) to outclass, surpass // vi to be in the dominant position; se ~ vi to control o.s.

domino [dɔmino] nm domino.

dommage [dɔmaʒ] nm (préjudice) harm, injury; (dégâts, pertes) damage q; c'est ~ de faire/que it's a shame ou pity to do/that; ~s-intérêts nmpl damages.

dompter [dɔ̃te] vt to tame; **dompteur, euse** nm/f trainer; liontamer.

don [dɔ̃] nm (cadeau) gift; (charité) donation; (aptitude) gift, talent; avoir des ~s pour to have a gift ou talent for.

donc [dɔ̃k] cj therefore, so; (après une digression) so, then.

donjon [dɔ̃ʒɔ̃] nm keep.

donné, e [dɔne] a (convenu) given; (pas cher): c'est ~ it's a gift // nf (MATH, gén) datum (pl data); étant ~ ... given ...

donner [dɔne] vt to give; (vieux habits etc) to give away; (spectacle) to put on; (film) to show; ~ qch à qn to give sb sth, give sth to sb; ~ sur (suj: fenêtre, chambre) to look (out) onto; ~ dans (piège etc) to fall into; se ~ à fond to give one's all; s'en ~ à cœur joie (fam) to have a great time.

dont [dɔ̃] pronom relatif **1** (appartenance: objets) whose, of which; (: êtres animés) whose; **la maison** ~ le toit est rouge the house the roof of which is red, the house whose roof is red; **l'homme** ~ **je connais la sœur** the man whose sister I know **2** (parmi lesquel(le)s): **2 livres**, ~ **l'un est ...** 2 books, one of which is ...; **il y avait plusieurs personnes**, ~ **Gabrielle** there were several people, among them Gabrielle; **10 blessés**, ~ **2 grièvement** 10 injured, 2 of them seriously **3** (complément d'adjectif, de verbe): **le fils** ~ **il est si fier** the son he's so proud of; **ce** ~ **je parle** what I'm talking about; voir adjectifs et verbes à complément prépositionnel: **responsable de, souffrir de** etc.

doré, e [dɔre] a golden; (avec dorure) gilt, gilded.

dorénavant [dɔrenavɑ̃] ad henceforth.

dorer [dɔre] vt (cadre) to gild; (faire) ~ (CULIN) to brown.

dorloter [dɔrlɔte] vt to pamper.

dormir [dɔrmir] vi to sleep; (être endormi) to be asleep.

dortoir [dɔrtwar] nm dormitory.

dorure [dɔʀyʀ] nf gilding.

dos [do] nm back; (de livre) spine; 'voir au ~' 'see over'; de ~ from the back.

dosage [dozaʒ] nm mixture.

dose [doz] nf dose.

doser [doze] vt to measure out; to mix in the correct proportions; (fig) to expend in the right amounts; to strike a balance between.

dossard [dosaʀ] nm number (worn by competitor).

dossier [dosje] nm (renseignements, fichier) file; (de chaise) back; (PRESSE) feature.

dot [dɔt] nf dowry.

doter [dɔte] vt to equip.

douane [dwan] nf (poste, bureau) customs pl; (taxes) (customs) duty; **douanier, ière** a customs cpd // nm customs officer.

double [dubl(ə)] a, ad double // nm (2 fois plus): le ~ (de) twice as much (ou many) (as); (autre exemplaire) duplicate, copy; (sosie) double; (TENNIS) doubles sg; en ~ (exemplaire) in duplicate; **faire ~ emploi** to be redundant.

doubler [duble] vt (multiplier par 2) to double; (vêtement) to line; (dépasser) to overtake, pass; (film) to dub; (acteur) to stand in for // vi to double.

doublure [dublyʀ] nf lining; (CINÉMA) stand-in.

douce [dus] a voir doux; **~âtre** a sickly sweet; **~ment** ad gently; slowly; **~reux, euse** a (péj) sugary; **douceur** nf softness; sweetness; mildness; gentleness; **douceurs** nfpl (friandises) sweets.

douche [duʃ] nf shower; **~s** nfpl (salle) shower room sg; se **doucher** vi to have ou take a shower.

doué, e [dwe] a gifted, talented; ~ de endowed with.

douille [duj] nf (ÉLEC) socket; (de projectile) case.

douillet, te [duje, -ɛt] a cosy; (péj) soft.

douleur [dulœʀ] nf pain; (chagrin) grief, distress; **douloureux, euse** a painful.

doute [dut] nm doubt; **sans** ~ ad no doubt; (probablement) probably.

douter [dute] vt to doubt; ~ **de** vt (allié) to doubt, have (one's) doubts about; (résultat) to be doubtful of; **se ~ de qch/que** to suspect sth/that; **je m'en doutais** I suspected as much.

douteux, euse [dutø, -øz] a (incertain) doubtful; (discutable) dubious, questionable; (péj) dubious-looking.

Douvres [duvʀ(ə)] n Dover.

doux, douce [du, dus] a (gén) soft; (sucré, agréable) sweet; (peu fort: moutarde, clément: climat) mild; (pas brusque) gentle.

douzaine [duzɛn] nf (12) dozen; (environ 12): une ~ (de) a dozen or so, twelve or so.

douze [duz] num twelve; **douzième** num twelfth.

doyen, ne [dwajɛ̃, -ɛn] nm/f (en âge, ancienneté) most senior member; (de faculté) dean.

dragée [dʀaʒe] nf sugared almond; (MÉD) (sugar-coated) pill.

dragon [dʀagɔ̃] nm dragon.

draguer [dʀage] vt (rivière) to dredge; to drag; (fam) to try to pick up.

dramatique [dʀamatik] a dramatic; (tragique) tragic // nf (TV) (television) drama.

dramaturge [dʀamatyʀʒ(ə)] nm dramatist, playwright.

drame [dʀam] nm (THÉÂTRE) drama.

drap [dʀa] nm (de lit) sheet; (tissu) woollen fabric.

drapeau, x [dʀapo] nm flag; **sous les ~x** with the colours, in the army.

dresser [dʀese] vt (mettre vertical, monter) to put up, erect; (fig: liste, bilan, contrat) to draw up; (animal) to train; se ~ vi (falaise, obstacle) to stand; to tower (up); (personne) to draw o.s. up; ~ **qn contre qn** to set sb against sb; ~ **l'oreille** to prick up one's ears.

drogue [dʀɔg] nf drug; **la ~ drugs** pl.

drogué, e [dʀɔge] nm/f drug addict.

droguer [dʀɔge] vt (victime) to drug; (malade) to give drugs to; ♦ vi (aux stupéfiants) to take drugs; (péj: de médicaments) to dose o.s. up.

droguerie [dʀɔgʀi] nf hardware shop.

droguiste [dʀɔgist(ə)] nm keeper (ou owner) of a hardware shop.

droit, e [dʀwa, dʀwat] a (non courbe) straight; (vertical) upright, straight; (fig: loyal) straight, straight(forward); (opposé à gauche) right, right-hand // ad straight // nm (prérogative) right; (taxe) duty, tax; (: d'inscription) fee; (JUR): **le ~ law** // nf (POL): **la ~e the right** (wing); **avoir le ~ de** to be allowed to; **avoir ~ à** to be entitled to; **être en ~ de** to have a ou the right to; **être dans son ~** to be within one's rights; **à ~e** on the right; (direction) (to the) right; **~s d'auteur** royalties.

droitier, ière [dʀwatje, -jɛʀ] nm/f right-handed person.

droiture [dʀwatyʀ] nf uprightness, straightness.

drôle [dʀol] a funny; **~ment** ad (très) terribly, awfully; **une ~ d'idée** a funny idea.

dromadaire [dʀɔmadɛʀ] nm dromedary.

dru, e [dʀy] a (cheveux) thick, bushy; (pluie) heavy.

du [dy] prép + dét, dét voir **de**.

dû, due [dy] vb voir **devoir** // a (somme) owing, owed; (: venant à échéance) due; (causé par): **~ à** due to // nm (pl somme) dues pl.

dubitatif, ive [dybitatif, -iv] a doubtful, dubious.

duc [dyk] nm duke; **duchesse** nf duchess.

dûment [dymã] ad duly.

Dunkerque [dœkɛʀk] n Dunkirk.

duo [dyo] nm (MUS) duet.

dupe [dyp] nf dupe // a: **(ne pas) être ~ de** (not) to be taken in by.

duplex [dyplɛks] nm (appartement) split-level apartment, duplex.

duplicata [dyplikata] nm duplicate.

duquel [dykɛl] prép + pronom voir **lequel**.

dur, e [dyʀ] a (pierre, siège, travail, problème) hard; (lumière, voix, climat) harsh; (sévère) hard, harsh; (cruel) hard(-hearted); (porte, col) stiff; (viande) tough // ad hard; **~ d'oreille** hard of hearing.

durant [dyʀã] prép (au cours de) during; (pendant) for; **des mois ~** for months.

durcir [dyʀsiʀ] vt, vi, **se ~** vi to harden.

durée [dyʀe] nf length; (d'une pile etc) life; (déroulement: des opérations etc) duration.

durement [dyʀmã] ad harshly.

durer [dyʀe] vi to last.

dureté [dyʀte] nf hardness; harshness; stiffness; toughness.

durit [dyʀit] nf ® (car radiator) hose.

dus etc vb voir **devoir**.

duvet [dyvɛ] nm down; (sac de couchage) down-filled sleeping bag.

dynamique [dinamik] a dynamic.

dynamisme [dinamism] nm dynamism.

dynamite [dinamit] nf dynamite.

dynamiter [dinamite] vt to (blow up with) dynamite.

dynamo [dinamo] nf dynamo.

dysenterie [disãtʀi] nf dysentery.

dyslexie [disleksi] nf dyslexia, word-blindness.

E

eau, x [o] nf water // nfpl waters; **prendre l'~** to leak, let in water; **tomber à l'~** (fig) to fall through; **~ de Cologne** Eau de Cologne; **~ courante** running water; **~ douce** fresh water; **~ de Javel** bleach;

minérale mineral water; ~ **plate** still water; ~ **salée** salt water; ~ **de toilette** toilet water; ~**-de-vie** nf brandy; ~**forte** nf etching.

ébahi, e [ebai] a dumbfounded.

ébattre [ebatʀ(ə)]: **s'~** vi to frolic.

ébaucher [eboʃe] vt to sketch out, outline; **s'~** vi to take shape.

ébène [eben] nf ebony.

ébéniste [ebenist(ə)] nm cabinetmaker.

éberlué, e [ebɛʀlɥe] a astounded.

éblouir [eblɥiʀ] vt to dazzle.

éblouissement [ebluismã] nm (faiblesse) dizzy turn.

éborgner [ebɔʀɲe] vt: ~ **qn** to blind sb in one eye.

éboueur [ebwœʀ] nm dustman (Brit), garbageman (US).

ébouillanter [ebujãte] vt to scald; (CULIN) to blanch.

éboulement [ebulmã] nm rock fall.

ébouler [ebule]: **s'~** vi to crumble, collapse.

éboulis [ebuli] nmpl fallen rocks.

ébouriffé, e [eburife] a tousled.

ébranler [ebʀãle] vt to shake; (rendre instable: mur) to weaken; **s'~** (partir) to move off.

ébrécher [ebʀeʃe] vt to chip.

ébriété [ebʀijete] nf: **en état d'~** in a state of intoxication.

ébrouer [ebʀue]: **s'~** vi to shake o.s.; (souffler) to snort.

ébruiter [ebʀɥite] vt to spread, disclose.

ébullition [ebylisjɔ̃] nf boiling point; **en ~** boiling; (fig) in an uproar.

écaille [ekaj] nf (de poisson) scale; (de coquillage) shell; (matière) tortoiseshell.

écailler [ekaje] vt (poisson) to scale; (huître) to open; **s'~** vi to flake ou peel (off).

écarlate [ekaʀlat] a scarlet.

écarquiller [ekaʀkije] vt: ~ **les yeux** to stare wide-eyed.

écart [ekaʀ] nm gap; (embardée) swerve; sideways leap; (fig) departure, deviation; **à l'~** ad out of the way; **à l'~ de** prép away from.

écarté, e [ekaʀte] a (lieu) out-of-the-way, remote; (ouvert): **les jambes** ~**es** legs apart; **les bras** ~**s** arms outstretched.

écarteler [ekaʀtəle] vt to quarter; (fig) to tear.

écarter [ekaʀte] vt (séparer) to move apart, separate; (éloigner) to push back, move away; (ouvrir: bras, jambes) to spread, open; (: rideau) to draw (back); (éliminer: candidat, possibilité) to dismiss; **s'~** vi to part; to move away; **s'~** de to wander from.

écervelé, e [esɛʀvəle] a scatterbrained, featherbrained.

échafaud [eʃafo] nm scaffold.

échafaudage [eʃafodaʒ] nm scaffolding.

échafauder [eʃafode] vt (plan) to construct.

échalote [eʃalɔt] nf shallot.

échancrure [eʃãkʀyʀ] nf (de robe) scoop neckline; (de côte, arête rocheuse) indentation.

échange [eʃãʒ] nm exchange; **en ~ de** in exchange ou return for.

échanger [eʃãʒe] vt: ~ **qch** (contre) to exchange sth (for).

échangeur nm (AUTO) interchange.

échantillon [eʃãtijɔ̃] nm sample.

échappée [eʃape] nf (vue) vista.

échappement [eʃapmã] nm (AUTO) exhaust.

échapper [eʃape]: ~ **à** vt (gardien) to escape (from); (punition, péril) to escape from; ~ **à qn** (détail, sens) to escape sb; (objet qu'on tient) to slip out of sb's hands; **s'~** vi to escape; **laisser** ~ (cri etc) to let out; **l'~ belle** to have a narrow escape.

écharde [eʃaʀd(ə)] nf splinter (of wood).

écharpe [eʃaʀp(ə)] nf scarf (pl scarves); (de maire) sash; (MÉD) sling.

échasse [eʃas] nf stilt.

échauffer [eʃofe] vt (métal, moteur) to overheat; (fig: exciter) to fire, excite; s'~ vi (SPORT) to warm up; (dans la discussion) to become heated.

échauffourée [eʃofuʀe] nf clash, brawl.

échéance [eʃeɑ̃s] nf (d'un paiement: date) settlement date; (: somme due) financial commitment(s); (fig) deadline; à brève/longue ~ a short/long-term // ad in the short/long run.

échéant [eʃeɑ̃]: le cas ~ ad if the case arises.

échec [eʃɛk] nm failure; (ÉCHECS) ~ et mat/au roi checkmate/check; ~s nmpl (jeu) chess sg; tenir en ~ to hold in check; faire ~ à to foil ou thwart.

échelle [eʃɛl] nf ladder; (fig, d'une carte) scale.

échelon [eʃlɔ̃] nm (d'échelle) rung; (ADMIN) grade.

échelonner [eʃlɔne] vt to space out.

échevelé, e [eʃəvle] a tousled, dishevelled; wild, frenzied.

échine [eʃin] nf backbone, spine.

échiquier [eʃikje] nm chessboard.

écho [eko] nm echo; ~s nmpl (potins) gossip sg, rumours.

échoir [eʃwaʀ] vi (dette) to fall due; (délais) to expire; ~ à vt to fall to.

échoppe [eʃɔp] nf stall, booth.

échouer [eʃwe] vi to fail; s'~ vi to run aground.

échu, e [eʃy] pp de **échoir**.

éclabousser [eklabuse] vt to splash.

éclair [eklɛʀ] nm (d'orage) flash of lightning, lightning q; (gâteau) éclair.

éclairage [eklɛʀaʒ] nm lighting.

éclaircie [eklɛʀsi] nf bright interval.

éclaircir [eklɛʀsiʀ] vt to lighten (fig) to clear up; to clarify; (CULIN) to thin (down); s'~ (ciel) to clear; s'~ la voix to clear one's throat; **éclaircissement** nm clearing up; clarification.

éclairer [eklɛʀe] vt (lieu) to light (up); (personne: avec une lampe etc) to light the way for; (fig) to enlighten; to shed light on // vi: ~

mal/bien to give a poor/good light; s'~ à l'électricité to have electric lighting.

éclaireur, euse [eklɛʀœʀ, -øz] nm/f (scout) (boy) scout/(girl) guide // nm (MIL) scout.

éclat [ekla] nm (de bombe, de verre) fragment; (du soleil, d'une couleur etc) brightness, brilliance; (d'une cérémonie) splendour; (scandale): faire un ~ to cause a commotion; ~s de voix shouts.

éclatant, e [eklatɑ̃, -ɑ̃t] a brilliant.

éclater [eklate] vi (pneu) to burst; (bombe) to explode; (guerre, épidémie) to break out; (groupe, parti) to break up; ~ en sanglots/de rire to burst out sobbing/laughing.

éclipse [eklips(ə)] nf eclipse.

éclipser [eklipse] vt: s'~ vi to slip away.

éclopé, e [eklɔpe] a lame.

éclore [eklɔʀ] vi (œuf) to hatch; (fleur) to open (out).

écluse [eklyz] nf lock.

écœurant, e [ekœʀɑ̃, -ɑ̃t] a (gâteau etc) sickly.

écœurer [ekœʀe] vt: ~ qn to make sb feel sick.

école [ekɔl] nf school; aller à l'~ to go to school; ~ normale teachers' training college; **écolier, ière** nm/f schoolboy/girl.

écologie [ekɔlɔʒi] nf ecology; environmental studies pl.

éconduire [ekɔ̃dɥiʀ] vt to dismiss.

économe [ekɔnɔm] a thrifty // nm/f (de lycée etc) bursar (Brit), treasurer (US).

économie [ekɔnɔmi] nf economy; (gain: d'argent, de temps etc) saving; (science) economics sg; ~s nfpl (pécule) savings; **économique** a (avantageux) economical; (ÉCON) economic.

économiser [ekɔnɔmize] vt, vi to save.

écoper [ekɔpe] vi to bale out; (fig) to cop it; ~ (de) vt to get.

écorce [ekɔʀs(ə)] nf bark; (de fruit)

peel.

écorcher [ekɔrʃe] vt (animal) to skin; (égratigner) to graze; **écorchure** nf graze.

écossais, e [ekɔsɛ, -ez] a Scottish // nm/f: E~, e Scot.

Écosse [ekɔs] nf: l'~ Scotland.

écosser [ekɔse] vt to shell.

écouler [ekule] vt to sell; to dispose of; s'~ vi (eau) to flow (out); (jours, temps) to pass (by).

écourter [ekurte] vt to curtail, cut short.

écoute [ekut] nf (RADIO, TV): temps/ heure d'~ (listening ou viewing) time/ hour; prendre l'~ to tune in; rester à l'~ (de) to stay tuned in (to); ~s téléphoniques phone tapping sg.

écouter [ekute] vt to listen to; **écouteur** nm (TÉL) receiver; (RADIO) headphones pl, headset.

écoutille [ekutij] nf hatch.

écran [ekrɑ̃] nm screen.

écrasant, e [ekrɑzɑ̃, -ɑ̃t] a overwhelming.

écraser [ekraze] vt to crush; (piéton) to run over; s'~ vi (fam) to pipe down; s'~ (au sol) to crash; s'~ contre to crash into.

écrémer [ekreme] vt to skim.

écrevisse [ekrəvis] nf crayfish inv.

écrier [ekrije]: s'~ vi to exclaim.

écrin [ekrɛ̃] nm case, box.

écrire [ekrir] vt to write; s'~ to write to each other; ça s'écrit comment? how is it spelt? **écrit** nm document; (examen) written paper; par écrit in writing.

écriteau, x [ekrito] nm notice, sign.

écriture [ekrityr] nf writing; (COMM) entry; ~s nfpl (COMM) accounts, books; l'É~, les É~s the Scriptures.

écrivain [ekrivɛ̃] nm writer.

écrou [ekru] nm nut.

écrouer [ekrue] vt to imprison; to remand in custody.

écrouler [ekrule]: s'~ vi to collapse.

écru, e [ekry] a (toile) raw, unbleached; (couleur) off-white, écru.

écueil [ekœj] nm reef; (fig) pitfall; stumbling block.

écuelle [ekɥɛl] nf bowl.

éculé, e [ekyle] a (chaussure) downat-heel; (fig: péj) hackneyed.

écume [ekym] nf foam; (CULIN) scum; **écumer** vt (CULIN) to skim; (fig) to plunder.

écureuil [ekyrœj] nm squirrel.

écurie [ekyri] nf stable.

écusson [ekysɔ̃] nm badge.

écuyer, ère [ekɥije, -ɛr] nm/f rider.

eczéma [ɛgzema] nm eczema.

édenté, e [edɑ̃te] a toothless.

E.D.F. sigle f (= Électricité de France) national electricity company.

édifier [edifje] vt to build, erect; (fig) to edify.

édiles [edil] nmpl city fathers.

édit [edi] nm edict.

éditer [edite] vt (publier) to publish; (: disque) to produce; **éditeur, trice** nm/f editor; publisher; **édition** nf editing q; edition; (industrie du livre) publishing.

édredon [edrədɔ̃] nm eiderdown.

éducatif, ive [edykatif, -iv] a educational.

éducation [edykasjɔ̃] nf education; (familiale) upbringing; (manières) (good) manners pl; ~ physique physical education.

édulcorer [edylkɔre] vt to sweeten; (fig) to tone down.

éduquer [edyke] vt to educate; (élever) to bring up; (faculté) to train.

effacé, e [efase] a unassuming.

effacer [efase] vt to erase, rub out; s'~ vi (inscription etc) to wear off; (pour laisser passer) to step aside.

effarer [efare] vt to alarm.

effaroucher [efaruʃe] vt to frighten ou scare away; to alarm.

effectif, ive [efɛktif, -iv] a real; effective // nm (MIL) strength; (SCOL) (pupil) numbers pl; **effectivement** ad effectively; (réellement) actually, really; (en effet) indeed.

effectuer [efɛktɥe] vt (opération) to

carry out; (déplacement, trajet) to make; (mouvement) to execute.

efféminé, e [efemine] a effeminate.

effervescent, e [efɛʀvesɑ̃, ɑ̃t] a effervescent; (fig) agitated.

effet [efɛ] nm (résultat, artifice) effect; (impression) impression; ~s nmpl (vêtements etc) things; **faire de l'~** (médicament, menace) to have an effect; **en ~** ad indeed.

efficace [efikas] a (personne) efficient; (action, médicament) effective.

effilé, e [efile] a slender; sharp; streamlined.

effiler [efile] vt (tissu) to fray.

effilocher [efilɔʃe]: **s'~** vi to fray.

efflanqué, e [eflɑ̃ke] a emaciated.

effleurer [eflœʀe] vt to brush (against); (sujet) to touch upon; (suj: idée, pensée): ~ **qn** to cross sb's mind.

effluves [eflyv] nmpl exhalation(s).

effondrer [efɔ̃dʀe]: **s'~** vi to collapse.

efforcer [efɔʀse]: **s'~ de** vt: **s'~ de faire** to try hard to do, try hard to.

effort [efɔʀ] nm effort.

effraction [efʀaksjɔ̃] nf: **s'intro- duire par ~** causes to break into.

effrayant, e [efʀɛjɑ̃, ɑ̃t] a frighten- ing.

effrayer [efʀeje] vt to frighten, scare.

effréné, e [efʀene] a wild.

effriter [efʀite]: **s'~** vi to crumble.

effroi [efʀwa] nm terror, dread q.

effronté, e [efʀɔ̃te] a insolent, bra- zen.

effroyable [efʀwajabl(ə)] a horrify- ing, appalling.

effusion [efyzjɔ̃] nf effusion; **sans ~ de sang** without bloodshed.

égal, e, aux [egal, -o] a equal; (plan: vitesse) even, level; (cons- tant: vitesse) steady; (équitable) even // nm/f equal; **être ~ à** (prix, nombre) to be equal to; **ça lui est ~** it's all the same to him; he doesn't mind; **sans ~** matchless, un- equalled; **à l'~ de** (comme) just

like; **d'~ à ~** as equals; **~ement** ad equally; evenly; steadily; (aussi) too, as well; **~er** vt to equal; **~iser** vt (sol, salaires) to level (out); (chances) to equalize // vi (SPORT) to equalize; **~ité** nf equality; evenness; steadiness; (MATH) identity; **être à ~ité** (de points) to be even.

égard [egaʀ] nm: **~s** nmpl consid- eration sg; **à cet ~** in this respect; **eu ~ à** in view of; **par ~ pour** out of consideration for; **sans ~ pour** without regard for; **à l'~ de** prép towards; concerning.

égarement [egaʀmɑ̃] nm distrac- tion; aberration.

égarer [egaʀe] vt to mislay; (morale- ment) to lead astray; **s'~** vi to get lost, lose one's way; (objet) to go astray; (dans une discussion) to wan- der.

égayer [egeje] vt (personne) to amuse; to cheer up; (récit, endroit) to brighten up, liven up.

églantine [eglɑ̃tin] nf wild ou dog rose.

églefin [egləfɛ̃] nm haddock.

église [egliz] nf church; **aller à l'~** to go to church.

égoïsme [egoism(ə)] nm selfishness; **égoïste** a selfish.

égorger [egɔʀʒe] vt to cut the throat of.

égosiller [egozije]: **s'~** vi to shout o.s. hoarse.

égout [egu] nm sewer.

égoutter [egute] vt (linge) to wring out; (vaisselle) to drain // vi, **s'~** vi to drip; **égouttoir** nm draining board; (mobile) draining rack.

égratigner [egʀatiɲe] vt to scratch; **égratignure** nf scratch.

égrillard, e [egʀijaʀ, -aʀd(ə)] a ribald.

Égypte [eʒipt(ə)] nf: **l'~** Egypt; **égyptien, ne** a, nm/f Egyptian.

eh [e] excl hey!: **~ bien** well.

éhonté, e [eɔ̃te] a shameless, bra- zen.

éjecter [eʒɛkte] vt (TECH) to eject;

(fam) to kick *ou* chuck out.

élaborer [elabɔʀe] *vt* to elaborate; *(projet, stratégie)* to work out; *(rapport)* to draft.

élaguer [elage] *vt* to prune.

élan [elɑ̃] *nm* (ZOOL) elk, moose; (SPORT: *avant le saut)* run up; *(d'objet en mouvement)* momentum; *(fig: de tendresse etc)* surge; prendre de l'~ to gather speed.

élancé, e [elɑ̃se] *a* slender.

élancement [elɑ̃smɑ̃] *nm* shooting pain.

élancer [elɑ̃se]: s'~ *vi* to dash, hurl o.s.; *(fig: arbre, clocher)* to soar (upwards).

élargir [elaʀʒiʀ] *vt* to widen; *(vêtement)* to let out; (JUR) to release; s'~ *vi* to widen; *(vêtement)* to stretch.

élastique [elastik] *a* elastic // *nm (de bureau)* rubber band; *(pour la couture)* elastic *q*.

électeur, trice [elɛktœʀ, -tʀis] *nm/f* elector, voter.

élection [elɛksjɔ̃] *nf* election.

électorat [elɛktɔʀa] *nm* electorate.

électricien, ne [elɛktʀisjɛ̃, -jɛn] *nm/f* electrician.

électricité [elɛktʀisite] *nf* electricity; allumer/éteindre l'~ to put on/off the light.

électrique [elɛktʀik] *a* electric(al).

électro... [elɛktʀɔ] *préfixe*: ~**choc** *nm* electric shock treatment; ~**ménager** *a, nm*: appareils ~**ménagers**, l'~**ménager** domestic (electrical) appliances.

électronique [elɛktʀɔnik] *a* electronic // *nf* electronics *sg*.

électrophone [elɛktʀɔfɔn] *nm* record player.

élégant, e [elegɑ̃, -ɑ̃t] *a* elegant; *(solution)* neat, elegant; *(attitude, procédé)* courteous, civilized.

élément [elemɑ̃] *nm* element; *(pièce)* component, part; **élémentaire** *a* elementary.

éléphant [elefɑ̃] *nm* elephant.

élevage [elvaʒ] *nm* breeding; *(de bovins)* cattle rearing.

élévation [elevasjɔ̃] *nf (gén)* elevation; *(voir élever)* raising; *(voir s'élever)* rise.

élevé, e [elve] *a (prix, sommet)* high; *(fig: noble)* elevated; bien/mal ~ well-/ill-mannered.

élève [elɛv] *nm/f* pupil.

élever [elve] *vt (enfant)* to bring up, raise; *(bétail, volaille)* to breed; *(abeilles)* to keep; *(hausser: taux, niveau)* to raise; *(fig: âme, esprit)* to raise; *(édifier: monument)* to put up, erect; s'~ *vi (avion, alpiniste)* to go up; *(niveau, température, aussi: cri etc)* to rise; *(survenir: difficultés)* to arise; s'~ à *(suj: frais, dégâts)* to amount to, add up to; s'~ contre qch to rise up against sth; ~ la voix to raise one's voice; **éleveur, euse** *nm/f* stockbreeder.

élimé, e [elime] *a* threadbare.

éliminatoire [eliminatwaʀ] *nf* (SPORT) heat.

éliminer [elimine] *vt* to eliminate.

élire [eliʀ] *vt* to elect.

elle [ɛl] *pronom (sujet: chose)* it; *(: chose)* it; *(complément)* her; it; ~s they; them; ~-même herself; itself; ~s-mêmes themselves; *voir* il.

élocution [elɔkysjɔ̃] *nf* delivery; défaut d'~ speech impediment.

éloge [elɔʒ] *nm* praise *(gén q)*; **élogieux, euse** *a* laudatory, full of praise.

éloigné, e [elwaɲe] *a* distant, far-off.

éloignement [elwaɲmɑ̃] *nm* removal; putting off; estrangement; *(fig)* distance.

éloigner [elwaɲe] *vt*: ~ qch *(de)* to move *ou* take sth away (from); *(personne)*: ~ qn *(de)* to take sb away *ou* remove sb (from); *(échéance)* to put off, postpone; *(soupçons, danger)* to ward off; s'~ *(de) (personne)* to go away (from); *(véhicule)* to move away (from); *(affectivement)* to become estranged (from).

élongation [elɔ̃gasjɔ̃] *nf* strained muscle.

éloquent, e [elɔkɑ̃, -ɑ̃t] *a* eloquent.

élu, e [ely] *pp de* élire // *nm/f* (*POL*) elected representative.

élucubrations [elykybʀasjɔ̃] *nfpl* wild imaginings.

éluder [elyde] *vt* to evade.

émacié, e [emasje] *a* emaciated.

émail, aux [emaj, -o] *nm* enamel.

émaillé, e [emaje] *a* (*fig*): ~ de dotted with.

émanciper [emɑ̃sipe] *vt* to emancipate; **s'~** *vi* (*fig*) to become emancipated *ou* liberated.

émaner [emane]: ~ **de** *vt* to come from; (*ADMIN*) to proceed from.

emballage [ɑ̃balaʒ] *nm* wrapping; packaging.

emballer [ɑ̃bale] *vt* to wrap (up); (*dans un carton*) to pack (up); (*fig: fam*) to thrill (to bits); **s'~** *vi* (*moteur*) to race; (*cheval*) to bolt; (*fig: personne*) to get carried away.

embarcadère [ɑ̃baʀkadɛʀ] *nm* wharf, pier.

embarcation [ɑ̃baʀkasjɔ̃] *nf* (small) boat, (small) craft *inv*.

embardée [ɑ̃baʀde] *nf*: **faire une** ~ to swerve.

embarquement [ɑ̃baʀkəmɑ̃] *nm* embarkation; loading; boarding.

embarquer [ɑ̃baʀke] *vt* (*personne*) to embark; (*marchandise*) to load; (*fam*) to cart off; to nick // *vi* (*passager*) to board; **s'~** *vi* to board; **s'~ dans** (*affaire, aventure*) to embark upon.

embarras [ɑ̃baʀa] *nm* (*obstacle*) hindrance; (*confusion*) embarrassment.

embarrassant, e [ɑ̃baʀasɑ̃, -ɑ̃t] *a* embarrassing.

embarrasser [ɑ̃baʀase] *vt* (*encombrer*) to clutter (up); (*gêner*) to hinder, hamper; (*fig*) to cause embarrassment to; to put in an awkward position.

embauche [ɑ̃boʃ] *nf* hiring; **bureau d'~** labour office.

embaucher [ɑ̃boʃe] *vt* to take on,
hire.

embaumer [ɑ̃bome] *vt* to embalm; to fill with its fragrance; ~ **la lavande** to be fragrant with (the scent of) lavender.

embellie [ɑ̃beli] *nf* brighter period.

embellir [ɑ̃beliʀ] *vt* to make more attractive; (*une histoire*) to embellish // *vi* to grow lovelier *ou* more attractive.

embêtements [ɑ̃bɛtmɑ̃] *nmpl* trouble *sg*.

embêter [ɑ̃bɛte] *vt* to bother; **s'~** *vi* (*s'ennuyer*) to be bored.

emblée [ɑ̃ble]: **d'~** *ad* straightaway.

emboîter [ɑ̃bwate] *vt* to fit together; **s'~** (**dans**) to fit (into); ~ **le pas à qn** to follow in sb's footsteps.

embonpoint [ɑ̃bɔ̃pwɛ̃] *nm* stoutness.

embouchure [ɑ̃buʃyʀ] *nf* (*GÉO*) mouth.

embourber [ɑ̃buʀbe]: **s'~** *vi* to get stuck in the mud.

embourgeoiser [ɑ̃buʀʒwaze]: **s'~** *vi* to adopt a middle-class outlook.

embouteillage [ɑ̃butejaʒ] *nm* traffic jam.

emboutir [ɑ̃butiʀ] *vt* (*heurter*) to crash into, ram.

embranchement [ɑ̃bʀɑ̃ʃmɑ̃] *nm* (*routier*) junction; (*classification*) branch.

embraser [ɑ̃bʀaze]: **s'~** *vi* to flare up.

embrasser [ɑ̃bʀase] *vt* to kiss; (*sujet, période*) to embrace, encompass; (*carrière, métier*) to enter upon.

embrasure [ɑ̃bʀazyʀ] *nf*: **dans l'~ de la porte** in the door(way).

embrayage [ɑ̃bʀejaʒ] *nm* clutch.

embrayer [ɑ̃bʀeje] *vi* (*AUTO*) to let in the clutch.

embrigader [ɑ̃bʀigade] *vt* to recruit.

embrocher [ɑ̃bʀoʃe] *vt* to put on a spit.

embrouiller [ɑ̃bʀuje] *vt* (*fils*) to tangle (up); (*fiches, idées, personne*) to muddle up; **s'~** *vi* (*personne*) to get in a muddle.

embruns [ɑ̃bʀœ̃] *nmpl* sea spray *sg*.

embûches [ɑ̃byʃ] *nfpl* pitfalls, traps.

embué, e [ɑ̃bɥe] *a* misted up.

embuscade [ɑ̃byskad] *nf* ambush.

éméché, e [emeʃe] *a* tipsy, merry.

émeraude [emʀod] *nf* emerald.

émerger [emɛʀʒe] *vi* to emerge; *(faire saillie, aussi fig)* to stand out.

émeri [emʀi] *nm*: **toile** *ou* **papier** *∼* emery paper.

émérite [emeʀit] *a* highly skilled.

émerveiller [emɛʀveje] *vt* to fill with wonder; **s'** *∼* to marvel at.

émetteur, trice [emɛtœʀ, -tʀis] *a* a transmitting; *(poste)* *∼* transmitter.

émettre [emɛtʀ(ə)] *vt (son, lumière)* to give out; *(message etc: RADIO)* to transmit; *(billet, timbre, emprunt)* to issue; *(hypothèse, avis)* to voice, put forward // *vi* to broadcast.

émeus *etc vb voir* **émouvoir**.

émeute [emøt] *nf* riot.

émietter [emjete] *vt* to crumble.

émigrer [emigʀe] *vi* to emigrate.

éminence [eminɑ̃s] *nf* distinction; *(colline)* knoll, hill; **Son E** *∼* his *ou* her) Eminence.

éminent, e [eminɑ̃, -ɑ̃t] *a* distinguished.

émission [emisjɔ̃] *nf* emission; transmission; issue; *(RADIO, TV)* programme, broadcast.

emmagasiner [ɑ̃magazine] *vt* to (put into) store; *(fig)* to store up.

emmailloter [ɑ̃majɔte] *vt* to wrap up.

emmanchure [ɑ̃mɑ̃ʃyʀ] *nf* armhole.

emmêler [ɑ̃mele] *vt* to tangle (up); *(fig)* to muddle up; **s'** *∼* *vi* to get into a tangle.

emménager [ɑ̃menaʒe] *vi* to move in; *∼* **dans** to move into.

emmener [ɑ̃mne] *vt* to take (with one); *(comme otage, capture)* to take away; *∼* **qn au cinéma** to take sb to the cinema.

emmerder [ɑ̃mɛʀde] *(fam!) vt* to bug, bother; **s'** *∼* *vi* to be bored stiff.

emmitoufler [ɑ̃mitufle] *vt* to wrap

up (warmly).

émoi [emwa] *nm* commotion; *(trouble)* agitation.

émoluments [emɔlymɑ̃] *nmpl* remuneration *sg*, fee *sg*.

émonder [emɔ̃de] *vt* to prune.

émotif, ive [emɔtif, -iv] *a* emotional.

émotion [emɔsjɔ̃] *nf* emotion.

émousser [emuse] *vt* to blunt; *(fig)* to dull.

émouvoir [emuvwaʀ] *vt (troubler)* to stir, affect; *(toucher, attendrir)* to move; *(indigner)* to rouse; **s'** *∼* *vi* to be affected; to be moved; to be roused.

empailler [ɑ̃paje] *vt* to stuff.

empaler [ɑ̃pale] *vt* to impale.

emparer [ɑ̃paʀe]: **s'** *∼* **de** *vt (objet)* to seize, grab; *(comme otage, MIL)* to seize; *(suj: peur etc)* to take hold of.

empâter [ɑ̃pɑte]: **s'** *∼* *vi* to thicken out.

empêchement [ɑ̃peʃmɑ̃] *nm* (unexpected) obstacle, hitch.

empêcher [ɑ̃peʃe] *vt* to prevent; *∼* **qn de faire** to prevent *ou* stop sb (from) doing; **il n'empêche que** nevertheless; **il n'a pas pu s'** *∼* **de rire** he couldn't help laughing.

empereur [ɑ̃pʀœʀ] *nm* emperor.

empeser [ɑ̃pəze] *vt* to starch.

empester [ɑ̃pɛste] *vi* to stink, reek.

empêtrer [ɑ̃petʀe] *vt*: **s'** *∼* **dans** *(fils etc)* to get tangled up in.

emphase [ɑ̃faz] *nf* pomposity, bombast.

empiéter [ɑ̃pjete] *vi*: *∼* **sur** to encroach upon.

empiffrer [ɑ̃pifʀe]: **s'** *∼* *vi (péj)* to stuff o.s.

empiler [ɑ̃pile] *vt* to pile (up).

empire [ɑ̃piʀ] *nm* empire; *(fig)* influence.

empirer [ɑ̃piʀe] *vi* to worsen, deteriorate.

emplacement [ɑ̃plasmɑ̃] *nm* site.

emplettes [ɑ̃plɛt] *nfpl* shopping *sg*.

emplir [ɑ̃pliʀ] *vt* to fill; **s'** *∼* **(de)** to fill (with).

emploi [ɑ̃plwa] *nm* use; (*COMM, ÉCON*) employment; (*poste*) job, situation; ~ **du temps** timetable, schedule.

employé, e [ɑ̃plwaje] *nm/f* employee; ~ **de bureau** office employee *ou* clerk.

employer [ɑ̃plwaje] *vt* (*outil, moyen, méthode, mot*) to use; (*ouvrier, main-d'œuvre*) to employ; **s'~ à faire** to apply *ou* devote o.s. to doing; **employeur, euse** *nm/f* employer.

empocher [ɑ̃pɔʃe] *vt* to pocket.

empoignade [ɑ̃pwaɲad] *nf* row, set-to.

empoigner [ɑ̃pwaɲe] *vt* to grab.

empoisonner [ɑ̃pwazɔne] *vt* to poison; (*empester: air, pièce*) to stink out; (*fam*): ~ **qn** to drive sb mad.

emporter [ɑ̃pɔrte] *vt* to take (with one); (*en dérobant ou enlevant, emmener: blessés, voyageurs*) to take away; (*arracher*) to tear off; (*avantage, approbation*) to win; **s'~** *vi* (*de colère*) to lose one's temper; **l'~ (sur)** to get the upper hand (of); (*méthode etc*) to prevail (over); **boissons à ~** take-away drinks.

empreint, e [ɑ̃prɛ̃, -ɛ̃t] *a*: ~ **de** marked with; tinged with // *nf* (*de pied, main*) print; (*fig*) stamp, mark; ~**e (digitale)** fingerprint.

empressé, e [ɑ̃prese] *a* attentive.

empressement [ɑ̃prɛsmɑ̃] *nm* (*hâte*) eagerness.

empresser [ɑ̃prese] **s'~** *vi*: **s'~ auprès de qn** to surround sb with attentions; **s'~ de faire** (*se hâter*) to hasten to do.

emprise [ɑ̃priz] *nf* hold, ascendancy.

emprisonner [ɑ̃prizɔne] *vt* to imprison.

emprunt [ɑ̃prœ̃] *nm* borrowing *q*, loan.

emprunté, e [ɑ̃prœ̃te] *a* (*fig*) ill-at-ease, awkward.

emprunter [ɑ̃prœ̃te] *vt* to borrow; (*itinéraire*) to take, follow; (*style,*

manière) to adopt, assume.

ému, e [emy] *pp* de **émouvoir** // *a* excited; touched; moved.

émulsion [emylsjɔ̃] *nf* (*cosmetic*) (water-based) lotion.

MOT-CLÉ

en [ɑ̃] ◆ *prép* **1** (*endroit, pays*) in; (*direction*) to; **habiter ~ France/ville** to live in France/town; **aller ~ France/ville** to go to France/town

2 (*moment, temps*) in; ~ **été/juin** in summer/June

3 (*moyen*) by; ~ **avion/taxi** by plane/taxi

4 (*composition*) made of; **c'est ~ verre** it's (made of) glass; **un collier ~ argent** a silver necklace

5 (*description, état*): **une femme (habillée) ~ rouge** a woman (dressed) in red; **peindre qch ~ rouge** to paint sth red; ~ **T/étoile** T-/star-shaped; ~ **chemise/ chaussettes** in one's shirt-sleeves/ socks; ~ **soldat** as a soldier; **cassé ~ plusieurs morceaux** broken into several pieces; ~ **réparation** being repaired, under repair; ~ **vacances** on holiday; ~ **deuil** in mourning; **le même ~ plus grand** the same but *ou* bigger

6 (*avec gérondif*) while; on; by; ~ **dormant** while sleeping, as one sleeps; ~ **sortant** on going out, as he *etc* went out; **sortir ~ courant** to run out

◆ *pronom* **1** (*indéfini*): **j'~ ai/veux** I have/want some; ~ **as-tu?** have you got any?; **je n'~ veux pas** I don't want any; **j'~ ai 2** I've got 2; **combien y ~ a-t-il?** how many (of them) are there?; **j'~ ai assez** I've got enough (of it *ou* them); (*j'en ai marre*) I've had enough

2 (*provenance*) from there; **j'~ viens** I've come from there

3 (*cause*): **il ~ est malade/perd le sommeil** he is ill/can't sleep because of it

4 (*complément de nom, d'adjectif,*

verbe): **j'~ connais les dangers** I know its *ou* the dangers; **j'~ suis fier/ai besoin** I am proud of it/need it; *voir le verbe ou l'adjectif lorsque 'en' correspond à 'de' introduisant un complément prépositionnel.*

E.N.A. [ena] *sigle f* (= *École Nationale d'Administration*) *one of the Grandes Écoles.*

encadrer [ãkadʀe] *vt* (*tableau, image*) to frame; (*fig: entourer*) to surround; (*personnel, soldats etc*) to train.

encaisse [ãkɛs] *nf* cash in hand; **~ or/métallique** gold/cash and silver reserves.

encaissé, e [ãkese] *a* steep-sided; with steep banks.

encaisser [ãkese] *vt* (*chèque*) to cash; (*argent*) to collect; (*fig: coup, défaite*) to take.

encan [ãkã]: **à l'~** *ad* by auction.

encart [ãkaʀ] *nm* insert.

encastrer [ãkastʀe] *vt*: **~ qch dans** (*mur*) to embed sth in(to); (*boîtier*) to fit sth into.

encaustique [ãkostik] *nf* polish, wax.

enceinte [ãsɛ̃t] *af*: **~ (de 6 mois)** (6 months) pregnant // *nf* (*mur*) wall; (*espace*) enclosure.

encens [ãsã] *nm* incense.

encercler [ãsɛʀkle] *vt* to surround.

enchaîner [ãʃene] *vt* to chain up; (*mouvements, séquences*) to link (together) // *vi* to carry on.

enchanté, e [ãʃãte] *a* delighted; enchanted; **~ (de faire votre connaissance)** pleased to meet you.

enchantement [ãʃãtmã] *nm* delight; (*magie*) enchantment.

enchâsser [ãʃase] *vt* to set.

enchère [ãʃɛʀ] *nf* bid; **mettre/vendre aux ~s** to put up for (sale by)/sell by auction.

enchevêtrer [ãʃvetʀe] *vt* to tangle (up).

enclencher [ãklãʃe] *vt* (*mécanisme*) to engage; **s'~** *vi* to engage.

enclin, e [ãklɛ̃, -in] *a*: **~ à** inclined *ou* prone to.

enclos [ãklo] *nm* enclosure.

enclume [ãklym] *nf* anvil.

encoche [ãkɔʃ] *nf* notch.

encoignure [ãkɔɲyʀ] *nf* corner.

encolure [ãkɔlyʀ] *nf* (*tour de cou*) collar size; (*col, cou*) neck.

encombrant, e [ãkɔ̃bʀã, -ãt] *a* cumbersome, bulky.

encombre [ãkɔ̃bʀ]: **sans ~** *ad* without mishap *ou* incident.

encombrer [ãkɔ̃bʀe] *vt* to clutter (up); (*gêner*) to hamper; **s'~ de** (*bagages etc*) to load *ou* burden o.s. with.

encontre [ãkɔ̃tʀ(ə)]: **à l'~ de** *prép* against, counter to.

<u>MOT-CLÉ</u>

encore [ãkɔʀ] *ad* **1** (*continuation*) still; **il y travaille ~** he's still working on it; **pas ~** not yet

2 (*de nouveau*) again; **j'irai ~ demain** I'll go again tomorrow; **~ une fois** (once) again; **~ deux jours** two more days

3 (*intensif*) even, still; **~ plus fort/mieux** even louder/better, louder/better still

4 (*restriction*) even so *ou* then, only; **~ pourrais-je le faire si ...** even so, I might be able to do it if ...; **si ~ if only**

encore que *cj* although.

encourager [ãkuʀaʒe] *vt* to encourage.

encourir [ãkuʀiʀ] *vt* to incur.

encre [ãkʀ(ə)] *nf* ink; **~ de Chine** Indian ink; **encrier** *nm* inkwell.

encroûter [ãkʀute]: **s'~** *vi* (*fig*) to get into a rut, get set in one's ways.

encyclopédie [ãsiklɔpedi] *nf* encyclopaedia.

endetter [ãdete] *vt*, **s'~** *vi* to get into debt.

endiablé, e [ãdjable] *a* furious; boisterous.

endiguer [ãdige] *vt* to dyke (up);

(fig) to check, hold back.

endimancher [ãdimãʃe] vt: s'~ to put on one's Sunday best.

endive [ãdiv] nf chicory q.

endoctriner [ãdɔktrine] vt to indoctrinate.

endommager [ãdɔmaʒe] vt to damage.

endormi, e [ãdɔrmi] a asleep.

endormir [ãdɔrmir] vt to put to sleep; *(suj: chaleur etc)* to send to sleep; *(MÉD: dent, nerf)* to anaesthetize; *(fig: soupçons)* to allay; s'~ vi to fall asleep, go to sleep.

endosser [ãdose] vt *(responsabilité)* to take, shoulder; *(chèque)* to endorse; *(uniforme, tenue)* to put on, don.

endroit [ãdrwa] nm place; *(opposé à l'envers)* right side; à l'~ the right way out; the right way up; à l'~ **de** prép regarding.

enduire [ãdɥir] vt to coat.

endurant, e [ãdyrã, -ãt] a tough, hardy.

endurcir [ãdyrsir] vt *(physiquement)* to toughen; *(moralement)* to harden; s'~ vi to become tougher; to become hardened.

endurer [ãdyre] vt to endure, bear.

énergie [enɛrʒi] nf *(PHYSIQUE)* energy; *(TECH)* power; *(morale)* vigour, spirit; **énergique** a energetic; vigorous; *(mesures)* drastic, stringent.

énergumène [enɛrgymɛn] nm rowdy character ou customer.

énerver [enɛrve] vt to irritate, annoy; s'~ vi to get excited, get worked up.

enfance [ãfãs] nf *(âge)* childhood; *(fig)* infancy; *(enfants)* children pl.

enfant [ãfã] nm/f child *(pl* children); ~ **de chœur** nm *(REL)* altar boy; **enfanter** vi to give birth // vt to give birth to; **enfantillage** nm *(péj)* childish behaviour q; **enfantin, e** a childlike; child cpd.

enfer [ãfɛr] nm hell.

enfermer [ãfɛrme] vt to shut up; *(à*

clef, interner)* to lock up.

enfiévré, e [ãfjevre] a *(fig)* feverish.

enfiler [ãfile] vt *(vêtement)* to slip on, slip into; *(insérer)*: ~ **qch dans** to stick sth into; *(rue, couloir)* to take; *(perles)* to string; *(aiguille)* to thread.

enfin [ãfɛ̃] ad at last; *(en énumérant)* lastly; *(de restriction, résignation)* still; well; *(pour conclure)* in a word.

enflammer [ãflame] vt to set fire to; *(MÉD)* to inflame; s'~ vi to catch fire; to become inflamed.

enflé, e [ãfle] a swollen.

enfler [ãfle] vi to swell (up).

enfoncer [ãfɔ̃se] vt *(clou)* to drive in; *(faire pénétrer)*: ~ **qch dans** to push *(ou* drive) sth into; *(forcer: porte)* to break open; *(: plancher)* to cause to cave in // vi *(dans la vase etc)* to sink in; *(sol, surface)* to give way; s'~ vi to sink in; s'~ **dans** to sink into; *(forêt, ville)* to disappear into.

enfouir [ãfwir] vt *(dans le sol)* to bury; *(dans un tiroir etc)* to tuck away.

enfourcher [ãfurʃe] vt to mount.

enfourner [ãfurne] vt to put in the oven.

enfreindre [ãfrɛ̃dr(ə)] vt to infringe, break.

enfuir [ãfɥir]: s'~ vi to run away ou off.

enfumer [ãfyme] vt to smoke out.

engageant, e [ãgaʒã, -ãt] a attractive, appealing.

engagement [ãgaʒmã] nm *(promesse, contrat, POL)* commitment; *(MIL: combat)* engagement.

engager [ãgaʒe] vt *(embaucher)* to take on, engage; *(commencer)* to start; *(lier)* to bind, commit; *(impliquer, entraîner)* to involve; *(investir)* to invest, lay out; *(faire intervenir)* to engage; *(inciter)* to urge; *(faire pénétrer)* to insert; s'~ vi *(faire o.s., get taken on; *(MIL)* to enlist; *(promettre, politiquement)* to commit o.s.; (*débuter*) to start (up); s'~ à faire to undertake to do; s'~ dans (*rue, passage*) to turn into; (*s'emboîter*) to engage into; (*fig: affaire, discussion*) to enter into, embark on.

engelures [ɑ̃ʒlyʀ] *nfpl* chilblains.

engendrer [ɑ̃ʒɑ̃dʀe] *vt* to father.

engin [ɑ̃ʒɛ̃] *nm* machine; instrument; vehicle; (*AVIAT*) aircraft *inv*; missile.

englober [ɑ̃glɔbe] *vt* to include.

engloutir [ɑ̃glutiʀ] *vt* to swallow up.

engoncé, e [ɑ̃gɔ̃se] *a*: ~ dans cramped in.

engorger [ɑ̃gɔʀʒe] *vt* to obstruct, block.

engouement [ɑ̃gumɑ̃] *nm* (sudden) passion.

engouffrer [ɑ̃gufʀe] *vt* to swallow up, devour; s'~ dans to rush into.

engourdir [ɑ̃guʀdiʀ] *vt* to numb; (*fig*) to dull, blunt; s'~ *vi* to go numb.

engrais [ɑ̃gʀɛ] *nm* manure; ~ (chimique) (chemical) fertilizer.

engraisser [ɑ̃gʀese] *vt* to fatten (up).

engrenage [ɑ̃gʀənaʒ] *nm* gears *pl*, gearing; (*fig*) chain.

engueuler [ɑ̃gœle] *vt* (*fam*) to bawl at.

enhardir [ɑ̃aʀdiʀ]: s'~ *vi* to grow bolder.

énigme [enigm(ə)] *nf* riddle.

enivrer [ɑ̃nivʀe] *vt*: s'~ to get drunk; s'~ de (*fig*) to become intoxicated with.

enjambée [ɑ̃ʒɑ̃be] *nf* stride.

enjamber [ɑ̃ʒɑ̃be] *vt* to stride over; (*suj: pont etc*) to span, straddle.

enjeu, x [ɑ̃ʒø] *nm* stakes *pl*.

enjoindre [ɑ̃ʒwɛ̃dʀ(ə)] *vt* to enjoin, order.

enjôler [ɑ̃ʒole] *vt* to coax, wheedle.

enjoliver [ɑ̃ʒɔlive] *vt* to embellish; **enjoliveur** *nm* (*AUTO*) hub cap.

enjoué, e [ɑ̃ʒwe] *a* playful.

enlacer [ɑ̃lase] *vt* (*étreindre*) to embrace, hug.

enlaidir [ɑ̃lediʀ] *vt* to make ugly // *vi* to become ugly.

enlèvement [ɑ̃lɛvmɑ̃] *nm* (*rapt*) abduction, kidnapping.

enlever [ɑ̃lve] *vt* (*ôter: gén*) to remove; (: *vêtement, lunettes*) to take off; (*emporter: ordures etc*) to take away; (*prendre*): ~ qch à qn to take sth (away) from sb; (*kidnapper*) to abduct, kidnap; (*obtenir: prix, contrat*) to win.

enliser [ɑ̃lize]: s'~ *vi* to sink, get stuck.

enluminure [ɑ̃lyminyʀ] *nf* illumination.

enneigé, e [ɑ̃neʒe] *a* snowy; snowed-up.

ennemi, e [ɛnmi] *a* hostile; (*MIL*) enemy *cpd* // *nm/f* enemy.

ennui [ɑ̃nɥi] *nm* (*lassitude*) boredom; (*difficulté*) trouble *q*; avoir des ~s to have problems; **ennuyer** *vt* to bother; (*lasser*) to bore; s'ennuyer *vi* to be bored; s'ennuyer de (*regretter*) to miss; **ennuyeux, euse** *a* boring, tedious; annoying.

énoncé [enɔ̃se] *nm* terms *pl*; wording.

énoncer [enɔ̃se] *vt* to say, express; (*conditions*) to set out, state.

enorgueillir [ɑ̃nɔʀgœjiʀ]: s'~ de *vt* to pride o.s. on; to boast.

énorme [enɔʀm(ə)] *a* enormous, huge; **énormément** *ad* enormously; énormément de neige/gens an enormous amount of snow/number of people.

enquérir [ɑ̃keʀiʀ]: s'~ de *vt* to inquire about.

enquête [ɑ̃kɛt] *nf* (*de journaliste, de police*) investigation; (*judiciaire, administrative*) inquiry; (*sondage d'opinion*) survey; **enquêter** *vi* to investigate; to hold an inquiry; to conduct a survey.

enquiers etc *vb* voir **enquérir**.

enraciné, e [ɑ̃ʀasine] *a* deep-rooted.

enragé, e [ɑ̃ʀaʒe] *a* (*MÉD*) rabid, with rabies; (*fig*) fanatical.

enrageant, e [ɑ̃ʀaʒɑ̃, -ɑ̃t] *a* infuriating.

enrager [ɑ̃ʀaʒe] *vi* to be in a rage.

enrayer [ɑ̃ʀeje] *vt* to check, stop; **s'~** *vi* (*arme à feu*) to jam.

enregistrement [ɑ̃ʀʒistʀəmɑ̃] *nm* recording; (*ADMIN*) registration; **~ des bagages** (*à l'aéroport*) baggage check-in.

enregistrer [ɑ̃ʀʒistʀe] *vt* (*MUS etc, remarquer, noter*) to record; (*fig: mémoriser*) to make a mental note of; (*ADMIN*) to register; (*bagages: par train*) to register; (*: à l'aéroport*) to check in.

enrhumer [ɑ̃ʀyme] **s'~** *vi* to catch a cold.

enrichir [ɑ̃ʀiʃiʀ] *vt* to make rich(er), (*fig*) to enrich; **s'~** *vi* to get rich(er).

enrober [ɑ̃ʀɔbe] *vt*: **~ qch de** to coat sth with; (*fig*) to wrap sth up in.

enrôler [ɑ̃ʀole] *vt* to enlist; **s'~ (dans)** to enlist (in).

enrouer [ɑ̃ʀwe]: **s'~** *vi* to go hoarse.

enrouler [ɑ̃ʀule] *vt* (*fil, corde*) to wind (up); **~ qch autour de** to wind sth (a)round; **s'~** *vi* to coil up; to wind.

ensanglanté, e [ɑ̃sɑ̃glɑ̃te] *a* covered with blood.

enseignant, e [ɑ̃sɛɲɑ̃, -ɑ̃t] *nm/f* teacher.

enseigne [ɑ̃sɛɲ] *nf* sign; **à telle ~ que** so much so that; **~ lumineuse** neon sign.

enseignement [ɑ̃sɛɲmɑ̃] *nm* teaching; (*ADMIN*) education.

enseigner [ɑ̃sɛɲe] *vt, vi* to teach; **~ qch à qn/à qn que** to teach sb sth/ sb that.

ensemble [ɑ̃sɑ̃bl(ə)] *ad* together // *nm* (*assemblage, MATH*) set; (*totalité*): **l'~ du/de la** the whole ou entire; (*unité, harmonie*) unity; **impression/idée d'~** overall ou general impression/ idea; **dans l'~** (*en gros*) on the whole.

ensemencer [ɑ̃smɑ̃se] *vt* to sow.

ensevelir [ɑ̃səvliʀ] *vt* to bury.

ensoleillé, e [ɑ̃sɔleje] *a* sunny.

ensommeillé, e [ɑ̃sɔmeje] *a*

drowsy.

ensorceler [ɑ̃sɔʀsəle] *vt* to enchant, bewitch.

ensuite [ɑ̃sɥit] *ad* then, next; (*plus tard*) afterwards, later; **~ de quoi** after which.

ensuivre [ɑ̃sɥivʀ(ə)]: **s'~** *vi* to follow, ensue.

entailler [ɑ̃taje] *vt* to notch; to cut.

entamer [ɑ̃tame] *vt* (*pain, bouteille*) to start; (*hostilités, pourparlers*) to open; (*fig: altérer*) to make a dent in; to shake; to damage.

entasser [ɑ̃tase] *vt* (*empiler*) to pile up, heap up; (*tenir à l'étroit*) to cram together; **s'~** *vi* to pile up; to cram.

entendre [ɑ̃tɑ̃dʀ(ə)] *vt* to hear; (*comprendre*) to understand; (*vouloir dire*) to mean; (*vouloir*): **être obéi/que** to mean to be obeyed/that; **j'ai entendu dire que** I've heard (it said) that; **s'~** *vi* (*sympathiser*) to get on; (*se mettre d'accord*) to agree; **s'~ à qch/à faire** (*être compétent*) to be good at sth/doing.

entendu, e [ɑ̃tɑ̃dy] *a* (*réglé*) agreed; (*au courant: air*) knowing; (**c'est**) **~** all right, agreed; **c'est ~** (*concession*) all right, granted; **bien ~** of course.

entente [ɑ̃tɑ̃t] *nf* understanding; (*accord, traité*) agreement; **à double ~** (*sens*) with a double meaning.

entériner [ɑ̃teʀine] *vt* to ratify, confirm.

enterrement [ɑ̃tɛʀmɑ̃] *nm* (*cérémonie*) funeral, burial.

enterrer [ɑ̃tɛʀe] *vt* to bury.

entêtant, e [ɑ̃tɛtɑ̃, -ɑ̃t] *a* heady.

entêté, e [ɑ̃tete] *a* stubborn.

en-tête [ɑ̃tɛt] *nm* heading; **papier à ~** headed notepaper.

entêter [ɑ̃tete]: **s'~** *vi*: **s'~ (à faire)** to persist (in doing).

enthousiasme [ɑ̃tuzjasm(ə)] *nm* enthusiasm; **enthousiasmer** *vt* to fill with enthusiasm; **s'enthousiasmer (pour qch)** to get enthusiastic (about sth).

enticher [ɑ̃tiʃe]: s'~ **de** vt to become infatuated with.

entier, ère [ɑ̃tje, -jɛʀ] a (non entamé, en totalité) whole; (total, complet) complete; (fig: caractère) unbending // nm (MATH) whole; en ~ totally, in its entirety; **lait** ~ full-cream milk; **entièrement** ad entirely, wholly.

entonner [ɑ̃tɔne] vt (chanson) to strike up.

entonnoir [ɑ̃tɔnwaʀ] nm funnel.

entorse [ɑ̃tɔʀs(ə)] nf (MÉD) sprain; (fig): ~ **au règlement** infringement of the rule.

entortiller [ɑ̃tɔʀtije] vt (envelopper) to wrap; (enrouler) to twist, wind; (duper) to deceive.

entourage [ɑ̃tuʀaʒ] nm circle; family (circle); entourage; (ce qui enclôt) surround.

entourer [ɑ̃tuʀe] vt to surround; (apporter son soutien à) to rally round; ~ **de** to surround with; (trait) to encircle with.

entourloupettes [ɑ̃tuʀlupɛt] nfpl mean tricks.

entracte [ɑ̃tʀakt(ə)] nm interval.

entraide [ɑ̃tʀɛd] nf mutual aid; **s'entraider** vi to help each other.

entrain [ɑ̃tʀɛ̃] nm spirit; **avec/sans** ~ spiritedly/half-heartedly.

entraînement [ɑ̃tʀɛnmɑ̃] nm training; (TECH) drive.

entraîner [ɑ̃tʀɛne] vt (tirer: wagons) to pull; (charrier) to carry ou drag along; (TECH) to drive; (emmener: personne) to take (off); (mener à l'assaut, influencer) to lead; (SPORT) to train; (impliquer) to entail; (causer) to lead to, bring about; ~ **qn à faire** (inciter) to lead sb to do; **s'~** vi (SPORT) to train; **s'~ à qch/à faire** to train o.s. for sth/to do; **entraîneur, euse** nm/f (SPORT) coach, trainer // nm (HIPPISME) trainer // nf (de bar) hostess.

entraver [ɑ̃tʀave] vt (circulation) to hold up; (action, progrès) to hinder.

entre [ɑ̃tʀ(ə)] prép between; (parmi)

among(st); **l'un d'~ eux/nous** one of them/us; ~ **eux** among(st) themselves.

entrebâillé, e [ɑ̃tʀəbaje] a half-open, ajar.

entrechoquer [ɑ̃tʀəʃɔke]: s'~ vi to knock ou bang together.

entrecôte [ɑ̃tʀəkot] nf entrecôte ou rib steak.

entrecouper [ɑ̃tʀəkupe] vt: ~ **qch de** to intersperse sth with.

entrecroiser [ɑ̃tʀəkʀwaze]: s'~ vi intertwine.

entrée [ɑ̃tʀe] nf entrance; (accès: au cinéma etc) admission; (billet) (admission) ticket; (CULIN) first course; **d'~** from the outset; ~ **en matière** introduction.

entrefaites [ɑ̃tʀəfɛt]: **sur ces** ~ ad at this juncture.

entrefilet [ɑ̃tʀəfilɛ] nm paragraph (short article).

entrejambes [ɑ̃tʀəʒɑ̃b] nm crotch.

entrelacer [ɑ̃tʀəlase] vt to intertwine.

entrelarder [ɑ̃tʀəlaʀde] vt to lard.

entremêler [ɑ̃tʀəmele] vt: ~ **qch de** to (inter)mingle sth with.

entremets [ɑ̃tʀəmɛ] nm (cream) dessert.

entremetteur, euse [ɑ̃tʀəmɛtœʀ, -øz] nm/f go-between.

entremise [ɑ̃tʀəmiz] nf intervention; **par l'~ de** through.

entreposer [ɑ̃tʀəpoze] vt to store, put into storage.

entrepôt [ɑ̃tʀəpo] nm warehouse.

entreprenant, e [ɑ̃tʀəpʀənɑ̃, -ɑ̃t] a (actif) enterprising; (trop galant) forward.

entreprendre [ɑ̃tʀəpʀɑ̃dʀ(ə)] vt (se lancer dans) to undertake; (commencer) to begin ou start (upon); (personne) to buttonhole; to tackle.

entrepreneur [ɑ̃tʀəpʀənœʀ] nm: ~ (en bâtiment) (building) contractor.

entreprise [ɑ̃tʀəpʀiz] nf (société) firm, concern; (action) undertaking, venture.

entrer [ɑ̃tʀe] vi to go (ou come) in,

enter // vt (INFORM) to enter, input; **(faire) ~ qch dans** to get sth into; **~ dans** (gén) to enter; (pièce) to go (ou come) into, enter; (club) to join; (heurter) to run into; (être une composante de) to go into; to form part of; **~ à l'hôpital** to go into hospital; **faire ~** (visiteur) to show in.

entresol [ãtʀəsɔl] nm mezzanine.

entre-temps [ãtʀətã] ad meanwhile.

entretenir [ãtʀətniʀ] vt to maintain; (famille, maitresse) to support, keep; **~ qn (de)** to speak to sb (about); **s'~ (de)** to converse (about).

entretien [ãtʀətjɛ̃] nm maintenance; (discussion) discussion, talk; (audience) interview.

entrevoir [ãtʀəvwaʀ] vt (à peine) to make out; (brièvement) to catch a glimpse of.

entrevue [ãtʀəvy] nf meeting; (audience) interview.

entrouvert, e [ãtʀuvɛʀ, -ɛʀt(ə)] a half-open.

énumérer [enymeʀe] vt to list, enumerate.

envahir [ãvaiʀ] vt to invade; (suj: inquiétude, peur) to come over; **envahissant, e** a (péj: personne) interfering, intrusive.

enveloppe [ãvlɔp] nf (de lettre) envelope; (TECH) casing; outer layer.

envelopper [ãvlɔpe] vt to wrap; (fig) to envelop, shroud.

envenimer [ãvnime] vt to aggravate.

envergure [ãvɛʀgyʀ] nf (fig) scope; calibre.

enverrai etc vb voir **envoyer**.

envers [ãvɛʀ] prép towards, to // nm other side; (d'une étoffe) wrong side; **à l'~** upside down; back to front; (vêtement) inside out.

envie [ãvi] nf (sentiment) envy; (souhait) desire, wish; **avoir ~ de (faire)** to feel like (doing); (plus fort) to want (to do); **avoir ~ que** to wish that; **ça lui fait ~** he would like that; **envier** vt to envy; **envieux, euse** a envious.

environ [ãviʀɔ̃] ad: **~ 3 h/2 km** (around) about 3 o'clock/2 km; **~s** nmpl surroundings.

environnement [ãviʀɔnmã] nm environment.

environner [ãviʀɔne] vt to surround.

envisager [ãvizaʒe] vt (examiner, considérer) to view, contemplate; (avoir en vue) to envisage.

envoi [ãvwa] nm (paquet) parcel, consignment.

envoler [ãvɔle]: **s'~** vi (oiseau) to fly away ou off; (avion) to take off; (papier, feuille) to blow away; (fig) to vanish (into thin air).

envoûter [ãvute] vt to bewitch.

envoyé, e [ãvwaje] nm/f (POL) envoy; (PRESSE) correspondent.

envoyer [ãvwaje] vt to send; (lancer) to hurl, throw; **~ chercher** to send for.

épagneul, e [epaɲœl] nm/f spaniel.

épais, se [epɛ, -ɛs] a thick; **épaisseur** nf thickness.

épancher [epãʃe]: **s'~** vi to open one's heart.

épanouir [epanwiʀ]: **s'~** vi (fleur) to bloom, open out; (visage) to light up; (fig) to blossom; to open out.

épargne [epaʀɲ(ə)] nf saving.

épargner [epaʀɲe] vt to save; (ne pas tuer ou endommager) to spare // vi to save; **~ qch à qn** to spare sb sth.

éparpiller [epaʀpije] vt to scatter; (pour répartir) to disperse; **s'~** vi to scatter; (fig) to dissipate one's efforts.

épars, e [epaʀ, -aʀs(ə)] a scattered.

épatant, e [epatã, -ãt] a (fam) super.

épater [epate] vt to amaze; to impress.

épaule [epol] nf shoulder.

épauler [epole] vt (aider) to back up, support; (arme) to raise (to one's shoulder) // vi to (take) aim.

épave [epav] nf wreck.

épée [epe] nf sword.

épeler [eple] vt to spell.

éperdu, e [epɛʀdy] a distraught, overcome; passionate; frantic.

éperon [epʀɔ̃] nm spur.

épi [epi] nm (de blé, d'orge) ear.

épice [epis] nf spice.

épicer [epise] vt to spice.

épicerie [episʀi] nf grocer's shop; (denrées) groceries pl; ~ **fine** delicatessen; **épicier, ière** nm/f grocer.

épidémie [epidemi] nf epidemic.

épier [epje] vt to spy on, watch closely; (occasion) to look out for.

épilepsie [epilɛpsi] nf epilepsy.

épiler [epile] vt (jambes) to remove the hair from; (sourcils) to pluck.

épilogue [epilɔg] nm (fig) conclusion, dénouement.

épiloguer [epilɔge] vi: ~ **sur** to hold forth on.

épinards [epinaʀ] nmpl spinach sg.

épine [epin] nf thorn, prickle; (d'oursin etc) spine; ~ **dorsale** backbone.

épingle [epɛ̃gl(ə)] nf pin; ~ **de nourrice** ou **de sûreté** ou **double** safety pin.

épingler [epɛ̃gle] vt (badge, décoration): ~ **qch sur** to pin sth on(to); (fam) to catch, nick.

épique [epik] a epic.

épisode [epizɔd] nm episode; **film/roman à** ~**s** serial; **épisodique** a occasional.

épître [epitʀ(ə)] nf epistle.

éploré, e [eplɔʀe] a tearful.

épluche-légumes [eplyʃlegym] nm inv (potato) peeler.

éplucher [eplyʃe] vt (fruit, légumes) to peel; (fig) to go over with a fine-tooth comb; **épluchures** nfpl peelings.

épointer [epwɛ̃te] vt to blunt.

éponge [epɔ̃ʒ] nf sponge; **éponger** vt (liquide) to mop up; (surface) to sponge; (fig: déficit) to soak up; **s'éponger le front** to mop one's brow.

épopée [epɔpe] nf epic.

époque [epɔk] nf (de l'histoire) age, era; (de l'année, la vie) time; **d'~ a**

(meuble) period cpd.

époumoner [epumɔne]: **s'~** vi to shout o.s. hoarse.

épouse [epuz] nf wife (pl wives).

épouser [epuze] vt to marry; (fig: idées) to espouse; (: forme) to fit.

épousseter [epuste] vt to dust.

époustouflant, e [epustuflã, -ãt] a staggering, mind-boggling.

épouvantable [epuvɑ̃tabl(ə)] a appalling, dreadful.

épouvantail [epuvɑ̃taj] nm (à moineaux) scarecrow.

épouvante [epuvɑ̃t] nf terror; **film d'~** horror film; **épouvanter** vt to terrify.

époux [epu] nm husband // nmpl (married) couple.

éprendre [epʀɑ̃dʀ(ə)]: **s'~ de** vt to fall in love with.

épreuve [epʀœv] nf (d'examen) test; (malheur, difficulté) trial, ordeal; (PHOTO) print; (TYPO) proof; (SPORT) event; **à l'~ des balles** bulletproof; **à toute ~** unfailing; **mettre à l'~** to put to the test.

épris, e [epʀi, -iz] vb voir **éprendre**.

éprouver [epʀuve] vt (tester) to test; (marquer, faire souffrir) to afflict, distress; (ressentir) to experience.

éprouvette [epʀuvɛt] nf test tube.

épuisé, e [epɥize] a exhausted; (livre) out of print.

épuisement [epɥizmɑ̃] nm exhaustion.

épuiser [epɥize] vt (fatiguer) to exhaust, wear ou tire out; (stock, sujet) to exhaust; **s'~** vi to wear ou tire o.s. out, exhaust o.s.; (stock) to run out.

épurer [epyʀe] vt (liquide) to purify; (parti etc) to purge; (langue, texte) to refine.

équateur [ekwatœʀ] nm equator; (**la république de**) **l'É~** Ecuador.

équation [ekwasjɔ̃] nf equation.

équerre [ekɛʀ] nf (à dessin) (set) square; (pour fixer) brace; **en ~** at right angles; **à l'~, d'~** straight.

équilibre [ekilibʀ(ə)] nm balance; (d'une balance) equilibrium; **garder/perdre l'~** to keep/lose one's balance; **être en ~** to be balanced; **équilibré, e** a (fig) well-balanced, stable; **équilibrer** vt to balance; **s'équilibrer** vi (poids) to balance; (fig: défauts etc) to balance each other out.

équipage [ekipaʒ] nm crew.

équipe [ekip] nf team; (bande: parfois péj) bunch.

équipé, e [ekipe] a: **bien/mal ~** well-/poorly-equipped.

équipée [ekipe] nf escapade.

équipement [ekipmɑ̃] nm equipment; **~s** nmpl amenities, facilities, installations.

équiper [ekipe] vt to equip; (voiture, cuisine) to equip, fit out; **~ qn/qch de** to equip sb/sth with.

équitable [ekitabl(ə)] a fair.

équitation [ekitɑsjɔ̃] nf (horse-)riding.

équivalent, e [ekivalɑ̃, -ɑ̃t] a, nm equivalent.

équivaloir [ekivalwaʀ]: **~ à** vt to be equivalent to.

équivoque [ekivɔk] a equivocal, ambiguous; (louche) dubious.

érable [eʀabl(ə)] nm maple.

érafler [eʀafle] vt to scratch; **éraflure** nf scratch.

éraillé, e [eʀaje] a (voix) rasping.

ère [eʀ] nf era; **en l'an 1050 de notre ~** in the year 1050 A.D.

érection [eʀɛksjɔ̃] nf erection.

éreinter [eʀɛ̃te] vt to exhaust, wear out.

ériger [eʀiʒe] vt (monument) to erect.

ermite [eʀmit] nm hermit.

éroder [eʀɔde] vt to erode.

érotique [eʀɔtik] a erotic.

errer [eʀe] vi to wander.

erreur [eʀœʀ] nf mistake, error; (morale) error; **faire ~** to be mistaken; **par ~** by mistake; **~ judiciaire** miscarriage of justice.

érudit, e [eʀydi, -it] nm/f scholar.

éruption [eʀypsjɔ̃] nf eruption; (MÉD) rash.

es vb voir **être**.

ès [ɛs] prép: **licencié ~ lettres/sciences** ≈ Bachelor of Arts/Science.

escabeau, x [ɛskabo] nm (tabouret) stool; (échelle) stepladder.

escadre [ɛskadʀ(ə)] nf (NAVIG) squadron; (AVIAT) wing.

escadrille [ɛskadʀij] nf (AVIAT) flight.

escadron [ɛskadʀɔ̃] nm squadron.

escalade [ɛskalad] nf climbing q; (POL etc) escalation.

escalader [ɛskalade] vt to climb.

escale [ɛskal] nf (NAVIG) call; port of call; (AVIAT) stop(over); **faire ~ à** to put in at; to stop over at.

escalier [ɛskalje] nm stairs pl; **dans l'~ ou les ~s** on the stairs; **~ roulant** escalator.

escamoter [ɛskamɔte] vt (esquiver) to get round, evade; (faire disparaître) to conjure away.

escapade [ɛskapad] nf: **faire une ~** to go on a jaunt; to run away ou off.

escargot [ɛskaʀgo] nm snail.

escarmouche [ɛskaʀmuʃ] nf skirmish.

escarpé, e [ɛskaʀpe] a steep.

escient [ɛsjɑ̃] nm: **à bon ~** advisedly.

esclaffer [ɛsklafe]: **s'~** vi to guffaw.

esclandre [ɛsklɑ̃dʀ(ə)] nm scene, fracas.

esclavage [ɛsklavaʒ] nm slavery.

esclave [ɛsklav] nm/f slave.

escompter [ɛskɔ̃te] vt (COMM) to discount; (espérer) to expect, reckon upon.

escorte [ɛskɔʀt(ə)] nf escort.

escouade [ɛskwad] nf squad.

escrime [ɛskʀim] nf fencing.

escrimer [ɛskʀime]: **s'~** vi: **s'~ à faire** to wear o.s. out doing.

escroc [ɛskʀo] nm swindler, conman.

escroquer [ɛskʀɔke] vt: **~ qn (de qch)/qch (à qn)** to swindle sb (of sth)/sth (out of sb); **escroquerie** nf swindle.

espace [εspas] *nm* space.

espacer [εspase] *vt* to space out; **s'~** *vi* (*visites etc*) to become less frequent.

espadon [εspadɔ̃] *nm* swordfish fin.

espadrille [εspadrij] *nf* rope-soled sandal.

Espagne [εspaɲ(ə)] *nf*: l'~ Spain; **espagnol, e** *a* Spanish // *nm/f*: Espagnol, e Spaniard // *nm* (*LING*) Spanish.

espagnolette [εspaɲɔlεt] *nf* (window) catch; **fermé à l'~** resting on the catch.

espèce [εspεs] *nf* (*BIO, BOT, ZOOL*) species *inv*; (*gén*: *sorte*) sort, kind, type; (*péj*): **~ de maladroit!** you clumsy oaf!; **en ~** in cash; **~s** *nfpl* (*COMM*) cash *sg*; **en l'~** *ad* in the case in point.

espérance [εsperãs] *nf* hope; **~ de vie** life expectancy.

espérer [εspere] *vt* to hope for; **j'espère (bien)** I hope so; **~ que/faire** to hope that/to do; **~ en** to trust in.

espiègle [εspjεgl(ə)] *a* mischievous.

espion, ne [εspjɔ̃, -ɔn] *nm/f* spy.

espionnage [εspjɔnaʒ] *nm* espionage, spying.

espionner [εspjɔne] *vt* to spy (up)on.

esplanade [εsplanad] *nf* esplanade.

espoir [εspwar] *nm* hope.

esprit [εspri] *nm* (*pensée, intellect*) mind; (*humour, ironie*) wit; (*mentalité, d'une loi etc, fantôme etc*) spirit; **faire de l'~** to try to be witty; **reprendre ses ~s** to come to; **perdre l'~** to lose one's mind.

esquimau, de, x [εskimo, -od] *a, nm/f* Eskimo // *nm* ice lolly (*Brit*), popsicle (*US*).

esquinter [εskɛ̃te] *vt* (*fam*) to mess up.

esquisse [εskis] *nf* sketch.

esquisser [εskise] *vt* to sketch; **s'~** *vi* (*amélioration*) to begin to be detectable; **~ un sourire** to give a vague smile.

esquiver [εskive] *vt* to dodge; **s'~** *vi*

to slip away.

essai [εsε] *nm* trying; testing; (*tentative*) attempt, try; (*RUGBY*) try; (*LITTÉRATURE*) essay; **~s** (*AUTO*) trials; **~ gratuit** (*COMM*) free trial; **à l'~** on a trial basis.

essaim [εsɛ̃] *nm* swarm.

essayer [εseje] *vt* (*gén*) to try; (*vêtement, chaussures*) to try (on); (*restaurant, méthode, voiture*) to try // *vi* to try; **~ de faire** to try ou attempt to do.

essence [εsãs] *nf* (*de voiture*) petrol (*Brit*), gas(oline) (*US*); (*extrait de plante, PHILOSOPHIE*) essence; (*espèce: d'arbre*) species *inv*.

essentiel, le [εsãsjεl] *a* essential; **c'est l'~** (*ce qui importe*) that's the main thing; **l'~ de** the main part of.

essieu, x [εsjø] *nm* axle.

essor [εsɔr] *nm* (*de l'économie etc*) rapid expansion.

essorer [εsɔre] *vt* (*en tordant*) to wring (out); (*par la force centrifuge*) to spin-dry; **essoreuse** *nf* mangle, wringer; spin-dryer.

essouffler [εsufle] *vt* to make breathless; **s'~** *vi* to get out of breath; (*fig*) to run out of steam.

essuie-glace [εsɥiglas] *nm inv* windscreen (*Brit*) ou windshield (*US*) wiper.

essuie-main [εsɥimɛ̃] *nm* hand towel.

essuyer [εsɥije] *vt* to wipe; (*fig*: *subir*) to suffer; **s'~** *vi* (*après le bain*) to dry o.s.; **~ la vaisselle** to dry up.

est [εst] *vb* [*v*] *voir* **être** // *nm* east // *a inv* east; (*région*) east(ern); **à l'~** in the east; (*direction*) to the east, east(wards); **à l'~ de** (to the) east of.

estafette [εstafεt] *nf* (*MIL*) dispatch rider.

estaminet [εstaminε] *nm* tavern.

estampe [εstãp] *nf* print, engraving.

estampille [εstãpij] *nf* stamp.

est-ce que [εskə] *ad*: **~ c'est cher/c'était bon?** is it expensive/was it good?; **quand est-ce qu'il part?**

when does he leave?, when is he leaving?: *voir aussi* **que**.

esthéticienne [ɛstetisjɛn] *nf* beautician.

esthétique [ɛstetik] *a* attractive; aesthetically pleasing.

estimation [ɛstimasjɔ̃] *nf* valuation; assessment.

estime [ɛstim] *nf* esteem, regard.

estimer [ɛstime] *vt* (*respecter*) to esteem; (*expertiser*) to value; (*évaluer*) to assess, estimate; (*penser*): ~ **que/être** to consider that/o.s. to be.

estival, e, aux [ɛstival, -o] *a* summer *cpd*.

estivant, e [ɛstivã, -ãt] *nm/f* (summer) holiday-maker.

estomac [ɛstɔma] *nm* stomach.

estomaqué, e [ɛstɔmake] *a* flabbergasted.

estomper [ɛstɔ̃pe] *vt* (*fig*) to blur, dim; **s'~** *vi* to soften; to become blurred.

estrade [ɛstrad] *nf* platform, rostrum.

estragon [ɛstragɔ̃] *nm* tarragon.

estropier [ɛstrɔpje] *vt* to cripple, maim; (*fig*) to twist, distort.

et [e] *cj* and; ~ **lui?** what about him?; ~ **alors!** so what!

étable [etabl(ə)] *nf* cowshed.

établi [etabli] *nm* (*work*)bench.

établir [etablir] *vt* (*papiers d'identité, facture*) to make out; (*liste, programme*) to draw up; (*entreprise, camp, gouvernement, artisan*) to set up; (*réputation, usage, fait, culpabilité*) to establish; **s'~** *vi* (*se faire: entente etc*) to be established; **s'~** (**à son compte**) to set up in business; **s'~** **à/près de** to settle in/near.

établissement [etablismã] *nm* making out; drawing up; setting up, establishing; (*entreprise, institution*) establishment; ~ **scolaire** school, educational establishment.

étage [etaʒ] *nm* (*d'immeuble*) storey, floor; (*de fusée*) stage; (*GÉO: de culture, végétation*) level; **à l'~** upstairs; **au 2ème ~** on the 2nd (*Brit*) ou 3rd (*US*) floor; **de bas ~** *a* of low quality.

étagère [etaʒɛr] *nf* (*rayon*) shelf; (*meuble*) shelves *pl*.

étai [etɛ] *nm* stay, prop.

étain [etɛ̃] *nm* tin; (*ORFÈVRERIE*) pewter *q*.

étais *etc vb voir* **être**.

étal [etal] *nm* stall.

étalage [etalaʒ] *nm* display; display window; **faire ~ de** to show off, parade.

étaler [etale] *vt* (*carte, nappe*) to spread (out); (*peinture, liquide*) to spread; (*échelonner: paiements, vacances*) to spread, stagger; (*marchandises*) to display; (*richesses, connaissances*) to parade; **s'~** *vi* (*liquide*) to spread out; (*fam*) to fall flat on one's face; **s'~ sur** (*suj: paiements etc*) to be spread out over.

étalon [etalɔ̃] *nm* (*mesure*) standard; (*cheval*) stallion.

étamer [etame] *vt* (*casserole*) to tin(plate); (*glace*) to silver.

étanche [etɑ̃ʃ] *a* (*récipient*) watertight; (*montre, vêtement*) waterproof.

étancher [etɑ̃ʃe] *vt*: ~ **sa soif** to quench one's thirst.

étang [etɑ̃] *nm* pond.

étant [etɑ̃] *vb voir* **être, donné**.

étape [etap] *nf* stage; (*lieu d'arrivée*) stopping place; (*CYCLISME*) staging point; **faire ~ à** to stop off at.

état [eta] *nm* (*POL, condition*) state; (*liste*) inventory, statement; **en mauvais ~** in poor condition; **en ~ (de marche)** in (working) order; **remettre en ~** to repair; **hors d'~** out of order; **être en ~/hors d'~ de faire** to be in a/in no fit state to do; **en tout ~ de cause** in any event; **être dans tous ses ~s** to be in a state; **faire ~ de** (*alléguer*) to put forward; **en ~ d'arrestation** under arrest; ~ **civil** civil status; ~ **des lieux** inventory of fixtures; ~**s**

d'âme moods; **étatiser** vt to bring under state control.

état-major [etamaʒɔʀ] nm (MIL) staff.

États-Unis [etazyni] nmpl: les ~ the United States.

étau, x [eto] nm vice (Brit), vise (US).

étayer [eteje] vt to prop ou shore up.

et c(a)etera [ɛtsetera], **etc.** ad et cetera, and so on, etc.

été [ete] pp de être // nm summer.

éteignoir [etɛɲwaʀ] nm (candle extinguisher; (péj) killjoy, wet blanket.

éteindre [etɛ̃dʀ(ə)] vt (lampe, lumière, radio) to turn ou switch off; (cigarette, incendie, bougie) to put out, extinguish; (JUR: dette) to extinguish; s'~ vi to go out; to go off; (mourir) to pass away; **éteint, e** (fig) lacklustre, dull; (volcan) extinct.

étendard [etãdaʀ] nm standard.

étendre [etãdʀ(ə)] vt (pâte, liquide) to spread; (carte etc) to spread out; (linge) to hang up; (bras, jambes, par terre: blessé) to stretch out; (diluer) to dilute, thin; (fig: agrandir) to extend; s'~ vi (augmenter, se propager) to spread; (terrain, forêt etc) to stretch; (s'allonger) to stretch out; (se coucher) to lie down; (fig: expliquer) to elaborate.

étendu, e [etãdy] a extensive // nf (d'eau, de sable) stretch, expanse; (importance) extent.

éternel, le [etɛʀnɛl] a eternal.

éterniser [etɛʀnize]: s'~ vi to last for ages; to stay for ages.

éternité [etɛʀnite] nf eternity.

éternuer [etɛʀnɥe] vi to sneeze.

êtes vb voir être.

éthique [etik] a ethical.

ethnie [etni] nf ethnic group.

éthylisme [etilism(ə)] nm alcoholism.

étiez vb voir être.

étinceler [etɛ̃sle] vi to sparkle.

étincelle [etɛ̃sɛl] nf spark.

étioler [etjɔle]: s'~ vi to wilt.

étiqueter [etikte] vt to label.

étiquette [etikɛt] nf label; (protocole): l'~ etiquette.

étirer [etiʀe] vt to stretch; s'~ vi (personne) to stretch; (convoi, route): s'~ sur to stretch out over.

étoffe [etɔf] nf material, fabric.

étoffer [etɔfe] vt, s'~ vi to fill out.

étoile [etwal] nf star; à la belle ~ in the open; ~ filante shooting star; ~ de mer starfish; **étoilé, e** a starry.

étole [etɔl] nf stole.

étonnant, e [etɔnã, -ãt] a amazing.

étonner [etɔne] vt to surprise, amaze; s'~ que/de to be amazed that/at; cela m'étonnerait (que) (j'en doute) I'd be very surprised (if).

étouffée [etufe]: à l'~ ad (CULIN) steamed; braised.

étouffer [etufe] vt to suffocate; (bruit) to muffle; (scandale) to hush up // vi to suffocate; s'~ vi (en mangeant etc) to choke.

étourderie [etuʀdəʀi] nf heedlessness ø; thoughtless blunder.

étourdi, e [etuʀdi] a (distrait) scatterbrained, heedless.

étourdir [etuʀdiʀ] vt (assommer) to stun, daze; (griser) to make dizzy ou giddy; **étourdissement** nm dizzy spell.

étourneau, x [etuʀno] nm starling.

étrange [etʀãʒ] a strange.

étranger, ère [etʀãʒe, -ɛʀ] a foreign; (pas de la famille, non familier) strange // nm/f foreigner; stranger // nm: à l'~ abroad; de l'~ from abroad; à ~ (fig) unfamiliar to; irrelevant to.

étranglement [etʀãgləmã] nm (d'une vallée etc) constriction.

étrangler [etʀãgle] vt to strangle; s'~ vi (en mangeant etc) to choke.

étrave [etʀav] nf stem.

MOT-CLÉ

être [ɛtʀ(ə)] ◆ nm being; ~ **humain** human being

◆ *vb avec attribut* **1** (*état, description*) to be; **il est instituteur** he is *ou* he's a teacher; **vous êtes grand/ intelligent/ fatigué** you are *ou* you're tall/clever/tired **2** (+ *à: appartenir*) to be; **le livre est à Paul** the book is Paul's *ou* belongs to Paul; **c'est à moi/eux** it is *ou* it's mine/theirs **3** (+ *de: provenance*) to be; **il est de Paris** he is from Paris; (: *appartenance*): **il est des nôtres** he is one of us **4** (*date*): **nous sommes le 10 janvier** it's the 10th of January (today) ◆ *vi* to be; **je ne serai pas ici demain** I won't be here tomorrow

◆ *vb auxiliaire* **1** to have; to be; **être arrivé/allé** to have arrived/ gone; **il est parti** he has left, he is gone **2** (*forme passive*) to be; **être fait par** to be made by; **il a été promu** he has been promoted **3** (+ *à: obligation*): **c'est à réparer** it needs repairing; **c'est à essayer** it should be tried

◆ *vb impersonnel* **1**: **il est** + *adjectif* **it is** + *adjective*; **il est impossible de le faire** it's impossible to do it **2** (*heure, date*): **il est 10 heures, c'est 10 heures** it is *ou* it's 10 o'clock **3** (*emphatique*): **c'est moi** it is; **c'est à lui de le faire** it's up to him to do it.

étreindre [etʀɛ̃dʀ(ə)] *vt* to clutch, grip; (*amoureusement, amicalement*) to embrace; **s'~** *vi* to embrace.
étrenner [etʀene] *vt* to use (*ou* wear) for the first time.
étrennes [etʀɛn] *nfpl* Christmas box *sg*.
étrier [etʀije] *nm* stirrup.
étriller [etʀije] *vt* (*cheval*) to curry; (*fam: battre*) to slaughter (*fig*).
étriqué, e [etʀike] *a* skimpy.
étroit, e [etʀwa, -wat] *a* narrow;

(*vêtement*) tight; (*fig: serré*) close, tight; **à l'~** cramped; **~ d'esprit** narrow-minded.
étude [etyd] *nf* studying; (*ouvrage, rapport*) study; (*de notaire: bureau*) office; (: *charge*) practice; (SCOL: *salle de travail*) study room; **~s** (SCOL) studies; **être à l'~** (*projet etc*) to be under consideration; **faire des ~s** (*de droit/médecine*) to study (law/medicine).
étudiant, e [etydjɑ̃, -ɑ̃t] *nm/f* student.
étudié, e [etydje] *a* (*démarche*) studied; (*système*) carefully designed; (*prix*) keen.
étudier [etydje] *vt, vi* to study.
étui [etɥi] *nm* case.
étuve [etyv] *nf* steamroom.
étuvée [etyve]: **à l'~** *ad* braised.
eu, eue [y] *pp* *de* avoir.
euh [ø] *excl* er.
Europe [øʀɔp] *nf*: **l'~** Europe; **européen, ne** *a, nm/f* European.
eus *etc* *vb voir* avoir.
eux [ø] *pronom* (*sujet*) they; (*objet*) them.
évacuer [evakɥe] *vt* to evacuate.
évader [evade]: **s'~** *vi* to escape.
évangile [evɑ̃ʒil] *nm* gospel.
évanouir [evanwiʀ]: **s'~** *vi* to faint; (*disparaître*) to vanish, disappear.
évanouissement [evanwismɑ̃] *nm* (*syncope*) fainting fit; (*dans un accident*) loss of consciousness.
évaporer [evapɔʀe]: **s'~** *vi* to evaporate.
évaser [evaze] *vt* (*tuyau*) to widen, open out; (*jupe, pantalon*) to flare.
évasif, ive [evazif, -iv] *a* evasive.
évasion [evazjɔ̃] *nf* escape.
évêché [eveʃe] *nm* bishopric; bishop's palace.
éveil [evɛj] *nm* awakening; **être en ~** to be alert.
éveillé, e [eveje] *a* awake; (*vif*) alert, sharp.
éveiller [eveje] *vt* to (a)waken; **s'~** *vi* to (a)waken; (*fig*) to be aroused.
événement [evɛnmɑ̃] *nm* event.

éventail [evãtaj] nm fan; (choix) range.

éventaire [evãtɛʀ] nm stall, stand.

éventer [evãte] vt (secret) to uncover; s'~ vi (parfum) to go stale.

éventrer [evãtʀe] vt to disembowel; (fig) to tear ou rip open.

éventualité [evãtɥalite] nf eventuality; possibility; dans l'~ de in the event of.

éventuel, le [evãtɥɛl] a possible; ~lement ad possibly.

évêque [evɛk] nm bishop.

évertuer [evɛʀtɥe]: s'~ vi: s'~ à faire to try very hard to do.

éviction [eviksjɔ̃] nf ousting; (de locataire) eviction.

évidemment [evidamã] ad obviously.

évidence [evidãs] nf obviousness; obvious fact; de toute ~ quite obviously ou evidently; en ~ conspicuous; mettre en ~ to highlight; to bring to the fore.

évident, e [evidã, -ãt] a obvious, evident.

évider [evide] vt to scoop out.

évier [evje] nm (kitchen) sink.

évincer [evɛ̃se] vt to oust.

éviter [evite] vt to avoid; ~ de faire/ que to not se passe to avoid doing/sth happening; ~ qch à qn to spare sb sth.

évolué, e [evɔlɥe] a advanced.

évoluer [evɔlɥe] vi (enfant, maladie) to develop; (situation, moralement) to evolve, develop; (aller et venir: danseur etc) to move about, circle; **évolution** nf development; evolution; **évolutions** nfpl movements.

évoquer [evɔke] vt to call to mind, evoke; (mentionner) to mention.

ex... [ɛks] préfixe ex-.

exact, e [ɛgzakt] a (précis) exact, accurate, precise; (correct) correct; (ponctuel) punctual; l'heure ~e the right ou exact time; **~ement** ad exactly, accurately, precisely; correctly; (c'est cela même) exactly.

ex aequo [ɛgzeko] a equally placed.

exagéré, e [ɛgzaʒeʀe] a (prix etc) excessive.

exagérer [ɛgzaʒeʀe] vt to exaggerate // vi (abuser) to go too far; to overstep the mark; (déformer les faits) to exaggerate.

exalter [ɛgzalte] vt (enthousiasmer) to excite, elate; (glorifier) to exalt.

examen [ɛgzamɛ̃] nm examination; (SCOL) exam, examination; à l'~ under consideration; (COMM) on approval.

examiner [ɛgzamine] vt to examine.

exaspérant, e [ɛgzaspeʀã, -ãt] a exasperating.

exaspérer [ɛgzaspeʀe] vt to exasperate; to exacerbate.

exaucer [ɛgzose] vt (vœu) to grant.

excédent [ɛksedã] nm surplus; en ~ surplus; ~ de bagages excess luggage.

excéder [ɛksede] vt (dépasser) to exceed; (agacer) to exasperate.

excellence [ɛkselãs] nf (titre) Excellency.

excellent, e [ɛkselã, -ãt] a excellent.

excentrique [ɛksãtʀik] a eccentric; (quartier) outlying.

excepté, e [ɛksɛpte] a, prép: les élèves ~s, ~ les élèves except for the pupils; ~ si except if.

exception [ɛksɛpsjɔ̃] nf exception; à l'~ de except for, with the exception of; d'~ (mesure, loi) special, exceptional; **exceptionnel, le** a exceptional.

excès [ɛksɛ] nm surplus // nmpl excesses; à l'~ to excess; ~ de vitesse speeding q; **excessif, ive** a excessive.

excitant, e [ɛksitã, -ãt] a exciting // nm stimulant.

excitation [ɛksitasjɔ̃] nf (état) excitement.

exciter [ɛksite] vt to excite; (suj: café etc) to stimulate; s'~ vi to get excited.

exclamation [ɛksklamasjɔ̃] nf exclamation.

exclamer [ɛksklame]: s'~ vi to exclaim.

exclure [ɛksklyʀ] vt (faire sortir) to expel; (ne pas compter) to exclude, leave out; (rendre impossible) to exclude, rule out; ce n'est pas exclu it's not impossible, I don't rule that out; **exclusif, ive** a exclusive; **exclusion** nf expulsion; à l'exclusion de with the exclusion ou exception of; **exclusivité** nf (COMM) exclusive rights pl; **film passant en exclusivité** à film showing only at.

excursion [ɛkskyʀsjɔ̃] nf (en autocar) excursion, trip; (à pied) walk, hike.

excuse [ɛkskyz] nf excuse; ~s nfpl apology sg, apologies.

excuser [ɛkskyze] vt to excuse; s'~ (de) to apologize (for); 'excusez-moi' 'I'm sorry'; (pour attirer l'attention) 'excuse me'.

exécrable [ɛgzekʀabl(ə)] a atrocious.

exécrer [ɛgzekʀe] vt to loathe, abhor.

exécuter [ɛgzekyte] vt (prisonnier) to execute; (tâche etc) to execute, carry out; (MUS: jouer) to perform, execute; (INFORM) to run; s'~ vi to comply; **exécutif, ive** a, nm (POL) executive; **exécution** nf execution; carrying out; **mettre à** exécution to carry out.

exemplaire [ɛgzɑ̃plɛʀ] nm copy.

exemple [ɛgzɑ̃pl(ə)] nm example; par ~ for instance, for example; donner l'~ to set an example; prendre ~ sur to take as a model; à l'~ de just like.

exempt, e [ɛgzɑ̃, -ɑ̃t] a: ~ de (sans) free from.

exercer [ɛgzɛʀse] vt (pratiquer) to exercise, practise; (prérogative) to exercise; (influence, contrôle) to exert; (former) to exercise, train; s'~ vi (sportif, musicien) to practise; (se faire sentir: pression etc) to be exerted.

exercice [ɛgzɛʀsis] nm (tâche, travail) exercise; l'~ exercise; (MIL)

drill; **en ~** (juge) in office; (médecin) practising.

exhaustif, ive [ɛgzostif, -iv] a exhaustive.

exhiber [ɛgzibe] vt (montrer: papiers, certificat) to present; produce; (péj) to display, flaunt; s'~ to parade; (suj: exhibitionniste) to expose o.s.

exhorter [ɛgzɔʀte] vt to urge.

exigeant, e [ɛgziʒɑ̃, -ɑ̃t] a demanding; (péj) hard to please.

exigence [ɛgziʒɑ̃s] nf demand, requirement.

exiger [ɛgziʒe] vt to demand, require.

exigu, ë [ɛgzigy] a (lieu) cramped, tiny.

exil [ɛgzil] nm exile; **~er** vt to exile; s'~er vi to go into exile.

existence [ɛgzistɑ̃s] nf existence.

exister [ɛgziste] vi to exist; **il existe un/des** there is a/are (some).

exonérer [ɛgzoneʀe] vt: ~ de to exempt from.

exorbité, e [ɛgzɔʀbite] a: **yeux ~s** bulging eyes.

exotique [ɛgzotik] a exotic.

expatrier [ɛkspatʀije] vt: s'~ to leave one's country.

expectative [ɛkspɛktativ] nf: **être dans l'~** to be still waiting.

expédient [ɛkspedjɑ̃] nm (péj) expedient; **vivre d'~s** to live by one's wits.

expédier [ɛkspedje] vt (lettre, paquet) to send; (troupes) to dispatch; (péj: travail etc) to dispose of, dispatch; **expéditeur, trice** nm/f sender.

expédition [ɛkspedisjɔ̃] nf sending; (scientifique, sportive, MIL) expedition.

expérience [ɛkspeʀjɑ̃s] nf (de la vie) experience; (scientifique) experiment.

expérimenté, e [ɛkspeʀimɑ̃te] a experienced.

expérimenter [ɛkspeʀimɑ̃te] vt to test out, experiment with.

expert, e [ɛkspɛʀ, -ɛʀt(ə)] a, nm expert; ~ **en assurances** insurance valuer; ~**-comptable** nm ≈ chartered accountant (Brit), ≈ certified public accountant (US).

expertise [ɛkspɛʀtiz] nf valuation; assessment; valuer's (ou assessor's) report; (JUR) (forensic) examination.

expertiser [ɛkspɛʀtize] vt (objet de valeur) to value; (voiture accidentée etc) to assess damage to.

expier [ɛkspje] vt to expiate, atone for.

expirer [ɛkspiʀe] vi (prendre fin, mourir) to expire; (respirer) to breathe out.

explicatif, ive [ɛksplikatif, -iv] a explanatory.

explication [ɛksplikɑsjɔ̃] nf explanation; (discussion) discussion; argument; ~ **de texte** (SCOL) critical analysis.

explicite [ɛksplisit] a explicit.

expliquer [ɛksplike] vt to explain; s'~ to explain (o.s.); (discuter) to discuss things; to have it out; **son erreur s'explique** one can understand his mistake.

exploit [ɛksplwa] nm exploit, feat.

exploitation [ɛksplwatɑsjɔ̃] nf exploitation; running; ~ **agricole** farming concern.

exploiter [ɛksplwate] vt (mine) to exploit, work; (entreprise, ferme) to run, operate; (clients, ouvriers, erreur, don) to exploit.

explorer [ɛksplɔʀe] vt to explore.

exploser [ɛksploze] vi to explode, blow up; (engin explosif) to go off; (fig: joie, colère) to burst out, explode; **explosif, ive** a, nm explosive; **explosion** nf explosion.

exportateur, trice [ɛkspɔʀtatœʀ, -tʀis] a export cpd, exporting // nm exporter.

exportation [ɛkspɔʀtɑsjɔ̃] nf exportation; export.

exporter [ɛkspɔʀte] vt to export.

exposant [ɛkspozɑ̃] nm exhibitor.

exposé, e [ɛkspoze] nm talk // a:

au sud facing south; **bien ~** well situated.

exposer [ɛkspoze] vt (marchandise) to display; (peinture) to exhibit, show; (parler de) to explain, set out; (mettre en danger, orienter, PHOTO) to expose; **exposition** nf (manifestation) exhibition; (PHOTO) exposure.

exprès [ɛkspʀɛ] ad (délibérément) on purpose; (spécialement) specially.

exprès, esse [ɛkspʀɛs] a (ordre, défense) express, formal // a inv, ad (PTT) express.

express [ɛkspʀɛs] a, nm: (café) ~ espresso (coffee); (train) ~ fast train.

expressément [ɛkspʀesemɑ̃] ad expressly; specifically.

expression [ɛkspʀesjɔ̃] nf expression.

exprimer [ɛkspʀime] vt (sentiment, idée) to express; (jus, liquide) to press out; s'~ vi (personne) to express o.s.

exproprier [ɛkspʀɔpʀije] vt to buy up by compulsory purchase, expropriate.

expulser [ɛkspylse] vt to expel; (locataire) to evict; (SPORT) to send off.

exquis, e [ɛkski, -iz] a exquisite; delightful.

exsangue [ɛksɑ̃g] a bloodless, drained of blood.

extase [ɛkstɑz] nf ecstasy; s'**extasier sur** to go into raptures over.

extension [ɛkstɑ̃sjɔ̃] nf (d'un muscle, ressort) stretching; (fig) extension; expansion.

exténuer [ɛkstenɥe] vt to exhaust.

extérieur, e [ɛksteʀjœʀ] a (porte, mur etc) outer, outside; (au dehors: escalier, w.-c.) outside; (commerce) foreign; (influences) external; (apparent: calme, gaieté etc) surface cpd (d'une maison, d'un récipient etc) outside, exterior; (apparence) exterior; (d'un groupe social): l'~ the outside world; à l'~ outside; (à l'étranger) abroad; **~ement** ad on the outside; (en apparence) on the surface.

exterminer [ɛkstɛʀmine] vt to exterminate, wipe out.

externat [ɛkstɛʀna] nm day school.

externe [ɛkstɛʀn(ə)] a external, outer // nm/f (MÉD) non-resident medical student (Brit), extern (US); (SCOL) day pupil.

extincteur [ɛkstɛ̃ktœʀ] nm (fire) extinguisher.

extinction [ɛkstɛ̃ksjɔ̃] nf: ~ de voix loss of voice.

extorquer [ɛkstɔʀke] vt to extort.

extorsion nf extortion.

extra [ɛkstʀa] a inv first-rate; top-quality // nm extra help.

extrader [ɛkstʀade] vt to extradite.

extraire [ɛkstʀɛʀ] vt to extract; **extrait** nm extract.

extraordinaire [ɛkstʀaɔʀdinɛʀ] a extraordinary; (POL: mesures etc) special.

extravagant, e [ɛkstʀavagɑ̃, -ɑ̃t] a extravagant; wild.

extraverti, e [ɛkstʀavɛʀti] a extrovert.

extrême [ɛkstʀɛm] a, nm extreme; **~ment** ad extremely; **~-onction** nf last rites pl; **E~-Orient** nm Far East.

extrémité [ɛkstʀemite] nf end; (situation) straits pl, plight; (geste désespéré) extreme action; **~s** nfpl (pieds et mains) extremities; à la dernière ~ on the point of death.

exutoire [ɛgzytwaʀ] nm outlet, release.

F

F abr de **franc**.

fa [fa] nm inv (MUS) F; (en chantant la gamme) fa.

fable [fabl(ə)] nf fable.

fabricant [fabʀikɑ̃] nm manufacturer.

fabrication [fabʀikasjɔ̃] nf manufacture.

fabrique [fabʀik] nf factory.

fabriquer [fabʀike] vt to make; (industriellement) to manufacture; (fig): **qu'est-ce qu'il fabrique?** what is he doing?

fabulation [fabylasjɔ̃] nf fantasizing.

fac [fak] abr f (fam: SCOL) de **faculté**.

façade [fasad] nf front, façade.

face [fas] nf face; (fig: aspect) side // a: **le côté ~** heads; **perdre la ~** to lose face; **en ~ de** prép opposite; (fig) in front of; **de ~** ad from the front; face on; **~ à** prép facing; (fig) faced with, in the face of; **faire ~ à** to face; **~ à ~** ad facing each other // nm inv encounter.

facétieux, euse [fasesjø, -øz] a mischievous.

fâché, e [faʃe] a angry; (désolé) sorry.

fâcher [faʃe] vt to anger; **se ~** vi to get angry; **se ~ avec** (se brouiller) to fall out with.

fâcheux, euse [faʃø, -øz] a unfortunate, regrettable.

facile [fasil] a easy; (accommodant) easy-going; **~ment** ad easily; **facilité** nf easiness; (disposition, don) aptitude; **facilités** nfpl facilities; **facilités de paiement** easy terms; **faciliter** vt to make easier.

façon [fasɔ̃] nf (manière) way; (d'une robe etc) making-up; cut; **~s** nfpl (péj) fuss sg; **de quelle ~?** (in) what way?; **de ~ à/à ce que so as to/that; **de toute ~** anyway, in any case.

façonner [fasɔne] vt (fabriquer) to manufacture; (travailler: matière) to shape, fashion; (fig) to mould, shape.

facteur, trice [faktœʀ, -tʀis] nm/f postman/woman (Brit), mailman/woman (US) // nm (MATH, fig: élément) factor; **~ d'orgues** organ builder; **~ de pianos** piano maker.

factice [faktis] a artificial.

faction [faksjɔ̃] nf faction; (MIL) guard ou sentry (duty); watch.

facture [faktyʀ] nf (à payer: gén)

bill; (: COMM) invoice; (d'un artisan, artiste) technique, workmanship; **facturer** vt to invoice.

facultatif, ive [fakyltatif, -iv] a optional; (arrêt de bus) request cpd.

faculté [fakylte] nf (intellectuelle, d'université) faculty; (pouvoir, possibilité) power.

fade [fad] a insipid.

fagot [fago] nm bundle of sticks.

faible [fɛbl(ə)] a weak; (voix, lumière, vent) faint; (rendement, intensité, revenu etc) low // nm weak point; (pour quelqu'un) weakness, soft spot; ~ d'esprit feeble-minded; **faiblesse** nf weakness; **faiblir** vi to weaken; (lumière) to dim; (vent) to drop.

faïence [fajɑ̃s] nf earthenware q; piece of earthenware.

faignant, e [fɛɲɑ̃, -ɑ̃t] nm/f = **fainéant, e**.

faille [faj] vb voir **falloir** // nf (GÉO) fault; (fig) flaw, weakness.

faillir [fajiʀ] vi: **j'ai failli tomber** I almost /ou nearly fell.

faillite [fajit] nf bankruptcy.

faim [fɛ̃] nf hunger; **avoir** ~ to be hungry; **rester sur sa** ~ (aussi fig) to be left wanting more.

fainéant, e [fɛneɑ̃, -ɑ̃t] nm/f idler, loafer.

MOT-CLÉ

faire [fɛʀ] ◆ vt 1 (fabriquer, être l'auteur de) to make; ~ du vin/une offre/un film to make wine/an offer/a film; ~ du bruit to make a noise

2 (effectuer: travail, opération) to do; **que faites-vous?** (quel métier etc) what do you do?; (quelle activité: au moment de la question) what are you doing?; ~ **la lessive** to do the washing

3 (études) to do; (sport, musique) to play; ~ **du droit/du français** to do law/French; ~ **du rugby/piano** to play rugby/the piano

4 (simuler): ~ **le malade/l'ignorant** to act the invalid/the fool

5 (transformer, avoir un effet sur): ~ **de qn un frustré/avocat** to make sb frustrated/a lawyer; **ça ne me fait rien** (m'est égal) I don't care ou mind; (me laisse froid) it has no effect on me; **ça ne fait rien** it doesn't matter; **que** (impliquer) to mean that

6 (calculs, prix, mesures): **2 et 2 font 4** 2 and 2 are ou make 4; **ça fait 10 m/15 F** it's 10 m/15 F; **je vous le fais 10 F** I'll let you have it for 10 F

7: **qu'a-t-il fait de sa valise?** what has he done with his case?

8: **ne** ~ **que**: il ne fait que critiquer (sans cesse) all he (ever) does is criticize; (seulement) he's only criticizing

9 (dire) to say; **'vraiment?' fit-il** 'really?' he said

10 (maladie) to have; ~ **du diabète** to have diabetes sg

◆ vi 1 (agir, s'y prendre) to act, to do; **il faut** ~ **vite** we (ou you etc) must act quickly; **comment a-t-il fait pour?** how did he manage to?; **faites comme chez vous** make yourself at home

2 (paraître) to look; ~ **vieux/démodé** to look old/old-fashioned; **ça fait bien** it looks good

◆ vb substitut to do; **ne le casse pas comme je l'ai fait** don't break it as I did; **je peux le voir? - faites!** can I see it? - please do!

◆ vb impersonnel 1: **il fait beau** etc the weather is fine etc; voir **jour, froid** etc

2 (temps écoulé, durée): **ça fait deux ans qu'il est parti** it's 2 years since he left; **ça fait 2 ans qu'il est** he's been there for 2 years

◆ vb semi-auxiliaire: ~ + infinitif 1 (action directe) to make; ~ **tomber/bouger qch** to make sth fall/move; ~ **démarrer un moteur/chauffer de l'eau** to start up an engine/heat some water; **cela fait dormir** it makes you sleep; ~ **travailler les** enfants to make the children work *ou* get the children to work

2 (*indirectement, par un intermédiaire*): ~ **réparer qch** to get *ou* have sth repaired; ~ **punir** les enfants to have the children punished

se faire *vi* **1** (*vin, fromage*) to mature

2: cela se fait beaucoup/ne se fait pas it's done a lot/not done

3: se ~ + *nom ou pronom*: se ~ une jupe to make o.s. a skirt; se ~ des amis to make friends; se ~ du souci to worry; il ne s'en fait pas he doesn't worry

4: se ~ + *adjectif* (*devenir*): se ~ vieux to be getting old; (*délibérément*): se ~ beau to do o.s. up

5: se ~ à (*s'habituer*) to get used to; je n'arrive pas à me ~ à la nourriture/au climat I can't get used to the food/climate

6: se ~ + *infinitif*: se ~ examiner la vue/opérer to have one's eyes tested/have an operation; se ~ couper les cheveux to get one's hair cut; il va se ~ tuer/punir he's going to get himself killed/get (himself) punished; il s'est fait aider he got somebody to help him; il s'est fait aider par Simon he got Simon to help him; se ~ faire un vêtement to get a garment made for o.s.

7 (*impersonnel*): comment se fait-il/ faisait-il que? how is it/was it that?

faire-part [fɛʀpaʀ] *nm inv* announcement (*of birth, marriage etc*).

faisable [fəzabl(ə)] *a* feasible.

faisan, e [fəzɑ̃, -an] *nm/f* pheasant.

faisandé, e [fəzɑ̃de] *a* high (*bad*).

faisceau, x [fɛso] *nm* (*de lumière etc*) beam; (*de branches etc*) bundle.

faisons *vb voir* **faire**.

fait [fɛ] *nm* (*événement*) event, occurrence; (*réalité, donnée*) fact; être le ~ de (*causé par*) to be the work of; être au ~ (de) to be informed (of);

au ~ (*à propos*) by the way; en venir au ~ to get to the point; de ~ (*opposé à: de droit*) de facto // ad in fact; du ~ de ceci/qu'il a menti because of *ou* on account of this/his having lied; de ce ~ for this reason; en ~ in fact; en ~ de repas by way of a meal; prendre ~ et cause pour qn to support sb, side with sb; prendre qn sur le ~ to catch sb in the act; ~ divers news item; les ~s et gestes de qn sb's actions *ou* doings.

fait, e [fɛ, fɛt] *a* (*mûr: fromage, melon*) ripe; c'est un ~ that's the end of.

faîte [fɛt] *nm* top; (*fig*) pinnacle, height.

faites *vb voir* **faire**.

fait-tout *nm inv*, **faitout** *nm* [fɛtu] stewpot.

falaise [falɛz] *nf* cliff.

fallacieux, euse [fa(l)lasjø, -øz] *a* fallacious; deceptive; illusory.

falloir [falwaʀ] *vb impersonnel*: il va ~ 100 F we'll (*ou* I'll) need 100 F; il doit ~ du temps that must take time; il me faudrait 100 F I would need 100 F; il vous faut tourner à gauche après l'église you have to turn left past the church; nous avons ce qu'il (nous) faut we have what we need; il faut qu'il parte/a fallu qu'il parte (*obligation*) he has to *ou* must leave/had to leave; il a fallu le faire it had to be done // s'en ~: il s'en est fallu de 100 F/5 minutes we (*ou* they) were 100 F short/5 minutes late (*ou* early); il s'en faut de beaucoup qu'il soit he is far from being; il s'en est fallu de peu que cela n'arrive it very nearly happened; ou peu s'en faut or as good as.

falot [falo, -ɔt] *a* dreary, colourless.

falsifier [falsifje] *vt* to falsify; to doctor.

famé, e [fame] *a*: mal ~ disreputable, of ill repute.

famélique [famelik] *a* half-starved.

fameux, euse [famø, -øz] *a* (*illustre*) famous; (*bon: repas, plat etc*) first-rate, first-class; (*valeur intensive*) real, downright.

familial, e, *aux* [familjal, -o] *a* family *cpd* // *nf* (*AUTO*) estate car (*Brit*), station wagon (*US*).

familiarité [familjarite] *nf* informality; familiarity; **~s** *nfpl* familiarities.

familier, ère [familje, -ɛʀ] *a* (*connu, impertinent*) familiar; (*dénotant une certaine intimité*) informal, friendly; (*LING*) informal, colloquial // *nm* regular (visitor).

famille [famij] *nf* family; **il a de la ~ à Paris** he has relatives in Paris.

famine [famin] *nf* famine.

fanal, aux [fanal, -o] *nm* beacon; lantern.

fanatique [fanatik] *a* fanatical // *nm/f* fanatic; **fanatisme** *nm* fanaticism.

faner [fane]: **se ~** *vi* to fade.

fanfare [fɑ̃faʀ] *nf* (*orchestre*) brass band; (*musique*) fanfare.

fanfaron, ne [fɑ̃faʀɔ̃, -ɔn] *nm/f* braggart.

fange [fɑ̃ʒ] *nf* mire.

fanion [fanjɔ̃] *nm* pennant.

fantaisie [fɑ̃tezi] *nf* (*spontanéité*) fancy, imagination; (*caprice*) whim; extravagance // *a*: **bijou/pain (de) ~** costume jewellery/fancy bread; **fantaisiste** *a* (*péj*) unorthodox, eccentric // *nm/f* (*de music-hall*) variety artist *ou* entertainer.

fantasme [fɑ̃tasm(ə)] *nm* fantasy.

fantasque [fɑ̃task(ə)] *a* a whimsical, capricious; fantastic.

fantastique [fɑ̃tastik] *a* fantastic.

fantôme [fɑ̃tom] *nm* ghost, phantom.

faon [fɑ̃] *nm* fawn.

farce [faʀs(ə)] *nf* (*viande*) stuffing; (*blague*) (practical) joke; (*THÉÂTRE*) farce; **farcir** *vt* (*viande*) to stuff.

fard [faʀ] *nm* make-up.

fardeau, x [faʀdo] *nm* burden.

farder [faʀde] *vt* to make up.

farfelu, e [faʀfəly] *a* hare-brained.

farine [faʀin] *nf* flour; **farineux, euse** (*sauce, pomme*) floury // *nmpl* (*aliments*) starchy foods.

farouche [faʀuʃ] *a* shy, timid; savage, wild; fierce.

fart [faʀ(t)] *nm* (ski) wax.

fascicule [fasikyl] *nm* volume.

fasciner [fasine] *vt* to fascinate.

fascisme [faʃism(ə)] *nm* fascism.

fasse *etc vb voir* **faire**.

faste [fast(ə)] *nm* splendour // *a*: **c'est un jour ~** it's his (*ou* our) lucky day.

fastidieux, euse [fastidjø, -øz] *a* tedious, tiresome.

fastueux, euse [fastɥø, -øz] *a* sumptuous, luxurious.

fat [fa] *am* conceited, smug.

fatal, e [fatal] *a* fatal; (*inévitable*) inevitable; **~ité** *nf* fate; fateful coincidence; inevitability.

fatidique [fatidik] *a* fateful.

fatigant, e [fatigɑ̃, -ɑ̃t] *a* tiring; (*agaçant*) tiresome.

fatigue [fatig] *nf* tiredness, fatigue.

fatigué, e [fatige] *a* tired.

fatiguer [fatige] *vt* to tire, make tired; (*TECH*) to put a strain on, strain; (*fig: importuner*) to wear out // *vi* (*moteur*) to labour, strain; **se ~** to get tired; to tire o.s. (out).

fatras [fatʀa] *nm* jumble, hotchpotch.

fatuité [fatɥite] *nf* conceitedness, smugness.

faubourg [fobuʀ] *nm* suburb.

fauché, e [foʃe] *a* (*fam*) broke.

faucher [foʃe] *vt* (*herbe*) to cut; (*champs, blés*) to reap; (*fig*) to cut down; to mow down.

faucille [fosij] *nf* sickle.

faucon [fokɔ̃] *nm* falcon, hawk.

faudra *vb voir* **falloir**.

faufiler [fofile] *vt* to tack, baste; **se ~** *vi*: **se ~ dans** to edge one's way into; **se ~ parmi/entre** to thread one's way among/between.

faune [fon] *nf* (*ZOOL*) wildlife, fauna.

faussaire [fosɛʀ] *nm* forger.

fausse [fos] a voir **faux**.

faussement [fosmɑ̃] ad (accuser) wrongly, wrongfully; (croire) falsely.

fausser [fose] vt (objet) to bend, buckle; (fig) to distort.

fausseté [foste] nf wrongness; falseness.

faut vb voir **falloir**.

faute [fot] nf (erreur) mistake, error; (péché, manquement) misdemeanour; (FOOTBALL etc) offence; (TENNIS) fault; c'est de sa/ma ~ it's his/my fault; être en ~ to be in the wrong; ~ de (temps, argent) for ou through lack of; sans ~ ad without fail; ~ de frappe typing error; ~ professionnelle professional misconduct q.

fauteuil [fotœj] nm armchair; ~ d'orchestre seat in the front stalls; ~ roulant wheelchair.

fauteur [fotœʀ] nm: ~ de troubles trouble-maker.

fautif, ive [fotif, -iv] a (incorrect) incorrect, inaccurate; (responsable) at fault, in the wrong; guilty.

fauve [fov] nm wildcat // a (couleur) fawn.

faux [fo] nf scythe.

faux, fausse [fo, fos] a (inexact) wrong; (piano, voix) out of tune; (falsifié) fake; forged; (sournois, postiche) false // ad (MUS) out of tune // nm (copie) fake, forgery; (opposé au vrai): le ~ falsehood; faire ~ bond à qn to stand sb up; ~ frais nmpl extras, incidental expenses; ~ pas tripping q; (fig) faux pas; ~ témoignage (délit) perjury; fausse alerte false alarm; fausse couche miscarriage; ~-filet nm sirloin; ~-fuyant nm equivocation; ~-monnayeur nm counterfeiter, forger.

faveur [favœʀ] nf favour; traitement de ~ preferential treatment; à la ~ de under cover of; thanks to; en ~ de in favour of.

favorable [favoʀabl(ə)] a favourable.

favori, te [favoʀi, -it] a, nm/f favour-

ite; ~s nmpl (barbe) sideboards (Brit), sideburns.

favoriser [favoʀize] vt to favour.

fébrile [febʀil] a feverish, febrile.

fécond, e [fekɔ̃, -ɔd] a fertile; **féconder** vt to fertilize; **fécondité** nf fertility.

fécule [fekyl] nf potato flour.

fédéral, e, aux [federal, -o] a federal.

fée [fe] nf fairy; ~rie nf enchantment; ~rique a magical, fairytale cpd.

feignant, e [fɛɲɑ̃, -ɑ̃t] nm/f = **fainéant, e**.

feindre [fɛ̃dʀ(ə)] vt to feign // vi to dissemble; ~ de faire to pretend to do.

feinte [fɛ̃t] nf (SPORT) dummy.

fêler [fele] vt to crack.

félicitations [felisitɑsjɔ̃] nfpl congratulations.

féliciter [felisite] vt: ~ qn (de) to congratulate sb (on); se ~ (de) to congratulate o.s. (on).

félin, e [felɛ̃, -in] a feline // nm (big) cat.

fêlure [felyʀ] nf crack.

femelle [fəmɛl] a, nf female.

féminin, e [feminɛ̃, -in] a feminine; (sexe) female; (équipe, vêtements etc) women's // nm feminine; **féministe** a feminist.

femme [fam] nf woman; (épouse) wife (pl wives); ~ de chambre, ~ de ménage cleaning lady.

fémur [femyʀ] nm femur, thighbone.

fendre [fɑ̃dʀ(ə)] vt (couper en deux) to split; (fissurer) to crack; (fig: traverser) to cut through; to cleave through; se ~ vi to crack.

fenêtre [f(ə)nɛtʀ(ə)] nf window.

fenouil [fənuj] nm fennel.

fente [fɑ̃t] nf (fissure) crack; (de boîte à lettres etc) slit.

féodal, e, aux [feodal, -o] a feudal.

fer [fɛʀ] nm iron; (de cheval) shoe; ~ à cheval horseshoe; ~ forgé wrought iron; ~ (à repasser) iron.

ferai etc vb voir **faire**.

fer-blanc [fɛʀblɑ̃] nm tin(plate).

férié, e [feʀje] a: **jour ~** public holiday.

ferions etc vb voir **faire**.

férir [feʀiʀ]: **sans coup ~** ad without meeting any opposition.

ferme [fɛʀm(ə)] a firm // ad (travailler etc) hard // nf (exploitation) farm; (maison) farmhouse.

fermé, e [fɛʀme] a closed, shut; (gaz, eau etc) off; (fig: personne) uncommunicative; (: milieu) exclusive.

fermenter [fɛʀmɑ̃te] vi to ferment.

fermer [fɛʀme] vt to close, shut; (cesser l'exploitation de) to close down, shut down; (eau, lumière, électricité, robinet) to put off, turn off; (aéroport, route) to close // vi to close, shut; to close down, shut down; **se ~** vi (yeux) to close, shut; (fleur, blessure) to close up.

fermeté [fɛʀməte] nf firmness.

fermeture [fɛʀmətyʀ] nf closing; shutting; closing ou shutting down; putting ou turning off; (dispositif) catch; fastening, fastener; **~ éclair** ® ou **à glissière** zip (fastener) (Brit), zipper (US).

fermier, ière [fɛʀmje, -jɛʀ] nm farmer // nf woman farmer; farmer's wife.

fermoir [fɛʀmwaʀ] nm clasp.

féroce [feʀɔs] a ferocious, fierce.

ferons vb voir **faire**.

ferraille [feʀaj] nf scrap iron; **mettre à la ~** to scrap.

ferré, e [feʀe] a hobnailed; steel-tipped; (fam): **~ en** well up on, hot at.

ferrer [feʀe] vt (cheval) to shoe.

ferronnerie [feʀɔnʀi] nf ironwork.

ferroviaire [feʀɔvjɛʀ] a rail(way) cpd (Brit), rail(road) cpd (US).

ferry-(boat) [feʀe(bot)] nm ferry.

fertile [fɛʀtil] a fertile; **~ en incidents** eventful, packed with incidents.

féru, e [feʀy] a: **~ de** with a keen interest in.

férule [feʀyl] nf: **être sous la ~ de**

qn to be under sb's (iron) rule.

fervent, e [fɛʀvɑ̃, -ɑ̃t] a fervent.

fesse [fɛs] nf buttock; **fessée** nf spanking.

festin [fɛstɛ̃] nm feast.

festival [fɛstival] nm festival.

festoyer [fɛstwaje] vi to feast.

fêtard [fɛtaʀ] nm (péj) high liver, merry-maker.

fête [fɛt] nf (religieuse) feast; (publique) holiday; (en famille etc) celebration; (kermesse) fête, fair, festival; (du nom) feast day, name day; **faire la ~** to live it up; **faire ~ à** qn to give sb a warm welcome; **les ~s (de fin d'année)** the festive season; **la salle/le comité des ~s** the village hall/festival committee; **~ foraine** (fun) fair; **la F~ Nationale** the national holiday; **fêter** vt to celebrate; (personne) to have a celebration for.

fétu [fety] nm: **~ de paille** wisp of straw.

feu [fø] a inv: **~ son père** his late father.

feu, x [fø] nm (gén) fire; (signal lumineux) light; (de cuisinière) ring; (sensation de brûlure) burning (sensation); **~x** nmpl (éclat, lumière) fire sg; (AUTO) (traffic) lights; **au ~!** (incendie) fire!; **à ~ doux/vif** over a slow/brisk heat; **à petit ~** (CULIN) over a gentle heat; (fig) slowly; **faire ~** to fire; **prendre ~** to catch fire; **mettre le ~ à** to set fire to; **faire du ~** to make a fire; **avez-vous du ~?** (pour cigarette) have you got a light?; **~ rouge/vert/orange** red/green/amber (Brit) ou yellow (US) light; **~ arrière** rear light; **~ d'artifice** firework; (spectacle) fireworks pl; **~ de joie** bonfire; **~x de brouillard** fog-lamps; **~x de croisement** dipped (Brit) ou dimmed (US) headlights; **~x de position** sidelights; **~x de route** headlights.

feuillage [fœjaʒ] nm foliage, leaves pl.

feuille [fœj] *nf* (*d'arbre*) leaf (*pl* leaves); (*de papier*) sheet; ~ d'impôts tax form; ~ de maladie *medical expenses claim form*; ~ de paie pay slip; ~ de vigne (*BOT*) vine leaf; (*sur statue*) fig leaf; ~ volante loose sheet.

feuillet [fœjɛ] *nm* leaf (*pl* leaves).

feuilleté, e [fœjte] *a* (*CULIN*) flaky; (*verre*) laminated.

feuilleter [fœjte] *vt* (*livre*) to leaf through.

feuilleton [fœjtɔ̃] *nm* serial.

feuillu, e [fœjy] *a* leafy // *nm* broadleaved tree.

feutre [føtr(ə)] *nm* felt; (*chapeau*) felt hat; (*aussi*: stylo-~) felt-tip pen.

feutré, e *a* feltlike; (*pas, voix*) muffled.

fève [fɛv] *nf* broad bean.

février [fevrije] *nm* February.

fi [fi] *excl*: faire ~ de to snap one's fingers at.

fiable [fjabl(ə)] *a* reliable.

fiacre [fjakr(ə)] *nm* (hackney) cab *ou* carriage.

fiançailles [fjɑ̃saj] *nfpl* engagement *sg*.

fiancé, e [fjɑ̃se] *nm/f* fiancé/fiancée // *a*: être ~ (à) to be engaged (to).

fiancer [fjɑ̃se]: se ~ *vi* to become engaged.

fibre [fibr(ə)] *nf* fibre; ~ de verre fibreglass, glass fibre.

ficeler [fisle] *vt* to tie up.

ficelle [fisɛl] *nf* string *q*; piece *ou* length of string.

fiche [fiʃ] *nf* (*pour fichier*) (index) card; (*formulaire*) form; (*ÉLEC*) plug.

ficher [fiʃe] *vt* (*dans un fichier*) to file; (*POLICE*) to put on file; (*planter*) to stick, drive; (*fam*) to do; to give; to stick *ou* shove; **fiche(-moi) le camp** (*fam*) clear off; **fiche-moi la paix** (*fam*) leave me alone; **se ~ de** (*fam*) to make fun of; not to care about.

fichier [fiʃje] *nm* file; card index.

fichu, e [fiʃy] *pp de* **ficher** (*fam*)

a (*fam*: *fini, inutilisable*) bust, done for; (: *intensif*) wretched, darned // *nm* (*foulard*) (head)scarf (*pl* scarves); **mal ~** (*fam*) feeling lousy; useless.

fictif, ive [fiktif, -iv] *a* fictitious.

fiction [fiksjɔ̃] *nf* fiction; (*fait imaginé*) invention.

fidèle [fidɛl] *a* faithful // *nm/f* (*REL*): **les ~s** the faithful; (*à l'église*) the congregation.

fief [fjɛf] *nm* fief; (*fig*) preserve; stronghold.

fier [fje]: **se ~ à** *vt* to trust.

fier, fière [fjɛr] *a* proud; ~**té** *nf* pride.

fièvre [fjɛvr(ə)] *nf* fever; **avoir de la ~/39 de ~** to have a high temperature/a temperature of 39°C; **fiévreux, euse** *a* feverish.

fifre [fifr(ə)] *nm* fife; fife-player.

figer [fiʒe] *vt* to congeal; (*fig: personne*) to freeze, root to the spot; **se ~** *vi* to congeal; to freeze; (*institutions etc*) to become set, stop evolving.

figue [fig] *nf* fig; **figuier** *nm* fig tree.

figurant, e [figyrɑ̃, -ɑ̃t] *nm/f* (*THÉÂTRE*) walk-on; (*CINÉMA*) extra.

figure [figyr] *nf* (*visage*) face; (*image, tracé, forme, personnage*) figure; (*illustration*) picture, diagram; **faire ~ de** to look like.

figuré, e [figyre] *a* (*sens*) figurative.

figurer [figyre] *vi* to appear // *vt* to represent; **se ~ que** to imagine that.

fil [fil] *nm* (*brin, fig: d'une histoire*) thread; (*du téléphone*) cable, wire; (*textile ou fibre*) linen; (*d'un couteau*) edge; **au ~ des années** with the passing of the years; **au ~ de l'eau** with the stream *ou* current; **coup de ~** phone call; ~ **à coudre** (sewing) thread; ~ **électrique** electric wire; ~ **de fer** wire; ~ **de fer barbelé** barbed wire; ~ **à pêche** fishing line; ~ **à plomb** plumbline.

filament [filamɑ̃] *nm* (*ÉLEC*) filament; (*de liquide*) trickle, thread.

filandreux, euse [filɑ̃drø, -øz] *a* stringy.

filasse [filas] *a inv* white blond.

filature [filatyʀ] *nf* (*fabrique*) mill; (*policière*) shadowing *q*, tailing *q*.

file [fil] *nf* line; (*AUTO*) lane; ~ **(d'attente)** queue (*BRIT*), line (*US*); **en ~** indienne in single file; **à la ~** *ad* (*d'affilée*) in succession.

filer [file] *vt* (*tissu, toile*) to spin; (*prendre en filature*) to shadow, tail; (*fam: donner*): ~ **qch à qn** to slip sb sth // *vi* (*bas, liquide, pâte*) to run; (*aller vite*) to fly past; (*fam: partir*) to make off; ~ **doux** to toe the line.

filet [file] *nm* net; (*CULIN*) fillet; (*d'eau, de sang*) trickle; ~ **(à provisions)** string bag.

filiale [filjal] *nf* (*COMM*) subsidiary.

filière [filjɛʀ] *nf:* passer par la ~ to go through the (administrative) channels; **suivre la ~** (*dans sa carrière*) to work one's way up (through the hierarchy).

filiforme [filifɔʀm(ə)] *a* spindly; threadlike.

filigrane [filigʀan] *nm* (*d'un billet, timbre*) watermark; **en ~** (*fig*) showing just beneath the surface.

fille [fij] *nf* girl; (*opposé à fils*) daughter; **vieille ~** old maid; ~-**mère** *nf* (*péj*) unmarried mother; **fillette** *nf* (little) girl.

filleul, e [fijœl] *nm/f* godchild, godson/daughter.

film [film] *nm* (*pour photo*) (roll of) film; (*œuvre*) film, picture, movie; (*couche*) film; ~ **muet/parlant** silent/talking picture ou movie; ~ **d'animation** animated film; ~ **policier** thriller.

filon [filɔ̃] *nm* vein, lode; (*fig*) lucrative line, money spinner.

fils [fis] *nm* son; ~ **de famille** moneyed young man; ~ **à papa** daddy's boy.

filtre [filtʀ(ə)] *nm* filter; ~ **à air** (*AUTO*) air filter; **filtrer** *vt* to filter; (*fig: candidats, visiteurs*) to screen //

vi to filter (through).

fin [fɛ̃] *nf* end; ~**s** *nfpl* (*but*) ends; **prendre ~** to come to an end; **mettre ~ à** to put an end to; **à la ~** *ad* in the end, eventually; **sans ~** *a* endless // *ad* endlessly.

fin, e [fɛ̃, fin] *a* (*papier, couche, fil*) thin; (*cheveux, poudre, pointe, visage*) fine; (*taille*) neat, slim; (*esprit, remarque*) subtle; shrewd // *ad* (*moudre, couper*) finely // *nf* (*alcool*) liqueur brandy; ~ **prêt** quite ready; **un ~ tireur** a crack shot; **avoir la vue/l'ouïe ~e** to have sharp ou keen eyes/ears; **vin ~** fine wine; ~ **gourmet** gourmet; **une ~e mouche** (*fig*) a sharp customer; ~**es herbes** mixed herbs.

final, e [final] *a*, *nf* final // *nm* (*MUS*) finale; **quarts de ~e** quarter finals; **8èmes/16èmes de ~e** 2nd/1st round (*in 5 round knock-out competition*); ~**ement** *ad* finally, in the end; (*après tout*) after all.

finance [finɑ̃s] *nf* finance; ~**s** *nfpl* (*situation*) finances; (*activités*) finance *sg*; **moyennant ~** for a fee; **financer** *vt* to finance; **financier, ière** *a* financial.

finaud, e [fino, -od] *a* wily.

finesse [fines] *nf* thinness; fineness; neatness, slimness; subtlety; shrewdness.

fini, e [fini] *a* finished; (*MATH*) finite; (*intensif*): **un menteur** ~ a liar through and through // *nm* (*d'un objet manufacturé*) finish.

finir [finiʀ] *vt* to finish // *vi* to finish, end; ~ **quelque part/par faire** to end ou finish up somewhere/doing; ~ **de faire** to finish doing; (*cesser*) to stop doing; **il finit par m'agacer** he's beginning to get on my nerves; ~ **en pointe/tragédie** to end in a point/in tragedy; **en ~ avec** to be ou have done with; **il va mal ~** he will come to a bad end.

finish [finiʃ] *nm* finishing; finish.

finlandais, e [fɛ̃lɑ̃dɛ, -ɛz] *a* Finnish // *nm/f*: **F~, e** Finn.

Finlande [fɛlɑ̃d] nf: la ~ Finland.
fiole [fjɔl] nf phial.
fioriture [fjɔrityr] nf embellishment, flourish.
firme [firm(ə)] nf firm.
fis vb voir **faire**.
fisc [fisk] nm tax authorities pl; ~al, e, aux a tax cpd, fiscal: ~alité f tax system; (charges) taxation.
fissure [fisyr] nf crack.
fissurer [fisyre] vt, se ~ vi to crack.
fiston [fistɔ̃] nm (fam) son, lad.
fit vb voir **faire**.
fixation [fiksasjɔ̃] nf fixing; fastening; setting; (de ski) binding; (PSYCH) fixation.
fixe [fiks(ə)] a fixed; (emploi) steady, regular // nm (salaire) basic salary; à heure ~ at a set time; menu à prix ~ set menu.
fixé, e [fikse] a: être ~ (sur) (savoir à quoi s'en tenir) to have made up one's mind (about); to know for certain (about).
fixer [fikse] vt (attacher): ~ qch (à/ sur) to fix ou fasten sth (to/onto); (déterminer) to fix, set; (CHIMIE, PHOTO) to fix; (regarder) to stare at; se ~ (s'établir) to settle down; se ~ sur (suj: attention) to focus on.
flacon [flakɔ̃] nm bottle.
flageller [flaʒele] vt to flog, scourge.
flageoler [flaʒɔle] vi (jambes) to sag.
flageolet [flaʒɔlɛ] nm (MUS) flageolet; (CULIN) dwarf kidney bean.
flagrant, e [flagrɑ̃, -ɑ̃t] a flagrant, blatant; en ~ délit in the act.
flair [flɛr] nm sense of smell; (fig) intuition; **flairer** vt (humer) to sniff (at); (détecter) to scent.
flamand, e [flamɑ̃, -ɑ̃d] a, nm (LING) Flemish // nm/f F~, e Fleming; les F~s the Flemish.
flamant [flamɑ̃] nm flamingo.
flambant [flɑ̃bɑ̃] ad: ~ neuf brand new.
flambé, e [flɑ̃be] a (CULIN) flambé // nf blaze; (fig) flaring-up, explosion.
flambeau, x [flɑ̃bo] nm (flaming)

torch.
flamber [flɑ̃be] vi to blaze (up).
flamboyer [flɑ̃bwaje] vi to blaze (up); to flame.
flamme [flam] nf flame; (fig) fire, fervour; en ~s on fire, ablaze.
flan [flɑ̃] nm (CULIN) custard tart ou pie.
flanc [flɑ̃] nm side; (MIL) flank; prêter le ~ à (fig) to lay o.s. open to.
flancher [flɑ̃ʃe] vi to fail, pack up; to quit.
flanelle [flanɛl] nf flannel.
flâner [flɑne] vi to stroll; **flânerie** nf stroll.
flanquer [flɑ̃ke] vt to flank; (fam: mettre) to chuck, shove; (: jeter): ~ par terre/à la porte to fling to the ground/chuck out.
flaque [flak] nf (d'eau) puddle; (d'huile, de sang etc) pool.
flash, pl flashes [flaʃ] nm (PHOTO) flash; ~ (d'information) newsflash.
flasque [flask(ə)] a flabby.
flatter [flate] vt to flatter; se ~ de qch to pride o.s. on sth; **flatterie** nf flattery q; **flatteur, euse** a flattering // nm/f flatterer.
fléau, x [fleo] nm scourge.
flèche [flɛʃ] nf arrow; (de clocher) spire; (de grue) jib; monter en ~ (fig) to soar, rocket; partir en ~ to be off like a shot; **fléchette** nf dart; **fléchettes** nfpl (jeu) darts sg.
fléchir [fleʃir] vt (corps, genou) to bend; (fig) to sway, weaken // vi (poutre) to sag, bend; (fig) to weaken, flag; to yield.
flemmard, e [flemar, -ard(ə)] nm/f lazybones sg, loafer.
flétrir [fletrir] vt, se ~ vi to wither.
fleur [flœr] nf flower; (d'un arbre) blossom; en ~ (arbre) in blossom; à ~ de terre just above the ground.
fleurer [flœre] vt: ~ la lavande to have the scent of lavender.
fleuri, e [flœri] a in flower ou bloom; surrounded by flowers; (fig) flowery; florid.

fleurir [flœʀiʀ] vi (rose) to flower; (arbre) to blossom; (fig) to flourish // vt (tombe) to put flowers on; (chambre) to decorate with flowers.

fleuriste [flœʀist(ə)] nm/f florist.

fleuron [flœʀɔ̃] nm jewel (fig).

fleuve [flœv] nm river.

flexible [flɛksibl(ə)] a flexible.

flexion [flɛksjɔ̃] nf flexing, bending.

flic [flik] nm (fam: péj) cop.

flipper [flipœʀ] nm pinball (machine).

flirter [flœʀte] vi to flirt.

flocon [flɔkɔ̃] nm flake.

floraison [flɔʀɛzɔ̃] nf flowering; blossoming; flourishing.

flore [flɔʀ] nf flora.

florissant, e [flɔʀisɑ̃, -ɑ̃t] vb voir **fleurir**.

flot [flo] nm flood, stream; ~s nmpl (de la mer) waves; être à ~ (NAVIG) to be afloat; (fig) to be on an even keel; entrer à ~s to stream ou pour in.

flotte [flɔt] nf (NAVIG) fleet; (fam) water; rain.

flottement [flɔtmɑ̃] nm (fig) wavering, hesitation.

flotter [flɔte] vi to float; (nuage, odeur) to drift; (drapeau) to fly; (vêtements) to hang loose; (monnaie) to float // vt to float; faire ~ to float; **flotteur** nm float.

flou, e [flu] a fuzzy, blurred; (fig) woolly, vague.

flouer [flue] vt to swindle.

fluctuation [flyktɥasjɔ̃] nf fluctuation.

fluet, te [flyɛ, -ɛt] a thin, slight.

fluide [flɥid] a (liquid) fluid; (circulation etc) flowing freely // nm fluid; (force) (mysterious) power.

fluor [flyɔʀ] nm fluorine.

fluorescent, e [flyɔʀesɑ̃, -ɑ̃t] a fluorescent.

flûte [flyt] nf flute; (verre) flute glass; (pain) long loaf (pl loaves); ~! drat it!; ~ à bec recorder.

flux [fly] nm incoming tide; (écoulement) flow; le ~ et le reflux the ebb and flow.

FM sigle f (= fréquence modulée) FM.

foc [fɔk] nm jib.

foi [fwa] nf faith; sous la ~ du serment under ou on oath; ajouter ~ à to lend credence to; digne de ~ reliable; sur la ~ de on the word ou strength of; être de bonne/mauvaise ~ to be sincere/insincere; ma ~... well...

foie [fwa] nm liver.

foin [fwɛ̃] nm hay; faire du ~ (fig: fam) to kick up a row.

foire [fwaʀ] nf fair; (fête foraine) (fun) fair; faire la ~ (fig: fam) to whoop it up; ~ (exposition) trade fair.

fois [fwa] nf time; une/deux ~ once/twice; 2 ~ 2 2 times 2; quatre ~ plus grand (que) four times as big (as); une ~ (passé) once; (futur) sometime; une ~ pour toutes once and for all; une ~ que once; des ~ (parfois) sometimes; à la ~ (ensemble) at once.

foison [fwazɔ̃] nf: une ~ de an abundance of; à ~ ad in plenty.

foisonner [fwazɔne] vi to abound.

fol [fɔl] a voir **fou**.

folâtrer [fɔlɑtʀe] vi to frolic (about).

folie [fɔli] nf (d'une décision, d'un acte) madness, folly; (état) madness, insanity; (acte) folly; la ~ des grandeurs delusions of grandeur; faire des ~s (en dépenses) to be extravagant.

folklorique [fɔlklɔʀik] a folk cpd; (fam) weird.

folle [fɔl] a, nf voir **fou**; ~ment ad (très) madly, wildly.

foncé, e [fɔ̃se] a dark.

foncer [fɔ̃se] vi to go darker; (fam: aller vite) to tear ou belt along; ~ sur to charge at.

foncier, ère [fɔ̃sje, -ɛʀ] a (honnêteté etc) basic, fundamental; (malhonnêteté) deep-rooted; (COMM) real estate cpd.

fonction [fɔ̃ksjɔ̃] nf (rôle, MATH,

LING) function; (_emploi, poste_) post, position; ~s (_professionnelles_) duties; **entrer** en ~s to take up one's post _ou_ duties; to take up office; **voiture de** ~ company car; **être** ~ **de** (_dépendre de_) to depend on; **en** ~ **de** (_par rapport à_) according to; **faire** ~ **de** to serve as; **la** ~ **publique** the state _ou_ civil (_Brit_) service.

fonctionnaire [fɔksjɔnɛʀ] _nm/f_ state employee, local authority employee; (_dans l'administration_) ≈ civil servant.

fonctionner [fɔksjɔne] _vi_ to work, function; (_entreprise_) to operate, function.

fond [fɔ̃] _nm voir aussi_ **fonds**; (_d'un récipient, trou_) bottom; (_d'une salle, scène_) back; (_d'un tableau, décor_) background; (_opposé à la forme_) content; (_SPORT_) **le** ~ long distance (running); **sans** ~ bottomless; **au** ~ **de** at the bottom of; at the back of; **à** ~ _ad_ (_connaître, soutenir_) thoroughly; (_appuyer, visser_) right down _ou_ home; **à** ~ (**de train**) _ad_ (_fam_) full tilt; **dans le** ~, **au** ~ _ad_ (_en somme_) basically, really; **de** ~ **en comble** _ad_ from top to bottom; ~ **sonore** background noise; ~ **de teint** (make-up) foundation.

fondamental, e, aux [fɔdamɑ̃tal, -o] _a_ fundamental.

fondant, e [fɔdɑ̃, -ɑ̃t] _a_ (_neige_) melting; (_poire_) that melts in the mouth.

fondateur, trice [fɔdatœʀ, -tʀis] _nm/f_ founder.

fondation [fɔdasjɔ̃] _nf_ founding; (_établissement_) foundation; ~s _nfpl_ (_d'une maison_) foundations.

fondé, e [fɔde] _a_ (_accusation etc_) well-founded; **être** ~ **à** to have grounds for _ou_ good reason to // _nm_: ~ **de pouvoir** authorized representative.

fondement [fɔdmɑ̃] _nm_ (_derrière_) behind; ~s _nmpl_ foundations; **sans**

~ _a_ (_rumeur etc_) groundless, unfounded.

fonder [fɔde] _vt_ to found; (_fig_) to base; **se** ~ **sur** (_suj: personne_) to base o.s. on.

fonderie [fɔdʀi] _nf_ smelting works _sg_.

fondre [fɔdʀ(ə)] _vt_ (_aussi_: **faire** ~) to melt; (_dans l'eau_) to dissolve; (_fig: mélanger_) to merge, blend // _vi_ to melt; to dissolve; (_fig_) to melt away; (_se précipiter_): ~ **sur** to swoop down on; ~ **en larmes** to burst into tears.

fonds [fɔ̃] _nm_ (_de bibliothèque_) collection; (_COMM_): ~ (**de commerce**) business // _nmpl_ (_argent_) funds; **à** ~ **perdus** _ad_ with little or no hope of getting the money back.

fondu, e [fɔdy] _a_ (_beurre, neige_) melted; (_métal_) molten // _nf_ (_CULIN_) fondue.

font _vb voir_ **faire**.

fontaine [fɔtɛn] _nf_ fountain; (_source_) spring.

fonte [fɔ̃t] _nf_ melting; (_métal_) cast iron; **la** ~ **des neiges** (the spring) thaw.

fonts baptismaux [fɔ̃batismo] _nmpl_ (baptismal) font _sg_.

foot [fut] _nm_ (_fam_) football.

football [futbol] _nm_ football, soccer; ~**eur** _nm_ footballer.

footing [futiŋ] _nm_ jogging; **faire du** ~ to go jogging.

for [fɔʀ] _nm_: **dans son** ~ **intérieur** in one's heart of hearts.

forain, e [fɔʀɛ̃, -ɛn] _a_ fairground _cpd_ // _nm_ stallholder; fairground entertainer.

forçat [fɔʀsa] _nm_ convict.

force [fɔʀs(ə)] _nf_ strength; (_puissance: surnaturelle etc_) power; (_PHYSIQUE, MÉCANIQUE_) force; ~s _nfpl_ (_physiques_) strength _sg_; (_MIL_) forces; **à** ~ **d'insister** by dint of insisting; **as he** (_ou_ I _etc_) kept on insisting; **de** ~ _ad_ forcibly, by force; **être de** ~ **à faire** to be up to doing; **de première ~** first class; **~ d'âme** fortitude; **les ~s de l'ordre** the police.

forcé, e [fɔrse] a forced; (unintended) inevitable.

forcément [fɔrsemã] ad necessarily; inevitably; (bien sûr) of course.

forcené, e [fɔrsəne] nm/f maniac.

forcer [fɔrse] vt (porte, serrure, plante) to force; (moteur, voix) to strain // vi (SPORT) to overtax o.s.; **~ la dose/l'allure** to overdo it/ increase the pace; **se ~ (pour faire)** to force o.s. (to do).

forcir [fɔrsir] vi (grossir) to broaden out; (vent) to increase.

forer [fɔre] vt to drill, bore.

forestier, ère [fɔrɛstje, -ɛr] a forest cpd.

forêt [fɔrɛ] nf forest.

foreuse [fɔrøz] nf (electric) drill.

forfait [fɔrfɛ] nm (COMM) fixed ou set price; all-in deal ou price; (crime) infamy; **déclarer ~** to withdraw; **travailler à ~** to work for a lump sum; **forfaitaire** a inclusive; set.

forfanterie [fɔrfãtri] nf boastfulness q.

forge [fɔrʒ(ə)] nf forge, smithy.

forger [fɔrʒe] vt to forge; (fig: personnalité) to form; (: prétexte) to contrive, make up.

forgeron [fɔrʒərɔ̃] nm (black)smith.

formaliser [fɔrmalize]: **se ~** vi: **se ~ (de)** to take offence (at).

format [fɔrma] nm size.

formater [fɔrmate] vt (disque) to format.

formation [fɔrmasjɔ̃] nf forming; training; (MUS) group; (MIL, AVIAT, GÉO) formation; **~ permanente** ou **continue** continuing education; **~ professionnelle** vocational training.

forme [fɔrm(ə)] nf (gén) form; (d'un objet) shape, form; **~s** nfpl (contours) manières) proprieties; (d'une femme) figure sg; **en ~ de poire** pear-shaped; **être en ~** (SPORT etc) to be on form; **en bonne et due**

in due form.

formel, le [fɔrmɛl] a (preuve, décision) definite, positive; (logique) formal; **~lement** ad (absolument) positively.

former [fɔrme] vt to form; (éduquer) to train; **se ~** vi to form.

formidable [fɔrmidabl(ə)] a tremendous.

formulaire [fɔrmylɛr] nm form.

formule [fɔrmyl] nf (gén) formula; (formulaire) form; **~ de politesse** polite phrase; letter ending.

formuler [fɔrmyle] vt (émettre: réponse, vœux) to formulate; (expliciter: sa pensée) to express.

fort, e [fɔr, fɔrt(ə)] a strong; (intensité, rendement) high, great; (corpulent) stout; (doué) good, able // ad (serrer, frapper) hard; (sonner) loud(ly); (beaucoup) greatly, very much; (très) very // nm (édifice) fort; (point fort) strong point, forte; **se faire ~ de ...** to claim one can ...; **au plus ~ de** (au milieu de) in the thick of; at the height of; **~e tête** rebel.

fortifiant [fɔrtifjã] nm tonic.

fortifier [fɔrtifje] vt to strengthen, fortify; (MIL) to fortify.

fortiori [fɔrtjɔri]: **à ~** ad all the more so.

fortuit, e [fɔrtɥi, -it] a fortuitous, chance cpd.

fortune [fɔrtyn] nf fortune; **faire ~** to make one's fortune; **de ~** a makeshift; chance cpd.

fortuné, e [fɔrtyne] a wealthy.

fosse [fos] nf (grand trou) pit; (tombe) grave; (d'orchestre) (orchestra) pit pl; **~ septique** septic tank.

fossé [fose] nm ditch; (fig) gulf, gap.

fossette [fosɛt] nf dimple.

fossile [fosil] nm fossil.

fossoyeur [foswajœr] nm gravedigger.

fou(fol), folle [fu, fɔl] a (dérèglé etc) wild, erratic; (fam: extrême, très grand) terrific, tremendous //

nm/f madman/woman // *nm* (*du roi*) jester; **être** ~ **de** to be mad *ou* crazy about; **faire le** ~ to act the fool; **avoir le** ~ **rire** to have the giggles.

foudre [fudʀ(ə)] *nf*: **la** ~ lightning; ~**s** *nfpl* (*colère*) wrath *sg*.

foudroyant, e [fudʀwajɑ̃, -ɑ̃t] *a* lightning *cpd*, stunning; (*maladie, poison*) violent.

foudroyer [fudʀwaje] *vt* to strike down; **être foudroyé(e)** to be struck by lightning; ~ **qn du regard** to glare at sb.

fouet [fwɛ] *nm* whip; (*CULIN*) whisk; **de plein** ~ *ad* (*se heurter*) head on; ~**ter** *vt* to whip; to whisk.

fougère [fuʒɛʀ] *nf* fern.

fougue [fug] *nf* ardour, spirit.

fouille [fuj] *nf* search; (*archéologiques*) ~**s** *nfpl* excavations.

fouiller [fuje] *vt* to search; (*creuser*) to dig // *vi* to rummage.

fouillis [fuji] *nm* jumble, muddle.

fouiner [fwine] *vi* (*péj*): ~ **dans** to nose around *ou* about in.

foulard [fulaʀ] *nm* scarf (*pl* scarves).

foule [ful] *nf* crowd; **la** ~ **crowds** *pl*; **les** ~**s** **the masses; une** ~ **de masses of.**

foulée [fule] *nf* stride.

fouler [fule] *vt* to press; (*sol*) to tread upon; **se** ~ *vi* (*fam*) to overexert o.s.; **se** ~ **la cheville** to sprain one's ankle; ~ **aux pieds** to trample underfoot.

foulure [fulyʀ] *nf* sprain.

four [fuʀ] *nm* oven; (*de potier*) kiln; (*THÉÂTRE: échec*) flop.

fourbe [fuʀb(ə)] *a* deceitful.

fourbu, e [fuʀby] *a* exhausted.

fourche [fuʀʃ(ə)] *nf* pitchfork; (*de bicyclette*) fork.

fourchette [fuʀʃɛt] *nf* fork; (*STATISTIQUE*) bracket, margin.

fourgon [fuʀgɔ̃] *nm* van; (*RAIL*) wag(g)on.

fourmi [fuʀmi] *nf* ant; ~**s** *nfpl* (*fig*) pins and needles; ~**lière** *nf* ant-hill.

fourmiller [fuʀmije] *vi* to swarm.

fournaise [fuʀnɛz] *nf* blaze; (*fig*) furnace, oven.

fourneau, x [fuʀno] *nm* stove.

fournée [fuʀne] *nf* batch.

fourni, e [fuʀni] *a* (*barbe, cheveux*) thick; (*magasin*): **bien** ~ (**en**) well stocked (with).

fournir [fuʀniʀ] *vt* to supply; (*preuve, exemple*) to provide, supply; (*effort*) to put in; **fournisseur, euse** *nm/f* supplier.

fourniture [fuʀnityʀ] *nf* supply(ing); ~**s** *nfpl* supplies.

fourrage [fuʀaʒ] *nm* fodder.

fourrager, ère [fuʀaʒe, -ɛʀ] *a* fodder *cpd*.

fourré, e [fuʀe] *a* (*bonbon etc*) filled; (*manteau etc*) fur-lined // *nm* thicket.

fourreau, x [fuʀo] *nm* sheath.

fourrer [fuʀe] *vt* (*fam*) to stick, shove; **se** ~ **dans/sous** to get into/under.

fourre-tout [fuʀtu] *nm inv* (*sac*) holdall; (*péj*) junk room (*ou* cupboard); (*fig*) rag-bag.

fourrière [fuʀjɛʀ] *nf* pound.

fourrure [fuʀyʀ] *nf* fur; (*sur l'animal*) coat.

fourvoyer [fuʀvwaje]: **se** ~ *vi* to go astray, stray.

foutre [futʀ(ə)] *vt* (*fam!*) = **ficher** (*fam*); **foutu, e** *a* (*fam!*) = **fichu, e** *a*.

foyer [fwaje] *nm* (*de cheminée*) hearth; (*famille*) family; (*maison*) home; (*de jeunes etc*) (social) club; hostel; (*salon*) foyer; (*OPTIQUE, PHOTO*) focus *sg*; **lunettes à double** ~ **bi-focal glasses.**

fracas [fʀaka] *nm* din; crash; roar.

fracasser [fʀakase] *vt* to smash.

fraction [fʀaksjɔ̃] *nf* fraction; **fractionner** *vt* to divide (up), split (up).

fracture [fʀaktyʀ] *nf* fracture; ~ **du crâne** fractured skull; ~ **de la jambe** broken leg.

fracturer [fʀaktyʀe] *vt* (*coffre, serrure*) to break open; (*os, membre*) to fracture.

fragile [fraʒil] a fragile, delicate; (fig) frail; **fragilité** nf fragility.

fragment [fragmã] nm (d'un objet) fragment, piece; (d'un texte) passage, extract.

fraîche [frɛʃ] a voir frais; **fraîcheur** nf coolness; freshness; **fraîchir** vi to get cooler; (vent) to freshen.

frais, fraîche [frɛ, frɛʃ] a fresh; (froid) cool // ad (récemment) newly, fresh(ly); **il fait ~** it's cool; **servir ~** serve chilled // nm: **mettre au ~** to put in a cool place; **prendre le ~** to take a breath of cool air // nmpl (débours) expenses; (COMM) costs; charges; **faire des ~** to spend; **se mettre en ~** to go to a lot of expense; **faire les ~ de** to bear the brunt of; **~ généraux** overheads; **~ de scolarité** school fees (Brit), tuition (US).

fraise [frɛz] nf strawberry; (TECH) countersink (bit); (de dentiste) drill; **~ des bois** wild strawberry.

framboise [frãbwaz] nf raspberry.

franc, franche [frã, frãʃ] a (personne) frank, straightforward; (visage) open; (net: refus, couleur) clear; (: coupure) clean; (intensif) downright; (exempt): **~ de port** postage paid // ad: **parler ~** to be frank ou candid // nm franc.

français, e [frãsɛ, -ɛz] a French // nm/f: **F~, e** Frenchman/woman // nm (LING) French; **les F~** the French.

France [frãs] nf: **la ~** France.

franche [frãʃ] a voir franc; **~ment** ad frankly; clearly; (tout à fait) downright.

franchir [frãʃir] vt (obstacle) to clear, get over; (seuil, ligne, rivière) to cross; (distance) to cover.

franchise [frãʃiz] nf frankness; (douanière, postale) exemption; (AS-SURANCES) excess.

franciser [frãsize] vt to gallicize, Frenchify.

franc-maçon [frãmasɔ̃] nm freemason.

franco [frãko] ad (COMM): **~ (de**

port) postage paid.

francophone [frãkɔfɔn] a French-speaking; **~phonie** nf French-speaking communities.

franc-parler [frãparle] nm inv outspokenness.

franc-tireur [frãtirœr] nm (MIL) irregular; (fig) freelance.

frange [frãʒ] nf fringe.

frangipane [frãʒipan] nf almond paste.

franquette [frãkɛt]: **à la bonne ~** ad without any fuss.

frappe [frap] nf (d'une dactylo, pianiste, machine à écrire) touch; (BOXE) punch.

frappé, e [frape] a iced.

frapper [frape] vt to hit, strike; (étonner) to strike; (monnaie) to strike, stamp; **se ~** vi (s'inquiéter) to get worked up; **~ dans ses mains** to clap one's hands; **~ du poing sur la table** to bang one's fist on the table; **frappé de stupeur** dumbfounded.

frasques [frask(ə)] nfpl escapades.

fraternel, le [fraternɛl] a brotherly, fraternal.

fraternité [fraternite] nf brotherhood.

fraude [frod] nf fraud; (SCOL) cheating; **passer qch en ~** to smuggle sth in (ou out); **~ fiscale** tax evasion; **frauder** vi, vt to cheat; **fraudeur, euse** nm/f cheat; fraudulent.

frayer [freje] vt to open up, clear // vi to spawn; (fréquenter): **~ avec** to mix with.

frayeur [frejœr] nf fright.

fredonner [frədɔne] vt to hum.

freezer [frizœr] nm freezing compartment.

frein [frɛ̃] nm brake; **~ à main** handbrake; **~s à disques/tambour** disc/drum brakes.

freiner [frene] vi to brake // vt (progrès etc) to check.

frelaté, e [frəlate] a adulterated; (fig) tainted.

frêle [frɛl] a frail, fragile.

frelon [frəlɔ̃] nm hornet.

frémir [fʀemiʀ] *vi* to tremble, shudder; to shiver; to quiver.

frêne [fʀɛn] *nm* ash.

frénétique [fʀenetik] *a* a frenzied, frenetic.

fréquemment [fʀekamɑ̃] *ad* frequently.

fréquent, e [fʀekɑ̃, -ɑ̃t] *a* frequent.

fréquentation [fʀekɑ̃tasjɔ̃] *nf* frequenting; seeing; **~s** *nfpl* company *sg*.

fréquenté, e [fʀekɑ̃te] *a*: **très ~** (very) busy; **mal ~** patronized by disreputable elements.

fréquenter [fʀekɑ̃te] *vt* (*lieu*) to frequent; (*personne*) to see; **se ~** to see each other.

frère [fʀɛʀ] *nm* brother.

fresque [fʀɛsk(ə)] *nf* (*ART*) fresco.

fret [fʀɛ] *nm* freight.

fréter [fʀete] *vt* to charter.

frétiller [fʀetije] *vi* to wriggle; to quiver; (*chien*) to wag its tail.

fretin [fʀətɛ̃] *nm*: **menu ~** small fry.

friable [fʀijabl(ə)] *a* crumbly.

friand, e [fʀijɑ̃, -ɑ̃d] *a*: **~ de** very fond of.

friandise [fʀijɑ̃diz] *nf* sweet.

fric [fʀik] *nm* (*fam*) cash, bread.

friche [fʀiʃ] *nf*: **en ~** *a*, *ad* (lying) fallow.

friction [fʀiksjɔ̃] *nf* (*massage*) rub, rub-down; (*TECH*, *fig*) friction; **frictionner** *vt* to rub (down); to massage.

frigidaire [fʀiʒidɛʀ] *nm* ® refrigerator.

frigide [fʀiʒid] *a* frigid.

frigo [fʀigo] *nm* fridge.

frigorifier [fʀigoʀifje] *vt* to refrigerate; **frigorifique** *a* refrigerating.

frileux, euse [fʀilø, -øz] *a* sensitive to (the) cold.

frimer [fʀime] *vi* to put on an act.

frimousse [fʀimus] *nf* (sweet) little face.

fringale [fʀɛ̃gal] *nf*: **avoir la ~** to be ravenous.

fringant, e [fʀɛ̃gɑ̃, -ɑ̃t] *a* dashing.

fripé, e [fʀipe] *a* crumpled.

fripon, ne [fʀipɔ̃, -ɔn] *a* roguish, mischievous // *nm/f* rascal, rogue.

fripouille [fʀipuj] *nf* scoundrel.

frire [fʀiʀ] *vt*, *vi*: **faire ~** to fry.

frisé, e [fʀize] *a* curly; curly-haired.

frisson [fʀisɔ̃] *nm* shudder, shiver; quiver; **frissonner** *vi* to shudder, shiver; to quiver.

frit, e [fʀi, fʀit] *pp de* **frire** // *nf*: **(pommes) ~es** chips (*Brit*), fries; **friteuse** *nf* chip pan; **friture** *nf* (*huile*) (deep) fat; (*plat*): **friture (de poissons)** fried fish; (*RADIO*) crackle.

frivole [fʀivɔl] *a* frivolous.

froid, e [fʀwa, fʀwad] *a*, *nm* cold; **il fait ~** it's cold; **avoir/prendre ~** to be/catch cold; **être en ~ avec** to be on bad terms with; **froidement** *ad* (*accueillir*) coldly; (*décider*) coolly.

froisser [fʀwase] *vt* to crumple (up), crease; (*fig*) to hurt, offend; **se ~** vi to crumple, crease; to take offence; **se ~ un muscle** to strain a muscle.

frôler [fʀole] *vt* to brush against; (*suj: projectile*) to skim past; (*fig*) to come very close to.

fromage [fʀɔmaʒ] *nm* cheese; **~ blanc** soft white cheese; **fromager, ère** *nm/f* cheese merchant.

froment [fʀɔmɑ̃] *nm* wheat.

froncer [fʀɔ̃se] *vt* to gather; **~ les sourcils** to frown.

frondaisons [fʀɔ̃dɛzɔ̃] *nfpl* foliage *sg*.

fronde [fʀɔ̃d] *nf* sling; (*fig*) rebellion, rebelliousness.

front [fʀɔ̃] *nm* forehead, brow; (*MIL*) front; **de ~** *ad* (*se heurter*) head-on; (*rouler*) together (i.e. 2 or 3 abreast); (*simultanément*) at once; **faire ~ à** to face up to; **~ de mer** (sea) front.

frontalier, ère [fʀɔ̃talje, -ɛʀ] *a* border *cpd*, frontier *cpd* // *nm/f*: (*travailleurs*) **~s** commuters from across the border.

frontière [fʀɔ̃tjɛʀ] *nf* frontier, border; (*fig*) frontier, boundary.

fronton [fʀɔ̃tɔ̃] *nm* pediment.

frotter [fʀɔte] *vi* to rub, scrape // *vt* to rub; (*pour nettoyer*) to rub (up); to scrub; ~ **une allumette** to strike a match.

fructifier [fʀyktifje] *vi* to yield a profit; **faire ~** to turn to good account.

fructueux, euse [fʀyktɥø, -øz] *a* fruitful; profitable.

fruit [fʀɥi] *nm* fruit *gén q*; ~**s de mer** seafood(s); ~**s secs** dried fruit *sg*; **fruité, e** *a* fruity; **fruitier, ère** *a*: **arbre fruitier** fruit tree // *nm/f* **fruiterer** (*Brit*), fruit merchant (*US*).

fruste [fʀyst(ə)] *a* unpolished, uncultivated.

frustrer [fʀystʀe] *vt* to frustrate.

fuel(-oil) [fjul(ɔjl)] *nm* fuel oil; heating oil.

fugace [fygas] *a* fleeting.

fugitif, ive [fyʒitif, -iv] *a* (*lueur, amour*) fleeting; (*prisonnier etc*) fugitive, runaway // *nm/f* fugitive.

fugue [fyg] *nf*: **faire une ~** to run away, abscond.

fuir [fɥiʀ] *vt* to flee from; (*éviter*) to shun // *vi* to run away; (*gaz, robinet*) to leak.

fuite [fɥit] *nf* flight; (*écoulement, divulgation*) leak; **être en ~** to be on the run; **mettre en ~** to put to flight.

fulgurant, e [fylgyʀɑ̃, -ɑ̃t] *a* lightning *cpd*, dazzling.

fulminer [fylmine] *vi* to thunder forth.

fumé, e [fyme] *a* (*CULIN*) smoked; (*verre*) tinted // *nf* smoke.

fume-cigarette [fymsigaʀɛt] *nm inv* cigarette holder.

fumer [fyme] *vi* to smoke; (*soupe*) to steam // *vt* to smoke; (*terre, champ*) to manure.

fûmes *etc vb voir* **être**.

fumet [fymɛ] *nm* aroma.

fumeur, euse [fymœʀ, -øz] *nm/f* smoker.

fumeux, euse [fymø, -øz] *a* (*péj*) woolly, hazy.

fumier [fymje] *nm* manure.

fumiste [fymist(ə)] *nm/f* (*péj*) shirker; phoney.

fumisterie [fymistəʀi] *nf* (*péj*) fraud, con.

funambule [fynɑ̃byl] *nm* tightrope walker.

funèbre [fynɛbʀ(ə)] *a* funeral *cpd*; (*fig*) doleful; funereal.

funérailles [fyneʀaj] *nfpl* funeral *sg*.

funeste [fynɛst(ə)] *a* disastrous; deathly.

fur [fyʀ]: **au ~ et à mesure** *ad* as one goes along; **au ~ et à mesure que** as.

furet [fyʀɛ] *nm* ferret.

fureter [fyʀte] *vi* (*péj*) to nose about.

fureur [fyʀœʀ] *nf* fury; (*passion*): ~ **de** passion for; **faire ~** to be all the rage.

furibond, e [fyʀibɔ̃, -bd] *a* furious.

furie [fyʀi] *nf* fury; (*femme*) shrew, vixen; **en ~** (*mer*) raging; **furieux, euse** *a* furious.

furoncle [fyʀɔ̃kl(ə)] *nm* boil.

furtif, ive [fyʀtif, -iv] *a* furtive.

fus *vb voir* **être**.

fusain [fyzɛ̃] *nm* (*ART*) charcoal.

fuseau, x [fyzo] *nm* (*pour filer*) spindle; (*pantalon*) (ski) pants; ~ **horaire** time zone.

fusée [fyze] *nf* rocket; ~ **éclairante** flare.

fuselé, e [fyzle] *a* slender; tapering.

fuser [fyze] *vi* (*rires etc*) to burst forth.

fusible [fyzibl(ə)] *nm* (*ÉLEC*: *fil*) fuse wire; (: *fiche*) fuse.

fusil [fyzi] *nm* (*de guerre, à canon rayé*) rifle, gun; (*de chasse, à canon lisse*) shotgun, gun; **fusillade** [-jad] *nf* gunfire *q*, shooting *q*; shooting battle; **fusiller** *vt* to shoot; **~ mitrailleur** *nm* machine gun.

fusionner [fyzjɔne] *vi* to merge.

fustiger [fystiʒe] *vt* to denounce.

fût [fy] *vb voir* **être** // *nm* (*tonneau*) barrel, cask.

futaie [fytɛ] *nf* forest, plantation.

futile [fytil] *a* futile; frivolous.

futur, e [fytyʀ] *a, nm* future.

fuyant, e [fɥijɑ̃, -ɑ̃t] *vb voir* **fuir** // *a* (*regard etc*) evasive; (*lignes etc*) receding; (*perspective*) vanishing.

fuyard, e [fɥijaʀ, -aʀd(ə)] *nm/f* runaway.

G

gabarit [gabaʀi] *nm* (*fig*) size; calibre.

gâcher [gɑʃe] *vt* (*gâter*) to spoil, ruin; (*gaspiller*) to waste.

gâchette [gɑʃɛt] *nf* trigger.

gâchis [gɑʃi] *nm* waste *q*.

gadoue [gadu] *nf* sludge.

gaffe [gaf] *nf* (*instrument*) boat hook; (*erreur*) blunder; **faire** ~ (*fam*) to be careful.

gage [gaʒ] *nm* (*dans un jeu*) forfeit; (*fig: de fidélité*) token; ~**s** *nmpl* (*salaire*) wages; (*garantie*) guarantee *sg*; **mettre en** ~ to pawn.

gager [gaʒe] *vt* to bet, wager.

gageure [gaʒyʀ] *nf:* **c'est une** ~ it's attempting the impossible.

gagnant, e [gaɲɑ̃, -ɑ̃t] *nm/f* winner.

gagne-pain [gaɲpɛ̃] *nm inv* job.

gagner [gaɲe] *vt* (*somme d'argent, revenu*) to earn; (*aller vers, atteindre*) to reach; (*envahir*) to overcome; to spread to // *vi* to win; (*fig*) to gain; ~ **du temps/de la place** to gain time/save space; ~ **sa vie** to earn one's living.

gai, e [ge] *a* gay, cheerful; (*un peu ivre*) merry.

gaieté [gete] *nf* cheerfulness; ~**s** *nfpl* (*souvent ironique*) delights; **de** ~ **de cœur** with a light heart.

gaillard, e [gajaʀ, -aʀd(ə)] *a* (*grivois*) bawdy, ribald // *nm* (*strapping*) fellow.

gain [gɛ̃] *nm* (*revenu*) earnings *pl*; (*bénéfice: gén pl*) profits *pl*; (*au jeu: gén pl*) winnings *pl*; (*fig: de temps, place*) saving; **avoir** ~ **de cause** to win the case; (*fig*) to be proved right.

gaine [gɛn] *nf* (*corset*) girdle; (*fourreau*) sheath.

galant, e [galɑ̃, -ɑ̃t] *a* (*courtois*) courteous, gentlemanly; (*entreprenant*) flirtatious, gallant; (*aventure, poésie*) amorous.

galbe [galb(ə)] *nm* curve(s); shapeliness.

galère [galɛʀ] *nf* galley.

galérer [galeʀe] *vi* (*fam*) to slog away, work hard.

galerie [galʀi] *nf* gallery; (*THÉÂTRE*) circle; (*de voiture*) roof rack; (*fig: spectateurs*) audience; ~ **marchande** shopping arcade; ~ **de peinture** (*private*) art gallery.

galet [galɛ] *nm* pebble; (*TECH*) wheel.

galette [galɛt] *nf* flat cake.

Galles [gal]: **le pays de** ~ Wales.

gallois, e [galwa, -waz] *a* (*langue*) Welsh // *nm/f*: **G**~, **e** Welshman/woman.

galon [galɔ̃] *nm* (*MIL*) stripe; (*décoratif*) piece of braid.

galop [galo] *nm* gallop.

galoper [galɔpe] *vi* to gallop.

galopin [galɔpɛ̃] *nm* urchin, ragamuffin.

galvauder [galvode] *vt* to debase.

gambader [gɑ̃bade] *vi* (*animal, enfant*) to leap about.

gamelle [gamɛl] *nf* mess tin; billy can.

gamin, e [gamɛ̃, -in] *nm/f* kid // *a* mischievous, playful.

gamme [gam] *nf* (*MUS*) scale; (*fig*) range.

gammé, e [game] *a*: **croix** ~**e** swastika.

gant [gɑ̃] *nm* glove; ~ **de toilette** (*face*) flannel (*Brit*), face cloth.

garage [gaʀaʒ] *nm* garage; **garagiste** *nm/f* garage owner; garage mechanic.

garant, e [gaʀɑ̃, -ɑ̃t] *nm/f* guarantor // *nm* guarantee; **se porter** ~ **de** to vouch for; to be answerable for.

garantie [gaʀɑ̃ti] *nf* guarantee; (*gage*) security, surety; (**bon de**) ~ guarantee *ou* warranty slip.

garantir [garɑ̃tir] *vt* to guarantee; (*protéger*): ~ **de** to protect from.

garçon [garsɔ̃] *nm* boy; (*célibataire*) bachelor; (*serveur*): ~ **(de café)** waiter; ~ **de courses** messenger; **garçonnet** *nm* small boy; **garçonnière** *nf* bachelor flat.

garde [gard(ə)] *nm* (*de prisonnier*) guard; (*de domaine etc*) warden; (*soldat, sentinelle*) guardsman // *nf* guarding; looking after; (*soldats, BOXE, ESCRIME*) guard; (*faction*) watch; (*TYPO*): **(page de)** ~ endpaper; flyleaf; **de** ~ *a, ad* on duty; **monter la** ~ to stand guard; **mettre en** ~ to warn; **prendre** ~ **(à)** to be careful (of); ~ **champêtre** *nm* rural policeman; ~ **du corps** *nm* bodyguard; ~ **des enfants** *nf* (*après divorce*) custody of the children; ~ **des Sceaux** *nm* ≈ Lord Chancellor (*Brit*), ≈ Attorney General (*US*); **à vue** *nf* (*JUR*) ≈ police custody; **être/se mettre au** ~-**à-vous** to be at/stand to attention.

garde... [gard(ə)] *préfixe*: ~-**barrière** *nm/f* level-crossing keeper; ~-**boue** *nm inv* mudguard; ~-**chasse** *nm* gamekeeper; ~-**fou** *nm* railing, parapet; ~-**malade** *nf* home nurse; ~-**manger** *nm inv* meat safe; pantry, larder.

garder [garde] *vt* (*conserver*) to keep; (*surveiller: enfants*) to look after; (*: immeuble, lieu, prisonnier*) to guard; ~ **le lit/la chambre** to stay in bed/indoors; **se** ~ *vi* (*aliment: se conserver*) to keep; **se** ~ **de faire** to be careful not to do; **pêche/chasse gardée** private fishing/hunting (ground).

garderie [gardəri] *nf* day nursery, crèche.

garde-robe [gardərɔb] *nf* wardrobe.

gardien, ne [gardjɛ̃, -jɛn] *nm/f* (*garde*) guard; (*de prison*) warder; (*de domaine, réserve*) warden; (*de musée etc*) attendant; (*de phare, cimetière*) keeper; (*d'immeuble*) caretaker; (*fig*) guardian; ~ **de but** goal-

keeper; ~ **de nuit** night watchman; ~ **de la paix** policeman.

gare [gar] *nf* (*railway*) station, train station (*US*) // *excl* watch out!; ~ **routière** bus station.

garer [gare] *vt* to park; **se** ~ *vi* to park; (*pour laisser passer*) to draw into the side.

gargariser [gargarize]: **se** ~ *vi* to gargle; **gargarisme** *nm* gargling *q*; gargle.

gargote [gargɔt] *nf* cheap restaurant.

gargouille [garguj] *nf* gargoyle.

gargouiller [garguje] *vi* to gurgle.

garnement [garnəmɑ̃] *nm* rascal, scallywag

garni, e [garni] *a* (*plat*) served with vegetables (*and chips or pasta or rice*) // *nm* furnished accommodation *q*.

garnir [garnir] *vt* (*orner*) to decorate; to trim; (*approvisionner*) to fill, stock; (*protéger*) to fit.

garnison [garnizɔ̃] *nf* garrison.

garniture [garnityr] *nf* (*CULIN*) vegetables *pl*; filling; (*décoration*) trimming; (*protection*) fittings *pl*; ~ **de frein** brake lining.

garrot [garo] *nm* (*MÉD*) tourniquet.

gars [ga] *nm* lad; guy.

Gascogne [gaskɔɲ] *nf* Gascony; **le golfe de** ~ **the** Bay of Biscay.

gas-oil [gazɔjl] *nm* diesel (oil).

gaspiller [gaspije] *vt* to waste.

gastronomique [gastrɔnɔmik] *a* gastronomic.

gâteau, x [gato] *nm* cake; ~ **sec** biscuit.

gâter [gate] *vt* to spoil; **se** ~ *vi* (*dent, fruit*) to go bad; (*temps, situation*) to change for the worse.

gâterie [gatri] *nf* little treat.

gâteux, euse [gatø, -øz] *a* senile.

gauche [goʃ] *a* left, left-hand; (*maladroit*) awkward, clumsy // *nf* (*POL*) left (wing); **à** ~ **on the left; (*direction*) to the left; **gaucher, ère** *a* left-handed; **gauchiste** *nm/f* leftist.

gaufre [gofr(ə)] *nf* waffle.

gaufrette [gofʀɛt] nf wafer.

gaulois, e [golwa, -waz] a Gallic; *(grivois)* bawdy // nmf: G~, e Gaul.

gausser [gose]: se ~ de vt to deride.

gaver [gave] vt to force-feed; *(fig)*: ~ de to cram with, fill up with.

gaz [gaz] nm inv gas.

gaze [gaz] nf gauze.

gazéifié, e [gazeifje] a aerated.

gazette [gazɛt] nf news sheet.

gazeux, euse [gazø, -øz] a gaseous; *(boisson)* fizzy; *(eau)* sparkling.

gazoduc [gazɔdyk] nm gas pipeline.

gazon [gazɔ̃] nm *(herbe)* turf; grass; *(pelouse)* lawn.

gazouiller [gazuje] vi to chirp; *(enfant)* to babble.

geai [ʒɛ] nm jay.

géant, e [ʒeɑ̃, -ɑ̃t] a gigantic, giant; *(COMM)* giant-size // nmf giant.

geindre [ʒɛ̃dʀ(ə)] vi to groan, moan.

gel [ʒɛl] nm frost; freezing.

gélatine [ʒelatin] nf gelatine.

gelée [ʒəle] nf jelly; *(gel)* frost.

geler [ʒəle] vt, vi to freeze; il gèle it's freezing; **gelures** nfpl frostbite sg.

gélule [ʒelyl] nf *(MÉD)* capsule.

Gémeaux [ʒemo] nmpl: les ~ Gemini.

gémir [ʒemiʀ] vi to groan, moan.

gemme [ʒɛm] nf gem(stone).

gênant, e [ʒɛnɑ̃, -ɑ̃t] a annoying, embarrassing.

gencive [ʒɑ̃siv] nf gum.

gendarme [ʒɑ̃daʀm(ə)] nm gendarme; **~rie** nf military police force in countryside and small towns; their police station or barracks.

gendre [ʒɑ̃dʀ(ə)] nm son-in-law.

gêne [ʒɛn] nf *(à respirer, bouger)* discomfort, difficulty; *(dérangement)* bother, trouble; *(manque d'argent)* financial difficulties pl ou straits pl; *(confusion)* embarrassment.

gêné, e [ʒene] a embarrassed.

gêner [ʒene] vt *(incommoder)* to bother; *(encombrer)* to hamper; to

be in the way; *(embarrasser)*: ~ qn to make sb feel ill-at-ease; se ~ vi to put o.s. out.

général, e, aux [ʒeneʀal, -o] a, nm general // nf: *(répétition)* le ~ final dress rehearsal; en ~ usually, in general; **~ement** ad generally.

généraliser [ʒeneʀalize] vt, vi to generalize; se ~ vi to become widespread.

généraliste [ʒeneʀalist(ə)] nmf general practitioner, G.P.

générateur, trice [ʒeneʀatœʀ, -tʀis] a: ~ de which causes // nf generator.

génération [ʒeneʀasjɔ̃] nf generation.

généreux, euse [ʒeneʀø, -øz] a generous.

générique [ʒeneʀik] nm *(CINÉMA)* credits pl, credit titles pl.

générosité [ʒeneʀozite] nf generosity.

genêt [ʒənɛ] nm broom q *(shrub)*.

génétique [ʒenetik] a genetic.

Genève [ʒənɛv] n Geneva.

génial, e, aux [ʒenjal, -o] a of genius; *(fam: formidable)* fantastic, brilliant.

génie [ʒeni] nm genius; *(MIL)*: le ~ the Engineers pl; ~ civil civil engineering.

genièvre [ʒənjɛvʀ(ə)] nm juniper.

génisse [ʒenis] nf heifer.

genou, x [ʒnu] nm knee; à ~x on one's knees; se mettre à ~x to kneel down.

genre [ʒɑ̃ʀ] nm kind, type, sort; *(allure)* manner; *(LING)* gender.

gens [ʒɑ̃] nmpl *(f in some phrases)* people pl.

gentil, le [ʒɑ̃ti, -ij] a kind; *(enfant: sage)* good; *(endroit etc)* nice; **gentillesse** nf kindness; **gentiment** ad kindly.

géographie [ʒeɔgʀafi] nf geography.

geôlier [ʒolje] nm jailer.

géologie [ʒeɔlɔʒi] nf geology.

géomètre [ʒeɔmɛtʀ(ə)] nmf: *(arpenteur-)* ~ (land) surveyor.

géométrie [ʒeɔmetri] *nf* geometry; **géométrique** *a* geometric.

gérance [ʒeʀɑ̃s] *nf* management; **mettre en ~ to** appoint a manager for.

géranium [ʒeʀanjɔm] *nm* geranium.

gérant, e [ʒeʀɑ̃, -ɑ̃t] *nm/f* manager/ manageress.

gerbe [ʒɛʀb(ə)] *nf* (*de fleurs*) spray; (*de blé*) sheaf (*pl* sheaves); (*fig*) shower, burst.

gercé, e [ʒɛʀse] *a* chapped.

gerçure [ʒɛʀsyʀ] *nf* crack.

gérer [ʒeʀe] *vt* to manage.

germain, e [ʒɛʀmɛ̃, -ɛn] *a:* **cousin ~ first** cousin.

germe [ʒɛʀm(ə)] *nm* germ.

germer [ʒɛʀme] *vi* to sprout; to germinate.

gésir [ʒeziʀ] *vi* to be lying (down); *voir aussi* **ci-gît.**

geste [ʒɛst(ə)] *nm* gesture; move; motion.

gestion [ʒɛstjɔ̃] *nf* management.

gibecière [ʒibsjɛʀ] *nf* gamebag.

gibet [ʒibɛ] *nm* gallows *pl.*

gibier [ʒibje] *nm* (*animaux*) game; (*fig*) prey.

giboulée [ʒibule] *nf* sudden shower.

gicler [ʒikle] *vi* to spurt, squirt.

gifle [ʒifl(ə)] *nf* slap (in the face); **gifler** *vt* to slap (in the face).

gigantesque [ʒigɑ̃tɛsk(ə)] *a* gigantic.

gigogne [ʒigɔɲ] *a:* **lits ~s** truckle (*Brit*) *ou* trundle beds.

gigot [ʒigo] *nm* leg (of mutton *ou* lamb).

gigoter [ʒigɔte] *vi* to wriggle (about).

gilet [ʒilɛ] *nm* waistcoat; (*pull*) cardigan; (*de corps*) vest; **~ pare-balles** bulletproof jacket; **~ de sauvetage** life jacket.

gingembre [ʒɛ̃ʒɑ̃bʀ(ə)] *nm* ginger.

girafe [ʒiʀaf] *nf* giraffe.

giratoire [ʒiʀatwaʀ] *a:* **sens ~** roundabout.

girouette [ʒiʀwɛt] *nf* weather vane *ou* cock.

gisait *etc vb voir* **gésir.**

gisement [ʒizmɑ̃] *nm* deposit.

gît *vb voir* **gésir.**

gitan, e [ʒitɑ̃, -an] *nm/f* gipsy.

gîte [ʒit] *nm* home; shelter; **~ (rural)** holiday cottage *ou* apartment.

givre [ʒivʀ(ə)] *nm* (hoar) frost.

glabre [glabʀ(ə)] *a* hairless; cleanshaven.

glace [glas] *nf* ice; (*crème glacée*) ice cream; (*verre*) sheet of glass; (*miroir*) mirror; (*de voiture*) window.

glacé, e [glase] *a* icy; (*boisson*) iced.

glacer [glase] *vt* to freeze; (*boisson*) to chill, ice; (*gâteau*) to ice; (*papier, tissu*) to glaze; (*fig*): **~ qn** to chill sb; to make sb's blood run cold.

glacial, e [glasjal] *a* icy.

glacier [glasje] *nm* (*GÉO*) glacier; (*marchand*) ice-cream maker.

glacière [glasjɛʀ] *nf* icebox.

glaçon [glasɔ̃] *nm* icicle; (*pour boisson*) ice cube.

glaise [glɛz] *nf* clay.

gland [glɑ̃] *nm* acorn; (*décoration*) tassel.

glande [glɑ̃d] *nf* gland.

glaner [glane] *vt, vi* to glean.

glapir [glapiʀ] *vi* to yelp.

glas [glɑ] *nm* knell, toll.

glauque [glok] *a* a dull blue-green.

glissant, e [glisɑ̃, -ɑ̃t] *a* slippery.

glissement [glismɑ̃] *nm:* **~ de terrain** landslide.

glisser [glise] *vi* (*avancer*) to glide *ou* slide along; (*coulisser, tomber*) to slide; (*déraper*) to slip; (*être glissant*) to be slippery // *vt* to slip; **se ~ dans** to slip into.

global, e, aux [glɔbal, -o] *a* overall.

globe [glɔb] *nm* globe.

globule [glɔbyl] *nm* (*du sang*) corpuscle.

globuleux, euse [glɔbylø, -øz] *a:* **yeux ~** protruding eyes.

gloire [glwaʀ] *nf* glory; (*mérite*) distinction, credit; (*personne*) celebrity.

glorieux, euse [glɔʀjø, -øz] *a* glorious.

glousser [gluse] *vi* to cluck; (*rire*) to

chuckle.

glouton, ne [glutɔ̃, -ɔn] *a* gluttonous.

gluant, e [glyɑ̃, -ɑ̃t] *a* sticky, gummy.

glycine [glisin] *nf* wisteria.

go [go]: **tout de** ~ *ad* straight out.

G.O. *sigle* = **grandes ondes**.

gobelet [gɔblɛ] *nm* tumbler; beaker; (*à dés*) cup.

gober [gɔbe] *vt* to swallow.

godasse [gɔdas] *nf* (*fam*) shoe.

godet [gɔdɛ] *nm* pot.

goéland [gɔelɑ̃] *nm* (sea)gull.

goélette [gɔelɛt] *nf* schooner.

goémon [gɔemɔ̃] *nm* wrack.

gogo [gogo]: **à** ~ *ad* galore.

goguenard, e [gɔgnaʀ, -aʀd(ə)] *a* mocking.

goinfre [gwɛ̃fʀ(ə)] *nm* glutton.

golf [gɔlf] *nm* golf; golf course.

golfe [gɔlf(ə)] *nm* gulf; bay.

gomme [gɔm] *nf* (*à effacer*) rubber (*Brit*), eraser; **gommer** *vt* to rub out (*Brit*), erase.

gond [gɔ̃] *nm* hinge; **sortir de ses** ~**s** (*fig*) to fly off the handle.

gondoler [gɔ̃dɔle]: **se** ~ *vi* to warp; to buckle.

gonflé, e [gɔ̃fle] *a* swollen; bloated.

gonfler [gɔ̃fle] *vt* (*pneu, ballon*) to inflate, blow up; (*nombre, importance*) to inflate // *vi* to swell (up); (*CULIN*: *pâte*) to rise.

gonzesse [gɔ̃zɛs] *nf* (*fam*) chick, bird (*Brit*).

goret [gɔʀɛ] *nm* piglet.

gorge [gɔʀʒ(ə)] *nf* (*ANAT*) throat; (*poitrine*) breast.

gorgé, e [gɔʀʒe] *a*: ~ **de** filled with; (*eau*) saturated with // *nf* mouthful; sip; gulp.

gorille [gɔʀij] *nm* gorilla; (*fam*) bodyguard.

gosier [gozje] *nm* throat.

gosse [gɔs] *nm/f* kid.

goudron [gudʀɔ̃] *nm* tar; **goudronner** *vt* to tar(mac) (*Brit*), asphalt (*US*).

gouffre [gufʀ(ə)] *nm* abyss, gulf.

goujat [guʒa] *nm* boor.

goulot [gulo] *nm* neck; **boire au** ~ to drink from the bottle.

goulu, e [guly] *a* greedy.

gourd, e [guʀ, guʀd(ə)] *a* numb (with cold).

gourde [guʀd(ə)] *nf* (*récipient*) flask; (*fam*) (clumsy) clot *ou* oaf // *a* oafish.

gourdin [guʀdɛ̃] *nm* club, bludgeon.

gourmand, e [guʀmɑ̃, -ɑ̃d] *a* greedy; **gourmandise** *nf* greed; (*bonbon*) sweet.

gousse [gus] *nf*: ~ **d'ail** clove of garlic.

goût [gu] *nm* taste; **de bon** ~ tasteful; **de mauvais** ~ tasteless; **prendre** ~ **à** to develop a taste *ou* a liking for.

goûter [gute] *vt* (*essayer*) to taste; (*apprécier*) to enjoy // *vi* to have (afternoon) tea // *nm* (afternoon) tea.

goutte [gut] *nf* drop; (*MÉD*) gout; (*alcool*) brandy.

goutte-à-goutte [gutagut] *nm* (*MÉD*) drip; **tomber** ~ to drip.

gouttière [gutjɛʀ] *nf* gutter.

gouvernail [guvɛʀnaj] *nm* rudder; (*barre*) helm, tiller.

gouvernante [guvɛʀnɑ̃t] *nf* governess.

gouverne [guvɛʀn(ə)] *nf*: **pour sa** ~ for his guidance.

gouvernement [guvɛʀnəmɑ̃] *nm* government; **gouvernemental, e, aux** *a* government *cpd*; pro-government.

gouverner [guvɛʀne] *vt* to govern.

grâce [gʀɑs] *nf* grace; favour; (*JUR*) pardon; ~**s** *nfpl* (*REL*) grace *sg*; **faire** ~ **à qn de qch** to spare sb sth; **rendre** ~(**s**) **à** to give thanks to; **demander** ~ to beg for mercy; ~ **à** *prép* thanks to; **gracier** *vt* to pardon; **gracieux, euse** *a* graceful.

grade [gʀad] *nm* rank; **monter en** ~ to be promoted.

gradé [gʀade] *nm* officer.

gradin [gʀadɛ̃] *nm* tier; step; ~**s** *nmpl* (*de stade*) terracing *sg*.

graduel, le [gradɥɛl] *a* gradual; progressive.

graduer [gradɥe] *vt* (*effort etc*) to increase gradually; (*règle, verre*) to graduate.

grain [grɛ̃] *nm* (*gén*) grain; (*NAVIG*) squall; ~ **de beauté** beauty spot; ~ **de café** coffee bean; ~ **de poivre** peppercorn; ~ **de poussière** speck of dust; ~ **de raisin** grape.

graine [grɛn] *nf* seed.

graissage [grɛsaʒ] *nm* lubrication, greasing.

graisse [grɛs] *nf* fat; (*lubrifiant*) grease; **graisser** *vt* to lubricate, grease; (*tacher*) to make greasy.

grammaire [gramɛr] *nf* grammar; **grammatical, e, aux** *a* grammatical.

gramme [gram] *nm* gramme.

grand, e [grɑ̃, grɑ̃d] *a* (*haut*) tall; (*gros, vaste, large*) big, large; (*long*) long; (*sens abstraits*) great // *ad*: ~ **ouvert** wide open; **au** ~ **air** in the open (air); **les** ~**s blessés** the severely injured; ~ **ensemble** housing scheme; ~ **magasin** department store; ~**e personne** grown-up; ~**e surface** hypermarket; ~**es écoles** prestige schools of university level; ~**es lignes** (*RAIL*) main lines; ~**es vacances** summer holidays; **grand-chose** *nm/f inv*: **pas grand-chose** not much; **Grande-Bretagne** *nf* (Great) Britain; **grandeur** *nf* (*dimension*) size; magnitude; (*fig*) greatness; **grandeur nature** life-size; **grandir** *vi* to grow // *vt*: **grandir qn** (*suj: vêtement, chaussure*) to make sb look taller; ~**mère** *nf* grandmother; ~**-messe** *nf* high mass; ~**-peine**: **à** ~**-peine** *ad* with difficulty; ~**père** *nm* grandfather; ~**-route** *nf* main road; ~**-rue** *nf* high street; ~**s-parents** *nmpl* grandparents.

grange [grɑ̃ʒ] *nf* barn.

granit(e) [granit] *nm* granite.

graphique [grafik] *a* graphic // *nm* graph.

grappe [grap] *nf* cluster; ~ **de raisin** bunch of grapes.

grappiller [grapije] *vt* to glean.

grappin [grapɛ̃] *nm* grapnel; **mettre le** ~ **sur** (*fig*) to get one's claws on.

gras, se [grɑ, grɑs] *a* (*viande, soupe*) fatty; (*personne*) fat; (*surface, main*) greasy; (*plaisanterie*) coarse; (*TYPO*) bold // *nm* (*CULIN*) fat; **faire la** ~**e matinée** to have a lie-in (*Brit*), sleep late (*US*); ~**sement** *ad*: ~**sement payé** handsomely paid; ~**souillet, te** *a* podgy, plump.

gratifier [gratifje] *vt*: ~ **qn de** to favour sb with; to reward sb with.

gratiné, e [gratine] *a* (*CULIN*) au gratin.

gratis [gratis] *ad* free.

gratitude [gratityd] *nf* gratitude.

gratte-ciel [gratsjɛl] *nm inv* skyscraper.

gratte-papier [gratpapje] *nm inv* (*péj*) penpusher.

gratter [grate] *vt* (*frotter*) to scrape; (*enlever*) to scrape off; (*bras, bouton*) to scratch.

gratuit, e [gratɥi, -ɥit] *a* (*entrée, billet*) free; (*fig*) gratuitous.

gravats [grava] *nmpl* rubble *sg*.

grave [grav] *a* (*maladie, accident*) serious, bad; (*sujet, problème*) serious, grave; (*air*) grave, solemn; (*voix, son*) deep, low-pitched; ~**ment** *ad* seriously; gravely.

graver [grave] *vt* to engrave.

gravier [gravje] *nm* gravel *q*; **gravillons** *nmpl* loose gravel *sg*.

gravir [gravir] *vt* to climb (up).

gravité [gravite] *nf* seriousness; gravity.

graviter [gravite] *vi* to revolve.

gravure [gravyr] *nf* engraving; (*reproduction*) print; plate.

gré [gre] *nm*: **à son** ~ to his liking; as he pleases; **au** ~ **de** according to, following; **contre le** ~ **de qn** against sb's will; **de son (plein)** ~ of one's own free will; **bon** ~ **mal** ~ like it or not; **de** ~ **ou de force**

whether one likes it or not; **savoir ~ à qn de qch** to be grateful to sb for sth.

grec, grecque [grɛk] *a* Greek; *(classique: vase etc)* Grecian // *nm* Greek.

Grèce [grɛs] *nf*: **la ~** Greece.

gréement [gremɑ̃] *nm* rigging.

greffer [grefe] *vt (BOT, MÉD: tissu)* to graft; *(MÉD: organe)* to transplant.

greffier [grefje] *nm* clerk of the court.

grêle [grɛl] *a (very) thin // nf* hail.

grêlé, e [grele] *a* pockmarked.

grêler [grele] *vb impersonnel*: **il grêle** it's hailing.

grêlon [grelɔ̃] *nm* hailstone.

grelot [grəlo] *nm* little bell.

grelotter [grəlɔte] *vi* to shiver.

grenade [grənad] *nf (explosive)* grenade; *(BOT)* pomegranate.

grenat [grəna] *a inv* dark red.

grenier [grənje] *nm* attic; *(de ferme)* loft.

grenouille [grənuj] *nf* frog.

grès [grɛ] *nm* sandstone; *(poterie)* stoneware.

grésiller [grezije] *vi* to sizzle; *(RADIO)* to crackle.

grève [grɛv] *nf (d'ouvriers)* strike; *(plage)* shore; **se mettre en/faire ~** to go on/be on strike; **~ de la faim** hunger strike; **~ du zèle** work-to-rule *(Brit)*, slowdown *(US)*.

grever [grəve] *vt* to put a strain on.

gréviste [grevist(ə)] *nm/f* striker.

gribouiller [gribuje] *vt* to scribble, scrawl.

grief [grijef] *nm* grievance; **faire ~ à qn de** to reproach sb for.

grièvement [grijɛvmɑ̃] *ad* seriously.

griffe [grif] *nf* claw; *(fig)* signature.

griffer [grife] *vt* to scratch.

griffonner [grifone] *vt* to scribble.

grignoter [griɲote] *vt* to nibble *ou* gnaw at.

gril [gril] *nm* steak *ou* grill pan.

grillade [grijad] *nf* grill.

grillage [grijaʒ] *nm (treillis)* wire

netting; wire fencing.

grille [grij] *nf (clôture)* railings; *(portail) (metal)* gate; *(d'égout) (metal)* grate; *(fig)* grid.

grille-pain [grijpɛ̃] *nm inv* toaster.

griller [grije] *vt (aussi: faire ~: pain)* to toast; *(: viande)* to grill; *(fig: ampoule etc)* to burn out, blow.

grillon [grijɔ̃] *nm* cricket.

grimace [grimas] *nf* grimace; *(pour faire rire)*: **faire des ~s** to pull *ou* make faces.

grimer [grime] *vt* to make up.

grimper [grɛ̃pe] *vi*, *vt* to climb.

grincer [grɛ̃se] *vi (porte, roue)* to grate; *(plancher)* to creak; **~ des dents** to grind one's teeth.

grincheux, euse [grɛ̃ʃø, -øz] *a* grumpy.

grippe [grip] *nf* flu, influenza; **grippé, e** *a*: **être grippé** to have flu.

gris, e [gri, griz] *a* grey; *(ivre)* tipsy; **faire ~e mine à** to pull a miserable *ou* wry face.

grisaille [grizaj] *nf* greyness, dullness.

griser [grize] *vt* to intoxicate.

grisonner [grizɔne] *vi* to be going grey.

grisou [grizu] *nm* firedamp.

grive [griv] *nf* thrush.

grivois, e [grivwa, -waz] *a* saucy.

Groenland [grɔɛnlɑ̃d] *nm* Greenland.

grogner [grɔɲe] *vi* to growl; *(fig)* to grumble.

groin [grwɛ̃] *nm* snout.

grommeler [grɔmle] *vi* to mutter to o.s.

gronder [grɔ̃de] *vi* to rumble; *(fig: révolte)* to be brewing // *vt* to scold.

gros, se [gro, gros] *a* big, large; *(obèse)* fat; *(travaux, dégâts)* extensive; *(large: trait, fil)* thick, heavy // *ad*: **risquer/ gagner ~** to risk/win a lot // *nm (COMM)*: **le ~ de** the wholesale business; **prix de ~** wholesale price; **par ~ temps/~se mer** in rough weather/heavy seas; **le ~ de**

the main body of; the bulk of; **en ~** roughly; (*COMM*) wholesale; **~ lot** jackpot; **~ mot** coarse word; **~ plan** (*PHOTO*) close-up; **~ sel** cooking salt; **~se caisse** big drum.

groseille [gʀozɛj] *nf*: **~** (**rouge**)/ (**blanche**) red/white currant; **~ à maquereau** gooseberry.

grosse [gʀos] *a voir* gros.

grossesse [gʀosɛs] *nf* pregnancy.

grosseur [gʀosœʀ] *nf* size; fatness; (*tumeur*) lump.

grossier, ière [gʀosje, -jɛʀ] *a* coarse; (*travail*) rough; crude; (*évident: erreur*) gross.

grossir [gʀosiʀ] *vi* (*personne*) to put on weight; (*fig*) to grow, get bigger; (*rivière*) to swell // *vt* to increase; to exaggerate; (*au microscope*) to magnify; (*suj: vêtement*): **~ qn** to make sb look fatter.

grossiste [gʀosist(ə)] *nm/f* wholesaler.

grosso modo [gʀosomodo] *ad* roughly.

grotte [gʀot] *nf* cave.

grouiller [gʀuje] *vi* to mill about; to swarm about; **~ de** to be swarming with.

groupe [gʀup] *nm* group.

groupement [gʀupmɑ̃] *nm* grouping; group.

grouper [gʀupe] *vt* to group; **se ~** *vi* to get together.

grue [gʀy] *nf* crane.

grumeaux [gʀymo] *nmpl* lumps.

gué [ge] *nm* ford; **passer à ~** to ford.

guenilles [gənij] *nfpl* rags.

guenon [gənɔ̃] *nf* female monkey.

guépard [gepaʀ] *nm* cheetah.

guêpe [gɛp] *nf* wasp.

guêpier [gepje] *nm* (*fig*) trap.

guère [gɛʀ] *ad* (*avec adjectif, adverbe*): **ne ... ~** hardly; (*avec verbe*): **ne ... ~** *tournure négative* + much; hardly ever; *tournure négative* + (*very*) long; **il n'y a ~ que/** de there's hardly anybody (*ou* anything) but/hardly any.

guéridon [geʀidɔ̃] *nm* pedestal table.

guérilla [geʀija] *nf* guerrilla warfare.

guérir [geʀiʀ] *vt* (*personne, maladie*) to cure; (*membre, plaie*) to heal // *vi* to recover, be cured; to heal; **guérison** *nf* curing; healing; recovery.

guérite [geʀit] *nf* sentry box.

guerre [gɛʀ] *nf* war; (*méthode*): **~ atomique** atomic warfare *q*; **en ~** at war; **faire la ~ à** to wage war against; **de ~ lasse** finally; **~ d'usure** war of attrition; **guerrier, ière** *a* warlike // *nm/f* warrior.

guet [gɛ] *nm*: **faire le ~** to be on the watch *ou* look-out.

guet-apens [gɛtapɑ̃] *nm* ambush.

guetter [gete] *vt* (*épier*) to watch (intently); (*attendre*) to watch (out) for; to be lying in wait for.

gueule [gœl] *nf* mouth; (*fam*) face; mouth; **ta ~!** (*fam*) shut up!; **~ de bois** (*fam*) hangover.

gueuler [gœle] *vi* (*fam*) to bawl.

gui [gi] *nm* mistletoe.

guichet [giʃɛ] *nm* (*de bureau, banque*) counter, window; (*d'une porte*) wicket, hatch; **les ~s** (*à la gare, au théâtre*) the ticket office.

guide [gid] *nm* guide.

guider [gide] *vt* to guide.

guidon [gidɔ̃] *nm* handlebars *pl*.

guignol [giɲɔl] *nm* ≈ Punch and Judy show; (*fig*) clown.

guillemets [gijmɛ] *nmpl*: **entre ~** in inverted commas.

guillotiner [gijɔtine] *vt* to guillotine.

guindé, e [gɛ̃de] *a* stiff, starchy.

guirlande [giʀlɑ̃d] *nf* garland; (*de papier*) paper chain.

guise [giz] *nf*: **à votre ~** as you wish *ou* please; **en ~ de** by way of.

guitare [gitaʀ] *nf* guitar.

gymnase [ʒimnɑz] *nm* gym(nasium).

gymnastique [ʒimnastik] *nf* gymnastics *sg*; (*au réveil etc*) keep-fit exercises *pl*.

gynécologie [ʒinekɔlɔʒi] *nf* gynaecology; **gynécologue** *nm/f* gynaecologist.

H

habile [abil] *a* skilful; (*malin*) clever; **~té** *nf* skill, skilfulness; cleverness.

habilité, e [abilite] *a*: **~ à faire** entitled to do, empowered to do.

habillé, e [abije] *a* dressed; (*chic*) dressy; (*TECH*): **~ de** covered with; encased in.

habillement [abijmɑ̃] *nm* clothes *pl*.

habiller [abije] *vt* to dress; (*fournir en vêtements*) to clothe; **s'~** *vi* to dress (o.s.); (*se déguiser, mettre des vêtements chic*) to dress up.

habit [abi] *nm* outfit; **~s** *nmpl* (*vêtements*) clothes; **~ (de soirée)** tails *pl*; evening dress.

habitant, e [abitɑ̃, -ɑ̃t] *nm/f* inhabitant; (*d'une maison*) occupant.

habitation [abitasjɔ̃] *nf* living; residence, home; house; **~s à loyer modéré (HLM)** low-rent housing *sg*.

habiter [abite] *vt* to live in; (*suj: sentiment*) to dwell in // *vi*: **~ à/dans** to live in *ou* at/in.

habitude [abityd] *nf* habit; **avoir l'~ de faire** to be in the habit of doing; (*expérience*) to be used to doing; **d'~** usually; **comme d'~** as usual.

habitué, e [abitye] *nm/f* regular visitor; regular (customer).

habituel, le [abituɛl] *a* usual.

habituer [abitye] *vt*: **~ qn à** to get sb used to; **s'~ à** to get used to.

'hache [ʼaʃ] *nf* axe.

'hacher [ʼaʃe] *vt* (*viande*) to mince; (*persil*) to chop.

'hachis [ʼaʃi] *nm* mince *q*.

'hachoir [ʼaʃwaR] *nm* chopper; (*meat*) mincer; chopping board.

'hagard, e [ʼagaR, -aRd(ə)] *a* wild, distraught.

'haie [ʼɛ] *nf* hedge; (*SPORT*) hurdle; (*fig: rang*) line, row.

'haillons [ʼajɔ̃] *nmpl* rags.

'haine [ʼɛn] *nf* hatred.

'hair [ʼaiR] *vt* to detest, hate.

'hâlé, e [ʼale] *a* (sun)tanned, sunburnt.

haleine [alɛn] *nf* breath; **hors d'~** out of breath; **tenir en ~** to hold spellbound; to keep in suspense; **de longue ~** a long-term.

'haler [ʼale] *vt* to haul in; to tow.

'haleter [ʼalte] *vt* to pant.

'hall [ʼol] *nm* hall.

'halle [ʼal] *nf* (covered) market; **~s** *nfpl* central food market *sg*.

hallucinant, e [alysinɑ̃, -ɑ̃t] *a* staggering.

hallucination [alysinasjɔ̃] *nf* hallucination.

'halte [ʼalt(ə)] *nf* stop, break; stopping place; (*RAIL*) halt // *excl* stop!; **faire ~** to stop.

haltère [altɛR] *nm* dumbbell, barbell; **(poids et) ~s** *nmpl* (*activité*) weight lifting *sg*.

'hamac [ʼamak] *nm* hammock.

'hameau, x [ʼamo] *nm* hamlet.

hameçon [amsɔ̃] *nm* (fish) hook.

'hanche [ʼɑ̃ʃ] *nf* hip.

handicapé, e [ʼɑ̃dikape] *nm/f* physically (*ou* mentally) handicapped person; **~ moteur** spastic.

'hangar [ʼɑ̃gaR] *nm* shed; (*AVIAT*) hangar.

'hanneton [ʼɑ̃tɔ̃] *nm* cockchafer.

'hanter [ʼɑ̃te] *vt* to haunt.

'hantise [ʼɑ̃tiz] *nf* obsessive fear.

'happer [ʼape] *vt* to snatch; (*suj: train etc*) to hit.

'haras [ʼaRɑ] *nm* stud farm.

'harassant, e [ʼaRasɑ̃, -ɑ̃t] *a* exhausting.

'harceler [ʼaRsəle] *vt* (*MIL, CHASSE*) to harass, harry; (*importuner*) to plague.

'hardi, e [ʼaRdi] *a* bold, daring.

'hareng [ʼaRɑ̃] *nm* herring.

'hargne [ʼaRɲ(ə)] *nf* aggressiveness.

'haricot [ʼaRiko] *nm* bean; **~ blanc** haricot bean; **~ vert** green bean.

harmonica [aRmɔnika] *nm* mouth organ.

harmonie [aʀmɔni] nf harmony.

'harnacher ['aʀnaʃe] vt to harness.

'harnais ['aʀnɛ] nm harness.

harpe ['aʀp(ə)] nf harp.

'harponner ['aʀpɔne] vt to harpoon; (fam) to collar.

hasard ['azaʀ] nm: le ~ chance, fate; un ~ a coincidence; a stroke of luck; au ~ aimlessly; at random; haphazardly; par ~ by chance; à tout ~ just in case; on the off chance (Brit).

hasarder ['azaʀde] vt (mot) to venture; (fortune) to risk.

'hâte ['ɑt] nf haste; à la ~ hurriedly, hastily; en ~ posthaste, with all possible speed; avoir ~ de to be eager ou anxious to; **'hâter** vt to hasten; **se hâter** vi to hurry.

'hâtif, ive ['ɑtif, -iv] a hurried; hasty; (légume) early.

'hausse ['os] nf rise, increase.

'hausser ['ose] vt to raise; ~ les épaules to shrug (one's shoulders).

'haut, e ['o, 'ot] a high; (grand) tall; (son, voix) high(-pitched) // ad high // nm top (part); de 3 m de ~ 3 m high, 3 m in height; des ~s et des bas ups and downs; en ~ lieu in high places; à ~e voix, (tout) ~ aloud, out loud; du ~ de from the top of; de ~ en bas from top to bottom; downwards; plus ~ higher up, further up; (dans un texte) above; (parler) louder; en ~ up above; at (ou to) the top; (dans une maison) upstairs; en ~ de at the top of.

'hautain, e ['otɛ̃, -ɛn] a haughty.

'hautbois ['obwa] nm oboe.

'haut-de-forme ['odfɔʀm(ə)] nm top hat.

'hauteur ['otœʀ] nf height; (fig) loftiness; haughtiness; à la ~ de (sur la même ligne) level with; by; (fig) equal to; à la ~ (fig) up to it.

'haut-fond ['ofɔ̃] nm shallow, shoal.

'haut-fourneau ['ofuʀno] nm blast ou smelting furnace.

'haut-le-cœur ['olkœʀ] nm inv retch, heave.

'haut-parleur ['opaʀlœʀ] nm (loud)speaker.

'havre ['ɑvʀ(ə)] nm haven.

'Haye ['ɛ] la: la ~ the Hague.

'hayon ['ɛjɔ̃] nm tailgate.

hebdo [ɛbdo] nm (fam) weekly.

hebdomadaire [ɛbdɔmadɛʀ] a, nm weekly.

héberger [ebɛʀʒe] vt to accommodate, lodge; (réfugiés) to take in.

hébété, e [ebete] a dazed.

hébreu, x [ebʀø] am, nm Hebrew.

hécatombe [ekatɔ̃b] nf slaughter.

hectare [ɛktaʀ] nm hectare.

hélas ['elɑs] excl alas! // ad unfortunately.

'héler ['ele] vt to hail.

hélice [elis] nf propeller.

hélicoptère [elikɔptɛʀ] nm helicopter.

helvétique [ɛlvetik] a Swiss.

hémicycle [emisikl(ə)] nm semicircle; (POL): l'~ = the benches (of the Commons) (Brit), = the floor of the House of Representatives (US).

hémorragie [emɔʀaʒi] nf bleeding q, haemorrhage.

hémorroïdes [emɔʀɔid] nfpl piles, haemorrhoids.

'hennir ['eniʀ] vi to neigh, whinny.

herbe [ɛʀb(ə)] nf grass; (CULIN, MÉD) herb; en ~ unripe; (fig) budding; **herbicide** nm weed-killer; **herboriste** nm/f herbalist.

'hère ['ɛʀ] nm: pauvre ~ poor wretch.

héréditaire [eʀeditɛʀ] a hereditary.

'hérisser ['eʀise] vt: ~ qn (fig) to ruffle sb; se ~ vi to bristle, bristle up.

'hérisson ['eʀisɔ̃] nm hedgehog.

héritage [eʀitaʒ] nm inheritance; (fig) heritage; legacy.

hériter [eʀite] vi: ~ de qch (de qn) to inherit sth (from sb); **héritier, ière** nm/f heir/heiress.

hermétique [ɛʀmetik] a airtight; watertight; (fig) abstruse; impenetrable.

hermine [ɛʀmin] *nf* ermine.

'hernie ['ɛʀni] *nf* hernia.

héroïne [eʀɔin] *nf* heroine; (*drogue*) heroin.

'héron ['eʀɔ̃] *nm* heron.

'héros ['eʀo] *nm* hero.

hésitation [ezitasjɔ̃] *nf* hesitation.

hésiter [ezite] *vi*: ~ (**à faire**) to hesitate (to do).

hétéroclite [eteʀɔklit] *a* heterogeneous; (*objets*) sundry.

'hêtre ['ɛtʀ(ə)] *nm* beech.

heure [œʀ] *nf* hour; (SCOL) period; (*moment*) time; **c'est l'~** it's time; **quelle ~ est-il?** what time is it? ; **2 ~s (du matin)** 2 o'clock (in the morning); **être à l'~** to be on time; (*montre*) to be right; **mettre à l'~** to set right; **à toute ~** at any time; **24 ~s sur 24** round the clock, 24 hours a day; **à l'~ qu'il est** at this time (of day); **by now; sur l'~** at once; **~s supplémentaires** overtime *sg*.

heureusement [œʀøzmɑ̃] *ad* (*par bonheur*) fortunately, luckily.

heureux, euse [œʀø, -øz] *a* happy; (*chanceux*) lucky, fortunate; (*judicieux*) fortunate.

'heurt ['œʀ] *nm* (*choc*) collision; ~s (*fig*) clashes.

'heurter ['œʀte] *vt* (*mur*) to strike, hit; (*personne*) to collide with; (*fig*) to go against, upset; **se ~ à** *vt* (*fig*) to come up against; **'heurtoir** *nm* door knocker.

hexagone [egzagɔn] *nm* hexagon; (*la France*) France (*because of its roughly hexagonal shape*).

hiberner [ibɛʀne] *vi* to hibernate.

'hibou, x ['ibu] *nm* owl.

'hideux, euse ['idø, -øz] *a* hideous.

hier [jɛʀ] *ad* yesterday; **toute la journée d'~** all day yesterday; **toute la matinée d'~** all yesterday morning.

'hiérarchie ['jeʀaʀʃi] *nf* hierarchy.

hilare [ilaʀ] *a* mirthful.

hippique [ipik] *a* equestrian, horse *cpd*.

hippodrome [ipɔdʀom] *nm* racecourse.

hippopotame [ipɔpɔtam] *nm* hippopotamus.

hirondelle [iʀɔ̃dɛl] *nf* swallow.

hirsute [iʀsyt] *a* hairy; shaggy; tousled.

'hisser ['ise] *vt* to hoist, haul up.

histoire [istwaʀ] *nf* (*science, événements*) history; (*anecdote, récit, mensonge*) story; (*affaire*) business *q*; ~s *nfpl* (*chichis*) fuss *q*; (*ennuis*) trouble *sg*; **historique** *a* historical; (*important*) historic.

hiver [ivɛʀ] *nm* winter; **~nal, e, aux** *a* winter *cpd*; wintry; **~ner** *vi* to winter.

HLM *sigle m ou f voir* **habitation**.

'hobby ['ɔbi] *nm* hobby.

'hocher ['ɔʃe] *vt*: **~ la tête** to nod; (*signe négatif ou dubitatif*) to shake one's head.

'hochet ['ɔʃɛ] *nm* rattle.

'hockey ['ɔkɛ] *nm*: ~ (**sur glace/gazon**) (ice/field) hockey.

'hold-up ['ɔldœp] *nm inv* hold-up.

'hollandais, e ['ɔlɑ̃dɛ, -ɛz] *a, nm* (LING) Dutch // *nm/f*: **H~, e** Dutchman/woman; **les H~** the Dutch.

'Hollande ['ɔlɑ̃d] *nf*: **la ~** Holland.

homard ['ɔmaʀ] *nm* lobster.

homéopathique [ɔmeɔpatik] *a* homoeopathic.

homicide [ɔmisid] *nm* murder; **~ involontaire** manslaughter.

hommage [ɔmaʒ] *nm* tribute; ~s *nmpl*: **présenter ses ~s** to pay one's respects; **rendre ~ à** to pay tribute *ou* homage to.

homme [ɔm] *nm* man; ~ **d'affaires** businessman; ~ **d'Etat** statesman; ~ **de main** hired man; ~ **de paille** stooge; **~-grenouille** *nm* frogman.

homogène [ɔmɔʒɛn] *a* homogeneous.

homologue [ɔmɔlɔg] *nm/f* counterpart, opposite number.

homologué, e [ɔmɔlɔge] *a* (SPORT) officially recognized, ratified; (*tarif*) authorized.

homonyme [ɔmɔnim] nm (LING) homonym; (d'une personne) namesake.

homosexuel, le [ɔmɔsɛksɥɛl] a homosexual.

'Hongrie ['5gʀi] nf: la ~ Hungary; **'hongrois, e** a, nm/f Hungarian.

honnête [ɔnɛt] a (intègre) honest; (juste, satisfaisant) fair; ~ment ad honestly; ~té nf honesty.

honneur [ɔnœʀ] nm honour; (mérite) credit; en l'~ de in honour of; (événement) on the occasion of; faire ~ à (engagements) to honour; (famille) to be a credit to; (fig: repas etc) to do justice to.

honorable [ɔnɔʀabl(ə)] a worthy, honourable; (suffisant) decent.

honoraire [ɔnɔʀɛʀ] a honorary; ~s nmpl fees pl; professeur ~ professor emeritus.

honorer [ɔnɔʀe] vt to honour; (estimer) to hold in high regard; (faire honneur à) to do credit to; s'~ de to pride o.s. upon; **honorifique** a honorary.

'honte ['5t] nf shame; **avoir** ~ de to be ashamed of; **faire** ~ à qn to make sb (feel) ashamed; **'honteux, euse** a ashamed; (conduite, acte) shameful, disgraceful.

hôpital, aux [ɔpital, -o] nm hospital.

'hoquet ['ɔkɛ] nm: avoir le ~ to have the hiccoughs; **'hoqueter** ['ɔkte] vi.

horaire [ɔʀɛʀ] a hourly // nm timetable, schedule; ~ **souple** flexitime; ~s nmpl (d'employé) hours.

horizon [ɔʀiz5] nm horizon; (paysage) landscape, view.

horizontal, e, aux [ɔʀiz5tal, -o] a horizontal.

horloge [ɔʀlɔʒ] nf clock; **horloger, ère** nm/f watchmaker; clockmaker; ~**rie** nf watch-making; watchmaker's (shop); clockmaker's (shop).

'hormis ['ɔʀmi] prép save.

horoscope [ɔʀɔskɔp] nm horoscope.

horreur [ɔʀœʀ] nf horror; avoir ~ de to loathe ou detest; **horrible** a horrible.

horripiler [ɔʀipile] vt to exasperate.

'hors ['ɔʀ] prép except (for); ~ de out of; ~ **pair** outstanding; ~ de propos inopportune; **être** ~ de soi to be beside o.s.; ~-**bord** nm inv speedboat (with outboard motor); ~-**concours** a ineligible to compete; ~ d'**œuvre** nm inv hors d'œuvre; ~-**jeu** nm inv offside; ~-**la-loi** nm inv outlaw; ~-**taxe** a (boutique, articles) duty-free.

hospice [ɔspis] nm (de vieillards) home.

hospitalier, ière [ɔspitalje, -jɛʀ] a (accueillant) hospitable; (MÉD: service, centre) hospital cpd.

hospitalité [ɔspitalite] nf hospitality.

hostie [ɔsti] nf host (REL).

hostile [ɔstil] a hostile; **hostilité** nf hostility.

hôte [ot] nm (maître de maison) host; (invité) guest.

hôtel [otɛl] nm hotel; **aller à l'**~ to stay in a hotel; ~ (**particulier**) (private) mansion; ~ **de ville** town hall; **hôtelier, ière** a hotel cpd // nm/f hotelier; ~**lerie** nf hotel business; (auberge) inn.

hôtesse [otɛs] nf hostess; ~ de l'**air** air stewardess.

'hotte ['ɔt] nf (panier) basket (carried on the back); (de cheminée) hood; ~ **aspirante** cooker hood.

houblon ['ubl5] nm (BOT) hop; (pour la bière) hops pl.

houille ['uj] nf coal; ~ **blanche** hydroelectric power.

houle ['ul] nf swell.

houlette [ulɛt] nf: sous la ~ de under the guidance of.

houleux, euse ['ulø, -øz] a heavy, swelling; (fig) stormy, turbulent.

houspiller ['uspije] vt to scold.

housse ['us] nf cover; dust cover; loose ou stretch cover.

houx ['u] nm holly.

'hublot ['yblo] nm porthole.

'**huche** ['yʃ] *nf*: ~ à **pain** bread bin.

'**huer** ['ɥe] *vt* to boo.

huile [ɥil] *nf* oil; ~ **de foie de morue** cod-liver oil; **huiler** *vt* to oil; **huileux, euse** *a* oily.

huis [ɥi] *nm*: à ~ **clos** in camera. =

huissier [ɥisje] *nm* usher; *(JUR)* = bailiff.

'**huit** ['ɥit] *num* eight; **samedi en** ~ a week on Saturday; **une huitaine de jours** a week or so; '**huitième** *num* eighth.

huître [ɥitʀ(ə)] *nf* oyster.

humain, e [ymɛ̃, -ɛn] *a* human; *(compatissant)* humane // *nm* **human** (being); **humanité** *nf* humanity.

humble [œ̃bl(ə)] *a* humble.

humecter [ymɛkte] *vt* to dampen.

humer ['yme] *vt* to smell; to inhale.

humeur [ymœʀ] *nf* mood; *(tempérament)* temper; *(irritation)* bad temper; **de bonne/mauvaise** ~ in a good/bad mood.

humide [ymid] *a* damp; *(main, yeux)* moist; *(climat, chaleur)* humid; *(saison, route)* wet.

humilier [ymilje] *vt* to humiliate.

humilité [ymilite] *nf* humility, humbleness.

humoristique [ymɔristik] *a* humorous; humoristic.

humour [ymuʀ] *nm* humour; **avoir de l'**~ to have a sense of humour; ~ **noir** sick humour.

hurlement ['yʀləmɑ̃] *nm* howling *q*, howl, yelling *q*, yell.

hurler ['yʀle] *vi* to howl, yell.

hurluberlu [yʀlybɛʀly] *nm* *(péj)* crank.

'**hutte** ['yt] *nf* hut.

hydratant, e [idʀatɑ̃, -ɑ̃t] *a (crème)* moisturizing.

hydrate [idʀat] *nm*: ~s **de carbone** carbohydrates.

hydraulique [idʀolik] *a* hydraulic.

hydravion [idʀavjɔ̃] *nm* seaplane.

hydrogène [idʀɔʒɛn] *nm* hydrogen.

hydroglisseur [idʀɔglisœʀ] *nm* hydroplane.

hygiénique [iʒjenik] *a* hygienic.

hymne [imn(ə)] *nm* hymn; ~ **national** national anthem.

hypermarché [ipɛʀmaʀʃe] *nm* hypermarket.

hypermétrope [ipɛʀmetʀɔp] *a* long-sighted.

hypnotiser [ipnotize] *vt* to hypnotize.

hypocrite [ipɔkʀit] *a* hypocritical.

hypothèque [ipɔtɛk] *nf* mortgage.

hypothèse [ipɔtɛz] *nf* hypothesis.

hystérique [isteʀik] *a* hysterical.

I

iceberg [isbɛʀg] *nm* iceberg.

ici [isi] *ad* here; **jusqu'**~ as far as this; until now; **d'**~ **là** by then; in the meantime; **d'**~ **peu** before long.

idéal, e, aux [ideal, -o] *a* ideal // *nm* ideal; ideals *pl*.

idée [ide] *nf* idea; **avoir dans l'**~ **que** to have an idea that; ~s **noires** black *ou* dark thoughts.

identifier [idãtifje] *vt* to identify; **s'**~ **à** *(héros etc)* to identify with.

identique [idãtik] *a*: ~ **(à)** identical (to).

identité [idãtite] *nf* identity.

idiot, e [idjo, idjɔt] *a* idiotic // *nm/f* idiot.

idole [idɔl] *nf* idol.

if [if] *nm* yew.

ignare [iɲaʀ] *a* ignorant.

ignifugé, e [iɲify3e] *a* fireproof(ed).

ignoble [iɲɔbl(ə)] *a* vile.

ignorant, e [iɲɔʀɑ̃, -ɑ̃t] *a* ignorant.

ignorer [iɲɔʀe] *vt (ne pas connaître)* not to know, be unaware *ou* ignorant of; *(être sans expérience de: plaisir, guerre etc)* not to know about, have no experience of; *(bouder: personne)* to ignore.

il [il] *pronom* he; *(animal, chose, en tournure impersonnelle)* it; ~s **they**; *voir aussi* **avoir**.

île [il] *nf* island; **les** ~s **anglonormandes** the Channel Islands; **les**

~s Britanniques the British Isles.

illégal, e, aux [ilegal, -o] *a* illegal.

illégitime [ileʒitim] *a* illegitimate.

illettré, e [iletʀe] *a, nm/f* illiterate.

illimité, e [ilimite] *a* unlimited.

illisible [ilizibl(ə)] *a* illegible; (*roman*) unreadable.

illumination [ilyminasjɔ̃] *nf* illumination, floodlighting; (*idée*) flash of inspiration.

illuminer [ilymine] *vt* to light up; (*monument, rue: pour une fête*) to illuminate, floodlight.

illusion [ilyzjɔ̃] *nf* illusion; se faire des ~s to delude o.s.; faire ~ to delude ou fool people; **illusionniste** *nm/f* conjuror.

illustration [ilystʀasjɔ̃] *nf* illustration.

illustre [ilystʀ(ə)] *a* illustrious.

illustré, e [ilystʀe] *a* illustrated // *nm* illustrated magazine; comic.

illustrer [ilystʀe] *vt* to illustrate; s'~ to become famous, win fame.

îlot [ilo] *nm* small island, islet; (*de maisons*) block.

ils [il] *pronom voir* il.

image [imaʒ] *nf* (*gén*) picture; (*comparaison, ressemblance, OPTIQUE*) image; ~ de marque brand image; (*fig*) public image.

imagination [imaʒinasjɔ̃] *nf* imagination; (*chimère*) fancy; avoir de l'~ to be imaginative.

imaginer [imaʒine] *vt* to imagine; (*inventer: expédient*) to devise, think up; s'~ *vt* (*se figurer: scène etc*) to imagine, picture; s'~ que to imagine that.

imbécile [ɛ̃besil] *a* idiotic // *nm/f* idiot.

imberbe [ɛ̃bɛʀb(ə)] *a* beardless.

imbiber [ɛ̃bibe] *vt* to moisten, wet; s'~ de to become saturated with.

imbu, e [ɛ̃by] *a:* ~ de full of.

imitateur, trice [imitatœʀ, -tʀis] *nm/f* (*gén*) imitator; (*MUSIC-HALL*) impersonator.

imitation [imitasjɔ̃] *nf* imitation; (*sketch*) imitation, impression; impersonation.

imiter [imite] *vt* to imitate; (*contrefaire*) to forge; (*ressembler à*) to look like.

immaculé, e [imakyle] *a* spotless; immaculate.

immatriculation [imatʀikylasjɔ̃] *nf* registration.

immatriculer [imatʀikyle] *vt* to register; faire/se faire ~ to register.

immédiat, e [imedja, -at] *a* immediate // *nm:* dans l'~ for the time being; **immédiatement** *ad* immediately.

immense [imɑ̃s] *a* immense.

immerger [imɛʀʒe] *vt* to immerse, submerge.

immeuble [imœbl(ə)] *nm* building; ~ locatif block of rented flats (*Brit*), rental building (*US*).

immigration [imigʀasjɔ̃] *nf* immigration.

immigré, e [imigʀe] *nm/f* immigrant.

imminent, e [iminɑ̃, -ɑ̃t] *a* imminent.

immiscer [imise]: s'~ *vi:* s'~ dans to interfere in ou with.

immobile [imɔbil] *a* still, motionless; (*fig*) unchanging.

immobilier, ière [imɔbilje, -jɛʀ] *a* property *cpd* // *nm:* l'~ the property business.

immobiliser [imɔbilize] *vt* (*gén*) to immobilize; (*circulation, véhicule, affaires*) to bring to a standstill; s'~ (*personne*) to stand still; (*machine, véhicule*) to come to a halt.

immonde [imɔ̃d] *a* foul.

immondices [imɔ̃dis] *nmpl* refuse *sg*; filth *sg*.

immoral, e, aux [imɔʀal, -o] *a* immoral.

immuable [imɥabl(ə)] *a* immutable; unchanging.

immunisé, e [imynize] *a:* ~ contre immune to.

immunité [imynite] *nf* immunity.

impact [ɛ̃pakt] *nm* impact.

impair, e [ɛ̃pɛʀ] *a* odd // *nm* faux

pas, blunder.

impardonnable [ɛ̃pardɔnabl(ə)] *a* unpardonable, unforgivable.

imparfait, e [ɛ̃parfɛ, -ɛt] *a* imperfect.

impartial, e, aux [ɛ̃parsjal, -o] *a* impartial, unbiased.

impartir [ɛ̃partir] *vt* to assign; to bestow.

impasse [ɛ̃pɑs] *nf* dead-end, cul-de-sac; (*fig*) deadlock.

impassible [ɛ̃pasibl(ə)] *a* impassive.

impatience [ɛ̃pasjɑ̃s] *nf* impatience.

impatient, e [ɛ̃pasjɑ̃, -ɑ̃t] *a* impatient; **impatienter** *vt* to irritate, annoy; **s'impatienter** to get impatient.

impayable [ɛ̃pɛjabl(ə)] *a* (*drôle*) priceless.

impeccable [ɛ̃pekabl(ə)] *a* faultless, impeccable; spotlessly clean; impeccably dressed; (*fam*) smashing.

impensable [ɛ̃pɑ̃sabl(ə)] *a* unthinkable; unbelievable.

impératif, ive [ɛ̃peratif, -iv] *a* imperative // *nm* (*LING*) imperative; **~s** *nmpl* requirements; demands.

impératrice [ɛ̃peratris] *nf* empress.

impérial, e, aux [ɛ̃perjal, -o] *a* imperial // *nf* top deck.

impérieux, euse [ɛ̃perjø, -øz] *a* (*caractère, ton*) imperious; (*obligation, besoin*) pressing, urgent.

impérissable [ɛ̃perisabl(ə)] *a* undying; imperishable.

imperméable [ɛ̃permeabl(ə)] *a* waterproof; (*GÉO*) impermeable; (*fig*): **~ à** impervious to // *nm* raincoat.

impertinent, e [ɛ̃pertinɑ̃, -ɑ̃t] *a* impertinent.

impétueux, euse [ɛ̃petɥø, -øz] *a* fiery.

impie [ɛ̃pi] *a* impious, ungodly.

impitoyable [ɛ̃pitwajabl(ə)] *a* pitiless, merciless.

implanter [ɛ̃plɑ̃te] *vt* (*usine, industrie, usage*) to establish; (*colons etc*) to settle; (*idée, préjugé*) to implant.

impliquer [ɛ̃plike] *vt* to imply; **~ qn** (**dans**) to implicate sb (in).

impoli, e [ɛ̃pɔli] *a* impolite, rude.

importance [ɛ̃pɔrtɑ̃s] *nf* importance; **sans ~** unimportant.

important, e [ɛ̃pɔrtɑ̃, -ɑ̃t] *a* important; (*en quantité*) considerable, sizeable; extensive; (*péj*: *airs, ton*) self-important // *nm*: **l'~** the important thing.

importateur, trice [ɛ̃pɔrtatœr, -tris] *nm/f* importer.

importation [ɛ̃pɔrtasjɔ̃] *nf* importation; introduction; (*produit*) import.

importer [ɛ̃pɔrte] *vt* (*COMM*) to import; (*maladies, plantes*) to introduce // *vi* (*être important*) to matter; **il importe qu'il fasse** it is important that he should do; **peu m'importe** I don't mind; I don't care; **peu importe** (que) it doesn't matter (if); *voir aussi* **n'importe**.

importun, e [ɛ̃pɔrtœ̃, -yn] *a* irksome, importunate; (*arrivée, visite*) inopportune, ill-timed // *nm* intruder; **importuner** *vt* to bother.

imposant, e [ɛ̃pozɑ̃, -ɑ̃t] *a* imposing.

imposer [ɛ̃poze] *vt* (*taxer*) to tax; **~ qch à qn** to impose sth on sb; **s'~** (*être nécessaire*) to be imperative; (*montrer sa prominence*) to stand out, emerge; (*artiste: se faire connaître*) to win recognition; **en ~ à** to impress.

imposition [ɛ̃pozisjɔ̃] *nf* (*ADMIN*) taxation.

impossible [ɛ̃pɔsibl(ə)] *a* impossible; **il m'est ~ de le faire** it is impossible for me to do it, I can't possibly do it; **faire l'~** to do one's utmost.

impôt [ɛ̃po] *nm* tax; (*taxes*) taxation; **taxes** *pl*; **~s** *nmpl* (*contributions*) tax *sg*; **payer 1000 F d'~s** to pay 1,000 F in tax; **~ sur le chiffre d'affaires** corporation (*Brit*) *ou* corporate (*US*) tax; **~ foncier** land tax; **~ sur le revenu** income tax.

impotent, e [ɛ̃pɔtɑ̃, -ɑ̃t] *a* disabled.

impraticable [ɛ̃pratikabl(ə)] *a* (*pro-*

jet) impracticable, unworkable; *(piste)* impassable.

imprécis, e [ɛ̃pʀesi, -iz] *a* imprecise.

imprégner [ɛ̃pʀeɲe] *vt (tissu, tampon)* to soak, impregnate; *(lieu, air)* to fill; **s'~ de** *(fig)* to absorb.

imprenable [ɛ̃pʀənabl(ə)] *a (forteresse)* impregnable; **vue ~** unimpeded outlook.

impression [ɛ̃pʀesjɔ̃] *nf* impression; *(d'un ouvrage, tissu)* printing; **faire bonne ~** to make a good impression.

impressionnant, e [ɛ̃pʀesjɔnɑ̃, -ɑ̃t] *a* impressive; upsetting.

impressionner [ɛ̃pʀesjɔne] *vt (frapper)* to impress; *(troubler)* to upset.

imprévisible [ɛ̃pʀevizibl(ə)] *a* unforeseeable.

imprévoyant, e [ɛ̃pʀevwajɑ̃, -ɑ̃t] *a* lacking in foresight; *(en matière d'argent)* improvident.

imprévu, e [ɛ̃pʀevy] *a* unforeseen, unexpected // *nm* unexpected incident; **en cas d'~** if anything unexpected happens.

imprimante [ɛ̃pʀimɑ̃t] *nf* printer; **~ matricielle** dot-matrix printer.

imprimé [ɛ̃pʀime] *nm (formulaire)* printed form; *(POSTES)* printed matter *q*.

imprimer [ɛ̃pʀime] *vt* to print; *(empreinte etc)* to imprint; *(publier)* to publish; *(communiquer: mouvement, impulsion)* to impart, transmit; **imprimerie** *nf* printing; *(établissement)* printing works *sg*; **imprimeur** *nm* printer.

impromptu, e [ɛ̃pʀɔ̃pty] *a* impromptu; sudden.

impropre [ɛ̃pʀɔpʀ(ə)] *a* inappropriate; **~ à** unsuitable for.

improviser [ɛ̃pʀɔvize] *vt, vi* to improvise.

improviste [ɛ̃pʀɔvist(ə)]: **à l'~** *ad* unexpectedly, without warning.

imprudence [ɛ̃pʀydɑ̃s] *nf* carelessness *q*; imprudence *q*.

imprudent, e [ɛ̃pʀydɑ̃, -ɑ̃t] *a (conducteur, geste, action)* careless; *(remarque)* unwise, imprudent; *(projet*

foolhardy.

impudent, e [ɛ̃pydɑ̃, -ɑ̃t] *a* impudent; brazen.

impudique [ɛ̃pydik] *a* shameless.

impuissant, e [ɛ̃pɥisɑ̃, -ɑ̃t] *a* a helpless; *(sans effet)* ineffectual; *(sexuellement)* impotent; **~ à faire** powerless to do.

impulsif, ive [ɛ̃pylsif, -iv] *a* impulsive.

impulsion [ɛ̃pylsjɔ̃] *nf (ÉLEC, instinct)* impulse; *(élan, influence)* impetus.

impunément [ɛ̃pynemɑ̃] *ad* with impunity.

imputer [ɛ̃pyte] *vt (attribuer)* to ascribe, impute; *(COMM)*: **~ à ou sur** to charge to.

inabordable [inabɔʀdabl(ə)] *a (cher)* prohibitive.

inaccessible [inaksesibl(ə)] *a* inaccessible; unattainable; *(insensible)*: **~ à** impervious to.

inachevé, e [inaʃve] *a* unfinished.

inadapté, e [inadapte] *a (gén)*: **~ à** not adapted to, unsuited to; *(PSYCH)* maladjusted.

inadmissible [inadmisibl(ə)] *a* inadmissible.

inadvertance [inadvɛʀtɑ̃s]: **par ~** *ad* inadvertently.

inaltérable [inalteʀabl(ə)] *a (matière)* stable; *(fig)* unchanging; **~ à** unaffected by.

inamovible [inamɔvibl(ə)] *a* fixed; *(JUR)* irremovable.

inanimé, e [inanime] *a (matière)* inanimate; *(évanoui)* unconscious; *(sans vie)* lifeless.

inanition [inanisjɔ̃] *nf*: **tomber d'~** to faint with hunger (and exhaustion).

inaperçu, e [inapɛʀsy] *a*: **passer ~** to go unnoticed.

inappréciable [inapʀesjabl(ə)] *a (service)* invaluable.

inapte [inapt(ə)] *a*: **~ à** incapable of; *(MIL)* unfit for.

inattaquable [inatakabl(ə)] *a (texte, preuve)* irrefutable.

inattendu, e [inatɑ̃dy] *a* unexpected.

inattentif, ive [inatɑ̃tif, -iv] *a* inattentive; ~ **à** (*dangers, détails*) heedless of; **inattention** *nf*: **faute d'inattention** careless mistake.

inaugurer [inɔgyʀe] *vt* (*monument*) to unveil; (*exposition, usine*) to open; (*fig*) to inaugurate.

inavouable [inavwabl(ə)] *a* shameful; undisclosable.

inavoué, e [inavwe] *a* unavowed.

incandescence [ɛ̃kɑ̃desɑ̃s] *nf*: **porter à ~** to heat white-hot.

incapable [ɛ̃kapabl(ə)] *a* incapable; **~ de faire** incapable of doing; (*empêché*) unable to do.

incapacité [ɛ̃kapasite] *nf* incapability; (*JUR*) incapacity.

incarner [ɛ̃kaʀne] *vt* to embody, personify; (*THÉÂTRE*) to play.

incartade [ɛ̃kaʀtad] *nf* prank.

incassable [ɛ̃kasabl(ə)] *a* unbreakable.

incendiaire [ɛ̃sɑ̃djɛʀ] *a* incendiary; (*fig*: *discours*) inflammatory // *nmf* fire-raiser, arsonist.

incendie [ɛ̃sɑ̃di] *nm* fire; ~ **criminel** arson *q*; ~ **de forêt** forest fire.

incendier [ɛ̃sɑ̃dje] *vt* (*mettre le feu à*) to set fire to, set alight; (*brûler complètement*) to burn down.

incertain, e [ɛ̃sɛʀtɛ̃, -ɛn] *a* uncertain; (*temps*) uncertain, unsettled; (*imprécis*: *contours*) indistinct, blurred; **incertitude** *nf* uncertainty.

incessamment [ɛ̃sesamɑ̃] *ad* very shortly.

incidemment [ɛ̃sidamɑ̃] *ad* in passing.

incident [ɛ̃sidɑ̃] *nm* incident; ~ **de parcours** minor hitch *ou* setback; ~ **technique** technical difficulties *pl*.

incinérer [ɛ̃sineʀe] *vt* (*ordures*) to incinerate; (*mort*) to cremate.

incisif, ive [ɛ̃siziv] *a* incisor.

inclinaison [ɛ̃klinɛzɔ̃] *nf* (*déclivité*: *d'une route etc*) incline; (*: d'un toit*) slope; (*état penché*) tilt.

inclination [ɛ̃klinasjɔ̃] *nf*: ~ **de (la**

tête) nod (of the head); ~ **(de buste)** bow.

incliner [ɛ̃kline] *vt* (*tête, bouteille*) to tilt // *vi*: ~ **à qch/à faire** to incline towards sth/doing; **s'~** (*devant*) to bow (before); (*céder*) to give in *ou* yield (to); ~ **la tête** *ou* **le front** to give a slight bow.

inclure [ɛ̃klyʀ] *vt* to include; (*joindre à un envoi*) to enclose; **jusqu'au 10 mars inclus** until 10th March inclusive.

incoercible [ɛ̃kɔɛʀsibl(ə)] *a* uncontrollable.

incohérent, e [ɛ̃kɔeʀɑ̃, -ɑ̃t] *a* inconsistent; incoherent.

incollable [ɛ̃kɔlabl(ə)] *a*: **il est ~** he's got all the answers.

incolore [ɛ̃kɔlɔʀ] *a* colourless.

incomber [ɛ̃kɔbe]: ~ **à** *vt* (*suj*: *devoirs, responsabilité*) to rest upon; (*: frais, travail*) to be the responsibility of.

incommensurable [ɛ̃kɔmɑ̃syʀabl(ə)] *a* immeasurable.

incommode [ɛ̃kɔmɔd] *a* inconvenient; (*posture, siège*) uncomfortable.

incommoder [ɛ̃kɔmɔde] *vt*: ~ **qn** to inconvenience sb; (*embarrasser*) to make sb feel uncomfortable.

incompétent, e [ɛ̃kɔpetɑ̃, -ɑ̃t] *a* incompetent.

incompris, e [ɛ̃kɔpʀi, -iz] *a* misunderstood.

inconcevable [ɛ̃kɔ̃svabl(ə)] *a* incredible.

inconciliable [ɛ̃kɔ̃siljabl(ə)] *a* irreconcilable.

inconditionnel, le [ɛ̃kɔ̃disjɔnɛl] *a* unconditional; (*partisan*) unquestioning.

inconduite [ɛ̃kɔ̃dɥit] *nf* wild behaviour *q*.

incongru, e [ɛ̃kɔ̃gʀy] *a* unseemly.

inconnu, e [ɛ̃kɔny] *a* unknown; new, strange // *nm/f* stranger; unknown person (*ou* artist etc) // *nm*: **l'~** the unknown // *nf* unknown.

inconsciemment [ɛ̃kɔ̃sjamɑ̃] *a* unconsciously.

inconscient, e [ɛ̃kɔ̃sjɑ̃, -ɑ̃t] *a* unconscious; *(irréfléchi)* thoughtless, reckless // *nm* (PSYCH): **l'~** the unconscious; **~ de** unaware of.

inconsidéré, e [ɛ̃kɔ̃sideʀe] *a* ill-considered.

inconsistant, e [ɛ̃kɔ̃sistɑ̃, -ɑ̃t] *a* flimsy, weak; runny.

incontestable [ɛ̃kɔ̃tɛstabl(ə)] *a* indisputable.

inconvenant, e [ɛ̃kɔ̃vnɑ̃, -ɑ̃t] *a* unseemly, improper.

inconvénient [ɛ̃kɔ̃venjɑ̃] *nm (d'une situation, d'un projet)* disadvantage, drawback; *(d'un remède, changement etc)* inconvenience; **si vous n'y voyez pas d'~** if you have no objections.

incorporer [ɛ̃kɔʀpɔʀe] *vt*: **~ qch à** to mix in (with); *(paragraphe etc)*: **~ (dans)** to incorporate (in); (MIL: *appeler*) to recruit, call up.

incorrect, e [ɛ̃kɔʀɛkt] *a (impropre, inconvenant)* improper; *(défectueux)* faulty; *(inexact)* incorrect; *(impoli)* impolite; *(déloyal)* underhand.

incrédule [ɛ̃kʀedyl] *a* incredulous; (REL) unbelieving.

increvable [ɛ̃kʀəvabl(ə)] *a (fam)* tireless.

incriminer [ɛ̃kʀimine] *vt (personne)* to incriminate; *(action, conduite)* to bring under attack; *(bonne foi, honnêteté)* to call into question.

incroyable [ɛ̃kʀwajabl(ə)] *a* incredible; unbelievable.

incruster [ɛ̃kʀyste] *vt (ART)* to inlay; **s'~** *vi (invité)* to take root; *(radiateur etc)* to become coated with fur *ou* scale.

incubateur [ɛ̃kybatœʀ] *nm* incubator.

inculpé, e [ɛ̃kylpe] *nm/f* accused.

inculper [ɛ̃kylpe] *vt*: **~ (de)** to charge (with).

inculquer [ɛ̃kylke] *vt*: **~ qch à** to inculcate sth in *ou* instil sth into.

inculte [ɛ̃kylt(ə)] *a* uncultivated; *(esprit, peuple)* uncultured; *(barbe)*

unkempt.

Inde [ɛ̃d] *nf*: **l'~** India.

indécis, e [ɛ̃desi, -iz] *a* indecisive; *(perplexe)* undecided.

indéfendable [ɛ̃defɑ̃dabl(ə)] *a* indefensible.

indéfini, e [ɛ̃defini] *a (imprécis, incertain)* undefined; *(illimité, LING)* indefinite; **~ment** *ad (abstraction faite de)* irrespective of; *(en plus de)* over and above.

indélébile [ɛ̃delebil] *a* indelible; **~ssable** *a* indefinable.

indélicat, e [ɛ̃delika, -at] *a* tactless; dishonest.

indemne [ɛ̃dɛmn(ə)] *a* unharmed.

indemniser [ɛ̃dɛmnize] *vt*: **~ qn (de)** to compensate sb (for).

indemnité [ɛ̃dɛmnite] *nf (dédommagement)* compensation *q*; *(allocation)* allowance; **~ de licenciement** redundancy payment.

indépendamment [ɛ̃depɑ̃damɑ̃] *ad* independently; **~ de** *(abstraction faite de)* irrespective of; *(en plus de)* over and above.

indépendance [ɛ̃depɑ̃dɑ̃s] *nf* independence.

indépendant, e [ɛ̃depɑ̃dɑ̃, -ɑ̃t] *a* independent; **~ de** independent of.

indescriptible [ɛ̃dɛskʀiptibl(ə)] *a* indescribable.

indétermination [ɛ̃detɛʀminasjɔ̃] *nf* indecision; indecisiveness.

indéterminé, e [ɛ̃detɛʀmine] *a* unspecified; indeterminate.

index [ɛ̃dɛks] *nm (doigt)* index finger; *(d'un livre etc)* index; **mettre à l'~** to blacklist.

indexé, e [ɛ̃dɛkse] *a (ÉCON)*: **~ (sur)** index-linked (to).

indicateur [ɛ̃dikatœʀ] *nm (POLICE)* informer; *(livre)* guide; directory; *(TECH)* gauge; indicator; **~ des chemins de fer** railway timetable.

indicatif, ive [ɛ̃dikatif, -iv] *a*: **à titre ~** for (your) information // *nm* (LING) indicative; *(RADIO)* theme *ou* signature tune; *(TÉL)* dialling code.

indication [ɛ̃dikasjɔ̃] *nf* indication; *(renseignement)* information *q*; **~s** *nfpl (directives)* instructions.

indice [ɛ̃dis] nm (marque, signe) indication, sign; (POLICE: lors d'une enquête) clue; (JUR: présomption) piece of evidence; (SCIENCE, ÉCON, TECH) index.

indicible [ɛ̃disibl(ə)] a inexpressible.

indien, ne [ɛ̃djɛ̃, -jɛn] a, nm/f Indian.

indifféremment [ɛ̃difeʀamã] ad (sans distinction) equally (well); indiscriminately.

indifférence [ɛ̃difeʀãs] nf indifference.

indifférent, e [ɛ̃difeʀã, -ãt] a (peu intéressé) indifferent.

indigence [ɛ̃diʒãs] nf poverty.

indigène [ɛ̃diʒɛn] a native, indigenous; local // nm/f native.

indigeste [ɛ̃diʒɛst(ə)] a indigestible.

indigestion [ɛ̃diʒɛstjɔ̃] nf indigestion q.

indigne [ɛ̃diɲ] a unworthy.

indigner [ɛ̃diɲe] vt: s'~ (de/ contre) to be indignant (at).

indiqué, e [ɛ̃dike] a (date, lieu) given; (adéquat, conseillé) suitable.

indiquer [ɛ̃dike] vt (désigner): ~ qch/qn à qn to point sth/sb out to sb; (suj: pendule, aiguille) to show; (suj: étiquette, plan) to show, indicate; (faire connaître: médecin, restaurant): ~ qch/qn à qn to tell sb of sth/sb; (renseigner sur) to point out, tell; (déterminer: date, lieu) to give, state; (dénoter) to indicate, point to.

indirect, e [ɛ̃diʀɛkt] a indirect.

indiscipline [ɛ̃disiplin] nf lack of discipline; **indiscipliné, e** a undisciplined; (fig) unmanageable.

indiscret, ète [ɛ̃diskʀɛ, -ɛt] a indiscreet.

indiscutable [ɛ̃diskytabl(ə)] a indisputable.

indispensable [ɛ̃dispãsabl(ə)] a indispensable; essential.

indisposer [ɛ̃dispoze] vt (incommoder) to upset; (déplaire à) to antagonize.

indistinct, e [ɛ̃distɛ̃(kt), -ɛ̃kt(ə)] a indis-tinct; **indistinctement** ad (voir, prononcer) indistinctly; (sans distinction) indiscriminately.

individu [ɛ̃dividy] nm individual.

individuel, le [ɛ̃dividɥɛl] a (gén) individual; (opinion, livret, contrôle, avantages) personal; **chambre ~le** single room; **maison ~le** detached house.

indolore [ɛ̃dɔlɔʀ] a painless.

indomptable [ɛ̃dɔ̃tabl(ə)] a untameable; (fig) invincible, indomitable.

Indonésie [ɛ̃dɔnezi] nf Indonesia.

indu, e [ɛ̃dy] a: à des heures ~es at some ungodly hour.

induire [ɛ̃dɥiʀ] vt: ~ qn en erreur to lead sb astray, mislead sb.

indulgent, e [ɛ̃dylʒã, -ãt] a (parent, regard) indulgent; (juge, examinateur) lenient.

indûment [ɛ̃dymã] ad wrongly; without due cause.

industrie [ɛ̃dystʀi] nf industry; **industriel, le** a industrial // nm industrialist; manufacturer.

inébranlable [inebʀãlabl(ə)] a (masse, colonne) solid; (personne, certitude, foi) steadfast, unwavering.

inédit, e [inedi, -it] a (correspondance etc) hitherto unpublished; (spectacle, moyen) novel, original.

ineffaçable [inefasabl(ə)] a indelible.

inefficace [inefikas] a (remède, moyen) ineffective; (machine, employé) inefficient.

inégal, e, aux [inegal, -o] a unequal; uneven.

inégalable [inegalabl(ə)] a matchless.

inégalé, e [inegale] a unmatched, unequalled.

inerte [inɛʀt(ə)] a lifeless; inert.

inestimable [inɛstimabl(ə)] a priceless; (fig: bienfait) invaluable.

inévitable [inevitabl(ə)] a unavoidable; (fatal, habituel) inevitable.

inexact, e [inɛgzakt] a inaccurate, inexact; unpunctual.

in extenso [inɛkstɛ̃so] ad in full.

in extremis [inɛkstʀemis] ad at the

last minute // a last-minute.

infaillible [ɛ̃fajibl(ə)] a infallible.

infâme [ɛ̃fɑm] a vile.

infanticide [ɛ̃fɑ̃tisid] nm/f child-murderer/eress // nm (meurtre) infanticide.

infarctus [ɛ̃faʀktys] nm: ~ (du myocarde) coronary (thrombosis).

infatigable [ɛ̃fatigabl(ə)] a tireless.

infect, e [ɛ̃fɛkt] a vile; foul; (repas, vin) revolting.

infecter [ɛ̃fɛkte] vt (atmosphère, eau) to contaminate; (MÉD) to infect; s'~ to become infected ou septic; **infection** [-sjɔ̃] nf infection.

inférieur, e [ɛ̃feʀjœʀ] a lower; (en qualité, intelligence) inferior; à (somme, quantité) less ou smaller than; (moins bon que) inferior to.

infernal, e, aux [ɛ̃fɛʀnal, -o] a (chaleur, rythme) infernal; (méchanceté, complot) diabolical.

infidèle [ɛ̃fidɛl] a unfaithful.

infiltrer [ɛ̃filtʀe]: s'~ vi: s'~ dans to penetrate into; (liquide) to seep into; (fig: noyauter) to infiltrate.

infime [ɛ̃fim] a minute, tiny; (inférieur) lowly.

infini, e [ɛ̃fini] a infinite // nm infinity; à l'~ (MATH) to infinity; (agrandir, varier) infinitely; (interminablement) endlessly; **infiniment** ad infinitely; **infinité** nf: une infinité de an infinite number of.

infinitif, ive [ɛ̃finitif] nm infinitive.

infirme [ɛ̃fiʀm(ə)] a disabled // nm/f disabled person; ~ de guerre war cripple.

infirmer [ɛ̃fiʀme] vt to invalidate.

infirmerie [ɛ̃fiʀməʀi] nf sick bay.

infirmier, ière [ɛ̃fiʀmje, -jɛʀ] nm/f nurse; **infirmière chef** sister; **infirmière visiteuse** = district nurse.

infirmité [ɛ̃fiʀmite] nf disability.

inflammable [ɛ̃flamabl(ə)] a (in)flammable.

inflation [ɛ̃flasjɔ̃] nf inflation.

inflexion [ɛ̃flɛksjɔ̃] nf inflexion; ~ de la tête slight nod (of the head).

infliger [ɛ̃fliʒe] vt: ~ qch (à qn) to inflict sth (on sb); (amende, sanction) to impose sth (on sb).

influence [ɛ̃flyɑ̃s] nf influence; (d'un médicament) effect; **influencer** vt to influence; **influent, e** a a influential.

influer [ɛ̃flye]: ~ sur vt to have an influence upon.

informaticien, ne [ɛ̃fɔʀmatisjɛ̃, -jɛn] nm/f computer scientist.

information [ɛ̃fɔʀmasjɔ̃] nf (renseignement) piece of information; (PRESSE, TV: nouvelle) item of news; ~s (TV) news sg; (diffusion de renseignements, INFORM) information; (JUR) inquiry, investigation; voyage d'~ fact-finding trip.

informatique [ɛ̃fɔʀmatik] nf (technique) data processing; (science) computer science // a computer cpd; **informatiser** vt to computerize.

informe [ɛ̃fɔʀm(ə)] a shapeless.

informer [ɛ̃fɔʀme] vt: ~ qn (de) to inform sb (of); s'~ (de/si) to inquire ou find out (about/whether ou if).

infortune [ɛ̃fɔʀtyn] nf misfortune.

infraction [ɛ̃fʀaksjɔ̃] nf offence; ~ à violation ou breach of; être en ~ to be in breach of the law.

infranchissable [ɛ̃fʀɑ̃ʃisabl(ə)] a impassable; (fig) insuperable.

infrastructure [ɛ̃fʀastʀyktyʀ] nf (AVIAT, MIL) ground installations pl; (ÉCON: touristique etc) infrastructure.

infuser [ɛ̃fyze] vt, vi (thé) to brew; (tisane) to infuse; **infusion** nf (tisane) herb tea.

ingénier [ɛ̃ʒenje]: s'~ vi: s'~ à faire to strive to do.

ingénierie [ɛ̃ʒeniʀi] nf engineering.

ingénieur [ɛ̃ʒenjœʀ] nm engineer; ~ du son sound engineer.

ingénieux, euse [ɛ̃ʒenjø, -øz] a ingenious, clever.

ingénu, e [ɛ̃ʒeny] a ingenuous, artless.

ingérer [ɛ̃ʒeʀe]: s'~ vi: s'~ dans to interfere in.

ingrat, e [ɛ̃gra, -at] a (personne) ungrateful; (sol) poor; (travail, sujet) thankless; (visage) unprepossessing.

ingrédient [ɛ̃gredjɑ̃] nm ingredient.

ingurgiter [ɛ̃gyʀʒite] vt to swallow.

inhabitable [inabitabl(ə)] a uninhabitable.

inhérent, e [inerɑ̃, -ɑ̃t] a: ~ à inherent in.

inhibition [inibisjɔ̃] nf inhibition.

inhumain, e [inymɛ̃, -ɛn] a inhuman.

inhumer [inyme] vt to inter, bury.

inimitié [inimitje] nf enmity.

initial, e, aux [inisjal, -o] a, nf initial.

initiateur, trice [inisjatœʀ, -tʀis] nm/f initiator; (d'une mode, technique) innovator, pioneer.

initiative [inisjativ] nf initiative.

initier [inisje] vt: ~ qn à to initiate sb into; (faire découvrir: art, jeu) to introduce sb to.

injecté, e [ɛ̃ʒɛkte] a: yeux ~s de sang bloodshot eyes.

injecter [ɛ̃ʒɛkte] vt to inject; **injection** [-sjɔ̃] nf injection; **à injection** a (AUTO) fuel injection cpd.

injure [ɛ̃ʒyʀ] nf insult, abuse q.

injurier [ɛ̃ʒyʀje] vt to insult, abuse; **injurieux, euse** a abusive, insulting.

injuste [ɛ̃ʒyst(ə)] a unjust, unfair; **injustice** nf injustice.

inlassable [ɛ̃lasabl(ə)] a tireless.

inné, e [ine] a innate, inborn.

innocent, e [inɔsɑ̃, -ɑ̃t] a innocent; **innocenter** vt to clear, prove innocent.

innombrable [inɔ̃bʀabl(ə)] a innumerable.

innommable [inɔmabl(ə)] a unspeakable.

innover [inɔve] vi to break new ground.

inoccupé, e [inɔkype] a unoccupied.

inoculer [inɔkyle] vt (volontairement) to inoculate; (accidentellement) to infect.

inodore [inɔdɔʀ] a (gaz) odourless; (fleur) scentless.

inoffensif, ive [inɔfɑ̃sif, -iv] a harmless, innocuous.

inondation [inɔ̃dasjɔ̃] nf flooding q; flood.

inonder [inɔ̃de] vt to flood; (fig) to inundate, overrun.

inopérant, e [inɔpeʀɑ̃, -ɑ̃t] a inoperative, ineffective.

inopiné, e [inɔpine] a unexpected, sudden.

inopportun, e [inɔpɔʀtœ̃, -yn] a ill-timed, untimely; inappropriate.

inoubliable [inublijabl(ə)] a unforgettable.

inouï, e [inwi] a unheard-of, extraordinary.

inox(ydable) [inɔks(idabl(ə))] a stainless.

inqualifiable [ɛ̃kalifjabl(ə)] a unspeakable.

inquiet, ète [ɛ̃kjɛ, -ɛt] a anxious.

inquiétant, e [ɛ̃kjetɑ̃, -ɑ̃t] a worrying, disturbing.

inquiéter [ɛ̃kjete] vt to worry; (harceler) to harass; s'~ to worry; s'~ de to worry about; (s'enquérir de) to inquire about.

inquiétude [ɛ̃kjetyd] nf anxiety.

insaisissable [ɛ̃sezisabl(ə)] a elusive.

insatisfait, e [ɛ̃satisfɛ, -ɛt] a (non comblé) unsatisfied; unfulfilled; (mécontent) dissatisfied.

inscription [ɛ̃skʀipsjɔ̃] nf inscription; (voir s'inscrire) enrolment; registration.

inscrire [ɛ̃skʀiʀ] vt (marquer: sur son calepin etc) to note ou write down; (: sur un mur, une affiche etc) to write; (: dans la pierre, le métal) to inscribe; (mettre: sur une liste, un budget etc) to put down; ~ qn à (club, école etc) to enrol sb at; s'~ (pour une excursion etc) to put one's name down; s'~ (à) (club, parti) to join; (université) to register ou enrol (at); (examen, concours) to register (for); s'~ en faux contre to challenge.

insecte [ɛ̃sɛkt(ə)] nm insect; **insec-**

ticide nm insecticide.

insensé, e [ɛ̃sɑ̃se] a mad.

insensibiliser [ɛ̃sɑ̃sibilize] vt to anaesthetize.

insensible [ɛ̃sɑ̃sibl(ə)] a (nerf, membre) numb; (dur, indifférent) insensitive; (imperceptible) imperceptible.

insérer [ɛ̃sere] vt to insert; s'~ dans to fit into; to come within.

insigne [ɛ̃siɲ] nm (d'un parti, club) badge // a distinguished; ~s nmpl (d'une fonction) insignia pl.

insignifiant, e [ɛ̃siɲifjɑ̃, -ɑ̃t] a insignificant; trivial.

insinuer [ɛ̃sinɥe] vt to insinuate, imply; s'~ dans (fig) to creep into.

insister [ɛ̃siste] vi to insist; (s'obstiner) to keep on; ~ sur (détail, note) to stress.

insolation [ɛ̃sɔlasjɔ̃] nf (MÉD) sunstroke q.

insolent, e [ɛ̃sɔlɑ̃, -ɑ̃t] a insolent.

insolite [ɛ̃sɔlit] a strange, unusual.

insomnie [ɛ̃sɔmni] nf insomnia q, sleeplessness q.

insondable [ɛ̃sɔ̃dabl(ə)] a unfathomable.

insonoriser [ɛ̃sɔnɔrize] vt to soundproof.

insouciant, e [ɛ̃susjɑ̃, -ɑ̃t] a carefree; (imprévoyant) heedless.

insoumis, e [ɛ̃sumi, -iz] a (caractère, enfant) refractory; (contrée, tribu) unsubdued.

insoupçonnable [ɛ̃supsɔnabl(ə)] a unsuspected; (personne) above suspicion.

insoutenable [ɛ̃sutnabl(ə)] a (argument) untenable; (chaleur) unbearable.

inspecter [ɛ̃spɛkte] vt to inspect.

inspecteur, trice [ɛ̃spɛktœr, -tris] nm/f inspector; ~ d'Académie (regional) director of education; ~ des finances ≈ tax inspector (Brit), Internal Revenue Service agent (US).

inspection [ɛ̃spɛksjɔ̃] nf inspection.

inspirer [ɛ̃spire] vt (gén) to inspire // vi (aspirer) to breathe in; s'~ de (suj: artiste) to draw one's inspiration from.

instable [ɛ̃stabl(ə)] a (meuble, équilibre) unsteady; (population, temps) unsettled; (régime, caractère) unstable.

installation [ɛ̃stalasjɔ̃] nf putting in ou up; fitting out; settling in; (appareils etc) fittings pl, installations pl; ~s nfpl equipment; facilities.

installer [ɛ̃stale] vt (loger): ~ qn to get sb settled; (placer) to put, place; (meuble, gaz, électricité) to put in; (rideau, étagère, tente) to put up; (appartement) to fit out; s'~ (artisan, dentiste etc) to set o.s. up; (se loger) to settle (o.s.); (emménager) to settle in; (sur un siège, à un emplacement) to settle (down); (fig: maladie, grève) to take a firm hold.

instamment [ɛ̃stamɑ̃] ad urgently.

instance [ɛ̃stɑ̃s] nf (ADMIN: autorité) authority; ~s nfpl (prières) entreaties; affaire en ~ matter pending; être en ~ de divorce to be awaiting a divorce.

instant [ɛ̃stɑ̃] nm moment, instant; dans un ~ in a moment; à l'~ this instant; à tout ou chaque ~ at any moment; constantly; pour l'~ for the moment, for the time being; par ~s at times; de tous les ~s perpetual.

instantané, e [ɛ̃stɑ̃tane] a (lait, café) instant; (explosion, mort) instantaneous // nm snapshot.

instar [ɛ̃star]: à l'~ de prép following the example of, like.

instaurer [ɛ̃stɔre] vt to institute.

instinct [ɛ̃stɛ̃] nm instinct.

instituer [ɛ̃stitɥe] vt to set up.

institut [ɛ̃stity] nm institute; ~ de beauté beauty salon; I~ Universitaire de Technologie (IUT) ≈ polytechnic.

instituteur, trice [ɛ̃stitytœr, -tris] nm/f (primary school) teacher.

institution [ɛ̃stitysjɔ̃] nf institution; (collège) private school.

instruction [ɛ̃stryksjɔ̃] nf (enseigne-

ment, savoir) education; (*JUR*) (preliminary) investigation and hearing; **~s** *nfpl* directions, instructions; **~ civique** civics *sg*.

instruire [ɛ̃stʀɥiʀ] (*élèves*) to teach; (*recrues*) to train; (*JUR: affaire*) to conduct the investigation for; **s'~** to educate o.s.; **instruit, e** educated.

instrument [ɛ̃stʀymɑ̃] *nm* instrument; **~ à cordes/vent** stringed/wind instrument; **~ de mesure** measuring instrument; **~ de musique** musical instrument; **~ de travail** (working) tool.

insu [ɛ̃sy] *nm*: **à l'~ de qn** without sb knowing (it).

insubmersible [ɛ̃sybmɛʀsibl(ə)] *a* unsinkable.

insubordination [ɛ̃sybɔʀdinasjɔ̃] *nf* rebelliousness; (*MIL*) insubordination.

insuccès [ɛ̃syksɛ] *nm* failure.

insuffisant, e [ɛ̃syfizɑ̃, -ɑ̃t] *a* insufficient; (*élève, travail*) inadequate.

insuffler [ɛ̃syfle] *vt* to blow; to inspire.

insulaire [ɛ̃sylɛʀ] *a* island *cpd*; (*attitude*) insular.

insuline [ɛ̃sylin] *nf* insulin.

insulte [ɛ̃sylt(ə)] *nf* insult; **insulter** *vt* to insult.

insupportable [ɛ̃sypɔʀtabl(ə)] *a* unbearable.

insurger [ɛ̃syʀʒe]: **s'~** *vi*: **s'~ (contre)** to rise up *ou* rebel (against).

insurmontable [ɛ̃syʀmɔ̃tabl(ə)] *a* (*difficulté*) insuperable; (*aversion*) unconquerable.

intact, e [ɛ̃takt] *a* intact.

intangible [ɛ̃tɑ̃ʒibl(ə)] *a* intangible; (*principe*) inviolable.

intarissable [ɛ̃taʀisabl(ə)] *a* inexhaustible.

intégral, e, aux [ɛ̃tegʀal, -o] *a* complete.

intégrant, e [ɛ̃tegʀɑ̃, -ɑ̃t] *a*: **faire partie ~e de** to be an integral part of.

intègre [ɛ̃tɛgʀ(ə)] *a* upright.

intégrer [ɛ̃tegʀe] *vt* to integrate; **s'~ à/dans** to become integrated into.

intellectuel, le [ɛ̃telɛktɥel] *a* intellectual // *nm/f* intellectual; (*péj*) highbrow.

intelligence [ɛ̃teliʒɑ̃s] *nf* intelligence; (*compréhension*): **l'~ de** the understanding of; (*complicité*): **regard d'~** glance of complicity; (*accord*): **vivre en bonne ~ avec qn** to be on good terms with sb.

intelligent, e [ɛ̃teliʒɑ̃, -ɑ̃t] *a* intelligent.

intempéries [ɛ̃tɑ̃peʀi] *nfpl* bad weather *sg*.

intempestif, ive [ɛ̃tɑ̃pɛstif, -iv] *a* untimely.

intenable [ɛ̃tnabl(ə)] *a* (*chaleur*) unbearable.

intendant, e [ɛ̃tɑ̃dɑ̃, -ɑ̃t] *nm/f* (*MIL*) quartermaster; (*SCOL*) bursar; (*d'une propriété*) steward.

intense [ɛ̃tɑ̃s] *a* intense; **intensif, ive** *a* intensive.

intenter [ɛ̃tɑ̃te] *vt*: **~ un procès contre** *ou* **à** to start proceedings against.

intention [ɛ̃tɑ̃sjɔ̃] *nf* intention; (*JUR*) intent; **avoir l'~ de faire** to intend to do; **à l'~ de** *prép* for (*renseignement*) the benefit of; (*film, ouvrage*) aimed at; **à cette ~** with this aim in view; **intentionné, e** *a*: **bien intentionné** well-meaning *ou* -intentioned; **mal intentionné** ill-intentioned.

intercaler [ɛ̃tɛʀkale] *vt* to insert.

intercepter [ɛ̃tɛʀsɛpte] *vt* to intercept; (*lumière, chaleur*) to cut off.

interchangeable [ɛ̃tɛʀʃɑ̃ʒabl(ə)] *a* interchangeable.

interclasse [ɛ̃tɛʀklɑs] *nm* (*SCOL*) break (between classes).

interdiction [ɛ̃tɛʀdiksjɔ̃] *nf* ban.

interdire [ɛ̃tɛʀdiʀ] *vt* to forbid; (*ADMIN*) to ban, prohibit; (*: journal, livre*) to ban; **~ à qn de faire** to forbid sb to do, prohibit sb from doing; (*suj: empêchement*) to pre-

vent sb from doing.
interdit, e [ɛ̃tɛʀdi, -it] *a* (*stupéfait*)
taken aback // *nm* prohibition.
intéressant, e [ɛ̃teʀesɑ̃, -ɑ̃t] *a*
interesting.
intéressé, e [ɛ̃teʀese] *a* (*parties*) involved, concerned; (*amitié, motifs*)
self-interested.
intéresser [ɛ̃teʀese] *vt* (*captiver*) to
interest; (*toucher*) to be of interest
to; (*ADMIN: concerner*) to affect,
concern; **s'~ à** to be interested in.
intérêt [ɛ̃teʀɛ] *nm* (*aussi COMM*) interest; (*égoisme*) self-interest; **avoir
~ à faire** to do well to do.
intérieur, e [ɛ̃teʀjœʀ] *a* (*mur, escalier, poche*) inside; (*commerce, politique*) domestic; (*cour, calme, vie*)
inner; (*navigation*) inland // *nm*
(*d'une maison, d'un récipient etc*) inside; (*d'un pays, aussi: décor,
mobilier*) interior; (*POL*): **l'I~** the
Interior; **à l'~ (de)** inside (of);
within.
intérim [ɛ̃teʀim] *nm* interim period;
assurer l'~ (de) to deputize (for);
par ~ interim.
intérioriser [ɛ̃teʀjɔʀize] *vt* to inter-
nalize.
interlocuteur, trice [ɛ̃tɛʀlɔkytœʀ,
-tʀis] *nm/f* speaker; **son ~** the person
he was speaking to.
interloquer [ɛ̃tɛʀlɔke] *vt* to take
aback.
intermède [ɛ̃tɛʀmɛd] *nm* interlude.
intermédiaire [ɛ̃tɛʀmedjɛʀ] *a* intermediate; middle; half-way // *nmf*
intermediary; (*COMM*) middleman;
sans ~ directly; **par l'~ de**
through.
intermittence [ɛ̃tɛʀmitɑ̃s] *nf*: **par
~** sporadically, intermittently.
internat [ɛ̃tɛʀna] *nm* (*SCOL*) boarding school.
international, e, aux [ɛ̃tɛʀnasjɔnal,
-o] *a, nm/f* international.
interne [ɛ̃tɛʀn(ə)] *a* internal // *nmf*
(*SCOL*) boarder; (*MÉD*) houseman.
interner [ɛ̃tɛʀne] *vt* (*POL*) to intern;
(*MÉD*) to confine to a mental institu-

tion.
interpeller [ɛ̃tɛʀpele] *vt* (*appeler*) to
call out to; (*apostropher*) to shout at;
(*POLICE*) to take in for questioning;
(*POL*) to question.
interphone [ɛ̃tɛʀfɔn] *nm* intercom.
interposer [ɛ̃tɛʀpoze] *vt* to inter-
pose; **s'~** *vi* to intervene; **par personnes interposées** through a third
party.
interprète [ɛ̃tɛʀpʀɛt] *nmf* inter-
preter; (*porte-parole*) spokesman.
interpréter [ɛ̃tɛʀpʀete] *vt* to interpret.
interrogateur, trice [ɛ̃tɛʀɔgatœʀ,
-tʀis] *a* questioning, inquiring.
interrogatif, ive [ɛ̃tɛʀɔgatif, -iv] *a*
(*LING*) interrogative.
interrogation [ɛ̃tɛʀɔgasjɔ̃] *nf* question; (*SCOL*) (written *ou* oral) test.
interrogatoire [ɛ̃tɛʀɔgatwaʀ] *nm*
(*POLICE*) questioning *q*; (*JUR*)
cross-examination.
interroger [ɛ̃tɛʀɔʒe] *vt* to question;
(*INFORM*) to consult; (*SCOL*) to test.
interrompre [ɛ̃tɛʀɔ̃pʀ(ə)] *vt* (*gén*)
to interrupt; (*travail, voyage*) to
break off, interrupt; **s'~** to break off.
interrupteur [ɛ̃tɛʀyptœʀ] *nm*
switch.
interruption [ɛ̃tɛʀypsjɔ̃] *nf* interruption; (*pause*) break.
interstice [ɛ̃tɛʀstis] *nm* crack; slit.
interurbain [ɛ̃tɛʀyʀbɛ̃] *nm* (*TÉL*)
long-distance call service // *a* (*TÉL*)
long-distance.
intervalle [ɛ̃tɛʀval] *nm* (*espace*)
space; (*de temps*) interval; **dans l'~**
in the meantime.
intervenir [ɛ̃tɛʀvəniʀ] *vi* (*gén*) to intervene; (*survenir*) to take place; **~
auprès de qn** to intervene with sb.
intervention [ɛ̃tɛʀvɑ̃sjɔ̃] *nf*
(*discours*) paper; **~ chirurgi-
cale** (surgical) operation.
intervertir [ɛ̃tɛʀvɛʀtiʀ] *vt* to invert
(the order of), reverse.
interview [ɛ̃tɛʀvju] *nf* interview.
intestin, e [ɛ̃tɛstɛ̃, -in] *a* internal //
nm intestine.

intime [ɛ̃tim] *a* intimate; (*vie, journal*) private; (*conviction*) inmost; (*dîner, cérémonie*) quiet // *nm/f* close friend.

intimer [ɛ̃time] *vt* (*JUR*) to notify; ~ à qn l'ordre de faire to order sb to do.

intimité [ɛ̃timite] *nf*: dans l'~ in private; (*sans formalités*) with only a few friends, quietly.

intitulé, e [ɛ̃tityle] *a* entitled.

intolérable [ɛ̃tɔleʀabl(ə)] *a* intolerable.

intoxication [ɛ̃tɔksikasjɔ̃] *nf*: ~ alimentaire food poisoning.

intoxiquer [ɛ̃tɔksike] *vt* to poison; (*fig*) to brainwash.

intraduisible [ɛ̃tʀadɥizibl(ə)] *a* untranslatable; (*fig*) inexpressible.

intraitable [ɛ̃tʀɛtabl(ə)] *a* inflexible, uncompromising.

intransigeant, e [ɛ̃tʀɑ̃ziʒɑ̃, -ɑ̃t] *a* intransigent; (*morale*) uncompromising.

intransitif, ive [ɛ̃tʀɑ̃zitif, -iv] *a* (*LING*) intransitive.

intrépide [ɛ̃tʀepid] *a* dauntless.

intrigue [ɛ̃tʀig] *nf* (*scénario*) plot.

intriguer [ɛ̃tʀige] *vi* to scheme // *vt* to puzzle, intrigue.

intrinsèque [ɛ̃tʀɛ̃sɛk] *a* intrinsic.

introduction [ɛ̃tʀɔdyksjɔ̃] *nf* introduction.

introduire [ɛ̃tʀɔdɥiʀ] *vt* to introduce; (*visiteur*) to show in; (*aiguille, clef*): ~ qch dans to insert ou introduce sth into; s'~ dans to gain entry into; to get o.s. accepted into; (*eau, fumée*) to get into.

introuvable [ɛ̃tʀuvabl(ə)] *a* which cannot be found; (*COMM*) unobtainable.

introverti, e [ɛ̃tʀɔvɛʀti] *a* introvert.

intrus, e [ɛ̃tʀy, -yz] *nm/f* intruder.

intrusion [ɛ̃tʀyzjɔ̃] *nf* intrusion; interference.

intuition [ɛ̃tɥisjɔ̃] *nf* intuition.

inusable [inyzabl(ə)] *a* hard-wearing.

inusité, e [inyzite] *a* rarely used.

inutile [inytil] *a* useless; (*superflu*) unnecessary; **inutilisable** *a* unusable.

invalide [ɛ̃valid] *a* disabled // *nm*: ~ de guerre disabled ex-serviceman.

invasion [ɛ̃vɑzjɔ̃] *nf* invasion.

invectiver [ɛ̃vɛktive] *vt* to hurl abuse at.

invendable [ɛ̃vɑ̃dabl(ə)] *a* unsaleable; unmarketable; **invendus** *nmpl* unsold goods.

inventaire [ɛ̃vɑ̃tɛʀ] *nm* inventory; (*COMM*: *liste*) stocklist; (*: opération*) stocktaking *q*; (*fig*) survey.

inventer [ɛ̃vɑ̃te] *vt* to invent; (*subterfuge*) to devise, invent; (*histoire, excuse*) to make up, invent; **inventeur** *nm* inventor; **inventif, ive** *a* inventive; **invention** [-sjɔ̃] *nf* invention.

inverse [ɛ̃vɛʀs(ə)] *a* reverse; opposite; inverse // *nm* inverse, reverse; dans l'ordre ~ in the reverse order; en sens ~ in (*ou* from) the opposite direction; ~**ment** *ad* conversely; **inverser** *vt* to invert, reverse; (*ÉLEC*) to reverse.

investir [ɛ̃vɛstiʀ] *vt* to invest; **investissement** *nm* investment; **investiture** *nf* investiture; (*à une élection*) nomination.

invétéré, e [ɛ̃vetere] *a* (*habitude*) ingrained; (*bavard, buveur*) inveterate.

invisible [ɛ̃vizibl(ə)] *a* invisible.

invitation [ɛ̃vitasjɔ̃] *nf* invitation.

invité, e [ɛ̃vite] *nm/f* guest.

inviter [ɛ̃vite] *vt* to invite; ~ qn à faire (*suj: chose*) to induce *ou* tempt sb to do.

involontaire [ɛ̃vɔlɔ̃tɛʀ] *a* (*mouvement*) involuntary; (*insulte*) unintentional; (*complice*) unwitting.

invoquer [ɛ̃vɔke] *vt* (*Dieu, muse*) to call upon, invoke; (*prétexte*) to put forward (as an excuse); (*loi, texte*) to refer to.

invraisemblable [ɛ̃vʀɛsɑ̃blabl(ə)] *a* unlikely, improbable; incredible.

iode [jɔd] *nm* iodine.

irai *etc vb voir* **aller.**

Irak [iʀak] *nm* Iraq.

Iran [iʀã] *nm* Iran.

irions *etc vb voir* **aller.**

irlandais, e [iʀlɑ̃dɛ, -ɛz] *a* Irish // *nm/f*: I~, e Irishman/woman; **les I~** *the* Irish.

Irlande [iʀlɑ̃d] *nf* Ireland; **~ du Nord** Northern Ireland.

ironie [iʀɔni] *nf* irony; **ironique** *a* ironical; **ironiser** *vi* to be ironical.

irons *etc vb voir* **aller.**

irradier [iʀadje] *vi* to radiate // *vt* (*aliment*) to irradiate.

irraisonné, e [iʀezɔne] *a* irrational, unreasoned.

irrationnel, le [iʀasjɔnɛl] *a* irrational.

irréalisable [iʀealizabl(ə)] *a* unrealizable; impracticable.

irrécupérable [iʀekypeʀabl(ə)] *a* unreclaimable, beyond repair; (*personne*) beyond redemption.

irrécusable [iʀekyzabl(ə)] *a* unimpeachable; incontestable.

irréductible [iʀedyktibl(ə)] *a* indomitable, implacable.

irréel, le [iʀeɛl] *a* unreal.

irréfléchi, e [iʀefleʃi] *a* thoughtless.

irrégularité [iʀegylaʀite] *nf* irregularity; unevenness *q*.

irrégulier, ière [iʀegylje, -jɛʀ] *a* irregular; uneven; (*élève, athlète*) erratic.

irrémédiable [iʀemedjabl(ə)] *a* irreparable.

irremplaçable [iʀɑ̃plasabl(ə)] *a* irreplaceable.

irréprochable [iʀepʀɔʃabl(ə)] *a* irreproachable, beyond reproach; (*tenue*) impeccable.

irrésistible [iʀezistibl(ə)] *a* irresistible; (*preuve, logique*) compelling.

irrespectueux, euse [iʀɛspɛktɥø, -øz] *a* disrespectful.

irriguer [iʀige] *vt* to irrigate.

irritable [iʀitabl(ə)] *a* irritable.

irriter [iʀite] *vt* to irritate.

irruption [iʀypsjɔ̃] *nf* irruption *q*; **faire ~** to burst into.

islamic [islamik] *a* Islamic.

Islande [islɑ̃d] *nf* Iceland.

isolant, e [izɔlɑ̃, -ɑ̃t] *a* insulating; (*insonorisant*) soundproofing.

isolation [izɔlasjɔ̃] *nf* insulation.

isolé, e [izɔle] *a* isolated; insulated.

isoler [izɔle] *vt* to isolate; (*prisonnier*) to put in solitary confinement; (*ville*) to cut off, isolate; (*ÉLEC*) to insulate; **isoloir** *nm* polling booth.

Israël [isʀaɛl] *nm* Israel; **israélien, ne** *a, nm/f* Israeli; **israélite** *a* Jewish // *nm/f* Jew/Jewess.

issu, e [isy] *a:* **~ de** descended from; (*fig*) stemming from // *nf* (*ouverture, sortie*) exit; (*solution*) way out, solution; (*dénouement*) outcome; **à l'~e de** at the conclusion *ou* close of; **rue sans ~e** dead end.

Italie [itali] *nf* Italy; **italien, ne** *a, nm, nf* Italian.

italique [italik] *nm*: **en ~ in** italics.

itinéraire [itineʀɛʀ] *nm* itinerary, route.

IUT *sigle m voir* **institut.**

ivoire [ivwaʀ] *nm* ivory.

ivre [ivʀ(ə)] *a* drunk; **~ de** (*colère, bonheur*) wild with; **ivresse** *nf* drunkenness; **ivrogne** *nm/f* drunkard.

J

jachère [ʒaʃɛʀ] *nf*: (être) **en ~** (to lie) fallow.

jacinthe [ʒasɛ̃t] *nf* hyacinth.

jack [ʒak] *nm* jack plug.

jadis [ʒadis] *ad* in times past, formerly.

jaillir [ʒajiʀ] *vi* (*liquide*) to spurt out; (*fig*) to burst out; to flood out.

jais [ʒɛ] *nm* jet; (**d'un noir) de ~** jet-black.

jalon [ʒalɔ̃] *nm* range pole; (*fig*) milestone; **jalonner** *vt* to mark out; (*fig*) to mark, punctuate.

jalousie [ʒaluzi] *nf* jealousy; (*store*) (venetian) blind.

jaloux, se [ʒalu, -uz] *a* jealous.

jamais [ʒamɛ] *ad* never; (*sans négation*) ever; **ne ... ~** never; **à ~ for**

ever.

jambe [ʒɑ̃b] *nf* leg.

jambon [ʒɑ̃bõ] *nm* ham.

jante [ʒɑ̃t] *nf* (wheel) rim.

janvier [ʒɑ̃vje] *nm* January.

Japon [ʒapõ] *nm* Japan; **japonais,** e *a, nm, nf* Japanese.

japper [ʒape] *vi* to yap, yelp.

jaquette [ʒakɛt] *nf* (de cérémonie) morning coat; (de dame) jacket.

jardin [ʒardɛ̃] *nm* garden; ~ **d'enfants** nursery school; **jardinage** *nm* gardening; **jardinier, ière** *nm/f* gardener // *nf* (de fenêtre) window box.

jarre [ʒar] *nf* (earthenware) jar.

jarret [ʒarɛ] *nm* back of knee, ham; (CULIN) knuckle, shin.

jarretelle [ʒartɛl] *nf* suspender (Brit), garter (US).

jarretière [ʒartjɛr] *nf* garter.

jaser [ʒaze] *vi* to chatter, prattle; (indiscrètement) to gossip.

jatte [ʒat] *nf* basin, bowl.

jauge [ʒoʒ] *nf* (instrument) gauge; **jauger** *vt* (fig) to size up.

jaune [ʒon] *a, nm* yellow // *ad* (fam): **rire** ~ to laugh on the other side of one's face; ~ **d'œuf** (egg) yolk; **jaunir** *vi, vt* to turn yellow.

jaunisse [ʒonis] *nf* jaundice.

Javel [ʒavɛl] *nf* voir **eau.**

javelot [ʒavlo] *nm* javelin.

jazz [dʒaz] *nm* jazz.

J.-C. *sigle voir* **Jésus-Christ.**

je, j' [ʒ(ə)] *pronom* I.

jean [dʒin] *nm* jeans *pl.*

Jésus-Christ [ʒezykri(st)] *n* Jesus Christ; **600 avant/après** ~ *ou* J.-C. 600 B.C./A.D.

jet [ʒɛ] *nm* (lancer) throwing q, throw; (jaillissement) jet; spurt; (de tuyau) nozzle; (avion) [dʒɛt] jet; **du premier** ~ at the first attempt *or* shot; ~ **d'eau** fountain; spray.

jetable [ʒətabl(ə)] *a* disposable.

jetée [ʒəte] *nf* jetty; pier.

jeter [ʒəte] *vt* (gén) to throw; (se défaire de) to throw away *ou* out; (son, lueur etc) to give out; ~ **qch à qn** to throw sth to sb; (de façon agressive)

to throw sth at sb; ~ **un coup d'œil** (à) to take a look (at); ~ **un sort à qn** to cast a spell on sb; **se** ~ **dans** (fleuve) to flow into.

jeton [ʒətõ] *nm* (au jeu) counter; (de téléphone) token.

jette etc *vb voir* **jeter.**

jeu, x [ʒø] *nm* (divertissement, TECH: d'une pièce) play; (TENNIS: partie, FOOTBALL etc: façon de jouer) game; (THÉÂTRE etc) acting; (au casino): **le** ~ gambling; (fonctionnement) working, interplay; (série d'objets, jouet) set; (CARTES) hand; **en** ~ at stake; at work; **remettre en** ~ to throw in; **entrer/mettre en** ~ to come/bring into play; ~ **de cartes** pack of cards; ~ **d'échecs** chess set; ~ **de hasard** game of chance; ~ **de mots** pun.

jeudi [ʒødi] *nm* Thursday.

jeun [ʒœ̃]: **à** ~ *ad* on an empty stomach.

jeune [ʒœn] *a* young; ~ **fille** *nf* girl; ~ **homme** *nm* young man.

jeûne [ʒøn] *nm* fast.

jeunesse [ʒœnɛs] *nf* youth; (aspect) youthfulness; youngness.

joaillerie [ʒɔajri] *nf* jewel trade; jewellery; **joaillier, ière** *nm/f* jeweller.

joie [ʒwa] *nf* joy.

joindre [ʒwɛ̃dr(ə)] *vt* to join; (à une lettre): ~ **qch à** to enclose sth with; (contacter) to contact, get in touch with; ~ **les mains** to put one's hands together; **se** ~ **à** to join.

joint, e [ʒwɛ̃, ʒwɛ̃t] *a*: **pièce** ~**e** enclosure // *nm* joint; (ligne de) join; ~ **de culasse** cylinder head gasket; ~ **de robinet** washer.

joli, e [ʒɔli] *a* pretty, attractive; **c'est du** ~! (ironique) that's very nice!; **c'est bien** ~, **mais...** that's all very well but...

jonc [ʒõ] *nm* (bul)rush.

joncher [ʒõʃe] *vt* (suj: choses) to be strewed on.

jonction [ʒõksjõ] *nf* joining; (point de) ~ junction.

jongleur, euse [ʒɔ̃glœr, -øz] nm/f juggler.

jonquille [ʒɔ̃kij] nf daffodil.

Jordanie [ʒɔʀdani] nf: la ~ Jordan.

joue [ʒu] nf cheek; **mettre en ~ to** take aim at.

jouer [ʒwe] vt to play; (somme d'argent, réputation) to stake, wager; (pièce, rôle) to perform; (film) to show; (simuler: sentiment) to affect, feign // vi to play; (THÉÂTRE, CINÉMA) to act, perform; (bois, parquet: se voiler) to warp; (clef, pièce: avoir du jeu) to be loose; ~ **sur** (miser) to gamble on; ~ **de** (MUS) to play; ~ **des coudes** to use one's elbows; ~ **à** (jeu, sport, roulette) to play; ~ **avec** (risquer) to gamble with; **se ~ de** (difficultés) to make light of; to deceive; ~ **un tour à qn** to play a trick on sb; ~ **serré** to play a close game; ~ **de malchance** to be dogged with ill-luck.

jouet [ʒwɛ] nm toy; **être le ~ de** (illusion etc) to be the victim of.

joueur, euse [ʒwœr, -øz] nm/f player; **être beau ~** to be a good loser.

joufflu, e [ʒufly] a chubby-cheeked.

joug [ʒu] nm yoke.

jouir [ʒwir]: ~ **de** to enjoy; **jouissance** nf pleasure; (JUR) use.

joujou [ʒuʒu] nm (fam) toy.

jour [ʒur] nm day; (opposé à la nuit) day, daytime; (clarté) daylight; (: aspect) light; (ouverture) opening; **au ~ le ~** from day to day; **de nos ~s** these days; **il fait ~** it's daylight; **au grand ~** (fig) in the open; **mettre au ~** to disclose; **mettre à ~** to update; **donner le ~ à** to give birth to; **voir le ~** to be born.

journal, aux [ʒurnal, -o] nm (news)paper; (personnel) journal, diary; **~ parlé/télévisé** radio/ television news sg; **~ de bord** log.

journalier, ière [ʒurnalje, -jɛr] a daily; (banal) everyday.

journalisme [ʒurnalism(ə)] nm journalism; **journaliste** nm/f journalist.

journée [ʒurne] nf day; **la ~ conti-** nue the 9 to 5 working day.

journellement [ʒurnɛlmɑ̃] ad daily.

joyau, x [ʒwajo] nm gem, jewel.

joyeux, euse [ʒwajø, -øz] a joyful, merry; **~ Noël!** merry Christmas!; **~ anniversaire!** happy birthday!

jubiler [ʒybile] vi to be jubilant, exult.

jucher [ʒyʃe] vt, vi to perch.

judas [ʒyda] nm (trou) spy-hole.

judiciaire [ʒydisjɛr] a judicial.

judicieux, euse [ʒydisjø, -øz] a judicious.

judo [ʒydo] nm judo.

juge [ʒyʒ] nm judge; **~ d'instruction** examining (Brit) ou committing (US) magistrate; **~ de paix** justice of the peace.

jugé [ʒyʒe]: **au ~** ad by guesswork.

jugement [ʒyʒmɑ̃] nm judgment; (JUR: au pénal) sentence; (: au civil) decision.

juger [ʒyʒe] vt to judge; **~ qn/qch satisfaisant** to consider sb/sth (to be) satisfactory; **~ bon de faire** to see fit to do; **~ de** to appreciate.

juif, ive [ʒuif, -iv] a Jewish // nm/f Jew/Jewess.

juillet [ʒyijɛ] nm July.

juin [ʒɥɛ̃] nm June.

jumeau, elle, x [ʒymo, -ɛl] a, nm/f twin; **jumelles** nfpl binoculars.

jumeler [ʒymle] vt to twin.

jumelle [ʒymɛl] a, nf voir **jumeau**.

jument [ʒymɑ̃] nf mare.

jungle [ʒɔ̃gl(ə)] nf jungle.

jupe [ʒyp] nf skirt.

jupon [ʒypɔ̃] nm waist slip.

juré, e [ʒyre] nm/f juror.

jurer [ʒyre] vt (obéissance etc) to swear, vow // vi (dire des jurons) to swear, curse; (dissoner): ~ (avec) to clash (with); (s'engager): ~ **de faire/que** to swear to do/that; (affirmer): ~ **que** to swear ou vouch that; ~ **de qch** (s'en porter garant) to swear to sth.

juridique [ʒyridik] a legal.

juron [ʒyrɔ̃] nm curse, swearword.

jury [ʒyri] nm jury; board.

jus [ʒy] nm juice; (de viande) gravy, (meat) juice; ~ **de fruit** fruit juice.

jusque [ʒysk(ə)]: **jusqu'à** prép (endroit) as far as, (up to; (moment) until, till; (limite) up to; ~ **sur/dans** up to; (y compris) even on/in; **jusqu'à ce que** until; **jusqu'à présent** until now.

juste [ʒyst(ə)] a (équitable) just, fair; (légitime) just, justified; (exact, vrai) right; (étroit, insuffisant) tight // ad tight; (chanter) in tune; (seulement) just; ~ **assez/au-dessus** just enough/above; **au** ~ exactly; **le** ~ **milieu** the happy medium; ~**ment** ad rightly; justly; (précisément) just, precisely; **justesse** nf (précision) accuracy; (d'une remarque) aptness; (d'une opinion) soundness; **de justesse** just.

justice [ʒystis] nf (équité) fairness, justice; (ADMIN) justice; **rendre la** ~ **to** dispense justice; **rendre** ~ **à** qn to do sb justice.

justicier, ière [ʒystisje, -jɛʀ] nm/f judge, righter of wrongs.

justifier [ʒystifje] vt to justify; ~ **de** vt to prove.

juteux, euse [ʒytø, -øz] a juicy.

juvénile [ʒyvenil] a young, youthful.

K

K [ka] nm (INFORM) K.

kaki [kaki] a inv khaki.

kangourou [kɑ̃guʀu] nm kangaroo.

karaté [kaʀate] nm karate.

karting [kaʀtiŋ] nm go-carting, karting.

kermesse [kɛʀmɛs] nf bazaar, (charity) fête; village fair.

kidnapper [kidnape] vt to kidnap.

kilogramme [kilɔgʀam] nm, **kilo** nm kilogramme.

kilométrage [kilɔmetʀaʒ] nm number of kilometres travelled; ≈ mileage.

kilomètre [kilɔmɛtʀ(ə)] nm kilometre.

kilométrique [kilɔmetʀik] a (distance) in kilometres.

kinésithérapeute [kineziteʀapøt] nm/f physiotherapist.

kiosque [kjɔsk(ə)] nm kiosk, stall.

klaxon [klaksɔn] nm horn; **klaxonner** vi, vt to hoot (Brit), honk (US).

km. abr de **kilomètre**; ~/h (= kilomètres/heure) ≈ m.p.h. (= miles per hour).

Ko [kao] nm (INFORM: = kilo-octet) K.

K.-O. [kao] a inv (knocked) out.

kyste [kist(ə)] nm cyst.

L

l' [l] dét voir **le**.

la [la] dét voir **le** // nm (MUS) A; (en chantant la gamme) la.

là [la] ad (voir aussi -ci, celui) there; (ici) here; (dans le temps) then; **elle n'est pas** ~ she isn't here; **c'est** ~ **que** this is where; ~ **où** where; **de** ~ **(fig)** hence; **par** ~ **(fig)** by that; **tout est** ~ **(fig)** that's what it's all about; ~**-bas** ad there.

label [label] nm stamp, seal.

labeur [labœʀ] nm toil q, toiling q.

labo [labo] abr m (= laboratoire) lab.

laboratoire [labɔʀatwaʀ] nm laboratory; ~ **de langues** language laboratory.

laborieux, euse [labɔʀjø, -øz] a (tâche) laborious; **classes** ~**euses** working classes.

labour [labuʀ] nm ploughing q; ~**s** nmpl ploughed fields; **cheval de** ~ plough- ou cart-horse; **bœuf de** ~ ox (pl oxen).

labourer [labuʀe] vt to plough; (fig) to make deep gashes ou furrows in.

labyrinthe [labiʀɛ̃t] nm labyrinth, maze.

lac [lak] nm lake.

lacer [lase] vt to lace ou do up.

lacérer [laseʀe] vt to tear to shreds.

lacet [lasɛ] nm (de chaussure) lace;

(de route) sharp bend; (piège) snare.

lâche [lɑʃ] a (poltron) cowardly; (desserré) loose, slack // nm/f coward.

lâcher [lɑʃe] nm (de ballons, oiseaux) release // vt to let go of; (ce qui tombe, abandonner) to drop; (oiseau, animal: libérer) to release, set free; (fig: mot, remarque) to let slip, come out with; (SPORT: distancer) to leave behind // vi (fil, amarres) to break, give way; (freins) to fail; ~ **les amarres** (NAVIG) to cast off (the moorings); ~ **les chiens** to unleash the dogs; ~ **prise** to let go.

lâcheté [lɑʃte] nf cowardice; lowness.

lacrymogène [lakʀimɔʒɛn] a: **gaz ~** teargas.

lacté, e [lakte] a (produit, régime) milk cpd.

lacune [lakyn] nf gap.

là-dedans [ladədɑ̃] ad inside (there), in it; (fig) in that; **là-dessous** ad underneath, under there; (fig) behind that; **là-dessus** ad on there; (fig) at that point; about that.

ladite [ladit] dét voir **ledit**.

lagune [lagyn] nf lagoon.

là-haut [lao] ad up there.

laïc [laik] a, nm/f = **laïque**.

laid, e [lɛ, lɛd] a ugly; **laideur** nf ugliness q.

lainage [lɛnaʒ] nm woollen garment; woollen material.

laine [lɛn] nf wool.

laïque [laik] a lay, civil; (SCOL) state cpd // nm/f layman/woman.

laisse [lɛs] nf (de chien) lead, leash; **tenir en ~** to keep on a lead ou leash.

laisser [lɛse] vt to leave // vb auxiliaire: ~ **qn faire** to let sb do; **se ~ aller** to let o.s. go; **laisse-toi faire** let me (ou him) do it; **~-aller** nm carelessness, slovenliness; **laissez-passer** nm inv pass.

lait [lɛ] nm milk; **frère/sœur de ~** foster brother/sister; ~ **condensé/ concentré** evaporated/condensed

milk; **laiterie** nf dairy; **laitier, ière** a dairy cpd // nm/f milkman/ dairywoman.

laiton [lɛtɔ̃] nm brass.

laitue [lɛty] nf lettuce.

laïus [lajys] nm (péj) spiel.

lambeau, x [lɑ̃bo] nm scrap; **en ~x** in tatters, tattered.

lambris [lɑ̃bʀi] nm panelling q.

lame [lam] nf blade; (vague) wave; (lamelle) strip; ~ **de fond** ground swell q; ~ **de rasoir** razor blade.

lamelle [lamɛl] nf thin strip ou blade.

lamentable [lamɑ̃tabl(ə)] a appalling; pitiful.

lamenter [lamɑ̃te]: **se ~** vi: **se ~ (sur)** to moan (over).

lampadaire [lɑ̃padɛʀ] nm (de salon) standard lamp; (dans la rue) street lamp.

lampe [lɑ̃p(ə)] nf lamp; (TECH) valve; ~ **de poche** torch (Brit), flashlight (US); ~ **à souder** blowlamp.

lampion [lɑ̃pjɔ̃] nm Chinese lantern.

lance [lɑ̃s] nf spear; ~ **d'incendie** fire hose.

lancée [lɑ̃se] nf: **être/continuer sur sa ~** to be under way/keep going.

lancement [lɑ̃smɑ̃] nm launching.

lance-pierres [lɑ̃spjɛʀ] nm inv catapult.

lancer [lɑ̃se] nm (SPORT) throwing q, throw // vt to throw; (émettre, projeter) to throw out, send out; (produit, fusée, bateau, artiste) to launch; (injure) to hurl, fling; (proclamation, mandat d'arrêt) to issue; ~ **qch à qn** to throw sth to sb; (de façon agressive) to throw sth at sb; **se ~ vi** (prendre de l'élan) to build up speed; (se précipiter): **se ~ sur ou contre** to rush at; **se ~ dans** (discussion) to launch into; (aventure) to embark on; ~ **du poids** nm putting the shot.

lancinant, e [lɑ̃sinɑ̃, -ɑ̃t] a (regrets etc) haunting; (douleur) shooting.

landau [lɑ̃do] nm pram (Brit), baby carriage (US).

lande [lɑ̃d] nf moor.

langage [lɑ̃gaʒ] nm language.

langer [lɑ̃ʒe] vt to change (the nappy (Brit) ou diaper (US) of).

langouste [lɑ̃gust(ə)] nf crayfish inv; **langoustine** nf Dublin Bay prawn.

langue [lɑ̃g] nf (ANAT, CULIN) tongue; (LING) language; tirer la ~ (à) to stick out one's tongue (at); de ~ française French-speaking; ~ maternelle native language, mother tongue; ~ verte slang; ~ vivante modern language.

langueur [lɑ̃gœʀ] nf languidness.

languir [lɑ̃giʀ] vi to languish; (conversation) to flag; **faire ~ qn** to keep sb waiting.

lanière [lanjɛʀ] nf (portable) lantern; (électrique) light, lamp; (de valise, bretelle) strap.

lanterne [lɑ̃tɛʀn(ə)] nf (portable) lantern; (électrique) light, lamp; (de voiture) (side)light.

laper [lape] vt to lap up.

lapidaire [lapidɛʀ] a (stone cpd; (fig) terse.

lapin [lapɛ̃] nm rabbit; (peau) rabbit-skin; (fourrure) cony.

Laponie [laponi] nf Lapland.

laps [laps] nm: ~ de temps space of time, time q.

laque [lak] nf lacquer; (brute) shellac; (pour cheveux) hair spray.

laquelle [lakɛl] pronom voir **lequel**.

larcin [laʀsɛ̃] nm theft.

lard [laʀ] nm (graisse) fat; (bacon) (streaky) bacon.

lardon [laʀdɔ̃] nm: ~s chopped bacon.

large [laʀʒ(ə)] a wide; broad; (fig) generous // ad: **calculer/voir ~** to allow extra/think big // nm (largeur): 5 m de ~ 5 m wide ou in width; (mer): le ~ the open sea; au ~ de off; ~ d'esprit broad-minded; ~ment ad widely; greatly; easily; generously; **largesse** nf generosity; largesses liberalities; **largeur** nf (qu'on mesure) width; (impression visuelle) wideness, width; breadth;

broadness.

larguer [laʀge] vt to drop; ~ les amarres to cast off (the moorings).

larme [laʀm(ə)] nf tear; (fig) drop; en ~s in tears; **larmoyer** vi (yeux) to water; (se plaindre) to whimper.

larvé, e [laʀve] a (fig) latent.

laryngite [laʀɛ̃ʒit] nf laryngitis.

las, lasse [lɑ, lɑs] a weary.

laser [lazɛʀ] nm: (rayon) ~ laser (beam); chaîne ~ compact disc (player); disque ~ compact disc.

lasse [lɑs] af voir **las**.

lasser [lɑse] vt to weary, tire; **se ~ de** to grow weary ou tired of.

latéral, e, aux [lateʀal, -o] a side cpd, lateral.

latin, e [latɛ̃, -in] a, nm, nf Latin.

latitude [latityd] nf latitude.

latte [lat] nf lath, slat; (de plancher) board.

lauréat, e [lɔʀea, -at] nm/f winner.

laurier [lɔʀje] nm (BOT) laurel; (CULIN) bay leaves pl; ~s nmpl (fig) laurels.

lavable [lavabl(ə)] a washable.

lavabo [lavabo] nm washbasin; ~s nmpl toilet sg.

lavage [lavaʒ] nm washing q, wash; ~ de cerveau brainwashing q.

lavande [lavɑ̃d] nf lavender.

lave [lav] nf lava q.

lave-glace [lavglas] nm windscreen (Brit) ou windshield (US) washer.

laver [lave] vt to wash; (tache) to wash off; **se** ~ vi to have a wash, wash; **se** ~ **les mains/dents** to wash one's hands/clean one's teeth; ~ **qn de** (accusation) to clear sb of; **laverie** nf: laverie (automatique) launderette.

lavette [lavɛt] nf dish cloth; (fam) drip.

laveur, euse [lavœʀ, -øz] nm/f cleaner.

lave-vaisselle [lavvɛsɛl] nm inv dishwasher.

lavoir [lavwaʀ] nm wash house.

laxatif, ive [laksatif, -iv] a, nm laxative.

MOT-CLÉ

le(l'), la, les [l(ǝ), la, le] ◆ article
défini **1** the; **le livre/la pomme/
l'arbre** the book/the apple/the tree;
les étudiants the students
2 (noms abstraits): **le courage/
l'amour/la jeunesse** courage/love/
youth
3 (indiquant la possession): **se casser la jambe** etc to break one's leg
etc; **levez la main** put your hand
up; **avoir les yeux gris/le nez
rouge** to have grey eyes/a red nose
4 (temps): **le matin/soir** in the
morning/evening; mornings/evenings;
le jeudi etc (d'habitude) on Thurs-
days etc; (ce jeudi-là etc) on (the)
Thursday
5 (distribution, évaluation) a, an; **10
F le mètre/kilo** 10 F a ou per
metre/kilo; **le tiers/quart de** a
third/quarter of
◆ pronom **1** (personne: mâle) him;
(: femelle) her; (: pluriel) them; **je
le/la/ les vois** I can see him/her/
them
2 (animal, chose: sing) it; (: pl)
them; **je le (la) vois** I can see
it; **je les vois** I can see them
3 (remplaçant une phrase): **je ne le
savais pas** I didn't know (about it);
il était riche et ne l'est plus he
was once rich but no longer is.

---

lécher [leʃe] vt to lick; (laper: lait,
eau) to lick ou lap up; ~ **les vitri-
nes** to go window-shopping.
leçon [l(ǝ)sɔ̃] nf lesson; **faire la ~** à
(fig) to give a lecture to; ~**s de
conduite** driving lessons.
lecteur, trice [lektœʀ, -tʀis] nm/f
reader; (d'université) foreign language assistant // nm (TECH): ~ **de
cassettes** cassette player; ~ **de disquette** disk drive.
lecture [lektyʀ] nf reading.
ledit [lǝdi], **ladite** [ladit] , mpl **lesdits** [ledi] , fpl **lesdites** [ledit] dét
the aforesaid.

légal, e, aux [legal, -o] a legal.
légende [leʒɑ̃d] nf (mythe) legend;
(de carte, plan) key; (de dessin) caption.
léger, ère [leʒe, -ɛʀ] a light; (bruit,
retard) slight; (superficiel) thoughtless; (volage) free and easy; flighty;
à la légère ad (parler, agir) rashly,
thoughtlessly; **légèrement** ad lightly;
thoughtlessly; slightly.
législatif, ive [leʒislatif, -iv] a legis-
lative; **législatives** nfpl general
election sg.
législature [leʒislatyʀ] nf legislature; term (of office).
légitime [leʒitim] a (JUR) lawful, legitimate; (fig) rightful, legitimate;
en état de ~ défense in self-
defence.
legs [leg] nm legacy.
léguer [lege] vt: ~ **qch à qn** (JUR)
to bequeath sth to sb; (fig) to hand
sth down ou pass sth on to sb.
légume [legym] nm vegetable.
lendemain [lɑ̃dmɛ̃] nm: **le ~** the
next ou following day; **le ~ matin/
soir** the next ou following morning/
evening; **le ~ de** the day after; **sans
~** short-lived.
lent, e [lɑ̃, lɑ̃t] a slow; **lentement**
ad slowly; **lenteur** nf slowness q.
lentille [lɑ̃tij] nf (OPTIQUE) lens sg;
(CULIN) lentil.
léopard [leɔpaʀ] nm leopard.
lèpre [lɛpʀ(ǝ)] nf leprosy.
lequel, laquelle [lǝkɛl, lakɛl], mpl
lesquels, fpl **lesquelles** [lekɛl]
(avec à, de: **auquel, duquel** etc)
pronom (interrogatif) which, which
one; (relatif: personne: sujet) who;
(: objet, après préposition) whom;
(: chose) which // a: **auquel cas** in
which case.
les [le] dét voir **le**.
lesbienne [lɛsbjɛn] nf lesbian.
lesdits [ledi], **lesdites** [ledit] dét
voir **ledit**.
léser [leze] vt to wrong.
lésiner [lezine] vi: ~ (**sur**) to skimp
(on).

lésion [lezjɔ̃] nf lesion, damage q.

lesquels, lesquelles [lekɛl] pronom voir **lequel**.

lessive [lesiv] nf (poudre) washing powder; (linge) washing q, wash.

lessiver [lesive] vt to wash.

lest [lɛst] nm ballast.

leste [lɛst(ə)] a sprightly, nimble.

lettre [lɛtʀ(ə)] nf letter; ~s nfpl literature sg; (SCOL) arts (subjects); à la ~ literally; en toutes ~s in full.

lettré, e [letʀe] a well-read.

leucémie [løsemi] nf leukaemia.

MOT-CLÉ

leur [lœʀ] ♦ a possessif their; ~ maison their house; ~s amis their friends
♦ pronom 1 (objet indirect) (to) them; je ~ ai dit la vérité I told them the truth; je le ~ ai donné I gave it to them, I gave them it
2 (possessif): le(la) ~, les ~s theirs.

---

leurre [lœʀ] nm (appât) lure; (fig) delusion; snare.

leurrer [lœʀe] vt to delude, deceive.

levain [ləvɛ̃] nm leaven.

levé, e [ləve] a: être ~ to be up.

levée [ləve] nf (POSTES) collection; (CARTES) trick; ~ de boucliers general outcry.

lever [ləve] vt (vitre, bras etc) to raise; (soulever de terre, supprimer: interdiction, siège) to lift; (séance) to close; (impôts, armée) to levy // vi to rise // nm: au ~ on getting up; le ~ du soleil sunrise.

levier [ləvje] nm lever.

lèvre [lɛvʀ(ə)] nf lip.

lévrier [levʀije] nm greyhound.

levure [ləvyʀ] nf yeast; ~ chimique baking powder.

lexique [lɛksik] nm vocabulary; lexicon.

lézard [lezaʀ] nm lizard.

lézarde [lezaʀd(ə)] nf crack.

liaison [ljɛzɔ̃] nf link; (amoureuse) affair; (PHONÉTIQUE) liaison; entrer/être en ~ avec to get/be in contact with.

liane [ljan] nf creeper.

liant, e [ljɑ̃, ɑ̃t] a sociable.

liasse [ljas] nf wad, bundle.

Liban [libɑ̃] nm: le ~ (the) Lebanon; **libanais, e** a, nm/f Lebanese.

libeller [libele] vt (chèque, mandat): ~ (au nom de) to make out (to); (lettre) to word.

libellule [libelyl] nf dragonfly.

libéral, e, aux [liberal, -o] a, nm/f liberal.

libérer [libere] vt (délivrer) to free, liberate; (: moralement, PSYCH) to liberate; (relâcher, dégager: gaz) to release; to discharge; se ~ vi (de rendez-vous) to get out of previous engagements.

liberté [libeʀte] nf freedom; (loisir) free time; ~s nfpl (privautés) liberties; mettre/être en ~ to set/be free; en ~ provisoire/surveillée/ conditionnelle on bail/probation/ parole; ~s individuelles personal freedom sg.

libraire [libʀɛʀ] nm/f bookseller.

librairie [libʀeʀi] nf bookshop.

libre [libʀ(ə)] a free; (route) clear; (place etc) vacant; empty; not engaged; not taken; (SCOL) non-state; de ~ (place) free; to qch/de faire free from sth/to do; ~ arbitre free will; ~-échange nm free trade; ~-service nm self-service store.

Libye [libi] nf: la ~ Libya.

licence [lisɑ̃s] nf (permis) permit; (diplôme) degree; (liberté) liberty; licence (Brit), license (US); licentiousness; **licencié, e** nm/f (SCOL): ~ ès lettres/en droit; ≈ Bachelor of Arts/Law; (SPORT) member of a sports federation.

licencier [lisɑ̃sje] vt (renvoyer) to dismiss; (débaucher) to make redun-

dant; to lay off.
licite [lisit] *a* lawful.
lie [li] *nf* dregs *pl*, sediment.
lié, e [lje] *a*: **très ~ avec** very friendly with *ou* close to; **~ par** (*serment*) bound by.
liège [ljɛʒ] *nm* cork.
lien [ljɛ̃] *nm* (*corde, fig: affectif*) bond; (*rapport*) link, connection; **~ de parenté** family tie.
lier [lje] *vt* (*attacher*) to tie up; (*joindre*) to link up; (*fig: unir, engager*) to bind; (*CULIN*) to thicken; **~ qch à** to tie *ou* link sth to; **~ conversation avec** to strike up a conversation with; **se ~ avec** to make friends with.
lierre [ljɛʀ] *nm* ivy.
liesse [ljɛs] *nf*: **être en ~** to be celebrating *ou* jubilant.
lieu, x [ljø] *nm* place // *nmpl* (*habitation*) premises; (*endroit: d'un accident etc*) scene *sg*; **en ~ sûr** in a safe place; **en premier/dernier ~** in the first place/lastly; **avoir ~** to take place; **avoir ~ de faire** to have grounds for doing; **tenir ~ de** to take the place of; to serve as; **donner ~ à** to give rise to; **au ~ de** instead of.
lieu-dit *nm* (*pl* lieux-dits) [ljødi] locality.
lieutenant [ljøtnɑ̃] *nm* lieutenant.
lièvre [ljɛvʀ(ə)] *nm* hare.
ligament [ligamɑ̃] *nm* ligament.
ligne [liɲ] *nf* (*gén*) line; (*TRANSPORTS*: liaison) service; (: *trajet*) route; (*silhouette*) figure; **entrer en ~ de compte** to come into it.
lignée [liɲe] *nf* line; lineage; descendants *pl*.
ligoter [ligɔte] *vt* to tie up.
ligue [lig] *nf* league; **se liguer contre** (*fig*) to combine against.
lilas [lila] *nm* lilac.
limace [limas] *nf* slug.
limaille [limɑj] *nf*: **~ de fer** iron filings *pl*.
limande [limɑ̃d] *nf* dab.

lime [lim] *nf* file; **~ à ongles** nail file; **limer** *vt* to file.
limier [limje] *nm* bloodhound; (*détective*) sleuth.
limitation [limitasjɔ̃] *nf*: **~ de vitesse** speed limit.
limite [limit] *nf* (*de terrain*) boundary; (*partie ou point extrême*) limit; **vitesse/charge ~** maximum speed/load; **cas ~** borderline case; **date ~** deadline.
limiter [limite] *vt* (*restreindre*) to limit, restrict; (*délimiter*) to border.
limitrophe [limitʀɔf] *a* border *cpd*.
limoger [limɔʒe] *vt* to dismiss.
limon [limɔ̃] *nm* silt.
limonade [limɔnad] *nf* lemonade.
lin [lɛ̃] *nm* flax.
linceul [lɛ̃sœl] *nm* shroud.
linge [lɛ̃ʒ] *nm* (*serviettes etc*) linen; (*pièce de tissu*) cloth; (*aussi: ~ de corps*) underwear; (*aussi: ~ de toilette*) towel; (*lessive*) washing.
lingerie [lɛ̃ʒʀi] *nf* lingerie, underwear.
lingot [lɛ̃go] *nm* ingot.
linguistique [lɛ̃gɥistik] *a* linguistic // *nf* linguistics *sg*.
lion, ne [ljɔ̃, ljɔn] *nm/f* lion/lioness; (*signe*): **le L~** Leo; **lionceau, x** [ljɔ̃so] *nm* lion cub.
liqueur [likœʀ] *nf* liqueur.
liquide [likid] *a* liquid // *nm* liquid; (*COMM*): **en ~** in ready money *ou* cash.
liquider [likide] *vt* (*société, biens, témoin gênant*) to liquidate; (*compte, problème*) to settle; (*COMM*: *articles*) to clear, sell off.
liquidités [likidite] *nfpl* (*COMM*) liquid assets.
lire [liʀ] *nf* (*monnaie*) lira // *vt, vi* to read.
lis *nm* [lis] = **lys**.
lisible [lizibl(ə)] *a* legible.
lisière [lizjɛʀ] *nf* (*de forêt*) edge; (*de tissu*) selvage.
lisons *vb voir* **lire**.
lisse [lis] *a* smooth.

liste [list(ə)] nf list; **faire la ~** de to list; **~ électorale** electoral roll.

listing [listiŋ] nm (INFORM) printout.

lit [li] nm (gén) bed; **faire son ~** to make one's bed; **aller/se mettre au ~** to go to/get into bed; **~ de camp** campbed; **~ d'enfant** cot (Brit), crib (US).

literie [litʀi] nf bedding, bedclothes pl.

litière [litjɛʀ] nf litter.

litige [litiʒ] nm dispute.

litre [litʀ(ə)] nm litre; (récipient) litre measure.

littéraire [liteʀɛʀ] a literary.

littéral, e, aux [liteʀal, -o] a literal.

littérature [liteʀatyʀ] nf literature.

littoral, aux [litoʀal, -o] nm coast.

liturgie [lityʀʒi] nf liturgy.

livide [livid] a livid, pallid.

livraison [livʀɛzɔ̃] nf delivery.

livre [livʀ(ə)] nm book // nf (poids, monnaie) pound; **~ de bord** logbook; **~ de poche** paperback (pocket size).

livré, e [livʀe] a: **~ à soi-même** left to o.s. ou one's own devices // nf livery.

livrer [livʀe] vt (COMM) to deliver; (otage, coupable) to hand over; (secret, information) to give away; se **~ à** (se confier) to confide in; (se rendre, s'abandonner) to give o.s. up to; (faire: pratiques, actes) to indulge in; (travail) to engage in; (: sport) to practise; (: enquête) to carry out.

livret [livʀe] nm booklet; (d'opéra) libretto (pl s); **~ de caisse d'épargne** (savings) bank-book; **~ de famille** (official) family record book; **~ scolaire** (school) report book.

livreur, euse [livʀœʀ, -øz] nm/f delivery boy ou man/girl ou woman.

local, e, aux [lokal, -o] a local // nm (salle) premises pl // nmpl premises.

localiser [lokalize] vt (repérer) to locate, place; (limiter) to confine.

localité [lokalite] nf locality.

locataire [lokatɛʀ] nm/f tenant; (de

chambre) lodger.

location [lokasjɔ̃] nf (par le locataire, le loueur) renting; (par le propriétaire) renting out, letting; (THÉÂTRE) booking office; **'~ de voitures'** 'car rental'.

locomotive [lokomotiv] nf locomotive, engine; (fig) pacesetter, pacemaker.

locution [lokysjɔ̃] nf phrase.

loge [lɔʒ] nf (THÉÂTRE: d'artiste) dressing room; (: de spectateurs) box; (de concierge, franc-maçon) lodge.

logement [lɔʒmɑ̃] nm accommodation q; flat (Brit), apartment (US); housing q.

loger [lɔʒe] vt to accommodate // vi to live; **trouver à se ~** to find accommodation; se **~ dans** (suj: balle, flèche) to lodge itself in; **logeur, euse** nm/f landlord/landlady.

logiciel [lɔʒisjɛl] nm software.

logique [lɔʒik] a logical // nf logic.

logis [lɔʒi] nm home; abode, dwelling.

loi [lwa] nf law; **faire la ~** to lay down the law.

loin [lwɛ̃] ad far; (dans le temps) a long way off; a long time ago; **plus ~** further; **~ de** far from; **au ~** far off; **de ~** ad from a distance; (fig: de beaucoup) by far; **il vient de ~** (fig) he's come a long way.

lointain, e [lwɛ̃tɛ̃, -ɛn] a faraway, distant; (dans le futur, passé) distant, far-off; (cause, parent) remote, distant // nm: **dans le ~** in the distance.

loir [lwaʀ] nm dormouse (pl -mice).

loisir [lwaziʀ] nm: **heures de ~** spare time; **~s** nmpl leisure sg; leisure activities; **avoir le ~ de faire** to have the time ou opportunity to do; **à ~** at leisure; at one's pleasure.

londonien, ne [lɔ̃dɔnjɛ̃, -jɛn] a London cpd, of London // nm/f: **L~,** ne Londoner.

Londres [lɔ̃dʀ(ə)] n London.

long, longue [lɔ̃, lɔ̃g] a long // ad:

en savoir ~ to know a great deal // nm: de 3 m de ~ 3 m long, 3 m in length // nf: à la longue in the long run; ne pas faire ~ feu not to last long; (tout) le ~ de (all) along; tout au ~ de (année, vie) throughout; de ~ en large (marcher) to and fro, up and down.

longer [lɔ̃ʒe] vt to go (ou walk ou drive) along(side); (suj: mur, route) to border.

longiligne [lɔ̃ʒiliɲ] a long-limbed.

longitude [lɔ̃ʒityd] nf longitude.

longitudinal, e, aux [lɔ̃ʒitydinal, -o] a (running) lengthways.

longtemps [lɔ̃tɑ̃] ad (for) a long time, (for) long; avant ~ before long; pour/pendant ~ for a long time; mettre ~ à faire to take a long time to do.

longue [lɔ̃g] af voir long; ~ment ad for a long time.

longueur [lɔ̃gœr] nf length; ~s nfpl (fig: d'un film etc) tedious parts; en ~ ad lengthwise; tirer en ~ to drag on; à ~ de journée all day long; ~ d'onde wavelength.

longue-vue [lɔ̃gvy] nf telescope.

lopin [lɔpɛ̃] nm: ~ de terre patch of land.

loque [lɔk] nf (personne) wreck; ~s nfpl (habits) rags.

loquet [lɔkɛ] nm latch.

lorgner [lɔrɲe] vt to eye; (fig) to have one's eye on.

lors [lɔr]: ~ de prép at the time of; during; ~ même que even though.

lorsque [lɔrsk(ə)] cj when, as.

losange [lɔzɑ̃ʒ] nm diamond; (GÉOM) lozenge.

lot [lo] nm (part) share; (de loterie) prize; (fig: destin) fate, lot; (COMM, INFORM) batch.

loterie [lɔtri] nf lottery; raffle.

loti, e [lɔti] a: bien/mal ~ well-/ badly off.

lotion [losjɔ̃] nf lotion.

lotir [lɔtir] vt (terrain) to divide into plots; to sell by lots; **lotissement** nm housing development; plot, lot.

loto [lɔto] nm lotto; numerical lottery.

louable [lwabl(ə)] a commendable.

louanges [lwɑ̃ʒ] nfpl praise sg.

loubard [lubar] nm (fam) lout.

louche [luʃ] a shady, fishy, dubious // nf ladle.

loucher [luʃe] vi to squint.

louer [lwe] vt (maison: suj: propriétaire) to let, rent (out); (: locataire) to rent; (voiture etc) to hire out (Brit), rent (out); to hire, rent; (réserver) to book; (faire l'éloge de) to praise; 'à louer' 'to let' (Brit), 'for rent' (US).

loup [lu] nm wolf (pl wolves).

loupe [lup] nf magnifying glass.

louper [lupe] vt (manquer) to miss.

lourd, e [lur, lurd(ə)] a, ad heavy; ~ de (conséquences, menaces) charged with; **lourdaud, e** a (péj) clumsy.

loutre [lutr(ə)] nf otter.

louve [luv] nf she-wolf.

louveteau, x [luvto] nm wolf-cub; (scout) cub (scout).

louvoyer [luvwaje] vi (NAVIG) to tack; (fig) to hedge, evade the issue.

lover [love]: se ~ vi to coil up.

loyal, e, aux [lwajal, -o] a (fidèle) loyal, faithful; (fair-play) fair; **loyauté** nf loyalty, faithfulness; fairness.

loyer [lwaje] nm rent.

lu, e [ly] pp de lire.

lubie [lybi] nf whim, craze.

lubrifiant [lybrifjɑ̃] nm lubricant.

lubrifier [lybrifje] vt to lubricate.

lubrique [lybrik] a lecherous.

lucarne [lykarn(ə)] nf skylight.

lucratif, ive [lykratif, -iv] a lucrative; profitable; à but non ~ non profit-making.

lueur [lɥœr] nf (chatoyante) glimmer q; (métallique, mouillée) gleam q; (rougeoyante, chaude) glow q; (pâle) (faint) light; (fig) glimmer; gleam.

luge [lyʒ] nf sledge (Brit), sled (US).

lugubre [lygybr(ə)] a gloomy; dismal.

MOT-CLÉ

---

lui [lɥi] *pronom* **1** (*objet indirect: mâle*) (to) him; (: *femelle*) (to) her; (: *chose, animal*) (to) it; **je** ~ **ai parlé** I have spoken to him (ou to her); **il** ~ **a offert un cadeau** he gave him (ou her) a present **2** (*après préposition, comparatif: personne*) him; (: *chose, animal*) it; **elle est contente de** ~ she is pleased with him; **je la connais mieux que** ~ I know her better than he does; I know him better than him **3** (*sujet, forme emphatique*) he; ~, **il est à Paris** HE is in Paris **4**: ~-**même** himself; itself.

luire [lɥir] *vi* to shine; to glow.

lumière [lymjɛr] *nf* light; ~**s** *nfpl* (*d'une personne*) wisdom *sg*; **mettre en** ~ (*fig*) to highlight; ~ **du jour/soleil** day/sunlight.

luminaire [lyminɛr] *nm* lamp, light.

lumineux, euse [lyminø, -øz] *a* (*émettant de la lumière*) luminous; (*éclairé*) illuminated; (*ciel, couleur*) bright; (*relatif à la lumière: rayon etc*) of light, light *cpd*; (*fig: regard*) radiant.

lunaire [lynɛr] *a* lunar, moon *cpd*.

lunatique [lynatik] *a* whimsical, temperamental.

lundi [lœdi] *nm* Monday; ~ **de Pâques** Easter Monday.

lune [lyn] *nf* moon; ~ **de miel** honeymoon.

lunette [lynɛt] *nf*: ~**s** *nfpl* glasses, spectacles, (*protectrices*) goggles; ~ **arrière** (*AUTO*) rear window; ~**s noires** dark glasses; ~**s de soleil** sunglasses.

lus *etc vb voir* **lire**.

lustre [lystr(ə)] *nm* (*de plafond*) chandelier; (*fig: éclat*) lustre.

lustrer [lystre] *vt* to shine.

lut *vb voir* **lire**.

luth [lyt] *nm* lute.

lutin [lytɛ̃] *nm* imp, goblin.

lutte [lyt] *nf* (*conflit*) struggle;

(*sport*) wrestling; **lutter** *vi* to fight, struggle.

luxe [lyks(ə)] *nm* luxury; **de** ~ a luxury *cpd*.

Luxembourg [lyksɑ̃bur] *nm*: **le** ~ Luxembourg.

luxer [lykse] *vt*: **se** ~ **l'épaule** to dislocate one's shoulder.

luxueux, euse [lyksɥø, -øz] *a* luxurious.

luxure [lyksyr] *nf* lust.

lycée [lise] *nm* secondary school; **lycéen, ne** *nm/f* secondary school pupil.

lyrique [lirik] *a* lyrical; (*OPÉRA*) lyric; **artiste** ~ opera singer.

lys [lis] *nm* lily.

M

M *abr de* **Monsieur**.

m' [m] *pronom voir* **me**.

ma [ma] *dét voir* **mon**.

macaron [makarɔ̃] *nm* (*gâteau*) macaroon; (*insigne*) (round) badge.

macaronis [makarɔni] *nmpl* macaroni *sg*.

macédoine [masedwan] *nf*: ~ **de fruits** fruit salad.

macérer [masere] *vi, vt* to macerate; (*dans du vinaigre*) to pickle.

mâcher [mɑʃe] *vt* to chew; **ne pas** ~ **ses mots** not to mince one's words.

machin [maʃɛ̃] *nm* (*fam*) thing(umajig).

machinal, e, aux [maʃinal, -o] *a* mechanical, automatic.

machination [maʃinasjɔ̃] *nf* scheming, frame-up.

machine [maʃin] *nf* machine; (*locomotive*) engine; (*fig: rouages*) machinery; ~ **à laver/coudre** washing/sewing machine; ~ **à écrire** typewriter; ~ **à sous** fruit machine; ~ **à vapeur** steam engine; ~**rie** *nf* machinery, plant; (*d'un navire*) engine room; **machinisme** *nm* mechanization; **machiniste** *nm* sbus, *métro*) driver.

mâchoire [mɑʃwaʀ] *nf* jaw; ~ **de frein** brake shoe.

mâchonner [mɑʃɔne] *vt* to chew (at).

maçon [masɔ̃] *nm* bricklayer; builder.

maçonnerie [masɔnʀi] *nf* (*murs*) brickwork; masonry, stonework; (*activité*) bricklaying; building.

maculer [makyle] *vt* to stain.

Madame [madam], *pl* **Mesdames** [medam], *nf*: ~ **X** Mrs X ['mɪsɪz]; **occupez-vous de ~/Monsieur/ Mademoiselle** please serve this lady/gentleman/(young) lady; **bonjour ~/Monsieur/Mademoiselle** good morning; (*ton déférent*) good morning Madam/Sir/Madam; (*le nom est connu*) good morning Mrs/Mr/ Miss X; **~/Monsieur/ Mademoiselle!** (*pour appeler*) Madam/Sir/Miss!; **~/Monsieur/ Mademoiselle** (*sur lettre*) Dear Madam/Sir/Madam; **chère ~/cher Monsieur/chère Mademoiselle** Dear Mrs/Mr/Miss X; **Mesdames** Ladies.

Mademoiselle [madmwazɛl], *pl* **Mesdemoiselles** [medmwazɛl] *nf* Miss; *voir aussi* **Madame**.

madère [madɛʀ] *nm* Madeira (wine).

magasin [magazɛ̃] *nm* (*boutique*) shop; (*entrepôt*) warehouse; (*d'une arme*) magazine; **en ~** (*COMM*) in stock.

magazine [magazin] *nm* magazine.

magicien, ne [maʒisjɛ̃, -jɛn] *nm/f* magician.

magie [maʒi] *nf* magic; **magique** *a* magic; (*enchanteur*) magical.

magistral, e, aux [maʒistral, -o] *a* (*œuvre, adresse*) masterly; (*ton*) authoritative; (*ex cathedra*) enseignement ~ lecturing, lectures *pl*.

magistrat [maʒistra] *nm* magistrate.

magnétique [maɲetik] *a* magnetic.

magnétiser [maɲetize] *vt* to magnetize; (*fig*) to mesmerize, hypnotize.

magnétophone [maɲetɔfɔn] *nm*

tape recorder; ~ **à cassettes** cassette recorder.

magnétoscope [maɲetɔskɔp] *nm* video-tape recorder.

magnifique [maɲifik] *a* magnificent.

magot [mago] *nm* (*argent*) pile (of money); nest egg.

magouille [maguj] *nf* scheming.

mai [mɛ] *nm* May.

maigre [mɛgʀ(ə)] *a* (very) thin, skinny; (*viande*) lean; (*fromage*) lowfat; (*végétation*) thin, sparse; (*fig*) poor, meagre, skimpy // *ad*: **faire ~** not to eat meat; **jours ~s** days of abstinence, fish days; **maigreur** *nf* thinness; **maigrir** *vi* to get thinner, lose weight.

maille [maj] *nf* stitch; ~ **à l'endroit/à l'envers** plain/purl stitch; **avoir ~ à partir avec qn** to have a brush with sb.

maillet [majɛ] *nm* mallet.

maillon [majɔ̃] *nm* link.

maillot [majo] *nm* (*aussi*: ~ **de corps**) vest; (*de danseur*) leotard; (*de sportif*) jersey; ~ **de bain** swimsuit; (*d'homme*) bathing trunks *pl*.

main [mɛ̃] *nf* hand; **à la ~** in one's hand; **se donner la ~** to hold hands; **donner ou tendre la ~ à qn** to hold out one's hand to sb; **se serrer la ~** to shake hands; **serrer la ~ à qn** to shake hands with sb; **sous la ~** to ou at hand; **attaque à ~ armée** armed attack; **à ~ droite/gauche** to the right/left; **à ~s remettre en ~s propres** to be delivered personally; **de première ~** (*COMM: voiture etc*) second-hand with only one previous owner; **mettre la dernière ~ à** to put the finishing touches to; **se faire/perdre la ~** to get one's hand in/lose one's touch; **avoir qch bien en ~** to have (got) the hang of sth.

main-d'œuvre [mɛ̃dœvʀ(ə)] *nf* manpower, labour.

main-forte [mɛ̃fɔʀt(ə)] *nf*: **prêter ~ à qn** to come to sb's assistance.

mainmise [mɛ̃miz] *nf* seizure; (*fig*): ~ **sur** complete hold on.

maint, e [mɛ̃, mɛ̃t] a many a; ~s many; à ~es reprises time and (time) again.

maintenant [mɛ̃tnɑ̃] ad now; (actuellement) nowadays.

maintenir [mɛ̃tniʀ] vt (retenir, soutenir) to support; (contenir: foule etc) to hold back; (conserver, affirmer) to maintain; se ~ vi to hold; to keep steady; to persist.

maintien [mɛ̃tjɛ̃] nm maintaining; (attitude) bearing.

maire [mɛʀ] nm mayor.

mairie [meʀi] nf (bâtiment) town hall; (administration) town council.

mais [me] cj but; ~ non! of course not!; ~ enfin but after all; (indignation) look here!; ~ encore? is that all?

mais [mais] nm maize (Brit), corn (US).

maison [mɛzɔ̃] nf house; (chez-soi) home; (COMM) firm // a inv (CULIN) home-made; made by the chef; (fig) in-house, own; à la ~ at home; (direction) home; ~ close ou de passe brothel; ~ de correction reformatory; ~ des jeunes ≈ youth club; ~ mère parent company; ~ de repos convalescent home; ~ de santé mental home; **maisonnée** nf household, family; **maisonnette** nf small house, cottage.

maître, esse [mɛtʀ(ə), mɛtʀɛs] nm/f master/mistress; (SCOL) teacher, schoolmaster/mistress // nm (peintre etc) master; (titre): M~ (Me) Maître, term of address gen for a barrister // nf (amante) mistress // a (principal, essentiel) main; être ~ de (soi-même, situation) to be in control of; une maîtresse femme a managing woman; ~ chanteur blackmailer; ~maîtresse d'école schoolmaster/mistress; ~ d'hôtel (domestique) butler; (d'hôtel) head waiter; ~ de maison host; ~ nageur lifeguard; maîtresse de maison hostess; housewife (pl wives).

maîtrise [mɛtʀiz] nf (aussi: ~ de

soi) self-control, self-possession; (habileté) skill, mastery; (suprématie) mastery, command; (diplôme) ≈ master's degree.

maîtriser [mɛtʀize] vt (cheval, incendie) to (bring under) control; (sujet) to master; (émotion) to control, master; se ~ to control o.s.

majestueux, euse [maʒɛstɥø, -øz] a majestic.

majeur, e [maʒœʀ] a (important) major; (JUR) of age; (fig) adult // nm (doigt) middle finger; en ~e partie for the most part.

majorer [maʒɔʀe] vt to increase.

majoritaire [maʒɔʀitɛʀ] a majority cpd.

majorité [maʒɔʀite] nf (gén) majority; (parti) party in power; en ~ mainly.

majuscule [maʒyskyl] a, nf: (lettre) ~ capital (letter).

mal, maux [mal, mo] nm (opposé au bien) evil; (tort, dommage) harm; (douleur physique) pain, ache; (maladie) illness, sickness a // ad badly // a (mauvais) bad, wrong; être ~ to be uncomfortable; être ~ avec qn to be on bad terms with sb; être au plus ~ (malade) to be at death's door; (brouillé) to be at daggers drawn; il a ~ compris he misunderstood; dire/penser du ~ de to speak/think ill of; ne voir aucun ~ à to see no harm in, see nothing wrong in; craignant ~ faire fearing he was doing the wrong thing; faire du ~ à qn to hurt sb; to harm sb; se faire ~ to hurt o.s.; se donner du ~ pour faire qch to go to a lot of trouble to do sth; ça fait ~ it hurts; j'ai ~ au dos my back hurts; avoir ~ à la tête/à la gorge/aux dents to have a headache/a sore throat/toothache; avoir le ~ du pays to be homesick; prendre ~ to be taken ill, feel unwell; ~ de mer seasickness; ~ en point a inv in a bad state; maux de ventre stomach ache sg; voir **coeur.**

malade [malad] *a* ill, sick; (*poitrine, jambe*) bad; (*plante*) diseased // *nm/f* invalid, sick person; (*à l'hôpital etc*) patient; **tomber ~** to fall ill; **être ~ du cœur** to have heart trouble *ou* a bad heart; **~ mental** mentally sick *ou* ill person.

maladie [maladi] *nf* (*spécifique*) disease, illness; (*mauvaise santé*) illness, sickness; **maladif, ive** *a* sickly; (*curiosité, besoin*) pathological.

maladresse [maladʀɛs] *nf* clumsiness *q*; (*gaffe*) blunder.

maladroit, e [maladʀwa, -wat] *a* clumsy.

malaise [malɛz] *nm* (*MÉD*) feeling of faintness; feeling of discomfort; (*fig*) uneasiness, malaise.

malaisé, e [malɛze] *a* difficult.

malappris, e [malapʀi, -iz] *nm/f* ill-mannered *ou* boorish person.

malaria [malaʀja] *nf* malaria.

malaxer [malakse] *vt* to knead; to mix.

malchance [malʃɑ̃s] *nf* misfortune, ill luck *q*; **par ~** unfortunately.

mâle [mal] *a* (*aussi ÉLEC, TECH*) male; (*viril: voix, traits*) manly // *nm* male.

malédiction [malediksjɔ̃] *nf* curse.

malencontreux, euse [malɑ̃kɔ̃tʀø, -øz] *a* unfortunate, untoward.

malentendu [malɑ̃tɑ̃dy] *nm* misunderstanding.

malfaçon [malfasɔ̃] *nf* fault.

malfaisant, e [malfəzɑ̃, -ɑ̃t] *a* evil, harmful.

malfaiteur [malfɛtœʀ] *nm* lawbreaker, criminal; burglar, thief (*pl* thieves).

malgache [malgaʃ] *a, nm/f* Madagascan, Malagasy // *nm* (*langue*) Malagasy.

malgré [malgʀe] *prép* in spite of, despite; **~ tout** all the same.

malheur [malœʀ] *nm* (*situation*) adversity, misfortune; (*événement*) misfortune; disaster, tragedy; **faire un ~** to be a smash hit; **malheu-**

reusement *ad* unfortunately; **malheureux, euse** *a* (*triste*) unhappy, miserable; (*infortuné, regrettable*) unfortunate; (*malchanceux*) unlucky; (*insignifiant*) wretched // *nm/f* poor soul; unfortunate creature; **les malheureux** the destitute.

malhonnête [malɔnɛt] *a* dishonest.

malice [malis] *nf* mischievousness; (*méchanceté*): **par ~** out of malice *ou* spite; **sans ~** guileless; **malicieux, euse** *a* mischievous.

malin, igne [malɛ̃, -iɲ] *a* (*futé: f gén:* **maline**) smart, shrewd; (*MÉD*) malignant.

malingre [malɛ̃gʀ] *a* puny.

malle [mal] *nf* trunk.

mallette [malɛt] *nf* (small) suitcase; overnight case; attaché case.

malmener [malməne] *vt* to manhandle; (*fig*) to give a rough handling to.

malodorant, e [malɔdɔʀɑ̃, -ɑ̃t] *a* foul- *ou* ill-smelling.

malotru [malɔtʀy] *nm* lout, boor.

malpropre [malpʀɔpʀ(ə)] *a* dirty.

malsain, e [malsɛ̃, -ɛn] *a* unhealthy.

malt [malt] *nm* malt.

Malte [malt(ə)] *nf* Malta.

maltraiter [maltʀɛte] *vt* (*brutaliser*) to manhandle, ill-treat.

malveillance [malvɛjɑ̃s] *nf* (*animosité*) ill will; (*intention de nuire*) malevolence; (*JUR*) malicious intent *q*.

malversation [malvɛʀsasjɔ̃] *nf* embezzlement.

maman [mamɑ̃] *nf* mum(my), mother.

mamelle [mamɛl] *nf* teat.

mamelon [mamlɔ̃] *nm* (*ANAT*) nipple; (*colline*) knoll, hillock.

mamie [mami] *nf* (*fam*) granny.

mammifère [mamifɛʀ] *nm* mammal.

manche [mɑ̃ʃ] *nf* (*de vêtement*) sleeve; (*d'un jeu, tournoi*) round; (*GÉO*): **la M~** the Channel // *nm* (*d'outil, casserole*) handle; (*de pelle, pioche etc*) shaft; **~ à balai** *nm* broomstick; (*AVIAT*, *INFORM*) joystick.

manchette [mɑ̃ʃɛt] *nf* (*de chemise*) cuff; (*coup*) forearm blow; (*titre*) headline.

manchon [mɑ̃ʃɔ̃] *nm* (*de fourrure*) muff.

manchot [mɑ̃ʃo] *nm* one-armed man; armless man; (*ZOOL*) penguin.

mandarine [mɑ̃daʀin] *nf* mandarin (orange), tangerine.

mandat [mɑ̃da] *nm* (*postal ou money order*); (*d'un député etc*) mandate; (*procuration*) power of attorney, proxy; (*POLICE*) warrant; ~ **d'amener** summons *sg*; ~ **d'arrêt** warrant for arrest; **mandataire** *nm/f* representative; proxy.

mander [mɑ̃de] *vt* to summon.

manège [manɛʒ] *nm* riding school; (*à la foire*) roundabout, merry-go-round; (*fig*) game, ploy.

manette [manɛt] *nf* lever, tap; ~ **de jeu** joystick.

mangeable [mɑ̃ʒabl(ə)] *a* edible, eatable.

mangeoire [mɑ̃ʒwaʀ] *nf* trough, manger.

manger [mɑ̃ʒe] *vt* to eat; (*ronger: suj: rouille etc*) to eat into *ou* away // *vi* to eat.

mangue [mɑ̃g] *nf* mango.

maniable [manjabl(ə)] *a* (*outil*) handy; (*voiture, voilier*) easy to handle.

maniaque [manjak] *a* finicky, fussy; suffering from a mania // *nm/f* maniac.

manie [mani] *nf* mania; (*tic*) odd habit.

manier [manje] *vt* to handle.

manière [manjɛʀ] *nf* (*façon*) way, manner; ~s *nfpl* (*attitude*) manners; (*chichis*) fuss *sg*; **de** ~ **à** so as to; **de telle** ~ **que** in such a way that; **de cette** ~ in this way *ou* manner; **d'une certaine** ~ in a way; **d'une** ~ **générale** generally speaking, as a general rule; **de toute** ~ in any

case.

maniéré, e [manjeʀe] *a* affected.

manifestant, e [manifɛstɑ̃, -ɑ̃t] *nm/f* demonstrator.

manifestation [manifɛstasjɔ̃] *nf* (*de joie, mécontentement*) expression, demonstration; (*symptôme*) outward sign; (*fête etc*) event; (*POL*) demonstration.

manifeste [manifɛst(ə)] *a* obvious, evident // *nm* manifesto (*pl* s).

manifester [manifɛste] *vt* (*volonté, intentions*) to show, indicate; (*joie, peur*) to express, show // *vi* to demonstrate; se ~ *vi* (*émotion*) to show *ou* express itself; (*difficultés*) to arise; (*symptômes*) to appear; (*témoin etc*) to come forward.

manigance [manigɑ̃s] *nf* scheme.

manipuler [manipyle] *vt* to handle; (*fig*) to manipulate.

manivelle [manivɛl] *nf* crank.

mannequin [mankɛ̃] *nm* (*COUTURE*) dummy; (*MODE*) model.

manœuvre [manœvʀ(ə)] *nf* (*gén*) manœuvre (*Brit*), maneuver (*US*) // *nm* labourer.

manœuvrer [manœvʀe] *vt* to manœuvre (*Brit*), maneuver (*US*); (*levier, machine*) to operate // *vi* to manœuvre.

manoir [manwaʀ] *nm* manor *ou* country house.

manque [mɑ̃k] *nm* (*insuffisance*): ~ **de** lack of; (*vide*) emptiness, gap; (*MÉD*) withdrawal; ~s *nmpl* (*lacunes*) faults, defects.

manqué, e [mɑ̃ke] *a* failed; **garçon** ~ tomboy.

manquer [mɑ̃ke] *vi* (*faire défaut*) to be lacking; (*être absent*) to be missing; (*échouer*) to fail // *vt* to miss // *vb impersonnel*: **il (nous) manque encore 100 F** we are still 100 F short; **il manque des pages (au livre)** there are some pages missing *ou* some pages are missing (from the book); **il/cela me manque** I miss him/this; ~ **à** *vt* (*règles etc*) to be in breach of, fail to observe; ~ **de** *vt* to lack; **il a manqué (de) se tuer** he very nearly got killed.

mansarde [mãsaʀd(ə)] *nf* attic.

mansuétude [mãsɥetyd] *nf* leniency.

manteau, x [mãto] *nm* coat; ~ **de cheminée** mantelpiece.

manucure [manykyʀ] *nf* manicurist.

manuel, le [manɥɛl] *a* manual // *nm* (*ouvrage*) manual, handbook.

manufacture [manyfaktyʀ] *nf* factory.

manufacturé, e [manyfaktyʀe] *a* manufactured.

manuscrit, e [manyskʀi, -it] *a* handwritten // *nm* manuscript.

manutention [manytãsjɔ̃] *nf* (*COMM*) handling; (*local*) storehouse.

mappemonde [mapmɔ̃d] *nf* (*plane*) map of the world; (*sphère*) globe.

maquereau, x [makʀo] *nm* (*ZOOL*) mackerel *inv*; (*fam*) pimp.

maquette [makɛt] *nf* (*d'un décor, bâtiment, véhicule*) (scale) model; (*d'une page illustrée*) paste-up.

maquillage [makijaʒ] *nm* making up; faking; (*crème etc*) make-up.

maquiller [makije] *vt* (*personne, visage*) to make up; (*truquer: passeport, statistique*) to fake; (: *voiture volée*) to do over (*respray etc*); **se** ~ *vi* to make up (o.'s face).

maquis [maki] *nm* (*GÉO*) scrub; (*MIL*) maquis, underground fighting q.

maraîcher, ère [maʀeʃe, maʀeʃɛʀ] *a*: **cultures maraîchères** market gardening *sg* // *nm/f* market gardener.

marais [maʀɛ] *nm* marsh, swamp.

marasme [maʀasm(ə)] *nm* stagnation, slump.

marathon [maʀatɔ̃] *nm* marathon.

marâtre [maʀɑtʀ(ə)] *nf* cruel mother.

maraudeur [maʀodœʀ] *nm* prowler.

marbre [maʀbʀ(ə)] *nm* (*pierre, statue*) marble; (*d'une table, commode*)

marble top; **marbrer** *vt* to mottle, blotch.

marc [maʀ] *nm* (*de raisin, pommes*) marc; ~ **de café** coffee grounds *pl* ou dregs *pl*.

marchand, e [maʀʃɑ̃, -ɑ̃d] *nm/f* shopkeeper, tradesman/woman; (*au marché*) stallholder // *a*: **prix/valeur** ~(**e**) market price/value; ~ **de charbon/vins** coal/wine merchant; ~/**e de couleurs** ironmonger (*Brit*), hardware dealer (*US*); ~/**e de fruits** fruiterer (*Brit*), fruit seller (*US*); ~/**e de journaux** newsagent; ~/**e de légumes** greengrocer (*Brit*), produce dealer (*US*); ~/**e de quatre saisons** costermonger (*Brit*), street vendor (selling fresh fruit and vegetables); ~/**e de tableaux** art dealer.

marchander [maʀʃɑ̃de] *vi* to bargain, haggle.

marchandise [maʀʃɑ̃diz] *nf* goods *pl*, merchandise *q*.

marche [maʀʃ(ə)] *nf* (*d'escalier*) step; (*activité*) walking; (*promenade, trajet, allure*) walk; (*démarche*) walk, gait; (*MIL etc, MUS*) march; (*fonctionnement*) running; (*progression*) progress; course; **ouvrir/fermer la** ~ to lead the way/bring up the rear; **dans le sens de la** ~ (*RAIL*) facing the engine; **en** ~ (*monter etc*) while the vehicle is moving ou in motion; **mettre en** ~ to start; **se mettre en** ~ (*personne*) to get moving; (*machine*) to start; ~ **arrière** reverse (gear); **faire** ~ **arrière** to reverse; (*fig*) to backtrack, back-pedal; ~ **à suivre** (correct) procedure; (*sur notice*) (step by step) instructions *pl*.

marché [maʀʃe] *nm* (*lieu, COMM, ÉCON*) market; (*ville*) trading centre; (*transaction*) bargain, deal; **M~ commun** Common Market; **faire du** ~ **noir** to buy and sell on the black market; ~ **aux puces** flea market.

marchepied [maʀʃəpje] *nm* (*RAIL*)

step; (fig) stepping stone.

marcher [marʃe] vi to walk; (MIL) to march; (aller: voiture, train, affaires) to go; (prospérer) to go well; (fonctionner) to work, run; (fam) to go along, agree; to be taken in; ~ **sur** to walk on; (mettre le pied sur) to step on ou in; (MIL) to march upon; ~ **dans** (herbe etc) to walk in ou on; (flaque) to step in; **faire** ~ **qn** to pull sb's leg; to lead sb up the garden path; **marcheur, euse** nm/f walker.

mardi [mardi] nm Tuesday; M~ **gras** Shrove Tuesday.

mare [mar] nf pond; ~ **de sang** pool of blood.

marécage [mareka3] nm marsh, swamp.

maréchal, aux [mareʃal, -o] nm marshal.

marée [mare] nf tide; (poissons) fresh (sea) fish; ~ **haute/basse** high/low tide; ~ **montante/descendante** rising/ebb tide.

marémotrice [maremotris] af tidal.

margarine [margarin] nf margarine.

marge [mar3(ə)] nf margin; **en** ~ **de** (fig) on the fringe of; cut off from; ~ **bénéficiaire** profit margin.

marguerite [margərit] nf marguerite, (oxeye) daisy; (d'imprimante) daisy-wheel.

mari [mari] nm husband.

mariage [marja3] nm (union, état, fig) marriage; (noce) wedding; ~ **civil/religieux** registry office (Brit) ou civil/church wedding.

marié, e [marje] a married // nm (bride)groom/bride; **les** ~**s** the bride and groom; **les (jeunes)** ~**s** the newly-weds.

marier [marje] vt to marry; (fig) to blend; **se** ~ **(avec)** to marry.

marin, e [marɛ̃, -in] a sea cpd, marine // nm sailor // nf navy; ~**e de guerre** navy; ~**e marchande** merchant navy.

marine [marin] af, nf voir **marin** // a inv navy (blue) // nm (MIL) marine.

marionnette [marjɔnɛt] nf puppet.

maritime [maritim] a sea cpd, maritime.

mark [mark] nm mark.

marmelade [marməlad] nf stewed fruit, compote; ~ **d'oranges** marmalade.

marmite [marmit] nf (cooking-)pot.

marmonner [marmɔne] vt, vi to mumble, mutter.

marmotte [marmɔt] nf marmot.

marmotter [marmɔte] vt to mumble.

Maroc [marɔk] nm: **le** ~ Morocco. **marocain, e** a, nm/f Moroccan.

maroquinerie [marɔkinri] nf leather craft; fine leather goods pl.

marquant, e [markɑ̃, -ɑ̃t] a outstanding.

marque [mark(ə)] nf mark; (SPORT, JEU: décompte des points) score; (COMM: de produits) brand; make; (: de disques) label; **de** ~ a (COMM) brand-name cpd; proprietary; (fig) high-class; distinguished; ~ **déposée** registered trademark; ~ **de fabrique** trademark.

marquer [marke] vt to mark; (inscrire) to write down; (bétail) to brand; (SPORT: but etc) to score; (: joueur) to mark; (accentuer: taille etc) to emphasize; (manifester: refus, intérêt) to show // vi (événement, personnalité) to stand out, be outstanding; (SPORT) to score; ~ **les points** (tenir la marque) to keep the score.

marqueterie [markɛtri] nf inlaid work, marquetry.

marquis [marki] nm marquis ou marquess/marchioness // nf (auvent) glass canopy ou awning.

marraine [marɛn] nf godmother.

marrant, e [marɑ̃, -ɑ̃t] a (fam) funny.

marre [mar] ad (fam): **en avoir** ~ **de** to be fed up with.

marrer [mare]: **se** ~ vi (fam) to have a (good) laugh.

marron [marɔ̃] nm (fruit) chestnut // a inv brown; **marronnier** nm chestnut (tree).

mars [mars] *nm* March.

marsouin [marswɛ̃] *nm* porpoise.

marteau, x [marto] *nm* hammer; *(de porte)* knocker; **~-piqueur** *nm* pneumatic drill.

marteler [martəle] *vt* to hammer.

martien, ne [marsjɛ̃, -jɛn] *a* Martian, *of ou* from Mars.

martinet [martinɛ] *nm (fouet)* small whip; *(ZOOL)* swift.

martyr, e [martir] *nm/f* martyr.

martyre [martir] *nm* martyrdom; *(fig: sens affaibli)* agony, torture.

martyriser [martirize] *vt (REL)* to martyr; *(fig)* to bully; *(enfant)* to batter, beat.

marxiste [marksist(ə)] *a, nm/f* Marxist.

masculin, e [maskylɛ̃, -in] *a* masculine; *(sexe, population)* male; *(équipe, vêtements)* men's; *(viril)* manly // *nm* masculine.

masque [mask(ə)] *nm* mask.

masquer [maske] *vt (cacher: paysage, porte)* to hide, conceal; *(dissimuler: vérité, projet)* to mask, obscure.

massacre [masakʀ(ə)] *nm* massacre, slaughter.

massacrer [masakʀe] *vt* to massacre, slaughter; *(fig: texte etc)* to murder.

massage [masaʒ] *nm* massage.

masse [mas] *nf* mass; **la ~** the masses *pl*; *(ÉLEC)* earth; *(maillet)* sledgehammer; **une ~ de** *(fam)* masses *ou* loads of; **en ~** *ad (en bloc)* in bulk; *(en foule)* en masse // *a (exécutions, production)* mass *cpd*.

masser [mase] *vt (assembler)* to gather; *(pétrir)* to massage; **se ~** *vi* to gather; **masseur, euse** *nm/f* masseur/masseuse.

massif, ive [masif, -iv] *a (porte)* solid, massive; *(visage)* heavy, large; *(bois, or)* solid; *(dose)* massive; *(déportations etc)* mass *cpd* // *nm (montagneux)* massif; *(de fleurs)* clump, bank.

massue [masy] *nf* club, bludgeon.

mastic [mastik] *nm (pour vitres)* putty; *(pour fentes)* filler.

mastiquer [mastike] *vt (aliment)* to chew, masticate; *(fente)* to fill; *(vitre)* to putty.

mat, e [mat] *a (couleur, métal* mat(t); *(bruit, son)* dull // *a inv (ÉCHECS)*: **être ~** to be checkmate.

mât [mɑ] *nm (NAVIG)* mast; *(poteau)* pole, post.

match [matʃ] *nm* match; **faire ~ nul** to draw; **~ aller** first leg; **~ retour** second leg, return match.

matelas [matla] *nm* mattress; **~ pneumatique** air bed *ou* mattress.

matelassé, e [matlase] *a* padded, quilted.

matelot [matlo] *nm* sailor, seaman.

mater [mate] *vt (personne)* to bring to heel, subdue; *(révolte)* to put down.

matérialiste [materjalist(ə)] *a* materialistic.

matériaux [materjo] *nmpl* material(s).

matériel, le [materjɛl] *a* material // *nm* equipment *q*; *(de camping etc)* gear *q*; **~ d'exploitation** *(COMM)* plant.

maternel, le [matɛrnɛl] *a (amour, geste)* motherly, maternal; *(grand-père, oncle)* maternal // *nf (aussi: école ~le)* (state) nursery school.

maternité [matɛrnite] *nf (établissement)* maternity hospital; *(état de mère)* motherhood, maternity; *(grossesse)* pregnancy.

mathématique [matematik] *a* mathematical; **~s** *nfpl (science)* mathematics *sg*.

matière [matjɛr] *nf (PHYSIQUE)* matter; *(COMM, TECH)* material, matter *q*; *(fig: d'un livre etc)* subject matter, material; *(SCOL)* subject; **en ~ de** as regards; **~s grasses** fat content *sg*; **~s premières** raw materials.

matin [matɛ̃] *nm, ad* morning; **du ~ au soir** from morning till night; **de**

bon *ou* **grand ~** early in the morning; **matinal, e, aux** *a* (*toilette, gymnastique*) morning cpd; (*de bonne heure*) early; **être matinal** (*personne*) to be up early; to be an early riser.

matinée [matine] *nf* morning; (*spectacle*) matinée.

matou [matu] *nm* tom(cat).

matraque [matʀak] *nf* club; (*de policier*) truncheon (*Brit*), billy (*US*).

matricule [matʀikyl] *nf* (*aussi:* registre ~) roll, register // *nm* (*aussi:* numéro ~: MIL) regimental number; (: ADMIN) reference number.

matrimonial, e, aux [matʀimɔnjal, -o] *a* marital, marriage cpd.

maudire [modiʀ] *vt* to curse.

maudit, e [modi, -it] *a* (*fam: satané*) blasted, confounded.

maugréer [mogʀee] *vi* to grumble.

maussade [mosad] *a* sullen.

mauvais, e [mɔvɛ, -ɛz] *a* bad; (*faux*): **le ~ numéro/moment** the wrong number/moment; (*méchant, malveillant*) malicious, spiteful // *ad*: **il fait ~** the weather is bad; **la mer est ~e** the sea is rough; **~ plaisant** hoaxer; **~e herbe** weed; **~e langue** gossip, scandalmonger (*Brit*); **~ passe** difficult situation; bad patch; **~e tête** rebellious *ou* headstrong customer.

maux [mo] *nmpl voir* **mal**.

maximum [maksimɔm] *a, nm* maximum; **au ~** *ad* (*le plus possible*) to the full; as much as one can; (*tout au plus*) at the (very) most *ou* maximum.

mayonnaise [majɔnɛz] *nf* mayonnaise.

mazout [mazut] *nm* (fuel) oil.

Me *abr de* **Maître**.

me, m' [m(ə)] *pronom* me; (*réfléchi*) myself.

mec [mɛk] *nm* (*fam*) bloke, guy.

mécanicien, ne [mekanisjɛ̃, -jɛn] *nm/f* mechanic; (RAIL) (train *ou* engine) driver.

mécanique [mekanik] *a* mechanical

// *nf* (*science*) mechanics sg; (*technologie*) mechanical engineering; (*mécanisme*) mechanism; (*engineering*): **works** pl; **ennui ~** engine trouble q.

mécanisme [mekanism(ə)] *nm* mechanism.

méchamment [meʃamɑ̃] *ad* nastily, maliciously, spitefully.

méchanceté [meʃɑ̃ste] *nf* nastiness, maliciousness; nasty *ou* spiteful *ou* malicious remark (*ou* action).

méchant, e [meʃɑ̃, -ɑ̃t] *a* nasty, malicious, spiteful; (*enfant: pas sage*) naughty; (*animal*) vicious; (*avant le nom: valeur péjorative*) nasty; miserable; (: *intensive*) terrific.

mèche [meʃ] *nf* (*de lampe, bougie*) wick; (*d'un explosif*) fuse; (*de vilebrequin, perceuse*) bit; (*de cheveux*) lock; **de ~ avec** in league with.

mécompte [mekɔ̃t] *nm* miscalculation; (*déception*) disappointment.

méconnaissable [mekɔnɛsabl(ə)] *a* unrecognizable.

méconnaître [mekɔnɛtʀ(ə)] *vt* (*ignorer*) to be unaware of; (*mésestimer*) to misjudge.

mécontent, e [mekɔ̃tɑ̃, -ɑ̃t] *a*: **~** (**de**) discontented *ou* dissatisfied *ou* displeased (with); (*contrarié*) annoyed (at); **mécontentement** *nm* dissatisfaction, discontent, displeasure; annoyance.

médaille [medaj] *nf* medal.

médaillon [medajɔ̃] *nm* (*portrait*) medallion; (*bijou*) locket.

médecin [medsɛ̃] *nm* doctor; **~ légiste** forensic surgeon.

médecine [medsin] *nf* medicine; **~ légale** forensic medicine.

média [medja] *nmpl*: **les ~** the media.

médiatique [medjatik] *a* media cpd.

médical, e, aux [medikal, -o] *a* medical.

médicament [medikamɑ̃] *nm* medicine, drug.

médiéval, e, aux [medjeval, -o] *a* medieval.

médiocre [medjɔkʀ(ə)] *a* mediocre, poor.

médire [mediʀ] *vi*: ~ **de** to speak ill of; **médisance** *nf* scandalmongering (*Brit*); piece of scandal *ou*: of malicious gossip.

méditer [medite] *vt* (*approfondir*) to meditate on, ponder (over); (*combiner*) to meditate *// vi* to meditate.

Méditerranée [mediteʀane] *nf*: **la (mer)** ~ the Mediterranean (Sea); **méditerranéen, ne** *a*, *nm/f* Mediterranean.

méduse [medyz] *nf* jellyfish.

meeting [mitiŋ] *nm* (*POL, SPORT*) rally.

méfait [mefɛ] *nm* (*faute*) misdemeanour, wrongdoing; ~**s** *nmpl* (*ravages*) ravages, damage *sg*.

méfiance [mefjɑ̃s] *nf* mistrust, distrust.

méfiant, e [mefjɑ̃, -ɑ̃t] *a* mistrustful, distrustful.

méfier [mefje]: **se** ~ *vi* to be wary; to be careful; **se** ~ **de** to mistrust, distrust, be wary of; (*faire attention*) to be careful about.

mégarde [megaʀd(ə)] *nf*: **par** ~ accidentally; by mistake.

mégère [meʒɛʀ] *nf* shrew.

mégot [mego] *nm* cigarette end.

meilleur, e [mejœʀ] *a, ad* better; (*valeur superlative*) best *// nm*: **le** ~ (*celui qui* ...) the best (one); (*ce qui* ...) the best *// nf*: **la** ~**e** the best (one); **le** ~ **des deux** the better of the two; **de** ~**e heure** earlier; ~ **marché** cheaper.

mélancolie [melɑ̃kɔli] *nf* melancholy, gloom; **mélancolique** *a* melancholic, melancholy.

mélange [melɑ̃ʒ] *nm* mixture.

mélanger [melɑ̃ʒe] *vt* (*substances*) to mix; (*vins, couleurs*) to blend; (*mettre en désordre*) to mix up, muddle (up).

mélasse [melas] *nf* treacle, molasses *sg*.

mêlée [mele] *nf* mêlée, scramble; (*RUGBY*) scrum(mage).

mêler [mele] *vt* (*substances, odeurs, races*) to mix; (*embrouiller*) to muddle (up), mix up; **se** ~ *vi* to mix; to mingle; **se** ~ **à** (*suj: personne*) to join; to mix with; (: *odeurs etc*) to mingle with; **se** ~ **de** (*suj: personne*) to meddle with, interfere in; ~ **qn à** (*affaire*) to get sb mixed up *ou* involved in.

mélodie [melɔdi] *nf* melody.

melon [məlɔ̃] *nm* (*BOT*) (honeydew) melon; (*aussi*: **chapeau** ~) bowler (hat).

membre [mɑ̃bʀ(ə)] *nm* (*ANAT*) limb; (*personne, pays, élément*) member *// a* member.

mémé [meme] *nf* (*fam*) granny.

MOT-CLÉ

---

même [mɛm] ♦ **a 1** (*avant le nom*) same; **en** ~ **temps** at the same time **2** (*après le nom: renforcement*): **il est la loyauté** ~ he is loyalty itself; **ce sont ses paroles/celles-là** ~ they are his very words/the very ones
♦ *pronom*: **le(la)** ~ the same one
♦ *ad* **1** (*renforcement*): **il n'a** ~ **pas pleuré** he didn't even cry; ~ **lui l'a dit** even HE said it; **ici** ~ at this very place
2: **à** ~: **à la bouteille** straight from the bottle; **à** ~ **la peau** next to the skin; **être à** ~ **de faire** to be in a position to do, be able to do
3: **de** ~: **faire de** ~ to do likewise; **lui de** ~ so does (*ou* did *ou*) he; **de** ~ **que** just as; **il en va de** ~ **pour** the same goes for.

---

mémento [memɛ̃to] *nm* (*agenda*) appointments diary; (*ouvrage*) summary.

mémoire [memwaʀ] *nf* memory *// nm* (*ADMIN, JUR*) memorandum (*pl* a); (*SCOL*) dissertation, paper; ~**s** *nmpl* memoirs; **à la** ~ **de** to the *ou* in memory of; **pour** ~ *ad* for the record; **de** ~ *ad* from memory; ~ **morte/vive** (*INFORM*) ROM/RAM.

menace [mənas] *nf* threat.

menacer [mənase] *vt* to threaten.

ménage [menaʒ] *nm* (*travail*) housekeeping, housework; (*couple*) (*married*) couple; (*famille*, *ADMIN*) household; **faire le ~ de** to do the housework.

ménagement [menaʒmɑ̃] *nm* care and attention; **~s** *nmpl* (*égards*) consideration *sg*, attention *sg*.

ménager [menaʒe] *vt* (*traiter*) to handle with tact; to treat considerately; (*utiliser*) to use sparingly; to use with care; (*prendre soin de*) to take (great) care of, look after; (*organiser*) to arrange; (*installer*) to put in; to make; **~ qch à qn** (*réserver*) to have sth in store for sb.

ménager, ère [menaʒe, -ɛʀ] *a* (*travail*) household *cpd*, domestic // *nf* housewife (*pl* wives).

mendiant, e [mɑ̃djɑ̃, -ɑ̃t] *nm/f* beggar.

mendier [mɑ̃dje] *vi* to beg // *vt* to beg (for).

menées [məne] *nfpl* intrigues.

mener [məne] *vt* to lead; (*enquête*) to conduct; (*affaires*) to manage // *vi*: **~ (à la marque)** to lead, be in the lead; **~ à/dans** (*emmener*) to take to/into; **~ qch à terme** *ou* **à bien** to see sth through (to a successful conclusion), complete sth successfully.

meneur, euse [mənœʀ, -øz] *nm/f* leader; (*péj*) agitator; **~ de jeu** host, quizmaster.

méningite [menɛ̃ʒit] *nf* meningitis *q*.

ménopause [menopoz] *nf* menopause.

menottes [mənɔt] *nfpl* handcuffs.

mensonge [mɑ̃sɔ̃ʒ] *nm* lie; lying *q*; **mensonger, ère** *a* false.

mensualité [mɑ̃sɥalite] *nf* monthly payment; monthly salary.

mensuel, le [mɑ̃sɥel] *a* monthly.

mensurations [mɑ̃syʀasjɔ̃] *nfpl* measurements.

mentalité [mɑ̃talite] *nf* mentality.

menteur, euse [mɑ̃tœʀ, -øz] *nm/f* liar.

menthe [mɑ̃t] *nf* mint.

mention [mɑ̃sjɔ̃] *nf* (*note*) note, comment; (*SCOL*): **~ bien** *etc* ≈ grade B *etc* (*ou* upper 2nd class *etc*) pass (*Brit*), ≈ pass with (high) honors (*US*); **mentionner** *vt* to mention.

mentir [mɑ̃tiʀ] *vi* to lie; to be lying.

menton [mɑ̃tɔ̃] *nm* chin.

menu, e [məny] *a* slim, slight; tiny; (*frais, difficulté*) minor // *ad* (*couper, hacher*) very fine // *nm* menu; **par le ~** (*raconter*) in minute detail; **~e monnaie** small change.

menuiserie [mənɥizʀi] *nf* (*travail*) joinery, carpentry; woodwork; (*local*) joiner's workshop; (*ouvrage*) woodwork *q*.

menuisier [mənɥizje] *nm* joiner, carpenter.

méprendre [mepʀɑ̃dʀ(ə)]: **se ~** *vi*: **se ~ sur** to be mistaken (about).

mépris [mepʀi] *nm* (*dédain*) contempt, scorn; (*indifférence*): **le ~ de** contempt *ou* disregard for; **au ~ de** regardless of, in defiance of.

méprisable [mepʀizabl(ə)] *a* contemptible, despicable.

méprise [mepʀiz] *nf* mistake, error; misunderstanding.

mépriser [mepʀize] *vt* to scorn, despise; (*gloire, danger*) to scorn, spurn.

mer [mɛʀ] *nf* sea; (*marée*) tide; **en ~** at sea; **prendre la ~** to put out to sea; **en haute** *ou* **pleine ~** off shore, on the open sea; **la ~ du Nord/ Rouge** the North/Red Sea.

mercantile [mɛʀkɑ̃til] *a* (*péj*) mercenary.

mercenaire [mɛʀsənɛʀ] *nm* mercenary, hired soldier.

mercerie [mɛʀsəʀi] *nf* haberdashery (*Brit*), notions (*US*); haberdasher's shop (*Brit*), notions store (*US*).

merci [mɛʀsi] *excl* thank you // *nf*: **à la ~ de qn/qch** at sb's mercy/the mercy of sth; **~ de** thank you for; **sans ~** merciless(ly).

mercredi [mɛʀkʀədi] *nm* Wednesday.

mercure [mɛRkyR] nm mercury.

merde [mɛRd(ə)] (fam!) nf shit (!) // excl (bloody) hell (!).

mère [mɛR] nf mother; ~ **célibataire** unmarried mother.

méridional, e, aux [meRidjɔnal, -o] a southern // nm/f Southerner.

meringue [məʀɛ̃g] nf meringue.

mérite [meRit] nm merit; le ~ (de ceci) **lui revient** the credit (for this) is his.

mériter [meRite] vt to deserve.

merlan [mɛRlɑ̃] nm whiting.

merle [mɛRl(ə)] nm blackbird.

merveille [mɛRvɛj] nf marvel, wonder; **faire** ~ to work wonders; **à** ~ perfectly, wonderfully.

merveilleux, euse [mɛRvɛjø, -øz] a marvellous, wonderful.

mes [me] dét voir **mon**.

mésange [mezɑ̃ʒ] nf tit(mouse) (pl mice).

mésaventure [mezavɑ̃tyR] nf misadventure, misfortune.

Mesdames voir **Madame**.

Mesdemoiselles voir **Mademoiselle**.

mésentente [mezɑ̃tɑ̃t] nf dissension, disagreement.

mesquin, e [mɛskɛ̃, -in] a mean, petty.

message [mesaʒ] nm message; **messager, ère** [-e, -ɛR] nm/f messenger.

messe [mɛs] nf mass; **aller à la** ~ to go to mass; ~ **de minuit** midnight mass.

Messieurs [mesjø] nmpl voir **Monsieur**.

mesure [məzyR] nf (évaluation, dimension) measurement; (étalon, récipient, contenu) measure; (MUS: cadence) time, tempo; (: division) bar; (retenue) moderation; (disposition) measure, step; **sur** ~ (costume) made-to-measure; **à la** ~ **de** (fig) worthy of; on the same scale as; **dans la** ~ **où** insofar as, inasmuch as; **à** ~ **que** as; **être en** ~ **de** to be in a position to.

mesurer [məzyRe] vt to measure;

(juger) to weigh up, assess; (limiter) to limit, ration; (modérer) to moderate; **se** ~ **avec** to have a confrontation with; to tackle; **il mesure 1 m 80** he's 1 m 80 tall.

met vb voir **mettre**.

métal, aux [metal, -o] nm `metal; ~**lique** a metallic.

météo [meteo] nf weather report; ≈ Met Office (Brit), ≈ National Weather Service (US).

météorologie [meteɔRɔlɔʒi] nf meteorology.

méthode [metɔd] nf method; (livre, ouvrage) manual, tutor.

métier [metje] nm (profession: gén) job; (: manuel) trade; (: artisanal) craft; (technique, expérience) (acquired) skill ou technique; (aussi: ~ **à tisser**) (weaving) loom.

métis, se [metis] a, nm/f half-caste, half-breed.

métisser [metise] vt to cross.

métrage [metRaʒ] nm (de tissu) length, ≈ yardage; (CINÉMA) footage, length; **long/moyen/court** ~ full-length/medium-length/short film.

mètre [mɛtR(ə)] nm metre; (règle) (metre) rule; (ruban) tape measure; **métrique** a metric.

métro [metRo] nm underground (Brit), subway.

métropole [metRɔpɔl] nf (capitale) metropolis; (pays) home country.

mets [mɛ] nm dish.

metteur [metœR] nm: ~ **en scène** (THÉÂTRE) producer; (CINÉMA) director; ~ **en ondes** producer.

MOT-CLÉ

mettre [mɛtR(ə)] vt **1** (placer) to put; ~ **en bouteille/en sac** to bottle/put in bags ou sacks

2 (vêtements: revêtir) to put on; (: porter) to wear; **mets ton gilet** put your cardigan on; **je ne mets plus mon manteau** I no longer wear my coat

3 (faire fonctionner: chauffage, électricité) to put on; (: reveil, mi-

nuteur) to set; (*installer: gaz, eau*) to put in, lay on; ~ **en marche** to start up

4 (*consacrer*): ~ **du temps à faire qch** to take time to do sth *ou* over sth

5 (*noter, écrire*) to say, put (down); **qu'est-ce qu'il a mis sur la carte?** what did he say *ou* write on the card?; **mettez au pluriel** ... **put** ... into the plural

6 (*supposer*): **mettons que** ... let's suppose ...

7: **y** ~ **du sien** to pull one's weight **se mettre** *vi* **1** (*se placer*): **vous pouvez vous** ~ **là** you can sit (*ou* stand) there; **où ça se met?** where does it go?; **se** ~ **au lit** to get into bed; **se** ~ **au piano** to sit down at the piano; **se** ~ **de l'encre sur les doigts** to get ink on one's fingers **2** (*s'habiller*): **se** ~ **en maillot de bain** to get into *ou* put on a swimsuit; **n'avoir rien à se** ~ to have nothing to wear

3: **se** ~ **à** to begin, start; **se** ~ **à faire** to begin *ou* start doing *ou* to do; **se** ~ **au piano** to start learning the piano; **se** ~ **au travail/à l'étude** to get down to work/one's studies

meuble [mœbl(ə)] *nm* piece of furniture; **furniture** *q* // *a* (*terre*) loose, friable; **meublé** *nm* furnished flatlet (*Brit*) *ou* room; **meubler** *vt* to furnish; (*fig*): **meubler qch (de)** to fill sth (with).

meugler [møgle] *vi* to low, moo.

meule [møl] *nf* (*à broyer*) millstone; (*à aiguiser*) grindstone; (*de foin, blé*) stack; (*de fromage*) round.

meunier, ière [mønje, -jɛʀ] *nm* miller // *nf* miller's wife.

meure *etc vb voir* **mourir**.

meurtre [mœʀtʀ(ə)] *nm* murder; **meurtrier, ière** [-ije] *a* (*arme etc*) deadly; (*fureur, instincts*) murderous // *nm/f* murderer/eress // *nf* (*ouverture*) loophole.

meurtrir [mœʀtʀiʀ] *vt* to bruise;

(*fig*) to wound; **meurtrissure** *nf* bruise; (*fig*) scar.

meus *etc vb voir* **mouvoir**.

meute [møt] *nf* pack.

Mexico [mɛksiko] *n* Mexico City.

Mexique [mɛksik] *nm:* **le** ~ Mexico.

MF *sigle f voir* **modulation**.

Mgr *abr de* **Monseigneur**.

mi [mi] *nm* (*MUS*) E; (*en chantant la gamme*) mi.

mi... [mi] *préfixe* half(-); mid-; **à la** ~**-janvier** in mid-January; **à** ~**-jambes/** -**corps** (up *ou* down) to the knees/waist; **à** ~**-hauteur/-pente** halfway up *ou* down/up *ou* down the hill.

miauler [mjole] *vi* to mew.

miche [miʃ] *nf* round *ou* cob loaf.

mi-chemin [miʃmɛ̃]: **à** ~ *ad* halfway, midway.

mi-clos, e [miklo, -kloz] *a* half-closed.

micro [mikʀo] *nm* mike, microphone; (*INFORM*) micro.

microbe [mikʀɔb] *nm* germ, microbe.

micro-onde [mikʀɔɔ̃d] *nf:* **four à** ~**s** microwave oven.

micro-ordinateur [mikʀɔɔʀdinatœʀ] *nm* microcomputer.

microscope [mikʀɔskɔp] *nm* microscope.

midi [midi] *nm* midday, noon; (*moment du déjeuner*) lunchtime; **à** ~ at 12 (o'clock) *ou* midday *ou* noon; (*sud*) south; **en plein** ~ (right) in the middle of the day; **facing south;** **le M~** the South (of France), the Midi.

mie [mi] *nf* crumb (of the loaf).

miel [mjɛl] *nm* honey.

mien, ne [mjɛ̃, mjɛn] *pronom:* **le** (*la*) ~(**ne**), **les** ~**s** mine; **les** ~**s** my family.

miette [mjɛt] *nf* (*du pain, gâteau*) crumb; (*fig: de la conversation etc*) scrap; **en** ~**s** (*fig*) in pieces *ou* bits.

MOT-CLÉ

---

mieux [mjø] ◆ *ad* **1** (*d'une meil-*

leure façon): ~ **(que)** better (than);
elle travaille/mange ~ she works/
eats better; **elle va** ~ she is better
2 *(de la meilleure façon)* best; **ce
que je sais le** ~ what I know best;
les livres les ~ **faits** the best made
books
3: de ~ **en** ~ better and better
◆ **a 1** *(plus à l'aise, en meilleure
forme)* better; **se sentir** ~ to feel
better
2 *(plus satisfaisant)* better; **c'est** ~
ainsi it's better like this; **c'est le** ~
des deux it's the better of the two;
le (la) ~, **les** ~ the best;
demandez-lui, c'est le ~ ask him,
it's the best thing
3 *(plus joli)* better-looking
4: au ~ at best; **au** ~ on the
best of terms with; **pour le** ~ for the
best
◆ *nm* **1** *(progrès)* improvement
2: de mon/ton ~ as best I/you can
(ou could); **faire de son** ~ to do
one's best.

mièvre [mjɛvʀ(ə)] *a* mawkish *(Brit)*,
sickly sentimental.

mignon, ne [miɲɔ̃, -ɔn] *a* sweet,
cute.

migraine [migʀɛn] *nf* headache; migraine.

mijoter [miʒɔte] *vt* to simmer; *(préparer avec soin)* to cook lovingly;
(affaire, projet) to plot, cook up // *vi*
to simmer.

mil [mil] *num* = **mille**.

milieu, x [miljø] *nm* *(centre)* middle; *(fig)* middle course *ou* way; happy medium; *(BIO, GEO)* environment; *(entourage social)* milieu;
background; circle; *(pègre)* **le** ~
the underworld; **au** ~ **de** in the
middle of; **au beau** *ou* **en plein** ~ **(de)**
right in the middle of.)

militaire [militɛʀ] *a* military, army
cpd // *nm* serviceman.

militant, e [militɑ̃, -ɑ̃t] *a, nm/f* militant.

militer [milite] *vi* to be a militant; ~

pour/contre *(suj: faits, raisons etc)*
to militate in favour of/against.

mille [mil] *num a ou* **une** thousand //
nm *(mesure)*: ~ **(marin)** nautical
mile; **mettre dans le** ~ to hit the
bull's-eye; to be bang on target;
~**feuille** *nm* cream *ou* vanilla slice;
millénaire *nm* millennium // *a*
thousand-year-old; *(fig)* ancient; ~
pattes *nm inv* centipede.

millésime [milezim] *nm* year; **mil-
lésimé, e** *a* vintage *cpd*.

millet [mijɛ] *nm* millet.

milliard [miljaʀ] *nm* milliard, thousand million *(Brit)*, billion *(US)*;
milliardaire *nm/f* multimillionaire
(Brit), billionaire *(US)*.

millier [milje] *nm* thousand; **un** ~
(de) a thousand *ou* so, about a thousand; **par** ~**s** in *(their)* thousands,
by the thousand.

milligramme [miligʀam] *nm* milligramme.

millimètre [milimɛtʀ(ə)] *nm* milli-
metre.

million [miljɔ̃] *nm* million; **deux** ~**s**
de two million; **millionnaire** *nm/f*
millionaire.

minable [minabl(ə)] *a* shabby
(-looking); pathetic.

mince [mɛ̃s] *a* thin; *(personne, taille)*
slim, slender; *(fig: profit, connaissances)* slight, small, weak // *excl*:
~ **alors!** drat it!, darn it! *(US)*;
minceur *nf* thinness; slimness, slen-
derness.

mine [min] *nf* *(physionomie)* expression, look; *(extérieur)* exterior, appearance; *(de crayon)* lead; *(gisement, exploitation, explosif, fig)*
mine; **avoir bonne** ~ *(personne)* to
look well; *(ironique)* to look an utter
idiot; **avoir mauvaise** ~ to look un-

well *ou* poorly; **faire ~ de faire** to make a pretence of doing; to make as if to do; **~ de rien** *ou* with a casual air; although you wouldn't think so.

miner [mine] *vt* (*saper*) to undermine, erode; (MIL) to mine.

minerai [minʀɛ] *nm* ore.

minéral, e, aux [mineʀal, -o] *a, nm* mineral.

minéralogique [mineʀalɔʒik] *a:* **numéro ~** registration number.

minet, te [minɛ, -ɛt] *nm/f* (*chat*) pussy-cat; (*péj*) young trendy.

mineur, e [minœʀ] *a* minor // *nm/f* (JUR) minor, person under age // *nm* (*travailleur*) miner.

miniature [minjatyʀ] *a, nf* miniature.

minibus [minibys] *nm* minibus.

mini-cassette [minikasɛt] *nf* cassette (recorder).

minier, ière [minje, -jɛʀ] *a* mining.

mini-jupe [miniʒyp] *nf* mini-skirt.

minime [minim] *a* minor, minimal.

minimiser [minimize] *vt* to minimize; (*fig*) to play down.

minimum [minimɔm] *a, nm* minimum; **au ~** (*au moins*) at the very least.

ministère [ministɛʀ] *nm* (*aussi* REL) ministry; (*cabinet*) government; **~ public** (JUR) Prosecution, State Prosecutor; **ministériel, le** *a* cabinet *cpd*; ministerial.

ministre [ministʀ(ə)] *nm* (*aussi* REL) minister; **~ d'État** senior minister.

Minitel [minitɛl] *nm* ® videotext terminal and service.

minorité [minɔʀite] *nf* minority; **être en ~** to be in the *ou* a minority; **mettre en ~** (POL) to defeat.

minoterie [minɔtʀi] *nf* flour-mill.

minuit [minɥi] *nm* midnight.

minuscule [minyskyl] *a* minute, tiny // *nf:* (*lettre*) **~** small letter.

minute [minyt] *nf* minute; (JUR: *original*) minute, draft; **à la ~** (*just*) this instant; there and then; **minuter** *vt* to time; **minuterie** *nf* time switch.

minutieux, euse [minysjø, -øz] *a* meticulous; minutely detailed.

mirabelle [miʀabɛl] *nf* (*cherry*) plum.

miracle [miʀakl(ə)] *nm* miracle.

mirage [miʀaʒ] *nm* mirage.

mire [miʀ] *nf:* **point de ~** target; (*fig*) focal point; **ligne de ~** line of sight.

miroir [miʀwaʀ] *nm* mirror.

miroiter [miʀwate] *vi* to sparkle, shimmer; **faire ~ qch à qn** to paint sth in glowing colours for sb, dangle sth in front of sb's eyes.

mis, e [mi, miz] *pp de* **mettre** // *a:* **bien ~** well dressed // *nf* (*argent: au jeu*) stake; (*tenue*) clothing; attire; **être de ~e** to be acceptable *ou* in season; **~ à feu** blast-off; **~e de fonds** capital outlay; **~en plis** set; **~e au point** (*fig*) clarification (*voir aussi* **point**); **~e en scène** production.

miser [mize] *vt* (*enjeu*) to stake, bet; **~ sur** *vt* (*cheval, numéro*) to bet on; (*fig*) to bank *ou* count on.

misérable [mizeʀabl(ə)] *a* (*lamentable, malheureux*) pitiful, wretched; (*pauvre*) poverty-stricken; (*insignifiant, mesquin*) miserable // *nm/f* wretch; (*miséreux*) poor wretch.

misère [mizeʀ] *nf* (*extreme*) poverty, destitution; **~s** *nfpl* woes, miseries; little troubles; **salaire de ~** starvation wage.

miséricorde [mizeʀikɔʀd(ə)] *nf* mercy, forgiveness.

missile [misil] *nm* missile.

mission [misjɔ̃] *nf* mission; **partir en ~** (ADMIN, POL) to go on an assignment; **missionnaire** *nm/f* missionary.

mit *vb voir* **mettre**.

mité, e [mite] *a* moth-eaten.

mi-temps [mitɑ̃] *nf* (SPORT: *période*) half (*pl* halves); (: *pause*) half-time; **à ~** *a, ad* part-time.

mitigé, e [mitiʒe] *a* lukewarm; mixed.

mitonner [mitɔne] *vt* to cook with loving care; *(fig)* to cook up quietly.
mitoyen, ne [mitwajɛ̃, -ɛn] *a* common, party *cpd.*
mitrailler [mitʀɑje] *vt* to machinegun; *(fig: photographier)* to take shot after shot of; to pelt, bombard; **mitraillette** *nf* submachine gun; **mitrailleuse** *nf* machine gun.
mi-voix [mivwa]: **à** ~ *ad* in a low *ou* hushed voice.
mixage [miksaʒ] *nm* (CINÉMA) (sound) mixing.
mixer [miksœʀ] *nm* (food) mixer.
mixte [mikst(ə)] *a* (gén) mixed; (SCOL) mixed, coeducational; **à usage** ~ dual-purpose.
mixture [mikstyʀ] *nf* mixture; *(fig)* concoction.
MLF *sigle m* = *Mouvement de libération de la femme.*
Mlle, *pl* **Mlles** *abr de* **Mademoiselle.**
MM *abr de* **Messieurs.**
Mme, *pl* **Mmes** *abr de* **Madame.**
Mo *abr de* **métro.**
mobile [mɔbil] *a* mobile; *(pièce de machine)* moving; *(élément de meuble etc)* movable // *nm* (motif) motive; *(œuvre d'art)* mobile.
mobilier, ière [mɔbilje, -jɛʀ] *a* (JUR) personal // *nm* furniture.
mobiliser [mɔbilize] *vt* (MIL, gén) to mobilize.
moche [mɔʃ] *a (fam)* rotten.
modalité [mɔdalite] *nf* form, mode; ~**s** *nfpl (d'un accord etc)* clauses, terms.
mode [mɔd] *nf* fashion // *nm (manière)* form, mode; **à la** ~ fashionable, in fashion; ~ **d'emploi** directions *pl* (for use).
modèle [mɔdɛl] *a, nm* model; *(qui pose: de peintre)* sitter; ~ **déposé** registered design; ~ **réduit** smallscale model.
modeler [mɔdle] *vt* (ART) to model, mould; *(suj: vêtement, érosion)* to mould, shape.
modem [mɔdɛm] *nm* modem.

modéré, e [mɔdeʀe] *a, nm/f* moderate.
modérer [mɔdeʀe] *vt* to moderate; **se** ~ *vi* to restrain o.s.
moderne [mɔdɛʀn(ə)] *a* modern // *nm* modern style; modern furniture; **moderniser** *vt* to modernize.
modeste [mɔdɛst(ə)] *a* modest; **modestie** *nf* modesty.
modifier [mɔdifje] *vt* to modify, alter; **se** ~ *vi* to alter.
modique [mɔdik] *a* modest.
modiste [mɔdist(ə)] *nf* milliner.
modulation [mɔdylasjɔ̃] *nf:* ~ **de fréquence** (FM *ou* MF) frequency modulation.
module [mɔdyl] *nm* module.
moelle [mwal] *nf* marrow.
moelleux, euse [mwalø, -øz] *a* soft; *(au goût, à l'ouïe)* mellow.
moellon [mwalɔ̃] *nm* rubble stone.
mœurs [mœʀ] *nfpl (conduite)* morals; *(manières)* manners; *(pratiques sociales, mode de vie)* habits.
mohair [mɔɛʀ] *nm* mohair.
moi [mwa] *pronom* me; *(emphatique):* ~, **je** ... for my part, I ..., I myself ....
moignon [mwaɲɔ̃] *nm* stump.
moi-même [mwamɛm] *pronom* myself; *(emphatique)* I myself.
moindre [mwɛ̃dʀ(ə)] *a* lesser; lower; **le(la)** ~, **les** ~**s** the least, the slightest.
moine [mwan] *nm* monk, friar.
moineau, x [mwano] *nm* sparrow.

─────────────

MOT-CLÉ

moins [mwɛ̃] ♦ *ad* **1** *(comparatif):* ~ **(que)** less (than); ~ **grand que** less tall than, not as tall as; ~ **je travaille, mieux je me porte** the less I work, the better I feel
2 *(superlatif):* **le** ~ (the) least; **c'est ce que j'aime le** ~ it's what I like (the) least; **le(la)** ~ **doué(e)** the least gifted; **au** ~, **du** ~ at least; **pour le** ~ at the very least
3: ~ **de** *(quantité)* less (than); *(nombre)* fewer (than); ~ **de sable**

d'eau less sand/water; ~ de livres/gens fewer books/people; ~ de 2 ans less than 2 years; ~ de midi not yet midday

4: de ~, en ~: 100 F/3 jours de ~ 100 F/3 days less; **3 livres en ~** 3 books fewer; 3 books too few; **de l'argent en ~** less money; **le soleil en ~** but for the sun, minus the sun; **de ~ en ~** less and less

5: à ~ de, à ~ que unless; **à ~ de faire** unless we do (*ou* he does *etc*); **à ~ que tu ne fasses** unless you do; **à ~ d'un accident** barring any accident

◆ *prép:* 4 ~ 2 4 minus 2; **il est ~ 5** it's 5 to; **il fait ~ 5** it's 5 (degrees) below (freezing), it's minus 5.

mois [mwa] *nm* month; ~ **double** (*COMM*) extra month's salary.

moisi [mwazi] *nm* mould, mildew; **odeur de ~** musty smell.

moisir [mwazir] *vi* to go mouldy; (*fig*) to rot; to hang about.

moisissure [mwazisyr] *nf* mould *q*.

moisson [mwasɔ̃] *nf* harvest; **moissonner** *vt* to harvest, reap; **moissonneuse** *nf* (*machine*) harvester.

moite [mwat] *a* sweaty, sticky.

moitié [mwatje] *nf* half (*pl* halves); **la ~ half; la ~ de** half (of); **la ~ du temps/ des gens** half the time/the people; **à la ~ de** halfway through; **à ~** half (*avant le verbe*); half- (*avant l'adjectif*); **de ~** by half; ~ ~ half-and-half.

mol [mɔl] *a voir* **mou.**

molaire [mɔlɛr] *nf* molar.

molester [mɔlɛste] *vt* to manhandle, maul (about).

molette [mɔlɛt] *nf* toothed *ou* cutting wheel.

molle [mɔl] *af voir* **mou;** ~ **ment** *ad* softly; (*péj*) sluggishly; (*protester*) feebly.

mollet [mɔlɛ] *nm* calf (*pl* calves) // *am:* **œuf ~** soft-boiled egg.

molletonné, e [mɔltɔne] *a* fleece-lined.

mollir [mɔlir] *vi* to give way; to relent; to go soft.

môme [mom] *nm/f* (*fam: enfant*) brat; (*: fille*) chick.

moment [mɔmɑ̃] *nm* moment; **ce n'est pas le ~** this is not the (right) time; **à un certain ~** at some point; **à un ~ donné** at a certain point; **pour un bon ~** for a good while; **pour le ~** for the moment, for the time being; **au ~ de** at the time of; **au ~ où, au ~ that** at a time when; **à tout ~** at any time *ou* moment; constantly, continually; **en ce ~** at the moment; at present; **sur le ~** at the time; **par ~s** now and then, at times; **du ~ où** *ou* **que** seeing that, since; **momentané, e** *a* temporary, momentary.

momie [mɔmi] *nf* mummy.

mon [mɔ̃], **ma** [ma], *pl* **mes** [me] *dét* my.

Monaco [mɔnako] *nm:* **le ~** Monaco.

monarchie [mɔnarʃi] *nf* monarchy.

monastère [mɔnastɛr] *nm* monastery.

monceau, x [mɔ̃so] *nm* heap.

mondain, e [mɔ̃dɛ̃, -ɛn] *a* society *cpd;* social; fashionable // *nf:* **M-e, la police ~e** ≈ the vice squad.

monde [mɔ̃d] *nm* world; (*haute société*): **le ~** (high) society; (*milieu*): **être du même ~** to move in the same circles; (*gens*): **il y a du ~** (*beaucoup de gens*) there are a lot of people; (*quelques personnes*) there are some people; **beaucoup/peu de ~** many/few people; **le meilleur** *etc* **du ~** the best *etc* in the world *ou* on earth; **mettre au ~** to bring into the world; **pas le moins du ~** not in the least; **se faire un ~ de qch** to make a great deal of fuss about sth; **mondial, e, aux** *a* (*population*) world *cpd;* (*influence*) world-wide; **mondialement** *ad* throughout the world.

monégasque [mɔnegask(ə)] *a* Monegasque, *ou* from Monaco.

monétaire [monetɛʀ] *a* monetary.

moniteur, trice [monitœʀ, -tʀis] *nm/f* (SPORT) instructor/instructress; (*de colonie de vacances*) supervisor // *nm* (*écran*) monitor.

monnaie [mɔnɛ] *nf* (*pièce*) coin; (ÉCON, *gén*: *moyen d'échange*) currency; (*petites pièces*): **avoir de la ~** to have (some) change; **faire de la ~** to get (some) change; **avoir/ faire la ~ de 20 F** to have change of/get change for 20 F; **rendre à qn la ~ (sur 20 F)** to give sb the change (out of *ou* from 20 F); **monnayer** *vt* to convert into cash; (*talent*) to capitalize on.

monologue [mɔnɔlɔg] *nm* monologue, soliloquy; **monologuer** *vi* to soliloquize.

monopole [mɔnɔpɔl] *nm* monopoly.

monotone [mɔnɔtɔn] *a* monotonous.

monseigneur [mɔ̃sɛɲœʀ] *nm* (*archevêque, évêque*) Your (*ou* His) Grace; (*cardinal*) Your (*ou* His) Eminence.

Monsieur [məsjø], *pl* **Messieurs** [mesjø] *titre* Mr [ˈmistəʳ] // *nm* (*homme quelconque*): **un/le m~** a/ the gentleman; *voir aussi* **Madame**.

monstre [mɔ̃stʀ(ə)] *nm* monster // *a*: **un travail ~** a fantastic amount of work; **an enormous job.**

mont [mɔ̃] *nm*: **par ~s et par vaux** up hill and down dale; **le M~ Blanc** Mont Blanc.

montage [mɔ̃taʒ] *nm* putting up; mounting; setting; assembly; (PHOTO) photomontage; (CINÉMA) editing.

montagnard, e [mɔ̃taɲaʀ, -aʀd(ə)] *a* mountain *cpd* // *nm/f* mountain-dweller.

montagne [mɔ̃taɲ] *nf* (*cime*) mountain; (*région*): **la ~** the mountains *pl*; **~s russes** big dipper *sg*, switchback *sg*.

montagneux, euse [mɔ̃taɲø, -øz] *a* mountainous; hilly.

montant, e [mɔ̃tɑ̃, -ɑ̃t] *a* rising;

(*robe, corsage*) high-necked // *nm* (*somme, total*) (sum) total, (total) amount; (*de fenêtre*) upright; (*de lit*) post.

mont-de-piété [mɔ̃dpjete] *nm* pawnshop.

monte-charge [mɔ̃tʃaʀʒ(ə)] *nm inv* goods lift, hoist.

montée [mɔ̃te] *nf* rising, rise; ascent, climb; (*chemin*) way up; (*côte*) hill; **au milieu de la ~** halfway up.

monter [mɔ̃te] *vt* (*escalier, côte*) to go (*ou* come) up; (*valise, paquet*) to take (*ou* bring) up; (*cheval*) to mount; (*étagère*) to raise; (*tente, échafaudage*) to put up; (*machine*) to assemble; (*bijou*) to mount, set; (COUTURE) to set in; to sew on; (CINÉMA) to edit; (THÉÂTRE) to put on, stage; (*société etc*) to set up // *vi* to go (*ou* come) up; (*avion etc*) to climb, go up; (*chemin, niveau, température*) to go up, rise; (*passager*) to get on; (*à cheval*): **~ bien/mal** to ride well/badly; **~ à pied** to walk up, go up on foot; **~ à bicyclette/ en voiture** to cycle/drive up, go up by bicycle/by car; **~ dans le train/ l'avion** to get into the train/plane, board the train/plane; **~ sur** to climb up onto; **~ à cheval** to get on *ou* mount a horse; **se ~ à** (*frais etc*) to add up to, come to.

monticule [mɔ̃tikyl] *nm* mound.

montre [mɔ̃tʀ(ə)] *nf* watch; **faire ~ de** to show, display; **contre la ~** (SPORT) against the clock; **~ bracelet** *nf* wrist watch.

montrer [mɔ̃tʀe] *vt* to show; **~ qch à qn** to show sb sth.

monture [mɔ̃tyʀ] *nf* (*bête*) mount; (*d'une bague*) setting; (*de lunettes*) frame.

monument [mɔnymɑ̃] *nm* monument; **~ aux morts** war memorial.

moquer [mɔke]: **se ~ de** *vt* to make fun of, laugh at; (*fam*: *se désintéresser de*) not to care about; (*tromper*): **se ~ de qn** to take sb for a ride.

moquette [mɔkɛt] nf fitted carpet.

moqueur, euse [mɔkœr, -øz] a mocking.

moral, e, aux [mɔral, -o] a moral // nm morale // nf (conduite) morals pl; (règles) moral code, ethic; (valeurs) moral standards pl, morality; (science) ethics sg, moral philosophy; (conclusion: d'une fable etc) moral; avoir le ~ à zéro to be really down; faire la ~e à to lecture, preach at; ~ité nf morality; (conduite) morals pl; (conclusion, enseignement) moral.

morceau, x [mɔrso] nm piece, bit; (d'une œuvre) passage, extract; (MUS) piece; (CULIN: de viande) cut; mettre en ~x to pull to pieces ou bits.

morceler [mɔrsəle] vt to break up, divide up.

mordant, e [mɔrdɑ̃, -ɑ̃t] a scathing, cutting; biting.

mordiller [mɔrdije] vt to nibble at, chew at.

mordre [mɔrdr(ə)] vt to bite; (suj: lime, vis) to bite into // vi (poisson) to bite; ~ sur (fig) to go over into, overlap into; ~ à l'hameçon to bite, rise to the bait.

mordu, e [mɔrdy] nm/f: un ~ du jazz a jazz fanatic.

morfondre [mɔrfɔdr(ə)]: se ~ vi to mope.

morgue [mɔrg(ə)] nf (arrogance) haughtiness; (lieu: de la police) morgue; (: à l'hôpital) mortuary.

morne [mɔrn(ə)] a dismal, dreary.

mors [mɔr] nm bit.

morse [mɔrs(ə)] nm (ZOOL) walrus; (TÉL) Morse (code).

morsure [mɔrsyr] nf bite.

mort [mɔr] nf death.

mort, e [mɔr, mɔrt(ə)] pp de mourir // a dead // nm/f (défunt) dead man/woman; (victime): il y a eu plusieurs ~s several people were killed, there were several killed // nm (CARTES) dummy; ~ ou vif dead or alive; ~ de peur/fatigue

frightened to death/dead tired.

mortalité [mɔrtalite] nf mortality, death rate.

mortel, le [mɔrtɛl] a (poison etc) deadly, lethal; (accident, blessure) fatal; (REL) mortal; (fig) deathly; deadly boring.

mortier [mɔrtje] nm (gén) mortar.

mort-né, e [mɔrne] a (enfant) stillborn.

mortuaire [mɔrtɥɛr] a funeral cpd.

morue [mɔry] nf (ZOOL) cod inv.

mosaïque [mɔzaik] nf (ART) mosaic; (fig) patchwork.

Moscou [mɔsku] n Moscow.

mosquée [mɔske] nf mosque.

mot [mo] nm word; (message) line, note; (bon mot etc) saying; sally; ~ à ~ a, ad word for word; ~s croisés crossword (puzzle) sg; ~ d'ordre watchword; ~ de passe password.

motard [mɔtar] nm biker; (policier) motorcycle cop.

motel [mɔtɛl] nm motel.

moteur, trice [mɔtœr, -tris] a (ANAT, PHYSIOL) motor; (TECH) driving; (AUTO): à 4 roues motrices 4-wheel drive // nm engine, motor; à ~ power-driven, motor.

motif [mɔtif] nm (cause) motive; (décoratif) design, pattern, motif; (d'un tableau) subject, motif; ~s nmpl (JUR) grounds pl; sans ~ a groundless.

motiver [mɔtive] vt (justifier) to justify, account for; (ADMIN, JUR, PSYCH) to motivate.

moto [mɔto] nf (motor)bike; ~cyclisme nm motorcycle racing; ~cycliste nm/f motorcyclist.

motorisé, e [mɔtɔrize] a (troupe) motorized; (personne) having transport ou a car.

motrice [mɔtris] a voir moteur.

motte [mɔt] nf: ~ de terre lump of earth, clod (of earth); ~ de gazon turf, sod; ~ de beurre lump of butter.

mou(mol), molle [mu, mɔl] a soft;

(*péj*) flabby; sluggish // *nm* (*abats*) lights *pl*, lungs *pl*; (*de la corde*): **avoir du ~** to be slack.

mouche [muʃ] *nf* fly.

moucher [muʃe] *vt* (*enfant*) to blow the nose of; (*chandelle*) to snuff (out); **se ~** *vi* to blow one's nose.

moucheron [muʃʀɔ̃] *nm* midge.

moucheté, e [muʃte] *a* dappled; flecked.

mouchoir [muʃwaʀ] *nm* handkerchief, hanky; **~ en papier** tissue, paper hanky.

moudre [mudʀ(ə)] *vt* to grind.

moue [mu] *nf* pout; **faire la ~** to pout; (*fig*) to pull a face.

mouette [mwɛt] *nf* (sea) gull.

moufle [mufl(ə)] *nf* (*gant*) mitt(en).

mouillé, e [muje] *a* wet.

mouiller [muje] *vt* (*humecter*) to wet, moisten; (*tremper*): **~ qn/qch** to make sb/sth wet; (*couper, diluer*) to water down; (*mine etc*) to lay // *vi* (*NAVIG*) to lie *ou* be at anchor; **se ~** to get wet; (*fam*) to commit o.s.; to get o.s. involved.

moule [mul] *nf* mussel // *nm* (*creux, CULIN*) mould; (*modèle plein*) cast; **~ à gâteaux** *nm* cake tin (*Brit*) *ou* pan (*US*).

moulent *vb voir* **moudre, mouler**.

mouler [mule] *vt* (*suj: vêtement*) to hug, fit closely round; **~ qch sur** (*fig*) to model sth on.

moulin [mulɛ̃] *nm* mill; **~ à café/à poivre** coffee/pepper mill; **~ à légumes** (vegetable) shredder; **~ à paroles** (*fig*) chatterbox; **~ à vent** windmill.

moulinet [mulinɛ] *nm* (*de treuil*) winch; (*de canne à pêche*) reel; (*mouvement*): **faire des ~s avec** qch to whirl sth around.

moulinette [mulinɛt] *nf* (vegetable) shredder.

moulu, e [muly] *pp de* **moudre**.

moulure [mulyʀ] *nf* (*ornement*) moulding.

mourant, e [muʀɑ̃, -ɑ̃t] *a* dying.

mourir [muʀiʀ] *vi* to die; (*civilisa-*

tion) to die out; **~ de froid/faim** to die of exposure/hunger; **~ de faim/d'ennui** (*fig*) to be starving/be bored to death; **~ d'envie de faire** to be dying to do.

mousse [mus] *nf* (*BOT*) moss; (*écume: sur l'eau, bière*) froth, foam; (*: shampooing*) lather; (*CULIN*) mousse // *nm* (*NAVIG*) ship's boy; **bas ~** stretch stockings; **~ carbonique** (fire-fighting) foam; **~ à raser** shaving foam.

mousseline [muslin] *nf* muslin; chiffon.

mousser [muse] *vi* to foam; to lather.

mousseux, euse [musø, -øz] *a* frothy // *nm*: (*vin*) **~** sparkling wine.

mousson [musɔ̃] *nf* monsoon.

moustache [mustaʃ] *nf* moustache; **~s** (*du chat*) whiskers *pl*.

moustiquaire [mustikɛʀ] *nf* mosquito net (*ou* screen).

moustique [mustik] *nm* mosquito.

moutarde [mutaʀd(ə)] *nf* mustard.

mouton [mutɔ̃] *nm* (*ZOOL, péj*) sheep *inv*; (*peau*) sheepskin; (*CULIN*) mutton.

mouvant, e [muvɑ̃, -ɑ̃t] *a* unsettled; changing; shifting.

mouvement [muvmɑ̃] *nm* (*gén, aussi: mécanisme*) movement; (*fig*) activity; impulse; gesture; (*MUS: rythme*) tempo (*pl* s); **en ~** in motion; to one move; **mouvementé, e** (*vie, poursuite*) eventful; (*réunion*) turbulent.

mouvoir [muvwaʀ] *vt* (*levier, membre*) to move; **se ~** *vi* to move.

moyen, ne [mwajɛ̃, -ɛn] *a* average; (*tailles, prix*) medium; (*de grandeur moyenne*) medium-sized // *nm* (*façon*) means *sg*, way // *nf* average; (*MATH*) mean; (*SCOL: à l'examen*) pass mark; (*AUTO*) average speed; **~s** (*capacités*) means; **au ~ de** by means of; **par tous les ~s** every possible means, every possible way; **par ses propres ~s** all by oneself; **en ~ne** on (an) average; **~ de**

transport means of transport; ~ âge Middle Ages; ~ne d'âge average age.

moyennant [mwajɛnɑ̃] *prép* (somme) for; (service, conditions) in return for; (travail, effort) with.

Moyen-Orient [mwajɛnɔʀjɑ̃] *nm*: le ~ the Middle East.

moyeu, x [mwajø] *nm* hub.

MST *sigle f* (= *maladie sexuellement transmissible*) sexually transmitted disease.

mû, mue [my] *pp de* mouvoir.

muer [mɥe] *vi* (oiseau, mammifère) to moult; (serpent) to slough; (jeune garçon): il mue his voice is breaking; se ~ en to transform into.

muet, te [mɥe, -ɛt] *a* dumb; (fig): ~ d'admiration *etc* speechless with admiration *etc*; (joie, douleur, CINÉMA) silent; (carte) blank // *nm/f* mute.

mufle [myfl(ə)] *nm* muzzle; (goujat) boor.

mugir [myʒiʀ] *vi* (taureau) to bellow; (vache) to low; (fig) to howl.

muguet [mygɛ] *nm* lily of the valley.

mule [myl] *nf* (ZOOL) (she-)mule.

mulet [mylɛ] *nm* (ZOOL) (he-)mule.

multiple [myltipl(ə)] *a* multiple, numerous; (varié) many, manifold // *nm* (MATH) multiple.

multiplication [myltiplikasjɔ̃] *nf* multiplication.

multiplier [myltiplije] *vt* to multiply; se ~ *vi* to multiply; to increase in number.

municipal, e, aux [mynisipal, -o] *a* municipal; town cpd, ~ borough cpd.

municipalité [mynisipalite] *nf* (corps municipal) town council, corporation.

munir [myniʀ] *vt*: ~ qn/qch de to equip sb/sth with.

munitions [mynisjɔ̃] *nfpl* ammunition *sg*.

mur [myʀ] *nm* wall; ~ du son sound barrier.

mûr, e [myʀ] *a* ripe; (personne) mature // *nf* blackberry; mulberry.

muraille [myʀɑj] *nf* (high) wall.

mural, e, aux [myʀal, -o] *a* wall cpd; mural.

murer [myʀe] *vt* (enclos) to wall (in); (porte, issue) to wall up; (personne) to wall up ou in.

muret [myʀɛ] *nm* low wall.

mûrir [myʀiʀ] *vi* (fruit, blé) to ripen; (abcès, furoncle) to come to a head; (fig: idée, personne) to mature // *vt* to ripen; to (make) mature.

murmure [myʀmyʀ] *nm* murmur; ~s (plaintes) murmurings, mutterings; **murmurer** *vi* to murmur; (se plaindre) to mutter, grumble.

muscade [myskad] *nf* (aussi: noix ~) nutmeg.

muscat [myska] *nm* muscat grape; muscatel (wine).

muscle [myskl(ə)] *nm* muscle; **musclé, e** *a* muscular; (fig) strong-arm.

museau, x [myzo] *nm* muzzle.

musée [myze] *nm* museum; art gallery.

museler [myzle] *vt* to muzzle; **muselière** *nf* muzzle.

musette [myzɛt] *nf* (sac) lunchbag // *a inv* (orchestre etc) accordion cpd.

musical, e, aux [myzikal, -o] *a* musical.

music-hall [myzikol] *nm* variety theatre; (genre) variety.

musicien, ne [myzisjɛ̃, -jɛn] *a* musical // *nm/f* musician.

musique [myzik] *nf* music; (fanfare) band; ~ de chambre chamber music.

musulman, e [myzylmɑ̃, -an] *a, nm/f* Moslem, Muslim.

mutation [mytasjɔ̃] *nf* (ADMIN) transfer.

mutilé, e [mytile] *nm/f* disabled person (through loss of limbs).

mutiler [mytile] *vt* to mutilate, maim.

mutin, e [mytɛ̃, -in] *a* (air, ton) mischievous, impish // *nm/f* (MIL, NAVIG) mutineer.

mutinerie [mytinʀi] *nf* mutiny.

mutisme [mytism(ə)] *nm* silence.

mutuel, le [mytɥɛl] *a* mutual //

mutual benefit society.

myope [mjɔp] *a* short-sighted.

myosotis [mjɔzɔtis] *nm* forget-me-not.

myrtille [miʀtij] *nf* bilberry.

mystère [mistɛʀ] *nm* mystery; **mystérieux, euse** *a* mysterious.

mystifier [mistifje] *vt* to fool; to mystify.

mythe [mit] *nm* myth.

mythologie [mitɔlɔʒi] *nf* mythology.

N

n' [n] *ad voir* **ne.**

nacelle [nasɛl] *nf* (*de ballon*) basket.

nacre [nakʀ(ə)] *nf* mother of pearl; **nacré, e** *a* pearly.

nage [naʒ] *nf* swimming; style of swimming, stroke; **traverser/s'éloigner à la ~** to swim across/away; **en ~** bathed in perspiration.

nageoire [naʒwaʀ] *nf* fin.

nager [naʒe] *vi* to swim; **nageur, euse** *nm/f* swimmer.

naguère [nagɛʀ] *ad* formerly.

naïf, ïve [naif, naiv] *a* naïve.

nain, e [nɛ̃, nɛn] *nm/f* dwarf.

naissance [nɛsɑ̃s] *nf* birth; **donner ~ à** to give birth to; (*fig*) to give rise to.

naître [nɛtʀ(ə)] *vi* to be born; (*fig*): **~ de** to arise from, be born out of; **il est né en 1960** he was born in 1960; **faire ~** (*fig*) to give rise to, arouse.

nana [nana] *nf* (*fam: fille*) chick, bird (*Brit*).

nantir [nɑ̃tiʀ] *vt*: **~ qn de** to provide sb with; **les nantis** (*péj*) the well-to-do.

nappe [nap] *nf* tablecloth; (*fig*) sheet; layer; **~ron** *nm* table-mat.

naquit *etc vb voir* **naître.**

narguer [naʀge] *vt* to taunt.

narine [naʀin] *nf* nostril.

narquois, e [naʀkwa, -waz] *a* derisive, mocking.

narrer [naʀe] *vt* to tell the story of, recount.

naseau, x [nazo] *nm* nostril.

natal, e [natal] *a* native.

natalité [natalite] *nf* birth rate.

natation [natasjɔ̃] *nf* swimming.

natif, ive [natif, -iv] *a* native.

nation [nasjɔ̃] *nf* nation.

national, e, aux [nasjɔnal, -o] *a* national // *nf*: (**route**) **~e** ≈ A road (*Brit*), ≈ state highway (*US*); **~iser** *vt* to nationalize; **~ité** *nf* nationality.

naturaliser [natyʀalize] *vt* to naturalize.

nature [natyʀ] *nf* nature // *a, ad* (*CULIN*) plain, without seasoning or sweetening; (*café, thé*) black, without sugar; **payer en ~** to pay in kind; **~ morte** still-life; **naturel, le** *a* (*gén, aussi: enfant*) natural // *nm* naturalness; disposition; nature; (*autochtone*) native; **naturellement** *ad* naturally; (*bien sûr*) of course.

naufrage [nofʀaʒ] *nm* (ship)wreck; (*fig*) wreck; **faire ~** to be shipwrecked.

nauséabond, e [nozeabɔ̃, -ɔd] *a* foul, nauseous.

nausée [noze] *nf* nausea.

nautique [notik] *a* nautical, water cpd.

nautisme [notism] *nm* water sports.

navet [navɛ] *nm* turnip.

navette [navɛt] *nf* shuttle; **faire la ~ (entre)** to go to and fro ou shuttle (between).

navigable [navigabl(ə)] *a* navigable.

navigateur [navigatœʀ] *nm* (*NAVIG*) seafarer, sailor; (*AVIAT*) navigator.

navigation [navigasjɔ̃] *nf* navigation, sailing; shipping.

naviguer [navige] *vi* to navigate, sail.

navire [naviʀ] *nm* ship.

navrer [navʀe] *vt* to upset, distress; **je suis navré** I'm so sorry.

ne, n' [n(ə)] *ad voir* **pas, plus, jamais** *etc*; (*explétif*) *non traduit.*

né, e [ne] *pp* (*voir* **naître**): **~ en 1960** born in 1960; **~e Scott** née

Scott.

néanmoins [neɑ̃mwɛ] ad nevertheless.

néant [neɑ̃] nm nothingness; réduire à ~ to bring to nought; (espoir) to dash.

nécessaire [nesesɛʁ] a necessary // nm necessary; (sac) kit; ~ de couture sewing kit; ~ de toilette toilet bag; **nécessité** nf necessity; **nécessiter** vt to require; **nécessiteux, euse** a needy.

nécrologique [nekʁɔlɔʒik] a: article ~ obituary; **rubrique** ~ obituary column.

néerlandais, e [neɛʁlɑ̃dɛ, -ɛz] a Dutch.

nef [nɛf] nf (d'église) nave.

néfaste [nefast(ə)] a baneful; ill-fated.

négatif, ive [negatif, iv] a negative // nm (PHOTO) negative.

négligé, e [neɡliʒe] a (en désordre) slovenly // nm (tenue) negligee.

négligent, e [neɡliʒɑ̃, -ɑ̃t] a careless; negligent.

négliger [neɡliʒe] vt (épouse, jardin) to neglect; (tenue) to be careless about; (avis, précautions) to disregard; ~ de faire to fail to do, not bother to do.

négoce [neɡɔs] nm trade.

négociant [neɡɔsjɑ̃] nm merchant.

négociation [neɡɔsjasjɔ̃] nf negotiation.

négocier [neɡɔsje] vi, vt to negotiate.

nègre [nɛɡʁ(ə)] nm Negro; ghost (writer).

négresse [neɡʁɛs] nf Negro woman.

neige [nɛʒ] nf snow; **neiger** vi to snow; **neigeux, euse** a snowy, snow-covered.

nénuphar [nenyfaʁ] nm water-lily.

néon [neɔ̃] nm neon.

néophyte [neɔfit] nm/f novice.

néo-zélandais, e [neozelɑ̃dɛ, -ɛz] a New Zealand cpd // : N~, e nm/f New Zealander.

nerf [nɛʁ] nm nerve; (fig) spirit,

stamina; **nerveux, euse** a nervous; (voiture) nippy, responsive; (tendineux) sinewy; **nervosité** nf excitability; state of agitation; nervousness.

nervure [nɛʁvyʁ] nf vein.

n'est-ce pas [nɛspa] ad isn't it?, won't you? etc, selon le verbe qui précède.

net, nette [nɛt] a (sans équivoque, distinct) clear; (évident) definite; (propre) neat, clean; (COMM: prix, salaire) net // ad (refuser) flatly; s'arrêter ~ to stop dead // nm: mettre au ~ to copy out; **nettement** ad clearly, distinctly; ~**teté** nf clearness.

nettoyage [nɛtwajaʒ] nm cleaning; ~ à sec dry cleaning.

nettoyer [nɛtwaje] vt to clean; (fig) to clean out.

neuf [nœf] num nine.

neuf, neuve [nœf, nœv] a new // nm: repeindre à ~ to redecorate; remettre à ~ to do up (as good as new); refurbish.

neutre [nøtʁ(ə)] a neutral; (LING) neuter // nm (LING) neuter.

neuve [nœv] a voir neuf.

neuvième [nœvjɛm] num ninth.

neveu, x [nəvø] nm nephew.

névrose, e [nevʁoze] a, nm/f neurotic.

nez [ne] nm nose; ~ à ~ avec face to face with; avoir du ~ to have flair.

ni [ni] cj: ~ l'un ~ l'autre ne sont neither one nor the other are; il n'a rien dit ~ fait he hasn't said or done anything.

niais, e [njɛ, ɛz] a silly, thick.

niche [niʃ] nf (du chien) kennel; (de mur) recess, niche.

nicher [niʃe] vi to nest.

nid [ni] nm nest; ~ de poule pothole.

nièce [njɛs] nf niece.

nier [nje] vt to deny.

nigaud, e [niɡo, -od] nm/f booby, fool.

Nil [nil] nm: le ~ the Nile.

n'importe [nɛ̃pɔʀt(ə)] ad: ~ qui/quoi/où anybody/anything/anywhere; ~ quand any time; ~ quel/quelle any; ~ lequel/ laquelle any (one); ~ comment (sans soin) carelessly.

niveau, x [nivo] nm level; (des élèves, études) standard; (avec) level (with); ~ (à bulle) spirit level; le ~ de la mer sea level; ~ de vie standard of living.

niveler [nivle] vt to level.

NN abr (= nouvelle norme) revised standard of hotel classification.

noble [nɔbl(ə)] a noble; **noblesse** nf nobility; (d'une action etc) nobleness.

noce [nɔs] nf wedding; (gens) wedding party (ou guests pl); faire la ~ (fam) to go on a binge; ~s d'or/ d'argent golden/silver wedding.

nocif, ive [nɔsif, -iv] a harmful, noxious.

noctambule [nɔktɑ̃byl] nm nightbird.

nocturne [nɔktyʀn(ə)] a nocturnal // nf late-night opening.

Noël [nɔɛl] nm Christmas.

nœud [nø] nm (de corde, du bois, NAVIG) knot; (ruban) bow; (fig: liens) bond, tie; ~ papillon bow tie.

noir, e [nwaʀ] a black; (obscur, sombre) dark // nm/f black man/woman, Negro/Negro woman // nm: dans le ~ in the dark; travail au ~ moonlighting // (MUS) crotchet (Brit), quarter note (US); ~ceur nf blackness; darkness; ~cir vt, vi to blacken.

noisette [nwazɛt] nf hazelnut.

noix [nwa] nf walnut; (CULIN): une ~ de beurre a knob of butter; ~ de cajou cashew nut; ~ de coco coconut.

nom [nɔ̃] nm name; (LING) noun; ~ d'emprunt assumed name; ~ de famille surname; ~ de jeune fille maiden name.

nombre [nɔ̃bʀ(ə)] nm number; venir en ~ to come in large numbers; depuis ~ d'années for many years; ils sont au ~ de 3 there are 3 of them; au ~ de mes amis among my friends.

nombreux, euse [nɔ̃bʀø, -øz] a many, numerous; (avec nom sg: foule etc) large; peu ~ few; small.

nombril [nɔ̃bʀi] nm navel.

nommer [nɔme] vt (baptiser, mentionner) to name; (qualifier) to call; (élire) to appoint, nominate; (se): il se nomme Pascal his name's Pascal, he's called Pascal.

non [nɔ̃] ad (réponse) no; (avec loin, sans, seulement) not; ~ que, ~ pas que not that; moi ~ plus neither do I, I don't either.

non-alcoolisé, e [nɔnalkɔlize] a non-alcoholic.

non-fumeur [nɔ̃fymœʀ] nm nonsmoker.

non-lieu [nɔ̃ljø] nm: il y a eu ~ the case was dismissed.

non-sens [nɔ̃sɑ̃s] nm absurdity.

nord [nɔʀ] nm North // a northern; north; au ~ (situation) in the north; (direction) to the north; au ~ de (to the) north of; ~-est nm North-East; ~-ouest nm North-West.

normal, e, aux [nɔʀmal, -o] a normal // nf: la ~e the norm, the average; ~ement ad (en général) normally; ~iser vt (COMM, TECH) to standardize.

normand, e [nɔʀmɑ̃, -ɑ̃d] a of Normandy.

Normandie [nɔʀmɑ̃di] nf Normandy.

norme [nɔʀm(ə)] nf norm; (TECH) standard.

Norvège [nɔʀvɛʒ] nf Norway; **norvégien, ne** a, nm, nf Norwegian.

nos [no] dét voir **notre**.

nostalgie [nɔstalʒi] nf nostalgia.

notable [nɔtabl(ə)] a notable, noteworthy; (marqué) noticeable, marked // nm prominent citizen.

notaire [nɔtɛʀ] nm notary; solicitor.

notamment [nɔtamɑ̃] ad in particular, among others.

note [nɔt] nf (écrite, MUS) note; (SCOL) mark (Brit), grade; (facture) bill; ~ **de service** memorandum.

noté, e [nɔte] a: **être bien/mal** ~ (employé etc) to have a good/bad record.

noter [nɔte] vt (écrire) to write down; (remarquer) to note, notice.

notice [nɔtis] nf summary, short article; (brochure) leaflet, instruction book.

notifier [nɔtifje] vt: ~ **qch à qn** to notify sb of sth, notify sth to sb.

notion [nɔsjɔ̃] nf notion, idea.

notoire [nɔtwar] a widely known; (en mal) notorious.

notre, nos [nɔtr(ə), no] dét our.

nôtre, nos [notr(ə)] pronom: **le/la** ~ ours; **les** ~**s** ours; (alliés etc) our own people; **soyez des** ~**s** join us // a ours.

nouer [nwe] vt to tie, knot; (fig: alliance etc) to strike up.

noueux, euse [nwø, -øz] a gnarled.

nouilles [nuj] nfpl noodles; pasta sg.

nourrice [nuris] nf wet-nurse.

nourrir [nurir] vt to feed; (fig: espoir) to harbour, nurse; **logé nourri** with board and lodging; **nourrissant, e** a nourishing, nutritious.

nourrisson [nurisɔ̃] nm (unweaned) infant.

nourriture [nurityr] nf food.

nous [nu] pronom (sujet) we; (objet) us; ~**-mêmes** pronom ourselves.

nouveau(nouvel), elle, x [nuvo, -ɛl] a new // nmf new pupil (ou employee) // nf (piece of) news sg; (LITTÉRATURE) short story; **de** ~, **à** ~ again; **je suis sans nouvelles de lui** I haven't heard from him; ~ **venu, nouvelle venue** nmf newcomer; **Nouvel An** New Year; ~**né, e** nmf newborn baby; **Nouvelle-Calédonie** nf New Caledonia; **Nouvelle-Zélande** nf New Zealand; ~**té** nf novelty; (COMM) new film (ou book ou creation etc).

novembre [nɔvɑ̃br(ə)] nm November.

novice [nɔvis] a inexperienced.

noyade [nwajad] nf drowning q.

noyau, x [nwajo] nm (de fruit) stone; (BIO, PHYSIQUE) nucleus; (ÉLEC, GÉO, fig: centre) core; ~**ter** vt (POL) to infiltrate.

noyer [nwaje] nm walnut (tree); (bois) walnut // vt to drown; (fig) to flood; to submerge; **se** ~ vi to be drowned, drown; (suicide) to drown o.s.

nu, e [ny] a naked; (membres) naked, bare; (chambre, fil, plaine) bare // nm (ART) nude; ~**pieds** a inv barefoot; ~**tête** a inv bareheaded; **se mettre** ~ to strip; **mettre à** ~ to bare.

nuage [nɥaʒ] nm cloud; **nuageux, euse** a cloudy.

nuance [nɥɑ̃s] nf (de couleur, sens) shade; **il y a une** ~ (**entre**) there's a slight difference (between); **nuancer** vt (opinion) to bring some reservations ou qualifications to.

nucléaire [nykleɛr] a nuclear.

nudiste [nydist(ə)] nmf nudist.

nudité [nydite] nf nudity.

nuée [nɥe] nf: **une** ~ **de** a cloud ou host ou swarm of.

nues [ny] nfpl: **tomber des** ~ to be taken aback; **porter qn aux** ~ to praise sb to the skies.

nuire [nɥir] vi to be harmful; ~ **à** to harm, do damage to; **nuisible** a harmful; **animal nuisible** pest.

nuit [nɥi] nf night; **il fait** ~ it's dark; **cette** ~ last night; tonight; ~ **blanche** sleepless night; ~ **de noces** wedding night.

nul, nulle [nyl] a (aucun) no; (minime) nil, non-existent; (non valable) null; (péj) useless, hopeless // pronom none, no one; **résultat** ~, **match** ~ draw; ~**le part** ad nowhere; ~**lement** ad by no means.

numérique [nymerik] a numerical.

numéro [nymero] nm number; (spectacle) act, turn; ~ **de téléphone** (tele)phone number; ~**ter** vt to number.

nuque [nyk] nf nape of the neck.

nutritif, ive [nytritif, -iv] a nutri-

tional; (aliment) nutritious.
nylon [nilɔ̃] nm nylon.

O

oasis [ɔazis] nf oasis (pl oases).

obéir [ɔbeir] vi to obey; ~ à to obey; (suj: moteur, véhicule) to respond to: **obéissant, e** a obedient.

objecter [ɔbʒɛkte] vt (prétexter) to plead, put forward as an excuse; ~ (à qn) que to object (to sb) that.

objecteur [ɔbʒɛktœr] nm: ~ de conscience conscientious objector.

objectif, ive [ɔbʒɛktif, -iv] a objective // nm (OPTIQUE, PHOTO) lens sg, objective; (MIL, fig) objective; ~ à focale variable zoom lens.

objection [ɔbʒɛksjɔ̃] nf objection.

objet [ɔbʒɛ] nm object; (d'une discussion, recherche) subject; être ou faire l'~ de (discussion) to be the subject of; (soins) to be given ou shown; **sans** ~ a purposeless; groundless; ~ **d'art** objet d'art; ~s **personnels** personal items; ~s **trouvés** lost property sg (Brit), lost-and-found sg (US).

obligation [ɔbligasjɔ̃] nf obligation; (COMM) bond, debenture; **obligatoire** a compulsory, obligatory.

obligé, e [ɔbliʒe] a (redevable): **être très** ~ **à qn** to be most obliged to sb; **obligeant, e** a obliging; kind.

obliger [ɔbliʒe] vt (contraindre): ~ **qn à faire** to force ou oblige sb to do; (JUR: engager) to bind; (rendre service) to oblige; **je suis bien obligé** I have to.

oblique [ɔblik] a oblique; **regard** ~ sidelong glance; **en** ~ ad diagonally; **obliquer** vi: **obliquer vers** to turn off towards.

oblitérer [ɔblitere] vt (timbre-poste) to cancel.

obscène [ɔpsɛn] a obscene.

obscur, e [ɔpskyr] a dark; (fig) obscure; lowly; ~**cir** vt to darken; (fig) to obscure; **s'**~**cir** vi to grow

dark; ~**ité** nf darkness; **dans l'**~**ité** in the dark, in darkness.

obséder [ɔpsede] vt to obsess, haunt.

obsèques [ɔpsɛk] nfpl funeral sg.

observateur, trice [ɔpsɛrvatœr, -tris] a observant, perceptive // nm/f observer.

observation [ɔpsɛrvasjɔ̃] nf observation; (d'un règlement etc) observance; (reproche) reproof.

observatoire [ɔpsɛrvatwar] nm observatory; (lieu élevé) observation post, vantage point.

observer [ɔpsɛrve] vt (regarder) to observe, watch; (examiner) to examine; (scientifiquement, aussi: règlement, jeûne etc) to observe; (surveiller) to watch; (remarquer) to observe, notice; **faire** ~ **qch à qn** (dire) to point out sth to sb.

obstacle [ɔpstakl(ə)] nm obstacle; (ÉQUITATION) jump, hurdle; **faire** ~ **à** (lumière) to block out; (projet) to hinder, put obstacles in the path of.

obstiné, e [ɔpstine] a obstinate.

obstiner [ɔpstine]: **s'**~ vi to insist, dig one's heels in; **s'**~ **à faire** to persist (obstinately) in doing; **s'**~ **sur qch** to keep working at sth, labour away at sth.

obstruer [ɔpstrye] vt to block, obstruct.

obtempérer [ɔptãpere] vi to obey.

obtenir [ɔptənir] vt to obtain, get; (total, résultat) to arrive at, reach; to achieve, obtain; ~ **de pouvoir faire** to obtain permission to do; ~ **de qn qu'il fasse** to get sb to agree to do; **obtention** nf obtaining.

obturateur [ɔptyratœr] nm (PHOTO) shutter.

obturer [ɔptyre] vt to close (up); (dent) to fill.

obus [ɔby] nm shell.

occasion [ɔkazjɔ̃] nf (aubaine, possibilité) opportunity; (circonstance) occasion; (COMM: article non neuf) secondhand buy; (: acquisition avantageuse) bargain; **à plusieurs** ~**s on**

several occasions; **être l'~ de** to occasion, give rise to; **à l'~** ad sometimes, on occasions; some time; **d'~** a, ad secondhand; **occasionnel, le** a (fortuit) chance cpd; (non régulier) occasional; casual.

occasionner [ɔkazjɔne] vt to cause, bring about; **~ qch à qn** to cause sb sth.

occident [ɔksidɑ̃] nm: **l'O~** the West; **occidental, e, aux** western; (POL) Western.

occupation [ɔkypasjɔ̃] nf occupation.

occupé, e [ɔkype] a (MIL, POL) occupied; (personne: affairé, pris) busy; (place, sièges) taken; (toilettes, ligne) engaged.

occuper [ɔkype] vt to occupy; (main-d'œuvre) to employ; **s'~ (à qch)** to occupy o.s. ou keep o.s. busy (with sth); **s'~ de** (être responsable de) to be in charge of; (se charger de: affaire) to take charge of, deal with; (: clients etc) to attend to; (s'intéresser à, pratiquer) to be involved in; **ça occupe trop de place** it takes up too much room.

occurrence [ɔkyʀɑ̃s] nf: **en l'~** in this case.

océan [ɔseɑ̃] nm ocean; **l'~ Indien** the Indian Ocean.

octet [ɔktɛt] nm byte.

octobre [ɔktɔbʀ(ə)] nm October.

octroyer [ɔktʀwaje] vt: **~ qch à qn** to grant sth to sb, grant sb sth.

oculiste [ɔkylist(ə)] nm/f eye specialist.

odeur [ɔdœʀ] nf smell.

odieux, euse [ɔdjø, -øz] a hateful.

odorant, e [ɔdɔʀɑ̃, -ɑ̃t] a sweet-smelling, fragrant.

odorat [ɔdɔʀa] nm (sense of) smell.

œil [œj], pl **yeux** [jø] nm eye; **à l'~** (fam) for free; **à l'~ nu** with the naked eye; **tenir qn à l'~** to keep an eye ou a watch on sb; **avoir l'~ à** to keep an eye on; **fermer les yeux (sur)** (fig) to turn a blind eye (to).

œillade [œjad] nf: **lancer une ~ à**

qn to wink at sb, give sb a wink; **faire des ~s à** to make eyes at.

œillères [œjɛʀ] nfpl blinkers (Brit), blinders (US).

œillet [œjɛ] nm (BOT) carnation.

œuf [œf,pl ø] nm egg; **~ dur** hard-boiled egg; **~ au plat** fried egg; **~s brouillés** scrambled eggs; **~ de Pâques** Easter egg.

œuvre [œvʀ(ə)] nf (tâche) task, undertaking; (ouvrage achevé, livre, tableau etc) work; (ensemble de la production artistique) works pl; (organisation charitable) charity // nm (d'un artiste) works pl; (CONSTR): **le gros ~** the shell; **être à l'~** to be at work; **mettre en ~** (moyens) to make use of; **~ d'art** work of art.

offense [ɔfɑ̃s] nf insult.

offenser [ɔfɑ̃se] vt to offend, hurt; (principes, Dieu) to offend against; **s'~ de** to take offence at.

offert, e [ɔfɛʀ, -ɛʀt(ə)] pp de **offrir**.

office [ɔfis] nm (charge) office; (agence) bureau, agency; (REL) service // nm ou nf (pièce) pantry; **faire ~ de** to act as; to do duty as; **d'~** ad automatically; **~ du tourisme** tourist bureau.

officiel, le [ɔfisjɛl] a, nm/f official.

officier [ɔfisje] nm officer // vi to officiate; **~ de l'état-civil** registrar.

officieux, euse [ɔfisjø, -øz] a unofficial.

officinal, e, aux [ɔfisinal, -o] a: **plantes ~es** medicinal plants.

officine [ɔfisin] nf (de pharmacie) dispensary; (bureau) agency, office.

offrande [ɔfʀɑ̃d] nf offering.

offre [ɔfʀ(ə)] nf offer; (aux enchères) bid; (ADMIN: soumission) tender; (ÉCON): **l'~** supply; **~ d'emploi** job advertised; **"~s d'emploi"** 'situations vacant'; **~ publique d'achat (O.P.A.)** takeover bid.

offrir [ɔfʀiʀ] vt: **~ (à qn)** to offer (to sb); (faire cadeau de) to give (to sb); **s'~** vi (occasion, paysage) to present itself // vt (vacances, voiture) to treat o.s. to; **~ (à qn) de faire**

qch to offer to do sth (for sb); ~ à boire à qn to offer sb a drink; s'~ comme guide/en otage to offer one's services as (a) guide/offer o.s. as hostage.

offusquer [ɔfyske] vt to offend.

ogive [ɔʒiv] nf: ~ nucléaire nuclear warhead.

oie [wa] nf (ZOOL) goose (pl geese).

oignon [ɔɲ5] nm (BOT, CULIN) onion; (de tulipe etc: bulbe) bulb; (MÉD) bunion.

oiseau, x [wazo] nm bird; ~ de proie bird of prey.

oiseux, euse [wazø, -øz] a pointless; trivial.

oisif, ive [wazif, -iv] a idle // nm/f (péj) man/woman of leisure.

oléoduc [ɔleɔdyk] nm (oil) pipeline.

olive [ɔliv] nf (BOT) olive; **olivier** nm olive tree.

olympique [ɔlɛ̃pik] a Olympic.

ombrage [ɔ̃bʀaʒ] nm (ombre) (leafy) shade; **ombragé, e** a shaded, shady; **ombrageux, euse** a (cheval) skittish, nervous; (personne) touchy, easily offended.

ombre [ɔ̃bʀ(ə)] nf (espace non ensoleillé) shade; (ombre portée, tache) shadow; à l'~ in the shade; tu me fais de l'~ you're in my light; ça nous donne de l'~ it gives us (some) shade; dans l'~ (fig) in obscurity; in the dark; ~ à paupières eyeshadow.

ombrelle [ɔ̃bʀɛl] nf parasol, sunshade.

omelette [ɔmlɛt] nf omelette.

omettre [ɔmɛtʀ(ə)] vt to omit, leave out.

omnibus [ɔmnibys] nm slow ou stopping train.

omoplate [ɔmɔplat] nf shoulder blade.

MOT-CLÉ

on [5] pronom

1 (indéterminé) you, one; ~ peut le faire ainsi you ou one can do it like this, it can be done like this

2 (quelqu'un): ~ les a attaqués they were attacked; ~ vous demande au téléphone there's a phone call for you, you're wanted on the phone

3 (nous) we; ~ va y aller demain we're going tomorrow

4 (les gens) they; autrefois, ~ croyait ... they used to believe ...

5: ~ ne peut plus ad: ~ ne peut plus stupide as stupid as can be.

---

oncle [5kl(ə)] nm uncle.

onctueux, euse [5ktɥø, -øz] a creamy, smooth; (fig) smooth, unctuous.

onde [5d] nf (PHYSIQUE) wave; sur les ~s on the radio; mettre en ~s to produce for the radio; sur ~s courtes (o.c.) on short wave sg; moyennes/ longues ~s medium/ long wave sg.

ondée [5de] nf shower.

on-dit [5di] nm inv rumour.

ondoyer [5dwaje] vi to ripple, wave.

onduler [5dyle] vi to undulate; (cheveux) to wave.

onéreux, euse [5neʀø, -øz] a costly; à titre ~ in return for payment.

ongle [5gl(ə)] nm (ANAT) nail; se faire les ~s to do one's nails.

onguent [5gã] nm ointment.

ont vb voir **avoir**.

O.N.U. [ɔny] sigle f voir **organisation**.

onze [5z] num eleven; **onzième** num eleventh.

O.P.A. sigle f voir **offre**.

opale [ɔpal] nf opal.

opaque [ɔpak] a opaque.

opéra [ɔpeʀa] nm opera; (édifice) opera house; **~-comique** nm light opera.

opérateur, trice [ɔpeʀatœʀ, -tʀis] nm/f operator; ~ (de prise de vues) cameraman.

opération [ɔpeʀasj5] nf operation; (COMM) dealing.

opératoire [ɔpeʀatwaʀ] a operating; (choc etc) post-operative.

opérer [ɔpere] vt (MÉD) to operate on; (faire, exécuter) to carry out, make // vi (remède: faire effet) to act, work; (procéder) to proceed; (MÉD) to operate; s'~ vi (avoir lieu) to occur, take place; se faire ~ to have an operation.

opiner [ɔpine] vi: ~ de la tête to nod assent.

opinion [ɔpinjɔ̃] nf opinion; l'~ (publique) public opinion.

opportun, e [ɔpɔrtœ̃, -yn] a timely, opportune; en temps ~ at the appropriate time.

opposant, e [ɔpozɑ̃, -ɑ̃t] a opposing; ~s nmpl opponents.

opposé, e [ɔpoze] a (direction, rive) opposite; (faction) opposing; (couleurs) contrasting; (opinions, intérêts) conflicting; (contre): ~ à opposed to, against // nm: l'~ the other ou opposite side (ou direction); (contraire) the opposite; à l'~ (fig) on the other hand; à l'~ de on the other ou opposite side from; (fig) contrary to, unlike.

opposer [ɔpoze] vt (personnes, armées, équipes) to oppose; (couleurs, termes, tons) to contrast; ~ qch à (comme obstacle, défense) to set sth against; (comme objection) to put sth forward against; s'~ (sens réciproque) to conflict; to clash; to contrast; s'~ à (interdire, empêcher) to oppose; (tenir tête à) to rebel against.

opposition [ɔpozisjɔ̃] nf opposition; par ~ à as opposed to, in contrast with; entrer en ~ avec to come into conflict with; être en ~ avec (idées, conduite) to be at variance with; faire ~ à un chèque to stop a cheque.

oppresser [ɔprese] vt to oppress; **oppression** nf oppression; (malaise) feeling of suffocation.

opprimer [ɔprime] vt to oppress; (liberté, opinion) to suppress, stifle; (suj: chaleur etc) to suffocate, oppress.

opter [ɔpte] vi: ~ pour to opt for; ~ entre to choose between.

opticien, ne [ɔptisjɛ̃, -ɛn] nm/f optician.

optimiste [ɔptimist(ə)] nm/f optimist // a optimistic.

option [ɔpsjɔ̃] nf option; matière à ~ (SCOL) optional subject.

optique [ɔptik] a (nerf) optic; (verres) optical // nf (PHOTO: lentilles etc) optics pl; (science, industrie) optics sg; (fig: manière de voir) perspective.

opulent, e [ɔpylɑ̃, -ɑ̃t] a wealthy, opulent; (formes, poitrine) ample, generous.

or [ɔr] nm gold // cj now, but; en ~ gold cpd; (fig) golden, marvellous.

orage [ɔraʒ] nm (thunder)storm; **orageux, euse** a stormy.

oraison [ɔrɛzɔ̃] nf orison, prayer; ~ funèbre funeral oration.

oral, e, aux [ɔral, -o] a, nm oral.

orange [ɔrɑ̃ʒ] nf, a inv orange; **oranger** nm orange tree.

orateur [ɔratœr] nm speaker; orator.

orbite [ɔrbit] nf (ANAT) (eye-) socket; (PHYSIQUE) orbit.

orchestre [ɔrkɛstr(ə)] nm orchestra; (de jazz, danse) band; (places) stalls pl (Brit), orchestra (US); **orchestrer** vt (MUS) to orchestrate; (fig) to mount, stage-manage.

orchidée [ɔrkide] nf orchid.

ordinaire [ɔrdinɛr] a ordinary; everyday; standard // nm ordinary; (menus) everyday fare // nf (essence) = two-star (petrol) (Brit), = regular (gas) (US); d'~ usually, normally; à l'~ usually, ordinarily.

ordinateur [ɔrdinatœr] nm computer; ~ domestique home computer; ~ individuel personal computer.

ordonnance [ɔrdɔnɑ̃s] nf organization; layout; (MÉD) prescription; (JUR) order; (MIL) orderly, batman (Brit).

ordonné, e [ɔrdɔne] a tidy, orderly; (MATH) ordered.

ordonner [ɔʀdɔne] vt (agencer) to organize, arrange; (donner un ordre): ~ à qn de faire to order sb to do; (REL) to ordain; (MÉD) to prescribe.

ordre [ɔʀdʀ(ə)] nm (gén) order; (propreté et soin) orderliness, tidiness; (nature): d'~ pratique of a practical nature; ~s nmpl (REL) holy orders; mettre en ~ to tidy (up), put in order; à l'~ de qn payable to sb; être aux ~s de qn/sous les ~s de qn to be at sb's disposal/under sb's command; jusqu'à nouvel ~ until further notice; dans le même ~ d'idées in this connection; donnez-nous un ~ de grandeur give us some idea as regards size (ou the amount); de premier ~ first-rate; ~ du jour (d'une réunion) agenda; (MIL) order of the day; à l'~ du jour (fig) topical.

ordure [ɔʀdyʀ] nf filth q; ~s (balayures, déchets) rubbish sg, refuse sg; ~s ménagères household refuse.

oreille [ɔʀɛj] nf (ANAT) ear; (de marmite, tasse) handle; avoir de l'~ to have a good ear (for music).

oreiller [ɔʀeje] nm pillow.

oreillons [ɔʀɛjɔ̃] nmpl mumps sg.

ores [ɔʀ]: d'~ et déjà ad already.

orfèvrerie [ɔʀfɛvʀəʀi] nf goldsmith's (ou silversmith's) trade; (ouvrage) gold (ou silver) plate.

organe [ɔʀgan] nm organ; (porte-parole) representative, mouthpiece.

organigramme [ɔʀganigʀam] nm organization chart; flow chart.

organique [ɔʀganik] a organic.

organisateur, trice [ɔʀganizatœʀ, -tʀis] nm/f organizer.

organisation [ɔʀganizasjɔ̃] nf organization; O~ des Nations Unies (O.N.U.) United Nations (Organization) (UN, UNO); O~ du traité de l'Atlantique Nord (O.T.A.N.) North Atlantic Treaty Organization (NATO).

organiser [ɔʀganize] vt to organize; (mettre sur pied; service etc) to set up; s'~ to get organized.

organisme [ɔʀganism(ə)] nm (BIO) organism; (corps, ADMIN) body.

organiste [ɔʀganist(ə)] nm/f organist.

orgasme [ɔʀgasm(ə)] nm orgasm, climax.

orge [ɔʀʒ(ə)] nf barley.

orgie [ɔʀʒi] nf orgy.

orgue [ɔʀg(ə)] nm organ; ~s nfpl organ sg.

orgueil [ɔʀgœj] nm pride; **orgueilleux, euse** a proud.

Orient [ɔʀjɑ̃] nm: l'~ the East, the Orient.

oriental, e, aux [ɔʀjɑ̃tal, -o] a oriental, eastern; (frontière) eastern.

orientation [ɔʀjɑ̃tasjɔ̃] nf positioning; orientation; (d'une maison etc) aspect; (d'un journal) leanings pl; avoir le sens de l'~ to have a (good) sense of direction; ~ professionnelle careers advising; careers advisory service.

orienté, e [ɔʀjɑ̃te] a (fig: article, journal) slanted; bien/mal ~ (appartement) well/badly positioned; ~ au sud facing south ou with a southern aspect.

orienter [ɔʀjɑ̃te] vt (placer, disposer: pièce mobile) to adjust, position; (tourner) to direct, turn; (voyageur, touriste, recherches) to direct; (fig: élève) to orientate; s'~ (se repérer) to find one's bearings; s'~ vers (fig) to turn towards.

originaire [ɔʀiʒinɛʀ] a: être ~ de to be a native of.

original, e, aux [ɔʀiʒinal, -o] a original; (bizarre) eccentric // nm/f eccentric // nm (document etc, ART) original; (dactylographie) top copy.

origine [ɔʀiʒin] nf origin; dès l'~ at ou from the outset; à l'~ originally; **originel, le** a original.

O.R.L. sigle nm/f de oto-rhino-laryngologiste.

orme [ɔʀm(ə)] nm elm.

ornement [ɔʀnəmɑ̃] nm ornament; (fig) embellishment, adornment.

orner [ɔʀne] vt to decorate, adorn.

ornière [ɔʀnjɛʀ] nf rut.

orphelin, e [ɔʀfəlɛ̃, -in] a orphan(ed) // nm/f orphan; ~ **de père/mère** fatherless/motherless; **orphelinat** nm orphanage.

orteil [ɔʀtɛj] nm toe; **gros** ~ big toe.

orthographe [ɔʀtɔgʀaf] nf spelling; **orthographier** vt to spell.

orthopédiste [ɔʀtɔpedist(ə)] nm/f orthopaedic specialist.

ortie [ɔʀti] nf (stinging) nettle.

os [ɔs, pl o] nm bone.

osciller [ɔsile] vi (pendule) to swing; (au vent etc) to rock; (TECH) to oscillate; (fig): ~ **entre** to waver ou fluctuate between.

osé, e [oze] a daring, bold.

oseille [ozɛj] nf sorrel.

oser [oze] vi, vt to dare; ~ **faire** to dare (to) do.

osier [ozje] nm willow; **d'**~, **en** ~ wicker(work).

ossature [ɔsatyʀ] nf (ANAT) frame, skeletal structure; (fig) framework.

osseux, euse [ɔsø, -øz] a bony; (tissu, maladie, greffe) bone cpd.

ostensible [ɔstɑ̃sibl(ə)] a conspicuous.

otage [ɔtaʒ] nm hostage; **prendre qn comme** ~ to take sb hostage.

O.T.A.N. [ɔtɑ̃] sigle f voir **organisation**.

otarie [ɔtaʀi] nf sea-lion.

ôter [ote] vt to remove; (soustraire) to take away; ~ **qch à qn** to take sth (away) from sb; ~ **qch à** to remove sth from.

otite [ɔtit] nf ear infection.

oto-rhino-(laryngologiste) [ɔtɔʀinɔ(laʀɛ̃gɔlɔʒist(ə))] nm/f ear nose and throat specialist.

ou [u] cj or; ~ ... ~ either ... or; ~ **bien** or (else).

MOT-CLÉ

---

où [u] ◆ pronom relatif **1** (position, situation) where, that (souvent omis); **la chambre** ~ **il était** the room (that) he was in, the room

where he was; **la ville** ~ **je l'ai rencontré** the town where I met him; **la place** ~ **la** the room he came out of; **le village d'**~ **je viens** the village I come from; **les villes par** ~ **il est passé** the towns he went through

2 (temps, état) that (souvent omis); **le jour** ~ **il est parti** the day (that) he left; **au prix** ~ **c'est** at the price it is

◆ ad **1** (interrogation) where; ~ **est-il/va-t-il?** where is he/is he going?; **par** ~? which way?; **d'**~ **vient que ...?** how come ...?

2 (position) where; **je sais** ~ **il est** I know where he is; ~ **que l'on aille** wherever you go.

---

ouate [wat] nf cotton wool (Brit), cotton (US); (bourre) padding, wadding.

oubli [ubli] nm (acte): **l'**~ **de** forgetting; (étourderie) forgetfulness q; (négligence) omission, oversight; (absence de souvenirs) oblivion.

oublier [ublije] vt (gén) to forget; (ne pas voir: erreurs etc) to miss; (ne pas mettre: virgule, nom) to leave out; (laisser quelque part: chapeau etc) to leave behind; **s'**~ to forget o.s.

oubliettes [ublijɛt] nfpl dungeon sg.

oublieux, euse [ublijø, -øz] a forgetful.

ouest [wɛst] nm west // a inv west; (région) western; **à l'**~ in the west; (to the) west, westwards; **à l'**~ **de** (to the) west of.

ouf [uf] excl phew!

oui [wi] ad yes.

ouï-dire [widiʀ]: **par** ~ ad by hearsay.

ouïe [wi] nf hearing; ~**s** nfpl (de poisson) gills.

ouïr [wiʀ] vt to hear; **avoir ouï dire que** to have heard it said that.

ouragan [uʀagɑ̃] nm hurricane.

ourlet [uʀlɛ] nm hem.

ours [uʀs] nm bear; ~ **brun/blanc**

brown/polar bear; ~ (en peluche) teddy (bear).

oursin [urSɛ̃] nm sea urchin.

ourson [urs5] nm (bear-)cub.

ouste [ust(ə)] excl hop it!

outil [uti] nm tool.

outiller [utije] vt (ouvrier, usine) to equip.

outrage [utraʒ] nm insult; **faire subir les derniers ~s à (femme)** to ravish; ~ **à la pudeur** indecent conduct q.

outrager [utraʒe] vt to offend gravely.

outrance [utrɑ̃s] : **à ~** ad excessively, to excess.

outre [utr(ə)] nf goatskin, water skin // prép besides // ad: **passer ~ à** to disregard, take no notice of; **en ~** besides, moreover; ~ **que** apart from the fact that; ~ **mesure** immoderately; unduly.

outre-Atlantique [utraatlɑ̃tik] ad across the Atlantic.

outre-Manche [utrəmɑ̃ʃ] ad across the Channel.

outremer [utrəmɛr] a inv ultramarine.

outre-mer [utrəmɛr] ad overseas.

outrepasser [utrəpase] vt to go beyond, exceed.

outrer [utre] vt to exaggerate; (choquer) to outrage.

ouvert, e [uvɛr, -ɛrt(ə)] pp de **ouvrir** // a open; (robinet, gaz etc) on; **ouvertement** ad openly.

ouverture [uvɛrtyr] nf opening; (MUS) overture; (PHOTO): ~ **(du diaphragme)** aperture; ~s nfpl (propositions) overtures; ~ **d'esprit** open-mindedness.

ouvrable [uvrabl(ə)] a: **jour ~** working day, weekday.

ouvrage [uvraʒ] nm (tâche, de tricot etc, MIL) work q; (texte, livre) work.

ouvragé, e [uvraʒe] a finely embroidered (ou worked ou carved).

ouvre-boîte(s) [uvrəbwat] nm inv tin (Brit) ou can opener.

ouvre-bouteille(s) [uvrəbutɛj] nm

inv bottle-opener.

ouvreuse [uvrøz] nf usherette.

ouvrier, ière [uvrije, -jɛr] nm/f worker // a working-class; industrial, labour cpd; **classe ouvrière** working class.

ouvrir [uvrir] vt (gén) to open; (brèche, passage, MÉD: abcès) to open up; (commencer l'exploitation de, créer) to open (up); (eau, électricité, chauffage, robinet) to turn on // vi to open; to open up; **s'~** vi to open; **s'~ à qn** to open one's heart to sb; ~ **l'appétit à qn** to whet sb's appetite.

ovaire [ovɛr] nm ovary.

ovale [oval] a oval.

ovni [ovni] sigle m (= objet volant non identifié) UFO.

oxyder [okside]: **s'~** vi to become oxidized.

oxygène [oksiʒɛn] nm oxygen; (fig): **cure d'~** fresh air cure.

oxygéné, e [oksiʒene] a: **eau ~e** hydrogen peroxide.

P

pacifique [pasifik] a peaceful // nm: **le P~, l'océan P~** the Pacific (Ocean).

pacte [pakt(ə)] nm pact, treaty.

pactiser [paktize] vi: ~ **avec** to come to terms with.

pagaie [pagɛ] nf paddle.

pagaille [pagaj] nf mess, shambles sg.

page [paʒ] nf page // nm page; **à la ~** (fig) up-to-date.

paie [pɛ] nf = **paye**.

paiement [pɛmɑ̃] nm = **payement**.

païen, ne [pajɛ̃, -jɛn] a, nm/f pagan, heathen.

paillard, e [pajar, -ard(ə)] a bawdy.

paillasson [pajas5] nm doormat.

paille [paj] nf straw; (défaut) flaw.

paillettes [pajɛt] nfpl (décoratives) sequins, spangles; **lessive en ~** soapflakes pl.

pain [pɛ̃] *nm* (*substance*) bread; (*unité*) loaf (*pl* loaves) (of bread); (*morceau*) ~ **de cire** *etc* bar of wax *etc*; ~ **bis/complet** brown/ wholemeal (*Brit*) *ou* wholewheat (*US*) bread; ~ **d'épice** gingerbread; ~ **grillé** toast; ~ **de mie** sandwich loaf; ~ **de sucre** sugar loaf.

pair, e [pɛʀ] *a* (*nombre*) even // *nm* peer; **aller de** ~ to go hand in hand *ou* together; **jeune fille au** ~ *au* pair.

paire [pɛʀ] *nf* pair.

paisible [pezibl(ə)] *a* peaceful, quiet.

paître [pɛtʀ(ə)] *vi* to graze.

paix [pɛ] *nf* peace; (*fig*) peacefulness, peace; **faire/avoir la** ~ to make/ have peace.

Pakistan [pakistɑ̃] *nm*: **le** ~ Pakistan.

palace [palas] *nm* luxury hotel.

palais [palɛ] *nm* palace; (*ANAT*) palate.

pale [pal] *nf* (*d'hélice, de rame*) blade.

pâle [pɑl] *a* pale; **bleu** ~ pale blue.

Palestine [palɛstin] *nf*: **la** ~ Palestine; **palestinien, ne** *a*, *nm/f* Palestinien.

palet [palɛ] *nm* disc, (*HOCKEY*) puck.

palette [palɛt] *nf* (*de peintre*) palette; (*produits*) range.

pâleur [palœʀ] *nf* paleness.

palier [palje] *nm* (*d'escalier*) landing; (*fig*) level, plateau; (*TECH*) bearing; **par** ~**s** in stages.

pâlir [paliʀ] *vi* to turn *ou* go pale; (*couleur*) to fade.

palissade [palisad] *nf* fence.

palliatif [paljatif] *nm* palliative; (*expédient*) stopgap measure.

pallier [palje] *vt*: ~ **à**; *vt* to offset, make up for.

palmarès [palmaʀɛs] *nm* record of achievements; (*SCOL*) prize list; (*SPORT*) list of winners.

palme [palm(ə)] *nf* (*symbole*) palm; (*de plongeur*) flipper; **palmé, e** *a* (*pattes*) webbed.

palmier [palmje] *nm* palm tree.

palombe [palɔ̃b] *nf* woodpigeon.

pâlot, e [pɑlo, -ɔt] *a* pale, peaky.

palourde [paluʀd(ə)] *nf* clam.

palper [palpe] *vt* to feel, finger.

palpitant, e [palpitɑ̃, -ɑ̃t] *a* thrilling.

palpiter [palpite] *vi* (*cœur, pouls*) to beat; (: *plus fort*) to pound, throb.

paludisme [palydism(ə)] *nm* malaria.

pamphlet [pɑ̃flɛ] *nm* lampoon, satirical tract.

pamplemousse [pɑ̃pləmus] *nm* grapefruit.

pan [pɑ̃] *nm* section, piece // *excl* bang!; ~ **de chemise** shirt tail.

panachage [panaʃaʒ] *nm* blend, mix.

panache [panaʃ] *nm* plume; (*fig*) spirit, panache.

panaché, e *a*: **glace** ~**e** mixed-flavour ice cream; **bière** ~**e** shandy.

pancarte [pɑ̃kaʀt(ə)] *nf* sign, notice; (*dans un défilé*) placard.

pancréas [pɑ̃kʀeas] *nm* pancreas.

pané, e [pane] *a* fried in breadcrumbs.

panier [panje] *nm* basket; **mettre au** ~ to chuck away; ~ **à provisions** shopping basket.

panique [panik] *nf*, *a* panic; **paniquer** *vi* to panic.

panne [pan] *nf* (*d'un mécanisme, moteur*) breakdown; **être/tomber en** ~ to have broken down/break down; **être en** ~ **d'essence** *ou* **sèche** to have run out of petrol (*Brit*) *ou* gas (*US*); ~ **d'électricité** *ou* **de courant** power *ou* electrical failure.

panneau, x [pano] *nm* (*écriteau*) sign, notice; (*de boiserie, de tapisserie etc*) panel; ~ **d'affichage** notice board; ~ **de signalisation** roadsign.

panonceau, x [panɔ̃so] *nm* sign.

panoplie [panɔpli] *nf* (*jouet*) outfit; (*d'armes*) display; (*fig*) array.

panorama [panɔʀama] *nm* panorama.

panse [pɑ̃s] *nf* paunch.

pansement [pɑ̃smɑ̃] *nm* dressing, bandage; ~ **adhésif** sticking plaster.

panser [pɑ̃se] *vt* (*plaie*) to dress, bandage; (*bras*) to put a dressing on, bandage; (*cheval*) to groom.

pantalon [pɑ̃talɔ̃] *nm* (*aussi*: ~s, **paire de** ~s) trousers *pl*, pair of trousers; ~ **de ski** ski pants *pl*.

pantelant, e [pɑ̃tlɑ̃, -ɑ̃t] *a* gasping for breath, panting.

panthère [pɑ̃tɛʀ] *nf* panther.

pantin [pɑ̃tɛ̃] *nm* jumping jack; (*péj*) puppet.

pantois [pɑ̃twa] *am*: **rester** ~ to be flabbergasted.

pantomime [pɑ̃tɔmim] *nf* mime; (*pièce*) mime show.

pantoufle [pɑ̃tufl(ə)] *nf* slipper.

paon [pɑ̃] *nm* peacock.

papa [papa] *nm* dad(dy).

pape [pap] *nm* pope.

paperasse [papʀas] *nf* (*péj*) bumf *q*, papers *pl*; ~**rie** *nf* (*péj*) red tape *q*; paperwork *q*.

papeterie [papetʀi] *nf* (*usine*) paper mill; (*magasin*) stationer's (shop).

papier [papje] *nm* paper; (*article*) article; ~s (*aussi*: ~s **d'identité**) (identity) papers; ~ **(d')aluminium** aluminium (*Brit*) *ou* aluminum (*US*) foil, tinfoil; ~ **buvard** blotting paper; ~ **carbone** carbon paper; ~ **hygiénique** toilet paper; ~ **journal** newsprint; (*pour emballer*) newspaper; ~ **à lettres** writing paper, notepaper; ~ **peint** wallpaper; ~ **de verre** sandpaper.

papillon [papijɔ̃] *nm* butterfly; (*fam: contravention*) (parking) ticket; (*TECH: écrou*) wing nut; ~ **de nuit** moth.

papilloter [papijɔte] *vi* to blink, flicker.

paquebot [pakbo] *nm* liner.

pâquerette [pakʀɛt] *nf* daisy.

Pâques [pak] *nm, nfpl* Easter.

paquet [pakɛ] *nm* packet; (*colis*) parcel; (*fig: tas*): ~ **de** pile *ou* heap of; ~**cadeau** *nm* gift-wrapped parcel.

par [paʀ] *prép* by; **finir** *etc* ~ to end *etc* with; ~ **amour** out of love; **passer** ~ **Lyon/la côte** to go via *ou* through Lyons/along by the coast; ~ **la fenêtre** (*jeter, regarder*) out of the window; 3 ~ **jour/personne** 3 a *ou* per day/head; 2 ~ 2 two at a time; in twos; ~ **ici** this way; (*dans le coin*) round here; ~**-ci, ~-là** here and there.

parabole [paʀabɔl] *nf* (*REL*) parable.

parachever [paʀaʃve] *vt* to perfect.

parachute [paʀaʃyt] *nm* parachute.

parachutiste [paʀaʃytist(ə)] *nm/f* parachutist; (*MIL*) paratrooper.

parade [paʀad] *nf* (*spectacle, défilé*) parade; (*ESCRIME, BOXE*) parry.

paradis [paʀadi] *nm* heaven, paradise.

paradoxe [paʀadɔks(ə)] *nm* paradox.

paraffine [paʀafin] *nf* paraffin.

parages [paʀaʒ] *nmpl*: **dans les** ~ **(de)** in the area *ou* vicinity (of).

paragraphe [paʀagʀaf] *nm* paragraph.

paraître [paʀɛtʀ(ə)] *vb avec attribut* to seem, look, appear // *vi* to appear; (*être visible*) to show; (*PRESSE, ÉDITION*) to be published, come out, appear; (*briller*) to show off // *vb impersonnel*: **il paraît que** it seems *ou* appears that, they say that; **il me paraît que** it seems to me that.

parallèle [paʀalɛl] *a* parallel; (*police, marché*) unofficial // *nm* (*comparaison*): **faire un** ~ **entre** to draw a parallel between; (*GÉO*) parallel // *nf* parallel line.

paralyser [paʀalize] *vt* to paralyze.

parapet [paʀapɛ] *nm* parapet.

parapher [paʀafe] *vt* to initial; to sign.

paraphrase [paʀafʀaz] *nf* paraphrase.

parapluie [paʀaplɥi] *nm* umbrella.

parasite [paʀazit] *nm* parasite; ~**s** (*TÉL*) interference *sg*.

parasol [paʀasɔl] *nm* parasol, sunshade.

paratonnerre [paratɔnɛr] *nm* lightning conductor.

paravent [paravɑ̃] *nm* folding screen.

parc [park] *nm* (public) park, gardens *pl*; (de château etc) grounds *pl*; (pour le bétail) pen, enclosure; (d'enfant) playpen; (MIL: entrepôt) depot; (ensemble d'unités) stock; (de voitures etc) fleet; (d'un pays) number of cars on the roads; ~ **de stationnement** car park.

parcelle [parsɛl] *nf* fragment, scrap; (de terrain) plot, parcel.

parce que [parskə] *cj* because.

parchemin [parʃəmɛ̃] *nm* parchment.

parc(o)mètre [park(ɔ)mɛtr(ə)] *nm* parking meter.

parcourir [parkurir] *vt* (trajet, distance) to cover; (article, livre) to skim *ou* glance through; (lieu) to go all over, travel up and down; (suj: frisson, vibration) to run through.

parcours [parkur] *nm* (trajet) journey; (itinéraire) route; (SPORT: terrain) course; (: tour) round; run, lap.

par-dessous [pardəsu] *prép, ad* under(neath).

pardessus [pardəsy] *nm* overcoat.

par-dessus [pardəsy] *prép* over (the top of) // *ad* over (the top); ~ **le marché** on top of all that.

par-devant [pardəvɑ̃] *prép* in the presence of, before // *ad* at the front; round the front.

pardon [pardɔ̃] *nm* forgiveness *q* // *excl* sorry!; (pour interpeller etc) excuse me!; **demander** ~ **à qn (de)** to apologize to sb (for); **je vous demande** ~ I'm sorry; excuse me.

pardonner [pardɔne] *vt* to forgive; ~ **qch à qn** to forgive sb for sth.

pare-balles [parbal] *a inv* bulletproof.

pare-boue [parbu] *nm inv* mudguard.

pare-brise [parbriz] *nm inv* wind-

screen (Brit), windshield (US).

pare-chocs [parʃɔk] *nm inv* bumper.

pareil, le [parɛj] *a* (identique) the same, alike; (similaire) similar; (tel): **un courage/livre** ~ such courage/a book, courage/a book like this; **de** ~**s livres** such books; **ses** ~**s** one's fellow men; one's peers; **ne pas avoir son(sa)** ~(le) to be second to none; ~ **à** the same as; similar to; **sans** ~ unparalleled, unequalled.

parent, e [parɑ̃, -ɑ̃t] *nm/f*: **un/une** ~**e** a relative *ou* relation // *a*: **être** ~ **de** to be related to; ~**s** *nmpl* (père et mère) parents; **parenté** *nf* (lien) relationship.

parenthèse [parɑ̃tɛz] *nf* (ponctuation) bracket, parenthesis; (MATH) bracket; (digression) parenthesis, digression; **ouvrir/fermer la** ~ to open/close the brackets; **entre** ~**s** in brackets; (fig) incidentally.

parer [pare] *vt* to adorn; (CULIN) to dress, trim; (éviter) to ward off.

pare-soleil [parsɔlɛj] *nm inv* sun visor.

paresse [parɛs] *nf* laziness; **paresseux, euse** *a* lazy; (fig) slow, sluggish.

parfaire [parfɛr] *vt* to perfect.

parfait, e [parfɛ, -ɛt] *a* perfect // *nm* (LING) perfect (tense); **parfaitement** *ad* perfectly // *excl* (most) certainly.

parfois [parfwa] *ad* sometimes.

parfum [parfœ̃] *nm* (produit) perfume, scent; (odeur: de fleur) scent, fragrance; (: de tabac, vin) aroma; (goût) flavour; (fig) aroma; **parfumé, e** *a* (fleur, fruit) fragrant; (femme) perfumed; **parfumé au café** coffee-flavoured; **parfumer** *vt* (suj: odeur, bouquet) to perfume; (mouchoir) to put scent *ou* perfume on; (crème, gâteau) to flavour; **parfumerie** *nf* (commerce) perfumery; (produits) perfumes *pl*; (boutique) perfume shop.

pari [pari] *nm* bet, wager; (SPORT)

bet.

paria [parja] *nm* outcast.

parier [parje] *vt* to bet.

Paris [pari] *n* Paris; **parisien, ne** *a* Parisian; (*GÉO, ADMIN*) Paris *cpd // nm/f:* **Parisien, ne** Parisian.

paritaire [pariter] *a* joint.

parjure [parʒyr] *nm* perjury; **se parjurer** *vi* to forswear *ou* perjure o.s.

parking [parkiŋ] *nm* (*lieu*) car park.

parlant, e [parlɑ̃, -ɑ̃t] *a* (*fig*) graphic, vivid; eloquent; (*CINÉMA*) talking.

parlement [parləmɑ̃] *nm* parliament; **parlementaire** *a* parliamentary // *nm/f* member of parliament.

parlementer [parləmɑ̃te] *vi* to negotiate, parley.

parler [parle] *vi* to speak; talk; (*avouer*) to talk; ~ (à qn) de to talk *ou* speak (to sb) about; ~ le/en français to speak French/in French; ~ affaires to talk business; ~ en dormant to talk in one's sleep; sans ~ de (*fig*) not to mention, to say nothing of; **tu parles!** you must be joking!

parloir [parlwar] *nm* (*de prison, d'hôpital*) visiting room; (*REL*) parlour.

parmi [parmi] *prép* among(st).

paroi [parwa] *nf* wall; (*cloison*) partition; ~ **rocheuse** rock face.

paroisse [parwas] *nf* parish.

parole [parɔl] *nf* (*faculté*): **la** ~ speech; (*mot, promesse*) word; ~**s** (*MUS*) words, lyrics; **tenir** ~ to keep one's word; **prendre la** ~ to speak; **demander la** ~ to ask for permission to speak; **je le crois sur** ~ I'll take his word for it.

parquer [parke] *vt* (*voiture, matériel*) to park; (*bestiaux*) to pen (in *ou* up).

parquet [parke] *nm* (*parquet*) floor; (*JUR*): **le** ~ the Public Prosecutor's department.

parrain [parɛ̃] *nm* godfather; (*d'un nouvel adhérent*) sponsor, proposer.

pars *vb voir* **partir**.

parsemer [parsəme] *vt* (*suj: feuilles, papiers*) to be scattered over; ~ **qch de** to scatter sth with.

part [par] *nf* (*qui revient à qn*) share; (*fraction, partie*) part; (*FINANCE*) (non-voting) share; **prendre** ~ **à** (*débat etc*) to take part in; (*soucis, douleur de qn*) to share in; **faire** ~ **de qch à qn** to announce sth to sb, inform sb of sth; **pour ma** ~ as for me, as far as I'm concerned; **à** ~ **entière** a full; **de la** ~ **de** (*au nom de*) on behalf of; (*donné par*) from; **de toute(s)** ~**(s)** from all sides *ou* quarters; **de** ~ **et d'autre** on both sides, on either side; **de** ~ **en** ~ right through; **d'une** ~ ... **d'autre** ~ on the one hand ... on the other hand; **à** ~ *ad* separately; (*de côté*) aside // *prép* apart from, except for // *a* exceptional, special; **faire la** ~ **des choses** to make allowances.

partage [partaʒ] *nm* dividing up; sharing (out) q, share-out; sharing; **recevoir qch en** ~ to receive sth as one's share (*ou* lot).

partager [partaʒe] *vt* to share; (*distribuer, répartir*) to share (out); (*morceler, diviser*) to divide (up); **se** ~ *vt* (*héritage etc*) to share between themselves (*ou* ourselves).

partance [partɑ̃s]: **en** ~ *ad* outbound, due to leave; **en** ~ **pour** (bound) for.

partant [partɑ̃] *vb voir* **partir** // *nm* (*SPORT*) starter; (*HIPPISME*) runner.

partenaire [partəner] *nm/f* partner.

parterre [parter] *nm* (*de fleurs*) (flower) bed; (*THÉÂTRE*) stalls *pl*.

parti [parti] *nm* (*POL*) party; (*décision*) course of action; (*personne à marier*) match; **tirer** ~ **de** to take advantage of, turn to good account; **prendre le** ~ **de qn** to stand up for sb, side with sb; **prendre** ~ (*pour/contre*) to take sides *ou* a stand (for/against); **prendre son** ~ **de** to come to terms with; ~ **pris** bias.

partial, e, aux [parsjal, -o] *a* biased, partial.

participant, e [partisipɑ̃, -ɑ̃t] *nm/f* participant; (*à un concours*) entrant.

participation [partisipasjɔ̃] *nf* participation; sharing; (*COMM*) interest; **la ~ aux bénéfices** profit-sharing.

participe [partisip] *nm* participle.

participer [partisipe]: **~ à** *vt* (*course, réunion*) to take part in; (*profits etc*) to share in; (*frais etc*) to contribute to; (*chagrin, succès de qn*) to share (in).

particularité [partikylarite] *nf* particularity; (*distinctive*) characteristic.

particule [partikyl] *nf* particle.

particulier, ière [partikylje, -jɛr] *a* (*personnel, privé*) private; (*spécial*) special, particular; (*caractéristique*) characteristic, distinctive; (*spécifique*) particular // *nm* (*individu: ADMIN*) private individual; **~ à** peculiar to; **en ~** *ad* (*surtout*) in particular, particularly; (*en privé*) in private; **particulièrement** *ad* particularly.

partie [parti] *nf* (*gén*) part; (*profession, spécialité*) field, subject; (*JUR etc*) protagonists) party; (*de cartes, tennis etc*) game; **une ~ de campagne/de pêche** an outing in the country/a fishing party ou trip; **en ~** partly, in part; **faire ~ de** to belong to; (*suj: chose*) to be part of; **prendre qn à ~** to take sb to task; (*malmener*) to set on sb; **en grande ~** largely, in the main; **~ civile** (*JUR*) party claiming damages in a criminal case.

partiel, le [parsjɛl] *a* partial // *nm* (*SCOL*) class exam.

partir [partir] *vi* (*gén*) to go; (*quitter*) to go, leave; (*s'éloigner*) to go (ou drive ou walk) away ou off; (*moteur*) to start; **~ de** (*lieu: quitter*) to leave; (*: commencer à*) to start from; (*date*) to run ou start from; **à ~ de** from.

partisan, e [partizɑ̃, -an] *nm/f* partisan // *a*: **être ~ de qch/faire** to be in favour of sth/doing.

partition [partisjɔ̃] *nf* (*MUS*) score.

partout [partu] *ad* everywhere; **~ où il allait** everywhere ou wherever he went; **trente ~** (*TENNIS*) thirty all.

paru *pp de* **paraître**.

parure [paryr] *nf* (*bijoux etc*) finery *q*; jewellery *q*; (*assortiment*) set.

parution [parysjɔ̃] *nf* publication, appearance.

parvenir [parvenir]: **~ à** *vt* (*atteindre*) to reach; (*réussir*): **~ à faire** to manage to do, succeed in doing; **faire ~ qch à qn** to have sth sent to sb.

parvis [parvi] *nm* square (*in front of a church*).

pas [pɑ] *ad voir le mot suivant* // *nm* (*allure, mesure*) pace; (*démarche*) tread; (*enjambée, DANSE*) step; (*bruit*) (foot)step; (*trace*) footprint; (*TECH: de vis, d'écrou*) thread; **~ à ~** step by step; **au ~** at walking pace; **à ~ de loup** stealthily; **faire les cent ~** to pace up and down; **faire les premiers ~** to make the first move; **sur le ~ de la porte** on the doorstep.

MOT-CLÉ

---

pas [pɑ] ◆ *nm voir le mot précédent*
◆ *ad* **1** (*en corrélation avec ne, non etc*) not; **il ne pleure ~** he does not ou doesn't cry; **he's not ou isn't crying; **il n'a ~ pleuré/ne pleura ~** he did not ou didn't/will not ou won't cry; **ils n'ont ~ de voiture/ d'enfants** they haven't got a car/any children, they have no car/children; **il m'a dit de ne ~ le faire** he told me not to do it; **non ~ que ...** not that ...

2 (*employé sans ne etc*): **~ moi** not me; **not I, I don't (ou can't etc)**; **~ pomme ~ mûre** an apple which isn't ripe; **~ plus tard qu'hier** only yesterday; **~ du tout** not at all

3: ~ **mal** not bad; not badly; ~ **mal de** quite a lot of.

passage [pasaʒ] nm (fait de passer) voir passer; (lieu, prix de la traversée, extrait de livre etc) passage; (chemin) way; **de ~** (touristes) passing through; (amants etc) casual; ~ **clouté** pedestrian crossing; '~ **interdit**' 'no entry'; **à niveau** level crossing; ~ **protégé** right of way over secondary road(s) on your right; ~ **souterrain** subway (Brit), underpass.

passager, e [pasaʒe, -ɛʀ] a (rue, endroit) busy // nm/f passenger; ~ **clandestin** stowaway.

passant, e [pasɑ̃, -ɑ̃t] a (rue, endroit) busy // nm/f passer-by; **en ~** in passing.

passe [pas] nf (SPORT, magnétique, NAVIG) pass // nm (passe-partout) master ou skeleton key; **être en ~ de faire** to be on the way to doing.

passé, e [pase] a (événement, temps) past; (couleur, tapisserie) faded // prép after // nm (aussi: LING) past (tense); ~ **de mode** out of fashion; ~ **composé** perfect (tense); ~ **simple** past historic.

passe-droit [pasdʀwa] nm special privilege.

passementerie [pasmɑ̃tʀi] nf trimmings pl.

passe-montagne [pasmɔ̃taɲ] nm balaclava.

passe-partout [paspaʀtu] nm inv master ou skeleton key // a inv all-purpose.

passe-passe [paspas] nm: **tour de ~** trick, sleight of hand q.

passeport [paspɔʀ] nm passport.

passer [pase] vi (se rendre, aller) to go; (voiture, piétons: défiler) to pass (by), go by; (faire une halte rapide: facteur, laitier etc) to come, call; (: pour rendre visite) to call ou drop in; (courant, air, lumière, franchir un obstacle etc) to get through; (accusé, projet de loi): ~ **devant** to

come before; (film, émission) to be on; (temps, jours) to pass, go by; (couleur, papier) to fade; (mode) to die out; (douleur) to pass, go away; (CARTES) to pass // (SCOL) to go up (to the next class) // vt (frontière, rivière etc) to cross; (douane) to go through; (examen) to sit, take; (visite médicale) to have; (journée, temps) to spend; (donner): ~ **qch à qn** to pass sth to sb; to give sb sth; (transmettre): ~ **qch à qn** to pass sth on to sb; (enfiler: vêtement) to slip on; (faire entrer, mettre): **(faire)** ~ **qch dans/par** to get sth into/through; (café) to pour the water on; (thé, soupe) to strain; (film, pièce) to show, put on; (disque) to play, put on; (marché, accord) to agree on; (tolérer): ~ **qch à qn** to let sb get away with sth; **se** ~ vi (avoir lieu: scène, action) to take place; (se dérouler: entretien etc) to go; (arriver): **que s'est-il passé?** what happened?; (s'écouler: semaine etc) to pass, go by; **se** ~ **de** vt to go ou do without; **se** ~ **les mains sous l'eau/de l'eau sur le visage** to put one's hands under the tap/run water over one's face; ~ **par** to go through; ~ **sur** vt (faute, détail inutile) to pass over; ~ **avant qch/qn** (fig) to come before sth/sb; **laisser** ~ (air, lumière, personne) to let through; (occasion) to let slip, miss; (erreur) to overlook; ~ **à la radio/télévision** to be on the radio/on television; ~ **pour riche** to be taken for a rich man; ~ **en seconde**, ~ **la seconde** (AUTO) to change into second; ~ **le balai/l'aspirateur** to sweep up/hoover; **je vous passe M. X** (je vous mets en communication avec lui) I'm putting you through to Mr X; (je lui passe l'appareil) here is Mr X, I'll hand you over to Mr X.

passerelle [pasʀɛl] nf footbridge; (de navire, avion) gangway.

passe-temps [pastɑ̃] nm inv pastime.

passette [pasɛt] nf (tea-)strainer.

passeur, euse [pasœʀ, -øz] nm/f smuggler.

passible [pasibl(ə)] a: ~ de liable to.

passif, ive [pasif, -iv] a passive // nm (LING) passive; (COMM) liabilities pl.

passion [pasjɔ̃] nf passion; **passionnant, e** a fascinating; **passionné, e** a passionate; impassioned; **passionner** vt (personne) to fascinate, grip; se passionner pour to take an avid interest in; to have a passion for.

passoire [paswaʀ] nf sieve; (à légumes) colander; (à thé) strainer.

pastèque [pastɛk] nf watermelon.

pasteur [pastœʀ] nm (protestant) minister, pastor.

pastille [pastij] nf (à sucer) lozenge, pastille; (de papier etc) (small) disc.

patate [patat] nf: ~ douce sweet potato.

patauger [patoʒe] vi (pour s'amuser) to splash about; (avec effort) to wade about.

pâte [pat] nf (à tarte) pastry; (à pain) dough; (à frire) batter; (substance molle) cream; ~s nfpl (macaroni etc) pasta sg; ~ d'amandes almond paste; ~ brisée shortcrust pastry; ~ de fruits crystallized fruit q; ~ à modeler modelling clay, Plasticine ® (Brit).

pâté [pate] nm (charcuterie) pâté; (tache) ink blot; (de sable) sandpie; ~ en croûte ≈ pork pie; ~ de maisons block of houses).

pâtée [pate] nf mash, feed.

patente [patɑ̃t] nf (COMM) trading licence.

patère [patɛʀ] nf (coat-)peg.

paternel, le [patɛʀnɛl] a (amour, soins) fatherly; (ligne, autorité) paternal.

pâteux, euse [patø, -øz] a thick, pasty.

pathétique [patetik] a moving.

patience [pasjɑ̃s] nf patience.

patient, e [pasjɑ̃, -ɑ̃t] a, nm/f patient.

patienter [pasjɑ̃te] vi to wait.

patin [patɛ̃] nm skate; (sport) skating; ~s (à glace) (ice) skates; ~ à roulettes roller skates.

patinage [patinaʒ] nm skating.

patiner [patine] vi to skate; (embrayage) to slip; (roue, voiture) to spin; se ~ vi (meuble, cuir) to acquire a sheen; **patineur, euse** nm/f skater; **patinoire** nf skating rink, (ice) rink.

pâtir [patiʀ]: ~ de vt to suffer because of.

pâtisserie [patisʀi] nf (boutique) cake shop; (métier) confectionery; (à la maison) pastry- ou cake-making, baking; ~s nfpl (gâteaux) pastries, cakes; **pâtissier, ière** nm/f pastrycook; confectioner.

patois [patwa] nm dialect, patois.

patrie [patʀi] nf homeland.

patrimoine [patʀimwan] nm inheritance, patrimony; (culture) heritage.

patriotique [patʀijɔtik] a patriotic.

patron, ne [patʀɔ̃, -ɔn] nm/f boss; (REL) patron saint // nm (COUTURE) pattern.

patronat [patʀɔna] nm employers pl.

patronner [patʀɔne] vt to sponsor, support.

patrouille [patʀuj] nf patrol.

patte [pat] nf (jambe) leg; (pied: de chien, chat) paw; (: d'oiseau) foot; (languette) strap.

pâturage [patyʀaʒ] nm pasture.

pâture [patyʀ] nf food.

paume [pom] nf palm.

paumé, e [pome] nm/f (fam) dropout.

paumer [pome] vt (fam) to lose.

paupière [popjɛʀ] nf eyelid.

pause [poz] nf (arrêt) break; (en parlant, MUS) pause.

pauvre [povʀ(ə)] a poor; ~té nf (état) poverty.

pavaner [pavane]: se ~ vi to strut about.

pavé, e [pave] a paved; cobbled // nm (bloc) paving stone; cobblestone;

(pavage) paving.

pavillon [pavijɔ̃] *nm (de banlieue)* small (detached) house; *(kiosque)* lodge; pavilion; *(drapeau)* flag.

pavoiser [pavwaze] *vt* to put out flags; *(fig)* to rejoice, exult.

pavot [pavo] *nm* poppy.

payant, e [pejɑ̃, -ɑ̃t] *a (spectateurs etc)* paying; *(fig: entreprise)* profitable; c'est ~ you have to pay, there is a charge.

paye [pɛj] *nf* pay, wages *pl*.

payement [pɛjmɑ̃] *nm* payment.

payer [peje] *vt (créancier, employé, loyer)* to pay; *(achat, réparations, fig: faute)* to pay for // *vi* to pay; *(métier)* to be well-paid; *(tactique etc)* to pay off; **il me l'a fait 10 F** he charged me 10 F for it; ~ **qch à qn** to buy sth for sb, buy sb sth; **cela ne le paie pas de mine** it doesn't look much.

pays [pei] *nm* country; land; region; village; **du ~** *a* local.

paysage [peizaʒ] *nm* landscape.

paysan, ne [peizɑ̃, -an] *nm/f* countryman/woman; farmer; *(péj)* peasant // *a* country *cpd*; farming; farmers'.

Pays-Bas [peiba] *nmpl*: **les ~** the Netherlands.

PC *nm (INFORM)* PC.

PDG *sigle m voir* **président.**

péage [peaʒ] *nm* toll; *(endroit)* tollgate; **pont à ~** toll bridge.

peau, x [po] *nf* skin; **gants de ~** fine leather gloves; ~ **de chamois** *(chiffon)* chamois leather, shammy; **P~-Rouge** *nm/f* Red Indian, redskin.

péché [peʃe] *nm* sin.

pêche [pɛʃ] *nf (sport, activité)* fishing; *(poissons pêchés)* catch; *(fruit)* peach; ~ **à la ligne** *(en rivière)* angling.

pécher [peʃe] *vi (REL)* to sin; *(fig: personne)* to err; *(: chose)* to be flawed.

pêcher [peʃe] *nm* peach tree // *vi* to go fishing // *vt* to catch; to fish for.

pécheur, eresse [peʃœʀ, peʃʀɛs] *nm/f* sinner.

pêcheur [peʃœʀ] *nm* fisherman; angler.

pécule [pekyl] *nm* savings *pl*, nest egg.

pécuniaire [pekynjɛʀ] *a* financial.

pédagogie [pedagɔʒi] *nf* educational methods *pl*, pedagogy; **pédagogique** *a* educational.

pédale [pedal] *nf* pedal.

pédalo [pedalo] *nm* pedal-boat.

pédant, e [pedɑ̃, -ɑ̃t] *a (péj)* pedantic.

pédestre [pedɛstʀ(ə)] *a*: **tourisme ~** hiking.

pédiatre [pedjatʀ(ə)] *nm/f* paediatrician, child specialist.

pédicure [pedikyʀ] *nm/f* chiropodist.

pègre [pɛgʀ(ə)] *nf* underworld.

peignais *etc vb voir* **peindre, peigner.**

peigne [pɛɲ] *nm* comb.

peigner [peɲe] *vt* to comb (the hair of); **se ~** *vi* to comb one's hair.

peignoir [pɛɲwaʀ] *nm* dressing gown; ~ **de bain** bathrobe.

peindre [pɛ̃dʀ(ə)] *vt* to paint; *(fig)* to portray, depict.

peine [pɛn] *nf (affliction)* sorrow, sadness *q*; *(mal, effort)* trouble *q*, effort; *(difficulté)* difficulty; *(punition, châtiment)* punishment; *(JUR)* sentence; **faire de la ~ à qn** to distress *ou* upset sb; **prendre la ~ de faire** to go to the trouble of doing; **se donner de la ~** to make an effort; **ce n'est pas la ~ de faire** there's no point in doing, it's not worth doing; **à ~** *ad* scarcely, hardly, barely; **à ~ ... que** hardly ... than; **défense d'afficher sous ~ d'amende** billposters will be fined; ~ **capitale** *ou* ~ **de mort** capital punishment, death sentence; **peiner** *vi* to work hard; to struggle; *(moteur, voiture)* to labour // *vt* to grieve, sadden.

peintre [pɛ̃tʀ(ə)] *nm* painter; ~ **en bâtiment** house painter.

peinture [pɛ̃tyʀ] *nf* painting;

(couche de couleur, couleur) paint; (surfaces peintes: aussi: ~s) paintwork; ~ mate/ brillante matt/ gloss paint; '~ fraîche' 'wet paint'.

péjoratif, ive [peʒɔʀatif, -iv] a pejorative, derogatory.

pelage [pəlaʒ] nm coat, fur.

pêle-mêle [pɛlmɛl] ad higgledy-piggledy.

peler [pəle] vt, vi to peel.

pèlerin [pɛlʀɛ̃] nm pilgrim.

pelle [pɛl] nf shovel; (d'enfant, de terrassier) spade; ~ **mécanique** mechanical shovel.

pellicule [pelikyl] nf film; ~s nfpl (MÉD) dandruff sg.

pelote [pəlɔt] nf (de fil, laine) ball; (d'épingles) pin cushion; ~ **basque** pelota.

peloton [pəlɔtɔ̃] nm group, squad; (CYCLISME) pack; ~ **d'exécution** firing squad.

pelotonner [pəlɔtɔne]: se ~ vi to curl (o.s.) up.

pelouse [pəluz] nf lawn.

peluche [pəlyʃ] nf: animal en ~ fluffy animal, soft toy.

pelure [pəlyʀ] nf peeling, peel q.

pénal, e, aux [penal, -o] a penal.

pénalité [penalite] nf penalty.

penaud, e [pəno, -od] a sheepish, contrite.

penchant [pɑ̃ʃɑ̃] nm tendency, propensity; liking, fondness.

pencher [pɑ̃ʃe] vi to tilt, lean over // vt to tilt; se ~ vi to lean over; (se baisser) to bend down; se ~ sur to bend over; (fig: problème) to look into; se ~ au dehors to lean out; ~ pour to be inclined to favour.

pendaison [pɑ̃dɛzɔ̃] nf hanging.

pendant [pɑ̃dɑ̃] nm: faire ~ à to match; to be the counterpart of // prép during; ~ que while.

pendentif [pɑ̃dɑ̃tif] nm pendant.

penderie [pɑ̃dʀi] nf wardrobe.

pendre [pɑ̃dʀ(ə)] vt, vi to hang; se ~ (à) (se suicider) to hang o.s. (on); ~ à to hang (down) from; ~ qch à to hang sth (up) on.

pendule [pɑ̃dyl] nf clock // nm pendulum.

pêne [pɛn] nm bolt.

pénétrer [penetʀe] vi, vt to penetrate; ~ dans to enter; (suj: projectile) to penetrate; (: air, eau) to come into, get into.

pénible [penibl(ə)] a (astreignant) hard; (affligeant) painful; (personne, caractère) tiresome; ~**ment** ad with difficulty.

péniche [peniʃ] nf barge.

pénicilline [penisilin] nf penicillin.

péninsule [penɛ̃syl] nf peninsula.

pénis [penis] nm penis.

pénitence [penitɑ̃s] nf (repentir) penitence; (peine) penance.

pénitencier [penitɑ̃sje] nm penitentiary.

pénombre [penɔ̃bʀ(ə)] nf half-light; darkness.

pensée [pɑ̃se] nf thought; (démarche, doctrine) thinking q; (BOT) pansy; en ~ in one's mind.

penser [pɑ̃se] vi to think // vt to think; (concevoir: problème, machine) to think out; ~ à to think of; (songer à: ami, vacances) to think of ou about; (réfléchir à: problème, offre) ~ à qch to think about sth ou think sth over; faire ~ à to remind one of; ~ **faire qch** to be thinking of doing sth, intend to do sth.

pension [pɑ̃sjɔ̃] nf (allocation) pension; (prix du logement) board and lodgings, bed and board; (maison particulière) boarding house; (hôtel) guesthouse, hotel; (école) boarding school; prendre qn en ~ to take sb (in) as a lodger; mettre en ~ to send to boarding school; ~ **alimentaire** (d'étudiant) living allowance; (de divorcée) maintenance allowance; alimony; ~ **complète** full board; ~ **de famille** boarding house, guesthouse; **pensionnaire** nm/f boarder; guest; **pensionnat** nm boarding school.

pente [pɑ̃t] nf slope; en ~ sloping.

Pentecôte [pɑ̃tkot] nf: la ~ Whitsun.

(Brit), Pentecost.

pénurie [penyri] nf shortage.

pépé [pepe] nm (fam) grandad.

pépin [pepɛ̃] nm (BOT: graine) pip; (ennui) snag, hitch.

pépinière [pepinjɛr] nf nursery.

perçant, e [pɛrsɑ̃, -ɑ̃t] a sharp, keen; piercing, shrill.

percée [pɛrse] nf (trouée) opening; (MIL, technologique) breakthrough; (SPORT) break.

perce-neige [pɛrsənɛʒ] nf inv snow-drop.

percepteur [pɛrsɛptœr] nm tax collector.

perception [pɛrsɛpsjɔ̃] nf perception; (d'impôts etc) collection; (bureau) tax office.

percer [pɛrse] vt to pierce; (ouverture etc) to make; (mystère, énigme) to penetrate // vi to come through; to break through; ~ **une dent** to cut a tooth.

perceuse [pɛrsøz] nf drill.

percevoir [pɛrsəvwar] vt (distinguer) to perceive, detect; (taxe, impôt) to collect; (revenu, indemnité) to receive.

perche [pɛrʃ(ə)] nf (bâton) pole.

percher [pɛrʃe] vt: ~ **qch sur** to perch sth on // vi, **se** ~ vi (oiseau) to perch; **perchoir** nm perch.

perçois etc vb voir **percevoir**.

percolateur [pɛrkɔlatœr] nm percolator.

perçu, e pp de **percevoir**.

percussion [pɛrkysjɔ̃] nf percussion.

percuter [pɛrkyte] vt to strike; (suj: véhicule) to crash into.

perdant, e [pɛrdɑ̃, -ɑ̃t] nm/f loser.

perdition [pɛrdisjɔ̃] nf: **en** ~ (NAVIG) in distress; **lieu de** ~ den of vice.

perdre [pɛrdr(ə)] vt to lose; (gaspiller: temps, argent) to waste; (personne: moralement etc) to ruin // vi to lose; (sur une vente etc) to lose out; **se** ~ vi (s'égarer) to get lost, lose one's way; (fig) to go to waste; to disappear, vanish.

perdrix [pɛrdri] nf partridge.

perdu, e [pɛrdy] pp de **perdre** // a (isolé) out-of-the-way; (COMM: emballage) non-returnable; (malade): **il est** ~ there's no hope left for him; **à vos moments** ~**s** in your spare time.

père [pɛr] nm father; ~**s** (ancêtres) forefathers; ~ **de famille** father; family man; **le** ~ **Noël** Father Christmas.

perfectionné, e [pɛrfɛksjɔne] a sophisticated.

perfectionner [pɛrfɛksjɔne] vt to improve, perfect.

perforatrice [pɛrfɔratris] nf (pour cartes) card-punch; (de bureau) punch.

perforer [pɛrfɔre] vt to perforate; to punch a hole (ou holes) in; (ticket, bande, carte) to punch.

performant, e [pɛrfɔrmɑ̃, -ɑ̃t] a: très ~ high-performance cpd.

perfusion [pɛrfyzjɔ̃] nf: **faire une** ~ **à qn** to put sb on a drip.

péril [peril] nm peril.

périmé, e [perime] a (out)dated; (ADMIN) out-of-date, expired.

périmètre [perimɛtr(ə)] nm perimeter.

période [perjɔd] nf period; **périodique** a (phases) periodic; (publication) periodical // nm periodical.

péripéties [peripesi] nfpl events, episodes.

périphérique [periferik] a (quartiers) outlying; (ANAT, TECH) peripheral; (station de radio) operating from outside France // nm (AUTO) ring road; (ORDIN) peripheral.

périple [peripl(ə)] nm journey.

périr [perir] vi to die, perish.

périssable [perisabl(ə)] a perishable.

perle [pɛrl(ə)] nf pearl; (de plastique, métal, sueur) bead.

perlé, e [pɛrle] a: **grève** ~**e** go-slow.

perler [pɛrle] vi to form in droplets.

permanence [pɛrmanɑ̃s] nf permanence; (local) (duty) office; emergency service; **assurer une ~** (service public, bureaux) to operate ou maintain a basic service; **être de ~** to be on call ou duty; **en ~** ad permanently; continuously.

permanent, e [pɛrmanã, -ãt] a permanent; (spectacle) continuous // nf perm.

perméable [pɛrmeabl(ə)] a (terrain) permeable; **~ à** (fig) receptive ou open to.

permettre [pɛrmɛtr(ə)] vt to allow, permit; **~ à qn de faire/qch** to allow sb to do/sth; **se ~ de faire** to take the liberty of doing; **permettez!** excuse me!

permis [pɛrmi] nm permit, licence; **~ de chasse** hunting permit; **~ (de conduire)** (driving) licence (Brit), (driver's) license (US); **~ de construire** planning permission (Brit), building permit (US); **~ d'inhumer** burial certificate; **~ de séjour** residence permit; **~ de travail** work permit.

permission [pɛrmisjɔ̃] nf permission; (MIL) leave; **en ~** on leave; **avoir la ~ de faire** to have permission to do.

permuter [pɛrmyte] vt to change around, permutate // vi to change, swap.

Pérou [peru] nm Peru.

perpétuel, le [pɛrpetɥɛl] a perpetual; (ADMIN etc) permanent; for life.

perpétuité [pɛrpetɥite] nf: **à ~** a, ad for life; **être condamné à ~** to receive a life sentence.

perplexe [pɛrplɛks(ə)] a perplexed, puzzled.

perquisitionner [pɛrkizisjɔne] vi to carry out a search.

perron [pɛrɔ̃] nm steps pl (in front of mansion etc).

perroquet [pɛrɔkɛ] nm parrot.

perruche [pɛryʃ] nf budgerigar (Brit), budgie (Brit), parakeet (US).

perruque [pɛryk] nf wig.

persan, e [pɛrsã, -an] a Persian.

persécuter [pɛrsekyte] vt to persecute.

persévérer [pɛrsevere] vi to persevere.

persiennes [pɛrsjɛn] nfpl (metal) shutters.

persiflage [pɛrsiflaʒ] nm mockery q.

persil [pɛrsi] nm parsley.

Persique [pɛrsik] a: **le golfe ~** the (Persian) Gulf.

persistant, e [pɛrsistã, -ãt] a persistent; (feuilles) evergreen.

persister [pɛrsiste] vi to persist; **~ à faire qch** to persist in doing sth.

personnage [pɛrsɔnaʒ] nm (notable) personality; figure; (individu) character, individual; (THÉÂTRE) character; (PEINTURE) figure.

personnalité [pɛrsɔnalite] nf personality; (personnage) prominent figure.

personne [pɛrsɔn] nf person // pronom nobody, no one; (quelqu'un) anybody, anyone; **~s** people pl; **il n'y a ~** there's nobody there, there isn't anybody there; **~ âgée** elderly person; **personnel, le** a personal // nm staff, personnel; **personnellement** ad personally.

perspective [pɛrspɛktiv] nf (ART) perspective; (vue, coup d'œil) view; (point de vue) viewpoint, angle; (chose escomptée, envisagée) prospect; **en ~** in prospect.

perspicace [pɛrspikas] a clear-sighted, gifted with (ou showing) insight.

persuader [pɛrsɥade] vt: **~ qn (de/de faire)** to persuade sb (of/to do).

perte [pɛrt(ə)] nf loss; (de temps) waste; (fig: morale) ruin; **à ~** (COMM) at a loss; **à ~ de vue** as far as the eye can (ou could) see; **~ sèche** dead loss; **~s blanches** (vaginal) discharge sg.

pertinemment [pɛrtinamã] ad to the point; full well.

pertinent, e [pɛrtinã, -ãt] a apt,

relevant.

perturbation [pɛrtyrbasjɔ̃] nf disruption; perturbation; (atmosphérique) atmospheric disturbance.

perturber [pɛrtyrbe] vt to disrupt; (PSYCH) to perturb, disturb.

pervers, e [pɛrvɛr, -ɛrs(ə)] a perverted, depraved; perverse.

pervertir [pɛrvɛrtir] vt to pervert.

pesant, e [pəzɑ̃, -ɑ̃t] a heavy; (fig) burdensome.

pesanteur [pəzɑ̃tœr] nf gravity.

pèse-personne [pɛzpɛrsɔn] nm (bathroom) scales pl.

peser [pəze] vt, vb avec attribut to weigh // vi to be heavy; (fig) to carry weight; **~ sur** (fig) to lie heavy on; to influence.

pessimiste [pesimist(ə)] a pessimistic // nm/f pessimist.

peste [pɛst(ə)] nf plague.

pester [pɛste] vi: **~ contre** to curse.

pétale [petal] nm petal.

pétanque [petɑ̃k] nf type of bowls.

pétarader [petarade] vi to backfire.

pétard [petar] nm banger (Brit), firecracker.

péter [pete] vi (fam: casser, sauter) to burst; to break; (fam!) to fart (!).

pétiller [petije] vi (flamme, bois) to crackle; (mousse, champagne) to bubble; (yeux) to sparkle.

petit, e [pəti, -it] a (gén) small; (main, objet, colline, en âge: enfant) small, little; (voyage) short, little; (bruit etc) faint, slight; (mesquin) mean // nm/f (d'un animal) young pl; **faire des ~s** to have kittens (ou puppies etc); **les tout-petits** the little ones, the tiny tots; **~ à ~** bit by bit, gradually; **~(e) ami/e** boyfriend/girlfriend; **les ~(e)s annonces** the small ads; **~ déjeuner** breakfast; **~ pain** (bread) roll; **~s pois** garden peas; **~-bourgeois, ~e-bourgeoise** a (péj) middle-class; **~e-fille** nf granddaughter; **~-fils** nm grandson; **~s-enfants** nmpl grandchildren.

pétition [petisjɔ̃] nf petition.

pétrin [petrɛ̃] nm kneading-trough; (fig): **dans le ~** in a jam ou fix.

pétrir [petrir] vt to knead.

pétrole [petrɔl] nm oil; (pour lampe, réchaud etc) paraffin (oil); **pétrolier, ière** a oil cpd // nm oil tanker.

MOT-CLÉ

---

peu [pø] ♦ ad 1 (modifiant verbe, adjectif, adverbe): **il boit ~** he doesn't drink (very) much; **il est ~ bavard** he's not very talkative; **~ avant/après** shortly before/afterwards

2 (modifiant nom): **~ de: ~ de gens/ d'arbres** few ou not (very) many people/trees; **il a ~ d'espoir** he hasn't (got) much hope, he has little hope; **pour ~ de temps** for (only) a short while

3: **~ à ~** little by little; **à ~ près** just about, more or less; **à ~ près 10 kg/10 F** approximately 10 kg/10 F ♦ nm

1: **le ~ de gens qui** the few people who; **le ~ de sable qui** what little sand, the little sand which

2: **un ~** a little; **un petit ~** a little bit; **un ~ d'espoir** a little hope

♦ pronom: **le ~ savent** few know (it); **avant ou sous ~** shortly, before long; **de ~** (only) just.

---

peuple [pœpl(ə)] nm people.

peupler [pœple] vt (pays, région) to populate; (étang) to stock; (suj: hommes, poissons) to inhabit; (fig: imagination, rêves) to fill.

peuplier [pøplije] nm poplar (tree).

peur [pœr] nf fear; **avoir ~ (de/de faire/ que)** to be frightened ou afraid (of/of doing/that); **faire ~ à** to frighten; **de ~ de/que** for fear of/that; **~eux, euse** a fearful, timorous.

peut vb voir **pouvoir**.

peut-être [pøtɛtr(ə)] ad perhaps, maybe; **~ que** perhaps, maybe; **~ bien qu'il fera/est** he may well do/be.

peux *etc vb voir* **pouvoir**.

phare [faʀ] *nm* (*en mer*) lighthouse; (*de véhicule*) headlight; **mettre ses** ~**s** to put on one's headlights; ~**s de recul** reversing lights.

pharmacie [faʀmasi] *nf* (*magasin*) chemist's (*Brit*); pharmacy; (*officine*) dispensary; (*de salle de bain*) medicine cabinet; **pharmacien, ne** *nm/f* pharmacist, chemist (*Brit*).

phase [faz] *nf* phase.

phénomène [fenɔmɛn] *nm* phenomenon (*pl* a); (*monstre*) freak.

philanthrope [filɑ̃tʀɔp] *nm/f* philanthropist.

philosophe [filɔzɔf] *nm/f* philosopher // a philosophical.

philosophie [filɔzɔfi] *nf* philosophy; **philosophique** a philosophical.

phobie [fɔbi] *nf* phobia.

phonétique [fɔnetik] *nf* phonetics *sg*.

phoque [fɔk] *nm* seal; (*fourrure*) sealskin.

phosphorescent, e [fɔsfɔʀesɑ̃, -ɑ̃t] a luminous.

photo [fɔto] *nf* photo(graph); **en** ~ in ou on a photograph; **prendre en** ~ to take a photo of; **aimer la/faire de la** ~ to like taking/take photos; ~ **d'identité** passport photograph.

photo... [fɔto] *préfixe:* ~**copie** *nf* photocopying; photocopy; ~**copier** *vt* to photocopy; ~**graphe** *nm/f* photographer; ~**graphie** *nf* (*procédé, technique*) photography; (*cliché*) photograph; ~**graphier** *vt* to photograph.

phrase [fʀaz] *nf* (*LING*) sentence; (*propos, MUS*) phrase.

physicien, ne [fizisjɛ̃, -ɛn] *nm/f* physicist.

physionomie [fizjɔnɔmi] *nf* face.

physique [fizik] a physical // *nf* physique // a physics *sg*; **au** ~ physically; ~**ment** ad physically.

piaffer [pjafe] *vi* to stamp.

piailler [pjaje] *vi* to squawk.

pianiste [pjanist(ə)] *nm/f* pianist.

piano [pjano] *nm* piano.

pianoter [pjanɔte] *vi* to tinkle away (at the piano); (*tapoter*): ~ **sur** to drum one's fingers on.

pic [pik] *nm* (*instrument*) pick(axe); (*montagne*) peak; (*ZOOL*) woodpecker; **à** ~ ad vertically; (*fig*) just at the right time.

pichet [piʃɛ] *nm* jug.

picorer [pikɔʀe] *vt* to peck.

picoter [pikɔte] *vt* (*suj: oiseau*) to peck // *vi* (*irriter*) to smart, prickle.

pie [pi] *nf* magpie; (*fig*) chatterbox // a inv (*cheval*) piebald.

pièce [pjɛs] *nf* (*d'un logement*) room; (*THÉÂTRE*) play; (*de mécanisme, machine*) part; (*de monnaie*) coin; (*COUTURE*) patch; (*document*) document; (*de drap, fragment, de collection*) piece; **dix francs** ~ ten francs each; **vendre à la** ~ to sell separately; **travailler/payer à la** ~ to do piecework/pay piece rate; **un maillot une** ~ a one-piece swimsuit; **un deux-**~**s cuisine** a two-room(ed) flat (*Brit*) ou apartment (*US*) with kitchen; ~ **à conviction** exhibit; ~ **d'eau** ornamental lake ou pond; ~ **d'identité:** **avez-vous une** ~ **d'identité?** have you got any (means of) identification?; ~ **montée** tiered cake; ~ **détachées** spares, (spare) parts; ~**s justificatives** supporting documents.

pied [pje] *nm* foot (*pl* feet); (*de verre*) stem; (*de table*) leg; (*de lampe*) base; (*plante*) plant; **à** ~ on foot; **à** ~ **sec** without getting one's feet wet; **au** ~ **de la lettre** literally; **au** ~ **en cap** from head to foot; **en** ~ (*portrait*) full-length; **avoir** ~ to be able to touch the bottom, not to be out of one's depth; **avoir le** ~ **marin** to be a good sailor; **sur** ~ (*debout, rétabli*) up and about; **mettre sur** ~ (*entreprise*) to set up; **mettre à** ~ to dismiss; to lay off; ~ **de vigne** vine.

piédestal, aux [pjedestal, -o] *nm* pedestal.

pied-noir [pjenwaʀ] *nm* Algerian-born Frenchman.

piège [pjɛʒ] nm trap; **prendre au ~** to trap; **piéger** vt (avec une bombe) to booby-trap; **lettre/voiture piégée** letter/car-bomb.

pierraille [pjɛrɑj] nf loose stones pl.

pierre [pjɛr] nf stone; **~ à briquet** flint; **~ fine** semiprecious stone; **~ de taille** freestone q; **~ tombale** tombstone.

pierreries [pjɛrri] nfpl gems, precious stones.

piétiner [pjetine] vi (trépigner) to stamp (one's foot); (marquer le pas) to stand about; (fig) to be at a standstill // vt (écraser) (pointu) stake.

piéton, ne [pjetɔ̃, -ɔn] nm/f pedestrian; **piétonnier, ière** a: **rue/zone piétonnière** pedestrian precinct.

pieu, x [pjø] nm (piquet) (pointu) stake.

pieuvre [pjœvr(ə)] nf octopus.

pieux, euse [pjø, -øz] a pious.

piffer [pife] vt (fam): **je ne peux pas le ~** I can't stand him.

pigeon [piʒɔ̃] nm pigeon.

piger [piʒe] vi, vt (fam) to understand.

pigiste [piʒist] nm/f freelance(r).

pignon [piɲɔ̃] nm (de mur) gable; (d'engrenage) cog(wheel), gearwheel.

pile [pil] nf (tas) pile; (ÉLEC) battery // ad (s'arrêter etc) dead; **à deux heures ~** at two on the dot; **jouer à ~ ou face** to toss up (for it); **~ ou face?** heads or tails?

piler [pile] vt to crush, pound.

pileux, euse [pilø, -øz] a: **système ~** (body) hair.

pilier [pilje] nm pillar.

piller [pije] vt to pillage, plunder, loot.

pilon [pilɔ̃] nm pestle.

pilote [pilɔt] nm (de char, voiture) driver // a pilot cpd; **~ de ligne/d'essai/de chasse** airline/test/fighter pilot; **~ de course** racing driver.

piloter [pilɔte] vt to pilot, fly; to drive.

pilule [pilyl] nf pill; **prendre la ~** to be on the pill.

piment [pimɑ̃] nm (BOT) pepper, capsicum; (fig) spice, piquancy.

pimpant, e [pɛ̃pɑ̃, -ɑ̃t] a spruce.

pin [pɛ̃] nm pine (tree); (bois) pine(wood).

pinard [pinar] nm (fam) (cheap) wine, plonk (Brit).

pince [pɛ̃s] nf (outil) pliers pl; (de homard, crabe) pincer, claw; (COUTURE: pli) dart; **~ à sucre/glace** sugar/ice tongs pl; **~ à épiler** tweezers pl; **~ à linge** clothes peg (Brit) ou pin (US).

pincé, e [pɛ̃se] a (air) stiff // nf: **une ~ de** a pinch of.

pinceau, x [pɛ̃so] nm (paint)brush.

pincer [pɛ̃se] vt to pinch; (MUS: cordes) to pluck; (fam) to nab.

pincettes [pɛ̃set] nfpl (pour le feu) (fire) tongs.

pinède [pined] nf pinewood, pine forest.

pingouin [pɛ̃gwɛ̃] nm penguin.

ping-pong [piŋpɔ̃g] nm table tennis.

pingre [pɛ̃gr(ə)] a niggardly.

pinson [pɛ̃sɔ̃] nm chaffinch.

pintade [pɛ̃tad] nf guinea-fowl.

pioche [pjɔʃ] nf pickaxe; **piocher** vt to dig up (with a pickaxe).

piolet [pjɔlɛ] nm ice axe.

pion [pjɔ̃] nm (ÉCHECS) pawn; (DAMES) piece.

pionnier [pjɔnje] nm pioneer.

pipe [pip] nf pipe.

pipeau, x [pipo] nm (reed-)pipe.

piquant, e [pikɑ̃, -ɑ̃t] a (barbe, rosier etc) prickly; (saveur, sauce) hot, pungent; (fig) racing; biting // nm (épine) thorn, prickle; (fig) spiciness, piquancy.

pique [pik] nf pike; (fig) cutting remark // nm (CARTES: couleur) spades pl; (: carte) spade.

pique-nique [piknik] nm picnic.

piquer [pike] vt (percer) to prick; (planter): **~ qch dans** to stick sth into; (MÉD) to give a jab to; (: animal blessé etc) to put to sleep; (suj: insecte, fumée, ortie) to sting;

poivre) to burn; (: *froid*) to bite; (COUTURE) to machine (stitch); (*intérêt etc*) to arouse; (*fam*) to pick up; (: *voler*) to pinch; (: *arrêter*) to nab // *vi* (*avion*) to go into a dive; se ~ de faire to pride o.s. on doing; ~ un galop/un cent mètres to break into a gallop/put on a sprint.

piquet [pikɛ] *nm* (*pieu*) post, stake; (*de tente*) peg; ~ de grève (strike-) picket; ~ d'incendie fire-fighting squad.

piqûre [pikyʀ] *nf* (*d'épingle*) prick; (*d'ortie*) sting; (*de moustique*) bite; (MÉD) injection, shot (US); (COUTURE) (straight) stitch; straight stitching; faire une ~ à qn to give sb an injection.

pirate [piʀat] *nm*, *a* pirate; ~ de l'air hijacker.

pire [piʀ] *a* worse; (*superlatif*): le (la) ~ ... the worst ... // *nm*: le ~ (de) the worst (of).

pis [pi] *nm* (*de vache*) udder; (*pire*): le ~ the worst // *a*, *ad* worse; **pis-aller** *nm inv* stopgap.

piscine [pisin] *nf* (swimming) pool; ~ couverte indoor (swimming) pool.

pissenlit [pisɑ̃li] *nm* dandelion.

pistache [pistaʃ] *nf* pistachio (nut).

piste [pist(ə)] *nf* (*d'un animal, sentier*) track, trail; (*indice*) lead; (*de stade, de magnétophone*) track; (*de cirque*) ring; (*de danse*) floor; (*de patinage*) rink; (*de ski*) run; (AVIAT) runway; ~ cyclable cycle track.

pistolet [pistolɛ] *nm* (*arme*) pistol, gun; (*à peinture*) spray gun; ~ à air comprimé airgun; **~-mitrailleur** *nm* submachine gun.

piston [pistɔ̃] *nm* (TECH) piston; **pistonner** *vt* (*candidat*) to , pull strings for.

piteux, euse [pitø, -øz] *a* pitiful, sorry (*avant le nom*).

pitié [pitje] *nf* pity; faire ~ to inspire pity; avoir ~ de (*compassion*) to pity, feel sorry for; (*merci*) to have pity ou mercy on.

piton [pitɔ̃] *nm* (*clou*) peg; ~ rocheux rocky outcrop.

pitoyable [pitwajabl(ə)] *a* pitiful.

pitre [pitʀ(ə)] *nm* clown; **pitrerie** *nf* tomfoolery *q*.

pittoresque [pitɔʀɛsk(ə)] *a* picturesque.

pivot [pivo] *nm* pivot; **pivoter** *vi* to swivel; to revolve.

P.J. *sigle f voir* police.

placard [plakaʀ] *nm* (*armoire*) cupboard; (*affiche*) poster, notice; **placarder** *vt* (*affiche*) to put up.

place [plas] *nf* (*emplacement, situation, classement*) place; (*de ville, village*) square; (*espace libre*) room, space; (*de parking*) space; (*siège: de train, cinéma, voiture*) seat; (*emploi*) job; en ~ (*mettre*) in its place; sur ~ on the spot; faire ~ à to give way to; faire de la ~ à to make room for; ça prend de la ~ it takes up a lot of room ou space; à la ~ de in place of, instead of; il y a 20 ~s assises/debout there are 20 seats/there is standing room for 20.

placement [plasmɑ̃] *nm* placing; (FINANCE) investment; bureau de ~ employment agency.

placer [plase] *vt* to place; (*convive, spectateur*) to seat; (*capital, argent*) to place, invest; (*dans la conversation*) to put ou get in; se ~ au premier rang to go and stand (*ou* sit) in the first row.

plafond [plafɔ̃] *nm* ceiling.

plafonner [plafone] *vi* to reach one's (ou a) ceiling.

plage [plaʒ] *nf* beach; (*d'un disque*) band, bracket; (*d'un disque*) track, band; ~ arrière (AUTO) parcel ou back shelf.

plagiat [plaʒja] *nm* plagiarism.

plaider [plede] *vi* (*avocat*) to plead; (*plaignant*) to go to court, litigate // *vt* to plead; ~ pour (*fig*) to speak for the defence; (*fig*) plea.

plaidoyer [plɛdwaje] *nm* (JUR) speech for the defence; (*fig*) plea.

plaie [plɛ] *nf* wound.

plaignant, e [plɛɲɑ̃, -ɑ̃t] *nm/f* plaintiff.

plaindre [plɛ̃dʀ(ə)] vt to pity, feel sorry for; se ~ vi (gémir) to moan; (protester, rouspéter): se ~ (à qn) (de) to complain (to sb) (about); (souffrir): se ~ de to complain of.

plaine [plɛn] nf plain.

plain-pied [plɛ̃pje]: de ~ (avec) on the same level (as).

plainte [plɛ̃t] nf (gémissement) moan, groan; (doléance) complaint; porter ~ to lodge a complaint.

plaire [plɛʀ] vi to be a success, be successful; to please; ~ à: cela me plaît I like it; se ~ quelque part to like being somewhere ou like it somewhere; s'il vous plaît please.

plaisance [plɛzɑ̃s] nf (aussi: navigation de ~) (pleasure) sailing, yachting.

plaisant, e [plɛzɑ̃, -ɑ̃t] a pleasant; (histoire, anecdote) amusing.

plaisanter [plɛzɑ̃te] vi to joke; **plaisanterie** nf joke; joking q.

plaise etc vb voir **plaire**.

plaisir [plɛziʀ] nm pleasure; faire ~ à qn (délibérément) to please sb, please sb; (suj: cadeau, nouvelle etc) ceci me fait ~ I'm delighted ou very pleased with this; pour le ou par ~ for pleasure.

plaît vb voir **plaire**.

plan, e [plɑ̃, -an] a flat // nm plan; (GÉOM) plane; (fig) level, plane; (CINÉMA) shot; au premier/second ~ in the foreground/middle distance; à l'arrière ~ in the background; ~ d'eau lake; pond.

planche [plɑ̃ʃ] nf (pièce de bois) plank, (wooden) board; (illustration) plate; les ~s (THÉÂTRE) the stage sg, the boards; ~ à repasser ironing board; ~ à roulettes skateboard; ~ de salut (fig) sheet anchor.

plancher [plɑ̃ʃe] nm floor; floorboards pl; (fig) minimum level // vi to work hard.

planer [plane] vi to glide; ~ sur (fig) to hang over; to hover above.

planète [planɛt] nf planet.

planeur [planœʀ] nm glider.

planification [planifikasjɔ̃] nf (economic) planning.

planifier [planifje] vt to plan.

planning [planiŋ] nm programme, schedule; ~ familial family planning.

plant [plɑ̃] nm seedling, young plant.

plante [plɑ̃t] nf plant; ~ d'appartement house ou pot plant; ~ du pied sole (of the foot).

planter [plɑ̃te] vt (plante) to plant; (enfoncer) to hammer ou drive in; (tente) to put up, pitch; (fam) to dump; to ditch; (fam: se tromper) to get it wrong.

plantureux, euse [plɑ̃tyʀø, -øz] a copious, lavish; (femme) buxom.

plaque [plak] nf plate; (de verglas, d'eczéma) patch; (avec inscription) plaque; ~ (minéralogique ou d'immatriculation) number (Brit) ou license (US) plate; ~ chauffante hotplate; ~ de chocolat bar of chocolate; ~ d'identité identity disc; ~ tournante (fig) centre.

plaqué, e [plake] a: ~ or/argent gold/silver-plated; ~ acajou veneered in mahogany.

plaquer [plake] vt (aplatir): ~ qch sur/contre to make sth stick ou cling to; (RUGBY) to bring down; (fam: laisser tomber) to drop.

plastic [plastik] nm plastic explosive.

plastique [plastik] a, nm plastic.

plastiquer [plastike] vt to blow up (with a plastic bomb).

plat, e [pla, -at] a flat; (cheveux) straight; (personne, livre) dull // nm (récipient, CULIN) dish; (d'un repas): le premier ~ the first course; à ~ ventre a face down; à ~ a, (pneu, batterie) flat; (personne) dead beat; ~ cuisiné pre-cooked meal; ~ du jour day's special (menu); ~ de résistance main course.

platane [platan] nm plane tree.

plateau, x [plato] nm (support) tray; (GÉO) plateau; (de tourne-

disques) turntable; (*CINÉMA*) set; ~ à fromages cheeseboard.

plate-bande [platbɑ̃d] *nf* flower bed.

plate-forme [platfɔʀm(ə)] *nf* platform; ~ **de forage/pétrolière** drilling/oil rig.

platine [platin] *nm* platinum // *nf* (*d'un tourne-disque*) turntable.

plâtras [plɑtʀɑ] *nm* rubble *q*.

plâtre [plɑtʀ(ə)] *nm* (*matériau*) plaster; (*statue*) plaster statue; (*MÉD*) (plaster) cast; **avoir un bras dans le ~** to have an arm in plaster.

plein, e [plɛ̃, -ɛn] *a* full; (*porte, roue*) solid; (*chienne, jument*) big (with young) // *nm*: **faire le ~** (*d'essence*) to fill up (with petrol); **à ~es mains** (*ramasser*) in handfuls; (*empoigner*) firmly; **à ~ régime** at maximum revs; (*fig*) full steam; **à ~ temps** full-time; **en ~ air** in the open air; **en ~ soleil** in direct sunlight; **en ~ nuit/rue** in the middle of the night/street; **en ~ jour** in broad daylight; **en ~ sur** right on; **~-emploi** *nm* full employment.

plénitude [plenityd] *nf* fullness.

pleurer [plœʀe] *vi* to cry; (*yeux*) to water // *vt* to mourn (for); **~ sur** *vt* to lament (over), to bemoan.

pleurnicher [plœʀniʃe] *vi* to snivel, whine.

pleurs [plœʀ] *nmpl*: **en ~** in tears.

pleut *vb voir* **pleuvoir**.

pleuvoir [pløvwaʀ] *vb impersonnel* to rain // *vi* (*fig*): **~ (sur)** to shower down (upon); **to be showered upon**; **il pleut** it's raining.

pli [pli] *nm* fold; (*de jupe*) pleat; (*de pantalon*) crease; (*aussi*: **faux ~**) crease; (*enveloppe*) envelope; (*lettre*) letter; (*CARTES*) trick.

pliant, e [plijɑ̃, -ɑ̃t] *a* folding // *nm* folding stool, campstool.

plier [plije] *vt* to fold; (*pour ranger*) to fold up; (*table pliante*) to fold down; (*genou, bras*) to bend // *vi* to bend; (*fig*) to yield; **se ~ à** to submit to.

plinthe [plɛ̃t] *nf* skirting board.

plisser [plise] *vt* (*rider, chiffonner*) to crease; (*jupe*) to put pleats in.

plomb [plɔ̃] *nm* (*métal*) lead; (*d'une cartouche*) (lead) shot; (*PÊCHE*) sinker; (*sceau*) (lead) seal; (*ÉLEC*) fuse.

plombage [plɔ̃baʒ] *nm* (*de dent*) filling.

plomber [plɔ̃be] *vt* (*canne, ligne*) to weight (with lead); (*dent*) to fill.

plomberie [plɔ̃bʀi] *nf* plumbing.

plombier [plɔ̃bje] *nm* plumber.

plongeant, e [plɔ̃ʒɑ̃, -ɑ̃t] *a* (*vue*) from above; (*tir, décolleté*) plunging.

plongée [plɔ̃ʒe] *nf* (*SPORT*) diving *q*; (*: sans scaphandre*) skin diving.

plongeoir [plɔ̃ʒwaʀ] *nm* diving board.

plongeon [plɔ̃ʒɔ̃] *nm* dive.

plonger [plɔ̃ʒe] *vi* to dive // *vt*: **~ qch dans** to plunge sth into.

ployer [plwaje] *vt* to bend // *vi* to sag; to bend.

plu *pp de* **plaire, pleuvoir**.

pluie [plɥi] *nf* rain; (*fig*): **~ de** shower of.

plume [plym] *nf* feather; (*pour écrire*) (pen) nib; (*fig*) pen.

plumer [plyme] *vt* to pluck.

plumier [plymje] *nm* pencil box.

plupart [plypaʀ]: **la ~** *pronom* the majority, most (of them); **la ~ des** most, the majority of; **la ~ du temps/d'entre nous** most of the time/of us; **pour la ~** *ad* for the most part, mostly.

pluriel [plyʀjɛl] *nm* plural.

MOT-CLÉ

plus ◆ *vb* [ply] *voir* **plaire**

◆ *ad* **1** [ply] (*forme négative*): **ne ... ~** no more, no longer; **je n'ai ~ d'argent** I've got no more money *ou* no money left; **il ne travaille ~** he's no longer working, he doesn't work any more

2 [ply, plyz + *voyelle*] (*comparatif*) more, ...+er; (*superlatif*): **le ~ the** most, the ...+est; **~ grand/**

intelligent (que) bigger/more intelligent (than); **le ~ grand/intelligent** the biggest/most intelligent; **tout au ~** at the very most
3 (*davantage*) more: **il travaille ~ (que)** he works more (than); **~ il travaille, ~ il est heureux** the more he works, the happier he is; **~ de pain** more bread; **~ de 10 personnes** more than 10 people, over 10 people; **3 heures de ~ que 3** 3 hours more than; **~ de** what's more, moreover; **3 kilos en ~** 3 kilos more; **en ~ de** in addition to; **de en ~** more and more; **~ ou moins** more or less; **ni ~ ni moins** no more, no less
◆ *prép* [plys]: **4 ~ 2** 4 plus 2

plusieurs [plyzjœr] *dét, pronom* several; **ils sont ~** there are several of them.

plus-que-parfait [plyskəparfɛ] *nm* pluperfect, past perfect.

plus-value [plyvaly] *nf* appreciation; capital gain; surplus.

plut *vb voir* **plaire**.

plutôt [plyto] *ad* rather; **je ferais ~ ceci** I'd rather *ou* sooner do this; **fais ~ comme ça** try this way instead; **~ que (de) faire** rather than *ou* instead of doing.

pluvieux, euse [plyvjø, -øz] *a* rainy, wet.

PMU *sigle m* (= *pari mutuel urbain*) *system of betting on horses*; (*café*) betting agency.

pneu [pnø] *nm* tyre (*Brit*), tire (*US*).

pneumatique [pnømatik] *nm* tyre (*Brit*), tire (*US*).

pneumonie [pnømɔni] *nf* pneumonia.

poche [pɔʃ] *nf* pocket; (*déformation*): **faire une/des ~(s) to bag**; (*sous les yeux*) bag, pouch; **de ~** pocket *cpd*.

pocher [pɔʃe] *vt* (*CULIN*) to poach.

pochette [pɔʃɛt] *nf* (*de timbres*) wallet, envelope; (*d'aiguilles etc*)

case; (*mouchoir*) breast pocket handkerchief; **~ de disque** record sleeve.

pochoir [pɔʃwar] *nm* (*ART*) stencil.

poêle [pwal] *nm* stove // *nf*: **~** (à *frire*) frying pan.

poêlon [pwalɔ̃] *nm* casserole.

poème [pɔɛm] *nm* poem.

poésie [pɔezi] *nf* (*poème*) poem; (*art*): **la ~** poetry.

poète [pɔɛt] *nm* poet.

poids [pwa] *nm* weight; (*SPORT*) shot; **vendre au ~** to sell by weight; **prendre du ~** to put on weight; **~ lourd** (*camion*) lorry (*Brit*), truck (*US*).

poignard [pwaɲar] *nm* dagger; **poignarder** *vt* to stab, knife.

poigne [pwaɲ] *nf* grip; (*fig*): **à ~** firm-handed.

poignée [pwaɲe] *nf* (*de sel etc, fig*) handful; (*de couvercle, porte*) handle; **~ de main** handshake.

poignet [pwaɲɛ] *nm* (*ANAT*) wrist; (*de chemise*) cuff.

poil [pwal] *nm* (*ANAT*) hair; (*de pinceau, brosse*) bristle; (*de tapis*) strand; (*pelage*) coat; **à ~** (*fam*) starkers; **au ~** (*fam*) hunky-dory; **poilu, e** *a* hairy.

poinçon [pwɛ̃sɔ̃] *nm* awl; bodkin; (*marque*) hallmark; **poinçonner** *vt* to stamp; to hallmark; (*billet*) to punch.

poing [pwɛ̃] *nm* fist.

point [pwɛ̃] *nm* (*marque, signe*) dot; (: *de ponctuation*) full stop, period (*US*); (*moment, de score etc, fig*: *question*) point; (*endroit*) spot; (*COUTURE, TRICOT*) stitch // *ad* = **pas**; **faire le ~** (*NAVIG*) to take a bearing; (*fig*) to take stock (of the situation); **en tout ~** in every respect; **sur le ~ de faire** (just) about to do; **à tel ~ que** so much so that; **mettre au ~** (*mécanisme, procédé*) to develop; (*appareil-photo*) to focus; (*affaire*) to settle; **à ~** (*CULIN*) medium; just right; **à ~** (*nommé*) just at the right time; **~ (de côté)** stitch (*pain*); **~ d'eau**

spring; water point; ~ d'exclamation exclamation mark; ~ faible weak point; ~ final full stop, period; ~ d'interrogation question mark; ~ mort (AUTO): au ~ mort in neutral; ~ de repère landmark; ~ de vente retail outlet; ~ de vue viewpoint; (fig: opinion) point of view; ~s de suspension suspension points.

pointe [pwɛ̃t] nf point; (fig): une ~ de a hint of; être à la ~ de (fig) to be in the forefront of; sur la ~ des pieds on tiptoe; en ~ ad (tailler) into a point // a pointed, tapered; de ~ a (technique) leading; heures/jours de ~ peak hours/days; ~ de vitesse burst of speed.

pointer [pwɛ̃te] vt (cocher) to tick off; (employés etc) to check in; (diriger: canon, doigt): ~ vers qch to point at sth // vi (employé) to clock in.

pointillé [pwɛ̃tije] nm (trait) dotted line.

pointilleux, euse [pwɛ̃tijø, -øz] a particular, pernickety.

pointu, e [pwɛ̃ty] a pointed; (clou) sharp; (voix) shrill; (analyse) precise.

pointure [pwɛ̃tyr] nf size.

point-virgule [pwɛ̃virgyl] nm semicolon.

poire [pwar] nf pear; (fam: péj) mug.

poireau, x [pwaro] nm leek.

poirier [pwarje] nm pear tree.

pois [pwa] nm (BOT) pea; (sur une étoffe) dot, spot; à ~ (cravate etc) spotted, polka-dot cpd.

poison [pwazɔ̃] nm poison.

poisse [pwas] nf rotten luck.

poisseux, euse [pwasø, -øz] a sticky.

poisson [pwasɔ̃] nm fish gén inv; les P~s (signe) Pisces; ~ d'avril! April fool!; ~ rouge goldfish; **poissonnerie** nf fish-shop; **poissonnier, ière** nm/f fishmonger (Brit), fish merchant (US).

poitrine [pwatrin] nf chest; (seins) bust, bosom; (CULIN) breast; ~ de bœuf brisket.

poivre [pwavr(ə)] nm pepper; **poivrier** nm (ustensile) pepperpot.

poivron [pwavrɔ̃] nm pepper, capsicum.

pôle [pol] nm (GÉO, ÉLEC) pole.

poli, e [pɔli] a polite; (lisse) smooth, polished.

police [pɔlis] nf police; **peine de simple ~** sentence given by magistrates' or police court; ~ d'assurance insurance policy; ~ **judiciaire (P.J.)** ≈ Criminal Investigation Department (Brit), ≈ Federal Bureau of Investigation (US); ~ **des mœurs** ≈ vice squad; ~ **secours** ≈ emergency services pl (Brit), paramedics pl (US).

policier, ière [pɔlisje, -jɛr] a police cpd // nm policeman; (aussi: **roman** ~) detective novel.

polio [pɔljo] nf polio.

polir [pɔlir] vt to polish.

polisson, ne [pɔlisɔ̃, -ɔn] a naughty.

politesse [pɔlitɛs] nf politeness.

politicien, ne [pɔlitisjɛ̃, -ɛn] nm/f politician.

politique [pɔlitik] a political // nf (science, pratique, activité) politics sg; (mesures, méthode) policies pl; **politiser** vt to politicize.

pollen [pɔlɛn] nm pollen.

pollution [pɔlysjɔ̃] nf pollution.

Pologne [pɔlɔɲ] nf: la ~ Poland; **polonais, e** a, nm (LING) Polish; **Polonais, e** nm/f Pole.

poltron, ne [pɔltrɔ̃, -ɔn] a cowardly.

poly... [pɔli] préfixe: **~copier** vt to duplicate.

Polynésie [pɔlinezi] nf: la ~ Polynesia.

polyvalent, e [pɔlivalɑ̃, -ɑ̃t] a versatile; multi-purpose.

pommade [pɔmad] nf ointment, cream.

pomme [pɔm] nf (BOT) apple; **tomber dans les ~s** (fam) to pass out;

~ **d'Adam** Adam's apple; ~ **d'arrosoir** (sprinkler) rose; ~ **de pin** pine ou fir cone; ~ **de terre** potato.

pommeau, x [pɔmo] nm (boule) knob; (de selle) pommel.

pommette [pɔmɛt] nf cheekbone.

pommier [pɔmje] nm apple tree.

pompe [pɔ̃p] nf pump; (faste) pomp (and ceremony); ~ **à essence** petrol pump; ~**s funèbres** funeral parlour sg, undertaker's sg.

pomper [pɔ̃pe] vt to pump; (évacuer) to pump out; (aspirer) to pump up; (absorber) to soak up.

pompeux, euse [pɔ̃pø, -øz] a pompous.

pompier [pɔ̃pje] nm fireman.

pompiste [pɔ̃pist(ə)] nm/f petrol (Brit) ou gas (US) pump attendant.

poncer [pɔ̃se] vt to sand (down).

ponctuation [pɔ̃ktɥasjɔ̃] nf punctuation.

ponctuel, le [pɔ̃ktɥɛl] a (à l'heure, aussi TECH) punctual; (fig: opération etc) one-off, single; (scrupuleux) punctilious, meticulous.

ponctuer [pɔ̃ktɥe] vt to punctuate.

pondéré, e [pɔ̃dere] a level-headed, composed.

pondre [pɔ̃dʀ(ə)] vt to lay; (fig) to produce.

poney [pɔnɛ] nm pony.

pont [pɔ̃] nm bridge; (AUTO) axle; (NAVIG) deck; **faire le** ~ to take the extra day off; ~ **de graissage** ramp (in garage); ~ **suspendu** suspension bridge; **P**~**s et Chaussées** highways department.

pont-levis [pɔ̃l(ə)vi] nm drawbridge.

pop [pɔp] a inv pop.

populace [pɔpylas] nf (péj) rabble.

populaire [pɔpylɛʀ] a popular; (manifestation) mass cpd; (milieux, clientèle) working-class.

population [pɔpylasjɔ̃] nf population.

populeux, euse [pɔpylø, -øz] a densely populated.

porc [pɔʀ] nm (ZOOL) pig; (CULIN) pork; (peau) pigskin.

porcelaine [pɔʀsəlɛn] nf porcelain, china; piece of china(ware).

porc-épic [pɔʀkepik] nm porcupine.

porche [pɔʀʃ(ə)] nm porch.

porcherie [pɔʀʃəʀi] nf pigsty.

pore [pɔʀ] nm pore.

pornographique [pɔʀnɔgʀafik] a (abr **porno**) pornographic.

port [pɔʀ] nm (NAVIG) harbour, port; (ville) port; (de l'uniforme etc) wearing; (pour lettre) postage; (pour colis, aussi: posture) carriage; ~ **d'arme** (JUR) carrying of a firearm.

portail [pɔʀtaj] nm gate; (de cathédrale) portal.

portant, e [pɔʀtɑ̃, -ɑ̃t] a: **bien/mal** ~ in good/poor health.

portatif, ive [pɔʀtatif, -iv] a portable.

porte [pɔʀt(ə)] nf door; (de ville, forteresse, SKI) gate; **mettre à la** ~ to throw out; ~ **d'entrée** front door; ~ **à** ~ nm door-to-door selling.

porte... [pɔʀt(ə)] préfixe: ~**à-faux** nm: **en** ~**-à-faux** cantilevered; (fig) in an awkward position; ~**avions** nm inv aircraft carrier; ~**bagages** nm inv luggage rack; ~**clefs** nm inv key ring; ~**documents** nm inv attaché ou document case.

portée [pɔʀte] nf (d'une arme) range; (fig) impact, import; scope, capability; (de chatte etc) litter; (MUS) stave, staff (pl staves); **à/hors de** ~ (de) within/out of reach (of); **à** ~ **de (la) main** within (arm's) reach; **à** ~ **de voix** within earshot; **à la** ~ **de qn** (fig) at sb's level, within sb's capabilities.

porte-fenêtre [pɔʀtfənɛtʀ(ə)] nf French window.

portefeuille [pɔʀtəfœj] nm wallet; (POL, BOURSE) portfolio.

porte-jarretelles [pɔʀtʒaʀtɛl] nm inv suspender belt.

portemanteau, x [pɔʀtmɑ̃to] nm coat hanger; coat rack.

porte-mine [pɔʀtəmin] nm propelling (Brit) ou mechanical (US) pencil.

porte-monnaie [pɔrtmɔnɛ] *nm inv* purse.

porte-parole [pɔrtparɔl] *nm inv* spokesman.

porter [pɔrte] *vt* to carry; (*sur soi: vêtement, barbe, bague*) to wear; (*fig: responsabilité etc*) to bear, carry; (*inscription, marque, titre, patronyme, suj: arbre: fruits, fleurs*) to bear; (*apporter*): ~ **qch quelque part/à qn** to take sth somewhere/to sb // *vi* (*voix, regard, canon*) to carry; (*coup, argument*) to hit home; ~ **sur** (*peser*) to rest on; (*accent*) to fall on; (*conférence etc*) to concern; (*heurter*) to strike; **se** ~ *vi* (*se sentir*): **se** ~ **bien/mal** to be well/unwell; **être porté à faire** to be apt *ou* inclined to do; **se faire** ~ **malade** to report sick; **la main à son chapeau** to raise one's hand to one's hat; ~ **son effort sur** to direct one's efforts towards; ~ **à croire** to lead one to believe.

porte-serviettes [pɔrtsɛrvjɛt] *nm inv* towel rail.

porteur [pɔrtœr] *nm* (*de bagages*) porter; (*de chèque*) bearer.

porte-voix [pɔrtvwa] *nm inv* megaphone.

portier [pɔrtje] *nm* doorman.

portière [pɔrtjɛr] *nf* door.

portillon [pɔrtijɔ̃] *nm* gate.

portion [pɔrsjɔ̃] *nf* (*part*) portion, share; (*partie*) portion, section.

portique [pɔrtik] *nm* (*RAIL*) gantry.

porto [pɔrto] *nm* port (wine).

portrait [pɔrtrɛ] *nm* portrait; photograph; ~**-robot** *nm* Identikit ® *ou* photo-fit ® picture.

portuaire [pɔrtɥɛr] *a* port *cpd*, harbour *cpd*.

portugais, e [pɔrtygɛ, -ɛz] *a, nm/f* Portuguese.

Portugal [pɔrtygal] *nm*: **le** ~ Portugal.

pose [poz] *nf* laying; hanging; (*attitude, d'un modèle*) pose; (*PHOTO*) exposure.

posé, e [poze] *a* serious.

poser [poze] *vt* (*déposer*): ~ **qch** (**sur**)/**qn à** to put sth down (on)/drop sb at; (*placer*): ~ **qch sur/quelque part** to put sth on/somewhere; (*installer: moquette, carrelage*) to lay; (*rideaux, papier peint*) to hang; (*question*) to ask; (*principe, conditions*) to lay *ou* set down; (*problème*) to formulate; (*difficulté*) to pose // *vi* (*modèle*) to pose; **se** ~ *vi* (*oiseau, avion*) to land; (*question*) to arise.

positif, ive [pozitif, -iv] *a* positive.

position [pozisjɔ̃] *nf* position; **prendre** ~ (*fig*) to take a stand.

posséder [posede] *vt* to own, possess; (*qualité, talent*) to have, possess; (*bien connaître: métier, langue*) to have mastered, have a thorough knowledge of; (*sexuellement, aussi: suj: colère etc*) to possess; **possession** *nf* ownership *q*; possession.

possibilité [posibilite] *nf* possibility; ~**s** *nfpl* (*moyens*) means; (*potentiel*) potential *sg*.

possible [posibl(ə)] *a* possible; (*projet, entreprise*) feasible // *nm*: **faire son** ~ to do all one can, do one's utmost; **le plus/moins de livres** ~ as many/few books as possible; **le plus/moins d'eau** ~ as much/little water as possible; **dès que** ~ as soon as possible.

postal, e, aux [pɔstal, -o] *a* postal.

poste [pɔst(ə)] *nf* (*service*) post, postal service; (*administration, bureau*) post office // *nm* (*fonction, MIL*) post; (*TÉL*) extension; (*de radio etc*) set; **mettre à la** ~ to post; ~**s, Télécommunications et Télédiffusion** (**P.T.T.**) *postal and telecommunications service*; ~ **d'essence** *nm* petrol *ou* filling station; ~ **d'incendie** *nm* fire point; ~ **de pilotage** *nm* cockpit; ~ (**de police**) *nm* police station; ~ **restante** *nf* poste restante (*Brit*), general delivery (*US*); ~ **de secours** *nm* first-aid post; ~ **de travail** *nm* work station.

poster vt [pɔste] to post // nm [pɔstɛʀ] poster.

postérieur, e [pɔsteʀjœʀ] a (date) later; (partie) back // nm (fam) behind.

posthume [pɔstym] a posthumous.

postiche [pɔstiʃ] nm hairpiece.

postuler [pɔstyle] vt (emploi) to apply for, put in for.

posture [pɔstyʀ] nf posture; position.

pot [po] nm jar, pot; (en plastique, carton) carton; (en métal) tin; boire ou prendre un ~ (fam) to have a drink; ~ (de chambre) (chamber) pot; ~ d'échappement exhaust pipe; ~ de fleurs plant pot, flowerpot; (plante) pot plant.

potable [pɔtabl(ə)] a: eau (non) ~ (not) drinking water.

potage [pɔtaʒ] nm soup; soup course.

potager, ère [pɔtaʒe, -ɛʀ] a (plante) edible, vegetable cpd; (jardin) ~ kitchen ou vegetable garden.

pot-au-feu [pɔtofø] nm inv (beef) stew.

pot-de-vin [pɔdvɛ̃] nm bribe.

pote [pɔt] nm (fam) pal.

poteau, x [pɔto] nm post; ~ indicateur signpost.

potelé, e [pɔtle] a plump, chubby.

potence [pɔtɑ̃s] nf gallows sg.

potentiel, le [pɔtɑ̃sjɛl] a, nm potential.

poterie [pɔtʀi] nf pottery; piece of pottery.

potier [pɔtje] nm potter.

potins [pɔtɛ̃] nmpl gossip sg.

potiron [pɔtiʀɔ̃] nm pumpkin.

pou, x [pu] nm louse (pl lice).

poubelle [pubɛl] nf (dust)bin.

pouce [pus] nm thumb.

poudre [pudʀ(ə)] nf powder; (fard) (face) powder; (explosif) gunpowder; en ~ : café en ~ instant coffee; lait en ~ dried ou powdered milk; **poudrier** nm (powder) compact.

pouffer [pufe] vi: ~ (de rire) to snigger; to giggle.

pouilleux, euse [pujø, -øz] a flea-

ridden; (fig) grubby; seedy.

poulailler [pulaje] nm henhouse.

poulain [pulɛ̃] nm foal; (fig) protégé.

poule [pul] nf (ZOOL) hen; (CULIN) (boiling) fowl.

poulet [pulɛ] nm chicken; (fam) cop.

poulie [puli] nf pulley; block.

pouls [pu] nm pulse; prendre le ~ de qn to feel sb's pulse.

poumon [pumɔ̃] nm lung.

poupe [pup] nf stern; en ~ astern.

poupée [pupe] nf doll.

poupon [pupɔ̃] nm babe-in-arms; **pouponnière** nf crèche, day nursery.

pour [puʀ] prép for // nm: le ~ et le contre the pros and cons; ~ faire (so as) to do, in order to do; ~ avoir fait for having done; ~ que so that, in order that; ~ 100 francs d'essence 100 francs' worth of petrol; ~ cent per cent; ~ ce qui est de as for.

pourboire [puʀbwaʀ] nm tip.

pourcentage [puʀsɑ̃taʒ] nm percentage.

pourchasser [puʀʃase] vt to pursue.

pourparlers [puʀpaʀle] nmpl talks, negotiations.

pourpre [puʀpʀ(ə)] a crimson.

pourquoi [puʀkwa] ad, cj why // nm inv: le ~ (de) the reason (for).

pourrai etc voir **pouvoir**.

pourri, e [puʀi] a rotten.

pourrir [puʀiʀ] vi to rot; (fruit) to go rotten ou bad // vt to rot; (fig) to spoil thoroughly; **pourriture** nf rot.

pourrons etc voir **pouvoir**.

poursuite [puʀsɥit] nf pursuit, chase; ~s (JUR) legal proceedings.

poursuivre [puʀsɥivʀ(ə)] vt to pursue, chase (after); (relancer) to hound, harry; (obséder) to haunt; (JUR) to bring proceedings against, prosecute; (: au civil) to sue; (but) to strive towards; (voyage, études) to carry on with, continue // vi to carry on, go on; se ~ vi to go on, continue.

pourtant [puʀtɑ̃] ad yet; c'est ~ facile (and) yet it's easy.

pourtour [puʀtuʀ] nm perimeter.

pourvoir [puʀvwaʀ] vt: ~ qch/qn de to equip sth/sb with // ~ à to provide for; (emploi) to fill; se ~ vi (JUR): se ~ en cassation to take one's case to the Court of Appeal.

pourvoyeur [puʀvwajœʀ] nm supplier.

pourvu, e [puʀvy] a: ~ de equipped with; ~ que cj (si) provided that, so long as; (espérons que) let's hope (that).

pousse [pus] nf growth; (bourgeon) shoot.

poussé, e [puse] a exhaustive.

poussée [puse] nf thrust; (coup) push; (MÉD) eruption; (fig) upsurge.

pousser [puse] vt to push; (inciter): ~ qn à to urge ou press sb to + infinitif; (acculer): ~ qn à to drive sb to; (émettre: cri etc) to give; (stimuler) to urge on; to drive hard; (poursuivre) to carry on (further) // vi to push; (croître) to grow; se ~ vi to move over; faire ~ (plante) to grow.

poussette [pusɛt] nf (voiture d'enfant) push chair (Brit), stroller (US).

poussière [pusjɛʀ] nf dust; (grain) speck of dust; **poussiéreux, euse** a dusty.

poussin [pusɛ̃] nm chick.

poutre [putʀ(ə)] nf beam; (en fer, ciment armé) girder.

---

pouvoir [puvwaʀ] ◆ nm power; (POL: dirigeants): le ~ those in power; les ~s publics the authorities; ~ d'achat purchasing power
◆ vb semi-auxiliaire 1 (être en état de) can, be able to; je ne peux pas le réparer I can't ou I am not able to repair it; (déçu de ne pas ~ le faire disappointed not to be able to do it
2 (avoir la permission) can, may, be allowed to; vous pouvez aller au cinéma you can ou may go to the pictures
3 (probabilité, hypothèse) may, might, could; il a pu avoir un accident he may ou might ou could have had an accident; il aurait pu le dire! he might ou could have said (so)!
◆ vb impersonnel may, might, could; il peut arriver que it may ou might ou could happen that
◆ vt can, be able to; j'ai fait tout ce que j'ai pu I did all I could; je n'en peux plus (épuisé) I'm exhausted; (à bout) I can't take any more
se pouvoir vi: il se peut que it may ou might be that; cela se pourrait that's quite possible.

prairie [pʀɛʀi] nf meadow.

praline [pʀalin] nf sugared almond.

praticable [pʀatikabl(ə)] a passable, practicable.

praticien, ne [pʀatisjɛ̃, -jɛn] nm/f practitioner.

pratique [pʀatik] nf practice // a practical.

pratiquement [pʀatikmɑ̃] ad (pour ainsi dire) practically, virtually.

pratiquer [pʀatike] vt to practise; (SPORT etc) to go in (for); to play; (intervention, opération) to carry out; (ouverture, abri) to make.

pré [pʀe] nm meadow.

préalable [pʀealabl(ə)] a preliminary; condition ~ (de) precondition (for), prerequisite (for); au ~ beforehand.

préambule [pʀeɑ̃byl] nm preamble; (fig) prelude; sans ~ straight away.

préavis [pʀeavi] nm notice; communication avec ~ (TÉL) personal ou person to person call.

précaution [pʀekosjɔ̃] nf precaution; avec ~ cautiously; par ~ as a precaution.

précédemment [pʀesedamɑ̃] ad before, previously.

précédent, e [pʀesedɑ̃, -ɑ̃t] a previous // nm precedent; sans ~ unprecedented; **le jour ~** the day before, the previous day.

précéder [presede] *vt* to precede; *(marcher ou rouler devant)* to be in front of.

précepteur, trice [preseptœr, -tris] *nm/f* (private) tutor.

prêcher [prefe] *vt* to preach.

précieux, euse [presjø, -øz] *a* precious, invaluable; *(style, écrivain)* précieux, precious.

précipice [presipis] *nm* drop, chasm; *(fig)* abyss.

précipitamment [presipitamɑ̃] *ad* hurriedly, hastily.

précipitation [presipitasjɔ̃] *nf* *(hâte)* haste; **~s** *(pluie)* rain.

précipité, e [presipite] *a* hurried, hasty.

précipiter [presipite] *vt* *(faire tomber)*: **~ qn/qch du haut de** ou **hurl sb/sth off** ou **from**; *(hâter: marche)* to quicken; *(: départ)* to hasten; **se ~** *vi* to speed up; **se ~ sur/vers** to rush at/towards.

précis, e [presi, -iz] *a* precise; *(tir, mesures)* accurate, precise // *nm* handbook; **précisément** *ad* precisely; **préciser** *vt (expliquer)* to be more specific about, clarify; *(spécifier)* to state, specify; **se préciser** *vi* to become clear(er); **précision** *nf* precision; accuracy; point ou detail *(made clear or to be clarified)*.

précoce [prekos] *a* early; *(enfant)* precocious; *(calvitie)* premature.

préconiser [prekɔnize] *vt* to advocate.

prédécesseur [predesesœr] *nm* predecessor.

prédilection [predileksjɔ̃] *nf*: **avoir une ~ pour** to be partial to; **de ~** favourite.

prédire [predir] *vt* to predict.

prédominer [predɔmine] *vi* to predominate; *(avis)* to prevail.

préface [prefas] *nf* preface.

préfecture [prefektyr] *nf* prefecture; **~ de police** police headquarters.

préférable [preferabl(ə)] *a* preferable.

préféré, e [prefere] *a, nm/f* favourite.

préférence [preferɑ̃s] *nf* preference; **de ~** preferably.

préférer [prefere] *vt*: **~ qn/qch (à)** to prefer sb/sth (to), like sb/sth better (than); **~ faire** to prefer to do; **je préférerais du thé** I would rather have tea, I'd prefer tea.

préfet [prefe] *nm* prefect.

préfixe [prefiks(ə)] *nm* prefix.

préhistorique [preistɔrik] *a* prehistoric.

préjudice [preʒydis] *nm* *(matériel)* loss; *(moral)* harm *q*; **porter ~ à** to harm, be detrimental to; **au ~ de** at the expense of.

préjugé [preʒyʒe] *nm* prejudice; **avoir un ~ contre** to be prejudiced ou biased against.

préjuger [preʒyʒe]: **~ de** *vt* to prejudge.

prélasser [prelase]: **se ~** *vi* to lounge.

prélèvement [prelevmɑ̃] *nm*: **faire un ~ de sang** to take a blood sample.

prélever [prelve] *vt* *(échantillon)* to take; *(argent)*: **~ (sur)** to deduct (from); *(: sur son compte)*: **~ (sur)** to withdraw (from).

prématuré, e [prematyre] *a* premature; *(retraite)* early // *nm* premature baby.

premier, ière [prəmje, -jɛr] *a* first; *(branche, marche)* bottom; *(fig)* basic; prime; initial // *nf (THÉÂTRE)* first night; *(AUTO)* first (gear); *(AVIAT, RAIL etc)* first class; *(CINÉMA)* première; *(exploit)* first; **le ~ venu** the first person to come along; **P~ Ministre** Prime Minister; **premièrement** *ad* firstly.

prémonition [premɔnisjɔ̃] *nf* premonition.

prémunir [premynir]: **se ~ vi**: **se ~ contre** to guard against.

prénatal, e [prenatal] *a (MÉD)*

antenatal.

prendre [prɑ̃dr(ə)] vt to take; (ôter): ~ **qch à** to take sth from; (aller chercher) to get, fetch; (se procurer) to get; (malfaiteur, poisson) to catch; (passager) to pick up; (personnel, aussi: couleur, goût) to take on; (locataire) to take in; (élève etc: traiter) to handle; (voix, ton) to put on; (coincer): **se ~ les doigts dans** to get one's fingers caught in // vi (liquide, ciment) to set; (greffe, vaccin) to take; (feu: foyer) to go; (: incendie) to start; (allumette) to light; (se diriger): **à gauche** to turn (to the) left; **à tout ~** on the whole, all in all; **se ~ pour** to think one is; **s'en ~ à** to attack; **se ~ d'amitié/d'affection pour** to befriend/become fond of; **s'y ~** (procéder) to set about it.

preneur [prənœr] nm: **être/trouver ~** to be willing to buy/find a buyer.

preniez, prenne etc vb voir **prendre**.

prénom [prenɔ̃] nm first ou Christian name.

prénuptial, e, aux [prenypsjal, -o] a premarital.

préoccupation [preɔkypasjɔ̃] nf (souci) concern; (idée fixe) preoccupation.

préoccuper [preɔkype] vt to concern; to preoccupy.

préparatifs [preparatif] nmpl preparations.

préparation [preparasjɔ̃] nf preparation; (SCOL) piece of homework.

préparer [prepare] vt to prepare; (café) to make; (examen) to prepare for; (voyage, entreprise) to plan; **se ~** vi (orage, tragédie) to brew, be in the air; **se ~ (à qch/faire)** to prepare (o.s.) ou get ready (for sth/to do); **~ qch à qn** (surprise etc) to have sth in store for sb.

prépondérant, e [prepɔ̃derɑ̃, -ɑ̃t] a major, dominating.

préposé, e [prepoze] a: **~ à** in charge of // nm/f employee; official;

attendant.

préposition [prepozisjɔ̃] nf preposition.

près [prɛ] ad near, close; **~ de** prép near (to), close to; (environ) nearly, almost; **de ~** ad closely; **à 5 kg ~** to within about 5 kg; **de cela ~ que** apart from the fact that.

présage [prezaʒ] nm omen.

présager [prezaʒe] vt to foresee.

presbyte [prɛsbit] a long-sighted.

presbytère [prɛsbiter] nm presbytery.

prescription [prɛskripsjɔ̃] nf (instruction) order, instruction; (MÉD, JUR) prescription.

prescrire [prɛskrir] vt to prescribe.

préséance [preseɑ̃s] nf precedence q.

présence [prezɑ̃s] nf presence; (au bureau etc) attendance; **~ d'esprit** presence of mind.

présent, e [prezɑ̃, -ɑ̃t] a, nm present; **à ~ (que)** now (that).

présentation [prezɑ̃tasjɔ̃] nf introduction; presentation; (allure) appearance.

présenter [prezɑ̃te] vt to present; (sympathie, condoléances) to offer; (soumettre) to submit; (invité, conférencier): **~ qn (à)** to introduce sb (to) // vi: **~ mal/bien** to have an unattractive/a pleasing appearance; **se ~** vi (sur convocation) to report, come; (à une élection) to stand; (occasion) to arise; **se ~ bien/mal** to look good/not too good; **se ~ à** (examen) to sit.

préservatif [prezɛrvatif] nm sheath, condom.

préserver [prezɛrve] vt: **~ de** to protect from; to save from.

président [prezidɑ̃] nm (POL) president; (d'une assemblée, COMM) chairman; **~ directeur général (PDG)** chairman and managing director.

présider [prezide] vt to preside over; (dîner) to be the guest of honour at; **~ à** vt to direct; to govern.

présomptueux, euse [prezɔ̃ptɥø, -øz] *a* presumptuous.

presque [prɛsk(ə)] *ad* almost, nearly; ~ **rien** hardly anything; ~ **pas hardly** (at all); ~ **pas de** hardly any.

presqu'île [prɛskil] *nf* peninsula.

pressant, e [prɛsɑ̃, -ɑ̃t] *a* urgent; **se faire** ~ to become insistent.

presse [prɛs] *nf* press; *(affluence):* **heures de** ~ busy times.

pressé, e [prese] *a* in a hurry; *(air)* hurried; *(besogne)* urgent; **orange** ~**e** fresh orange juice.

pressentiment [presɑ̃timɑ̃] *nm* foreboding, premonition.

pressentir [presɑ̃tir] *vt* to sense; *(prendre contact avec)* to approach.

presse-papiers [prɛspapje] *nm inv* paperweight.

presser [prese] *vt (fruit, éponge)* to squeeze; *(bouton)* to press; *(allure, affaire)* to speed up; *(inciter):* ~ **qn de faire** to urge ou press sb to do *// vi* to be urgent; **rien ne presse** there's no hurry; **se** ~ *vi (se hâter)* to hurry (up); **se** ~ **contre qn** to squeeze up against sb.

pressing [prɛsiŋ] *nm* steam-pressing; *(magasin)* dry-cleaner's.

pression [prɛsjɔ̃] *nf* pressure; **faire** ~ **sur** to put pressure on; ~ **artérielle** blood pressure.

pressoir [prɛswar] *nm (wine ou oil etc)* press.

pressurer [prɛsyre] *vt (fig)* to squeeze.

prestance [prɛstɑ̃s] *nf* presence, imposing bearing.

prestataire [prɛstatɛr] *nm/f* supplier.

prestation [prɛstasjɔ̃] *nf (allocation)* benefit; *(d'une entreprise)* service provided; *(d'un artiste)* performance.

prestidigitateur, trice [prɛstidiʒitatœr, -tris] *nm/f* conjurer.

prestigieux, euse [prɛstiʒjø, -øz] *a* prestigious.

présumer [prezyme] *vt:* ~ **que** to presume ou assume that; ~ **de** to

overrate.

présupposer [presypoze] *vt* to suppose.

prêt, e [prɛ, prɛt] *a* ready *// nm* lending *q*; loan; **prêt-à-porter** *nm* ready-to-wear ou off-the-peg (Brit) clothes *pl*.

prétendant [pretɑ̃dɑ̃] *nm* pretender; *(d'une femme)* suitor.

prétendre [pretɑ̃dʁ(ə)] *vt (affirmer):* ~ **que** to claim that; *(avoir l'intention de):* ~ **faire qch** to mean ou intend to do sth; ~ **à** *vt (droit, titre)* to lay claim to; **prétendu, e** *a (supposé)* so-called.

prête-nom [prɛtnɔ̃] *nm (péj)* figurehead.

prétentieux, euse [pretɑ̃sjø, -øz] *a* pretentious.

prétention [pretɑ̃sjɔ̃] *nf* claim; pretentiousness.

prêter [prete] *vt (livres, argent):* ~ **qch (à qn)** to lend sth (to); *(supposer):* ~ **à qn** *(caractère, propos)* to attribute to sb *// vi (aussi: se ~: tissu, cuir)* to give; ~ **à** *(commentaires etc)* to be open to, give rise to; **se à qch** to go along with; ~ **à qn** *(ma-nigances etc)* to go along with; ~ **assistance à** to give help to; ~ **attention à** to pay attention to; ~ **serment** to take the oath; ~ **l'oreille** to listen.

prétexte [pretɛkst(ə)] *nm* pretext, excuse; **sous aucun** ~ on no account; **prétexter** *vt* to give as a pretext ou an excuse.

prêtre [prɛtʁ(ə)] *nm* priest.

preuve [prœv] *nf* proof; *(indice)* proof, evidence *q*; **faire** ~ **de** to show; **faire ses** ~**s** to prove o.s. (ou itself).

prévaloir [prevalwar] *vi* to prevail; **se** ~ **de** *vt* to take advantage of; to pride o.s. on.

prévenant, e [prevnɑ̃, -ɑ̃t] *a* thoughtful, kind.

prévenir [prevnir] *vt (avertir):* ~ **qn (de)** to warn sb (about); *(informer):* ~ **qn (de)** to tell ou inform sb (about); (éviter) to avoid, prevent; (anticiper) to forestall; to anticipate.

prévention [prevɑ̃sjɔ̃] nf prevention; ~ routière road safety.

prévenu, e [prevny] nm/f (JUR) defendant, accused.

prévision [previzjɔ̃] nf: ~s predictions; forecast sg; en ~ de in anticipation of; ~s météorologiques weather forecast sg.

prévoir [prevwar] vt (deviner) to foresee; (s'attendre à) to expect, reckon on; (prévenir) to anticipate; (organiser) to plan; (préparer, réserver) to allow; prévu pour 10h scheduled for 10 o'clock.

prévoyance [prevwajɑ̃s] nf: caisse de ~ contingency fund.

prévoyant, e [prevwajɑ̃, -ɑ̃t] a gifted with (ou showing) foresight.

prévu, e [prevy] pp de prévoir.

prier [prije] vi to pray // vt (Dieu) to pray to; (implorer) to beg; (demander): ~ qn de faire to ask sb to do; se faire ~ to need coaxing ou persuading; je vous en prie (allez-y) please do; (de rien) don't mention it.

prière [prijɛr] nf prayer; '~ de faire ...' 'please do ...'.

primaire [primɛr] a primary; (péj) simple-minded; simplistic // nm (SCOL) primary education.

prime [prim] nf (bonification) bonus; (subside) allowance; (COMM: cadeau) free gift; (ASSURANCES, BOURSE) premium // a: de ~ abord at first glance.

primer [prime] vt (l'emporter sur) to prevail over; (récompenser) to award a prize to // vi to dominate; to prevail.

primeurs [primœr] nfpl early fruits and vegetables.

primevère [primvɛr] nf primrose.

primitif, ive [primitif, -iv] a primitive; (originel) original.

prince, esse [prɛ̃s, prɛ̃sɛs] nm/f prince/princess.

principal, e, aux [prɛ̃sipal, -o] a principal, main // nm (SCOL) princi-

pal, head(master); (essentiel) main thing.

principe [prɛ̃sip] nm principle; pour le ~ on principle; de ~ a (accord, hostilité) automatic; par ~ on principle; en ~ (habituellement) as a rule; (théoriquement) in principle.

printemps [prɛ̃tɑ̃] nm spring.

priorité [priɔrite] nf (AUTO): avoir la ~ (sur) to have right of way (over); ~ à droite right of way to vehicles coming from the right.

pris, e [pri, priz] pp de prendre // a (place) taken; (journée, mains) full; (billets) sold; (personne) busy; avoir le nez/la gorge ~ (e) to have a stuffy nose/a hoarse throat; être ~ de panique to be panic-stricken.

prise [priz] nf (d'une ville) capture; (PÊCHE, CHASSE) catch; (de judo ou catch, point d'appui ou pour empoigner) hold; (ÉLEC: fiche) plug; (: femelle) socket; être aux ~s avec to be grappling with; ~ de courant power point; ~ multiple adaptor; ~ de sang blood test; ~ de terre earth; ~ de vue (photo) shot.

priser [prize] vt (tabac, héroïne) to take; (estimer) to prize, value // vi to take snuff.

prison [prizɔ̃] nf prison; aller/être en ~ to go to/be in prison ou jail; faire de la ~ to serve time; **prisonnier, ière** nm/f prisoner // a captive.

prit vb voir prendre.

privé, e [prive] a private; en ~ in private.

priver [prive] vt: ~ qn de to deprive sb of; se ~ de to go ou do without.

privilège [privilɛʒ] nm privilege.

prix [pri] nm (valeur) price; (récompense, SCOL) prize; hors de ~ exorbitantly priced; à aucun ~ not at any price; à tout ~ at all costs; ~ d'achat/de vente/de revient purchasing/selling/cost price.

probable [prɔbabl(ə)] a likely, probable; ~ment ad probably.

probant, e [prɔbɑ̃, -ɑ̃t] a convincing.

problème [problɛm] nm problem.

procédé [prosede] nm (méthode) process; (comportement) behaviour q.

procéder [prosede] vi to proceed; to behave; ~ à vt to carry out.

procès [prosɛ] nm trial; (poursuites) proceedings pl; être en ~ avec to be involved in a lawsuit with.

processus [prosesys] nm process.

procès-verbal, aux [prosɛvɛrbal, -o] nm (constat) statement; (aussi: P.V.): avoir un ~ to get a parking ticket; to be booked; (de réunion) minutes pl.

prochain, e [proʃɛ̃, -ɛn] a next; (proche) impending; near // nm fellow man; la ~e fois/semaine ~e next time/week; **prochainement** ad soon, shortly.

proche [proʃ] a nearby; (dans le temps) imminent; (parent, ami) close; ~s nmpl close relatives; être ~ (de) to be near, be close (to); de ~ en ~ gradually; le P~ Orient the Middle East.

proclamer [proklame] vt to proclaim.

procuration [prokyrasjɔ̃] nf proxy; power of attorney.

procurer [prokyre] vt: ~ qch à qn (fournir) to obtain sth for sb; (causer: plaisir etc) to bring sb sth; se ~ vt to get.

procureur [prokyrœr] nm public prosecutor.

prodige [prodiʒ] nm marvel, wonder; (personne) prodigy.

prodigue [prodig] a generous; extravagant; fils ~ prodigal son.

prodiguer [prodige] vt (argent, biens) to be lavish with; (soins, attentions): ~ qch à qn to give sb sth.

producteur, trice [prodyktœr, -tris] nm/f producer.

production [prodyksjɔ̃] nf (gén) production; (rendement) output.

produire [produir] vt to produce; se ~ vi (acteur) to perform, appear; (événement) to happen, occur.

produit [produi] nm (gén) product; ~s agricoles farm produce sg; ~ d'entretien cleaning product.

prof [prof] nm (fam) teacher.

profane [profan] a (REL) secular // nm/f layman.

proférer [profere] vt to utter.

professer [profese] vt to teach.

professeur [profesœr] nm teacher; (titulaire d'une chaire) professor; ~ (de faculté) (university) lecturer.

profession [profesjɔ̃] nf profession; sans ~ unemployed; **professionnel, le** a, nm/f professional.

profil [profil] nm profile; (d'une voiture) line, contour; de ~ in profile; ~er vt to streamline.

profit [profi] nm (avantage) benefit, advantage; (COMM, FINANCE) profit; au ~ de in aid of; tirer ~ de to profit from.

profitable [profitabl(ə)] a beneficial; profitable.

profiter [profite] vi: ~ de to take advantage of; to make the most of; ~ à to benefit; to be profitable to.

profond, e [profɔ̃, -ɔ̃d] a deep; (méditation, mépris) profound; **fondeur** nf depth.

progéniture [proʒenityr] nf offspring inv.

programme [program] nm programme; (TV, RADIO) programmes pl; (SCOL) syllabus, curriculum; (INFORM) program; **programmer** vt (TV, RADIO) to put on, show; (INFORM) to program; **programmeur, euse** nm/f programmer.

progrès [progrɛ] nm progress q; faire des ~ to make progress.

progresser [progrese] vi to progress; (troupes etc) to make headway ou progress; **progressif, ive** a progressive.

prohiber [proibe] vt to prohibit, ban.

proie [prwa] nf prey q.

projecteur [proʒɛktœr] nm projector; (de théâtre, cirque) spotlight.

projectile [proʒɛktil] nm missile.

projection [proʒɛksjɔ̃] nf projection;

showing; **conférence avec ~s** lecture with slides (ou a film).

projet [prɔʒɛ] nm plan; (ébauche) draft; **~ de loi** bill.

projeter [prɔʒte] vt (envisager) to plan; (film, photos) to project; (passer) to show; (ombre, lueur) to throw, cast; (jeter) to throw up (ou off ou out).

prolixe [prɔliks(ə)] a verbose.

prolongations [prɔlɔ̃gasjɔ̃] nfpl (FOOTBALL) extra time sg.

prolongement [prɔlɔ̃ʒmɑ̃] nm extension; **~s** (fig) repercussions, effects; **dans le ~ de** running on from.

prolonger [prɔlɔ̃ʒe] vt (débat, séjour) to prolong; (délai, billet, rue) to extend; (suj: chose) to be a continuation ou an extension of; **se ~** vi to go on.

promenade [prɔmnad] nf walk (ou drive ou ride); **faire une ~** to go for a walk; **une ~ en voiture/à vélo** a drive/(bicycle) ride.

promener [prɔmne] vt (chien) to take out for a walk; (doigts, regard): **~ qch sur** to run sth over; **se ~** vi to go for (ou be out for) a walk.

promesse [prɔmɛs] nf promise.

promettre [prɔmɛtr(ə)] vt to promise // vi to be ou look promising; **~ à qn de faire** to promise sb that one will do.

promiscuité [prɔmiskɥite] nf crowding; lack of privacy.

promontoire [prɔmɔ̃twar] nm headland.

promoteur, trice [prɔmɔtœr, -tris] nm/f (instigateur) instigator, promoter; **~ (immobilier)** property developer (Brit), real estate promoter (US).

promotion [prɔmɔsjɔ̃] nf promotion.

promouvoir [prɔmuvwar] vt to promote.

prompt, e [prɔ̃, prɔ̃t] a swift, rapid.

prôner [prone] vt to advocate.

pronom [prɔnɔ̃] nm pronoun.

prononcer [prɔnɔ̃se] vt (son, mot,

jugement) to pronounce; (dire) to utter; (allocution) to deliver; **se ~** vi to reach a decision, give a verdict; **se ~ sur** to give an opinion on; **se ~ contre** to come down against; **prononciation** nf pronunciation.

pronostic [prɔnɔstik] nm (MÉD) prognosis (pl oses); (fig: aussi: **~s**) forecast.

propagande [prɔpagɑ̃d] nf propaganda.

propager [prɔpaʒe] vt, **se ~** vi to spread.

prophète [prɔfɛt] nm prophet.

prophétie [prɔfesi] nf prophecy.

propice [prɔpis] a favourable.

proportion [prɔpɔrsjɔ̃] nf proportion; **toute(s) ~(s) gardée(s)** making due allowance(s).

propos [prɔpo] nm (paroles) talk q, remark; (intention) intention, aim; (sujet): **à quel ~?** what about?; **à ~ de** about, regarding; **à tout ~** for no reason at all; **à ~** ad by the way; (opportunément) at the right moment.

proposer [prɔpoze] vt (suggérer): **~ qch (à qn)/de faire** to suggest sth (to sb)/doing, propose sth (to sb) to do; (offrir): **~ qch à qn/de faire** to offer sb sth/to do; (candidat) to put forward; (loi, motion) to propose: **se ~** (pour faire) to offer one's services; **se ~ de faire** to intend ou propose to do; **proposition** nf suggestion; proposal; offer; (LING) clause.

propre [prɔpr(ə)] a clean; (net) neat, tidy; (possessif) own; (sens) literal; (particulier): **~ à** peculiar to; (approprié): **~ à** suitable for; (de nature à): **~ à faire** likely to do // nm: **recopier au ~** to make a fair copy of; **~ment** ad cleanly; neatly, tidily; **le village ~ment dit** the village itself; **à ~ment parler** strictly speaking; **~té** nf cleanliness; neatness; tidiness.

propriétaire [prɔprijetɛr] nm/f owner; (pour le locataire) landlord/lady.

propriété [prɔprijete] nf (gén) property; (droit) ownership; (objet, meuble, terres) property gén q.

propulser [prɔpylse] vt (missile) to propel; (projeter) to hurl, fling.

proroger [prɔrɔʒe] vt to put back, defer; (prolonger) to extend.

proscrire [prɔskrir] vt (bannir) to banish; (interdire) to ban, prohibit.

prose [proz] nf prose (style).

prospecter [prɔspɛkte] vt to prospect; (COMM) to canvass.

prospectus [prɔspɛktys] nm leaflet.

prospère [prɔspɛr] a prosperous.

prosterner [prɔstɛrne]: se ~ vi to bow low, prostrate o.s.

prostituée [prɔstitɥe] nf prostitute.

protecteur, trice [prɔtɛktœr, -tris] a protective; (air, ton: péj) patronizing // nm/f protector.

protection [prɔtɛksjɔ̃] nf protection; (d'un personnage influent: aide) patronage.

protéger [prɔteʒe] vt to protect; se ~ de/contre to protect o.s. from.

protéine [prɔtein] nf protein.

protestant, e [prɔtɛstɑ̃, -ɑ̃t] a, nm/f Protestant.

protestation [prɔtɛstasjɔ̃] nf (plainte) protest.

protester [prɔtɛste] vi: ~ (contre) to protest (against ou about); ~ de (son innocence, sa loyauté) to protest.

prothèse [prɔtɛz] nf artificial limb, prosthesis; ~ dentaire denture.

protocole [prɔtɔkɔl] nm (fig) etiquette.

proue [pru] nf bow(s pl), prow.

prouesse [prues] nf feat.

prouver [pruve] vt to prove.

provenance [prɔvnɑ̃s] nf origin; (de mot, coutume) source; avion en ~ de plane (arriving) from.

provenir [prɔvnir]: ~ de vt to come from; (résulter de) to be the result of.

proverbe [prɔvɛrb(ə)] nm proverb.

province [prɔvɛ̃s] nf province.

proviseur [prɔvizœr] nm = head-

(teacher) (Brit), ≈ principal (US).

provision [prɔvizjɔ̃] nf (réserve) stock, supply; (avance: à un avocat, avoué) retainer, retaining fee; (COMM) funds pl (in account); reserve; (vivres) provisions, food q.

provisoire [prɔvizwar] a temporary; (JUR) provisional.

provoquer [prɔvɔke] vt (inciter): ~ qn à to incite sb to; (défier) to provoke; (causer) to cause, bring about.

proxénète [prɔksenɛt] nm procurer.

proximité [prɔksimite] nf nearness, closeness; (dans le temps) imminence, closeness; à ~ near ou close by; à ~ de near (to), close to.

prude [pryd] a prudish.

prudemment [prydamɑ̃] ad carefully, cautiously; wisely, sensibly.

prudence [prydɑ̃s] nf carefulness; caution; avec ~ carefully, cautiously; par (mesure de) ~ as a precaution.

prudent, e [prydɑ̃, -ɑ̃t] a (pas téméraire) careful, cautious; (: en général) safety-conscious; (sage, conseillé) wise, sensible; (réservé) cautious.

prune [pryn] nf plum.

pruneau, x [pryno] nm prune.

prunelle [prynɛl] nf pupil; eye.

prunier [prynje] nm plum tree.

psaume [psom] nm psalm.

pseudonyme [psødɔnim] nm (gén) fictitious name; (d'écrivain) pseudonym, pen name; (de comédien) stage name.

psychanalyste [psikanalist(ə)] nm/f psychoanalyst.

psychiatre [psikjatr(ə)] nm/f psychiatrist.

psychiatrique [psikjatrik] a psychiatric.

psychique [psiʃik] a psychological.

psychologie [psikɔlɔʒi] nf psychology; **psychologique** a psychological; **psychologue** nm/f psychologist.

P.T.T. sigle fpl voir poste.

pu pp de **pouvoir**.

puanteur [pɥɑ̃tœʀ] nf stink, stench.

pub [pœb] abr f (fam: = publicité): la ~ advertising.

public, ique [pyblik] a public; (école, instruction) state cpd // nm public; (assistance) audience; **en** ~ in public.

publicitaire [pyblisitɛʀ] a advertising cpd; (film, voiture) publicity cpd.

publicité [pyblisite] nf (méthode, profession) advertising; (annonce) advertisement; (révélations) publicity.

publier [pyblije] vt to publish.

publique [pyblik] af voir **public**.

puce [pys] nf flea; (INFORM) chip; ~s nfpl (marché) flea market sg.

pucelle [pysɛl] af: être ~ to be a virgin.

pudeur [pydœʀ] nf modesty.

pudique [pydik] a (chaste) modest; (discret) discreet.

puer [pɥe] (péj) vi to stink.

puériculture [pɥeʀikyltʀis] nf p(a)ediatric nurse.

puériculture [pɥeʀikyltyʀ] nf p(a)ediatric nursing; infant care.

puéril, e [pɥeʀil] a childish.

pugilat [pyʒila] nm (fist) fight.

puis [pɥi] vb voir **pouvoir** // ad then.

puiser [pɥize] vt: ~ (dans) to draw (from).

puisque [pɥisk(ə)] cj since.

puissance [pɥisɑ̃s] nf power; **en** ~ a potential.

puissant, e [pɥisɑ̃, -ɑ̃t] a powerful.

puisse etc vb voir **pouvoir**.

puits [pɥi] nm well; ~ **de mine** mine shaft.

pull(-over) [pyl(ɔvɛʀ)] nm sweater.

pulluler [pylyle] vi to swarm.

pulpe [pylp(ə)] nf pulp.

pulvérisateur [pylveʀizatœʀ] nm spray.

pulvériser [pylveʀize] vt to pulverize; (liquide) to spray.

punaise [pynɛz] nf (ZOOL) bug; (clou) drawing pin (Brit), thumbtack (US).

punch [pɔ̃ʃ] nm (boisson) punch;

[pœnʃ] (BOXE, fig) punch.

punir [pyniʀ] vt to punish; **punition** nf punishment.

pupille [pypij] nf (ANAT) pupil; nmf (enfant) ward; ~ **de l'État** child in care.

pupitre [pypitʀ(ə)] nm (SCOL) desk; (REL) lectern; (de chef d'orchestre) rostrum.

pur, e [pyʀ] a pure; (vin) undiluted; (whisky) neat; **en** ~e **perte** to no avail.

purée [pyʀe] nf: ~ (**de pommes de terre**) mashed potatoes pl; ~ **de marrons** chestnut purée.

purger [pyʀʒe] vt (radiateur) to drain; (circuit hydraulique) to bleed; (MÉD, POL) to purge; (JUR: peine) to serve.

purin [pyʀɛ̃] nm liquid manure.

pur-sang [pyʀsɑ̃] nm inv thoroughbred.

pusillanime [pyzilanim] a fainthearted.

putain [pytɛ̃] nf (fam!) whore (!).

puzzle [pœzl(ə)] nm jigsaw (puzzle).

P.V. sigle m = **procès-verbal**.

pyjama [piʒama] nm pyjamas pl.

pyramide [piʀamid] nf pyramid.

Pyrénées [piʀene] nfpl: les ~ the Pyrenees.

Q

QG [kyʒe] voir **quartier**.

QI [kyi] sigle m (= quotient intellectuel) IQ.

quadragénaire [kadʀaʒenɛʀ] nmf man/woman in his/her forties.

quadriller [kadʀije] vt (papier) to mark out in squares; (POLICE) to keep under tight control.

quadruple [k(w)adʀypl(ə)] nm: le ~ **de** four times as much as; **quadruplés, ées** nm/fpl quadruplets, quads.

quai [ke] nm (de port) quay; (de gare) platform; être à ~ (navire) to be alongside; (train) to be in the station.

qualifier [kalifje] vt, se ~ vi (SPORT) to qualify; ~ **qch/qn de** to describe sth/sb as.

qualité [kalite] nf quality; (titre, fonction) position.

quand [kɑ̃] cj, ad when; ~ **je serai riche** when I'm rich; ~ **même** all the same; really; ~ **bien même** even though.

quant [kɑ̃]: ~ **à** prép as for, as to; regarding.

quant-à-soi [kɑ̃taswa] nm: **rester sur son** ~ to remain aloof.

quantité [kɑ̃tite] nf quantity, amount; (SCIENCE) quantity; (grand nombre): **une ou des ~(s) de** a great deal of.

quarantaine [karɑ̃ten] nf (MÉD) quarantine; **avoir la** ~ (âge) to be around forty; **une ~ (de)** forty or so, about forty.

quarante [karɑ̃t] num forty.

quart [kar] nm (fraction, partie) quarter; (surveillance) watch; **un ~ de beurre** a quarter kilo of butter; **un ~ de vin** a quarter litre of wine; **une livre un ~ ou et ~** one and a quarter pounds; **le ~ de** a quarter of; ~ **d'heure** quarter of an hour.

quartier [kartje] nm (de ville) district, area; (de bœuf) quarter; (de fruit, fromage) piece; ~**s** nmpl (MIL, BLASON) quarters; **cinéma de** ~ local cinema; **avoir** ~ **libre** (fig) to be free; ~ **général (QG)** headquarters (HQ).

quartz [kwarts] nm quartz.

quasi [kazi] ad almost, nearly; ~**ment** ad almost, nearly.

quatorze [katɔrz(ə)] num fourteen.

quatre [katr(ə)] num four; **à** ~ **pattes** on all fours; **tiré à** ~ **épingles** dressed up to the nines; **faire les** ~ **cent coups** to get a bit wild; **se mettre en** ~ **pour qn** to go out of one's way for sb; ~ **à** ~ (monter, descendre) four at a time; ~**vingt-dix** num ninety; ~**vingts** num eighty; **quatrième** num fourth.

quatuor [kwatɥɔr] nm quartet(te).

MOT-CLÉ

que [kə] ♦ cj **1** (introduisant complétive) that; **il sait** ~ **tu es là** he knows (that) you're here; **je veux** ~ **tu acceptes** I want you to accept; **il a dit** — **oui** he said he would (ou it was etc)

2 (reprise d'autres conjonctions): **quand il rentrera et qu'il aura mangé** when he gets back and (when) he has eaten; **si vous y allez ou** ~ **vous** ... if you go there or if you ...

3 (en tête de phrase: hypothèse, souhait etc): **qu'il le veuille ou non** whether he likes it or not; **qu'il fasse ce qu'il voudra!** let him do as he pleases!

4 (après comparatif) than; as; voir **plus, aussi, autant** etc

5 (seulement): **ne ... ~** only; **il ne boit** ~ **de l'eau** he only drinks water ♦ ad (exclamation): **qu'il ou qu'est-ce qu'il est bête/court vite!** he's so silly!/he runs so fast!; ~ **de livres!** what a lot of books!

♦ pronom **1** (relatif: personne) whom; (: chose) that, which; **l'homme** ~ **je vois** the man (whom) I see; **le livre** ~ **tu vois** the book (that ou which) you see; **un jour** ~ **j'étais** ... a day when I was ...

2 (interrogatif) what; ~ **fais-tu?, qu'est-ce que tu fais?** what are you doing?; **qu'est-ce que c'est?** what is it?, what's that?; ~ **faire?** what can one do?

MOT-CLÉ

quel, quelle [kɛl] a **1** (interrogatif: personne) who; (: chose) what; which; ~ **est cet homme?** who is this man?; ~ **est ce livre?** what is this book?; ~ **livre/ homme?** what book/man?; (parmi un certain nombre) which book/man?; ~**s acteurs préférez-vous?** which actors do you

prefer; **dans ~s pays êtes-vous allé?** which *ou* what countries did you go to?
2 *(exclamatif):* **~le surprise!** what a surprise!
3: ~(le) que soit: ~ que soit le coupable whoever is guilty; **~ que soit votre avis** whatever your opinion.

quelconque [kɛlkɔ̃k] *a (médiocre)* indifferent, poor; *(sans attrait)* ordinary, plain; *(indéfini):* **un ami/pretexte ~** some friend/pretext or other.

MOT-CLÉ

quelque [kɛlkə] ◆ *a* **1** some; a few; *(tournure interrogative)* any; **~ espoir** some hope; **il a ~s amis** he has a few *ou* some friends; **a-t-il ~s amis?** has he any friends?; **les ~s livres qui** the few books which; **20 kg et ~(s)** a bit over 20 kg
2: ~ ... que *(+ subjonctif)* **~ livre qu'il choisisse** whatever *(ou* whichever) book he chooses
3: ~ chose something; *(tournure interrogative)* anything; **~ chose d'autre** something else; anything else; **~ part** somewhere; anywhere; **en ~ sorte** as it were
◆ *ad* **1** *(environ):* **~ 100 mètres** some 100 metres.
2: ~ peu rather, somewhat.

quelquefois [kɛlkəfwa] *ad* sometimes.

quelques-uns, -unes [kɛlkəzœ̃, -yn] *pronom* a few, some.

quelqu'un [kɛlkœ̃] *pronom* someone, somebody, *tournure interrogative* + anyone *ou* anybody; **~ d'autre** someone *ou* somebody else; anybody else.

quémander [kemɑ̃de] *vt* to beg for.

qu'en dira-t-on [kɑ̃diratɔ̃] *nm inv:* **le ~** gossip, what people say.

querelle [kərɛl] *nf* quarrel.

quereller [kərele]: **se ~** *vi* to quar-

rel.

qu'est-ce que *(ou* **qui)** [kɛskə(ki)] *voir* **que**, **qui**.

question [kɛstjɔ̃] *nf (gén)* question; *(fig)* matter; issue; **il a été ~ de we** *(ou* they) spoke about; **de quoi est-il ~?** what is it about?; **il n'en est pas ~** ~ there's no question of it; **hors de ~** out of the question; **remettre en ~** to question.

questionnaire [kɛstjɔnɛr] *nm* questionnaire; **questionner** *vt* to question.

quête [kɛt] *nf* collection; *(recherche)* quest, search; **faire la ~** *(à l'église)* to take the collection; *(artiste)* to pass the hat round; **quêter** *vi* à l'église) to take the collection.

quetsche [kwɛtʃ(ə)] *nf* damson.

queue [kø] *nf* tail; *(fig: du classement)* bottom; *(: de poêle)* handle; *(: de fruit, feuille)* stalk; *(: de train, colonne, file)* rear; **faire la ~** to queue (up); **~ de cheval** ponytail; **~-de-pie** *nf (habit)* tails *pl*, tail coat.

qui [ki] *pronom (personne)* who, *prép* + whom; *(chose, animal)* which, that; **qu'est-ce ~ est sur la table?** what is on the table?; **~ est-ce qui?** who?; **~ est-ce que?** who?; whom?; **à ~ est ce sac?** whose bag is this?; **à ~ parlais-tu?** who were you talking to?, to whom were you talking?; **amenez ~ vous voulez** bring who you like; **~ que ce soit** whoever it may be.

quiconque [kikɔ̃k] *pronom (celui qui)* whoever, anyone who; *(personne)* anyone, anybody.

quiétude [kjetyd] *nf (d'un lieu)* quiet, tranquillity; **en toute ~** in complete peace.

quille [kij] *nf:* **(jeu de) ~s** skittles *sg* (*Brit*), bowling (*US*).

quincaillerie [kɛ̃kajri] *nf (ustensiles)* hardware; *(magasin)* hardware shop; **quincaillier, ière** *nm/f* hardware dealer.

quinine [kinin] *nf* quinine.

quinquagénaire [kɛ̃kaʒenɛʀ] *nm/f* man/woman in his/her fifties.

quintal, aux [kɛ̃tal, o] *nm* quintal *(100 kg)*.

quinte [kɛ̃t] *nf*: ~ **(de toux)** coughing fit.

quintuple [kɛ̃typl(ə)] *nm*: le ~ de five times as much as; **quintuplés, ées** *nm/fpl* quintuplets, quins.

quinzaine [kɛ̃zɛn] *nf*: une ~ (de) about fifteen, fifteen or so; une ~ (de jours) a fortnight, two weeks.

quinze [kɛ̃z] *num* fifteen; demain en ~ a fortnight ou two weeks tomorrow; dans ~ jours in a fortnight('s time), in two weeks(' time).

quiproquo [kipʀɔko] *nm* misunderstanding.

quittance [kitãs] *nf* (reçu) receipt; (facture) bill.

quitte [kit] *a*: être ~ envers qn to be no longer in sb's debt; (fig) to be quits with sb; être ~ de (obligation) to be clear of; en être ~ à bon compte to have got off lightly; ~ à faire even if it means doing.

quitter [kite] *vt* to leave; (espoir, illusion) to give up; (vêtement) to take off; se ~ vi (couples, interlocuteurs) to part; ne quittez pas (au téléphone) hold the line.

qui-vive [kiviv] *nm*: être sur le ~ to be on the alert.

quoi [kwa] *pronom (interrogatif)* what; ~ de neuf? what's the news?; as-tu de ~ écrire? have you anything to write with?; il n'a pas de ~ se l'acheter he can't afford it; qu'il arrive whatever happens; ~ qu'il en soit be that as it may; que ce soit anything at all; **'il n'y a pas de ~'** (please) don't mention it; à ~ bon? what's the use?; en ~ puis-je vous aider? how can I help you?

quoique [kwak(ə)] *cj* (al)though.

quolibet [kɔlibɛ] *nm* gibe, jeer.

quote-part [kɔtpaʀ] *nf* share.

quotidien, ne [kɔtidjɛ̃, -ɛn] *a* daily; (banal) everyday // *nm (journal)* daily (paper).

R

r. *abr de* route, rue.

rab [ʀab] *abr nm (fam) de* **rabiot.**

rabâcher [ʀabaʃe] *vt* to keep on repeating.

rabais [ʀabɛ] *nm* reduction, discount.

rabaisser [ʀabese] *vt (rabattre)* to reduce; (dénigrer) to belittle.

rabattre [ʀabatʀ(ə)] *vt (couvercle, siège)* to pull down; (gibier) to drive; se ~ vi (bords, couvercle) to fall shut; (véhicule, coureur) to cut in; se ~ sur *vt* to fall back on.

rabbin [ʀabɛ̃] *nm* rabbi.

rabiot [ʀabjo] *nm (fam)* extra, more.

râblé, e [ʀɑble] *a* stocky.

rabot [ʀabo] *nm* plane.

rabougri, e [ʀabugʀi] *a* stunted.

rabrouer [ʀabʀue] *vt* to snub.

racaille [ʀakaj] *nf (péj)* rabble, riffraff.

raccommoder [ʀakɔmɔde] *vt* to mend, repair; (chaussette etc) to darn.

raccompagner [ʀakɔ̃paɲe] *vt* to take ou see back.

raccord [ʀakɔʀ] *nm* link.

raccorder [ʀakɔʀde] *vt* to join (up), link up; (suj: pont etc) to connect, link.

raccourci [ʀakuʀsi] *nm* short cut.

raccourcir [ʀakuʀsiʀ] *vt* to shorten.

raccrocher [ʀakʀɔʃe] *vt (tableau)* to hang back up; (récepteur) to put down // *vi (TEL)* to hang up, ring off; se ~ à *vt* to cling to, hang on to.

race [ʀas] *nf* race; (d'animaux, fig) breed; (ascendance) stock, race; de ~ a purebred, pedigree.

rachat [ʀaʃa] *nm* buying; buying back.

racheter [ʀaʃte] *vt (article perdu)* to buy another; (davantage) ~ du lait/3 œufs to buy more milk/another 3 eggs ou 3 more eggs; (après avoir vendu) to buy back; (d'occasion) buy; (COMM: part, firme) to buy up; (: pension, rente) to redeem; se ~ vi (fig) to make amends.

racial, e, aux [ʀasjal, -o] a racial.

racine [ʀasin] nf root; ~ carrée/cubique square/cube root.

raciste [ʀasist(ə)] a, nmf raci(al)ist.

racket [ʀakɛt] nm racketeering q.

racler [ʀakle] vt (surface) to scrape; (tache, boue) to scrape off.

racoler [ʀakɔle] vt (attirer: suj: prostituée) to solicit; (: parti, marchand) to tout for.

racontars [ʀakɔ̃taʀ] nmpl gossip sg.

raconter [ʀakɔ̃te] vt: ~ qch (à qn) (décrire) to relate (to sb), tell (sb) about; (dire) to tell (sb).

racorni, e [ʀakɔʀni] a hard(ened).

radar [ʀadaʀ] nm radar.

rade [ʀad] nf (natural) harbour; rester en ~ (fig) to be left stranded.

radeau, x [ʀado] nm raft.

radiateur [ʀadjatœʀ] nm radiator, heater; (AUTO) radiator; ~ électrique/à gaz electric/gas heater ou fire.

radiation [ʀadjasjɔ̃] nf (voir radier) striking off q; (PHYSIQUE) radiation.

radical, e, aux [ʀadikal, -o] a radical.

radier [ʀadje] vt to strike off.

radieux, euse [ʀadjø, -øz] a radiant; brilliant, glorious.

radin, e [ʀadɛ̃, -in] a (fam) stingy.

radio [ʀadjo] nf radio; (MÉD) X-ray // nm radio operator; à la ~ on the radio.

radio... [ʀadjo] préfixe: ~actif, ive a radioactive; **radiodiffuser** vt to broadcast; ~**graphie** nf radiography; (photo) X-ray photograph; ~**phonique** a radio cpd; ~**télévisé, e** a broadcast on radio and television.

radis [ʀadi] nm radish.

radoter [ʀadɔte] vi to ramble on.

radoucir [ʀadusiʀ]: se ~ vi (se réchauffer) to become milder; (se calmer) to calm down; to soften.

rafale [ʀafal] nf (vent) gust (of wind); (tir) burst of gunfire.

raffermir [ʀafɛʀmiʀ] vt, se ~ vi (tissus, muscle) to firm up; (fig) to strengthen.

raffiner [ʀafine] vt to refine; **raffinerie** nf refinery.

raffoler [ʀafɔle]: ~ de vt to be very keen on.

rafle [ʀafl(ə)] nf (de police) raid.

rafler [ʀafle] vt (fam) to swipe, nick.

rafraîchir [ʀafʀeʃiʀ] vt (atmosphère, température) to cool (down); (aussi: mettre à ~) to chill; (fig: rénover) to brighten up; se ~ vi to grow cooler; to freshen up; to refresh o.s; **rafraîchissant, e** a refreshing; **rafraîchissement** nm cooling; (boisson) cool drink; **rafraîchissements** (boissons, fruits etc) refreshments.

rage [ʀaʒ] nf (MÉD): la ~ rabies; (fureur) rage, fury; faire ~ to rage; ~ de dents (raging) toothache.

ragot [ʀago] nm (fam) malicious gossip q.

ragoût [ʀagu] nm (plat) stew.

raide [ʀɛd] a (tendu) taut, tight; (escarpé) steep; (droit: cheveux) straight; (ankylosé, dur, guindé) stiff; (fam) steep, stiff; flat broke // ad (en pente) steeply; ~ **mort** stone dead; **raidir** vt (muscles) to stiffen; (câble) to pull taut; se **raidir** vi to stiffen; to become taut; (personne) to tense up; to brace o.s.

raie [ʀɛ] nf (ZOOL) skate, ray; (rayure) stripe; (des cheveux) parting.

raifort [ʀɛfɔʀ] nm horseradish.

rail [ʀaj] nm rail; (chemins de fer) railways pl; par ~ by rail.

railler [ʀaje] vt to scoff at, jeer at.

rainure [ʀenyʀ] nf groove; slot.

raisin [ʀezɛ̃] nm (aussi: ~s) grapes pl; ~s secs raisins.

raison [ʀezɔ̃] nf reason; avoir ~ to be right; donner ~ à qn to agree with sb; to prove sb right; se faire une ~ to learn to live with it; perdre la ~ to become insane; to take leave of one's senses; ~ de plus a the more reason; **à plus forte ~** all the more so; **en ~ de** because of; according to; in proportion to; **à ~ de** at the rate of; **~ sociale** corporate name; **raisonnable** a reasonable, sensible.

raisonnement [rɛzɔnmɑ̃] nm reasoning; arguing; argument.

raisonner [rɛzɔne] vi (penser) to reason; (argumenter, discuter) to argue // vt (personne) to reason with.

rajeunir [raʒœnir] vt (suj: coiffure, robe) to make sb look younger; (suj: cure etc) to rejuvenate; (fig) to give a new lease to; to inject new blood into // vi to become (ou look) younger.

rajouter [raʒute] vt: **~ du sel/un œuf** to add some more salt/another egg.

rajuster [raʒyste] vt (vêtement) to straighten, tidy; (salaires) to adjust; (machine) to readjust.

ralenti [ralɑ̃ti] nm: **au ~** (AUTO): **tourner au ~** to tick over, idle; (CINÉMA) in slow motion; (fig) at a slower pace.

ralentir [ralɑ̃tir] vt, vi, **se ~** vi to slow down.

râler [rale] vi to groan; (fam) to grouse, moan and (groan).

rallier [ralje] vt (rassembler) to rally; (rejoindre) to rejoin; (gagner à sa cause) to win over; **se ~ à** (avis) to come over ou round to.

rallonge [ralɔ̃ʒ] nf (de table) (extra) leaf (pl leaves); (argent etc) extra q.

rallonger [ralɔ̃ʒe] vt to lengthen.

rallye [rali] nm rally; (POL) march.

ramassage [ramasaʒ] nm: **~ scolaire** school bus service.

ramassé, e [ramase] a (trapu) squat.

ramasser [ramase] vt (objet tombé ou par terre, fam) to pick up; (recueillir) to collect; (récolter) to gather; **se ~** vi (sur-même) to huddle up; to crouch; **ramassis** nm (péj) bunch; jumble.

rambarde [rɑ̃bard(ə)] nf guardrail.

rame [ram] nf (aviron) oar; (de métro) train; (de papier) ream.

rameau, x [ramo] nm (small) branch; **les R~x** (REL) Palm Sunday sg.

ramener [ramne] vt to bring back; (recouvrir) to take back; (rabattre: couverture, visière): **~ qch sur** to pull sth back over; **~ qch à** (réduire à, aussi MATH) to reduce sth to.

ramer [rame] vi to row.

ramollir [ramɔlir] vt to soften; **se ~** vi to go soft.

ramoner [ramɔne] vt to sweep.

rampe [rɑ̃p] nf (d'escalier) banister (pl s); (dans un garage, d'un terrain) ramp; (THÉÂTRE): **la ~** the footlights pl; **~ de lancement** launching pad.

ramper [rɑ̃pe] vi to crawl.

rancard [rɑ̃kar] nm (fam) date; tip.

rancart [rɑ̃kar] nm: **mettre au ~** to scrap.

rance [rɑ̃s] a rancid.

rancœur [rɑ̃kœr] nf rancour.

rançon [rɑ̃sɔ̃] nf ransom; (fig) price.

rancune [rɑ̃kyn] nf grudge, rancour; **garder ~ à qn (de qch)** to bear sb a grudge (for sth); **sans ~!** no hard feelings!; **rancunier, ière** a vindictive, spiteful.

randonnée [rɑ̃dɔne] nf ride; (à pied) walk, ramble; hike, hiking q.

rang [rɑ̃] nm (rangée) row; (grade, classement) rank; **~s** (MIL) ranks; **se mettre en ~s/sur un ~** to get into ou form rows/a line; **au premier ~** in the first row; (fig) ranking first.

rangé, e [rɑ̃ʒe] a (sérieux) orderly, steady.

rangée [rɑ̃ʒe] nf row.

ranger [rɑ̃ʒe] vt (classer, grouper) to order, arrange; (mettre à sa place) to put away; (voiture dans la rue) to park; (mettre de l'ordre dans) to tidy up; (arranger) to arrange; (fig: classer): **~ qn/qch parmi** to rank sb/sth among; **se ~** vi (véhicule, conducteur) to pull over ou in; (piéton) to step aside; (s'assagir) to settle down; se ~ à (avis) to come round to.

ranimer [ranime] vt (personne) to bring round; (forces, courage) to restore; (troupes etc) to kindle new life in; (douleur, souvenir) to revive; (feu) to rekindle.

rapace [rapas] nm bird of prey.

râpe [ʀɑp] nf (CULIN) grater.

râpé, e [ʀɑpe] a (tissu) threadbare.

râper [ʀɑpe] vt (CULIN) to grate.

rapetisser [raptise] vt to shorten.

rapide [rapid] a fast; (prompt) quick // nm express (train); (de cours d'eau) rapid; ~ment ad fast; quickly.

rapiécer [rapjese] vt to patch.

rappel [rapɛl] nm (THÉÂTRE) curtain call; (MÉD: vaccination) booster; (ADMIN: de salaire) back pay g; (d'une aventure, d'un nom) reminder.

rappeler [raple] vt to call back; (ambassadeur, MIL) to recall; (faire se souvenir): ~ qch à qn to remind sb of sth; se ~ vt (se souvenir de) to remember, recall.

rapport [ʀapɔʀ] nm (compte rendu) report; (profit) yield, return; revenue; (lien, analogie) relationship; (MATH, TECH) ratio (pl s); ~s (entre personnes, pays) relations; avoir ~ à to have something to do with; être en ~ avec (idée de corrélation) to be related to; être/se mettre en ~ avec qn to be/get in touch with sb; par ~ à in relation to; ~s (sexuels) (sexual) intercourse sg.

rapporter [ʀapɔʀte] vt (rendre, ramener) to bring back; (apporter davantage) to bring more; (suj: investissement) to yield; (: activité) to bring in; (relater) to report // vi (investissement) to give a good return ou yield; (: activité) to be very profitable; ~ qch à (fig: rattacher) to relate sth to; se ~ à (correspondre à) to relate to; s'en ~ à to rely on; **rapporteur, euse** nm/f (de

procès, commission) reporter; (péj) telltale // nm (GÉOM) protractor.

rapprochement [ʀapʀɔʃmɑ̃] nm (de nations, familles) reconciliation; (analogie, rapport) parallel.

rapprocher [ʀapʀɔʃe] vt (chaise d'une table): ~ qch (de) to bring sth closer (to); (deux objets) to bring closer together; (réunir) to bring together; (comparer) to establish a parallel between; se ~ vi to draw closer ou nearer; se ~ de to come closer to; (présenter une analogie avec) to be close to.

rapt [ʀapt] nm abduction.

raquette [ʀakɛt] nf (de tennis) racket; (de ping-pong) bat; (à neige) snowshoe.

rare [ʀɑʀ] a rare; (main-d'œuvre, denrées) scarce; (cheveux, herbe) sparse.

rarement [ʀɑʀmɑ̃] ad rarely, seldom.

ras, e [ʀɑ, ʀɑz] a (tête, cheveux) close-cropped; (poil, herbe) short // ad short; **en** ~ **campagne** in open country; **à** ~ **bords** to the brim; **au** ~ **de** level with; **en avoir** ~ **le bol** (fam) to be fed up; ~ **du cou** (pull, robe) crew-neck.

rasade [ʀazad] nf glassful.

raser [ʀɑze] vt (barbe, cheveux) to shave off; (menton, personne) to shave; (fam: ennuyer) to bore; (démolir) to raze (to the ground); (frôler) to graze, skim; se ~ vi to shave; (fam) to be bored (to tears); **rasoir** nm razor.

rassasier [ʀasazje] vt to satisfy.

rassemblement [ʀasɑ̃bləmɑ̃] nm (groupe) gathering; (POL) union.

rassembler [ʀasɑ̃ble] vt (réunir) to assemble, gather; (regrouper, amasser) to gather together, collect; se ~ vi to gather.

rassis, e [ʀasi, -iz] a (pain) stale.

rassurer [ʀasyʀe] vt to reassure; se ~ vi to be reassured; rassure-toi don't worry.

rat [ʀa] nm rat.

rate [ʀat] *nf* spleen.

raté, e [ʀate] *a* (*tentative*) unsuccessful, failed // *nm/f* failure // *nm* misfiring *q*.

râteau, x [ʀɑto] *nm* rake.

râtelier [ʀɑtəlje] *nm* rack; (*fam*) false teeth *pl*.

rater [ʀate] *vi* (*affaire, projet etc*) to go wrong, fail // *vt* (*cible, train, occasion*) to miss; (*démonstration, plat*) to spoil; (*examen*) to fail.

ration [ʀasjɔ̃] *nf* ration; (*fig*) share.

ratisser [ʀatise] *vt* (*allée*) to rake; (*feuilles*) to rake up; (*suj: armée, police*) to comb.

R.A.T.P. *sigle f* (= *Régie autonome des transports parisiens*) *Paris transport authority*.

rattacher [ʀataʃe] *vt* (*animal, cheveux*) to tie up again; (*incorporer: ADMIN etc*): ~ **qch à** to join sth to; (*fig: relier*): ~ **qch à** to link sth with; (: *lier*): ~ **qn à** to bind ou tie sb to.

rattraper [ʀatʀape] *vt* (*fugitif*) to recapture; (*empêcher de tomber*) to catch (hold of); (*atteindre, rejoindre*) to catch up with; (*réparer: imprudence, erreur*) to make up for; se ~ *vi* to make good one's losses; to make up for it; se ~ (**à**) (*se raccrocher*) to stop o.s. falling (by catching hold of).

rature [ʀatyʀ] *nf* deletion, erasure.

rauque [ʀok] *a* raucous; hoarse.

ravages [ʀavaʒ] *nmpl*: **faire des ~** to wreak havoc.

ravaler [ʀavale] *vt* (*mur, façade*) to restore; (*déprécier*) to lower.

ravi, e [ʀavi] *a*: **être ~ de/que** to be delighted with/that.

ravin [ʀavɛ̃] *nm* gully, ravine.

ravir [ʀaviʀ] *vt* (*enchanter*) to delight; (*enlever*): ~ **qch à qn** to rob sb of sth; **à** ~ *ad* beautifully.

raviser [ʀavize]: se ~ *vi* to change one's mind.

ravissant, e [ʀavisɑ̃, -ɑ̃t] *a* delightful.

ravisseur, euse [ʀavisœʀ, -øz] *nm/f*

abductor, kidnapper.

ravitailler [ʀavitaje] *vt* to resupply; (*véhicule*) to refuel; se ~ *vi* to get fresh supplies.

raviver [ʀavive] *vt* (*feu, douleur*) to revive; (*couleurs*) to brighten up.

rayé, e [ʀeje] *a* (à *rayures*) striped.

rayer [ʀeje] *vt* (*érafler*) to scratch; (*barrer*) to cross out; (*d'une liste*) to cross off.

rayon [ʀɛjɔ̃] *nm* (*de soleil etc*) ray; (*GEOM*) radius; (*de roue*) spoke; (*étagère*) shelf (de *rayons*); (*de grand magasin*) department; **dans un ~ de** within a radius of; ~ **d'action** range; ~ **de soleil** sunbeam; ~**s X** X-rays.

rayonnement [ʀɛjɔnmɑ̃] *nm* radiation; (*fig*) radiance; influence.

rayonner [ʀɛjɔne] *vi* (*chaleur, énergie*) to radiate; (*fig*) to shine forth; to be radiant; (*touriste*) to go touring (*from one base*).

rayure [ʀɛjyʀ] *nf* (*motif*) stripe; (*éraflure*) scratch; (*rainure, d'un fusil*) groove.

raz-de-marée [ʀɑdmaʀe] *nm inv* tidal wave.

ré [ʀe] *nm* (*MUS*) D; (*en chantant la gamme*) re.

réacteur [ʀeaktœʀ] *nm* jet engine.

réaction [ʀeaksjɔ̃] *nf* reaction; moteur à ~ jet engine.

réadapter [ʀeadapte] *vt* to readjust; (*MÉD*) to rehabilitate; se ~ (**à**) to readjust (to).

réagir [ʀeaʒiʀ] *vi* to react.

réalisateur, trice [ʀealizatœʀ, -tʀis] *nm/f* (*TV, CINÉMA*) director.

réalisation [ʀealizasjɔ̃] *nf* carrying out; realization; fulfilment; achievement; production; (*œuvre*) production; creation; work.

réaliser [ʀealize] *vt* (*projet, opération*) to carry out, realize; (*rêve, souhait*) to realize, fulfil; (*exploit*) to achieve; (*achat, vente*) to make; (*film*) to produce; (*se rendre compte de, COMM: bien, capital*) to realize; se ~ *vi* to be realized.

realiste [realist(ə)] a realistic.

réalité [realite] nf reality; **en ~** in (actual) fact; **dans la ~** in reality.

réanimation [reanimasjɔ̃] nf resuscitation; **service de ~** intensive care unit.

réarmer [rearme] vt (arme) to reload // vi (état) to rearm.

rébarbatif, ive [rebarbatif, -iv] a forbidding.

rebattu, e [rəbaty] a hackneyed.

rebelle [rəbɛl] nm/f rebel // a (troupes) rebel; (enfant) rebellious; (mèche etc) unruly; **~ à** unamenable to.

rebeller [rəbele]: **se ~** vi to rebel.

rebondi, e [rəbɔ̃di] a rounded, chubby.

rebondir [rəbɔ̃dir] vi (ballon: au sol) to bounce; (: contre un mur) to rebound; (fig) to get moving again; **rebondissement** nm new development.

rebord [rəbɔr] nm edge.

rebours [rəbur]: **à ~** ad the wrong way.

rebrousse-poil [rəbruspwal]: **à ~** ad the wrong way.

rebrousser [rəbruse] vt: **~ chemin** to turn back.

rebut [rəby] nm: **mettre au ~** to scrap.

rebuter [rəbyte] vt to put off.

récalcitrant, e [rekalsitrɑ̃, -ɑ̃t] a refractory.

recaler [rəkale] vt (SCOL) to fail.

récapituler [rekapityle] vt to recapitulate; to sum up.

receler [rəsəle] vt (produit d'un vol) to receive; (malfaiteur) to harbour; (fig) to conceal; **receleur, euse** nm/f receiver.

récemment [resamɑ̃] ad recently.

recenser [rəsɑ̃se] vt (population) to take a census of; (inventorier) to list.

récent, e [resɑ̃, -ɑ̃t] a recent.

récépissé [resepise] nm receipt.

récepteur [reseptœr] nm receiver; **~ (de radio)** radio set ou receiver.

réception [resepsjɔ̃] nf receiving q;

(accueil) reception, welcome; (bureau) reception desk; (réunion mondaine) reception, party; **réceptionniste** nm/f receptionist.

recette [rəsɛt] nf (CULIN) recipe; (fig) formula, recipe; (COMM) takings pl; **~s** nfpl (COMM: rentrées) receipts.

receveur, euse [rəsvœr, -øz] nm/f (des contributions) tax collector; (des postes) postmaster/mistress; (d'autobus) conductor/conductress.

recevoir [rəsvwar] vt to receive; (client, patient) to see // vi to receive visitors; to see parties; to see patients etc; **se ~** vi (athlète) to land; **être reçu** (à un examen) to pass.

rechange [rəʃɑ̃ʒ]: **de ~** (pièces, roue) spare; (fig: solution) alternative; **des vêtements de ~** a change of clothes.

rechaper [rəʃape] vt to remould, retread.

réchapper [reʃape]: **~ de ou à** vt (accident, maladie) to come through.

recharge [rəʃarʒ] nf refill.

recharger [rəʃarʒe] vt (camion, fusil, appareil-photo) to reload; (briquet, stylo) to refill; (batterie) to recharge.

réchaud [reʃo] nm (portable) stove; plate-warmer.

réchauffer [reʃofe] vt (plat) to reheat; (mains, personne) to warm; **se ~** vi (température) to get warmer.

rêche [rɛʃ] a rough.

recherche [rəʃɛrʃ(ə)] nf (action): **la ~ de** the search for; (raffinement) affectedness, studied elegance; (scientifique etc): **la ~** research; **~s** nfpl (de la police) investigations; (scientifiques) research sg; **se mettre à la ~ de** to go in search of.

recherché, e [rəʃɛrʃe] a (rare, demandé) much sought-after; (raffiné) studied, affected.

rechercher [rəʃɛrʃe] vt (objet égaré, personne) to look for; (causes, nouveau procédé) to try to find; (bonheur, amitié) to seek.

rechute [rəʃyt] nf (MÉD) relapse.

récidiver [residive] vi to commit a subsequent offence; (fig) to do it again.

récif [resif] nm reef.

récipient [resipjɑ̃] nm container.

réciproque [resiprɔk] a reciprocal.

récit [resi] nm story.

récital [resital] nm recital.

réciter [resite] vt to recite.

réclamation [reklamasjɔ̃] nf complaint; **~s** (bureau) complaints department sg.

réclame [reklam] nf ad, advert(isement); **article en ~** special offer.

réclamer [reklame] vt (aide, nourriture etc) to ask for; (revendiquer) to claim, demand; (nécessiter) to demand, require // vi to complain.

réclusion [reklyzjɔ̃] nf imprisonment.

recoin [rəkwɛ̃] nm nook, corner; (fig) hidden recess.

reçois etc vb voir **recevoir**.

récolte [rekɔlt(ə)] nf harvesting; gathering; (produits) harvest, crop; (fig) crop, collection.

récolter [rekɔlte] vt to harvest, gather (in); (fig) to collect; to get.

recommandé [rəkɔmɑ̃de] nm (POSTES): **en ~** by registered mail.

recommander [rəkɔmɑ̃de] vt to recommend; (suj: qualités etc) to commend; (POSTES) to register; se **~ de qn** to give sb's name as a reference.

recommencer [rəkɔmɑ̃se] vt (reprendre: lutte, séance) to resume, start again; (refaire: travail, explications) to start afresh, start (over) again; (récidiver: erreur) to make again // vi to start again; (récidiver) to do it again.

récompense [rekɔ̃pɑ̃s] nf reward; (prix) award; **récompenser** (): vt récompenser qn (de ou pour) to reward sb (for).

réconcilier [rekɔ̃silje] vt to reconcile; se **~** (avec) to be reconciled with).

reconduire [rəkɔ̃dɥir] vt (raccompagner) to take ou see back; (JUR, POL: renouveler) to renew.

réconfort [rekɔ̃fɔr] nm comfort.

réconforter [rekɔ̃fɔrte] vt (consoler) to comfort; (revigorer) to fortify.

reconnaissance [rəkɔnɛsɑ̃s] nf recognition; acknowledgement; (gratitude) gratitude, gratefulness; (MIL) reconnaissance, recce.

reconnaissant, e [rəkɔnɛsɑ̃, -ɑ̃t] a grateful.

reconnaître [rəkɔnɛtr(ə)] vt to recognize; (MIL: lieu) to reconnoitre; (JUR: enfant, dette, droit) to acknowledge; **~ que** to admit ou acknowledge that; **~ qn/qch à** to recognize sb/sth by.

reconstituer [rəkɔ̃stitɥe] vt (monument ancien) to recreate; (fresque, vase brisé) to piece together, reconstitute; (événement, accident) to reconstruct; (fortune, patrimoine) to rebuild.

reconstruire [rəkɔ̃strɥir] vt to rebuild.

record [rəkɔr] nm, a record.

recoupement [rəkupmɑ̃] nm: par **~** by cross-checking.

recouper [rəkupe]: se **~** vi (témoignages) to tie ou match up.

recourbé, e [rəkurbe] a curved; hooked; bent.

recourir [rəkurir]: **~ à** vt (ami, agence) to turn ou appeal to; (force, ruse, emprunt) to resort to.

recours [rəkur] nm (JUR) appeal; avoir **~ à** = recourir à; en dernier **~** as a last resort; **~ en grâce** plea for clemency.

recouvrer [rəkuvre] vt (vue, santé etc) to recover, regain; (impôts) to collect; (créance) to recover.

recouvrir [rəkuvrir] vt (couvrir à nouveau) to re-cover; (couvrir entièrement, aussi fig) to cover; (cacher, masquer) to conceal, hide; se **~** vi (se superposer) to overlap.

récréation [rekreasjɔ̃] nf recreation, entertainment; (SCOL) break.

récrier [rekrije]: se ~ vi to exclaim.

récriminations [rekriminasjɔ̃] nfpl remonstrations, complaints.

recroqueviller [rəkrɔkvije]: se ~ vi (feuilles) to curl ou shrivel up; (personne) to huddle up.

recrudescence [rəkrydesɑ̃s] nf fresh outbreak.

recrue [rəkry] nf recruit.

recruter [rəkryte] vt to recruit.

rectangle [rɛktɑ̃gl(ə)] nm rectangle; **rectangulaire** a rectangular.

recteur [rɛktœr] nm ≈ (regional) director of education (Brit); ≈ state superintendent of education (US).

rectifier [rɛktifje] vt (tracé, virage) to straighten; (calcul, adresse) to correct; (erreur, faute) to rectify.

rectiligne [rɛktiliɲ] a straight; (GÉOM) rectilinear.

reçu, e [rəsy] pp de recevoir // a (admis, consacré) accepted // nm (COMM) receipt.

recueil [rəkœj] nm collection.

recueillir [rəkœjir] vt to collect; (voix, suffrages) to win; (accueillir: réfugiés, chat) to take in; se ~ vi to gather one's thoughts; to meditate.

recul [rəkyl] nm retreat; recession; decline; (d'arme à feu) recoil, kick; avoir un mouvement de ~ to recoil; prendre du ~ to stand back.

reculé, e [rəkyle] a remote.

reculer [rəkyle] vi to move back, back away; (AUTO) to reverse, back (up); (fig) to be (on the) decline; to be losing ground; (: se dérober) to shrink back // vt to move back; to reverse, back (up); (fig: possibilités, limites) to extend; (: date, décision) to postpone.

reculons [rəkylɔ̃]: à ~ ad backwards.

récupérer [rekypere] vt to recover, get back; (heures de travail) to make up; (déchets) to salvage; (délinquant etc) to rehabilitate // vi to recover.

récurer [rekyre] vt to scour.

récuser [rekyze] vt to challenge; se ~ vi to decline to give an opinion.

reçut vb voir recevoir.

recycler [rəsikle] vt (SCOL) to re-orientate; (employés) to retrain; (TECH) to recycle.

rédacteur, trice [redaktœr, -tris] nm/f (journaliste) writer; subeditor; (d'ouvrage de référence) editor, compiler; ~ en chef chief editor; ~ publicitaire copywriter.

rédaction [redaksjɔ̃] nf writing; (rédacteurs) editorial staff; (bureau) editorial office(s); (SCOL: devoir) essay, composition.

reddition [redisjɔ̃] nf surrender.

redemander [rədmɑ̃de] vt to ask again for; to ask for more of.

redescendre [rədesɑ̃dr(ə)] vi to go back down // vt (pente etc) to go down.

redevable [rədvabl(ə)] a: être ~ de qch à qn (somme) to owe sb sth; (fig) to be indebted to sb for sth.

redevance [rədvɑ̃s] nf (TÉL) rental charge; (TV) licence fee.

rédiger [rediʒe] vt to write; (contrat) to draw up.

redire [rədir] vt to repeat; trouver à ~ à to find fault with.

redoublé, e [rəduble] a: à coups ~s even harder, twice as hard.

redoubler [rəduble] vi (tempête, violence) to intensify; (SCOL) to repeat a year; ~ de vt to be twice as + adjectif.

redoutable [rədutabl(ə)] a formidable, fearsome.

redouter [rədute] vt to fear; (appréhender) to dread.

redresser [rədrese] vt (arbre, mât) to set upright; (pièce tordue) to straighten out; (situation, économie) to put right; (objet penché) to right itself; (personne) to sit (ou stand) up (straight).

réduction [redyksjɔ̃] nf reduction.

réduire [reduir] vt to reduce; (prix, dépenses) to cut, reduce; (MÉD:

fracture) to set; se ~ à (*revenir à*) to boil down to; se ~ en (*se transformer en*) to be reduced to.

réduit [redɥi] *nm* tiny room; recess.

rééducation [reedykasjɔ̃] *nf* (*d'un membre*) re-education; (*de délinquants, d'un blessé*) rehabilitation; ~ de la parole speech therapy.

réel, le [reɛl] *a* real.

réellement [reɛlmã] *ad* really.

réévaluer [reevalɥe] *vt* to revalue.

réexpédier [reɛkspedje] *vt* (à l'envoyeur) to return, send back; (au destinataire) to send on, forward.

refaire [rəfɛr] *vt* (*faire de nouveau, recommencer*) to do again; (*réparer, restaurer*) to do up.

réfection [refɛksjɔ̃] *nf* repair.

réfectoire [refɛktwar] *nm* refectory.

référence [referãs] *nf* reference; ~s (*recommandations*) reference sg.

référer [refere]: se ~ à *vt* to refer to; en ~ à qn to refer the matter to sb.

réfléchi, e [reflefi] *a* (*caractère*) thoughtful; (*action*) well-thought-out; (*LING*) reflexive.

réfléchir [reflefir] *vt* to reflect // *vi* to think; ~ à ou sur to think about.

reflet [rəflɛ] *nm* reflection; (*sur l'eau etc*) sheen *q*, glint.

refléter [rəflete] *vt* to reflect; se ~ *vi* to be reflected.

réflexe [reflɛks(ə)] *nm, a* reflex.

réflexion [reflɛksjɔ̃] *nf* (*de la lumière etc, pensée*) reflection; (*fait de penser*) thought; (*remarque*) remark; ~ faite, à la ~ on reflection.

refluer [rəflye] *vi* to flow back; (*foule*) to surge back.

reflux [rəfly] *nm* (*de la mer*) ebb.

réforme [refɔrm(ə)] *nf* reform; (*REL*): la R~ the Reformation.

réformer [refɔrme] *vt* to reform; (*MIL*) to declare unfit for service.

refouler [rəfule] *vt* (*envahisseurs*) to drive back; (*liquide*) to force back; (*fig*) to suppress; (*PSYCH*) to repress.

réfractaire [refraktɛr] *a*: être à

to resist.

refrain [rəfrɛ̃] *nm* (*MUS*) refrain, chorus; (*air, fig*) tune.

refréner, réfréner [rəfrene, refrene] *vt* to curb, check.

réfrigérateur [refriʒeratœr] *nm* refrigerator, fridge.

refroidir [rəfrwadir] *vt* to cool // *vi* to cool (down); se ~ *vi* (*prendre froid*) to catch a chill; (*temps*) to get cooler ou colder; (*fig*) to cool (off);

refroidissement *nm* (*grippe etc*) chill.

refuge [rəfyʒ] *nm* refuge; (*pour piétons*) (traffic) island.

réfugié, e [refyʒje] *a, nm/f* refugee.

réfugier [refyʒje]: se ~ *vi* to take refuge.

refus [rəfy] *nm* refusal; ce n'est pas de ~ I won't say no, it's welcome.

refuser [rəfyze] *vt* to refuse; (*SCOL: candidat*) to fail; ~ qch à qn to refuse sb sth; ~ du monde to have to turn people away; se ~ à faire to refuse to do.

regagner [rəgɑɲe] *vt* (*argent, faveur*) to win back; (*lieu*) to get back to; ~ le temps perdu to make up (for) lost time.

regain [rəgɛ̃] *nm* (*renouveau*): un ~ de renewed + *nom*.

régal [regal] *nm* treat.

régaler [regale]: se ~ *vi* to have a delicious meal; (*fig*) to enjoy o.s.

regard [rəgar] *nm* (*coup d'œil*) look, glance; (*expression*) look in (one's) eye; au ~ de (*loi, morale*) from the point of view of; en ~ (*vis à vis*) opposite; en ~ de in comparison with.

regardant, e [rəgardã, -ãt] *a*: très/peu ~ (*sur*) quite fussy/very free (about); (*économe*) very tightfisted/quite generous (with).

regarder [rəgarde] *vt* (*examiner, observer, lire*) to look at; (*film, télévision, match*) to watch; (*envisager: situation, avenir*) to view; (*considérer: son intérêt etc*) to be concerned with; (*être orienté vers*): ~ (*vers*) to face; (*concerner*) to concern *vi* to look; ~ à vt (dépense) to be fussy with ou over; ~ qn/qch comme to regard sb/sth as.

régie [ʀeʒi] nf (COMM, INDUSTRIE) state-owned company; (THÉÂTRE, CINÉMA) production; (RADIO, TV) control room.

regimber [ʀəʒɛ̃be] vi to balk, jib.

régime [ʀeʒim] nm (POL) régime; (ADMIN: carcéral, fiscal etc) system; (MÉD) diet; (TECH) (engine) speed; (fig) rate, pace; (de bananes, dattes) bunch; se mettre au/suivre un ~ to go on/be on a diet.

régiment [ʀeʒimɑ̃] nm regiment; (fig: fam): un ~ de an army of.

région [ʀeʒjɔ̃] nf region; **régional, e, aux** a regional.

régir [ʀeʒiʀ] vt to govern.

régisseur [ʀeʒisœʀ] nm (d'un domaine) steward; (CINÉMA, TV) assistant director; (THÉÂTRE) stage manager.

registre [ʀeʒistʀ(ə)] nm (livre) register; logbook; ledger; (MUS, LING) register.

réglage [ʀeglaʒ] nm adjustment; tuning.

règle [ʀɛgl(ə)] nf (instrument) ruler; (loi, prescription) rule; ~s nfpl (PHYSIOL) period sg; en ~ (papiers d'identité) in order; en ~ générale as a (general) rule; ~ à calcul slide rule.

réglé, e [ʀegle] a well-ordered; steady; (papier) ruled; (arrangé) settled.

règlement [ʀɛgləmɑ̃] nm (paiement) settlement; (arrêté) regulation; (règles, statuts) regulations pl, rules pl; **réglementaire** a conforming to the regulations; (tenue) regulation cpd.

réglementer [ʀɛgləmɑ̃te] vt to regulate.

régler [ʀegle] vt (mécanisme, machine) to regulate, adjust; (moteur) to tune; (thermostat etc) to set, adjust; (conflit, facture) to settle; (fournisseur) to settle up with.

réglisse [ʀeglis] nf liquorice.

règne [ʀɛɲ] nm (d'un roi etc, fig) reign; (BIO): le ~ végétal/animal the vegetable/animal kingdom.

régner [ʀeɲe] vi (roi) to rule, reign; (fig) to reign.

regorger [ʀəgɔʀʒe] vi: ~ de to overflow with, be bursting with.

regret [ʀəgʀɛ] nm regret; à ~ with regret; avec ~ regretfully; être au ~ de devoir faire to regret having to do.

regrettable [ʀəgʀetabl(ə)] a regrettable.

regretter [ʀəgʀete] vt to regret; (personne) to miss; je regrette I'm sorry.

regrouper [ʀəgʀupe] vt (grouper) to group together; (contenir) to include, comprise; se ~ vi to gather (together).

régulier, ière [ʀegylje, -jɛʀ] a (gén) regular; (vitesse, qualité) steady; (répartition, pression, paysage) even; (TRANSPORTS: ligne, service) scheduled, regular; (légal, réglementaire) lawful, in order; (fam: correct) straight, on the level; **régulièrement** ad regularly; steadily; evenly; normally.

rehausser [ʀəose] vt to heighten, raise.

rein [ʀɛ̃] nm kidney; ~s nmpl (dos) back sg.

reine [ʀɛn] nf queen.

reine-claude [ʀɛnklod] nf greengage.

réintégrer [ʀeɛ̃tegʀe] vt (lieu) to return to; (fonctionnaire) to reinstate.

rejaillir [ʀəʒajiʀ] vi to splash up; ~ sur to splash up onto; (fig) to rebound on; to fall upon.

rejet [ʀəʒɛ] nm (action, aussi MÉD) rejection.

rejeter [ʀəʒte] vt (relancer) to throw back; (vomir) to bring ou throw up; (écarter) to reject; (déverser) to throw out, discharge; ~ la responsabilité de qch sur qn to lay the responsibility for sth at sb's door.

rejoindre [ʀəʒwɛ̃dʀ(ə)] vt (famille,

régiment) to rejoin, return to; (*lieu*) to get (back) to; (*suj: route etc*) to meet, join; (*rattraper*) to catch up (with); se ~ *vi* to meet; **je te rejoins au café** I'll see ou meet you at the café.

réjouir [ʀeʒwiʀ] *vt* to delight; se ~ *vi* to be delighted; to rejoice; **réjouissances** *nfpl* (*joie*) rejoicing *sg*; (*fête*) festivities.

relâche [ʀəlɑʃ]: **faire** ~ *vi* (CI-NÉMA) to be closed; **sans** ~ *ad* without respite ou a break.

relâché, e [ʀəlɑʃe] *a* loose, lax.

relâcher [ʀəlɑʃe] *vt* (*étreinte*) to loosen; se ~ *vi* to loosen; (*discipline*) to become slack ou lax; (*élève etc*) to slacken off.

relais [ʀəlɛ] *nm* (SPORT): (**course de**) ~ relay (race); **équipe de** ~ shift team; (SPORT) relay team; **prendre le** ~ (**de**) to take over (from); ~ **routier** ≈ transport café (*Brit*), ≈ truck stop (*US*).

relancer [ʀəlɑ̃se] *vt* (*balle*) to throw back; (*moteur*) to restart; (*fig*) to boost, revive; (*personne*): ~ **qn** to pester sb.

relater [ʀəlate] *vt* to relate, recount.

relatif, ive [ʀəlatif, -iv] *a* relative.

relation [ʀəlɑsjɔ̃] *nf* (*récit*) account, report; (*rapport*) relation(ship); ~**s** *nfpl* (*rapports*) relations; relationship *sg*; (*connaissances*) connections; **être/entrer en** ~(**s**) **avec** to be in contact with.

relaxer [ʀəlakse] *vt* to relax; (JUR) to discharge; se ~ *vi* to relax.

relayer [ʀəleje] *vt* (*collaborateur, coureur etc*) to relieve; se ~ *vi* (*dans une activité*) to take it in turns.

reléguer [ʀəlege] *vt* to relegate.

relent(s) [ʀəlɑ̃] *nm(pl)* (foul) smell.

relevé, e [ʀəlve] *a* (*manches*) rolled-up; (*sauce*) highly-seasoned // *nm* (*lecture*) reading; (*liste*) statement; list; (*facture*) account; ~ **de compte** bank statement.

relève [ʀəlɛv] *nf* relief; relief team (ou troops *pl*); **prendre la** ~ to take over.

relever [ʀəlve] *vt* (*statue, meuble*) to stand up again; (*personne tombée*) to help up; (*vitre, niveau de vie*) to raise; (*col*) to turn up; (*style, conversation*) to elevate; (*plat, sauce*) to season; (*sentinelle, équipe*) to relieve; (*fautes, points*) to pick out; (*constater: traces etc*) to find, pick up; (*répliquer à: remarque*) to react to, reply to; (: *défi*) to accept, take up; (*noter: adresse etc*) to take down, note; (: *plan*) to sketch; (: *cotes etc*) to plot; (*compteur*) to read; (*ramasser: copies*) to collect, take in; ~ **de** *vt* (*maladie*) to be recovering from; (*être du ressort de*) to be a matter for; (ADMIN: *dépendre de*) to come under; (*fig*) to pertain to; se ~ *vi* (*se remettre debout*) to get up; ~ **qn de** (*fonctions*) to relieve sb of; ~ **la tête** to look up; to hold up one's head.

relief [ʀəljɛf] *nm* relief; ~**s** *nmpl* (*restes*) remains; **mettre en** ~ (*fig*) to bring out, highlight.

relier [ʀəlje] *vt* to link up; (*livre*) to bind; ~ **qch à** to link sth to.

religieux, euse [ʀəliʒjø, -øz] *a* religious // *nm* monk // *nf* nun; (*gâteau*) cream bun.

religion [ʀəliʒjɔ̃] *nf* religion; (*piété, dévotion*) faith.

relire [ʀəliʀ] *vt* (*à nouveau*) to reread, read again; (*vérifier*) to read over.

reliure [ʀəljyʀ] *nf* binding.

reluire [ʀəlɥiʀ] *vi* to gleam.

remanier [ʀəmanje] *vt* to reshape, recast; (POL) to reshuffle.

remarquable [ʀəmaʀkabl(ə)] *a* remarkable.

remarque [ʀəmaʀk(ə)] *nf* remark; (*écrite*) note.

remarquer [ʀəmaʀke] *vt* (*voir*) to notice; se ~ *vi* to be noticeable; **faire** ~ (**à qn**) **que** to point out (to sb) that; **faire** ~ **qch** (**à qn**) to point sth out (to sb); **remarquez, ...** mind you ....

remblai [ʀɑ̃blɛ] nm embankment.

rembourrer [ʀɑ̃buʀe] vt to stuff; (dossier, vêtement, souliers) to pad.

remboursement [ʀɑ̃buʀsəmɑ̃] nm repayment; **envoi contre ~** cash on delivery.

rembourser [ʀɑ̃buʀse] vt to pay back, repay.

remède [ʀəmɛd] nm (médicament) medicine; (traitement, fig) remedy, cure.

remémorer [ʀəmemɔʀe]: **se ~** vt to recall, recollect.

remerciements [ʀəmɛʀsimɑ̃] nmpl thanks.

remercier [ʀəmɛʀsje] vt to thank; (congédier) to dismiss; **~ qn de/ d'avoir fait** to thank sb for/for having done.

remettre [ʀəmɛtʀ(ə)] vt (vêtement): **~ qch** to put sth back on; (replacer): **~ qch quelque part** to put sth back somewhere; (ajouter): **~ du sel/un sucre** to add more salt/ another lump of sugar; (ajourner): **~ qch (à)** to postpone sth (until); **~ qch à qn** (rendre, restituer) to give sth back to sb; (donner, confier: paquet, argent) to hand over sth to sb, deliver sth to sb; (: prix, décoration) to present sb with sth; **se ~** vi to get better, recover; **se ~ de** to recover from, get over; **s'en ~ à** to leave it (up) to.

remise [ʀəmiz] nf delivery; presentation; (rabais) discount; (local) shed; **~ en jeu** (FOOTBALL) throw-in; **~ de peine** reduction of sentence.

remontant [ʀəmɔ̃tɑ̃] nm tonic, pick-me-up.

remonte-pente [ʀəmɔ̃tpɑ̃t] nm ski-lift.

remonter [ʀəmɔ̃te] vi to go back up; (jupe) to ride up // vt (pente) to go up; (fleuve) to sail (ou swim etc) up; (manches, pantalon) to roll up; (col) to turn up; (niveau, limite) to raise; (fig: personne) to buck up; (moteur, meuble) to put back together, reassemble; (montre, mécanisme) to wind up; **~ le moral à qn** to raise sb's spirits; **~ à** (dater de) to date ou go back to.

remontrance [ʀəmɔ̃tʀɑ̃s] nf reproof, reprimand.

remontrer [ʀəmɔ̃tʀe] vt (fig): **en ~ à** to prove one's superiority over.

remords [ʀəmɔʀ] nm remorse q; **avoir des ~** to feel remorse.

remorque [ʀəmɔʀk(ə)] nf trailer; **être en ~** to be on tow; **remorquer** vt to tow; **remorqueur** nm tug(boat).

remous [ʀəmu] nm (d'un navire) (back)wash q; (de rivière) swirl, eddy // nmpl (fig) stir sg.

remparts [ʀɑ̃paʀ] nmpl walls, ramparts.

remplaçant, e [ʀɑ̃plasɑ̃, ɑ̃t] nm/f replacement, stand-in; (THÉÂTRE) understudy; (SCOL) supply teacher.

remplacement [ʀɑ̃plasmɑ̃] nm replacement; (job) replacement work q.

remplacer [ʀɑ̃plase] vt to replace; (tenir lieu de) to take the place of; **~ qch/qn par** to replace sth/sb with.

rempli, e [ʀɑ̃pli] a (emploi du temps) full, busy; **~ de** full of, filled with.

remplir [ʀɑ̃pliʀ] vt to fill (up); (questionnaire) to fill out ou up; (obligations, fonction, condition) to fulfil; **se ~** vi to fill up.

remporter [ʀɑ̃pɔʀte] vt (marchandise) to take away; (fig) to win, achieve.

remuant, e [ʀəmɥɑ̃, ɑ̃t] a restless.

remue-ménage [ʀəmymenaʒ] nm inv commotion.

remuer [ʀəmɥe] vt to move; (café, sauce) to stir // vi, **se ~** vi to move.

rémunérer [ʀemyneʀe] vt to remunerate.

renard [ʀənaʀ] nm fox.

renchérir [ʀɑ̃ʃeʀiʀ] vi (fig): **~ (sur)** to add something (to).

rencontre [ʀɑ̃kɔ̃tʀ(ə)] nf meeting; (imprévue) encounter; **aller à la ~ de qn** to go and meet sb.

rencontrer [ʀɑ̃kɔ̃tʀe] *vt* to meet; (*mot, expression*) to come across; (*difficultés*) to meet with; **se ~ à** to meet; (*véhicules*) to collide.

rendement [ʀɑ̃dmɑ̃] *nm* (*d'un travailleur, d'une machine*) output; (*d'une culture*) yield; (*d'un investissement*) return; **à plein ~** at full capacity.

rendez-vous [ʀɑ̃devu] *nm* (*rencontre*) appointment; (: *d'amoureux*) date; (*lieu*) meeting place; **donner ~ à qn** to arrange to meet sb; **avoir/prendre ~ (avec)** to have/make an appointment (with).

rendre [ʀɑ̃dʀ(ə)] *vt* (*livre, argent etc*) to give back, return; (*visite etc*) to return; (*sang, aliments*) to bring up; (*exprimer, traduire*) to render; (*faire devenir*): **~ qn célèbre/qch possible** to make sb famous/sth possible; **se ~** *vi* (*capituler*) to surrender, give o.s. up; (*aller*): **se ~ quelque part** to go somewhere; **se ~ compte de qch** to realize sth.

rênes [ʀɛn] *nfpl* reins.

renfermé, e [ʀɑ̃fɛʀme] *a* (*fig*) withdrawn // *nm*: **sentir le ~** to smell stuffy.

renfermer [ʀɑ̃fɛʀme] *vt* to contain.

renflement [ʀɑ̃fləmɑ̃] *nm* bulge.

renflouer [ʀɑ̃flue] *vt* to refloat; (*fig*) to set back on its (*ou his/her etc*) feet.

renfoncement [ʀɑ̃fɔ̃smɑ̃] *nm* recess.

renforcer [ʀɑ̃fɔʀse] *vt* to reinforce.

renfort [ʀɑ̃fɔʀ]: **~s** *nmpl* reinforcements; **à grand ~ de** with a great deal of.

renfrogné, e [ʀɑ̃fʀɔɲe] *a* sullen.

rengaine [ʀɑ̃gɛn] *nf* (*péj*) old tune.

renier [ʀənje] *vt* (*parents*) to disown, repudiate; (*foi*) to renounce.

renifler [ʀənifle] *vi, vt* to sniff.

renne [ʀɛn] *nm* reindeer *inv*.

renom [ʀənɔ̃] *nm* reputation; (*célébrité*) renown; **renommé, e** *a* celebrated, renowned // *nf* fame.

renoncer [ʀənɔ̃se] *vi*: **~ à** *vt* to give up; **~ à faire** to give up the idea of doing.

renouer [ʀənwe] *vt*: **~ avec** (*tradition*) to revive; (*habitude*) to take up again; **~ avec qn** to take up with sb again.

renouveler [ʀənuvle] *vt* to renew; (*exploit, méfait*) to repeat; **se ~** *vi* (*incident*) to recur, happen again; **renouvellement** *nm* renewal; recurrence.

rénover [ʀenɔve] *vt* (*immeuble*) to renovate, do up; (*enseignement*) to reform; (*quartier*) to redevelop.

renseignement [ʀɑ̃sɛɲmɑ̃] *nm* information, piece of information; (**guichet des**) **~s** information desk.

renseigner [ʀɑ̃sɛɲe] *vt*: **~ qn (sur)** to give information to sb (about); **se ~** *vi* to ask for information, make inquiries.

rentable [ʀɑ̃tabl(ə)] *a* profitable.

rente [ʀɑ̃t] *nf* income; pension; government stock *ou* bond; **rentier, ière** *nm/f* person of private means.

rentrée [ʀɑ̃tʀe] *nf*: **~ (d'argent)** cash *q* coming in; **la ~ (des classes)** the start of the new school year.

rentrer [ʀɑ̃tʀe] *vi* (*entrer de nouveau*) to go (*ou* come) back in; (*entrer*) to go (*ou* come) in; (*revenir chez soi*) to go (*ou* come) (back) home; (*air, clou: pénétrer*) to go in; (*revenu, argent*) to come in // *vt* (*foins*) to bring in; (*véhicule*) to put away; (*chemise dans pantalon etc*) to tuck in; (*griffes*) to draw in; (*fig: larmes, colère etc*) to hold back; **~ le ventre** to pull in one's stomach; **~ dans** (*heurter*) to crash into; **~ dans l'ordre** to be back to normal; **~ dans ses frais** to recover one's expenses.

renversant, e [ʀɑ̃vɛʀsɑ̃, -ɑ̃t] *a* astounding.

renverse [ʀɑ̃vɛʀs(ə)]: **à la ~** *ad* backwards.

renverser [ʀɑ̃vɛʀse] *vt* (*faire tomber: chaise, verre*) to knock over, overturn; (*piéton*) to knock down; (*liquide, contenu*) to spill, upset; (*retourner*) to turn upside down; (: *ordre des mots etc*) to reverse; (*fig*: *gouvernement etc*) to overthrow; (*stupéfier*) to bowl over; se ~ vi to fall over; to overturn; to spill.

renvoi [ʀɑ̃vwa] *nm* (*référence*) cross-reference; (*éructation*) belch.

renvoyer [ʀɑ̃vwaje] *vt* to send back; (*congédier*) to dismiss; (*lumière*) to reflect; (*son*) to echo; (*ajourner*): ~ qch (à) to put sth off ou postpone sth (until); ~ qn à (*fig*) to refer sb to.

repaire [ʀəpɛʀ] *nm* den.

répandre [ʀepɑ̃dʀ(ə)] *vt* (*renverser*) to spill; (*étaler, diffuser*) to spread; (*lumière*) to shed; (*chaleur, odeur*) to give off; se ~ vi to spill; to spread; **répandu, e** a (*opinion, usage*) widespread.

réparation [ʀepaʀasjɔ̃] *nf* repair.

réparer [ʀepaʀe] *vt* to repair; (*fig*: *offense*) to make up for, atone for; (: *oubli, erreur*) to put right.

repartie [ʀəpaʀti] *nf* retort; **avoir de la ~** to be quick at repartee.

repartir [ʀəpaʀtiʀ] *vi* to set off again; to leave again; (*fig*) to get going again; ~ **à zéro** to start from scratch (again).

répartir [ʀepaʀtiʀ] *vt* (*pour attribuer*) to share out; (*pour disperser, disposer*) to divide up; (*poids, chaleur*) to distribute; se ~ vt (*travail, rôles*) to share out between themselves; **répartition** *nf* sharing out; dividing up; distribution.

repas [ʀəpa] *nm* meal.

repasser [ʀəpase] *vi* to come (ou go) back // *vt* (*vêtement, tissu*) to iron; (*examen*) to retake, resit; (*film*) to show again; (*leçon, rôle: revoir*) to go over (again).

repêcher [ʀəpeʃe] *vt* (*noyé*) to recover the body of; (*candidat*) to pass (*by inflating marks*).

repentir [ʀəpɑ̃tiʀ] *nm* repentance; se ~ vi to repent; se ~ **de** to repent of.

répercuter [ʀepɛʀkyte] *vt* (*information, hausse des prix*) to pass on; se ~ vi (*bruit*) to reverberate; (*fig*): se ~ **sur** to have repercussions on.

repère [ʀəpɛʀ] *nm* mark; (*monument etc*) landmark.

repérer [ʀəpeʀe] *vt* (*erreur, connaissance*) to spot; (*abri, ennemi*) to locate; se ~ vi to find one's way about.

répertoire [ʀepɛʀtwaʀ] *nm* (*liste*) (alphabetical) list; (*carnet*) index notebook; (*d'un artiste*) repertoire.

répéter [ʀepete] *vt* to repeat; (*préparer*: *leçon*: *aussi vi*) to learn, go over; (*THÉÂTRE*) to rehearse; se ~ vi (*redire*) to repeat o.s.; (*se reproduire*) to be repeated; recur.

répétition [ʀepetisjɔ̃] *nf* repetition; (*THÉÂTRE*) rehearsal; ~ **générale** final dress rehearsal.

répit [ʀepi] *nm* respite.

replet, ète [ʀəplɛ, -ɛt] *a* chubby.

replier [ʀəplije] *vt* (*rabattre*) to fold down ou over; se ~ vi (*troupes, armée*) to withdraw, fall back.

réplique [ʀeplik] *nf* (*repartie, fig*) reply; (*THÉÂTRE*) line; (*copie*) replica.

répliquer [ʀeplike] *vi* to reply; (*riposter*) to retaliate.

répondre [ʀepɔ̃dʀ(ə)] *vi* to answer, reply; (*freins, mécanisme*) to respond; ~ **à** vt to reply to, answer; (*avec impertinence*): ~ **à qn** to answer sb back; (*affection, salut*) to return; (*provocation, suj*: *mécanisme etc*) to respond to; (*correspondre à*: *besoin*) to answer; (: *conditions*) to meet; (: *description*) to match; ~ **de** to answer for.

réponse [ʀepɔ̃s] *nf* answer, reply; **en** ~ **à** in reply to.

reportage [ʀəpɔʀtaʒ] *nm* (*bref*) report; (*écrit*: *documentaire*) story; article; (*en direct*) commentary; (*genre, activité*): **le** ~ reporting.

reporter *nm* [ʀəpɔʀtɛʀ] reporter // *vt* [ʀəpɔʀte] (*total*): ~ **qch sur** to carry sth forward ou over; (*ajourner*):

~ **qch (à)** to postpone sth (until); (*transférer*): ~ **qch sur** to transfer sth to; **se** ~ **à** (*époque*) to think back to; (*document*) to refer to.

repos [rəpo] *nm* rest; (*fig*) peace (and quiet); peace of mind; (*MIL*): ~! stand at ease!; **en** ~ at rest; **de tout** ~ safe.

reposant, e [rəpozɑ̃, -ɑ̃t] *a* restful.

reposer [rəpoze] *vt* (*verre, livre*) to put down; (*délasser*) to rest; (*problème*) to reformulate // *vi* (*liquide, pâte*) to settle, rest; ~ **sur** to be built on; (*fig*) to rest on; **se** ~ *vi* to rest; **se** ~ **sur qn** to rely on sb.

repoussant, e [rəpusɑ̃, -ɑ̃t] *a* repulsive.

repousser [rəpuse] *vi* to grow again // *vt* to repel, repulse; (*offre*) to turn down, reject; (*tiroir, personne*) to push back; (*différer*) to put off.

reprendre [rəprɑ̃dr(ə)] *vt* (*prisonnier, ville*) to recapture; (*objet prêté, donné*) to take back; (*chercher*): **je viendrai te** ~ **à 4h** I'll come and fetch you at 4; (*se resservir de*): ~ **du pain/un œuf** to take (ou eat) more bread/another egg; (*firme, entreprise*) to take over; (*travail, promenade*) to resume; (*emprunter: argument, idée*) to take up, use; (*refaire: article etc*) to go over again; (*jupe etc*) to alter; (*émission, pièce*) to put on again; (*réprimander*) to tell off; (*corriger*) to correct // *vi* (*classes, pluie*) to start (up) again; (*activités, travaux, combats*) to resume, start (up) again; (*affaires, industrie*) to pick up; (*dire*): **reprit-il** he went on; **se** ~ *vi* (*se ressaisir*) to recover; **s'y** ~ to make another attempt; ~ **des forces** to recover one's strength; ~ **courage** to take new heart; ~ **la route** to set off again; ~ **haleine** *ou* **son souffle** to get one's breath back.

représailles [rəprezaj] *nfpl* reprisals.

représentant, e [rəprezɑ̃tɑ̃, -ɑ̃t] *nm/f* representative.

représentation [rəprezɑ̃tasjɔ̃] *nf* (*symbole, image*) representation; (*spectacle*) performance.

représenter [rəprezɑ̃te] *vt* to represent; (*donner: pièce, opéra*) to perform; **se** ~ *vt* (*se figurer*) to imagine; to visualize.

répression [represjɔ̃] *nf* (*voir réprimer*) suppression; repression.

réprimer [reprime] *vt* (*émotions*) to suppress; (*peuple etc*) to repress.

repris [rəpri] *nm*: ~ **de justice** ex-prisoner, ex-convict.

reprise [rəpriz] *nf* (*recommencement*) resumption; recovery; (*TV*) repeat; (*CINÉMA*) rerun; (*AUTO*) acceleration *q*; (*COMM*) trade-in, part exchange; **à plusieurs** ~**s** on several occasions.

repriser [rəprize] *vt* to darn; to mend.

reproche [rəprɔʃ] *nm* (*remontrance*) reproach; **faire des** ~**s à qn** to reproach sb; **sans** ~(**s**) beyond reproach.

reprocher [rəprɔʃe] *vt*: ~ **qch à qn** to reproach *ou* blame sb for sth; ~ **qch à** (*machine, théorie*) to have sth against.

reproduction [rəprodyksjɔ̃] *nf* reproduction.

reproduire [rəprodɥir] *vt* to reproduce; **se** ~ *vi* (*BIO*) to reproduce; (*recommencer*) to recur, re-occur.

reptile [rɛptil] *nm* reptile.

repu, e [rəpy] *a* satisfied, sated.

républicain, e [repyblikɛ̃, -ɛn] *a, nm/f* republican.

république [repyblik] *nf* republic.

répugnant, e [repynɑ̃, -ɑ̃t] *a* repugnant; loathsome.

répugner [repyne]: ~ **à** *vt*: ~ **à qn** to repel *ou* disgust sb; ~ **à faire** to be loath *ou* reluctant to do.

réputation [repytasjɔ̃] *nf* reputation; **réputé, e** *a* renowned.

requérir [rekerir] *vt* (*nécessiter*) to require, call for; (*JUR: peine*) to call for, demand.

requête [rəkɛt] *nf* request; (*JUR*) petition.

requin [ʀəkɛ̃] nm shark.

requis, e [ʀəki, -iz] a required.

R.E.R. sigle m (= réseau express régional) Greater Paris high speed train service.

rescapé, e [ʀɛskape] nm/f survivor.

rescousse [ʀɛskus] nf: aller à la ~ de qn to go to sb's aid ou rescue.

réseau, x [ʀezo] nm network.

réservation [ʀezɛʀvɑsjɔ̃] nf booking, reservation.

réserve [ʀezɛʀv(ə)] nf (retenue) reserve; (entrepôt) storeroom; (restriction, d'Indiens) reservation; (de pêche, chasse) preserve; sous ~ de subject to; sans ~ ad unreservedly; de ~ (provisions etc) in reserve.

réservé, e [ʀezɛʀve] a (discret) reserved; (chasse, pêche) private.

réserver [ʀezɛʀve] vt to reserve; (chambre, billet etc) to book, reserve; (garder): ~ qch pour/à to keep ou save sth for; ~ qch à qn to reserve ou (ou book) sth for sb.

réservoir [ʀezɛʀvwaʀ] nm tank.

résidence [ʀezidɑ̃s] nf residence; ~ secondaire second home; (en) ~ surveillée (under) house arrest; **résidentiel, le** a residential.

résider [ʀezide] vi: ~ à/dans/en to reside in; ~ dans (fig) to lie in.

résidu [ʀezidy] nm residue q.

résigner [ʀezine]: se ~ vi: ~ (à qch/à faire) to resign o.s. (to sth/to doing).

résilier [ʀezilje] vt to terminate.

résistance [ʀezistɑ̃s] nf resistance; (de réchaud, bouilloire: fil) element.

résistant, e [ʀezistɑ̃, -ɑ̃t] a (personne) robust, tough; (matériau) strong, hard-wearing.

résister [ʀeziste] vi to resist; ~ à vt (assaut, tentation) to resist; (effort, souffrance) to withstand; (désobéir à) to stand up to, oppose.

résolu, e [ʀezɔly] pp de **résoudre** // a: être ~ à qch/faire to be set upon sth/doing.

résolution [ʀezɔlysjɔ̃] nf solving; (fermeté, décision) resolution.

résolve etc vb voir **résoudre**.

résonner [ʀezɔne] vi (cloche, pas) to reverberate, resound; (salle) to be resonant; ~ de to resound with.

résorber [ʀezɔʀbe]: se ~ vi (fig) to be reduced; to be absorbed.

résoudre [ʀezudʀ(ə)] vt to solve; se ~ à faire to bring o.s. to do.

respect [ʀɛspɛ] nm respect; tenir en ~ to keep at bay.

respecter [ʀɛspɛkte] vt to respect.

respectueux, euse [ʀɛspɛktɥø, -øz] a respectful; ~ de respectful of.

respiration [ʀɛspiʀɑsjɔ̃] nf breathing q; ~ artificielle artificial respiration.

respirer [ʀɛspiʀe] vi to breathe; (fig) to get one's breath; to breathe again // vi (air) to breathe in, inhale; (manifester: santé, calme etc) to exude.

resplendir [ʀɛsplɑ̃diʀ] vi to shine; (fig): ~ (de) to be radiant (with).

responsabilité [ʀɛspɔ̃sabilite] nf responsibility; (légale) liability.

responsable [ʀɛspɔ̃sabl(ə)] a responsible // nm/f (du ravitaillement etc) person in charge; (de parti, syndicat) official; ~ de responsible for; (chargé de) in charge of, responsible for.

ressaisir [ʀəsɛziʀ]: se ~ vi to regain one's self-control.

ressasser [ʀəsase] vt to keep going over.

ressemblance [ʀəsɑ̃blɑ̃s] nf resemblance, similarity, likeness.

ressemblant, e [ʀəsɑ̃blɑ̃, -ɑ̃t] a (portrait) lifelike, true to life.

ressembler [ʀəsɑ̃ble]: ~ à vt to be like; to resemble; (visuellement) to look like; se ~ vi to be (ou look) alike.

ressemeler [ʀəsəmle] vt to (re)sole.

ressentiment [ʀəsɑ̃timɑ̃] nm resentment.

ressentir [ʀəsɑ̃tiʀ] vt to feel; se ~ de to feel (ou show) the effects of.

resserrer [ʀəseʀe] vt (nœud, boulon) to tighten (up); (fig: liens) to strengthen; se ~ vi (vallée) to narrow.

resservir [RəsɛRviR] vi to do ou serve again // vt: ~ **qn** (d'un plat) to give sb a second helping of (a dish).

ressort [RəsɔR] nm (pièce) spring; (force morale) spirit; (recours): **en dernier** ~ as a last resort; (compétence): **être du** ~ **de** to fall within the competence of.

ressortir [RəsɔRtiR] vi to go (ou come) out (again); (contraster) to stand out; ~ **de** to emerge from; **faire** ~ (fig: souligner) to bring out.

ressortissant, e [RəsɔRtisɑ̃, -ɑ̃t] nm/f national.

ressource [RəsuRs(ə)] nf: **avoir la** ~ **de** to have the possibility of; **leur seule** ~ **était de** the only course open to them was to; ~**s** nfpl resources.

ressusciter [Resysite] vt (fig) to revive, bring back // vi to rise (from the dead).

restant, e [Rɛstɑ̃, -ɑ̃t] a remaining // nm: **le** ~ (**de**) the remainder (of); **un** ~ **de** (de trop) some left-over.

restaurant [RɛstɔRɑ̃] nm restaurant.

restauration [RɛstɔRɑsjɔ̃] nf restoration; (hôtellerie) catering; ~ **rapide** fast food.

restaurer [RɛstɔRe] vt to restore; se ~ vi to have something to eat.

reste [Rɛst(ə)] nm (restant): **le** ~ (**de**) the rest (of); (de trop): **un** ~ (**de**) some left over; (vestige): **un** ~ **de** a remnant ou last trace of; (MATH) remainder; ~**s** nmpl left-overs; (d'une cité etc, dépouille mortelle) remains; **du** ~, **au** ~ ad besides, moreover.

rester [Rɛste] vi to stay, remain; (subsister) to remain, be left; (durer) to last, live on // vb impersonnel: **il reste du pain/2 œufs** there's some bread/there are 2 eggs left (over); **il me reste assez de temps** I have enough time left; **ce qui reste à faire** what remains to be done; **restons-en là** let's leave it at that.

restituer [Rɛstitɥe] vt (objet, somme): ~ **qch** (à qn) to return sth (to sb); (TECH) to release; (: son) to reproduce.

restoroute [RɛstɔRut] nm motorway (Brit) ou highway (US) restaurant.

restreindre [RɛstRɛ̃dR(ə)] vt to restrict, limit.

restriction [RɛstRiksjɔ̃] nf restriction; ~**s** (mentales) reservations.

résultat [Rezylta] nm result; (d'élection etc) results pl.

résulter [Rezylte]: ~ **de** vt to result from, be the result of.

résumé [Rezyme] nm summary, résumé.

résumer [Rezyme] vt (texte) to summarize; (récapituler) to sum up; se ~ à to come down to.

résurrection [RezyRɛksjɔ̃] nf resurrection; (fig) revival.

rétablir [Retablir] vt to restore, reestablish; se ~ vi (guérir) to recover; (silence, calme) to return, be restored; **rétablissement** nm restoring; recovery; (SPORT) pull-up.

retaper [Rətape] vt (maison, voiture etc) to do up; (fam: revigorer) to buck up; (redactylographier) to retype.

retard [RətaR] nm (d'une personne attendue) lateness q; (sur l'horaire, un programme) delay; (fig: scolaire, mental etc) backwardness; **en** ~ (de 2 heures) (2 hours) late; **avoir du** ~ to be late; (sur un programme) to be behind (schedule); **prendre du** ~ (train, avion) to be delayed; (montre) to lose (time); **sans** ~ ad without delay.

retardement [Rətardəmɑ̃]: **à** ~ a delayed action cpd; **bombe à** ~ **time** bomb.

retarder [RətaRde] vt (sur un horaire): ~ **qn** (d'une heure) to delay sb (an hour); (départ, date): ~ **qch** (de 2 jours) to put back (by 2 days), delay sth (for ou by 2 days); (horloge) to put back // vi (montre) to be slow; to lose (time).

retenir [rətniːr] vt (garder, retarder) to keep, detain; (maintenir: objet qui glisse, fig: colère, larmes) to hold back; (: objet suspendu) to hold; (fig: empêcher d'agir): ~ qn (de faire) to hold sb back (from doing); (se rappeler) to retain; (réserver) to reserve; (accepter) to accept; (prélever): ~ qch (sur) to deduct sth (from); se ~ vi (se raccrocher): se ~ à to hold onto; (se contenir): se ~ de faire to restrain o.s. from doing; ~ son souffle to hold one's breath.

retentir [rətɑ̃tiːr] vi to ring out; (salle): ~ de to ring ou resound with.

retentissant, e [rətɑ̃tisɑ̃, -ɑ̃t] a resounding; (fig) impact-making.

retentissement [rətɑ̃tismɑ̃] nm repercussion; effect, impact; stir.

retenue [rətny] nf (prélèvement) deduction; (SCOL) detention; (modération) (self-)restraint; (réserve) reserve, reticence.

réticence [retisɑ̃s] nf hesitation, reluctance ø.

rétine [retin] nf retina.

retiré, e [rətire] a secluded; remote.

retirer [rətire] vt to withdraw; (vêtement, lunettes) to take off, remove; (extraire): ~ qch de to take sth out of, remove sth from; (: prendre: bagages, billets) to collect, pick up.

retombées [rətɔ̃be] nfpl (radioactives) fallout sg; (fig) fallout: spin-offs.

retomber [rətɔ̃be] vi (à nouveau) to fall again; (atterrir: après un saut etc) to land; (tomber, redescendre) to fall back; (pendre) to fall, hang (down); (échoir): ~ sur qn to fall on sb.

rétorquer [retɔrke] vt: ~ (à qn) que to retort (to sb) that.

retors, e [rətɔr, -ɔrs(ə)] a wily.

rétorsion [retɔrsjɔ̃] nf: mesures de ~ reprisals.

retoucher [rətuʃe] vt (photographie) to touch up; (texte, vêtement) to al-

ter.

retour [rətuːr] nm return; au ~ when we (ou they etc) get (ou got) back; (en route) on the way back; être de ~ (de) to be back (from); par ~ du courrier by return of post.

retourner [rəturne] vt (dans l'autre sens: matelas, crêpe, foin, terre) to turn (over); (: caisse) to turn upside down; (: sac, vêtement) to turn inside out; (émouvoir: personne) to shake; (renvoyer, restituer): ~ qch à qn to return sth to sb // vi (aller, revenir): ~ quelque part/à to go back ou return somewhere/to; ~ à (état, activité) to return to, go back to; se ~ vi to turn over; (tourner la tête) to turn round; se ~ contre (fig) to turn against; savoir de quoi il retourne to know what it is all about.

retracer [rətrase] vt to relate, recount.

retrait [rətrɛ] nm (voir retirer) withdrawal; collection; en ~ set back; ~ du permis (de conduire) disqualification from driving (Brit), revocation of driver's license (US).

retraite [rətrɛt] nf (d'une armée, REL, refuge) retreat; (d'un employé) retirement; (revenu) pension; prendre sa ~ to retire; ~ anticipée early retirement; **retraité, e** a retired // nm/f pensioner.

retrancher [rətrɑ̃ʃe] vt (passage, détails) to take out, remove; (nombre, somme): ~ qch de to take ou deduct sth from; (couper) to cut off; se ~ derrière/dans to take refuge behind/in.

retransmettre [rətrɑ̃smɛtr(ə)] vt (RADIO) to broadcast; (TV) to show.

rétrécir [retresir] vt (vêtement) to take in // vi to shrink; se ~ vi to narrow.

rétribution [retribysjɔ̃] nf payment.

rétro [retro] a inv: la mode ~ the nostalgia vogue.

rétrograde [retrograd] a reactionary, backward-looking.

rétrograder [retrɔgrade] *vi* (*économie*) to regress; (*AUTO*) to change down.

rétroprojecteur [retrɔprɔʒɛktœr] *nm* overhead projector.

rétrospective [retrɔspɛktiv] *nf*; retrospective exhibition/season; ~**ment** *ad* in retrospect.

retrousser [rətruse] *vt* to roll up.

retrouvailles [rətruvɑj] *nfpl* reunion *sg*.

retrouver [rətruve] *vt* (*fugitif, objet perdu*) to find; (*occasion*) to find again; (*calme, santé*) to regain; (*revoir*) to see again; (*rejoindre*) to meet (again), join; se ~ *vi* to meet (again); (*s'orienter*) to find one's way; se ~ **quelque part** to find o.s. somewhere; **s'y** ~ (*rentrer dans ses frais*) to break even.

rétroviseur [retrɔvizœr] *nm* (rearview) mirror.

réunion [reynjɔ̃] *nf* bringing together; joining; (*séance*) meeting.

réunir [reynir] *vt* (*convoquer*) to call together; (*rassembler*) to gather together; (*cumuler*) to combine; (*rapprocher*) to bring together (again), reunite; (*rattacher*) to join (together); se ~ *vi* (*se rencontrer*) to meet.

réussi, e [reysi] *a* successful.

réussir [reysir] *vi* to succeed, be successful; (*à un examen*) to pass; (*plante, culture*) to thrive, do well // *vt* to make a success of; ~ **à faire** to succeed in doing; ~ **à qn** to go right for sb; (*aliment*) to agree with sb.

réussite [reysit] *nf* success; (*CARTES*) patience.

revaloir [rəvalwar] *vt*: **je vous revaudrai cela** I'll repay you some day; (*en mal*) I'll pay you back for this.

revaloriser [rəvalɔrize] *vt* (*monnaie*) to revalue; (*salaires*) to raise the level of.

revanche [rəvɑ̃ʃ] *nf* revenge; **en** ~ on the other hand.

rêve [rɛv] *nm* dream; (*activité psychique*): **le** ~ dreaming.

revêche [rəvɛʃ] *a* surly, sour-tempered.

réveil [revɛj] *nm* (*d'un dormeur*) waking up q; (*fig*) awakening; (*pendule*) alarm (clock); (*MIL*) reveille; **au** ~ on waking (up).

réveille-matin [revɛjmatɛ̃] *nm inv* alarm clock.

réveiller [revɛje] *vt* (*personne*) to wake up; (*fig*) to awaken, revive; se ~ *vi* to wake up; (*fig*) to reawaken.

réveillon [revɛjɔ̃] *nm* Christmas Eve; (*de la Saint-Sylvestre*) New Year's Eve; **réveillonner** *vi* to celebrate Christmas Eve (*ou* New Year's Eve).

révélateur, trice [revelatœr, -tris] *a*: ~ (**de qch**) revealing (sth) // *nm* (*PHOTO*) developer.

révéler [revele] *vt* (*gén*) to reveal; (*faire connaître au public*): ~ **qn/qch** to make sb/sth widely known, bring sb/sth to the public's notice; se ~ *vi* to be revealed, reveal itself // *vb avec attribut* to prove (to be).

revenant, e [rəvnɑ̃, -ɑ̃t] *nm/f* ghost.

revendeur, euse [rəvɑ̃dœr, -øz] *nm/f* (*détaillant*) retailer; (*d'occasions*) secondhand dealer.

revendication [rəvɑ̃dikɑsjɔ̃] *nf* claim, demand; **journée de** ~ day of action.

revendiquer [rəvɑ̃dike] *vt* to claim, demand; (*responsabilité*) to claim.

revendre [rəvɑ̃dr(ə)] *vt* (*d'occasion*) to resell; (*détailler*) to sell; **à** ~ (*en abondance*) to spare.

revenir [rəvnir] *vi* to come back; (*CULIN*): **faire** ~ to brown; (*coûter*): ~ **cher/à 100 F** (**à qn**) to cost (sb) a lot/100 F; ~ **à** (*études, projet*) to return to, go back to; (*équivaloir à*) to amount to; ~ **à qn** (*part, honneur*) to go to sb, be sb's; (*souvenir, nom*) to come back to sb; ~ **de** (*fig: maladie, étonnement*) to recover from; ~ **sur** (*question, su-*

jet) to go back over; (*engagement*) to go back on; ~ **à la charge** to return to the attack; ~ **à soi** to come round; **n'en pas** ~: **je n'en reviens pas** I can't get over it; ~ **sur ses pas** to retrace one's steps; **cela revient à dire que/au même** it amounts to saying that/the same thing.

revenu [ʀəvny] *nm* income; (*de l'État*) revenue; (*d'un capital*) yield; ~**s** *nmpl* income *sg*.

rêver [ʀeve] *vi*, *vt* to dream; ~ **de/à** to dream of.

réverbère [ʀeveʀbɛʀ] *nm* street lamp *ou* light.

réverbérer [ʀeveʀbeʀe] *vt* to reflect.

révérence [ʀeveʀɑ̃s] *nf* (*salut*) bow; (: *de femme*) curtsey.

rêverie [ʀɛvʀi] *nf* daydreaming *q*, daydream.

revers [ʀəvɛʀ] *nm* (*de feuille*, *main*) back; (*d'étoffe*) wrong side; (*de pièce*, *médaille*) back, reverse; (*TENNIS*, *PING-PONG*) backhand; (*de veston*) lapel; (*de pantalon*) turn-up; (*fig*: *échec*) setback.

revêtement [ʀəvɛtmɑ̃] *nm* (*de paroi*) facing; (*des sols*) flooring; (*de chaussée*) surface; (*de tuyau etc*: *enduit*) coating.

revêtir [ʀəvetiʀ] *vt* (*habit*) to don, put on; (*fig*) to take on; ~ **qn de** (*fig*) to endow *ou* invest sb with; ~ **qch de** to cover sth with; (*fig*) to cloak sth in.

rêveur, euse [ʀɛvœʀ, -øz] *a* dreamy // *nm/f* dreamer.

revient [ʀəvjɛ̃] *vb voir* **revenir**.

revigorer [ʀəvigɔʀe] *vt* to invigorate, brace up; to revive, buck up.

revirement [ʀəviʀmɑ̃] *nm* change of mind; (*d'une situation*) reversal.

réviser [ʀevize] *vt* (*texte*, *SCOL*: *matière*) to revise; (*machine*, *installation*, *moteur*) to overhaul, service; (*JUR*: *procès*) to review.

révision [ʀevizjɔ̃] *nf* revision; auditing *q*; overhaul; servicing *q*; review; **la** ~ **des 10 000 km** (*AUTO*) the 10,000 km service.

revivre [ʀəvivʀ(ə)] *vi* (*reprendre des forces*) to come alive again; (*traditions*) to be revived // *vt* (*épreuve*, *moment*) to relive.

revoir [ʀəvwaʀ] *vt* to see again; (*réviser*) to revise // *nm*: **au** ~ goodbye.

révoltant, e [ʀevɔltɑ̃, -ɑ̃t] *a* revolting; appalling.

révolte [ʀevɔlt(ə)] *nf* rebellion, revolt.

révolter [ʀevɔlte] *vt* to revolt; to outrage, appal; **se** ~ (**contre**) to rebel (against).

révolu, e [ʀevɔly] *a* past; (*ADMIN*): **âgé de 18 ans** ~**s** over 18 years of age; **après 3 ans** ~**s** when 3 full years have passed.

révolution [ʀevɔlysjɔ̃] *nf* revolution; **révolutionnaire** *a*, *nm/f* revolutionary.

revolver [ʀevɔlvɛʀ] *nm* gun; (*à barillet*) revolver.

révoquer [ʀevɔke] *vt* (*fonctionnaire*) to dismiss; (*arrêt*, *contrat*) to revoke.

revue [ʀəvy] *nf* (*inventaire*, *examen*, *MIL*) review; (*périodique*) review, magazine; (*de music-hall*) variety show; **passer en** ~ to review; to go through.

rez-de-chaussée [ʀedʃose] *nm inv* ground floor.

RF *sigle* = **République Française**.

RFA *sigle f* = **République fédérale d'Allemagne**.

Rhin [ʀɛ̃] *nm*: **le** ~ the Rhine.

rhinocéros [ʀinɔseʀɔs] *nm* rhinoceros.

Rhône [ʀon] *nm*: **le** ~ the Rhone.

rhubarbe [ʀybaʀb(ə)] *nf* rhubarb.

rhum [ʀɔm] *nm* rum.

rhumatisme [ʀymatism(ə)] *nm* rheumatism *q*.

rhume [ʀym] *nm* cold; ~ **de cerveau** head cold; **le** ~ **des foins** hay fever.

ri [ʀi] *pp de* **rire**.

riant, e [ʀjɑ̃, -ɑ̃t] *a* smiling, cheerful.

ricaner [ʀikane] *vi* (*avec méchanceté*) to snigger; (*bêtement*) to giggle.

riche [ʀiʃ] a (gén) rich; (personne, pays) rich, wealthy; ~ **de** full of; rich in; **richesse** nf wealth; (fig) richness; **richesses** nfpl wealth sg; treasures.

ricin [ʀisɛ̃] nm: **huile de** ~ castor oil.

ricocher [ʀikɔʃe] vi: ~ (**sur**) to rebound (off); (sur l'eau) to bounce (on ou off).

ricochet [ʀikɔʃɛ] nm: **faire des** ~s to skip stones; **par** ~ ad on the rebound; (fig) as an indirect result.

rictus [ʀiktys] nm grin; (snarling) grimace.

ride [ʀid] nf wrinkle; (fig) ripple.

rideau, x [ʀido] nm curtain; (POL): **le** ~ **de fer** the Iron Curtain.

rider [ʀide] vt to wrinkle; (eau) to ripple; **se** ~ vi to become wrinkled.

ridicule [ʀidikyl] a ridiculous ♦ nm: **le** ~ ridicule; **se ridiculiser** vi to make a fool of o.s.

MOT-CLÉ

rien [ʀjɛ̃] ♦ pronom

1: (**ne**) ... ~ nothing, tournure négative + anything; **qu'est-ce que vous avez?** - ~ what have you got? - nothing; **il n'a** ~ **dit/fait** he said/did nothing; he hasn't said/done anything; **il n'a** ~ (n'est pas blessé) he's all right; **de** ~! not at all!

2 (quelque chose): **a-t-il jamais** ~ **fait pour nous?** has he ever done anything for us?

3: ~ **de:** ~ **d'intéressant** nothing interesting; ~ **d'autre** nothing else; ~ **du tout** nothing at all

4: ~ **que** just, only; nothing but; ~ **que pour lui faire plaisir** only ou just to please him; ~ **que la vérité** nothing but the truth; ~ **que cela** that alone

♦ nm: **un petit** ~ (cadeau) a little something; **des** ~s trivia pl; **un** ~ **de** a hint of; **en un** ~ **de temps** in no time at all.

---

rieur, euse [ʀjœʀ, -øz] a cheerful.

rigide [ʀiʒid] a stiff; (fig) rigid; strict.

rigole [ʀigɔl] nf (conduit) channel; (filet d'eau) rivulet.

rigoler [ʀigɔle] vi (rire) to laugh; (s'amuser) to have (some) fun; (plaisanter) to be joking ou kidding.

rigolo, ote [ʀigɔlo, -ɔt] a (fam) funny ♦ nm/f comic; (péj) fraud, phoney.

rigoureux, euse [ʀiguʀø, -øz] a (morale) rigorous, strict; (personne) stern, strict; (climat, châtiment) rigorous, harsh; (interdiction, neutralité) strict.

rigueur [ʀigœʀ] nf rigour; strictness; harshness; **être de** ~ to be the rule; **à la** ~ at a pinch; **tenir** ~ **à qn de qch** to hold sth against sb.

rime [ʀim] nf rhyme.

rinçage [ʀɛ̃saʒ] nm rinsing (out); (opération) rinse.

rincer [ʀɛ̃se] vt to rinse; (récipient) to rinse out.

ring [ʀiŋ] nm (boxing) ring.

ringard, e [ʀɛ̃gaʀ, -aʀd(ə)] a old-fashioned.

rions vb voir **rire**.

riposter [ʀipɔste] vi to retaliate ♦ vt: ~ **que** to retort that; ~ **à** vt to counter; to reply to.

rire [ʀiʀ] vi to laugh; (se divertir) to have fun ♦ nm laugh; **le** ~ laughter; ~ **de** vt to laugh at; **pour** ~ (pas sérieusement) for a joke ou a laugh.

risée [ʀize] nf: **être la** ~ **de** to be the laughing stock of.

risible [ʀizibl(ə)] a laughable.

risque [ʀisk(ə)] nm risk; **le** ~ **danger**; **à ses** ~s **et périls** at his own risk.

risqué, e [ʀiske] a risky; (plaisanterie) risqué, daring.

risquer [ʀiske] vt to risk; (allusion, question) to venture, hazard; **ça ne risque rien** it's quite safe; ~ **de:** il risque de se tuer he could get himself killed; ce qui risque de se pro-

duire what might *ou* could well happen; **il ne risque pas de recommencer** there's no chance of him doing that again; **se ~ à faire** (*tenter*) to venture *ou* dare to do.

rissoler [ʀisɔle] *vi, vt*: **(faire) ~ to** brown.

ristourne [ʀistuʀn(ə)] *nf* rebate.

rite [ʀit] *nm* rite; (*de fleuve*) bank.

rivage [ʀivaʒ] *nm* shore.

rival, e, aux [ʀival, -o] *a, nm/f* rival.

rivaliser [ʀivalize] *vi*: **~ avec** to rival, vie with; (*être comparable*) to hold its own against, compare with.

rivalité [ʀivalite] *nf* rivalry.

rive [ʀiv] *nf* shore; (*de fleuve*) bank.

river [ʀive] *vt* (*clou, pointe*) to clinch; (*plaques*) to rivet together.

riverain, e [ʀivʀɛ̃, -ɛn] *nm/f* riverside (*ou* lakeside) resident; local resident.

rivet [ʀivɛ] *nm* rivet.

rivière [ʀivjɛʀ] *nf* river.

rixe [ʀiks(ə)] *nf* brawl, scuffle.

riz [ʀi] *nm* rice.

R.N. *sigle f de* **route nationale**.

robe [ʀɔb] *nf* dress; (*de juge, d'ecclésiastique*) gown; (*de professeur*) gown; (*pelage*) coat; **~ de soirée/de mariée** evening/wedding dress; **~ de chambre** dressing gown; **~ de grossesse** maternity dress.

robinet [ʀɔbinɛ] *nm* tap.

robot [ʀɔbo] *nm* robot.

robuste [ʀɔbyst(ə)] *a* robust, sturdy.

roc [ʀɔk] *nm* rock.

rocaille [ʀɔkaj] *nf* loose stones *pl*, rocky *ou* stony ground; (*jardin*) rockery, rock garden.

roche [ʀɔʃ] *nf* rock.

rocher [ʀɔʃe] *nm* rock.

rocheux, euse [ʀɔʃø, -øz] *a* rocky.

rodage [ʀɔdaʒ] *nm*: **en ~** (*AUTO*) running in.

roder [ʀɔde] *vt* (*AUTO*) to run in.

rôder [ʀode] *vi* to roam about; (*de façon suspecte*) to lurk (about *ou* around); **rôdeur, euse** *nm/f*

prowler.

rogne [ʀɔɲ] *nf*: **être en ~** to be in a temper.

rogner [ʀɔɲe] *vt* to clip; **~ sur** (*fig*) to cut down *ou* back on.

rognons [ʀɔɲɔ̃] *nmpl* kidneys.

roi [ʀwa] *nm* king; **le jour** *ou* **la fête des R~s, les R~s** Twelfth Night.

roitelet [ʀwatlɛ] *nm* wren.

rôle [ʀol] *nm* role; (*contribution*) part.

romain, e [ʀɔmɛ̃, -ɛn] *a, nm/f* Roman.

roman, e [ʀɔmɑ̃, -an] *a* (*ARCHIT*) Romanesque // *nm* novel; **~ d'espionnage** spy novel *ou* story; **~ photo** romantic picture story.

romance [ʀɔmɑ̃s] *nf* ballad.

romancer [ʀɔmɑ̃se] *vt* to make into a novel; to romanticize.

romancier, ière [ʀɔmɑ̃sje, -jɛʀ] *nm/f* novelist.

romanesque [ʀɔmanɛsk(ə)] *a* (*fantastique*) fantastic; storybook *cpd*; (*sentimental*) romantic.

roman-feuilleton [ʀɔmɑ̃fœjtɔ̃] *nm* serialized novel.

romanichel, le [ʀɔmaniʃɛl] *nm/f* gipsy.

romantique [ʀɔmɑ̃tik] *a* romantic.

romarin [ʀɔmaʀɛ̃] *nm* rosemary.

rompre [ʀɔ̃pʀ(ə)] *vt* to break; (*entretien, fiançailles*) to break off // *vi* (*fiancés*) to break it off; **se ~** *vi* to break; (*MÉD*) to burst, rupture.

rompu, e [ʀɔ̃py] *a*: **~ à** with wide experience of; inured to.

ronces [ʀɔ̃s] *nfpl* brambles.

ronchonner [ʀɔ̃ʃɔne] *vi* (*fam*) to grouse, grouch.

rond, e [ʀɔ̃, ʀɔ̃d] *a* round; (*joues, mollets*) well-rounded; (*fam: ivre*) tight // *nm* (*cercle*) ring; (*fam: sou*): **je n'ai plus un ~** I haven't a penny left // *nf* (*gén: de surveillance*) rounds *pl*, patrol; (*danse*) round (dance); (*MUS*) semibreve (*Brit*), whole note (*US*); **en ~** (*s'asseoir, danser*) in a ring; **à la ~e** (*alen-*

tour): **à 10 km à la ~e** for 10 km round; **rondelet, te** *a* plump.

rondelle [rɔ̃dɛl] *nf* (TECH) washer; (*tranche*) slice, round.

rondement [rɔ̃dmɑ̃] *ad* briskly, frankly.

rondin [rɔ̃dɛ̃] *nm* log.

rond-point [rɔ̃pwɛ̃] *nm* roundabout.

ronéotyper [rɔneɔtipe] *vt* to duplicate.

ronfler [rɔ̃fle] *vi* to snore; (*moteur, poêle*) to hum; to roar.

ronger [rɔ̃ʒe] *vt* to gnaw (at); (*suj: vers, rouille*) to eat into; **se ~ les sangs** to worry o.s. sick; **se ~ les ongles** to bite one's nails; **rongeur** *nm* rodent.

ronronner [rɔ̃rɔne] *vi* to purr.

roquet [rɔkɛ] *nm* nasty little lapdog.

roquette [rɔkɛt] *nf* rocket.

rosace [rozas] *nf* (*vitrail*) rose window.

rosbif [rɔsbif] *nm*: **du ~** roasting beef; (*cuit*) roast beef; **un ~** a joint of beef.

rose [roz] *nf* rose // *a* pink.

rosé, e [roze] *a* pinkish; (*vin*) ~ rosé.

roseau, x [rozo] *nm* reed.

rosée [roze] *nf* dew.

roseraie [rozrɛ] *nf* rose garden.

rosier [rozje] *nm* rosebush, rose tree.

rosse [rɔs] *nf* (*péj: cheval*) nag // *a* nasty, vicious.

rossignol [rɔsiɲɔl] *nm* (ZOOL) nightingale.

rot [ro] *nm* belch; (*de bébé*) burp.

rotatif, ive [rɔtatif, -iv] *a* rotary.

rotation [rɔtasjɔ̃] *nf* rotation; (*fig*) rotation, swap-around; turnover.

roter [rɔte] *vi* (*fam*) to burp, belch.

rôti [roti] *nm*: **du ~** roasting meat; (*cuit*) roast meat; **un ~ de bœuf/porc** a joint of beef/pork.

rotin [rɔtɛ̃] *nm* rattan (cane); **fauteuil en ~** cane (arm)chair.

rôtir [rotiʀ] *vi, vt* (*aussi*: **faire ~**) to roast; **rôtisserie** *nf* steakhouse; roast meat counter (*ou* shop);

rôtissoire *nf* (roasting) spit.

rotule [rɔtyl] *nf* kneecap, patella.

roturier, ière [rɔtyrje, -jɛr] *nm/f* commoner.

rouage [rwaʒ] *nm* cog(wheel), gearwheel; (*de montre*) part; (*fig*) cog.

roucouler [rukule] *vi* to coo.

roue [ru] *nf* wheel; **~ dentée** cogwheel; **~ de secours** spare wheel.

roué, e [rwe] *a* wily.

rouer [rwe] *vt*: **~ qn de coups** to give sb a thrashing.

rouet [rwe] *nm* spinning wheel.

rouge [ruʒ] *a, nm/f* red // *nm* red; (*fard*) rouge; (*vin*) ~ red wine; **sur la liste ~** ex-directory (*Brit*), unlisted (*US*); **passer au ~** (*signal*) to go red; (*automobiliste*) to go through a red light; ~ **(à lèvres)** lipstick; **~-gorge** *nm* robin (redbreast).

rougeole [ruʒɔl] *nf* measles *sg*.

rougeoyer [ruʒwaje] *vi* to glow red.

rouget [ruʒɛ] *nm* mullet.

rougeur [ruʒœr] *nf* redness.

rougir [ruʒir] *vi* (*de honte, timidité*) to blush, flush; (*de plaisir, colère*) to flush; (*fraise, tomate*) to go *ou* turn red; (*ciel*) to redden.

rouille [ruj] *nf* rust.

rouillé, e [ruje] *a* rusty.

rouiller [ruje] *vt* to rust // *vi* to rust, go rusty; **se ~** *vi* to rust.

roulant, e [rulɑ̃, -ɑ̃t] *a* (*meuble*) on wheels; (*surface, trottoir*) moving.

rouleau, x [rulo] *nm* (*papier, tissu, SPORT*) roll; (*de machine à écrire*) roller, platen; (*à mise en plis, à peinture, vague*) roller; ~ **compresseur** steamroller; ~ **à pâtisserie** rolling pin.

roulement [rulmɑ̃] *nm* (*bruit*) rumbling *q*, rumble; (*rotation*) rotation; turnover; **par ~** *ou* **a rota** (*Brit*) *ou* **rotation** (*US*) basis; ~ **(à billes)** ball bearings *pl*; ~ **de tambour** drum roll.

rouler [rule] *vt* to roll; (*papier, tapis*) to roll up; (CULIN: *pâte*) to roll out; (*fam*) to do, con // *vi* (*bille, boule*) to roll; (*voiture, train*) to go;

run; *(automobiliste)* to drive; *(cycliste)* to ride; *(bateau)* to roll; *(tonnerre)* to rumble, roll; se ~ dans *(boue)* to roll in; *(couverture)* to roll o.s. (up) in.

roulette [Rulɛt] *nf (de table, fauteuil)* castor; *(de pâtissier)* pastry wheel; *(jeu)*: la ~ roulette; à ~s on castors.

roulis [Ruli] *nm* roll(ing).

roulotte [Rulɔt] *nf* caravan.

Roumanie [Rumani] *nf* Rumania.

rouquin, e [Rukɛ̃, -in] *nm/f (péj)* redhead.

rouspéter [Ruspete] *vi (fam)* to moan.

rousse [Rus] *a voir roux.*

roussi [Rusi] *nm*: ça sent le ~ there's a smell of burning; *(fig)* I can smell trouble.

roussir [RusiR] *vt* to scorch // *vi (feuilles)* to go *ou* turn brown; *(CULIN)*: faire ~ to brown.

route [Rut] *nf* road; *(fig: chemin)* way; *(itinéraire, parcours)* route; *(fig: voie)* road, path; **par (la)** ~ by road; **il y a 3h de** ~ it's a 3-hour ride *ou* journey; **en** ~ on the way; **mettre en** ~ to start up; se **mettre en** ~ to set off; **faire** ~ **vers** to head towards; ~ **nationale** ≈ A road *(Brit)*, ≈ state highway *(US)*; **routier, ière** a road *cpd* // *nm (camionneur)* (long-distance) lorry *(Brit) ou* truck *(US)* driver; *(restaurant)* ≈ transport café *(Brit)*, ≈ truck stop *(US)* // *nf (voiture)* touring car.

routine [Rutin] *nf* routine; **routinier, ière** a *(péj)* humdrum; addicted to routine.

rouvrir [RuvRiR] *vt, vi,* se ~ *vi* to re-open, open again.

roux, rousse [Ru, Rus] a red; *(personne)* red-haired // *nm/f* redhead.

royal, e, aux [Rwajal, -o] a royal; *(fig)* princely.

royaume [Rwajom] *nm* kingdom; *(fig)* realm; **le R~-Uni** the United Kingdom.

royauté [Rwajote] *nf (dignité)* kingship; *(régime)* monarchy.

ruban [Rybɑ̃] *nm (gén)* ribbon; *(d'acier)* strip; ~ **adhésif** adhesive tape.

rubéole [Rybeɔl] *nf* German measles *sg*, rubella.

rubis [Rybi] *nm* ruby.

rubrique [RybRik] *nf (titre, catégorie)* heading; *(PRESSE: article)* column.

ruche [Ryʃ] *nf* hive.

rude [Ryd] a *(barbe, toile)* rough; *(métier, tâche)* hard, tough; *(climat)* severe, harsh; *(bourru)* harsh, rough; *(fruste)* rugged, tough; *(fam)* jolly good; ~**ment** ad; *(fam: très)* terribly; *(: beaucoup)* terribly hard.

rudimentaire [Rydimɑ̃tɛR] a rudimentary, basic.

rudoyer [Rydwaje] *vt* to treat harshly.

rue [Ry] *nf* street.

ruée [Rye] *nf* rush.

ruelle [Ryɛl] *nf* alley(-way).

ruer [Rye] *vi (cheval)* to kick out; se ~ *vi*: se ~ **sur** to pounce on; se ~ **vers/ dans/hors de** to rush *ou* dash towards/into/out of.

rugby [Rygbi] *nm* Rugby (football).

rugir [RyʒiR] *vi* to roar.

rugueux, euse [Rygø, -øz] a rough.

ruine [Ruin] *nf* ruin; ~**s** *nfpl* ruins.

ruiner [Ruine] *vt* to ruin.

ruisseau, x [Ruiso] *nm* stream, brook.

ruisseler [Ruisle] *vi* to stream.

rumeur [RymœR] *nf (bruit confus)* rumbling; hubbub *g*; murmur(ing); *(nouvelle)* rumour.

ruminer [Rymine] *vt (herbe)* to ruminate; *(fig)* to ruminate on *ou* over, chew over.

rupture [RyptyR] *nf (de câble, digue)* breaking; *(de tendon)* rupture, tearing; *(de négociations etc)* breakdown; *(de contrat)* breach; *(séparation, désunion)* break-up, split.

rural, e, aux [RyRal, -o] a rural, country *cpd*.

ruse [ʀyz] *nf*: la ~ cunning, craftiness; trickery; **une** ~ a trick, a ruse; **rusé, e** *a* cunning, crafty.

russe [ʀys] *a, nm, nf* Russian.

Russie [ʀysi] *nf*: la ~ Russia.

rustique [ʀystik] *a* rustic.

rustre [ʀystʀ(ə)] *nm* boor.

rutilant, e [ʀytilɑ̃, -ɑ̃t] *a* gleaming.

rythme [ʀitm(ə)] *nm* rhythm; (*vitesse*) rate; (: *de la vie*) pace, tempo.

S

s' [s] *pronom voir* **se**.

sa [sa] *dét voir* **son**.

S.A. *sigle voir* **société**.

sable [sɑbl(ə)] *nm* sand; ~**s mouvants** quicksand(s).

sablé [sɑble] *nm* shortbread biscuit.

sabler [sɑble] *vt* to sand; (*contre le verglas*) to grit; ~ **le champagne** to drink champagne.

sablier [sɑblije] *nm* hourglass; (*de cuisine*) egg timer.

sablonneux, euse [sɑblɔnø, -øz] *a* sandy.

saborder [sabɔʀde] *vt* (*navire*) to scuttle; (*fig*) to wind up, shut down.

sabot [sabo] *nm* clog; (*de cheval, bœuf*) hoof; ~ **de frein** brake shoe.

saboter [sabɔte] *vt* to sabotage.

sac [sak] *nm* bag; (*à charbon etc*) sack; **mettre à** ~ to sack; ~ **à provisions/de voyage** shopping/travelling bag; ~ **de couchage** sleeping bag; ~ **à dos** rucksack; ~ **à main** handbag.

saccade [sakad] *nf* jerk.

saccager [sakaʒe] *vt* (*piller*) to sack; (*dévaster*) to create havoc in.

saccharine [sakaʀin] *nf* saccharin(e).

sacerdoce [sasɛʀdɔs] *nm* priesthood; (*fig*) calling, vocation.

sache *etc vb voir* **savoir**.

sachet [saʃɛ] *nm* (small) bag; (*de lavande, poudre, shampooing*) sachet; ~ **de thé** tea bag.

sacoche [sakɔʃ] *nf* (*gén*) bag; (*de bicyclette*) saddlebag.

sacre [sakʀ(ə)] *nm* coronation; consecration.

sacré, e [sakʀe] *a* sacred; (*fam: satané*) blasted; (*: fameux*): **un** ~ ... a heck of a ...

sacrement [sakʀəmɑ̃] *nm* sacrament.

sacrifice [sakʀifis] *nm* sacrifice.

sacrifier [sakʀifje] *vt* to sacrifice; ~ **à** *vt* to conform to.

sacristie [sakʀisti] *nf* sacristy; (*culte protestant*) vestry.

sadique [sadik] *a* sadistic.

sage [saʒ] *a* wise; (*enfant*) good // *nm* wise man; sage.

sage-femme [saʒfam] *nf* midwife (*pl* wives).

sagesse [saʒɛs] *nf* wisdom.

Sagittaire [saʒitɛʀ] *nm*: le ~ Sagittarius.

Sahara [saaʀa] *nm*: le ~ the Sahara (desert).

saignant, e [sɛɲɑ̃, -ɑ̃t] *a* (*viande*) rare.

saignée [seɲe] *nf* (*fig*) heavy losses *pl*.

saigner [seɲe] *vi* to bleed // *vt* to bleed; (*animal*) to kill (by bleeding); ~ **du nez** to have a nosebleed.

saillie [saji] *nf* (*sur un mur etc*) projection; (*trait d'esprit*) witticism.

saillir [sajiʀ] *vi* to project, stick out; (*veine, muscle*) to bulge.

sain, e [sɛ̃, sɛn] *a* healthy; (*lectures*) wholesome; ~ **et sauf** safe and sound, unharmed; ~ **d'esprit** sound in mind, sane.

saindoux [sɛ̃du] *nm* lard.

saint, e [sɛ̃, sɛ̃t] *a* holy; (*fig*) saintly // *nm/f* saint; le **S**~ **Esprit** the Holy Spirit *ou* Ghost; la **S**~**e Vierge** the Blessed Virgin; la **S**~**Sylvestre** New Year's Eve; **sainteté** *nf* holiness.

sais *etc vb voir* **savoir**.

saisie [sezi] *nf* seizure; ~ (**de données**) (data) capture.

saisir [seziʀ] *vt* to take hold of, grab

(fig: occasion) to seize; *(comprendre)* to grasp; *(entendre)* to get, catch; *(données)* to capture; *(suj: émotions)* to take hold of, come over; *(CULIN)* to fry quickly; *(fig: biens, publication)* to seize; *(: juridiction)*: ~ **un tribunal d'une affaire** to submit *ou* refer a case to a court; **se** ~ **de** *vt* to seize; **saisissant, e** *a* startling, striking.

saison [sɛzɔ̃] *nf* season; **morte** ~ slack season; **saisonnier, ière** *a* seasonal.

sait *vb voir* **savoir**.

salade [salad] *nf* *(BOT)* lettuce *etc*; *(CULIN)* (green) salad; *(fam)* tangle, muddle; ~ **de fruits** fruit salad; **saladier** *nm* (salad) bowl.

salaire [salɛʀ] *nm* *(annuel, mensuel)* salary; *(hebdomadaire, journalier)* pay, wages *pl*; *(fig)* reward; ~ **de base** basic salary *(ou* wage); ~ **minimum interprofessionnel de croissance (SMIC)** index-linked guaranteed minimum wage.

salarié, e [salaʀje] *nm/f* salaried employee; wage-earner.

salaud [salo] *nm* *(fam!)* sod (!), bastard (!).

sale [sal] *a* dirty, filthy.

salé, e [sale] *a* *(liquide, saveur)* salty; *(CULIN)* salted; *(fig)* spicy; steep.

saler [sale] *vt* to salt.

saleté [salte] *nf* *(état)* dirtiness; *(crasse)* dirt, filth; *(tache etc)* dirt *q*; *(fig)* dirty trick; rubbish *q*; filth *q*.

salière [saljɛʀ] *nf* saltcellar.

salin, e [salɛ̃, -in] *a* saline // *nf* saltworks *sg*; salt marsh.

salir [saliʀ] *vt* to (make) dirty; *(fig)* to soil the reputation of; **se** ~ *vi* to get dirty; **salissant, e** *a* *(tissu)* which shows the dirt; *(métier)* dirty, messy.

salle [sal] *nf* room; *(d'hôpital)* ward; *(de restaurant)* dining room; *(d'un cinéma)* auditorium; *(: public)* audience; **faire** ~ **comble** to have a full house; ~ **d'attente** waiting room; ~

de bain(s) bathroom; ~ **de classe** classroom; ~ **commune** *(d'hôpital)* ward; ~ **de concert** concert hall; ~ **de consultation** consulting room; ~ **d'eau** shower-room; ~ **d'embarquement** *(à l'aéroport)* departure lounge; ~ **de jeux** games room; playroom; ~ **à manger** dining room; ~ **d'opération** *(MÉD)* operating theatre; ~ **de séjour** living room; ~ **de spectacle** theatre; cinema; ~ **des ventes** saleroom.

salon [salɔ̃] *nm* lounge, sitting room; *(mobilier)* lounge suite; *(exposition)* exhibition, show; ~ **de thé** tearoom.

salopard [salɔpaʀ] *nm* *(fam!)* bastard (!).

salope [salɔp] *nf* *(fam!)* bitch (!).

saloperie [salɔpʀi] *nf* *(fam!)* filth *q*; dirty trick; rubbish *q*.

salopette [salɔpɛt] *nf* dungarees *pl*; *(d'ouvrier)* overall(s).

salsifis [salsifi] *nm* salsify.

salubre [salybʀ(ə)] *a* healthy, salubrious.

saluer [salɥe] *vt* *(pour dire bonjour, fig)* to greet; *(pour dire au revoir)* to take one's leave; *(MIL)* to salute.

salut [saly] *nm* *(sauvegarde)* safety; *(REL)* salvation; *(geste)* wave; *(parole)* greeting; *(MIL)* salute // *excl* *(fam)* hi (there).

salutations [salytasjɔ̃] *nfpl* greetings; **recevez mes** ~ **distinguées** *ou* **respectueuses** yours faithfully.

samedi [samdi] *nm* Saturday.

SAMU [samy] *sigle m* (= *service d'assistance médicale d'urgence*) ≈ ambulance (service) *(Brit)*, ≈ paramedics *pl (US)*.

sanction [sɑ̃ksjɔ̃] *nf* sanction; *(fig)* penalty; **sanctionner** *vt* *(loi, usage)* to sanction; *(punir)* to punish.

sandale [sɑ̃dal] *nf* sandal.

sandwich [sɑ̃dwitʃ] *nm* sandwich.

sang [sɑ̃] *nm* blood; **en** ~ covered in blood; **se faire du mauvais** ~ to fret, get in a state.

sang-froid [sɑ̃fʀwa] *nm* calm, sangfroid; **de** ~ in cold blood.

sanglant, e [sɑ̃glɑ̃, -ɑ̃t] *a* bloody, covered in blood; (*combat*) bloody.

sangle [sɑ̃gl(ə)] *nf* strap.

sanglier [sɑ̃glije] *nm* (wild) boar.

sanglot [sɑ̃glo] *nm* sob.

sangloter [sɑ̃glɔte] *vi* to sob.

sangsue [sɑ̃sy] *nf* leech.

sanguin, e [sɑ̃gɛ̃, -in] *a* blood *cpd*; (*fig*) fiery.

sanguinaire [sɑ̃ginɛʀ] *a* blood-thirsty; bloody.

sanisette [sanizɛt] *nf* (automatic) public toilet.

sanitaire [sanitɛʀ] *a* health *cpd*; **~s** *nmpl* bathroom *sg*.

sans [sɑ̃] *prép* without; **~ qu'il se aperçoive** without him *ou* his noticing; **~-abri** *nmpl* homeless; **~-façon** *a inv* fuss-free; free and easy; **~-gêne** *a inv* inconsiderate; **~-logis** *nmpl* homeless.

santé [sɑ̃te] *nf* health; **en bonne ~** in good health; **boire à la ~ de qn** to drink (to) sb's health; **'à la ~ de'** 'here's to'; **à ta/votre ~!** cheers!

saoudien, ne [saudjɛ̃, -jɛn] *a* Saudi Arabian // *nm/f*: **S~(ne)** Saudi Arabian.

saoul, e [su, sul] *a* = **soûl, e**.

saper [sape] *vt* to undermine, sap.

sapeur [sapœʀ] *nm* sapper; **~-pompier** *nm* fireman.

saphir [safiʀ] *nm* sapphire.

sapin [sapɛ̃] *nm* fir (tree); (*bois*) fir; **~ de Noël** Christmas tree.

sarcastique [saʀkastik] *a* sarcastic.

sarcler [saʀkle] *vt* to weed.

Sardaigne [saʀdɛɲ] *nf*: **la ~** Sardinia.

sardine [saʀdin] *nf* sardine.

S.A.R.L. *sigle voir* **société**.

sas [sas] *nm* (*de sous-marin, d'engin spatial*) airlock; (*d'écluse*) lock.

satané, e [satane] *a* confounded.

satellite [satelit] *nm* satellite.

satin [satɛ̃] *nm* satin.

satire [satiʀ] *nf* satire; **satirique** *a* satirical.

satisfaction [satisfaksjɔ̃] *nf* satisfaction.

satisfaire [satisfɛʀ] *vt* to satisfy; **~**

à *vt* (*engagement*) to fulfil; (*revendications, conditions*) to satisfy, meet; to comply with; **satisfaisant, e** *a* satisfactory; (*qui fait plaisir*) satisfying; **satisfait, e** *a* satisfied; **satisfait de** happy *ou* satisfied with.

saturer [satyʀe] *vt* to saturate.

sauce [sos] *nf* sauce; (*avec un rôti*) gravy; **saucière** *nf* sauceboat.

saucisse [sosis] *nf* sausage.

saucisson [sosisɔ̃] *nm* (slicing) sausage.

sauf [sof] *prép* except; **~ si** (*à moins que*) unless; **~ erreur** if I'm not mistaken; **~ avis contraire** unless you hear to the contrary.

sauf, sauve [sof, sov] *a* unharmed, unhurt; (*fig: honneur*) intact, saved; **laisser la vie sauve à qn** to spare sb's life.

sauge [soʒ] *nf* sage.

saugrenu, e [sogʀəny] *a* preposterous.

saule [sol] *nm* willow (tree).

saumon [somɔ̃] *nm* salmon *inv*.

saumure [somyʀ] *nf* brine.

sauna [sona] *nm* sauna.

saupoudrer [sopudʀe] *vt*: **~ qch de** to sprinkle sth with.

saur [sɔʀ] *am*: **hareng ~** smoked *ou* red herring, kipper.

saurai *etc vb voir* **savoir**.

saut [so] *nm* jump; (*discipline sportive*) jumping; **faire un ~ chez qn** to pop over to sb's (place); **au ~ du lit** on getting out of bed; **~ en hauteur/longueur** high/long jump; **~ à la corde** skipping; **~ à la perche** pole vaulting; **~ périlleux** somersault.

saute [sot] *nf* sudden change.

saute-mouton [sotmutɔ̃] *nm*: **jouer à ~** to play leapfrog.

sauter [sote] *vi* to jump, leap; (*exploser*) to blow up, explode; (: *fusibles*) to blow; (*se rompre*) to snap, burst; (*se détacher*) to pop off) // *vt* to jump (over), leap (over); (*fig: omettre*) to skip, miss (out); **faire ~** to blow up; to burst open;

(CULIN) to sauté; ~ **au cou de qn** to fly into sb's arms.

sauterelle [sotʀɛl] *nf* grasshopper.

sautiller [sotije] *vi* to hop; to skip.

sautoir [sotwaʀ] *nm*: ~ **(de perles)** string of pearls.

sauvage [sovaʒ] *a* (*gén*) wild; (*peuplade*) savage; (*farouche*) unsociable; (*barbare*) wild, savage; (*non officiel*) unauthorized, unofficial // *nm/f* savage; (*timide*) unsociable type.

sauve [sov] *af voir* **sauf**.

sauvegarde [sovgaʀd(ə)] *nf* safeguard; **sauvegarder** *vt* to safeguard; (*INFORM: enregistrer*) to save; (*: copier*) to back up.

sauve-qui-peut [sovkipø] *excl* run for your life!

sauver [sove] *vt* to save; (*porter secours à*) to rescue; (*récupérer*) to salvage, rescue; **se** ~ *vi* (*s'enfuir*) to run away; (*fam: partir*) to be off; **sauvetage** *nm* rescue; **sauveteur** *nm* rescuer; **sauvette**: **à la sauvette** *ad* (*vendre*) without authorization; (*se marier etc*) hastily, hurriedly; **sauveur** *nm* saviour (*Brit*), savior (*US*).

savais etc *vb voir* **savoir**.

savamment [savamā] *ad* (*avec érudition*) learnedly; (*habilement*) skillfully, cleverly.

savant, e [savā, -āt] *a* scholarly, learned; (*calé*) clever // *nm* scientist.

saveur [savœʀ] *nf* flavour, (*fig*) savour.

savoir [savwaʀ] *vt* to know; (*être capable de*): **il sait nager** he can swim // *nm* knowledge; **se** ~ *vi* (*être connu*) to be known; **à** ~ *a* that is, namely; **faire** ~ **qch à qn** to let sb know sth; **pas que je sache** not as far as I know.

savon [savɔ̃] *nm* (*produit*) soap; (*morceau*) bar of soap; (*fam*): **passer un** ~ **à qn** to give sb a good dressing-down; **savonnette** *nf* bar of soap; **savonneux, euse** *a* soapy.

savons *vb voir* **savoir**.

savourer [savure] *vt* to savour.

savoureux, euse [savuʀø, -øz] *a* tasty; (*fig*) spicy, juicy.

saxo(phone) [saksɔ(fɔn)] *nm* sax(o-phone).

scabreux, euse [skabʀø, -øz] *a* risky; (*indécent*) improper, shocking.

scandale [skɑ̃dal] *nm* scandal; (*tapage*): **faire du** ~ to make a scene, create a disturbance; **faire** ~ to scandalize people; **scandaleux, euse** *a* scandalous, outrageous.

scandinave [skɑ̃dinav] *a*, *nm/f* Scandinavian.

Scandinavie [skɑ̃dinavi] *nf* Scandinavia.

scaphandre [skafɑ̃dʀ(ə)] *nm* (*de plongeur*) diving suit; (*de cosmonaute*) space-suit.

scarabée [skaʀabe] *nm* beetle.

sceau, x [so] *nm* seal; (*fig*) stamp, mark.

scélérat, e [selɛʀa, -at] *nm/f* villain.

sceller [sele] *vt* to seal.

scénario [senaʀjo] *nm* (*CINÉMA*) scenario; script; (*fig*) scenario.

scène [sɛn] *nf* (*gén*) scene; (*estrade, fig: théâtre*) stage; **entrer en** ~ to come on stage; **mettre en** ~ (*THÉÂTRE*) to stage; (*CINÉMA*) to direct; (*fig*) to present, introduce.

sceptique [sɛptik] *a* sceptical.

schéma [ʃema] *nm* (*diagramme*) diagram, sketch; (*fig*) outline; pattern; **schématique** *a* diagrammatic(al), schematic; (*fig*) oversimplified.

sciatique [sjatik] *nf* sciatica.

scie [si] *nf* saw; ~ **à découper** fretsaw; ~ **à métaux** hacksaw.

sciemment [sjamɑ̃] *ad* knowingly.

science [sjɑ̃s] *nf* science; (*savoir*) knowledge; (*savoir-faire*) art, skill; ~**s naturelles** (*SCOL*) natural science *sg*, biology *sg*; **scientifique** *a* scientific // *nm/f* scientist; science student.

scier [sje] *vt* to saw; (*retrancher*) to saw off; **scierie** *nf* sawmill.

scinder [sēde] *vt*, **se** ~ *vi* to split

(up).

scintiller [sɛ̃tije] *vi* to sparkle.

scission [sisjɔ̃] *nf* split.

sciure [sjyr] *nf*: ~ (de bois) sawdust.

sclérose [skleroz] *nf*: ~ en plaques multiple sclerosis.

scolaire [skɔlɛr] *a* school *cpd*; (*péj*) schoolish; **scolariser** *vt* to provide with schooling (*ou* schools); **scolarité** *nf* schooling.

scooter [skutœr] *nm* (motor) scooter.

score [skɔr] *nm* score.

scorpion [skɔrpjɔ̃] *nm* (*signe*): le S~ Scorpio.

Scotch [skɔtʃ] *nm* ® adhesive tape.

scout, e [skut] *a, nm* scout.

script [skript] *nm* printing; (*CINÉMA*) (shooting) script; **~-girl** [-gœrl] *nf* continuity girl.

scrupule [skrypyl] *nm* scruple.

scruter [skryte] *vt* to scrutinize; (*l'obscurité*) to peer into.

scrutin [skrytɛ̃] *nm* (*vote*) ballot; (*ensemble des opérations*) poll.

sculpter [skylte] *vt* to sculpt; (*suj: érosion*) to carve; **sculpteur** *nm* sculptor.

sculpture [skyltyr] *nf* sculpture; ~ sur bois wood carving.

MOT-CLÉ

se, s' [s(ə)] *pronom* **1** (*emploi réfléchi*) oneself, *m* himself, *f* herself, non humain itself; (*pl*) themselves: ~ **voir comme l'on est** to see o.s. as one is

2 (*réciproque*) one another, each other; **ils s'aiment** they love one another *ou* each other

3 (*passif*): **cela ~ répare facilement** it is easily repaired

4 (*possessif*): ~ **casser la jambe/laver les mains** to break one's leg/wash one's hands; *autres emplois pronominaux: voir le verbe en question*

séance [seɑ̃s] *nf* (*d'assemblée, ré-*créative) meeting, session; (*de tribunal*) sitting, session; (*musicale, CINÉMA, THÉÂTRE*) performance; ~ **tenante** forthwith.

seau, x [so] *nm* bucket, pail.

sec, sèche [sɛk, sɛʃ] *a* dry; (*raisins, figues*) dried; (*cœur, personne: insensible*) hard, cold // *nm*: **tenir au** ~ to keep in a dry place // *ad* hard; **je le bois** ~ I drink it straight *ou* neat; **à** ~ a dried up

sécateur [sekatœr] *nm* secateurs *pl* (*Brit*), shears *pl*.

sèche [sɛʃ] *af voir* **sec**.

sèche-cheveux [sɛʃʃəvø] *nm inv* hair-drier.

sécher [seʃe] *vt* to dry; (*dessécher: peau, blé*) to dry (out); (: *étang*) to dry up // *vi* to dry; to dry out; to dry up; (*fam: candidat*) to be stumped; **se** ~ (*après le bain*) to dry o.s.

sécheresse [sɛʃrɛs] *nf* dryness; (*absence de pluie*) drought.

séchoir [seʃwar] *nm* drier.

second, e [s(ə)gɔ̃, -ɔ̃d] *a* second // *nm* (*assistant*) second in command; (*NAVIG*) first mate // *nf* second; **voyager en** ~ to travel second-class; **de ~e main** second-hand; **secondaire** *a* secondary; **seconder** *vt* to assist.

secouer [s(ə)kwe] *vt* to shake; (*passagers*) to rock; (*traumatiser*) to shake (up).

secourir [s(ə)kurir] *vt* (*aller sauver*) to (go and) rescue; (*prodiguer des soins à*) to help, assist; (*venir en aide à*) to assist, aid; **secourisme** *nm* first aid; life saving.

secours [s(ə)kur] *nm* help, aid, assistance // *nmpl* aid *sg*; **au** ~! help!; **appeler au** ~ to shout *ou* call for help; **porter** ~ **à** qn to give sb assistance, help sb; **les premiers** ~ first aid *sg*.

secousse [s(ə)kus] *nf* jolt, bump; (*électrique*) shock; (*fig: psychologique*) jolt, shock; ~ **sismique** *ou* **tellurique** earth tremor.

secret, ète [s(ə)krɛ, -ɛt] *a* secret; (*fig: renfermé*) reticent, reserved //

secret *nm* secret; (*discrétion absolue*): le ~ secrecy; au ~ in solitary confinement.

secrétaire [səkretɛr] *nm/f* secretary // *nm* (*meuble*) writing desk; ~ de direction private *ou* personal secretary; ~ d'État junior minister; **secrétariat** *nm* (*profession*) secretarial work; (*bureau*) office; (: *d'organisation internationale*) secretariat.

secteur [sɛktœr] *nm* sector; (*ADMIN*) district; (*ÉLEC*): branché sur le ~ plugged into the mains (supply).

section [sɛksjɔ̃] *nf* section; (*de parcours d'autobus*) fare stage; (*MIL*: *unité*) platoon; **sectionner** *vt* to sever.

Sécu [seky] *abr f de* **sécurité sociale.**

séculaire [sekylɛr] *a* secular; (*très vieux*) age-old.

sécuriser [sekyrize] *vt* to give a feeling of) security to.

sécurité [sekyrite] *nf* safety; security; système de ~ safety system; être en ~ to be safe; la ~ routière road safety; la ~ sociale ≈ (the) Social Security (*Brit*), ≈ Welfare (*US*).

sédition [sedisjɔ̃] *nf* insurrection; sedition.

séduction [sedyksjɔ̃] *nf* seduction; (*charme, attrait*) appeal, charm.

séduire [seduir] *vt* to charm; (*femme: abuser de*) to seduce; **séduisant, e** *a* (*femme*) seductive; (*homme, offre*) very attractive.

ségrégation [segregasjɔ̃] *nf* segregation.

seigle [sɛgl(ə)] *nm* rye.

seigneur [sɛɲœr] *nm* lord.

sein [sɛ̃] *nm* breast; (*entrailles*) womb; au ~ de *prép* (*équipe, institution*) within; (*flots, bonheur*) in the midst of.

séisme [seism(ə)] *nm* earthquake.

seize [sɛz] *num* sixteen; **seizième** *num* sixteenth.

séjour [seʒur] *nm* stay; (*pièce*) living room; ~ner *vi* to stay.

sel [sɛl] *nm* salt; (*fig*) wit; spice; ~ de cuisine/de table cooking/table salt.

sélection [selɛksjɔ̃] *nf* selection; **sélectionner** *vt* to select.

self-service [sɛlfsɛrvis] *a*, *nm* self-service.

selle [sɛl] *nf* saddle; ~s *nfpl* (*MÉD*) stools; **seller** *vt* to saddle.

sellette [sɛlɛt] *nf*: être sur la ~ to be on the carpet.

selon [səlɔ̃] *prép* according to; (*en se conformant à*) in accordance with; ~ que according to whether; ~ moi as I see it.

semaine [səmɛn] *nf* week; en ~ during the week, on weekdays.

semblable [sɑ̃blabl(ə)] *a* similar; (*de ce genre*) of ~s mésaventures such mishaps // *nm* fellow creature *ou* man; ~ à similar to, like.

semblant [sɑ̃blɑ̃] *nm*: un ~ de vérité a semblance of truth; faire ~ (de faire) to pretend (to do).

sembler [sɑ̃ble] *vb avec attribut* to seem // *vb impersonnel*: il semble (bien) que/inutile de il (really) seems *ou* appears that/useless to; il me semble que it seems to me that; I think (that); comme bon lui semble as he sees fit.

semelle [səmɛl] *nf* sole; (*intérieure*) insole, inner sole.

semence [səmɑ̃s] *nf* (*graine*) seed.

semer [səme] *vt* to sow; (*fig: éparpiller*) to scatter; (: *confusion*) to spread; (: *poursuivants*) to lose, shake off; **semé de** (*difficultés*) riddled with.

semestre [səmɛstr(ə)] *nm* half-year; (*SCOL*) semester.

séminaire [seminɛr] *nm* seminar.

semi-remorque [səmirəmɔrk(ə)] *nm* articulated lorry (*Brit*), semi (trailer) (*US*).

semonce [səmɔ̃s] *nf*: un coup de ~ a shot across the bows.

semoule [səmul] *nf* semolina.

sempiternel, le [sɛ̃pitɛrnɛl] *a* eternal, never-ending.

sénat [sena] nm Senate; **sénateur** nm Senator.

sens [sãs] nm (PHYSIOL, instinct) sense; (signification) meaning, sense; (direction) direction; **à mon ~** to my mind; **reprendre ses ~** to regain consciousness; **dans le ~ des aiguilles d'une montre** clockwise; **~ commun** common sense; **~ dessus dessous** upside down; **~ interdit**, **~ unique** one-way street.

sensass [sãsas] a (fam) fantastic.

sensation [sãsasjɔ̃] nf sensation; **à ~** (péj) sensational.

sensé, e [sãse] a sensible.

sensibiliser [sãsibilize] vt: **~ qn à** to make sb sensitive to.

sensibilité [sãsibilite] nf sensitivity.

sensible [sãsibl(ə)] a sensitive; (aux sens) perceptible; (appréciable: différence, progrès) noticeable, appreciable; **~ment** ad (notablement) appreciably, noticeably; (à peu près): **ils ont ~ment le même poids** they weigh approximately the same; **~rie** nf sentimentality; squeamishness.

sensuel, le [sãsɥɛl] a sensual; sensuous.

sentence [sãtãs] nf (jugement) sentence; (adage) maxim.

sentier [sãtje] nm path.

sentiment [sãtimã] nm feeling; **recevez mes ~s respectueux** yours faithfully; **sentimental, e, aux** a sentimental; (vie, aventure) love cpd.

sentinelle [sãtinɛl] nf sentry.

sentir [sãtir] vt (par l'odorat) to smell; (par le goût) to taste; (au toucher, fig) to feel; (répandre une odeur de) to smell of; (: ressemblance) to smell like; (avoir la saveur de) to taste of; to taste like // vi to smell; **~ mauvais** to smell bad; **se ~ bien** to feel good; **se ~ mal** (être indisposé) to feel unwell ou ill; **se ~ le courage/la force de faire** to feel brave/strong enough to do; **il ne peut pas le ~** (fam) he can't

stand him.

séparation [separasjɔ̃] nf separation; (cloison) division, partition; **~ de corps** legal separation.

séparé, e [separe] a (appartements, pouvoirs) separate; (époux) separated; **~ment** ad separately.

séparer [separe] vt (gén) to separate; (suj: divergences etc) to divide; to drive apart; (: différences, obstacles) to stand between; (détacher): **~ qch de** to pull sth (off) from; (diviser): **~ qch** to divide; **~ une pièce en deux** to divide a room into two; **se ~** vi (époux, amis, adversaires) to separate, part; (se diviser: route, tige etc) to divide; (se détacher) to split off (from); to come off; **se ~ de** (époux) to separate ou part from; (employé, objet personnel) to part with.

sept [sɛt] num seven.

septembre [sɛptãbr(ə)] nm September.

septentrional, e, aux [sɛptãtrijɔnal, -o] a northern.

septicémie [sɛptisemi] nf blood poisoning, septicaemia.

septième [sɛtjɛm] num seventh.

septique [sɛptik] a: **fosse ~** septic tank.

sépulture [sepyltyr] nf burial; burial place, grave.

séquelles [sekɛl] nfpl after-effects; (fig) aftermath sg; consequences.

séquestrer [sekɛstre] vt (personne) to confine illegally; (biens) to impound.

serai etc vb voir **être**.

serein, e [sərɛ̃, -ɛn] a serene; (jugement) dispassionate.

serez vb voir **être**.

sergent [sɛrʒã] nm sergeant.

série [seri] nf (de questions, d'accidents) series inv; (de clés, casseroles, outils) set; (catégorie: SPORT) rank; class; **en ~** in quick succession; (COMM) mass cpd; **de ~** a standard; **hors ~** (COMM) custom-built; (*fig*) outstanding.

sérieusement [serjøzmɑ̃] *ad* seriously; reliably; responsibly.

sérieux, euse [serjø, -øz] *a* serious; (*élève, employé*) reliable, responsible; (*client, maison*) reliable, dependable // *nm* seriousness; reliability; **garder son ~** to keep a straight face; **prendre qch/qn au ~** to take sth/sb seriously.

serin [sərɛ̃] *nm* canary.

seringue [sərɛ̃g] *nf* syringe.

serions *vb voir* **être**.

serment [sermɑ̃] *nm* (*juré*) oath; (*promesse*) pledge, vow.

sermon [sermɔ̃] *nm* sermon.

serpent [serpɑ̃] *nm* snake; **~ à sonnettes** rattlesnake.

serpenter [serpɑ̃te] *vi* to wind.

serpentin [serpɑ̃tɛ̃] *nm* (*tube*) coil; (*ruban*) streamer.

serpillière [serpijɛr] *nf* floorcloth.

serre [ser] *nf* (*AGR*) greenhouse; **~s** *nfpl* (*griffes*) claws, talons.

serré, e [sere] *a* (*réseau*) dense; (*écriture*) close; (*habits*) tight; (*fig: lutte, match*) tight, close-fought; (*passagers etc*) (tightly) packed.

serrer [sere] *vt* (*tenir*) to grip *ou* hold tight; (*comprimer, coincer*) to squeeze; (*poings, mâchoires*) to clench; (*suj: vêtement*) to be too tight for; (*à fit tightly*); (*rapprocher*) to close up, move closer together; (*ceinture, nœud, frein, vis*) to tighten // *vi*: **~ à droite** to keep *ou* get over to the right; **se ~** *vi* (*se rapprocher*) to squeeze up; **se ~ contre qn** to huddle up to sb; **~ la main à qn** to shake sb's hand; **~ qn dans ses bras** to hug sb, clasp sb in one's arms.

serrure [seryr] *nf* lock.

serrurier [seryrje] *nm* locksmith.

sert *etc vb voir* **servir**.

sertir [sertir] *vt* (*pierre*) to set.

servante [servɑ̃t] *nf* (maid)servant.

serveur, euse [servœr, -øz] *nm/f* waiter/waitress.

serviable [servjabl(ə)] *a* obliging, willing to help.

service [servis] *nm* (*gén*) service; (*série de repas*): **premier ~** first sitting; (*assortiment de vaisselle*) set, service; (*bureau: de la vente etc*) department, section; (*travail*): **pendant le ~** on duty; **~s** *nmpl* (*travail, ÉCON*) services; **faire le ~** to serve; **rendre ~ à** to help; **rendre un ~ à qn** to do sb a favour; **mettre en ~** to put into service *ou* operation; **hors ~** out of order; **après vente** after-sales service; **~ militaire** military service; **~ d'ordre** police (*ou* stewards) in charge of maintaining order; **~s secrets** secret service *sg*.

serviette [servjɛt] *nf* (*de table*) (table) napkin, serviette; (*de toilette*) towel; (*porte-documents*) briefcase; **~ hygiénique** sanitary towel.

servir [servir] *vt* (*gén*) to serve; (*au restaurant*) to wait on; (*au magasin*) to serve, attend to; (*fig: aider*): **qn** to aid sb; to serve sb's interests; (*COMM: rente*) to pay // *vi* (*TENNIS*) to serve; (*CARTES*) to deal; **vous êtes servi?** are you being served?; **se ~** *vi* (*prendre d'un plat*) to help o.s.; **se ~ de** (*plat*) to help o.s. to; (*voiture, outil, relations*) to use; **~ à qn** (*diplôme, livre*) to be of use to sb; **~ à qch/faire** (*outil etc*) to be used for sth/doing; **à quoi cela sert-il (de faire)?** what's the use (of doing)?; **cela ne sert à rien** it's no use; **~ (à qn)** **de** to serve as (for sb); **~ à dîner (à qn)** to serve dinner (to sb).

serviteur [servitœr] *nm* servant.

servitude [servityd] *nf* servitude; (*fig*) constraint.

ses [se] *dét voir* **son**.

seuil [sœj] *nm* doorstep; (*fig*) threshold.

seul, e [sœl] *a* (*sans compagnie*) alone; (*avec nuance affective: isolé*) lonely; (*unique*): **un ~ livre** only one book, a single book; **le ~ livre** the only book; **~ ce livre, ce livre**

~ this book alone, only this book // *ad* (*vivre*) alone, on one's own; **parler tout** ~ to talk to oneself; **faire qch (tout)** ~ to do sth (all) on one's own *ou* (all) by oneself // *nm, nf*: **il en reste un(e) ~(e)** there's only one left; **à lui (tout)** ~ single-handed, on his own.

seulement [sœlmɑ̃] *ad* only; **non ~ ... mais aussi *ou* encore** not only ... but also.

sève [sɛv] *nf* sap.

sévère [sevɛʀ] *a* severe.

sévices [sevis] *nmpl* (physical) cruelty *q*, ill treatment *q*.

sévir [seviʀ] *vi* (*punir*) to use harsh measures, crack down; (*suj: fléau*) to rage, be rampant.

sevrer [səvʀe] *vt* (*enfant etc*) to wean.

sexe [sɛks(ə)] *nm* sex; (*organe mâle*) member.

sexuel, le [sɛksɥɛl] *a* sexual.

seyant, e [sɛjɑ̃, -ɑ̃t] *a* becoming.

shampooing [ʃɑ̃pwɛ̃] *nm* shampoo; **se faire un** ~ to shampoo one's hair.

short [ʃɔʀt] *nm* (pair of) shorts *pl*.

MOT-CLÉ

si [si] ◆ *nm* (*MUS*) B; (*en chantant la gamme*) ti
◆ *ad* **1** (*oui*) yes
2 (*tellement*) so; ~ **gentil/rapidement** so kind/fast; (*tant et*) ~ **bien que** so much so that; ~ **rapide qu'il soit** however fast he may be
◆ *cj* if; ~ **tu veux** if you want; **je me demande** ~ I wonder if *ou* whether; ~ **seulement** if only.

Sicile [sisil] *nf*: **la** ~ Sicily.

SIDA [sida] *sigle m* (= *syndrome immuno-déficitaire acquis*) AIDS *sg*.

sidéré, e [sideʀe] *a* staggered.

sidérurgie [sideʀyʀʒi] *nf* steel industry.

siècle [sjɛkl(ə)] *nm* century; (*époque*) age.

siège [sjɛʒ] *nm* seat; (*d'entreprise*) head office; (*d'organisation*) headquarters *pl*; (*MIL*) siege; ~ **social** registered office.

siéger [sjeʒe] *vi* to sit.

sien, ne [sjɛ̃, sjɛn] *pronom*: **le(la) ~(ne), les ~s(~nes)** his; hers; its; **faire des ~nes** (*fam*) to be up to one's (usual) tricks; **les ~s** (*sa famille*) one's family.

sieste [sjɛst(ə)] *nf* (afternoon) snooze *ou* nap, siesta; **faire la** ~ to have a snooze *ou* nap.

sieur [sjœʀ] *nm*: **le ~ Thomas** Master Thomas.

sifflement [sifləmɑ̃] *nm* whistle, whistling *q*; wheezing *q*; hissing *q*.

siffler [sifle] *vi* (*gén*) to whistle; (*en respirant*) to wheeze; (*serpent, vapeur*) to hiss // *vt* (*chanson*) to whistle; (*chien etc*) to whistle for; (*fille*) to whistle at; (*pièce, orateur*) to hiss, boo; (*faute*) to blow one's whistle at; (*fin du match, départ*) to blow one's whistle for; (*fam: verre*) to guzzle.

sifflet [siflɛ] *nm* whistle; **coup de** ~ whistle.

siffloter [siflɔte] *vi, vt* to whistle.

sigle [sigl(ə)] *nm* acronym.

signal, aux [siɲal, -o] *nm* (*signe convenu, appareil*) signal; (*indice, écriteau*) sign; **donner le** ~ **de** to give the signal for; ~ **d'alarme** alarm signal; **signaux (lumineux)** (*AUTO*) traffic signals.

signalement [siɲalmɑ̃] *nm* description, particulars *pl*.

signaler [siɲale] *vt* to indicate; to announce; to report; (*faire remarquer*): ~ **qch à qn/(à qn) que** to point out sth to sb/(to sb) that; **se** ~ **(par)** to distinguish o.s. (by).

signaliser [siɲalize] *vt* to put up roadsigns on; to put signals on.

signature [siɲatyʀ] *nf* signature (*action*), signing.

signe [siɲ] *nm* sign; (*TYPO*) mark; **faire un** ~ **de la main** to give a sign with one's hand; **faire** ~ **à qn** (*fig*) to get in touch with sb; **faire** ~

à qn d'entrer to motion (to) sb to come in.

signer [siɲe] *vt* to sign; **se** ~ *vi* to cross o.s.

signet [siɲɛ] *nm* bookmark.

significatif, ive [siɲifikatif, -iv] *a* significant.

signification [siɲifikasjɔ̃] *nf* meaning.

signifier [siɲifje] *vt* (*vouloir dire*) to mean; (*faire connaître*): ~ **qch** (à **qn**) to make sth known (to sb); (*JUR*): ~ **qch à qn** to serve notice of sth on sb.

silence [silɑ̃s] *nm* silence; (*MUS*) rest; **garder le** ~ to keep silent, say nothing; **passer sous** ~ to pass over (in silence); **silencieux, euse** *a* quiet, silent // *nm* silencer.

silex [silɛks] *nm* flint.

silhouette [silwɛt] *nf* outline, silhouette; (*lignes, contour*) outline; (*figure*) figure.

silicium [silisjɔm] *nm* silicon; **plaquette de** ~ silicon chip.

sillage [sijaʒ] *nm* wake; (*fig*) trail.

sillon [sijɔ̃] *nm* furrow; (*de disque*) groove; **sillonner** *vt* to criss-cross.

simagrées [simagʀe] *nfpl* fuss *sg*; airs and graces.

similaire [similɛʀ] *a* similar; **similicuir** *nm* imitation leather; **similitude** *nf* similarity.

simple [sɛ̃pl(ə)] *a* (*gén*) simple; (*non multiple*) single; ~**s** *nmpl* (*MÉD*) medicinal plants; ~ **messieurs** (*TENNIS*) men's singles *sg*; **un** ~ **particulier** an ordinary citizen; ~ **d'esprit** *nm/f* simpleton; ~ **soldat** private.

simulacre [simylakʀ(ə)] *nm* (*péj*): **un** ~ **de** a pretence of.

simuler [simyle] *vt* to sham, simulate.

simultané, e [simyltane] *a* simultaneous.

sincère [sɛ̃sɛʀ] *a* sincere, genuine; **sincérité** *nf* sincerity.

sine qua non [sinekwanɔn] *a*: **condition** ~ indispensable condition.

singe [sɛ̃ʒ] *nm* monkey; (*de grande taille*) ape.

singer [sɛ̃ʒe] *vt* to ape, mimic.

singeries [sɛ̃ʒʀi] *nfpl* antics; (*simagrées*) airs and graces.

singulariser [sɛ̃gylaʀize] *vt* to mark out; **se** ~ *vi* to call attention to o.s.

singularité [sɛ̃gylaʀite] *nf* peculiarity.

singulier, ière [sɛ̃gylje, -jɛʀ] *a* remarkable, singular // *nm* singular.

sinistre [sinistʀ(ə)] *a* sinister // *nm* (*incendie*) blaze; (*catastrophe*) disaster; (*ASSURANCES*) damage (*giving rise to a claim*); **sinistré, e** *a* disaster-stricken // *nm/f* disaster victim.

sinon [sinɔ̃] *cj* (*autrement*, *sans quoi*) otherwise, or else; (*sauf*) except, other than; (*si ce n'est*) if not.

sinueux, euse [sinɥø, -øz] *a* winding; (*fig*) tortuous.

sinus [sinys] *nm* (*ANAT*) sinus; (*GÉOM*) sine; **sinusite** *nf* sinusitis.

siphon [sifɔ̃] *nm* (*tube, d'eau gazeuse*) siphon; (*d'évier etc*) U-bend.

sirène [siʀɛn] *nf* siren; ~ **d'alarme** air-raid siren; fire alarm.

sirop [siʀo] *nm* (à *diluer: de fruit etc*) syrup; (*boisson*) fruit drink; (*pharmaceutique*) syrup, mixture.

siroter [siʀote] *vt* to sip.

sis, e [si, siz] *a* located.

sismique [sismik] *a* seismic.

site [sit] *nm* (*paysage, environnement*) setting; (*d'une ville etc: emplacement*) site; ~ (*pittoresque*) beauty spot; ~**s touristiques** places of interest.

sitôt [sito] *ad*: ~ **parti** as soon as he etc had left; ~ **après** straight after; **pas de** ~ not for a long time.

situation [sitɥasjɔ̃] *nf* (*gén*) situation; (*d'un édifice, d'une ville*) situation, position; location.

situé, e [sitɥe] *a*: **bien** ~ well situated; ~ à situated at.

situer [sitɥe] *vt* to site, situate; (*en pensée*) to set, place; **se** ~ *vi*: **se** ~ **à/près de** to be situated at/near.

six [sis] *num* six; **sixième** *num* sixth.

ski [ski] nm (objet) ski; (sport) skiing; **faire du ~** to ski; **~ de fond** cross-country skiing; **~ nautique** water-skiing; **~ de piste** downhill skiing; **~ de randonnée** cross-country skiing; **skier** vi to ski; **skieur, euse** nm/f skier.

slip [slip] nm (sous-vêtement) pants pl, briefs pl; (de bain: d'homme) trunks pl; (: du bikini) (bikini) briefs pl.

slogan [slɔgɑ̃] nm slogan.

S.M.I.C. [smik] sigle m voir **salaire**.

smoking [smɔkiŋ] nm dinner ou evening suit.

S.N.C.F. sigle f (= société nationale des chemins de fer français) French railways.

snob [snɔb] a snobbish // nm/f snob.

sobre [sɔbʀ(ə)] a temperate, abstemious; (élégance, style) sober; **~ de** (gestes, compliments) sparing of.

sobriquet [sɔbʀikɛ] nm nickname.

social, e, aux [sɔsjal, -o] a social.

socialisme [sɔsjalism(ə)] nm socialism; **socialiste** nm/f socialist.

société [sɔsjete] nf society; (sportive) club; (COMM) company; **la ~ d'abondance/de consommation** the affluent/consumer society; **~ anonyme (S.A.)** ≈ limited (Brit) ou incorporated (US) company; **~ à responsabilité limitée (S.A.R.L.)** type of limited liability company (with non-negotiable shares).

sociologie [sɔsjɔlɔʒi] nf sociology.

socle [sɔkl(ə)] nm (de colonne, statue) plinth, pedestal; (de lampe) base.

socquette [sɔkɛt] nf ankle sock.

sœur [sœʀ] nf sister; (religieuse) nun, sister.

soi [swa] pronom oneself; **cela va de ~** that ou it goes without saying; **~-disant** a inv so-called // ad supposedly.

soie [swa] nf silk; (de porc, sanglier: poil) bristle; **~-rie** nf (tissu) silk.

soif [swaf] nf thirst; **avoir ~** to be thirsty; **donner ~ à qn** to make sb thirsty.

soigné, e [swaɲe] a (tenue) well-groomed, neat; (travail) careful, meticulous; (fam) whopping; stiff.

soigner [swaɲe] vt (malade, maladie: suj: docteur) to treat; (suj: infirmière, mère) to nurse, look after; (blessé) to tend; (travail, détails) to take care over; (jardin, chevelure, invités) to look after.

soigneux, euse [swaɲø, -øz] a (propre) tidy, neat; (méticuleux) painstaking, careful; **~ de** careful with.

soi-même [swamɛm] pronom oneself.

soin [swɛ̃] nm (application) care; (propreté, ordre) tidiness, neatness; **~s** nmpl (à un malade, blessé) treatment sg, medical attention sg; (attentions, prévenance) care and attention sg; (hygiène) care sg; **prendre ~ de** to take care of, look after; **prendre ~ de faire** to take care to do; **les premiers ~s** first aid sg; **aux bons ~s de** c/o, care of.

soir [swaʀ] nm evening; **ce ~** this evening, tonight; **demain ~** tomorrow evening, tomorrow night.

soirée [swaʀe] nf evening; (réception) party.

soit [swa] vb voir **être** // cj (à savoir) namely; (ou): **~ ... ~ ...** either ... or // ad so be it, very well; **~ que ... ~ que ou ou que** whether ... or whether.

soixantaine [swasɑ̃tɛn] nf: **une ~** (de) sixty or so, about sixty; **avoir la ~** (âge) to be around sixty.

soixante [swasɑ̃t] num sixty; **~-dix** seventy.

soja [sɔʒa] nm soya; (graines) soya beans pl.

sol [sɔl] nm ground; (de logement) floor; (revêtement) flooring q; (territoire, AGR, GÉO) soil; (MUS) G; (: en chantant la gamme) so(h).

solaire [sɔlɛʀ] a solar, sun cpd.

soldat [sɔlda] nm soldier.

solde [sɔld(ə)] nf pay // nm (COMM)

balance; ~s nmpl ou nfpl (COMM) sale goods; sales; **en ~ at** sale price.

solder [sɔlde] vt (compte) to settle; (marchandise) to sell at sale price, sell off; **se ~ par** (fig) to end in; **article soldé (à) 10 F** item reduced to 10 F.

sole [sɔl] nf sole inv (fish).

soleil [sɔlɛj] nm sun; (lumière) sun(light); (temps ensoleillé) sun(shine); (BOT) sunflower; **il fait du ~** it's sunny; **au ~** in the sun.

solennel, le [sɔlanɛl] a solemn; ceremonial; **solennité** nf (d'une fête) solemnity.

solfège [sɔlfɛʒ] nm rudiments pl of music; (exercices) ear training q.

solidaire [sɔlidɛʀ] a (personnes) who stand together, who show solidarity; (pièces mécaniques) interdependent; **être ~ de** (collègues) to stand by; **solidarité** nf solidarity; interdependence; **par solidarité (avec)** in sympathy (with).

solide [sɔlid] a (mur, maison, meuble) solid, sturdy; (connaissances, argument) sound; (personne, estomac) robust, sturdy // nm solid.

soliste [sɔlist(ə)] nm/f soloist.

solitaire [sɔlitɛʀ] a (sans compagnie) solitary, lonely; (lieu) lonely // nm/f recluse; loner.

solitude [sɔlityd] nf loneliness; (paix) solitude.

solive [sɔliv] nf joist.

sollicitations [sɔlisitasjɔ̃] nfpl entreaties, appeals; enticements; (TECH) stress sg.

solliciter [sɔlisite] vt (personne) to appeal to; (emploi, faveur) to seek; (suj: occupations, attractions etc): ~ **qn** to appeal to sb's curiosity etc; to entice sb; to make demands on sb's time.

sollicitude [sɔlisityd] nf concern.

soluble [sɔlybl(ə)] a soluble.

solution [sɔlysjɔ̃] nf solution; ~ **de facilité** easy way out.

solvable [sɔlvabl(ə)] a solvent.

sombre [sɔ̃bʀ(ə)] a dark; (fig)

gloomy.

sombrer [sɔ̃bʀe] vi (bateau) to sink; ~ **dans** (misère, désespoir) to sink into.

sommaire [sɔmɛʀ] a (expéditif) summary // nm summary.

sommation [sɔmasjɔ̃] nf (JUR) summons sg; (avant de faire feu) warning.

somme [sɔm] nf (MATH) sum; (fig) amount; (argent) sum, amount // nm: **faire un ~** to have a (short) nap; **en ~** ad all in all; **~ toute** ad all in all.

sommeil [sɔmɛj] nm sleep; **avoir ~** to be sleepy; **sommeiller** vi to doze; (fig) to lie dormant.

sommelier [sɔməlje] nm wine waiter.

sommer [sɔme] vt: ~ **qn de faire** to command ou order sb to do; (JUR) to summon sb to do.

sommes vb voir **être**.

sommet [sɔme] nm top; (d'une montagne) summit, top; (fig: de la perfection, gloire) height.

sommier [sɔmje] nm (bed) base.

sommité [sɔmite] nf prominent person, leading light.

somnambule [sɔmnãbyl] nm/f sleepwalker.

somnifère [sɔmnifɛʀ] nm sleeping drug q (ou pill).

somnoler [sɔmnɔle] vi to doze.

somptueux, euse [sɔ̃ptɥø, -øz] a sumptuous; lavish.

son [sɔ̃], sa [sa], pl ses [se] dét (antécédent humain mâle) his; (: femelle) her; (: valeur indéfinie) one's, his/her; (: non humain) its.

son [sɔ̃] nm sound; (de blé) bran.

sondage [sɔ̃daʒ] nm: ~ **(d'opinion)** (opinion) poll.

sonde [sɔ̃d] nf (NAVIG) lead ou sounding line; (MÉD) probe; catheter; feeding tube; (TECH) borer, driller; (pour fouiller etc) probe.

sonder [sɔ̃de] vt (NAVIG) to sound; (atmosphère, plaie, bagages etc) to probe; (TECH) to bore, drill; (fig) to sound out; to probe.

songe [sɔ̃ʒ] nm dream.

songer [sɔ̃ʒe] vi: ~ à (penser à) to think of; ~ que to consider that; to think that; **songeur, euse** a pensive.

sonnant, e [sɔnɑ̃, -ɑ̃t] a: à 8 heures ~es on the stroke of 8.

sonné, e [sɔne] a (fam) cracked; il est midi ~ it's gone twelve.

sonner [sɔne] vi to ring // vt (cloche) to ring; (glas, tocsin) to sound; (portier, infirmière) to ring for; (messe) to ring the bell for; ~ faux (instrument) to sound out of tune; (rire) to ring false; ~ les heures to strike the hours.

sonnerie [sɔnri] nf (son) ringing; (sonnette) bell; (mécanisme d'horloge) striking mechanism; ~ d'alarme alarm bell.

sonnette [sɔnɛt] nf bell; ~ d'alarme alarm bell; ~ de nuit night-bell.

sono [sɔno] abr f de **sonorisation**.

sonore [sɔnɔr] a (voix) sonorous, ringing; (salle, métal) resonant; (ondes, film, signal) sound cpd.

sonorisation [sɔnɔrizasjɔ̃] nf (installations) public address system, P.A. system.

sonorité [sɔnɔrite] nf (de piano, violon) tone; (de voix, mot) sonority; (d'une salle) resonance; acoustics pl.

sont vb voir **être**.

sophistiqué, e [sɔfistike] a sophisticated.

sorbet [sɔrbɛ] nm water ice, sorbet.

sorcellerie [sɔrsɛlri] nf witchcraft q.

sorcier, ière [sɔrsje, -jɛr] nm/f sorcerer/witch ou sorceress.

sordide [sɔrdid] a sordid; squalid.

sornettes [sɔrnɛt] nfpl twaddle sg.

sort [sɔr] nm (fortune, destinée) fate; (condition, situation) lot; (magique) curse, spell; **tirer au** ~ to draw lots.

sorte [sɔrt(ə)] nf sort, kind; **de la** ~ ad in that way; **de (telle)** ~ **que, en** ~ **que** so that; so much so that;

faire en ~ **que** to see to it that.

sortie [sɔrti] nf (issue) way out, exit; (MIL) sortie; (fig: verbale) outburst; sally; (promenade) outing; (le soir: au restaurant etc) night out; (COMM: somme): ~s items of expenditure; outgoings sans sg; ~ de bain (vêtement) bathrobe; ~ de secours emergency exit.

sortilège [sɔrtilɛʒ] nm (magic) spell.

sortir [sɔrtir] vi (gén) to come out; (partir, se promener, aller au spectacle etc) to go out; (numéro gagnant) to come up // vt (gén) to take out; (produit, ouvrage, modèle) to bring out; (INFORM) to output; (: sur papier) to print out; (fam: expulser) to throw out; ~ de (gén) to leave; (endroit) to go ou (come) out of, leave; (rainure etc) to come out of; (cadre, compétence) to be outside; se ~ de (affaire, situation) to get out of; **s'en** ~ (malade) to pull through; (d'une difficulté etc) to get by.

sosie [sɔzi] nm double.

sot, sotte [so, sɔt] a silly, foolish // nm/f fool; **sottise** nf silliness, foolishness; silly ou foolish thing.

sou [su] nm: **près de ses** ~s tight-fisted; **sans le** ~ penniless.

soubresaut [subrəso] nm start; jolt.

souche [suʃ] nf (d'arbre) stump; (de carnet) counterfoil (Brit); stub; **de vieille** ~ of old stock.

souci [susi] nm (inquiétude) worry; (préoccupation) concern; (BOT) marigold; **se faire du** ~ to worry.

soucier [susje]: **se** ~ **de** vt to care about.

soucieux, euse [susjø, -øz] a concerned, worried.

soucoupe [sukup] nf saucer; ~ **volante** flying saucer.

soudain, e [sudɛ̃, -ɛn] a (douleur, mort) sudden // ad suddenly, all of a sudden.

soude [sud] nf soda.

souder [sude] vt (avec fil à souder)

to solder; (*par soudure autogène*) to weld; (*fig*) to bind together.

soudoyer [sudwaje] *vt* (*péj*) to bribe.

soudure [sudyʀ] *nf* soldering; welding; (*joint*) soldered joint; weld.

souffert, e [sufɛʀ, -ɛʀt(ə)] *pp de* **souffrir**.

souffle [sufl(ə)] *nm* (*en expirant*) breath; (*en soufflant*) puff, blow; (*respiration*) breathing; (*d'explosion, de ventilateur*) blast; (*du vent*) blowing; **être à bout de** ~ to be out of breath; **un** ~ **d'air ou de vent** a breath of air, a puff of wind.

soufflé, e [sufle] *a* (*fam*: *stupéfié*) staggered // *nm* (*CULIN*) soufflé.

souffler [sufle] *vi* (*gén*) to blow; (*haleter*) to puff (and blow) // *vt* (*feu, bougie*) to blow out; (*chasser: poussière etc*) to blow away; (*TECH: verre*) to blow; (*suj: explosion*) to destroy (with its blast); (*dire*): ~ **qch à qn** to whisper sth to sb; (*fam: voler*): ~ **qch à qn** to pinch sth from sb.

soufflet [sufle] *nm* (*instrument*) bellows *pl*; (*gifle*) slap in the face.

souffleur [sufœʀ] *nm* (*THÉÂTRE*) prompter.

souffrance [sufʀɑ̃s] *nf* suffering; **en** ~ (*marchandise*) awaiting delivery; (*affaire*) pending.

souffrant, e [sufʀɑ̃, -ɑ̃t] *a* unwell.

souffre-douleur [sufʀədulœʀ] *nm inv* butt, underdog.

souffrir [sufʀiʀ] *vi* to suffer; to be in pain // *vt* to suffer, endure; (*supporter*) to bear, stand; (*admettre: exception etc*) to allow ou admit of; ~ **de** (*maladie, froid*) to suffer from.

soufre [sufʀ(ə)] *nm* sulphur.

souhait [swe] *nm* wish; **tous nos** ~**s de** good wishes ou our best wishes for; **riche etc à** ~ as rich etc as one could wish; **à vos** ~**s!** bless you!

souhaitable [swɛtabl(ə)] *a* desirable.

souhaiter [swete] *vt* to wish for; ~ **la bonne année à qn** to wish sb a happy New Year.

souiller [suje] *vt* to dirty, soil; (*fig*) to sully, tarnish.

soûl, e [su, sul] *a* drunk // *nm*: **tout son** ~ to one's heart's content.

soulagement [sulaʒmɑ̃] *nm* relief.

soulager [sulaʒe] *vt* to relieve.

soûler [sule] *vt*: ~ **qn** to get sb drunk; (*suj: boisson*) to make sb drunk; (*fig*) to make sb's head spin ou reel; **se** ~ to get drunk.

soulever [sulve] *vt* to lift; (*vagues, poussière*) to send up; (*peuple*) to stir up (to revolt); (*enthousiasme*) to arouse; (*question, débat*) to raise; **se** ~ *vi* (*peuple*) to rise up; (*personne couchée*) to lift o.s. up; **cela me soulève le cœur** it makes me feel sick.

soulier [sulje] *nm* shoe.

souligner [suliɲe] *vt* to underline; (*fig*) to emphasize; to stress.

soumettre [sumɛtʀ(ə)] *vt* (*pays*) to subject, subjugate; (*rebelle*) to put down, subdue; ~ **qn/qch à** to subject sb/sth to; ~ **qch à qn** (*projet etc*) to submit sth to sb; **se** ~ (**à**) to submit (to).

soumis, e [sumi, -iz] *a* submissive; **revenus** ~ **à l'impôt** taxable income.

soumission [sumisjɔ̃] *nf* submission; (*docilité*) submissiveness; (*COMM*) tender.

soupape [supap] *nf* valve.

soupçon [supsɔ̃] *nm* suspicion; (*petite quantité*): **un** ~ **de** a hint ou touch of; **soupçonner** *vt* to suspect; **soupçonneux, euse** *a* suspicious.

soupe [sup] *nf* soup; ~ **au lait** *a inv* quick-tempered.

souper [supe] *vi* to have supper // *nm* supper.

soupeser [supəze] *vt* to weigh in one's hand(s); (*fig*) to weigh up.

soupière [supjɛʀ] *nf* (soup) tureen.

soupir [supiʀ] *nm* sigh; (*MUS*) crotchet rest.

soupirail, aux [supiʀaj, -o] nm (small) basement window.

soupirer [supiʀe] vi to sigh; ~ après qch to yearn for sth.

souple [supl(ə)] a supple; (fig: règlement, caractère) flexible; (: démarche, taille) lithe, supple.

source [suʀs(ə)] nf (point d'eau) spring; (d'un cours d'eau, fig) source; **de bonne ~** on good authority.

sourcil [suʀsij] nm (eye)brow.

sourciller [suʀsije] vi: **sans ~** without turning a hair ou batting an eyelid.

sourcilleux, euse [suʀsijø, -øz] a pernickety.

sourd, e [suʀ, suʀd(ə)] a deaf; (bruit, voix) muffled; (douleur) dull; (lutte) silent, hidden // nm/f deaf person.

sourdine [suʀdin] nf (MUS) mute; **en ~** ad softly, quietly.

sourd-muet, sourde-muette [suʀmyɛ, suʀdmyɛt] a deaf-and-dumb // nm/f deaf-mute.

souriant, e [suʀjɑ̃, -ɑ̃t] a cheerful.

souricière [suʀisjɛʀ] nf mousetrap; (fig) trap.

sourire [suʀiʀ] nm smile // vi to smile; ~ **à qn** to smile at sb; (fig) to appeal to sb; to smile on sb; **garder le ~** to keep smiling.

souris [suʀi] nf mouse (pl mice).

sournois, e [suʀnwa, -waz] a deceitful, underhand.

sous [su] prép (gén) under; ~ **la pluie/ le soleil** in the rain/sunshine; ~ **terre a, ad** underground; ~ **peu** ad shortly, before long.

sous-alimenté, e [suzalimɑ̃te] a undernourished.

sous-bois [subwa] nm inv undergrowth.

souscrire [suskʀiʀ]: ~ **à** vt to subscribe to.

sous-directeur, trice [sudiʀɛktœʀ, -tʀis] nm/f assistant manager/ manageress.

sous-entendre [suzɑ̃tɑ̃dʀ(ə)] vt to imply, infer; **sous-entendu, e** a implied; (LING) understood // nm innuendo, insinuation.

sous-estimer [suzɛstime] vt to under-estimate.

sous-jacent, e [suʒasɑ̃, -ɑ̃t] a underlying.

sous-louer [sulwe] vt to sublet.

sous-main [sumɛ̃] nm inv desk blotter; **en ~** ad secretly.

sous-marin, e [sumaʀɛ̃, -in] a (flore, volcan) submarine; (navigation, pêche, explosif) underwater // nm submarine.

sous-officier [suzɔfisje] nm ≈ noncommissioned officer (N.C.O.).

sous-produit [supʀɔdɥi] nm byproduct; (fig: péj) pale imitation.

soussigné, e [susiɲe] a: **je ~** I the undersigned.

sous-sol [susɔl] nm basement.

sous-titre [sutitʀ(ə)] nm subtitle.

soustraction [sustʀaksjɔ̃] nf subtraction.

soustraire [sustʀɛʀ] vt to subtract, take away; (dérober): ~ **qch à qn** to remove sth from sb; ~ **qn à** (danger) to shield sb from; **se ~ à** (autorité etc) to elude, escape from.

sous-traitant [sutʀɛtɑ̃] nm subcontractor.

sous-vêtements [suvɛtmɑ̃] nmpl underwear sg.

soutane [sutan] nf cassock, soutane.

soute [sut] nf hold.

soutènement [sutɛnmɑ̃] nm: **mur de ~** retaining wall.

souteneur [sutnœʀ] nm procurer.

soutenir [sutniʀ] vt to support; (assaut, choc) to stand up to, withstand; (intérêt, effort) to keep up; (assurer): ~ **que** to maintain that; ~ **la comparaison avec** to bear ou stand comparison with; **soutenu, e** a (efforts) sustained, unflagging; (style) elevated.

souterrain, e [sutɛʀɛ̃, -ɛn] a underground // nm underground passage.

soutien [sutjɛ̃] nm support; ~ **de famille** breadwinner.

soutien-gorge [sutjɛ̃gɔrʒ(ə)] nm bra.

soutirer [sutire] vt: ~ qch à qn to squeeze ou get sth out of sb.

souvenir [suvnir] nm (réminiscence) memory; (objet) souvenir // vb: se ~ de vt to remember; se ~ que to remember that; en ~ de in memory ou remembrance of.

souvent [suvɑ̃] ad often; peu ~ seldom, infrequently.

souverain, e [suvrɛ̃, -ɛn] a sovereign; (fig: mépris) supreme // nm/f sovereign, monarch.

soviétique [sɔvjetik] a Soviet // nm/f: S~ Soviet citizen.

soyeux, euse [swajø, øz] a silky.

soyons etc vb voir **être**.

spacieux, euse [spasjø, -øz] a spacious; roomy.

spaghettis [spageti] nmpl spaghetti sg.

sparadrap [sparadra] nm sticking plaster (Brit), bandaid ® (US).

spatial, e, aux [spasjal, -o] a (AVIAT) space cpd.

speaker, ine [spikœr, -krin] nm/f announcer.

spécial, e, aux [spesjal, -o] a special; (bizarre) peculiar; ~ement a especially, particularly; (tout exprès) specially.

spécialiser [spesjalize]: se ~ vi to specialize.

spécialiste [spesjalist(ə)] nm/f specialist.

spécialité [spesjalite] nf speciality; (SCOL) special field.

spécifier [spesifje] vt to specify, state.

spécimen [spesimɛn] nm specimen; (revue etc) specimen ou sample copy.

spectacle [spɛktakl(ə)] nm (tableau, scène) sight; (représentation) show; (industrie) show business; **spectaculaire** a spectacular.

spectateur, trice [spɛktatœr, -tris] nm/f (CINÉMA etc) member of the audience; (SPORT) spectator; (d'un

événement) onlooker, witness.

spéculer [spekyle] vi to speculate; ~ sur (COMM) to speculate in; (réfléchir) to speculate on.

spéléologie [speleɔlɔʒi] nf potholing.

sperme [spɛrm(ə)] nm semen, sperm.

sphère [sfɛr] nf sphere.

spirale [spiral] nf spiral.

spirituel, le [spirituɛl] a spiritual; (fin, piquant) witty.

spiritueux [spiritɥø] nm spirit.

splendide [splɑ̃did] a splendid; magnificent.

spontané, e [spɔ̃tane] a spontaneous.

sport [spɔr] nm sport // a inv (vêtement) casual; **faire du** ~ to do sport; ~s **d'hiver** winter sports; **sportif, ive** a (journal, association, épreuve) sports cpd; (allure, démarche) athletic; (attitude, esprit) sporting.

spot [spɔt] nm (lampe) spot(light); (annonce): ~ (**publicitaire**) commercial (break).

square [skwar] nm public garden(s).

squelette [skəlɛt] nm skeleton; **squelettique** a scrawny; (fig) skimpy.

stabiliser [stabilize] vt to stabilize; (terrain) to consolidate.

stable [stabl(ə)] a stable, steady.

stade [stad] nm (SPORT) stadium; (phase, niveau) stage.

stage [staʒ] nm training period; training course; **stagiaire** nm/f, a trainee.

stalle [stal] nf stall, box.

stand [stɑ̃d] nm (d'exposition) stand; (de foire) stall; ~ **de tir** (à la foire, SPORT) shooting range.

standard [stɑ̃dar] a inv standard // nm switchboard; **standardiste** nm/f switchboard operator.

standing [stɑ̃diŋ] nm standing; **immeuble de grand** ~ block of luxury flats (Brit), condo(minium) (US).

starter [starter] nm (AUTO) choke.

station [stɑsjɔ̃] nf station; (de bus

stop; (de villégiature) resort; (posture): la ~ debout standing, an upright posture; ~ de ski ski resort; ~ de taxis taxi rank (Brit) ou stand (US).

stationnement [stasjɔnmɑ̃] nm parking.

stationner [stasjɔne] vi to park.

station-service [stasjɔsɛrvis] nf service station.

statistique [statistik] a (science) statistics sg; (rapport, étude) statistic // a statistical.

statue [staty] nf statue.

statuer [statɥe] vi: ~ sur to rule on, give a ruling on.

statut [staty] nm status; ~s nmpl (JUR, ADMIN) statutes; **statutaire** a statutory.

Sté abr de **société**.

steak [stɛk] nm steak.

sténo... [steno] préfixe: ~(dactylo) nf shorthand typist (Brit), stenographer (US); ~(graphie) nf shorthand.

stéréo(phonique) [stereɔ(fɔnik)] a stereo(phonic).

stérile [steril] a sterile; (terre) barren; (fig) fruitless, futile.

stérilet [sterilɛ] nm coil, loop.

stériliser [sterilize] vt to sterilize.

stigmates [stigmat] nmpl scars, marks.

stimulant [stimylɑ̃] nm (fig) stimulus (pl i), incentive.

stimuler [stimyle] vt to stimulate.

stipuler [stipyle] vt to stipulate.

stock [stɔk] nm stock; ~ d'or (FINANCE) gold reserves pl; ~er vt to stock.

stop [stɔp] nm (AUTO: écriteau) stop sign; (: signal) brake-light.

stopper [stɔpe] vt to stop, halt; (COUTURE) to mend // vi to stop, halt.

store [stɔr] nm blind; (de magasin) shade, awning.

strabisme [strabism(ə)] nm squinting.

strapontin [strapɔ̃tɛ̃] nm jump ou foldaway seat.

stratégie [strateʒi] nf strategy; **stratégique** a strategic.

stressant, e [strɛsɑ̃, -ɑ̃t] a stressful.

strict, e [strikt(ə)] a strict; (tenue, décor) severe, plain; son droit le plus ~ his most basic right; le ~ nécessaire/ minimum the bare essentials/minimum.

strie [stri] nf streak.

strophe [strɔf] nf verse, stanza.

structure [stryktyr] nf structure; ~s d'accueil reception facilities.

studieux, euse [stydjø, -øz] a studious; devoted to study.

studio [stydjo] nm (logement) (one-roomed) flatlet (Brit) ou apartment (US); (d'artiste, TV etc) studio (pl s).

stupéfait, e [stypefɛ, -ɛt] a astonished.

stupéfiant [stypefjɑ̃] nm (MÉD) drug, narcotic.

stupéfier [stypefje] vt to stupefy; (étonner) to stun, astonish.

stupeur [stypœr] nf astonishment.

stupide [stypid] a stupid; **stupidité** nf stupidity; stupid thing to do ou say).

style [stil] nm style; meuble de ~ piece of period furniture.

stylé, e [stile] a well-trained.

stylo [stilo] nm: ~ (à encre) (fountain) pen; ~ (à) bille ball-point pen.

su, e [sy] pp de **savoir** // nm: au ~ de with the knowledge of.

suave [sɥav] a sweet; (goût) mellow.

subalterne [sybaltɛrn(ə)] a (employé, officier) junior; (rôle) subordinate, subsidiary // nm/f subordinate.

subconscient [sypkɔ̃sjɑ̃] nm subconscious.

subir [sybir] vt (affront, dégâts) to suffer; (influence, charme) to be under; (opération, châtiment) to undergo.

subit, e [sybi, -it] a sudden; **subitement** ad suddenly, all of a sudden.

subjectif, ive [sybʒɛktif, -iv] a subjective.

subjonctif [sybʒɔ̃ktif] *nm* subjunctive.

submerger [sybmɛrʒe] *vt* to submerge; (*fig*) to overwhelm.

subordonné, e [sybɔrdɔne] *a, nm/f* subordinate; **~ à** subordinate to; subject to, depending on.

subornation [sybɔrnasjɔ̃] *nf* bribing.

subrepticement [sybrɛptismɑ̃] *ad* surreptitiously.

subside [sypsid] *nm* grant.

subsidiaire [sypsidjɛr] *a*: **question ~** deciding question.

subsister [sybziste] *vi* (*rester*) to remain, subsist; (*vivre*) to live; (*survivre*) to live on.

substance [sypstɑ̃s] *nf* substance.

substituer [sypstitɥe] *vt*: **~ qn/qch à** to substitute sth/sb for; **se ~ à qn** (*évincer*) to substitute o.s. for sb.

substitut [sypstity] *nm* (*JUR*) deputy public prosecutor; (*succédané*) substitute.

subtil, e [syptil] *a* subtle.

subtiliser [syptilize] *vt*: **~ qch (à qn)** to spirit sth away (from sb).

subvenir [sybvənir]: **~ à** *vt* to meet.

subvention [sybvɑ̃sjɔ̃] *nf* subsidy, grant; **subventionner** *vt* to subsidize.

suc [syk] *nm* (*BOT*) sap; (*de viande, fruit*) juice.

succédané [syksedane] *nm* substitute.

succéder [syksede]: **~ à** *vt* (*directeur, roi etc*) to succeed; (*venir après: dans une série*) to follow, succeed; **se ~** *vi* (*accidents, années*) to follow one another.

succès [syksɛ] *nm* success; **avoir du ~** to be a success, be successful; **~ de librairie** bestseller; **~** (*féminins*) conquests; **à ~** successful.

succession [syksɛsjɔ̃] *nf* (*série, POL*) succession; (*JUR: patrimoine*) estate, inheritance.

succomber [sykɔ̃be] *vi* to die, succumb; (*fig*) **~ à** to give way to, succumb to.

succursale [sykyrsal] *nf* branch.

sucer [syse] *vt* to suck.

sucette [sysɛt] *nf* (*bonbon*) lollipop; (*de bébé*) dummy (*Brit*), pacifier (*US*).

sucre [sykr(ə)] *nm* (*substance*) sugar; (*morceau*) lump of sugar, sugar lump *ou* cube; **~ en morceaux/cristallisé/en poudre** lump/granulated/caster sugar; **~ d'orge** barley sugar; **sucré, e** *a* (*produit alimentaire*) sweetened; (*au goût*) sweet; (*péj*) sugary, honeyed; **sucrer** *vt* (*thé, café*) to sweeten, put sugar in; **sucreries** *nfpl* (*bonbons*) sweets, sweet things; **sucrier** *nm* (*récipient*) sugar bowl.

sud [syd] *nm*: **le ~** the south // *a inv* south; (*côte*) south, southern; **au ~** (*situation*) in the south; (*direction*) to the south; **au ~ de** (*direction*) to the south of; **~-africain, e** *a, nm/f* South African; **~-américain, e** *a, nm/f* South American.

sud-est [sydɛst] *nm, a inv* south-east.

sud-ouest [sydwɛst] *nm, a inv* south-west.

Suède [sɥɛd] *nf*: **la ~** Sweden; **suédois, e** *a* Swedish // *nm/f*: **Suédois, e** Swede // *nm* (*LING*) Swedish.

suer [sɥe] *vi* to sweat; (*suinter*) to ooze.

sueur [sɥœr] *nf* sweat; **en ~** sweating, in a sweat.

suffire [syfir] *vi* (*être assez*): **~ (à qn/pour qn/pour faire)** to be enough *ou* sufficient (for sb/for sth/to do); **cela suffit pour les irriter/qu'ils se fâchent** it's enough to annoy them/for them to get angry; **il suffit d'une négligence/qu'on oublie pour que ...** it only takes one act of carelessness/one only needs to forget for ....

suffisamment [syfizamɑ̃] *ad* sufficiently, enough; **~ de** sufficient, enough.

suffisant, e [syfizɑ̃, -ɑ̃t] *a* (*temps, ressources*) sufficient; (*résultats*) satisfactory; (*vaniteux*) self-important, bumptious.

suffixe [syfiks(ə)] *nm* suffix.

suffoquer [syfɔke] *vt* to choke, suffocate; (*stupéfier*) to stagger, astound // *vi* to choke, suffocate.

suffrage [syfraʒ] *nm* (*POL: voix*) vote; (*du public etc*) approval *pl.*

suggérer [sygʒere] *vt* to suggest; **suggestion** *nf* suggestion.

suicide [sɥisid] *nm* suicide.

suicider [sɥiside]: **se ~** *vi* to commit suicide.

suie [sɥi] *nf* soot.

suinter [sɥɛ̃te] *vi* to ooze.

suis *vb voir* **être suivre**.

suisse [sɥis] *a* Swiss // *nm*: **S~** Swiss *pl inv*; (*bedeau*) ≈ verger // *nf*: **la S~** Switzerland; **la S~ romande/allemande** French-speaking/German-speaking Switzerland; **Suissesse** *nf* Swiss (woman *ou* girl).

suite [sɥit] *nf* (*continuation: d'énumération etc*) rest, remainder; (*de feuilleton*) continuation; (*second film etc sur le même thème*) sequel; (*série: de maisons, succès*) **une ~ de** a series *ou* succession of; (*MATH*) series *sg*; (*conséquence*) result; (*ordre, liaison logique*) coherence; (*appartement, MUS*) suite; (*escorte*) retinue, suite; **~s** *nfpl* (*d'une maladie etc*) effects; **prendre la ~ de** (*directeur etc*) to succeed, take over from; **donner ~ à** (*requête, projet*) to follow up; **faire ~ à** to follow; (*faisant*) **à votre lettre du** further to your letter of; **de ~** *ad* (*d'affilée*) in succession; (*immédiatement*) at once; **par la ~** afterwards, subsequently; **à la ~** *ad* one after the other; **à la ~ de** (*derrière*) behind; (*en conséquence de*) following; **par ~ de** owing to, as a result of.

suivant, e [sɥivã, -ãt] *a* next, following; (*ci-après*): **l'exercice ~** the following exercise // *prép* (*selon*) according to; **au ~!** next!

suivi, e [sɥivi] *a* (*régulier*) regular; (*cohérent*) consistent, coherent; **très/peu ~** (*cours*) well-/poorly-attended.

suivre [sɥivʀ(ə)] *vt* (*gén*) to follow;

(*SCOL: cours*) to attend; (: *programme*) to keep up with; (*COMM: article*) to continue to stock // *vi* to follow; (*élève*) to attend; to keep up; **se ~** *vi* (*accidents etc*) to follow one after the other; (*raisonnement etc*) to be coherent; **faire ~** (*lettre*) to forward; **~ son cours** (*suj: enquête etc*) to run *ou* take its course; **'à ~'** 'to be continued'.

sujet, te [syʒɛ, -ɛt] *a*: **être ~ à** (*vertige etc*) to be liable *ou* subject to // *nm/f* (*d'un souverain*) subject // *nm* subject; **au ~ de** *prép* about; **à caution** *a* questionable; **~ de conversation** topic *ou* subject of conversation; **~ d'examen** (*SCOL*) examination question; examination paper.

summum [sɔmɔm] *nm*: **le ~ de** the height of.

superbe [sypɛrb(ə)] *a* magnificent, superb.

super(carburant) [sypɛr(karbyrã)] *nm* ≈ 4-star petrol (*Brit*), ≈ high-octane gasoline (*US*).

supercherie [sypɛrʃəri] *nf* trick.

superficie [sypɛrfisi] *nf* (*surface*) area; (*fig*) surface.

superficiel, le [sypɛrfisjɛl] *a* superficial.

superflu, e [sypɛrfly] *a* superfluous.

supérieur, e [sypɛrjœr] *a* (*lèvre, étages, classes*) upper; (*plus élevé: température, niveau*): **~ (à)** higher (than); (*meilleur: qualité, produit*): **~ (à)** superior (to); (*excellent, hautain*) superior // *nm, nf* superior; **à l'étage ~** on the next floor up; **supériorité** *nf* superiority.

superlatif [sypɛrlatif] *nm* superlative.

supermarché [sypɛrmarʃe] *nm* supermarket.

superposer [sypɛrpoze] *vt* (*faire chevaucher*) to superimpose; **lits superposés** bunk beds.

superproduction [sypɛrprodyksjɔ̃] *nf* (*film*) spectacular.

superpuissance [sypɛrpɥisãs] *nf*

super-power.

superstitieux, euse [syperstisjø, -øz] a superstitious.

superviser [sypervize] vt to supervise.

suppléant, e [sypleã, -ãt] a (juge, fonctionnaire) deputy cpd; (professeur) supply cpd // nm/f deputy: supply teacher.

suppléer [syplee] vt (ajouter: mot manquant etc) to supply, provide; (compenser: lacune) to fill in; (: défaut) to make up for; (remplacer) to stand in for; ~ à vt to make up for; to substitute for.

supplément [syplemã] nm supplement; (de frites etc) extra portion; un ~ de travail extra ou additional work; ceci est en ~ (au menu etc) this is extra, there is an extra charge for this; **supplémentaire** a additional, further; (train, bus) relief cpd, extra.

supplications [syplikasjõ] nfpl pleas, entreaties.

supplice [syplis] nm (peine corporelle) torture q; form of torture; (douleur physique, morale) torture, agony.

supplier [syplije] vt to implore, beseech.

supplique [syplik] nf petition.

support [sypɔr] nm support; (pour livre, outils) stand.

supportable [sypɔrtabl(ə)] a (douleur) bearable.

supporter nm [sypɔrtɛr] supporter, fan // vt [sypɔrte] (poids, poussée) to support; (conséquences, épreuve) to bear, endure; (défauts, personne) to put up with; (suj: chose: chaleur etc) to withstand; (suj: personne: chaleur, vin) to be able to take.

supposé, e [sypoze] a (nombre) estimated; (auteur) supposed.

supposer [sypoze] vt to suppose; (impliquer) to presuppose; à ~ que supposing (that).

suppositoire [sypozitwar] nm suppository.

suppression [sypresjõ] nf removal; deletion; cancellation; suppression.

supprimer [syprime] vt (cloison, cause, anxiété) to remove; (clause, mot) to delete; (congés, service d'autobus etc) to cancel; (emplois, privilèges, témoin gênant) to do away with.

supputer [sypyte] vt to calculate.

suprême [syprɛm] a supreme.

sur, e [syr] a sour.

MOT-CLÉ

sur [syr] prép 1 (position) on; (pardessus) over; (au-dessus) above; pose-le ~ la table put it on the table; je n'ai pas d'argent ~ moi I haven't any money on me

2 (direction) towards; en allant ~ Paris going towards Paris; ~ votre droite on ou to your right

3 (à propos de) on, about; un livre/ une conférence ~ Balzac a book/ lecture on ou about Balzac

4 (proportion, mesures) out of; by; un ~ 10 one in 10; (SCOL) one out of 10; 4 m ~ 2 4 m by 2

sur ce ad hereupon.

---

sûr, e [syr] a sure, certain; (digne de confiance) reliable; (sans danger) safe; ~ de soi self-confident; le plus ~ est de the safest thing is to; ~ et certain absolutely certain.

suranné, e [syrane] a outdated, outmoded.

surbaissé, e [syrbese] a lowered, low.

surcharge [syrʃarʒ(ə)] nf (de passagers, marchandises) excess load; (correction) alteration.

surcharger [syrʃarʒe] vt to overload.

surchoix [syrʃwa] a inv top-quality.

surclasser [syrklase] vt to outclass.

surcroît [syrkrwa] nm: un ~ de additional + nom; par ou de ~ moreover; en ~ in addition.

surdité [syrdite] nf deafness.

surélever [syrelve] vt to raise,

heighten.

sûrement [syrmɑ̃] *ad* reliably; safely, securely; (*certainement*) certainly.

surenchère [syrɑ̃ʃɛr] *nf* (*aux enchères*) higher bid; (*sur prix fixe*) overbid; (*fig*) overstatement; outbidding tactics *pl*; **surenchérir** *vi* to bid higher; (*fig*) to try and outbid each other.

surent *vb voir* **savoir**.

surestimer [syrɛstime] *vt* to overestimate.

sûreté [syrte] *nf* (*voir sûr*) reliability; safety; (*JUR*) guaranty; surety; mettre en ~ to put in a safe place; pour plus de ~ as an extra precaution; to be on the safe side.

surf [syrf] *nm* surfing.

surface [syrfas] *nf* surface; (*superficie*) surface area; faire ~ to surface; en ~ *ad* near the surface; (*fig*) superficially.

surfait, e [syrfɛ, -ɛt] *a* overrated.

surfin, e [syrfɛ̃, -in] *a* superfine.

surgelé, e [syrʒəle] *a* (deep-)frozen.

surgir [syrʒir] *vi* to appear suddenly; (*jaillir*) to shoot up; (*fig: problème, conflit*) to arise.

surhumain, e [syrymɛ̃, -ɛn] *a* superhuman.

surimpression [syrɛ̃prɛsjɔ̃] *nf* (*PHOTO*) double exposure; en ~ superimposed.

sur-le-champ [syrləʃɑ̃] *ad* immediately.

surlendemain [syrlɑ̃dmɛ̃] *nm*: le ~ (soir) two days later (in the evening); le ~ de two days after.

surligneur [syrliɲœr] *nm* highlighter (pen).

surmener [syrməne] *vt*, **se ~** *vi* to overwork.

surmonter [syrmɔ̃te] *vt* (*suj: coupole etc*) to top; (*vaincre*) to overcome.

surnager [syrnaʒe] *vi* to float.

surnaturel, le [syrnatyrɛl] *a, nm* supernatural.

surnom [syrnɔ̃] *nm* nickname.

surnombre [syrnɔ̃br(ə)] *nm*: être en ~ to be too many (*ou* one too many).

surpeuplé, e [syrpœ̃ple] *a* overpopulated.

sur-place [syrplas] *nm*: faire du ~ to mark time.

surplomber [syrplɔ̃be] *vi* to be overhanging // *vt* to overhang; to tower above.

surplus [syrply] *nm* (*COMM*) surplus; (*reste*): ~ de bois wood left over.

surprenant, e [syrprənɑ̃, -ɑ̃t] *a* amazing.

surprendre [syrprɑ̃dr(ə)] *vt* (*étonner, prendre à l'improviste*) to surprise; (*tomber sur: intrus etc*) to catch; (*fig*) to detect; to chance upon; to overhear.

surpris, e [syrpri, -iz] *a*: ~ (de/que) surprised (at/that).

surprise [syrpriz] *nf* surprise; faire une ~ à qn to give sb a surprise; **surprise-partie** [syrprizparti] *nf* party.

sursaut [syrso] *nm* start, jump; ~ de (*énergie, indignation*) sudden fit *ou* burst of; en ~ *ad* with a start; **sursauter** *vi* to (give a) start, jump.

surseoir [syrswar]: ~ à *vt* to defer.

sursis [syrsi] *nm* (*JUR: gén*) suspended sentence; (*à l'exécution capitale, aussi fig*) reprieve; (*MIL*) deferment.

surtaxe [syrtaks(ə)] *nf* surcharge.

surtout [syrtu] *ad* (*avant tout, d'abord*) above all; (*spécialement, particulièrement*) especially; ~, ne dites rien! whatever you do don't say anything!; ~ pas! certainly *ou* definitely not!; ~ que ... especially as ...

surveillance [syrvɛjɑ̃s] *nf* watch; (*POLICE, MIL*) surveillance; sous ~ médicale under medical supervision.

surveillant, e [syrvɛjɑ̃, -ɑ̃t] *nm/f* (*de prison*) warder; (*SCOL*) monitor; (*de travaux*) supervisor, overseer.

surveiller [syrveje] *vt* (*enfant,*

élèves, bagages) to watch, keep an eye on; (*malade*) to watch over; (*prisonnier, suspect*) to keep a watch on; (*territoire, bâtiment*) to (keep) watch over; (*travaux, cuisson*) to supervise; (*SCOL: examen*) to invigilate; **se** ~ *vi* to keep a check *ou* watch on o.s.; ~ **son langage/sa ligne** to watch one's language/figure.

survenir [syrvənir] *vi* (*incident, retards*) to occur, arise; (*événement*) to take place; (*personne*) to appear, arrive.

survêt(ement) [syrvɛt(mã)] *nm* tracksuit.

survie [syrvi] *nf* survival; (*REL*) afterlife.

survivant, e [syrvivã, -ãt] *nm/f* survivor.

survivre [syrvivR(ə)] *vi* to survive; ~ **à** *vt* (*accident etc*) to survive; (*personne*) to outlive.

survoler [syrvole] *vt* to fly over; (*fig: livre*) to skim through.

survolté, e [syrvolte] *a* (*fig*) worked up.

sus [sy(s)]: **en** ~ **de** *prép* in addition to, over and above; **en** ~ *ad* in addition; ~ **à** *excl:* ~ **au tyran!** at the tyrant!

susceptible [syseptibl(ə)] *a* touchy, sensitive; ~ **d'amélioration** that can be improved, open to improvement; ~ **de faire** able to do; liable to do.

susciter [sysite] *vt* (*admiration*) to arouse; (*obstacles, ennuis*) ~ (**à qn**) to create (for sb).

suspect, e [syspɛ(kt), -ɛkt(ə)] *a* suspicious; (*témoignage, opinions*) suspect // *nm/f* suspect.

suspecter [syspɛkte] *vt* to suspect; (*honnêteté de qn*) to question, have one's suspicions about.

suspendre [syspãdR(ə)] *vt* (*accrocher: vêtement*): ~ **qch (à)** to hang sth up (on); (*fixer: lustre etc*): ~ **qch à** to hang sth from; (*interrompre, démettre*) to suspend; (*remettre*) to defer; **se** ~ **à** to hang

from.

suspendu, e [syspãdy] *a* (*accroché*): ~ **à** hanging on (ou from); (*perché*): ~ **au-dessus de** suspended over.

suspens [syspã]: **en** ~ *ad* (*affaire*) in abeyance; **tenir en** ~ to keep in suspense.

suspense [syspãs] *nm* suspense.

suspension [syspãsjõ] *nf* suspension; ~ **d'audience** adjournment.

sut *vb voir* **savoir**.

suture [sytyR] *nf:* **point de** ~ stitch.

svelte [svɛlt(ə)] *a* slender, svelte.

S.V.P. *sigle (= s'il vous plait)* please.

syllabe [silab] *nf* syllable.

sylviculture [silvikyltyR] *nf* forestry.

symbole [sɛbɔl] *nm* symbol; **symbolique** *a* symbolic(al); (*geste, offrande*) token *cpd*; (*salaire, dommage-intérêts*) nominal; **symboliser** *vt* to symbolize.

symétrique [simetRik] *a* symmetrical.

sympa [sɛpa] *a inv (abr de* **sympathique**.

sympathie [sɛpati] *nf* (*inclination*) liking; (*affinité*) fellow feeling; (*condoléances*) sympathy; **accueillir avec** ~ (*projet*) to receive favourably; **croyez à toute ma** ~ you have my deepest sympathy.

sympathique [sɛpatik] *a* nice, friendly; likeable; pleasant.

sympathisant, e [sɛpatizã, -ãt] *nm/f* sympathizer.

sympathiser [sɛpatize] *vi* (*voisins etc: s'entendre*) to get on (*Brit*) *ou* along (*US*) (well).

symphonie [sɛfɔni] *nf* symphony.

symptôme [sɛptom] *nm* symptom.

synagogue [sinagɔg] *nf* synagogue.

syncope [sɛkɔp] *nf* (*MÉD*) blackout; **tomber en** ~ to faint, pass out.

syndic [sɛdik] *nm* managing agent.

syndical, e, aux [sɛdikal, -o] *a* (trade-)union *cpd*; ~**iste** *nm/f* trade unionist.

syndicat [sɛdika] *nm* (*d'ouvriers, employés*) (trade) union; (*autre asso-*

ciation d'intérêts) union, association; ~ **d'initiative** tourist office.

syndiqué, e [sɛ̃dike] *a* belonging to a (trade) union; **non** ~ non-union.

syndiquer [sɛ̃dike]: **se** ~ *vi* to form a trade union; *(adhérer)* to join a trade union.

synonyme [sinɔnim] *a* synonymous // *nm* synonym; **~ de** synonymous with.

syntaxe [sɛ̃taks(ə)] *nf* syntax.

synthèse [sɛ̃tɛz] *nf* synthesis *(pl* es).

synthétique [sɛ̃tetik] *a* synthetic.

Syrie [siʀi] *nf:* **la** ~ Syria.

systématique [sistematik] *a* systematic.

système [sistɛm] *nm* system; **le** ~ **D** resourcefulness.

T

t' [t(ə)] *pronom voir* **te**.

ta [ta] *dét voir* **ton**.

tabac [taba] *nm* tobacco; tobacconist's (shop); ~ **blond/brun** light/dark tobacco; ~ **à priser** snuff.

table [tabl(ə)] *nf* table; **à** ~! dinner *etc* is ready!; **se mettre à** ~ to sit down to eat; *(fig: fam)* to come clean; **mettre la** ~ to lay the table; **faire** ~ **rase** de to make a clean sweep of; ~ **des matières** (table of) contents *pl;* ~ **de nuit** *ou* **de chevet** bedside table.

tableau, x [tablo] *nm* painting; *(reproduction, fig)* picture; *(panneau)* board; *(schéma)* table, chart; ~ **d'affichage** notice board; ~ **de bord** dashboard; *(AVIAT)* instrument panel; ~ **noir** blackboard.

tabler [table] *vi:* ~ **sur** to bank on.

tablette [tablɛt] *nf (planche)* shelf *(pl* shelves); ~ **de chocolat** bar of chocolate.

tableur [tablœʀ] *nm* spreadsheet.

tablier [tablije] *nm* apron.

tabouret [tabuʀɛ] *nm* stool.

tac [tak] *nm:* **du** ~ **au** ~ tit for tat.

tache [taʃ] *nf (saleté)* stain, mark;

(ART, de couleur, lumière) spot; splash, patch.

tâche [taʃ] *nf* task; **travailler à la** ~ to do piecework.

tacher [taʃe] *vt* to stain, mark; *(fig)* to sully, stain.

tâcher [taʃe] *vi:* ~ **de faire** to try *ou* endeavour to do.

tacot [tako] *nm (péj)* banger *(Brit)*, (old) heap.

tact [takt] *nm* tact; **avoir du** ~ to be tactful.

tactique [taktik] *a* tactical // *nf (technique)* tactics *sg; (plan)* tactic.

taie [tɛ] *nf:* ~ **(d'oreiller)** pillowslip, pillowcase.

taille [taj] *nf* cutting; pruning; *(milieu du corps)* waist; *(hauteur)* height; *(grandeur)* size; **de** ~ **à faire** capable of doing; **de** ~ *a* sizeable.

taille-crayon(s) [tajkʀɛjɔ̃] *nm* pencil sharpener.

tailler [taje] *vt (pierre, diamant)* to cut; *(arbre, plante)* to prune; *(vêtement)* to cut out; *(crayon)* to sharpen.

tailleur [tajœʀ] *nm (couturier)* tailor; *(vêtement)* suit; **en** ~ *(assis)* cross-legged.

taillis [taji] *nm* copse.

taire [tɛʀ] *vt* to keep to o.s., conceal // *vi:* **faire** ~ **qn** to make sb be quiet; *(fig)* to silence sb; **se** ~ *vi* to be silent *ou* quiet.

talc [talk] *nm* talc, talcum powder.

talent [talɑ̃] *nm* talent.

talon [talɔ̃] *nm* heel; *(de chèque, billet)* stub, counterfoil *(Brit);* ~**s plats/aiguilles** flat/stiletto heels.

talonner [talɔne] *vt* to follow hard behind; *(fig)* to hound.

talus [taly] *nm* embankment.

tambour [tɑ̃buʀ] *nm (MUS, aussi TECH)* drum; *(musicien)* drummer; *(porte)* revolving door *(pl* s).

tamis [tami] *nm* sieve.

Tamise [tamiz] *nf:* **la** ~ the Thames.

tamisé, e [tamize] *a (fig)* subdued, soft.

tamiser [tamize] vt to sieve, sift.

tampon [tɑ̃pɔ̃] nm (de coton, d'ouate) wad, pad; (amortisseur) buffer; (bouchon) plug, stopper; (cachet, timbre) stamp; (mémoire) ~ (INFORM) buffer; (hygiénique) tampon; **tamponner** vt (timbres) to stamp; (heurter) to crash ou ram into; **tamponneuse** a: autos tamponneuses dodgems.

tandis [tɑ̃di]: ~ que cj while.

tanguer [tɑ̃ge] vi to pitch (and toss).

tanière [tanjɛʁ] nf lair, den.

tanné, e [tane] a weather-beaten.

tanner [tane] vt to tan.

tant [tɑ̃] ad so much; ~ de (sable, eau) so much; (gens, livres) so many; ~ que cj as long as; ~ que (comparatif) as much as; ~ mieux that's great; so much the better; ~ pis never mind; too bad.

tante [tɑ̃t] nf aunt.

tantôt [tɑ̃to] ad (parfois) ~ ... now ... now; (cet après-midi) this afternoon.

tapage [tapaʒ] nm uproar, din.

tapageur, euse [tapaʒœʁ, -øz] a loud, flashy; noisy.

tape [tap] nf slap.

tape-à-l'œil [tapalœj] a inv flashy, showy.

taper [tape] vt (porte) to bang, slam; (dactylographier) to type (out); (fam: emprunter): ~ qn de 10 F to touch sb for 10 F // vi (soleil) to beat down; ~ sur qn to thump sb; (fig) to run sb down; ~ sur qch to hit sth; to bang on sth; ~ à (porte etc) to knock on; ~ dans vt (se servir) to dig into; ~ des mains/pieds to clap one's hands/stamp one's feet; ~ à (la machine) to type; se ~ un travail to land o.s. with a job.

tapi, e [tapi] a crouching, cowering; hidden away.

tapis [tapi] nm carpet; (de table) cloth; mettre sur le ~ (fig) to bring up for discussion; ~ roulant conveyor belt; ~ de sol (de tente) groundsheet.

tapisser [tapise] vt (avec du papier peint) to paper; (recouvrir): ~ qch (de) to cover sth with).

tapisserie [tapisʁi] nf (tenture, broderie) tapestry; (papier peint) wallpaper.

tapissier, ière [tapisje, -jɛʁ] nm/f: ~-(-décorateur) upholsterer (and decorator).

tapoter [tapɔte] vt to pat, tap.

taquiner [takine] vt to tease.

tarabiscoté, e [taʁabiskɔte] a overornate, fussy.

tard [taʁ] ad late; plus ~ later (on); au plus ~ at the latest; sur le ~ late in life.

tarder [taʁde] vi (chose) to be a long time coming; (personne): ~ à faire to delay doing; il me tarde d'être I am longing to be; sans (plus) ~ without (further) delay.

tardif, ive [taʁdif, -iv] a late.

targuer [taʁge]: se ~ de vt to boast about.

tarif [taʁif] nm (liste) price list; tariff; (barème) rates pl; fares pl; tariff; (prix) rate; fare.

tarir [taʁiʁ] vi to dry up, run dry.

tarte [taʁt(ə)] nf tart.

tartine [taʁtin] nf slice of bread; ~ de miel slice of bread and honey; **tartiner** vt to spread; fromage à tartiner cheese spread.

tartre [taʁtʁ(ə)] nm (des dents) tartar; (de chaudière) fur, scale.

tas [tɑ] nm heap, pile; (fig): un ~ de heaps of, lots of; en ~ in a heap ou pile; formé sur le ~ trained on the job.

tasse [tɑs] nf cup; ~ à café coffee cup.

tassé, e [tɑse] a: bien ~ (café etc) strong.

tasser [tɑse] vt (terre, neige) to pack down; (entasser): ~ qch dans to cram sth into; se ~ vi (terrain) to settle; (fig) to sort itself out, settle down.

tâter [tɑte] vt to feel; (fig) to try out; ~ de (prison etc) to have a taste of;

se ~ (hésiter) to be in two minds.

tatillon, ne [tatijɔ̃, -ɔn] a pernickety.

tâtonnement [tɑtɔnmɑ̃] nm: par ~s (fig) by trial and error.

tâtonner [tɑtɔne] vi to grope one's way along.

tâtons [tɑtɔ̃]: à ~ ad: chercher/avancer à ~ to grope around for/grope one's way forward.

tatouer [tatwe] vt to tattoo.

taudis [todi] nm hovel, slum.

taule [tol] nf (fam) nick (fam), prison.

taupe [top] nf mole.

taureau, x [tɔʀo] nm bull; (signe): le T~ Taurus.

tauromachie [tɔʀɔmaʃi] nf bullfighting.

taux [to] nm rate; (d'alcool) level; ~ d'intérêt interest rate.

taxe [taks] nf tax; (douanière) duty; ~ de séjour tourist tax; ~ à la valeur ajoutée (T.V.A.) value added tax (V.A.T.).

taxer [takse] vt (personne) to tax; (produit) to put a tax on; (fig): ~ qn de to call sb + attribut; to accuse sb of, tax sb with.

taxi [taksi] nm taxi.

tchao [tʃao] excl (fam) bye(-bye)!

Tchécoslovaquie [tʃekɔslɔvaki] nf Czechoslovakia; **tchèque** a, nm, nf Czech.

te, t' [t(ə)] pronom you; (réfléchi) yourself.

technicien, ne [tɛknisjɛ̃, -jɛn] nm/f technician.

technique [tɛknik] a technical // nf technique; ~ment ad technically.

technologie [tɛknɔlɔʒi] nf technology; **technologique** a technological.

teck [tɛk] nm teak.

teignais etc vb voir teindre.

teindre [tɛ̃dʀ(ə)] vt to dye.

teint, e [tɛ̃, tɛ̃t] a dyed // nm (du visage) complexion; colour // nf shade; **grand** ~ a inv colourfast.

teinté, e [tɛ̃te] a: ~ de (fig) tinged with.

teinter [tɛ̃te] vt to tint; (bois) to stain; **teinture** nf dyeing; (substance) dye; (MÉD) tincture.

teinturerie [tɛ̃tyʀʀi] nf dry cleaner's.

teinturier [tɛ̃tyʀje] nm dry cleaner's.

tel, telle [tɛl] a (pareil) such; (comme): ~ un/des ... like a/like ...; (indéfini) such-and-such a, a given; (intensif): un ~/de ~s ... such (a)/such ...; **rien de** ~ nothing like it, no such thing; ~ **que** cj like, such as; ~ **quel** as it is ou stands (ou was etc).

télé [tele] abr f (= télévision) TV, telly (Brit); (poste) TV (set), telly; à la ~ on TV, on telly.

télé... [tele] préfixe: **~benne** ~, **cabine** nf (benne) cable car; **~commande** nf remote control; **~copie** nf fax; **~distribution** nf cable TV; **~frique** nm = **~phérique**; **~gramme** nm = télégram.

télégraphe [telegraf] nm telegraph; **télégraphier** vt to telegraph, cable.

téléguider [telegide] vt to operate by remote control, radio-control.

téléjournal [teleʒuʀnal] nm TV news magazine programme.

télématique [telematik] nf telematics sg.

téléobjectif [teleɔbʒɛktif] nm telephoto lens sg.

téléphérique [teleferik] nm cablecar.

téléphone [telefɔn] nm telephone; **avoir le** ~ to be on the (tele)phone; **au** ~ on the phone; **téléphoner** vi to telephone, ring; to make a phone call; **téléphoner à** to phone, call up; **téléphonique** a (tele)phone cpd.

télescope [telɛskɔp] nm telescope.

télescoper [telɛskɔpe] vt to smash up; se ~ (véhicules) to concertina.

télescripteur [teleskʀiptœʀ] nm teleprinter.

télésiège [telesjɛʒ] nm chairlift.

téléski [teleski] nm ski-tow.

téléspectateur, trice [telespɛktateœr, -trɛs] nm/f (television) viewer.

téléviseur [televizœr] nm television set.

télévision [televizjɔ̃] nf television; à la ~ on television.

télex [telɛks] nm telex.

telle [tɛl] a voir **tel**.

tellement [tɛlmã] ad (tant) so much; (si) so; ~ de (sable, eau) so much; (gens, livres) so many; il s'est endormi ~ il était fatigué he was so tired (that) he fell asleep; pas ~ not (all) that much; not (all) that + adjectif.

téméraire [temerɛr] a reckless, rash; **témérité** [temerite] nf recklessness, rashness.

témoignage [temwaɲaʒ] nm (JUR: déclaration) testimony q, evidence q; (: faits) evidence q; (rapport, récit) account; (fig: d'affection etc) token, mark; expression.

témoigner [temwaɲe] vt (intérêt, gratitude) to show // vi (JUR) to testify, give evidence; ~ de vt to bear witness to, testify to.

témoin [temwɛ̃] nm witness; (fig) testimony // a control cpd, test cpd; appartement ~ show flat (Brit); être ~ de to witness; ~ oculaire eyewitness.

tempe [tãp] nf temple.

tempérament [tãperamã] nm temperament, disposition; à ~ (vente) on deferred (payment) terms; (achat) by instalments, hire purchase cpd.

température [tãperatyr] nf temperature; avoir ou faire de la ~ to be running ou have a temperature.

tempéré, e [tãpere] a temperate.

tempête [tãpɛt] nf storm; ~ de sable/ neige sand/snowstorm.

temple [tãpl(ə)] nm temple; (protestant) church.

temporaire [tãpɔrɛr] a temporary.

temps [tã] nm (atmosphérique) weather; (durée) time; (époque) time, times pl; (LING) tense; (MUS) beat; (TECH) stroke; il fait beau/

mauvais ~ the weather is fine/bad; avoir le ~/tout le ~ to have time/ plenty of time; en ~ de paix/guerre in peacetime/wartime; en ~ utile ou voulu in due time ou course; de ~ en ~, de ~ à autre from time to time; à ~ (partir, arriver) in time; à ~ partiel ad, a part-time; dans le ~ at one time; de tout ~ always; ~ d'arrêt pause, halt; ~ mort (COMM) slack period.

tenable [tənabl(ə)] a bearable.

tenace [tənas] a tenacious, persistent.

tenailler [tənaje] vt (fig) to torment.

tenailles [tənaj] nfpl pincers.

tenais etc vb voir **tenir**.

tenancier, ière [tənãsje, -jɛr] nm/f manager/manageress.

tenant, e [tənã, -ãt] nm/f (SPORT): ~ du titre title-holder.

tendance [tãdãs] nf (opinions) leanings pl, sympathies pl; (inclination) tendency; (évolution) trend; avoir ~ à to have a tendency to, tend to.

tendeur [tãdœr] nm (attache) elastic strap.

tendre [tãdr(ə)] a tender; (bois, roche, couleur) soft // vt (élastique, peau) to stretch, draw tight; (muscle) to tense; (donner): ~ qch à qn to hold sth out to sb; (fig: piège) to set, lay; se ~ vi (corde) to tighten; (relations) to become strained; ~ à qch/à faire to tend towards sth/to do; ~ l'oreille to prick up one's ears; ~ la main/le bras to hold out one's hand/stretch out one's arm; ~ment ad tenderly; **tendresse** nf tenderness.

tendu, e [tãdy] pp de **tendre** // a tight; tensed; strained.

ténèbres [tenɛbr(ə)] nfpl darkness sg.

teneur [tənœr] nf content; (d'une lettre) terms pl, content.

tenir [tənir] vt to hold; (magasin, hôtel) to run; (promesse) to keep // vi to hold; (neige, gel) to last; se ~ vi (avoir lieu) to be held, take place;

(être: personne) to stand; se ~
droit to stand up *(ou* sit up)
straight; **bien se** ~ to behave well;
se ~ **à qch** to hold on to sth; **s'en**
~ **à qch** to confine o.s. to sth; to
stick to sth; ~ **à** *vt* to be attached
to; to care about; to depend on; to
stem from; ~ **à faire** to want to do;
~ **de** *vt* to partake of; to take after;
ça ne tient qu'à lui it is entirely up
to him; ~ **qn pour** to take sb for; ~
qch de qn *(histoire)* to have heard
ou learnt sth from sb; *(qualité, défaut)* to have inherited *ou* got sth
from sb; ~ **les comptes** to keep the
books; ~ **le coup** to hold out; ~ **au
chaud** to keep hot; **tiens/ tenez,
voilà le stylo** there's the pen!;
tiens, Alain! look, here's Alain!;
tiens? *(surprise)* really?

tennis [tenis] *nm* tennis; *(court)* tennis court // *nmpl ou fpl (aussi:*
chaussures de ~) tennis *ou* gym
shoes; ~ **de table** table tennis;
~**man** *nm* tennis player.

tension [tɑ̃sjɔ̃] *nf* tension; *(fig)* tension; strain; *(MÉD)* blood pressure;
faire *ou* **avoir de la** ~ to have high
blood pressure.

tentation [tɑ̃tasjɔ̃] *nf* temptation.

tentative [tɑ̃tativ] *nf* attempt, bid.

tente [tɑ̃t] *nf* tent.

tenter [tɑ̃te] *vt (éprouver, attirer)*
to tempt; *(essayer)*: ~ **qch/ou de faire** to
attempt *ou* try sth/to do; ~ **sa
chance** to try one's luck.

tenture [tɑ̃tyʀ] *nf* hanging.

tenu, e [təny] *pp de* **tenir** // *a (maison, comptes)*: **bien** ~ well-kept;
(obligé): ~ **de faire** under an obligation to do // *nf (action de tenir)* running; keeping; holding; *(vêtements)*
clothes *pl*, gear; *(allure)* dress *g*, appearance; *(comportement)* manners
pl, behaviour; **en petite** ~ scantily
dressed *ou* clad; ~**e de route**
(AUTO) road-holding; ~**e de soirée**
evening dress.

ter [tɛʀ] *a*: **16** ~ **16b** *ou* B.

térébenthine [teʀebɑ̃tin] *nf*: *(essence de)* ~ (oil of) turpentine.

terme [tɛʀm(ə)] *nm* term; *(fin)* end;
à court/long ~ *a* short-/long-term
ou -range // *ad* in the short/long term;
avant ~ *(MÉD) ad* prematurely;
mettre un ~ **à** to put an end *ou* a
stop to.

terminaison [tɛʀminɛzɔ̃] *nf* *(LING)*
ending.

terminal, e, aux [tɛʀminal, -o] *a*
final // *nm* terminal // *nf (SCOL)* ≈
sixth form *ou* year *(Brit)* ≈ twelfth
grade *(US)*.

terminer [tɛʀmine] *vt* to end; *(travail, repas)* to finish; **se** ~ *vi* to end.

terne [tɛʀn(ə)] *a* dull.

ternir [tɛʀniʀ] *vt* to dull; *(fig)* to
sully, tarnish; **se** ~ *vi* to become
dull.

terrain [tɛʀɛ̃] *nm (sol, fig)* ground;
(COMM) land *q*, plot of (land); site;
sur le ~ *(fig)* on the field; ~ **de
football/rugby** football/rugby pitch
(Brit) ou field *(US)*; ~ **d'aviation**
airfield; ~ **de camping** campsite; ~
de golf golf course; ~ **de jeu** games
field; playground; ~ **de sport** sports
ground; ~ **vague** waste ground *q*.

terrasse [tɛʀas] *nf* terrace; **à la** ~
(café) outside.

terrassement [tɛʀasmɑ̃] *nm* earth-
moving, earthworks *pl*; embankment.

terrasser [tɛʀase] *vt (adversaire)* to
floor; *(suj: maladie etc)* to lay low.

terre [tɛʀ] *nf (gén, aussi ÉLEC)*
earth; *(substance)* soil, earth; *(opposé à mer)* land *q*; *(contrée)* land;
~**s** *nfpl (terrains)* lands, land *sg*; **en**
~ *(pipe, poterie)* clay *cpd*; **à** ~ *ou*
par ~ *(mettre, être)* on the ground
(ou floor); *(jeter, tomber)* to the
ground, down; ~ **cuite** earthenware;
terracotta; **la** ~ **ferme** dry land; ~
glaise clay; ~ **à** ~ *a inv* down-to-
earth.

terreau [tɛʀo] *nm* compost.

terre-plein [tɛʀplɛ̃] *nm* platform.

terrer [tɛʀe]: **se** ~ *vi* to hide away;
to go to ground.

terrestre [tɛʀɛstʀ(ə)] *a (surface)*

earth's, of the earth; (*BOT, ZOOL, MIL*) land *cpd*; (*REL*) earthly, worldly.

terreur [tɛʀœʀ] *nf* terror *q*.

terrible [tɛʀibl(ə)] *a* terrible, dreadful; (*fam*) terrific.

terrien, ne [tɛʀjɛ̃, -jɛn] *a*: **propriétaire ~** landowner // *nm/f* (*non martien etc*) earthling.

terrier [tɛʀje] *nm* burrow, hole; (*chien*) terrier.

terril [tɛʀil] *nm* slag heap.

terrine [tɛʀin] *nf* (*récipient*) terrine; (*CULIN*) pâté.

territoire [tɛʀitwaʀ] *nm* territory.

terroir [tɛʀwaʀ] *nm* (*AGR*) soil; region.

terrorisme [tɛʀɔʀism(ə)] *nm* terrorism; **terroriste** *nm/f* terrorist.

tertiaire [tɛʀsjɛʀ] *a* tertiary // *nm* (*ÉCON*) service industries *pl*.

tertre [tɛʀtʀ(ə)] *nm* hillock, mound.

tes [te] *dét voir* **ton**.

tesson [tesɔ̃] *nm*: **~ de bouteille** piece of broken bottle.

test [tɛst] *nm* test.

testament [tɛstamɑ̃] *nm* (*JUR*) will; (*REL*) Testament; (*fig*) legacy.

tester [tɛste] *vt* to test.

testicule [tɛstikyl] *nm* testicle.

tétanos [tetanos] *nm* tetanus.

têtard [tɛtaʀ] *nm* tadpole.

tête [tɛt] *nf* head; (*cheveux*) hair *q*; (*visage*) face; **de ~** (*wagon etc*) front *cpd* // *ad* (*calculer*) in one's head, mentally; **tenir ~ à qn** to stand up to sb; **la ~ en bas** with one's head down; **la ~ la première** (*tomber*) headfirst; **faire une ~** (*FOOTBALL*) to head the ball; **faire la ~** (*fig*) to sulk; **en ~** (*SPORT*) in the lead; at the front; **en ~ à ~** in private, alone together; **de la ~ aux pieds** from head to toe; **~ de lecture** (*playback*) head; **~ de liste** (*POL*) chief candidate; **~ de série** (*TENNIS*) seeded player, seed; **~-à-queue** *nm inv*: **faire un ~-à-queue** to spin round.

téter [tete] *vt*: **~ (sa mère)** to suck

at one's mother's breast, feed.

tétine [tetin] *nf* teat; (*sucette*) dummy (*Brit*), pacifier (*US*).

têtu, e [tety] *a* stubborn, pigheaded.

texte [tɛkst(ə)] *nm* text.

textile [tɛkstil] *a* textile *cpd* // *nm* textile; textile industry.

texture [tɛkstyʀ] *nf* texture.

TGV *sigle m* (= *train à grande vitesse*) high-speed train.

thé [te] *nm* tea; **prendre le ~** to have tea; **faire le ~** to make the tea.

théâtral, e, aux [teatʀal, -o] *a* theatrical.

théâtre [teatʀ(ə)] *nm* theatre; (*œuvres*) plays *pl*, dramatic works *pl*; (*fig*: *lieu*): **le ~ de** the scene of; (*péj*) histrionics *pl*, playacting; **faire du ~** to be on the stage; to do some acting.

théière [tejɛʀ] *nf* teapot.

thème [tɛm] *nm* theme; (*SCOL*: *traduction*) prose (composition).

théologie [teɔlɔʒi] *nf* theology.

théorie [teɔʀi] *nf* theory; **théorique** *a* theoretical.

thérapie [teʀapi] *nf* therapy.

thermal, e, aux [tɛʀmal, -o] *a*: **station ~e** spa; **cure ~e** water cure.

thermes [tɛʀm(ə)] *nmpl* thermal baths.

thermomètre [tɛʀmɔmɛtʀ(ə)] *nm* thermometer.

thermos ® [tɛʀmos] *nm ou nf*: (**bouteille**) **~** vacuum *ou* Thermos ® flask.

thermostat [tɛʀmosta] *nm* thermostat.

thèse [tɛz] *nf* thesis (*pl* theses).

thon [tɔ̃] *nm* tuna (fish).

thym [tɛ̃] *nm* thyme.

tibia [tibja] *nm* shinbone, tibia; shin.

tic [tik] *nm* tic, (nervous) twitch; (*de langage etc*) mannerism.

ticket [tikɛ] *nm* ticket; **~ de quai** platform ticket.

tiède [tjɛd] *a* lukewarm; tepid; (*vent, air*) mild, warm; **tiédir** *vi* to cool; to grow warmer.

tien, tienne [tjɛ̃, tjɛn] *pronom*: le ~ (la tienne), les ~s (tiennes) yours; à la tienne! cheers!

tiens [tjɛ̃] *vb, excl voir* tenir.

tiercé [tjɛrse] *nm* system of forecast betting giving first 3 horses.

tiers, tierce [tjɛr, tjɛrs(ə)] *a* third // *nm* (JUR) third party; (*fraction*) third; le ~ monde the third world.

tige [tiʒ] *nf* stem; (*bois*) rod.

tignasse [tiɲas] *nf* (*péj*) mop of hair.

tigre [tigr(ə)] *nm* tiger.

tigré, e [tigre] *a* striped; spotted.

tilleul [tijœl] *nm* lime (tree), linden (tree); (*boisson*) lime(-blossom) tea.

timbale [tɛ̃bal] *nf* (metal) tumbler; ~s *nfpl* (MUS) timpani, kettledrums.

timbre [tɛ̃br(ə)] *nm* (*tampon*) stamp; (*aussi*: ~-poste) (postage) stamp; (MUS: de voix, instrument) timbre, tone.

timbré, e [tɛ̃bre] *a* (*fam*) daft.

timbrer [tɛ̃bre] *vt* to stamp.

timide [timid] *a* shy; timid; (*timoré*) timid, timorous; ~ment *ad* shyly; timidly; **timidité** *nf* shyness; timidity.

tins *etc vb voir* tenir.

tintamarre [tɛ̃tamar] *nm* din, uproar.

tinter [tɛ̃te] *vi* to ring, chime; (*argent, clefs*) to jingle.

tir [tir] *nm* (*sport*) shooting; (*fait ou manière de tirer*) firing *q*; (*stand*) shooting gallery; à l'arc archery; ~ au pigeon clay pigeon shooting.

tirage [tiraʒ] *nm* (*action*) printing; (PHOTO) print; (*de journal*) circulation; (*de livre*) (print-)run; edition; (*de cheminée*) draught; (*de loterie*) draw; (*désaccord*) friction; ~ au sort drawing lots.

tirailler [tiraje] *vt* to pull at, tug at // *vi* to fire at random.

tirant [tirɑ̃] *nm*: ~ d'eau draught.

tire [tir] *nf*: vol à la ~ pickpocketing.

tiré, e [tire] *a* (*traits*) drawn // *nm* (COMM) drawee; ~ par les che-

veux far-fetched.

tire-au-flanc [tiroflɑ̃] *nm inv* (*péj*) skiver.

tire-bouchon [tirbuʃɔ̃] *nm* corkscrew.

tirelire [tirlir] *nf* moneybox.

tirer [tire] *vt* (*gén*) to pull; (*extraire*): ~ qch de to take ou pull sth out of; to get sth out of; to extract sth from; (*tracer: ligne, trait*) to draw, trace; (*fermer: rideau*) to draw, close; (*choisir: carte, conclusion, aussi* COMM: *chèque*) to draw; (*en faisant feu: balle, coup*) to fire; (: *animal*) to shoot; (*journal, livre, photo*) to print; (FOOTBALL: *corner etc*) to take // *vi* (*faire feu*) to fire; (*faire du tir,* FOOTBALL) to shoot; (*cheminée*) to draw; se ~ *vi* (*fam*) to push off; s'en ~ to pull through, get off; ~ sur to pull on ou at; to shoot ou fire at; (*pipe*) to draw on; (*fig: avoisiner*) to verge ou border on; ~ qn de (*embarras etc*) to help ou get sb out of; ~ à l'arc/la carabine to shoot with a bow and arrow/ with a rifle.

tiret [tire] *nm* dash.

tireur, euse [tirœr, -øz] *nm/f* gunman; (COMM) drawer; ~ d'élite marksman.

tiroir [tirwar] *nm* drawer; ~-caisse *nm* till.

tisane [tizan] *nf* herb tea.

tisonnier [tizɔnje] *nm* poker.

tisser [tise] *vt* to weave; **tisserand** *nm* weaver.

tissu [tisy] *nm* fabric, material, cloth *q*; (ANAT, BIO) tissue.

tissu-éponge [tisyepɔ̃ʒ] *nm* (terry) towelling *q*.

titre [titr(ə)] *nm* (*gén*) title; (*de journal*) headline; (*diplôme*) qualification; (COMM) security; en ~ (*champion*) official; à juste ~ with just cause, rightly; à quel ~? on what grounds?; à aucun ~ on no account; au même ~ (que) in the same way (as); à ~ d'information for (your) information; à ~ gracieux free of charge; à ~ **d'essai** on a trial basis; à ~ **privé** in a private capacity; ~ **de propriété** title deed; ~ **de transport** ticket.

tituber [titybe] *vi* to stagger (along).

titulaire [titylɛʀ] (*ADMIN*) *a* appointed, with tenure // *nm* incumbent; **être** ~ **de** (*poste*) to hold; (*permis*) to be the holder of.

toast [tost] *nm* slice *ou* piece of toast; (*de bienvenue*) (welcoming) toast; **porter un** ~ **à qn** to propose *ou* drink a toast to sb.

toboggan [tɔbɔgɑ̃] *nm* toboggan; (*jeu*) slide.

tocsin [tɔksɛ̃] *nm* alarm (bell).

toge [tɔʒ] *nf* toga; (*de juge*) gown.

toi [twa] *pronom* you.

toile [twal] *nf* (*matériau*) cloth *g*; (*bâche*) piece of canvas; (*tableau*) canvas; ~ **d'araignée** cobweb; ~ **cirée** oilcloth; ~ **de fond** (*fig*) backdrop.

toilette [twalɛt] *nf* wash; (*habits*) outfit; dress *g*; ~**s** *nfpl* (w.-c.) toilet *sg*; **faire sa** ~ to have a wash, get washed; **articles de** ~ toiletries.

toi-même [twamɛm] *pronom* yourself.

toiser [twaze] *vt* to eye up and down.

toison [twazɔ̃] *nf* (*de mouton*) fleece; (*cheveux*) mane.

toit [twa] *nm* roof; ~ **ouvrant** sunroof.

toiture [twatyʀ] *nf* roof.

tôle [tol] *nf* (*plaque*) steel *ou* iron sheet; ~ **ondulée** corrugated iron.

tolérable [tɔleʀabl(ə)] *a* tolerable, bearable.

tolérant, e [tɔleʀɑ̃, -ɑ̃t] *a* tolerant.

tolérer [tɔleʀe] *vt* to tolerate; (*ADMIN: hors taxe etc*) to allow.

tollé [tɔle] *nm* outcry.

tomate [tɔmat] *nf* tomato.

tombe [tɔ̃b] *nf* (*sépulture*) grave; (*avec monument*) tomb.

tombeau, x [tɔ̃bo] *nm* tomb.

tombée [tɔ̃be] *nf*: **à la** ~ **de la nuit** at the close of day, at nightfall.

tomber [tɔ̃be] *vi* to fall; **laisser** ~

to drop; ~ **sur** *vt* (*rencontrer*) to come across; (*attaquer*) to set about; ~ **de fatigue/sommeil** to drop from exhaustion/be falling asleep on one's feet; **ça tombe bien** that's come at the right time; **il est bien tombé** he's been lucky.

tome [tɔm] *nm* volume.

ton, ta, *pl* **tes** [tɔ̃, ta, te] *dét* your.

ton [tɔ̃] *nm* (*gén*) tone; (*MUS*) key; (*couleur*) shade, tone; **de bon** ~ in good taste.

tonalité [tɔnalite] *nf* (*au téléphone*) dialling tone; (*MUS*) key; (*fig*) tone.

tondeuse [tɔ̃døz] *nf* (*à gazon*) (lawn)mower; (*du coiffeur*) clippers *pl*; (*pour la tonte*) shears *pl*.

tondre [tɔ̃dʀ(ə)] *vt* (*pelouse, herbe*) to mow; (*haie*) to cut, clip; (*mouton, toison*) to shear; (*cheveux*) to crop.

tonifier [tɔnifje] *vt* (*peau, organisme*) to tone up.

tonique [tɔnik] *a* fortifying // *nm* tonic.

tonne [tɔn] *nf* metric ton, tonne.

tonneau, x [tɔno] *nm* (*à vin, cidre*) barrel; (*NAVIG*) ton; **faire des** ~**x** (*voiture, avion*) to roll over.

tonnelle [tɔnɛl] *nf* bower, arbour.

tonner [tɔne] *vi* to thunder; **il tonne** it is thundering, there's some thunder.

tonnerre [tɔnɛʀ] *nm* thunder.

tonus [tɔnys] *nm* dynamism.

top [tɔp] *nm*: **au 3ème** ~ at the 3rd stroke.

topinambour [tɔpinɑ̃buʀ] *nm* Jerusalem artichoke.

toque [tɔk] *nf* (*de fourrure*) fur hat; ~ **de jockey/juge** jockey's/judge's cap; ~ **de cuisinier** chef's hat.

toqué, e [tɔke] *a* (*fam*) cracked.

torche [tɔʀʃ(ə)] *nf* torch.

torchon [tɔʀʃɔ̃] *nm* cloth, duster; (*à vaisselle*) tea towel *ou* cloth.

tordre [tɔʀdʀ(ə)] *vt* (*chiffon*) to wring; (*barre, fig: visage*) to twist; **se** ~ *vi* (*barre*) to bend; (*roue*) to twist, buckle; (*ver, serpent*) to writhe; **se** ~ **le pied/ bras** to twist one's foot/arm.

tordu, e [tɔʀdy] a (fig) warped, twisted.

tornade [tɔʀnad] nf tornado.

torpille [tɔʀpij] nf torpedo; **torpiller** vt to torpedo.

torréfier [tɔʀefje] vt to roast.

torrent [tɔʀɑ̃] nm torrent.

torse [tɔʀs(ə)] nm (ANAT) torso; chest.

torsion [tɔʀsjɔ̃] nf twisting; torsion.

tort [tɔʀ] nm (défaut) fault; (préjudice) wrong q; ~s mpl (JUR) fault sg; **avoir** ~ to be wrong; **être dans son** ~ to be in the wrong; **donner** ~ **à qn** to lay the blame on sb; (fig) to prove sb wrong; **causer du** ~ **à** to harm; to be harmful ou detrimental to; **à** ~ wrongly; **à** ~ **et à travers** wildly.

torticolis [tɔʀtikɔli] nm stiff neck.

tortiller [tɔʀtije] vt to twist; to twiddle; **se** ~ vi to wriggle, squirm.

tortionnaire [tɔʀsjɔnɛʀ] nm torturer.

tortue [tɔʀty] nf tortoise.

tortueux, euse [tɔʀtɥø, -øz] a (rue) twisting; (fig) tortuous.

torture [tɔʀtyʀ] nf torture; **torturer** vt to torture; (fig) to torment.

tôt [to] ad early; ~ **ou tard** sooner or later; **si** ~ so early; (déjà) so soon; **au plus** ~ at the earliest; **il eut** ~ **fait de faire** he soon did.

total, e, aux [tɔtal, -o] a, nm total; **au** ~ in total ou all; **faire le** ~ to work out the total, add up; **~ement** ad totally, completely; **~iser** vt to total (up).

totalité [tɔtalite] nf: **la** ~ **de** all of, the total amount (ou number) of; the whole + sg; **en** ~ entirely.

toubib [tubib] nm (fam) doctor.

touchant, e [tuʃɑ̃, -ɑ̃t] a touching.

touche [tuʃ] nf (de piano, de machine à écrire) key; (PEINTURE etc) stroke, touch; (fig de nostalgie) touch, hint; (FOOTBALL: aussi: remise en ~) throw-in; (aussi: ligne de ~) touch-line.

toucher [tuʃe] nm touch // vt to touch; (palper) to feel; (atteindre: d'un coup de feu etc) to hit; (concerner) to concern, affect; (contacter) to reach, contact; (recevoir: récompense) to receive, get; (: salaire) to draw, get; (: chèque) to cash; **au** ~ to the touch; **se** ~ (être en contact) to touch; **~ à** to touch; (concerner) to have to do with, concern; **je vais lui en** ~ **un mot** I'll have a word with him about it; **~ à sa fin** to be drawing to a close.

touffe [tuf] nf tuft.

touffu, e [tufy] a thick, dense.

toujours [tuʒuʀ] ad always; (encore) still; (constamment) forever; ~ **plus nombreux** more and more; **pour** ~ forever; ~ **est-il que** the fact remains that; **essaie** ~ (you can) try anyway.

toupet [tupɛ] nm (fam) cheek.

toupie [tupi] nf (spinning) top.

tour [tuʀ] nf tower; (immeuble) high-rise block (Brit) ou building (US); (ÉCHECS) castle, rook // nm (excursion) stroll, walk; run, ride; trip; (SPORT: aussi: ~ **de piste**) lap; (d'être servi ou de jouer etc, tournure, de vis ou clef) turn; (de roue etc) revolution; (circonférence): **de 3 m** ~ 3 m round, with a circumference ou girth of 3 m; (POL: aussi: ~ **de scrutin**) ballot; (ruse, de prestidigitation) trick; (de potier) wheel; (à bois, métaux) lathe; **faire le** ~ **de** to go round; (à pied) to walk round; **c'est au** ~ **de Renée** it's Renée's turn; **à** ~ **de rôle**, **à** ~ **de rôle**, **à** ~ **de rôle** in turn; ~ **de taille/tête** waist/head measurement; ~ **de chant** song recital; ~ **de contrôle** nf control tower; ~ **de garde** spell of duty; ~ **d'horizon** (fig) general survey.

tourbe [tuʀb(ə)] nf peat.

tourbillon [tuʀbijɔ̃] nm whirlwind; (d'eau) whirlpool; (fig) whirl, swirl; **tourbillonner** vi to whirl (round).

tourelle [tuʀɛl] nf turret.

tourisme [turism(ə)] *nm* tourism;
agence de ~ tourist agency; **faire
du ~** to go sightseeing; to go touring; **touriste** *nmf* tourist; **touristique** *a* tourist *cpd*; (*région*) touristic.

tourment [turmɑ̃] *nm* torment.

tourmenter [turmɑ̃te] *vt* to torment; **se ~** *vi* to fret, worry *vo*.

tournant [turnɑ̃] *nm* (*de route*)
bend; (*fig*) turning point.

tournebroche [turnəbrɔʃ] *nm*
roasting spit.

tourne-disque [turnədisk(ə)] *nm*
record player.

tournée [turne] *nf* (*du facteur etc*)
round; (*d'artiste, politicien*) tour;
(*au café*) round (of drinks).

tourner [turne] *vt* to turn; (*sauce,
mélange*) to stir; (*contourner*) to get
round; (*CINÉMA*) to shoot; to make
// to turn; (*moteur*) to run; (*compteur*) to tick away; (*lait etc*) to turn
(sour); **se ~** *vi* to turn round; **se ~
vers** to turn to; to turn towards;
bien ~ to turn out well; **~ autour
de** to go round; (*péj*) to hang about;
~ à/en to turn into; **~ le dos à** to
turn one's back on; **to have one's
back to; **~ de l'œil** to pass out.

tournesol [turnəsɔl] *nm* sunflower.

tournevis [turnəvis] *nm* screw-
driver.

tourniquet [turnike] *nm* (*pour arroser*) sprinkler; (*portillon*) turnstile;
(*présentoir*) revolving stand, spinner.

tournoi [turnwa] *nm* tournament.

tournoyer [turnwaje] *vi* to whirl
round; to swirl round.

tournure [turnyr] *nf* (*LING*) turn of
phrase; form; phrasing; (*évolution*):
la ~ de qch the way sth is develop-
ing; (*aspect*): **la ~ de** the look of;
d'esprit turn *ou* cast of mind; **la ~
des événements** the turn of events.

tourte [turt(ə)] *nf* pie.

tous *dét* [tu] , *pronom* [tus] *voir*
tout.

Toussaint [tusɛ̃] *nf*: **la ~** All Saints'
Day.

tousser [tuse] *vi* to cough.

tout, e, *pl* **tous, toutes** [tu, tut,
tus] ♦ *a*

1 (*avec article sing*) all; **~ le lait**
all the milk; **~e la nuit** all night, the
whole night; **~ le livre** the whole
book; **~ un pain** a whole loaf; **~ le
temps** all the time; the whole time;
c'est ~ le contraire it's quite the
opposite

2 (*avec article pl*) every; all; **tous
les livres** all the books; **toutes les
nuits** every night; **toutes les fois**
every time; **toutes les trois/deux
semaines** every third/other *ou* second week, every three/two weeks;
tous les deux both *ou* each of us (*ou*
them *ou* you); **toutes les 3** all 3 of
us (*ou* them *ou* you)

3 (*sans article*): **à ~ âge** at any
age; **pour ~e nourriture, il avait
... ** his only food was ...

♦ *pronom* everything, all; **il a ~
fait** he's done everything; **je les
vois tous** I can see them all *ou* all of
them; **nous y sommes tous allés**
all of us went, we all went; **en ~** in
all; **~ ce qu'il sait** all he knows

♦ *nm* whole; **le ~** all of it (*ou*
them); **le ~ est de ...** the main
thing is to ...; **pas du ~** not at all

♦ *ad* **1** (*très, complètement*) very;
~ près very near; **le ~ premier** the
very first; **~ seul** all alone; **le livre
~ entier** the whole book; **~ en haut**
right at the top; **~ droit** straight
ahead

2: **~ en** while; **~ en travaillant**
while working, as he *etc* works

3: **~ d'abord** first of all; **~ à coup**
suddenly; **~ à fait** absolutely; **~ à
l'heure** a short while ago; (*futur*) in
a short while, shortly; **à ~ à
l'heure!** see you later!; **~ de
même** all the same; **~ le monde**
pronom everybody; **~ de suite** immediately, straight away; **~ terrain,
tous terrains** *a inv* all-terrain.

toutefois [tutfwa] *ad* however.

toux [tu] *nf* cough.

toxicomane [tɔksikɔman] *nm/f* drug addict.

trac [tʀak] *nm* nerves *pl*.

tracasser [tʀakase] *vt* to worry, bother; to harass.

trace [tʀas] *nf* (*empreintes*) tracks *pl*; (*marques, aussi fig*) mark; (*restes, vestige*) trace; (*indice*) sign; ~s de pas footprints.

tracé [tʀase] *nm* line; layout.

tracer [tʀase] *vt* to draw; (*mot*) to trace; (*piste*) to open up.

tract [tʀakt] *nm* tract, pamphlet.

tractations [tʀaktasjɔ̃] *nfpl* dealings, bargaining *sg*.

tracteur [tʀaktœʀ] *nm* tractor.

traction [tʀaksjɔ̃] *nf*: ~ **avant/arrière** front-wheel/rear-wheel drive.

tradition [tʀadisjɔ̃] *nf* tradition; **traditionnel, le** *a* traditional.

traducteur, trice [tʀadyktœʀ, -tʀis] *nm/f* translator.

traduction [tʀadyksjɔ̃] *nf* translation.

traduire [tʀadɥiʀ] *vt* to translate; (*exprimer*) to render, convey.

trafic [tʀafik] *nm* traffic; ~ **d'armes** arms dealing; **trafiquant, e** *nm/f* trafficker; dealer; **trafiquer** *vt* (*péj*) to doctor, tamper with.

tragédie [tʀaʒedi] *nf* tragedy.

tragique [tʀaʒik] *a* tragic.

trahir [tʀaiʀ] *vt* to betray; (*fig*) to give away, reveal; **trahison** *nf* betrayal; (*JUR*) treason.

train [tʀɛ̃] *nm* (*RAIL*) train; (*allure*) pace; (*fig: ensemble*) set; **mettre qch en** ~ to get sth under way; **mettre qn en** ~ to put sb in good spirits; **se mettre en** ~ to get started; to warm up; **se sentir en** ~ to feel in good form; ~ **d'atterrissage** undercarriage; ~ **autos-couchettes** car-sleeper train; ~ **électrique** (*jouet*) (electric) train set; ~ **de vie** style of living.

traîne [tʀɛn] *nf* (*de robe*) train; **être à la** ~ to be in tow; to lag behind.

traîneau, x [tʀɛno] *nm* sleigh, sledge.

traînée [tʀene] *nf* streak, trail; (*péj*) slut.

traîner [tʀene] *vt* (*remorque*) to pull; (*enfant, chien*) to drag ou trail along // *vi* (*être en désordre*) to be around; (*marcher*) to dawdle (along); (*vagabonder*) to hang about; (*agir lentement*) to idle about; (*durer*) to drag on; **se** ~ *vi* to drag o.s. along; ~ **les pieds** to drag one's feet.

train-train [tʀɛ̃tʀɛ̃] *nm* humdrum routine.

traire [tʀɛʀ] *vt* to milk.

trait [tʀɛ] *nm* (*ligne*) line; (*de dessin*) stroke; (*caractéristique*) feature, trait; ~s *nmpl* (*du visage*) features; **d'un** ~ (*boire*) in one gulp; **de** ~ *a* (*animal*) draught; **avoir** ~ **à** to concern; ~ **d'union** hyphen; (*fig*) link.

traitant, e [tʀɛtɑ̃, -ɑ̃t] *a*: **votre médecin** ~ your usual *ou* family doctor; **crème** ~**e** conditioning cream.

traite [tʀɛt] *nf* (*COMM*) draft; (*AGR*) milking; **d'une** ~ without stopping; **la** ~ **des noirs** the slave trade.

traité [tʀɛte] *nm* treaty.

traitement [tʀɛtmɑ̃] *nm* treatment; processing; (*salaire*) salary; ~ **de données/texte** data/word processing.

traiter [tʀɛte] *vt* (*gén*) to treat; (*TECH, INFORM*) to process; (*affaire*) to deal with, handle; (*qualifier*): ~ **qn d'idiot** to call sb a fool // *vi* to deal; ~ **de** *vt* to deal with.

traiteur [tʀɛtœʀ] *nm* caterer.

traître, esse [tʀɛtʀ(ə), -tʀɛs] *a* (*dangereux*) treacherous // *nm* traitor.

trajectoire [tʀaʒɛktwaʀ] *nf* path.

trajet [tʀaʒɛ] *nm* journey; (*itinéraire*) route; (*fig*) path, course.

trame [tʀam] *nf* (*de tissu*) weft; (*fig*) framework; texture.

tramer [tʀame] *vt* to plot, hatch.

trampolino [tʀɑ̃polino] *nm* trampoline.

tramway [tʀamwɛ] *nm* tram(way);

tram(car) (Brit), streetcar (US).

tranchant, e [trɑ̃ʃɑ̃, -ɑ̃t] a sharp; (fig) peremptory // nm (d'un couteau) cutting edge; (de la main) edge.

tranche [trɑ̃ʃ] nf (morceau) slice; (arête) edge; (partie) section; (série) block; issue; bracket.

tranché, e [trɑ̃ʃe] a (couleurs) distinct, sharply contrasted; (opinions) clear-cut, definite // nf trench.

trancher [trɑ̃ʃe] vt to cut, sever; (fig: résoudre) to settle // vi to take a decision; ~ avec to contrast sharply with.

tranquille [trɑ̃kil] a calm, quiet, (enfant, élève) quiet; (rassuré) easy in one's mind, with one's mind at rest; **se tenir ~** (enfant) to be quiet; **laisse-moi/ laisse-ça ~** leave me/it alone; **tranquillité** nf quietness; peace (and quiet).

transat [trɑ̃zat] nm deckchair.

transborder [trɑ̃sbɔrde] vt to tran(s)ship.

transférer [trɑ̃sfere] vt to transfer; **transfert** nm transfer.

transfigurer [trɑ̃sfigyre] vt to transform.

transformation [trɑ̃sfɔrmasjɔ̃] nf transformation; (RUGBY) conversion.

transformer [trɑ̃sfɔrme] vt to transform, alter; (matière première, appartement, RUGBY) to convert; ~ en to transform into; to turn into; to convert into.

transfusion [trɑ̃sfyzjɔ̃] nf: ~ sanguine blood transfusion.

transgresser [trɑ̃sgrese] vt to contravene, disobey.

transi, e [trɑ̃zi] a numb (with cold), chilled to the bone.

transiger [trɑ̃ziʒe] vi to compromise.

transistor [trɑ̃zistɔr] nm transistor.

transit [trɑ̃zit] nm transit; ~**er** vi to pass in transit.

transitif, ive [trɑ̃zitif, -iv] a transitive.

transition [trɑ̃zisjɔ̃] nf transition; **transitoire** a transitional; transient.

translucide [trɑ̃slysid] a translucent.

transmetteur [trɑ̃smetœr] nm transmitter.

transmettre [trɑ̃smetr(ə)] vt (passer): ~ qch à qn to pass sth on to sb; (TECH, TÉL, MÉD) to transmit; (TV, RADIO: retransmettre) to broadcast.

transmission [trɑ̃smisjɔ̃] nf transmission.

transparaître [trɑ̃sparetr(ə)] vi to show (through).

transparence [trɑ̃sparɑ̃s] nf transparency; **par ~** (regarder) against the light; (voir) showing through.

transparent, e [trɑ̃sparɑ̃, -ɑ̃t] a transparent.

transpercer [trɑ̃sperse] vt to go through, pierce.

transpiration [trɑ̃spirasjɔ̃] nf perspiration.

transpirer [trɑ̃spire] vi to perspire.

transplanter [trɑ̃splɑ̃te] vt (MÉD, BOT) to transplant; (personne) to uproot.

transport [trɑ̃spɔr] nm transport; ~**s en commun** public transport sg.

transporter [trɑ̃spɔrte] vt to carry, move; (COMM) to transport, convey; **transporteur** nm haulage contractor (Brit), trucker (US).

transversal, e, aux [trɑ̃sversal, -o] a transverse, cross(-); cross-country; running at right angles.

trapèze [trapez] nm (au cirque) trapeze.

trappe [trap] nf trap door.

trapu, e [trapy] a squat, stocky.

traquenard [traknar] nm trap.

traquer [trake] vt to track down; (harceler) to hound.

traumatiser [tromatize] vt to traumatize.

travail, aux [travaj, -o] nm (gén) work; (tâche, métier) work a job; (ÉCON, MÉD) labour // nmpl (de réparation, agricoles etc) work sg; (sur route) roadworks pl; (de construction) building (work); **être sans ~** (employé) to be out of work ou unem-

ployed; ~ **(au) noir** moonlighting;
travaux des champs farmwork sg;
travaux dirigés (SCOL) supervised
practical work sg; **travaux forcés**
hard labour sg; **travaux manuels**
(SCOL) handicrafts; **travaux ménagers** housework sg.

travailler [tʀavaje] vi to work; (bois)
to warp // vt (bois, métal) to work;
(objet d'art, discipline, fig: influencer) to work on; **cela le travaille** it
is on his mind; ~ **à** to work on; (fig:
contribuer à) to work towards; **travailleur, euse** a hard-working //
nm/f worker; **travailliste** a ~ Labour cpd.

travée [tʀave] nf row; (ARCHIT)
bay; span.

travers [tʀavɛʀ] nm fault, failing; **en
~ (de)** across; **au ~ (de)** through;
de ~ a askew // ad sideways; (fig)
the wrong way; **à ~** through; **regarder de ~** (fig) to look askance at.

traverse [tʀavɛʀs(ə)] nf (de voie ferrée) sleeper; **chemin de ~** shortcut.

traversée [tʀavɛʀse] nf crossing.

traverser [tʀavɛʀse] vt (gén) to
cross; (ville, tunnel, aussi: percer,
fig) to go through; (suj: ligne, trait)
to run across.

traversin [tʀavɛʀsɛ̃] nm bolster.

travestir [tʀavɛstiʀ] vt (vérité) to
misrepresent; se ~ vi to dress up; to
dress as a woman.

trébucher [tʀebyʃe] vi: ~ **(sur)** to
stumble (over), trip (against).

trèfle [tʀɛfl(ə)] nm (BOT) clover;
(CARTES: couleur) clubs pl; (:
carte) club.

treille [tʀɛj] nf vine arbour; climbing
vine.

treillis [tʀeji] nm (métallique) wire-
mesh.

treize [tʀɛz] num thirteen; **treizième** num thirteenth.

tréma [tʀema] nm diaeresis.

tremblement [tʀɑ̃bləmɑ̃] nm: ~ **de
terre** earthquake.

trembler [tʀɑ̃ble] vi to tremble,
shake; ~ **de** (froid, fièvre) to shiver

ou tremble with; (peur) to shake ou
tremble with; ~ **pour qn** to fear for
sb.

trémousser [tʀemuse]: se ~ vi to
jig about, wriggle about.

trempe [tʀɑ̃p] nf (fig): **de cette/sa
~** of this/his calibre.

trempé, e [tʀɑ̃pe] a soaking (wet),
drenched; (TECH) tempered.

tremper [tʀɑ̃pe] vt to soak, drench;
(aussi: **faire ~**, **mettre à ~**) to
soak; (plonger): ~ **qch dans** to dip
sth in(to) // vi to soak; (fig): ~ **dans**
to be involved ou have a hand in; se
~ vi to have a quick dip; **trempette**
nf: **faire trempette** to go paddling.

tremplin [tʀɑ̃plɛ̃] nm springboard;
(SKI) ski-jump.

trentaine [tʀɑ̃tɛn] nf: **une ~ (de)**
thirty or so, about thirty; **avoir la ~**
(âge) to be around thirty.

trente [tʀɑ̃t] num thirty; **trentième**
num thirtieth.

trépied [tʀepje] nm tripod.

trépigner [tʀepiɲe] vi to stamp
(one's feet).

très [tʀɛ] ad very; much + pp, highly
+ pp.

trésor [tʀezɔʀ] nm treasure; (AD-
MIN) finances pl; funds pl; **T~** (public) public revenue.

trésorerie [tʀezɔʀʀi] nf (gestion) accounts pl; (bureaux) accounts department; **difficultés de ~** cash problems, shortage of cash ou funds.

trésorier, ière [tʀezɔʀje, -jɛʀ] nm/f
treasurer.

tressaillir [tʀesajiʀ] vi to shiver,
shudder; to quiver.

tressauter [tʀesote] vi to start,
jump.

tresse [tʀɛs] nf braid, plait.

tresser [tʀese] vt (cheveux) to braid,
plait; (fil, jonc) to plait; (corbeille)
to weave; (corde) to twist.

tréteau, x [tʀeto] nm trestle.

treuil [tʀœj] nm winch.

trêve [tʀɛv] nf (MIL, POL) truce;
(fig) respite; ~ **de ...** enough of
this ....

tri [tʀi] nm sorting out q; selection; (POSTES) sorting; sorting office.

triangle [tʀijɑ̃gl(ə)] nm triangle.

tribord [tʀibɔʀ] nm: à ~ to starboard, on the starboard side.

tribu [tʀiby] nf tribe.

tribunal, aux [tʀibynal, -o] nm (JUR) court; (MIL) tribunal.

tribune [tʀibyn] nf (estrade) platform, rostrum; (débat) forum; (d'église, de tribunal) gallery; (de stade) stand.

tribut [tʀiby] nm tribute.

tributaire [tʀibytɛʀ] a: être ~ de to be dependent on.

tricher [tʀiʃe] vi to cheat.

tricolore [tʀikɔlɔʀ] a three-coloured; (français) red, white and blue.

tricot [tʀiko] nm (technique, ouvrage) knitting q; (tissu) knitted fabric; (vêtement) jersey, sweater.

tricoter [tʀikɔte] vt to knit.

trictrac [tʀiktʀak] nm backgammon.

tricycle [tʀisikl(ə)] nm tricycle.

triennal, e, aux [tʀiɛnal, -o] a three-yearly; three-year.

trier [tʀije] vt to sort out; (POSTES, fruits) to sort.

trimestre [tʀimɛstʀ(ə)] nm (SCOL) term; (COMM) quarter; **trimestriel, le** a quarterly; (SCOL) end-of-term.

tringle [tʀɛ̃gl(ə)] nf rod.

trinquer [tʀɛ̃ke] vi to clink glasses.

triomphe [tʀijɔ̃f] nm triumph.

triompher [tʀijɔ̃fe] vi to triumph, win; ~ de to triumph over, overcome.

tripes [tʀip] nfpl (CULIN) tripe sg.

triple [tʀipl(ə)] a triple; treble // nm: le ~ (de) (comparaison) three times as much (as); en ~ exemplaire in triplicate; **triplés, ées** nm/fpl triplets; **tripler** vi, vt to triple, treble.

tripoter [tʀipɔte] vt to fiddle with.

trique [tʀik] nf cudgel.

triste [tʀist(ə)] a sad; (péj): ~ personnage/affaire sorry individual/affair; **tristesse** nf sadness.

trivial, e, aux [tʀivjal, -o] a coarse, crude; (commun) mundane.

troc [tʀɔk] nm barter.

trognon [tʀɔɲɔ̃] nm (de fruit) core; (de légume) stalk.

trois [tʀwa] num three; **troisième** num third; ~-**quarts** nmpl: les ~-quarts de three-quarters of.

trombe [tʀɔ̃b] nf: des ~s d'eau a downpour; en ~ like a whirlwind.

trombone [tʀɔ̃bɔn] nm (MUS) trombone; (de bureau) paper clip.

trompe [tʀɔ̃p] nf (d'éléphant) trunk; (MUS) trumpet, horn.

tromper [tʀɔ̃pe] vt to deceive; (vigilance, poursuivants) to elude; se ~ vi to make a mistake, be mistaken; se ~ de voiture/jour to take the wrong car/get the day wrong; se ~ de 3 cm/20 F to be out by 3 cm/20 F; **tromperie** nf deception, trickery q.

trompette [tʀɔ̃pɛt] nf trumpet; en ~ (nez) turned-up.

tronc [tʀɔ̃] nm (BOT, ANAT) trunk; (d'église) collection box.

tronçon [tʀɔ̃sɔ̃] nm section.

tronçonner [tʀɔ̃sɔne] vt to saw up.

trône [tʀon] nm throne.

trop [tʀo] ad vb +, too much, too + adjectif, adverbe; ~ (nombreux) too many; ~ peu (nombreux) too few; ~ (souvent) too often; ~ (longtemps) (for) too long; ~ de (nombre) too many; (quantité) too much; de ~, en ~: des livres en ~ a few books too many; du lait en ~ too much milk; 3 livres/3 F de ~ = 3 books too many/3 F too much.

tropical, e, aux [tʀɔpikal, -o] a tropical.

tropique [tʀɔpik] nm tropic.

trop-plein [tʀɔplɛ̃] nm (tuyau) overflow ou outlet (pipe); (liquide) overflow.

troquer [tʀɔke]: ~ qch contre to barter ou trade sth for; (fig) to swap sth for.

trot [tʀo] nm trot.

trotter [tʀɔte] vi to trot; (fig) to scamper along (ou about).

trottiner [tʀɔtine] vi (fig) to scamper

along (*ou* about).

trottinette [trɔtinɛt] *nf* (child's) scooter.

trottoir [trɔtwar] *nm* pavement; **faire le ~** (*péj*) to walk the streets; **~ roulant** moving walkway, travellator.

trou [tru] *nm* hole; (*fig*) gap; (*COMM*) deficit; **~ d'air** air pocket; **~ de mémoire** blank, lapse of memory; **le ~ de la serrure** the keyhole.

trouble [trubl(ə)] *a* (*liquide*) cloudy; (*image, mémoire*) indistinct, hazy; (*affaire*) shady, murky // *nm* (*désarroi*) agitation; (*embarras*) confusion; (*zizanie*) unrest, discord; **~s** *nmpl* (*POL*) disturbances, troubles, unrest *sg*; (*MÉD*) trouble *sg*, disorders.

troubler [truble] *vt* (*embarrasser*) to confuse, disconcert; (*émouvoir*) to agitate; to disturb; (*perturber: ordre etc*) to disrupt; (*liquide*) to make cloudy; **se ~** *vi* (*personne*) to become flustered *ou* confused.

trouée [true] *nf* gap; (*MIL*) breach.

trouer [true] *vt* to make a hole (*ou* holes) in; (*fig*) to pierce.

trouille [truj] *nf* (*fam*): **avoir la ~** to be scared to death.

troupe [trup] *nf* troop; **~ (de théâtre)** (theatrical) company.

troupeau, x [trupo] *nm* (*de moutons*) flock; (*de vaches*) herd.

trousse [trus] *nf* case, kit; (*d'écolier*) pencil case; (*de docteur*) instrument case; **aux ~s de** (*fig*) on the heels *ou* tail of; **~ à outils** toolkit; **~ de toilette** toilet bag.

trousseau, x [truso] *nm* (*de mariée*) trousseau; **~ de clefs** bunch of keys.

trouvaille [truvaj] *nf* find.

trouver [truve] *vt* to find; (*rendre visite*): **aller/venir ~ qn** to go and see sb; **je trouve que** I find *ou* think that; **~ à boire/critiquer** to find something to drink/criticize; **se ~** *vi* (*être*) to be; (*être soudain*) to find o.s.; **il se trouve que** it happens

that, it turns out that; **se ~ bien** to feel well; **se ~ mal** to pass out.

truand [tryɑ̃] *nm* villain, crook.

truander [tryɑ̃de] *vt* to cheat.

truc [tryk] *nm* (*astuce*) way, device; (*de cinéma, prestidigitateur*) trick effect; (*chose*) thing, thingumajig; **avoir le ~** to have the knack.

truchement [tryʃmɑ̃] *nm*: **par le ~ de qn** through (the intervention of) sb.

truelle [tryɛl] *nf* trowel.

truffe [tryf] *nf* truffle; (*nez*) nose.

truffé, e [tryfe] *a*: **~ de** (*fig*) peppered with; bristling with.

truie [trɥi] *nf* sow.

truite [trɥit] *nf* trout *inv*.

truquer [tryke] *vt* (*élections, serrure, dés*) to fix; (*CINÉMA*) to use special effects in.

T.S.V.P. *sigle* (= *tournez s.v.p.*) P.T.O.

T.T.C. *sigle* = *toutes taxes comprises*.

tu [ty] *pronom* you.

tu, e [ty] *pp de* **taire**.

tuba [tyba] *nm* (*MUS*) tuba; (*SPORT*) snorkel.

tube [tyb] *nm* tube; pipe; (*chanson, disque*) hit song *ou* record.

tuer [tɥe] *vt* to kill; **se ~** *vi* to be killed; (*suicide*) to kill o.s.; **tuerie** *nf* slaughter *q*.

tue-tête [tytɛt]: **à ~** *ad* at the top of one's voice.

tueur [tɥœr] *nm* killer; **~ à gages** hired killer.

tuile [tɥil] *nf* tile; (*fam*) spot of bad luck, blow.

tulipe [tylip] *nf* tulip.

tuméfié, e [tymefje] *a* puffy, swollen.

tumeur [tymœr] *nf* growth, tumour.

tumulte [tymylt(ə)] *nm* commotion.

tumultueux, euse [tymyltɥø, -øz] *a* stormy, turbulent.

tunique [tynik] *nf* tunic.

Tunisie [tynizi] *nf*: **la ~** Tunisia; **tunisien, ne** *a, nm/f* Tunisian.

tunnel [tynɛl] *nm* tunnel.

turbulences [tyrbylɑ̃s] *nfpl* (*AVIAT*)

turbulence sg.

turbulent, e [tyrbylɑ̃, -ɑ̃t] *a* boisterous, unruly.

turc, turque [tyrk(ə)] *a* Turkish // *nm/f:* T~, **Turque** Turk/Turkish woman // *nm* (LING) Turkish.

turf [tyrf] *nm* racing; ~**iste** *nm/f* racegoer.

Turquie [tyrki] *nf:* la ~ Turkey.

turquoise [tyrkwaz] *nf, a inv* turquoise.

tus *etc vb voir* taire.

tutelle [tytɛl] *nf* (JUR) guardianship; (POL) trusteeship; **sous la ~ de** (fig) under the supervision of.

tuteur [tytœr] *nm* (JUR) guardian; (de plante) stake, support.

tutoyer [tytwaje] *vt:* ~ **qn** to address sb as 'tu'.

tuyau, x [tɥijo] *nm* pipe; (flexible) tube; (fam) tip; gen *q.;* ~ **d'arrosage** hosepipe; ~ **d'échappement** exhaust pipe; ~**terie** *nf* piping *q.*

T.V.A. *sigle f voir* **taxe.**

tympan [tɛ̃pɑ̃] *nm* (ANAT) eardrum.

type [tip] *nm* type; (fam) chap, guy // *a* typical, standard.

typé [tipe] *a* ethnic (euph).

typhoïde [tifɔid] *nf* typhoid.

typique [tipik] *a* typical.

tyran [tirɑ̃] *nm* tyrant.

tzigane [dzigan] *a* gipsy, tzigane.

U

ulcère [ylsɛr] *nm* ulcer.

ulcérer [ylsere] *vt* (fig) to sicken, appal.

ultérieur, e [ylterjœr] *a* later, subsequent; **remis à une date ~e** postponed to a later date.

ultime [yltim] *a* final.

ultra... [yltra] *préfixe:* ~**moderne/-rapide** ultra-modern/-fast.

un, une [œ̃, yn] ♦ *article indéfini* a; (devant voyelle) an; ~ **garçon/vieillard** a boy/an old man; **une fille** a girl

♦ *pronom* one; l'~ **des meilleurs** one of the best; l'~ ..., **l'autre** the one ..., the other; **les ~s ..., les autres** some ..., others; l'~ **et l'autre** both (of them); l'~ **ou l'autre** either (of them); l'~ **l'autre, les ~s les autres** each other, one another; **pas ~ seul** not a single one; ~ **par ~** one by one

♦ *num* one; **une pomme seulement** one apple only.

unanime [ynanim] *a* unanimous; **unanimité** *nf:* **à l'unanimité** unanimously.

uni, e [yni] *a* (ton, tissu) plain; (surface) smooth, even; (famille) close(-knit); (pays) united.

unifier [ynifje] *vt* to unite, unify.

uniforme [ynifɔrm(ə)] *a* (mouvement) regular, uniform; (surface, ton) even; (objets, maisons) uniform // *nm* uniform; **uniformiser** *vt* to make uniform; (systèmes) to standardize.

union [ynjɔ̃] *nf* union; ~ **de consommateurs** consumers' association; l'**U~ soviétique** the Soviet Union.

unique [ynik] *a* (seul) only; (le même): **un prix/système** ~ a single price/system; (exceptionnel) unique; **fils/fille** ~ only son/daughter, only child; ~**ment** *ad* only, solely; (juste) only, merely.

unir [ynir] *vt* (nations) to unite; (éléments, couleurs) to combine; (en mariage) to unite, join together; ~ **qch à** to unite sth with; to combine sth with; s'~ to unite; (en mariage) to be joined together.

unité [ynite] *nf* (harmonie, cohésion) unity; (COMM, MIL, de mesure, MATH) unit.

univers [ynivɛr] *nm* universe.

universel, le [ynivɛrsɛl] *a* universal; (esprit) all-embracing.

universitaire [ynivɛrsitɛr] *a* university *cpd;* (diplôme, études) academic, university *cpd* // *nm/f* academic.

université [ynivɛrsite] nf university.

urbain, e [yrbɛ̃, -ɛn] a urban, city cpd; town cpd; (poli) urbane; **urbanisme** nm town planning.

urgence [yrʒɑ̃s] nf urgency; (MÉD etc) emergency; **d'~** a emergency cpd // ad as a matter of urgency.

urgent, e [yrʒɑ̃, -ɑ̃t] a urgent.

urine [yrin] nf urine; **urinoir** nm (public) urinal.

urne [yrn(ə)] nf (électorale) ballot box; (vase) urn.

URSS [fareois: yrs] sigle f: **l'~** the USSR.

urticaire [yrtikɛr] nf nettle rash.

us [ys] nmpl: **~ et coutumes** (habits and) customs.

USA sigle mpl: les **~** the USA.

usage [yzaʒ] nm (emploi, utilisation) use; (coutume) custom; (LING): **l'~** usage; **à l'~** de (pour) (for use of); **en ~** in use; **hors d'~** out of service; wrecked; **à ~ interne** to be taken; **à ~ externe** for external use only.

usagé, e [yzaʒe] a (usé) worn; (d'occasion) used.

usager, ère [yzaʒe, -ɛr] nm/f user.

usé, e [yze] a worn; (banal) hackneyed.

user [yze] vt (outil) to wear down; (vêtement) to wear out; (matière) to wear away; (consommer: charbon etc) to use; **s'~** vi to wear; to wear out; (fig) to decline; **~ de** vt (moyen, procédé) to use, employ; (droit) to exercise.

usine [yzin] nf factory; **~ marémotrice** tidal power station.

usiner [yzine] vt (TECH) to machine.

usité, e [yzite] a common.

ustensile [ystɑ̃sil] nm implement; **~ de cuisine** kitchen utensil.

usuel, le [yzɥɛl] a everyday, common.

usure [yzyr] nf wear; worn state.

ut [yt] nm (MUS) C.

utérus [yterys] nm uterus, womb.

utile [ytil] a useful.

utilisation [ytilizasjɔ̃] nf use.

utiliser [ytilize] vt to use.

utilitaire [ytilitɛr] a utilitarian; (objets) practical.

utilité [ytilite] nf usefulness q; use; **reconnu d'~ publique** state-approved.

V

va vb voir **aller**.

vacance [vakɑ̃s] nf (ADMIN) vacancy; **~s** nfpl holiday(s pl), vacation sg; **prendre des/ses ~s** to take a holiday/one's holiday(s); **aller en ~s** to go on holiday; **vacancier, ière** nm/f holiday-maker.

vacant, e [vakɑ̃, -ɑ̃t] a vacant.

vacarme [vakarm(ə)] nm row, din.

vaccin [vaksɛ̃] nm vaccine; (opération) vaccination; **vaccination** nf vaccination; **vacciner** vt to vaccinate; (fig) to make immune.

vache [vaʃ] nf (ZOOL) cow; (cuir) cowhide // a (fam) rotten; mean; **vachement** ad (fam) damned, hellish.

vaciller [vasije] vi to sway, wobble; (bougie, lumière) to flicker; (fig) to be failing, falter.

va-et-vient [vaevjɛ̃] nm inv (de personnes, véhicules) comings and goings pl, to-ings and fro-ings pl.

vagabond [vagabɔ̃] nm (rôdeur) tramp, vagrant; (voyageur) wanderer.

vagabonder [vagabɔ̃de] vi to roam, wander.

vagin [vaʒɛ̃] nm vagina.

vague [vag] nf wave // a vague; (regard) faraway; (manteau, robe) loose(-fitting); (quelconque): **un ~ bureau/cousin** some office/cousin or other; **~ de fond** nf ground swell.

vaillant, e [vajɑ̃, -ɑ̃t] a (courageux) gallant; (robuste) hale and hearty.

vaille vb voir **valoir**.

vain, e [vɛ̃, vɛn] a vain; **en ~** ad in vain.

vaincre [vɛ̃kr(ə)] vt to defeat; (fig)

to conquer, overcome; **vaincu**, **e** nm/f defeated party; **vainqueur** nm victor; (SPORT) winner.

vais vb voir **aller**.

vaisseau, **x** [veso] nm (ANAT) vessel; (NAVIG) ship, vessel; ~ **spatial** spaceship.

vaisselier [vɛsəlje] nm dresser.

vaisselle [vɛsɛl] nf (service) crockery; (plats etc à laver) (dirty) dishes pl; (lavage) washing-up (Brit), dishes pl.

val, **vaux** [val, vo] nm valley.

valable [valabl(ə)] a valid; (acceptable) decent, worthwhile.

valent etc vb voir **valoir**.

valet [valɛ] nm valet; (CARTES) jack.

valeur [valœʀ] nf (gén) value; (mérite) worth, merit; (COMM: titre) security; **mettre en** ~ (terrain, région) to develop; (fig) to highlight; to show off to advantage; **avoir de la** ~ to be valuable; **sans** ~ worthless; **prendre de la** ~ to go up ou gain in value.

valide [valid] a (en bonne santé) fit; (valable) valid; **valider** vt to validate.

valions vb voir **valoir**.

valise [valiz] nf (suit)case.

vallée [vale] nf valley.

vallon [valɔ̃] nm small valley.

valoir [valwaʀ] vi (être valable) to hold, apply // vt (prix, valeur, effort) to be worth; (causer): ~ **qch à qn** to earn sb sth; **se** ~ vi to be of equal merit; (péj) to be two of a kind; **faire** ~ (droits, prérogatives) to assert; **faire** ~ **que** to point out that; **à** ~ **sur** to be deducted from; **vaille que vaille** somehow or other; **cela ne me dit rien qui vaille** I don't like the look of it at all; **ce climat ne me vaut rien** this climate doesn't suit me; **la peine to be worth the trouble ou worth it; ~ mieux: il vaut mieux se taire** it's better to say nothing; **ça ne vaut**

rien it's worthless; **que vaut ce candidat?** how good is this applicant?

valoriser [valɔʀize] vt (ÉCON) to develop (the economy of); (PSYCH) to increase the standing of.

valse [vals(ə)] nf waltz.

valu, **e** [valy] pp de **valoir**.

vandale [vɑ̃dal] nm/f vandal; **vandalisme** nm vandalism.

vanille [vanij] nf vanilla.

vanité [vanite] nf vanity; **vaniteux**, **euse** a vain, conceited.

vanne [van] nf gate; (fig) joke.

vannerie [vanʀi] nf basketwork.

vantail, **aux** [vɑ̃taj, -o] nm door, leaf (pl leaves).

vantard, **e** [vɑ̃taʀ, -aʀd(ə)] a boastful.

vanter [vɑ̃te] vt to speak highly of, vaunt; **se** ~ vi to boast, brag; **se** ~ **de** to pride o.s. on; (péj) to boast of.

vapeur [vapœʀ] nf steam; (émanation) vapour, fumes pl; ~**s** nfpl (bouffées) vapours; **à** ~ steampowered, steam cpd; **cuit à la** ~ steamed.

vapocuiseur [vapɔkɥizœʀ] nm pressure cooker.

vaporeux, **euse** [vapɔʀø, -øz] a (flou) hazy, misty; (léger) filmy.

vaporisateur [vapɔʀizatœʀ] nm spray.

vaporiser [vapɔʀize] vt (parfum etc) to spray.

varappe [vaʀap] nf rock climbing.

vareuse [vaʀøz] nf (blouson) pea jacket; (d'uniforme) tunic.

variable [vaʀjabl(ə)] a variable; (temps, humeur) changeable; (divers: résultats) varied, various.

varice [vaʀis] nf varicose vein.

varicelle [vaʀisɛl] nf chickenpox.

varié, **e** [vaʀje] a varied; (divers) various.

varier [vaʀje] vi to vary; (temps, humeur) to change // vt to vary.

variété [vaʀjete] nf variety.

variole [vaʀjɔl] nf smallpox.

vas vb voir **aller**.

vase [vɑz] *nm* vase // *nf* silt, mud.

vaseux, euse [vɑzø, -øz] *a* silty, muddy; (*fig: confus*) woolly, hazy; (: *fatigué*) peaky; woozy.

vasistas [vazistas] *nm* fanlight.

vaste [vast(ə)] *a* vast, immense.

vaudrai *etc vb voir* **valoir**.

vaurien, ne [voʀjɛ̃, -ɛn] *nm/f* good-for-nothing, guttersnipe.

vaut *vb voir* **valoir**.

vautour [votuʀ] *nm* vulture.

vautrer [votʀe]: **se ~** *vi*: **se ~ dans/sur** to wallow in/sprawl on.

vaux [vo] *pl de* **val** // *vb voir* **valoir**.

veau, x [vo] *nm* (*ZOOL*) calf (*pl* calves); (*CULIN*) veal; (*peau*) calf-skin.

vécu, e [veky] *pp de* **vivre**.

vedette [vədɛt] *nf* (*artiste etc*) star; (*canot*) patrol boat; launch.

végétal, e, aux [veʒetal, -o] *a* vegetable // *nm* vegetable, plant.

végétarien, ne [veʒetaʀjɛ̃, -ɛn] *a, nm/f* vegetarian.

végétation [veʒetasjɔ̃] *nf* vegetation; **~s** *nfpl* (*MÉD*) adenoids.

véhicule [veikyl] *nm* vehicle; **~ utilitaire** commercial vehicle.

veille [vɛj] *nf* (*garde*) watch; (*PSYCH*) wakefulness; (*jour*): **la ~ (de)** the day before; (*veiller*): **la veille** the previous evening; **à la ~ de** on the eve of.

veillée [veje] *nf* (*soirée*) evening; (*réunion*) evening gathering; **~ (mortuaire)** watch.

veiller [veje] *vi* to stay up; to be awake; to be on watch // *vt* (*malade, mort*) to watch over, sit up with; **~ à** *vt* to attend to, see to; **~ à ce que** to make sure that; **~ sur** *vt* to keep a watch on; **veilleur de nuit** *nm* night watchman.

veilleuse [vɛjøz] *nf* (*lampe*) night light; (*AUTO*) sidelight; (*flamme*) pilot light; **en ~** *a, ad* (*lampe*) dimmed.

veine [vɛn] *nf* (*ANAT, du bois etc*) vein; (*filon*) vein, seam; (*fam: chance*): **avoir de la ~** to be lucky.

velléités [veleite] *nfpl* vague impulses.

vélo [velo] *nm* bike, cycle; **faire du ~** to go cycling.

vélomoteur [velomotœʀ] *nm* moped.

velours [vəluʀ] *nm* velvet; **~ côtelé** corduroy.

velouté, e [vəlute] *a* (*au toucher*) velvety; (*à la vue*) soft, mellow; (*au goût*) smooth, mellow.

velu, e [vəly] *a* hairy.

venais *etc vb voir* **venir**.

venaison [vənɛzɔ̃] *nf* venison.

vendange [vɑ̃dɑ̃ʒ] *nf* (*opération, période: aussi: ~s*) grape harvest; (*raisins*) grape crop, grapes *pl*.

vendanger [vɑ̃dɑ̃ʒe] *vi* to harvest the grapes.

vendeur, euse [vɑ̃dœʀ, -øz] *nm/f* (*de magasin*) shop assistant; (*COMM*) salesman/woman // *nm* (*JUR*) vendor, seller; **~ de journaux** newspaper seller.

vendre [vɑ̃dʀ(ə)] *vt* to sell; **~ qch à qn** to sell sth to sb; **'à ~'** 'for sale'.

vendredi [vɑ̃dʀədi] *nm* Friday; **V~ saint** Good Friday.

vénéneux, euse [venenø, -øz] *a* poisonous.

vénérien, ne [veneʀjɛ̃, -ɛn] *a* venereal.

vengeance [vɑ̃ʒɑ̃s] *nf* vengeance *q*, revenge *q*.

venger [vɑ̃ʒe] *vt* to avenge; **se ~** *vi* to avenge o.s.; **se ~ de qch** to avenge o.s. for sth; to take one's revenge for sth; **se ~ de qn** to take revenge on sb; **se ~ sur** to take revenge on; to take it out on.

venimeux, euse [vənimø, -øz] *a* poisonous, venomous; (*fig: haineux*) venomous, vicious.

venin [vənɛ̃] *nm* venom, poison.

venir [vəniʀ] *vi* to come; **~ de** to come from; **~ de faire**: **je viens d'y aller/de le voir** I've just been there/seen him; **s'il vient à pleuvoir** if it should rain; **j'en viens à croire que** I have come to believe that; **faire ~** (*docteur, plombier*) to call (out).

vent [vɑ̃] *nm* wind; **il y a du ~** it's windy; **c'est du ~** it's all hot air; **au ~** to windward; **sous le ~** to leeward; **avoir le ~ debout/arrière** to head into the wind/have the wind astern; **dans le ~** (*fam*) trendy.

vente [vɑ̃t] *nf* sale; **la ~** (*activité*) selling; (*secteur*) sales *pl*; **mettre en ~** to put on sale; (*objets personnels*) to put up for sale; **~ de charité** jumble sale; **~ aux enchères** auction sale.

venteux, euse [vɑ̃tø, -øz] *a* windy.

ventilateur [vɑ̃tilatœʀ] *nm* fan.

ventiler [vɑ̃tile] *vt* to ventilate; (*total, statistiques*) to break down.

ventouse [vɑ̃tuz] *nf* (*de caoutchouc*) suction pad; (*ZOOL*) sucker.

ventre [vɑ̃tʀ(ə)] *nm* (*ANAT*) stomach; (*fig*) belly; **avoir mal au ~** to have stomach ache (*Brit*) ou a stomach ache (*US*).

ventriloque [vɑ̃tʀilɔk] *nm/f* ventriloquist.

venu, e [vəny] *pp de* **venir** // *a*: **être mal ~ à** to do faire to have no grounds for doing, be in no position to do // *nf* coming.

ver [vɛʀ] *nm voir aussi* **vers**; worm; (*des fruits etc*) maggot; (*du bois*) woodworm *q*; **~ luisant** glow-worm; **~ à soie** silkworm; **~ solitaire** tapeworm; **~ de terre** earthworm.

verbaliser [vɛʀbalize] *vi* (*POLICE*) to book ou report an offender.

verbe [vɛʀb(ə)] *nm* verb.

verdeur [vɛʀdœʀ] *nf* (*vigueur*) vigour, vitality; (*crudité*) forthrightness.

verdict [vɛʀdik(t)] *nm* verdict.

verdir [vɛʀdiʀ] *vi, vt* to turn green.

verdure [vɛʀdyʀ] *nf* greenery.

véreux, euse [veʀø, -øz] *a* worm-eaten; (*malhonnête*) shady, corrupt.

verge [vɛʀʒ(ə)] *nf* (*ANAT*) penis; (*baguette*) stick, cane.

verger [vɛʀʒe] *nm* orchard.

verglacé, e [vɛʀglase] *a* icy, iced-over.

verglas [vɛʀgla] *nm* (black) ice.

vergogne [vɛʀgɔɲ]: **sans ~** *ad* shamelessly.

véridique [veʀidik] *a* truthful.

vérification [veʀifikasjɔ̃] *nf* checking *q*, check.

vérifier [veʀifje] *vt* to check; (*corroborer*) to confirm, bear out.

véritable [veʀitabl(ə)] *a* real; (*ami, amour*) true.

vérité [veʀite] *nf* truth; (*d'un portrait romanesque*) lifelikeness; (*sincérité*) truthfulness, sincerity.

vermeil, le [vɛʀmɛj] *a* ruby red.

vermine [vɛʀmin] *nf* vermin *pl*.

vermoulu, e [vɛʀmuly] *a* worm-eaten, with woodworm.

verni, e [vɛʀni] *a* (*fam*) lucky; **cuir ~** patent leather.

vernir [vɛʀniʀ] *vt* (*bois, tableau, ongles*) to varnish; (*poterie*) to glaze.

vernis [vɛʀni] *nm* (*enduit*) varnish; glaze; (*fig*) veneer; **~ à ongles** nail polish ou varnish.

vernissage [vɛʀnisaʒ] *nm* varnishing; glazing; (*d'une exposition*) preview.

vérole [veʀɔl] *nf* (*variole*) smallpox.

verrai *etc vb voir* **voir**.

verre [vɛʀ] *nm* glass; (*de lunettes*) lens *sg*; **boire** *ou* **prendre un ~** to have a drink; **~s de contact** contact lenses.

verrerie [vɛʀʀi] *nf* (*fabrique*) glassworks *sg*; (*activité*) glass-making; (*objets*) glassware.

verrière [vɛʀjɛʀ] *nf* (*grand vitrage*) window; (*toit vitré*) glass roof.

verrons *etc vb voir* **voir**.

verrou [vɛʀu] *nm* (*targette*) bolt; (*fig*) constriction; **mettre qn sous les ~s** to put sb behind bars; **verrouillage** *nm* locking; **verrouiller** *vt* to lock; to bolt.

verrue [vɛʀy] *nf* wart.

vers [vɛʀ] *nm* line // *nmpl* (*poésie*) verse *sg* // *prép* (*en direction de*) toward(s); (*près de*) around (about); (*temporel*) about, around.

versant [vɛʀsɑ̃] *nm* slopes *pl*, side.

versatile [vɛʀsatil] *a* fickle, changeable.

verse [vɛʀs(ə)]: à ~ ad: il pleut à ~ it's pouring (with rain).

Verseau [vɛʀso] nm: le ~ Aquarius.

versement [vɛʀsəmã] nm payment; en 3 ~s in 3 instalments.

verser [vɛʀse] vt (liquide, grains) to pour; (larmes, sang) to shed; (argent) to pay // vi (véhicule) to overturn; (fig): ~ dans to lapse into.

verset [vɛʀsɛ] nm verse.

version [vɛʀsjɔ̃] nf version; (SCOL) translation (into the mother tongue).

verso [vɛʀso] nm back; voir au ~ see over(leaf).

vert, e [vɛʀ, vɛʀt(ə)] a green; (vin) young; (vigoureux) sprightly; (cru) forthright // nm green.

vertèbre [vɛʀtɛbʀ(ə)] nf vertebra (pl ae).

vertement [vɛʀtəmã] ad (réprimander) sharply.

vertical, e, aux [vɛʀtikal, -o] a, nf vertical; à la ~e vertically; ~ement ad vertically.

vertige [vɛʀtiʒ] nm (peur du vide) vertigo; (étourdissement) dizzy spell; (fig) fever; **vertigineux, euse** a breathtaking.

vertu [vɛʀty] nf virtue; en ~ de prép in accordance with; ~eux, euse a virtuous.

verve [vɛʀv(ə)] nf witty eloquence; être en ~ to be in brilliant form.

verveine [vɛʀvɛn] nf (BOT) verbena, vervain; (infusion) verbena tea.

vésicule [vezikyl] nf vesicle; ~ biliaire gall-bladder.

vessie [vesi] nf bladder.

veste [vɛst(ə)] nf jacket; ~ droite/croisée single/double-breasted jacket.

vestiaire [vɛstjɛʀ] nm (au théâtre etc) cloakroom; (de stade etc) changing-room (Brit), locker-room (US).

vestibule [vɛstibyl] nm hall.

vestige [vɛstiʒ] nm relic; (fig) vestige; ~s nmpl remains.

veston [vɛstɔ̃] nm jacket.

vêtement [vɛtmã] nm garment, item of clothing; ~s nmpl clothes.

vétérinaire [veteʀinɛʀ] nm/f, vet, veterinary surgeon.

vêtir [vetiʀ] vt to clothe, dress.

veto [veto] nm veto; opposer un ~ à to veto.

vêtu, e [vety] pp de **vêtir**.

vétuste [vetyst(ə)] a ancient, time-worn.

veuf, veuve [vœf, vœv] a widowed // nm widower // nf widow.

veuille, veuillez etc vb voir **vouloir**.

veule [vøl] a spineless.

veux vb voir **vouloir**.

vexations [vɛksasjɔ̃] nfpl humiliations.

vexer [vɛkse] vt to hurt, upset; se ~ vi to be hurt, get upset.

viabiliser [vjabilize] vt to provide with services (water etc).

viable [vjabl(ə)] a viable.

viager, ère [vjaʒe, -ɛʀ] a: rente viagère life annuity.

viande [vjãd] nf meat.

vibrer [vibʀe] vi to vibrate; (son, voix) to be vibrant; (fig) to be stirred; faire ~ to (cause to) vibrate; to stir, thrill.

vice [vis] nm vice; (défaut) fault; ~ de forme legal flaw ou irregularity.

vice... [vis] préfixe vice-.

vichy [viʃi] nm (toile) gingham.

vicié, e [visje] a (air) polluted, tainted; (JUR) invalidated.

vicieux, euse [visjø, -øz] a (pervers) dirty(-minded); nasty; (fautif) incorrect, wrong.

vicinal, e, aux [visinal, -o] a: chemin ~ by-road, byway.

victime [viktim] nf victim; (d'accident) casualty.

victoire [viktwaʀ] nf victory.

vidange [vidãʒ] nf (d'un fossé, réservoir) emptying; (AUTO) oil change; (de lavabo: bonde) waste outlet; ~s nfpl (matières) sewage sg; **vidanger** vt to empty.

vide [vid] a empty // nm (PHYSI-

QUE) vacuum; (espace) (empty) space, gap; (futilité, néant) void; **avoir peur du ~** to be afraid of heights; **emballé sous ~** vacuum packed; **à ~ ad** (sans occupants) empty; (sans charge) unladen.

vidéo [video] nf video / a: **cassette ~** video cassette.

vide-ordures [vidɔʀdyʀ] nm inv (rubbish) chute.

vide-poches [vidpɔʃ] nm inv (tiny); (AUTO) glove compartment.

vider [vide] vt to empty; (CULIN: volaille, poisson) to gut, clean out; **se ~ vi** to empty; **les lieux** to quit ou vacate the premises; **videur** nm (de boîte de nuit) bouncer.

vie [vi] nf life (pl lives); **être en ~** to be alive; **sans ~** lifeless; **à ~** for life.

vieil [vjɛj] a voir **vieux**.

vieillard [vjɛjaʀ] nm old man; les **~s** old people, the elderly.

vieille [vjɛj] a, nf voir **vieux**.

vieilleries [vjɛjʀi] nfpl old things.

vieillesse [vjɛjɛs] nf old age.

vieillir [vjɛjiʀ] vi (prendre de l'âge) to grow old; (population, vin) to age; (doctrine, auteur) to become dated // vt to age; **vieillissement** nm growing old; ageing.

Vienne [vjɛn] nf Vienna.

vienne, viens etc vb voir **venir**.

vierge [vjɛʀʒ(ə)] a virgin; (page) clean, blank // nf virgin; (signe): **V~** Virgo; **~ de** (sans) free from, unsullied by.

Viet-Nam, Vietnam [vjɛtnam] nm Vietnam.

vietnamien, ne [vjɛtnamjɛ̃, -jɛn] a, nm/f Vietnamese.

vieux(vieil), vieille [vjø, vjɛj] a old // nm/f old man/woman // nmpl old people; **mon ~/ma vieille** (fam) old man/girl; **prendre un coup de ~** to put years on; **~ garçon** nm bachelor; **~ jeu** a inv old-fashioned;

vent, émotion) keen; (fort: regret, déception) great, deep; (vivant): **brûlé ~** burnt alive; **de vive voix** personally; **piquer qn au ~** to cut sb to the quick; **à ~** (plaie) open; **avoir les nerfs à ~** to be on edge.

vigie [viʒi] nf look-out; look-out post.

vigne [viɲ] nf (plante) vine; (plantation) vineyard.

vigneron [viɲʀɔ̃] nm wine grower.

vignette [viɲɛt] nf (motif) vignette; (de marque) manufacturer's label ou seal; (ADMIN) = (road) tax disc (Brit), ≈ license plate sticker (US); price label (on medicines for reimbursement by Social Security).

vignoble [viɲɔbl(ə)] nm (plantation) vineyard; (vignes d'une région) vineyards pl.

vigoureux, euse [viguʀø, -øz] a vigorous, robust.

vigueur [vigœʀ] nf vigour; **entrer en ~** to come into force; **en ~** current.

vil, e [vil] a vile, base; **à ~ prix** at a very low price.

vilain, e [vilɛ̃, -ɛn] a (laid) ugly; (affaire, blessure) nasty; (pas sage: enfant) naughty.

vilebrequin [vilbʀəkɛ̃] nm (outil) (bit-)brace.

villa [vila] nf (detached) house.

village [vilaʒ] nm village; **villageois, e** a village cpd // nm/f villager.

ville [vil] nf town; (importante) city; (administration): **la ~** ≈ the Corporation; ≈ the (town) council.

villégiature [vileʒjatyʀ] nf holiday; (holiday) resort.

vin [vɛ̃] nm wine; **avoir le ~ gai** to get happy after a few drinks; **d'honneur** reception (with wine and snacks); **~ ordinaire** table wine; **~ de pays** local wine.

vinaigre [vinɛgʀ(ə)] nm vinegar; **vinaigrette** nf vinaigrette, French dressing.

vindicatif, ive [vɛ̃dikatif, -iv] a vindictive.

vineux, euse [vinø, -øz] a win(e)y.

vingt [vɛ̃, vɛ̃t] num twenty; **vingtaine** nf: **une vingtaine (de)** about twenty, twenty or so; **vingtième** num twentieth.

vinicole [vinikɔl] a wine cpd, wine-growing.

vins etc vb voir **venir**.

vinyle [vinil] nm vinyl.

viol [vjɔl] nm (d'une femme) rape; (d'un lieu sacré) violation.

violacé, e [vjɔlase] a purplish, mauvish.

violemment [vjɔlamɑ̃] ad violently.

violence [vjɔlɑ̃s] nf violence.

violent, e [vjɔlɑ̃, -ɑ̃t] a violent; (remède) drastic.

violer [vjɔle] vt (femme) to rape; (sépulture, loi, traité) to violate.

violet, te [vjɔlɛ, -ɛt] a, nm purple, mauve // nf (fleur) violet.

violon [vjɔlɔ̃] nm violin; (fam: prison) lock-up.

violoncelle [vjɔlɔ̃sɛl] nm cello.

violoniste [vjɔlɔnist(ə)] nm/f violinist.

vipère [vipɛr] nf viper, adder.

virage [viraʒ] nm (d'un véhicule) turn; (d'une route, piste) bend; (fig: POL) about-turn.

virée [vire] nf (courte) run; (: à pied) walk; (longue) trip; hike, walking tour.

virement [virmɑ̃] nm (COMM) transfer.

virent vb voir aussi **voir**.

virer [vire] vt (COMM): ~ **qch** (sur) to transfer sth (into) // vi to turn; (CHIMIE) to change colour; ~ **de bord** to tack.

virevolter [virvɔlte] vi to twirl around.

virgule [virgyl] nf comma; (MATH) point.

viril, e [viril] a (propre à l'homme) masculine; (énergique, courageux) manly, virile.

virtuel, le [virtɥɛl] a potential; (théorique) virtual.

virtuose [virtɥoz] nm/f (MUS) virtuoso; (gén) master.

virus [virys] nm virus.

vis vb [vi] voir **voir**, **vivre** // nf [vis] screw.

visa [viza] nm (sceau) stamp; (validation de passeport) visa.

visage [vizaʒ] nm face.

vis-à-vis [vizavi] ad face to face // nm person opposite; house etc opposite; ~ **de** prép opposite; (fig) vis-à-vis; en ~ facing each other.

viscéral, e, aux [viseral, -o] a (fig) deep-seated, deep-rooted.

visée [vize]: ~**s** nfpl (intentions) designs.

viser [vize] vi to aim // vt to aim at; (concerner) to be aimed ou directed at; (apposer un visa sur) to stamp, visa; ~ **à qch/faire** to aim at sth/doing ou to do.

viseur [vizœr] nm (d'arme) sights pl; (PHOTO) viewfinder.

visibilité [vizibilite] nf visibility.

visible [vizibl(ə)] a visible; (disponible): est-il ~? can he see me?, will he see visitors?

visière [vizjɛr] nf (de casquette) peak; (qui s'attache) eyeshade.

vision [vizjɔ̃] nf vision; (sens) (eye)sight, vision; (fait de voir): **la ~ de** the sight of.

visite [vizit] nf visit; (visiteur) visitor; (médicale, à domicile) visit, call; **la ~** (MÉD) medical examination; **faire une ~ à qn** to call on sb, pay sb a visit; **rendre ~ à qn** to visit sb, pay sb a visit; **être en ~ (chez qn)** to be visiting (sb); **heures de ~** (hôpital, prison) visiting hours.

visiter [vizite] vt to visit; (musée, ville) to visit, go round; **visiteur, euse** nm/f visitor.

vison [vizɔ̃] nm mink.

visser [vise] vt: ~ **qch** (fixer, serrer) to screw sth on.

visuel, le [vizɥɛl] a visual.

vit vb voir **voir** **vivre**.

vital, e, aux [vital, -o] a vital.

vitamine [vitamin] nf vitamin.

vite [vit] *ad* (*rapidement*) quickly, fast; (*sans délai*) quickly; soon; **faire ~ to act quickly; to be quick.**

vitesse [vites] *nf* speed; (*AUTO: dispositif*) gear; **prendre qn de ~ to** outstrip sb; get ahead of sb; **prendre de la ~** to pick up (*or* gather speed); **à toute ~** at full *ou* top speed.

viticole [vitikɔl] *a* wine *cpd*, wine-growing.

viticulteur [vitikyltœr] *nm* wine grower.

vitrage [vitraʒ] *nm* glass *q*; (*rideau*) net curtain.

vitrail, aux [vitraj, -o] *nm* stained-glass window.

vitre [vitr(ə)] *nf* (*window*) pane; (*de portière, voiture*) window.

vitré, e [vitre] *a* glass *cpd*.

vitrer [vitre] *vt* to glaze.

vitreux, euse [vitrø, -øz] *a* (*terne*) glassy.

vitrine [vitrin] *nf* (*devanture*) (shop) window; (*étalage*) display; (*petite armoire*) display cabinet; **~ publicitaire** display case, showcase.

vitupérer [vitypere] *vi* to rant and rave.

vivace *a* [vivas] (*arbre, plante*) hardy; (*fig*) indestructible, inveterate.

vivacité [vivasite] *nf* liveliness, vivacity; sharpness; brilliance.

vivant, e [vivã, -ãt] *a* (*qui vit*) living, alive; (*animé*) lively; (*preuve, exemple*) living // *nm*: **du ~ de qn** in sb's lifetime.

vivats [viva] *nmpl* cheers.

vive [viv] *af voir vif* // *vb voir* **vivre** // *excl*: **~ le roi!** long live the king!; **~ment** *ad* vivaciously; sharply // *excl*: **~ment les vacances!** roll on the holidays!

viveur [vivœr] *nm* (*péj*) high liver, pleasure-seeker.

vivier [vivje] *nm* fish tank; fishpond.

vivifiant, e [vivifjã, -ãt] *a* invigorating.

vivions *vb voir* **vivre**.

vivre [vivr(ə)] *vi, vt* to live; **~s** *nmpl*

provisions, food supplies; **il vit encore** he is still alive; **se laisser ~ to** take life as it comes; **ne plus ~** (*être anxieux*) to live on one's nerves; **il a vécu** (*eu une vie aventureuse*) he has seen life; **être facile à ~** to be easy to get on with; **faire ~ qn** (*pourvoir à sa subsistance*) to provide (a living) for sb.

vlan [vlã] *excl* wham!, bang!

vocable [vɔkabl(ə)] *nm* term.

vocabulaire [vɔkabylɛr] *nm* vocabulary.

vocation [vɔkasjɔ̃] *nf* vocation, calling.

vociférer [vɔsifere] *vi, vt* to scream.

vodka [vɔdka] *nf* vodka.

vœu, x [vø] *nm* wish; (*à Dieu*) vow; **faire ~ de** to take a vow of; **~x de bonne année** best wishes for the New Year.

vogue [vɔg] *nf* fashion, vogue.

voguer [vɔge] *vi* to sail.

voici [vwasi] *prép* (*pour introduire, désigner*) here + *sg*, here are + *pl*; **et ~ que ...** and now it (*ou* he) ...; *voir aussi* **voilà**.

voie [vwa] *nf* way; (*RAIL*) track, line; (*AUTO*) lane; **être en bonne ~** to be going well; **mettre qn sur la ~** to put sb on the right track; **être en ~ d'achèvement/de renovation** to be nearing completion/in the process of renovation; **par/en ~ buccale** *ou* **orale** orally; **à ~ étroite** narrow-gauge; **~ d'eau** (*NAVIG*) leak; **~ ferrée** track; railway line; **~ de garage** (*RAIL*) siding.

voilà [vwala] *prép* (*en désignant*) there is + *sg*, there are + *pl*; **les ~** *ou* **voici** there they are; **en ~ ~** *ou* **voici un** here's one, there's one; **~ ~** *ou* **voici deux ans** two years ago; **~ ~** *ou* **voici deux ans que** it's two years since; **et ~!** there we are!; **~ tout** that's all; **'~ ~** *ou* **voici'** (*en offrant etc*) 'there *ou* here you are'.

voile [vwal] *nm* veil; (*tissu léger*) net // *nf* sail; (*sport*) sailing.

voiler [vwale] *vt* to veil; (*fausser: roue*) to buckle; (*: bois*) to warp; **se ~ vi** (*lune, regard*) to mist over; (*voix*) to become husky; (*roue, disque*) to buckle; (*planche*) to warp.

voilier [vwalje] *nm* sailing ship; (*de plaisance*) sailing boat.

voilure [vwalyʀ] *nf* (*de voilier*) sails *pl*.

voir [vwaʀ] *vi, vt* to see; **se ~ vt**: **se ~ critiquer/transformer** to be criticized/transformed; **cela se voit** (*cela arrive*) it happens; (*c'est visible*) that's obvious, it shows; **~ venir** (*fig*) to wait and see; **faire ~ qch à qn** to show sb sth; **en faire ~ à qn** (*fig*) to give sb a hard time; **ne pas pouvoir ~ qn** (*fig*) not to be able to stand sb; **voyons!** let's see now; (*indignation etc*) come (along) now!; **avoir quelque chose à ~ avec** to have something to do with.

voire [vwaʀ] *ad* indeed; nay; or even.

voisin, e [vwazɛ̃, -in] *a* (*proche*) neighbouring; (*contigu*) next; (*ressemblant*) connected // *nm/f* neighbour; **voisinage** *nm* (*proximité*) proximity; (*environs*) vicinity; (*quartier, voisins*) neighbourhood.

voiture [vwatyʀ] *nf* car; (*wagon*) coach, carriage; **~ d'enfant** pram (*Brit*), baby carriage (*US*); **~ de sport** sports car; **~-lit** *nf* sleeper.

voix [vwa] *nf* voice; (*POL*) vote; **à haute ~** aloud; **à ~ basse** in a low voice; **à 2/4 ~** (*MUS*) in 2/4 parts; **avoir ~ au chapitre** to have a say in the matter.

vol [vɔl] *nm* (*mode de locomotion*) flying; (*trajet, voyage, groupe d'oiseaux*) flight; (*larcin*) theft; **à ~ d'oiseau** as the crow flies; **au ~**: **attraper qch au ~** to catch sth as it flies past; **en ~** in flight; **~ libre** hang-gliding; **~ à main armée** armed robbery; **~ à voile** gliding.

volage [vɔlaʒ] *a* fickle.

volaille [vɔlaj] *nf* (*oiseaux*) poultry *pl*; (*viande*) poultry *q*; (*oiseau*) fowl.

volant, e [vɔlɑ̃, -ɑ̃t] *a voir* **feuille**

etc // *nm* (*d'automobile*) (steering) wheel; (*de commande*) wheel; (*objet lancé*) shuttlecock; (*bande de tissu*) flounce.

volcan [vɔlkɑ̃] *nm* volcano.

volée [vɔle] *nf* (*TENNIS*) volley; **~ de coups/de flèches** volley of blows/arrows; **à la ~**: **rattraper à la ~** to catch in mid air; **à toute ~** (*sonner les cloches*) vigorously; (*lancer un projectile*) with full force.

voler [vɔle] *vi* (*avion, oiseau, fig*) to fly; (*voleur*) to steal // *vt* (*objet*) to steal; (*personne*) to rob; **~ qch à qn** to steal sth from sb.

volet [vɔlɛ] *nm* (*de fenêtre*) shutter; (*de feuillet, document*) section.

voleter [vɔlte] *vi* to flutter (about).

voleur, euse [vɔlœʀ, -øz] *nm/f* thief (*pl* thieves) // *a* thieving.

volontaire [vɔlɔ̃tɛʀ] *a* (*caractère, personne: décidé*) self-willed // *nm/f* volunteer.

volonté [vɔlɔ̃te] *nf* (*faculté de vouloir*) will; (*énergie, fermeté*) will(power); (*souhait, désir*) wish; **à ~** as much as one likes; **bonne ~** goodwill, willingness; **mauvaise ~** lack of goodwill, unwillingness.

volontiers [vɔlɔ̃tje] *ad* (*de bonne grâce*) willingly; (*avec plaisir*) willingly, gladly; (*habituellement, souvent*) readily, willingly.

volt [vɔlt] *nm* volt.

volte-face [vɔltəfas] *nf inv* about-turn.

voltige [vɔltiʒ] *nf* (*ÉQUITATION*) trick riding; (*au cirque*) acrobatics *sg*.

voltiger [vɔltiʒe] *vi* to flutter (about).

volume [vɔlym] *nm* volume; (*GÉOM: solide*) solid; **volumineux, euse** *a* voluminous, bulky.

volupté [vɔlypte] *nf* sensual delight ou pleasure.

vomir [vɔmiʀ] *vi* to vomit, be sick // *vt* to vomit, bring up; (*fig*) to belch out, spew out; (*exécrer*) to loathe, abhor.

vont [vɔ̃] *vb voir* **aller**.

vos [vo] *dét voir* **votre**.

vote [vɔt] *nm* vote; ~ **par correspondance/procuration** postal/proxy vote.

voter [vɔte] *vi* to vote // *vt* (*loi, décision*) to vote for.

votre [vɔtr(ə)], *pl* **vos** [vo] *dét* your.

vôtre [votr(ə)] *pronom*: **le** ~, **la** ~, **les** ~**s** yours; **les** ~**s** (*fig*) your family *ou* folks; **à la** ~ (*toast*) your (good) health!

voudrai *etc vb voir* **vouloir**.

voué, e [vwe] *a*: ~ **à** doomed to.

vouer [vwe] *vt*: ~ **qch à** (*Dieu/un saint*) to dedicate sth to; ~ **sa vie à** (*étude, cause etc*) to devote one's life to; ~ **une amitié éternelle à qn** to vow undying friendship to sb.

MOT-CLÉ

vouloir [vulwar] ◆ *nm*: **le bon** ~ **de qn** sb's goodwill; sb's pleasure

◆ *vt* **1** (*exiger, désirer*) to want; ~ **faire/que qn fasse** to want to do/sb to do; **voulez-vous du thé?** would you like *ou* do you want some tea?; **que me veut-il?** what does he want with me?; **sans le** ~ (*involontairement*) without meaning to, unintentionally; **je voudrais ceci/faire** I would *ou* I'd like this/to do

2 (*consentir*): **je veux bien** (*bonne volonté*) I'll be happy to; (*concession*) fair enough, that's fine; **oui, si on veut** (*en quelque sorte*) yes, if you like; **veuillez attendre** please wait; **veuillez agréer** ... (*formule épistolaire*) yours faithfully

3: **en** ~ **à**: **en** ~ **à qn** to bear sb a grudge; **s'en** ~ (**de**) to be annoyed with o.s. (for); **il en veut à mon argent** he's after my money

4: ~ **de**: **l'entreprise ne veut plus de lui** the firm doesn't want him any more; **elle ne veut pas de son aide** she doesn't want his help

5: ~ **dire** to mean.

voulu, e [vuly] *a* (*requis*) required, requisite; (*délibéré*) deliberate, inten-

tional.

vous [vu] *pronom* you; (*objet indirect*) (to) you; (*réfléchi*) yourself (*pl* yourselves); (*réciproque*) each other; ~**-même** yourself; ~**-mêmes** yourselves.

voûte [vut] *nf* vault.

voûter [vute] *vt*: **se** ~ *vi* (*dos, personne*) to become stooped.

vouvoyer [vuvwaje] *vt*: ~ **qn** to address sb as 'vous'.

voyage [vwajaʒ] *nm* journey, trip; (*fait de voyager*): **le** ~ travel(ling); **partir/ être en** ~ to go off/be away on a journey *ou* trip; **faire bon** ~ to have a good journey; ~ **d'agrément/d'affaires** pleasure/business trip; ~ **de noces** honeymoon; ~ **organisé** package tour.

voyager [vwajaʒe] *vi* to travel; **voyageur, euse** *nm/f* traveller; (*passager*) passenger.

voyant, e [vwajɑ̃, -ɑ̃t] *a* (*couleur*) loud, gaudy // *nm* (*signal*) (warning) light // *nf* clairvoyant.

voyelle [vwajɛl] *nf* vowel.

voyons *etc vb voir* **voir**.

voyou [vwaju] *nm* lout, hoodlum; (*enfant*) guttersnipe.

vrac [vrak]: **en** ~ *ad* higgledy-piggledy; (*COMM*) in bulk.

vrai, e [vre] *a* (*véridique: récit, faits*) true; (*non factice, authentique*) real; **à** ~ **dire** to tell the truth.

vraiment [vrɛmɑ̃] *ad* really.

vraisemblable [vrɛsɑ̃blabl(ə)] *a* likely, probable.

vraisemblance [vrɛsɑ̃blɑ̃s] *nf* likelihood; (*romanesque*) verisimilitude.

vrille [vrij] *nf* (*de plante*) tendril; (*outil*) gimlet; (*spirale*) spiral; (*AVIAT*) spin.

vrombir [vrɔ̃bir] *vi* to hum.

vu [vy] *prép* (*en raison de*) in view of; ~ **que** in view of the fact that.

vu, e [vy] *pp de* **voir** // *a*: **bien/mal** ~ (*fig*) well/poorly thought of; good/bad form.

vue [vy] *nf* (*fait de voir*): **la** ~ **de** the sight of; (*sens, faculté*) (eye)sight; *(panorama, image, photo)* view; **~s** *nfpl (idées)* views; *(dessein)* designs; **hors de ~** out of sight; **tirer à ~** to shoot on sight; **à ~ d'œil** *ad* visibly; at a quick glance; **en ~** *(visible)* in sight; *(COMM)* in the public eye; **en ~ de faire** with a view to doing.

vulgaire [vylgɛʀ] *a (grossier)* vulgar, coarse; *(trivial)* commonplace, mundane; *(péj: quelconque)*: **de ~s touristes** common tourists; *(BOT, ZOOL: non latin)* common; **vulgariser** *vt* to popularize.

vulnérable [vylnɛʀabl(ə)] *a* vulnerable.

W X Y Z

wagon [vagɔ̃] *nm (de voyageurs)* carriage; *(de marchandises)* truck, wagon; **~-citerne** *nm* tanker; **~-lit** *nm* sleeper, sleeping car; **~-restaurant** *nm* restaurant *ou* dining car.

wallon, ne [walɔ̃, -ɔn] *a* Walloon.

waters [watɛʀ] *nmpl* toilet *sg*.

watt [wat] *nm* watt.

w.-c. [vese] *nmpl* toilet *sg*, lavatory *sg*.

week-end [wikɛnd] *nm* weekend.

western [wɛstɛʀn] *nm* western.

whisky, *pl* **whiskies** [wiski] *nm* whisky.

xérès [gzeʀɛs] *nm* sherry.

xylophone [ksilɔfɔn] *nm* xylophone.

y [i] *ad (à cet endroit)* there; *(dessus)* on it *(ou* them); *(dedans)* in it

(ou them) // *pronom (about* ou on *ou* of) it : *vérifier la syntaxe du verbe employé*; **j'~** **pense** I'm thinking about it; *voir aussi* **aller, avoir.**

yacht [jɔt] *nm* yacht.

yaourt [jauʀt] *nm* yoghurt.

yeux [jø] *pl de* **œil.**

yoga [jɔga] *nm* yoga.

yoghourt [jɔguʀt] *nm* = **yaourt.**

yougoslave [jugɔslav] *a, nm/f* Yugoslav(ian).

Yougoslavie [jugɔslavi] *nf* Yugoslavia.

zèbre [zɛbʀ(ə)] *nm (ZOOL)* zebra.

zébré, e [zebʀe] *a* striped, streaked.

zèle [zɛl] *nm* zeal; **faire du ~** *(péj)* to be over-zealous.

zéro [zeʀo] *nm* zero, nought *(Brit)*; **au-dessous de ~** below zero (Centigrade) *ou* freezing; **partir de ~** to start from scratch; **trois (buts) à ~** 3 (goals) to nil.

zeste [zɛst(ə)] *nm* peel, zest.

zézayer [zezeje] *vi* to have a lisp.

zigzag [zigzag] *nm* zigzag.

zinc [zɛ̃g] *nm (CHIMIE)* zinc; *(comptoir)* bar, counter.

zizanie [zizani] *nf*: **semer la ~** to stir up ill-feeling.

zodiaque [zɔdjak] *nm* zodiac.

zona [zona] *nm* shingles *sg.*

zone [zon] *nf* zone, area; *(quartiers)*: **la ~** the slum belt; **~ bleue** ≈ restricted parking area.

zoo [zoo] *nm* zoo.

zoologie [zɔɔlɔʒi] *nf* zoology; **zoologique** *a* zoological.

zut [zyt] *excl* dash (it)! *(Brit)*, nuts! *(US).*

ENGLISH - FRENCH
ANGLAIS - FRANÇAIS
A

A [eɪ] n (MUS) la m; (AUT): ~ **road** route nationale.

a (before vowel or silent h: **an**) [æ, æn] indefinite article **1** un(e); ~ **book** un livre; **an apple** une pomme; **she's** ~ **doctor** elle est médecin

2 (instead of the number 'one') un(e); ~ **year ago** il y a un an; ~ **hundred/thousand** etc **pounds** cent/mille etc livres

3 (in expressing ratios, prices etc): **3** ~ **day/week** 3 par jour/semaine; **10 km an hour** 10 km à l'heure; **30p** ~ **kilo** 30p le kilo.

A.A. n abbr = Alcoholics Anonymous; (Brit: =Automobile Association) ≈TCF m.

A.A.A. n abbr (US: =American Automobile Association) ≈TCF m.

aback [ə'bæk] ad: **to be taken** ~ être stupéfait(e).

abandon [ə'bændən] vt abandonner // n abandon m; **with** ~ avec désinvolture.

abashed [ə'bæʃt] a confus(e), embarrassé(e).

abate [ə'beɪt] vi s'apaiser, se calmer.

abbey ['æbɪ] n abbaye f.

abbot ['æbət] n père supérieur.

abbreviation [əbriːvɪ'eɪʃən] n abréviation f.

abdicate ['æbdɪkeɪt] vt, vi abdiquer.

abdomen ['æbdəmən] n abdomen m.

abduct [æb'dʌkt] vt enlever.

aberration [æbə'reɪʃən] n anomalie f.

abet [ə'bet] vt see **aid**.

abeyance [ə'beɪəns] n: **in** ~ (law) en désuétude; (matter) en suspens.

abide [ə'baɪd] vt: **I can't** ~ **it/him** je ne peux pas le souffrir or supporter; **to** ~ **by** vt fus observer, respecter.

ability [ə'bɪlɪtɪ] n compétence f; capacité f; (skill) talent m.

abject ['æbdʒɛkt] a (poverty) sordide; (apology) plat(e).

ablaze [ə'bleɪz] a en feu, en flammes.

able ['eɪbl] a compétent(e); **to be** ~ **to do sth** pouvoir faire qch, être capable de faire qch; **ably** ad avec compétence or talent, habilement.

abnormal [æb'nɔ:məl] a anormal(e).

aboard [ə'bɔ:d] ad à bord // prep à bord de.

abode [ə'bəud] n: **of no fixed** ~ sans domicile fixe.

abolish [ə'bɔlɪʃ] vt abolir.

aborigine [æbə'rɪdʒɪnɪ] n aborigène m/f.

abort [ə'bɔ:t] vt faire avorter; ~**ion** [ə'bɔ:ʃən] n avortement m; **to have an** ~**ion** se faire avorter; ~**ive** a manqué(e).

abound [ə'baund] vi abonder; **to** ~ **in** abonder en, regorger de.

about [ə'baut] ♦ ad **1** (approximately) environ, à peu près; ~ **a hundred/ thousand** etc environ cent/mille etc, une centaine/un millier etc; **it takes** ~ **10 hours** ça prend environ or à peu près 10 heures; **at** ~ **2 o'clock** vers 2 heures; **I've just finished** j'ai presque fini

2 (referring to place) çà et là, de côté et d'autre; **to run** ~ courir çà et là; **to walk** ~ se promener, aller et venir

3: **to be** ~ **to do sth** être sur le point de faire qch

♦ prep **1** (relating to) au sujet de, à propos de; **a book** ~ **London** un livre sur Londres; **what is it** ~? de quoi s'agit-il?; **we talked** ~ **it** nous en avons parlé; **what** or **how** ~ **doing this?** et si nous faisions ceci? **2** (referring to place) dans; **to walk** ~ **the town** se promener dans la ville.

about turn n demi-tour m.

above [ə'bʌv] ad au-dessus // prep au-dessus de; **mentioned** ~ mentionné ci-dessus; ~ **all** par-dessus tout, surtout; ~**board** a franc(franche), loyal(e), honnête.

abrasive [ə'breɪzɪv] a abrasif(ive); (fig) caustique, agressif(ive).

abreast [ə'brest] ad de front; **to keep** ~ **of** se tenir au courant de.

abridge [ə'brɪdʒ] vt abréger.

abroad [ə'brɔːd] ad à l'étranger.

abrupt [ə'brʌpt] a (steep, blunt) abrupt(e); (sudden, gruff) brusque.

abscess ['æbsɪs] n abcès m.

abscond [əb'skɒnd] vi disparaître, s'enfuir.

absence ['æbsəns] n absence f.

absent ['æbsənt] a absent(e); ~**ee** [-'tiː] n absent(e); ~**-minded** a distrait(e).

absolute ['æbsəluːt] a absolu(e); ~**ly** [-'luːtlɪ] ad absolument.

absolve [əb'zɔlv] vt: **to** ~ **sb (from)** (sin etc) absoudre qn (de); **to** ~ **sb from** (oath) délier qn de.

absorb [əb'zɔːb] vt absorber; **to be** ~**ed in a book** être plongé dans un livre; ~**ent cotton** n (US) coton m hydrophile.

absorption [əb'zɔːpʃən] n absorption f; amortissement m; intégration f; (fig) concentration f.

abstain [əb'steɪn] vi: **to** ~ (**from**) s'abstenir (de).

abstemious [əb'stiːmɪəs] a sobre, frugal(e).

abstract ['æbstrækt] a abstrait(e).

absurd [əb'sɜːd] a absurde.

abuse n [ə'bjuːs] abus m, insultes fpl, injures fpl // vt [ə'bjuːz] abuser de; **abusive** a grossier(ère), inju-

rieux(euse).

abysmal [ə'bɪzməl] a exécrable; (ignorance etc) sans bornes.

abyss [ə'bɪs] n abîme m, gouffre m.

AC abbr (=alternating current) courant alternatif.

academic [ækə'dɛmɪk] a universitaire; (pej: issue) oiseux(euse), purement théorique // n universitaire m/f.

academy [ə'kædəmɪ] n (learned body) académie f; (school) collège m; ~ **of music** conservatoire m.

accelerate [æk'sɛləreɪt] vt, vi accélérer; **accelerator** n accélérateur m.

accent ['æksɛnt] n accent m.

accept [ək'sɛpt] vt accepter; ~**able** a acceptable; ~**ance** n acceptation f.

access ['æksɛs] n accès m; ~**ible** [æk'sɛsəbl] a accessible.

accessory [æk'sɛsərɪ] n accessoire m; **toilet accessories** npl articles mpl de toilette.

accident ['æksɪdənt] n accident m; (chance) hasard m; **by** ~ par hasard; accidentellement; ~**al** [-'dɛntl] a accidentel(le); ~**ally** [-'dɛntəlɪ] ad accidentellement; ~**-prone** a sujet(te) aux accidents.

acclaim [ə'kleɪm] n acclamation f.

accommodate [ə'kɔmədeɪt] vt loger, recevoir; (oblige, help) obliger.

accommodating [ə'kɔmədeɪtɪŋ] a obligeant(e), arrangeant(e).

accommodation [əkɔmə'deɪʃən] n (US: ~s) logement m.

accompany [ə'kʌmpənɪ] vt accompagner.

accomplice [ə'kʌmplɪs] n complice m/f.

accomplish [ə'kʌmplɪʃ] vt accomplir; ~**ment** n accomplissement m; réussite f, résultat m; ~**ments** npl talents mpl.

accord [ə'kɔːd] n accord m // vt accorder; **of his own** ~ de son plein gré; ~**ance** n: **in** ~**ance with** conformément à; ~**ing to** prep selon; ~**ingly** ad en conséquence.

accordion [ə'kɔːdɪən] n accordéon m.

accost [ə'kɔst] vt aborder.

account [ə'kaunt] n (COMM) compte m; (report) compte rendu; récit m; ~s npl comptabilité f, comptes; of little ~ de peu d'importance; on ~ en acompte; on no ~ en aucun cas; on ~ of à cause de; to take into ~, take ~ of tenir compte de; to ~ for vt fus expliquer, rendre compte de; ~**able** a responsable.

accountancy [ə'kauntənsɪ] n comptabilité f.

accountant [ə'kauntənt] n comptable m/f.

account number n (at bank etc) numéro m de compte.

accumulate [ə'kju:mjuleit] vt accumuler, amasser // vi s'accumuler, s'amasser.

accuracy ['ækjurəsɪ] n exactitude f, précision f.

accurate ['ækjurɪt] a exact(e), précis(e); ~**ly** ad avec précision.

accusation [ækju'zeɪʃən] n accusation f.

accuse [ə'kju:z] vt accuser; ~**d** n accusé/e.

accustom [ə'kʌstəm] vt accoutumer, habituer; ~**ed** a (usual) habituel(le); ~**ed to** habitué(e) or accoutumé(e) à.

ace [eis] n as m.

ache [eik] n mal m, douleur f // vi (be sore) faire mal, être douloureux(euse); my head ~s j'ai mal à la tête.

achieve [ə'tʃi:v] vt (aim) atteindre; (victory, success) remporter, obtenir; (task) accomplir; ~**ment** n exploit m, réussite f.

acid ['æsɪd] a, n acide (m); ~ **rain** n pluies fpl acides.

acknowledge [ək'nɔlɪdʒ] vt (letter: also: ~ **receipt of**) accuser réception de; (fact) reconnaître; ~**ment** n accusé m de réception.

acne ['æknɪ] n acné m.

acorn ['eikɔ:n] n gland m.

acoustic [ə'ku:stɪk] a acoustique; ~**s** n, npl acoustique f.

acquaint [ə'kweɪnt] vt: to ~ sb with sth mettre qn au courant de qch; to be ~**ed with** (person) connaître; ~**ance** n connaissance f.

acquire [ə'kwaɪə*] vt acquérir.

acquit [ə'kwɪt] vt acquitter; to ~ o.s. well bien se comporter, s'en tirer très honorablement; ~**tal** n acquittement m.

acre ['eikə*] n acre f (= 4047 m²).

acrid ['ækrɪd] a âcre.

acrobat ['ækrəbæt] n acrobate m/f.

across [ə'krɔs] prep (on the other side) de l'autre côté de; (crosswise) en travers de // ad de l'autre côté; en travers; to run/swim ~ traverser en courant/à la nage; ~ **from** en face de.

acrylic [ə'krɪlɪk] a, n acrylique (m).

act [ækt] n acte m, action f; (THEATRE) acte; (in music-hall etc) numéro m; (LAW) loi f // vi agir; (THEATRE) jouer; (pretend) jouer la comédie // vt (part) jouer, tenir; to ~ as servir de; ~**ing** a suppléant(e), par intérim // n (of actor) jeu m; (activity): to do some ~**ing** faire du théâtre or du cinéma).

action ['ækʃən] n action f; (MIL) combat(s) m(pl); (LAW) procès m, action en justice; out of ~ hors de combat; hors d'usage; to take ~ agir, prendre des mesures; ~ **replay** n (TV) répétition f d'une séquence.

activate ['æktɪveɪt] vt (mechanism) actionner, faire fonctionner; (CHEM, PHYSICS) activer.

active ['æktɪv] a actif(ive); (volcano) en activité; ~**ly** ad activement.

activity [æk'tɪvɪtɪ] n activité f.

actor ['æktə*] n acteur m.

actress ['æktrɪs] n actrice f.

actual ['æktjuəl] a réel(le), véritable; ~**ly** ad réellement, véritablement; en fait.

acumen ['ækjumən] n perspicacité f.

acute [ə'kju:t] a aigu(ë); (mind, observer) pénétrant(e).

ad [æd] n abbr of **advertisement**.

A.D. ad abbr (= Anno Domini) ap. J.-C.

adamant ['ædəmənt] a inflexible.

adapt [ə'dæpt] vt adapter // vi: to ~ (to) s'adapter (à); ~**able** a (device) adaptable; (person) qui s'adapte facilement; ~**er** or ~**or** n (ELEC) adapteur m.

add [æd] vt ajouter; (figures: also: to ~ up) additionner // vi to ~ to (increase) ajouter à, accroître; it doesn't ~ up (fig) cela ne rime à rien.

adder ['ædə*] n vipère f.

addict ['ædɪkt] n intoxiqué/e; (fig) fanatique m/f; ~**ed** [ə'dɪktɪd] a: to be ~**ed** to (drink etc) être adonné/e à; (fig: football etc) être un fanatique de; ~**ion** [ə'dɪkʃən] n (MED) dépendance f; ~**ive** a qui crée une dépendance.

addition [ə'dɪʃən] n addition f; in ~ de plus; de surcroit; in ~ to en plus de; ~**al** a supplémentaire.

additive ['ædɪtɪv] n additif m.

address [ə'drɛs] n adresse f; (talk) discours m, allocution f // vt adresser; (speak to) s'adresser à.

adept ['ædɛpt] a: ~ at expert(e) à or en.

adequate ['ædɪkwɪt] a adéquat(e); suffisant(e); compétent(e).

adhere [əd'hɪə*] vi: to ~ to adhérer à; (fig: rule, decision) se tenir à.

adhesive [əd'hi:zɪv] a adhésif(ive) // n adhésif m; ~ **tape** n (Brit) ruban adhésif; (US: MED) sparadrap m.

adjective ['ædʒɛktɪv] n adjectif m.

adjoining [ə'dʒɔɪnɪŋ] a voisin(e), adjacent(e), attenant(e).

adjourn [ə'dʒɜːn] vt ajourner // vi suspendre la séance; lever la séance; clore la session; (go) se retirer.

adjudicate [ə'dʒuːdɪkeɪt] vi se prononcer.

adjust [ə'dʒʌst] vt ajuster, régler; rajuster // vi: to ~ (to) s'adapter (à); ~**able** a réglable.

ad-lib [æd'lɪb] vt, vi improviser // ad: ad lib à volonté, à discrétion.

administer [əd'mɪnɪstə*] vt administrer; (justice) rendre.

administration [ədmɪnɪs'treɪʃən] n administration f.

administrative [əd'mɪnɪstrətɪv] a administratif(ive).

admiral ['ædmərəl] n amiral m; **A~ty** n (Brit: also: **A~ty Board**) ministère m de la Marine.

admiration [ædmə'reɪʃən] n admiration f.

admire [əd'maɪə*] vt admirer.

admission [əd'mɪʃən] n admission f; (to exhibition, night club etc) entrée f; (confession) aveu m.

admit [əd'mɪt] vt laisser entrer; admettre; (agree) reconnaître, admettre; to ~ to vt reconnaître, avouer; ~**tance** n admission f, (droit m d')entrée f; ~**tedly** ad il faut en convenir.

admonish [əd'mɒnɪʃ] vt donner un avertissement à; réprimander.

ad nauseam [æd 'nɔːzɪæm] ad (repeat, talk) à satiété.

ado [ə'duː] n: without (any) more ~ sans plus de cérémonies.

adolescence [ædəu'lɛsnt] n adolescence f.

adolescent [ædəu'lɛsnt] a, n adolescent(e).

adopt [ə'dɒpt] vt adopter; ~**ed** a adoptif(ive), adopté(e); ~**ion** [ə'dɒpʃən] n adoption f.

adore [ə'dɔː*] vt adorer.

adorn [ə'dɔːn] vt orner.

Adriatic (Sea) [eɪdrɪ'ætɪk('siː)] n Adriatique f.

adrift [ə'drɪft] ad à la dérive.

adult ['ædʌlt] n adulte m/f.

adultery [ə'dʌltərɪ] n adultère m.

advance [əd'vɑːns] n avance f // vt avancer // vi s'avancer; in ~ en avance, d'avance; ~**d** a avancé(e); (SCOL: studies) supérieur(e).

advantage [əd'vɑːntɪdʒ] n (also TENNIS) avantage m; to take ~ of profiter de.

advent ['ædvənt] n avènement m, venue f; **A~** Avent m.

adventure [əd'vεntʃə*] *n* aventure *f.*

adverb ['ædvə:b] *n* adverbe *m.*

adverse ['ædvə:s] *a* contraire, adverse; **~ to** hostile à.

advert ['ædvə:t] *n abbr (Brit)* of **advertisement**.

advertise ['ædvətaɪz] *vi (vt)* faire de la publicité *or* de la réclame (pour); mettre une annonce (pour vendre); **to ~ for** *(staff)* faire paraître une annonce pour trouver.

advertisement [əd'və:tɪsmənt] *n (COMM)* réclame *f*, publicité *f*; *(in classified ads)* annonce *f.*

advertiser ['ædvətaɪzə*] *n (in newspaper etc)* annonceur *m.*

advertising ['ædvətaɪzɪŋ] *n* publicité *f*, réclame *f.*

advice [əd'vaɪs] *n* conseils *mpl*; *(notification)* avis *m*; **piece of ~** conseil; **to take legal ~** consulter un avocat.

advisable [əd'vaɪzəbl] *a* recommandable, indiqué(e).

advise [əd'vaɪz] *vt* conseiller; **to ~ sb of sth** aviser *or* informer qn de qch; **to ~ against sth/doing sth** déconseiller qch/conseiller de ne pas faire qch; **~dly** [-'vaɪzdlɪ] *ad (deliberately)* délibérément; **~r** *n* conseiller/ère; **advisory** [-ərɪ] *a* consultatif(ive).

advocate *n* ['ædvəkɪt] *(upholder)* défenseur *m*, avocat/e ♦ *vt* ['ædvəkeɪt] recommander, prôner; **to be an ~ of** être partisan/e de.

aerial ['εərɪəl] *n* antenne *f* // *a* aérien(ne).

aerobics [εə'rəubɪks] *n* aérobic *m.*

aeroplane ['εərəpleɪn] *n (Brit)* avion *m.*

aerosol ['εərəsɔl] *n* aérosol *m.*

aesthetic [ɪs'θεtɪk] *a* esthétique.

afar [ə'fɑ:*] *ad*: **from ~** de loin.

affair [ə'fεə*] *n* affaire *f*; *(also*: love ~) liaison *f*; aventure *f.*

affect [ə'fεkt] *vt* affecter.

affection [ə'fεkʃən] *n* affection *f*; **~ate** *a* affectueux(euse).

affirmation [æfə'meɪʃən] *n* affirma-

tion *f*, assertion *f.*

affix [ə'fɪks] *vt* apposer, ajouter.

afflict [ə'flɪkt] *vt* affliger.

affluence ['æfluəns] *n* abondance *f*, opulence *f.*

affluent ['æfluənt] *a* abondant(e); opulent(e); *(person)* dans l'aisance, riche.

afford [ə'fɔ:d] *vt* se permettre; avoir les moyens d'acheter *or* d'entretenir; *(provide)* fournir, procurer.

afield [ə'fi:ld] *ad*: **far ~** loin.

afloat [ə'fləut] *a, ad* à flot; **to stay ~** surnager.

afoot [ə'fut] *ad*: **there is something ~** il se prépare quelque chose.

afraid [ə'freɪd] *a* effrayé(e); **to be ~ of or to** avoir peur de; **I am ~ that** je crains que + *sub.*

afresh [ə'frεʃ] *ad* de nouveau, à nouveau.

Africa ['æfrɪkə] *n* Afrique *f*; **~n** *a* africain(e) // *n* Africain/e.

aft [ɑ:ft] *ad* à l'arrière, vers l'arrière.

after ['ɑ:ftə*] *prep, ad* après // *cj* après que, après avoir *or* être + *pp*; **what/who are you ~?** que/qui cherchez-vous?; **~ he left/having done** après qu'il fut parti/après avoir fait; **ask ~ him** demandez de ses nouvelles; **~ all** après tout; **~ you!** après vous, Monsieur *or* Madame *etc*); **~effects** *npl* répercussions *fpl*; *(of illness)* séquelles *fpl*, suites *fpl*; **~life** *n* vie future; **~math** *n* conséquences *fpl*; **in the ~math of** dans les mois *ou* années *etc* qui suivirent, au lendemain de; **~noon** *n* après-midi *m or f*; **~s** *n (col: dessert)* dessert *m*; **~sales service** *n (Brit: for car, washing machine etc)* service *m* après-vente (S.A.V.); **~shave (lotion)** *n* after-shave *m*; **~thought** *n*: **I had an ~thought** il m'est venu une idée après coup; **~wards** *ad* après.

again [ə'gεn] *ad* de nouveau; **to do sth ~** refaire qch; **not ~ ~ ne ... ne ... plus**; **~ and ~** à plusieurs reprises.

against [ə'gεnst] *prep* contre.

age [eɪdʒ] n âge m // vt, vi vieillir; it's been ~s since ça fait une éternité que — ne; he is 20 years ~ il a 20 ans; to come of ~ atteindre sa majorité; ~d 10 âgé de 10 ans; the ~d ['eɪdʒɪd] les personnes âgées; ~ group n tranche f d'âge; ~ limit n limite f d'âge.

agency ['eɪdʒənsɪ] n agence f; through or by the ~ of par l'entremise or l'action de.

agenda [ə'dʒɛndə] n ordre m du jour.

agent ['eɪdʒənt] n agent m.

aggregate ['ægrɪgeɪt] n ensemble m, total m.

aggressive [ə'grɛsɪv] a agressif(ive).

aggrieved [ə'griːvd] a chagriné(e), affligé(e).

aghast [ə'gɑːst] a consterné(e), atterré(e).

agitate ['ædʒɪteɪt] vt rendre inquiet(ète) or agité(e); agiter; to ~ for faire campagne pour.

ago [ə'gəʊ] ad: 2 days ~ il y a deux jours; not long ~ il n'y a pas longtemps; how long ~? il y a combien de temps (de cela)?

agog [ə'gɒg] a en émoi.

agonizing ['ægənaɪzɪŋ] a angoissant(e); déchirant(e).

agony ['ægənɪ] n grande souffrance or angoisse.

agree [ə'griː] vt (price) convenir de // vi: to ~ (with) (person) être d'accord (avec); (statements etc) concorder (avec); (LING) s'accorder (avec); to ~ to do accepter de or consentir à faire; to ~ to sth consentir à qch; to ~ that (admit) convenir or reconnaître que; garlic doesn't ~ with me je ne supporte pas l'ail; ~able a agréable; (willing) consentant(e), d'accord; ~d a (time, place) convenu(e); ~ment n accord m; ~ment d'accord.

agricultural [ægrɪ'kʌltʃərəl] a agricole.

agriculture ['ægrɪkʌltʃə*] n agricul-

ture f.

aground [ə'graʊnd] ad: to run ~ s'échouer.

ahead [ə'hɛd] ad en avant; devant; ~ of devant; (fig: schedule etc) en avance sur; ~ of time en avance; go right or straight ~ allez tout droit; they were (right) ~ of us ils nous précédaient (de peu), ils étaient (juste) devant nous.

aid [eɪd] n aide f // vt aider; in ~ of en faveur de; to ~ and abet (LAW) se faire le complice de.

aide [eɪd] n (person) collaborateur/trice, assistant/e.

AIDS [eɪdz] n abbr (=acquired immune deficiency syndrome) SIDA m.

ailing ['eɪlɪŋ] a malade.

ailment ['eɪlmənt] n petite maladie, affection f.

aim [eɪm] vt: to ~ sth at (such as gun, camera) braquer or pointer qch sur, diriger qch contre; (missile) lancer qch à or contre or en direction de; (remark, blow) destiner or adresser qch à // vi (also: to take ~) viser // n but m; (fig) viser (à); avoir pour but or ambition; to ~ to do avoir l'intention de faire; ~less a sans but.

ain't [eɪnt] (col) =am not, aren't, isn't.

air [ɛə*] n air m // vt aérer; (grievances, ideas) exposer (librement) // cpd (currents, attack etc) aérien(ne); to throw sth into the ~ jeter qch en l'air; to be on the ~ (RADIO, TV: programme) être diffusé(e); (: station) diffuser; ~bed n matelas m pneumatique; ~borne a en vol; aéroporté(e); ~ conditioning n climatisation f; ~craft n, pl inv avion m; ~craft carrier n porte-avions m inv; ~field n terrain m d'aviation; A~ Force n Armée f de l'air; ~ freshener n désodorisant m; ~gun n fusil m à air comprimé; ~ hostess n (Brit) hôtesse f de l'air; ~ letter n (Brit) aérogramme m; ~lift n pont aérien

~line n ligne aérienne, compagnie f d'aviation; ~liner n avion m de ligne; ~lock n sas m; ~mail n: by ~mail par avion; (letter) par avion; ~mattress n matelas m pneumatique; ~plane n (US) avion m; ~port n aéroport m; ~ raid n attaque aérienne; ~sick a: to be ~sick avoir le mal de l'air; ~strip n terrain m d'atterrissage; ~terminal n aérogare f; ~tight a hermétique; ~ traffic controller n aiguilleur m du ciel; ~y a bien aéré(e); (manners) dégagé(e).

aisle [ail] n (of church) allée centrale; nef latérale.

ajar [ə'dʒɑː*] a entrouvert(e).

akin [ə'kɪn] a: ~ to (similar) qui tient de or ressemble à.

alacrity [ə'lækrɪtɪ] n empressement m.

alarm [ə'lɑːm] n alarme f // vt alarmer; ~ clock n réveille-matin m, réveil m.

alas [ə'læs] excl hélas!

albeit [ɔːl'biːɪt] cj (although) bien que + sub, encore que + sub.

album ['ælbəm] n album m; (L.P.) 33 tours m inv.

alcohol ['ælkəhɒl] n alcool m; ~ic [-'hɒlɪk] a, n alcoolique (m/f).

alderman ['ɔːldəmən] n conseiller municipal m (en Angleterre).

ale [eɪl] n bière f.

alert [ə'lɜːt] a alerte, vif(vive), vigilant(e) // n alerte f // vt alerter; (fig) éveiller l'attention de; on the ~ sur le qui-vive, (MIL) en état d'alerte.

algebra ['ældʒɪbrə] n algèbre m.

Algeria [æl'dʒɪərɪə] n Algérie f.

alias ['eɪlɪæs] ad alias // n faux nom, nom d'emprunt.

alibi ['ælɪbaɪ] n alibi m.

alien ['eɪlɪən] n étranger/ère // a: ~ (to) étranger(ère) (à); ~ate vt aliéner; s'aliéner.

alight [ə'laɪt] a, ad en feu // vi mettre pied à terre; (passenger) descendre; (bird) se poser.

alike [ə'laɪk] a semblable, pareil(le) // ad de même; to look ~ se ressem-

bler.

alimony ['ælɪmənɪ] n (payment) pension f alimentaire.

alive [ə'laɪv] a vivant(e); (active) plein(e) de vie.

all [ɔːl] ♦ a (singular) tout(e); (plural) tous(toutes); ~ day tout le jour; ~ night toute la nuit; ~ men tous les hommes; ~ five tous les cinq; ~ the food toute la nourriture; ~ the books tous les livres; ~ the time tout le temps; ~ his life toute sa vie
♦ pronoun 1 tout; I ate it ~, I ate ~ of it j'ai tout mangé; ~ of us went nous y sommes tous allés; ~ of the boys went tous les garçons y sont allés
2 (in phrases): above ~ surtout, par-dessus tout; after ~ après tout; at ~: not at ~ (in answer to question) pas du tout; (in answer to thanks) je vous en prie!; I'm not at ~ tired je ne suis pas du tout fatigué(e); anything at ~ will do n'importe quoi fera l'affaire; in ~ tout compté, en fin de compte
♦ ad: ~ alone tout(e) seul(e); it's not as hard as ~ that ce n'est pas si difficile que ça; ~ the more/the better d'autant plus/mieux; ~ but presque, pratiquement; the score is 2 ~ le score est 2 partout.

allay [ə'leɪ] vt (fears) apaiser, calmer.

all clear n (after attack etc, also fig) fin f d'alerte.

allege [ə'ledʒ] vt alléguer, prétendre; ~dly [ə'ledʒɪdlɪ] ad à ce que l'on prétend, paraît-il.

allegiance [ə'liːdʒəns] n fidélité f, obéissance f.

allergic [ə'lɜːdʒɪk] a: ~ to allergique à.

allergy ['ælədʒɪ] n allergie f.

alleviate [ə'liːvɪeɪt] vt soulager, adoucir.

alley ['ælɪ] n ruelle f; (in garden) allée f.

alliance [ə'laɪəns] n alliance f.

allied ['ælaɪd] a allié(e).

all-in ['ɔ:lɪn] a (Brit: also ad: charge) tout compris; ~ **wrestling** n catch m.

all-night ['ɔ:l'naɪt] a ouvert(e) ou qui dure toute la nuit.

allocate ['æləkeɪt] vt (share out) répartir, distribuer; (duties): to ~ sth to assigner or attribuer qch à; (sum, time): to ~ sth to allouer qch à; to ~ sth for affecter qch à.

allot [ə'lɒt] vt (share out) répartir, distribuer; (time): to ~ sth to allouer qch à; (duties): to ~ sth to assigner qch à; ~ment n (share) part f; (garden) lopin m de terre (loué à la municipalité).

all-out ['ɔ:laut] a (effort etc) total(e) // ad: **all out** à fond.

allow [ə'lau] vt (practice, behaviour) permettre, autoriser; (sum to spend etc) accorder; allouer; (sum, time estimated) compter, prévoir; (concede): to ~ that convenir que; to ~ sb to do permettre à qn de faire, autoriser qn à faire; he is ~ed to — on lui permet de —; to ~ for vt fus tenir compte de; ~ance n (money received) allocation f; subside m; indemnité f; (TAX) somme f déductible du revenu imposable, abattement m; to make ~ances for tenir compte de.

alloy ['ælɔɪ] n alliage m.

all right ['ɔ:l'raɪt] ad (feel, work) bien; (as answer) d'accord.

all-round ['ɔ:l'raund] a compétent(e) dans tous les domaines; (athlete etc) complet(ète).

all-time ['ɔ:l'taɪm] a (record) sans précédent, absolu(e).

allude [ə'lu:d] vi: to ~ to faire allusion à.

alluring [ə'ljuərɪŋ] a séduisant(e), alléchant(e).

ally ['ælaɪ] n allié m.

almighty [ɔ:l'maɪtɪ] a tout-puissant.

almond ['ɑ:mənd] n amande f.

almost ['ɔ:lməust] ad presque.

alms [ɑ:mz] npl aumône(s) f.

aloft [ə'lɒft] ad en haut, en l'air; (NAUT) dans la mâture.

alone [ə'ləun] a, ad seul(e); to leave sb ~ laisser qn tranquille; to leave sth ~ ne pas toucher à qch; let ~ — sans parler de; encore moins —.

along [ə'lɒŋ] prep le long de // ad: is he coming ~? vient-il avec nous?; he was hopping/limping ~ il venait or avançait en sautillant/boitant; ~ with en compagnie de; avec, en plus de; all ~ (all the time) depuis le début; ~side prep le long de; au côté de // ad à bord à bord; côte à côte.

aloof [ə'lu:f] a, à distance, à l'écart.

aloud [ə'laud] ad à haute voix.

alphabet ['ælfəbet] n alphabet m; ~ical [-'betɪkəl] a alphabétique.

alpine ['ælpaɪn] a alpin(e), alpestre.

Alps [ælps] npl: the ~ les Alpes fpl.

already [ɔ:l'redɪ] ad déjà.

alright ['ɔ:l'raɪt] a (Brit) = **all right**.

Alsatian [æl'seɪʃən] n (dog) berger allemand.

also ['ɔ:lsəu] ad aussi.

altar ['ɔltə*] n autel m.

alter ['ɔltə*] vt, vi changer, modifier.

alternate [ɔl'tə:nɪt] a alterné(e), alternant(e), alternatif(ive) // vi ['ɔltə:neɪt] alterner; on ~ days un jour sur deux, tous les deux jours; **alternating** a (current) alternatif(ive).

alternative [ɔl'tə:nətɪv] a (solutions) interchangeable, possible; (solution) autre, de remplacement // n (choice) alternative f; (other possibility) solution f de remplacement or de rechange, autre possibilité f; ~ly ad: ~ly one could une autre or l'autre solution serait de.

alternator ['ɔltə:neɪtə*] n (AUT) alternateur m.

although [ɔ:l'ðəu] cj bien que + sub.

altitude ['æltɪtju:d] n altitude f.

alto ['æltəu] n (female) contralto m;

(male) haute-contre f.

altogether [ɔːltə'geðə*] ad entièrement, tout à fait; (on the whole) tout compte fait; (in all) en tout.

aluminium [ælju'mɪnɪəm] , (US) **aluminum** [ə'luːmɪnəm] n aluminium m.

always ['ɔːlweɪz] ad toujours.

am [æm] vb see **be**.

a.m. ad abbr (=ante meridiem) du matin.

amalgamate [ə'mælgəmeɪt] vt, vi fusionner.

amateur ['æmətə*] n amateur m // a (SPORT) amateur inv; ~ish a (pej) d'amateur.

amaze [ə'meɪz] vt stupéfier; to be ~d (at) être surpris(e) or étonné(e) (de); ~ment n stupéfaction f, stupeur f; **amazing** a étonnant(e); exceptionnel(le).

ambassador [æm'bæsədə*] n ambassadeur m.

amber ['æmbə*] n ambre m; at ~ (Brit AUT) à l'orange.

ambiguous [æm'bɪgjuəs] a ambigu(ë).

ambition [æm'bɪʃən] n ambition f.

ambitious [æm'bɪʃəs] a ambitieux(euse).

amble ['æmbl] vi (also: to ~ along) aller d'un pas tranquille.

ambulance ['æmbjuləns] n ambulance f.

ambush ['æmbuʃ] n embuscade f // vt tendre une embuscade à.

amenable [ə'miːnəbl] a: ~ to (advice etc) disposé(e) à écouter ou suivre.

amend [ə'mend] vt (law) amender; (text) corriger; to make ~s réparer ses torts, faire amende honorable.

amenities [ə'miːnɪtɪz] npl aménagements mpl (prévus pour le loisir des habitants).

America [ə'merɪkə] n Amérique f; ~n a américain(e) // n Américain/e.

amiable ['eɪmɪəbl] a aimable, affable.

amicable ['æmɪkəbl] a amical(e).

amid(st) [ə'mɪd(st)] prep parmi, au milieu de.

amiss [ə'mɪs] a, ad: there's something ~ il y a quelque chose qui ne va pas or qui cloche; to take sth ~ prendre qch mal or de travers.

ammonia [ə'məunɪə] n (gas) ammoniac m; (liquid) ammoniaque f.

ammunition [æmju'nɪʃən] n munitions fpl.

amok [ə'mɒk] ad: to run ~ être pris(e) d'un accès de folie furieuse.

among(st) [ə'mʌŋ(st)] prep parmi, entre.

amorous ['æmərəs] a amoureux(euse).

amount [ə'maunt] n (sum) somme f, montant m; (quantity) quantité f // vi: to ~ to (total) s'élever à; (be same as) équivaloir à, revenir à.

amp(ère) ['æmp(εə*)] n ampère m.

ample ['æmpl] a ample; spacieux(euse); (enough): this is ~ c'est largement suffisant; to have ~ time/room avoir bien assez de temps/place.

amplifier ['æmplɪfaɪə*] n amplificateur m.

amuck [ə'mʌk] ad =amok.

amuse [ə'mjuːz] vt amuser; ~ment n amusement m; ~ment arcade n salle f de jeu.

an [æn] indefinite article see **a**.

anaemic [ə'niːmɪk] a anémique.

anaesthetic [ænɪs'θetɪk] a, n anesthésique (m).

analog(ue) ['ænəlɒg] a (watch, computer) analogique.

analyse ['ænəlaɪz] vt (Brit) analyser.

analysis, pl **analyses** [ə'næləsɪs, -siːz] n analyse f.

analyst ['ænəlɪst] n (POL etc) spécialiste m/f; (US) psychanalyste m/f.

analyze ['ænəlaɪz] vt (US) =**analyse**.

anarchist ['ænəkɪst] n, a anarchiste (m/f).

anarchy ['ænəkɪ] n anarchie f.

anathema [ə'næθɪmə] n: it is ~ to him il a cela en abomination.

anatomy [ə'nætəmɪ] n anatomie f.

ancestor ['ænsɪstə*] n ancêtre m, aïeul m.

anchor ['æŋkə*] n ancre f // vi (also: **to drop** ~) jeter l'ancre, mouiller // vt mettre à l'ancre; **to weigh** ~ lever l'ancre.

anchovy ['æntʃəvɪ] n anchois m.

ancient ['eɪnʃənt] a ancien(ne), antique; (fig) d'un âge vénérable, antique.

ancillary [æn'sɪlərɪ] a auxiliaire.

and [ænd] cj et; ~ **so on** et ainsi de suite; **try** ~ **come** essayez de venir; **he talked** ~ **talked** il n'a pas arrêté de parler; **better** ~ **better** de mieux en mieux.

anew [ə'njuː] ad à nouveau.

angel ['eɪndʒəl] n ange m.

anger ['æŋgə*] n colère f // vt mettre en colère, irriter.

angina [æn'dʒaɪnə] n angine f de poitrine.

angle ['æŋgl] n angle m; **from their** ~ de leur point de vue; ~**r** n pêcheur/euse à la ligne.

Anglican ['æŋglɪkən] a, n anglican(e).

angling ['æŋglɪŋ] n pêche f à la ligne.

Anglo- ['æŋgləu] prefix anglo(-).

angry ['æŋgrɪ] a en colère, furieux(euse); **to be** ~ **with sb/at sth** être furieux contre qn/de qch; **to get** ~ se fâcher, se mettre en colère; **to make sb** ~ mettre qn en colère.

anguish ['æŋgwɪʃ] n angoisse f.

angular ['æŋgjulə*] a anguleux(euse).

animal ['ænɪməl] n animal m // a animal(e).

animate vt ['ænɪmeɪt] animer // a ['ænɪmɪt] animé(e), vivant(e); ~**d** a animé(e).

aniseed ['ænɪsiːd] n anis m.

ankle ['æŋkl] n cheville f; ~ **sock** n socquette f.

annex n ['æneks] (also: Brit: **annexe**) annexe f // vt [ə'neks] annexer.

anniversary [ænɪ'vɔːsərɪ] n anniver-

saire m.

announce [ə'nauns] vt annoncer; (birth, death) faire part de; ~**ment** n annonce f; (for births etc: in newspaper) avis m de faire-part; (: letter, card) faire-part m; ~**r** n (RADIO, TV: between programmes) speaker/ine; (: in a programme) présentateur/trice.

annoy [ə'nɔɪ] vt agacer, ennuyer, contrarier; **don't get** ~**ed!** ne vous fâchez pas!; ~**ance** n mécontentement m, contrariété f; (cause of) ennui m; ~**ing** a agaçant(e), contrariant(e).

annual ['ænjuəl] a annuel(le) // n (BOT) plante annuelle; (book) album m.

annul [ə'nʌl] vt annuler; (law) abroger.

annum ['ænəm] n see **per**.

anonymous [ə'nɔnɪməs] a anonyme.

anorak ['ænəræk] n anorak m.

another [ə'nʌðə*] a: ~ **book** (one more) un autre livre, encore un livre, un livre de plus; (a different one) un autre livre // pronoun un(e) autre, encore un(e), un de plus; see also **one**.

answer ['aːnsə*] n réponse f; solution f // vi répondre // vt (reply to) répondre à; (problem) résoudre; (prayer) exaucer; **to** ~ **the phone** répondre (au téléphone); **in** ~ **to your letter** suite à or en réponse à votre lettre; **to** ~ **the bell** or **the door** aller or venir ouvrir (la porte); **to** ~ **back** vi répondre, répliquer; **to** ~ **for** vt fus répondre de, se porter garant de; être responsable de; **to** ~ **to** vt fus (description) répondre or correspondre à; ~**able** a; ~**able** (**to sb/for sth**) responsable (devant qn/de qch); ~**ing machine** n répondeur m automatique.

ant [ænt] n fourmi f.

antagonism [æn'tægənɪzm] n antagonisme m.

antagonize [æn'tægənaɪz] vt éveiller l'hostilité de, contrarier.

Antarctic [æntˈɑːktɪk] n: the ~ l'Antarctique m.

antenatal [ˈæntɪˈneɪtl] a prénatal(e); ~ **clinic** n service m de consultation prénatale.

anthem [ˈænθəm] n motet m; **national** ~ hymne national.

anthology [ænˈθɒlədʒɪ] n anthologie f.

antibiotic [æntɪbaɪˈɒtɪk] a, n antibiotique (m).

antibody [ˈæntɪbɒdɪ] n anticorps m.

anticipate [ænˈtɪsɪpeɪt] vt s'attendre à; prévoir; (wishes, request) aller au devant de, devancer.

anticipation [æntɪsɪˈpeɪʃən] n attente f.

anticlimax [ˈæntɪˈklaɪmæks] n réalisation décevante d'un événement que l'on escomptait important, intéressant etc.

anticlockwise [ˈæntɪˈklɒkwaɪz] a, ad dans le sens inverse des aiguilles d'une montre.

antics [ˈæntɪks] npl singeries fpl.

antifreeze [ˈæntɪfriːz] n antigel m.

antihistamine [æntɪˈhɪstəmiːn] n antihistaminique m.

antiquated [ˈæntɪkweɪtɪd] a vieilli(e), suranné(e), vieillot(te).

antique [ænˈtiːk] n objet m d'art ancien, meuble ancien or d'époque, antiquité f // a ancien(ne); (premediaeval) antique; ~ **shop** n magasin m d'antiquités.

anti-Semitism [æntɪˈsemɪtɪzəm] n antisémitisme m.

antiseptic [æntɪˈseptɪk] a, n antiseptique (m).

antisocial [ˈæntɪˈsəʊʃəl] a peu liant(e), sauvage, insociable; (against society) antisocial(e).

antlers [ˈæntləz] npl bois mpl, ramure f.

anvil [ˈænvɪl] n enclume f.

anxiety [æŋˈzaɪətɪ] n anxiété f; (keenness): ~ **to do** grand désir or impatience f de faire.

anxious [ˈæŋkʃəs] a anxieux(euse), (très) inquiet(ète); (keen): ~ **to do/**

that qui tient beaucoup à faire/à ce que; impatient(e) de faire/que.

KEYWORD

---

any [ˈenɪ] ◆ a **1** (in questions etc: singular) du, de l', de la; (: plural) des; **have you** ~ **butter/children/ink?** avez-vous du beurre/des enfants/de l'encre?
2 (with negative) de, d'; **I haven't** ~ **money/books** je n'ai pas d'argent/de livres
3 (no matter which) n'importe quel(le); **choose** ~ **book you like** vous pouvez choisir n'importe quel livre
4 (in phrases): **in** ~ **case** de toute façon; ~ **day now** d'un jour à l'autre; **at** ~ **moment** à tout moment, d'un instant à l'autre; **at** ~ **rate** en tout cas
◆ pronoun **1** (in questions etc) en; **have you got** ~? est-ce que vous en avez?; **can** ~ **of you sing?** est-ce que parmi vous il y en a qui chantent?
2 (with negative) en; **I haven't** ~ **(of them)** je n'en ai pas, je n'en ai aucun
3 (no matter which one(s)) n'importe lequel (or laquelle); **take** ~ **of those books (you like)** vous pouvez prendre n'importe lequel de ces livres
◆ ad **1** (in questions etc): **do you want** ~ **more soup/sandwiches?** voulez-vous encore de la soupe/des sandwichs?; **are you feeling** ~ **better?** est-ce que vous vous sentez mieux?
2 (with negative): **I can't hear him** ~ **more** je ne l'entends plus; **don't wait** ~ **longer** n'attendez pas plus longtemps.

---

anybody [ˈenɪbɒdɪ] pronoun n'importe qui; (in interrogative sentences) quelqu'un; (in negative sentences): **I don't see** ~ je ne vois personne.

anyhow ['ɛnɪhau] *ad* (*at any rate*) de toute façon, quand même; (*haphazard*) n'importe comment.

anyone ['ɛnɪwʌn] *pronoun* = **anybody**.

anything ['ɛnɪθɪŋ] *pronoun* (*see anybody*) n'importe quoi; quelque chose; ne ~ rien.

anyway ['ɛnɪweɪ] *ad* de toute façon.

anywhere ['ɛnɪwɛə*] *ad* (*see anybody*) n'importe où; quelque part; I don't see him ~ je ne le vois nulle part.

apart [ə'pɑːt] *ad* (*to one side*) à part; de côté; à l'écart; (*separately*) séparément; **with one's legs ~** les jambes écartées; **10 miles ~** à 10 milles l'un de l'autre; **to take ~** démonter; **~ from** *prep* à part, excepté.

apartheid [ə'pɑːteɪt] *n* apartheid *m*.

apartment [ə'pɑːtmənt] *n* (*US*) appartement *m*, logement *m*; **~ building** *n* (*US*) immeuble *m*; maison divisée en appartements.

ape [eɪp] *n* (*grand*) singe *m* // *vt* singer.

aperture ['æpətjuə*] *n* orifice *m*, ouverture *f*; (*PHOT*) ouverture (du diaphragme).

apex ['eɪpɛks] *n* sommet *m*.

apiece [ə'piːs] *ad* (*for each person*) chacun(e).

apologetic [əpɔlə'dʒɛtɪk] *a* (*tone, letter*) d'excuse.

apologize [ə'pɔlədʒaɪz] *vi*: **to ~ (for sth to sb)** s'excuser (de qch auprès de qn), présenter des excuses (à qn pour qch).

apology [ə'pɔlədʒɪ] *n* excuses *fpl*.

apostle [ə'pɔsl] *n* apôtre *m*.

apostrophe [ə'pɔstrəfɪ] *n* apostrophe *f*.

appalling [ə'pɔːlɪŋ] *a* épouvantable; (*stupidity*) consternant(e).

apparatus [æpə'reɪtəs] *n* appareil *m*, dispositif *m*; (*in gymnasium*) agrès *mpl*.

apparel [ə'pærl] *n* (*US*) habillement *m*.

apparent [ə'pærənt] *a* apparent(e); **~ly** *ad* apparemment.

appeal [ə'piːl] *vi* (*LAW*) faire or interjeter appel // *n* (*LAW*) appel *m*; (*request*) prière *f*; appel *m*; (*charm*) attrait *m*, charme *m*; **to ~ for** demander (instamment); implorer; **to ~ to** (*subj: person*) faire appel à; (*subj: thing*) plaire à; **it doesn't ~ to me** cela ne m'attire pas; **~ing** *a* (*nice*) attrayant(e); (*touching*) attendrissant(e).

appear [ə'pɪə*] *vi* apparaître, se montrer; (*LAW*) comparaître; (*publication*) paraître, sortir, être publié(e); (*seem*) paraître, sembler; **it would ~ that** il semble que; **to ~ in Hamlet** jouer dans Hamlet; **to ~ on TV** passer à la télé; **~ance** *n* apparition *f*; parution *f*; (*look, aspect*) apparence *f*, aspect *m*.

appease [ə'piːz] *vt* apaiser, calmer.

appendicitis [əpɛndɪ'saɪtɪs] *n* appendicite *f*.

appendix [ə'pɛndɪks], *pl* **appendices** [-siːz] *n* appendice *m*.

appetite ['æpɪtaɪt] *n* appétit *m*.

appetizer ['æpɪtaɪzə*] *n* amuse-gueule *m*.

applaud [ə'plɔːd] *vt*, *vi* applaudir.

applause [ə'plɔːz] *n* applaudissements *mpl*.

apple ['æpl] *n* pomme *f*; **~ tree** *n* pommier *m*.

appliance [ə'plaɪəns] *n* appareil *m*.

applicant ['æplɪkənt] *n*: **~ (for)** (*post*) candidat(e) (à).

application [æplɪ'keɪʃən] *n* application *f*; (*for a job, a grant etc*) demande *f*; candidature *f*; **~ form** *n* formulaire *m* de demande.

applied [ə'plaɪd] *a* appliqué(e).

apply [ə'plaɪ] *vt* (*paint, ointment*): **to ~ (to)** appliquer (sur); (*theory, technique*): **to ~ (to)** appliquer (à) // *vi*: **to ~ (to)** (*ask*) s'adresser à; (*be suitable for, relevant to*) s'appliquer à; se rapporter à; être valable pour; **to ~ (for)** (*permit, grant*) faire une demande (en vue d'obtenir); (*job*) poser sa candidature (pour), faire une demande d'emploi (concernant).

to ~ the brakes actionner les freins, freiner; to ~ o.s. to s'appliquer à.

appoint [ə'pɔɪnt] vt nommer, engager; (date, place) fixer, désigner; ~ment n nomination f; rendez-vous m; to make an ~ment (with) prendre rendez-vous (avec).

appraisal [ə'preɪzl] n évaluation f.

appreciate [ə'priːʃɪeɪt] vt (like) apprécier, faire cas de; (be aware of) comprendre; se rendre compte de // vi (FINANCE) prendre de la valeur.

appreciation [əpriːʃɪ'eɪʃən] n appréciation f; reconnaissance f; (COMM) hausse f, valorisation f.

appreciative [ə'priːʃɪətɪv] a (person) sensible; (comment) élogieux(euse).

apprehensive [æprɪ'hensɪv] a inquiet(ète), appréhensif(ive).

apprentice [ə'prentɪs] n apprenti m; ~ship n apprentissage m.

approach [ə'prəʊtʃ] vi approcher // vt (come near) approcher de; (ask, apply to) s'adresser à; (subject, passer-by) aborder // n approche f; accès m, abord m; démarche f (auprès de qn); démarche (intellectuelle); ~able a accessible.

appropriate [ə'prəʊprɪɪt] a opportun(e); qui convient, approprié(e) // vt [ə'prəʊprɪeɪt] (take) s'approprier.

approval [ə'pruːvəl] n approbation f; on ~ (COMM) à l'examen.

approve [ə'pruːv] vt approuver; to ~ of vt fus approuver; ~d school n (Brit) centre m d'éducation surveillée.

approximate a [ə'prɔksɪmɪt] approximatif(ive); ~ly ad approximativement.

apricot ['eɪprɪkɔt] n abricot m.

April ['eɪprəl] n avril m; ~ Fool's Day n le premier avril.

apron ['eɪprən] n tablier m.

apt [æpt] a (suitable) approprié(e); (likely): ~ to do susceptible de faire; ayant tendance à faire.

aqualung ['ækwəlʌŋ] n scaphandre m autonome.

aquarium [ə'kwɛərɪəm] n aquarium m.

Aquarius [ə'kwɛərɪəs] n le Verseau.

Arab ['ærəb] n Arabe m/f.

Arabian [ə'reɪbɪən] a arabe.

Arabic ['ærəbɪk] a arabe // n arabe m; ~ numerals chiffres mpl arabes.

arbitrary ['ɑːbɪtrərɪ] a arbitraire.

arbitration [ɑːbɪ'treɪʃən] n arbitrage m.

arcade [ɑː'keɪd] n arcade f; (passage with shops) passage m, galerie f.

arch [ɑːtʃ] n arche f; (of foot) cambrure f, voûte f plantaire // vt arquer, cambrer // a malicieux(euse).

archaeologist [ɑːkɪ'ɔlədʒɪst] n archéologue m/f.

archaeology [ɑːkɪ'ɔlədʒɪ] n archéologie f.

archbishop [ɑːtʃ'bɪʃəp] n archevêque m.

arch-enemy ['ɑːtʃ'enəmɪ] n ennemi m de toujours or par excellence.

archeology etc [ɑːkɪ'ɔlədʒɪ] (US) = **archaeology** etc.

archer ['ɑːtʃə*] n archer m; ~y n tir m à l'arc.

architect ['ɑːkɪtekt] n architecte m; ~ure ['ɑːkɪtektʃə*] n architecture f.

archives ['ɑːkaɪvz] npl archives fpl.

archway ['ɑːtʃweɪ] n voûte f, porche voûté or cintré.

Arctic ['ɑːktɪk] a arctique // n: the ~ l'Arctique m.

ardent ['ɑːdənt] a fervent(e).

are [ɑː*] vb see **be**.

area ['ɛərɪə] n (GEOM) superficie f; (zone) région f; (: smaller) secteur m.

aren't [ɑːnt] = **are not**.

Argentina [ɑːdʒən'tiːnə] n Argentine f; **Argentinian** [-'tɪnɪən] a argentin(e) // n Argentin(e).

arguably [ə'gjuːəblɪ] ad: it is ~ — on peut soutenir que c'est —.

argue ['ɑːgjuː] vi (quarrel) se disputer; (reason) argumenter; to ~ that objecter or alléguer que, donner comme argument que.

argument ['ɑ:gjumənt] n (*reasons*) argument m; (*quarrel*) dispute f, discussion f; (*debate*) discussion f, controverse f; ~**ative** [-'mentətiv] a ergoteur(euse), raisonneur(euse).

Aries ['ɛəriz] n le Bélier.

arise, pt **arose**, pp **arisen** [ə'raiz, ə'rəuz, ə'rizn] vi survenir, se présenter; **to** ~ **from** résulter de.

aristocrat ['ærɪstəkræt] n aristocrate m/f.

arithmetic [ə'riθmətik] n arithmétique f.

ark [ɑ:k] n: **Noah's A~** l'Arche f de Noé.

arm [ɑ:m] n bras m // vt armer; ~**s** npl (*weapons, HERALDRY*) armes fpl; ~ **in** ~ bras dessus bras dessous.

armaments ['ɑ:məmənts] npl armements mpl.

arm: ~**chair** n fauteuil m; ~**ed** a armé(e); ~**ed robbery** n vol m à main armée.

armour, (*US*) **armor** ['ɑ:mə*] n armure f; (*also*: ~-**plating**) blindage m; (*MIL: tanks*) blindés mpl; ~**ed car** n véhicule blindé; ~**y** n arsenal m.

armpit ['ɑ:mpit] n aisselle f.

armrest ['ɑ:mrest] n accoudoir m.

army ['ɑ:mi] n armée f.

aroma [ə'rəumə] n arôme m.

arose [ə'rəuz] pt of **arise**.

around [ə'raund] ad (*tout*) autour; dans les parages // prep autour de; (*fig: about*) environ; vers.

arouse [ə'rauz] vt (*sleeper*) éveiller; (*curiosity, passions*) éveiller, susciter; exciter.

arrange [ə'reindʒ] vt arranger; (*programme*) arrêter, convenir de; **to** ~ **to do sth** prévoir de faire qch; ~**ment** n arrangement m; (*plans etc*): ~**ments** dispositions fpl.

array [ə'rei] n: ~ **of** déploiement m or étalage m de.

arrears [ə'riəz] npl arriéré m; **to be in** ~ **with one's rent** devoir un ar-

riéré de loyer.

arrest [ə'rest] vt arrêter; (*sb's attention*) retenir, attirer // n arrestation f; **under** ~ en état d'arrestation.

arrival [ə'raivl] n arrivée f; (*COMM*) arrivage m; (*person*) arrivant/e; **new** ~ nouveau venu, nouvelle venue.

arrive [ə'raiv] vi arriver.

arrogant ['ærəgənt] a arrogant(e).

arrow ['ærəu] n flèche f.

arse [ɑ:s] n (*col!*) cul m (!).

arson ['ɑ:sn] n incendie criminel.

art [ɑ:t] n art m; (*craft*) métier m; **A~s** npl (*SCOL*) les lettres fpl.

artefact ['ɑ:tifækt] n objet fabriqué.

artery ['ɑ:təri] n artère f.

art gallery n musée d'art; (*small and private*) galerie f de peinture.

arthritis [ɑ:'θraitis] n arthrite f.

artichoke ['ɑ:titʃəuk] n artichaut m; **Jerusalem** ~ topinambour m.

article ['ɑ:tikl] n article m; (*Brit LAW: training*): ~**s** npl =stage m; ~ **of clothing** vêtement m.

articulate a [ɑ:'tikjulit] (*person*) qui s'exprime clairement et aisément; (*speech*) bien articulé(e), prononcé(e) clairement // vi [ɑ:'tikjuleit] articuler, parler distinctement; ~**d lorry** n (*Brit*) (camion m) semi-remorque m.

artificial [ɑ:ti'fiʃəl] a artificiel(le).

artist ['ɑ:tist] n artiste m/f; ~**ic** [ɑ:'tistik] a artistique; ~**ry** n art m, talent m.

artless ['ɑ:tlis] a naïf(naïve), simple, ingénu(e).

art school n =école f des beaux-arts.

<hr>

KEYWORD

<hr>

as [æz] ◆ cj **1** (*referring to time*) comme, alors que; à mesure que; **he came in** ~ **I was leaving** il est arrivé comme je partais; ~ **the years went by** à mesure que les années passaient; ~ **from tomorrow** à partir de demain

2 (*in comparisons*): ~ **big** ~ aussi

grand que; **twice ~ big** = deux fois plus grand que; **~ much** *or* **many ~** autant que; **~ much money/ many books** = autant d'argent/de livres que; **~ soon** = dès que

3 (*since, because*) comme, puisque; **he left early, ~ he had to be home by 10** comme il a dû or puisqu'il devait être de retour avant 10h il est parti tôt

4 (*referring to manner, way*) comme; **do ~ you wish** faites comme vous voudrez

5 (*concerning*): **~ for** *or* **to that** quant à cela, pour ce qui est de cela

6: **~ if** *or* **though** comme si; **he looked ~ if he was ill** il avait l'air d'être malade; *see also* **long, such, well**

♦ *prep*: **he works ~ a driver** il travaille comme chauffeur; **~ chairman of the company, he** — en tant que président de la compagnie, il —; **dressed up ~ a cowboy** déguisé en cowboy; **he gave me it ~ a present** il me l'a offert, il m'en a fait cadeau.

---

a.s.a.p. *abbr* (=*as soon as possible*) dès que possible.

ascend [ə'sɛnd] *vt* gravir.

ascent [ə'sɛnt] *n* ascension *f*.

ascertain [æsə'teɪn] *vt* s'assurer de, vérifier; établir.

ash [æʃ] *n* (*dust*) cendre *f*; (*also*: **~ tree**) frêne *m*.

ashamed [ə'ʃeɪmd] *a* honteux(euse), confus(e); **to be ~ of** avoir honte de.

ashen ['æʃn] *a* (*pale*) cendreux(euse), blême.

ashore [ə'ʃɔː] *ad* à terre.

ashtray ['æʃtreɪ] *n* cendrier *m*.

Ash Wednesday *n* mercredi *m* des cendres.

Asia ['eɪʃə] *n* Asie *f*; **~n** *n* Asiatique *m/f // a* asiatique.

aside [ə'saɪd] *ad* de côté; à l'écart // *n* aparté *m*.

ask [ɑːsk] *vt* demander; (*invite*) invi-

ter; **to ~ sb sth/to do sth** demander à qn qch/de faire qch; **to ~ sb about sth** questionner qn au sujet de qch; **se renseigner auprès de qn au sujet de qch; to ~ (sb) a question** poser une question (à qn); **to ~ sb out to dinner** inviter qn au restaurant; **to ~ after** *vt fus* demander des nouvelles de; **to ~ for** *vt fus* demander.

askance [ə'skɑːns] *ad*: **to look ~ at sb** regarder qn de travers *or* d'un œil désapprobateur.

askew [ə'skjuː] *ad* de travers, de guinguois.

asleep [ə'sliːp] *a* endormi(e); **to be ~** dormir, être endormi; **to fall ~** s'endormir.

asparagus [əs'pærəgəs] *n* asperges *fpl*.

aspect ['æspɛkt] *n* aspect *m*; (*direction in which a building etc faces*) orientation *f*, exposition *f*.

aspersions [əs'pɜːʃənz] *npl*: **to cast ~ on** dénigrer.

aspire [əs'paɪə] *vi*: **to ~ to** aspirer à.

aspirin ['æsprɪn] *n* aspirine *f*.

ass [æs] *n* âne *m*; (*col*) imbécile *m/f*; (*US col!*) cul *m* (!).

assailant [ə'seɪlənt] *n* agresseur *m*; assaillant *m*.

assassinate [ə'sæsɪneɪt] *vt* assassiner; **assassination** [əsæsɪ'neɪʃən] *n* assassinat *m*.

assault [ə'sɔːlt] *n* (*MIL*) assaut *m*; (*gen: attack*) agression *f // vt* attaquer; (*sexually*) violenter.

assemble [ə'sɛmbl] *vt* assembler // *vi* s'assembler, se rassembler.

assembly [ə'sɛmbli] *n* (*meeting*) rassemblement *m*; (*construction*) assemblage *m*; **~ line** *n* chaîne *f* de montage.

assent [ə'sɛnt] *n* assentiment *m*, consentement *m*.

assert [ə'sɜːt] *vt* affirmer, déclarer; établir.

assess [ə'sɛs] *vt* évaluer, estimer; (*tax, damages*) établir *or* fixer le montant de; (*property etc: for tax*) calculer la valeur imposable de; **~ment** n évaluation f, estimation f; **~or** n expert m (en matière d'impôt et d'assurance).

asset ['æset] n avantage m, atout m; **~s** pl capital m; avoir(s) m(pl); actif m.

assign [ə'saɪn] vt (date) fixer, arrêter; (task): to **~** sth to assigner qch à; (resources): to **~** sth to affecter qch à; (cause, meaning): to **~** sth to attribuer qch à; **~ment** n tâche f, mission f.

assist [ə'sɪst] vt aider, assister, secourir; **~ance** n aide f, assistance f, secours mpl; **~ant** n assistant/e, adjoint/e; (Brit: also: shop **~ant**) vendeur/euse.

associate a n, [ə'səufɪt] associé(e) // vb [ə'səufɪeɪt] vt associer // vi: to **~ with** sb fréquenter qn.

association [əsəusɪ'eɪʃən] n association f.

assorted [ə'sɔːtɪd] a assorti(e).

assortment [ə'sɔːtmənt] n assortiment m.

assume [ə'sjuːm] vt supposer; (responsibilities etc) assumer; (attitude, name) prendre, adopter; **~d name** n nom m d'emprunt.

assumption [ə'sʌmpʃən] n supposition f, hypothèse f.

assurance [ə'ʃuərəns] n assurance f.

assure [ə'ʃuə] vt assurer.

astern [ə'stɜːn] ad à l'arrière.

asthma ['æsmə] n asthme m.

astonish [ə'stɒnɪʃ] vt étonner, stupéfier; **~ment** n étonnement m.

astound [ə'staʊnd] vt stupéfier, sidérer.

astray [ə'streɪ] ad: to go **~** s'égarer; (fig) quitter le droit chemin.

astride [ə'straɪd] ad à cheval // prep à cheval sur.

astrology [əs'trɒlədʒɪ] n astrologie f.

astronaut ['æstrənɔːt] n astronaute m/f.

astronomy [əs'trɒnəmɪ] n astronomie f.

astute [əs'tjuːt] a astucieux(euse).

asylum [ə'saɪləm] n asile m.

━━━━━━━━━━━━━━━━
KEYWORD
━━━━━━━━━━━━━━━━

at [æt] prep
1 (referring to position, direction) à; **~** the top au sommet; **~** home/school à la maison or chez soi/à l'école; **~** the baker's à la boulangerie, chez le boulanger; to look **~** sth regarder qch

2 (referring to time) à; **~** 4 o'clock à 4 heures; **~** Christmas à Noël; **~** night la nuit; **~** times par moments, parfois

3 (referring to rates, speed etc) à; **~** £1 a kilo une livre le kilo; two **~** a time deux à la fois; **~** 50 km/h à 50 km/h

4 (referring to manner): **~** a stroke d'un seul coup; **~** peace en paix

5 (referring to activity): to be **~** work être à l'œuvre, travailler; to play **~** cowboys jouer aux cowboys; to be good **~** sth être bon en qch

6 (referring to cause): shocked/surprised/annoyed **~** sth choqué par/étonné de/agacé par qch; I went **~** his suggestion j'y suis allé sur son conseil.

ate [eɪt] pt of eat.

atheist ['eɪθɪɪst] n athée m/f.

Athens ['æθɪnz] n Athènes f.

athlete ['æθliːt] n athlète m/f.

athletic [æθ'letɪk] a athlétique; **~s** n athlétisme m.

Atlantic [ət'læntɪk] a atlantique // n: the **~** (Ocean) l'Atlantique m, l'océan m Atlantique.

atlas ['ætləs] n atlas m.

atmosphere ['ætməsfɪə] n atmosphère f.

atom ['ætəm] n atome m; **~ic** [ə'tɒmɪk] a atomique; **~(ic) bomb** n bombe f atomique; **~izer** ['ætəmaɪzə] n atomiseur m.

atone [ə'təun] vi: to **~** for expier, racheter.

atrocious [ə'trəuʃəs] a (very bad) atroce, exécrable.

attach [ə'tætʃ] *vt* (*gen*) attacher; (*document, letter*) joindre; (*employee, troops*) affecter; **to be ~ed to sb/sth** (*to like*) être attaché à qch.

attaché case [ə'tæʃeɪ-] *n* mallette *f*, attaché-case *m*.

attachment [ə'tætʃmənt] *n* (*tool*) accessoire *m*; (*love*): **~ (to)** affection *f* (pour), attachement *m* (à).

attack [ə'tæk] *vt* attaquer; (*task etc*) s'attaquer à // *n* attaque *f*; (*also*: **heart ~**) crise *f* cardiaque.

attain [ə'teɪn] *vt* (*also*: **to ~ to**) parvenir à, atteindre; acquérir; **~ments** *npl* connaissances *fpl*, résultats *mpl*.

attempt [ə'tɛmpt] *n* tentative *f* // *vt* essayer, tenter; **to make an ~ on sb's life** attenter à la vie de qn.

attend [ə'tɛnd] *vt* (*course*) suivre; (*meeting, talk*) assister à; (*school, church*) aller à, fréquenter; (*patient*) soigner, s'occuper de; **to ~ to** *vt fus* (*needs, affairs etc*) s'occuper de; (*customer*) s'occuper de, servir; **~ance** *n* (*being present*) présence *f*; (*people present*) assistance *f*; **~ant** *n* employé/e; gardien/ne // *a* concomitant(e), qui accompagne *ou* s'ensuit.

attention [ə'tɛnʃən] *n* attention *f*; **~!** (*MIL*) garde-à-vous!; **for the ~ of** (*ADMIN*) à l'attention de.

attentive [ə'tɛntɪv] *a* attentif(ive); (*kind*) prévenant(e).

attic ['ætɪk] *n* grenier *m*, combles *mpl*.

attitude ['ætɪtjuːd] *n* attitude *f*, manière *f*; pose *f*, maintien *m*.

attorney [ə'tɜːnɪ] *n* (*lawyer*) avoué *m*; (*having proxy*) mandataire *m*; **A~ General** *n* (*Brit*) ≈procureur général; (*US*) ≈garde des Sceaux, ministre *m* de la Justice.

attract [ə'trækt] *vt* attirer; **~ion** [ə'trækʃən] *n* (*gen pl*: *pleasant things*) attraction *f*, attrait *m*; (*PHYSICS*) attraction *f*; (*fig*: *towards sth*) attirance *f*; **~ive** *a* séduisant(e), at-

trayant(e).

attribute *n* ['ætrɪbjuːt] attribut *m* // *vt* [ə'trɪbjuːt]: **to ~ sth to** attribuer qch à.

attrition [ə'trɪʃən] *n*: **war of ~** guerre *f* d'usure.

aubergine ['əʊbəʒiːn] *n* aubergine *f*.

auction ['ɔːkʃən] *n* (*also*: **sale by ~**) vente *f* aux enchères // *vt* (*also*: **to sell by ~**) vendre aux enchères; (*also*: **to put up for ~**) mettre aux enchères; **~eer** [-'nɪə] *n* commissaire-priseur *m*.

audience ['ɔːdɪəns] *n* (*people*) assistance *f*, auditoire *m*; auditeurs *mpl*; spectateurs *mpl*; (*interview*) audience *f*.

audio-visual [ɔːdɪəʊ'vɪzjʊəl] *a* audio-visuel(le); **~ aids** *npl* supports *ou* moyens audiovisuels.

audit ['ɔːdɪt] *vt* vérifier, apurer.

audition [ɔː'dɪʃən] *n* audition *f*.

auditor ['ɔːdɪtə*] *n* vérificateur *m* des comptes.

augur ['ɔːgə*] *vi*: **it ~s well** c'est bon signe *ou* de bon augure.

August ['ɔːgəst] *n* août *m*.

aunt [ɑːnt] *n* tante *f*; **~ie, ~y** *n diminutive of* **aunt**.

au pair ['əʊ'pɛə*] *n* (*also*: **~ girl**) jeune fille *f* au pair.

aura ['ɔːrə] *n* atmosphère *f*.

auspicious [ɔːs'pɪʃəs] *a* de bon augure, propice.

austerity [ɔs'tɛrɪtɪ] *n* austérité *f*.

Australia [ɔs'treɪlɪə] *n* Australie *f*; **~n** *a* australien(ne) // *n* Australien/ne.

Austria ['ɔstrɪə] *n* Autriche *f*; **~n** *a* autrichien(ne) // *n* Autrichien/ne.

authentic [ɔː'θɛntɪk] *a* authentique.

author ['ɔːθə*] *n* auteur *m*.

authoritarian [ɔːθɔrɪ'tɛərɪən] *a* autoritaire.

authoritative [ɔː'θɔrɪtətɪv] *a* (*account*) digne de foi; (*study, treatise*) qui fait autorité; (*manner*) autoritaire.

authority [ɔː'θɔrɪtɪ] *n* autorité *f*; (*permission*) autorisation (formelle)

the authorities *npl* les autorités *fpl*, l'administration *f*.

authorize ['ɔːθəraɪz] *vt* autoriser.

auto ['ɔːtəu] *n* (*US*) auto *f*, voiture *f*.

autobiography [ɔːtəbaɪ'ɔgrəfɪ] *n* autobiographie *f*.

autograph ['ɔːtəgrɑːf] *n* autographe *m* // *vt* signer, dédicacer.

automatic [ɔːtə'mætɪk] *a* automatique // *n* (*gun*) automatique *m*; (*Brit AUT*) voiture *f* à transmission automatique; **~ally** *ad* automatiquement.

automation [ɔːtə'meɪʃən] *n* automatisation *f*.

automobile ['ɔːtəməbiːl] *n* (*US*) automobile *f*.

autonomy [ɔː'tɔnəmɪ] *n* autonomie *f*.

autumn ['ɔːtəm] *n* automne *m*.

auxiliary [ɔːg'zɪlɪərɪ] *a*, *n* auxiliaire (*m/f*).

Av. *abbr of* avenue.

avail [ə'veɪl] *vt*: to ~ o.s. of user de; profiter de // *n*: to no ~ sans résultat, en vain, en pure perte.

available [ə'veɪləbl] *a* disponible.

avalanche ['ævəlɑːnʃ] *n* avalanche *f*.

Ave. *abbr of* avenue.

avenge [ə'vɛndʒ] *vt* venger.

avenue ['ævənjuː] *n* avenue *f*.

average ['ævərɪdʒ] *n* moyenne *f* // *a* moyen(ne) // *vt* (*a certain figure*) atteindre or faire *etc* en moyenne; **on ~** en moyenne; **to ~ out** *vi*: to ~ **out at** représenter en moyenne, donner une moyenne de.

averse [ə'vəːs] *a*: **to be ~ to sth/doing** éprouver une forte répugnance envers qch/à faire.

avert [ə'vəːt] *vt* prévenir, écarter; (*one's eyes*) détourner.

aviary ['eɪvɪərɪ] *n* volière *f*.

avocado [ævə'kɑːdəu] *n* (*also*: *Brit* **~ pear**) avocat *m*.

avoid [ə'vɔɪd] *vt* éviter.

await [ə'weɪt] *vt* attendre.

awake [ə'weɪk] *a* éveillé(e); (*fig*) en éveil // *vb* (*pt* **awoke**, *pp* **awoken**, **awaked**) *vt* éveiller // *vi* s'éveiller; **to be ~** être réveillé(e); **he was still ~** il ne dormait pas encore.

award [ə'wɔːd] *n* récompense *f*, prix *m* // *vt* (*prize*) décerner; (*LAW*: *damages*) accorder.

aware [ə'wɛə] *a*: ~ **of** (*conscious*) conscient(e) de; (*informed*) au courant de; **to become ~ of** avoir conscience de, prendre conscience de; se rendre compte de; **~ness** *n* le fait d'être conscient, au courant *etc*.

awash [ə'wɔʃ] *a* recouvert(e) (d'eau); ~ **with** inondé(e) de.

away [ə'weɪ] *a*, *ad* (au) loin; absent(e); **two kilometres ~** à (une distance de) deux kilomètres, à deux kilomètres de distance; **two hours ~ by car** à deux heures de voiture or de route; **the holiday was two weeks ~** il restait deux semaines jusqu'aux vacances; **he's ~ for a week** il est parti (pour) une semaine; **to take ~** *vt* emporter; **to pedal/work/laugh** *etc* ~ la particule indique la constance et l'énergie de l'action: **il pédalait** *etc* **tant qu'il pouvait**; **to fade** *etc* ~ la particule renforce l'idée de la disparition, l'éloignement; ~ **game** *n* (*SPORT*) match *m* à l'extérieur.

awe [ɔː] *n* respect mêlé de crainte, effroi mêlé d'admiration; **~-inspiring**, **~some** *a* impressionnant(e).

awful ['ɔːfəl] *a* affreux(euse); **~ly** *ad* (*very*) terriblement, vraiment.

awhile [ə'waɪl] *ad* un moment, quelque temps.

awkward ['ɔːkwəd] *a* (*clumsy*) gauche, maladroit(e); (*inconvenient*) malaisé(e), d'emploi malaisé, peu pratique; (*embarrassing*) gênant(e), délicat(e).

awning ['ɔːnɪŋ] *n* (*of tent*) auvent *m*; (*of shop*) store *m*; (*of hotel etc*) marquise *f* (de toile).

awoke, awoken [ə'wəuk, -kən] *pt*, *pp* of **awake**.

awry [ə'raɪ] *ad*, *a* de travers; **to go ~** mal tourner.

axe, (*US*) **ax** [æks] *n* hache *f* // *vt*

(employee) renvoyer; *(project etc)* abandonner; *(jobs)* supprimer.

axis, pl **axes** ['æksɪs, -siːz] n axe m.

axle ['æksl] n *(also:* ~**-tree**) essieu m.

ay(e) [aɪ] *excl (yes)* oui.

B

B [biː] n *(MUS)* si m.

B.A. *abbr see* **bachelor**.

baby ['beɪbɪ] n bébé m; ~ **carriage** n *(US)* voiture f d'enfant; ~**-sit** vi garder les enfants; ~**-sitter** n babysitter m/f.

bachelor ['bætʃələ*] n célibataire m; **B~ of Arts/Science (B.A./B.Sc.)** ≈ licencié(e) ès or en lettres/sciences.

back [bæk] n *(of person, horse)* dos m; *(of hand)* dos, revers m; *(of house)* derrière m; *(of car, train)* arrière m; *(of chair)* dossier m; *(of page)* verso m; *(FOOTBALL)* arrière m // vt *(candidate: also:* ~ **up)** soutenir, appuyer; *(horse: at races)* parier or miser sur; *(car)* (faire) reculer // vi *(also:* ~ **up)** *(car etc)* faire marche arrière // a *(in compounds)* de derrière, à l'arrière; ~ **seats/wheels** *(AUT)* sièges mpl/roues fpl arrière; ~ **payments/rent** arriéré m de paiements/loyer // ad *(not forward)* en arrière; *(returned)*: **he's** ~ il est rentré, il est de retour; **he ran** ~ il est revenu en courant; *(restitution)*: **throw the ball** ~ renvoie la balle; **can I have it** ~? puis-je le ravoir?; *(again)*: **he called** ~ il a rappelé; **to** ~ **down** vi rabattre de ses prétentions; **to** ~ **out** vi *(of promise)* se dédire; **to** ~ **up** vt *(candidate etc)* soutenir, appuyer; *(COMPUT)* sauvegarder; ~**bencher** n *(Brit)* membre m du parlement sans portefeuille; ~**bone** n colonne vertébrale, épine dorsale; ~**cloth** n toile f de fond; ~**date** vt *(letter)* antidater; ~**dated pay rise** augmentation f avec effet rétroactif; ~**drop** n =

~**cloth**; ~**fire** vi *(AUT)* pétarader; *(plans)* mal tourner; ~**ground** n arrière-plan m; *(of events)* situation f, conjoncture f; *(basic knowledge)* éléments mpl de base; *(experience)* formation f; **family** ~**ground** milieu familial; ~**hand** n *(TENNIS: also:* ~**hand stroke)** revers m; ~**handed** a *(fig)* déloyal(e); équivoque; ~**hander** n *(Brit: bribe)* pot-de-vin m; ~**ing** n *(fig)* soutien m, appui m; ~**lash** n contre-coup m, répercussion f; ~**log** n *(of work)* travail en retard; *(of magazine etc)* vieux numéro; ~**pack** n sac m à dos; ~**pay** n rappel m de salaire; ~**side** n *(col)* derrière m, postérieur m; ~**stage** ad derrière la scène, dans la coulisse; ~**stroke** n dos crawlé; ~**up** a *(train, plane)* supplémentaire, de réserve; *(COMPUT)* de sauvegarde // n *(support)* appui m, soutien m; *(also:* ~**up file)** sauvegarde f; ~**ward** a *(movement)* en arrière; *(person, country)* arriéré(e); attardé(e); ~**wards** ad *(move, go)* en arrière; *(read a list)* à l'envers, à rebours; *(fall)* à la renverse; *(walk)* à reculons; ~**water** n *(fig)* coin reculé; bled perdu; ~**yard** n arrière-cour f.

bacon ['beɪkən] n bacon m, lard m.

bad [bæd] a mauvais(e); *(child)* vilain(e); *(meat, food)* gâté(e), avarié(e); **his** ~ **leg** sa jambe malade; **to go** ~ *(meat, food)* se gâter; *(milk)* tourner.

bade [bæd] pt of **bid**.

badge [bædʒ] n insigne m; *(of policeman)* plaque f.

badger ['bædʒə*] n blaireau m.

badly ['bædlɪ] ad *(work, dress etc)* mal; ~ **wounded** grièvement blessé; **he needs it** ~ il en a absolument besoin; ~ **off** a, ad dans la gêne.

badminton ['bædmɪntən] n badminton m.

bad-tempered ['bæd'tɛmpəd] a ayant mauvais caractère; de mauvaise humeur.

baffle ['bæfl] vt (puzzle) déconcerter.

bag [bæg] n sac m; (of hunter) gibecière f; chasse f // vi (col: take) empocher; s'approprier; ~s of (col: lots of) des masses de; ~**gage** n bagages mpl; ~**gy** a avachi(e), qui fait des poches; ~**pipes** npl cornemuse f.

bail [beɪl] n caution f // vt (prisoner: also: **grant ~ to**) mettre en liberté sous caution; (boat: also: ~ **out**) écoper; **on ~** (prisoner) sous caution; **to ~ out** (prisoner) payer la caution de; see also **bale**.

bailiff ['beɪlɪf] n huissier m.

bait [beɪt] n appât m // vt appâter; (fig) tourmenter.

bake [beɪk] vt (faire) cuire au four // vi cuire (au four); faire de la pâtisserie; ~**d beans** npl haricots blancs à la sauce tomate; ~**r** n boulanger m; ~**ry** n boulangerie f; boulangerie industrielle; **baking** n cuisson f.

balance ['bæləns] n équilibre m; (COMM: sum) solde m; (scales) balance f // vt mettre ou faire tenir en équilibre; (pros and cons) peser; (budget) équilibrer; (account) balancer; (compensate) compenser, contrebalancer; ~ **of trade/payments** balance commerciale/des comptes or paiements; ~**d** (personality, diet) équilibré(e); ~ **sheet** n bilan m.

balcony ['bælkənɪ] n balcon m.

bald [bɔːld] a chauve; (tyre) lisse.

bale [beɪl] n balle f, ballot m; **to ~ out** vi (of a plane) sauter en parachute.

baleful ['beɪlful] a funeste, maléfique.

ball [bɔːl] n boule f; (football) ballon m; (for tennis, golf) balle f; (dance) bal m.

ballast ['bæləst] n lest m.

ball bearings npl roulement m à billes.

ballerina [bælə'riːnə] n ballerine f.

ballet ['bæleɪ] n ballet m; (art) danse f (classique).

balloon [bə'luːn] n ballon m; (in comic strip) bulle f.

ballot ['bælət] n scrutin m.

ball-point pen ['bɔːlpɔɪnt-] n stylo m à bille.

ballroom ['bɔːlrum] n salle f de bal.

balm [bɑːm] n baume m.

ban [bæn] n interdiction f // vt interdire.

banana [bə'nɑːnə] n banane f.

band [bænd] n bande f; (at a dance) orchestre m; (MIL) musique f, fanfare f; **to ~ together** vi se liguer.

bandage ['bændɪdʒ] n bandage m, pansement m.

bandaid ['bændeɪd] n (US) pansement adhésif.

bandwagon ['bændwægən] n: **to jump on the ~** (fig) monter dans or prendre le train en marche.

bandy ['bændɪ] vt (jokes, insults) échanger.

bandy-legged ['bændɪ'legɪd] a aux jambes arquées.

bang [bæŋ] n détonation f; (of door) claquement m; (blow) coup (violent) // vt frapper (violemment); (door) claquer // vi détoner, claquer.

bangle ['bæŋgl] n bracelet m.

bangs [bæŋz] npl (US: fringe) frange f.

banish ['bænɪʃ] vt bannir.

banister(s) ['bænɪstə(z)] n(pl) rampe f (d'escalier).

bank [bæŋk] n banque f; (of river, lake) bord m, rive f; (of earth) talus m, remblai m // vi (AVIAT) virer sur l'aile; **to ~ on** vt fus miser or tabler sur; ~ **account** n compte m en banque; ~ **card** n carte f d'identité bancaire; ~**er** n banquier m; ~**er's card** = ~ **card**; **B~ holiday** n (Brit) jour férié (où les banques sont fermées); ~**ing** n opérations fpl de banquier; profession f de banquier; ~**note** n billet m de banque; ~ **rate** n taux m de l'escompte.

bankrupt ['bæŋkrʌpt] a en faillite; **to go ~** faire faillite; ~**cy** n faillite f.

bank statement n relevé m de compte.

banner ['bænə*] n bannière f.

baptism ['bæptizəm] n baptême m.

bar [ba:*] n barre f; (of window etc) barreau m; (of chocolate) tablette f, plaque f; (fig) obstacle m; mesure f d'exclusion; (pub) bar m; (counter: in pub) comptoir m, bar; (MUS) mesure f // vt (road) barrer; (window) munir de barreaux; (person) exclure; (activity) interdire; ~ of soap savonnette f; the B~ (LAW) le barreau; barrier; ~s (prisoner) sous les verrous; ~ none sans exception.

barbaric [ba:'bærik] a barbare.

barbecue ['ba:bikju:] n barbecue m.

barbed wire ['ba:bd-] n fil m de fer barbelé.

barber ['ba:bə*] n coiffeur m (pour hommes).

bar code n (on goods) code m à barres.

bare [bɛə*] a nu(e) // vt mettre à nu, dénuder; (teeth) montrer; ~back ad à cru, sans selle; ~faced a impudent(e), effronté(e); ~foot a nu-pieds, (les) pieds nus; ~ly ad à peine.

bargain ['ba:gin] n (transaction) marché m; (good buy) affaire f, occasion f // vi (haggle) marchander; (trade) négocier, traiter; into the ~ par-dessus le marché; to ~ for vt fus: he got more than he ~ed for il ne s'attendait pas à un coup pareil.

barge [ba:dʒ] n péniche f; to ~ in vi (walk in) faire irruption; (interrupt talk) intervenir mal à propos; to ~ into vt fus rentrer dans.

bark [ba:k] n (of tree) écorce f; (of dog) aboiement m // vi aboyer.

barley ['ba:li] n orge f.

barmaid ['ba:meid] n serveuse f (de bar), barmaid f.

barman ['ba:mən] n serveur m (de bar), barman m.

barn [ba:n] n grange f.

barometer [bə'rɔmitə*] n baromètre m.

baron ['bærən] n baron m; ~ess n baronne f.

barracks ['bærəks] npl caserne f.

barrage ['bæra:ʒ] n (MIL) tir m de barrage; (dam) barrage m; (fig) pluie f.

barrel ['bærəl] n tonneau m; (of gun) canon m.

barren ['bærən] a stérile; (hills) aride.

barricade [bæri'keid] n barricade f.

barrier ['bæriə*] n barrière f.

barring ['ba:riŋ] prep sauf.

barrister ['bæristə*] n (Brit) avocat (plaidant).

barrow ['bærəu] n (cart) charrette f à bras.

bartender ['ba:tendə*] n (US) serveur m (de bar), barman m.

barter ['ba:tə*] vt: to ~ sth for échanger qch contre.

base [beis] n base f // vt: to ~ sth on baser ou fonder qch sur // a vile(e), bas(se).

baseball ['beisbɔ:l] n base-ball m.

basement ['beismənt] n sous-sol m.

bases ['beisi:z] npl of **basis**; ['beisiz] npl of **base**.

bash [bæʃ] vt (col) frapper, cogner.

bashful ['bæʃful] a timide; modeste.

basic ['beisik] a fondamentale(e), de base; réduit(e) au minimum, rudimentaire; ~ally [-li] ad fondamentalement, à la base; en fait, au fond.

basil ['bæzl] n basilic m.

basin ['beisn] n (vessel, also GEO) cuvette f, bassin m; (also: wash~) lavabo m.

basis, pl **bases** ['beisis, -si:z] n base f.

bask [ba:sk] vi: to ~ in the sun se chauffer au soleil.

basket ['ba:skit] n corbeille f; (with handle) panier m; ~ball n basketball m.

bass [beis] n (MUS) basse f.

bassoon [bə'su:n] n basson m.

bastard ['ba:stəd] n enfant naturel(le), bâtard/e; (col!) salaud m (!).

bat [bæt] n chauve-souris f; (for base-

ball etc) batte *f*; *(Brit: for table tennis)* raquette *f* // *vi*: he didn't ~ an eyelid il n'a pas sourcillé *or* bronché.

batch [bætʃ] *n (of bread)* fournée *f*; *(of papers)* liasse *f*.

bated ['beɪtɪd] *adj*: with ~ breath en retenant son souffle.

bath [bɑːθ, *pl* bɑːðz] *n see also* **baths**; bain *m*; *(bathtub)* baignoire *f* // *vt* baigner, donner un bain à; to have a ~ prendre un bain.

bathe [beɪð] *vi* se baigner // *vt* baigner.

bathing ['beɪðɪŋ] *n* baignade *f*; ~ **cap** *n* bonnet *m* de bain; ~ **costume**, *(US)* ~ **suit** *n* maillot *m* (de bain).

bath: ~**robe** *n* peignoir *m* de bain; ~**room** *n* salle *f* de bains.

baths [bɑːðz] *npl* établissement *m* de bains-(douches).

bath towel *n* serviette *f* de bain.

baton ['bætən] *n* bâton *m*; *(MUS)* baguette *f*; *(club)* matraque *f*.

batter ['bætə*] *vt* battre // *n* pâte *f* à frire; ~**ed** *a (hat, pan)* cabossé(e).

battery ['bætərɪ] *n* batterie *f*; *(of torch)* pile *f*.

battle ['bætl] *n* bataille *f*, combat *m* // *vi* se battre, lutter; ~**field** *n* champ *m* de bataille; ~**ship** *n* cuirassé *m*.

bawdy ['bɔːdɪ] *a* paillard(e).

bawl [bɔːl] *vi* hurler, brailler.

bay [beɪ] *n (of sea)* baie *f*; to hold sb at ~ tenir qn à distance *or* en échec.

bay window *n* baie vitrée.

bazaar [bə'zɑː*] *n* bazar *m*; vente *f* de charité.

b. & b., B. & B. *abbr see* **bed**.

BBC *n abbr (= British Broadcasting Corporation)* office de la radiodiffusion et télévision britannique.

B.C. *ad abbr (= before Christ)* av. J.-C.

be [biː], *pt* **was, were**, *pp* **been** ♦ *auxiliary vb* **1** *(with present participle: forming continuous tenses)*:

what are you doing? que faites-vous?; **they're coming tomorrow** ils viennent demain; **I've been waiting for you for 2 hours** je t'attends depuis 2 heures

2 *(with pp: forming passives)* être; **to ~ killed** être tué(e); **he was nowhere to ~ seen** on ne le voyait nulle part

3 *(in tag questions)*: **it was fun, wasn't it?** c'était drôle, n'est-ce pas?; **she's back, is she?** elle est rentrée, n'est-ce pas *or* alors?

4 *(+ to + infinitive)*: **the house is to ~ sold** la maison doit être vendue; **he's not to open it** il ne doit pas l'ouvrir

♦ *vb + complement* **1** *(gen)* être; **I'm English** je suis anglais(e); **I'm tired** je suis fatigué(e); **I'm hot/cold** j'ai chaud/froid; **he's a doctor** il est médecin; **2 and 2 are 4** 2 et 2 font 4

2 *(of health)* aller; **how are you?** comment allez-vous?; **I'm better now** je vais mieux maintenant; **he's very ill** il est très malade

3 *(of age)* avoir; **how old are you?** quel âge avez-vous?; **I'm sixteen (years old)** j'ai seize ans

4 *(cost)* coûter; **how much was the meal?** combien a coûté le repas?; **that'll ~ £5, please** ça fera 5 livres, s'il vous plaît

♦ *vi* **1** *(exist, occur etc)* être, exister; **the best singer that ever was** le meilleur chanteur qui ait jamais existé; ~ **that as it may** quoi qu'il en soit; **so** ~ **it** soit

2 *(referring to place)* se trouver; **I won't ~ here tomorrow** je ne serai pas là demain; **Edinburgh is in Scotland** Édimbourg *or* se trouve en Écosse

3 *(referring to movement)* aller; **where have you been?** où êtes-vous allé(s)?

♦ *impersonal vb* **1** *(referring to time, distance)* être; **it's 5 o'clock** il est 5 heures; **it's the 28th of April**

c'est le 28 avril; **it's 10 km to the village** le village est à 10 km
2 (*referring to the weather*) faire; **it's too hot/cold** il fait trop chaud/froid; **it's windy** il y a du vent
3 (*emphatic*) **it's me/the postman** c'est moi/le facteur.

beach [biːtʃ] *n* plage *f* // *vt* échouer.

beacon ['biːkən] *n* (*lighthouse*) fanal *m*; (*marker*) balise *f*.

bead [biːd] *n* perle *f*.

beak [biːk] *n* bec *m*.

beaker ['biːkə*] *n* gobelet *m*.

beam [biːm] *n* poutre *f*; (*of light*) rayon *m* // *vi* rayonner.

bean [biːn] *n* haricot *m*; (*of coffee*) grain *m*; **runner ~** haricot *m* (à rames); **broad ~** fève *f*; **~sprouts** *npl* germes *mpl* de soja.

bear [bɛə*] *n* ours *m* // *vb* (*pt* **bore**, *pp* **borne**) *vt* porter; (*endure*) supporter // *vi*: **to ~ right/left** obliquer à droite/gauche, se diriger vers la droite/gauche; **to ~ out** corroborer, confirmer; **to ~ up** *vi* (*person*) tenir le coup.

beard [biəd] *n* barbe *f*.

bearer ['bɛərə*] *n* porteur *m*.

bearing ['bɛərɪŋ] *n* maintien *m*, allure *f*; (*connection*) rapport *m*; **~s** *npl* (*also*: **ball ~s**) roulement *m* (à billes); **to take a ~** faire le point; **to find one's ~s** s'orienter.

beast [biːst] *n* bête *f*; **~ly** *a* infect(e).

beat [biːt] *n* battement *m*; (*MUS*) temps *m*, mesure *f*; (*of policeman*) ronde *f* // *vt* (*pt* **beat**, *pp* **beaten**) battre; **off the ~en track** hors des chemins ou sentiers battus; **to ~ time** battre la mesure; **~ it!** (*col*) fiche(-moi) le camp!; **to ~ off** *vt* repousser; **to ~ up** *vt* (*col: person*) tabasser; (*eggs*) battre; **~ing** *n* raclée *f*.

beautiful ['bjuːtɪful] *a* beau(belle); **~ly** *ad* admirablement.

beauty ['bjuːtɪ] *n* beauté *f*; **~ salon** *n* institut *m* de beauté; **~ spot** *n*

grain *m* de beauté; (*Brit TOURISM*) site naturel (d'une grande beauté).

beaver ['biːvə*] *n* castor *m*.

became [bɪ'keɪm] *pt of* **become**.

because [bɪ'kɔz] *cj* parce que; **~ of** *prep* à cause de.

beck [bɛk] *n*: **to be at sb's ~ and call** être à l'entière disposition de qn.

beckon ['bɛkən] *vt* (*also*: **~ to**) faire signe de (venir) à.

become [bɪ'kʌm] *vt* (*irg: like come*) devenir; **to ~ thin** maigrir.

becoming [bɪ'kʌmɪŋ] *a* (*behaviour*) convenable, bienséant(e); (*clothes*) seyant(e).

bed [bɛd] *n* lit *m*; (*of flowers*) parterre *m*; (*of coal, clay*) couche *f*; **to go to ~** aller se coucher; **single ~** lit à une place; **double ~** grand lit; **~ and breakfast** (b. & b.) *n* (*terms*) chambre et petit déjeuner; **~clothes** *npl* couvertures *fpl* et draps *mpl*; **~ding** *n* literie *f*.

bedlam ['bɛdləm] *n* chahut *m*, cirque *m*.

bedraggled [bɪ'drægld] *a* dépenaillé(e), les vêtements en désordre.

bed: **~ridden** *a* cloué(e) au lit; **~room** *n* chambre *f* (à coucher); **~side** *n*: **at sb's ~side** au chevet de qn; **~sit(ter)** *n* (*Brit*) chambre meublée, studio *m*; **~spread** *n* couvre-lit *m*, dessus-de-lit *m*; **~time** *n* heure *f* du coucher.

bee [biː] *n* abeille *f*.

beech [biːtʃ] *n* hêtre *m*.

beef [biːf] *n* bœuf *m*; **roast ~** rosbif *m*; **~burger** *n* hamburger *m*; **~eater** *n* hallebardier de la Tour de Londres.

beehive ['biːhaɪv] *n* ruche *f*.

beeline ['biːlaɪn] *n*: **to make a ~ for** se diriger tout droit vers.

been [biːn] *pp of* **be**.

beer [biə*] *n* bière *f*.

beetle ['biːtl] *n* scarabée *m*.

beetroot ['biːtruːt] *n* (*Brit*) betterave *f*.

before [bɪ'fɔː*] *prep* (*in time*) avant; (*in space*) devant // *cj* avant que +

sub; avant de // *ad* avant; ~ **going** avant de partir; ~ **she goes** avant qu'elle (ne) parte; **the week** ~ la semaine précédente *or* d'avant; **I've seen it** ~ je l'ai déjà vu; ~**hand** *ad* au préalable, à l'avance.

beg [beg] *vi* mendier // *vt* mendier; *(favour)* quémander, solliciter; *(entreat)* supplier.

began [bɪ'gæn] *pt of* **begin**.

beggar ['begə*] *n* mendiant/e.

begin [bɪ'gɪn], *pt* **began**, *pp* **begun** *vt, vi* commencer; **to** ~ **doing** *or* **to do sth** commencer à *or* par faire qch; ~**ner** *n* débutant/e; ~**ning** *n* commencement *m*, début *m*.

begun [bɪ'gʌn] *pp of* **begin**.

behalf [bɪ'hɑ:f] *n*: **on** ~ **of** de la part de; au nom de; pour le compte de.

behave [bɪ'heɪv] *vi* se conduire, se comporter; *(well: also: ~ o.s.)* se conduire bien *or* comme il faut.

behaviour, *(US)* **behavior** [bɪ'heɪvjə*] *n* comportement *m*, conduite *f*.

behead [bɪ'hed] *vt* décapiter.

beheld [bɪ'held] *pt, pp of* **behold**.

behind [bɪ'haɪnd] *prep* derrière; *(time)* en retard sur // *ad* derrière; en retard // *n* derrière *m*; **to be** ~ *(schedule)* être en retard; ~ **the scenes** dans les coulisses.

behold [bɪ'həuld] *vt (irg: like hold)* apercevoir, voir.

beige [beɪʒ] *a* beige.

being [bɪ'ɪŋ] *n* être *m*; **to come into** ~ prendre naissance.

Beirut [beɪ'ru:t] *n* Beyrouth.

belated [bɪ'leɪtɪd] *a* tardif(ive).

belch [beltʃ] *vi* avoir un renvoi, roter // *vt (also:* ~ **out: smoke etc)** vomir, cracher.

belfry ['belfrɪ] *n* beffroi *m*.

Belgian ['beldʒən] *a* belge, de Belgique // *n* Belge *m/f*.

Belgium ['beldʒəm] *n* Belgique *f*.

belie [bɪ'laɪ] *vt* démentir.

belief [bɪ'li:f] *n (opinion)* conviction *f*; *(trust, faith)* foi *f*; *(acceptance as true)* croyance *f*.

believe [bɪ'li:v] *vt, vi* croire; **to** ~ **in** *(God)* croire en; *(method, ghosts)* croire à; ~**r** *n (in idea, activity)* ~**r** in partisan/e de; *(REL)* croyant/e.

belittle [bɪ'lɪtl] *vt* déprécier, rabaisser.

bell [bel] *n* cloche *f*; *(small)* clochette *f*, grelot *m*; *(on door)* sonnette *f*; *(electric)* sonnerie *f*.

bellow ['beləu] *vi* mugir.

bellows ['beləuz] *npl* soufflet *m*.

belly ['belɪ] *n* ventre *m*.

belong [bɪ'lɒŋ] *vi*: **to** ~ **to** appartenir à; *(club etc)* faire partie de; **this book** ~**s here** ce livre va ici; ~**ings** *npl* affaires *fpl*, possessions *fpl*.

beloved [bɪ'lʌvɪd] *a* (bien-)aimé(e).

below [bɪ'ləu] *prep* sous, au-dessous de // *ad* en dessous; en contre-bas; **see** ~ voir plus bas *or* plus loin *or* ci-dessous.

belt [belt] *n* ceinture *f*; *(TECH)* courroie *f* // *vt (thrash)* donner une raclée à; ~**way** *n (US AUT)* route *f* de ceinture; *(: motorway)* périphérique *m*.

bemused [bɪ'mju:zd] *a* stupéfié(e).

bench [bentʃ] *n* banc *m*; *(in workshop)* établi *m*; **the B~** *(LAW)* la magistrature, la Cour.

bend [bend] *vb (pt, pp* **bent**) *vt* courber; *(leg, arm)* plier // *vi* se courber // *n (Brit: in road)* virage *m*, tournant *m*; *(in pipe, river)* coude *m*; **to** ~ **down** *vi* se baisser; **to** ~ **over** *vi* se pencher.

beneath [bɪ'ni:θ] *prep* sous, au-dessous de; *(unworthy of)* indigne de // *ad* dessous, au-dessous, en bas.

benefactor ['benɪfæktə*] *n* bienfaiteur *m*.

beneficial [benɪ'fɪʃəl] *a* salutaire; avantageux(euse).

benefit ['benɪfɪt] *n* avantage *m*, profit *m*; *(allowance of money)* allocation *f* // *vt* faire du bien à, profiter à // *vi*: **he'll** ~ **from it** cela lui fera du bien, il y gagnera *or* s'en trouvera bien.

benevolent [bɪ'nevələnt] *a* bienveilant(e).

benign [bɪˈnaɪn] a (person, smile) bienveillant(e), affable; (MED) bénin(igne).

bent [bɛnt] pt, pp of bend // n inclination f, penchant m // a (col: dishonest) véreux(euse); **to be ~ on** être résolu(e) à.

bequest [bɪˈkwɛst] n legs m.

bereaved [bɪˈriːvd] n: the ~ la famille du disparu.

beret [ˈbɛreɪ] n béret m.

berm [bəːm] n (US AUT) accotement m.

berry [ˈbɛrɪ] n baie f.

berserk [bəˈsəːk] a: **to go ~** être pris(e) d'une rage incontrôlable; se déchaîner.

berth [bəːθ] n (bed) couchette f; (for ship) poste m d'amarrage, mouillage m // vi (in harbour) venir à quai; (at anchor) mouiller.

beseech [bɪˈsiːtʃ], pt, pp **besought** vt implorer, supplier.

beset, pt, pp **beset** [bɪˈsɛt] vt assaillir.

beside [bɪˈsaɪd] prep à côté de; **to be ~ o.s.** (with anger) être hors de soi; **that's ~ the point** cela n'a rien à voir.

besides [bɪˈsaɪdz] ad en outre, de plus // prep en plus de; excepté.

besiege [bɪˈsiːdʒ] vt (town) assiéger; (fig) assaillir.

besought [bɪˈsɔːt] pt, pp of beseech.

best [bɛst] a meilleur(e) // ad le mieux; **the ~ part of** (quantity) le plus clair de, la plus grande partie de; **at ~** au mieux; **to make the ~ of sth** s'accommoder de qch (du mieux que l'on peut); **to do one's ~** faire de son mieux; **to the ~ of my knowledge** pour autant que je sache; **to the ~ of my ability** du mieux que je pourrai; **~ man** n garçon m d'honneur.

bestow [bɪˈstəu] vt accorder; (title) conférer.

bet [bɛt] n pari m // vt, vi (pt, pp bet

or **betted**) parier.

betray [bɪˈtreɪ] vt trahir; **~al** n trahison f.

better [ˈbɛtə*] a meilleur(e) // ad mieux // vt améliorer // n: **to get the ~ of** triompher de, l'emporter sur; **you had ~ do it** il vous feriez mieux de le faire; **he thought ~ of it** il s'est ravisé; **to get ~** aller mieux; s'améliorer; **~ off** a plus à l'aise financièrement; (fig): **you'd be ~ off this way** vous vous en trouveriez mieux ainsi.

betting [ˈbɛtɪŋ] n paris mpl; **~ shop** n (Brit) bureau m de paris.

between [bɪˈtwiːn] prep entre // ad au milieu; dans l'intervalle.

beverage [ˈbɛvərɪdʒ] n boisson f (gén sans alcool).

bevy [ˈbɛvɪ] n: **a ~ of** un essaim ou une volée de.

beware [bɪˈwɛə*] vi: **to ~ (of)** prendre garde (à).

bewildered [bɪˈwɪldəd] a dérouté(e), ahuri(e).

bewitching [bɪˈwɪtʃɪŋ] a enchanteur(teresse).

beyond [bɪˈjɔnd] prep (in space) au-delà de; (exceeding) au-dessus de // ad au-delà; **~ doubt** hors de doute.

bias [ˈbaɪəs] n (prejudice) préjugé m, parti pris; (preference) prévention f; **~(s)ed** a partial(e), montrant un parti pris.

bib [bɪb] n bavoir m, bavette f.

Bible [ˈbaɪbl] n Bible f.

bicarbonate of soda [baɪˈkɑːbənɪt-] n bicarbonate m de soude.

bicker [ˈbɪkə*] vi se chamailler.

bicycle [ˈbaɪsɪkl] n bicyclette f.

bid [bɪd] n offre f; (at auction) enchère f; (attempt) tentative f // vb (pt bid ou bade, pp bid ou bidden) vi faire une enchère ou offre // vt faire une enchère ou offre de; **to ~ sb good day** souhaiter le bonjour à qn; **~der** n: **the highest ~der** le plus offrant; **~ding** n enchères fpl.

bide [baɪd] vt: **to ~ one's time** attendre son heure.

bifocals [baɪˈfəʊklz] npl verres mpl à double foyer, lunettes bifocales.

big [bɪg] a grand(e); gros(se).

big dipper [-ˈdɪpə*] n montagnes fpl russes.

bigheaded [ˈbɪgˈhedɪd] a prétentieux(euse).

bigot [ˈbɪgət] n fanatique m/f, sectaire m/f; ~**ed** a fanatique, sectaire; ~**ry** n fanatisme m, sectarisme m.

big top n grand chapiteau.

bike [baɪk] n vélo m, bécane f.

bikini [bɪˈkiːnɪ] n bikini m.

bilingual [baɪˈlɪŋgwəl] a bilingue.

bill [bɪl] n note f, facture f; (POL) projet m de loi; (US: banknote) billet m (de banque); (of bird) bec m; 'post no ~s' 'défense d'afficher'; to fit or fill the ~ (fig) faire l'affaire; ~**board** n panneau m d'affichage.

billet [ˈbɪlɪt] n cantonnement m (chez l'habitant).

billfold [ˈbɪlfəʊld] n (US) portefeuille m.

billiards [ˈbɪljədz] n (jeu m de) billard m.

billion [ˈbɪljən] n (Brit) billion m (million de millions); (US) milliard m.

bin [bɪn] n boîte f; (also: dust~) poubelle f; (for coal) coffre m.

bind [baɪnd], pt, pp bound vt attacher; (book) relier; (oblige) obliger, contraindre; ~**ing** n (of book) reliure f // a (contract) constituant une obligation.

binge [bɪndʒ] n (col): to go on a ~ aller faire la bringue.

bingo [ˈbɪŋgəʊ] n sorte de jeu de loto pratiqué dans des établissements publics.

binoculars [bɪˈnɒkjʊləz] npl jumelles fpl.

bio... [baɪə'...] prefix: ~**chemistry** n biochimie f; ~**graphy** [baɪˈɒgrəfɪ] n biographie f; ~**logical** a biologique; ~**logy** [baɪˈɒlədʒɪ] n biologie f.

birch [bəːtʃ] n bouleau m.

bird [bəːd] n oiseau m; (Brit col:

girl) nana f; ~**'s-eye view** n vue f à vol d'oiseau; (fig) vue d'ensemble or générale; ~ **watcher** n ornithologue m/f amateur.

Biro [ˈbaɪərəʊ] n ® stylo m à bille.

birth [bəːθ] n naissance f; ~ **certificate** n acte m de naissance; ~ **control** n limitation f des naissances; méthode(s) contraceptive(s); ~**day** n anniversaire m; ~ **rate** n (taux m de) natalité f.

biscuit [ˈbɪskɪt] n (Brit) biscuit m.

bisect [baɪˈsɛkt] vt couper or diviser en deux.

bishop [ˈbɪʃəp] n évêque m.

bit [bɪt] n pt of bite // n morceau m; (of tool) mèche f; (of horse) mors m; (COMPUT) élément m binaire; **a** ~ **of** un peu de; **a** ~ **mad** un peu fou; ~ **by** ~ petit à petit.

bitch [bɪtʃ] n (dog) chienne f; (col!) salope f (!), garce f.

bite [baɪt] vt, vi (pt bit, pp bitten) mordre // n morsure f; (insect ~) piqûre f; (mouthful) bouchée f; **let's have a** ~ **(to eat)** mangeons un morceau; **to** ~ **one's nails** se ronger les ongles.

bitter [ˈbɪtə*] a amer(ère); (wind, criticism) cinglant(e) // n (Brit: beer) bière f (à forte teneur en houblon); ~**ness** n amertume f; goût amer.

blab [blæb] vi jaser, trop parler.

black [blæk] a noir(e) // n (colour) noir m; (person): **B**~ noir/e // vt (shoes) cirer; (Brit INDUSTRY) boycotter; **to give sb a** ~ **eye** pocher l'œil à qn, faire un œil au beurre noir à qn; ~ **and blue** a couvert(e) de bleus; **to be in the** ~ (in credit) être créditeur(trice); ~**berry** n mûre f; ~**bird** n merle m; ~**board** n tableau noir; ~**currant** n cassis m; ~**en** vt noircir; ~ **ice** n verglas m; ~**leg** n (Brit) briseur m de grève, jaune m; ~**list** n liste noire; ~**mail** n chantage m // vt faire chanter, soumettre au chantage; ~ **market** n marché noir; ~**out** n panne f d'électricité; (fainting) syncope f; **the B~ Sea** n la mer Noire; ~ **sheep** n brebis galeuse; ~**smith** n forgeron m; ~ **spot** n (AUT) point noir.

bladder ['blædə*] n vessie f.

blade [bleɪd] n lame f; (of oar) plat m; ~ **of grass** brin m d'herbe.

blame [bleɪm] n faute f, blâme m // vt: to ~ **sb/sth for sth** attribuer à qn/qch la responsabilité de qch; reprocher qch à qn/qch; **who's to ~?** qui est le fautif ou coupable ou responsable?

bland [blænd] a affable; (taste) doux(douce), fade.

blank [blæŋk] a blanc(blanche); (look) sans expression, dénué(e) d'expression // n espace m vide, blanc m; (cartridge) cartouche f à blanc; ~ **cheque** n chèque m en blanc.

blanket ['blæŋkɪt] n couverture f.

blare [blɛə*] vi beugler.

blast [bla:st] n souffle m; explosion f // vt faire sauter ou exploser; ~**-off** n (SPACE) lancement m.

blatant ['bleɪtənt] a flagrant(e), criant(e).

blaze [bleɪz] n (fire) incendie m, (fig) flamboiement m // vi (fire) flamber; (fig) flamboyer, resplendir // vt: to ~ **a trail** (fig) montrer la voie.

blazer ['bleɪzə*] n blazer m.

bleach [bli:tʃ] n (also: **household** ~) eau f de Javel // vt (linen) blanchir; ~**ed** a (hair) oxygéné(e), décoloré(e); ~**ers** npl (US SPORT) gradins mpl (en plein soleil).

bleak [bli:k] a morne, désolé(e).

bleary-eyed ['blɪərɪ'aɪd] a aux yeux pleins de sommeil.

bleat [bli:t] vi bêler.

bleed, pt, pp **bled** [bli:d, bled] vt, vi saigner; **my nose is** ~**ing** je saigne du nez.

bleeper ['bli:pə*] n (device) bip m.

blemish ['blɛmɪʃ] n défaut m.

blend [blend] n mélange m // vt mélanger // vi (colours etc) se mélanger, se fondre, s'allier.

bless, pt, pp **blessed** or **blest** [bles, blest] vt bénir; ~**ing** n bénédiction f; bienfait m.

blew [blu:] pt of **blow**.

blight [blaɪt] vt (hopes etc) anéantir, briser.

blimey ['blaɪmɪ] excl (Brit col) mince alors!

blind [blaɪnd] a aveugle // n (for window) store m // vt aveugler; ~ **alley** n impasse f; ~ **corner** n (Brit) virage m sans visibilité; ~**fold** n bandeau m // a, ad les yeux bandés // vt bander les yeux à; ~**ly** ad aveuglément; ~**ness** n cécité f, (fig) aveuglement m; ~ **spot** n (AUT etc) angle mort.

blink [blɪŋk] vi cligner des yeux, (light) clignoter; ~**ers** npl œillères fpl.

bliss [blɪs] n félicité f, bonheur m sans mélange.

blister ['blɪstə*] n (on skin) ampoule f, cloque f; (on paintwork) boursouflure f // vi (paint) se boursoufler, se cloquer.

blithely ['blaɪðlɪ] ad joyeusement.

blitz [blɪts] n bombardement (aérien).

blizzard ['blɪzəd] n blizzard m, tempête f de neige.

bloated ['bləutɪd] a (face) bouffi(e); (stomach) gonflé(e).

blob [blɔb] n (drop) goutte f; (stain, spot) tache f.

block [blɔk] n bloc m; (in pipes) obstruction f; (toy) cube m; (of buildings) pâté m (de maisons) // vt bloquer; ~**age** [-'keɪd] n blocus m // vt faire le blocus de; ~**buster** n (film, book) grand succès; ~ **of flats** n (Brit) immeuble (locatif); ~ **letters** npl majuscules fpl.

bloke [bləuk] n (Brit col) type m.

blonde [blɔnd] a, n blond(e).

blood [blʌd] n sang m; ~ **donor** n donneur/euse de sang; ~ **group** n groupe sanguin; ~**hound** n limier m; ~ **poisoning** n empoisonnement m du sang; ~ **pressure** n tension f (artérielle); **~shed** n effusion f de sang, carnage m; **~shot** a: **~shot eyes** yeux injectés de sang; **~stream** n sang m, système sanguin; **~ test** n prise f de sang; **~thirsty** a sanguinaire; **~y** a sanglant(e); (Brit col): **this ~y ... ce** foutu ..., ce putain de ... (!); **~y strong/good** vachement or sacrément fort/bon; **~y-minded** a (Brit col) contrariant(e), obstiné(e).

bloom [blu:m] n fleur f; (fig) épanouissement m // vi être en fleur; (fig) s'épanouir; être florissant(e).

blossom ['blɔsəm] n fleur(s f(pl)) // vi être en fleur; (fig) s'épanouir.

blot [blɔt] n tache f // vt tacher; **to ~ out** vt (memories) effacer; (view) cacher, masquer; (nation, city) annihiler.

blotchy ['blɔtʃɪ] a (complexion) couvert(e) de marbrures.

blotting paper n ['blɔtɪŋ-] n buvard m.

blouse [blauz] n (feminine garment) chemisier m, corsage m.

blow [bləu] n coup m // vb (pt blew, pp blown [blu:, bləun]) vi souffler // vt (fuse) faire sauter; **to ~ one's nose** se moucher; **to ~ a whistle** siffler; **to ~ away** vt chasser, faire s'envoler; **to ~ down** vt faire tomber, renverser; **to ~ off** vt emporter; **to ~ out** vi éclater, sauter; **to ~ over** vi s'apaiser; **to ~ up** vi exploser, sauter // vt faire sauter; (tyre) gonfler; (PHOT) agrandir; **~dry** n brushing m; **~lamp** n (Brit) chalumeau m; **~out** n (of tyre) éclatement m; **~torch** n = **~lamp.**

blue [blu:] a bleu(e); **~ film/joke** film m/histoire f pornographique; **to come out of the ~** (fig) être complètement inattendu; **to have the ~s** avoir le cafard; **~bottle** n mouche f à viande; **~jeans** npl blue-jeans mpl; **~print** n (fig) projet m, plan(s pl).

bluff [blʌf] vi bluffer // n bluff m; **to call sb's ~** mettre qn au défi d'exé-

cuter ses menaces.

blunder ['blʌndə*] n gaffe f, bévue f // vi faire une gaffe or une bévue.

blunt [blʌnt] a émoussé(e), peu tranchant(e); (person) brusque, ne mâchant pas ses mots // vt émousser.

blur [blə:*] n tache or masse floue or confuse // vt brouiller, rendre flou(e).

blurb [blə:b] n notice f publicitaire; (for book) texte m de présentation.

blurt [blə:t]: **to ~ out** vt (reveal) lâcher; (say) balbutier, dire d'une voix entrecoupée.

blush [blʌʃ] vi rougir // n rougeur f.

blustery ['blʌstərɪ] a (weather) à bourrasques.

boar [bɔ:*] n sanglier m.

board [bɔ:d] n planche f; (on wall) panneau m; (committee) conseil m, comité m; (in firm) conseil m d'administration // vt (ship) monter à bord de; (train) monter dans; (NAUT, AVIAT): **on ~** à bord; **full ~** (Brit) pension complète; **half ~** (Brit) demi-pension f; **~ and lodging** n chambre f avec pension; **which goes by the ~** (fig) qu'on laisse tomber, qu'on abandonne; **to ~ up** vt (door) condamner (au moyen de planches, de tôle); **~er** n pensionnaire m/f; (SCOL) interne m/f, pensionnaire; **~ing card** n (AVIAT, NAUT) carte f d'embarquement; **~ing house** n pension f; **~ing school** n internat m, pensionnat m; **~ room** n salle f du conseil d'administration.

boast [bəust] vi: **to ~** (about or of) se vanter (de) // vt s'enorgueillir de // n vantardise f; sujet m d'orgueil or de fierté.

boat [bəut] n bateau m; (small) canot m; barque f; **~er** n (hat) canotier m; **~swain** ['bəusn] n maître m d'équipage.

bob [bɔb] vi (boat, cork on water: also: **~ up and down**) danser, se balancer // n (Brit col) = shilling; **to ~ up** vi surgir or apparaître brusquement.

bobby ['bɔbɪ] n (Brit col) = agent m

(de police).

bobsleigh ['bɔbsleɪ] n bob m.

bode [bəud] vi: **to ~ well/ill (for)** être de bon/mauvais augure (pour).

bodily ['bɔdɪlɪ] a corporel(le) // ad physiquement; dans son entier or ensemble; en personne.

body ['bɔdɪ] n corps m; (of car) carrosserie f; (of plane) fuselage m; (fig: society) organe m, organisme m; (fig: quantity) ensemble m, masse f; (of wine) corps m; **~-building** n culturisme m; **~guard** n garde m du corps; **~work** n carrosserie f.

bog [bɔg] n tourbière f // vt: **to get ~ged down** (fig) s'enliser.

boggle ['bɔgl] vi: **the mind ~s** c'est incroyable, on en reste sidéré.

bogus ['bəugəs] a bidon inv; fantôme.

boil [bɔɪl] vt (faire) bouillir // vi bouillir // n (MED) furoncle m; **to come to the (Brit) or a (US) ~** bouillir; **to ~ down** vi (fig): **to ~ down to** se réduire or ramener à; **to ~ over** vi déborder; **~ed egg** n œuf m à la coque; **~ed potatoes** npl pommes fpl à l'anglaise or à l'eau; **~er** n chaudière f; **~er suit** n (Brit) bleu m de travail, combinaison f; **~ing point** n point m d'ébullition.

boisterous ['bɔɪstərəs] a bruyant(e), tapageur(euse).

bold [bəuld] a hardi(e), audacieux(euse); (pej) effronté(e); (outline, colour) franc(franche), tranché(e), marqué(e).

bollard ['bɔləd] n (Brit AUT) borne lumineuse or de signalisation.

bolster ['bəulstə*] n traversin m; **to ~ up** vt soutenir.

bolt [bəult] n verrou m; (with nut) boulon m // ad: **~ upright** droit(e) comme un piquet // vt verrouiller; (food) engloutir // vi se sauver, filer (comme une flèche).

bomb [bɔm] n bombe f // vt bombarder; **~ disposal unit** n section f de

déminage; **~er** n (AVIAT) bombardier m; **~shell** n (fig) bombe f.

bona fide ['bəunə'faɪdɪ] a de bonne foi; (offer) sérieux(euse).

bond [bɔnd] n lien m; (binding promise) engagement m, obligation f; (COMM) obligation f; **in ~** (of goods) en douane.

bondage ['bɔndɪdʒ] n esclavage m.

bone [bəun] n os m; (of fish) arête f // vt désosser; ôter les arêtes de; **~ idle** a, **~ lazy** a fainéant(e).

bonfire ['bɔnfaɪə*] n feu m (de joie); (for rubbish) feu.

bonnet ['bɔnɪt] n bonnet m; (Brit: of car) capot m.

bonus ['bəunəs] n prime f, gratification f.

bony ['bəunɪ] a (arm, face, MED: tissue) osseux(euse); (meat) plein(e) d'os; (fish) plein d'arêtes.

boo [bu:] excl hou!, peuh! // vt huer.

booby trap ['bu:bɪ-] n engin piégé.

book [buk] n livre m; (of stamps etc) carnet m; (COMM): **~s** comptes mpl, comptabilité f // vt (ticket) prendre; (seat, room) réserver; (driver) dresser un procès-verbal à; (football player) prendre le nom de; **~case** n bibliothèque f (meuble); **~ing office** n (Brit) bureau m de location; **~-keeping** n comptabilité f; **~let** n brochure f; **~maker** n bookmaker m; **~seller** n libraire m/f; **~shop** n, **~store** n librairie f.

boom [bu:m] n (noise) grondement m; (busy period) boom m, vague f de prospérité f // vi gronder; prospérer.

boon [bu:n] n bénédiction f, grand avantage.

boost [bu:st] n stimulant m, remontant m // vt stimuler; **~er** n (MED) rappel m.

boot [bu:t] n botte f; (for hiking) chaussure f (de marche); (for football etc) soulier m; (Brit: of car) coffre m // vt (COMPUT) remettre à zéro; **to ~** (in addition) par-dessus le marché, en plus.

booth [bu:ð] n (at fair) baraque (foraine); (of cinema, telephone etc) cabine f; (also: **voting** ~) isoloir m.

booty ['buːtɪ] n butin m.

booze [buːz] n (col) boissons fpl alcooliques, alcool m.

border ['bɔːdə*] n bordure f; bord m; (of a country) frontière f; the B~s la région frontière entre l'Écosse et l'Angleterre; **to ~ on** vt fus être voisin(e) de, toucher à; **~line** n (fig) ligne f de démarcation; **~line case** n cas m limite.

bore [bɔː*] pt of **bear** // vt (hole) percer; (person) ennuyer, raser // n (person) raseur/euse; (of gun) calibre m; **to be ~d** s'ennuyer; **~dom** n ennui m; **boring** a ennuyeux(euse).

born [bɔːn] a: **to be ~** naître; **I was ~ in 1960** je suis né en 1960.

borne [bɔːn] pp of **bear**.

borough ['bʌrə] n municipalité f.

borrow ['bɔrəu] vt: **to ~ sth (from sb)** emprunter qch (à qn).

bosom ['buzəm] n poitrine f; (fig) sein m.

boss [bɔs] n patron/ne // vt commander; **~y** a autoritaire.

bosun ['bəusn] n maître m d'équipage.

botany ['bɔtənɪ] n botanique f.

botch [bɔtʃ] vt (also: **~ up**) saboter, bâcler.

both [bəuθ] a les deux, l'un(e) et l'autre // pronoun: ~ **(of them)** les deux, tous(toutes) (les) deux, l'un(e) et l'autre; ~ **of us went, we ~ went** nous y sommes allés (tous) les deux // ad: **they sell ~ the fabric and the finished curtains** ils vendent (et) le tissu et les rideaux (finis), ils vendent à la fois le tissu et les rideaux (finis).

bother ['bɔðə*] vt (worry) tracasser; (needle, bait) importuner, ennuyer; (disturb) déranger // vi (also: ~ **o.s.**) se tracasser, se faire du souci // n: **it is a ~ to have to do** c'est vraiment ennuyeux d'avoir à faire; **it's no ~** aucun problème; **to ~**

doing prendre la peine de faire.

bottle ['bɔtl] n bouteille f; (baby's) biberon m // vt mettre en bouteille(s); **to ~ up** vt refouler, contenir; **~neck** n étranglement m; **~opener** n ouvre-bouteille m.

bottom ['bɔtəm] n (of container, sea etc) fond m; (buttocks) derrière m; (of page, list) bas m; (of chair) siège m // a du fond; du bas.

bough [bau] n branche f, rameau m.

bought [bɔːt] pt, pp of **buy**.

boulder ['bəuldə*] n gros rocher.

bounce [bauns] vi (ball) rebondir; (cheque) être refusé (étant sans provision) // vt faire rebondir // n (rebound) rebond m; **~r** n (col) videur m.

bound [baund] pt, pp of **bind** // n (gen pl) limite f; (leap) bond m // vt (leap) bondir; (limit) borner // a: **to be ~ to do sth** (obliged) être obligé(e) or avoir obligation de faire qch; **he's ~ to fail** (likely) il est sûr d'échouer, son échec est inévitable or assuré; ~ **for** à destination de; **out of ~s** dont l'accès est interdit.

boundary ['baundrɪ] n frontière f.

bout [baut] n période f; (of malaria etc) accès m, crise f, attaque f; (BOXING etc) combat m, match m.

bow [bəu] n nœud m; (weapon) arc m; (MUS) archet m; [bau] (with body) révérence f, inclination f (du buste or corps); (NAUT: also: ~s) proue f // vi [bau] faire une révérence, s'incliner; (yield): **to ~ to** or **before** s'incliner devant, se soumettre à.

bowels [bauəlz] npl intestins mpl; (fig) entrailles fpl.

bowl [bəul] n (for eating) bol m; (for washing) cuvette f; (ball) boule f; (of pipe) fourneau m // vi (CRICKET) lancer (la balle); ~**s** n (jeu m de) boules fpl.

bow-legged ['bəu'lɛgd] a aux jambes arquées.

bowler ['bəulə*] n (CRICKET) lanceur m (de la balle); (Brit: also:

hat) (chapeau m) melon m.

bowling ['bəʊlɪŋ] n (game) jeu m de boules; jeu m de quilles; ~ **alley** n bowling m; ~ **green** n terrain m de boules (gazonné et carré).

bow tie n nœud m papillon.

box [bɔks] n boîte f; (also: **card-board** ~) carton m; (THEATRE) loge f // vt mettre en boîte; (SPORT) boxer avec // vi boxer, faire de la boxe; ~**er** n (person) boxeur m; ~**ing** n (SPORT) boxe f; **B**~**ing Day** n (Brit) le lendemain m de Noël; ~**ing gloves** npl gants mpl de boxe; ~**ing ring** n ring m; ~ **office** n bureau m de location; ~ **room** n débarras m; chambrette f.

boy [bɔɪ] n garçon m.

boycott ['bɔɪkɔt] n boycottage m // vt boycotter.

boyfriend ['bɔɪfrɛnd] n (petit) ami.

B.R. abbr of British Rail.

bra [brɑ:] n soutien-gorge m.

brace [breɪs] n attache f, agrafe f; (on teeth) appareil m (dentaire); (tool) vilbrequin m // vt consolider, soutenir; ~**s** npl (Brit) bretelles fpl; **to** ~ **o.s.** (fig) se préparer mentalement.

bracelet ['breɪslɪt] n bracelet m.

bracing ['breɪsɪŋ] a tonifiant(e), tonique.

bracken ['brækən] n fougère f.

bracket ['brækɪt] n (TECH) tasseau m, support m; (group) classe f, tranche f; (also: **brace** ~) accolade f; (also: **round** ~) parenthèse f; (also: **square** ~) crochet m // vt mettre entre parenthèse(s).

brag [bræg] vi se vanter.

braid [breɪd] n (trimming) galon m; (of hair) tresse f, natte f.

brain [breɪn] n cerveau m; ~**s** npl cervelle f; **he's got** ~**s** il est intelligent; ~**child** n invention personnelle; ~**wash** vt faire subir un lavage de cerveau à; ~**wave** n idée géniale; ~**y** a intelligent(e), doué(e).

brake [breɪk] n (on vehicle) frein m // vt, vi freiner; ~ **fluid** n liquide m de

freins; ~ **light** n feu m de stop.

bramble ['bræmbl] n (bush) ronce f; (berry) mûre f sauvage.

bran [bræn] n son m.

branch [brɑ:ntʃ] n branche f; (COMM) succursale f // vi bifurquer.

brand [brænd] n marque (commerciale) // vt (cattle) marquer (au fer rouge).

brand-new ['brænd'nju:] a tout(e) neuf(neuve), flambant neuf(neuve).

brandy ['brændɪ] n cognac m, fine f.

brash [bræʃ] a effronté(e).

brass [brɑ:s] n cuivre (jaune), laiton m; **the** ~ (MUS) les cuivres; ~ **band** n fanfare f.

brassière ['bræsɪə*] n soutien-gorge m.

brat [bræt] n (pej) mioche m/f, môme m/f.

brave [breɪv] a courageux(euse), brave // n guerrier indien // vt braver, affronter; ~**ry** n bravoure f, courage m.

brawl [brɔ:l] n rixe f, bagarre f.

brawn [brɔ:n] n muscle m; (meat) fromage m de tête.

bray [breɪ] vi braire.

brazen ['breɪzn] a impudent(e), effronté(e) // vt: **to** ~ **it out** payer d'effronterie, crâner.

brazier ['breɪzɪə*] n brasero m.

Brazil [brə'zɪl] n Brésil m.

breach [bri:tʃ] vt ouvrir une brèche dans // n (gap) brèche f; (breaking): ~ **of contract** rupture f de contract; ~ **of the peace** attentat m à l'ordre public.

bread [brɛd] n pain m; ~ **and butter** n tartines (beurrées); (fig) subsistance f; ~**bin**, (US) ~**box** n boîte f à pain; (bigger) huche f à pain; ~**crumbs** npl miettes fpl de pain; (CULIN) chapelure f, panure f; ~**line** n: **to be on the** ~**line** être sans le sou or dans l'indigence.

breadth [brɛtθ] n largeur f.

breadwinner ['brɛdwɪnə*] n soutien m de famille.

break [breɪk] vb (pt **broke**, pp **bro-**

ken vt casser, briser; (promise) rompre; (law) violer // n (gap) brèche f; (fracture) cassure f (rest) interruption f, arrêt m; (: short) pause f; (: at school) récréation f; (chance) chance f, occasion f favorable; to ~ one's leg etc se casser la jambe etc; to ~ a record battre un record; to ~ the news to sb annoncer la nouvelle à qn; to ~ down vt (figures, data) décomposer, analyser // vi s'effondrer; (MED) faire une dépression (nerveuse); (AUT) tomber en panne; to ~ even vi rentrer dans ses frais; to ~ free or loose vi se dégager, s'échapper; to ~ in vt (horse etc) dresser // vi (burglar) entrer par effraction; to ~ into vt fus (house) s'introduire or pénétrer par effraction dans; to ~ off vi (speaker) s'interrompre; (branch) se rompre; to ~ open vt (door etc) forcer, fracturer; to ~ out vi éclater, se déclarer; to ~ out in spots se couvrir de boutons; to ~ up vi (partnership) cesser, prendre fin; (friends) se séparer // vt fracasser, casser; (fight etc) interrompre, faire cesser; ~age n casse f; ~down n (AUT) panne f; (in communications) rupture f; (MED: also: nervous ~down) dépression f (nerveuse); ~down van n (Brit) dépanneuse f; ~er n brisant m.

breakfast ['brɛkfəst] n petit déjeuner m.

break: ~-in n cambriolage m; ~ing and entering n (LAW) effraction f; ~-through n percée f; ~-water n brise-lames m inv, digue f.

breast [brɛst] n (of woman) sein m; (chest) poitrine f; ~-feed vt, vi (irg: like feed) allaiter; ~-stroke n brasse f.

breath [brɛθ] n haleine f, souffle m; out of ~ à bout de souffle, essoufflé(e).

Breathalyser ['brɛθəlaɪzə*] n ® alcootest m.

breathe [bri:ð] vt, vi respirer; to ~ in vt, vi aspirer, inspirer; to ~ out vt, vi expirer; ~r n moment m de repos or de répit; **breathing** n respiration f.

breathless ['brɛθlɪs] a essoufflé(e), haletant(e); oppressé(e).

breath-taking ['brɛθteɪkɪŋ] a stupéfiant(e), à vous couper le souffle.

breed [bri:d] vb (pt, pp bred [brɛd]) vt élever, faire l'élevage de // vi se reproduire // n race f, variété f; ~ing n reproduction f; élevage m; (upbringing) éducation f.

breeze [bri:z] n brise f.

breezy ['bri:zi] a frais(fraîche); aéré(e); désinvolte, jovial(e).

brevity ['brɛvɪtɪ] n brièveté f.

brew [bru:] vt (tea) faire infuser; (beer) brasser; (plot) tramer, préparer // vi (tea) infuser; (beer) fermenter; (fig) se préparer, couver; ~er n brasseur m; ~ery n brasserie f (fabrique).

bribe [braɪb] n pot-de-vin m // vt acheter; soudoyer; ~ry n corruption f.

brick [brɪk] n brique f; ~layer n maçon m; ~work n briqueterie f.

bridal ['braɪdl] a nuptial(e).

bride [braɪd] n mariée f, épouse f; ~groom n marié m, époux m; ~smaid n demoiselle f d'honneur.

bridge [brɪdʒ] n pont m; (NAUT) passerelle f (de commandement); (of nose) arête f; (CARDS, DENTISTRY) bridge m // vt (river) construire un pont sur; (gap) combler.

bridle ['braɪdl] n bride f // vt refréner, mettre la bride à; (horse) brider; ~ path n piste or allée cavalière.

brief [bri:f] a bref(brève) // n (LAW) dossier m, cause f // vt donner des instructions à; ~s npl slip m; ~case n serviette f; porte-documents m inv; ~ing n instructions fpl; ~ly ad brièvement.

bright [braɪt] a brillant(e); (room,

weather) clair(e); *(person)* intelligent(e), doué(e); *(colour)* vif(vive); **~en** *(also:* **~en up)** *vt (room)* éclaircir; *(person)* retrouver un peu de sa gaieté.

brilliance ['brɪljəns] *n* éclat *m*.

brilliant ['brɪljənt] *a* brillant(e).

brim [brɪm] *n* bord *m*.

brine [braɪn] *n* eau salée; *(CULIN)* saumure *f*.

bring [brɪŋ], *pt, pp* **brought** *vt (thing)* apporter; *(person)* amener; **to ~ about** *vt* provoquer, entraîner; **to ~ back** *vt* rapporter; ramener; **to ~ down** *vt* abaisser; faire s'effondrer; **to ~ forward** *vt* avancer; **to ~ off** *vt (task, plan)* réussir, mener à bien; **to ~ out** *vt (meaning)* faire ressortir, mettre en relief; **to ~ round** *or* **to** *vt (unconscious person)* ranimer; **to ~ up** *vt* élever; *(question)* soulever; *(food: vomit)* vomir, rendre.

brink [brɪŋk] *n* bord *m*.

brisk [brɪsk] *a* vif(vive).

bristle ['brɪsl] *n* poil *m* // *vi* se hérisser.

Britain ['brɪtən] *n (also:* **Great ~)** Grande-Bretagne *f*.

British ['brɪtɪʃ] *a* britannique; **the ~** *npl* les Britanniques *mpl*; **the ~ Isles** *npl* les Îles *fpl* Britanniques; **B~ Rail (B.R.)** *n* ≈ S.N.C.F. *f*.

Briton ['brɪtən] *n* Britannique *m/f*.

Brittany ['brɪtənɪ] *n* Bretagne *f*.

brittle ['brɪtl] *a* cassant(e), fragile.

broach [brəʊtʃ] *vt (subject)* aborder.

broad [brɔːd] *a* large; *(distinction)* général(e); *(accent)* prononcé(e); **in ~ daylight** en plein jour; **~cast** *n* émission *f* // *vb (pt, pp* **broadcast)** *vt* radiodiffuser; téléviser // *vi* émettre; **~en** *vt* élargir // *vi* s'élargir; **~ly** *ad* en gros, généralement; **~-minded** *a* large d'esprit.

broccoli ['brɒkəlɪ] *n* brocoli *m*.

brochure ['brəʊʃjʊə*] *n* prospectus *m*, dépliant *m*.

broil [brɔɪl] *vt* griller.

broke [brəʊk] *pt of* **break** // *a (col)* fauché(e).

broken ['brəʊkən] *pp of* **break** // *a:* **~ leg** *etc* jambe *etc* cassée; **in ~ English** dans un anglais approximatif *or* hésitant; **~-hearted** *a* (ayant) le cœur brisé.

broker ['brəʊkə*] *n* courtier *m*.

brolly ['brɒlɪ] *n (Brit col)* pépin *m*, parapluie *m*.

bronchitis [brɒŋ'kaɪtɪs] *n* bronchite *f*.

bronze [brɒnz] *n* bronze *m*.

brooch [brəʊtʃ] *n* broche *f*.

brood [bruːd] *n* couvée *f* // *vi (hen, storm)* couver; *(person)* méditer (sombrement), ruminer.

brook [brʊk] *n* ruisseau *m*.

broom [brʊm] *n* balai *m*; **~stick** *n* manche *m* à balai.

Bros. *abbr* = **Brothers**.

broth [brɒθ] *n* bouillon *m* de viande et de légumes.

brothel ['brɒθl] *n* maison close, bordel *m*.

brother ['brʌðə*] *n* frère *m*; **~-in-law** *n* beau-frère *m*.

brought [brɔːt] *pt, pp of* **bring**.

brow [braʊ] *n* front *m*; *(rare, gen:* **eye~)** sourcil *m*; *(of hill)* sommet *m*.

brown [braʊn] *a* brun(e), marron *inv* // *n (colour)* brun *m* // *vt* brunir; *(CULIN)* faire dorer, faire roussir; **~ bread** *n* pain *m* bis.

brownie ['braʊnɪ] *n* jeannette *f*, éclaireuse (cadette).

brown paper *n* papier *m* d'emballage.

brown sugar *n* cassonade *f*.

browse [braʊz] *vi (among books)* bouquiner, feuilleter les livres.

bruise [bruːz] *n* bleu *m*, ecchymose *f*, contusion *f* // *vt* contusionner, meurtrir.

brunette [bruː'net] *n* (femme) brune.

brunt [brʌnt] *n:* **the ~ of** *(attack, criticism etc)* le plus gros de.

brush [brʌʃ] n brosse f; (quarrel) accrochage m, prise f de bec // vt brosser; (also: ~ past, ~ against) effleurer, frôler; **to ~ aside** vt écarter, balayer; **to ~ up** vt (knowledge) rafraîchir, réviser; **~wood** n broussailles fpl, taillis m.

Brussels ['brʌslz] n Bruxelles; ~ **sprout** n chou m de Bruxelles.

brutal ['bru:tl] a brutal(e).

brute [bru:t] n brute f // a: **by ~ force** par la force.

B.Sc. abbr see **bachelor**.

bubble ['bʌbl] n bulle f // vi bouillonner, faire des bulles; (sparkle, fig) pétiller; ~ **bath** n bain moussant.

buck [bʌk] n mâle m (d'un lapin, lièvre, daim etc); (US col) dollar m // vi ruer, lancer une ruade; **to pass the ~** (to sb) se décharger de la responsabilité (sur qn); **to ~ up** vi (cheer up) reprendre du poil de la bête, se remonter.

bucket ['bʌkɪt] n seau m.

buckle ['bʌkl] n boucle f // vt boucler, attacher; (warp) tordre, gauchir; (: wheel) voiler.

bud [bʌd] n bourgeon m; (of flower) bouton m // vi bourgeonner; (flower) éclore.

Buddhism ['budɪzəm] n bouddhisme m.

budding ['bʌdɪŋ] a (poet etc) en herbe; (passion etc) naissant(e).

buddy ['bʌdɪ] n (US) copain m.

budge [bʌdʒ] vt faire bouger // vi bouger.

budgerigar ['bʌdʒərɪgɑː*] n perruche f.

budget ['bʌdʒɪt] n budget m // vi: **to ~ for sth** inscrire qch au budget.

budgie ['bʌdʒɪ] n = **budgerigar**.

buff [bʌf] a (couleur f) chamois m // n (enthusiast) mordu(e).

buffalo, pl ~ or ~es ['bʌfələu] n buffle m; (US) bison m.

buffer ['bʌfə*] n tampon m; (COMPUT) mémoire f tampon.

buffet n ['bufei] (food, Brit: bar) buffet m // vt ['bʌfɪt] gifler, frapper;

secouer, ébranler; ~ **car** n (Brit RAIL) voiture-buffet f.

bug [bʌg] n (insect) punaise f; (: gen) insecte m, bestiole f; (: germ) virus m, microbe m; (: spy device) dispositif m d'écoute (électronique), micro clandestin // vt garnir de dispositifs d'écoute.

bugle ['bju:gl] n clairon m.

build [bɪld] n (of person) carrure f, charpente f // vt (pt, pp built) construire, bâtir; **to ~ up** vt accumuler, amasser; accroître; ~**er** n entrepreneur m; ~**ing** n construction f; bâtiment m, construction; (habitation, offices) immeuble m; ~**ing society** n (Brit) société f de crédit immobilier.

built [bɪlt] pt, pp of **build**; ~**-in** (cupboard) encastré(e); (device) incorporé(e); intégré(e); ~**-up area** n agglomération (urbaine); zone urbanisée.

bulb [bʌlb] n (BOT) bulbe m, oignon m; (ELEC) ampoule f.

bulge [bʌldʒ] n renflement m, gonflement m // vi faire saillie; présenter un renflement; **to be bulging with** être plein(e) à craquer de.

bulk [bʌlk] n masse f, volume m; **in ~** (COMM) en vrac; **the ~ of** la plus grande ou grosse partie de; ~**y** a volumineux(euse), encombrant(e).

bull [bul] n taureau m; ~**dog** n bouledogue m.

bulldozer ['buldəuzə*] n bulldozer m.

bullet ['bulɪt] n balle f (de fusil etc).

bulletin ['bulɪtɪn] n bulletin m, communiqué m.

bulletproof ['bulɪtpru:f] a (car) blindé(e); (vest etc) pare-balles inv.

bullfight ['bulfaɪt] n corrida f, course f de taureaux; ~**er** n torero m; ~**ing** n tauromachie f.

bullion ['buljən] n or m or argent m en lingots.

bullock ['bulək] n bœuf m.

bullring ['bulrɪŋ] n arènes fpl.

bull's-eye ['bulzaɪ] n centre m (de la

cible).

bully ['buli] *n* brute *f*, tyran *m* // *vt* tyranniser, rudoyer; *(frighten)* intimider.

bum [bʌm] *n* (*col: backside*) derrière *m*; *(tramp)* vagabond/e, traînesavates *m/f inv.*

bumblebee ['bʌmblbi:] *n* bourdon *m*.

bump [bʌmp] *n* (*blow*) coup *m*, choc *m*; *(jolt)* cahot *m*; (*on road etc, on head*) bosse *f* // *vt* heurter, cogner; **to ~ into** *vt fus* rentrer dans, tamponner; *(col)* rencontrer par hasard; **~er** *n* pare-chocs *m inv* // *a*: **~er crop/harvest** récolte/moisson exceptionnelle.

bumptious ['bʌmpʃəs] *a* suffisant(e), prétentieux(euse).

bumpy ['bʌmpɪ] *a* cahoteux(euse).

bun [bʌn] *n* petit pain au lait; *(of hair)* chignon *m*.

bunch [bʌntʃ] *n* (*of flowers*) bouquet *m*; *(of keys)* trousseau *m*; *(of bananas)* régime *m*; *(of people)* groupe *m*; **~ of grapes** grappe *f* de raisin.

bundle ['bʌndl] *n* paquet *m* // *vt* (*also: ~ up*) faire un paquet de; *(put)*: **to ~ sth/sb into** fourrer or enfourner qch/qn dans.

bungalow ['bʌŋgələu] *n* bungalow *m*.

bungle ['bʌŋgl] *vt* bâcler, gâcher.

bunion ['bʌnjən] *n* oignon *m* (au pied).

bunk [bʌŋk] *n* couchette *f*; **~ beds** *npl* lits superposés.

bunker ['bʌŋkə*] *n* (*coal store*) soute *f* à charbon; *(MIL, GOLF)* bunker *m*.

bunny ['bʌnɪ] *n* (*also: ~ rabbit*) Jeannot *m* lapin.

bunting ['bʌntɪŋ] *n* pavoisement *m*, drapeaux *mpl*.

buoy [bɔɪ] *n* bouée *f*; **to ~ up** *vt* faire flotter; *(fig)* soutenir, épauler; **~ant** *a* (*carefree*) gai(e), plein(e) d'entrain.

burden ['bə:dn] *n* fardeau *m*, charge *f* // *vt* charger; *(oppress)* accabler, surcharger.

bureau, *pl* **~x** [bjuə'rəu, -z] *n* (Brit:

writing desk) bureau *m*, secrétaire *m*; (*US: chest of drawers*) commode *f*; *(office)* bureau, office *m*.

bureaucracy [bjuə'rɔkrəsɪ] *n* bureaucratie *f*.

burglar ['bə:glə*] *n* cambrioleur *m*; **~ alarm** sonnerie *f* d'alarme; **~y** *n* cambriolage *m*.

Burgundy ['bə:gəndɪ] *n* Bourgogne *f*.

burial ['berɪəl] *n* enterrement *m*.

burly ['bə:lɪ] *a* de forte carrure, costaud(e).

Burma ['bə:mə] *n* Birmanie *f*.

burn [bə:n] *vt, vi* (*pt, pp* **burned** or **burnt**) brûler *n* brûlure *f*; **to ~ down** *vt* incendier, détruire par le feu; **~er** *n* brûleur *m*.

burnt [bə:nt] *pt, pp* of **burn**.

burrow ['bʌrəu] *n* terrier *m* // *vt* creuser.

bursar ['bə:sə*] *n* économe *m/f*; (Brit: student) boursier/ère; **~y** *n* (Brit) bourse *f* (d'études).

burst [bə:st] *vb* (*pt, pp* **burst**) *vt* crever; faire éclater // *vi* éclater; *(tyre)* crever // *n* explosion *f*; (*also: ~ pipe*) rupture *f*; fuite *f*; **to ~ into flames** s'enflammer soudainement; **to ~ out laughing** éclater de rire; **to ~ing with** être plein (à craquer) de; regorger de; **to ~ into** *vt fus* (*room etc*) faire irruption dans; **to ~ open** *vi* s'ouvrir violemment or soudainement.

bury ['berɪ] *vt* enterrer.

bus, ~es [bʌs, 'bʌsɪz] *n* autobus *m*.

bush [buʃ] *n* buisson *m*; *(scrub land)* brousse *f*; **to beat about the ~** tourner autour du pot.

bushy ['buʃɪ] *a* broussailleux(euse), touffu(e).

busily ['bɪzɪlɪ] *ad* activement.

business ['bɪznɪs] *n* (*matter, firm*) affaire *f*; *(trading)* affaires *fpl*; *(job, duty)* travail *m*; **to be away on ~** être en déplacement d'affaires; **it's none of my ~** cela ne me regarde pas, ce ne sont pas mes affaires; **he means ~** il ne plaisante pas, il est

sérieux; ~**like** a sérieux(euse); efficace; ~**man/woman** n homme/
femme d'affaires; ~ **trip** n voyage
m d'affaires.
busker ['bʌskə*] n (Brit) musicien
ambulant.
bus-stop ['bʌsstɔp] n arrêt m d'autobus.
bust [bʌst] n buste m // a (col: broken) fichu(e), fini(e); **to go** ~ faire
faillite.
bustle ['bʌsl] n remue-ménage m, affairement m // vi s'affairer, se démener.
busy ['bɪzɪ] a occupé(e); (shop,
street) très fréquenté(e) // vt: **to** ~
o.s. s'occuper; ~**body** n mouche f du
coche, âme f charitable; ~ **signal** n (US TEL) tonalité f occupé inv.

KEYWORD

---

but [bʌt] ◆ cj mais; **I'd love to
come,** ~ **I'm busy** j'aimerais venir
mais je suis occupé
◆ prep (apart from, except) sauf,
excepté; **we've had nothing** ~
trouble nous n'avons eu que des ennuis; **no-one** ~ **him** can do it lui
seul peut le faire; ~ **for you/your
help** sans toi/ton aide; **anything** ~
that tout sauf or excepté ça, tout
mais pas ça
◆ ad (just, only) ne ... que; **she's** ~
a child elle n'est qu'une enfant; **had
I** ~ **known** si seulement j'avais su;
all ~ **finished** pratiquement terminé.

butcher ['butʃə*] n boucher m // vt
massacrer; (cattle etc for meat)
tuer.
butler ['bʌtlə*] n maître m d'hôtel.
butt [bʌt] n (cask) gros tonneau;
(thick end) gros bout; (of gun)
crosse f; (of cigarette) mégot m;
(Brit fig: target) cible f // vt donner
un coup de tête à; **to** ~ **in** vi (interrupt) s'immiscer dans la conversation.
butter ['bʌtə*] n beurre m // vt beur-

rer; ~**cup** n bouton m d'or.
butterfly ['bʌtəflaɪ] n papillon m;
(SWIMMING: also: ~ **stroke**) brasse
f papillon inv.
buttocks ['bʌtəks] npl fesses fpl.
button ['bʌtn] n bouton m // vt (also:
~ **up**) boutonner // vi se boutonner.
buttress ['bʌtrɪs] n contrefort m.
buxom ['bʌksəm] a aux formes
avantageuses or épanouies.
buy [baɪ] vb (pt, pp bought) vt acheter; **to** ~ **sb sth/sth from sb** acheter qch à qn; **to** ~ **sb a drink** offrir
un verre or à boire à qn; ~**er** n
acheteur/euse.
buzz [bʌz] n bourdonnement m; (col:
phone call) coup m de fil // vi bourdonner.
buzzer ['bʌzə*] n timbre m électrique.
buzz word n (col) mot m à la
mode.

KEYWORD

---

by [baɪ] ◆ prep 1 (referring to
cause, agent) par, de; **killed** ~
lightning tué par la foudre; **surrounded** ~ **a fence** entouré d'une
barrière; **a painting** ~ **Picasso** un
tableau de Picasso
2 (referring to method, manner,
means): ~ **bus/car** en autobus/
voiture; ~ **train** par le or en train;
to pay ~ **cheque** payer par chèque;
~ **saving hard, he ...** à force d'économiser, il ...
3 (via, through) par; **we came** ~
Dover nous sommes venus par Douvres
4 (close to, past) à côté de; **the
house** ~ **the school** la maison à
côté de l'école; **a holiday** ~ **the sea**
des vacances au bord de la mer; **she
sat** ~ **his bed** elle était assise à son
chevet; **she went** ~ **me** elle est passée à côté de moi; **I go** ~ **the post
office every day** je passe devant la
poste tous les jours
5 (with time: not later than) avant;
(: during): ~ **daylight** à la lumière

du jour; **by night** la nuit, de nuit; ~ 4 o'clock avant 4 heures; ~ **this time tomorrow** d'ici demain à la même heure; **the time I got here** it was too late lorsque je suis arrivé c'était déjà trop tard
6 (amount) à; ~ **the kilo/metre** au kilo/au mètre; **paid** ~ **the hour** payé à l'heure
7 (MATH, measure): **to divide/multiply** ~ **3** diviser/multiplier par 3; **a room 3 metres** ~ **4** une pièce de 3 mètres sur 4; **it's broader** ~ **a metre** c'est plus large d'un mètre; **one** ~ **one** un à un; **little** ~ **little** petit à petit, peu à peu
8 (according to) d'après, selon; **it's 3 o'clock** ~ **my watch** il est 3 heures d'après ma montre; **it's all right** ~ **me** je n'ai rien contre
9: (all) ~ **oneself** etc tout(e) seul(e)
10: ~ **the way** au fait, à propos
♦ ad **1** see go, pass etc
2: ~ **and** ~ un peu plus tard, bientôt; ~ **and large** dans l'ensemble.

---

bye(-bye) ['baɪ('baɪ)] excl au revoir!, salut!

bye(e)-law ['baɪlɔ:] n arrêté municipal.

by-election ['baɪɪlekʃən] n (Brit) élection (législative) partielle.

bygone ['baɪɡɒn] a passé(e) // n: let ~s be ~s passons l'éponge, oublions le passé.

bypass ['baɪpɑ:s] n (route f de) contournement m; (MÉD) pontage m // vt éviter.

by-product ['baɪprɒdʌkt] n sous-produit m, dérivé m; (fig) conséquence f secondaire, retombée f.

bystander ['baɪstændə*] n spectateur/trice, badaud/e.

byte [baɪt] n (COMPUT) octet m.

byword ['baɪwɜ:d] n: **to be a** ~ **for** être synonyme de (fig).

by-your-leave ['baɪ'jɔ:li:v] n: without so much as a ~ sans même demander la permission.

C

C [si:] n (MUS) do m.

C.A. abbr of **chartered accountant**.

cab [kæb] n taxi m; (of train, truck) cabine f; (horse-drawn) fiacre m.

cabaret ['kæbəreɪ] n attractions fpl, spectacle m de cabaret.

cabbage ['kæbɪdʒ] n chou m.

cabin ['kæbɪn] n cabane f, hutte f; (on ship) cabine f.

cabinet ['kæbɪnɪt] n (POL) cabinet m; (furniture) petit meuble à tiroirs et rayons; (also: **display** ~) vitrine f, petite armoire vitrée; ~**-maker** n ébéniste m.

cable ['keɪbl] n câble m // vt câbler, télégraphier; ~**-car** n téléphérique m; ~ **television** n télévision f par câble.

cache [kæʃ] n cachette f.

cackle ['kækl] vi caqueter.

cactus ['kæktəs], pl **cacti** [-taɪ] n cactus m.

cadet [kə'det] n (MIL) élève m officier.

cadge [kædʒ] vt se faire donner.

café ['kæfeɪ] n ≈ café-(restaurant) m (sans alcool).

cage [keɪdʒ] n cage f.

cagey ['keɪdʒɪ] a (col) réticent(e); méfiant(e).

cagoule [kə'ɡu:l] n K-way m ®.

Cairo ['kaɪərəu] n le Caire.

cajole [kə'dʒəul] vt couvrir de flatteries ou de gentillesses.

cake [keɪk] n gâteau m; ~ **of soap** savonnette f; ~**d** a: ~**d with** raidi(e) par, couvert(e) d'une croûte de.

calculate ['kælkjuleɪt] vt calculer; **calculation** [-'leɪʃən] n calcul m; **calculator** n machine f à calculer, calculatrice f.

calendar ['kæləndə*] n calendrier m; ~ **year** n année civile.

calf [kɑ:f], pl **calves** n (of cow) veau m; (of other animals) petit m; (also:

~**skin**) veau m, vachette f; (ANAT) mollet m.

calibre, (US) **caliber** ['kælibə*] n calibre m.

call [kɔ:l] vt (gen, also TEL) appeler // vi appeler; (visit: also: ~ **in**, ~ **round**): **to** ~ (**for**) passer (prendre) // n (shout) appel m, cri m; (visit) visite f; (also: **telephone** ~) coup m de téléphone; communication f; **she's** ~**ed Suzanne** elle s'appelle Suzanne; **to be on** ~ être de permanence; **to** ~ **back** vi (return) repasser; (TEL) rappeler; **to** ~ **for** vt fus demander; **to** ~ **off** vt annuler; **to** ~ **on** vt fus (visit) rendre visite à, passer voir; (request): **to** ~ **on sb to do** inviter qn à faire; **to** ~ **out** vi pousser un cri or des cris; **to** ~ **up** vt (MIL) mobiliser; ~**box** n (Brit) cabine f téléphonique; ~**er** n personne f qui appelle; visiteur m; ~ **girl** n call-girl f; ~**in** n (US: phone-in) programme m à ligne ouverte; ~**ing** n vocation f; (trade, occupation) état m; ~**ing card** n (US) carte f de visite.

callous ['kæləs] a dur(e), insensible.

calm [kɑ:m] a calme // n calme m // vt calmer, apaiser; **to** ~ **down** vi se calmer, s'apaiser // vt calmer, apaiser.

Calor gas ['kælə*-] n ® butane m, butagaz m ®.

calorie ['kælərɪ] n calorie f.

calves [kɑ:vz] npl of **calf**.

camber ['kæmbə*] n (of road) bombement m.

Cambodia [kæm'bəudjə] n Cambodge m.

came [keɪm] pt of **come**.

camel ['kæməl] n chameau m.

cameo ['kæmɪəu] n camée m.

camera ['kæmərə] n appareil-photo m; (also: **cine-~**, **movie~**) caméra f; **in** ~ à huis clos, en privé; ~**man** n caméraman m.

camouflage ['kæməflɑ:ʒ] n camouflage m // vt camoufler.

camp [kæmp] n camp m // vi camper.

campaign [kæm'peɪn] n (MIL, POL etc) campagne f // vi (also fig) faire campagne.

campbed ['kæmp'bed] n (Brit) lit m de camp.

camper ['kæmpə*] n campeur/euse.

camping ['kæmpɪŋ] n camping m; **to go** ~ faire du camping.

campsite ['kæmpsaɪt] n campement m.

campus ['kæmpəs] n campus m.

can [kæn] auxiliary vb see next headword // n (of milk, oil, water) bidon m; (tin) boîte f de conserve // vt mettre en conserve.

─────────────────
KEYWORD
─────────────────

can [kæn] ♦ n, vt see previous headword

♦ auxiliary vb (negative **cannot**, **can't**; conditional and pt **could**) **1** (be able to) pouvoir; **you** ~ **do it if you try** vous pouvez le faire si vous essayez; **I** ~**'t hear you** je ne t'entends pas

2 (know how to) savoir; **I** ~ **swim/play tennis/drive** je sais nager/jouer au tennis/conduire; ~ **you speak French?** parlez-vous français?

3 (may) pouvoir; ~ **I use your phone?** puis-je me servir de votre téléphone?

4 (expressing disbelief, puzzlement etc): **it** ~**'t be true!** ce n'est pas possible!; **what CAN he want?** qu'est-ce qu'il peut bien vouloir?

5 (expressing possibility, suggestion etc): **he could be in the library** il est peut-être dans la bibliothèque; **she could have been delayed** il se peut qu'elle ait été retardée

─────────────────

Canada ['kænədə] n Canada m.

Canadian [kə'neɪdɪən] a canadien(ne) // n Canadien/ne.

canal [kə'næl] n canal m.

canary [kə'nɛərɪ] n canari m, serin m.

cancel ['kænsəl] vt annuler; (train)

supprimer; (*party, appointment*) décommander; (*cross out*) barrer, rayer; (*stamp*) oblitérer; ~**lation** [-'leɪʃən] *n* annulation *f*; suppression *f*; oblitération *f*; (*TOURISM*) réservation annulée.

cancer ['kænsə] *n* cancer *m*; C~ (*sign*) le Cancer.

candid ['kændɪd] *a* (très) franc(franche), sincère.

candidate ['kændɪdeɪt] *n* candidat/e.

candle ['kændl] *n* bougie *f*; (*of tallow*) chandelle *f*; (*in church*) cierge *m*; by ~**light** à la lumière d'une bougie; (*dinner*) aux chandelles; ~**stick** *n* (*also: ~ holder*) bougeoir *m*; (*bigger, ornate*) chandelier *m*.

candour ['kændə] (*US*) **candor** *n* (grande) franchise *or* sincérité.

candy ['kændɪ] *n* sucre candi; (*US*) bonbon *m*; ~**-floss** *n* (*Brit*) barbe *f* à papa.

cane [keɪn] *n* canne *f* // *vt* (*Brit SCOL*) administrer des coups de bâton à.

canister ['kænɪstə] *n* boîte *f*.

cannabis ['kænəbɪs] *n* (*drug*) cannabis *m*; (*also: ~ plant*) chanvre indien.

canned ['kænd] *a* (*food*) en boîte, en conserve.

cannon [kænən], *pl* ~ *or* ~**s** ['kænən] *n* (*gun*) canon *m*.

cannot ['kænɔt] = **can not**.

canny ['kænɪ] *a* madré(e), finaud(e).

canoe [kə'nuː] *n* pirogue *f*; (*SPORT*) canoë *m*.

canon ['kænən] *n* (*clergyman*) chanoine *m*; (*standard*) canon *m*.

can opener [-'əupnə] *n* ouvre-boîte *m*.

canopy ['kænəpɪ] *n* baldaquin *m*; dais *m*.

can't [kænt] = **can not**.

cantankerous [kæn'tæŋkərəs] *a* querelleur(euse), acariâtre.

canteen [kæn'tiːn] *n* cantine *f*; (*Brit: of cutlery*) ménagère *f*.

canter ['kæntə] *n* petit galop.

canvas ['kænvəs] *n* (*gen*) toile *f*.

canvassing ['kænvəsɪŋ] *n* (*POL*) prospection électorale, démarchage électoral; (*COMM*) démarchage, prospection.

canyon ['kænjən] *n* cañon *m*, gorge (profonde).

cap [kæp] *n* casquette *f*; (*of pen*) capuchon *m*; (*of bottle*) capsule *f* // *vt* capsuler; (*outdo*) surpasser.

capability [keɪpə'bɪlɪtɪ] *n* aptitude *f*, capacité *f*.

capable ['keɪpəbl] *a* capable.

capacity [kə'pæsɪtɪ] *n* capacité *f*, contenance *f*; aptitude *f*.

cape [keɪp] *n* (*garment*) cape *f*; (*GEO*) cap *m*.

capital ['kæpɪtl] *n* (*also: ~ city*) capitale *f*; (*money*) capital *m*; (*also: ~ letter*) majuscule *f*; ~ **gains tax** *n* impôt *m* sur les plus-values; ~**ism** *n* capitalisme *m*; ~**ist** *a*, capitaliste (*m/f*); ~**ize**: to ~**ize** on *vt fus* profiter de; ~ **punishment** *n* peine capitale.

Capricorn ['kæprɪkɔːn] *n* le Capricorne.

capsize [kæp'saɪz] *vt* faire chavirer // *vi* chavirer.

capsule ['kæpsjuːl] *n* capsule *f*.

captain ['kæptɪn] *n* capitaine *m*.

caption ['kæpʃən] *n* légende *f*.

captive ['kæptɪv] *a, n* captif(ive).

capture ['kæptʃə] *vt* capturer, prendre; (*attention*) capter // *n* capture *f*; (*data*) ~ saisie *f* de données.

car [kɑː] *n* voiture *f*, auto *f*.

carafe [kə'ræf] *n* carafe *f*.

caramel ['kærəməl] *n* caramel *m*.

caravan ['kærəvæn] *n* caravane *f*; ~ **site** *n* (*Brit*) camping *m* pour caravanes.

carbohydrates [kɑːbəu'haɪdreɪts] *npl* (*foods*) aliments *mpl* riches en hydrate de carbone.

carbon ['kɑːbən] *n* carbone *m*; ~ **paper** *n* papier *m* carbone.

carburettor, (*US*) **carburetor** [kɑːbju'rɛtə] *n* carburateur *m*.

card [kɑːd] *n* carte *f*; ~**board** *n* carton *m*; ~ **game** *n* jeu *m* de cartes.

cardiac ['kɑːdiæk] a cardiaque.

cardigan ['kɑːdɪgən] n cardigan m.

cardinal ['kɑːdɪnl] a cardinal(e) // n cardinal m.

card index ['kɑːdɪndeks] n fichier m (alphabétique).

care [kɛə*] n soin m, attention f; (worry) souci m // vi: to ~ about se soucier de, s'intéresser à; ~ of (c/o) chez, aux bons soins de; in sb's ~ à la garde de qn, confié à qn; **to take** ~ **(to do)** faire attention à (faire); **to take** ~ **of** vt s'occuper de, prendre soin de; **to** ~ **for** vt fus s'occuper de; (like) aimer; **I don't** ~ ça m'est bien égal, peu m'importe.

career [kə'rɪə*] n carrière f // vi (also: ~ **along**) aller à toute allure.

carefree ['kɛəfriː] a sans souci, insouciant(e).

careful ['kɛəful] a soigneux(euse); (cautious) prudent(e); (be ~!) (fais) attention!; ~**ly** ad avec soin, soigneusement; prudemment.

careless ['kɛəlɪs] a négligent(e); (heedless) insouciant(e).

caress [kə'rɛs] n caresse f // vt caresser.

caretaker ['kɛəteɪkə*] n gardien m, concierge m/f.

car-ferry ['kɑːferɪ] n (on sea) ferry(-boat) m; (on river) bac m.

cargo, pl ~**es** ['kɑːgəu] n cargaison f, chargement m.

car hire n location f de voiture.

Caribbean [kærɪ'biːən] a: **the** ~ **(Sea)** la mer des Antilles or Caraïbes.

caring ['kɛərɪŋ] a (person) bienveillant(e); (society, organization) humanitaire.

carnal ['kɑːnl] a charnel(le).

carnation [kɑː'neɪʃən] n œillet m.

carnival ['kɑːnɪvəl] n (public celebration) carnaval m; (US: funfair) fête foraine.

carol ['kærəl] n: **(Christmas)** ~ chant m de Noël.

carp [kɑːp] n (fish) carpe f; **to** ~ **at** vt fus critiquer.

car park n (Brit) parking m, parc m de stationnement.

carpenter ['kɑːpɪntə*] n charpentier m.

carpentry ['kɑːpɪntrɪ] n charpenterie f, métier m de charpentier; (woodwork: at school etc) menuiserie f.

carpet ['kɑːpɪt] n tapis m // vt recouvrir (d'un tapis); ~ **slippers** npl pantoufles fpl; ~ **sweeper** n balai m mécanique.

carriage ['kærɪdʒ] n (of goods) transport m; (: cost) port m; (of typewriter) chariot m; (bearing) maintien m, port m; ~ **return** n (on typewriter etc) retour m de chariot; ~**way** n (Brit: part of road) chaussée f.

carrier ['kærɪə*] n transporteur m, camionneur m; (MED) porteur/euse; (NAUT) porte-avions m inv; ~ **bag** n (Brit) sac m en papier or en plastique.

carrot ['kærət] n carotte f.

carry ['kærɪ] vt (subj: person) porter; (: vehicle) transporter; (a motion, bill) voter, adopter; (involve: responsibilities etc) comporter, impliquer // vi (sound) porter; **to be** or **get carried away** (fig) s'emballer, s'enthousiasmer; **to** ~ **on** vi: **to** ~ **on with sth/doing** continuer qch/à faire // vt entretenir, poursuivre; **to** ~ **out** vt (orders) exécuter; (investigation) effectuer; ~**cot** n porte-bébé m; ~**on** n (col: fuss) histoires fpl.

cart [kɑːt] n charrette f // vt transporter.

carton ['kɑːtən] n (box) carton m; (of yogurt) pot m (en carton); (of cigarettes) cartouche f.

cartoon [kɑː'tuːn] n (PRESS) dessin m (humoristique); (satirical) caricature f; (comic strip) bande dessinée; (CINEMA) dessin animé.

cartridge ['kɑːtrɪdʒ] n (for gun, pen) cartouche f; (for camera) chargeur m; (music tape) cassette f.

carve [kɑːv] vt (meat) découper; (wood, stone) tailler, sculpter; **to** ~

up vt découper; (fig: country) morceler; **carving** n (in wood etc) sculpture f; **carving knife** n couteau m à découper.

car wash n station f de lavage (de voitures).

case [keɪs] n cas m; (LAW) affaire f, procès m; (box) caisse f, boîte f, étui m; (Brit: also: suit~) valise f; **he hasn't put forward his ~ very well** ses arguments ne sont guère convaincants; **in ~** en cas de; **in ~ he** au cas où il; **just in ~** à tout hasard.

cash [kæʃ] n argent m; (COMM: argent liquide, numéraire m; liquidités fpl; (COMM: in payment) argent comptant, espèces fpl // vt encaisser; **to pay (in) ~** payer (en argent) comptant; **~ on delivery (C.O.D.)** (COMM) payable ou paiement à la livraison; **~book** n livre m de caisse; **~ card** n carte f de retrait; **~ desk** n (Brit) caisse f; **~ dispenser** n guichet m automatique de banque.

cashew [kæˈʃuː] n (also: ~ nut) noix f de cajou.

cashier [kæˈʃɪə*] n caissier/ère.

cashmere [ˈkæʃmɪə*] n cachemire m.

cash register n caisse enregistreuse.

casing [ˈkeɪsɪŋ] n revêtement (protecteur), enveloppe (protectrice).

casino [kəˈsiːnəu] n casino m.

cask [kɑːsk] n tonneau m.

casket [ˈkɑːskɪt] n coffret m; (US: coffin) cercueil m.

casserole [ˈkæsərəul] n cocotte f; (food) ragoût m (en cocotte).

cassette [kæˈsɛt] n cassette f, musicassette f; **~ player** n lecteur m de cassettes; **~ recorder** n magnétophone m à cassettes.

cast [kɑːst] vb (pt, pp cast) vt (throw) jeter; (shed) perdre; se dépouiller de; (metal) couler, fondre; (THEATRE): **to ~ sb as Hamlet** attribuer à qn le rôle d'Hamlet // n

(THEATRE) distribution f; (mould) moule m; (plaster): **to ~ plaster** m; **to ~ one's vote** voter, exprimer son suffrage; **to ~ off** vi (NAUT) larguer les amarres.

castaway [ˈkɑːstəweɪ] n naufragé/e.

caster sugar [ˈkɑːstə*-] n (Brit) sucre m semoule.

casting [ˈkɑːstɪŋ] a: **~ vote** (Brit) voix prépondérante (pour départager).

cast iron n fonte f.

castle [ˈkɑːsl] n château-fort m; (manor) château m.

castor [ˈkɑːstə*] n (wheel) roulette f; **~ oil** n huile f de ricin.

castrate [kæsˈtreɪt] vt châtrer.

casual [ˈkæʒjul] a (by chance) de hasard, fait(e) au hasard, fortuit(e); (irregular: work etc) temporaire; (unconcerned) désinvolte; **~ wear** n vêtements mpl sport im; **~ly** ad avec désinvolture, négligemment; fortuitement.

casualty [ˈkæʒjultɪ] n accidenté/e, blessé/e; (dead) victime f, mort/e.

cat [kæt] n chat m.

catalogue, (US) **catalog** [ˈkætələg] n catalogue m // vt cataloguer.

catalyst [ˈkætəlɪst] n catalyseur m.

catapult [ˈkætəpʌlt] n lance-pierres im inv, fronde m; (HISTORY) catapulte f.

catarrh [kəˈtɑː*] n rhume m chronique, catarrhe f.

catastrophe [kəˈtæstrəfɪ] n catastrophe f.

catch [kætʃ] vb (pt, pp caught) vt (ball, train, thief, cold) attraper; (person: by surprise) prendre, surprendre; (understand) saisir; (get entangled) accrocher // vi (fire) prendre // n (fish etc caught) prise f; (thief etc caught) capture f; (trick) attrape f; (TECH) loquet m; cliquet m; **to ~ sb's attention** ou **eye** attirer l'attention de qn; **to ~ fire** prendre feu; **to ~ sight of** apercevoir; **to ~ on** vi saisir; (grow popular) prendre; **to ~ up** vi se rattraper, combler son retard // vt (also: ~ **up with**) rattraper.

catching ['kætʃɪŋ] a (MED) contagieux(euse).

catchment area ['kætʃmənt-] n (Brit SCOL) aire f de recrutement; (GEO) bassin m hydrographique.

catch phrase n slogan m; expression toute faite.

catchy ['kætʃɪ] a (tune) facile à retenir.

category ['kætɪgərɪ] n catégorie f.

cater ['keɪtə*] vi (provide food): to ~ (for) préparer des repas (pour), se charger de la restauration (pour); to ~ for vt fus (Brit: needs) satisfaire, pourvoir à; (: readers, consumers) s'adresser à, pourvoir aux besoins de; ~**er** n traiteur m; fournisseur m; ~**ing** n restauration f; approvisionnement m, ravitaillement m.

caterpillar ['kætəpɪlə*] n chenille f; ~ **track** n chenille f.

cathedral [kə'θi:drəl] n cathédrale f.

catholic ['kæθəlɪk] a éclectique; universel(le); libéral(e); **C~** a, n (REL) catholique (m/f).

cat's-eye n (Brit AUT) (clou m à) catadioptre m.

cattle ['kætl] npl bétail m, bestiaux mpl.

catty ['kætɪ] a méchant(e).

caucus ['kɔ:kəs] n (POL: group) comité local d'un parti politique; (: US) comité électoral (pour désigner des candidats).

caught [kɔ:t] pt, pp of **catch**.

cauliflower ['kɒlɪflauə*] n chou-fleur m.

cause [kɔ:z] n cause f // vt causer.

caution ['kɔ:ʃən] n prudence f; (warning) avertissement m // vt avertir, donner un avertissement à.

cautious ['kɔ:ʃəs] a prudent(e).

cavalry ['kævəlrɪ] n cavalerie f.

cave [keɪv] n caverne f, grotte f; to ~ **in** vi (roof etc) s'effondrer; ~ **man** n homme m des cavernes.

caviar(e) ['kævɪa:*] n caviar m.

cavort [kə'vɔ:t] vi cabrioler, faire des cabrioles.

CB n abbr (= Citizens' Band (Radio)) CB f.

CBI n abbr (= Confederation of British Industries) groupement du patronat.

cc abbr = carbon copy, cubic centimetres.

cease [si:s] vt, vi cesser; ~**fire** n cessez-le-feu m; ~**less** a incessant(e), continuel(le).

cedar ['si:də*] n cèdre m.

ceiling ['si:lɪŋ] n plafond m.

celebrate ['selɪbreɪt] vt, vi célébrer; ~**d** a célèbre; **celebration** [-'breɪʃən] n célébration f.

celery ['selərɪ] n céleri m (en branches).

cell [sel] n (gen) cellule f; (ELEC) élément m (de pile).

cellar ['selə*] n cave f.

'cello ['tʃeləu] n violoncelle m.

Celt [kelt, selt] n Celte m/f.

Celtic ['keltɪk, 'seltɪk] a celte.

cement [sə'ment] n ciment m // vt cimenter; ~ **mixer** n bétonnière f.

cemetery ['semɪtrɪ] n cimetière m.

censor ['sensə*] n censeur m // vt censurer; ~**ship** n censure f.

censure ['senʃə*] vt blâmer, critiquer.

census ['sensəs] n recensement m.

cent [sent] n (US: coin) cent m (= 1:100 du dollar); see also **per**.

centenary [sen'ti:nərɪ] n centenaire m.

center ['sentə*] n (US) = **centre**.

centi... ['sentɪ] prefix: ~**grade** a centigrade; ~**metre**, (US) ~**meter** n centimètre m.

centipede ['sentɪpi:d] n mille-pattes m inv.

central ['sentrəl] a central(e); **C~ America** n Amérique centrale; ~ **heating** n chauffage central.

centre ['sentə*] n centre m // vt centrer; (PHOT) cadrer; ~**forward** n (SPORT) avant-centre m; ~**half** n (SPORT) demi-centre m.

century ['sentjurɪ] n siècle m; **20th**

~ XXe siècle.

ceramic [sɪ'ræmɪk] *a* céramique.

cereal ['sɪ:rɪəl] *n* céréale *f*.

ceremony ['serɪmənɪ] *n* cérémonie *f*; **to stand on** ~ faire des façons.

certain ['sə:tən] *a* certain(e); **to make** ~ s'assurer de; **for** ~ certainement, sûrement; ~**ly** *ad* certainement; ~**ty** *n* certitude *f*.

certificate [sə'tɪfɪkɪt] *n* certificat *m*.

certified ['sə:tɪfaɪd]: ~ **mail** *n* (US): **by** ~ **mail** en recommandé, avec avis de réception; ~ **public accountant** *n* (US) expert-comptable *m*.

cervical ['sə:vɪkl] *a*: ~ **cancer** cancer *m* du col de l'utérus; ~ **smear** frottis vaginal.

cervix ['sə:vɪks] *n* col *m* de l'utérus.

cesspit ['sespɪt] *n* fosse *f* d'aisance.

cf. *abbr* (= *compare*) cf., voir.

ch. *abbr* (= *chapter*) chap.

chafe [tʃeɪf] *vt* irriter, frotter contre.

chaffinch ['tʃæfɪntʃ] *n* pinson *m*.

chain [tʃeɪn] *n* (*gen*) chaîne *f* // *vt* (*also*: ~ **up**) enchaîner, attacher (avec une chaîne); ~ **reaction** *n* réaction *f* en chaîne; **to** ~ **smoke** *vi* fumer cigarette sur cigarette; ~ **store** *n* magasin *m* à succursales multiples.

chair [tʃeə*] *n* chaise *f*; (*armchair*) fauteuil *m*; (*of university*) chaire *f* // *vt* (*meeting*) présider; ~**lift** *n* télé-siège *m*; ~**man** *n* président *m*.

chalice ['tʃælɪs] *n* calice *m*.

chalk [tʃɔ:k] *n* craie *f*.

challenge ['tʃælɪndʒ] *n* défi *m* // *vt* défier; (*statement, right*) mettre en question, contester; **to** ~ **sb to do** mettre qn au défi de faire; **challenging** *a* de défi, provoca-teur(trice).

chamber ['tʃeɪmbə*] *n* chambre *f*; ~ **of commerce** chambre de commerce; ~**maid** *n* femme *f* de chambre; ~ **music** *n* musique *f* de chambre.

champagne [ʃæm'peɪn] *n* champa-gne *m*.

champion ['tʃæmpɪən] *n* champion; ne; ~**ship** *n* championnat *m*.

chance [tʃɑ:ns] *n* hasard *m*; (*opportunity*) occasion *f*, possibilité *f*; (*hope, likelihood*) chance *f* // *vt*: **to** ~ **it** risquer (le coup), essayer // *a* fortuit(e), de hasard; **to take a** ~ prendre un risque; **by** ~ par hasard.

chancellor ['tʃɑ:nsələ*] *n* chancelier *m*; **C**~ **of the Exchequer** *n* (*Brit*) chancelier de l'Échiquier.

chandelier [ʃændə'lɪə*] *n* lustre *m*.

change [tʃeɪndʒ] *vt* (*alter, replace, COMM: money*) changer; (*switch, substitute*) gear, hands, trains, clothes, one's name etc) changer de; (*transform*): **to** ~ **sb into** changer ou transformer qn en *vi* (*gen*) changer; (*change clothes*) se changer; (*be transformed*): **to** ~ **into** se changer ou transformer en // *n* changement *m*; (*money*) monnaie *f*; **to** ~ **one's mind** changer d'avis; **a** ~ **of clothes** des vêtements de rechange; **for a** ~ pour changer; ~**able** *a* (*weather*) variable; ~ **machine** *n* distributeur *m* de monnaie; ~**over** *n* (*to new system*) changement *m*, passage *n*.

changing ['tʃeɪndʒɪŋ] *a* changeant(e); ~ **room** *n* (*Brit: in shop*) salon *m* d'essayage; (: *SPORT*) vestiaire *m*.

channel ['tʃænl] *n* (*TV*) chaîne *f*; (*waveband, groove, fig: medium*) canal *m*; (*of river, sea*) chenal *m* // *vt* canaliser; **through the usual** ~**s** en suivant la filière habituelle; **the (English) C**~ la Manche; **the C**~ **Islands** les îles de la Manche, les îles anglo-normandes.

chant [tʃɑ:nt] *n* chant *m*; mélopée *f*; psalmodie *f* // *vt* chanter; scander; psalmodier.

chaos ['keɪɔs] *n* chaos *m*.

chap [tʃæp] *n* (*Brit col: man*) type *m*.

chapel ['tʃæpl] *n* chapelle *f*.

chaplain ['tʃæplɪn] *n* aumônier *m*.

chapped ['tʃæpt] *a* (*skin, lips*) gercé(e).

chapter ['tʃæptə*] n chapitre m.

char [tʃɑ:*] vt (burn) carboniser // (Brit) = **charlady**.

character ['kærɪktə*] n caractère m; (in novel, film) personnage m; (eccentric) numéro m, phénomène m; ~**istic** [-'rɪstɪk] a, n caractéristique (f).

charcoal ['tʃɑ:kəul] n charbon m de bois.

charge [tʃɑ:dʒ] n accusation f; (LAW) inculpation f; (cost) prix (demandé); (of gun, battery, MIL: attack) charge f // vt (LAW): **to ~ sb (with)** inculper qn (de); (gun, battery, MIL: enemy) charger; (customer, sum) faire payer // vi (gen with: up, along etc) foncer; ~**s** npl: **bank ~s** frais mpl de banque; **is there a ~?** doit-on payer?; **to reverse the ~s** (TEL) téléphoner en PCV; **to take ~ of** se charger de; **to be in ~ of** être responsable de, s'occuper de; **to ~ an expense (up) to sb** mettre une dépense sur le compte de qn; ~ **card** n carte f de client (émise par un grand magasin).

charity ['tʃærɪtɪ] n charité f; institution f charitable or de bienfaisance, œuvre f de charité).

charlady ['tʃɑ:leɪdɪ] n (Brit) femme f de ménage.

charm [tʃɑ:m] n charme m // vt charmer, enchanter; ~**ing** a charmant(e).

chart [tʃɑ:t] n tableau m, diagramme m; graphique m; (map) carte marine // vt dresser or établir la carte de.

charter ['tʃɑ:tə*] vt (plane) affréter // n (document) charte f; ~**ed accountant** n (Brit) expert-comptable m; ~ **flight** n charter m.

chase [tʃeɪs] vt poursuivre, pourchasser // n poursuite f, chasse f.

chasm ['kæzəm] n gouffre m, abîme m.

chat [tʃæt] vi (also: **have a ~**) bavarder, causer // n conversation f; ~

show n (Brit) entretien télévisé.

chatter ['tʃætə*] vi (person) bavarder // n bavardage m; **my teeth are ~ing** je claque des dents; ~**box** n moulin m à paroles.

chatty ['tʃætɪ] a (style) familier(ère); (person) enclin(e) à bavarder.

chauffeur ['ʃəufə*] n chauffeur m (de maître).

chauvinist ['ʃəuvɪnɪst] n (male ~) phallocrate m; (nationalist) chauvin(e).

cheap [tʃi:p] a bon marché inv, pas cher(chère); (joke) facile, d'un goût douteux; (poor quality) à bon marché, de qualité médiocre // ad à bon marché, pour pas cher; ~**en** vt rabaisser, déprécier; ~**er** a moins cher(chère); ~**ly** ad à bon marché, à bon compte.

cheat [tʃi:t] vi tricher // vt tromper, duper; (rob) escroquer // n tricheur/euse; escroc m; (trick) duperie f, tromperie f.

check [tʃek] vt vérifier; (passport, ticket) contrôler; (halt) enrayer; (restrain) maîtriser // n vérification f; contrôle m; (curb) frein m; (bill) addition f; (pattern: gen pl) carreaux mpl; (US) = **cheque** // a (also: ~**ed**: pattern, cloth) à carreaux; **to ~ in** vi (in hotel) remplir sa fiche (d'hôtel); (at airport) se présenter à l'enregistrement // vt (luggage) (faire) enregistrer; **to ~ out** vi (in hotel) régler sa note // vt (luggage) retirer; **to ~ up** vi: **to ~ up (on sth)** vérifier (qch); **to ~ up on sb** se renseigner sur le compte de qn; ~**ered** a (US) = **chequered**; ~**ers** n (US) jeu m de dames; ~**in (desk)** n enregistrement m; ~**ing account** n (US: current account) compte courant; ~**mate** n échec et mat m; ~**out** n caisse f (dans un supermarché); ~**point** n contrôle m; ~**room** n (US: left-luggage office) consigne f; ~**up** n (MED) examen médical, check-up m.

cheek [tʃi:k] n joue f; (impudence)

toupet m, culot m; ~**bone** n pommette f; ~**y** a effronté(e), culotté(e).

cheep [tʃi:p] vi piauler.

cheer [tʃɪə*] vt acclamer, applaudir; (gladden) réjouir, réconforter // vi applaudir // n (gen pl) acclamations fpl, applaudissements mpl; bravos mpl, hourras mpl; ~**s!** : (à votre) santé!; **to** ~ **up** vi se dérider, se reprendre courage // vt remonter le moral à or de, dérider, égayer; ~**ful** a gai(e), joyeux(euse).

cheerio ['tʃɪərɪ'əu] excl (Brit) salut!, au revoir!

cheese [tʃi:z] n fromage m; ~**board** n plateau m à fromages.

cheetah ['tʃi:tə] n guépard m.

chef [ʃef] n chef (cuisinier).

chemical ['kemɪkəl] a chimique // n produit m chimique.

chemist ['kemɪst] n (Brit: pharmacist) pharmacien/ne; (scientist) chimiste m/f; ~**ry** n chimie f; ~'**s** (shop) n (Brit) pharmacie f.

cheque [tʃek] n (Brit) chèque m; ~**book** n chéquier m, carnet m de chèques; ~ **card** n carte f (d'identité) bancaire.

chequered ['tʃekəd] a (fig) varié(e).

cherish ['tʃerɪʃ] vt chérir; (hope etc) entretenir.

cherry ['tʃerɪ] n cerise f.

chess [tʃes] n échecs mpl; ~**board** n échiquier m; ~**man** n pièce f (de jeu d'échecs).

chest [tʃest] n poitrine f; (box) coffre m, caisse f; ~ **of drawers** n commode f.

chestnut ['tʃesnʌt] n châtaigne f; (also: ~ **tree**) châtaignier m.

chew [tʃu:] vt mâcher; ~**ing gum** n chewing-gum m.

chic [ʃi:k] a chic inv, élégant(e).

chick [tʃɪk] n poussin m; (US col) pépée f.

chicken ['tʃɪkɪn] n poulet m; **to** ~ **out** vi (col) se dégonfler; ~**pox** n varicelle f.

chicory ['tʃɪkərɪ] n (for coffee) chicorée f; (salad) endive f.

chief [tʃi:f] n chef m // a principal(e); ~ **executive** n directeur général; ~**ly** ad principalement, surtout.

chiffon ['ʃɪfɔn] n mousseline f de soie.

chilblain ['tʃɪlbleɪn] n engelure f.

child, pl ~**ren** [tʃaɪld, 'tʃɪldrən] n enfant m/f; ~**birth** n accouchement m; ~**hood** n enfance f; ~**ish** a puéril(e), enfantin(e); ~**like** a innocent(e), pur(e); ~ **minder** n (Brit) garde f d'enfants.

Chile ['tʃɪlɪ] n Chili m.

chill [tʃɪl] n froid m; (MED) refroidissement m, coup m de froid // a froid(e), glacial(e) // vt faire frissonner; refroidir; (CULIN) mettre au frais, rafraîchir.

chil(l)i ['tʃɪlɪ] n piment m (rouge).

chilly ['tʃɪlɪ] a froid(e), glacé(e); (sensitive to cold) frileux(euse); **to feel** ~ avoir froid.

chime [tʃaɪm] n carillon m // vi carillonner, sonner.

chimney ['tʃɪmnɪ] n cheminée f; ~ **sweep** n ramoneur m.

chimpanzee [tʃɪmpæn'zi:] n chimpanzé m.

chin [tʃɪn] n menton m.

China ['tʃaɪnə] n Chine f.

china ['tʃaɪnə] n porcelaine f; (vaisselle f en) porcelaine.

Chinese [tʃaɪ'ni:z] a chinois(e) // n, pl inv Chinois/e; (LING) chinois m.

chink [tʃɪŋk] n (opening) fente f, fissure f; (noise) tintement m.

chip [tʃɪp] n (gen pl: CULIN) frite f (: US: also: **potato** ~) chip m; (of wood) copeau m; (of glass, stone) éclat m; (also: **micro**~) puce f // vt (cup, plate) ébrécher; **to** ~ **in** vi mettre son grain de sel.

chiropodist [kɪ'rɔpədɪst] n (Brit) pédicure m/f.

chirp [tʃə:p] vi pépier, gazouiller.

chisel ['tʃɪzl] n ciseau m.

chit [tʃɪt] n mot m, note f.

chitchat ['tʃɪttʃæt] n bavardage m.

chivalry ['ʃɪvəlrɪ] n chevalerie f; esprit m chevaleresque.

chives [tʃaɪvz] npl ciboulette f, civette f.

chock [tʃɔk] n cale f; **~-a-block**, **~-full** a plein(e) à craquer.

chocolate ['tʃɔklɪt] n chocolat m.

choice [tʃɔɪs] n choix m // a de choix.

choir ['kwaɪə*] n chœur m, chorale f; **~boy** n jeune choriste m.

choke [tʃəuk] vi étouffer // vt étrangler; étouffer; (block) boucher, obstruer // n (AUT) starter m.

choose [tʃuːz], pt chose, pp chosen vt choisir; **to do** décider de faire, juger bon de faire.

choosy ['tʃuːzɪ] a: **(to be) ~** (faire le) difficile.

chop [tʃɔp] vt (wood) couper (à la hache); (CULIN: also: ~ **up**) couper (fin), émincer, hacher (en morceaux) // n coup m (de hache, du tranchant de la main); (CULIN) côtelette f; **~s** npl (jaws) mâchoires fpl; babines fpl.

chopper ['tʃɔpə*] n (helicopter) hélicoptère m, hélico m.

choppy ['tʃɔpɪ] a (sea) un peu agité(e).

chopsticks ['tʃɔpstɪks] npl baguettes fpl.

chord [kɔːd] n (MUS) accord m.

chore [tʃɔː*] n travail m de routine; **household ~s** tâches mpl du ménage.

chortle ['tʃɔːtl] vi glousser.

chorus ['kɔːrəs] n chœur m; (repeated part of song, also fig) refrain m.

chose [tʃəuz] pt of **choose**.

chosen ['tʃəuzn] pp of **choose**.

Christ [kraɪst] n Christ m.

christen ['krɪsn] vt baptiser.

Christian ['krɪstɪən] a, n chrétien(ne); **~ity** [-'ænɪtɪ] n christianisme m; chrétienté f; **~ name** n prénom m.

Christmas ['krɪsməs] n Noël m or f; **Merry ~!** joyeux Noël!; **~ card** n carte f de Noël; **~ Day** n le jour de Noël; **~ Eve** n la veille de Noël; la nuit de Noël; **~ tree** n arbre m de Noël.

chrome [krəum], **chromium** ['krəumɪəm] n chrome m.

chronic ['krɔnɪk] a chronique.

chronicle ['krɔnɪkl] n chronique f.

chronological [krɔnə'lɔdʒɪkəl] a chronologique.

chrysanthemum [krɪ'sænθəməm] n chrysanthème m.

chubby ['tʃʌbɪ] a potelé(e), rondelet(te).

chuck [tʃʌk] vt lancer, jeter; **to ~ out** vt flanquer dehors or à la porte; **to ~ (up)** (Brit) lâcher, plaquer.

chuckle ['tʃʌkl] vi glousser.

chug [tʃʌg] vi faire teuf-teuf; souffler.

chum [tʃʌm] n copain/copine.

chunk [tʃʌŋk] n gros morceau; (of bread) quignon m.

church [tʃəːtʃ] n église f; **~yard** n cimetière m.

churlish ['tʃəːlɪʃ] a grossier(ère); hargneux(euse).

churn [tʃəːn] n (for butter) baratte f; (for transport: also: **milk ~**) (grand) bidon à lait; **to ~ out** vt débiter.

chute [ʃuːt] n glissoire f; (also: rubbish ~) vide-ordures m inv; (Brit: children's slide) toboggan m.

chutney ['tʃʌtnɪ] n condiment m à base de fruits.

CIA n abbr (US: = Central Intelligence Agency) CIA f.

CID n abbr (Brit = Criminal Investigation Department) ≈ P.J. f (= police judiciaire).

cider ['saɪdə*] n cidre m.

cigar [sɪ'gɑː*] n cigare m.

cigarette [sɪgə'rɛt] n cigarette f; **~ case** n étui m à cigarettes; **~ end** n mégot m.

cinder ['sɪndə*] n cendre f.

Cinderella [sɪndə'rɛlə] n Cendrillon f.

cine ['sɪnɪ]: **~-camera** n (Brit) caméra f; **~-film** n (Brit) film m.

cinema ['sɪnəmə] n cinéma m.

cinnamon ['sɪnəmən] n cannelle f.

cipher ['saɪfə*] n code secret; (fig:

faceless employee etc) numéro *m*.

circle ['sə:kl] *n* cercle *m*; (*in cinema*) balcon *m* // *vi* faire *or* décrire des cercles // *vt* (*surround*) entourer, encercler; (*move round*) faire le tour de, tourner autour de.

circuit ['sə:kɪt] *n* circuit *m*; ~**ous** [sə:'kjuːtəs] *a* indirect(e), qui fait un détour.

circular ['sə:kjulə*] *a*, *n* circulaire (*f*).

circulate ['sə:kjulɛɪt] *vi* circuler // *vt* faire circuler; **circulation** [-'leɪʃən] *n* circulation *f*; (*of newspaper*) tirage *m*.

circumflex ['sə:kəmflɛks] *n* (*also*: ~ **accent**) accent *m* circonflexe.

circumstances ['sə:kəmstənsɪz] *npl* circonstances *fpl*; (*financial condition*) moyens *mpl*, situation financière.

circumvent [sə:kəm'vɛnt] *vt* tourner.

circus ['sə:kəs] *n* cirque *m*.

cistern ['sɪstən] *n* réservoir *m* (d'eau); (*in toilet*) réservoir de la chasse d'eau.

citizen ['sɪtɪzn] *n* (*POL*) citoyen/ne; (*resident*): **the ~s of this town** les habitants de cette ville; ~**ship** *n* citoyenneté *f*.

citrus fruit ['sɪtrəs-] *n* agrume *m*.

city ['sɪtɪ] *n* ville *f*, cité *f*; **the C~** la Cité de Londres (*centre des affaires*).

civic ['sɪvɪk] *a* civique; ~ **centre** *n* (*Brit*) centre administratif (municipal).

civil ['sɪvl] *a* civil(e); poli(e); civil; ~ **engineer** *n* ingénieur civil; ~**ian** [sɪ'vɪlɪən] *a*, *n* civil(e).

civilization [sɪvɪlaɪ'zeɪʃən] *n* civilisation *f*.

civilized ['sɪvɪlaɪzd] *a* civilisé(e); (*fig*) où règnent les bonnes manières, empreint(e) d'une courtoisie de bon ton.

civil: ~ **law** *n* code civil; (*study*) droit civil; ~ **servant** *n* fonctionnaire *m/f*; **C~ Service** *n* fonction publique, administration *f*; ~ **war** *n*

guerre civile.

clad [klæd] *a*: ~ (**in**) habillé(e) (de).

claim [kleɪm] *vt* revendiquer; demander, prétendre à; déclarer, prétendre // *vi* (*for insurance*) faire une déclaration de sinistre // *n* revendication *f*; demande *f*; prétention *f*; déclaration *f*; (*right*) droit *m*, titre *m*; (*insurance*) ~ demande *f* d'indemnisation, déclaration *f* de sinistre; ~**ant** *n* (*ADMIN, LAW*) requérant/e.

clairvoyant [klɛə'vɔɪənt] *n* voyant/e, extra-lucide *m/f*.

clam [klæm] *n* palourde *f*.

clamber ['klæmbə*] *vi* grimper, se hisser.

clammy ['klæmɪ] *a* humide et froid(e) (au toucher), moite.

clamour, (*US*) **clamor** ['klæmə*] *vi*: **to ~ for** réclamer à grands cris.

clamp [klæmp] *n* étau *m* à main; agrafe *f*, crampon *m* // *vt* serrer; cramponner; **to ~ down on** *vt fus* sévir contre, prendre des mesures draconiennes à l'égard de.

clan [klæn] *n* clan *m*.

clang [klæŋ] *n* bruit *m* *or* fracas *m* métallique.

clap [klæp] *vi* applaudir; ~**ping** *n* applaudissements *mpl*.

claret ['klærət] *n* (vin *m* de) bordeaux *m* (rouge).

clarinet [klærɪ'nɛt] *n* clarinette *f*.

clarity ['klærɪtɪ] *n* clarté *f*.

clash [klæʃ] *n* choc *m*; (*fig*) conflit *m* // *vi* se heurter; être *or* entrer en conflit.

clasp [klɑːsp] *n* fermoir *m* // *vt* serrer, étreindre.

class [klɑːs] *n* (*gen*) classe *f* // *vt* classer, classifier.

classic ['klæsɪk] *a* classique *m*; ~**al** *a* classique.

classified ['klæsɪfaɪd] *a* (*information*) secret(ète); ~ **advertisements**, ~ **ads** *npl* petites annonces.

classmate ['klɑːsmeɪt] *n* camarade *m/f* de classe.

classroom ['klɑːsrum] *n* (salle *f* de)

classe f.

clatter ['klætə*] n cliquetis m // vi cliqueter.

clause [klɔ:z] n clause f; (LING) proposition f.

claw [klɔ:] n griffe f; (of bird of prey) serre f; (of lobster) pince f; to ~ at vt essayer de griffer or déchirer.

clay [kleɪ] n argile f.

clean [kli:n] a propre; (clear, smooth) net(te) // ad nettoyer; to ~ out vt nettoyer (à fond); to ~ up vt nettoyer; (fig) remettre de l'ordre dans; ~er n (person) nettoyeur/euse, femme f de ménage; (also: dry ~er) teinturier/ière; (product) détachant m; ~ing n nettoyage m; ~liness ['klɛnlɪnɪs] n propreté f.

cleanse [klɛnz] vt nettoyer; purifier; ~r n détergent m; (for face) démaquillant m; **cleansing department** n (Brit) service m de voirie.

clean-shaven ['kli:n'ʃeɪvn] a rasé(e) de près.

clear [klɪə*] a clair(e); (road, way) libre, dégagé(e) // vt dégager, déblayer, débarrasser; faire évacuer; (COMM: goods) liquider; (cheque) compenser; (LAW: suspect) innocenter; (obstacle) franchir or sauter sans heurter // vi (weather) s'éclaircir; (fog) se dissiper // ad: ~ of à distance de, à l'écart de; to ~ the table débarrasser la table, desservir; to ~ up vi s'éclaircir, se dissiper // vt ranger, mettre en ordre; (mystery) éclaircir, résoudre; ~ance n (removal) déblayage m (free space) dégagement m; (permission) autorisation f; ~-cut a précise(e), nettement défini(e); ~ing n (in forest) clairière f; ~ing bank n (Brit) banque f qui appartient à une chambre de compensation; ~ly ad clairement, de toute évidence; ~way n (Brit) route f à stationnement interdit.

cleaver ['kli:və*] n fendoir m, couperet m.

clef [klɛf] n (MUS) clé f.

cleft [klɛft] n (in rock) crevasse f, fissure f.

clench [klɛntʃ] vt serrer.

clergy ['klə:dʒɪ] n clergé m; ~man n ecclésiastique m.

clerical ['klɛrɪkəl] a de bureau, d'employé de bureau; (REL) clérical(e), du clergé.

clerk [klɑ:k, (US) klə:rk] n employé/e de bureau; (US: salesman/woman) vendeur/euse.

clever ['klɛvə*] a (mentally) intelligent(e); (deft, crafty) habile, adroit(e); (device, arrangement) ingénieux(euse), astucieux(euse).

click [klɪk] vi faire un bruit sec or un déclic // vt: to ~ one's tongue faire claquer sa langue; to ~ one's heels claquer des talons.

client ['klaɪənt] n client/e.

cliff [klɪf] n falaise f.

climate ['klaɪmɪt] n climat m.

climax ['klaɪmæks] n apogée m, point culminant; (sexual) orgasme m.

climb [klaɪm] vi grimper, monter // vt gravir, escalader, monter sur // n montée f, escalade f; ~-down n reculade f, dérobade f; ~er n (also: rock ~er) grimpeur/euse, varappeur/euse; ~ing n (also: rock ~ing) escalade f, varappe f.

clinch [klɪntʃ] vt (deal) conclure, sceller.

cling [klɪŋ], pt, pp **clung** vi: to ~ (to) se cramponner (à), s'accrocher (à); (of clothes) coller (à).

clinic ['klɪnɪk] n centre médical.

clink [klɪŋk] vi tinter, cliqueter.

clip [klɪp] n (for hair) barrette f; (also: paper ~) trombone m; (holding hose etc) collier m or bague f (métallique) de serrage // vt (also: ~ together: papers) attacher; (hair, nails) couper; (hedge) tailler; ~pers npl tondeuse f; (also: nail ~pers) coupe-ongles m inv; ~ping n (from newspaper) coupure f de journal.

cloak [kləuk] n grande cape // vt (fig)

masquer, cacher; **~room** n (for coats etc) vestiaire m; (Brit: W.C.) toilettes fpl.

clock [klɔk] n (large) horloge f; (small) pendule f; to ~ in or on vi pointer (en arrivant); to ~ off or out vi pointer (en partant); **~wise** ad dans le sens des aiguilles d'une montre; **~work** n mouvement m (d'horlogerie); rouages mpl, mécanisme m à mécanique.

clog [klɔg] n sabot m // vt boucher, encrasser // vi se boucher, s'encrasser.

cloister ['klɔɪstə*] n cloître m.

close a, ad and derivatives [kləus] a (near): ~ (to) près (de), proche (de); (writing, texture) serré(e); (watch) étroit(e), strict(e); (examination) attentif(ive), minutieux(euse); (weather) lourd(e), étouffant(e) // ad près, à proximité; **~ to** prep près de; ~ by, ~ at hand a, ad tout(e) près; a ~ friend un ami intime; to have a ~ shave (fig) l'échapper belle // vb and derivatives [kləuz] vt fermer // vi (shop etc) fermer; (lid, door etc) se fermer; (end) se terminer, se conclure // n (end) conclusion f; to ~ down vt, vi fermer (définitivement); **~d** a fermé(e); **~d shop** n organisation f qui n'admet que des travailleurs syndiqués; **~-knit** a (family, community) très uni(e); **~ly** ad (examine, watch) de près.

closet ['klɔzɪt] n (cupboard) placard m, réduit m.

close-up ['kləusʌp] n gros plan.

closure ['kləuʒə*] n fermeture f.

clot [klɔt] n (gen: blood) caillot m; (col: person) ballot m // vi (blood) former des caillots; (: external bleeding) se coaguler.

cloth [klɔθ] n (material) tissu m, étoffe f; (also: tea~) torchon m; lavette f.

clothe [kləuð] vt habiller, vêtir; **~s** npl vêtements mpl, habits mpl; **~s brush** n brosse f à habits; **~s line**

n corde f (à linge); **~s peg**, (US) **~s pin** n pince f à linge.

clothing ['kləuðɪŋ] n =**clothes**.

cloud [klaud] n nuage m; **~y** a nuageux(euse), couvert(e); (liquid) trouble.

clout [klaut] vt flanquer une taloche à.

clove [kləuv] n clou m de girofle; ~ of garlic gousse f d'ail.

clover ['kləuvə*] n trèfle m.

clown [klaun] n clown m // vi (also: ~ about, ~ around) faire le clown.

cloying ['klɔɪɪŋ] a (taste, smell) écœurant(e).

club [klʌb] n (society) club m; (weapon) massue f, matraque f; (also: golf ~) club // vt matraquer // vi: to ~ together s'associer; **~s** npl (CARDS) trèfle m; ~ car n (US RAIL) wagon-restaurant m; **~house** n pavillon m.

cluck [klʌk] vi glousser.

clue [klu:] n indice m; (in crosswords) définition f; I haven't a ~ je n'en ai pas la moindre idée.

clump [klʌmp] n: ~ of trees bouquet m d'arbres.

clumsy ['klʌmzɪ] a (person) gauche, maladroit(e); (object) malcommode, peu maniable.

clung [klʌŋ] pt, pp of **cling**.

cluster ['klʌstə*] n (petit) groupe // vi se rassembler.

clutch [klʌtʃ] n (grip, grasp) étreinte f, prise f; (AUT) embrayage m // vt agripper, serrer fort; to ~ at se cramponner à.

clutter ['klʌtə*] vt encombrer.

CND abbr = Campaign for Nuclear Disarmament.

Co. abbr of county, company.

c/o abbr = care of) c/o, aux bons soins de.

coach [kəutʃ] n (bus) autocar m; (horse-drawn) diligence f; (of train) voiture f, wagon m; (SPORT: trainer) entraîneur/euse // vt entraîner; **~ trip** n excursion f en car.

coal [kəul] n charbon m; ~ **face** n

front *m* de taille; ~**field** *n* bassin houiller.

coalition [kəuə'lɪʃən] *n* coalition *f*.

coalman, coal merchant ['kəulmən, 'kəulmɜ:tʃənt] *n* charbonnier *m*, marchand *m* de charbon.

coalmine ['kəulmaɪn] *n* mine *f* de charbon.

coarse [kɔ:s] *a* grossier(ère), rude.

coast [kəust] *n* côte *f* // *vi* (*with cycle etc*) descendre en roue libre; ~**al** *a* côtier(ère); ~**guard** *n* garde-côte *m*; ~**line** *n* côte *f*, littoral *m*.

coat [kəut] *n* manteau *m*; (*of animal*) pelage *m*, poil *m*; (*of paint*) couche *f* // *vt* couvrir, enduire; ~ **of arms** *n* blason *m*, armoiries *fpl*; ~**hanger** *n* cintre *m*; ~**ing** *n* couche *f*, enduit *m*.

coax [kəuks] *vt* persuader par des cajoleries.

cob [kɔb] *n* see **corn**.

cobbler ['kɔblə*] *n* cordonnier *m*.

cobbles, cobblestones ['kɔblz, 'kɔblstəunz] *npl* pavés (ronds).

cobweb ['kɔbweb] *n* toile *f* d'araignée.

cocaine [kə'keɪn] *n* cocaïne *f*.

cock [kɔk] *n* (*rooster*) coq *m*; (*male bird*) mâle *m* // *vt* (*gun*) armer; ~**erel** *n* jeune coq *m*; ~**-eyed** *a* (*fig*) de travers; qui louche; qui ne tient pas debout (*fig*).

cockle ['kɔkl] *n* coque *f*.

cockney ['kɔknɪ] *n* cockney *m/f* (*habitant des quartiers populaires de l'East End de Londres*), ≈ faubourien *m*.

cockpit ['kɔkpɪt] *n* (*in aircraft*) poste *m* de pilotage, cockpit *m*.

cockroach ['kɔkrəutʃ] *n* cafard *m*.

cocktail ['kɔkteɪl] *n* cocktail *m*; ~ **cabinet** *n* (meuble-)bar *m*; ~ **party** *n* cocktail *m*.

cocoa ['kəukəu] *n* cacao *m*.

coconut ['kəukənʌt] *n* noix *f* de coco.

cod [kɔd] *n* morue (fraîche), cabillaud *m*.

C.O.D. *abbr* of **cash on delivery**.

code [kəud] *n* code *m*.

cod-liver oil *n* huile *f* de foie de morue.

coercion [kəu'ɜ:ʃən] *n* contrainte *f*.

coffee ['kɔfɪ] *n* café *m*; ~ **bar** *n* (*Brit*) café *m*; ~ **break** *n* pause-café *f*; ~**pot** *n* cafetière *f*; ~ **table** *n* (petite) table basse.

coffin ['kɔfɪn] *n* cercueil *m*.

cog [kɔg] *n* dent *f* (d'engrenage).

cogent ['kəudʒənt] *a* puissant(e), convaincant(e).

coil [kɔɪl] *n* rouleau *m*, bobine *f*; (*one loop*) anneau *m*, spire *f*; (*contraceptive*) stérilet *m* // *vt* enrouler.

coin [kɔɪn] *n* pièce *f* de monnaie // *vt* (*word*) inventer; ~**age** *n* monnaie *f*, système *m* monétaire; ~**-box** *n* (*Brit*) cabine *f* téléphonique.

coincide [kəuɪn'saɪd] *vi* coïncider; ~**nce** [kəu'ɪnsɪdəns] *n* coïncidence *f*.

coke [kəuk] *n* coke *m*.

colander ['kɔləndə*] *n* passoire *f* (à légumes).

cold [kəuld] *a* froid(e) // *n* froid *m*; (*MED*) rhume *m*; **it's** ~ il fait froid; **to be** ~ avoir froid; **to catch** ~ prendre *or* attraper froid; **to catch a** ~ attraper un rhume; **in** ~ **blood** de sang-froid; ~ **sore** *n* bouton *m* de fièvre.

coleslaw ['kəulslɔ:] *n* sorte de salade de chou cru.

colic ['kɔlɪk] *n* colique *f* (*pl*).

collapse [kə'læps] *vi* s'effondrer, s'écrouler // *n* effondrement *m*, écroulement *m*.

collapsible [kə'læpsəbl] *a* pliant(e); télescopique.

collar ['kɔlə*] *n* (*of coat, shirt*) col *m*; ~**bone** *n* clavicule *f*.

collateral [kɔ'lætərl] *n* nantissement *m*.

colleague ['kɔli:g] *n* collègue *m/f*.

collect [kə'lekt] *vt* rassembler; ramasser; (*as a hobby*) collectionner; (*Brit*: *call and pick up*) (passer) prendre; (*mail*) faire la levée de, ramasser; (*money owed*) encaisser; (*donations, subscriptions*) recueillir //

vi se rassembler; s'amasser; **to call ~** (*US TEL*) téléphoner en PCV; **~ion** [kə'lɛkʃən] *n* collection *f*; levée *f*; (*for money*) collecte *f*, quête *f*.

collector [kə'lɛktə*] *n* collectionneur *m*; (*of taxes*) percepteur *m*.

college ['kɔlɪdʒ] *n* collège *m*.

collide [kə'laɪd] *vi*: **to ~ (with)** entrer en collision (avec).

collie ['kɔlɪ] *n* (*dog*) colley *m*.

colliery ['kɔlɪərɪ] *n* mine *f* de charbon, houillère *f*.

collision [kə'lɪʒən] *n* collision *f*, heurt *m*.

colloquial [kə'ləukwɪəl] *a* familier(ère).

colon ['kəulən] *n* (*sign*) deux-points *mpl*; (*MED*) côlon *m*.

colonel ['kə:nl] *n* colonel *m*.

colonial [kə'ləunɪəl] *a* colonial(e).

colony ['kɔlənɪ] *n* colonie *f*.

colour, (*US*) **color** ['kʌlə*] *n* couleur *f* // *vt* colorer; peindre; (*with crayons*) colorier; (*news*) fausser, exagérer // *vi* (*blush*) rougir; **~s** *npl* (*of party, club*) couleurs *fpl*; **~ bar** *n* discrimination raciale (*dans un établissement etc*); **~-blind** *a* daltonien(ne); **~ed** *a* coloré(e); (*photo*) en couleur // *n*: **~eds** personnes *fpl* de couleur; **~ film** *n* (*for camera*) pellicule *f* (en) couleur; **~ful** *a* coloré(e), vif(vive); (*personality*) pittoresque, haut(e) en couleurs; **~ing** *n* colorant *m*; (*complexion*) teint *m*; **~ scheme** *n* combinaison *f* de(s) couleurs; **~ television** *n* télévision *f* en couleur.

colt [kəult] *n* poulain *m*.

column ['kɔləm] *n* colonne *f*; **~ist** ['kɔləmnɪst] *n* rédacteur/trice d'une rubrique.

coma ['kəumə] *n* coma *m*.

comb [kəum] *n* peigne *m* // *vt* (*hair*) peigner; (*area*) ratisser, passer au peigne fin.

combat ['kɔmbæt] *n* combat *m* // *vt* combattre, lutter contre.

combination [kɔmbɪ'neɪʃən] *n* (*gen*) combinaison *f*.

combine *vb* [kəm'baɪn] *vt* combiner; (*one quality with another*) joindre (à), allier (à) // *vi* s'associer; (*CHEM*) se combiner // *n* ['kɔmbaɪn] association *f*; (*ECON*) trust *m*; **~ (harvester)** *n* moissonneuse-batteuse(-lieuse) *f*.

come [kʌm], *pt* **came**, *pp* **come** *vi* venir; arriver; **to ~ to** (*decision etc*) parvenir à, arriver à; **to ~ undone/ loose** se défaire/desserrer; **to ~ about** *vi* se produire, arriver; **to ~ across** *vt fus* rencontrer par hasard, tomber sur; **to ~ along** *vi* (*button*) se détacher; **to ~ away** *vi* partir, s'en aller; se détacher; **to ~ back** *vi* revenir; **to ~ by** *vt fus* (*acquire*) obtenir, se procurer; **to ~ down** *vi* descendre; (*prices*) baisser; (*buildings*) s'écrouler; être démoli(e); **to ~ forward** *vi* s'avancer; se présenter; s'annoncer; **to ~ from** *vt fus* être originaire de; venir de; **to ~ in** *vi* entrer; **to ~ in for** *vt fus* (*criticism etc*) être l'objet de; **to ~ into** *vt fus* (*money*) hériter de; **to ~ off** *vi* (*button*) se détacher; (*stain*) s'enlever; (*attempt*) réussir; **to ~ on** *vi* (*pupil, work, project*) faire des progrès, avancer; (*lights, electricity*) s'allumer; (*central heating*) se mettre en marche; **~ on!** viens!, allons!, allez!; **to ~ out** *vi* sortir; (*book*) paraître; (*strike*) cesser le travail, se mettre en grève; **to ~ round** *vi* (*after faint, operation*) revenir à soi, reprendre connaissance; **to ~ to** *vi* revenir à soi; **to ~ up** *vi* monter; **to ~ up against** *vt fus* (*resistance, difficulties*) rencontrer; **to ~ up with** *vt fus*: **he came up with an idea** il a eu une idée, il a proposé quelque chose; **to ~ upon** *vt fus* tomber sur; **~-back** *n* (*THEATRE etc*) rentrée *f*.

comedian [kə'mi:dɪən] *n* (*in music hall etc*) comique *m*; (*THEATRE*) comédien *m*.

comedown ['kʌmdaun] *n* déchéance *f*.

comedy ['kɒmɪdɪ] n comédie f.

comeuppance [kʌm'ʌpəns] n: to get one's ~ recevoir ce qu'on mérite.

comfort ['kʌmfət] n confort m, bien-être m; (solace) consolation f, réconfort m ♦ vt consoler, réconforter; ~s npl aises fpl; ~able a confortable; ~ably ad (sit) confortablement; (live) à l'aise; ~ station n (US) toilettes fpl.

comic ['kɒmɪk] a (also: ~al) comique // n comique m; (magazine) illustré m; ~ strip n bande dessinée.

coming ['kʌmɪŋ] n arrivée f ♦ a prochain(e), à venir; ~(s) and going(s) n(pl) va-et-vient m inv.

comma ['kɒmə] n virgule f.

command [kə'mɑːnd] n ordre m, commandement m; (MIL: authority) commandement; (mastery) maîtrise f // vt (troops) commander; (be able to get) (pouvoir) disposer de, avoir à sa disposition; (deserve) avoir droit à; ~eer [kɒmən'dɪə] vt réquisitionner (par la force); ~er n chef m, (MIL) commandant m.

commando [kə'mɑːndəʊ] n commando m; membre m d'un commando.

commemorate [kə'meməreɪt] vt commémorer.

commence [kə'mens] vt, vi commencer.

commend [kə'mend] vt louer; recommander.

commensurate [kə'menʃərɪt] a: ~ with en proportion de, proportionné(e) à.

comment ['kɒment] n commentaire m // vi: to ~ (on) faire des remarques (sur); ~ary ['kɒmənt(ə)rɪ] n commentaire m; (SPORT) reportage m (en direct); ~ator ['kɒmənteɪtə*] n commentateur m; reporter m.

commerce ['kɒmə:s] n commerce m.

commercial [kə'mə:ʃəl] a commercial(e) // n (TV: also: ~ break) annonce f publicitaire, spot m (publici-

taire).

commiserate [kə'mɪzəreɪt] vi: to ~ with sb témoigner de la sympathie pour qn.

commission [kə'mɪʃən] n (committee, fee) commission f // vt (MIL) nommer (à un commandement); (work of art) commander, charger un artiste de l'exécution de; out of ~ (NAUT) hors de service; ~aire [kəmɪʃə'nɛə*] n (Brit: at shop, cinema etc) portier m (en uniforme); ~er n membre m d'une commission; (POLICE) préfet m (de police).

commit [kə'mɪt] vt (act) commettre; (to sb's care) confier (à); to ~ o.s. (to do) s'engager (à faire); to ~ suicide se suicider; ~ment n engagement m; (obligation) responsabilité(s) f(pl).

committee [kə'mɪtɪ] n comité m.

commodity [kə'mɒdɪtɪ] n produit m, marchandise f, article m; (food) denrée f.

common ['kɒmən] a (gen, also pej) commun(e); (usual) courant(e) // n terrain communal; the C~s npl (Brit) la chambre des Communes; in ~ en commun; ~er n roturier/ière; ~ law n droit coutumier; ~ly ad communément, généralement; couramment; C~ Market n Marché commun; ~place a banal(e), ordinaire; ~room n salle commune; (SCOL) salle des professeurs; ~ sense n bon sens; the C~wealth n le Commonwealth.

commotion [kə'məʊʃən] n désordre m, tumulte m.

communal ['kɒmju:nl] a (life) communautaire; (for common use) commun(e).

commune n ['kɒmju:n] (group) communauté f // vi [kə'mju:n]: to ~ with converser intimement avec; communier avec.

communicate [kə'mju:nɪkeɪt] vt, vi communiquer.

communication [kəmju:nɪ'keɪʃən] n communication f; ~ cord n (Brit) sonnette f d'alarme.

communion [kə'mju:nɪən] n (also: Holy C~) communion f.

communism ['kɔmjunɪzəm] n communisme m; **communist** a, n communiste (m/f).

community [kə'mju:nɪtɪ] n communauté f; ~ **centre** n foyer socio-éducatif, centre m de loisirs; ~ **chest** n (US) fonds commun.

commutation ticket [kɔmju'teɪʃən-] n (US) carte f d'abonnement.

commute [kə'mju:t] vi faire le trajet journalier (de son domicile à un lieu de travail assez éloigné) // vt (LAW) commuer; ~r n banlieusard/e (qui ... see vi).

compact a [kəm'pækt] compact(e) // n ['kɔmpækt] (also: powder ~) poudrier m; ~ **disk** n disque compact.

companion [kəm'pænjən] n compagnon/compagne; ~**ship** n camaraderie f.

company ['kʌmpənɪ] n (also COMM, MIL, THEATRE) compagnie f; to keep sb ~ tenir compagnie à qn; ~ **secretary** n (COMM) secrétaire général (d'une société).

comparative [kəm'pærətɪv] a comparatif(ive); (relative) relatif(ive); ~**ly** ad (relatively) relativement.

compare [kəm'pεə*] vt: to ~ sth/sb with/to comparer qch/qn avec or et/à // vi: to ~ (with) se comparer (à); être comparable (à); **comparison** [-'pærɪsn] n comparaison f.

compartment [kəm'pɔ:tmənt] n (also RAIL) compartiment m.

compass ['kʌmpəs] n boussole f; ~**es** npl compas m.

compassion [kəm'pæʃən] n compassion f, humanité f.

compatible [kəm'pætɪbl] a compatible.

compel [kəm'pεl] vt contraindre, obliger; ~**ling** a (fig: argument) irrésistible.

compendium [kəm'pεndɪəm] n

abrégé m.

compensate ['kɔmpənseɪt] vt indemniser, dédommager // vi: to ~ for compenser; **compensation** [-'seɪʃən] n compensation f; (money) dédommagement m, indemnité f.

compete [kəm'pi:t] vi (take part) concourir; (vie): to ~ (with) rivaliser (avec), faire concurrence (à).

competence ['kɔmpɪtəns] n compétence f, aptitude f.

competent ['kɔmpɪtənt] a compétent(e), capable.

competition [kɔmpɪ'tɪʃən] n compétition f, concours m; (ECON) concurrence f.

competitive [kəm'petɪtɪv] a (ECON) concurrentiel(le); (sport) de compétition.

competitor [kəm'petɪtə*] n concurrent/e.

complacency [kəm'pleɪsnsɪ] n contentement m de soi, vaine complaisance.

complain [kəm'pleɪn] vi: to ~ (about) se plaindre (de); (in shop etc) réclamer (au sujet de); ~**t** n plainte f; réclamation f; (MED) affection f.

complement ['kɔmplɪmənt] n complément m; (especially of ship's crew etc) effectif complet // ['kɔmplɪment] vt (enhance) compléter; ~**ary** [kɔmplɪ'mentərɪ] a complémentaire.

complete [kəm'pli:t] a complet(ète) // vt achever, parachever; (a form) remplir; ~**ly** ad complètement; **completion** n achèvement m.

complex ['kɔmplεks] a, n complexe (m).

complexion [kəm'plεkʃən] n (of face) teint m; (of event etc) aspect m, caractère m.

compliance [kəm'plaɪəns] n (submission) docilité f; (agreement): ~ with le fait de se conformer à.

complicate ['kɔmplɪkeɪt] vt compliquer; ~**d** a compliqué(e); **complication** [-'keɪʃən] n complication f.

compliment n ['kɔmplɪmənt] compliment m // vt ['kɔmplɪment] complimenter; ~s npl compliments mpl, hommages mpl; vœux mpl; to pay sb a ~ faire or adresser un compliment à qn; ~ary [-'mentərɪ] a flatteur(euse); (free) à titre gracieux; ~ary ticket n billet m de faveur.

comply [kəm'plaɪ] vi: to ~ with se soumettre à, se conformer à.

component [kəm'pəunənt] n composant m, élément m.

compose [kəm'pəuz] vt composer; to ~ o.s. se calmer, se maîtriser; prendre une contenance; ~d a calme, posé(e); ~r n (MUS) compositeur m.

composition [kɔmpə'zɪʃən] n composition f.

composure [kəm'pəuʒə*] n calme m, maîtrise f de soi.

compound ['kɔmpaund] n (CHEM, LING) composé m; (enclosure) enclos m, enceinte f // a composé(e); ~ **fracture** n fracture compliquée.

comprehend [kɔmprɪ'hend] vt comprendre; **comprehension** [-'henʃən] n compréhension f.

comprehensive [kɔmprɪ'hensɪv] a (très) complet(ète); ~ **policy** n (INSURANCE) assurance f tous risques; ~ **(school)** n (Brit) école secondaire non sélective avec libre circulation d'une section à l'autre, ≈ C.E.S. m.

compress vt [kəm'pres] comprimer // n ['kɔmpres] (MED) compresse f.

comprise [kəm'praɪz] vt (also: be ~d of) comprendre.

compromise ['kɔmprəmaɪz] n compromis m // vt compromettre // vi transiger, accepter un compromis.

compulsion [kəm'pʌlʃən] n contrainte f, force f.

compulsive [kəm'pʌlsɪv] a (PSYCH) compulsif(ive).

compulsory [kəm'pʌlsərɪ] a obligatoire.

computer [kəm'pju:tə*] n ordinateur m; (mechanical) calculatrice f; ~ize

vt traiter or automatiser par ordinateur; ~ **programmer** n programmeur/euse; ~ **programming** n programmation f; ~ **science, computing** n informatique f.

comrade ['kɔmrɪd] n camarade m/f.

con [kɔn] vt duper; escroquer // n escroquerie f.

conceal [kən'si:l] vt cacher, dissimuler.

conceit [kən'si:t] n vanité f, suffisance f, prétention f; ~ed a vaniteux(euse), suffisant(e).

conceive [kən'si:v] vt, vi concevoir.

concentrate ['kɔnsəntreɪt] vi se concentrer // vt concentrer.

concentration [kɔnsən'treɪʃən] n concentration f; ~ **camp** n camp m de concentration.

concept ['kɔnsept] n concept m.

concern [kən'sɜ:n] n affaire f; (COMM) entreprise f, firme f; (anxiety) inquiétude f, souci m // vt concerner; to be ~ed (about) s'inquiéter (de), être inquiet (au sujet de); ~ing prep en ce qui concerne, à propos de.

concert ['kɔnsət] n concert m; ~ed [kən'sɜ:tɪd] a concerté(e); ~ **hall** n salle f de concert.

concertina [kɔnsə'ti:nə] n concertina m // vi se télescoper, se caramboler.

concerto [kən'tʃə:təu] n concerto m.

conclude [kən'klu:d] vt conclure; **conclusion** [-'klu:ʒən] n conclusion f; **conclusive** [-'klu:sɪv] a concluant(e), définitif(ive).

concoct [kən'kɔkt] vt confectionner, composer; ~ion [-'kɔkʃən] n mélange m.

concourse ['kɔnkɔ:s] n (hall) hall m, salle f des pas perdus.

concrete ['kɔnkri:t] n béton m // a concret(ète) // a en béton.

concur [kən'kə:*] vi être d'accord.

concurrently [kən'kʌrntlɪ] ad simultanément.

concussion [kən'kʌʃən] n (MED) commotion (cérébrale).

condemn [kən'dɛm] vt condamner.

condensation [kɔndɛn'seɪʃən] n condensation f.

condense [kən'dɛns] vi se condenser // vt condenser; **~d milk** n lait concentré (sucré).

condition [kən'dɪʃən] n condition f // vt déterminer, conditionner; **on ~ that** à condition que + sub, à condition de; **~al** a conditionnel(le); **~er** n (for hair) baume démêlant.

condolences [kən'dəʊlənsɪz] npl condoléances fpl.

condom ['kɔndɔm] n préservatif m.

condominium [kɔndə'mɪnɪəm] n (US: building) immeuble m (en copropriété); (: rooms) appartement m (dans un immeuble en copropriété).

condone [kən'dəʊn] vt fermer les yeux sur, approuver (tacitement).

conducive [kən'dju:sɪv] a: **~ to** favorable à, qui contribue à.

conduct n ['kɔndʌkt] conduite f // vt [kən'dʌkt] (manage) mener, diriger; (MUS) diriger; **to ~ o.s.** se conduire, se comporter; **~ed tour** n voyage organisé; visite guidée; **~or** n (of orchestra) chef m d'orchestre; (on bus) receveur m; (US: on train) chef m de train; (ELEC) conducteur m; **~ress** n (on bus) receveuse f.

cone [kəʊn] n cône m; (for icecream) cornet m; (BOT) pomme f de pin, cône.

confectioner [kən'fɛkʃənə*] n (of cakes) pâtissier/ière; (of sweets) confiseur/euse; **~'s (shop)** n confiserie(-pâtisserie); **~y** n pâtisserie f; confiserie f.

confer [kən'fə:*] vt: **to ~ sth on** conférer qch à // vi conférer, s'entretenir.

conference ['kɔnfərəns] n conférence f.

confess [kən'fɛs] vt confesser, avouer // vi se confesser; **~ion** [kən'fɛʃən] n confession f.

confetti [kən'fɛtɪ] n confettis mpl.

confide [kən'faɪd] vi: **to ~ in** s'ou-

vrir à, se confier à.

confidence ['kɔnfɪdns] n confiance f; (also: self-~) assurance f, confiance en soi; (secret) confidence f; **in ~** (speak, write) en confidence, confidentiellement; **~ trick** n escroquerie f; **confident** a sûr(e), assuré(e); **confidential** [kɔnfɪ'dɛnʃəl] a confidentiel(le).

confine [kən'faɪn] vt limiter, borner; (shut up) confiner, enfermer; **~s** ['kɔnfaɪnz] npl confins mpl, bornes fpl; **~d** a (space) restreint(e), réduit(e); **~ment** n emprisonnement m, détention f; (MIL) consigne f (au quartier); (MED) accouchement m.

confirm [kən'fə:m] vt (report, REL) confirmer; (appointment) ratifier; **~ation** [kɔnfə'meɪʃən] n confirmation f; **~ed** a invétéré(e), incorrigible.

confiscate ['kɔnfɪskeɪt] vt confisquer.

conflict n ['kɔnflɪkt] conflit m, lutte f // vi [kən'flɪkt] être or entrer en conflit; (opinions) s'opposer, se heurter; **~ing** a contradictoire.

conform [kən'fɔ:m] vi: **to ~ (to)** se conformer (à).

confound [kən'faʊnd] vt confondre.

confront [kən'frʌnt] vt confronter, mettre en présence; (enemy, danger) affronter, faire face à; **~ation** [kɔnfrən'teɪʃən] n confrontation f.

confuse [kən'fju:z] vt embrouiller, (one thing with another) confondre; **~d** a (person) dérouté(e), désorienté(e); **confusing** a peu clair(e), déroutant(e); **confusion** [-'fju:ʒən] n confusion f.

congeal [kən'dʒi:l] vi (blood) se coaguler.

congenial [kən'dʒi:nɪəl] a sympathique, agréable.

congested [kən'dʒɛstɪd] a (MED) congestionné(e); (fig) surpeuplé(e); congestionné; bloqué(e).

congestion [kən'dʒɛstʃən] n congestion f; (fig) encombrement m.

congratulate [kən'grætjʊleɪt] vt: to

~ sb (on) féliciter qn (de); **congratulations** [-'leɪʃənz] npl félicitations fpl.

congregate ['kɔŋgrɪgeɪt] vi se rassembler, se réunir.

congregation [kɔŋgrɪ'geɪʃən] n assemblée f (des fidèles).

congress ['kɔŋgres] n congrès m; ~**man** n (US) membre m du Congrès.

conjunction [kən'dʒʌŋkʃən] n conjonction f.

conjunctivitis [kəndʒʌŋktɪ'vaɪtɪs] n conjonctivite f.

conjure ['kʌndʒə*] vt faire apparaître (par la prestidigitation) // vi faire des tours de passe-passe; **to ~ up** vt (ghost, spirit) faire apparaître; (memories) évoquer; ~**r** n prestidigitateur m, illusionniste m/f.

conk out [kɔŋk-] vi (col) tomber ou rester en panne.

conman ['kɔnmæn] n escroc m.

connect [kə'nekt] vt joindre, relier; (ELEC) connecter; (fig) établir un rapport entre, faire un rapprochement entre // vi (train): **to ~ with** assurer la correspondance avec; **to be ~ed with** avoir un rapport avec, avoir des rapports avec, être en relation avec; (related) être allié(e) à, être parent(e) avec; ~**ion** [-ʃən] n relation f, lien m; (ELEC) connexion f; (TEL) communication f; **in ~ion with** à propos de.

connive [kə'naɪv] vi: **to ~ at** se faire le complice de.

conquer ['kɔŋkə*] vt conquérir; (feelings) vaincre, surmonter.

conquest ['kɔŋkwest] n conquête f.

cons [kɔnz] npl see **convenience**, **pro**.

conscience ['kɔnʃəns] n conscience f.

conscientious [kɔnʃɪ'enʃəs] a consciencieux(euse); (scruple, objection) de conscience.

conscious ['kɔnʃəs] a conscient(e); ~**ness** n conscience f; (MED) connaissance f.

conscript ['kɔnskrɪpt] n conscrit m.

consent [kən'sent] n consentement m // vi: **to ~ (to)** consentir (à).

consequence ['kɔnsɪkwəns] n suites fpl, conséquence f; importance f.

consequently ['kɔnsɪkwəntlɪ] ad par conséquent, donc.

conservation [kɔnsə'veɪʃən] n préservation f, protection f.

conservative [kən'sə:vətɪv] a conservateur(trice); (cautious) prudent(e); **C~** a, n (Brit POL) conservateur(trice).

conservatory [kən'sə:vətrɪ] n (greenhouse) serre f.

conserve [kən'sə:v] vt conserver, préserver; (supplies, energy) économiser // n confiture f, conserve f (de fruits).

consider [kən'sɪdə*] vt considérer, réfléchir à; (take into account) penser à, prendre en considération; (regard, judge) considérer, estimer; **to ~ doing sth** envisager de faire qch.

considerable [kən'sɪdərəbl] a considérable; **considerably** ad nettement.

considerate [kən'sɪdərɪt] a prévenant(e), plein(e) d'égards.

consideration [kənsɪdə'reɪʃən] n considération f; (reward) rétribution f, rémunération f.

considering [kən'sɪdərɪŋ] prep étant donné.

consign [kən'saɪn] vt expédier, livrer; ~**ment** n arrivage m, envoi m.

consist [kən'sɪst] vi: **to ~ of** consister en, se composer de.

consistency [kən'sɪstənsɪ] n consistance f; (fig) cohérence f.

consistent [kən'sɪstənt] a logique, cohérent(e); ~ **with** compatible avec, en accord avec.

consolation [kɔnsə'leɪʃən] n consolation f.

consonant ['kɔnsənənt] n consonne f.

conspicuous [kən'spɪkjuəs] a voyant(e), qui attire la vue ou l'attention.

conspiracy [kən'spɪrəsɪ] n conspiration f, complot m.

constable ['kʌnstəbl] n (Brit) ≈ agent m de police, gendarme m ; **chief ~** ≈ préfet m de police.

constabulary [kən'stæbjʊlərɪ] n = police f, gendarmerie f.

constant ['kɒnstənt] a constant(e); incessant(e); **~ly** ad constamment, sans cesse.

constipated ['kɒnstɪpeɪtɪd] a constipé(e).

constipation [kɒnstɪ'peɪʃən] n constipation f.

constituency [kən'stɪtjuənsɪ] n circonscription électorale.

constituent [kən'stɪtjuənt] n électeur/trice; (part) élément constitutif, composant m.

constitution [kɒnstɪ'tjuːʃən] n constitution f; **~al** a constitutionnel(le).

constraint [kən'streɪnt] n contrainte f.

construct [kən'strʌkt] vt construire; **~ion** [-ʃən] n construction f; **~ive** a constructif(ive).

construe [kən'struː] vt analyser, expliquer.

consul ['kɒnsl] n consul m; **~ate** ['kɒnsjʊlɪt] n consulat m.

consult [kən'sʌlt] vt consulter // vi consulter; se consulter; **~ant** n (MED) médecin consultant; (other specialist) consultant m, (expert-)conseil m; **~ing room** n (Brit MED) cabinet m de consultation.

consume [kən'sjuːm] vt consommer; **~r** n consommateur/trice; **~r goods** npl biens mpl de consommation; **~r society** n société f de consommation.

consummate ['kɒnsʌmeɪt] vt consommer.

consumption [kən'sʌmpʃən] n consommation f; (MED) consomption f (pulmonaire).

cont. abbr = continued.

contact ['kɒntækt] n contact m; (per-

son) connaissance f, relation f // vt se mettre en contact or en rapport avec; **~ lenses** npl verres mpl de contact.

contagious [kən'teɪdʒəs] a contagieux(euse).

contain [kən'teɪn] vt contenir; **to ~ o.s.** se contenir, se maîtriser; **~er** n récipient m; (for shipping etc) container m.

contaminate [kən'tæmɪneɪt] vt contaminer.

cont'd abbr = continued.

contemplate ['kɒntəmpleɪt] vt contempler; (consider) envisager.

contemporary [kən'tempərərɪ] a contemporain(e); (design, wallpaper) moderne // n contemporain/e.

contempt [kən'tempt] n mépris m, dédain m; **~ of court** (LAW) outrage m à l'autorité de la justice; **~uous** a dédaigneux(euse), méprisant(e).

contend [kən'tend] vt: **to ~ that** soutenir or prétendre que // vi: **to ~ with** rivaliser avec, lutter avec; **~er** n prétendant/e; adversaire m/f.

content [kən'tent] a content(e), satisfait(e) // vt contenter, satisfaire // ['kɒntent] n contenu m; teneur f; **~s** npl contenu m; (table of) **~s** table f des matières; **~ed** a content(e), satisfait(e).

contention [kən'tenʃən] n dispute f, contestation f; (argument) assertion f, affirmation f.

contest n ['kɒntest] combat m, lutte f; (competition) concours m // vt [kən'test] contester, discuter; (compete for) disputer; **~ant** [kən'testənt] n concurrent/e; (in fight) adversaire m/f.

context ['kɒntekst] n contexte m.

continent ['kɒntɪnənt] n continent m; **the C~** (Brit) l'Europe continentale; **~al** [-'nentl] a continental(e) // n Européen/ne (continental(e)); **~al quilt** n (Brit) couette f.

contingency [kən'tɪndʒənsɪ] n éventualité f, événement imprévu; **~**

plan n plan m d'urgence.

continual [kən'tinjuəl] a continuel(le).

continuation [kəntinju'eiʃən] n continuation f; (after interruption) reprise f; (of story) suite f.

continue [kən'tinju:] vi continuer // vt continuer; (start again) reprendre.

continuous [kən'tinjuəs] a continu(e), permanent(e); ~ **stationery** n papier m en continu.

contort [kən'tɔ:t] vt tordre, crisper.

contour ['kɔntuə] n contour m, profil m; (also: ~ **line**) courbe f de niveau.

contraband ['kɔntrəbænd] n contrebande f.

contraceptive [kɔntrə'sɛptiv] a contraceptif(ive), anticonceptionnel(le) // n contraceptif m.

contract n ['kɔntrækt] contrat m // vb [kən'trækt] vi (become smaller) se contracter, se resserrer; (COMM): **to** ~ **to do sth** s'engager (par contrat) à faire qch; ~**ion** [-ʃən] n contraction f; ~**or** n entrepreneur m.

contradict [kɔntrə'dikt] vt contredire; (be contrary to) démentir, être en contradiction avec.

contraption [kən'træpʃən] n (pej) machin m, truc m.

contrary ['kɔntrəri] a contraire, opposé(e); ['kɔntrɛəri] (perverse) contrariant(e), entêté(e) // n contraire m; **on the** ~ au contraire; **unless you hear to the** ~ sauf avis contraire.

contrast n ['kɔntrɑ:st] contraste m // vt [kən'trɑ:st] mettre en contraste, contraster.

contribute [kən'tribju:t] vi contribuer // vt: **to** ~ **£10/an article to** donner 10 livres/un article à; **to** ~ **to** (gen) contribuer à; (newspaper) collaborer à; **contribution** [kɔntri'bju:ʃən] n contribution f; **contributor** n (to newspaper) collaborateur/trice.

contrive [kən'traiv] vt combiner, inventer // vi: **to** ~ **to do** s'arranger pour faire, trouver le moyen de faire.

control [kən'trəul] vt maîtriser; (check) contrôler // n contrôle m, autorité f; maîtrise f; ~**s** npl commandes fpl; **everything is under** ~ tout va bien, j'ai (or il a etc) la situation en main; **to be in** ~ **of** être maître de, maîtriser; être responsable de; **the car went out of** ~ j'ai (or il a etc) perdu le contrôle du véhicule; ~ **panel** n tableau m de commande; ~ **room** n salle f des commandes; (RADIO, TV) régie f; ~ **tower** n (AVIAT) tour f de contrôle.

controversial [kɔntrə'və:ʃl] a discutable, controversé(e).

controversy ['kɔntrəvə:si] n controverse f, polémique f.

convalesce [kɔnvə'lɛs] vi relever de maladie, se remettre (d'une maladie).

convene [kən'vi:n] vt convoquer, assembler // vi se réunir, s'assembler.

convenience [kən'vi:niəns] n commodité f; **at your** ~ quand or comme cela vous convient; **all modern** ~**s, all mod cons** avec tout le confort moderne, tout confort.

convenient [kən'vi:niənt] a commode.

convent ['kɔnvənt] n couvent m.

convention [kən'vɛnʃən] n convention f; ~**al** a conventionnel(le).

conversant [kən'və:snt] a: **to be** ~ **with** s'y connaître en; être au courant de.

conversation [kɔnvə'seiʃən] n conversation f.

converse [kən'və:s] n contraire m, inverse m // [kən'və:s] s'entretenir; ~**ly** [-'və:sli] ad inversement, réciproquement.

convert vt [kən'və:t] (REL, COMM) convertir; (alter) transformer, aménager // n ['kɔnvə:t] converti/e; ~**ible** a convertible // n (voiture f) décapotable f.

convey [kən'vei] vt transporter; (thanks) transmettre; (idea) communiquer; ~**or belt** n convoyeur m, tapis roulant.

convict vt [kən'vɪkt] déclarer (or reconnaître) coupable // n ['kɒnvɪkt] forçat m, convict m; ~ion [-ʃən] n condamnation f; (belief) conviction f.

convince [kən'vɪns] vt convaincre, persuader; **convincing** a persuasif(ive), convaincant(e).

convoluted [kɒnvə'luːtɪd] a (argument) compliqué(e).

convulse [kən'vʌls] vt ébranler; **to be ~d with laughter** se tordre de rire.

coo [kuː] vi roucouler.

cook [kuk] vt (faire) cuire // vi cuire; (person) faire la cuisine // n cuisinier/ière; **~book** n livre m de cuisine; **~er** n cuisinière f; **~ery** n cuisine f; **~ery book** (Brit) = **~book**; **~ie** n (US) biscuit m, petit gâteau sec; **~ing** n cuisine f.

cool [kuːl] a frais (fraîche); (not afraid) calme; (unfriendly) froid(e); (impertinent) effronté(e) // vt, vi rafraîchir, refroidir.

coop [kuːp] n poulailler m // vt: **to ~ up** (fig) cloîtrer, enfermer.

cooperate [kəu'ɒpəreɪt] vi coopérer, collaborer; **cooperation** [-'reɪʃən] n coopération f, collaboration f.

cooperative [kəu'ɒpərətɪv] a coopératif(ive) // n coopérative f.

coordinate vt [kəu'ɔːdɪneɪt] coordonner // n [kəu'ɔːdɪnət] (MATH) coordonnée f; **~s** npl (clothes) ensemble m, coordonnés mpl.

cop [kɒp] n (col) flic m.

cope [kəup] vi se débrouiller; **to ~ with** faire face à; s'occuper de.

copper ['kɒpə*] n cuivre m; (col: policeman) flic m; **~s** npl petite monnaie.

coppice ['kɒpɪs] n, **copse** [kɒps] n taillis m.

copy ['kɒpɪ] n copie f; (book etc) exemplaire m // vt copier; **~right** n droit m d'auteur, copyright m.

coral ['kɒrəl] n corail m.

cord [kɔːd] n corde f; (fabric) velours côtelé; whipcord m; corde f.

cordial ['kɔːdɪəl] a cordial(e), chaleureux(euse) // n sirop m; cordial m.

cordon ['kɔːdn] n cordon m; **to ~ off** vt boucler (par cordon de police).

corduroy ['kɔːdərɔɪ] n velours côtelé.

core [kɔː*] n (of fruit) trognon m, cœur m; (TECH) noyau m // vt enlever le trognon or le cœur de.

cork [kɔːk] n liège m; (of bottle) bouchon m; **~screw** n tire-bouchon m.

corn [kɔːn] n (Brit: wheat) blé m; (US: maize) maïs m; (on foot) cor m; **~ on the cob** (CULIN) épi m de maïs au naturel.

corned beef ['kɔːnd-] n corned-beef m.

corner ['kɔːnə*] n coin m; (AUT) tournant m, virage m // vt acculer, mettre au pied du mur; coincer; (COMM: market) accaparer // vi prendre un virage; **~stone** n pierre f angulaire.

cornet ['kɔːnɪt] n (MUS) cornet m à pistons; (Brit: of ice-cream) cornet (de glace).

cornflakes ['kɔːnfleɪks] npl cornflakes mpl.

cornflour ['kɔːnflauə*] n (Brit) farine f de maïs, maizena f ®.

cornstarch ['kɔːnstɑːtʃ] n (US) = **cornflour**.

Cornwall ['kɔːnwəl] n Cornouailles f.

corny ['kɔːnɪ] a (col) rebattu(e), galvaudé(e).

coronary ['kɒrənərɪ] n: **~ (thrombosis)** infarctus m (du myocarde), thrombose f coronaire.

coronation [kɒrə'neɪʃən] n couronnement m.

coronet ['kɒrənɪt] n couronne f.

corporal ['kɔːpərəl] n caporal m, brigadier m // a: **~ punishment** châtiment corporel.

corporate ['kɔːpərɪt] a en commun, constitué(e) (en corporation).

corporation [kɔːpə'reɪʃən] n (of town) municipalité f, conseil municipal; (COMM) société f.

corps [kɔː*], pl **corps** [kɔːz] n corps

m.

corpse [kɔ:ps] n cadavre m.

correct [kə'rekt] a (accurate) correct(e), exact(e); (proper) correct, convenable // vt corriger; **~ion** [-ʃən] n correction f.

correspond [kɔrɪs'pɔnd] vi correspondre; **~ence** n correspondance f; **~ence course** n cours m par correspondance; **~ent** n correspondant/e.

corridor ['kɔridɔ:*] n couloir m, corridor m.

corrode [kə'rəud] vt corroder, ronger // vi se corroder.

corrugated ['kɔrəgeitid] a plissé(e); cannelé(e); ondulé(e); **~ iron** n tôle ondulée.

corrupt [kə'rʌpt] a corrompu(e) // vt corrompre; **~ion** [-ʃən] n corruption f.

Corsica ['kɔ:sikə] n Corse f.

cortège [kɔ:'teiʒ] n cortège m (gén funèbre).

cosh [kɔʃ] n (Brit) matraque f.

cosmetic [kɔz'metik] n produit m de beauté, cosmétique m.

cosset ['kɔsit] vt choyer, dorloter.

cost [kɔst] n coût m // vb (pt, pp **cost**) vi coûter // vt établir or calculer le prix de revient de; **~s** npl (LAW) dépens mpl; it **~s** £5/too much cela coûte cinq livres/trop cher; at all **~s** coûte que coûte, à tout prix.

co-star ['kəustɑ:*] n partenaire m/f.

cost-effective [kɔsti'fektiv] a rentable.

costly ['kɔstli] a coûteux(euse).

cost-of-living [kɔstɔv'liviŋ] a: **~ allowance** indemnité f de vie chère; **~ index** n indice m du coût de la vie.

cost price n (Brit) prix coûtant or de revient.

costume ['kɔstju:m] n costume m; (lady's suit) tailleur m; (Brit: also: **swimming ~**) maillot m (de bain); **~ jewellery** n bijoux mpl de fantaisie.

cosy, (US) **cozy** ['kəuzi] a douil-

let(te).

cot [kɔt] n (Brit: child's) lit m d'enfant, petit lit; (US: campbed) lit de camp.

cottage ['kɔtidʒ] n petite maison (à la campagne), cottage m; **~ cheese** n fromage blanc (maigre); **~ industry** n industrie familiale or artisanale; **~ pie** n ≈ hachis m Parmentier.

cotton ['kɔtn] n coton m; **to ~ on to** vt fus (col) piger; **~ candy** n (US) barbe f à papa; **~ wool** n (Brit) ouate f, coton m hydrophile.

couch [kautʃ] n canapé m; divan m // vt coucher, exprimer.

couchette [ku:'ʃet] n couchette f.

cough [kɔf] vi tousser // n toux f; **~ drop** n pastille f pour or contre la toux.

could [kud] pt of **can**; **~n't** = **could not.**

council ['kaunsl] n conseil m; **city or town ~** conseil municipal; **~ estate** n (Brit) (quartier m or zone f de) logements loués à/par la municipalité; **~ house** n (Brit) maison f (à loyer modéré) louée par la municipalité; **~lor** n conseiller/ère.

counsel ['kaunsl] n avocat/e; consultation f, délibération f; **~lor** n conseiller/ère.

count [kaunt] vt, vi compter // n compte m; (nobleman) comte m; **to ~ on** vt fus compter sur; **~down** n compte m à rebours.

countenance ['kauntinəns] n expression f // vt approuver.

counter ['kauntə*] n comptoir m; (in post office, bank) guichet m; (in game) jeton m // vt aller à l'encontre de, opposer; (blow) parer // ad: **~ to** à l'encontre de; contrairement à; **~act** vt neutraliser, contrebalancer; **~espionage** n contre-espionnage m.

counterfeit ['kauntəfit] n faux m, contrefaçon f // vt contrefaire // a faux(fausse).

counterfoil ['kauntəfɔil] n talon m,

souche f.

countermand [kauntə'mɑːnd] vt annuler.

counterpart ['kauntəpɑːt] n (of document etc) double m; (of person) homologue m/f.

countess ['kauntɪs] n comtesse f.

countless ['kauntlɪs] a innombrable.

country ['kʌntrɪ] n pays m; (native land) patrie f; (as opposed to town) campagne f; (region) région f, pays; ~ **dancing** n (Brit) danse f folklorique; ~ **house** n manoir m, (petit) château; **~man** n (national) compatriote m; (rural) habitant m de la campagne, campagnard m; **~side** n campagne f.

county ['kauntɪ] n comté m.

coup, **~s** [kuː, -z] n beau coup; (also: ~ d'état) coup d'État.

couple ['kʌpl] n couple m // vt (carriages) atteler; (TECH) coupler; (ideas, names) associer; **a ~ of** deux.

coupon ['kuːpɔn] n coupon m, bon-prime m, bon-réclame m; (COMM) coupon.

courage ['kʌrɪdʒ] n courage m.

courgette [kuə'ʒet] n (Brit) courgette f.

courier ['kurɪə*] n messager m, courrier m; (for tourists) accompagnateur/trice.

course [kɔːs] n cours m; (of ship) route f; (for golf) terrain m; (part of meal) plat m; **first ~** n entrée f, of ad bien sûr; **~ of action** parti m, ligne f de conduite; **~ of lectures** série f de conférences; **~ of treatment** (MED) traitement m.

court [kɔːt] n cour f; (LAW) cour, tribunal m; (TENNIS) court m // vt (woman) courtiser, faire la cour à; **to take to ~** actionner or poursuivre en justice.

courteous ['kɔːtɪəs] a courtois(e), poli(e).

courtesy ['kɔːtəsɪ] n courtoisie f, politesse f; **by ~ of** avec l'aimable autorisation de.

court-house ['kɔːthaus] n (US) palais m de justice.

courtier ['kɔːtɪə*] n courtisan m, dame f de cour.

court-martial, pl **courts-martial** ['kɔːt'mɑːʃəl] n cour martiale, conseil m de guerre.

courtroom ['kɔːtrum] n salle f de tribunal.

courtyard ['kɔːtjɑːd] n cour f.

cousin ['kʌzn] n cousin/e; **first ~** cousin/e germain(e).

cove [kəuv] n petite baie, anse f.

covenant ['kʌvənənt] n contrat m, engagement m.

cover ['kʌvə*] vt couvrir // n (for bed, of book, COMM) couverture f; (of pan) couvercle m; (over furniture) housse f; (shelter) abri m; **to take ~** (shelter) se mettre à l'abri; **under ~** à l'abri; **under ~ of darkness** à la faveur de la nuit; **under separate ~** (COMM) sous pli séparé; **to ~ up for sb** couvrir qn; **~age** n reportage m; (INSURANCE) couverture f; **~ charge** n couvert m (supplément à payer); **~ing** n couverture f, enveloppe f; **~ing letter**, (US) **~ letter** n lettre explicative; **~ note** n (INSURANCE) police f provisoire.

covert ['kʌvət] a (threat) voilé(e), caché(e); (attack) indirect(e); (glance) furtif/ive.

cover-up ['kʌvərʌp] n tentative f pour étouffer une affaire.

covet ['kʌvɪt] vt convoiter.

cow [kau] n vache f // cpd femelle // vt effrayer, intimider.

coward ['kauəd] n lâche m/f; **~ice** [-ɪs] n lâcheté f; **~ly** a lâche.

cowboy ['kaubɔɪ] n cow-boy m.

cower ['kauə*] vi se recroqueviller; trembler.

coxswain ['kɔksn] n (abbr: cox) barreur m; (of ship) patron m.

coy [kɔɪ] a faussement effarouché(e) or timide.

cozy ['kəuzɪ] a (US) = **cosy**.

CPA n abbr (US) of **certified public**

accountant.

crab [kræb] n crabe m; ~ **apple** n pomme f sauvage.

crack [kræk] n fente f, fissure f; fêlure f; lézarde f; (noise) craquement m, coup (sec); (joke) plaisanterie f; (col: attempt): **to have a ~** at essayer // vt fendre, fissurer; fêler; lézarder; (whip) faire claquer; (nut) casser // a (athlete) de première classe, d'élite; **to ~ down on** vt fus mettre un frein à; **to ~ up** vi être au bout de son rouleau, flancher; ~**er** n pétard m; biscuit (salé), craquelin m.

crackle [ˈkrækl] vi crépiter, grésiller.

cradle [ˈkreidl] n berceau m.

craft [krɑːft] n métier (artisanal); (cunning) ruse f, astuce f; (boat) embarcation f, barque f; ~**sman** n artisan m, ouvrier (qualifié); ~**smanship** n métier m, habileté f; ~**y** a rusé(e), malin(igne), astucieux(euse).

crag [kræg] n rocher escarpé.

cram [kræm] vt (fill): **to ~ sth with** bourrer qch de; (put): **to ~ sth into** fourrer qch dans // vi (for exams) bachoter.

cramp [kræmp] n crampe f // vt gêner, entraver; ~**ed** a à l'étroit, très serré(e).

cranberry [ˈkrænbəri] n canneberge f.

crane [krein] n grue f.

crank [kræŋk] n manivelle f; (person) excentrique m/f; ~**shaft** n vilebrequin m.

cranny [ˈkræni] n see **nook**.

crash [kræʃ] n fracas m; (of car, plane) collision f // vt (plane) écraser // vi (plane) s'écraser; (two cars) se percuter, s'emboutir; (fig) s'effondrer; **to ~ into** se jeter or se fracasser contre; ~ **course** n cours intensif; ~ **helmet** n casque (protecteur); ~ **landing** n atterrissage forcé or en catastrophe.

crate [kreit] n cageot m.

cravat(e) [krəˈvæt] n foulard (noué autour du cou).

crave [kreiv] vt, vi: **to ~ (for)** avoir une envie irrésistible de.

crawl [krɔːl] vi ramper; (vehicle) avancer au pas // n (SWIMMING) crawl m.

crayfish [ˈkreifiʃ] n (pl inv) (freshwater) écrevisse f; (saltwater) langoustine f.

crayon [ˈkreiən] n crayon m (de couleur).

craze [kreiz] n engouement m.

crazy [ˈkreizi] a fou(folle); ~ **paving** n dallage irrégulier (en pierres plates).

creak [kriːk] vi grincer; craquer.

cream [kriːm] n crème f // a (colour) crème inv; ~ **cake** n (petit) gâteau à la crème; ~ **cheese** n fromage m à la crème, fromage blanc; ~**y** a crémeux(euse).

crease [kriːs] n pli m // vt froisser, chiffonner // vi se froisser, se chiffonner.

create [kriːˈeit] vt créer; **creation** [-ʃən] n création f; **creative** a créateur(trice).

creature [ˈkriːtʃə*] n créature f.

crèche, creche [kreʃ] n garderie f, crèche f.

credence [ˈkriːdns] n: **to lend** or **give ~ to** ajouter foi à.

credentials [kriˈdenʃlz] npl (papers) références fpl.

credit [ˈkredit] n crédit m // vt (COMM) créditer; (believe: also: **give ~ to**) ajouter foi à, croire; ~**s** npl (CINEMA) générique m; **to ~ sb with** (fig) prêter or attribuer à qn; **to be in ~** (person, bank account) être créditeur(trice); ~ **card** n carte f de crédit; ~**or** n créancier/ière.

creed [kriːd] n croyance f, credo m, principes mpl.

creek [kriːk] n crique f, anse f; (US) ruisseau m, petit cours d'eau.

creep [kriːp], pt, pp **crept** vi ramper; (fig) se faufiler, se glisser; (plant) grimper; ~**er** n plante grimpante; ~**y** a (frightening) qui fait frissonner, qui donne la chair de poule.

cremate [krɪ'meɪt] vt incinérer.

crematorium, pl **crematoria** [kremə'tɔːrɪəm, -'tɔːrɪə] n four m crématoire.

crêpe [kreɪp] n crêpe m; ~ **bandage** n (Brit) bande f Velpeac ®.

crept [krept] pt, pp of **creep.**

crescent [kresnt] n croissant m; rue f (en arc de cercle).

cress [kres] n cresson m.

crest [krest] n crête f; ~**fallen** a déconfit(e), découragé(e).

crevice [krevɪs] n fissure f, lézarde f, fente f.

crew [kruː] n équipage m; **to have a ~-cut** avoir les cheveux en brosse; ~**-neck** n col ras.

crib [krɪb] n lit m d'enfant // vt (col) copier.

crick [krɪk] n crampe f.

cricket ['krɪkɪt] n (insect) grillon m, cri-cri m inv; (game) cricket m.

crime [kraɪm] n crime m; **criminal** ['krɪmɪnl] a, n criminel(le).

crimson ['krɪmzn] a cramoisi(e).

cringe [krɪndʒ] vi avoir un mouvement de recul; (fig) s'humilier, ramper.

crinkle ['krɪŋkl] vt froisser, chiffonner.

cripple ['krɪpl] n boiteux/euse, infirme m/f // vt estropier, paralyser.

crisis, pl **crises** ['kraɪsɪs, -siːz] n crise f.

crisp [krɪsp] a croquant(e); (fig) vif(vive); brusque; ~**s** npl (Brit) (pommes) chips fpl.

criss-cross ['krɪskrɔs] a entrecroisé(e).

criterion, pl **criteria** [kraɪ'tɪərɪən, -'tɪərɪə] n critère m.

critic ['krɪtɪk] n critique m/f; ~**al** a critique; (speak etc) sévèrement; ~**ally ill** gravement malade; ~**ism** ['krɪtɪsɪzm] n critique f; ~**ize** ['krɪtɪsaɪz] vt critiquer.

croak [krəʊk] vi (frog) coasser;

(raven) croasser.

crochet ['krəʊʃeɪ] n travail m au crochet.

crockery ['krɔkərɪ] n vaisselle f.

crocodile ['krɔkədaɪl] n crocodile m.

crocus ['krəʊkəs] n crocus m.

croft [krɔft] n (Brit) petite ferme.

crony ['krəʊnɪ] n copain/copine.

crook [krʊk] n escroc m; (of shepherd) houlette f; ~**ed** ['krʊkɪd] a courbé(e), tordu(e); (action) malhonnête.

crop [krɔp] n (produce) culture f; (amount produced) récolte f; (riding ~) cravache f; **to ~ up** vi surgir, se présenter, survenir.

cross [krɔs] n croix f; (BIOL) croisement m // vt (street etc) traverser; (arms, legs, BIOL) croiser; (cheque) barrer // a en colère, fâché(e); **to o.s.** se signer, faire le signe de (la) croix; **to ~ out** vt barrer, biffer; **to ~ over** vt traverser; ~**bar** n barre transversale; ~**country (race)** n cross(-country) m; ~**examine** vt (LAW) faire subir un examen contradictoire à; ~**eyed** a qui louche; ~**fire** n feux croisés; ~**ing** n croisement m, carrefour m; (sea passage) traversée f; (also: pedestrian ~**ing**) passage clouté; ~**ing-guard** n (US) contractuel/le qui fait traverser la rue aux enfants; ~ **purposes** npl: **to be at ~ purposes** ne pas parler de la même chose; ~**reference** n renvoi m, référence f; ~**roads** n carrefour m; ~ **section** n (BIOL) coupe transversale; (in population) échantillon m; ~**walk** n (US) passage clouté; ~**wind** n vent m de travers; ~**wise** ad en travers; ~**word** n mots croisés mpl.

crotch [krɔtʃ] n (of garment) entrejambes m inv.

crotchety ['krɔtʃɪtɪ] a (person) grognon(ne), grincheux(euse).

crouch [kraʊtʃ] vi s'accroupir; se tapir; se ramasser.

crow [krəʊ] n (bird) corneille f; (of

cock) chant *m* du coq, cocorico *m* // *vi* (*cock*) chanter; (*fig*) pavoiser, chanter victoire.

crowbar ['krəubɑ:*] *n* levier *m*.

crowd [kraud] *n* foule *f* // *vt* bourrer, remplir // *vi* affluer, s'attrouper, s'entasser; ~ed a bondé(e), plein(e); ~ed with plein de.

crown [kraun] *n* couronne *f*; (*of head*) sommet *m* de la tête, calotte crânienne; (*of hat*) fond *m*; (*of hill*) sommet *m* // *vt* couronner; ~ **jewels** *npl* joyaux *mpl* de la Couronne; ~ **prince** *n* prince héritier.

crow's feet *npl* pattes *fpl* d'oie (*fig*).

crucial ['kru:ʃl] *a* crucial(e), décisif(ive).

crucifixion [kru:sɪ'fɪkʃən] *n* crucifiement *m*, crucifixion *f*.

crude [kru:d] *a* (*materials*) brut(e); non raffiné(e); (*fig*: *basic*) rudimentaire, sommaire; (: *vulgar*) cru(e), grossier(ère); ~ (**oil**) *n* (pétrole) brut *m*.

cruel ['kruəl] *a* cruel(le); ~**ty** *n* cruauté *f*.

cruet ['kru:ɪt] *n* huilier *m*; vinaigrier *m*.

cruise [kru:z] *n* croisière *f* // *vi* (*ship*) croiser; (*car*) rouler; (*aircraft*) voler; (*taxi*) être en maraude; ~**r** *n* croiseur *m*.

crumb [krʌm] *n* miette *f*.

crumble ['krʌmbl] *vt* émietter // *vi* s'émietter; (*plaster etc*) s'effriter; (*land, earth*) s'ébouler; (*building*) s'écrouler, crouler; (*fig*) s'effondrer; **crumbly** *a* friable.

crumpet ['krʌmpɪt] *n* petite crêpe (épaisse).

crumple ['krʌmpl] *vt* froisser, friper.

crunch [krʌntʃ] *vt* croquer; (*underfoot*) faire craquer, écraser; faire crisser // *n* (*fig*) instant *m* ou moment *m* critique, moment de vérité; ~**y** *a* croquant(e), croustillant(e).

crusade [kru:'seɪd] *n* croisade *f*.

crush [krʌʃ] *n* foule *f*, cohue *f* // *vt* écraser; (*crumple*) froisser.

crust [krʌst] *n* croûte *f*.

crutch [krʌtʃ] *n* béquille *f*.

crux [krʌks] *n* point crucial.

cry [kraɪ] *vi* pleurer; (*shout: also*: ~ **out**) crier // *n* cri *m*; **to** ~ **off** *vi* se dédire; se décommander.

cryptic ['krɪptɪk] *a* énigmatique.

crystal ['krɪstl] *n* cristal *m*; ~-**clear** *a* clair(e) comme de l'eau de roche.

cub [kʌb] *n* petit *m* (*d'un animal*); (*also*: ~ **scout**) louveteau *m*.

Cuba ['kju:bə] *n* Cuba *m*.

cubbyhole ['kʌbɪhəul] *n* cagibi *m*.

cube [kju:b] *n* cube *m* // *vt* (*MATH*) élever au cube; **cubic** *a* cubique; ~ **metre** *etc* = mètre *m etc* cube; **cubic capacity** *n* cylindrée *f*.

cubicle ['kju:bɪkl] *n* box *m*, cabine *f*.

cuckoo ['kuku:] *n* coucou *m*; ~ **clock** *n* (pendule *f* à) coucou *m*.

cucumber ['kju:kʌmbə*] *n* concombre *m*.

cuddle ['kʌdl] *vt* câliner, caresser // *vi* se blottir l'un contre l'autre.

cue [kju:] *n* (*snooker*) ~ queue *f* de billard; (*THEATRE etc*) signal *m*.

cuff [kʌf] *n* (*Brit: of shirt, coat etc*) poignet *m*, manchette *f*; (*US: of trousers*) revers *m*; **off the** ~ *ad* de chic, à l'improviste; ~**link** *n* bouton *m* de manchette.

cul-de-sac ['kʌldəsæk] *n* cul-de-sac *m*, impasse *f*.

cull [kʌl] *vt* sélectionner.

culminate ['kʌlmɪneɪt] *vi*: **to** ~ **in** finir *ou* se terminer par; (*end in*) mener à; **culmination** ['neɪʃən] *n* point culminant.

culottes [kju:'lɔts] *npl* jupe-culotte *f*.

culpable ['kʌlpəbl] *a* coupable.

culprit ['kʌlprɪt] *n* coupable *m/f*.

cult [kʌlt] *n* culte *m*.

cultivate ['kʌltɪveɪt] *vt* (*also fig*) cultiver; **cultivation** ['veɪʃən] *n* culture *f*.

cultural ['kʌltʃərəl] *a* culturel(le).

culture ['kʌltʃə*] *n* (*also fig*) culture *f*; ~**d** *a* cultivé(e).

cumbersome ['kʌmbəsəm] *a* encombrant(e), embarrassant(e).

cunning [ˈkʌnɪŋ] n ruse f, astuce f // a rusé(e), malin(igne).

cup [kʌp] n tasse f; (prize, event) coupe f; (of bra) bonnet m.

cupboard [ˈkʌbəd] n placard m.

cup-tie [ˈkʌptaɪ] n (Brit) match m de coupe.

curate [ˈkjuərɪt] n vicaire m.

curator [kjuəˈreɪtə*] n conservateur m (d'un musée etc).

curb [kə:b] vt refréner, mettre un frein à // n frein m (fig); (US) = **kerb**.

curdle [ˈkə:dl] vi (se) cailler.

cure [kjuə*] vt guérir; (CULIN) saler; fumer; sécher // n remède m.

curfew [ˈkə:fju:] n couvre-feu m.

curio [ˈkjuərɪəʊ] n bibelot m, curiosité f.

curiosity [kjuərɪˈɒsɪtɪ] n curiosité f.

curious [ˈkjuərɪəs] a curieux(euse).

curl [kə:l] n boucle f (de cheveux) // vt, vi boucler; (tightly) friser; to ~ up s'enrouler; se pelotonner; ~er n bigoudi m, rouleau m.

curly [ˈkə:lɪ] a bouclé(e); frisé(e).

currant [ˈkʌrnt] n raisin m de Corinthe, raisin sec.

currency [ˈkʌrnsɪ] n monnaie f; to gain ~ (fig) s'accréditer.

current [ˈkʌrnt] n courant m // a courant(e); ~ **account** n (Brit) compte courant; ~ **affairs** npl questions fpl d'actualité f; ~**ly** ad actuellement.

curriculum, pl ~s or **curricula** [kəˈrɪkjuləm, -lə] n programme m d'études; ~ **vitae (CV)** n curriculum vitae (C.V.) m.

curry [ˈkʌrɪ] n curry m // vt: to ~ **favour with** chercher à gagner la faveur or à s'attirer les bonnes grâces de.

curse [kə:s] vi jurer, blasphémer // vt maudire // n malédiction f; fléau m.

cursor [ˈkə:sə*] n (COMPUT) curseur m.

cursory [ˈkə:sərɪ] a superficiel(le), hâtif(ive).

curt [kə:t] a brusque, sec(sèche).

curtail [kə:ˈteɪl] vt (visit etc) écour-

ter; (expenses etc) réduire.

curtain [ˈkə:tn] n rideau m.

curts(e)y [ˈkə:tsɪ] n révérence f // vi faire une révérence.

curve [kə:v] n courbe f; (in the road) tournant m, virage m // vi se courber; (road) faire une courbe.

cushion [ˈkuʃən] n coussin m // vt (shock) amortir.

custard [ˈkʌstəd] n (for pouring) crème anglaise.

custodian [kʌsˈtəudɪən] n gardien; ne; (of collection etc) conservateur/trice.

custody [ˈkʌstədɪ] n (of child) garde f; (of offenders) détention préventive.

custom [ˈkʌstəm] n coutume f, usage m; (LAW) droit coutumier, coutume; (COMM) clientèle f; ~**ary** a habituel(le).

customer [ˈkʌstəmə*] n client/e.

customized [ˈkʌstəmaɪzd] a (car etc) construit(e) sur commande.

custom-made [ˈkʌstəmˈmeɪd] a (clothes) fait(e) sur mesure; (other goods) hors série, fait(e) sur commande.

customs [ˈkʌstəmz] npl douane f; ~ **officer** n douanier m.

cut [kʌt] vb (pt, pp cut) vt couper; (meat) découper; (shape, make) tailler; couper; creuser; graver; (reduce) réduire // vi couper; (intersect) se couper // n (gen) coupure f; (of clothes) coupe f; (of jewel) taille f; (in salary etc) réduction f; (of meat) morceau m; to ~ a tooth percer une dent; to ~ **down** vt fus (tree etc) couper, abattre; (reduce: also: ~ **down on**) réduire; to ~ **off** vt couper; (fig) isoler; to ~ **out** vt couper; découper; tailler; to ~ **up** vt (paper, meat) découper; ~**back** n réduction f.

cute [kju:t] a mignon(ne), adorable; (clever) rusé(e), astucieux(euse).

cuticle [ˈkju:tɪkl] n (on nail): ~ **remover** n repousse-peaux m inv.

cutlery [ˈkʌtlərɪ] n couverts mpl.

cutlet ['kʌtlɪt] n côtelette f.

cut: ~**out** n coupe-circuit m inv; (cardboard ~) découpage m; ~ **price,** (US) ~**rate** a au rabais, à prix réduit; ~ **throat** n assassin m // a acharné(e).

cutting ['kʌtɪŋ] a tranchant(e), coupant(e); (fig) cinglant(e), mordant(e) // n (Brit: from newspaper) coupure f (de journal).

CV n abbr of **curriculum vitae**.

cwt abbr of **hundredweight(s)**.

cyanide ['saɪənaɪd] n cyanure m.

cycle ['saɪkl] n cycle m // vi faire de la bicyclette.

cycling ['saɪklɪŋ] n cyclisme m.

cyclist ['saɪklɪst] n cycliste m/f.

cygnet ['sɪgnɪt] n jeune cygne m.

cylinder ['sɪlɪndə*] n cylindre m; ~**head gasket** n joint m de culasse.

cymbals ['sɪmblz] npl cymbales fpl.

cynic ['sɪnɪk] n cynique m/f; ~**al** a cynique; ~**ism** ['sɪnɪsɪzəm] n cynisme m.

Cypriot ['sɪprɪət] a cypriote, chypriote // n Cypriote m/f, Chypriote m/f.

Cyprus ['saɪprəs] n Chypre f.

cyst [sɪst] n kyste m.

cystitis [sɪs'taɪtɪs] n cystite f.

czar [za:*] n tsar m.

Czech [tʃɛk] a tchèque // n Tchèque m/f; (LING) tchèque m.

Czechoslovakia [tʃɛkəslə'vækɪə] n Tchécoslovaquie f; ~**n** a tchécoslovaque // n Tchécoslovaque m/f.

D

D [di:] n (MUS) ré m.

dab [dæb] vt (eyes, wound) tamponner; (paint, cream) appliquer (par petites touches or rapidement).

dabble ['dæbl] vi: to ~ **in** faire or se mêler or s'occuper un peu de.

dad, daddy [dæd, 'dædɪ] n papa m.

daffodil ['dæfədɪl] n jonquille f.

daft [dɑ:ft] a idiot(e), stupide.

dagger ['dægə*] n poignard m.

daily ['deɪlɪ] a quotidien(ne), journalier(ère) // n quotidien m // ad tous les jours.

dainty ['deɪntɪ] a délicat(e), mignon(ne).

dairy ['dɛərɪ] n (shop) crèmerie f, laiterie f; (on farm) laiterie // a laitier(ère); ~ **produce** n produits laitiers.

dais ['deɪɪs] n estrade f.

daisy ['deɪzɪ] n pâquerette f; ~ **wheel** n (on printer) marguerite f.

dale [deɪl] n vallon m.

dam [dæm] n barrage m // vt endiguer.

damage ['dæmɪdʒ] n dégâts mpl, dommages mpl; (fig) tort m // vt endommager, abîmer; (fig) faire du tort à; ~**s** npl (LAW) dommages-intérêts mpl.

damn [dæm] vt condamner; (curse) maudire // n (col): **I don't give a** ~ je m'en fous // a (col: also: ~**ed**): **this** ~ ... ce sacré or foutu ...; ~ **(it)!** zut!

damp [dæmp] a humide // n humidité f // vt (also: ~**en:** cloth, rag) humecter; (enthusiasm etc) refroidir.

damson ['dæmzən] n prune f de Damas.

dance [dɑ:ns] n danse f; (ball) bal m // vi danser; ~ **hall** n salle f de bal, dancing m; ~**r** n danseur/euse.

dancing ['dɑ:nsɪŋ] n danse f.

dandelion ['dændɪlaɪən] n pissenlit m.

dandruff ['dændrəf] n pellicules fpl.

Dane [deɪn] n Danois/e.

danger ['deɪndʒə*] n danger m; **there is a** ~ **of fire** il y a (un) risque d'incendie; **in** ~ en danger; **he was in** ~ **of falling** il risquait de tomber; ~**ous** a dangereux(euse).

dangle ['dæŋgl] vt balancer; (fig) faire miroiter // vi pendre, se balancer.

Danish ['deɪnɪʃ] a danois(e) // n (LING) danois m.

dapper ['dæpə*] a pimpant(e).

dare [dɛə*] vt: **to ~ sb to do** défier qn or mettre qn au défi de faire // vi: **to ~ (to) do sth** oser faire qch; **I ~ say** (*I suppose*) il est probable (que); **~devil** n casse-cou m inv.

daring a hardi(e), audacieux(euse) // n audace f, hardiesse f.

dark [dɑːk] a (*night, room*) obscur(e), sombre; (*colour, complexion*) foncé(e), sombre; (*fig*) sombre // n: **in the ~** dans le noir; **in the ~ about** (*fig*) ignorant tout de; **after ~** après la tombée de la nuit; **~en** vt obscurcir, assombrir // vi s'obscurcir, s'assombrir; **~ glasses** npl lunettes noires; **~ness** n obscurité f; **~ room** n chambre noire.

darling [dɑːlɪŋ] a, n chéri(e).

darn [dɑːn] vt repriser.

dart [dɑːt] n fléchette f // vi: **to ~ towards** se précipiter or s'élancer vers; **to ~ away/along** partir/passer comme une flèche; **~s** n jeu m de fléchettes; **~board** n cible f (de jeu de fléchettes).

dash [dæʃ] n (*sign*) tiret m; (*small quantity*) goutte f, larme f // vt (*missile*) jeter or lancer violemment; (*hopes*) anéantir // vi: **to ~ towards** se précipiter or se ruer vers; **to ~ away** or **off** vi partir à toute allure.

dashboard [dæʃbɔːd] n (*AUT*) tableau m de bord.

dashing [dæʃɪŋ] a fringant(e).

data [deɪtə] npl données fpl; **~ base** n base f de données; **~ processing** n traitement m (électronique) de l'information.

date [deɪt] n date f; rendez-vous m; (*fruit*) datte f // vt dater; **~ of birth** date de naissance; **to ~** ad à ce jour; **out of ~** périmé(e); **up to ~** à la page; mis(e) à jour; moderne; **~d** a démodé(e).

daub [dɔːb] vt barbouiller.

daughter [dɔːtə*] n fille f; **~in-law** n belle-fille f, bru f.

daunting [dɔːntɪŋ] a intimidant(e), décourageant(e).

dawdle [dɔːdl] vi traîner, lambiner.

dawn [dɔːn] n aube f, aurore f // vi (*day*) se lever, poindre; (*fig*) naître, se faire jour; **it ~ed on him that ...** il lui vint à l'esprit que ...

day [deɪ] n jour m; (*as duration*) journée f; (*period of time, age*) époque f, temps m; **the ~ before** la veille, le jour précédent; **the ~ after, the following ~** le lendemain, le jour suivant; **the ~ after tomorrow** après-demain; **the ~ before yesterday** avant-hier; **by ~** de jour; **~break** n point m du jour; **~dream** vi rêver (tout éveillé); **~light** n (lumière f du) jour m; **~ return** n (*Brit*) billet m d'aller-retour (valable pour la journée); **~time** n jour m, journée f; **~-to-~** a journalier(ère).

daze [deɪz] vt (*subj: drug*) hébéter; (: *blow*) étourdir // n: **in a ~** hébété(e); étourdi(e).

dazzle [dæzl] vt éblouir, aveugler.

DC abbr = *direct current* courant continu.

deacon [diːkən] n diacre m.

dead [dɛd] a mort(e); (*numb*) engourdi(e), insensible // ad absolument, complètement; **he was shot ~** il a été tué d'un coup de revolver; **on time** à l'heure pile; **~ tired** éreinté(e), complètement fourbu(e); **to stop ~** s'arrêter pile or net; **the ~ les morts; ~en** vt (*blow, sound*) amortir; (*make numb*) endormir, rendre insensible; **~ end** n impasse f; **~ heat** n (*SPORT*): **to finish in a ~ heat** terminer ex-aequo; **~line** n date f or heure f limite; **~lock** n impasse f (*fig*); **~ loss** n: **to be a ~ loss** (*col: person*) n'être bon(bonne) à rien; (*thing*) ne rien valoir; **~ly** a mortel(le); (*weapon*) meurtrier(ère); **~pan** a impassible.

deaf [dɛf] a sourd(e); **~en** vt rendre sourd; (*fig*) assourdir; **~ness** n surdité f; **~-mute** n sourd/e-muet/te.

deal [diːl] n affaire f, marché m // vt (*pt, pp* **dealt** [dɛlt]) (*blow*) porter; (*cards*) donner, distribuer; **a great**

~ (of) beaucoup (de); **to ~ in** vt fus faire le commerce de; **to ~ with** vt fus (COMM) traiter avec; (handle) s'occuper ou se charger de; (be about: book etc) traiter de; **~er** n marchand m; **~ings** npl (COMM) transactions fpl; (relations) relations fpl, rapports mpl.

dean [di:n] n (REL, Brit SCOL) doyen m; (US SCOL) conseiller/ère (principal(e)) d'éducation.

dear [dɪə*] a cher(chère); (expensive) cher, coûteux(euse) // n: **my ~** mon cher/ma chère; **~ me!** mon Dieu!; **D~ Sir/Madam** (in letter) Monsieur/Madame; **~ly** ad (love) tendrement; (pay) cher.

death [dɛθ] n mort f; (ADMIN) décès m; **~ certificate** n acte m de décès; **~ duties** npl (Brit) droits mpl de succession; **~ly** a de mort; **~ penalty** n peine f de mort; **~ rate** n (taux m de) mortalité f.

debar [dɪ'bɑ:*] vt: **to ~ sb from doing** interdire à qn de faire.

debase [dɪ'beɪs] vt (currency) déprécier, dévaloriser; (person) abaisser, avilir.

debate [dɪ'beɪt] n discussion f, débat m // vt discuter, débattre.

debit ['dɛbɪt] n débit m // vt: **to ~ a sum to sb or to sb's account** porter une somme au débit de qn, débiter qn d'une somme.

debt [dɛt] n dette f; **to be in ~** avoir des dettes, être endetté(e); **~or** n débiteur/trice.

debunk [dɪ'bʌŋk] vt (theory, claim) montrer le ridicule de.

decade ['dɛkeɪd] n décennie f, décade f.

decadence ['dɛkədəns] n décadence f.

decaffeinated [dɪ'kæfɪneɪtɪd] a décaféiné(e).

decanter [dɪ'kæntə*] n carafe f.

decay [dɪ'keɪ] n décomposition f, pourrissement m; (fig) déclin m, délabrement m; (also: **tooth ~**) carie f (dentaire) // vi (rot) se décomposer,

pourrir; (fig) se délabrer; décliner; se détériorer.

deceased [dɪ'si:st] n défunt/e.

deceit [dɪ'si:t] n tromperie f, supercherie f; **~ful** a trompeur(euse).

deceive [dɪ'si:v] vt tromper.

December [dɪ'sɛmbə*] n décembre m.

decent ['di:sənt] a décent(e), convenable; **they were very ~ about it** ils se sont montrés très chics.

deception [dɪ'sɛpʃən] n tromperie f.

deceptive [dɪ'sɛptɪv] a trompeur(euse).

decide [dɪ'saɪd] vt (person) décider; (question, argument) trancher, régler // vi se décider, décider; **to ~ to do/ that** décider de faire/que; **to ~ on** décider, se décider pour; **~d** a (resolute) résolu(e), décidé(e); (clear, definite) net(te), marqué(e); **~dly** [-dɪdlɪ] ad résolument; incontestablement, nettement.

deciduous [dɪ'sɪdjuəs] a à feuilles caduques.

decimal ['dɛsɪməl] a décimal(e) // n décimale f; **~ point** n ≈ virgule f.

decipher [dɪ'saɪfə*] vt déchiffrer.

decision [dɪ'sɪʒən] n décision f.

decisive [dɪ'saɪsɪv] a décisif(ive).

deck [dɛk] n (NAUT) pont m; (of bus): **top ~** impériale f; (of cards) jeu m; **~chair** n chaise longue.

declaration [dɛklə'reɪʃən] n déclaration f.

declare [dɪ'klɛə*] vt déclarer.

decline [dɪ'klaɪn] n (decay) déclin m; (lessening) baisse f // vt refuser, décliner // vi décliner; être en baisse, baisser.

decorate ['dɛkəreɪt] vt (adorn, give a medal to) décorer; (paint and paper) peindre et tapisser; **decoration** [-'reɪʃən] n (medal etc, adornment) décoration f; **decorator** n peintre m en bâtiment.

decoy ['di:kɔɪ] n piège m.

decrease n ['di:kri:s] diminution f // vt, vi [di:'kri:s] diminuer.

decree [dɪ'kri:] n (POL, REL) décret

m; *(LAW)* arrêt m, jugement m; ~ **nisi** n jugement m provisoire de divorce.

dedicate ['dedikeit] *vt* consacrer; *(book etc)* dédier.

dedication [dedi'keiʃən] n *(devotion)* dévouement m.

deduce [di'dju:s] *vt* déduire, conclure.

deduct [di'dʌkt] *vt*: **to ~ sth (from)** déduire qch (de), retrancher qch (de); *(from wage etc)* prélever qch (sur), retenir qch (sur); **~ion** [di'dʌkʃən] n *(deducting, deducing)* déduction f; *(from wage etc)* prélèvement m, retenue f.

deed [di:d] n action f, acte m; *(LAW)* acte notarié, contrat m.

deep [di:p] a *(water, sigh, sorrow, thoughts)* profond(e); *(voice)* grave; **4 metres ~** de 4 mètres de profondeur // *ad*: **spectators stood 20 ~** il y avait 20 rangs de spectateurs; **~en** *vt (hole)* approfondir // *vi (s'approfondir; (darkness)* s'épaissir; **~-freeze** vt congélateur m // vt congeler; **~-fry** vt faire frire (en friteuse); **~ly** *ad (breathe)* profondément; *(interested, moved)* vivement; *(grateful)* profondément, infiniment; **~-sea diving** n plongée sous-marine.

deer [diə*] n *(pl inv)*: **the ~** les cervidés mpl *(ZOOL)*; **(red) ~** cerf m; **(fallow) ~** daim m; **(roe) ~** chevreuil m.

deface [di'feis] *vt* dégrader; barbouiller; rendre illisible.

default [di'fɔ:lt] *vi (LAW)* faire défaut; *(gen)* manquer à ses engagements // n *(COMPUT: also: ~ value)* valeur f par défaut; **by ~** *(LAW)* par défaut, par contumace; *(SPORT)* par forfait.

defeat [di'fi:t] n défaite f // *vt (team, opponents)* battre; *(fig: plans, efforts)* faire échouer.

defect n ['di:fekt] défaut m // *vi* [di'fekt]: **to ~ to the enemy** passer à l'ennemi; **~ive** [di'fektiv] a défec-

tueux(euse).

defence [di'fens] n défense f; **in ~ of** pour défendre; **~less** a sans défense.

defend [di'fend] *vt* défendre; **~ant** n défendeur/deresse; *(in criminal case)* accusé/e, prévenu/e; **~er** n défenseur m.

defense [di'fens] n *(US)* = **defence**.

defer [di'fə:*] *vt (postpone)* différer, ajourner // *vi*: **to ~ to** déférer à, s'en remettre à.

defiance [di'faiəns] n défi m; **in ~** of au mépris de.

defiant [di'faiənt] a provocant(e), de défi; *(person)* rebelle, intraitable.

deficiency [di'fiʃənsi] n insuffisance f, déficience f; carence f.

deficit ['defisit] n déficit m.

defile vb [di'fail] *vt* souiller // *vi* défiler // n ['di:fail] défilé m.

define [di'fain] *vt* définir.

definite ['definit] a *(fixed)* défini(e), (bien) déterminé(e); *(clear, obvious)* net(te), manifeste; **he was ~ about** it il a été catégorique sur ce point; **~ly** *ad* sans aucun doute.

definition [defi'niʃən] n définition f.

deflate [di:'fleit] *vt* dégonfler.

deflect [di'flekt] *vt* détourner, faire dévier.

deformed [di'fɔ:md] a difforme.

defraud [di'frɔ:d] *vt* frauder; **to ~ sb of sth** escroquer qch à qn.

defrost [di:'frɒst] *vt (fridge)* dégivrer; *(US: demister)* dispositif m anti-buée *inv.*

deft [deft] a adroit(e), preste.

defunct [di'fʌŋkt] a défunt(e).

defuse [di:'fju:z] *vt* désamorcer.

defy [di'fai] *vt* défier; *(efforts etc)* résister à.

degenerate *vi* [di'dʒenəreit] dégénérer // a [di'dʒenərit] dégénéré(e).

degree [di'gri:] n degré m; grade m (universitaire); **a (first) ~ in maths** une licence en maths; **by ~s** *(gradually)* par degrés; **to some ~** jusqu'à un certain point, dans une certaine mesure.

dehydrated [di:har'dreitid] a déshydraté(e); (milk, eggs) en poudre.

de-ice [di:'aɪs] vt (windscreen) dégivrer.

deign [deɪn] vi: to ~ to do daigner faire.

deity ['di:ɪtɪ] n divinité f; dieu m, déesse f.

dejected [dɪ'dʒektɪd] a abattu(e), déprimé(e).

delay [dɪ'leɪ] vt retarder // vi s'attarder // n délai m, retard m.

delectable [dɪ'lektəbl] a délicieux(euse).

delegate n ['delɪgɪt] délégué/e // vt ['delɪgeɪt] déléguer.

delete [dɪ'li:t] vt rayer, supprimer.

deliberate a [dɪ'lɪbərɪt] (intentional) délibéré(e); (slow) mesuré(e) // vi [dɪ'lɪbəreɪt] délibérer, réfléchir; ~ly ad (on purpose) exprès, délibérément.

delicacy ['delɪkəsɪ] n délicatesse f; (food) mets fin or délicat, friandise f.

delicate ['delɪkɪt] a délicat(e).

delicatessen [delɪkə'tesn] n épicerie fine.

delicious [dɪ'lɪʃəs] a délicieux(euse).

delight [dɪ'laɪt] n (grande) joie, grand plaisir // vt enchanter; to ~ in prendre grand plaisir à // vt enchanter; ~ed a: ~ed (at or with/to do) ravi(e) (de/de faire); ~ful a adorable, merveilleux(euse); délicieux(euse).

delinquent [dɪ'lɪŋkwənt] a, n délinquant(e).

delirious [dɪ'lɪrɪəs] a: to be ~ délirer.

deliver [dɪ'lɪvə*] vt (mail) distribuer; (goods) livrer; (message) remettre; (speech) prononcer; (warning, ultimatum) lancer; (free) délivrer; (MED) accoucher; ~y n distribution f; livraison f; (of speaker) élocution f; (MED) accouchement m.

delude [dɪ'lu:d] vt tromper, leurrer.

delusion [dɪ'lu:ʒən] n illusion f.

delve [delv] vi: to ~ into fouiller dans.

demand [dɪ'mɑ:nd] vt réclamer, exiger // n exigence f; (claim) revendication f; (ECON) demande f; in ~ demandé(e), recherché(e); on ~ sur demande; ~ing a (boss) exigeant(e); (work) astreignant(e).

demean [dɪ'mi:n] vt: to ~ o.s. s'abaisser.

demeanour, (US) **demeanor** [dɪ'mi:nə*] n comportement m; maintien m.

demented [dɪ'mentɪd] a dément(e), fou(folle).

demise [dɪ'maɪz] n décès m.

demister [di:'mɪstə*] n (AUT) dispositif m anti-buée inv.

demo ['demau] n abbr (col: = demonstration) manif f.

democracy [dɪ'mɔkrəsɪ] n démocratie f.

democrat ['deməkræt] n démocrate m/f; ~ic [deməʊ'krætɪk] a démocratique.

demolish [dɪ'mɔlɪʃ] vt démolir.

demonstrate ['demənstreɪt] vt démontrer, prouver // vi: to ~ (for/against) manifester (en faveur de/contre); **demonstration** [-'streɪʃən] n démonstration f, manifestation f; **demonstrator** n (POL) manifestant/e.

demote [dɪ'məut] vt rétrograder.

demure [dɪ'mjuə*] a sage, réservé(e); d'une modestie affectée.

den [den] n tanière f, antre m.

denatured alcohol [di:'neɪtʃəd-] n (US) alcool m à brûler.

denial [dɪ'naɪəl] n démenti m; dénégation f.

denim ['denɪm] n coton émerisé; ~s npl (blue-)jeans mpl.

Denmark ['denmɑ:k] n Danemark m.

denomination [dɪnɔmɪ'neɪʃən] n (money) valeur f; (REL) confession f; culte m.

denounce [dɪ'nauns] vt dénoncer.

dense [dens] a dense; (stupid) obtus(e), dur(e) or lent(e) à la compre-nette.

density ['densɪtɪ] n densité f.

dent [dent] n bosse f // vt (also:

make a ~ **in** cabosser.

dental ['dɛntl] *a* dentaire; ~ **sur-geon** *n* (chirurgien/ne) dentiste.

dentist ['dɛntɪst] *n* dentiste *m/f*; ~**ry** *n* art *m* dentaire.

denture(s) ['dɛntʃə(z)] *n(pl)* dentier *m*.

deny [dɪ'naɪ] *vt* nier; (*refuse*) refuser.

deodorant [diː'əʊdərənt] *n* désodorisant *m*, déodorant *m*.

depart [dɪ'pɑːt] *vi* partir; to ~ **from** (*fig: differ from*) s'écarter de.

department [dɪ'pɑːtmənt] *n* (*COMM*) rayon *m*; (*SCOL*) section *f*; (*POL*) ministère *m*, département *m*; ~ **store** *n* grand magasin.

departure [dɪ'pɑːtʃə*] *n* départ *m*; (*fig*): ~ **from** écart *m* par rapport à; **a new** ~ une nouvelle voie; ~ **lounge** *n* (*at airport*) salle *f* de départ.

depend [dɪ'pɛnd] *vi*: to ~ **on** dépendre de; (*rely on*) compter sur; it ~**s** cela dépend; ~**ing on the result** ... selon le résultat ...; ~**able** *a* sûr(e), digne de confiance; ~**ant** *n* personne *f* à charge; ~**ent** *a*: to be ~**ent** (**on**) dépendre (de) // *n* = ~**ant**.

depict [dɪ'pɪkt] *vt* (*in picture*) représenter; (*in words*) (dé)peindre, décrire.

depleted [dɪ'pliːtɪd] *a* (considérablement) réduit(e) or diminué(e).

deploy [dɪ'plɔɪ] *vt* déployer.

deport [dɪ'pɔːt] *vt* déporter; expulser.

deportment [dɪ'pɔːtmənt] *n* maintien *m*, tenue *f*.

deposit [dɪ'pɔzɪt] *n* (*CHEM, COMM, GEO*) dépôt *m*; (*of ore, oil*) gisement *m*; (*part payment*) arrhes *fpl*, acompte *m*; (*on bottle etc*) consigne *f*; (*for hired goods etc*) cautionnement *m*, garantie *f* // *vt* déposer; mettre or laisser en dépôt; fournir or donner un acompte; laisser en garantie; ~ **account** *n* compte *m* de dépôt.

depot ['dɛpəʊ] *n* dépôt *m*.

depress [dɪ'prɛs] *vt* déprimer; (*press down*) appuyer sur, abaisser; ~**ed** *a* (*person*) déprimé(e), abattu(e); (*area*) en déclin, touché(e) par le sous-emploi; ~**ing** *a* déprimant(e); ~**ion** [dɪ'prɛʃən] *n* dépression *f*.

deprivation [dɛprɪ'veɪʃən] *n* privation *f*; (*loss*) perte *f*.

deprive [dɪ'praɪv] *vt*: to ~ **sb of** priver qn de; enlever à qn; ~**d** *a* déshérité(e).

depth [dɛpθ] *n* profondeur *f*; **in the** ~**s of** au fond de; au cœur de; au plus profond de.

deputize ['dɛpjʊtaɪz] *vi*: to ~ **for** assurer l'intérim de.

deputy ['dɛpjʊtɪ] *a*: ~ **head** directeur adjoint, sous-directeur *m* // *n* (*replacement*) suppléant(e), intérimaire *m/f*; (*second in command*) adjoint•e.

derail [dɪ'reɪl] *vt*: to be ~**ed** dérailler.

derby ['dɜːbɪ] *n* (*US: bowler hat*) (chapeau *m*) melon *m*.

derelict ['dɛrɪlɪkt] *a* abandonné(e), à l'abandon.

deride [dɪ'raɪd] *vt* railler.

derisory [dɪ'raɪsərɪ] *a* (*sum*) dérisoire; (*smile, person*) moqueur(euse).

derive [dɪ'raɪv] *vt*: to ~ **sth from** tirer qch de; trouver qch dans // *vi*: to ~ **from** provenir de, dériver de.

derogatory [dɪ'rɒgətərɪ] *a* désobligeant(e); péjoratif(ive).

derv [dɜːv] *n* (*Brit*) gas-oil *m*.

descend [dɪ'sɛnd] *vt, vi* descendre; to ~ **from** descendre de, être issu de.

descent [dɪ'sɛnt] *n* descente *f*; (*origin*) origine *f*.

describe [dɪs'kraɪb] *vt* décrire; **description** [-'krɪpʃən] *n* description *f*; (*sort*) sorte *f*, espèce *f*.

desecrate ['dɛsɪkreɪt] *vt* profaner.

desert *n* ['dɛzət] désert *m* // *vb* [dɪ'zɜːt] *vt* déserter, abandonner // *vi* (*MIL*) déserter; ~**er** *n* déserteur *m*;

~ **island** *n* île déserte; ~**s** *npl*: **to get one's just** ~**s** n'avoir que ce qu'on mérite.

deserve [dɪ'zə:v] *vt* mériter; **deserving** *a* (*person*) méritant(e); (*action, cause*) méritoire.

design [dɪ'zaɪn] *n* (*sketch*) plan *m*, dessin *m*; (*layout, shape*) conception *f*, ligne *f*; (*pattern*) dessin *m*, motif(s) *m(pl)*; (*COMM*) esthétique industrielle; (*intention*) dessein *m* // *vt* dessiner; concevoir; **to have** ~**s on** avoir des visées sur.

designer [dɪ'zaɪnə*] *n* (*ART, TECH*) dessinateur/trice; (*fashion*) modéliste *m/f*.

desire [dɪ'zaɪə*] *n* désir *m* // *vt* désirer, vouloir.

desk [dɛsk] *n* (*in office*) bureau *m*; (*for pupil*) pupitre *m*; (*Brit: in shop, restaurant*) caisse *f*; (*in hotel, at airport*) réception *f*.

desolate ['dɛsəlɪt] *a* désolé(e).

despair [dɪs'pɛə*] *n* désespoir *m* // *vi*: **to** ~ **of** désespérer de.

despatch [dɪs'pætʃ] *n*, *vt* = **dispatch**.

desperate ['dɛspərɪt] *a* désespéré(e); (*fugitive*) prêt(e) à tout; ~**ly** *ad* désespérément; (*very*) terriblement, extrêmement.

desperation [dɛspə'reɪʃən] *n* désespoir *m*; **in** ~ à bout de nerf; en désespoir de cause.

despicable [dɪs'pɪkəbl] *a* méprisable.

despise [dɪs'paɪz] *vt* mépriser, dédaigner.

despite [dɪs'paɪt] *prep* malgré, en dépit de.

despondent [dɪs'pɔndənt] *a* découragé(e), abattu(e).

dessert [dɪ'zə:t] *n* dessert *m*; ~**spoon** *n* cuiller *f* à dessert.

destination [dɛstɪ'neɪʃən] *n* destination *f*.

destiny ['dɛstɪnɪ] *n* destinée *f*, destin *m*.

destitute ['dɛstɪtju:t] *a* indigent(e).

destroy [dɪs'trɔɪ] *vt* détruire; ~**er** *n*

(*NAUT*) contre-torpilleur *m*.

destruction [dɪs'trʌkʃən] *n* destruction *f*.

detach [dɪ'tætʃ] *vt* détacher; ~**ed** *a* (*attitude*) détaché(e); ~**ed house** *n* pavillon *m*, maison(nette) (individuelle); ~**ment** *n* (*MIL*) détachement *m*; (*fig*) détachement, indifférence *f*.

detail ['di:teɪl] *n* détail *m* // *vt* raconter en détail, énumérer; **in** ~ en détail; ~**ed** *a* détaillé(e).

detain [dɪ'teɪn] *vt* retenir; (*in captivity*) détenir; (*in hospital*) hospitaliser.

detect [dɪ'tɛkt] *vt* déceler, percevoir; (*MED, POLICE*) dépister; (*MIL, RADAR, TECH*) détecter; ~**ion** [dɪ'tɛkʃən] *n* découverte *f*; dépistage *m*; détection *f*; ~**ive** *n* agent *m* de la sûreté, policier *m*; **private** ~**ive** détective privé; ~**ive story** *n* roman policier.

detention [dɪ'tɛnʃən] *n* détention *f*; (*SCOL*) retenue *f*, consigne *f*.

deter [dɪ'tə:*] *vt* dissuader.

detergent [dɪ'tə:dʒənt] *n* détersif *m*, détergent *m*.

deteriorate [dɪ'tɪərɪəreɪt] *vi* se détériorer, se dégrader.

determine [dɪ'tə:mɪn] *vt* déterminer; **to** ~ **to do** résoudre de faire, se déterminer à faire; ~**d** *a* (*person*) déterminé(e).

deterrent [dɪ'tɛrənt] *n* effet *m* de dissuasion; force *f* de dissuasion.

detour ['di:tuə*] *n* détour *m*; (*US AUT: diversion*) déviation *f*.

detract [dɪ'trækt] *vi*: **to** ~ **from** (*quality, pleasure*) diminuer; (*reputation*) porter atteinte à.

detriment ['dɛtrɪmənt] *n*: **to the** ~ **of** au détriment de, au préjudice de; ~**al** [dɛtrɪ'mɛntl] *a*: ~**al to** préjudiciable *or* nuisible à.

devaluation [dɪvælju'eɪʃən] *n* dévaluation *f*.

devastating ['dɛvəsteɪtɪŋ] *a* dévastateur(trice).

develop [dɪ'vɛləp] *vt* (*gen*) développer; (*habit*) contracter; (*resources*) mettre en valeur, exploiter // *vi* se développer; (*situation, disease: evolve*) évoluer; (*facts, symptoms: appear*) se manifester, se produire; ~**ing country** pays m en voie de développement; ~**ment** n développement m; (*of affair, case*) rebondissement m, fait(s) nouveau(x).

device [dɪ'vaɪs] n (*apparatus*) engin m, dispositif m.

devil [ˈdɛvl] n diable m; démon m.

devious [ˈdiːvɪəs] a (*means*) détourné(e); (*person*) sournois(e), dissimulé(e).

devise [dɪ'vaɪz] vt imaginer, concevoir.

devoid [dɪ'vɔɪd] a: ~ **of** dépourvu(e) de, dénué(e) de.

devolution [diːvəˈluːʃən] n (POL) décentralisation f.

devote [dɪ'vəut] vt: **to** ~ **sth to** consacrer qch à; ~**d** a dévoué(e); **to be** ~**d to** (*book etc*) être consacré à; ~**e** [dɪvəuˈtiː] n (REL) adepte m/f; (MUS, SPORT) fervent(e).

devotion [dɪ'vəuʃən] n dévouement m, attachement m; (REL) dévotion f, piété f.

devour [dɪ'vauə*] vt dévorer.

devout [dɪ'vaut] a pieux(euse), dévot(e).

dew [djuː] n rosée f.

DHSS n abbr (Brit: = Department of Health and Social Security) ≈ ministère de la Santé et de la Sécurité Sociale.

diabetes [daɪəˈbiːtiːz] n diabète m; **diabetic** [-ˈbɛtɪk] a, n diabétique (m/f).

diabolical [daɪəˈbɒlɪkl] a (col: weather) atroce; (: behaviour) infernal(e).

diagnosis, pl **diagnoses** [daɪəgˈnəusɪs, -siːz] n diagnostic m.

diagonal [daɪˈægənl] a diagonal(e) // n diagonale f.

diagram [ˈdaɪəgræm] n diagramme m, schéma m; graphique m.

dial [ˈdaɪəl] n cadran m // vt (num-

ber) faire, composer.

dialect [ˈdaɪəlɛkt] n dialecte m.

dialling: ~ **code** (US) **dial**, **code** n indicatif m (téléphonique); ~ **tone**, (US) **dial tone** n tonalité f.

dialogue [ˈdaɪəlɒg] n dialogue m.

diameter [daɪˈæmɪtə*] n diamètre m.

diamond [ˈdaɪəmənd] n diamant m; (shape) losange m; ~**s** npl (CARDS) carreau m.

diaper [ˈdaɪəpə*] n (US) couche f.

diaphragm [ˈdaɪəfræm] n diaphragme m.

diarrhoea, (US) **diarrhea** [daɪəˈriːə] n diarrhée f.

diary [ˈdaɪərɪ] n (daily account) journal m; (book) agenda m.

dice [daɪs] n (pl inv) dé m // vt (CULIN) couper en dés or en cubes.

dictate [dɪkˈteɪt] vt dicter // n [ˈdɪkteɪt] injonction f.

dictation [dɪkˈteɪʃən] n dictée f.

dictator [dɪkˈteɪtə*] n dictateur m; ~**ship** n dictature f.

dictionary [ˈdɪkʃənrɪ] n dictionnaire m.

did [dɪd] pt of **do**.

didn't = **did not**.

die [daɪ] vi mourir; **to be dying for sth** avoir une envie folle de qch; **to be dying to do sth** mourir d'envie de faire qch; **to** ~ **away** vi s'éteindre; **to** ~ **down** vi se calmer, s'apaiser; **to** ~ **out** vi disparaître, s'éteindre.

diehard [ˈdaɪhɑːd] n réactionnaire m/f, jusqu'au-boutiste m/f.

Diesel [ˈdiːzəl]: ~ **engine** n moteur m diesel; ~ (**oil**) n carburant m diesel.

diet [ˈdaɪət] n alimentation f; (restricted food) régime m // vi (also: **be on a** ~) suivre un régime.

differ [ˈdɪfə*] vi: **to** ~ **from** sth être différent de; différer de; **to** ~ **from sb over sth** ne pas être d'accord avec qn au sujet de qch; ~**ence** n différence f; (quarrel) différend m, désaccord m; ~**ent** a différent(e); ~**entiate** [-ˈrɛnʃɪeɪt] vi se différencier; to ~**entiate between** faire une différence entre.

difficult ['dɪfɪkəlt] a difficile; ~**y** n difficulté f.

diffident ['dɪfɪdənt] a qui manque de confiance or d'assurance.

dig [dɪg] vt (pt, pp **dug**) (hole) creuser; (garden) bêcher // n (prod) coup m de coude; (fig) coup de griffe or de patte; **to** ~ **in** vi (MIL: also: o.s. **in**) se retrancher; (col: eat) attaquer un repas etc); **to** ~ **into** (snow, soil) creuser; **to** ~ **one's nails into** enfoncer ses ongles dans; **to** ~ **up** vt déterrer.

digest vt [daɪ'dʒɛst] digérer // n ['daɪdʒɛst] sommaire m, résumé m; ~**ion** [dɪ'dʒɛstʃən] n digestion f.

digit ['dɪdʒɪt] n chiffre m (de 0 à 9); (finger) doigt m; ~**al** a digital(e); à affichage numérique or digital.

dignified ['dɪgnɪfaɪd] a digne.

dignity ['dɪgnɪtɪ] n dignité f.

digress [daɪ'grɛs] vi: **to** ~ **from** s'écarter de, s'éloigner de.

digs [dɪgz] npl (Brit col) piaule f, chambre meublée.

dilapidated [dɪ'læpɪdeɪtɪd] a délabré(e).

dilemma [daɪ'lɛmə] n dilemme m.

diligent ['dɪlɪdʒənt] a appliqué(e), assidu(e).

dilute [daɪ'lu:t] vt diluer.

dim [dɪm] a (light, eyesight) faible; (memory, outline) vague, indécis(e); (stupid) borné(e), obtus(e) // vt (light) réduire, baisser.

dime [daɪm] n (US) = 10 cents.

dimension [daɪ'mɛnʃən] n dimension f.

diminish [dɪ'mɪnɪʃ] vt, vi diminuer.

diminutive [dɪ'mɪnjutɪv] a minuscule, tout(e) petit(e).

dimmers ['dɪməz] npl (US AUT) phares mpl code inv; feux mpl de position.

dimple ['dɪmpl] n fossette f.

din [dɪn] n vacarme m.

dine [daɪn] vi dîner; ~**r** n (person) dîneur/euse; (RAIL) = **dining car**.

dinghy ['dɪŋgɪ] n youyou m; (also: **rubber** ~) canot m pneumatique; (also: **sailing** ~) voilier m, dériveur m.

dingy ['dɪndʒɪ] a miteux(euse), minable.

dining ['daɪnɪŋ] cpd: ~ **car** n (Brit) wagon-restaurant m; ~ **room** n salle f à manger.

dinner ['dɪnə*] n dîner m; (public) banquet m; ~'**s ready!** à table!; ~ **jacket** n smoking m; ~ **party** n dîner m; ~ **time** n heure f du dîner.

dint [dɪnt] n: **by** ~ **of** (doing) à force de (faire).

dip [dɪp] n déclivité f; (in sea) baignade f, bain m // vt tremper, plonger; (Brit AUT: lights) mettre en code, baisser // vi plonger.

diploma [dɪ'pləumə] n diplôme m.

diplomacy [dɪ'pləuməsɪ] n diplomatie f.

diplomat ['dɪpləmæt] n diplomate m; ~**ic** [dɪplə'mætɪk] a diplomatique.

dipstick ['dɪpstɪk] n (AUT) jauge f de niveau d'huile.

dire [daɪə*] a terrible, extrême, affreux(euse).

direct [daɪ'rɛkt] a direct(e) // vt diriger, adresser; **can you** ~ **me to ...?** pouvez-vous m'indiquer le chemin de ...?

direction [dɪ'rɛkʃən] n direction f; **sense of** ~ sens m de l'orientation; ~**s** npl (advice) indications fpl; ~**s for use** mode m d'emploi.

directly [dɪ'rɛktlɪ] ad (in straight line) directement, tout droit; (at once) tout de suite, immédiatement.

director [dɪ'rɛktə*] n directeur m; administrateur m; (THEATRE) metteur m en scène; (CINEMA, TV) réalisateur/trice.

directory [dɪ'rɛktərɪ] n annuaire m.

dirt [də:t] n saleté f; crasse f; ~-**cheap** a (ne) coûtant presque rien; ~**y** a sale // vt salir; ~**y trick** coup tordu.

disability [dɪsə'bɪlɪtɪ] n invalidité f, infirmité f.

disabled [dɪs'eɪbld] *a* infirme, invalide; (*maimed*) mutilé(e); (*through illness, old age*) impotent(e).

disadvantage [dɪsəd'vɑːntɪdʒ] *n* désavantage *m*, inconvénient *m*.

disagree [dɪsə'griː] *vi* (*differ*) ne pas concorder; (*be against, think otherwise*): **to ~ (with)** ne pas être d'accord (avec); **~able** *a* désagréable; **~ment** *n* désaccord *m*, différend *m*.

disappear [dɪsə'pɪə*] *vi* disparaître; **~ance** *n* disparition *f*.

disappoint [dɪsə'pɔɪnt] *vt* décevoir; **~ed** *a* déçu(e); **~ing** *a* décevant(e); **~ment** *n* déception *f*.

disapproval [dɪsə'pruːvəl] *n* désapprobation *f*.

disapprove [dɪsə'pruːv] *vi*: **to ~ of** désapprouver.

disarm [dɪs'ɑːm] *vt* désarmer; **~ament** *n* désarmement *m*.

disarray [dɪsə'reɪ] *n*: **in ~** (*army, organization*) en déroute; (*hair, clothes*) en désordre.

disaster [dɪ'zɑːstə*] *n* catastrophe *f*, désastre *m*.

disband [dɪs'bænd] *vt* démobiliser; disperser // *vi* se séparer; se disperser.

disbelief ['dɪsbə'liːf] *n* incrédulité *f*.

disc [dɪsk] *n* disque *m*; (*COMPUT* = **disk**.

discard [dɪs'kɑːd] *vt* (*old things*) se défaire de; (*fig*) écarter, renoncer à.

discern [dɪ'sɜːn] *vt* discerner, distinguer; **~ing** *a* judicieux(euse), perspicace.

discharge *vt* [dɪs'tʃɑːdʒ] (*duties*) s'acquitter de; (*waste etc*) déverser, décharger; (*ELEC, MED*) émettre; (*patient*) renvoyer (chez lui); (*employee, soldier*) congédier, licencier; (*defendant*) relaxer, élargir // *n* ['dɪstʃɑːdʒ] (*ELEC, MED*) émission *f*; (*dismissal*) renvoi *m*; licenciement *m*; élargissement *m*.

discipline ['dɪsɪplɪn] *n* discipline *f*.

disc jockey *n* disque-jockey *m*.

disclaim [dɪs'kleɪm] *vt* désavouer, dénier.

disclose [dɪs'kləʊz] *vt* révéler, divulguer; **disclosure** [-'kləʊʒə*] *n* révélation *f*, divulgation *f*.

disco ['dɪskəʊ] *n abbr of* **discothèque**.

discomfort [dɪs'kʌmfət] *n* malaise *m*, gêne *f*; (*lack of comfort*) manque *m* de confort.

disconcert [dɪskən'sɜːt] *vt* déconcerter.

disconnect [dɪskə'nekt] *vt* détacher; (*ELEC, RADIO*) débrancher; (*gas, water*) couper.

disconsolate [dɪs'kɒnsəlɪt] *a* inconsolable.

discontent [dɪskən'tent] *n* mécontentement *m*; **~ed** *a* mécontent(e).

discontinue [dɪskən'tɪnjuː] *vt* cesser, interrompre.

discord ['dɪskɔːd] *n* discorde *f*, dissension *f*; (*MUS*) dissonance *f*.

discothèque [dɪs'kəʊtek] *n* discothèque *f*.

discount *n* ['dɪskaʊnt] remise *f*, rabais *m* // *vt* [dɪs'kaʊnt] ne pas tenir compte de.

discourage [dɪs'kʌrɪdʒ] *vt* décourager.

discover [dɪs'kʌvə*] *vt* découvrir; **~y** *n* découverte *f*.

discredit [dɪs'kredɪt] *vt* mettre en doute; discréditer.

discreet [dɪ'skriːt] *a* discret(ète).

discrepancy [dɪ'skrepənsɪ] *n* divergence *f*, contradiction *f*.

discriminate [dɪ'skrɪmɪneɪt] *vi*: **to ~ between** établir une distinction entre, faire la différence entre; **to ~ against** pratiquer une discrimination contre; **discriminating** *a* qui a du discernement; **discrimination** [-'neɪʃən] *n* discrimination *f*; (*judgment*) discernement *m*.

discuss [dɪs'kʌs] *vt* discuter de; (*debate*) discuter; **~ion** [dɪs'kʌʃən] *n* discussion *f*.

disdain [dɪs'deɪn] *n* dédain *m*.

disease [dɪ'ziːz] *n* maladie *f*.

disembark [dɪsɪm'bɑːk] *vt, vi* débarquer.

disengage [dɪsɪn'geɪdʒ] *vt* dégager; (*TECH*) déclencher; **to ~ the clutch** (*AUT*) débrayer.

disfigure [dɪs'fɪgə*] *vt* défigurer.

disgrace [dɪs'greɪs] *n* honte *f*; (*disfavour*) disgrâce *f* // *vt* déshonorer, couvrir de honte; **~ful** *a* scandaleux(euse), honteux(euse).

disgruntled [dɪs'grʌntld] *a* mécontent(e).

disguise [dɪs'gaɪz] *n* déguisement *m* // *vt* déguiser; **in ~** déguisé(e).

disgust [dɪs'gʌst] *n* dégoût *m*, aversion *f* // *vt* dégoûter, écœurer; **~ing** *a* dégoûtant(e); révoltant(e).

dish [dɪʃ] *n* plat *m*; **to do or wash the ~es** faire la vaisselle; **to ~ up** *vt* servir; **~cloth** *n* (*for drying*) torchon *m*; (*for washing*) lavette *f*.

dishearten [dɪs'hɑ:tn] *vt* décourager.

dishevelled [dɪ'ʃevld] *a* ébouriffé(e); décoiffé(e); débraillé(e).

dishonest [dɪs'ɔnɪst] *a* malhonnête.

dishonour, (*US*) **dishonor** [dɪs'ɔnə*] *n* déshonneur *m*; **~able** *a* déshonorant(e).

dish towel *n* (*US*) torchon *m*.

dishwasher [dɪʃwɒʃə*] *n* lave-vaisselle *m*; (*person*) plongeur/euse.

disillusion [dɪsɪ'lu:ʒən] *vt* désabuser, désenchanter.

disincentive [dɪsɪn'sentɪv] *n*: **to be a ~** être démotivant(e); **to be a ~ to sb** démotiver qn.

disinfect [dɪsɪn'fekt] *vt* désinfecter; **~ant** *n* désinfectant *m*.

disintegrate [dɪs'ɪntɪgreɪt] *vi* se désintégrer.

disinterested [dɪs'ɪntrəstɪd] *a* désintéressé(e).

disjointed [dɪs'dʒɔɪntɪd] *a* décousu(e), incohérent(e).

disk [dɪsk] *n* (*COMPUT*) disquette *f*; **single-/double-sided ~** disquette une face/double face; **~ drive** *n* lecteur *m* de disque *or* disquette, drive *m*; **~ette** *n* (*US*) = **disk**.

dislike [dɪs'laɪk] *n* aversion *f*, antipathie *f* // *vt* ne pas aimer.

dislocate ['dɪslɔkeɪt] *vt* disloquer; déboîter; désorganiser.

dislodge [dɪs'lɔdʒ] *vt* déplacer, faire bouger; (*enemy*) déloger.

disloyal [dɪs'lɔɪəl] *a* déloyal(e).

dismal ['dɪzml] *a* lugubre, maussade.

dismantle [dɪs'mæntl] *vt* démonter; (*fort, warship*) démanteler.

dismay [dɪs'meɪ] *n* consternation *f*.

dismiss [dɪs'mɪs] *vt* congédier, renvoyer; (*idea*) écarter; (*LAW*) rejeter // *vi* (*MIL*) rompre les rangs; **~al** *n* renvoi *m*.

dismount [dɪs'maunt] *vi* mettre pied à terre.

disobedience [dɪsə'bi:dɪəns] *n* désobéissance *f*.

disobedient [dɪsə'bi:dɪənt] *a* désobéissant(e).

disobey [dɪsə'beɪ] *vt* désobéir à.

disorder [dɪs'ɔ:də*] *n* désordre *m*; (*rioting*) désordres *mpl*; (*MED*) troubles *mpl*; **~ly** *a* en désordre; désordonné(e).

disorientated [dɪs'ɔ:rɪenteɪtɪd] *a* désorienté(e).

disown [dɪs'əun] *vt* renier.

disparaging [dɪs'pærɪdʒɪŋ] *a* désobligeant(e).

dispassionate [dɪs'pæʃənət] *a* calme, froid(e); impartial(e), objectif(ive).

dispatch [dɪs'pætʃ] *vt* expédier, envoyer // *n* envoi *m*, expédition *f*; (*MIL, PRESS*) dépêche *f*.

dispel [dɪs'pel] *vt* dissiper, chasser.

dispensary [dɪs'pensərɪ] *n* pharmacie *f*; (*in chemist's*) officine *f*.

dispense [dɪs'pens] *vt* distribuer, administrer; **to ~ with** *vt fus* se passer de; **~r** *n* (*container*) distributeur *m*; **dispensing chemist** *n* (*Brit*) pharmacie *f*.

disperse [dɪs'pə:s] *vt* disperser; (*knowledge*) disséminer // *vi* se disperser.

dispirited [dɪs'pɪrɪtɪd] *a* découragé(e), déprimé(e).

displace [dɪs'pleɪs] *vt* déplacer.

display [dɪs'pleɪ] *n* étalage *m*; déploiement m; affichage m; (screen) écran m de visualisation, visuel m; (of feeling) manifestation f; (pej) ostentation f // vt montrer; (goods) mettre à l'étalage, exposer; (results, departure times) faire étalage de.

displease [dɪs'pliːz] vt mécontenter, contrarier; ~d with mécontent(e) de; **displeasure** ['pleʒə*] n mécontentement m.

disposable [dɪs'pəuzəbl] a (pack etc) jetable; (income) disponible; ~ **nappy** n couche f à jeter, couche-culotte f.

disposal [dɪs'pəuzl] n (availability, arrangement) disposition f; (of property) disposition f, cession f; (of rubbish) évacuation f, destruction f; at one's ~ à sa disposition.

dispose [dɪs'pəuz] vt disposer; **to** ~ **of** vt (time, money) disposer de; (unwanted goods) se débarrasser de, se défaire de; (problem) expédier; ~**d** a: ~**d to do** disposé(e) à faire; **disposition** [-'zɪʃən] n disposition f; (temperament) naturel m.

disprove [dɪs'pruːv] vt réfuter.

dispute [dɪs'pjuːt] n discussion f; (also: **industrial** ~) conflit m // vt contester; (matter) discuter; (victory) disputer.

disqualify [dɪs'kwɔlɪfaɪ] vt (SPORT) disqualifier; **to** ~ **sb for sth/from doing** rendre qn inapte à qch/à faire; signifier à qn l'interdiction de faire; **to** ~ **sb (from driving)** retirer à qn son permis (de conduire).

disquiet [dɪs'kwaɪət] n inquiétude f, trouble m.

disregard [dɪsrɪ'gɑːd] vt ne pas tenir compte de.

disrepair [dɪsrɪ'pɛə*] n mauvais état; **to fall into** ~ (building) tomber en ruine.

disreputable [dɪs'rɛpjutəbl] a (person) de mauvaise réputation; (behaviour) déshonorant(e).

disrupt [dɪs'rʌpt] vt (plans) déranger; (conversation) interrompre.

dissatisfaction [dɪssætɪs'fækʃən] n mécontentement m, insatisfaction f.

dissect [dɪ'sɛkt] vt disséquer.

dissent [dɪ'sɛnt] n dissentiment m, différence f d'opinion.

dissertation [dɪsə'teɪʃən] n mémoire m.

disservice [dɪs'səːvɪs] n: **to do sb a** ~ rendre un mauvais service à qn; desservir qn.

dissimilar [dɪ'sɪmɪlə*] a: ~ **(to)** dissemblable (à), différent (e) (de).

dissipate ['dɪsɪpeɪt] vt dissiper; (energy, efforts) disperser.

dissolute ['dɪsəluːt] a débauché(e), dissolu(e).

dissolve [dɪ'zɔlv] vt dissoudre // vi se dissoudre, fondre; (fig) disparaître.

distance ['dɪstns] n distance f; **in the** ~ au loin.

distant ['dɪstnt] a lointain(e), éloigné(e); (manner) distant(e), froid(e).

distaste [dɪs'teɪst] n dégoût m; ~**ful** a déplaisant(e), désagréable.

distended [dɪs'tɛndɪd] a (stomach) dilaté(e).

distil [dɪs'tɪl] vt distiller; ~**lery** n distillerie f.

distinct [dɪs'tɪŋkt] a distinct(e); (preference, progress) marqué(e); **as** ~ **from** par opposition à; ~**ion** [dɪs'tɪŋkʃən] n distinction f; (in exam) mention f très bien; ~**ive** a distinctif(ive).

distinguish [dɪs'tɪŋgwɪʃ] vt distinguer, différencier; ~**ed** a (eminent) distingué(e); ~**ing** a (feature) distinctif(ive), caractéristique.

distort [dɪs'tɔːt] vt déformer.

distract [dɪs'trækt] vt distraire, déranger; ~**ed** a éperdu(e), égaré(e); ~**ion** [dɪs'trækʃən] n distraction f; égarement m.

distraught [dɪs'trɔːt] a éperdu(e).

distress [dɪs'trɛs] n détresse f; (pain) douleur f // vt affliger; ~**ing** a douloureux(euse), pénible.

distribute [dɪs'trɪbjuːt] vt distribuer; **distribution** [-'bjuːʃən] n distribution f; **distributor** n distributeur m.

district ['dɪstrɪkt] n (of country) région f; (of town) quartier m; (ADMIN) district m; **~ attorney** n (US) = procureur m de la République; **~ nurse** n (Brit) infirmière visiteuse.

distrust [dɪs'trʌst] n méfiance f, doute m // vt se méfier de.

disturb [dɪs'tɜ:b] vt troubler; (inconvenience) déranger; **~ance** n dérangement m; (political etc) troubles mpl; (by drunks etc) tapage m; **~ed** a (worried, upset) agité(e), troublé(e); **to be emotionally ~ed** avoir des problèmes affectifs; **~ing** a troublant(e), inquiétant(e).

disuse [dɪs'ju:s] n: **to fall into ~** tomber en désuétude.

disused [dɪs'ju:zd] a désaffecté(e).

ditch [dɪtʃ] n fossé m // vt (col) abandonner.

dither ['dɪðə*] vi hésiter.

ditto ['dɪtəʊ] ad idem.

dive [daɪv] n plongeon m; (of submarine) plongée f; (AVIAT) piqué m; (pej) bouge m // vi plonger; **~r** n plongeur m.

diversion [daɪ'vɜːʃən] n (Brit AUT) déviation f; (distraction, MIL) diversion f.

divert [daɪ'vɜːt] vt (traffic) dévier; (river) détourner; (amuse) divertir.

divide [dɪ'vaɪd] vt diviser; (separate) séparer // vi se diviser; **~d highway** n (US) route f à quatre voies.

dividend ['dɪvɪdɛnd] n dividende m.

divine [dɪ'vaɪn] a divin(e).

diving ['daɪvɪŋ] n plongée (sous-marine); **~ board** n plongeoir m.

divinity [dɪ'vɪnɪtɪ] n divinité f; théologie f.

division [dɪ'vɪʒən] n division f; séparation f.

divorce [dɪ'vɔːs] n divorce m // vt divorcer d'avec; **~d** a divorcé(e); **~e** [-'si:] n divorcé/e.

D.I.Y. n abbr (Brit) of **do-it-yourself**.

dizzy ['dɪzɪ] a (height) vertigineux(euse); **to make sb ~** donner le vertige à qn; **to feel ~** avoir la tête qui tourne.

DJ n abbr of **disc jockey**.

KEYWORD

---

do [du:] ♦ n (col: party etc) soirée f, fête f

♦ vb (pt **did**, pp **done**) **1** (in negative constructions) non traduit; I **don't understand** je ne comprends pas

2 (to form questions) non traduit; **didn't you know?** vous ne le saviez pas?; **why didn't you come?** pourquoi n'êtes-vous pas venu?

3 (for emphasis, in polite expressions): **she does seem rather late** je trouve qu'elle est bien en retard; **~ sit down/ help yourself** asseyez-vous/servez-vous je vous en prie

4 (used to avoid repeating vb): **she swims better than I ~** elle nage mieux que moi; **~ you agree?** – **yes, I ~/no, I don't** vous êtes d'accord? – oui/non; **she lives in Glasgow** – **so ~ I** elle habite Glasgow – moi aussi; **who broke it?** – **I did** qui l'a cassé? – c'est moi

5 (in question tags): **he laughed, didn't he?** il a ri, n'est-ce pas?; **I don't know him, ~ I?** je ne le connais pas, je crois

♦ vt (gen: carry out, perform etc) faire; **what are you doing tonight?** qu'est-ce que vous faites ce soir?; **to ~ the cooking/washing-up** faire la cuisine/la vaisselle; **to ~ one's teeth/hair/nails** se brosser les dents/se coiffer/se faire les ongles; **the car was ~ing 100** la voiture faisait du 100 (à l'heure)

♦ vi **1** (act, behave) faire; **~ as I ~** faites comme moi

2 (get on, fare) marcher; **the firm is ~ing well** l'entreprise marche bien; **how ~ you ~?** comment allez-vous? (on being introduced) enchanté(e)

3 (suit) aller; **will it ~?** est-ce que ça ira?

4 (*be sufficient*) suffire, aller; **will £10 ~?** est-ce que 10 livres suffiront?; **that'll ~** ça suffit, ça ira; **that'll ~!** (*in annoyance*) ça va or suffit comme ça!; **to make ~ (with)** se contenter (de)

to do away with *vt fus* supprimer
to do up *vt* (*laces, dress*) attacher; (*buttons*) boutonner; (*zip*) fermer; (*renovate: room*) refaire; (*: house*) remettre à neuf

to do with *vt fus* (*need*): **I could ~ with a drink/some help** quelque chose à boire/un peu d'aide ne serait pas de refus; (*be connected*): **that has nothing to ~ with you** cela ne vous concerne pas; **I won't have anything to ~ with it** je ne veux pas m'en mêler

to do without *vi* s'en passer ♦ *vt fus* se passer de.

dock [dɔk] *n* dock *m*; (*LAW*) banc *m* des accusés // *vi* se mettre à quai; **~er** *n* docker *m*; **~yard** *n* chantier *m* de construction navale.

doctor ['dɔktə*] *n* médecin *m*, docteur *m*; (*Ph.D. etc*) docteur // *vt* falsifier; (*drink*) frelater; **D~ of Philosophy (Ph.D.)** *n* doctorat *m*; titulaire *m/f* d'un doctorat.

doctrine ['dɔktrɪn] *n* doctrine *f*.

document ['dɔkjumənt] *n* document *m*; **~ary** [-'mɛntərɪ] *a*, *n* documentaire (*m*).

dodge [dɔdʒ] *n* truc *m*; combine *f* // *vt* esquiver, éviter.

doe [dəu] *n* (*deer*) biche *f*; (*rabbit*) lapine *f*.

does [dʌz] *vb see* **do**; **doesn't** = **does not**.

dog [dɔg] *n* chien/ne // *vt* suivre de près; poursuivre, harceler; **~ collar** *n* collier *m* de chien; (*fig*) faux-col *m* d'ecclésiastique; **~-eared** *a* corné(e).

dogged ['dɔgɪd] *a* obstiné(e), opiniâtre.

dogsbody ['dɔgzbɔdɪ] *n* bonne *f* à tout faire, tâcheron *m*.

doings ['duːɪŋz] *npl* activités *fpl*.

do-it-yourself [ˈduːɪtjɔːˈself] *n* bricolage *m*.

doldrums ['dɔldrəmz] *npl*: **to be in the ~** avoir le cafard; être dans le marasme.

dole [dəul] *n* (*Brit: payment*) allocation *f* de chômage; **on the ~** au chômage; **to ~ out** *vt* donner au compte-goutte.

doleful ['dəulful] *a* triste, lugubre.

doll [dɔl] *n* poupée *f*; **to ~ o.s. up** se faire beau(belle).

dollar ['dɔlə*] *n* dollar *m*.

dolphin ['dɔlfɪn] *n* dauphin *m*.

domestic [dəˈmɛstɪk] *a* (*duty, happiness*) familial(e); (*policy, affairs, flights*) intérieur(e); (*animal*) domestique.

dominant ['dɔmɪnənt] *a* dominant(e).

dominate ['dɔmɪneɪt] *vt* dominer; **domineering** [-'nɪərɪŋ] *a* dominateur(trice), autoritaire.

dominion [dəˈmɪnɪən] *n* domination *f*; territoire *m*; dominion *m*.

domino, **~es** ['dɔmɪnəu] *n* domino *m*; **~es** *n* (*game*) dominos *mpl*.

don [dɔn] *n* (*Brit*) professeur *m* d'université.

donate [dəˈneɪt] *vt* faire don de, donner.

done [dʌn] *pp of* **do**.

donkey ['dɔŋkɪ] *n* âne *m*.

donor ['dəunə*] *n* (*of blood etc*) donneur/euse; (*to charity*) donateur/trice.

don't [dəunt] *vb* = **do not**.

doodle ['duːdl] *vi* griffonner, gribouiller.

doom [duːm] *n* destin *m*; ruine *f* // *vt*: **to be ~ed (to failure)** être voué(e) à l'échec; **~sday** *n* le Jugement dernier.

door [dɔː*] *n* porte *f*; **~bell** *n* sonnette *f*; **~man** *n* (*in hotel*) portier *m*; (*in block of flats*) concierge *m*; **~mat** *n* paillasson *m*; **~step** *n* pas *m* de (la) porte, seuil *m*; **~way** *n* (embrasure *f* de) porte *f*.

dope [dəup] n (col) drogue f // vt (horse etc) doper.

dopey ['dəupɪ] a (col) à moitié endormi(e).

dormant ['dɔ:mənt] a assoupi(e), en veilleuse; (rule, law) inapplicable(e).

dormitory ['dɔ:mɪtrɪ] n dortoir m.

dose [dəus] n dose f; (bout) attaque f.

doss house ['dɔs-] n (Brit) asile m de nuit.

dot [dɔt] n point m // vt: ~ted with parsemé(e) de; on the ~ à l'heure tapante.

dote [dəut]: to ~ on vt fus être fou(folle) de.

dot-matrix printer [dɔt'meɪtrɪks-] n imprimante matricielle.

dotted line ['dɔtɪd-] n ligne pointillée.

double ['dʌbl] a double // ad (fold) en deux; (twice): to cost ~ (sth) coûter le double (de qch) or deux fois plus (que qch) // n double m; (CINEMA) doublure f // vt doubler; (fold) plier en deux // vi doubler; on the ~, (Brit) at the ~ au pas de course; ~s n (TENNIS) double m; ~ bass n contrebasse f; ~ bed n grand lit; ~-breasted a croisé(e); ~cross n vt doubler, trahir; ~decker n autobus m à impériale; ~ glazing n (Brit) double vitrage m; ~ room n chambre f pour deux personnes; **doubly** ad doublement, deux fois plus.

doubt [daut] n doute m // vt douter de; to ~ that douter que; ~ful a douteux(euse); (person) incertain(e); ~less ad sans doute, sûrement.

dough [dəu] n pâte f; ~nut n beignet m.

douse [dauz] vt (drench) tremper, inonder; (extinguish) éteindre.

dove [dʌv] n colombe f.

Dover ['dəuvə*] n Douvres.

dovetail ['dʌvteɪl] vi (fig) concorder.

dowdy ['daudɪ] a démodé(e); mal fagoté(e).

down [daun] n (fluff) duvet m // ad en bas // prep en bas de // vt (col: drink) vider; ~ with X! à bas X!; ~-and-out n clochard/e; ~-at-heel a éculé(e); (fig) miteux(euse); ~cast a démoralisé(e); ~fall n chute f; ruine f; ~hearted a découragé(e); ~hill ad: to go ~hill descendre; ~ payment n acompte m; ~pour n pluie torrentielle, déluge m; ~right a franc(franche); (refusal) catégorique; ~stairs ad au rez-de-chaussée; à l'étage inférieur; ~stream ad en aval; ~-to-earth a terre à terre inv; ~town ad en ville; ~ under ad en Australie (or Nouvelle Zélande); ~ward ['daunwəd] a, ad, ~wards ['daunwədz] ad vers le bas.

dowry ['dauri] n dot f.

doz. abbr of **dozen**.

doze [dəuz] vi sommeiller; to ~ off vi s'assoupir.

dozen ['dʌzn] n douzaine f; a ~ books une douzaine de livres; ~s of des centaines ou des milliers de.

Dr. abbr of **doctor, drive** (n).

drab [dræb] a terne, morne.

draft [drɑːft] n brouillon m; (COMM) traite f; (US MIL) contingent m; (: call-up) conscription f // vt faire le brouillon de; see also **draught**.

draftsman n (US) = **draughts-man**.

drag [dræg] vt traîner; (river) draguer // vi traîner // n (col) raseur/euse; corvée f; (women's clothing): in ~ (en) travesti; to ~ on vi s'éterniser.

dragon ['drægən] n dragon m.

dragonfly ['drægənflaɪ] n libellule f.

drain [dreɪn] n égout m; (on resources) saignée f // vt (land, marshes) drainer, assécher; (vegetables) égoutter; (reservoir etc) vider // vi (water) s'écouler; ~age n système m d'égouts; ~ing board, (US) ~board n égouttoir m; ~pipe n tuyau m d'écoulement.

dram [dræm] n petit verre.

drama ['drɑːmə] n (art) théâtre m, art m dramatique; (play) pièce f.

(*event*) drame *m*; ~**tic** [drə'mætɪk] *a* dramatique; spectaculaire; ~**tist** ['dræmətɪst] *n* auteur *m* dramatique; ~**tize** *vt* (*events*) dramatiser; (*adapt: for TV/cinema*) adapter pour la télévision/pour l'écran.

drank [dræŋk] *pt* of **drink**.

drape [dreɪp] *vt* draper; ~**s** *npl* (*US*) rideaux *mpl*; ~**r** *n* (*Brit*) marchand/e de nouveautés.

drastic ['dræstɪk] *a* sévère; énergique.

draught, (*US*) **draft** [drɑ:ft] *n* courant *m* d'air; (*NAUT*) tirant *m* d'eau; ~**s** *n* (*Brit*) (jeu *m* de) dames *fpl*; on ~ (*beer*) à la pression; ~**board** *n* (*Brit*) damier *m*.

draughtsman, (*US*) **draftsman** ['drɑ:ftsmən] *n* dessinateur/trice (industriel(le)).

draw [drɔ:] *vb* (*pt* drew, *pp* drawn) *vt* tirer; (*attract*) attirer; (*picture*) dessiner; (*line, circle*) tracer; (*money*) retirer // *vi* (*SPORT*) faire match nul // *n* match nul; tirage au sort, loterie *f*; to ~ **near** *vi* s'approcher; approcher; to ~ **out** *vi* (*lengthen*) s'allonger // *vt* (*money*) retirer; to ~ **up** *vi* (*stop*) s'arrêter // *vt* (*document*) établir, dresser; ~**back** *n* inconvénient *m*, désavantage *m*; ~**bridge** *n* pont-levis *m*.

drawer [drɔ:*] *n* tiroir *m*; ['drɔ:ə*] (*of cheque*) tireur *m*.

drawing ['drɔ:ɪŋ] *n* dessin *m*; ~**board** *n* planche *f* à dessin; ~**pin** *n* (*Brit*) punaise *f*; ~**room** *n* salon *m*.

drawl [drɔ:l] *n* accent traînant.

drawn [drɔ:n] *pp* of **draw**.

dread [dred] *n* épouvante *f*, effroi *m* // *vt* redouter, appréhender; ~**ful** *a* épouvantable, affreux(euse).

dream [dri:m] *n* rêve *m* // *vt, vi* (*pt, pp* **dreamed** *or* **dreamt** [dremt]) rêver; ~**y** *a* rêveur(euse).

dreary ['drɪərɪ] *a* triste; monotone.

dredge [dredʒ] *vt* draguer.

dregs [dregz] *npl* lie *f*.

drench [drentʃ] *vt* tremper.

dress [dres] *n* robe *f*; (*clothing*) habillement *m*, tenue *f* // *vi* s'habiller; *vt* habiller; (*wound*) panser; (*food*) préparer; to get ~**ed** s'habiller; to ~ **up** *vi* s'habiller; (*in fancy dress*) se déguiser; ~ **circle** *n* (*Brit*) premier balcon; ~**er** *n* (*THEATRE*) habilleur/euse; (*furniture*) vaisselier *m*; ~**ing** *n* (*MED*) pansement *m*; (*CULIN*) sauce *f*, assaisonnement *m*; ~**ing gown** *n* (*Brit*) robe *f* de chambre; ~**ing room** *n* (*THEATRE*) loge *f*; (*SPORT*) vestiaire *m*; ~**ing table** *n* coiffeuse *f*; ~**maker** *n* couturière *f*; ~**making** *n* couture *f*; ~ **rehearsal** *n* (répétition) générale; ~**y** *a* (*col: clothes*) (qui fait) habillé(e).

drew [dru:] *pt* of draw.

dribble ['drɪbl] *vi* tomber goutte à goutte; (*baby*) baver // *vt* (*ball*) dribbler.

dried [draɪd] *a* (*fruit, beans*) sec(sèche); (*eggs, milk*) en poudre.

drier ['draɪə*] *n* = **dryer**.

drift [drɪft] *n* (*of current etc*) force *f*; direction *f*; (*of sand etc*) amoncellement *m*; (*of snow*) rafale *f*; coulée *f*; (: *on ground*) congère *f*; (*general meaning*) sens général // *vi* (*boat*) aller à la dérive, dériver; (*sand, snow*) s'amonceler, s'entasser; ~**wood** *n* bois flotté.

drill [drɪl] *n* perceuse *f*; (*bit*) foret *m*; (*of dentist*) roulette *f*, fraise *f*; (*MIL*) exercice *m* // *vt* percer // *vi* (*for oil*) faire un *or* des forage(s).

drink [drɪŋk] *n* boisson *f* // *vt, vi* (*pt* **drank**, *pp* **drunk**) boire; to have a ~ boire quelque chose, boire un verre; prendre l'apéritif; a ~ of water un verre d'eau; ~**er** *n* buveur/euse; ~**ing water** *n* eau *f* potable.

drip [drɪp] *n* bruit *m* d'égouttement, goutte *f*; (*MED*) goutte-à-goutte *m inv*; perfusion *f* // *vi* tomber goutte à goutte; (*washing*) s'égoutter; (*wall*) suinter; ~**dry** *a* (*shirt*) sans repassage; ~**ping** *n* graisse *f* de rôti.

drive [draɪv] *n* promenade *f* or trajet *m* en voiture; (*also:* ~**way**) allée *f* (*energy*) dynamisme *m*, énergie *f*; (*PSYCH*) besoin *m*; pulsion *f*; (*push*) effort (concerté); campagne *f* (*SPORT*) drive *m*; (*TECH*) entraînement *m*; traction *f*; transmission *f*; (*also*: disk ~) lecteur *m* de disquette // *vb* (*pt* drove, *pp* driven) *vt* (*vehicle*; (*nail*) enfoncer; (*push*) chasser, pousser; (*TECH*: *motor*) actionner; entraîner // *vi* (*AUT*: at controls) conduire; (: *travel*) aller en voiture; **left-/right-hand** ~ conduite *f* à gauche/droite; **to** ~ **sb mad** rendre qn fou (folle).

drivel ['drɪvl] *n* (*col*) idioties *fpl*.

driven ['drɪvn] *pp* of **drive**.

driver ['draɪvə*] *n* conducteur/trice; (*of taxi, bus*) chauffeur *m*; ~'**s license** *n* (*US*) permis *m* de conduire.

driveway ['draɪvweɪ] *n* allée *f*.

driving ['draɪvɪŋ] *n* conduite *f*; ~ **instructor** *n* moniteur *m* d'auto-école; ~ **lesson** *n* leçon *f* de conduite; ~ **licence** *n* (*Brit*) permis *m* de conduire; ~ **mirror** *n* rétroviseur *m*; ~ **school** *n* auto-école *f*; ~ **test** *n* examen *m* du permis de conduire.

drizzle ['drɪzl] *n* bruine *f*, crachin *m*.

droll [drəʊl] *a* drôle.

drone [drəʊn] *n* bourdonnement *m*.

drool [druːl] *vi* baver.

droop [druːp] *vi* s'affaisser; tomber.

drop [drɒp] *n* goutte *f*; (*fall*) baisse *f*; (*also*: **parachute** ~) saut *m*; (*of cliff*) dénivellation *f*; à-pic *m* // *vt* laisser tomber; (*voice, eyes, price*) baisser; (*set down from car*) déposer // *vi* tomber; ~**s** *npl* (*MED*) gouttes; **to** ~ **off** *vi* (*sleep*) s'assoupir // *vt* (*passenger*) déposer; **to** ~ **out** *vi* (*withdraw*) se retirer; (*student etc*) abandonner, décrocher; ~**out** *n* marginal/e; (*from studies*) drop-out *m/f*; ~**pings** *npl* crottes *fpl*.

drought [draʊt] *n* sécheresse *f*.

drove [drəʊv] *pt* of **drive**.

drown [draʊn] *vt* noyer // *vi* se noyer.

drowsy ['draʊzɪ] *a* somnolent(e).

drudgery ['drʌdʒərɪ] *n* corvée *f*.

drug [drʌg] *n* médicament *m*; (*narcotic*) drogue *f* // *vt* droguer; ~ **addict** *n* toxicomane *m/f*; ~**gist** *n* (*US*) pharmacien/ne-droguiste; ~**store** *n* (*US*) pharmacie-droguerie *f*, drugstore *m*.

drum [drʌm] *n* tambour *m*; (*for oil, petrol*) bidon *m* // *vi* tambouriner; ~**s** *npl* batterie *f*; ~**mer** *n* (joueur *m* de tambour.

drunk [drʌŋk] *pp* of **drink** // *a* ivre, soûl(e) // *n* (*also*: ~**ard**) soûlard/e; homme/femme soûl(e); ~**en** *a* ivre, soûl(e); ivrogne, d'ivrogne.

dry [draɪ] *a* sec(sèche); (*day*) sans pluie *f*; (*clothes*) sec; **to** ~ **up** *vi* se tarir; ~-**cleaner's** *n* teinturerie *f*; ~-**er** *n* séchoir *m*; (*US*: *spin-dryer*) essoreuse *f*; ~ **goods store** *n* (*US*) magasin *m* de nouveautés; ~**ness** *n* sécheresse *f*; ~ **rot** *n* pourriture sèche (*du bois*).

dual ['djuəl] *a* double; ~ **carriageway** *n* (*Brit*) route *f* à quatre voies or à chaussées séparées.

dubbed [dʌbd] *a* (*CINEMA*) doublé(e); (*nicknamed*) surnommé(e).

dubious ['djuːbɪəs] *a* hésitant(e), incertain(e); (*reputation, company*) douteux(euse).

duchess ['dʌtʃɪs] *n* duchesse *f*.

duck [dʌk] *n* canard *m* // *vi* se baisser vivement, baisser subitement la tête; ~**ling** *n* caneton *m*.

duct [dʌkt] *n* conduite *f*, canalisation *f*; (*ANAT*) conduit *m*.

dud [dʌd] *n* (*shell*) obus non éclaté; (*object, tool*): **it's a** ~ c'est de la camelote, ça ne marche pas // *a* (*Brit*: *cheque*) sans provision; (: *note, coin*) faux(fausse).

due [djuː] *a* (*expected*) dû(due); (*fitting*) qui convient // *n* dû *m* // *ad*: ~ **north** droit vers le nord; ~**s** *npl* (*for club, union*) cotisation *f*; (*in harbour*) droits *mpl* de port); **in** ~ **course** en temps utile or voulu; finalement; ~ **to** dû(due) à; causé(e) par; **he's** ~ **to finish tomorrow**

normalement il doit finir demain.

duet [dju:'et] n duo m.

duffel [dʌfl] a: ~ **bag** sac m marin; ~ **coat** duffel-coat m.

dug [dʌg] pt, pp of **dig**.

duke [dju:k] n duc m.

dull [dʌl] a ennuyeux(euse); terne; (sound, pain) sourd(e); (weather, day) gris(e), maussade; (blade) émoussé(e) // vt (pain, grief) atténuer; (mind, senses) engourdir.

duly ['dju:lɪ] ad (on time) en temps voulu; (as expected) comme il se doit.

dumb [dʌm] a muet(te); (stupid) bête; **dumbfounded** [dʌm'faundɪd] a sidéré(e).

dummy ['dʌmɪ] n (tailor's model) mannequin m; (SPORT) feinte f; (Brit: for baby) tétine f // a faux(fausse), factice.

dump [dʌmp] n tas m d'ordures; (place) décharge (publique); (MIL) dépôt m // vt (put down) déposer; déverser; (get rid of) se débarrasser de; ~**ing** n (ECON) dumping m; (of rubbish) 'no ~ing' 'décharge interdite'.

dumpling ['dʌmplɪŋ] n boulette f (de pâte).

dumpy ['dʌmpɪ] a courtaud(e), boulot(te).

dunce [dʌns] n âne m, cancre m.

dung [dʌŋ] n fumier m.

dungarees [dʌŋgə'ri:z] npl bleus(s) m(pl); salopette f.

dungeon ['dʌndʒən] n cachot m.

Dunkirk [dʌn'kə:k] n Dunkerque.

duplex ['du:plɛks] n (US) maison jumelée; (: apartment) duplex m.

duplicate n ['dju:plɪkət] double m, copie exacte // a ['dju:plɪkət] faire en double de; (on machine) polycopier.

durable ['djuərəbl] a durable; (clothes, metal) résistant(e), solide.

duration [djuə'reɪʃən] n durée f.

duress [djuə'rɛs] n: **under** ~ sous la contrainte.

during ['djuərɪŋ] prep pendant, au cours de.

dusk [dʌsk] n crépuscule m.

dust [dʌst] n poussière f // vt (furniture) essuyer, épousseter; (cake etc): **to** ~ **with** saupoudrer de; ~**bin** n (Brit) poubelle f; ~**er** n chiffon m; ~ **jacket** n jacquette f; ~**man** n (Brit) boueux m, éboueur m; ~**y** a poussiéreux(euse).

Dutch [dʌtʃ] a hollandais(e), néerlandais(e) // n (LING) hollandais m; **the** ~ npl les Hollandais; **to go** ~ partager les frais; ~**man/woman** n Hollandais/e.

dutiful ['dju:tɪful] a (child) respectueux(euse).

duty ['dju:tɪ] n devoir m; (tax) droit m, taxe f; **duties** npl fonctions fpl; **on** ~ de service; (at night etc) de garde; **off** ~ libre, pas de service or de garde; ~**-free** a exempté(e) de douane, hors-taxe.

duvet ['du:veɪ] n (Brit) couette f.

dwarf [dwɔ:f] n nain/e // vt écraser.

dwell, pt, pp **dwelt** [dwɛl, dwɛlt] vi demeurer; **to** ~ **on** vt fus s'étendre sur; ~**ing** n habitation f, demeure f.

dwindle ['dwɪndl] vi diminuer, décroître.

dye [daɪ] n teinture f // vt teindre.

dying ['daɪɪŋ] a mourant(e), agonisant(e).

dyke [daɪk] n (Brit) digue f.

dynamic [daɪ'næmɪk] a dynamique.

dynamite ['daɪnəmaɪt] n dynamite f.

dynamo ['daɪnəməu] n dynamo f.

dyslexia [dɪs'lɛksɪə] n dyslexie f.

E

E [i:] n (MUS) mi m.

each [i:tʃ] a chaque // pronoun chacun(e); ~ **one** chacun(e); **they hate** ~ **other** ils se détestent (mutuellement); **you are jealous of** ~ **other** vous êtes jaloux l'un de l'autre; **they have 2 books** ~ ils ont 2 livres chacun.

eager [i:gə*] a impatient(e); avide;

ardent(e), passionné(e); to be ~ for désirer vivement, être avide de.

eagle ['i:gl] n aigle m.

ear [ɪə*] n oreille f; (of corn) épi m; ~ache n douleurs fpl aux oreilles; ~drum n tympan m.

earl [ə:l] n comte m.

earlier ['ə:lɪə*] a (date etc) plus rapproché(e). (edition etc) plus ancien(ne), antérieur(e) // ad plus tôt.

early ['ə:lɪ] ad tôt, de bonne heure; (ahead of time) en avance // a précoce; anticipé(e); qui se manifeste (or se fait) tôt or de bonne heure; to have an ~ night se coucher tôt or de bonne heure; in the ~ or ~ in the spring/19th century au début du commencement du printemps/19ème siècle; ~ retirement n retraite anticipée.

earmark ['ɪəmɑ:k] vt: to ~ sth for réserver or destiner qch à.

earn [ə:n] vt gagner; (COMM: yield) rapporter.

earnest ['ə:nɪst] a sérieux(euse); in ~ ad sérieusement, pour de bon.

earnings ['ə:nɪŋz] npl salaire m; gains mpl.

earphones ['ɪəfəunz] npl écouteurs mpl.

earring ['ɪərɪŋ] n boucle f d'oreille.

earshot ['ɪəʃɔt] n: out of/within ~ hors de portée/à portée de la voix.

earth [ə:θ] n (gen; also ELEC: Brit) terre f; (of fox etc) terrier m // vt (Brit: ELEC) relier à la terre; ~enware n poterie f; faïence f // a de terre, en terre cuite; ~quake n tremblement m de terre, séisme m; ~y a (fig) terre à terre inv; truculent(e).

ease [i:z] n facilité f, aisance f // vt (soothe) calmer; (loosen) relâcher, détendre; (help pass): to ease sth in/out faire pénétrer/sortir qch délicatement or avec douceur; faciliter la pénétration/la sortie de qch; at ~ à l'aise; (MIL) au repos; to ~ off or up vi diminuer; ralentir; se détendre.

easel ['i:zl] n chevalet m.

east [i:st] n est m // a d'est // ad à l'est, vers l'est; the E~ l'Orient m.

Easter ['i:stə*] n Pâques fpl; ~ egg n œuf m de Pâques.

easterly ['i:stəlɪ] a d'est.

eastern ['i:stən] a de l'est, oriental(e).

East Germany n Allemagne f de l'Est.

eastward(s) ['i:stwəd(z)] ad vers l'est, à l'est.

easy ['i:zɪ] a facile; (manner) aisé(e) // ad: to take it or things ~ ne pas se fatiguer; ne pas (trop) s'en faire; ~ chair n fauteuil m; ~-going a accommodant(e), facile à vivre.

eat [i:t], pt ate, pp eaten [i:t, ɛt, 'i:tn] vt, vi manger; to ~ into, to ~ away at vt fus ronger, attaquer.

eaves [i:vz] npl avant-toit m.

eavesdrop ['i:vzdrɔp] vi: to ~ (on a conversation) écouter (une conversation) de façon indiscrète.

ebb [ɛb] n reflux m // vi refluer; (fig: also: ~ away) décliner.

ebony ['ɛbənɪ] n ébène f.

eccentric [ɪk'sɛntrɪk] a, n excentrique (m/f).

echo, ~es ['ɛkəu] n écho m // vt répéter; faire chorus avec // vi résonner; faire écho.

eclipse [ɪ'klɪps] n éclipse f.

ecology [ɪ'kɔlədʒɪ] n écologie f.

economic [i:kə'nɔmɪk] a économique; (business etc) rentable; ~al a économique; (person) économe; ~s n économie f politique.

economize [ɪ'kɔnəmaɪz] vi économiser, faire des économies.

economy [ɪ'kɔnəmɪ] n économie f.

ecstasy ['ɛkstəsɪ] n extase f.

eczema ['ɛksɪmə] n eczéma m.

edge [ɛdʒ] n bord m; (of knife etc) tranchant m, fil m // vt border; on ~ (fig) = edgy; to ~ away from s'éloigner furtivement de; ~ways ad latéralement; he couldn't get a word in ~ways il ne pouvait pas placer un mot.

edgy ['edʒɪ] a crispé(e), tendu(e).

edible ['edɪbl] a comestible; (*meal*) mangeable.

edict ['iːdɪkt] n décret m.

Edinburgh ['edɪnbərə] n Édimbourg.

edit ['edɪt] vt éditer; ~**ion** [ɪ'dɪʃən] n édition f; ~**or** n (*in newspaper*) rédacteur/trice; rédacteur/trice en chef; (*of sb's work*) éditeur/trice; ~**orial** [-'tɔːrɪəl] a de la rédaction, éditorial(e) // n éditorial m.

educate ['edjukeɪt] vt instruire, éduquer.

education [edju'keɪʃən] n éducation f; (*schooling*) enseignement m, instruction f; ~**al** a pédagogique; scolaire; instructif(ive).

EEC n abbr (= *European Economic Community*) C.E.E. f (= *Communauté économique européenne*).

eel [iːl] n anguille f.

eerie ['ɪərɪ] a inquiétant(e), spectral(e), surnaturel(le).

effect [ɪ'fekt] n effet m // vt effectuer; ~**s** npl (*THEATRE*) effets mpl; **to take ~** (*law*) entrer en vigueur, prendre effet; (*drug*) agir, faire son effet; **in ~** en fait, en réalité; ~**ive** a efficace; (*in reality*) effectif(ive); ~**ively** ad efficacement; (*in reality*) effectivement; ~**iveness** n efficacité f.

effeminate [ɪ'femɪnɪt] a efféminé(e).

efficiency [ɪ'fɪʃənsɪ] n efficacité f; rendement m.

efficient [ɪ'fɪʃənt] a efficace.

effort ['efət] n effort m.

effusive [ɪ'fjuːsɪv] a expansif(ive), chaleureux(euse).

e.g. ad abbr (= *exempli gratia*) par exemple, p. ex.

egg [eg] n œuf m; **to ~ on** vt pousser; ~**cup** n coquetier m; ~**plant** n (*esp US*) aubergine f; ~**shell** n coquille f d'œuf.

ego ['iːgəu] n moi m.

egotism ['egəutɪzəm] n égotisme m.

egotist ['egəutɪst] n égocentrique m/ f.

Egypt ['iːdʒɪpt] n Égypte f; ~**ian** [ɪ'dʒɪpʃən] a égyptien(ne) // n

Égyptien/ne.

eiderdown ['aɪdədaun] n édredon m.

eight [eɪt] num huit; ~**een** num dix-huit; ~**h** a, n huitième (m); ~**y** num quatre-vingt(s).

Eire ['ɛərə] n République f d'Irlande.

either ['aɪðə*] a l'un ou l'autre; (*both, each*) chaque; **on ~ side** de chaque côté // pronoun: ~ (**of them**) l'un ou l'autre; **I don't like ~** je n'aime ni l'un ni l'autre // ad non plus; **no, I don't ~** moi non plus // cj: ~ **good or bad** ou bon ou mauvais, soit bon soit mauvais.

eject [ɪ'dʒekt] vt expulser; éjecter.

eke [iːk]: **to ~ out** vt faire durer; augmenter.

elaborate a [ɪ'læbərɪt] compliqué(e), recherché(e), minutieux(euse) // vb [ɪ'læbəreɪt] vt élaborer // vi entrer dans les détails.

elapse [ɪ'læps] vi s'écouler, passer.

elastic [ɪ'læstɪk] a, n élastique (m); ~ **band** a (*Brit*) élastique m.

elated [ɪ'leɪtɪd] a transporté(e) de joie.

elbow ['elbəu] n coude m.

elder ['eldə*] a aîné(e) // n (*tree*) sureau m; **one's ~s** ses aînés; ~**ly** a âgé(e) // npl: **the ~ly** les personnes âgées.

eldest ['eldɪst] a, n: **the ~** (*child*) l'aîné(e) (des enfants).

elect [ɪ'lekt] vt élire; **to ~ to do** choisir de faire // a: **the president ~** le président désigné; ~**ion** [ɪ'lekʃən] n élection f; ~**ioneering** [ɪlekʃə'nɪərɪŋ] n propagande électorale, manœuvres électorales; ~**or** n électeur/trice; ~**orate** n électorat m.

electric [ɪ'lektrɪk] a électrique; ~**al** a électrique; ~ **blanket** n couverture chauffante; ~ **fire** n radiateur m électrique.

electrician [ɪlek'trɪʃən] n électricien m.

electricity [ɪlek'trɪsɪtɪ] n électricité f.

electrify [ɪ'lektrɪfaɪ] vt (*RAIL*) électrifier; (*audience*) électriser.

electronic [ɪlek'trɔnɪk] a électronique; **~s** *n* électronique *f*.

elegant ['elɪɡənt] *a* élégant(e).

element ['elɪmənt] *n* (*gen*) élément *m*; (*of heater, kettle etc*) résistance *f*; **~ary** [-'mentərɪ] *a* élémentaire; (*school, education*) primaire.

elephant ['elɪfənt] *n* éléphant *m*.

elevate ['elɪveɪt] *vt* élever.

elevator ['elɪveɪtə*] *n* élévateur *m*, monte-charge *m inv*; (*US: lift*) ascenseur *m*.

eleven [ɪ'levn] *num* onze; **~ses** *npl* (*Brit*) ≈ pause-café *f*; **~th** *a* onzième.

elicit [ɪ'lɪsɪt] *vt*: **to ~ (from)** obtenir (de), arracher (à).

eligible ['elɪdʒəbl] *a* éligible; (*for membership*) admissible.

elm [elm] *n* orme *m*.

elongated ['iːlɔŋɡeɪtɪd] *a* étiré(e), allongé(e).

elope [ɪ'ləup] *vi* (*lovers*) s'enfuir (ensemble).

eloquent ['elakwant] *a* éloquent(e).

else [els] *ad* d'autre; **something ~** quelque chose d'autre, autre chose; **somewhere ~** ailleurs, autre part; **everywhere ~** partout ailleurs; **nobody ~** personne d'autre; **where ~?** à quel autre endroit?; **little ~** pas grand-chose d'autre; **~where** *ad* ailleurs, autre part.

elude [ɪ'luːd] *vt* échapper à; (*question*) éluder.

elusive [ɪ'luːsɪv] *a* insaisissable.

emaciated [ɪ'meɪsɪeɪtɪd] *a* émacié(e), décharné(e).

emancipate [ɪ'mænsɪpeɪt] *vt* émanciper.

embankment [ɪm'bæŋkmənt] *n* (*of road, railway*) remblai *m*, talus *m*; (*riverside*) berge *f*, quai *m*; (*dyke*) digue *f*.

embark [ɪm'bɑːk] *vi*: **to ~ (on)** (s')embarquer (à bord de *or* sur) // *vt* embarquer; **to ~ on** (*fig*) se lancer *or* s'embarquer dans; **~ation** [emba'keɪʃən] *n* embarquement *m*.

embarrass [ɪm'bærəs] *vt* embarrasser, gêner; **~ed** *a* gêné(e); **~ing** *a*

gênant(e), embarrassant(e); **~ment** *n* embarras *m*, gêne *f*.

embassy ['embəsɪ] *n* ambassade *f*.

embed [ɪm'bed] *vt* enfoncer; sceller.

embers ['embəz] *npl* braise *f*.

embezzle [ɪm'bezl] *vt* détourner.

embitter [ɪm'bɪtə*] *vt* aigrir; envenimer.

embody [ɪm'bɔdɪ] *vt* (*features*) réunir, comprendre; (*ideas*) formuler, exprimer.

embossed [ɪm'bɔst] *a* repoussé(e); gaufré(e).

embrace [ɪm'breɪs] *vt* embrasser, étreindre; (*include*) embrasser, couvrir // *vi* s'étreindre, s'embrasser // *n* étreinte *f*.

embroider [ɪm'brɔɪdə*] *vt* broder; (*fig: story*) enjoliver; **~y** *n* broderie *f*.

emerald ['emərəld] *n* émeraude *f*.

emerge [ɪ'məːdʒ] *vi* apparaître, surgir.

emergence [ɪ'məːdʒəns] *n* apparition *f*.

emergency [ɪ'məːdʒənsɪ] *n* urgence *f*; **in an ~** en cas d'urgence; **~ cord** *n* (*US*) sonnette *f* d'alarme; **~ exit** *n* sortie *f* de secours; **~ landing** *n* atterrissage forcé; **the ~ services** *npl* (*fire, police, ambulance*) les services *mpl* d'urgence.

emery board ['eməɪ-] *n* lime *f* à ongles (*en carton émerisé*).

emigrate ['emɪɡreɪt] *vi* émigrer.

eminent ['emɪnənt] *a* éminent(e).

emit [ɪ'mɪt] *vt* émettre.

emotion [ɪ'məuʃən] *n* émotion *f*; **~al** *a* (*person*) émotif(ive), très sensible; (*scene*) émouvant(e); (*tone, speech*) qui fait appel aux sentiments.

emperor ['empərə*] *n* empereur *m*.

emphasis ['emfəsɪs], *pl* **-ases** [-siːz] *n* accent *m*; force *f*, insistance *f*.

emphasize ['emfəsaɪz] *vt* (*syllable, word, point*) appuyer *or* insister sur; (*feature*) souligner, accentuer.

emphatic [em'fætɪk] *a* (*strong*) énergique, vigoureux(euse); (*unambi-*

guous, clear) catégorique; ~**ally** *ad* avec vigueur or énergie; catégoriquement.

empire ['empaɪə*] *n* empire *m*.

employ [ɪm'plɔɪ] *vt* employer; ~**ee** [-'i:] *n* employé(e), ~**er** *n* employeur/euse; ~**ment** *n* emploi *m*; ~**ment agency** *n* agence *f* or bureau *m* de placement.

empower [ɪm'pauə*] *vt*: to ~ sb to do autoriser or habiliter qn à faire.

empress ['emprɪs] *n* impératrice *f*.

empty ['emptɪ] *a* vide; (*threat, promise*) en l'air, vain(e) // *vt* vider; *vi* se vider; (*liquid*) s'écouler // *n* (*bottle*) bouteille *f* vide; ~**handed** *a* les mains vides.

emulate ['emjuleɪt] *vt* rivaliser avec, imiter.

emulsion [ɪ'mʌlʃən] *n* émulsion *f*; ~ (**paint**) *n* peinture mate.

enable [ɪ'neɪbl] *vt*: to ~ sb to do permettre à qn de faire.

enact [ɪn'ækt] *vt* (*law*) promulguer; (*play*) jouer, représenter.

enamel [ɪ'næməl] *n* émail *m*.

encased [ɪn'keɪst] *a*: ~ in enfermé(e) dans, recouvert(e) de.

enchant [ɪn'tʃɑ:nt] *vt* enchanter; ~**ing** *a* ravissant(e), enchanteur(eresse).

encl. *abbr* (= *enclosed*) annexe(s).

enclose [ɪn'kləuz] *vt* (*land*) clôturer; (*letter etc*): to ~ (**with**) joindre (à); **please find** ~**d** veuillez trouver ci-joint.

enclosure [ɪn'kləuʒə*] *n* enceinte *f*; (*COMM*) annexe *f*.

encompass [ɪn'kʌmpəs] *vt* encercler, entourer; (*include*) contenir, inclure.

encore [ɔŋ'kɔ:*] *excl, n* bis (*m*).

encounter [ɪn'kauntə*] *n* rencontre *f* // *vt* rencontrer.

encourage [ɪn'kʌrɪdʒ] *vt* encourager; ~**ment** *n* encouragement *m*.

encroach [ɪn'krəutʃ] *vi*: to ~ (**up**)**on** empiéter sur.

encyclop(a)edia [ensaɪkləu'pi:dɪə] *n* encyclopédie *f*.

end [end] *n* (*gen, also*: *aim*) fin *f*; (*of table, street etc*) bout *m*, extrémité *f* // *vt* terminer; (*also*: **bring to an** ~, **put an** ~ **to**) mettre fin à // *vi* se terminer, finir; **in the** ~ finalement; **on** ~ (*object*) debout, dressé(e); **to stand on** ~ (*hair*) se dresser sur la tête; **for 5 hours on** ~ durant 5 heures d'affilée or de suite; **to** ~ **up** *vi*: **to** ~ **up in** finir or se terminer par; (*place*) finir or aboutir à.

endanger [ɪn'deɪndʒə*] *vt* mettre en danger.

endearing [ɪn'dɪərɪŋ] *a* attachant(e).

endeavour, (*US*) **endeavor** [ɪn'devə*] *n* tentative *f*, effort *m* // *vi*: **to** ~ **to do** tenter or s'efforcer de faire.

ending ['endɪŋ] *n* dénouement *m*, conclusion *f*; (*LING*) terminaison *f*.

endive ['endaɪv] *n* chicorée *f*.

endless ['endlɪs] *a* sans fin, interminable; (*patience, resources*) inépuisable, sans limites.

endorse [ɪn'dɔ:s] *vt* (*cheque*) endosser; (*approve*) appuyer, approuver, sanctionner; ~**ment** *n* (*on driving licence*) contravention portée au permis de conduire.

endow [ɪn'dau] *vt* (*provide with money*) faire une donation à, doter; (*equip*): **to** ~ **with** gratifier de, doter de.

endure [ɪn'djuə*] *vt* supporter, endurer // *vi* durer.

enemy ['enəmɪ] *a, n* ennemi(e).

energetic [enə'dʒetɪk] *a* énergique; actif(ive); qui fait se dépenser (physiquement).

energy ['enədʒɪ] *n* énergie *f*.

enforce [ɪn'fɔ:s] *vt* (*LAW*) appliquer, faire respecter; ~**d** *a* forcé(e).

engage [ɪn'geɪdʒ] *vt* engager; (*MIL*) engager le combat avec // *vi* (*TECH*) s'enclencher, s'engrener; **to** ~ **in** se lancer dans; ~**d** *a* (*Brit*: *busy, in use*) occupé(e); (*betrothed*) fiancé(e); **to get** ~**d** se fiancer; ~**d tone** *n* (*Brit TEL*) tonalité *f* occupé or pas libre; ~**ment** *n* obligation *f*,

engagement m; rendez-vous m inv; (to marry) fiançailles fpl; (MIL) combat m; ~**ment ring** n bague f de fiançailles.

engaging [ɪn'geɪdʒɪŋ] a engageant(e), attirant(e).

engender [ɪn'dʒɛndə*] vt produire, causer.

engine ['ɛndʒɪn] n (AUT) moteur m; (RAIL) locomotive f; ~ **driver** n mécanicien m.

engineer [ɛndʒɪ'nɪə*] n ingénieur m; (US RAIL) mécanicien m; ~**ing** n engineering m, ingénierie f; (of bridges, ships) génie m; (of machine) mécanique f.

England ['ɪŋglənd] n Angleterre f.

English ['ɪŋglɪʃ] a anglais(e); n (LING) anglais m; **the** ~ npl les Anglais; **the** ~ **Channel** ≈ la Manche; ~**man/woman** n Anglais/e.

engraving [ɪn'greɪvɪŋ] n gravure f.

engrossed [ɪn'grəust] a: ~ **in** absorbé(e) par, plongé(e) dans.

engulf [ɪn'gʌlf] vt engloutir.

enhance [ɪn'hɑ:ns] vt rehausser, mettre en valeur.

enjoy [ɪn'dʒɔɪ] vt aimer, prendre plaisir à; (have: health, fortune) jouir de; (: success) connaître; **to o.s.** s'amuser; ~**able** a agréable; ~**ment** n plaisir m.

enlarge [ɪn'lɑ:dʒ] vt accroître; (PHOT) agrandir // vi: **to** ~ **on** (subject) s'étendre sur.

enlighten [ɪn'laɪtn] vt éclairer; ~**ed** a éclairé(e); ~**ment** n: **the E~ment** (HISTORY) ≈ le Siècle des lumières.

enlist [ɪn'lɪst] vt recruter; (support) s'assurer // vi s'engager.

enmity ['ɛnmɪtɪ] n inimitié f.

enormous [ɪ'nɔ:məs] a énorme.

enough [ɪ'nʌf] a, n: ~ **time/books** assez or suffisamment de temps/livres; **have you got** ~? (en) avez-vous assez? // ad: **big** ~ assez or suffisamment grand; **he has not worked** ~ il n'a pas assez or suffisamment travaillé; ~! assez!, ça

suffit!; **that's** ~, **thanks** cela suffit or c'est assez, merci; **I've had** ~ **of him** j'en ai assez de lui; ..., **which**, **funnily** ~ ..., qui, chose curieuse.

enquire [ɪn'kwaɪə*] vt, vi = **inquire**.

enrage [ɪn'reɪdʒ] vt mettre en fureur or en rage, rendre furieux(euse).

enrol [ɪn'rəul] vt inscrire // vi s'inscrire; ~**ment** n inscription f.

ensign (NAUT) ['ɛnsən] enseigne f, pavillon m; (MIL) ['ɛnsaɪn] porte-étendard m.

ensue [ɪn'sju:] vi s'ensuivre, résulter.

ensure [ɪn'ʃuə*] vt assurer; garantir; **to** ~ **that** s'assurer que.

entail [ɪn'teɪl] vt entraîner, nécessiter.

entangle [ɪn'tæŋgl] vt emmêler, embrouiller.

enter ['ɛntə*] vt (room) entrer dans, pénétrer dans; (club, army) entrer à; (competition) s'inscrire à or pour; (sb for a competition) (faire) inscrire; (write down) inscrire, noter; (COMPUT) entrer, introduire // vi entrer; **to** ~ **for** vt fus s'inscrire à, se présenter pour or à; **to** ~ **into** vt fus (explanation) se lancer dans; (debate) prendre part à; (agreement) conclure; **to** ~ **(up)on** vt fus commencer.

enterprise ['ɛntəpraɪz] n entreprise f; (esprit m d')initiative f; **free** ~ libre entreprise; **private** ~ entreprise privée.

enterprising ['ɛntəpraɪzɪŋ] a entreprenant(e), dynamique.

entertain [ɛntə'teɪn] vt amuser, distraire; (invite) recevoir (à dîner); (idea, plan) envisager; ~**er** n artiste m/f de variétés; ~**ing** a amusant(e), distrayant(e); ~**ment** n (amusement) distraction f, divertissement m, amusement m; (show) spectacle m.

enthralled [ɪn'θrɔ:ld] a captivé(e).

enthusiasm [ɪn'θu:zɪæzəm] n enthousiasme m.

enthusiast [ɪn'θu:zɪæst] n enthousiaste m/f; ~**ic** [-'æstɪk] a enthousiaste; **to be ~ic about** être enthousiasmé(e) par.

entice [ɪn'taɪs] vt attirer, séduire.

entire [ɪn'taɪə*] a (tout) (entier(ère)); **~ly** ad entièrement, complètement; **~ty** [ɪn'taɪərətɪ] n: **in its ~ty** dans sa totalité.

entitle [ɪn'taɪtl] vt (allow): **to ~ sb to do** donner (le) droit à qn de faire; **to ~ sb to sth** donner droit à qch à qn; **~d** a (book) intitulé(e); **to be ~d to do** avoir le droit de ou être habilité à faire.

entrance n ['entrns] entrée f // vt [ɪn'trɑːns] enchanter, ravir; **to gain ~ to** (university etc) être admis à; **~ examination** n examen m d'entrée; **~ fee** n droit m d'inscription; (to museum etc) prix m d'entrée; **~ ramp** n (US AUT) bretelle f d'accès.

entrant ['entrnt] n participant/e, concurrent/e.

entreat [en'triːt] vt supplier.

entrenched [en'trentʃt] a retranché(e).

entrepreneur [ɔntrəprə'nə:*] n entrepreneur m.

entrust [ɪn'trʌst] vt: **to ~ sth to sb** confier qch à.

entry ['entrɪ] n entrée f; (in register) inscription f; **no ~** défense d'entrer, entrée interdite; (AUT) sens interdit; **~ form** n feuille f d'inscription; **~ phone** n interphone m (à l'entrée d'un immeuble).

envelop [ɪn'vɛləp] vt envelopper.

envelope ['envələup] n enveloppe f.

envious ['envɪəs] a envieux(euse).

environment [ɪn'vaɪərnmənt] n milieu m; environnement m; **~al** [-'mentl] a écologique; du milieu.

envisage [ɪn'vɪzɪdʒ] vt envisager; prévoir.

envoy ['envɔɪ] n envoyé/e.

envy ['envɪ] n envie f // vt envier; **to ~ sb sth** envier qch à qn.

epic ['epɪk] n épopée f // a épique.

epidemic [epɪ'demɪk] n épidémie f.

epilepsy ['epɪlepsɪ] n épilepsie f.

episode ['epɪsəud] n épisode m.

epistle [ɪ'pɪsl] n épître f.

epitome [ɪ'pɪtəmɪ] n résumé m; quintessence f, type m; **epitomize** vt résumer; illustrer, incarner.

equable ['ekwəbl] a égal(e); de tempérament égal.

equal ['iːkwl] a égal(e) // n égal/e // vt égaler; **~ to** (task) à la hauteur de; **~ity** [iː'kwɔlɪtɪ] n égalité f; **~ize** vt, vi égaliser; **~izer** n but égalisateur; **~ly** ad également; (just as) tout aussi.

equanimity [ɛkwə'nɪmɪtɪ] n égalité f d'humeur.

equate [ɪ'kweɪt] vt: **to ~ sth with** comparer qch à; assimiler qch à; **equation** [ɪ'kweɪʃən] n (MATH) équation f.

equator [ɪ'kweɪtə*] n équateur m.

equilibrium [iːkwɪ'lɪbrɪəm] n équilibre m.

equip [ɪ'kwɪp] vt équiper; **to be well ~ped** (office etc) être bien équipé(e); **he is well ~ped for the job** il a les compétences ou les qualités requises pour ce travail; **~ment** n équipement m; (electrical etc) appareillage m, installation f.

equities ['ekwɪtɪz] npl (Brit COMM) actions cotées en Bourse.

equivalent [ɪ'kwɪvəlnt] a: **~ (to)** équivalent(e) à // n équivalent m.

equivocal [ɪ'kwɪvəkl] a équivoque; (open to suspicion) douteux(euse).

era ['ɪərə] n ère f, époque f.

eradicate [ɪ'rædɪkeɪt] vt éliminer.

erase [ɪ'reɪz] vt effacer; **~r** n gomme f.

erect [ɪ'rekt] a droit(e) // vt construire; (monument) ériger; élever; (tent etc) dresser; **~ion** [ɪ'rekʃən] n érection f.

ermine ['ɜːmɪn] n hermine f.

erode [ɪ'rəud] vt éroder; (metal) ronger.

erotic [ɪ'rɔtɪk] a érotique.

err [əː*] vi se tromper; (REL) pécher.

errand ['ernd] n course f, commission f.

erratic [ɪ'rætɪk] a irrégulier(ère); inconstant(e).

error ['ɛrə*] n erreur f.

erupt [ı'rʌpt] vi entrer en éruption; (fig) éclater; ~**ion** [ı'rʌpʃən] n éruption f.

escalate ['ɛskəleıt] vi s'intensifier.

escalator ['ɛskəleıtə*] n escalier roulant.

escapade [ɛskə'peıd] n fredaine f; équipée f.

escape [ı'skeıp] n évasion f; fuite f; (of gas etc) échappement m; fuite // vi s'échapper, fuir, (from jail) s'évader; (gas) s'en tirer; (leak) s'échapper; fuir // vt échapper à; **to** ~ **from** (person) échapper à; (place) s'échapper de; (fig) fuir; **escapism** n évasion f (fig).

escort n ['ɛskɔ:t] escorte f // vt [ı'skɔ:t] escorter.

Eskimo ['ɛskıməu] n Esquimau/de.

especially [ı'spɛʃlı] ad particulièrement; surtout; exprès.

espionage ['ɛspıənɑ:ʒ] n espionnage m.

Esquire [ı'skwaıə*] n (abbr Esq.): **J. Brown,** ~ **Monsieur J. Brown.**

essay ['ɛseı] n (SCOL) dissertation f; (LITERATURE) essai m.

essence ['ɛsns] n essence f.

essential [ı'sɛnʃl] a essentiel(le); (basic) fondamental(e) // n élément essentiel; ~**s** éléments essentiels; ~**ly** ad essentiellement.

establish [ı'stæblıʃ] vt établir; (business) fonder, créer; (one's power etc) asseoir, affirmer; ~**ment** n établissement m; création f; **the E**~**ment** les pouvoirs établis; l'ordre établi, les milieux dirigeants.

estate [ı'steıt] n domaine m, propriété f; biens mpl, succession f; ~ **agent** n agent immobilier; ~ **car** n (Brit) break m.

esteem [ı'sti:m] n estime f // vt estimer; apprécier.

esthetic [ıs'θɛtık] a (US) = **aesthetic.**

estimate n ['ɛstımət] estimation f; (COMM) devis m // vt ['ɛstımeıt] esti-

mer; **estimation** [-'meıʃən] n opinion f; estime f.

estranged [ı'streındʒd] a séparé(e); dont on s'est séparé(e).

etc abbr (= et cetera) etc.

etching ['ɛtʃıŋ] n eau-forte f.

eternal [ı'tə:nl] a éternel(le).

eternity [ı'tə:nıtı] n éternité f.

ethical ['ɛθıkl] a moral(e).

ethics ['ɛθıks] n éthique f // npl moralité f.

Ethiopia [i:θı'əupıə] n Éthiopie f.

ethnic ['ɛθnık] a ethnique.

ethos ['i:θɔs] n génie m.

etiquette ['ɛtıkɛt] n convenances fpl, étiquette f.

Eurocheque ['juərəutʃɛk] n eurochèque m.

Europe ['juərəp] n Europe f; ~**an** [-'pi:ən] a européen(ne) // n Européen/ne.

evacuate [ı'vækjueıt] vt évacuer.

evade [ı'veıd] vt échapper à; (question etc) éluder; (duties) se dérober à.

evaporate [ı'væpəreıt] vi s'évaporer // vt faire évaporer; ~**d milk** n lait condensé non sucré.

evasion [ı'veıʒən] n dérobade f; faux-fuyant m.

eve [i:v] n: **on the** ~ **of** à la veille de.

even ['i:vn] a régulier(ère), égal(e); (number) pair(e) // ad même; ~ **if** même si + indic; ~ **though** quand (bien) même + cond, alors même que + cond; ~ **more** encore plus; ~ **so** quand même; **not** ~ pas même; **to get** ~ **with sb** prendre sa revanche sur qn; **to** ~ **out** vi s'égaliser.

evening ['i:vnıŋ] n soir m; (as duration, event) soirée f; **in the** ~ le soir; ~ **class** n cours m du soir; ~ **dress** n (man's) habit m de soirée, smoking m; (woman's) robe f de soirée.

event [ı'vɛnt] n événement m; (SPORT) épreuve f; **in the** ~ **of** en cas de; ~**ful** a mouvementé(e).

eventual [ı'vɛntʃuəl] a final(e); ~**ity**

[-'æliti] n possibilité f, éventualité f; **~ly** ad finalement.

ever ['ɛvə*] ad jamais; (at all times) toujours; **the best** ~ le meilleur qu'on ait jamais vu; **have you seen it?** l'as-tu déjà vu?, as-tu eu l'occasion or t'est-il arrivé de le voir?; ~ **since** ad depuis // cj depuis que; **~green** n arbre m à feuilles persistantes; **~lasting** a éternel(le).

every ['ɛvrɪ] a chaque; ~ **day** tous les jours, chaque jour; ~ **other/third day** tous les deux/trois jours; ~ **other car** une voiture sur deux; **now and then** de temps en temps; **~body** pronoun tout le monde, tous pl; **~day** a quotidien(ne); de tous les jours; **~one** = **~body**; **~thing** pronoun tout; **~where** ad partout.

evict [ɪ'vɪkt] vt expulser.

evidence ['ɛvɪdns] n (proof) preuve(s) f(pl); (of witness) témoignage m; (sign): **to show** ~ of donner des signes de; **to give** ~ témoigner, déposer.

evident ['ɛvɪdnt] a évident(e); **~ly** ad de toute évidence.

evil ['iːvl] a mauvais(e) // n mal m.

evoke [ɪ'vəuk] vt évoquer.

evolution [iːvə'luːʃən] n évolution f.

evolve [ɪ'vɔlv] vt élaborer // vi évoluer, se transformer.

ewe [juː] n brebis f.

ex- [ɛks] prefix ex-.

exact [ɪg'zækt] a exact(e) // vt: **to** ~ **sth (from)** extorquer qch (à); exiger qch (de); **~ing** a exigeant(e); (work) fatigant(e); **~ly** ad exactement.

exaggerate [ɪg'zædʒəreɪt] vt, vi exagérer; **exaggeration** [-'reɪʃən] n exagération f.

exalted [ɪg'zɔːltɪd] a élevé(e); (person) haut placé(e); (elated) exalté(e).

exam [ɪg'zæm] n abbr (SCOL) of **examination**.

examination [ɪgzæmɪ'neɪʃən] n (SCOL, MED) examen m.

examine [ɪg'zæmɪn] vt (gen) examiner; (SCOL, LAW: person) interroger; (at customs: luggage) inspecter; **~r** n examinateur m.

example [ɪg'zaːmpl] n exemple m; **for** ~ par exemple.

exasperate [ɪg'zaːspəreɪt] vt exaspérer; **exasperation** [ɪgzaːspə'reɪʃən] n exaspération f, irritation f.

excavate ['ɛkskəveɪt] vt excaver; (object) mettre au jour.

exceed [ɪk'siːd] vt dépasser; (one's powers) outrepasser; **~ingly** ad excessivement.

excellent ['ɛksələnt] a excellent(e).

except [ɪk'sɛpt] prep (also: ~ **for**, ~ **ing**) sauf, excepté, à l'exception de // vt excepter; ~ **if/when** sauf si/ quand; ~ **that** excepté que, si ce n'est que; **~ion** [ɪk'sɛpʃən] n exception f; **to take** ~ **to** s'offusquer de; **~ional** [ɪk'sɛpʃənl] a exceptionnel(le).

excerpt ['ɛksəːpt] n extrait m.

excess [ɪk'sɛs] n excès m; ~ **baggage** n excédent m de bagages; ~ **fare** n supplément m; **~ive** a excessif(ive).

exchange [ɪks'tʃeɪndʒ] n échange m; (also: **telephone** ~) central m // vt: **to** ~ **(for)** échanger (contre); ~ **rate** n taux m des changes.

Exchequer [ɪks'tʃɛkə*] n: **the** ~ (Brit) l'Échiquier m, ≈ le ministère des Finances.

excise ['ɛksaɪz] n taxe f.

excite [ɪk'saɪt] vt exciter; **to get** ~ **d** s'exciter; **~ment** n excitation f; **exciting** a passionnant(e).

exclaim [ɪk'skleɪm] vi s'exclamer; **exclamation** [ɛksklə'meɪʃən] n exclamation f; **exclamation mark** n point m d'exclamation.

exclude [ɪk'skluːd] vt exclure.

exclusive [ɪk'skluːsɪv] a exclusif(ive); (club, district) sélect(e); (item of news) en exclusivité; ~ **of VAT** TVA non comprise.

excruciating [ɪk'skruːʃɪeɪtɪŋ] a atroce, déchirant(e).

excursion [ɪk'skəːʃən] n excursion f.

excuse n [ɪkˈskjuːs] excuse f // vt [ɪkˈskjuːz] excuser; **to ~ sb from** (activity) dispenser qn de; **~ me!** excusez-moi!, pardon!; **now if you will ~ me, ...** maintenant, si vous (le) permettez ....

ex-directory [ˈɛksdɪˈrɛktərɪ] a (Brit) sur la liste rouge.

execute [ˈɛksɪkjuːt] vt exécuter.

execution [ɛksɪˈkjuːʃən] n exécution f; **~er** n bourreau m.

executive [ɪgˈzɛkjutɪv] n (COMM) cadre m; (POL) exécutif m // a exécutif(ive).

exemplify [ɪgˈzɛmplɪfaɪ] vt illustrer.

exempt [ɪgˈzɛmpt] a: **~ from** exempté(e) or dispensé(e) de // vt: **to ~ sb from** exempter or dispenser qn de.

exercise [ˈɛksəsaɪz] n exercice m // vt exercer; (patience etc) faire preuve de; (dog) promener // vi prendre de l'exercice; **~ book** n cahier m.

exert [ɪgˈzɜːt] vt exercer, employer; **to ~ o.s.** se dépenser; **~ion** [-ʃən] n effort m.

exhaust [ɪgˈzɔːst] n (also: **~ fumes**) gaz mpl d'échappement; (also: **~ pipe**) tuyau m d'échappement // vt épuiser; **~ed** a épuisé(e); **~ion** [ɪgˈzɔːstʃən] n épuisement m; **nervous ~ion** fatigue nerveuse; surmenage mental; **~ive** a très complet(ète).

exhibit [ɪgˈzɪbɪt] n (ART) pièce f or objet m exposé(e); (LAW) pièce à conviction // vt exposer; (courage, skill) faire preuve de; **~ion** [ɛksɪˈbɪʃən] n exposition f.

exhilarating [ɪgˈzɪləreɪtɪŋ] a grisant(e); stimulant(e).

exile [ˈɛksaɪl] n exil m; (person) exilé/e // vt exiler.

exist [ɪgˈzɪst] vi exister; **~ence** n existence f; **to be in ~ence** exister; **~ing** a actuel(le).

exit [ˈɛksɪt] n sortie f // vi (COMPUT, THEATRE) sortir; **~ ramp** n (US AUT) bretelle f d'accès.

exodus [ˈɛksədəs] n exode m.

exonerate [ɪgˈzɔnəreɪt] vt: **to ~ from** disculper de.

exotic [ɪgˈzɔtɪk] a exotique.

expand [ɪkˈspænd] vt agrandir; accroître, étendre // vi (trade etc) se développer, s'accroître; s'étendre; (gas, metal) se dilater.

expanse [ɪkˈspæns] n étendue f.

expansion [ɪkˈspænʃən] n développement m, accroissement m; dilatation f.

expect [ɪkˈspɛkt] vt (anticipate) s'attendre à, s'attendre à ce que + sub; (count on) compter sur, escompter; (hope for) espérer; (require) demander, exiger; (suppose) supposer; (await, also baby) attendre // vi: **to be ~ing** être enceinte; **to ~ sb to do** s'attendre à ce que qn fasse; attendre de qn qu'il fasse; **~ancy** n (anticipation) attente f; **life ~ancy** espérance f de vie; **~ant mother** n future maman; **~ation** [ɛkspɛkˈteɪʃən] n attente f, prévisions fpl; espérance(s) f(pl).

expedience, expediency [ɪkˈspiːdɪəns, ɪkˈspiːdɪənsɪ] n: **for the sake of ~** parce que c'est plus commode.

expedient [ɪkˈspiːdɪənt] a indiqué(e), opportun(e); commode // n expédient m.

expedition [ɛkspəˈdɪʃən] n expédition f.

expel [ɪkˈspɛl] vt chasser, expulser; (SCOL) renvoyer, exclure.

expend [ɪkˈspɛnd] vt consacrer; (use up) dépenser; **~able** a remplaçable; **~iture** [ɪkˈspɛndɪtʃə*] n dépense f, dépenses fpl.

expense [ɪkˈspɛns] n dépense f; frais mpl; (high cost) coût m; **~s** npl (COMM) frais mpl; **at the ~ of** aux dépens de; **~ account** n (note f de) frais mpl.

expensive [ɪkˈspɛnsɪv] a cher(chère), coûteux(euse); **to be ~** coûter cher.

experience [ɪkˈspɪərɪəns] n expérience f // vt connaître; éprouver; ~d a expérimenté(e).

experiment [ɪk'sperɪmənt] n expérience f // vi faire une expérience; to ~ with expérimenter.

expert ['ekspə:t] a expert(e) // n expert m; ~ise [-'ti:z] n (grande) compétence.

expire [ɪk'spaɪə*] vi expirer; **expiry** n expiration f.

explain [ɪk'spleɪn] vt expliquer; **explanation** [eksplə'neɪʃən] n explication f; **explanatory** [ɪk'splænətrɪ] a explicatif(ive).

explicit [ɪk'splɪsɪt] a explicite; (definite) formel(le).

explode [ɪk'spləud] vi exploser // vt faire exploser.

exploit n ['eksplɔɪt] exploit m // vt [ɪk'splɔɪt] exploiter; ~ation [-'teɪʃən] n exploitation f.

exploratory [ɪk'splɔrətrɪ] a (fig: talks) préliminaire.

explore [ɪk'splɔ:*] vt explorer; (possibilities) étudier, examiner; ~r n explorateur/trice.

explosion [ɪk'spləuʒən] n explosion f.

explosive [ɪk'spləusɪv] a explosif(ive) // n explosif m.

exponent [ɪk'spəunənt] n (of school of thought etc) interprète m, représentant m.

export vt [ek'spɔ:t] exporter // n ['ekspɔ:t] exportation f // cpd d'exportation; ~er n exportateur m.

expose [ɪk'spəuz] vt exposer; (unmask) démasquer, dévoiler; ~d a (position) exposé(e).

exposure [ɪk'spəuʒə*] n exposition f; (PHOT) (temps m de) pose f; (: shot) pose; **suffering from ~** (MED) souffrant des effets du froid et de l'épuisement; ~ **meter** n posemètre m.

expound [ɪk'spaund] vt exposer.

express [ɪk'spres] a (definite) formel(le), exprès(esse); (Brit: letter etc) exprès inv // n (train) rapide m // ad (send) exprès // vt exprimer;

~**ion** [ɪk'spreʃən] n expression f; ~**ly** ad expressément, formellement; ~**way** n (US: urban motorway) voie f express (à plusieurs files).

exquisite [ek'skwɪzɪt] a exquis(e).

extend [ɪk'stend] vt (visit, street) prolonger; (building) agrandir; (offer) présenter, offrir // vi (land) s'étendre.

extension [ɪk'stenʃən] n prolongation f; agrandissement m; (building) annexe f; (to wire, table) rallonge f; (telephone: in offices) poste m; (: in private house) téléphone m supplémentaire.

extensive [ɪk'stensɪv] a étendu(e), vaste; (damage, alterations) considérable; (inquiries) approfondi(e); (use) largement répandu(e); **he's travelled ~** il a beaucoup voyagé.

extent [ɪk'stent] n étendue f; **to some ~** dans une certaine mesure; **to what ~?** dans quelle mesure?, jusqu'à quel point?; **to the ~ of ...** au point de ....

extenuating [ɪk'stenjueɪtɪŋ] a: ~ **circumstances** circonstances atténuantes.

exterior [ek'stɪərɪə*] a extérieur(e), du dehors // n extérieur m; dehors m.

external [ek'stə:nl] a externe.

extinct [ɪk'stɪŋkt] a éteint(e).

extinguish [ɪk'stɪŋgwɪʃ] vt éteindre; ~**er** n extincteur m.

extort [ɪk'stɔ:t] vt: **to ~ sth (from)** extorquer qch (à); ~**ionate** [ɪk'stɔ:ʃnət] a exorbitant(e).

extra ['ekstrə] a supplémentaire, de plus // ad (in addition) en plus // n supplément m; (THEATRE) figurant/e.

extra... ['ekstrə] prefix extra....

extract vt [ɪk'strækt] extraire; (tooth) arracher; (money, promise) soutirer // n ['ekstrækt] extrait m.

extracurricular ['ekstrəkə'rɪkjulə*] a parascolaire.

extradite ['ekstrədaɪt] vt extrader.

extramarital [ekstrə'mærɪtl] a extra-conjugal(e).

extramural [ɛkstrəˈmjuərl] a hors-faculté *inv*.

extraordinary [ɪkˈstrɔːdɪnrɪ] a extraordinaire.

extravagance [ɪkˈstrævəgəns] n prodigalités *fpl*; *(thing bought)* folie f, dépense excessive *or* exagérée.

extravagant [ɪkˈstrævəgənt] a extravagant(e); *(in spending)* prodigue, dépensier(ère); dispendieux(euse).

extreme [ɪkˈstriːm] a, n extrême *(m)*; ~**ly** ad extrêmement.

extricate [ˈɛkstrɪkeɪt] vt: to ~ sth (from) dégager qch (de).

extrovert [ˈɛkstrəvɜːt] n extraverti-e.

eye [aɪ] n œil m *(pl* yeux); *(of needle)* trou m, chas m // vt examiner; **to keep an ~ on** surveiller; ~**ball** n globe m oculaire; ~**bath** n œillère f *(pour bains d'œil)*; ~**brow** n sourcil m; ~**brow pencil** n crayon m à sourcils; ~**drops** npl gouttes *fpl* pour les yeux; ~**lash** n cil m; ~**lid** n paupière f; ~**liner** n eye-liner m; ~**opener** n révélation f; ~**shadow** n ombre f à paupières; ~**sight** n vue f; ~**sore** n horreur f, chose f qui dépare *or* enlaidit; ~ **witness** n témoin m oculaire.

F

F [ɛf] n *(MUS)* fa m.
fable [ˈfeɪbl] n fable f.
fabric [ˈfæbrɪk] n tissu m.
fabrication [fæbrɪˈkeɪʃən] n invention(s) f(pl), fabulation f; fait m *(or* preuve f) forgé(e) de toutes pièces.
fabulous [ˈfæbjuləs] a fabuleux(euse); *(col: super)* formidable.
face [feɪs] n visage m, figure f; expression f; *(of clock)* cadran m; *(of building)* façade f; *(side, surface)* face f // vt faire face à; ~ **down** *(person)* à plat ventre; *(card)* face en dessous; **to make *or* pull a ~** faire une grimace; **in the ~ of** *(difficulties etc)* face à, devant; **on the ~**

of it à première vue; ~ **to** ~ face à face; **to** ~ **up to** vt fus faire face à, affronter; ~ **cloth** n *(Brit)* gant m de toilette; ~ **cream** n crème f pour le visage; ~ **lift** n lifting m; *(of building etc)* ravalement m, retapage m.

face value n *(of coin)* valeur nominale; **to take sth at** ~ *(fig)* prendre qch pour argent comptant.

facilities [fəˈsɪlɪtɪz] npl installations *fpl*, équipement m; **credit** ~ facilités *fpl* de paiement.

facing [ˈfeɪsɪŋ] prep face à, en face de // n *(of wall etc)* revêtement m; *(SEWING)* revers m.

facsimile [fækˈsɪmɪlɪ] n *(document)* télécopie f; *(machine)* télécopieur m.

fact [fækt] n fait m; **in** ~ en fait.

factor [ˈfæktə*] n facteur m.

factory [ˈfæktərɪ] n usine f, fabrique f.

factual [ˈfæktjuəl] a basé(e) sur les faits.

faculty [ˈfækəltɪ] n faculté f; *(US: teaching staff)* corps enseignant.

fad [fæd] n manie f, engouement m.

fade [feɪd] vi se décolorer, passer; *(light, sound, hope)* s'affaiblir, disparaître; *(flower)* se faner.

fag [fæg] n *(col: cigarette)* sèche f.

fail [feɪl] vt *(exam)* échouer à; *(candidate)* recaler; *(subj: courage, memory)* faire défaut à // vi échouer; *(supplies)* manquer; *(eyesight, health, light)* baisser, s'affaiblir; **to** ~ **to do sth** *(neglect)* négliger de faire qch; *(be unable)* ne pas arriver *or* parvenir à faire qch; **without** ~ à coup sûr; sans faute; ~**ing** n défaut m // prep faute de; ~**ure** [ˈfeɪljə*] n échec m; *(person)* raté(e); *(mechanical etc)* défaillance f.

faint [feɪnt] a faible; *(recollection)* vague; *(mark)* à peine visible // n évanouissement m // vi s'évanouir; **to feel** ~ défaillir.

fair [fɛə*] a équitable, juste, impartial(e); *(hair)* blond(e); *(skin, complexion)* pâle, blanc(blanche);

(weather) beau(belle); (good enough) assez bon(ne); (sizeable) considérable // ad (play) franc-jeu // foire f; (Brit: funfair) fête (foraine); ~ly ad équitablement; (quite) assez; ~ness n justice f, équité f, impartialité f.

fairy ['fɛərɪ] n fée f; ~ **tale** n conte m de fées.

faith [feɪθ] n foi f; (trust) confiance f; (sect) culte m, religion f; ~**ful** a fidèle; ~**fully** ad fidèlement.

fake [feɪk] n (painting etc) faux m; (photo) trucage m; (person) imposteur m // a faux(fausse); simulé(e) // vt simuler; (photo) truquer; (story) fabriquer.

falcon ['fɔ:lkən] n faucon m.

fall [fɔ:l] n chute f; (US: autumn) automne m // vi (pt fell, pp fallen) tomber; ~s npl (waterfall) chute f d'eau, cascade f; **to** ~ **flat** vi (on one's face) tomber de tout son long, s'étaler; (joke) tomber à plat; (plan) échouer; **to** ~ **back** vi reculer, se retirer; **to** ~ **back on** vt fus se rabattre sur; **to** ~ **behind** vi prendre du retard; **to** ~ **down** vi (person) tomber; (building, hopes) s'effondrer, s'écrouler; **to** ~ **for** vt fus (trick) se laisser prendre à; (person) tomber amoureux de; **to** ~ **in** vi s'effondrer; (MIL) se mettre en rangs; **to** ~ **off** vi tomber; (diminish) baisser, diminuer; **to** ~ **out** vi (friends etc) se brouiller; **to** ~ **through** vi (plan, project) tomber à l'eau.

fallacy ['fæləsɪ] n erreur f, illusion f.

fallen ['fɔ:lən] pp of **fall**.

fallout ['fɔ:laʊt] n retombées (radioactives); ~ **shelter** n abri m antiatomique.

fallow ['fæləʊ] a en jachère; en friche.

false [fɔ:ls] a faux(fausse); **under** ~ **pretences** sous un faux prétexte; ~ **teeth** npl (Brit) fausses dents.

falter ['fɔ:ltə*] vi chanceler, vaciller.

fame [feɪm] n renommée f, renom m.

familiar [fə'mɪlɪə*] a familier(ère);

to be ~ **with** (subject) connaître; ~**ity** [fəmɪlɪ'ærɪtɪ] n familiarité f.

family ['fæmɪlɪ] n famille f.

famine ['fæmɪn] n famine f.

famished ['fæmɪʃt] a affamé(e).

famous ['feɪməs] a célèbre; ~**ly** ad (get on) fameusement, à merveille.

fan [fæn] n (folding) éventail m; (ELEC) ventilateur m; (person) fan m, admirateur/trice; supporter m/f // vt éventer; (fire, quarrel) attiser; **to** ~ **out** vi se déployer (en éventail).

fanatic [fə'nætɪk] n fanatique m/f.

fan belt n courroie f de ventilateur.

fanciful ['fænsɪful] a fantaisiste.

fancy ['fænsɪ] n fantaisie f, envie f; imagination f // a (de) fantaisie inv // vt (feel like, want) avoir envie de; (imagine) imaginer; **to take a** ~ **to** se prendre d'affection pour; s'enticher de; ~ **dress** n déguisement m, travesti m; ~-**dress ball** n bal masqué or costumé.

fang [fæŋ] n croc m; (of snake) crochet m.

fantastic [fæn'tæstɪk] a fantastique.

fantasy ['fæntəsɪ] n imagination f, fantaisie f; fantasme m; chimère f.

far [fɑ:*] a: **the** ~ **side/end** l'autre côté/bout // ad loin; ~ **away**, ~ **off** au loin, dans le lointain; ~ **better** beaucoup mieux; ~ **from** loin de; **by** ~ de loin, de beaucoup; **go as** ~ **as the farm** allez jusqu'à la ferme; **as** ~ **as I know** pour autant que je sache; ~**away** a lointain(e).

farce [fɑ:s] n farce f.

farcical ['fɑ:sɪkl] a grotesque.

fare [fɛə*] n (on trains, buses) prix m du billet; (in taxi) prix de la course; (food) table f, chère f; **half** ~ demitarif; **full** ~ plein tarif.

Far East n: **the** ~ l'Extrême-Orient m.

farewell [fɛə'wel] excl, n adieu m.

farm [fɑ:m] n ferme f // vt cultiver; ~**er** n fermier/ère; cultivateur/trice; ~**hand** n ouvrier/ère agricole; ~**house** n (maison f de) ferme f; ~**ing** n agriculture f; ~ **worker**

= ~**hand**; ~**yard** n cour f de ferme.

far-reaching ['fɑː'riːtʃɪŋ] a d'une grande portée.

fart [fɑːt] (col!) n pet m // vi péter.

farther ['fɑːðəᵣ] ad plus loin // a plus éloigné(e), plus lointain(e).

farthest ['fɑːðɪst] superlative of far.

fascinate ['fæsɪneɪt] vt fasciner; **fascinating** a fascinant(e).

fascism ['fæʃɪzəm] n fascisme m.

fashion ['fæʃən] n mode f; (manner) façon f, manière f // vt façonner; **in ~** à la mode; **out of ~** démodé(e) // ~**able** a à la mode; **~ show** n défilé m de mannequins or de mode.

fast [fɑːst] a rapide; (clock): **to be ~** avancer; (dye, colour) grand or bon teint inv // ad vite, rapidement; (stuck, held) solidement // n jeûne m // vi jeûner; **~ asleep** profondément endormi.

fasten ['fɑːsn] vt attacher, fixer; (coat) attacher, fermer // vi se fermer, s'attacher; **~er**, **~ing** n fermeture f, attache f.

fast food n fast food m, restauration f rapide.

fastidious [fæs'tɪdɪəs] a exigeant(e), difficile.

fat [fæt] a gros(se) // n graisse f; (on meat) gras m.

fatal ['feɪtl] a mortel(le); fatal(e); désastreux(euse); **~ity** [fə'tælɪtɪ] n (road death etc) victime f, décès m.

fate [feɪt] n destin m; (of person) sort m; **~ful** a fatidique.

father ['fɑːðəᵣ] n père m; **~-in-law** n beau-père m; **~ly** a paternel(le).

fathom ['fæðəm] n brasse f (= 1828 mm) // vt (mystery) sonder, pénétrer.

fatigue [fə'tiːg] n fatigue f; (MIL) corvée f.

fatten ['fætn] vt, vi engraisser.

fatty ['fætɪ] a (food) gras(se) // n (col) gros/grosse.

fatuous ['fætjʊəs] a stupide.

faucet ['fɔːsɪt] n (US) robinet m.

fault [fɔːlt] n faute f; (defect) défaut

m; (GEO) faille f // vt trouver des défauts à, prendre en défaut; **it's my ~** c'est de ma faute; **to find ~ with** trouver à redire or à critiquer à; **at ~** fautif(ive), coupable; **to a ~** à l'excès; **~less** a sans fautes; impeccable; irréprochable; **~y** a défectueux(euse).

fauna ['fɔːnə] n faune f.

faux pas ['fəʊ'pɑː] n impair m, bévue f, gaffe f.

favour, (US) **favor** ['feɪvəᵣ] n faveur f; (help) service m // vt (proposition) être en faveur de; (pupil etc) favoriser; (team, horse) donner gagnant; **to do sb a ~** rendre un service à qn; **to find ~ with** trouver grâce aux yeux de; **in ~ of** en faveur de; **~able** a favorable; (price) avantageux(euse); **~ite** [-rɪt] a, n favori(te).

fawn [fɔːn] n faon m // a (also: **~-coloured**) fauve // vi: **to ~ (up)on** flatter servilement.

fax [fæks] n (document) télécopie f; (machine) télécopieur m.

FBI n abbr (US: = Federal Bureau of Investigation) F.B.I. m.

fear [fɪəᵣ] n crainte f, peur f // vt craindre; **for ~ of** de peur que + sub or de + infinitive; **~ful** a craintif(ive); (sight, noise) affreux(euse), épouvantable.

feasible ['fiːzəbl] a faisable, réalisable.

feast [fiːst] n festin m, banquet m; (REL: also: **~ day**) fête f // vi festoyer.

feat [fiːt] n exploit m, prouesse f.

feather ['feðəᵣ] n plume f.

feature ['fiːtʃəᵣ] n caractéristique f; (article) chronique m, rubrique f // vt (subj: film) avoir pour vedette(s) // vi figurer (en bonne place); **~s** npl (of face) traits -mpl; **~ film** n film principal.

February ['februərɪ] n février m.

fed [fed] pt, pp of **feed**.

federal ['fedərəl] a fédéral(e).

fed-up [fed'ʌp] a: **to be ~** en avoir

marre or plein le dos.

fee [fi:] n rémunération f; (of doctor, lawyer) honoraires mpl; (of school, college etc) frais mpl de scolarité; (for examination) droits mpl.

feeble ['fi:bl] a faible.

feed [fi:d] n (of baby) tétée f; (of animal) fourrage m; pâture f; (on printer) mécanisme m d'alimentation // vt (pt, pp fed) nourrir; (baby) allaiter; donner le biberon à; (horse etc) donner à manger à; (machine) alimenter; (data, information) to ~ into fournir à; to ~ on vt fus se nourrir de; ~back n feed-back m; ~ing bottle n (Brit) biberon m.

feel [fi:l] n sensation f // vt (pt, pp felt) toucher; tâter, palper; (cold, pain) sentir; (grief, anger) ressentir, éprouver; (think, believe): to ~ (that) trouver que; to ~ hungry/ cold avoir faim/froid; to ~ lonely/ better se sentir seul/mieux; I don't ~ well je ne me sens pas bien; to ~ like (want) avoir envie de; to ~ about or around vt fouiller, tâtonner; ~er n (of insect) antenne f; to put out ~ers or a ~er tâter le terrain; ~ing n sensation f, sentiment m.

feet [fi:t] npl of foot.

feign [fein] vt feindre, simuler.

fell [fel] pt of fall // vt (tree) abattre.

fellow ['feləu] n type m; compagnon m; (of learned society) membre m // cpd: ~ countryman n compatriote m; ~ men npl semblables mpl; ~ship n association f; amitié f, camaraderie f; sorte de bourse universitaire.

felony ['feləni] n crime m, forfait m.

felt [felt] pt, pp of feel // n feutre m; ~-tip pen n stylo-feutre m.

female ['fi:meil] n (ZOOL) femelle f; (pej: woman) bonne femme // a (BIOL, ELEC) femelle; (sex, character) féminin(e); (vote etc) des femmes.

feminine ['feminin] a féminin(e).

feminist ['feminist] n féministe m/f.

fence [fens] n barrière f; (col: person) receleur/euse // vt (also: ~ in) clôturer // vi faire de l'escrime; **fencing** n escrime m.

fend [fend] vi: to ~ for o.s. se débrouiller (tout seul); to ~ off vt (attack etc) parer.

fender ['fendə*] n garde-feu m inv; (US) gardeboue m inv; pare-chocs m inv.

ferment vi ['fə:ment] fermenter // n ['fə:ment] agitation f, effervescence f.

fern [fə:n] n fougère f.

ferocious [fə'rəuʃəs] a féroce.

ferret ['ferit] n furet m.

ferry ['feri] n (small) bac m; (large: also: ~boat) ferry(-boat) m // vt transporter.

fertile ['fə:tail] a fertile; (BIOL) fécond(e); **fertilizer** ['fə:tilaizə*] n engrais m.

fester ['festə*] vi suppurer.

festival ['festivəl] n (REL) fête f; (ART, MUS) festival m.

festive ['festiv] a de fête; the ~ season (Brit: Christmas) la période des fêtes.

festivities [fes'trvitiz] npl réjouissances fpl.

festoon [fes'tu:n] vt: to ~ with orner de.

fetch [fetʃ] vt aller chercher; (sell for) se vendre.

fetching ['fetʃiŋ] a charmant(e).

fête [feit] n fête f, kermesse f.

feud [fju:d] n dispute f, dissension f.

feudal ['fju:dl] a féodal(e).

fever ['fi:və*] n fièvre f; ~ish a fiévreux(euse), fébrile.

few [fju:] a peu de; they were ~ ils étaient peu (nombreux); a ~ a quelques // pronoun quelques-uns; ~er a moins de; moins (nombreux).

fiancé [fi'ɑ̃:ŋsei] n fiancé m; ~e n fiancée f.

fib [fib] n bobard m.

fibre, (US) **fiber** ['faibə*] n fibre f; ~glass n fibre de verre.

fickle ['fikl] a inconstant(e), volage, capricieux(euse).

fiction ['fɪkʃən] n romans mpl, littérature f romanesque; fiction f; ~**al** a fictif(ive).

fictitious [fɪk'tɪʃəs] a fictif(ive), imaginaire.

fiddle ['fɪdl] n (MUS) violon m; (cheating) combine f; escroquerie f // vt (Brit: accounts) falsifier, maquiller; **to ~ with** vt fus tripoter.

fidget ['fɪdʒɪt] vi se trémousser, remuer.

field [fi:ld] n champ m; (fig) domaine m, champ; (SPORT: ground) terrain m; ~ **marshal** n maréchal m; ~**work** n travaux mpl pratiques (sur le terrain).

fiend [fi:nd] n démon m.

fierce [fɪəs] a (look) féroce, sauvage; (wind, attack) (très) violent(e); (fighting, enemy) acharné(e).

fiery ['faɪərɪ] a ardent(e), brûlant(e); fougueux(euse).

fifteen [fɪf'ti:n] num quinze.

fifth [fɪfθ] a, n cinquième m/f.

fifty ['fɪftɪ] num cinquante; ~~ a: a ~~ **chance** une chance etc sur deux // ad moitié-moitié.

fig [fɪg] n figue f.

fight [faɪt] n bagarre f; (MIL) combat m; (against cancer etc) lutte f // vb (pt, pp **fought**) vt se battre contre; (cancer, alcoholism) combattre, lutter contre // vi se battre; ~**er** n lutteur m; (plane) chasseur m; ~**ing** n combats mpl.

figment ['fɪgmənt] n: a ~ **of the imagination** une invention.

figurative ['fɪgjurətɪv] a figuré(e).

figure ['fɪgə*] n (DRAWING, GEOM) figure f; (number, cipher) chiffre m; (body, outline) silhouette f, ligne f, formes fpl // vt (US) supposer // vi (appear) figurer; (US: make sense) s'expliquer; **to ~ out** vt arriver à comprendre; calculer; ~**head** n (NAUT) figure f de proue; (pej) prête-nom m; ~ **of speech** n figure f de rhétorique.

file [faɪl] n (tool) lime f; (dossier) dossier m; (folder) dossier, chemise

f; (with hinges) classeur m; (COMPUT) fichier m; (row) file f // vt (nails, wood) limer; (papers) classer; (LAW: claim) faire enregistrer; déposer // vi: **to ~ in/out** entrer/sortir l'un derrière l'autre; **to ~ past** défiler devant.

filing ['faɪlɪŋ] n (travaux mpl de) classement m; ~ **cabinet** n classeur m (meuble).

fill [fɪl] vt remplir // n: **to eat one's ~** manger à sa faim; **to ~ in** vt (hole) boucher; (form) remplir; **to ~ up** vt remplir; **to ~ it up, please** (AUT) le plein, s'il vous plaît.

fillet ['fɪlɪt] n filet m; ~ **steak** n filet m de bœuf, tournedos m.

filling ['fɪlɪŋ] n (CULIN) garniture f, farce f; (for tooth) plombage m; ~ **station** n station f d'essence.

film [fɪlm] n film m; (PHOT) pellicule f, film // vt (scene) filmer; ~ **star** n vedette f de cinéma; ~**strip** n (film m pour) projection f fixe.

filter ['fɪltə*] n filtre m // vt filtrer; ~ **lane** n (Brit AUT) voie f de sortie; ~**-tipped** a à bout filtre.

filth [fɪlθ] n saleté f; ~**y** a sale, dégoûtant(e); (language) ordurier(ère).

fin [fɪn] n (of fish) nageoire f.

final ['faɪnl] a final(e), dernier(ère); définitif(ive) // n (SPORT) finale f; ~**s** npl (SCOL) examens mpl de dernière année; ~**e** [fɪ'nɑ:lɪ] n finale m; ~**ize** vt mettre au point; ~**ly** ad (lastly) en dernier lieu; (eventually) enfin, finalement.

finance [faɪ'næns] n finance f; ~**s** npl finances fpl // vt financer.

financial [faɪ'nænʃəl] a financier(ère).

find [faɪnd] vt (pt, pp **found**) trouver; (lost object) retrouver // n trouvaille f, découverte f; **to ~ sb guilty** (LAW) déclarer qn coupable; **to ~ out** vt se renseigner sur; (truth, secret) découvrir; (person) démasquer; **to ~ out about** se renseigner sur; (by chance) apprendre; ~**ings** npl (LAW) conclusions fpl, verdict *m*; (of report) constatations *fpl*.

fine [faɪn] *a* beau(belle); excellent(e); (thin, subtle) fin(e) // *ad* (well) très bien; (small) fin, finement // *n* (LAW) amende *f*; contravention *f* // *vt* (LAW) condamner à une amende; donner une contravention à; **to be** ~ (weather) faire beau; ~ **arts** *npl* beaux-arts *mpl*.

finery ['faɪnərɪ] *n* parure *f*.

finger ['fɪŋgə*] *n* doigt *m* // *vt* palper, toucher; **little/index** ~ auriculaire *m*/index *m*; ~**nail** *n* ongle *m* (de la main); ~**print** *n* empreinte digitale; ~**tip** *n* bout *m* du doigt.

finicky ['fɪnɪkɪ] *a* tatillon(ne), méticuleux(euse); minutieux(euse).

finish ['fɪnɪʃ] *n* fin *f*; (SPORT) arrivée *f*; (polish etc) finition *f* // *vt* finir, terminer // *vi* finir, se terminer; (session) s'achever; **to** ~ **doing sth** finir de faire qch; **to** ~ **third** arriver *or* terminer troisième; **to** ~ **off** *vt* finir, terminer; (kill) achever; **to** ~ **up** *vi, vt* finir; ~**ing line** *n* ligne *f* d'arrivée; ~**ing school** *n* institution privée (pour jeunes filles).

finite ['faɪnaɪt] *a* fini(e); (verb) conjugué(e).

Finland ['fɪnlənd] *n* Finlande *f*.

Finn [fɪn] *n* Finnois/e; Finlandais/e; ~**ish** *a* finnois(e); finlandais(e) // *n* (LING) finnois *m*.

fir [fə:*] *n* sapin *m*.

fire ['faɪə*] *n* feu *m*; incendie *m* // *vt* (discharge): **to** ~ **a gun** tirer un coup de feu; (fig) enflammer, animer; (dismiss) mettre à la porte, renvoyer // *vi* tirer, faire feu; **on** ~ en feu; ~ **alarm** *n* avertisseur *m* d'incendie; ~**arm** *n* arme *f* à feu; ~ **brigade**, (US) ~ **department** *n* (régiment *m* de sapeurs-)pompiers *mpl*; ~ **engine** *n* pompe *f* à incendie; ~ **escape** *n* escalier *m* de secours; ~ **extinguisher** *n* extincteur *m*; ~**man** *n* pompier *m*; ~**place** *n* cheminée *f*; ~**side** *n* foyer *m*, coin *m* du feu; ~ **station** *n* caserne *f* de pompiers; ~**wood** *n* bois *m* de

chauffage; ~**work** *n* feu *m* d'artifice; ~**works** *npl* (display) feu(x) d'artifice.

firing ['faɪərɪŋ] *n* (MIL) feu *m*, tir *m*; ~ **squad** *n* peloton *m* d'exécution.

firm [fə:m] *n* compagnie *f*, firme *f*; ~**ly** *ad* fermement.

first [fə:st] *a* premier(ère) // *ad* (before others) le premier, la première; (before other things) en premier, d'abord; (when listing reasons etc) en premier lieu, premièrement // *n* (person: in race) premier/ère; (SCOL) mention *f* très bien; (AUT) première *f*; **at** ~ au commencement, au début; ~ **of all** tout d'abord, pour commencer; ~ **aid** *n* premiers secours *or* soins; ~-**aid kit** *n* trousse *f* à pharmacie; ~-**class** *a* de première classe; ~-**hand** *a* de première main; ~ **lady** *n* (US) femme *f* du président; ~**ly** *ad* premièrement, en premier lieu; ~ **name** *n* prénom *m*; ~-**rate** *a* excellent(e).

fish [fɪʃ] *n* (pl inv) poisson *m*; poissons *mpl* // *vi, vt* pêcher; **to go** ~**ing** aller à la pêche; ~**erman** *n* pêcheur *m*; ~ **farm** *n* établissement *m* piscicole; ~ **fingers** *npl* (Brit) bâtonnets de poisson (congelés); ~**ing boat** *n* barque *f* de pêche; ~**ing line** *n* ligne *f* (de pêche); ~**ing rod** *n* canne *f* à pêche; ~**monger** *n* marchand *m* de poisson; ~**monger's (shop)** *n* poissonnerie *f*; ~ **sticks** *npl* (US) = ~ **fingers**; ~**y** *a* (fig) suspect(e), louche.

fist [fɪst] *n* poing *m*.

fit [fɪt] *a* (MED, SPORT) en (bonne) forme; (proper) convenable; approprié(e) // *vt* (subj: clothes) aller à; (adjust) ajuster; (put in, attach) installer, poser; adapter; (equip) équiper, garnir, munir // *vi* (clothes) aller; (parts) s'adapter; (in space, gap) entrer, s'adapter // *n* (MED) accès *m*, crise *f*; (of coughing) quinte *f*; ~ **to en état de**; ~ **for digne de**; apte à; **a** ~ **of anger** un accès de colère; **this dress is a tight/good** ~

cette robe est un peu juste/(me) ou très bien; **by ~s and starts** par à-coups; **to ~ in** vi s'accorder; s'adapter; **to ~ out** (Brit: also: **~ up**) vt équiper; **~ful** a intermittent(e); **~ment** n meuble encastré, élément m; **~ness** n (MED) forme physique; (of remark) à-propos m, justesse f; **~ted carpet** n moquette f; **~ted kitchen** n cuisine équipée; **~ter** n monteur m; (DRESSMAKING) essayeur/euse; **~ting** a approprié(e) // n (of dress) essayage m; (of piece of equipment) pose f, installation f; **~ting room** n cabine f d'essayage; **~tings** npl installations fpl.

five [faɪv] num cinq; **~r** n (col: Brit) billet m de cinq livres; (: US) billet de cinq dollars.

fix [fɪks] vt fixer; arranger; (mend) réparer // n: **to be in a ~** être dans le pétrin; **to ~ up** vt (meeting) arranger; **to ~ sb up with sth** faire avoir qch à qn; **~ation** [-'eɪʃən] n (PSYCH) fixation f; (fig) obsession f; **~ed** [fɪkst] a (prices etc) fixe; **~ture** ['fɪkstʃə*] n installation f (fixe); (SPORT) rencontre f (au programme).

fizz [fɪz] vi pétiller.

fizzle ['fɪzl] vi pétiller; **to ~ out** vi rater.

fizzy ['fɪzɪ] a pétillant(e); gazeux(euse).

flabbergasted ['flæbəgɑːstɪd] a sidéré(e), ahuri(e).

flabby ['flæbɪ] a mou(molle).

flag [flæg] n drapeau m; (also: **~stone**) dalle f // vi faiblir; fléchir; **to ~ down** vt héler, faire signe de (s'arrêter) à.

flagpole ['flægpəul] n mât m.

flair [flɛə*] n flair m.

flak [flæk] n (MIL) tir antiaérien; (col: criticism) critiques fpl.

flake [fleɪk] n (of rust, paint) écaille f; (of snow, soap powder) flocon m // vi (also: **~ off**) s'écailler.

flamboyant [flæm'bɔɪənt] a flam-

boyant(e), éclatant(e); (person) haut(e) en couleur.

flame [fleɪm] n flamme f.

flamingo [flə'mɪŋɡəu] n flamant m (rose).

flammable ['flæməbl] a inflammable.

flan [flæn] n (Brit) tarte f.

flank [flæŋk] n flanc m // vt flanquer.

flannel ['flænl] n (Brit: also: **face ~**) gant m de toilette; (fabric) flanelle f; **~s** npl pantalon m de flanelle.

flap [flæp] n (of pocket, envelope) rabat m // vt (wings) battre (de) // vi (sail, flag) claquer; (col: also: **be in a ~**) paniquer.

flare [flɛə*] n fusée éclairante; (in skirt etc) évasement m; **to ~ up** vi s'embraser; (fig: person) se mettre en colère, s'emporter; (: revolt) éclater.

flash [flæʃ] n éclair m; (also: **news ~**) flash m (d'information); (PHOT) flash m // vt (switch on) allumer (brièvement); (send: message) câbler // vi briller; jeter des éclairs; (light on ambulance etc) clignoter; **in a ~** en un clin d'œil; **to ~ one's headlights** faire un appel de phares; **he ~ed by** or **past** il passa (devant nous) comme un éclair; **~bulb** n ampoule f de flash; **~cube** n cube-flash m; **~light** n lampe f de poche.

flashy ['flæʃɪ] a (pej) tape-à-l'œil inv, tapageur(euse).

flask [flɑːsk] n flacon m, bouteille f; (also: **vacuum ~**) bouteille f thermos ®.

flat [flæt] a plat(e); (tyre) dégonflé(e), à plat; (denial) catégorique; (MUS) bémolisé(e); (: voice) faux(fausse) // n (Brit: apartment) appartement m; (AUT) crevaison f; (MUS) bémol m; **to work ~ out** travailler d'arrache-pied; **~ly** ad catégoriquement; **~ten** vt (also: **~ten out**) aplatir.

flatter ['flætə*] vt flatter; **~ing** a flatteur(euse); **~y** n flatterie f.

flaunt [flɔːnt] vt faire étalage de.

flavour, (*US*) **flavor** ['fleɪvə*] *n* goût *m*, saveur *f*; (*of ice cream etc*) parfum *m* // *vt* parfumer; **vanilla~ed** à l'arôme de vanille, vanillé(e); **~ing** *n* arôme *m* (synthétique).

flaw [flɔ:] *n* défaut *m*.

flax [flæks] *n* lin *m*; **~en** *a* blond(e).

flea [fli:] *n* puce *f*.

fleck [flɛk] *n* tacheture *f*; moucheture *f*.

flee, *pt*, *pp* **fled** [fli:, flɛd] *vt* fuir, s'enfuir de // *vi* fuir, s'enfuir.

fleece [fli:s] *n* toison *f* // *vt* (*col*) voler, filouter.

fleet [fli:t] *n* flotte *f*; (*of lorries etc*) parc *m*, convoi *m*.

fleeting ['fli:tɪŋ] *a* fugace, fugitif(ive); (*visit*) très bref(brève).

Flemish ['flɛmɪʃ] *a* flamand(e).

flesh [flɛʃ] *n* chair *f*; **~ wound** *n* blessure superficielle.

flew [flu:] *pt of* **fly**.

flex [flɛks] *n* fil *m* or câble *m* électrique (souple) // *vt* fléchir; (*muscles*) tendre; **~ible** *a* flexible.

flick [flɪk] *n* petite tape; chiquenaude *f*; sursaut *m*; **to ~ through** *vt fus* feuilleter.

flicker ['flɪkə*] *vi* vaciller.

flier ['flaɪə*] *n* aviateur *m*.

flight [flaɪt] *n* vol *m*; (*escape*) fuite *f*; (*also:* **~ of steps**) escalier *m*; **~ attendant** *n* (*US*) steward *m*, hôtesse *f* de l'air; **~ deck** *n* (*AVIAT*) poste *m* de pilotage; (*NAUT*) pont *m* d'envol.

flimsy ['flɪmzɪ] *a* (*partition, fabric*) peu solide, mince; (*excuse*) pauvre, mince.

flinch [flɪntʃ] *vi* tressaillir; **to ~ from** se dérober à, reculer devant.

fling, *pt*, *pp* **flung** [flɪŋ, flʌŋ] *vt* jeter, lancer.

flint [flɪnt] *n* silex *m*; (*in lighter*) pierre *f* (à briquet).

flip [flɪp] *n* chiquenaude *f*.

flippant ['flɪpənt] *a* désinvolte, irrévérencieux(euse).

flipper ['flɪpə*] *n* (*of seal etc*) nageoire *f*; (*for swimming*) palme *f*.

flirt [flə:t] *vi* flirter // *n* flirteuse *f*.

flit [flɪt] *vi* voleter.

float [fləʊt] *n* flotteur *m*; (*in procession*) char *m*; (*money*) réserve *f* // *vi* flotter // *vt* faire flotter; (*loan, business*) lancer.

flock [flɒk] *n* troupeau *m*; (*of people*) foule *f*.

flog [flɒg] *vt* fouetter.

flood [flʌd] *n* inondation *f*; (*of words, tears etc*) flot *m*, torrent *m* // *vt* inonder; **~ing** *n* inondation *f*; **~light** *n* projecteur *m* // *vt* éclairer aux projecteurs, illuminer.

floor [flɔ:*] *n* sol *m*; (*storey*) étage *m*; (*fig: at meeting*): **the ~** l'assemblée *f*, les membres *mpl* de l'assemblée // *vt* terrasser; **on the ~** par terre; **ground ~,** (*US*) **first ~** rez-de-chaussée *m*; **first ~,** (*US*) **second ~** premier étage; **~board** *n* planche *f* (*du plancher*); **~ show** *n* spectacle *m* de variétés.

flop [flɒp] *n* fiasco *m*.

floppy ['flɒpɪ] *a* lâche, flottant(e); **~ (disk)** *n* (*COMPUT*) disquette *f*.

flora ['flɔ:rə] *n* flore *f*.

florid ['flɒrɪd] *a* (*complexion*) fleurie(e); (*style*) plein(e) de fioritures.

florist ['flɒrɪst] *n* fleuriste *m/f*.

flounce [flaʊns] *n* volant *m*.

flounder ['flaʊndə*] *vi* patauger // *n* (*ZOOL*) flet *m*.

flour ['flaʊə*] *n* farine *f*.

flourish ['flʌrɪʃ] *vi* prospérer // *n* fioriture *f*; (*of trumpets*) fanfare *f*.

flout [flaʊt] *vt* se moquer de, faire fi de.

flow [fləʊ] *n* flot *m*; courant *m*; circulation *f*; (*tide*) flux *m* // *vi* couler; (*traffic*) s'écouler; (*robes, hair*) flotter; **~ chart** *n* organigramme *m*.

flower ['flaʊə*] *n* fleur *f* // *vi* fleurir; **~ bed** *n* plate-bande *f*; **~pot** *n* pot *m* (à fleurs); **~y** *a* fleuri(e).

flown [fləʊn] *pp of* **fly**.

flu [flu:] *n* grippe *f*.

fluctuate ['flʌktjueɪt] *vi* varier, fluctuer.

fluency ['flu:ənsɪ] *n* facilité *f*.

fluent ['fluːənt] a (speech) coulant(e), aisé(e); **he speaks ~ French** il parle le français couramment.

fluff [flʌf] n duvet m; peluche f; **~y** a duveteux(euse); pelucheux(euse).

fluid ['fluːɪd] a, n fluide (m).

fluke [fluːk] n (col: luck) coup m de veine.

flung [flʌŋ] pt, pp of **fling**.

fluoride ['fluəraɪd] n fluor m.

flurry ['flʌrɪ] n (of snow) rafale f, bourrasque f; **~ of activity/ excitement** affairement m/excitation f soudain(e).

flush [flʌʃ] n rougeur f; excitation f; (fig: of youth, beauty etc) éclat m // vt nettoyer à grande eau // vi rougir // a: **~ with** au ras de, de niveau avec; **to ~ the toilet** tirer la chasse (d'eau); **to ~ out** vt débusquer; **~ed** a (tout(e)) rouge.

flustered ['flʌstəd] a énervé(e).

flute [fluːt] n flûte f.

flutter ['flʌtə*] n agitation f; (of wings) battement m // vi battre des ailes, voleter.

flux [flʌks] n: **in a state of ~** fluctuant sans cesse.

fly [flaɪ] n (insect) mouche f; (on trousers: also: **flies**) braguette f // vb (pt **flew**, pp **flown**) vt piloter; (passengers, cargo) transporter par avion; (distances) parcourir // vi voler; (passengers) aller en avion; (escape) s'enfuir, fuir; (flag) se déployer; **to ~ away** or **off** vi (bird, insect) s'envoler; **~ing** n (activity) aviation f // a: **~ing visit** visite f éclair inv; **with ~ing colours** haut la main; **~ing saucer** n soucoupe volante; **~ing start** n: **to get off to a ~ing start** faire un excellent départ; **~over** n (Brit: bridge) sautde-mouton m; **~sheet** n (for tent) double toit m.

foal [fəul] n poulain m.

foam [fəum] n écume f; (on beer) mousse f; (also: **plastic ~**) mousse cellulaire or de plastique // vi écumer; (soapy water) mousser; **~ rubber** n caoutchouc m mousse.

fob [fɔb] vt: **to ~ sb off with** refiler à qn; se débarrasser de qn avec.

focus ['fəukəs] n (pl: **~es**) foyer m; (of interest) centre m // vt (field glasses etc) mettre au point // vi: **to ~ (on)** (with camera) régler la mise au point (sur); (person) fixer son regard (sur); **in ~** au point; **out of ~** pas au point.

fodder ['fɔdə*] n fourrage m.

foe [fəu] n ennemi m.

fog [fɔg] n brouillard m; **~gy** a: **it's ~gy** il y a du brouillard; **~lamp** n (AUT) phare m anti-brouillard.

foil [fɔɪl] vt déjouer, contrecarrer // n feuille f de métal; (kitchen ~) papier m d'alu(minium); (FENCING) fleuret m.

fold [fəuld] n (bend, crease) pli m; (AGR) parc m à moutons; (fig) bercail m // vt plier; **to ~ up** vi (business) fermer boutique // vt (map etc) plier, replier; **~er** n (for papers) chemise f; classeur m; (brochure) dépliant m; **~ing** a (chair, bed) pliant(e).

foliage ['fəulɪɪdʒ] n feuillage m.

folk [fəuk] npl gens mpl // a folklorique; **~s** npl famille f, parents mpl; **~lore** ['fəuklɔː*] n folklore m; **~ song** n chanson f folklorique.

follow ['fɔləu] vt suivre // vi suivre; (result) s'ensuivre; **he ~ed suit** il fit de même; **to ~ up** vt (victory) tirer parti de; (letter, offer) donner suite à; (case) suivre; **~er** n disciple m/f, partisan/e; **~ing** a suivant(e) // n partisans mpl, disciples mpl.

folly ['fɔlɪ] n inconscience f; sottise f.

fond [fɔnd] a (memory, look) tendre, affectueux(euse); **to be ~ of** aimer beaucoup.

fondle ['fɔndl] vt caresser.

food [fuːd] n nourriture f; **~ mixer** n mixer m; **~ poisoning** n intoxication f alimentaire; **~ processor** n robot m de cuisine; **~stuffs** npl denrées fpl alimentaires.

fool [fu:l] n idiot/e; (HISTORY: of king) bouffon m, fou m; (CULIN: purée f de fruits à la crème // vt berner, duper // vi (also: ~ around) faire l'idiot or l'imbécile; ~**hardy** a téméraire, imprudent(e); ~**ish** a idiot(e), stupide; imprudent(e); écervelé(e); ~**proof** a (plan etc) infaillible.

foot [fut] n (pl: **feet**) pied m; (measure) pied (= 304 mm; 12 inches); (of animal) patte f // vt (bill) casquer, payer; **on** ~ à pied; ~**age** n (CINEMA: length) ~ métrage m; (: material) séquences fpl; ~**ball** n ballon m (de football); (sport: Brit) football m; (: US) football américain; ~**baller** (Brit) = ~**ball player**; ~**ball ground** n terrain m de football; ~**ball player** n joueur m de football; ~**brake** n frein m à pied; ~**bridge** n passerelle f; ~**hills** npl contreforts mpl; ~**hold** n prise f (de pied); ~**ing** n (fig) position f; **to lose one's** ~**ing** perdre pied; ~**lights** npl rampe f; ~**man** n laquais m; ~**note** n note f (en bas de page); ~**path** n sentier m; (in street) trottoir m; ~**print** n trace f (de pied); ~**step** n pas m; ~**wear** n chaussure(s) f(pl).

KEYWORD

for [fɔ:*] ◆ prep 1 (indicating destination, intention, purpose) pour; the **train** ~ **London** le train pour or (à destination) de Londres; **he went** ~ **the paper** il est allé chercher le journal; **it's time** ~ **lunch** c'est l'heure du déjeuner; **what's it** ~? ça sert à quoi?; **what** ~? (why) pourquoi?

2 (on behalf of, representing) pour; the **MP** ~ **Hove** le député de Hove; **to work** ~ **sb/sth** travailler pour qn/qch; **G** ~ **George** G comme Georges

3 (because of) pour; ~ **this reason** pour cette raison; ~ **fear of being criticized** de peur d'être critiqué

4 (with regard to) pour; **it's cold** ~

July il fait froid pour juillet; **a gift** ~ **languages** un don pour les langues

5 (in exchange for): **I sold it** ~ **£5** je l'ai vendu 5 livres; **to pay 50 pence** ~ **a ticket** payer 50 pence un billet

6 (in favour of) pour; **are you** ~ **or against us?** êtes-vous pour ou contre nous?

7 (referring to distance) pendant, sur; **there are roadworks** ~ **5 km** il y a des travaux sur or pendant 5 km; **we walked** ~ **miles** nous avons marché pendant des kilomètres

8 (referring to time) pendant; depuis; pour; **he was away** ~ **2 years** il a été absent pendant 2 ans; **she will be away** ~ **a month** elle sera absente (pendant) un mois; **I have known her** ~ **years** je la connais depuis des années; **can you do it** ~ **tomorrow?** est-ce que tu peux le faire pour demain?

9 (with infinitive clauses): **it is not** ~ **me to decide** ce n'est pas à moi de décider; **it would be best** ~ **you to leave** le mieux serait que vous partiez; **there is still time** ~ **you to do it** il vous reste encore le temps de le faire; ~ **this to be possible** ... pour que cela soit possible ...

10 (in spite of): ~ **all his work/ efforts** malgré tout son travail/tous ses efforts; ~ **all his complaints,** **he's very fond of her** il a beau se plaindre, il l'aime beaucoup

◆ cj (since, as: rather formal) car.

forage ['fɔrɪdʒ] n fourrage m.

foray ['fɔreɪ] n incursion f.

forbid, pt forbad(e), pp forbidden [fə'bɪd, -'bæd, -'bɪdn] vt défendre, interdire; **to** ~ **sb to do** défendre or interdire à qn de faire; ~**den** a défendu(e); ~**ding** a d'aspect or d'allure sévère ou sombre.

force [fɔ:s] n force f // vt forcer; the **F**~**s** npl (Brit) l'armée f; **in** ~ en force; **to come into** ~ entrer en vigueur; **~-feed** vt nourrir de force; **~ful** a énergique, volontaire.

forcibly ['fɔːsəblɪ] ad par la force, de force; (vigorously) énergiquement.

ford [fɔːd] n gué m.

fore [fɔː*] n: to the ~ en évidence.

forearm ['fɔːrɑːm] n avant-bras m inv.

foreboding [fɔː'bəudɪŋ] n pressentiment m (néfaste).

forecast ['fɔːkɑːst] n prévision f // vt (irg: like cast) prévoir.

forecourt ['fɔːkɔːt] n (of garage) devant m.

forefathers ['fɔːfɑːðəz] npl ancêtres mpl.

forefinger ['fɔːfɪŋgə*] n index m.

forefront ['fɔːfrʌnt] n: in the ~ of au premier rang ou plan de.

forego vt = forgo.

foregone ['fɔːgɔn] a: it's a ~ conclusion c'est à prévoir, c'est couru d'avance.

foreground ['fɔːgraund] n premier plan.

forehead ['fɔrɪd] n front m.

foreign ['fɔrɪn] a étranger(ère); (trade) extérieur(e); **~-er** n étranger/ère; ~ **secretary** n (Brit) ministre m des Affaires étrangères; **F~ Office** n (Brit) ministère m des Affaires étrangères.

foreleg ['fɔːleg] n patte f de devant; jambe antérieure.

foreman ['fɔːmən] n contremaître m.

foremost ['fɔːməust] a le(la) plus en vue; premier(ère) // ad: **first and ~** avant tout, tout d'abord.

forensic [fə'rensɪk] a: ~ **medicine** médecine légale.

forerunner ['fɔːrʌnə*] n précurseur m.

foresee, pt **foresaw**, pp **foreseen** [fɔː'siː, -'sɔː, -'siːn] vt prévoir; **~able** a prévisible.

foreshadow [fɔː'ʃædəu] vt présager, annoncer, laisser prévoir.

foresight ['fɔːsaɪt] n prévoyance f.

forest ['fɔrɪst] n forêt f.

forestall [fɔː'stɔːl] vt devancer.

forestry ['fɔrɪstrɪ] n sylviculture f.

foretaste ['fɔːteɪst] n avant-goût m.

foretell, pt, pp **foretold** [fɔː'tel, -'təuld] vt prédire.

forever [fə'rɛvə*] ad pour toujours; (fig) continuellement.

foreword ['fɔːwəːd] n avant-propos m inv.

forfeit ['fɔːfɪt] n prix m, rançon f // vt perdre; (one's life, health) payer de.

forgave [fə'geɪv] pt of **forgive**.

forge [fɔːdʒ] n forge f // vt (signature) contrefaire; (wrought iron) forger; to ~ **documents** fabriquer de faux papiers; to ~ **money** (Brit) fabriquer de la fausse monnaie; to ~ **ahead** vi pousser de l'avant, prendre de l'avance; **~r** n faussaire m; **~ry** n faux m, contrefaçon f.

forget [fə'get], pt **forgot**, pp **forgotten**, vi, vt oublier; **~ful** a distrait(e), étourdi(e); **~ful of** oublieux(euse) de; **~-me-not** n myosotis m.

forgive [fə'gɪv], pt **forgave**, pp **forgiven** vt pardonner; to ~ **sb for sth** pardonner qch à qn; **~ness** n pardon m.

forgo [fɔː'gəu], pt **forwent**, pp **forgone** vt renoncer à.

forgot [fə'gɔt] pt of **forget**.

forgotten [fə'gɔtn] pp of **forget**.

fork [fɔːk] n (for eating) fourchette f; (for gardening) fourche f; (of roads) bifurcation f; (of railways) embranchement m // vi (road) bifurquer; to ~ **out** (col: pay) vt allonger, se fendre de // vi casquer; **~-lift truck** n chariot élévateur.

forlorn [fə'lɔːn] a (person) abandonné(e); (place) désert(e); (attempt, hope) désespéré(e).

form [fɔːm] n forme f; (SCOL) classe f; (questionnaire) formulaire m // vt former; **in top** ~ en pleine forme.

formal ['fɔːməl] a (offer, receipt) en bonne et due forme; (person) cérémonieux(euse); (dinner) officiel(le); (ART, PHILOSOPHY) formel(le); **~ly** ad officiellement; formellement;

cérémonieusement.

format ['fɔːmæt] *n* format *m* // *vt* (*COMPUT*) formater.

formation [fɔːˈmeɪʃən] *n* formation *f*.

formative ['fɔːmətɪv] *a*: ~ **years** années *fpl* d'apprentissage (*fig*) or de formation.

former ['fɔːmə*] *a* ancien(ne) (*before n*), précédent(e); **the ~ ... the** latter le premier ... le second, celui-là ... celui-ci; **~ly** *ad* autrefois.

formidable ['fɔːmɪdəbl] *a* redoutable.

formula ['fɔːmjulə] *n* formule *f*.

forsake, *pt* **forsook**, *pp* **forsaken** [fəˈseɪk, -ˈsuk, -ˈseɪkən] *vt* abandonner.

fort [fɔːt] *n* fort *m*.

forte ['fɔːtɪ] *n* (point) fort *m*.

forth [fɔːθ] *ad* en avant; **to go back and ~** aller et venir; **and so ~** et ainsi de suite; (*character*) ouvert(e), communicatif(ive); **~right** *a* franc(franche), direct(e); **~with** *ad* sur le champ.

fortify ['fɔːtɪfaɪ] *vt* fortifier; **fortified wine** *n* vin liquoreux or de liqueur.

fortnight ['fɔːtnaɪt] *n* quinzaine *f*, quinze jours *mpl*; **~ly** *a* bimensuel(le) // *ad* tous les quinze jours.

fortunate ['fɔːtʃnɪt] *a*: **it is ~ that** c'est une chance que; **~ly** *ad* heureusement.

fortune ['fɔːtʃən] *n* chance *f*; (*wealth*) fortune *f*; **~teller** *n* diseuse *f* de bonne aventure.

forty ['fɔːtɪ] *num* quarante.

forward ['fɔːwəd] *a* (*ahead of schedule*) en avance; (*movement, position*) en avant, vers l'avant; (*not shy*) ouvert(e); direct(e); effronté(e) *n* (*SPORT*) avant *m* // *vt* (*letter*) faire suivre; (*parcel, goods*) expédier; (*fig*) promouvoir, contribuer au développement or à l'avancement de; **to move ~** avancer; **~(s)** *ad* en avant.

forwent [fɔːˈwent] *pt* of **forgo**.

fossil ['fɔsl] *a*, *n* fossile (*m*).

fought [fɔːt] *pt*, *pp* of **fight**.

foul [faul] *a* (*weather, smell, food*) infect(e); (*language*) ordurier(ère); (*deed*) infâme // *n* (*FOOTBALL*) faute *f* // *vt* salir, encrasser; (*football player*) commettre une faute sur.

found [faund] *pt*, *pp* of **find** // *vt* (*establish*) fonder; **~ation** [-ˈdeɪʃən] *n* (*act*) fondation *f*; (*base*) fondement *m*; (*also*: **~ation cream**) fond *m* de teint; **~ations** *npl* (*of building*) fondations *fpl*.

founder ['faundə*] *n* fondateur *m* // *vi* couler, sombrer.

foundry ['faundrɪ] *n* fonderie *f*.

fount [faunt] *n* source *f*.

fountain ['fauntɪn] *n* fontaine *f*; **~ pen** *n* stylo *m* (à encre).

four [fɔː*] *num* quatre; **on all ~s** à quatre pattes; **~poster** *n* (*also*: **~poster bed**) lit *m* à baldaquin; **~some** ['fɔːsəm] *n* partie *f* à quatre; sortie *f* à quatre; **~teen** *num* quatorze; **~th** *num* quatrième.

fowl [faul] *n* volaille *f*.

fox [fɔks] *n* renard *m* // *vt* mystifier.

foyer ['fɔɪeɪ] *n* vestibule *m*; (*THEATRE*) foyer *m*.

fraction ['frækʃən] *n* fraction *f*.

fracture ['fræktʃə*] *n* fracture *f*.

fragile ['frædʒaɪl] *a* fragile.

fragment ['frægmənt] *n* fragment *m*.

fragrant ['freɪgrənt] *a* parfumé(e), odorant(e).

frail [freɪl] *a* fragile, délicat(e).

frame [freɪm] *n* charpente *f*; (*of picture*) cadre *m*; (*of door, window*) encadrement *m*, chambranle *m*; (*of spectacles*: *also*: **~s**) monture *f* // *vt* encadrer; **~ of mind** disposition *f* d'esprit; **~work** *n* structure *f*.

France [frɑːns] *n* France *f*.

franchise ['fræntʃaɪz] *n* (*POL*) droit *m* de vote; (*COMM*) franchise *f*.

frank [fræŋk] *a* franc(franche) // *vt* (*letter*) affranchir; **~ly** *ad* franchement.

frantic ['fræntɪk] a frénétique.

fraternity [frə'tɜːnɪtɪ] n (club) communauté f, confrérie f; (spirit) fraternité f.

fraud [frɔːd] n supercherie f, fraude f, tromperie f; imposteur m.

fraught [frɔːt] a: ~ with chargé(e) de, plein(e) de.

fray [freɪ] n bagarre f // vi s'effilocher; tempers were ~ed les gens commençaient à s'énerver.

freak [friːk] n (also cpd) phénomène m, créature ou événement exceptionnel par sa rareté, son caractère d'anomalie.

freckle ['frekl] n tache f de rousseur.

free [friː] a libre; (gratis) gratuit(e); (liberal) généreux(euse), large // vt (prisoner etc) libérer; (jammed object or person) dégager; (obof charge), for ~ ad gratuitement; ~dom ['friːdəm] n liberté f; ~-for-all n mêlée générale; ~ gift n prime f; ~hold n propriété foncière libre; ~ kick n coup franc; ~lance a indépendant(e); ~ly ad librement; ~mason n franc-maçon m; ~masonry n franc-maçonnerie f; ~ post n franchise postale; ~-range a (hen, eggs) de ferme; ~ trade n libre-échange m; ~way n (US) autoroute f; ~wheel vi descendre en roue libre; ~ will n libre arbitre m; of one's own ~ will de son plein gré.

freeze [friːz] vb (pt froze, pp frozen) vi geler // vt geler; (food) congeler; (prices, salaries) bloquer, geler // n gel m; blocage m; ~-dried a lyophilisé(e); ~r n congélateur m.

freezing ['friːzɪŋ] a: ~ cold a glacial(e); ~ point n point m de congélation; 3 degrees below ~ 3 degrés au-dessous de zéro.

freight [freɪt] n (goods) fret m, cargaison f; (money charged) fret, prix m du transport; ~ train n (US) train m de marchandises.

French [frentʃ] a français(e) // n

(LING) français m; the ~ npl les Français; ~ bean n haricot vert; ~ fried potatoes, (US) ~ fries npl (pommes de terre fpl) frites fpl; ~man n Français m; ~ window n porte-fenêtre f; ~woman n Française f.

frenzy ['frenzɪ] n frénésie f.

frequent a ['friːkwənt] fréquent(e) // vt [frɪ'kwent] fréquenter; ~ly ad fréquemment.

fresh [freʃ] a frais(fraîche); (new) nouveau(nouvelle); (cheeky) familier(ère), culotté(e); (air, wind, air) fraîchir; to ~en up vi faire un brin de toilette; ~er n (Brit SCOL: col) bizuth m, étudiant(e) de 1ère année; ~ly ad nouvellement, récemment; ~man n (US) = ~er; ~ness n fraîcheur f; ~water a (fish) d'eau douce.

fret [fret] vi s'agiter, se tracasser.

friar ['fraɪə*] n moine m, frère m.

friction ['frɪkʃən] n friction f.

Friday ['fraɪdɪ] n vendredi m.

fridge [frɪdʒ] n (Brit) frigo m, frigidaire m ®.

fried [fraɪd] pt, pp of fry // a frite(e); ~ egg œuf m sur le plat.

friend [frend] n ami(e); ~ly a amical(e); gentil(le); ~ship n amitié f.

frieze [friːz] n frise f, bordure f.

fright [fraɪt] n peur f, effroi m; to take ~ prendre peur, s'effrayer; ~en vt effrayer, faire peur à; ~ened a: to be ~ened (of) avoir peur (de); ~ening a effrayant(e); ~ful a affreux(euse).

frigid ['frɪdʒɪd] a (woman) frigide.

frill [frɪl] n (of dress) volant m; (of shirt) jabot m.

fringe [frɪndʒ] n frange f; (edge: of forest etc) bordure f; (fig): on the ~ en marge; ~ benefits npl avantages sociaux or en nature.

frisk [frɪsk] vt fouiller.

frisky ['frɪskɪ] a vif(vive), sémillant(e).

fritter ['frɪtə*] n beignet m; to ~ away vt gaspiller.

frivolous ['frɪvələs] a frivole.

frizzy ['frɪzɪ] a crépu(e).

fro [frəʊ] see **to**.

frock [frɒk] n robe f.

frog [frɒg] n grenouille f; ~ **man** n homme-grenouille m.

frolic ['frɒlɪk] vi folâtrer, batifoler.

KEYWORD

from [frɒm] prep **1** (indicating starting place, origin etc) de; **where do you come** ~?, **where are you** ~? d'où venez-vous?; ~ **London to Paris** de Londres à Paris; **a letter** ~ **my sister** une lettre de ma sœur; **to drink** ~ **the bottle** boire à (même) la bouteille

2 (indicating time) (à partir) de; **one o'clock** ~ **or until or till two** de une heure à deux heures; ~ **January** (**on**) à partir de janvier

3 (indicating distance) de; **the hotel is one kilometre** ~ **the beach** l'hôtel est à un kilomètre de la plage

4 (indicating price, number etc) de; **the interest rate was increased** ~ **9% to 10%** le taux d'intérêt a augmenté de 9 à 10%

5 (indicating difference) de; **he can't tell red** ~ **green** il ne peut pas distinguer le rouge du vert

6 (because of, on the basis of): ~ **what he says** d'après ce qu'il dit; **weak** ~ **hunger** affaibli par la faim.

front [frʌnt] n (of house, dress) devant m; (of coach, train) avant m; (of book) couverture f; (promenade: also: **sea** ~) bord m de mer; (MIL, POL, METEOROLOGY) front m; (fig: appearances) contenance f, façade f // a de avant; premier(ère); **in** ~ (**of**) devant; ~ **door** n porte f d'entrée; (of car) portière f avant; ~**ier** ['frʌntɪə*] n frontière f; ~ **page** n première page f; ~ **room** n (Brit) pièce f de devant, salon m; ~**wheel drive** n traction f avant.

frost [frɒst] n gel m, gelée f; (also: **hoar**~) givre m; ~**bite** n gelures

fpl; ~**ed** a (glass) dépoli(e); ~**y** a (window) couvert(e) de givre; (welcome) glacial(e).

froth ['frɒθ] n mousse f; écume f.

frown [fraʊn] vi froncer les sourcils.

froze [frəʊz] pt of **freeze**; ~**n** pp of **freeze** // a (food) congelé(e).

fruit [fru:t] n (pl inv) fruit m; ~**erer** n fruitier m, marchand de fruits; ~**erer's (shop)** n fruiterie f; ~**ful** a fructueux(euse); (plant, soil) fécond(e); ~**ion** [fru:'ɪʃən] n: **to come to** ~ **ion** se réaliser; ~ **juice** n jus m de fruit; ~ **machine** n (Brit) machine f à sous; ~ **salad** n salade f de fruits.

frustrate [frʌs'treɪt] vt frustrer; (plot, plans) faire échouer; ~**d** a frustré(e).

fry [fraɪ], pt, pp **fried** vt (faire) frire; **the small** ~ le menu fretin; ~**ing pan** n poêle f (à frire).

ft. abbr of **foot, feet**.

fuddy-duddy ['fʌdɪdʌdɪ] n (pej) vieux schnock.

fudge [fʌdʒ] n (CULIN) sorte de confiserie à base de sucre, de beurre et de lait.

fuel [fjʊəl] n (for heating) combustible m; (for propelling) carburant m; ~ **tank** n cuve f à mazout, citerne f; (in vehicle) réservoir m de or à carburant.

fugitive ['fju:dʒɪtɪv] n fugitif/ive.

fulfil [fʊl'fɪl] vt (function) remplir; (order) exécuter; (wish, desire) satisfaire, réaliser; ~**ment** n (of wishes) réalisation f.

full [fʊl] a plein(e); (details, information) complet(ète); (skirt) ample, large // ad: **to know** ~ **well that** savoir fort bien que; **I'm** ~ (**up**) j'ai bien mangé; ~ **employment** plein emploi; **a** ~ **two hours** deux bonnes heures; **at** ~ **speed** à toute vitesse; **in** ~ (reproduce, quote) intégralement; (write name etc) en toutes lettres; **to pay in** ~ tout payer; ~ **moon** n pleine lune; ~**scale** a (attack, war) complet(ète), total(e);

(model) grandeur nature *inv*; ~ **stop** *n* point *m*; ~-**time** *a*, *ad* (work) à plein temps // *n* (SPORT) fin *f* du match; ~**y** *ad* entièrement, complètement; ~-**y-fledged** *a* (teacher, barrister) diplômé(e); (citizen, member) à part entière.

fulsome ['fulsəm] *a* (pej: praise, gratitude) excessif(ive).

fumble ['fʌmbl] *vi* fouiller, tâtonner; **to ~ with** *vt fus* tripoter.

fume [fju:m] *vi* rager; ~**s** *npl* vapeurs *fpl*, émanations *fpl*, gaz *mpl*.

fun [fʌn] *n* amusement *m*, divertissement *m*; **to have ~** s'amuser; **for ~** pour rire; **to make ~ of** *vt fus* se moquer de.

function ['fʌŋkʃən] *n* fonction *f*; cérémonie *f*, soirée officielle // *vi* fonctionner; ~**al** *a* fonctionnel(le).

fund [fʌnd] *n* caisse *f*, fonds *m*; (source, store) source *f*, mine *f*; ~**s** *npl* fonds *mpl*.

fundamental [fʌndə'mɛntl] *a* fondamental(e).

funeral ['fju:nərəl] *n* enterrement *m*, obsèques *fpl* (more formal occasion); ~ **parlour** *n* dépôt *m* mortuaire; ~ **service** *n* service *m* funèbre.

fun fair *n* (Brit) fête (foraine).

fungus, *pl* **fungi** ['fʌŋgəs, -gai] *n* champignon *m*; (mould) moisissure *f*.

funnel ['fʌnl] *n* entonnoir *m*; (of ship) cheminée *f*.

funny ['fʌni] *a* amusant(e), drôle; (strange) curieux(euse), bizarre.

fur [fə:*] *n* fourrure *f*; (Brit: in kettle etc) dépôt *m* de) tartre *m*; ~ **coat** *n* manteau *m* de fourrure.

furious ['fjuəriəs] *a* furieux(euse); (effort) acharné(e).

furlong ['fə:lɔŋ] *n* = 201.17 *m* (terme d'hippisme).

furlough ['fə:ləu] *n* permission *f*, congé *m*.

furnace ['fə:nis] *n* fourneau *m*.

furnish ['fə:niʃ] *vt* meubler; (supply) fournir; ~**ings** *npl* mobilier *m*, articles *mpl* d'ameublement.

furniture ['fə:nitʃə*] *n* meubles *mpl*, mobilier *m*; **piece of ~** meuble *m*.

furrow ['fʌrəu] *n* sillon *m*.

furry ['fə:ri] *a* (animal) à fourrure; (toy) en peluche.

further ['fə:ðə*] *a* supplémentaire, autre; nouveau(nouvelle); plus loin // *ad* plus loin; (more) davantage; (moreover) de plus // *vt* faire avancer or progresser, promouvoir; ~ **education** *n* enseignement *m* postscolaire (recyclage, formation professionnelle); ~**more** [fə:ðə'mɔ:*] *ad* de plus, en outre.

furthest ['fə:ðist] *superlative of* **far**.

fury ['fjuəri] *n* fureur *f*.

fuse [fju:z] *n* fusible *m*; (for bomb etc) amorce *f*, détonateur *m* // *vt*, *vi* (metal) fondre; (fig) fusionner; **the lights have ~d** (Brit) les plombs ont sauté; ~ **box** *n* boîte *f* à fusibles.

fuss [fʌs] *n* chichis *mpl*, façons *fpl*, embarras *mpl*; (complaining) histoire(s) *f(pl)*; **to make a ~** faire des façons *etc*; ~**y** *a* (person) tatillon(ne), difficile; chichiteux(euse); (dress, style) tarabiscoté(e).

future ['fju:tʃə*] *a* futur(e) // *n* avenir *m*; (LING) futur *m*; **in (the) ~** à l'avenir.

fuze [fju:z] (US) = **fuse**.

fuzzy ['fʌzi] *a* (PHOT) flou(e); (hair) crépu(e).

G

G [dʒi:] *n* (MUS) sol *m*.

gabble ['gæbl] *vi* bredouiller; jacasser.

gable ['geibl] *n* pignon *m*.

gadget ['gædʒit] *n* gadget *m*.

Gaelic ['geilik] *a*, *n* (LING) gaélique (*m*).

gag [gæg] *n* bâillon *m*; (joke) gag *m* // *vt* bâillonner.

gaiety ['geiəti] *n* gaieté *f*.

gaily ['geili] *ad* gaiement.

gain [gein] *n* gain *m*, profit *m* // *vt*

gait // vi (*watch*) avancer; **to ~ in/by** gagner en/à; **to ~ 3lbs** (in weight) prendre 3 livres.

gait [geɪt] n démarche f.

gal. abbr of gallon.

gale [geɪl] n rafale f de vent; coup m de vent.

gallant [ˈgælənt] a vaillant(e), brave; (*towards ladies*) empressé(e), galant(e).

gall bladder [ˈgɔːlblædə*] n vésicule f biliaire.

gallery [ˈgælərɪ] n galerie f; (*also: art ~*) musée m; (*: private*) galerie.

galley [ˈgælɪ] n (*ship's kitchen*) cambuse f; (*ship*) galère f.

Gallic [ˈgælɪk] a gaulois(e), français(e); (*charm*) latin(e).

gallon [ˈgælən] n gallon m (= 8 pints; Brit = 4.543 l; US = 3.785 l).

gallop [ˈgæləp] n galop m // vi galoper.

gallows [ˈgæləʊz] n potence f.

gallstone [ˈgɔːlstəʊn] n calcul m (biliaire).

galore [gəˈlɔː*] ad en abondance, à gogo (col).

galvanize [ˈgælvənaɪz] vt galvaniser; (*fig*): **to ~ sb into action** galvaniser qn.

gambit [ˈgæmbɪt] n (*fig*): (*opening*) **~** manœuvre f stratégique.

gamble [ˈgæmbl] n pari m, risque calculé // vt, vi jouer; **to ~ on** (*fig*) miser sur; **~r** n joueur m; **gambling** n jeu m.

game [geɪm] n jeu m; (*event*) match m; (*HUNTING*) gibier m // a brave; (*ready*): **to be ~ (for sth/to do)** être prêt(e) (à qch/à faire); **a ~ of football/tennis** une partie de football/tennis; **big ~** gros gibier; **~keeper** n garde-chasse m.

gammon [ˈgæmən] n (*bacon*) quartier m de lard fumé; (*ham*) jambon fumé.

gamut [ˈgæmət] n gamme f.

gang [gæŋ] n bande f, groupe m // vi: **to ~ up on sb** se liguer contre qn.

gangster [ˈgæŋstə*] n gangster m.

gangway [ˈgæŋweɪ] n passerelle f; (*Brit: of bus*) couloir central.

gaol [dʒeɪl] n, vt (*Brit*) = **jail**.

gap [gæp] n trou m; (*in time*) intervalle m; (*fig*) lacune f; vide m.

gape [geɪp] vi être ou rester bouche bée; **gaping** a (*hole*) béant(e).

garage [ˈgærɑːʒ] n garage m.

garbage [ˈgɑːbɪdʒ] n ordures fpl, détritus mpl; **~ can** n (US) poubelle f, boîte f à ordures.

garbled [ˈgɑːbld] a déformé(e); faussé(e).

garden [ˈgɑːdn] n jardin m; **~er** n jardinier m; **~ing** n jardinage m.

gargle [ˈgɑːgl] vi se gargariser.

gargoyle [ˈgɑːgɔɪl] n gargouille f.

garish [ˈgɛərɪʃ] a criard(e), voyant(e).

garland [ˈgɑːlənd] n guirlande f; couronne f.

garlic [ˈgɑːlɪk] n ail m.

garment [ˈgɑːmənt] n vêtement m.

garrison [ˈgærɪsn] n garnison f.

garrulous [ˈgærʊləs] a volubile, loquace.

garter [ˈgɑːtə*] n jarretière f; (US) jarretelle f.

gas [gæs] n, pl gases n; (US: gasoline) essence f ou d'asphyxier; (MIL) gazer; **~ cooker** n (Brit) cuisinière f à gaz; **~ cylinder** n bouteille f de gaz; **~ fire** n radiateur m à gaz.

gash [gæʃ] n entaille f; (on face) balafre f.

gasket [ˈgæskɪt] n (AUT) joint m de culasse.

gas mask n masque m à gaz.

gas meter n compteur m à gaz.

gasoline [ˈgæsəliːn] n (US) essence f.

gasp [gɑːsp] vi haleter; (fig) avoir le souffle coupé; **to ~ out** vt (say) dire dans un souffle or d'une voix entrecoupée.

gas ring n brûleur m.

gassy [ˈgæsɪ] a gazeux(euse).

gas tap n bouton m (de cuisinière à gaz); (on pipe) robinet m à gaz.

gate [geɪt] n (of garden) portail m; (of farm) barrière f; (of building) porte f; (of lock) vanne f; ~**crash** vt (Brit) s'introduire sans invitation dans; ~**way** n porte f.

gather ['gæðə*] vt (flowers, fruit) cueillir; (pick up) ramasser; (assemble) rassembler, réunir; recueillir; (understand) comprendre // vi (assemble) se rassembler; to ~ **speed** prendre de la vitesse; ~**ing** n rassemblement m.

gaudy ['gɔːdɪ] a voyant(e).

gauge [geɪdʒ] n (standard measure) calibre m; (RAIL) écartement m; (instrument) jauge f // vt jauger.

Gaul [gɔːl] n (country) Gaule f; (person) Gaulois(e).

gaunt [gɔːnt] a décharné(e); (grim, desolate) désolé(e).

gauntlet ['gɔːntlɪt] n (fig): to run the ~ through an angry crowd se frayer un passage à travers une foule hostile; to throw down the ~ jeter le gant.

gauze [gɔːz] n gaze f.

gave [geɪv] pt of **give**.

gay [geɪ] a (person) gai(e), réjoui(e); (colour) gai, vif(vive); (col) homosexuel(le).

gaze [geɪz] n regard m fixe // vi: to ~ at fixer du regard.

gazetteer [gæzə'tɪə*] n dictionnaire m géographique.

GB abbr of **Great Britain**.

GCE n abbr (Brit) = General Certificate of Education.

GCSE n abbr (Brit) = General Certificate of Secondary Education.

gear [gɪə*] n matériel m, équipement m; attirail m; (TECH) engrenage m; (AUT) vitesse f // vt (fig: adapt): to ~ **sth to** adapter qch à; **top** or (US) **high**/**low**/**bottom** ~ quatrième (or cinquième)/deuxième/première vitesse; in ~ en prise; ~ **box** n boîte f de vitesse; ~ **lever**, (US) ~ **shift** n levier m de vitesse.

geese [giːs] npl of **goose**.

gel [dʒɛl] n gelée f; (CHEM) colloïde m.

gelignite ['dʒɛlɪgnaɪt] n plastic m.

gem [dʒɛm] n pierre précieuse.

Gemini ['dʒɛmɪnaɪ] n les Gémeaux mpl.

gender ['dʒɛndə*] n genre m.

general ['dʒɛnərl] n général m // a général(e); in ~ en général; ~ **delivery** n (US) poste restante; ~ **election** n (Brit) législative(s); ~**ize** vi généraliser; ~**ly** ad généralement; ~ **practitioner** (G.P.) n généraliste m/f.

generate ['dʒɛnəreɪt] vt engendrer; (electricity) produire.

generation [dʒɛnə'reɪʃən] n génération f.

generator ['dʒɛnəreɪtə*] n générateur m.

generosity [dʒɛnə'rɔsɪtɪ] n générosité f.

generous ['dʒɛnərəs] a généreux(euse); (copious) copieux(euse).

genetic [dʒɪ'nɛtɪk] a génétique.

Geneva [dʒɪ'niːvə] n Genève.

genial ['dʒiːnɪəl] a cordial(e), chaleureux(euse); (climate) clément(e).

genitals ['dʒɛnɪtlz] npl organes génitaux.

genius ['dʒiːnɪəs] n génie m.

gent [dʒɛnt] n abbr of **gentleman**.

genteel [dʒɛn'tiːl] a de bon ton, distingué(e).

gentle ['dʒɛntl] a doux(douce).

gentleman ['dʒɛntlmən] n monsieur m; (well-bred man) gentleman m.

gently ['dʒɛntlɪ] ad doucement.

gentry ['dʒɛntrɪ] n petite noblesse.

gents [dʒɛnts] n W.C. mpl (pour hommes).

genuine ['dʒɛnjuɪn] a véritable, authentique; sincère.

geography [dʒɪ'ɔgrəfɪ] n géographie f.

geology [dʒɪ'ɔlədʒɪ] n géologie f.

geometric(al) [dʒɪə'mɛtrɪk(l)] a géométrique.

geometry [dʒɪ'ɔmɪtrɪ] n géométrie f.

geranium [dʒɪ'reɪnjəm] n géranium m.

geriatric [dʒɛrɪ'ætrɪk] a gériatrique.

germ [dʒəːm] n (MED) microbe;

(BIO, fig) germe m.

German ['dʒə:mən] a allemand(e) // n Allemand/e; (LING) allemand m; ~ **measles** n rubéole f.

Germany ['dʒə:mənı] n Allemagne f.

gesture ['dʒestjə*] n geste m.

KEYWORD

get [gɛt], pt, pp **got**, pp **gotten** (US) vi 1 (become, be) devenir; to ~ **old/tired** devenir vieux/fatigué, vieillir/se fatiguer; to ~ **drunk** s'enivrer; to ~ **killed** se faire tuer; **when do I** ~ **paid?** quand est-ce que je serai payé?; **it's** ~**ting late** il se fait tard

2 (go): to ~ **to/from** aller à/de; to ~ **home** rentrer chez soi; **how did you** ~ **here?** comment es-tu arrivé ici?

3 (begin) commencer or se mettre à; **I'm** ~**ting to like him** je commence à l'apprécier; **let's** ~ **going** or **started** allons-y

4 (modal auxiliary vb): **you've got to do it** il faut que vous le fassiez; **I've got to tell the police** je dois le dire à la police

◆ vt

1: to ~ **sth done** (do) faire qch; (have done) faire faire qch; to ~ **one's hair cut** se faire couper les cheveux; to ~ **sb to do sth** faire faire qch à qn; to ~ **sb drunk** enivrer qn

2 (obtain: money, permission, results) obtenir, avoir; (find: job, flat) trouver; (fetch: person, doctor, object) aller chercher; to ~ **sth for sb** procurer qch à qn; ~ **me Mr Jones, please** (on phone) passez-moi Mr Jones, s'il vous plaît; **can I** ~ **you a drink?** est-ce que je peux vous servir à boire?

3 (receive: present, letter) recevoir, avoir; (acquire: reputation) avoir; (~ prize) obtenir; **what did you** ~ **for your birthday?** qu'est-ce que tu as eu pour ton anniversaire?

4 (catch) prendre, saisir, attraper;

(hit: target etc) atteindre; to ~ **sb by the arm/throat** prendre or saisir or attraper qn par le bras/à la gorge; ~ **him!** arrête-le!

5 (take, move) faire parvenir; **do you think we'll** ~ **it through the door?** on arrivera à le faire passer par la porte?; **I'll** ~ **you there somehow** je me débrouillerai pour t'y emmener

6 (catch, take: plane, bus etc) prendre

7 (understand) comprendre, saisir; (hear) entendre; **I've got it!** j'ai compris!, je saisis!; **I didn't** ~ **your name** je n'ai pas entendu votre nom

8 (have, possess): **to have got** avoir; **how many have you got?** vous en avez combien?

to get about vi se déplacer; (news) se répandre

to get along vi (agree) s'entendre; (depart) s'en aller; (manage) = **to get by**

to get at vt fus (attack) s'en prendre à; (reach) attraper, atteindre

to get away vi partir, s'en aller; (escape) s'échapper

to get away with vt fus en être quitte pour; le faire passer or pardonner

to get back vi (return) rentrer ◆ vt récupérer, recouvrer

to get by vi (pass) passer; (manage) se débrouiller

to get down vi, vt fus descendre ◆ vt descendre; (depress) déprimer

to get down to vt fus (work) se mettre à (faire)

to get in vi rentrer; (train) arriver

to get into vt fus entrer dans; (car, train etc) monter dans; (clothes) mettre, enfiler, endosser; to ~ **into bed/a rage** se mettre au lit/en colère

to get off vi (from train etc) descendre; (depart: person, car) s'en aller; (escape) s'en tirer ◆ vt (remove: clothes, stain) enlever ◆ vt fus (train, bus) descendre de

to get on vi (at exam etc) se débrouiller; (agree): **to ~ on (with)** s'entendre (avec) ◆ vt fus monter dans; (horse) monter sur

to get out vi sortir; (of vehicle) descendre ◆ vt sortir

to get out of vt fus sortir de; (duty etc) échapper à, se soustraire à

to get over vt fus (illness) se remettre de

to get round vt fus contourner; (fig: person) entortiller

to get through vi (TEL) avoir la communication; **to ~ through to sb** atteindre qn

to get together vi se réunir ◆ vt assembler

to get up vi (rise) se lever ◆ vt fus monter

to get up to vt fus (reach) arriver à; (prank etc) faire.

getaway [gɛtəweɪ] n fuite f.

get-up [ˈgɛtʌp] n (col) accoutrement m.

geyser [ˈgiːzə*] n chauffe-eau m inv; (GEO) geyser m.

Ghana [ˈgɑːnə] n Ghana m.

ghastly [ˈgɑːstlɪ] a atroce, horrible; (pale) livide, blême.

gherkin [ˈgəːkɪn] n cornichon m.

ghost [gəust] n fantôme m, revenant m.

giant [ˈdʒaɪənt] n géant/e // a géant(e), énorme.

gibberish [ˈdʒɪbərɪʃ] n charabia m.

gibe [dʒaɪb] n sarcasme m.

giblets [ˈdʒɪblɪts] npl abats mpl.

Gibraltar [dʒɪˈbrɔːltə*] n Gibraltar m.

giddy [ˈgɪdɪ] a (dizzy): **to be ~** avoir le vertige; (height) vertigineux(euse).

gift [gɪft] n cadeau m, présent m; (donation, ability) don m; **~ed** a doué(e); **~ token** or **voucher** n chèque-cadeau m.

gigantic [dʒaɪˈgæntɪk] a gigantesque.

giggle [ˈgɪgl] vi pouffer, ricaner sottement.

gill [dʒɪl] n (measure) = 0.25 pints

(Brit = 0.148 l, US = 0.118 l).

gills [gɪlz] npl (of fish) ouïes fpl, branchies fpl.

gilt [gɪlt] n dorure f // a doré(e); **~-edged** a (COMM) de premier ordre.

gimmick [ˈgɪmɪk] n truc m.

gin [dʒɪn] n (liquor) gin m.

ginger [ˈdʒɪndʒə*] n gingembre m; **~ ale**, **~ beer** n boisson gazeuse au gingembre; **~bread** n pain m d'épices.

gingerly [ˈdʒɪndʒəlɪ] ad avec précaution.

gipsy [ˈdʒɪpsɪ] n gitan/e, bohémien/ne.

giraffe [dʒɪˈrɑːf] n girafe f.

girder [ˈgəːdə*] n poutrelle f.

girdle [ˈgəːdl] n (corset) gaine f.

girl [gəːl] n fille f, fillette f; (young unmarried woman) jeune fille; (daughter) fille; **an English ~** une jeune Anglaise; **~friend** n (of girl) amie f; (of boy) petite amie.

giro [ˈdʒaɪrəu] n (bank) ~ virement m bancaire; (post office ~) mandat m.

girth [gəːθ] n circonférence f; (of horse) sangle f.

gist [dʒɪst] n essentiel m.

give [gɪv] vb (pt gave, pp given) vt donner // vi (break) céder; (stretch: fabric) se prêter; **to ~ sb sth**, **~ sth to sb** donner qch à qn; **to ~ a cry/sigh** pousser un cri/un soupir; **to ~ away** vt donner; (give free) faire cadeau de; (betray) donner, trahir; (disclose) révéler; (bride) conduire à l'autel; **to ~ back** vt rendre; **to ~ in** vi céder // vt donner; **to ~ off** vt dégager; **to ~ out** vt distribuer; annoncer; **to ~ up** vi renoncer // vt renoncer à; **to ~ up smoking** arrêter de fumer; **to ~ o.s. up** se rendre; **to ~ way** vi céder; (Brit AUT) céder la priorité.

glacier [ˈglæsɪə*] n glacier m.

glad [glæd] a content(e).

gladly [ˈglædlɪ] ad volontiers.

glamorous [ˈglæmərəs] a séduisant(e).

glamour ['glæmə*] n éclat m, prestige m.

glance [glɑːns] n coup m d'œil // vi: to ~ at jeter un coup d'œil à; to ~ off vt fus (bullet) ricocher sur; **glancing** a (blow) oblique.

gland [glænd] n glande f.

glare [glɛə*] n lumière éblouissante // vi briller d'un éclat aveuglant; to ~ at lancer un or des regard(s) furieux à; **glaring** a (mistake) criant(e), qui saute aux yeux.

glass [glɑːs] n verre m; (also: looking ~) miroir m; ~es npl lunettes fpl; ~ware n verrerie f; ~y a (eyes) vitreux(euse).

glaze [gleɪz] vt (door) vitrer; (pottery) vernir // n vernis m.

glazier ['gleɪzɪə*] n vitrier m.

gleam [gliːm] n lueur f; rayon m // vi luire, briller; ~ing a luisant(e).

glean [gliːn] vt (information) recueillir.

glee [gliː] n joie f.

glen [glɛn] n vallée f.

glib [glɪb] a qui a du bagou; facile.

glide [glaɪd] vi glisser; (AVIAT, birds) planer; ~r n (AVIAT) planeur m; **gliding** n (AVIAT) vol m à voile.

glimmer ['glɪmə*] n lueur f.

glimpse [glɪmps] n vision passagère, aperçu m // vt entrevoir, apercevoir.

glint [glɪnt] vi étinceler.

glisten ['glɪsn] vi briller, luire.

glitter ['glɪtə*] vi scintiller, briller // n scintillement m.

gloat [gləut] vi: to ~ (over) jubiler (à propos de).

global ['gləubl] a mondial(e).

globe [gləub] n globe m.

gloom [gluːm] n obscurité f; (sadness) tristesse f, mélancolie f; ~y a sombre, triste, mélancolique.

glorious ['glɔːrɪəs] a glorieux(euse); splendide.

glory ['glɔːrɪ] n gloire f; splendeur f // vi: to ~ in se glorifier de.

gloss [glɔs] n (shine) brillant m, vernis m; ~ over vt fus glisser sur.

glossary ['glɔsərɪ] n glossaire m.

glossy ['glɔsɪ] a brillant(e), luisant(e).

glove [glʌv] n gant m; ~ compartment n (AUT) boîte f à gants, videpoches m inv.

glow [gləu] vi rougeoyer; (face) rayonner // n rougeoiement m.

glower ['glauə*] vi: to ~ (at) lancer des regards mauvais (à).

glue [gluː] n colle f // vt coller.

glum [glʌm] a maussade, morose.

glut [glʌt] n surabondance f.

glutton ['glʌtn] n glouton/ne; a ~ for work un bourreau de travail.

gnarled [nɑːld] a noueux(euse).

gnat [næt] n moucheron m.

gnaw [nɔː] vt ronger.

go [gəu] vb (pt **went**, pp **gone**) vi aller; (depart) partir, s'en aller; (work) marcher; (be sold): to ~ for £10 se vendre 10 livres; (fit, suit): to ~ with aller avec; (become): to ~ pale/mouldy pâlir/moisir; (break etc) céder // n (pl: ~es): to have a ~ (at) essayer (de faire); to be on the ~ être en mouvement; whose ~ is it? à qui est-ce de jouer?; he's going to do il va faire, il est sur le point de faire; to ~ for a walk aller se promener; to ~ dancing aller danser; how did it ~? comment est-ce que ça s'est passé?; to ~ round the back/by the shop passer par derrière/devant le magasin; to ~ about: (rumour) se répandre // vt fus: how do I ~ about this? comment dois-je m'y prendre (pour faire ceci)?; to ~ ahead vi (make progress) avancer; (get going) aller; to ~ along vi aller, avancer // vt fus longer, parcourir; to ~ away vi partir, s'en aller; to ~ back vi rentrer; revenir; (go again) retourner; to ~ back on vt fus (promise) revenir sur; to ~ by vi (years, time) passer, s'écouler // vt fus s'en tenir à, en croire; to ~ down vi descendre; (ship) couler; (sun) se coucher // vt fus descendre; to ~ for vt fus (fetch) aller chercher; (like) aimer; (attack) s'en prendre à; attaquer; **to ~ in** vi entrer; **to ~ in for** vt fus (competition) se présenter à; (like) aimer; **to ~ into** vt fus entrer dans; (investigate) étudier, examiner; **to ~ off** vi partir, s'en aller; (food) se gâter; (explode) sauter; (event) se dérouler // vt fus se passer de; **the gun went off** le coup est parti; **to ~ on** vi continuer; (happen) se passer; **to ~ on doing** continuer à faire; **to ~ out** vi sortir; (fire, light) s'éteindre; **to ~ over** vt fus (check) revoir, vérifier; **to ~ through** vt fus (town etc) traverser; **to ~ up** vi monter; (price) augmenter // vt fus gravir; **to ~ without** vt fus se passer de.

goad [gəud] vt aiguillonner.

go-ahead ['gəuəhɛd] a dynamique, entreprenant(e) // n feu vert.

goal [gəul] n but m; **~keeper** n gardien m de but; **~post** n poteau m de but.

goat [gəut] n chèvre f.

gobble ['gɔbl] vt (also: ~ **down**, ~ **up**) engloutir.

god [gɔd] n dieu m; **G~** n Dieu m; **~child** n filleul(e); **~daughter** n filleule f; **~dess** n déesse f; **~father** n parrain m; **~forsaken** a maudit(e); **~mother** n marraine f; **~send** n aubaine f; **~son** n filleul m.

goggles ['gɔglz] npl lunettes fpl (protectrices) (de motocycliste etc).

going ['gəuɪŋ] n (conditions) état m du terrain // a: **the ~ rate** le tarif (en vigueur).

gold [gəuld] n or m // a en or; **~en** a (made of gold) en or; (in colour) doré(e); **~fish** n poisson m rouge; **~-plated** a plaqué(e) or inv; **~smith** n orfèvre m.

golf [gɔlf] n golf m; **~ ball** n balle f de golf; (on typewriter) boule m; **~ club** n club m de golf; (stick) club m, crosse f de golf; **~ course** n terrain m de golf; **~er** n joueur/euse de golf.

gone [gɔn] pp of **go** // a parti(e).

good [gud] a bon(ne); (kind) gentil(le); (child) sage // n bien m; **~s** npl marchandise f, articles mpl; **~!** bon!, très bien!; **to be ~ at** être bon en; **to be ~ for** être bon pour vous; **it's ~ for you** c'est bon pour vous; **would you be ~ enough to ...?** auriez-vous la bonté ou l'amabilité de ...?; **a ~ deal (of)** beaucoup (de); **a ~ many** beaucoup (de); **to make ~** vi (succeed) faire son chemin, réussir // vt (deficit) combler; (losses) compenser; **it's no ~ complaining** cela ne sert à rien de se plaindre; **for ~** pour de bon, une fois pour toutes; **~ morning/afternoon!** bonjour!; **~ evening!** bonsoir!; **~ night!** bonsoir!; (on going to bed) bonne nuit!; **~bye** excl au revoir!; **G~ Friday** n Vendredi saint; **~-looking** a bien inv; **~-natured** a qui a un bon naturel; (discussion) enjoué(e); **~ness** n (of person) bonté f; **for ~ness sake!** je vous en prie!; **~ness gracious!** mon Dieu!; **~s train** n (Brit) train m de marchandises; **~will** n bonne volonté; (COMM) réputation f (auprès de la clientèle).

goose [gu:s], pl **geese** n oie f.

gooseberry ['guzbəri] n groseille f à maquereau; **to play ~** tenir la chandelle.

gooseflesh ['gu:sflɛʃ] n, **goose pimples** ['gu:spɪmplz] npl chair f de poule.

gore [gɔ:*] vt encorner // n sang m.

gorge [gɔ:dʒ] n gorge f // vt: **to ~ o.s. (on)** se gorger (de).

gorgeous ['gɔ:dʒəs] a splendide, superbe.

gorilla [gə'rɪlə] n gorille m.

gorse [gɔ:s] n ajoncs mpl.

gory ['gɔ:rɪ] a sanglant(e).

go-slow ['gəu'sləu] n (Brit) grève perlée.

gospel ['gɔspl] n évangile m.

gossip ['gɔsɪp] n bavardages mpl; commérage m, cancans mpl; (person) commère f // vi bavarder; (mali-

ciously) cancaner, faire des commérages.
got [gɔt] _pt, pp of_ **get**; **~ten** (US) _pp
of_ **get**.

gout [gaut] _n_ goutte _f_.

govern ['gʌvn] _vt_ gouverner.

governess ['gʌvnis] _n_ gouvernante
_f_.

government _n_ gouvernement _m_; (_Brit: ministers_) ministère _m_.

governor ['gʌvnə*] _n_ (_of state,
bank_) gouverneur _m_; (_of school, hos-
pital_) administrateur _m_.

gown [gaun] _n_ robe _f_; (_of teacher,
Brit: of judge_) toge _f_.

G.P. _n abbr of_ **general practitioner**.

grab [græb] _vt_ saisir, empoigner;
(_property, power_) se saisir de.

grace [greis] _n_ grâce _f_ // _vt_ honorer;
5 days' ~ répit _m_ de 5 jours; to ~
dire le bénédicité; (_after meal_)
dire les grâces; **~ful** _a_ gra-
cieux(euse), élégant(e); **gracious**
['greifəs] _a_ bienveillant(e); de bonne
grâce; miséricordieux(euse).

grade [greid] _n_ (_COMM_) qualité _f_;
calibre _m_; catégorie _f_; (_in hierarchy_)
grade _m_, échelon _m_; (_US SCOL_) note
_f_; classe _f_ // _vt_ classer; calibrer; graduer; **~ crossing** _n_ (US) passage _m_
à niveau; **~ school** _n_ (US) école _f_
primaire.

gradient ['greidiənt] _n_ inclinaison _f_,
pente _f_.

gradual ['grædjuəl] _a_ graduel(le),
progressif(ive); **~ly** _ad_ peu à peu,
graduellement.

graduate _n_ ['grædjuit] diplômé/e
d'université // _vi_ ['grædjueit] obtenir
un diplôme d'université; **graduation**
[-'eifən] _n_ cérémonie _f_ de remise des
diplômes.

graffiti [grə'fi:ti] _npl_ graffiti _mpl_.

graft [grɑ:ft] _n_ (_AGR, MED_) greffe _f_;
(_bribery_) corruption _f_ // _vt_ greffer;
hard ~ _n_ (_col_) boulot acharné.

grain [grein] _n_ grain _m_.

gram [græm] _n_ gramme _m_.

grammar ['græmə*] _n_ grammaire _f_;
~ school _n_ (_Brit_) ≈ lycée _m_.

grammatical [grə'mætikl] _a_ gram-
matical(e).

gramme [græm] _n_ = **gram**.

grand [grænd] _a_ magnifique, splendide; noble; **~children** _npl_ petits-
enfants _mpl_; **~dad** _n_ grand-papa _m_;
~daughter _n_ petite-fille _f_;
~father _n_ grand-père _m_; **~ma** _n_ grand-
maman _f_; **~mother** _n_ grand-mère
_f_; **~pa** _n_ = **~dad**; **~parents** _npl_
grand-père _m_ et grand-mère _f_; **~
piano** _n_ piano _m_ à queue; **~son** _n_
petit-fils _m_; **~stand** _n_ (_SPORT_) tribune _f_.

granite ['grænit] _n_ granit _m_.

granny ['græni] _n_ grand-maman _f_.

grant [grɑ:nt] _vt_ accorder; (_a re-
quest_) accéder à; (_admit_) concéder //
_n_ (_SCOL_) bourse _f_; (_ADMIN_) subside
_m_, subvention _f_; **to take sth for
~ed** considérer qch comme acquis.

granulated ['grænjuleitid] _a_: ~ **sugar** _n_ sucre _m_ en poudre.

grape [greip] _n_ raisin _m_.

grapefruit ['greipfru:t] _n_ pamplemousse _m_.

graph [grɑ:f] _n_ graphique _m_, courbe
_f_; **~ic** _a_ graphique; (_vivid_) vi-
vant(e); **~ics** _n_ arts _mpl_ graphiques //
npl graphisme _m_.

grapple ['græpl] _vi_: **to ~ with** être
aux prises avec.

grasp [grɑ:sp] _vt_ saisir // _n_ (_grip_)
prise _f_; (_fig_) emprise _f_, pouvoir _m_;
compréhension _f_, connaissance _f_;
~ing _a_ avide.

grass [grɑ:s] _n_ herbe _f_; **~hopper** _n_
sauterelle _f_; **~roots** _a_ de base; **~
snake** _n_ couleuvre _f_.

grate [greit] _n_ grille _f_ de cheminée //
_vi_ grincer // _vt_ (_CULIN_) râper.

grateful ['greitful] _a_ reconnais-
sant(e).

grater ['greitə*] _n_ râpe _f_.

gratify ['grætifai] _vt_ faire plaisir à;
(_whim_) satisfaire.

grating ['greitiŋ] _n_ (_iron bars_) grille
_f_ // _a_ (_noise_) grinçant(e).

gratitude ['grætɪtjuːd] n gratitude f.

gratuity [grə'tjuːɪtɪ] n pourboire m.

grave [greɪv] n tombe f // a grave, sérieux(euse).

gravel ['grævl] n gravier m.

gravestone ['greɪvstəʊn] n pierre tombale.

graveyard ['greɪvjɑːd] n cimetière m.

gravity ['grævɪtɪ] n (PHYSICS) gravité f; pesanteur f; (seriousness) gravité.

gravy ['greɪvɪ] n jus m (de viande); sauce f.

gray [greɪ] a = **grey**.

graze [greɪz] vi paître, brouter // vt (touch lightly) frôler, effleurer; (scrape) écorcher // n écorchure f.

grease [griːs] n (fat) graisse f; (lubricant) lubrifiant m // vt graisser; lubrifier; ~proof paper n (Brit) papier sulfurisé; **greasy** a gras(se), graisseux(euse).

great [greɪt] a grand(e); (col) formidable; **G~ Britain** n Grande-Bretagne f; ~**grandfather** n arrière-grand-père m; ~**grandmother** n arrière-grand-mère f; ~**ly** ad très, grandement; (with verbs) beaucoup; ~**ness** n grandeur f.

Greece [griːs] n Grèce f.

greed [griːd] n (also: ~iness) avidité f; (for food) gourmandise f; ~**y** a avide; gourmand(e).

Greek [griːk] a grec(grecque) // n Grec/Grecque; (LING) grec m.

green [griːn] a vert(e); (inexperienced) (bien) jeune, naïf(ïve) // n vert m; (stretch of grass) pelouse f; (also: village ~) = place f du village; ~s npl légumes verts; ~ **belt** n (round town) ceinture verte; ~ **card** n (AUT) carte verte; ~**ery** n verdure f; ~**gage** n reine-claude f; ~**grocer** n (Brit) marchand m de fruits et légumes; ~**house** n serre f.

Greenland ['griːnlənd] n Groenland m.

greet [griːt] vt accueillir; ~**ing** n sa-

lutation f; ~**ing(s) card** n carte f de vœux.

grenade [grə'neɪd] n grenade f.

grew [gruː] pt of **grow**.

grey [greɪ] a gris(e); (dismal) sombre; ~**hound** n lévrier m.

grid [grɪd] n grille f; (ELEC) réseau m.

grief [griːf] n chagrin m, douleur f.

grievance ['griːvəns] n doléance f, grief m.

grieve [griːv] vi avoir du chagrin; se désoler // vt faire de la peine à, affliger; **to ~ for sb** (dead person) pleurer qn.

grievous ['griːvəs] a: ~ **bodily harm** (LAW) coups mpl et blessures fpl.

grill [grɪl] n (on cooker) gril m // vt (Brit) griller; (question) cuisiner.

grille [grɪl] n grillage m; (AUT) calandre f.

grim [grɪm] a sinistre, lugubre.

grimace [grɪ'meɪs] n grimace f // vi grimacer, faire une grimace.

grimy ['graɪmɪ] a crasseux(euse).

grin [grɪn] n large sourire m // vi sourire.

grind [graɪnd] vt (pt, pp **ground**) écraser; (coffee, pepper etc) moudre; (US: meat) hacher; (make sharp) aiguiser // n (work) corvée f; **to ~ one's teeth** grincer des dents.

grip [grɪp] n étreinte f, poigne f; prise f; (holdall) sac m de voyage // vt saisir, empoigner; étreindre; **to come to ~s with** en venir aux prises avec.

gripping ['grɪpɪŋ] a prenant(e), palpitant(e).

grisly ['grɪzlɪ] a sinistre, macabre.

gristle ['grɪsl] n cartilage m (de poulet etc).

grit [grɪt] n gravillon m; (courage) cran m // vt (road) sabler; **to ~ one's teeth** serrer les dents.

groan [grəʊn] n gémissement m; grognement m // vi gémir; grogner.

grocer ['grəʊsə*] n épicier m; ~**ies** npl provisions fpl.

groin [grɔɪn] n aine f.

groom [gru:m] n palefrenier m; (also: **bride~**) marié m // vt (horse) panser; (fig): to ~ sb for former ou pour.

groove [gru:v] n sillon m, rainure f.

grope [grəup] vi tâtonner; to ~ vt fus chercher à tâtons.

gross [grəus] a grossier(ère); (COMM) brut(e); ~**ly** ad (greatly) très, grandement.

grotto ['grɔtəu] n grotte f.

ground [graund] pt, pp of **grind** // n sol m, terre f; (land) terrain m, terres fpl; (SPORT) terrain; (US: also: ~ **wire**) terre; (reason: gen pl) raison f // vt (plane) empêcher de décoller, retenir au sol; (US: ELEC) équiper d'une prise de terre // vi (ship) s'échouer; ~**s** npl (of coffee etc) marc m; (gardens etc) parc m, domaine m; on the ~, to the ~ par terre; to gain/lose ~ gagner/perdre du terrain; ~ **cloth** n (US) = ~**sheet**; ~**ing** n (in education) connaissances fpl de base; ~**less** a sans fondement; ~**sheet** n (Brit) tapis m de sol; ~ **staff** n équipage m au sol; ~ **swell** n lame f ou vague f de fond; ~**work** n préparation f.

group [gru:p] n groupe m // vt (also: ~ **together**) grouper // vi (also: ~ **together**) se grouper.

grouse [graus] n (pl inv) (bird) grouse f // vi (complain) rouspéter, râler.

grove [grəuv] n bosquet m.

grovel ['grɔvl] vi ramper.

grow [grəu], pt **grew**, pp **grown** (plant) pousser, croître; (person) grandir; (increase) augmenter, se développer; (become): to ~ **rich/weak** s'enrichir/s'affaiblir // vt cultiver, faire pousser; to ~ **up** vi grandir; ~**er** n producteur m; ~**ing** a (fear, amount) croissant(e), grandissant(e).

growl [graul] vi grogner.

grown [grəun] pp of **grow** // a adulte; ~**-up** n adulte m/f, grande personne.

growth [grəuθ] n croissance f, développement m; (what has grown) pousse f; poussée f; (MED) grosseur f, tumeur f.

grub [grʌb] n larve f; (col: food) bouffe f.

grubby ['grʌbɪ] a crasseux(euse).

grudge [grʌdʒ] n rancune f // vt: to ~ **sb sth** donner qch à qn à contrecœur; reprocher qch à qn; to bear **sb a** ~ (for) garder rancune or en vouloir à qn (de).

gruelling ['gruəlɪŋ] a exténuant(e).

gruesome ['gru:səm] a horrible.

gruff [grʌf] a bourru(e).

grumble ['grʌmbl] vi rouspéter, ronchonner.

grumpy ['grʌmpɪ] a grincheux(euse).

grunt [grʌnt] vi grogner.

G-string ['dʒi:strɪŋ] n (garment) cache-sexe m inv.

guarantee [gærən'ti:] n garantie f // vt garantir.

guard [gɑ:d] n garde f; (one man) garde m; (Brit RAIL) chef m de train // vt garder, surveiller; ~**ed** a (fig) prudent(e); ~**ian** n gardien/ne; (of minor) tuteur/trice; ~**'s van** n (Brit RAIL) fourgon m.

guerrilla [gə'rɪlə] n guérillero m; ~ **warfare** n guérilla f.

guess [gɛs] vi deviner // vt (US) croire, penser; ~ n supposition f, hypothèse f; ~**work** n hypothèse f.

guest [gɛst] n invité/e; (in hotel) client/e; ~**house** n pension f; ~ **room** n chambre f d'amis.

guffaw [gʌ'fɔ:] n // vi pouffer de rire.

guidance ['gaɪdəns] n conseils mpl.

guide [gaɪd] n (person, book etc) guide m; (also: **girl** ~) guide f // vt guider; ~**book** n guide m; ~ **dog** n chien m d'aveugle; ~**lines** npl (fig) instructions générales, conseils mpl.

guild [gɪld] n corporation f; cercle m, association f.

guile [gaɪl] n astuce f.

guillotine ['gɪləti:n] n guillotine f.

guilt [gɪlt] n culpabilité f; ~**y** a coupable.

guinea pig ['gɪnɪpɪg] n cobaye m.

guise [gaɪz] n aspect m, apparence f.

guitar [gɪ'tɑ:*] n guitare f.

gulf [gʌlf] n golfe m; (abyss) gouffre m.

gull [gʌl] n mouette f.

gullet ['gʌlɪt] n gosier m.

gullible ['gʌlɪbl] a crédule.

gully ['gʌlɪ] n ravin m; ravine f; couloir m.

gulp [gʌlp] vi avaler sa salive; (from emotion) avoir la gorge serrée // vt (also: ~ **down**) avaler.

gum [gʌm] n (ANAT) gencive f; (glue) colle f; (sweet) boule f de gomme; (also: **chewing-~**) chewing-gum m // vt coller; ~**boots** npl (Brit) bottes fpl en caoutchouc.

gun [gʌn] n (small) revolver m, pistolet m; (rifle) fusil m, carabine f; (cannon) canon m; ~**boat** n canonnière f; ~**fire** n fusillade f; ~**man** n bandit armé; ~**ner** n artilleur m; ~**point** n: at ~**point** sous la menace du pistolet (or fusil); ~**powder** n poudre f à canon; ~**shot** n coup m de feu; ~**smith** n armurier m.

gurgle ['gə:gl] vi gargouiller.

guru ['guru:] n gourou m.

gush [gʌʃ] vi jaillir; (fig) se répandre en effusions.

gusset ['gʌsɪt] n gousset m, soufflet m.

gust [gʌst] n (of wind) rafale f; (of smoke) bouffée f.

gusto ['gʌstəu] n enthousiasme m.

gut [gʌt] n intestin m, boyau m; (MUS etc) boyau; ~s npl (courage) cran m.

gutter ['gʌtə*] n (of roof) gouttière f; (in street) caniveau m.

guy [gaɪ] n (also: ~**rope**) corde f; (col: man) type m; (figure) effigie f de Guy Fawkes.

guzzle ['gʌzl] vi s'empiffrer // vt avaler gloutonnement.

gym [dʒɪm] n (also: **gymnasium**) gymnase m; (also: **gymnastics**)

gym f; ~ **shoes** npl chaussures fpl de gym(nastique); ~ **slip** n (Brit) tunique f d'écolière.

gymnast ['dʒɪmnæst] n gymnaste m/f; ~**ics** [-'næstɪks] n, npl gymnastique f.

gynaecologist, (US) **gynecologist** [gaɪnɪ'kɔlədʒɪst] n gynécologue m/f.

gypsy ['dʒɪpsɪ] n = **gipsy**.

gyrate [dʒaɪ'reɪt] vi tournoyer.

H

haberdashery ['hæbə'dæʃərɪ] n (Brit) mercerie f.

habit ['hæbɪt] n habitude f; (costume) habit m, tenue f.

habitual [hə'bɪtjuəl] a habituel(le); (drinker, liar) invétéré(e).

hack [hæk] vt hacher, tailler // n (cut) entaille f; (blow) coup m; (pej: writer) nègre m.

hackneyed ['hæknɪd] a usé(e), rebattu(e).

had [hæd] pt, pp of **have**.

haddock, pl ~ or ~**s** ['hædək] n églefin m; **smoked** ~ haddock m.

hadn't ['hædnt] = **had not**.

haemorrhage, (US) **hemorrhage** ['hemərɪdʒ] n hémorragie f.

haggle ['hægl] vi marchander.

Hague [heɪg] n: **The** ~ La Haye.

hail [heɪl] n grêle f // vt (call) héler; (greet) acclamer // vi grêler; ~**stone** n grêlon m.

hair [hɛə*] n cheveux mpl; (single hair: on head) cheveu m; (: on body) poil m; **to do one's** ~ se coiffer; ~**brush** n brosse f à cheveux; ~**cut** n coupe f (de cheveux); ~**do** ['hɛədu:] n coiffure f; ~**dresser** n coiffeur/euse; ~**-dryer** n sèche-cheveux m, séchoir m; ~**grip** n pince f à cheveux; ~**pin** n épingle f à cheveux; ~**pin bend**, (US) ~**pin curve** n virage m en épingle à cheveux; ~**raising** a à (vous) faire dresser les cheveux sur la tête; ~**remover** n dépilateur m; ~ **spray** n laque f (pour les cheveux); ~**style** n coiffure f; ~**y** a poilu(e); chevelu(e); (fig) effrayant(e).

hake [heɪk] n colin m, merlu m.

half [hɑːf] n (pl halves) moitié f // a demi(e) // ad (à) moitié, à demi; ~-**an-hour** une demi-heure; ~ **a dozen** une demi-douzaine; ~ **a pound** une demi-livre; ~ **: 250 g; two and a** ~ deux et demi; **a week and a** ~ une semaine et demie; ~ (**of it**) la moitié; ~ (**of**) la moitié de, la moitié; **to cut sth in** ~ couper qch en deux; ~ **asleep** à moitié endormi(e); ~-**back** n (SPORT) demi m; ~-**breed, caste** n métis/se; ~-**hearted** a tiède, sans enthousiasme; ~-**hour** n demi-heure f; ~-**mast**: **at** ~-**mast** (flag) en berne, à mi-mât; ~**penny** ['heɪpnɪ] n (Brit) demi-penny m; (**at**) ~-**price** à moitié prix; ~ **term** n (Brit SCOL) congé m de demi-trimestre; ~-**time** n mi-temps f; ~**way** ad à mi-chemin.

halibut ['hælɪbət] n (pl inv) flétan m.

hall [hɔːl] n salle f; (entrance way) hall m, entrée f; (corridor) couloir m; (mansion) château m, manoir m; ~ **of residence** n (Brit) pavillon m or résidence f universitaire.

hallmark ['hɔːlmɑːk] n poinçon m; (fig) marque f.

hallo ['hʌ'ləu] excl = **hello**.

Hallowe'en [ˌhæləu'iːn] n veille f de la Toussaint.

hallucination [həluːsɪ'neɪʃən] n hallucination f.

hallway ['hɔːlweɪ] n vestibule m, couloir m.

halo ['heɪləu] n (of saint etc) auréole f; (of sun) halo m.

halt [hɔːlt] n halte f, arrêt m // vt faire arrêter // vi faire halte, s'arrêter.

halve [hɑːv] vt (apple etc) partager or diviser en deux; (expense) réduire de moitié.

halves [hɑːvz] npl of **half**.

ham [hæm] n jambon m.

hamburger ['hæmbəːgə*] n hamburger m.

hamlet ['hæmlɪt] n hameau m.

hammer ['hæmə*] n marteau m // vt (fig) éreinter, démolir // vi (on door) frapper à coups redoublés.

hammock ['hæmək] n hamac m.

hamper ['hæmpə*] vt gêner // n panier m (d'osier).

hamster ['hæmstə*] n hamster m.

hand [hænd] n main f; (of clock) aiguille f; (handwriting) écriture f; (at cards) jeu m; (worker) ouvrier/ère // vt passer, donner; **to give sb a** ~ donner un coup de main à qn; **at** ~ à portée de la main; (work) en cours; **to be on** ~ (person) être disponible; (emergency services) se tenir prêt(e) (à intervenir); **to** ~ (information etc) sous la main, à portée de la main; **on the one** ~ ..., **on the other** ~ d'une part ..., d'autre part; **to** ~ **in** vt remettre; **to** ~ **out** vt distribuer; **to** ~ **over** vt transmettre; céder; ~**bag** n sac m à main; ~**book** n manuel m; ~**brake** n frein m à main; ~**cuffs** npl menottes fpl; ~**ful** n poignée f.

handicap ['hændɪkæp] n handicap m // vt handicaper; **mentally/physically** ~**ped** a handicapé(e) mentalement/physiquement.

handicraft ['hændɪkrɑːft] n travail m d'artisanat, technique artisanale.

handiwork ['hændɪwəːk] n ouvrage m; (pej) œuvre f.

handkerchief ['hæŋkətʃɪf] n mouchoir m.

handle ['hændl] n (of door etc) poignée f; (of cup etc) anse f; (of knife etc) manche m; (of saucepan) queue f; (for winding) manivelle // vt toucher, manier; (deal with) s'occuper de; (treat: people) traiter; '~ **with care**' 'fragile'; **to fly off the** ~ s'énerver; ~**bar(s)** n(pl) guidon m.

hand: ~**luggage** n bagages mpl à main; ~**made** a fait(e) à la main; ~**out** n documentation f, prospectus m; ~**rail** n rampe f, main courante f;

~**shake** n poignée f de main.

handsome ['hænsəm] a beau(belle); généreux(euse); considérable.

handwriting ['hændraɪtɪŋ] n écriture f.

handy ['hændɪ] a (person) adroit(e); (close at hand) sous la main; (convenient) pratique; **handyman** n bricoleur m; (servant) homme à tout faire.

hang [hæŋ], pt, pp **hung** vt accrocher; (criminal: pt, pp **hanged**) pendre // vi pendre; (hair, drapery) tomber; to **get** the ~ of (doing) sth (col) attraper le coup pour faire qch; to ~ **about** vi flâner, traîner; to ~ **on** vi (wait) attendre; to ~ **up** vi (TEL) raccrocher // vt accrocher, suspendre.

hangar ['hæŋə*] n hangar m.

hanger ['hæŋə*] n cintre m, portemanteau m.

hanger-on [hæŋər'ɔn] n parasite m.

hang-gliding ['hæŋglaɪdɪŋ] n vol m libre or sur aile delta.

hangover ['hæŋəʊvə*] n (after drinking) gueule f de bois.

hang-up ['hæŋʌp] n complexe m.

hanker ['hæŋkə*] vi: to ~ **after** avoir envie de.

hankie, hanky ['hæŋkɪ] n abbr of **handkerchief**.

haphazard [hæp'hæzəd] a fait(e) au hasard, fait(e) au petit bonheur.

happen ['hæpən] vi arriver; se passer, se produire; as it ~s justement; ~**ing** n événement m.

happily ['hæpɪlɪ] ad heureusement.

happiness ['hæpɪnɪs] n bonheur m.

happy ['hæpɪ] a heureux(euse); ~ **with** (arrangements etc) satisfait(e) de; ~ **birthday!** bon anniversaire!; ~**-go-lucky** a insouciant(e).

harass ['hærəs] vt accabler, tourmenter; ~**ment** n tracasseries fpl.

harbour, (US) **harbor** ['hɑ:bə*] n port m // vt héberger, abriter.

hard [hɑ:d] a dur(e) // ad (work) dur; (think, try) sérieusement; to look ~ at regarder fixement; regarder de près; no ~ **feelings!** sans rancune!; to be ~ of **hearing** être dur(e) d'oreille; to be ~ **done by** être traité(e) injustement; ~**back** n livre relié; ~ **cash** n espèces fpl; ~ **disk** n (COMPUT) disque dur; ~**en** vt durcir; (fig) endurcir // vi durcir; ~**-headed** a réaliste; décidé(e); ~ **labour** n travaux forcés.

hardly ['hɑ:dlɪ] ad (scarcely) à peine; it's ~ the case ce n'est guère le cas; that can ~ be true cela ne peut tout de même pas être vrai; ~ **anywhere/ever** presque nulle part/ jamais.

hardship ['hɑ:dʃɪp] n épreuves fpl; privations fpl.

hard-up [hɑ:d'ʌp] a (col) fauché(e).

hardware ['hɑ:dwɛə*] n quincaillerie f; (COMPUT) matériel m; ~ **shop** n quincaillerie f.

hard-wearing [hɑ:d'wɛərɪŋ] a solide.

hard-working [hɑ:d'wə:kɪŋ] a travailleur(euse).

hardy ['hɑ:dɪ] a robuste; (plant) résistant(e) au gel.

hare [hɛə*] n lièvre m; ~**-brained** a farfelu(e); écervelé(e).

harm [hɑ:m] n mal m; (wrong) tort m // vt (person) faire du mal or du tort à; (thing) endommager; out of ~'s **way** à l'abri du danger, en lieu sûr; ~**ful** a nuisible; ~**less** a inoffensif(ive); sans méchanceté.

harmony ['hɑ:mənɪ] n harmonie f.

harness ['hɑ:nɪs] n harnais m // vt (horse) harnacher; (resources) exploiter.

harp [hɑ:p] n harpe f // vi: to ~ **on about** parler tout le temps de.

harrowing ['hærəʊɪŋ] a déchirant(e).

harsh [hɑ:ʃ] a (hard) dur(e); (severe) sévère; (unpleasant: sound) discordant(e); (: colour) criard(e); cru(e); (: wine) âpre.

harvest ['hɑ:vɪst] n (of corn) moisson f; (of fruit) récolte f; (of grapes) vendange f // vi, vt moissonner; récolter; vendanger.

has [hæz] *vb see* **have**.

hash [hæʃ] *n* (CULIN) hachis *m*; (fig: mess) gâchis *m*.

hasn't ['hæznt] = **has not**.

hassle ['hæsl] *n* chamaillerie *f*.

haste [heɪst] *n* hâte *f*; précipitation *f*; **~n** ['heɪsn] *vt* hâter, accélérer // *vi* se hâter, s'empresser; **hastily** *ad* à la hâte; précipitamment; **hasty** *a* hâtif(ive); précipité(e).

hat [hæt] *n* chapeau *m*.

hatch [hætʃ] *n* (NAUT: also: ~way) écoutille *f*; (also: **service ~**) passe-plats *m inv* // *vi* éclore // *vt* faire éclore; (plot) tramer.

hatchback ['hætʃbæk] *n* (AUT) modèle *m* avec hayon arrière.

hatchet ['hætʃit] *n* hachette *f*.

hate [heɪt] *vt* haïr, détester // *n* haine *f*; **~ful** *a* odieux(euse), détestable.

hatred ['heɪtrid] *n* haine *f*.

hat trick *n* (SPORT, also fig) triplé *m* (3 buts réussis au cours du même match etc).

haughty ['hɔːtɪ] *a* hautain(e), arrogant(e).

haul [hɔːl] *vt* traîner, tirer // *n* (of fish) prise *f*; (of stolen goods etc) butin *m*; **~age** *n* transport routier; **~ier**, (US) **~er** *n* transporteur (routier), camionneur *m*.

haunch [hɔːntʃ] *n* hanche *f*.

haunt [hɔːnt] *vt* (subj: ghost, fear) hanter; (: person) fréquenter // *n* repaire *m*.

KEYWORD

have [hæv], *pt*, *pp* had ◆ auxiliary *vb* **1** (gen) avoir; être; **to ~ arrived/gone** être arrivé(e)/allé(e); **to ~ eaten/slept** avoir mangé/ dormi; **he has been promoted** il a été promu

2 (in tag questions): **you've done it, ~n't you?** vous l'avez fait, n'est-ce pas?

3 (in short answers and questions): **no I ~n't!/yes we ~!** mais non!/

mais si!; **so I ~!** ah oui!; oui c'est vrai!; **I've been there before, ~ you?** j'y suis déjà allé, et vous?

◆ *modal auxiliary vb* (be obliged): **to ~ (got) to do sth** devoir faire qch; être obligé(e) de faire qch; **she has (got) to do it** elle doit le faire, il faut qu'elle le fasse; **you ~n't to tell her** vous ne devez pas le lui dire

◆ *vt* **1** (possess, obtain) avoir; **he has (got) blue eyes/dark hair** il a les yeux bleus/les cheveux bruns; **may I ~ your address?** puis-je avoir votre adresse?

2 (+ noun: take, hold etc): **to ~ breakfast/a bath/a shower** prendre le petit déjeuner/un bain/une douche; **to ~ dinner/lunch** dîner/déjeuner; **to ~ a swim** nager; **to ~ a meeting** se réunir; **to ~ a party** organiser une fête

3: **to ~ sth done** faire faire qch; **to ~ one's hair cut** se faire couper les cheveux; **to ~ sb do sth** faire faire qch à qn

4 (experience, suffer) avoir; **to ~ a cold/flu** avoir un rhume/la grippe; **to ~ an operation** se faire opérer

5 (col: dupe) avoir; **he's been had** il s'est fait avoir ou roulé

to have out *vt*: **to ~ it out with sb** (settle a problem etc) s'expliquer (franchement) avec qn.

---

haven ['heɪvn] *n* port *m*; (fig) havre *m*.

haven't ['hævnt] = **have not**.

haversack ['hævəsæk] *n* sac *m* à dos.

havoc ['hævək] *n* ravages *mpl*.

hawk [hɔːk] *n* faucon *m*.

hay [heɪ] *n* foin *m*; **~ fever** *n* rhume *m* des foins; **~stack** *n* meule *f* de foin.

haywire ['heɪwaɪə*] *a* (col): **to ~** perdre la tête; mal tourner.

hazard ['hæzəd] *n* hasard *m*; danger *m*, risque *m* // *vt* risquer, hasarder; **~ warning** *n* (AUT) feux *mpl* de détresse

haze [heɪz] *n* brume *f*.

hazelnut ['heɪzlnʌt] *n* noisette *f*.

hazy ['heɪzɪ] *a* brumeux(euse); (*idea*) vague; (*photograph*) flou(e).

he [hi:] *pronoun* il; **it is ~ who ...** c'est lui qui ...

head [hɛd] *n* tête *f*; (*leader*) chef *m* // (*of list*) être en tête de; (*group*) être à la tête de; **~s or tails** pile ou face; **~ first** la tête la première; **~ over heels in love** follement ou éperdument amoureux(euse); **to ~ the ball** faire une tête; **to ~ for** *vt fus* se diriger vers; **~ache** n mal *m* de tête; **~dress** *n* coiffure *f*; **~ing** n titre *m*; rubrique *f*; (*Brit*) = **~light**; **~land** *n* promontoire *m*, cap *m*; **~light** n phare *m*; **~line** n titre *m*; **~long** *ad* (*fall*) la tête la première; (*rush*) tête baissée; **~master** n directeur *m*, proviseur *m*; **~mistress** n directrice *f*; **~office** n bureau central; **~on** *a* (*collision*) de plein fouet; **~phones** *npl* casque *m* (à écouteurs); **~quarters (HQ)** *npl* bureau ou siège central; (*MIL*) quartier général; **~rest** *n* appui-tête *m*; **~room** *n* (*in car*) hauteur *f* de plafond; (*under bridge*) hauteur limite; dégagement *m*; **~scarf** *n* foulard *m*; **~strong** a têtu(e), entêté(e); **~waiter** n maître *m* d'hôtel; **~way** n: **to make ~way** avancer, faire des progrès; **~wind** n vent *m* contraire; **~y** a capiteux(euse); enivrant(e).

heal [hi:l] *vt, vi* guérir.

health [hɛlθ] *n* santé *f*; **~ food shop** *n* magasin *m* diététique; **the H~ Service** *n* (*Brit*) ≈ la Sécurité Sociale; **~y** a (*person*) en bonne santé; (*climate, food, attitude etc*) sain(e).

heap [hi:p] *n* tas *m*, monceau *m* // *vt* entasser, amonceler.

hear, *pt, pp* **heard** [hɪə*, hə:d] *vt* entendre; (*news*) apprendre; (*lecture*) assister à, écouter // *vi* entendre; **to ~ about** avoir des nouvelles de; entendre parler de; **to ~ from sb** rece-

voir des nouvelles de qn; **~ing** *n* (*sense*) ouïe *f*; (*of witnesses*) audition *f*; (*of a case*) audience *f*; **~ing aid** *n* appareil *m* acoustique; **~say**: **by ~say** *ad* par ouï-dire *m*.

hearse [hə:s] *n* corbillard *m*.

heart [hɑːt] *n* cœur *m*; **~s** *npl* (*CARDS*) cœur; **at ~** au fond; **by ~** (*learn, know*) par cœur; **~ attack** *n* crise *f* cardiaque; **~beat** n battement *m* de cœur; **~broken** a: **to be ~broken** avoir beaucoup de chagrin; **~burn** n brûlures *fpl* d'estomac; **~ failure** n arrêt *m* du cœur; **~felt** a sincère.

hearth [hɑːθ] *n* foyer *m*, cheminée *f*.

heartily ['hɑːtɪlɪ] *ad* chaleureusement; (*laugh*) de bon cœur; (*eat*) de bon appétit; **to agree ~** être entièrement d'accord.

hearty ['hɑːtɪ] *a* chaleureux(euse); robuste, vigoureux(euse).

heat [hi:t] *n* chaleur *f*; (*fig*) ardeur *f*; feu *m*; (*SPORT*: *also*: **qualifying ~**) éliminatoire // *vt* chauffer; **to ~ up** *vi* (*liquids*) chauffer; (*room*) se réchauffer // *vt* réchauffer; **~ed** a chauffé(e); (*fig*) passionné(e), échauffé(e), excité(e); **~er** n appareil *m* de chauffage; radiateur *m*.

heath [hi:θ] *n* (*Brit*) lande *f*.

heathen ['hi:ðn] *a, n* païen(ne).

heather ['hɛðə*] *n* bruyère *f*.

heating ['hi:tɪŋ] *n* chauffage *m*.

heatstroke ['hi:tstrəuk] *n* coup *m* de chaleur.

heatwave ['hi:tweɪv] *n* vague *f* de chaleur.

heave [hi:v] *vt* soulever (avec effort) // *vi* se soulever; (*retch*) avoir des haut-le-cœur // *n* (*push*) poussée *f*.

heaven ['hɛvn] *n* ciel *m*, paradis *m*; **~ly** a céleste, divin(e).

heavily ['hɛvɪlɪ] *ad* lourdement; (*drink, smoke*) beaucoup; (*sleep, sigh*) profondément.

heavy ['hɛvɪ] *a* lourd(e); (*work, sea, rain, eater*) gros(se); (*drinker, smoker*) grand(e); **~ goods vehicle (HGV)** *n* poids lourd (PL);

~**weight** n (SPORT) poids lourd.

Hebrew ['hi:bru:] a hébraïque // n (LING) hébreu m.

Hebrides ['hɛbrɪdi:z] npl: the ~ les Hébrides fpl.

heckle ['hɛkl] vt interpeller (un orateur).

hectic ['hɛktɪk] a agité(e), trépidant(e).

he'd [hi:d] = **he would, he had.**

hedge [hɛdʒ] n haie f // vi se défiler; to ~ one's bets (fig) se couvrir.

hedgehog ['hɛdʒhɔg] n hérisson m.

heed [hi:d] vt (also: take ~ of) tenir compte de, prendre garde à; ~**less** a insouciant(e).

heel [hi:l] n talon m // vt (shoe) retalonner.

hefty ['hɛftɪ] a (person) costaud(e); (parcel) lourd(e); (piece, price) gros(se).

heifer ['hɛfə*] n génisse f.

height [haɪt] n (of person) taille f, grandeur f; (of object) hauteur f; (of plane, mountain) altitude f; (high ground) hauteur, éminence f; (of glory) sommet m; (: of stupidity) comble m; ~**en** vt hausser, surélever; (fig) augmenter.

heir [ɛə*] n héritier m; ~**ess** n héritière f; ~**loom** n meuble m (or bijou m or tableau m) de famille.

held [hɛld] pt, pp of **hold.**

helicopter ['hɛlɪkɔptə*] n hélicoptère m.

hell [hɛl] n enfer m; ~! (col) merde!

he'll [hi:l] = **he will, he shall.**

hellish ['hɛlɪʃ] a infernal(e).

hello [hə'ləu] excl bonjour!; salut! (to sb one addresses as 'tu'); (surprise) tiens!

helm [hɛlm] n (NAUT) barre f.

helmet ['hɛlmɪt] n casque m.

help [hɛlp] n aide f; (charwoman) femme f de ménage; (assistant etc) employé(e) // vt aider; ~! au secours!; ~ **yourself** (to bread) servez-vous (de pain); he can't ~ it il n'y peut rien; ~**er** n aide m/f, assistant(e); ~**ful** a serviable, obli-

geant(e); (useful) utile; ~**ing** n portion f; ~**less** a impuissant(e); faible.

hem [hɛm] n ourlet m // vt ourler; **to** ~ **in** vt cerner.

he-man ['hi:mæn] n macho m.

hemorrhage ['hɛmərɪdʒ] n (US) = **haemorrhage.**

hen [hɛn] n poule f.

hence [hɛns] ad (therefore) d'où, de là; 2 years ~ d'ici 2 ans; ~**forth** ad dorénavant.

henchman ['hɛntʃmən] n (pej) acolyte m, séide m.

henpecked ['hɛnpɛkt] a dominé par sa femme.

her [hə:*] pronoun (direct) la, l' + vowel or h mute; (indirect) lui; (stressed, after prep) elle; see note at she // a sa(son), ses pl; see also me, my.

herald ['hɛrəld] n héraut m // vt annoncer.

herb [hə:b] n herbe f.

herd [hə:d] n troupeau m.

here [hɪə*] ad ici // excl tiens!, tenez!; ~! présent!; ~ **is,** ~ **are** voici; ~'s my sister voici ma sœur; ~/ he/she **is** le/la voici; ~ **she comes** la voici qui vient; ~**after** ad après, plus tard; ci-après // n: **the** ~**after** l'au-delà m; ~**by** ad (in letter) par la présente.

hereditary [hɪ'rɛdɪtrɪ] a héréditaire.

heredity [hɪ'rɛdɪtɪ] n hérédité f.

heresy ['hɛrəsɪ] n hérésie f.

hermit ['hə:mɪt] n ermite m.

hernia ['hə:nɪə] n hernie f.

hero, pl ~**es** [hɪərəu] n héros m.

heroin ['hɛrəuɪn] n héroïne f.

heroine ['hɛrəuɪn] n héroïne f.

heron ['hɛrən] n héron m.

herring ['hɛrɪŋ] n hareng m.

hers [hə:z] pronoun le(la) sien(ne), les siens(siennes); see also **mine.**

herself [hə:'sɛlf] pronoun (reflexive) se; (emphatic) elle-même; (after prep) elle; see also **oneself.**

he's [hi:z] = **he is, he has.**

hesitant ['hɛzɪtənt] a hésitant(e), indécis(e).

hesitate ['hezɪteɪt] *vi*: to ~ (about/ to do) hésiter (sur/à faire); **hesitation** ['-teɪʃən] *n* hésitation *f*.

heyday ['heɪdeɪ] *n*: the ~ of l'âge d'or de, les beaux jours de.

HGV *n abbr of* **heavy goods vehicle.**

hi [haɪ] *excl* salut!

hiatus [haɪ'eɪtəs] *n* trou *m*, lacune *f*; (LING) hiatus *m*.

hibernate ['haɪbəneɪt] *vi* hiberner.

hiccough, hiccup ['hɪkʌp] *vi* hoqueter // *n* hoquet *m*.

hide [haɪd] *n* (skin) peau *f* // *vb* (pt **hid**, pp **hidden** [hɪd, 'hɪdn]) *vt*: to ~ **sth** (from sb) cacher qch (à qn) // *vi*: to ~ (from sb) se cacher (de qn); ~**-and-seek** *n* cache-cache *m*; ~**away** *n* cachette *f*.

hideous ['hɪdɪəs] *a* hideux(euse); atroce.

hiding ['haɪdɪŋ] *n* (beating) correction *f*, volée *f* de coups; **to be in** ~ (concealed) se tenir caché(e).

hierarchy ['haɪərɑːkɪ] *n* hiérarchie *f*.

hi-fi ['haɪfaɪ] *n* hi-fi *f inv* // *a* hi-fi *inv*.

high [haɪ] *a* haut(e); (speed, respect, number) grand(e); (price) élevé(e); (wind) fort(e), violent(e); (voice) aigu(aiguë) // *ad* haut, en haut; 20 m ~ haut(e) de 20 m; ~**boy** *n* (US: tallboy) commode (haute); ~**brow** *a*, *n* intellectuel(le); ~**chair** *n* chaise haute (pour enfant); ~**er education** *n* études supérieures; ~**er-handed** *a* très autoritaire; très cavalier(ère); ~**jack** = **hijack**; ~ **jump** *n* (SPORT) saut *m* en hauteur; **the H~lands** *npl* les Highlands *mpl*; ~**light** *n* (fig: of event) point culminant // *vt* faire ressortir, souligner; ~**ly** *ad* très, fort, hautement; ~**ly strung** *a* nerveux(euse), toujours tendu(e); ~**ness** *n* hauteur *f*; **Her H~ness** son Altesse *f*; ~**pitched** *a* aigu(aiguë); ~**rise block** *n* tour *f* (d'habitation); ~ **school** *n* lycée *m*; (US) établissement *m* d'enseignement supérieur; ~ **season** *n* (Brit) haute saison; ~ **street** *n* (Brit)

grand-rue *f*.

highway ['haɪweɪ] *n* grand'route *f*, route nationale; **H~ Code** *n* (Brit) code *m* de la route.

hijack ['haɪdʒæk] *vt* détourner (par la force); ~**er** *n* pirate *m* de l'air.

hike [haɪk] *vi* aller à pied // *n* excursion *f* à pied, randonnée *f*; (in prices) hausse *f*, augmentation *f*; ~**r** *n* promeneur/euse, excursionniste *m/f*.

hilarious [hɪ'leərɪəs] *a* (behaviour, event) désopilant(e).

hill [hɪl] *n* colline *f*; (fairly high) montagne *f*; (on road) côte *f*; ~**side** *n* (flanc *m* de) coteau *m*; ~**y** *a* vallonné(e); montagneux(euse).

hilt [hɪlt] *n* (of sword) garde *f*; **to the** ~ (fig: support) à fond.

him [hɪm] *pronoun* (direct) le, l' + vowel or h mute; (stressed, indirect, after prep) lui; see also **me**; ~**self** *pronoun* (reflexive) se; (emphatic) lui-même; (after prep) lui; see also **oneself**.

hind [haɪnd] *a* de derrière // *n* biche *f*.

hinder ['hɪndə*] *vt* gêner; (delay) retarder; (prevent): to ~ **sb** from doing empêcher qn de faire; **hindrance** ['hɪndrəns] *n* gêne *f*, obstacle *m*.

hindsight ['haɪndsaɪt] *n*: **with** ~ avec du recul, rétrospectivement.

Hindu ['hɪnduː] *n* Hindou/e.

hinge [hɪndʒ] *n* charnière *f* // *vi* (fig): to ~ on dépendre de.

hint [hɪnt] *n* allusion *f*; (advice) conseil *m* // *vt*: to ~ **that** insinuer que // *vi*: to ~ **at** faire une allusion à.

hip [hɪp] *n* hanche *f*.

hippopotamus, *pl* ~**es** or **hippopotami** [hɪpə'pɔtəməs, -'pɔtəmaɪ] *n* hippopotame *m*.

hire ['haɪə*] *vt* (Brit: car, equipment) louer; (worker) embaucher, engager // *n* location *f*; **for** ~ à louer; (taxi) libre; ~ **purchase (H.P.)** *n* (Brit) achat *m* (or vente *f*) à tempérament or crédit.

his [hɪz] *pronoun* le(la) sien(ne), les

siens(siennes) // *a* son(sa), ses *pl*; *see also* **my, mine**.

hiss [hɪs] *vi* siffler.

historic(al) [hɪ'stɒrɪk(l)] *a* historique.

history ['hɪstərɪ] *n* histoire *f*.

hit [hɪt] *vt* (*pt, pp* **hit**) frapper; (*knock against*) cogner; (*reach: target*) atteindre, toucher; (*collide with: car*) entrer en collision avec, heurter; (*fig: affect*) toucher; (*find*) tomber sur // *n* coup *m*; (*success*) coup réussi; succès *m*; (*song*) chanson *f* à succès, tube *m*; **to ~ it off with sb** bien s'entendre avec qn; **~-and-run driver** *n* chauffard *m*.

hitch [hɪtʃ] *vt* (*fasten*) accrocher, attacher; (*also:* **~ up**) remonter d'une saccade // *n* (*difficulty*) anicroche *f*, contretemps *m*; **to ~ a lift** faire du stop.

hitch-hike ['hɪtʃhaɪk] *vi* faire de l'auto-stop; **~r** *n* auto-stoppeur/euse.

hi-tech ['haɪtɛk] *a* à la pointe de la technologie, technologiquement avancé(e) // *n* high-tech *m*.

hitherto [hɪðə'tu:] *ad* jusqu'ici.

hive [haɪv] *n* ruche *f*; **to ~ off** *vt* mettre à part, séparer.

H.M.S. *abbr* = His (Her) Majesty's Ship.

hoard [hɔ:d] *n* (*of food*) provisions *fpl*, réserves *fpl*; (*of money*) trésor *m* // *vt* amasser.

hoarding ['hɔ:dɪŋ] *n* (*Brit: for posters*) panneau *m* d'affichage *or* publicitaire.

hoarfrost ['hɔ:frɒst] *n* givre *m*.

hoarse [hɔ:s] *a* enroué(e).

hoax [həʊks] *n* canular *m*.

hob [hɒb] *n* plaque chauffante.

hobble ['hɒbl] *vi* boitiller.

hobby ['hɒbɪ] *n* passe-temps favori; **~-horse** *n* (*fig*) dada *m*.

hobo ['həʊbəʊ] *n* (*US*) vagabond *m*.

hockey ['hɒkɪ] *n* hockey *m*.

hoe [həʊ] *n* houe *f*, binette *f*.

hog [hɒg] *n* sanglier *m* // *vt* (*fig*) accaparer; **to go the whole ~** aller jusqu'au bout.

hoist [hɔɪst] *n* palan *m* // *vt* hisser.

hold [həʊld] *vb* (*pt, pp* **held**) *vt* tenir; (*contain*) contenir; (*keep back*) retenir; (*believe*) maintenir; considérer; (*possess*) avoir; détenir // *vi* (*withstand pressure*) tenir (bon); (*be valid*) valoir // *n* prise *f*; (*fig*) influence *f*; (*NAUT*) cale *f*; **~ the line!** (*TEL*) ne quittez pas!; **to ~ one's own** (*fig*) (bien) se défendre; (*sick person*) se maintenir; **to catch** *or* **get** (**a**) **~ of** saisir; **to get ~ of** (*fig*) trouver; **to ~ back** *vt* retenir; (*secret*) cacher; **to ~ down** *vt* (*person*) maintenir à terre; (*job*) occuper; **to ~ off** *vt* tenir à distance; **to ~ on** *vi* tenir bon; (*wait*) attendre; **~ on!** (*TEL*) ne quittez pas!; **to ~ on to** *vt fus* se cramponner à; (*keep*) conserver, garder; **to ~ out** *vt* offrir // *vi* (*resist*) tenir bon; **to ~ up** *vt* (*raise*) lever; (*support*) soutenir; (*delay*) retarder; **~all** *n* (*Brit*) fourre-tout *m inv*; **~er** *n* (*of ticket, record*) détenteur/trice; (*of office, title etc*) titulaire *m/f*; **~ing** *n* (*share*) intérêts *mpl*; (*farm*) ferme *f*; **~up** *n* (*robbery*) hold-up *m*; (*delay*) retard *m*; (*Brit: in traffic*) embouteillage *m*.

hole [həʊl] *n* trou *m*.

holiday ['hɒlɪdɪ] *n* vacances *fpl*; (*day off*) jour *m* de congé; (*public*) jour férié; **on ~** en congé; **~ camp** *n* (*for children*) colonie *f* de vacances; (*also:* **~ centre**) camp *m* de vacances; **~maker** *n* (*Brit*) vacancier/ère; **~ resort** *n* centre *m* de villégiature *or* de vacances.

holiness ['həʊlɪnɪs] *n* sainteté *f*.

Holland ['hɒlənd] *n* Hollande *f*.

hollow ['hɒləʊ] *a* creux(euse); (*fig*) faux(fausse) // *n* creux *m*; (*in land*) dépression *f* (*de terrain*), cuvette *f* // *vt*: **to ~ out** *vt* creuser, évider.

holly ['hɒlɪ] *n* houx *m*.

holocaust ['hɒləkɔ:st] *n* holocauste *m*.

holster ['həʊlstə*] *n* étui *m* de revolver.

holy ['həʊlɪ] *a* saint(e); (*bread, wa-*

ter) bénit(e); (*ground*) sacré(e); **H~ Ghost** *or* **Spirit** *n* Saint-Esprit *m*.

home [həʊm] *n* foyer *m*, maison *f*; (*country*) pays natal, patrie *f*; (*institution*) maison *f* // *a* de famille; (ECON, POL) national(e), intérieur(e) // *ad* chez soi, à la maison; au pays natal; (*right in: nail etc*) à fond; **at ~** chez soi, à la maison; **to go** (*or* **come**) **~** rentrer (chez soi), rentrer à la maison (*or* au pays); **make yourself at ~** faites comme chez vous; **~ address** *n* domicile permanent; **~ computer** *n* ordinateur *m* domestique; **~land** *n* patrie *f*; **~less** *a* sans foyer; sans abri; **~ly** *a* simple, sans prétention; accueillant(e); **~-made** *a* fait(e) à la maison; **H~ Office** *n* (*Brit*) Ministère *m* de l'Intérieur; **~ rule** *n* autonomie *f*; **H~ Secretary** *n* (*Brit*) ministre *m* de l'Intérieur; **~sick** *a*: **to be ~sick** avoir le mal du pays; s'ennuyer de sa famille; **~ town** *n* ville natale; **~ward** ['həʊmwəd] *a* (*journey*) du retour; **~work** *n* devoirs *mpl*.

homogeneous [hɒməʊ'dʒiːnɪəs] *a* homogène.

homosexual [hɒməʊ'sɛksjʊəl] *a, n* homosexuel(le).

honest ['ɒnɪst] *a* honnête; (*sincere*) franc(franche); **~ly** *ad* honnêtement; franchement; **~y** *n* honnêteté *f*.

honey ['hʌnɪ] *n* miel *m*; **~comb** *n* rayon *m* de miel; **~moon** *n* lune *f* de miel; (*trip*) voyage *m* de noces; **~suckle** *n* (BOT) chèvrefeuille *m*.

honk [hɒŋk] *vi* klaxonner.

honorary ['ɒnərərɪ] *a* honoraire; (*duty, title*) honorifique.

honour, (US) **honor** ['ɒnə*] *vt* honorer // *n* honneur *m*; **~able** *a* honorable; **~s degree** *n* (SCOL) licence *avec mention*.

hood [hʊd] *n* capuchon *m*; (*Brit AUT*) capote *f*; (*US AUT*) capot *m*.

hoodlum ['huːdləm] *n* truand *m*.

hoodwink ['hʊdwɪŋk] *vt* tromper.

hoof [huːf] , *pl* **~s** *or* **hooves** *n* sabot *m*.

hook [hʊk] *n* crochet *m*; (*on dress*) agrafe *f*; (*for fishing*) hameçon *m* // *vt* accrocher; (*dress*) agrafer.

hooligan ['huːlɪgən] *n* voyou *m*.

hoop [huːp] *n* cerceau *m*.

hoot [huːt] *vi* (AUT) klaxonner; (*siren*) mugir; **~er** *n* (*Brit AUT*) klaxon *m*; (NAUT) sirène *f*.

hoover ® ['huːvə*] (*Brit*) *n* aspirateur *m* // *vt* passer l'aspirateur dans *or* sur.

hooves [huːvz] *npl of* **hoof**.

hop [hɒp] *vi* sauter; (*on one foot*) sauter à cloche-pied.

hope [həʊp] *vt, vi* espérer // *n* espoir *m*; **I ~ so** je l'espère; **I ~ not** j'espère que non; **~ful** *a* (*person*) plein(e) d'espoir; (*situation*) prometteur(euse), encourageant(e); **~fully** *ad* avec espoir, avec optimisme; avec un peu de chance; **~less** *a* désespéré(e); (*useless*) nul(le).

hops [hɒps] *npl* houblon *m*.

horizon [hə'raɪzn] *n* horizon *m*; **~tal** [hɒrɪ'zɒntl] *a* horizontal(e).

horn [hɔːn] *n* corne *f*; (MUS: *also*: **French ~**) cor *m*; (AUT) klaxon *m*.

hornet ['hɔːnɪt] *n* frelon *m*.

horny ['hɔːnɪ] *a* corné(e); (*hands*) calleux(euse); (*col*) en rut, excité(e).

horoscope ['hɒrəskəʊp] *n* horoscope *m*.

horrendous [hə'rɛndəs] *a* horrible, affreux(euse).

horrible ['hɒrɪbl] *a* horrible, affreux(euse).

horrid ['hɒrɪd] *a* méchant(e), désagréable.

horrify ['hɒrɪfaɪ] *vt* horrifier.

horror ['hɒrə*] *n* horreur *f*; **~ film** *n* film *m* d'épouvante.

horse [hɔːs] *n* cheval *m*; **~back**: **on ~back** à cheval; **~ chestnut** *n* marron *m* d'(Inde); **~man/woman** *n* cavalier/ière; **~power** (h.p.) *n* puissance *f* (en chevaux); **~racing** *n* courses *fpl* de chevaux; **~radish** *n* raifort *m*; **~shoe** *n* fer *m* à cheval.

hose [həuz] *n* (*also*: ~**pipe**) tuyau *m*; (*also*: **garden** ~) tuyau d'arrosage.

hosiery ['həuziəri] *n* (*in shop*) (rayon *m* des) bas *mpl*.

hospitable ['hospitəbl] *a* hospitalier(ère).

hospital ['hospitl] *n* hôpital *m*; **in** ~ à l'hôpital.

hospitality [hospi'tæliti] *n* hospitalité *f*.

host [həust] *n* hôte *m*; (*in hotel etc*) patron *m*; (REL) hostie *f*; (*large number*): **a** ~ **of** une foule de.

hostage ['hostidʒ] *n* otage *m*.

hostel ['hostl] *n* foyer *m*; (*also*: **youth** ~) auberge *f* de jeunesse.

hostess ['həustis] *n* hôtesse *f*.

hostile ['hostail] *a* hostile.

hostility [ho'stiliti] *n* hostilité *f*.

hot [hot] *a* chaud(e); (*as opposed to only warm*) très chaud; (*spicy*) fort(e), (*fig*) acharné(e), brûlant(e), violent(e), passionné(e); **to be** ~ (*person*) avoir chaud; (*object*) être (très) chaud; (*weather*) faire chaud; ~**bed** *n* (*fig*) foyer *m*, pépinière *f*; ~ **dog** *n* hot-dog *m*.

hotel [həu'tel] *n* hôtel *m*.

hot: ~**headed** *a* impétueux(euse); ~**house** *n* serre chaude; ~ **line** *n* (POL) téléphone *m* rouge, ligne directe; ~**ly** *ad* passionnément, violemment; ~**plate** *n* (*on cooker*) plaque chauffante; ~**water bottle** *n* bouillotte *f*.

hound [haund] *vt* poursuivre avec acharnement // *n* chien courant.

hour ['auə*] *n* heure *f*; ~**ly** *a, ad* toutes les heures; (*rate*) horaire; ~**ly paid** *a* payé(e) à l'heure.

house *n* [haus] (*pl*: ~**s** ['hauziz]) maison *f*; (POL) chambre *f*; (THEATRE) salle *f*; auditoire *m* // *vt* [hauz] (*person*) loger, héberger; **on the** ~ (*fig*) aux frais de la maison; ~**boat** *n* bateau (aménagé en habitation); ~**breaking** *n* cambriolage *m* (avec effraction); ~**coat** *n* peignoir *m*; ~**hold** *n* famille *f*, maisonnée *f*; mé-

nage *m*; ~**keeper** *n* gouvernante *f*; ~**keeping** *n* (*work*) ménage *m*; ~**keeping** (*money*) argent *m* du ménage; ~**-warming party** *n* pendaison *f* de crémaillère; ~**wife** *n* ménagère *f*; femme *f* au foyer; ~**work** *n* (travaux *mpl* du) ménage *m*.

housing ['hauziŋ] *n* logement *m*; ~ **development**, (*Brit*) ~ **estate** *n* cité *f*; lotissement *m*.

hovel ['hovl] *n* taudis *m*.

hover ['hovə*] *vi* planer; ~**craft** *n* aéroglisseur *m*.

how [hau] *ad* comment; ~ **are you?** comment allez-vous?; ~ **do you do?** bonjour; enchanté(e); ~ **far is it to ...?** combien y a-t-il jusqu'à ...?; ~ **long have you been here?** depuis combien de temps êtes-vous là?; ~ **lovely!** que *or* comme c'est joli!; ~ **many/much?** combien?; ~ **many people/much milk** combien de gens/lait; ~ **old are you?** quel âge avez-vous?; ~**ever** *ad* de quelque façon *or* manière que + *sub*; (+ *adjective*) quelque *or* si ... que + *sub*; (*in questions*) comment // *cj* pourtant, cependant.

howl ['haul] *vi* hurler.

h.p., H.P. *abbr* of **hire purchase, horsepower.**

HQ *abbr* of **headquarters.**

hub [hʌb] *n* (*of wheel*) moyeu *m*; (*fig*) centre *m*, foyer *m*.

hubbub ['hʌbʌb] *n* brouhaha *m*.

hub cap *n* enjoliveur *m*.

huddle ['hʌdl] *vi*: **to** ~ **together** se blottir les uns contre les autres.

hue [hju:] *n* teinte *f*, nuance *f*; ~ **and cry** *n* (*fig*) clameur *f*.

huff [hʌf] *n*: **in a** ~ fâché(e).

hug [hʌg] *vt* serrer dans ses bras; (*shore, kerb*) serrer // *n* étreinte *f*.

huge [hju:dʒ] *a* énorme, immense.

hulk [hʌlk] *n* (*ship*) vieux rafiot (*car, building*) carcasse *f*; (*person*) mastodonte *m*, malabar *m*.

hull [hʌl] *n* (*of ship, nuts*) coque *f*.

hullo [hə'ləu] *excl* = **hello.**

hum [hʌm] *vt* (*tune*) fredonner // *vi* fredonner; (*insect*) bourdonner; (*plane, tool*) vrombir.

human ['hju:mən] *a* humain(e) // *n* être humain.

humane [hju:'meɪn] *a* humain(e), humanitaire.

humanitarian [hju:mænɪ'tɛərɪən] *a* humanitaire.

humanity [hju:'mænɪtɪ] *n* humanité *f*.

humble ['hʌmbl] *a* humble, modeste // *vt* humilier.

humbug ['hʌmbʌg] *n* fumisterie *f*.

humdrum ['hʌmdrʌm] *a* monotone, routinier(ère).

humid ['hju:mɪd] *a* humide.

humiliate [hju:'mɪlɪeɪt] *vt* humilier; **humiliation** [-'eɪʃən] *n* humiliation *f*.

humility [hju:'mɪlɪtɪ] *n* humilité *f*.

humorous ['hju:mərəs] *a* humoristique; (*person*) plein(e) d'humour.

humour, (*US*) **humor** ['hju:mə*] *n* humour *m*; (*mood*) humeur *f* // *vt* (*person*) faire plaisir à; se prêter aux caprices de.

hump [hʌmp] *n* bosse *f*.

hunch [hʌntʃ] *n* bosse *f*; (*premonition*) intuition *f*; **~back** *n* bossu(e); **~ed** *a* arrondi(e), voûté(e).

hundred ['hʌndrəd] *num* cent; **~s of** des centaines de; **~weight** *n* (*Brit*) = 50.8 kg; 112 lb; (*US*) = 45.3 kg; 100 lb.

hung [hʌŋ] *pt, pp of* **hang**.

Hungary ['hʌŋgərɪ] *n* Hongrie *f*.

hunger ['hʌŋgə*] *n* faim *f* // *vi*: **to ~ for** avoir faim, désirer ardemment.

hungry ['hʌŋgrɪ] *a* affamé(e); **to be ~** avoir faim.

hunk [hʌŋk] *n* (*of bread etc*) gros morceau.

hunt [hʌnt] *vt* (*seek*) chercher; (*SPORT*) chasser // *vi* chasser // *n* chasse *f*; **~er** *n* chasseur *m*; **~ing** *n* chasse *f*.

hurdle ['hə:dl] *n* (*SPORT*) haie *f*; (*fig*) obstacle *m*.

hurl [hə:l] *vt* lancer (avec violence).

hurrah, **hurray** [hu'rɑː, hu'reɪ] *n* hourra *m*.

hurricane ['hʌrɪkən] *n* ouragan *m*.

hurried ['hʌrɪd] *a* pressé(e), précipité(e); (*work*) fait(e) à la hâte; **~ly** *ad* précipitamment, à la hâte.

hurry ['hʌrɪ] *n* hâte *f*, précipitation *f* // *vb* (*also*: **~ up**) *vi* se presser, se dépêcher // *vt* (*person*) faire presser, faire se dépêcher; (*work*) presser, faire se dépêcher; **to be in a ~** être pressé(e); **to do sth in a ~** faire qch en vitesse; **to ~ in/out** entrer/sortir précipitamment.

hurt [hə:t] *vt* (*pt, pp* **hurt**) (*cause pain to*) faire mal à; (*injure, fig*) blesser // *vi* faire mal // *a* blessé(e); **~ful** *a* (*remark*) blessant(e).

hurtle ['hə:tl] *vi*: **to ~** passer en trombe; **to ~ down** dégringoler.

husband ['hʌzbənd] *n* mari *m*.

hush [hʌʃ] *n* calme *m*, silence *m* // *vt* faire taire; **~!** chut!

husk [hʌsk] *n* (*of wheat*) balle *f*; (*of rice, maize*) enveloppe *f*.

husky ['hʌskɪ] *a* rauque // *n* chien *m* esquimau *or* de traîneau.

hustle ['hʌsl] *vt* pousser, bousculer // *n* bousculade *f*; **~ and bustle** *n* tourbillon *m* (d'activité).

hut [hʌt] *n* hutte *f*; (*shed*) cabane *f*.

hutch [hʌtʃ] *n* clapier *m*.

hyacinth ['haɪəsɪnθ] *n* jacinthe *f*.

hydrant ['haɪdrənt] *n* prise *f* d'eau; (*also*: **fire ~**) bouche *f* d'incendie.

hydraulic [haɪ'drɔ:lɪk] *a* hydraulique.

hydroelectric [haɪdrəʊɪ'lɛktrɪk] *a* hydro-électrique.

hydrofoil ['haɪdrəfɔɪl] *n* hydrofoil *m*.

hydrogen ['haɪdrədʒən] *n* hydrogène *m*.

hyena [haɪ'i:nə] *n* hyène *f*.

hygiene ['haɪdʒi:n] *n* hygiène *f*.

hymn [hɪm] *n* hymne *m*; cantique *m*.

hype [haɪp] *n* (*col*) campagne *f* publicitaire.

hypermarket ['haɪpəmɑːkɪt] *n* hypermarché *m*.

hyphen ['haɪfn] *n* trait *m* d'union.

hypnotize ['hɪpnətaɪz] *vt* hypnotiser.

hypocrisy [hɪ'pɒkrəsɪ] *n* hypocrisie *f*.

hypocrite ['hɪpəkrɪt] *n* hypocrite *m/f*; **hypocritical** [-'krɪtɪk] *a* hypocrite.

hypothesis, *pl* **hypotheses** [haɪ'pɒθɪsɪs, -siːz] *n* hypothèse *f*.

hysterical [hɪ'sterɪkl] *a* hystérique.

hysterics [hɪ'sterɪks] *npl* (*violente*) crise de nerfs; (*laughter*) crise de rire.

I

I [aɪ] *pronoun* je; (*before vowel*) j'; (*stressed*) moi.

ice [aɪs] *n* glace *f*; (*on road*) verglas *m* // *vt* (*cake*) glacer; (*drink*) faire rafraîchir // *vi* (*also*: ~ **over**) geler; (*also*: ~ **up**) se givrer; ~ **axe** *n* piolet *m*; ~**berg** *n* iceberg *m*; ~**box** *n* (*US*) réfrigérateur *m*; (*ice compartiment*) *m* à glace *f*; (*insulated box*) glacière *f*; ~ **cream** *n* glace *f*; ~ **cube** *n* glaçon *m*; ~ **hockey** *n* hockey *m* sur glace.

Iceland ['aɪslənd] *n* Islande *f*.

ice: ~ **lolly** *n* (*Brit*) esquimau *m*; ~ **rink** *n* patinoire *f*; ~ **skating** *n* patinage *m* (sur glace).

icicle ['aɪsɪkl] *n* glaçon *m* (*naturel*).

icing ['aɪsɪŋ] *n* (*AVIAT etc*) givrage *m*; (*CULIN*) glaçage *m*; ~ **sugar** *n* (*Brit*) sucre *m* glace.

icy ['aɪsɪ] *a* glacé(e); (*road*) verglacé(e); (*weather, temperature*) glacial(e).

I'd [aɪd] = I would, I had.

idea [aɪ'dɪə] *n* idée *f*.

ideal [aɪ'dɪəl] *n* idéal *m* // *a* idéal(e).

identical [aɪ'dentɪkl] *a* identique.

identification [aɪdentɪfɪ'keɪʃən] *n* identification *f*; **means of** ~ pièce *f* d'identité.

identify [aɪ'dentɪfaɪ] *vt* identifier.

identikit picture [aɪ'dentɪkɪt-] *n* portrait-robot *m*.

identity [aɪ'dentɪtɪ] *n* identité *f*; ~ **card** *n* carte *f* d'identité.

idiom ['ɪdɪəm] *n* langue *f*, idiome *m*; (*phrase*) expression *f* idiomatique.

idiosyncrasy [ɪdɪə'sɪŋkrəsɪ] *n* particularité *f*, caractéristique *f*.

idiot ['ɪdɪət] *n* idiot, imbécile *m/f*; ~**ic** [-'ɔtɪk] *a* idiot(e), bête, stupide.

idle ['aɪdl] *a* sans occupation, désœuvré(e); (*lazy*) oisif(ive), paresseux(euse); (*unemployed*) au chômage; (*question, pleasures*) vain(e), futile // *vi* (*engine*) tourner au ralenti; **to** ~ **away the time** passer son temps à ne rien faire; **to lie** ~ être arrêté, ne pas fonctionner.

idol ['aɪdl] *n* idole *f*; ~**ize** *vt* idolâtrer, adorer.

i.e. *ad abbr* (= id est) c'est-à-dire.

if [ɪf] *cj* si; ~ **so** si c'est le cas; ~ **not** sinon; ~ **only** si seulement.

ignite [ɪg'naɪt] *vt* mettre le feu à, enflammer // *vi* s'enflammer.

ignition [ɪg'nɪʃən] *n* (*AUT*) allumage *m*; **to switch on/off the** ~ mettre/couper le contact; ~ **key** *n* (*AUT*) clé *f* de contact.

ignorant ['ɪgnərənt] *a* ignorant(e); **to be** ~ **of** (*subject*) ne rien connaître en; (*events*) ne pas être au courant de.

ignore [ɪg'nɔː] *vt* ne tenir aucun compte de, ne pas relever; (*person*) faire semblant de ne pas reconnaître; (*fact*) méconnaître.

ill [ɪl] *a* (*sick*) malade; (*bad*) mauvais(e) // *n* mal *m* // *ad*: **to speak** *etc* ~ **of** dire etc du mal de; **to take** or **be taken** ~ tomber malade; ~-**advised** (*decision*) peu judicieux(euse); (*person*) malavisé(e); ~-**at-ease** a mal à l'aise.

I'll [aɪl] = I will, I shall.

illegal [ɪ'liːgl] *a* illégal(e).

illegible [ɪ'ledʒɪbl] *a* illisible.

illegitimate [ɪlɪ'dʒɪtɪmət] *a* illégitime.

ill-fated [ɪl'feɪtɪd] *a* malheureux(euse); (*day*) néfaste.

ill feeling *n* ressentiment *m*, rancune *f*.

illiterate [ɪ'lɪtərət] *a* illettré(e); (*letter*) plein(e) de fautes.

illness [ˈɪlnɪs] n maladie f.

ill-treat [ɪlˈtriːt] vt maltraiter.

illuminate [ɪˈluːmɪneɪt] vt (room, street) éclairer; (building) illuminer.

illumination [-ˈneɪʃən] n éclairage m; illumination f.

illusion [ɪˈluːʒən] n illusion f; **to be under the ~ that** s'imaginer or croire que.

illustrate [ˈɪləstreɪt] vt illustrer; **illustration** [-ˈstreɪʃən] n illustration f.

ill will n malveillance f.

I'm [aɪm] =I am.

image [ˈɪmɪdʒ] n image f; (public face) image de marque; **~ry** n images fpl.

imaginary [ɪˈmædʒɪnərɪ] a imaginaire.

imagination [ɪmædʒɪˈneɪʃən] n imagination f.

imaginative [ɪˈmædʒɪnətɪv] a imaginatif(ive); plein(e) d'imagination.

imagine [ɪˈmædʒɪn] vt s'imaginer; (suppose) imaginer, supposer.

imbalance [ɪmˈbæləns] n déséquilibre m.

imitate [ˈɪmɪteɪt] vt imiter; **imitation** [-ˈteɪʃən] n imitation f.

immaculate [ɪˈmækjulət] a impeccable; (REL) immaculé(e).

immaterial [ɪməˈtɪərɪəl] a sans importance, insignifiant(e).

immature [ɪməˈtjuə*] a (fruit) qui n'est pas mûr(e); (person) qui manque de maturité.

immediate [ɪˈmiːdɪət] a immédiat(e); **~ly** ad (at once) immédiatement; **~ly next to** juste à côté de.

immense [ɪˈmɛns] a immense, énorme.

immerse [ɪˈmɜːs] vt immerger, plonger.

immersion heater [ɪˈmɜːʃən] n (Brit) chauffe-eau m électrique.

immigrant [ˈɪmɪgrənt] n immigrant/e; immigré/e.

immigration [ɪmɪˈgreɪʃən] n immigration f.

imminent [ˈɪmɪnənt] a imminent(e).

immoral [ɪˈmɔrl] a immoral(e).

immortal [ɪˈmɔːtl] a, n immortel(le).

immune [ɪˈmjuːn] a: **~ (to)** immunisé(e) (contre).

immunity [ɪˈmjuːnɪtɪ] n immunité f.

imp [ɪmp] n lutin m; (child) petit diable.

impact [ˈɪmpækt] n choc m, impact m; (fig) impact.

impair [ɪmˈpɛə*] vt détériorer, diminuer.

impart [ɪmˈpɑːt] vt communiquer, transmettre; confier, donner.

impartial [ɪmˈpɑːʃl] a impartial(e).

impassable [ɪmˈpɑːsəbl] a infranchissable; (road) impraticable.

impassive [ɪmˈpæsɪv] a impassible.

impatience [ɪmˈpeɪʃəns] n impatience f.

impatient [ɪmˈpeɪʃənt] a impatient(e); **to get** or **grow ~** s'impatienter.

impeccable [ɪmˈpɛkəbl] a impeccable, parfait(e).

impede [ɪmˈpiːd] vt gêner.

impediment [ɪmˈpɛdɪmənt] n obstacle m; (also: **speech ~**) défaut m d'élocution.

impending [ɪmˈpɛndɪŋ] a imminent(e).

imperative [ɪmˈpɛrətɪv] a nécessaire; urgent(e), pressant(e); (tone) impérieux(euse) // n (LING) impératif m.

imperfect [ɪmˈpɜːfɪkt] a imparfait(e); (goods etc) défectueux(euse) // n (LING) imparfait m.

imperial [ɪmˈpɪərɪəl] a impérial(e); (measure) légal(e).

impersonal [ɪmˈpɜːsənl] a impersonnel(le).

impersonate [ɪmˈpɜːsəneɪt] vt se faire passer pour; (THEATRE) imiter.

impertinent [ɪmˈpɜːtɪnənt] a impertinent(e), insolent(e).

impervious [ɪmˈpɜːvɪəs] a imperméable; (fig): **~ to** insensible à; inaccessible à.

impetuous [ɪmˈpɛtjuəs] a impétueux(euse), fougueux(euse).

impetus ['ɪmpətəs] *n* impulsion *f*; (*of runner*) élan *m*.

impinge [ɪm'pɪndʒ]: **to ~ on** *vt fus* (*person*) affecter, toucher; (*rights*) empiéter sur.

implement *n* ['ɪmplɪmənt] outil *m*, instrument *m*; (*for cooking*) ustensile *m // vt* ['ɪmplɪment] exécuter, mettre à effet.

implicit [ɪm'plɪsɪt] *a* implicite; (*complete*) absolu(e), sans réserve.

imply [ɪm'plaɪ] *vt* suggérer, laisser entendre; indiquer, supposer.

impolite [ɪmpə'laɪt] *a* impoli(e).

import *vt* [ɪm'pɔːt] importer *// n* ['ɪmpɔːt] (*COMM*) importation *f*; (*meaning*) portée *f*, signification *f*.

importance [ɪm'pɔːtns] *n* importance *f*.

important [ɪm'pɔːtnt] *a* important(e).

importer [ɪm'pɔːtə*] *n* importateur/trice.

impose [ɪm'pəuz] *vt* imposer *// vi*: **to ~ on sb** abuser de la gentillesse (*or* crédulité) de qn.

imposing [ɪm'pəuzɪŋ] *a* imposant(e), impressionnant(e).

imposition [ɪmpə'zɪʃən] *n* (*of tax etc*) imposition *f*; **to be an ~ on** (*person*) abuser de la gentillesse *or* la bonté de.

impossible [ɪm'pɒsɪbl] *a* impossible.

impotent ['ɪmpətnt] *a* impuissant(e).

impound [ɪm'paund] *vt* confisquer, saisir.

impoverished [ɪm'pɒvərɪʃt] *a* pauvre, appauvri(e).

impractical [ɪm'præktɪkl] *a* pas pratique; (*person*) qui manque d'esprit pratique.

impregnable [ɪm'pregnəbl] *a* (*fortress*) imprenable; (*fig*) inattaquable; irréfutable.

impress [ɪm'pres] *vt* impressionner, faire impression sur; (*mark*) imprimer, marquer; **to ~ sth on sb** faire bien comprendre qch à qn.

impression [ɪm'preʃən] *n* impression *f*; (*of stamp, seal*) empreinte *f*; **to be under the ~ that** avoir l'impression que.

impressive [ɪm'presɪv] *a* impressionnant(e).

imprint ['ɪmprɪnt] *n* (*PUBLISHING*) notice *f*.

imprison [ɪm'prɪzn] *vt* emprisonner, mettre en prison.

improbable [ɪm'prɒbəbl] *a* improbable; (*excuse*) peu plausible.

improper [ɪm'prɒpə*] *a* incorrect(e); (*unsuitable*) déplacé(e), de mauvais goût; indécent(e).

improve [ɪm'pruːv] *vt* améliorer *// vi* s'améliorer; (*pupil etc*) faire des progrès; **~ment** *n* amélioration *f*; progrès *m*.

improvise ['ɪmprəvaɪz] *vt*, *vi* improviser.

impudent ['ɪmpjudnt] *a* impudent(e).

impulse ['ɪmpʌls] *n* impulsion *f*; **on ~** impulsivement, sur un coup de tête.

impulsive [ɪm'pʌlsɪv] *a* impulsif(ive).

KEYWORD

in [ɪn] ♦ *prep* **1** (*indicating place, position*) dans; **~ the house/the fridge** dans la maison/le frigo; **~ the garden** dans le *or* au jardin; **~ town** en ville; **~ the country** à la campagne; **~ school** à l'école; **~ here/there** ici/là

2 (*with place names: of town, region, country*): **London** à Londres; **~ England** en Angleterre; **~ Japan** au Japon; **~ the United States** aux États-Unis

3 (*indicating time: during*): **~ spring** au printemps; **~ summer** en été; **~ May/1992** en mai/1992; **~ the afternoon** (dans) l'après-midi; **at 4 o'clock ~ the afternoon** à 4 heures de l'après-midi

4 (*indicating time: in the space of*) en; (: *future*) dans; **I did it ~ 3 hours/days** je l'ai fait en 3 heures/jours; **I'll see you ~ 2 weeks or ~**

2 weeks' time je te verrai dans 2 semaines
5 (*indicating manner etc*) à; ~ a **loud/ soft voice** à voix haute/basse; ~ **pencil** au crayon; ~ **French** en français; **the boy** ~ **the blue shirt** le garçon à *or* avec la chemise bleue
6 (*indicating circumstances*): ~ **the sun** au soleil; ~ **the shade** à l'ombre; ~ **the rain** sous la pluie
7 (*indicating mood, state*): ~ **tears** en larmes; ~ **anger** sous le coup de la colère; ~ **despair** au désespoir; ~ **good condition** en bon état; **to live** ~ **luxury** vivre dans le luxe
8 (*with ratios, numbers*): 1 ~ 10 (**households**), 1 (**household**) ~ 10 1 (ménage) sur 10; **20 pence** ~ **the pound** 20 pence par livre sterling; **they lined up** ~ **twos** ils se mirent en rangs (deux) par deux; ~ **hundreds** par centaines
9 (*referring to people, works*): **the disease is common** ~ **children** c'est une maladie courante chez les enfants; ~ (**the works of**) **Dickens** chez Dickens, dans (l'œuvre de) Dickens
10 (*indicating profession etc state*): **to be** ~ **teaching** être dans l'enseignement
11 (*after superlative*) de; **the best pupil** ~ **the class** le meilleur élève de la classe
12 (*with present participle*): ~ **saying this** en disant ceci
◆ *ad*: **to be** ~ (*person: at home, work*) être là; (*train, ship, plane*) être arrivé(e); (*in fashion*) être à la mode; **to ask sb** ~ inviter qn à entrer; **to run/limp** etc ~ entrer en courant/boitant etc
◆ *n*: **the ~s and outs** (*of proposal, situation etc*) les tenants et aboutissants (de).

in., ins *abbr of* **inch(es)**.
inability [ɪnəˈbɪlɪtɪ] *n* incapacité *f*.
inaccurate [ɪnˈækjʊrət] *a* inexact(e); (*person*) qui manque de précision.

inadequate [ɪnˈædɪkwət] *a* insuffisant(e), inadéquat(e).
inadvertently [ɪnədˈvɜːtntlɪ] *ad* par mégarde.
inane [ɪˈneɪn] *a* inepte, stupide.
inanimate [ɪnˈænɪmət] *a* inanimé(e).
inappropriate [ɪnəˈprəʊprɪət] *a* inopportun(e), mal à propos; (*word, expression*) impropre.
inarticulate [ɪnɑːˈtɪkjʊlət] *a* (*person*) qui s'exprime mal; (*speech*) indistinct(e).
inasmuch as [ɪnəzˈmʌtʃæz] *ad* dans la mesure où; (*seeing that*) attendu que.
inauguration [ɪnɔːgjʊˈreɪʃən] *n* inauguration *f*; (*of president, official*) investiture *f*.
in-between [ɪnbɪˈtwiːn] *a* entre les deux.
inborn [ɪnˈbɔːn] *a* (*feeling*) inné(e); (*defect*) congénital(e).
inbred [ɪnˈbred] *a* inné(e), naturel(le); (*family*) consanguin(e).
Inc. *abbr of* **incorporated**.
incapable [ɪnˈkeɪpəbl] *a* incapable.
incapacitate [ɪnkəˈpæsɪtet] *vt*: **to** ~ **sb from doing** rendre qn incapable de faire.
incense *n* [ˈɪnsɛns] encens *m* // *vt* [ɪnˈsɛns] (*anger*) mettre en fureur.
incentive [ɪnˈsɛntɪv] *n* encouragement *m*, raison *f* de se donner de la peine.
incessant [ɪnˈsɛsnt] *a* incessant(e); ~**ly** *ad* sans cesse, constamment.
inch [ɪntʃ] *n* pouce *m* (= 25 mm; 12 *in a foot*); **within an** ~ **of** à deux doigts de; **he didn't give an** ~ (*fig*) il n'a pas voulu céder d'un pouce *or* faire la plus petite concession; **to** ~ **forward** *vi* avancer petit à petit.
incidence [ˈɪnsɪdns] *n* (*of crime, disease*) fréquence *f*.
incident [ˈɪnsɪdnt] *n* incident *m*; (*in book*) péripétie *f*.
incidental [ɪnsɪˈdentl] *a* accessoire; (*unplanned*) accidentel(le); ~ **to** qui accompagne; ~**ly** [-ˈdɛntəlɪ] *ad* (*by the way*) à propos.

incipient [ɪn'sɪpɪənt] *a* naissant(e).

inclination [ɪnklɪ'neɪʃən] *n* inclination *f*.

incline *n* ['ɪnklaɪn] pente *f*, plan incliné // *vb* [ɪn'klaɪn] *vt* incliner // *vi*: **to ~ to** avoir tendance à; **to be ~d to do** être enclin(e) à faire; avoir tendance à faire.

include [ɪn'kluːd] *vt* inclure, comprendre; **including** *prep* y compris.

inclusive [ɪn'kluːsɪv] *a* inclus(e), compris(e) // *ad*: **~ of tax** etc taxes etc comprises.

income ['ɪnkʌm] *n* revenu *m*; **~ tax** *n* impôt *m* sur le revenu.

incompetent [ɪn'kɒmpɪtnt] *a* incompétent(e), incapable.

incomplete [ɪnkəm'pliːt] *a* incomplet(ète).

incongruous [ɪn'kɒŋgruəs] *a* peu approprié(e), *(remark, act)* incongru(e), déplacé(e).

inconsistency [ɪnkən'sɪstənsɪ] *n (of actions etc)* inconséquence *f*; *(of work)* irrégularité *f*; *(of statement etc)* incohérence *f*.

inconsistent [ɪnkən'sɪstnt] *a* inconséquent(e); irrégulier(ère); peu cohérent(e).

inconspicuous [ɪnkən'spɪkjuəs] *a* qui passe inaperçu(e), *(colour, dress)* discret(ète).

inconvenience [ɪnkən'viːnjəns] *n* inconvénient *m*; *(trouble)* dérangement *m* // *vt* déranger.

inconvenient [ɪnkən'viːnjənt] *a* malcommode, *(time, place)* mal choisi(e), qui ne convient pas.

incorporate [ɪn'kɔːpəreɪt] *vt* incorporer; *(contain)* contenir; **~d a: ~d company** *(US: abbr* Inc.*)* = société *f* anonyme (S.A.).

incorrect [ɪnkə'rekt] *a* incorrect(e); *(opinion, statement)* inexact(e).

increase *n* ['ɪnkriːs] augmentation *f* // *vi, vt* [ɪn'kriːs] augmenter.

increasing [ɪn'kriːsɪŋ] *a (number)* croissant(e); **~ly** *ad* de plus en plus.

incredible [ɪn'kredɪbl] *a* incroyable.

incredulous [ɪn'kredjuləs] *a* incrédule.

increment ['ɪnkrɪmənt] *n* augmentation *f*.

incubator ['ɪnkjubeɪtə*] *n* incubateur *m*; *(for babies)* couveuse *f*.

incumbent [ɪn'kʌmbənt] *n (REL)* titulaire *m/f* // *a*: **it is ~ on him to** ... il lui incombe *or* appartient de ....

incur [ɪn'kɜː*] *vt (expenses)* encourir; *(anger, risk)* s'exposer à; *(debt)* contracter; *(loss)* subir.

indebted [ɪn'detɪd] *a*: **to be ~ to sb (for)** être redevable à qn (de).

indecent [ɪn'diːsnt] *a* indécent(e), inconvenant(e); **~ assault** *n (Brit)* attentat *m* à la pudeur; **~ exposure** *n* outrage *m (public)* à la pudeur.

indecisive [ɪndɪ'saɪsɪv] *a* indécis(e); *(discussion)* peu concluant(e).

indeed [ɪn'diːd] *ad* en effet; d'ailleurs; vraiment; **yes ~!** certainement!

indefinite [ɪn'defɪnɪt] *a* indéfini(e); *(answer)* vague; *(period, number)* indéterminé(e); **~ly** *ad (wait)* indéfiniment.

indemnity [ɪn'demnɪtɪ] *n (insurance)* assurance *f*, garantie *f*; *(compensation)* indemnité *f*.

independence [ɪndɪ'pendns] *n* indépendance *f*.

independent [ɪndɪ'pendnt] *a* indépendant(e); **to become ~** s'affranchir.

index ['ɪndeks] *n (pl: ~es: in book)* index *m*; *(: in library etc)* catalogue *m*; *(pl: indices* ['ɪndɪsiːz]*) (ratio, sign)* indice *m*; **~ card** *n* fiche *f*; **~ finger** *n* index *m*; **~-linked**, *(US)* **~ed** *a* indexé(e) *(sur le coût de la vie etc)*.

India [ɪ'ndɪə] *n* Inde *f*; **~n a** indien(ne) // *n* Indien(ne); **Red ~n** Indien/ne (d'Amérique).

indicate ['ɪndɪkeɪt] *vt* indiquer; **indication** [-'keɪʃən] *n* indication *f*, signe *m*.

indicative [ɪn'dɪkətɪv] *a* indicatif(ive) // *n (LING)* indicatif *m*; **~ of**

symptomatique de.

indicator ['ɪndɪkeɪtə*] n (sign) indicateur m; (AUT) clignotant m.

indices ['ɪndɪsi:z] npl of **index**.

indictment [ɪn'daɪtmənt] n accusation f.

indifference [ɪn'dɪfrəns] n indifférence f.

indifferent [ɪn'dɪfrənt] a indifférent(e); (poor) médiocre, quelconque.

indigenous [ɪn'dɪdʒɪnəs] a indigène.

indigestion [ɪndɪ'dʒestʃən] n indigestion f, mauvaise digestion.

indignant [ɪn'dɪgnənt] a: ~ (at or about sth/with sb) indigné(e) (de qch/contre qn).

indignity [ɪn'dɪgnɪtɪ] n indignité f, affront m.

indirect [ɪndɪ'rekt] a indirect(e).

indiscreet [ɪndɪs'kri:t] a indiscret(ète); (rash) imprudent(e).

indiscriminate [ɪndɪs'krɪmɪnət] a (person) qui manque de discernement; (admiration) aveugle; (killings) commis(e) au hasard.

indisputable [ɪndɪs'pju:təbl] a incontestable, indiscutable.

individual [ɪndɪ'vɪdjuəl] n individu m // a individuel(le); (characteristic) particulier(ère), original(e).

indoctrination [ɪndɒktrɪ'neɪʃən] n endoctrinement m.

Indonesia [ɪndə'ni:zɪə] n Indonésie f.

indoor ['ɪndɔ:*] a d'intérieur; (swimming pool) couvert(e); (games) pratiqué(e) en salle; ~s ad à l'intérieur; (at home) à la maison.

induce [ɪn'dju:s] vt persuader; (bring about) provoquer; ~ment n incitation f; (incentive) but m; (pej: bribe) pot-de-vin m.

induction [ɪn'dʌkʃən] n (MED: of birth) accouchement provoqué; ~ course n (Brit) stage m de mise au courant.

indulge [ɪn'dʌldʒ] vt (whim) céder à, satisfaire; (child) gâter // vi: to ~ in s'offrir qch, se permettre qch;

se livrer à qch; ~nce n fantaisie f (que l'on s'offre); (leniency) indulgence f; ~nt a indulgent(e).

industrial [ɪn'dʌstrɪəl] a industriel(le); (injury) du travail; (dispute) ouvrier(ère); ~ action n action revendicative; ~ estate n (Brit) zone industrielle; ~ist n industriel m; ~ park n (US) = ~ estate.

industrious [ɪn'dʌstrɪəs] a travailleur(euse).

industry ['ɪndəstrɪ] n industrie f; (diligence) zèle m, application f.

inebriated [ɪ'ni:brɪeɪtɪd] a ivre.

inedible [ɪn'edɪbl] a immangeable; (plant etc) non comestible.

ineffective [ɪnɪ'fektɪv], **ineffectual** [ɪnɪ'fektʃuəl] a inefficace; (person) incompétent(e).

inefficiency [ɪnɪ'fɪʃənsɪ] n inefficacité f.

inefficient [ɪnɪ'fɪʃənt] a inefficace.

inequality [ɪnɪ'kwɔlɪtɪ] n inégalité f.

inescapable [ɪnɪ'skeɪpəbl] a inéluctable, inévitable.

inevitable [ɪn'evɪtəbl] a inévitable; **inevitably** ad inévitablement.

inexpensive [ɪnɪk'spensɪv] a bon marché inv.

inexperienced [ɪnɪks'pɪərɪənst] a inexpérimenté(e).

infallible [ɪn'fælɪbl] a infaillible.

infamous ['ɪnfəməs] a infâme, abominable.

infancy ['ɪnfənsɪ] n petite enfance, bas âge; (fig) enfance, débuts mpl.

infant ['ɪnfənt] n (baby) nourrisson m; (young child) petit(e) enfant; ~ school n (Brit) classes fpl préparatoires (entre 5 et 7 ans).

infatuated [ɪn'fætjueɪtɪd] a: ~ with entiché(e) de.

infatuation [ɪnfætju'eɪʃən] n toquade f; engouement m.

infect [ɪn'fekt] vt infecter, contaminer; ~ion [ɪn'fekʃən] n infection f; contagion f; ~ious [ɪn'fekʃəs] a infectieux(euse); (also fig) contagieux(euse).

infer [ɪn'fə:*] vt conclure, déduire.
inferior [ɪn'fɪərɪə*] a inférieur(e);
(goods) de qualité inférieure // n
inférieur/e; (in rank) subalterne m/f;
~**ity** [ɪnfɪərɪ'ɔrətɪ] n infériorité f;
~**ity complex** n complexe m d'infériorité.
inferno [ɪn'fə:nəu] n enfer m; brasier m.
infertile [ɪn'fə:taɪl] a stérile.
in-fighting ['ɪnfaɪtɪŋ] n querelles fpl
internes.
infinite ['ɪnfɪnɪt] a infini(e).
infinitive [ɪn'fɪnɪtɪv] n infinitif m.
infinity [ɪn'fɪnɪtɪ] n infinité f; (also
MATH) infini m.
infirmary [ɪn'fə:mərɪ] n hôpital m;
(in school, factory) infirmerie f.
infirmity [ɪn'fə:mɪtɪ] n infirmité f.
inflamed [ɪn'fleɪmd] a enflammée(e).
inflammable [ɪn'flæməbl] a (Brit)
inflammable.
inflammation [ɪnflə'meɪʃən] n inflammation f.
inflatable [ɪn'fleɪtəbl] a gonflable.
inflate [ɪn'fleɪt] vt (tyre, balloon)
gonfler; (fig) grossir; gonfler; faire
monter; **inflation** [ɪn'fleɪʃən] n
(ECON) inflation f; **inflationary**
[ɪn'fleɪʃnərɪ] a inflationniste.
inflict [ɪn'flɪkt] vt: to ~ on infliger à.
influence ['ɪnfluəns] n influence f //
vt influencer; **under the** ~ **of drink**
en état d'ébriété.
influential [ɪnflu'enʃl] a influent(e).
influenza [ɪnflu'enzə] n grippe f.
influx ['ɪnflʌks] n afflux m.
inform [ɪn'fɔ:m] vt: to ~ sb (of) informer ou avertir qn (de) // vi: to ~
on sb dénoncer qn, informer contre
qn; to ~ sb about renseigner qn
sur, mettre qn au courant de.
informal [ɪn'fɔ:ml] a (person, manner) simple, sans façon; (visit, discussion) dénué(e) de formalités; (announcement, invitation) non officiel(le); ~**ity** [-'mælɪtɪ] n simplicité
f, absence f de cérémonie; caractère
non officiel.
informant [ɪn'fɔ:mənt] n informa-

teur/trice.
information [ɪnfə'meɪʃən] n information f; renseignements mpl;
(knowledge) connaissances fpl; **a
piece of** ~ un renseignement; ~
office n bureau m de renseignements.
informative [ɪn'fɔ:mətɪv] a instructif(ive).
informer [ɪn'fɔ:mə*] n dénonciateur/
trice; (also: police ~) indicateur/
trice.
infringe [ɪn'frɪndʒ] vt enfreindre //
vi: to ~ on empiéter sur; ~**ment**
n: ~**ment** (**of**) infraction f (à).
infuriating [ɪn'fjuərɪeɪtɪŋ] a exaspérant(e).
ingenious [ɪn'dʒi:njəs] a ingénieux(euse).
ingenuity [ɪndʒɪ'nju:ɪtɪ] n ingéniosité
f.
ingenuous [ɪn'dʒenjuəs] a naïf(ïve),
ingénu(e).
ingot ['ɪŋgət] n lingot m.
ingrained [ɪn'greɪnd] a enraciné(e).
ingratiate [ɪn'greɪʃɪeɪt] vt: to ~ o.s.
with s'insinuer dans les bonnes grâces de, se faire bien voir de.
ingredient [ɪn'gri:dɪənt] n ingrédient
m; élément m.
inhabit [ɪn'hæbɪt] vt habiter.
inhabitant [ɪn'hæbɪtnt] n habitant/e.
inhale [ɪn'heɪl] vt inhaler; (perfume)
respirer // vi (in smoking) avaler la
fumée.
inherent [ɪn'hɪərənt] a: ~ (**in** or
to) inhérent(e) (à).
inherit [ɪn'herɪt] vt hériter (de);
~**ance** n héritage m.
inhibit [ɪn'hɪbɪt] vt (PSYCH) inhiber;
to ~ **sb from doing** empêcher ou retenir qn de faire; ~**ion** [-'bɪʃən] n inhibition f.
inhuman [ɪn'hju:mən] a inhumain(e).
initial [ɪ'nɪʃl] a initial(e) // n initiale f
// vt parafer; ~**s** npl initiales fpl; (as
signature) parafe m; ~**ly** ad initialement, au début.
initiate [ɪ'nɪʃɪeɪt] vt (start) entre-

prendre; amorcer; lancer; (person) initier.

initiative [ɪˈnɪʃɪtɪv] n initiative f.

inject [ɪnˈdʒɛkt] vt (liquid) injecter; (person) faire une piqûre à; **~ion** [ɪnˈdʒɛkʃən] n injection f, piqûre f.

injure [ˈɪndʒə*] vt blesser; (wrong) faire du tort à; (damage: reputation etc) compromettre; **~d** a blessé(e).

injury [ˈɪndʒərɪ] n blessure f; (wrong) tort m; **~ time** n (SPORT) arrêts mpl de jeu.

injustice [ɪnˈdʒʌstɪs] n injustice f.

ink [ɪŋk] n encre f.

inkling [ˈɪŋklɪŋ] n soupçon m, vague idée f.

inlaid [ˈɪnleɪd] a incrusté(e); (table etc) marqueté(e).

inland a [ˈɪnlənd] intérieur(e) // ad [ɪnˈlænd] à l'intérieur, dans les terres; **I~ Revenue** n (Brit) fisc m.

in-laws [ˈɪnlɔːz] npl beaux-parents mpl; belle famille.

inlet [ˈɪnlɛt] n (GEO) crique f.

inmate [ˈɪnmeɪt] n (in prison) détenu/e; (in asylum) interné/e.

inn [ɪn] n auberge f.

innate [ɪˈneɪt] a inné(e).

inner [ˈɪnə*] a intérieur(e); **~ city** n centre m de zone urbaine; **~ tube** n (of tyre) chambre f à air.

innings [ˈɪnɪŋz] n (CRICKET) tour m de batte.

innocence [ˈɪnəsns] n innocence f.

innocent [ˈɪnəsnt] a innocent(e).

innocuous [ɪˈnɔkjuəs] a inoffensif(ive).

innuendo, ~es [ɪnjuˈɛndəu] n insinuation f, allusion (malveillante).

innumerable [ɪˈnjuːmrəbl] a innombrable.

inordinately [ɪˈnɔːdɪnɪtlɪ] ad démesurément.

in-patient [ˈɪnpeɪʃənt] n malade hospitalisé(e).

input [ˈɪnput] n (ELEC) énergie f, puissance f; (of machine) consommation f; (of computer) information fournie.

inquest [ˈɪnkwɛst] n enquête (crimi-

nelle).

inquire [ɪnˈkwaɪə*] vi demander // vt demander, s'informer de; **to ~ about** s'informer de, se renseigner sur; **to ~ into** vt fus faire une enquête sur; **inquiry** n demande f de renseignements; (LAW) enquête f, investigation f; **inquiry office** n (Brit) bureau m de renseignements.

inquisitive [ɪnˈkwɪzɪtɪv] a curieux(euse).

inroad [ˈɪnrəud] n incursion f.

insane [ɪnˈseɪn] a fou(folle); (MED) aliéné(e).

insanity [ɪnˈsænɪtɪ] n folie f; (MED) aliénation (mentale).

inscription [ɪnˈskrɪpʃən] n inscription f; dédicace f.

inscrutable [ɪnˈskruːtəbl] a impénétrable.

insect [ˈɪnsɛkt] n insecte m; **~icide** [ɪnˈsɛktɪsaɪd] n insecticide m.

insecure [ɪnsɪˈkjuə*] a peu solide; peu sûr(e); (person) anxieux(euse).

insensible [ɪnˈsɛnsɪbl] a insensible; (unconscious) sans connaissance.

insensitive [ɪnˈsɛnsɪtɪv] a insensible.

insert vt [ɪnˈsəːt] insérer // n [ˈɪnsəːt] insertion f; **~ion** [ɪnˈsəːʃən] n insertion f.

in-service [ɪnˈsəːvɪs] a (training) continu(e), en cours d'emploi; (course) d'initiation; de perfectionnement; de recyclage.

inshore [ɪnˈʃɔː*] a côtier(ère) // ad près de la côte; vers la côte.

inside [ˈɪnˈsaɪd] n intérieur m // a intérieur(e) // ad à l'intérieur, dedans // prep à l'intérieur de; (of time): **~ 10 minutes** en moins de 10 minutes; **~s** mpl (col) intestins mpl; **~ forward** n (SPORT) intérieur m; **~ lane** n (AUT: in Britain) voie f de gauche; **~ out** ad à l'envers; (know) à fond; **to turn ~ out** retourner.

insight [ˈɪnsaɪt] n perspicacité f; (glimpse, idea) aperçu m.

insignificant [ɪnsɪgˈnɪfɪknt] a insignifiant(e).

insincere [ɪnsɪn'sɪə*] a hypocrite.

insinuate [ɪn'sɪnjueɪt] vt insinuer.

insist [ɪn'sɪst] vi insister; **to ~ on doing** insister pour faire; **to ~ that** insister pour que; (claim) maintenir or soutenir que; **~ent** a insistant(e), pressant(e).

insole ['ɪnsəʊl] n semelle intérieure; (fixed part of shoe) première f.

insolent ['ɪnsələnt] a insolent(e).

insomnia [ɪn'sɒmnɪə] n insomnie f.

inspect [ɪn'spekt] vt inspecter; (ticket) contrôler; **~ion** [ɪn'spekʃən] n inspection f; contrôle m; **~or** n inspecteur/trice; (Brit: on buses, trains) contrôleur/euse.

inspire [ɪn'spaɪə*] vt inspirer.

install [ɪn'stɔːl] vt installer; **~ation** [ɪnstə'leɪʃən] n installation f.

instalment, (US) **installment** [ɪn'stɔːlmənt] n acompte m, versement partiel; (of TV serial etc) épisode m; **in ~s** (pay) à tempérament; (receive) en plusieurs fois.

instance ['ɪnstəns] n exemple m; **for ~** par exemple; **in many ~s** dans bien des cas; **in the first ~** tout d'abord, en premier lieu.

instant ['ɪnstənt] n instant m // a immédiat(e); urgent(e); (coffee, food) instantané(e), en poudre; **~ly** ad immédiatement, tout de suite.

instead [ɪn'sted] ad au lieu de cela; **~ of** au lieu de; **~ of sb** à la place de qn.

instep ['ɪnstep] n cou-de-pied m; (of shoe) cambrure f.

instil [ɪn'stɪl] vt: **to ~ (into)** inculquer (à); (courage) insuffler (à).

instinct ['ɪnstɪŋkt] n instinct m.

institute ['ɪnstɪtjuːt] n institut m // vt instituer, établir; (inquiry) ouvrir; (proceedings) entamer.

institution [ɪnstɪ'tjuːʃən] n institution f; établissement m (scolaire); établissement (psychiatrique).

instruct [ɪn'strʌkt] vt instruire, former; **to ~ sb in sth** enseigner qch à qn; **to ~ sb to do** charger qn or ordonner à qn de faire;

~ion [ɪn'strʌkʃən] n instruction f; **~ions** npl directives fpl; **~ions (for use)** mode m d'emploi; **~or** n professeur m; (for skiing, driving) moniteur m.

instrument ['ɪnstrʊmənt] n instrument m; **~al** [-'mentl] a: **to be ~al in** contribuer à; **~ panel** n tableau m de bord.

insufficient [ɪnsə'fɪʃənt] a insuffisant(e).

insular ['ɪnsjʊlə*] a insulaire; (outlook) étroit(e); (person) aux vues étroites.

insulate ['ɪnsjʊleɪt] vt isoler; (against sound) insonoriser; **insulating tape** n ruban isolant; **insulation** [-'leɪʃən] n isolation f; insonorisation f.

insulin ['ɪnsjʊlɪn] n insuline f.

insult n ['ɪnsʌlt] insulte f, affront m // vt [ɪn'sʌlt] insulter, faire un affront à.

insuperable [ɪn'sjuːprəbl] a insurmontable.

insurance [ɪn'ʃʊərəns] n assurance f; **fire/life ~** assurance-incendie/-vie; **~ policy** n police f d'assurance.

insure [ɪn'ʃʊə*] vt assurer.

intact [ɪn'tækt] a intact(e).

intake ['ɪnteɪk] n (TECH) admission f; adduction f; (of food) consommation f; (Brit SCOL): **an ~ of 200 a year** 200 admissions fpl par an.

integral ['ɪntɪɡrəl] a intégral(e); (part) intégrant(e).

integrate ['ɪntɪɡreɪt] vt intégrer // vi s'intégrer.

integrity [ɪn'tɛɡrɪtɪ] n intégrité f.

intellect ['ɪntəlekt] n intelligence f; **~ual** [-'lektjʊəl] a, n intellectuel(le).

intelligence [ɪn'telɪdʒəns] n intelligence f; (MIL etc) informations fpl, renseignements mpl.

intelligent [ɪn'telɪdʒənt] a intelligent(e).

intend [ɪn'tend] vt (gift etc): **to ~ sth for** destiner qch à; **to ~ to do** avoir l'intention de faire; **~ed** a (insult) intentionnel(le); (journey) projeté(e); (effect) voulu(e).

intense [ɪn'tens] a intense; (person)

véhément(e); **~ly** ad intensément; profondément.

intensive [ɪnˈtɛnsɪv] a intensif(ive); **~ care unit** n service m de réanimation.

intent [ɪnˈtɛnt] n intention f // a attentif(ive), absorbé(e); **to all ~s and purposes** en fait, pratiquement; **to be ~ on doing sth** être (bien) décidé à faire qch.

intention [ɪnˈtɛnʃən] n intention f; **~al** a intentionnel(le), délibéré(e).

intently [ɪnˈtɛntlɪ] ad attentivement.

interact [ɪntərˈækt] vi avoir une action réciproque.

interchange n [ˈɪntətʃeɪndʒ] (exchange) échange m; (on motorway) échangeur m // vt [ɪntəˈtʃeɪndʒ] échanger; mettre à la place l'une de l'autre; **~able** a interchangeable.

intercom [ˈɪntəkɔm] n interphone m.

intercourse [ˈɪntəkɔːs] n rapports mpl.

interest [ˈɪntrɪst] n intérêt m; (COMM: stake, share) intérêts mpl // vt intéresser; **~ed** a intéressé(e); **to be ~ed in** s'intéresser à; **~ing** a intéressant(e); **~ rate** n taux m d'intérêt.

interfere [ɪntəˈfɪə*] vi: **to ~ in** (quarrel, other people's business) se mêler à; **to ~ with** (plans) tripoter, toucher à; (plans) contrecarrer; (duty) être en conflit avec.

interference [ɪntəˈfɪərəns] n (gen) intrusion f; (PHYSICS) interférence f; (RADIO, TV) parasites mpl.

interim [ˈɪntərɪm] a provisoire; (post) intérimaire // n: **in the ~** dans l'intérim.

interior [ɪnˈtɪərɪə*] n intérieur m // a intérieur(e).

interlock [ɪntəˈlɔk] vi s'enclencher.

interloper [ˈɪntələupə*] n intrus/e.

interlude [ˈɪntəluːd] n intervalle m; (THEATRE) intermède m.

intermediate [ɪntəˈmiːdɪət] a intermédiaire; (SCOL: course, level) moyen(ne).

intermission [ɪntəˈmɪʃən] n pause f;

(THEATRE, CINEMA) entracte m.

intern [ɪnˈtəːn] vt interner // n [ˈɪntəːn] (US) interne m/f.

internal [ɪnˈtəːnl] a interne; (dispute, reform etc) intérieur(e); **~ly** ad intérieurement; **'not to be taken ~ly'** 'pour usage externe'; **I~ Revenue Service (IRS)** n (US) fisc m.

international [ɪntəˈnæʃənl] a international(e).

interplay [ˈɪntəpleɪ] n effet m réciproque, jeu m.

interpret [ɪnˈtəːprɪt] vt interpréter // vi servir d'interprète; **~er** n interprète m/f.

interrelated [ɪntərɪˈleɪtɪd] a en corrélation, en rapport étroit.

interrogate [ɪnˈtɛrəugeɪt] vt interroger; (suspect etc) soumettre à un interrogatoire; **interrogation** [-ˈgeɪʃən] n interrogation f; interrogatoire m; **interrogative** [ɪntəˈrɔgətɪv] a interrogateur(trice).

interrupt [ɪntəˈrʌpt] vt interrompre; **~ion** [-ˈrʌpʃən] n interruption f.

intersect [ɪntəˈsɛkt] vt couper, croiser // vi (roads) se croiser, se couper; **~ion** [-ˈsɛkʃən] n intersection f; (of roads) croisement m.

intersperse [ɪntəˈspəːs] vt: **to ~ with** parsemer de.

intertwine [ɪntəˈtwaɪn] vt entrelacer // vi s'entrelacer.

interval [ˈɪntəvl] n intervalle m; (Brit: SCOL) récréation f; (: THEATRE) entracte m; (: SPORT) mi-temps f; **at ~s** par intervalles.

intervene [ɪntəˈviːn] vi (time) s'écouler (entre-temps); (event) survenir; (person) intervenir; **intervention** [-ˈvɛnʃən] n intervention f.

interview [ˈɪntəvjuː] n (RADIO, TV etc) interview f; (for job) entrevue f // vt interviewer; avoir une entrevue avec; **~er** n interviewer m.

intestine [ɪnˈtɛstɪn] n intestin m.

intimacy [ˈɪntɪməsɪ] n intimité f.

intimate a [ˈɪntɪmət] a intime; (knowledge) approfondi(e) // vt [ˈɪntɪmeɪt] suggérer, laisser entendre; (announce) faire savoir.

into ['ɪntu:] prep dans; ~ **pieces/ French** en morceaux/français.

intolerable [ɪn'tɔlərəbl] a intolérable.

intolerance [ɪn'tɔlərns] n intolérance f.

intolerant [ɪn'tɔlərnt] a: ~ **of** intolérant(e) en; (MED) intolérant à.

intoxicate [ɪn'tɔksɪkeɪt] vt enivrer; ~**d** a ivre; **intoxication** [-'keɪʃən] n ivresse f.

intractable [ɪn'træktəbl] a (child, temper) indocile, insoumis; (e) (problem) insoluble.

intransitive [ɪn'trænsɪtɪv] a intransitif(ive).

intravenous [ɪntrə'vi:nəs] a intraveineux(euse).

in-tray ['ɪntreɪ] n courrier m 'arrivée'.

intricate ['ɪntrɪkət] a complexe, compliqué(e).

intrigue [ɪn'tri:g] n intrigue f // vt intriguer // vi intriguer, comploter; **intriguing** a fascinant(e).

intrinsic [ɪn'trɪnsɪk] a intrinsèque.

introduce [ɪntrə'dju:s] vt introduire; to ~ sb (to sb) présenter qn (à qn); to ~ sb to (pastime, technique) initier qn à; **introduction** [-'dʌkʃən] n introduction f; (of person) présentation f; **introductory** a préliminaire, d'introduction.

intrude [ɪn'tru:d] vi (person) être importun(e); to ~ **on** (conversation etc) s'immiscer dans; ~**r** n intrus/e.

intuition [ɪntju:'ɪʃən] n intuition f.

inundate ['ɪnʌndeɪt] vt: to ~ **with** inonder de.

invade [ɪn'veɪd] vt envahir.

invalid n ['ɪnvəlɪd] malade m/f; (with disability) invalide m/f // a [ɪn'vælɪd] (not valid) invalide, non valide.

invaluable [ɪn'væljuəbl] a inestimable, inappréciable.

invariably [ɪn'vɛərɪəblɪ] ad invariablement; toujours.

invasion [ɪn'veɪʒən] n invasion f.

invent [ɪn'vɛnt] vt inventer; ~**ion**

[ɪn'vɛnʃən] n invention f; ~**ive** a inventif(ive); ~**or** n inventeur/trice.

inventory ['ɪnvəntrɪ] n inventaire m.

invert [ɪn'və:t] vt intervertir; (cup, object) retourner; ~**ed commas** npl (Brit) guillemets mpl.

invest [ɪn'vɛst] vt investir // vi faire un investissement.

investigate [ɪn'vɛstɪgeɪt] vt étudier, examiner; (crime) faire une enquête sur; **investigation** [-'geɪʃən] n examen m; (of crime) enquête f, investigation f.

investment [ɪn'vɛstmənt] n investissement m, placement m.

investor [ɪn'vɛstə*] n épargnant/e; actionnaire m/f.

invidious [ɪn'vɪdɪəs] a injuste; (task) déplaisant(e).

invigilate [ɪn'vɪdʒɪleɪt] vt surveiller // vi (in exam) être de surveillance.

invigorating [ɪn'vɪgəreɪtɪŋ] a vivifiant(e); stimulant(e).

invisible [ɪn'vɪzɪbl] a invisible; ~ **ink** n encre f sympathique.

invitation [ɪnvɪ'teɪʃən] n invitation f.

invite [ɪn'vaɪt] vt inviter; (opinions etc) demander; (trouble) chercher; **inviting** a engageant(e), attrayant(e); (gesture) encourageant(e).

invoice ['ɪnvɔɪs] n facture f.

involuntary [ɪn'vɔləntrɪ] a involontaire.

involve [ɪn'vɔlv] vt (entail) entraîner, nécessiter; (associate): to ~ **sb** (in) impliquer qn (dans), mêler qn (à); faire participer qn (à); ~**d** a complexe; to feel ~**d** se sentir concerné(e); ~**ment** n mise f en jeu; implication f; ~**ment (in)** participation f (à); rôle m (dans).

inward ['ɪnwəd] a (movement) vers l'intérieur; (thought, feeling) profond(e); intime; ~(**s**) ad vers l'intérieur.

I/O abbr (COMPUT: = input/output) E/S.

iodine ['aɪəudi:n] n iode m.

iota [aɪ'əutə] n (fig) brin m, grain m.

IOU n abbr (= I owe you) reconnaissance f de dette.

IQ n abbr (= intelligence quotient) Q.I. m (= quotient intellectuel).

IRA n abbr (= Irish Republican Army) IRA f.

Iran [ɪˈrɑːn] n Iran m.

Iraq [ɪˈrɑːk] n Irak m.

irate [aɪˈreɪt] a courroucé(e).

Ireland [ˈaɪələnd] n Irlande f.

iris [ˈaɪrɪs], **~es** [ˈaɪrɪs, -ɪz] n iris m.

Irish [ˈaɪrɪʃ] a irlandais(e) // npl: the ~ les Irlandais; **~man** n Irlandais m; **~ Sea** n mer f d'Irlande; **~woman** n Irlandaise f.

irksome [ˈəːksəm] a ennuyeux(euse).

iron [ˈaɪən] n (for clothes) fer m à repasser // a de or en fer // vt (clothes) repasser; **to ~ out** vt (crease) faire disparaître au fer; (fig) aplanir; faire disparaître; **the ~ curtain** n le rideau de fer.

ironic(al) [aɪˈrɒnɪk(l)] a ironique.

ironing [ˈaɪənɪŋ] n repassage m; **~ board** n planche f à repasser.

ironmonger [ˈaɪənmʌŋgəʳ] n (Brit) quincailler m; **~'s (shop)** n quincaillerie f.

irony [ˈaɪərənɪ] n ironie f.

irrational [ɪˈræʃənl] a irrationnel(le); déraisonnable; qui manque de logique.

irregular [ɪˈregjʊləʳ] a irrégulier(ère).

irrelevant [ɪˈreləvənt] a sans rapport, hors de propos.

irresistible [ɪrɪˈzɪstɪbl] a irrésistible.

irrespective [ɪrɪˈspektɪv]: **~ of** prep sans tenir compte de.

irresponsible [ɪrɪˈspɒnsɪbl] a (act) irréfléchi(e); (person) qui n'a pas le sens des responsabilités.

irrigate [ˈɪrɪgeɪt] vt irriguer; **irrigation** [-ˈgeɪʃən] n irrigation f.

irritable [ˈɪrɪtəbl] a irritable.

irritate [ˈɪrɪteɪt] vt irriter; **irritating** a irritant(e); **irritation** [-ˈteɪʃən] n irritation f.

IRS n abbr of Internal Revenue Service.

is [ɪz] vb see **be**.

Islam [ˈɪzlɑːm] n Islam m.

island [ˈaɪlənd] n île f; (also: traffic ~) refuge m (pour piétons); **~er** n habitant/e d'une île, insulaire m/f.

isle [aɪl] n île f.

isn't [ˈɪznt] = **is not**.

isolate [ˈaɪsəleɪt] vt isoler; **~d** a isolé(e).

Israel [ˈɪzreɪl] n Israël m; **~i** [ɪzˈreɪlɪ] a israélien(ne) // n Israélien(ne).

issue [ˈɪʃuː] n question f, problème m; (outcome) résultat m, issue f; (of banknotes etc) émission f; (of newspaper etc) numéro m; (offspring) descendance f // vt (rations, equipment) distribuer; (orders) donner; (book) faire paraître, publier; (banknotes, cheques, stamps) émettre, mettre en circulation; **at ~** en jeu, en cause; **to take ~ with sb (over)** exprimer son désaccord avec qn (sur).

KEYWORD

it [ɪt] pronoun **1** (specific: subject) il(elle); (: direct object) le(la), l'; (: indirect object) lui; **~'s on the table** c'est sur la (or elle) est sur la table; about/from/of ~ en; I spoke to him about ~ je lui en ai parlé; **what did you learn from ~?** qu'est-ce que vous en avez retiré?; I'm proud of ~ j'en suis fier; **in/to ~ y**; put the book in ~ mettez-y le livre; he agreed to ~ il y a consenti; did you go to ~? (party, concert etc) est-ce que vous y êtes allé(s)? **2** (impersonal) il; ce; **~'s raining** il pleut; **~'s Friday tomorrow** demain c'est vendredi or nous sommes vendredi; **~'s 6 o'clock** il est 6 heures; **who is ~? - ~'s me** qui est-ce? - c'est moi.

Italian [ɪˈtæljən] a italien(ne) // n Italien/ne; (LING) italien m.

italic [ɪˈtælɪk] a italique.

Italy [ˈɪtəlɪ] n Italie f.

itch [ɪtʃ] n démangeaison f // vi (person) éprouver des démangeaisons; (part of body) démanger; **I'm ~ing to do** j'ai envie me démange de faire; **~y** a qui démange; **to be ~y** to ~.

it'd ['ɪtd] = **it would, it had**.

item ['aɪtəm] n (gen) article m; (on agenda) question f, point m; (in programme) numéro m; (also: **news ~**) nouvelle f; **~ize** vt détailler, spécifier.

itinerary [aɪ'tɪnərərɪ] n itinéraire m.

it'll ['ɪtl] = **it will, it shall**.

its [ɪts] a son(sa), ses pl.

it's [ɪts] = **it is, it has**.

itself [ɪt'self] pronoun (emphatic) lui-même(elle-même); (reflexive) se.

ITV n abbr (Brit: = Independent Television) chaîne fonctionnant en concurrence avec la BBC.

I.U.D. n abbr (= intra-uterine device) DIU m (dispositif intra-utérin), stérilet m.

I've [aɪv] = **I have**.

ivory ['aɪvərɪ] n ivoire m.

ivy ['aɪvɪ] n lierre m.

J

jab [dʒæb] vt: **to ~ sth into** enfoncer or planter qch dans // n coup m; (MED: col) piqûre f.

jack [dʒæk] n (AUT) cric m; (CARDS) valet m; **to ~ up** vt soulever (au cric).

jackal ['dʒækl] n chacal m.

jackdaw ['dʒækdɔ:] n choucas m.

jacket ['dʒækɪt] n veste f, veston m.

jack-knife ['dʒæknaɪf] vi: **the lorry ~d** la remorque (du camion) s'est mise en travers.

jack plug n (ELEC) jack m.

jackpot ['dʒækpɔt] n gros lot.

jaded ['dʒeɪdɪd] a éreinté(e), fatigué(e).

jagged ['dʒægɪd] a dentelé(e).

jail [dʒeɪl] n prison f // vt emprisonner, mettre en prison; **~er** n geôlier/ière.

jam [dʒæm] n confiture f; (of shoppers etc) cohue f; (also: **traffic ~**) embouteillage m // vt (passage etc) encombrer, obstruer; (mechanism, drawer etc) bloquer, coincer; (RADIO) brouiller // vi (mechanism, sliding part) se coincer, se bloquer; (gun) s'enrayer; **to ~ sth into** entasser or comprimer qch dans; enfoncer qch dans.

jangle ['dʒæŋgl] vi cliqueter.

janitor ['dʒænɪtə*] n (caretaker) huissier m; concierge m.

January ['dʒænjuərɪ] n janvier m.

Japan [dʒə'pæn] n Japon m; **~ese** [dʒæpə'ni:z] a japonais(e) // n (pl inv) Japonais/e; (LING) japonais m.

jar [dʒɑ:*] n (glass) pot m, bocal m // vi (sound) produire un son grinçant or discordant; (colours etc) détonner, jurer.

jargon ['dʒɑ:gən] n jargon m.

jaundice ['dʒɔ:ndɪs] n jaunisse f; **~d** a (fig) envieux(euse), désapprobateur(trice).

jaunt [dʒɔ:nt] n balade f; **~y** a enjoué(e); désinvolte.

javelin ['dʒævlɪn] n javelot m.

jaw [dʒɔ:] n mâchoire f.

jay [dʒeɪ] n geai m.

jaywalker ['dʒeɪwɔ:kə*] n piéton indiscipliné.

jazz [dʒæz] n jazz m; **to ~ up** vt animer, égayer.

jealous ['dʒeləs] a jaloux(euse); **~y** n jalousie f.

jeans [dʒi:nz] npl (blue-)jean m.

jeer [dʒɪə*] vi: **to ~ (at)** huer; se moquer cruellement (de), railler.

jelly ['dʒelɪ] n gelée f; **~fish** n méduse f.

jeopardy ['dʒepədɪ] n: **to be in ~** être en danger or péril.

jerk [dʒə:k] n secousse f, saccade f; sursaut m, spasme m // vt donner une secousse à // vi (vehicles) cahoter.

jerkin ['dʒə:kɪn] n blouson m.

jersey ['dʒə:zɪ] n tricot m.

jest [dʒest] n plaisanterie f.

jet [dʒet] n (gas, liquid) jet m;

(AVIAT) avion *m* à réaction, jet *m*; **~-black** *a* (d'un noir) de jais; **~ engine** *n* moteur *m* à réaction; **~ lag** *n* décalage *m* horaire.

jettison ['dʒetɪsn] *vt* jeter par-dessus bord.

jetty ['dʒetɪ] *n* jetée *f*, digue *f*.

Jew ['dʒuː] *n* Juif *m*.

jewel ['dʒuːəl] *n* bijou *m*, joyau *m*; **~ler** *n* bijoutier/ère, joaillier *m*; **~ler's (shop)** *n* bijouterie *f*, joaillerie *f*; **~lery** *n* bijoux *mpl*.

Jewess ['dʒuːɪs] *n* Juive *f*.

Jewish ['dʒuːɪʃ] *a* juif(juive).

jib [dʒɪb] *n* (NAUT) foc *m*.

jibe [dʒaɪb] *n* sarcasme *m*.

jiffy ['dʒɪfɪ] *n* (col): **in a ~** en un clin d'œil.

jig [dʒɪg] *n* gigue *f*.

jigsaw ['dʒɪgsɔː] *n* (also: ~ **puzzle**) puzzle *m*.

jilt [dʒɪlt] *vt* laisser tomber, plaquer.

jingle ['dʒɪŋgl] *n* (advert) couplet *m* publicitaire // *vi* cliqueter, tinter.

jinx [dʒɪŋks] *n* (col) (mauvais) sort *m*.

jitters ['dʒɪtəz] *npl* (col): **to get the ~** avoir la trouille ou la frousse.

job [dʒɔb] *n* travail *m*; (employment) emploi *m*, poste *m*, place *f*; it's a good ~ **that** — c'est heureux ou c'est une chance que —; **just the ~**! (c'est) juste ou exactement ce qu'il faut!; **~ centre** *n* (Brit) agence *f* pour l'emploi; **~less** *a* sans travail, au chômage.

jockey ['dʒɔkɪ] *n* jockey *m* // *vi*: **to ~ for position** manœuvrer pour être bien placé.

jocular ['dʒɔkjʊlə*] *a* jovial(e), enjoué(e); facétieux(euse).

jog [dʒɔg] *vt* secouer // *vi* (SPORT) faire du footing; **to ~ along** vi cahoter; trotter; **~ging** *n* footing *m*.

join [dʒɔɪn] *vt* unir, assembler; (become member of) s'inscrire à; (meet) rejoindre, retrouver; (queue) se joindre à // *vi* (roads, rivers) se rejoindre, se rencontrer // *n* raccord *m*; **to ~ in** vi se mettre de la partie // *vt* fus se mêler à; (thanks etc) s'asso-

cier à; **to ~ up** vi s'engager.

joiner ['dʒɔɪnə*] *n* menuisier *m*; **~y** *n* menuiserie *f*.

joint [dʒɔɪnt] *n* (TECH) jointure *f*, joint *m*; (ANAT) articulation *f*, jointure; (Brit: CULIN) rôti *m*; (col: place) boîte *f* // *a* commun(e); **~ account** *n* (with bank etc) compte joint; **~ly** *ad* ensemble, en commun.

joist [dʒɔɪst] *n* solive *f*.

joke [dʒəʊk] *n* plaisanterie *f*; (also: **practical ~**) farce *f* // *vi* plaisanter; **to play a ~ on** jouer un tour à, faire une farce à; **~r** *n* plaisantin *m*, blagueur/euse; (CARDS) joker *m*.

jolly ['dʒɔlɪ] *a* gai(e), enjoué(e) // *ad* (col) rudement, drôlement.

jolt [dʒəʊlt] *n* cahot *m*, secousse *f* // *vt* cahoter, secouer.

Jordan ['dʒɔːdən] *n* Jordanie *f*.

jostle ['dʒɔsl] *vt* bousculer, pousser.

jot [dʒɔt] *n*: **not one ~** pas un brin; **to ~ down** vi inscrire rapidement, noter; **~ter** *n* (Brit) cahier *m* (de brouillon); bloc-notes *m*.

journal ['dʒɜːnl] *n* journal *m*; **~ism** *n* journalisme *m*; **~ist** *n* journaliste *m/f*.

journey ['dʒɜːnɪ] *n* voyage *m*; (distance covered) trajet *m* // *vi* voyager.

joy [dʒɔɪ] *n* joie *f*; **~ful**, **~ous** *a* joyeux(euse); **~ ride** *n* virée *f* (gén avec une voiture volée); **~stick** *n* (AVIAT, COMPUT) manche à balai.

J.P. *n abbr see* **justice**.

Jr, Jun., Junr *abbr of* **junior**.

jubilant ['dʒuːbɪlnt] *a* triomphant(e), réjoui(e).

judge [dʒʌdʒ] *n* juge *m* // *vt* juger; **judg(e)ment** *n* jugement *m*; (punishment) châtiment *m*.

judicial [dʒuː'dɪʃl] *a* judiciaire.

judiciary [dʒuː'dɪʃɪərɪ] *n* (pouvoir *m*) judiciaire *m*.

judo ['dʒuːdəʊ] *n* judo *m*.

jug [dʒʌg] *n* pot *m*, cruche *f*.

juggernaut ['dʒʌgənɔːt] *n* (Brit: huge truck) mastodonte *m*.

juggle ['dʒʌgl] *vi* jongler; **~r** *n* jon-

gleur *m.*

Jugoslav *etc* ['ju:gəʊslɑ:v] = **Yugoslav** *etc.*

juice [dʒu:s] *n* jus *m.*

juicy ['dʒu:sɪ] *a* juteux(euse).

jukebox ['dʒu:kbɒks] *n* juke-box *m.*

July [dʒu:'laɪ] *n* juillet *m.*

jumble ['dʒʌmbl] *n* fouillis *m* // *vt* (*also*: ~ **up**) mélanger, brouiller; ~ **sale** *n* (*Brit*) vente *f* de charité.

jumbo ['dʒʌmbəʊ] *a*: ~ **jet** avion géant, gros porteur (à réaction).

jump [dʒʌmp] *vi* sauter, bondir; (*start*) sursauter; (*increase*) monter en flèche // *vt* sauter, franchir // *n* saut *m*, bond *m*; sursaut *m.*

jumper ['dʒʌmpə*] *n* (*Brit*: *pullover*) pull-over *m*; (*US*: *dress*) robe-chasuble *f*; ~ **cables** *npl* (*US*) = **jump leads.**

jump leads *npl* (*Brit*) câbles *mpl* de démarrage.

jumpy ['dʒʌmpɪ] *a* nerveux(euse), agité(e).

junction ['dʒʌŋkʃən] *n* (*Brit*: *of roads*) carrefour *m*; (*of rails*) embranchement *m.*

juncture ['dʒʌŋktʃə*] *n*: **at this** ~ à ce moment-là, sur ces entrefaites.

June [dʒu:n] *n* juin *m.*

jungle ['dʒʌŋgl] *n* jungle *f.*

junior ['dʒu:nɪə*] *a*, *n*: **he's** ~ **to me** (**by 2 years**), **he's my** ~ (**by 2 years**) il est mon cadet (de 2 ans), il est plus jeune que moi (de 2 ans); **he's** ~ **to me** (*seniority*) il est en dessous de moi (dans la hiérarchie), j'ai plus d'ancienneté que lui; ~ **school** *n* (*Brit*) école *f* primaire, cours moyen.

junk [dʒʌŋk] *n* (*rubbish*) bric-à-brac *m inv*; ~ **food** *n* snacks *mpl* (vite prêts); ~ **shop** *n* (boutique *f* de) brocanteur *m.*

juror ['dʒʊərə*] *n* juré *m.*

jury ['dʒʊərɪ] *n* jury *m.*

just [dʒʌst] *a* juste // *ad*: **he's** ~ **done it/left** il vient de le faire/partir; ~ **as I expected** exactement *or* précisément comme je m'y attendais; ~

right/two o'clock exactement *or* juste ce qu'il faut/deux heures; **she's** ~ **as clever as you** elle est tout aussi intelligente que vous; **it's** ~ **as well that** ... heureusement que ...; ~ **as he was leaving** au moment *or* à l'instant précis où il partait; ~ **before/enough/here** juste avant/assez/là; **it's** ~ **me/a mistake** ce n'est que moi/(rien) qu'une erreur; ~ **missed/caught** manqué/attrapé de justesse; ~ **listen to this!** écoutez un peu ça!

justice ['dʒʌstɪs] *n* justice *f*; **J~ of the Peace** (*J.P.*) juge *m* de paix.

justify ['dʒʌstɪfaɪ] *vt* justifier.

jut [dʒʌt] *vi* (*also*: ~ **out**) dépasser, faire saillie.

juvenile ['dʒu:vənaɪl] *a* juvénile; (*court, books*) pour enfants // *n* adolescent/e.

K

K *abbr* (= *one thousand*) K; (= *kilobyte*) Ko.

kangaroo [kæŋgə'ru:] *n* kangourou *m.*

karate [kə'rɑ:tɪ] *n* karaté *m.*

kebab [kə'bæb] *n* kébab *m.*

keel [ki:l] *n* quille *f*; **on an even** ~ (*fig*) à flot.

keen [ki:n] *a* (*interest, desire, competition*) vif(vive); (*eye, intelligence*) pénétrant(e); (*edge*) effilé(e); (*eager*) plein(e) d'enthousiasme; **to be** ~ **to do** *or* **on doing sth** désirer vivement faire qch, tenir beaucoup à faire qch; **to be** ~ **on sth/sb** aimer beaucoup qch/qn.

keep [ki:p] *vb* (*pt, pp* **kept**) *vt* (*retain, preserve*) garder; (*hold back*) retenir; (*a shop, the books, a diary, a promise*) tenir; (*feed: one's family etc*) entretenir, assurer la subsistance de; (*chickens, bees etc*) élever // *vi* (*food*) se conserver; (*remain: in a certain state or place*) rester // *n* (*of castle*) donjon *m*; (*food etc*) enough for his ~ assez pour (assurer) sa subsistance; (col): **for ~s** pour de bon, pour toujours; **to ~ doing sth** continuer à faire qch; faire qch continuellement; **to ~ sth from doing/sth from happening** empêcher qn de faire or que qn (ne) fasse/que qch (n')arrive; **to ~ sb happy/a place tidy** faire que qn soit content/qu'un endroit reste propre; **to ~ sth to o.s.** garder qch pour soi, tenir qch secret; **to ~ sth (back) from sb** cacher qch à qn; **to ~ time** (clock) être à l'heure, ne pas retarder; **to ~ on** vi continuer; **to ~ on doing** continuer à faire; **to ~ out** vt empêcher d'entrer; '~ **out**' 'défense d'entrer'; **to ~ up** vi se maintenir // vt continuer, maintenir; **to ~ up with** se maintenir au niveau de; **~er** n gardien/ne; **~fit** n gymnastique f de maintien; **~ing** n (care) garde f; **in ~ing with** à l'avenant de; en accord avec; **~sake** n souvenir m.

keg [keg] n barrique f, tonnelet m.

kennel ['kɛnl] n niche f; **~s** npl chenil m.

kept [kɛpt] pt, pp of **keep**.

kerb [kə:b] n (Brit) bordure f du trottoir.

kernel ['kə:nl] n amande f; (fig) noyau m.

kettle ['kɛtl] n bouilloire f.

kettle drums npl timbales fpl.

key [ki:] n (gen, MUS) clé f; (of piano, typewriter) touche f // vt (also: ~ in) introduire au clavier; **~board** n clavier m; **~ed up** a (person) surexcité(e); **~hole** n trou m de la serrure; **~note** n (fig) note dominante; **~ ring** n porte-clés m.

khaki ['kɑːkɪ] a, n kaki (m).

kick [kɪk] vt donner un coup de pied à // vi (horse) ruer // n coup m de pied; (of rifle) recul m; (thrill): **he does it for ~s** il le fait parce que ça l'excite, il le fait pour le plaisir; **to ~ off** vi (SPORT) donner le coup d'envoi.

kid [kɪd] n (col: child) gamin/e, gosse m/f; (animal, leather) chevreau m // vi (col) plaisanter, blaguer.

kidnap ['kɪdnæp] vt enlever, kidnapper; **~per** n ravisseur/euse; **~ping** n enlèvement m.

kidney ['kɪdnɪ] n (ANAT) rein m; (CULIN) rognon m.

kill [kɪl] vt tuer; (fig) faire échouer; détruire; supprimer // n mise f à mort; **~er** n tueur/euse; meurtrier/ère; **~ing** n meurtre m; tuerie f, massacre m; **~joy** n rabat-joie m/f.

kiln [kɪln] n four m.

kilo ['kiːləʊ] n kilo m; **~byte** n (COMPUT) kilo-octet m; **~gram(me)** ['kɪləʊgræm] n kilogramme m; **~metre**, (US) **~meter** ['kɪləmiːtə*] n kilomètre m; **~watt** ['kɪləʊwɔt] n kilowatt m.

kilt [kɪlt] n kilt m.

kin [kɪn] n see **next, kith**.

kind [kaɪnd] a gentil(le), aimable // n sorte f, espèce f; (species) genre m; **to be two of a ~** se ressembler; **in ~** (COMM) en nature.

kindergarten ['kɪndəgɑːtn] n jardin m d'enfants.

kind-hearted [kaɪnd'hɑːtɪd] a bon(bonne).

kindle ['kɪndl] vt allumer, enflammer.

kindly ['kaɪndlɪ] a bienveillant(e), plein(e) de gentillesse // ad avec bonté; **will you ~** ... auriez-vous la bonté or l'obligeance de ...

kindness ['kaɪndnɪs] n bonté f, gentillesse f.

kindred ['kɪndrɪd] a apparenté(e); **~ spirit** âme f sœur.

king [kɪŋ] n roi m; **~dom** n royaume m; **~fisher** n martin-pêcheur m; **~-size** a long format inv; format géant inv.

kinky ['kɪŋkɪ] a (fig) excentrique; aux goûts spéciaux.

kiosk ['kiːɒsk] n kiosque m; (Brit TEL) cabine f (téléphonique).

kipper ['kɪpə*] n hareng fumé et salé.

kiss [kɪs] n baiser m // vt embrasser;
to ~ (each other) s'embrasser.

kit [kɪt] n équipement m, matériel m;
(set of tools etc) trousse f; (for assembly) kit m.

kitchen ['kɪtʃɪn] n cuisine f; ~ **sink**
n évier m.

kite [kaɪt] n (toy) cerf-volant m.

kith [kɪθ] n: ~ **and kin** parents et
amis mpl.

kitten ['kɪtn] n petit chat, chaton m.

kitty ['kɪtɪ] n (money) cagnotte f.

knack [næk] n: to have the ~ (of
doing) avoir le coup (pour faire);
there's a ~ il y a un coup à prendre
or une combine.

knapsack ['næpsæk] n musette f.

knead [niːd] vt pétrir.

knee [niː] n genou m; ~**cap** n rotule
f.

kneel, pt, pp **knelt** [niːl, nɛlt] vi
(also: ~ **down**) s'agenouiller.

knell [nɛl] n glas m.

knew [njuː] pt of **know**.

knickers ['nɪkəz] npl (Brit) culotte f
(de femme).

knife [naɪf] n (pl **knives**) couteau m
// vt poignarder, frapper d'un coup de
couteau.

knight [naɪt] n chevalier m; (CHESS)
cavalier m; ~**hood** n (title): to get
a ~**hood** être fait chevalier.

knit [nɪt] vt tricoter; (fig): to ~ **together** vt unir // vi (broken bones) se
ressouder; ~**ting** n tricot m; ~**ting
needle** n aiguille f à tricoter;
~**wear** n tricots mpl, lainages mpl.

knives [naɪvz] npl of **knife**.

knob [nɔb] n bouton m.

knock [nɔk] vt frapper; heurter;
(fig: col) dénigrer // vi (at door etc):
to ~ **at/on** frapper à/sur // n coup m;
to ~ **down** vt renverser; to ~ **off**
vi (col: finish) s'arrêter (de travailler); to ~ **out** vt assommer; (BOX-
ING) mettre k.o.; to ~ **over** vt
(person) renverser; (object) faire
tomber; ~**er** n (on door) heurtoir m;
~**-kneed** a aux genoux cagneux;
~**out** n (BOXING) knock-out m,

K.-O. m.

knot [nɔt] n (gen) nœud m // vt
nouer; ~**ty** a (fig) épineux(euse).

know [nəu] vt (pt **knew**, pp **known**)
savoir; (person, place) connaître; to
~ **how to do** savoir (comment)
faire; to ~ **how to swim** savoir nager; to ~ **about/of sth** être au courant de/connaître qch; to ~ **about or
of sb** avoir entendu parler de qn;
~**-all** n je-sais-tout m/f; ~**how** n
savoir-faire m, technique f, compétence f; ~**ing** a (look etc) enten-
du(e); ~**ingly** ad sciemment;
(smile, look) d'un air entendu.

knowledge ['nɔlɪdʒ] n connaissance
f; (learning) connaissances, savoir
m; ~**able** a bien informé(e).

known [nəun] pp of **know**.

knuckle ['nʌkl] n articulation f (des
phalanges), jointure f.

Koran [kɔ'rɑːn] n Coran m.

Korea [kə'rɪə] n Corée f.

kosher ['kəuʃə] a kascher inv.

L

lab [læb] n abbr (= laboratory) labo
m.

label ['leɪbl] n étiquette f; (brand: of
record) marque f // vt étiqueter.

laboratory [lə'bɔrətərɪ] n laboratoire
m.

labour, (US) **labor** ['leɪbə*] n (task)
travail m; (also: ~ **force**) main-
d'œuvre f; (MED) travail, accouchement m // vi: to ~ (**at**) travailler
dur (à), peiner (sur); **in** ~ (MED)
en travail; **L~, the L~ party** (Brit)
le parti travailliste, les travaillistes
mpl; ~**ed** a lourd(e), labo-
rieux(euse); ~**er** n manœuvre m;
(on farm) ouvrier m agricole.

lace [leɪs] n dentelle f; (of shoe etc)
lacet m // vt (shoe) lacer.

lack [læk] n manque m // vt manque
de; **through** or **for** ~ **of** faute de,
par manque de; **to be ~ing** manquer,
faire défaut; **to be ~ing in**

manquer de.

lackadaisical [lækə'deızıkl] *a* nonchalant(e), indolent(e).

lacquer ['lækə*] *n* laque *f*.

lad [læd] *n* garçon *m*, gars *m*.

ladder ['lædə*] *n* échelle *f*; (Brit: in tights) maille filée // *vt, vi* (Brit: tights) filer.

laden ['leıdn] *a*: ~ (with) chargé(e) (de).

ladle ['leıdl] *n* louche *f*.

lady ['leıdı] *n* dame *f*; dame (du monde); L~ Smith lady Smith; the ladies' (room) les toilettes *fpl* des dames; ~**bird**, (US) ~**bug** *n* coccinelle *f*; ~-**in-waiting** *n* dame *f* d'honneur; ~**like** *a* distingué(e); ~**ship** *n*: your ~**ship** Madame la comtesse (or la baronne etc).

lag [læg] *vi* (also: ~ **behind**) rester en arrière, traîner // *vt* (pipes) calorifuger.

lager ['lɑːgə*] *n* bière blonde.

lagoon [lə'guːn] *n* lagune *f*.

laid [leıd] *pt, pp* of **lay**; ~ **back** *a* (col) relaxe, décontracté(e).

lain [leın] *pp* of **lie**.

lair [lɛə*] *n* tanière *f*, gîte *m*.

laity ['leıətı] *n* laïques *mpl*.

lake [leık] *n* lac *m*.

lamb [læm] *n* agneau *m*.

lame [leım] *a* boiteux(euse).

lament [lə'mɛnt] *vt* pleurer, se lamenter sur.

laminated ['læmıneıtıd] *a* laminé(e) (windscreen) (en verre) feuilleté.

lamp [læmp] *n* lampe *f*.

lampoon [læm'puːn] *n* pamphlet *m*.

lamp: ~**post** *n* (Brit) réverbère *m*; ~**shade** *n* abat-jour *m inv*.

lance [lɑːns] *n* lance *f* // *vt* (MED) inciser; ~ **corporal** *n* (Brit) (soldat *m* de) première classe *m*.

land [lænd] *n* (as opposed to sea) terre *f* (ferme); (country) pays *m*; (soil) terre; terrain *m*; (estate) terre(s), domaine(s) *m(pl)* // *vi* (from ship) débarquer; (AVIAT) atterrir; (fig: fall) (re)tomber // *vt* (obtain)

décrocher; (passengers, goods) débarquer; **to** ~ **up** *vi* atterrir, (finir par) se retrouver; ~**ing** *n* atterrissage *m*; débarquement *m*; (of staircase) palier *m*; ~**ing stage** *n* (Brit) débarcadère *m*, embarcadère *m*; ~**lady** *n* propriétaire *f*, logeuse *f*; ~**lord** *n* propriétaire *m*, logeur *m*; (of pub etc) patron *m*; ~**mark** *n* (point *m* de) repère *m*; **to be a** ~**mark** (fig) faire date or époque; ~**owner** *n* propriétaire foncier or terrien.

landscape ['lænskeıp] *n* paysage *m*.

landslide ['lændsleıd] *n* (GEO) glissement *m* (de terrain); (fig: POL) raz-de-marée électoral).

lane [leın] *n* (in country) chemin *m*; (in town) ruelle *f*; (AUT) voie *f*; file *f*; (in race) couloir *m*.

language ['læŋgwıdʒ] *n* langue *f*; (way one speaks) langage *m*; **bad** ~ grossièretés *fpl*, langage grossier; ~ **laboratory** *n* laboratoire *m* de langues.

languid ['læŋgwıd] *a* languissant(e); langoureux(euse).

lank [læŋk] *a* (hair) raide et terne.

lanky ['læŋkı] *a* grand(e) et maigre, efflanqué(e).

lantern ['læntn] *n* lanterne *f*.

lap [læp] *n* (of track) tour *m* (de piste); (of body): **in** or **on** one's ~ sur les genoux // *vt* (also: ~ **up**) laper // *vi* (waves) clapoter.

lapel [lə'pɛl] *n* revers *m*.

Lapland ['læplænd] *n* Laponie *f*.

lapse [læps] *n* défaillance *f* // *vi* (LAW) cesser d'être en vigueur; se périmer; **to** ~ **into bad habits** prendre de mauvaises habitudes; ~ **of time** laps *m* de temps, intervalle *m*.

larceny ['lɑːsənı] *n* vol *m*.

lard [lɑːd] *n* saindoux *m*.

larder ['lɑːdə*] *n* garde-manger *m inv*.

large [lɑːdʒ] *a* grand(e); (person, animal) gros(grosse); **at** ~ (free) en liberté; (generally) en général; pour la plupart; ~**ly** *ad* en grande partie.

lark [lɑːk] n (bird) alouette f; (joke) blague f, farce f; **to ~ about** vi faire l'idiot, rigoler.

laryngitis [lærɪn'dʒaɪtɪs] n laryngite f.

laser ['leɪzə*] n laser m; **~ printer** n imprimante f laser.

lash [læʃ] n coup m de fouet; (also: eyelash) cil m // vt fouetter; (tie) attacher; **to ~ out** vi: **to ~ out** (at or against sb/sth) attaquer violemment (qn/qch); **to ~ out** (on sth) (col: spend) se fendre (de qch).

lass [læs] n (jeune) fille f.

lasso [læ'suː] n lasso m.

last [lɑːst] a dernier(ère) // ad en dernier // vi durer; **~ week** la semaine dernière; **~ night** hier soir; la nuit dernière; **at ~** enfin; **~ but one** avant-dernier(ère); **~-ditch** a (attempt) ultime, désespéré(e); **~ing** a durable; **~ly** ad en dernier lieu, pour finir; **~-minute** a de dernière minute.

latch [lætʃ] n loquet m.

late [leɪt] a (not on time) en retard; (far on in day etc) avancé(e); tardif(ive); (recent) récent(e), dernier; (former) ancien(ne); (dead) défunt(e) // ad tard; (behind time, schedule) en retard; **of ~** dernièrement; **in ~ May** vers la fin (du mois) de mai; **the ~ Mr X** feu M. X; **~comer** n retardataire m/f; **~ly** ad récemment.

later ['leɪtə*] a (date etc) ultérieur(e); (version etc) plus récent(e) // ad plus tard; **~ on** plus tard.

lateral ['lætərl] a latéral(e).

latest ['leɪtɪst] a tout(e) dernier(ère); **at the ~** au plus tard.

lathe [leɪð] n tour m.

lather ['lɑːðə*] n mousse f (de savon).

Latin ['lætɪn] n latin m // a latin(e); **~ America** n Amérique latine; **~ American** a d'Amérique latine.

latitude ['lætɪtjuːd] n latitude f.

latter ['lætə*] a deuxième, dernier(ère) // n: **the ~** ce dernier, celui-ci; **~ly** ad dernièrement, récemment.

lattice ['lætɪs] n treillis m; treillage m.

laudable ['lɔːdəbl] a louable.

laugh [lɑːf] n rire m // vi rire; **to ~ at** vi fus se moquer de; (joke) rire de; **to ~ off** vt écarter ou rejeter par une plaisanterie ou par une boutade; **~able** a risible, ridicule; **~ing stock** n: **the ~ing stock of** la risée de; **~ter** n rire m; rires mpl.

launch [lɔːntʃ] n lancement m; (boat) chaloupe f; (also: **motor ~**) vedette f // vt (ship, rocket, plan) lancer; **~(ing) pad** n rampe f de lancement.

launder ['lɔːndə*] vt blanchir.

launderette [lɔːn'drɛt], (US) **laundromat** ['lɔːndrəmæt] n laverie f (automatique).

laundry ['lɔːndrɪ] n blanchisserie f; (clothes) linge m.

laureate ['lɔːrɪət] a see **poet**.

laurel ['lɔrl] n laurier m.

lava ['lɑːvə] n lave f.

lavatory ['lævətərɪ] n toilettes fpl.

lavender ['lævəndə*] n lavande f.

lavish ['lævɪʃ] a copieux(euse), somptueux(euse); (giving freely): **~ with** prodigue de // vt: **to ~ sth on sb** prodiguer qch à qn; (money, gifts) dépenser qch sans compter pour qn/qch.

law [lɔː] n loi f; (science) droit m; **~-abiding** a respectueux(euse) des lois; **~ and order** n l'ordre public; **~ court** n tribunal m, cour f de justice; **~ful** a légal(e); permis(e).

lawn [lɔːn] n pelouse f; **~mower** n tondeuse f à gazon; **~ tennis** n tennis m.

law school n faculté f de droit.

lawsuit ['lɔːsuːt] n procès m.

lawyer ['lɔːjə*] n (consultant, with company) juriste m; (for sales, wills etc) ≈ notaire m; (partner, in court) ≈ avocat m.

lax [læks] a relâché(e).

laxative ['læksətɪv] n laxatif m.

laxity ['læksɪtɪ] n relâchement m.

lay [leɪ] pt of **lie** // a laïque; profane // vt (pt, pp **laid**) poser, mettre; (eggs) pondre; (trap) tendre; (plans) élaborer; **to ~ the table** mettre la table; **to ~ aside** or **by** vt mettre de côté; **to ~ down** vt poser; **to ~ down the law** faire la loi; **to ~ off** vt (workers) licencier; **to ~ on** vt (water, gas) mettre, installer; (provide) fournir; (paint) étaler; **to ~ out** vt (design) dessiner, concevoir; (display) disposer; (spend) dépenser; **to ~ up** vt (to store) amasser; (car) remiser; (ship) désarmer; (subj: illness) forcer à s'aliter; **~about** n fainéant/e; **~-by** n (Brit) aire f de stationnement (sur le bas-côté).

layer ['leɪə*] n couche f.

layman ['leɪmən] n laïque m; profane m.

layout ['leɪaut] n disposition f, plan m, agencement m; (PRESS) mise f en page.

laze [leɪz] vi paresser.

lazy ['leɪzɪ] a paresseux(euse).

lb. abbr of **pound** (weight).

lead [li:d] n (front position) tête f; (distance, time ahead) avance f; (clue) piste f; (to battery) raccord m; (ELEC) fil m; (for dog) laisse f; (THEATRE) rôle principal; [led] vb (pt, pp **led**) vt mener, conduire; (induce) amener; (be leader of) être à la tête de; (SPORT) être en tête // vi mener, être en tête; **to ~ astray** détourner qn du droit chemin; **to ~ away** vt emmener; **to ~ back** vt: **to ~ back to** ramener à; **to ~ on** vt (tease) faire marcher; **to ~ on to** vt (induce) amener à; **to ~ to** vt fus mener à; conduire à; aboutir à; **to ~ up to** vt fus conduire à.

leaden ['lɛdn] a (sky, sea) de plomb; (heavy: footsteps) lourd(e).

leader ['li:də*] n chef m; dirigeant/e, leader m; (in newspaper) éditorial

m; **~ship** n direction f; qualités fpl de chef.

leading ['li:dɪŋ] a de premier plan; principal(e); **~ man/lady** n (THEATRE) vedette (masculine)/(féminine); **~ light** n (person) vedette f, sommité f.

leaf [li:f], pl **leaves** n feuille f; (of table) rallonge f // vi: **to ~ through** sth feuilleter qch; **to turn over a new ~** changer de conduite or d'existence.

leaflet ['li:flit] n prospectus m, brochure f; (POL, REL) tract m.

league [li:g] n ligue f; (FOOTBALL) championnat m; (measure) lieue f; **to be in ~ with** avoir partie liée avec, être de mèche avec.

leak [li:k] n (out, also fig) fuite f; (in pipe, liquid etc) infiltration f // vi (pipe, liquid etc) fuir; (shoes) prendre l'eau // vt (liquid) répandre; (information) divulguer; **to ~ out** vi fuir; être divulgué(e).

lean [li:n] a maigre // vb (pt, pp **leaned** or **leant** [lɛnt]) vt: **to ~ sth on sth** appuyer qch sur qch // vi (slope) pencher; (rest): **to ~ against** s'appuyer contre; être appuyé(e) contre; **to ~ on** s'appuyer sur; **to ~ back/forward** vi se pencher en arrière/avant; **to ~ out** vi se pencher au dehors; **to ~ over** vi se pencher; **~-to** n appentis m.

leap [li:p] n bond m, saut m // vi (pt, pp **leaped** or **leapt** [lɛpt]) bondir, sauter; **~frog** n jeu m de saute-mouton; **~ year** n année f bissextile.

learn, pt, pp **learned** or **learnt** [lə:n, -t] vt, vi apprendre; **to ~ how to do sth** apprendre à faire qch; **~ed** ['lə:nɪd] a érudit(e), savant(e); **~er** n débutant/e; (Brit: also: **~er driver**) (conducteur/trice) débutant(e); **~ing** n savoir m.

lease [li:s] n bail m // vt louer à bail.

leash [li:ʃ] n laisse f.

least [li:st] a: **the ~ +** noun le(la) plus petit(e), le(la) moindre; (smallest amount of) le moins de; **the ~ +**

adjective le(la) moins; **the ~ money** le moins d'argent; **at ~** au moins; **not in the ~** pas le moins du monde.

leather ['lɛðə*] n cuir m.

leave [li:v] vb (pt, pp **left**) vt laisser; (go away from) quitter // vi partir, s'en aller // n (time off) congé m; (MIL, also: consent) permission f; **to be left** rester; **there's some milk left over** il reste du lait; **on ~** en permission; **to ~ behind** vt (person, object) laisser; **to ~ out** vt oublier, omettre; **~ of absence** n congé exceptionnel; (MIL) permission spéciale.

leaves [li:vz] npl of **leaf**.

Lebanon ['lɛbənən] n Liban m.

lecherous ['lɛtʃərəs] a lubrique.

lecture ['lɛktʃə*] n conférence f; (SCOL) cours (magistral) m // vi donner des cours; enseigner // vt (scold) sermonner, réprimander; **to ~ on** faire un cours (or son cours) sur; **to give a ~ on** faire une conférence sur; faire or donner un cours sur.

lecturer ['lɛktʃərə*] n (speaker) conférencier/ère; (Brit: at university) professeur m (d'université), ≈ maître assistant, maître de conférences.

led [lɛd] pt, pp of **lead**.

ledge [lɛdʒ] n (of window, on wall) rebord m; (of mountain) saillie f, corniche f.

ledger ['lɛdʒə*] n registre m, grand livre.

lee [li:] n côté m sous le vent.

leech [li:tʃ] n sangsue f.

leek [li:k] n poireau m.

leer [liə*] vi: **to ~ at sb** regarder qn d'un air mauvais or concupiscent.

leeway ['li:weɪ] n (fig): **to have some ~** avoir une certaine liberté d'action.

left [lɛft] pt, pp of **leave** // a gauche // ad à gauche // n gauche f; **on the ~, to the ~** à gauche; **the L~** (POL) la gauche; **~-handed** a gaucher(ère); **~-hand side** n gauche f,

côté m gauche; **~-luggage (office)** n (Brit) consigne f; **~-overs** npl restes mpl; **~-wing** a (POL) de gauche.

leg [lɛg] n jambe f; (of animal) patte f; (of furniture) pied m; (CULIN: of chicken) cuisse f; **1st/2nd ~** (SPORT) match m aller/retour; (of journey) 1ère/2ème étape.

legacy ['lɛgəsɪ] n héritage m, legs m.

legal ['li:gl] a légal(e); **~ holiday** n (US) jour férié; **~ tender** n monnaie légale.

legend ['lɛdʒənd] n légende f.

legible ['lɛdʒəbl] a lisible.

legislation [lɛdʒɪs'leɪʃən] n législation f; **legislature** ['lɛdʒɪslətʃə*] n corps législatif.

legitimate [lɪ'dʒɪtɪmət] a légitime.

leg-room ['lɛgru:m] n place f pour les jambes.

leisure ['lɛʒə*] n loisir m, temps m libre; (also: ~**s**) loisirs mpl; **at ~** (à) loisir; à tête reposée; **~ centre** n centre m de loisirs; **~ly** a tranquille; fait(e) sans se presser.

lemon ['lɛmən] n citron m; **~ade** [-'neɪd] n limonade f; **~ tea** n thé m au citron.

lend [lɛnd], pt, pp **lent** vt: **to ~ sth (to sb)** prêter qch (à qn).

length [lɛŋθ] n longueur f; (section: of road, pipe etc) morceau m, bout m; **at ~** (at last) enfin, à la fin; (lengthily) longuement; **~en** vt allonger, prolonger // vi s'allonger; **~ways** ad dans le sens de la longueur, en long; **~y** a (très) long(longue).

lenient ['li:nɪənt] a indulgent(e), clément(e).

lens [lɛnz] n lentille f; (of spectacles) verre m; (of camera) objectif m.

Lent [lɛnt] n Carême m.

lent [lɛnt] pt, pp of **lend**.

lentil ['lɛntl] n lentille f.

Leo ['li:əu] n le Lion.

leotard ['li:ətɑ:d] n maillot m (de danseur etc).

leper ['lɛpə*] n lépreux/euse.

leprosy ['leprəsɪ] n lèpre f.

lesbian ['lezbɪən] n lesbienne f.

less [les] a moins de // pronoun, ad moins; ~ than that/you moins que cela/vous; ~ than half moins de la moitié; ~ than ever moins que jamais; ~ and ~ de moins en moins; the ~ he works ... moins il travaille ....

lessen ['lesn] vi diminuer, s'amoindrir, s'atténuer // vt diminuer, réduire, atténuer.

lesser ['lesə*] a moindre; to a ~ extent à un degré moindre.

lesson ['lesn] n leçon f.

lest [lest] cj de peur de + infinitive, de peur que + sub.

let, pt, pp **let** [let] vt laisser; (Brit: lease) louer; (US) louer; to ~ sb do sth laisser qn faire qch; to ~ sb know sth faire savoir qch à qn, prévenir qn de qch; he ~ me go il m'a laissé partir; ~'s go allons-y; ~ him come qu'il vienne; 'to ~' 'à louer'; to ~ down vt (lower) baisser; (dress) rallonger; (hair) défaire; (disappoint) décevoir; to ~ go vi lâcher prise // vt lâcher; to ~ in vt laisser entrer; (visitor etc) faire entrer; to ~ off vt laisser partir; (firework etc) faire partir; (smell etc) dégager; to ~ on vi (col) dire; to ~ out vt laisser sortir; (dress) élargir; (scream) laisser échapper; to ~ up vi diminuer, s'arrêter.

lethal ['li:θl] a mortel(le), fatal(e).

letter ['letə*] n lettre f; ~ bomb n lettre piégée; ~box n (Brit) boîte f aux or à lettres; ~ing n lettres fpl; caractères mpl.

lettuce ['letɪs] n laitue f, salade f.

leukaemia, (US) **leukemia** [lu:'ki:mɪə] n leucémie f.

level ['levl] a plat(e), plan(e), uni(e); horizontal(e) // n niveau m; (flat place) terrain plat; (also: spirit ~) niveau à bulle // vt niveler, aplanir; to be ~ with être au même niveau que; 'A' ~s npl (Brit) = baccalauréat m; 'O' ~s npl (Brit) =

B.E.P.C; on the ~ à l'horizontale; (fig: honest) régulier(ère); to ~ off or ~ out (prices etc) se stabiliser; ~ crossing n (Brit) passage m à niveau; ~-headed a équilibré(e).

lever ['li:və*] n levier m // vt: to ~ up/out soulever/extraire au moyen d'un levier; ~age n: ~age (on or with) prise f (sur).

levy ['levɪ] n taxe f, impôt m // vt prélever, imposer; percevoir.

lewd [lu:d] a obscène, lubrique.

liability [laɪə'bɪlɪtɪ] n responsabilité f; (handicap) handicap m; **liabilities** npl obligations fpl, engagements mpl; (on balance sheet) passif m.

liable ['laɪəbl] a (subject): ~ to sujet(te) à; passible de; (responsible): ~ (for) responsable (de); (likely): ~ to do susceptible de faire.

liaison [li:'eɪzɔn] n liaison f.

liar ['laɪə*] n menteur/euse.

libel ['laɪbl] n écrit m diffamatoire; diffamation f // vt diffamer.

liberal ['lɪbərl] a libéral(e); (generous): ~ with prodigue de, généreux(euse) avec.

liberty ['lɪbətɪ] n liberté f; to be at ~ to do être libre de faire.

Libra ['li:brə] n la Balance.

librarian [laɪ'brɛərɪən] n bibliothécaire m/f.

library ['laɪbrərɪ] n bibliothèque f.

libretto [lɪ'brɛtəu] n livret m.

Libya ['lɪbɪə] n Libye f.

lice [laɪs] npl of **louse**.

licence, (US) **license** ['laɪsns] n autorisation f, permis m; (COMM) licence f; (RADIO, TV) redevance f; (also: driving ~, (US) driver's ~) permis m (de conduire); (excessive freedom) licence; ~ number n numéro m d'immatriculation; ~ plate n plaque f minéralogique.

license ['laɪsns] n (US) = **licence** // vt donner une licence à; ~d a (for alcohol) patenté(e) (pour la vente des spiritueux.

lick [lɪk] vt lécher.

licorice ['lɪkərɪs] n = **liquorice**.

lid [lɪd] n couvercle m.

lie [laɪ] n mensonge m // vi mentir; (pt lay, pp lain) (rest) être étendu(e) or allongé(e) or couché(e); (in grave) être enterré(e), reposer; (of object: be situated) se trouver, être; **to ~ low** (fig) se cacher; **to ~ about** vi traîner; **to have a ~ down** (Brit) s'allonger, se reposer; **to have a ~-in** (Brit) faire la grasse matinée.

lieutenant [lɛf'tɛnənt, (US) luː'tɛnənt] n lieutenant m.

life [laɪf], pl **lives** n vie f; **~ assurance** n (Brit) assurance-vie f; **~belt** n (Brit) bouée f de sauvetage; **~boat** n canot m or chaloupe f de sauvetage; **~guard** n surveillant m de baignade; **~ insurance** n = **life assurance**; **~ jacket** n gilet m or ceinture f de sauvetage; **~less** a sans vie, inanimé(e); (dull) qui manque de vie or de vigueur; **~like** a qui semble vrai(e) or vivant(e); ressemblant(e); **~long** a de toute une vie, de toujours; **~ preserver** n (US) gilet m or ceinture f de sauvetage; bouée f de sauvetage; **~saver** n surveillant m de baignade; **~ sentence** n condamnation f à vie or à perpétuité; **~sized** a grandeur nature inv; **~ span** n (durée f de) vie f; **~style** n style m or mode m de vie; **~ support system** n (MED) respirateur artificiel; **~time** n: in his **~time** de son vivant; once in a **~time** une fois dans la or dans une vie.

lift [lɪft] vt soulever, lever; (steal) prendre, voler // vi (fog) se lever // n (Brit: elevator) ascenseur m; **to give sb a ~** (Brit) emmener or prendre qn en voiture; **~-off** n décollage m.

light [laɪt] n lumière f; (daylight) lumière, jour m; (lamp) lampe f; (AUT: traffic ~, rear ~) feu m; (: headlamp) phare m; (for cigarette etc) have you got a ~? avez-vous du feu? // vt (pt, pp **lighted** or **lit**) (candle, cigarette, fire) allumer; (room) éclairer // a (room, colour) clair(e); (not heavy, also fig) léger(ère); **to come to ~** être dévoilé(e) or découvert(e); **to ~ up** vi s'allumer; (face) s'éclairer // vt (illuminate) éclairer, illuminer; **~ bulb** n ampoule f; **~en** vi s'éclairer // vt (give light to) éclairer; (make lighter) éclaircir; (make less heavy) alléger; **~er** n (also: **cigarette ~er**) briquet m; (: in car) allume-cigare m inv; (boat) péniche f; **~-headed** a étourdi(e), écervelé(e); **~-hearted** a gai(e), joyeux(euse), enjoué(e); **~house** n phare m; **~ing** n (on road) éclairage m; (in theatre) éclairages; **~ly** ad légèrement; **to get off ~ly** s'en tirer à bon compte; **~ness** n clarté f; (in weight) légèreté f.

lightning [ˈlaɪtnɪŋ] n éclair m, foudre f; **~ conductor**, (US) **~ rod** n paratonnerre m.

light pen n crayon m optique.

lightweight [ˈlaɪtweɪt] a (suit) léger(ère); (boxer) poids léger inv // n (BOXING) poids léger.

like [laɪk] vt aimer (bien) // prep comme // a semblable, pareil(le) // n: the **~un**(e) pareil(le) or semblable; le(la) pareil(le) (pej) (d')autres du même genre or acabit; his **~s and dislikes** ses goûts mpl or préférences fpl; **I would ~**, **I'd ~** je voudrais, j'aimerais; **would you ~ a coffee?** voulez-vous du café? **to be/look ~ sb/sth** ressembler à qn/qch; **that's just ~ him** c'est bien de lui, ça lui ressemble; **do it ~ this** fais-le comme ceci; **nothing ~ ...** rien de tel que ...; **~able** a sympathique, agréable.

likelihood [ˈlaɪklɪhʊd] n probabilité f.

likely [ˈlaɪklɪ] a probable; plausible; **he's ~ to leave** il va sûrement partir, il risque fort de partir; **not ~!** pas de danger!

likeness [ˈlaɪknɪs] n ressemblance f.

likewise ['laɪkwaɪz] *ad* de même, pareillement.

liking ['laɪkɪŋ] *n* affection *f*, penchant *m*; goût *m*.

lilac ['laɪlək] *n* lilas *m* // *a* lilas *inv*.

lily ['lɪlɪ] *n* lis *m*; ~ **of the valley** *n* muguet *m*.

limb [lɪm] *n* membre *m*.

limber ['lɪmbə*]: **to** ~ **up** *vi* se dégourdir, se mettre en train.

limbo ['lɪmbəu] *n*: **to be in** ~ (*fig*) être tombé(e) dans l'oubli.

lime [laɪm] *n* (*tree*) tilleul *m*; (*fruit*) lime *f*; (*GEO*) chaux *f*.

limelight ['laɪmlaɪt] *n*: **in the** ~ (*fig*) en vedette, au premier plan.

limerick ['lɪmərɪk] *n* poème *m* humoristique (de 5 vers).

limestone ['laɪmstəun] *n* pierre *f* à chaux; (*GEO*) calcaire *m*.

limit ['lɪmɪt] *n* limite *f* // *vt* limiter; ~**ed** *a* limité(e), restreint(e); **to be** ~**ed to** se limiter à, ne concerner que; ~**ed (liability) company (Ltd)** *n* (*Brit*) ≈ société *f* anonyme (S.A.).

limp [lɪmp] *n*: **to have a** ~ boiter // *vi* boiter // *a* mou(molle).

limpet ['lɪmpɪt] *n* patelle *f*.

line [laɪn] *n* (*gen*) ligne *f*; (*rope*) corde *f*; (*wire*) fil *m*; (*of poem*) vers *m*; (*row*, *series*) rangée *f*, file *f*, queue *f*; (*COMM*: *series of goods*) article *m(pl)* // *vt* (*clothes*): **to** ~ (**with**) doubler (de); (*box*): **to** ~ (**with**) garnir *or* tapisser (de); (*subj*: *trees*, *crowd*) border; **in his** ~ **of business** dans sa partie, dans son rayon; **in** ~ **with** en accord avec; **to** ~ **up** *vi* s'aligner, se mettre en rang(s) // *vt* aligner.

lined [laɪnd] *a* (*face*) ridé(e), marqué(e); (*paper*) réglé(e).

linen ['lɪnɪn] *n* linge *m* (de corps *or* de maison); (*cloth*) lin *m*.

liner ['laɪnə*] *n* paquebot *m* de ligne.

linesman ['laɪnzmən] *n* (*TENNIS*) juge *m* de ligne; (*FOOTBALL*) juge de touche.

line-up ['laɪnʌp] *n* file *f*; (*SPORT*)

(*composition f* de l')équipe *f*.

linger ['lɪŋgə*] *vi* s'attarder; traîner; (*smell*, *tradition*) persister.

lingo, ~**es** ['lɪŋgəu] *n* (*pej*) jargon *m*.

linguistics [lɪŋ'gwɪstɪks] *n* linguistique *f*.

lining ['laɪnɪŋ] *n* doublure *f*.

link [lɪŋk] *n* (*of a chain*) maillon *m*; (*connection*) lien *m*, rapport *m* // *vt* relier, lier, unir; ~**s** *npl* (*GOLF*) (terrain *m* de) golf *m*; **to** ~ **up** *vt* relier // *vi* se rejoindre; s'associer.

lino ['laɪnəu], **linoleum** [lɪ'nəulɪəm] *n* linoléum *m*.

lion ['laɪən] *n* lion *m*; ~**ess** *n* lionne *f*.

lip [lɪp] *n* lèvre *f*; (*of cup etc*) rebord *m*; ~**read** *vi* lire sur les lèvres; ~ **salve** *n* pommade *f* rosat *or* pour les lèvres; ~ **service** *n*: **to pay** ~ **service to sth** ne reconnaître le mérite de qch que pour la forme; ~**stick** *n* rouge *m* à lèvres.

liqueur [lɪ'kjuə*] *n* liqueur *f*.

liquid ['lɪkwɪd] *n* liquide *m* // *a* liquide.

liquidize ['lɪkwɪdaɪz] *vt* (*CULIN*) passer au mixer; ~**r** *n* mixer *m*.

liquor ['lɪkə*] *n* spiritueux *m*, alcool *m*; ~ **store** *n* (*US*) magasin *m* de vins et spiritueux.

liquorice ['lɪkərɪs] *n* réglisse *f*.

lisp [lɪsp] *n* zézaiement *m*.

list [lɪst] *n* liste *f*; (*of ship*) inclinaison *f* // *vt* (*write down*) inscrire; faire la liste de; (*enumerate*) énumérer // *vi* (*ship*) gîter, donner de la bande.

listen ['lɪsn] *vi* écouter; **to** ~ **to** écouter; ~**er** *n* auditeur/trice.

listless ['lɪstlɪs] *a* indolent(e), apathique.

lit [lɪt] *pt*, *pp* of **light**.

liter ['li:tə*] *n* (*US*) = **litre**.

literacy ['lɪtərəsɪ] *n* degré *m* d'alphabétisation, fait *m* de savoir lire et écrire.

literal ['lɪtərl] *a* littéral(e).

literary ['lɪtərərɪ] *a* littéraire.

literate ['lɪtərət] *a* qui sait lire et

écrire, instruit(e).

literature ['lɪtərɪtʃə*] n littérature f; (brochures etc) copie f publicitaire, prospectus mpl.

lithe [laɪð] a agile, souple.

litigation [lɪtɪ'geɪʃən] n litige m; contentieux m.

litre, (US) liter ['li:tə*] n litre m.

litter ['lɪtə*] n (rubbish) détritus mpl, ordures fpl; (young animals) portée f; ~ bin n (Brit) boîte f à ordures, poubelle f; ~ed a: ~ed with jonché(e) de, couvert(e) de.

little ['lɪtl] a (small) petit(e); (not much): it's ~ c'est peu; ~ milk peu de lait // ad peu; a ~ un peu (de); ~ by ~ petit à petit, peu à peu.

live vi [lɪv] vivre; (reside) vivre, habiter // a [laɪv] (animal) vivant(e), en vie; (wire) sous tension; (broadcast) transmis(e) en direct; to ~ down vt faire oublier (avec le temps); to ~ on vt fus (food) vivre de // vi survivre; to ~ together vi vivre ensemble, cohabiter; to ~ up to vt fus se montrer à la hauteur de.

livelihood ['laɪvlɪhud] n moyens mpl d'existence.

lively ['laɪvlɪ] a vif(vive), plein(e) d'entrain.

liven up ['laɪvn'ʌp] vt animer.

liver ['lɪvə*] n foie m.

livery ['lɪvərɪ] n livrée f.

lives [laɪvz] npl of **life**.

livestock ['laɪvstɔk] n cheptel m, bétail m.

livid ['lɪvɪd] a livide, blafard(e); (furious) furieux(euse), furibond(e).

living ['lɪvɪŋ] a vivant(e), en vie // n: to earn or make a ~ gagner sa vie; ~ conditions npl conditions fpl de vie; ~ room n salle f de séjour; ~ wage n salaire m permettant de vivre (décemment).

lizard ['lɪzəd] n lézard m.

load [ləud] n (weight) poids m; (thing carried) chargement m, charge f; (ELEC, TECH) charge // vt (also: ~ up): to ~ (with) (lorry, ship) charger de; (gun, camera)

charger (avec); (COMPUT) charger; a ~ of, ~s of (fig) un or des tas de, des masses de; ~ed a (dice) pipé(e); (question) insidieux(euse); (col: rich) bourré(e) de fric; (: drunk) bourré; ~ing bay n aire f de chargement.

loaf [ləuf], pl **loaves** n pain m miche, f // vi (also: ~ about, ~ around) fainéanter, traîner.

loan [ləun] n prêt m // vt prêter; on ~ prêté(e), en prêt.

loath [ləuθ] a: to be ~ to do répugner à faire.

loathe [ləuð] vt détester, avoir en horreur.

loaves [ləuvz] npl of **loaf**.

lobby ['lɔbɪ] n hall m, entrée f; (POL) groupe m de pression, lobby m // vt faire pression sur.

lobster ['lɔbstə*] n homard m.

local ['ləukl] a local(e) // n (pub) pub m or café m du coin; the ~npl les gens du pays or du coin; ~ call n communication urbaine; ~ government n administration locale or municipale.

locality [ləu'kælɪtɪ] n région f, environs mpl; (position) lieu m.

locate [ləu'keɪt] vt (find) trouver, repérer; (situate) situer.

location [ləu'keɪʃən] n emplacement m; on ~ (CINEMA) en extérieur.

loch [lɔx] n lac m, loch m.

lock [lɔk] n (of door, box) serrure f; (of canal) écluse f; (of hair) mèche f, boucle f // vt (with key) fermer à clé; (immobilize) bloquer // vi (door etc) fermer à clé; (wheels) se bloquer.

locker ['lɔkə*] n casier m.

locket ['lɔkɪt] n médaillon m.

locksmith ['lɔksmɪθ] n serrurier m.

lock-up ['lɔkʌp] n box m.

locomotive [ləukə'məutɪv] n locomotive f.

locum ['ləukəm] n (MED) suppléant/e (de médecin).

lodge [lɔdʒ] n pavillon m (de gardien); (FREEMASONRY) loge f // vi

(person): to ~ (with) être logé(e) (chez); être en pension (chez) // vt (appeal etc) présenter; déposer; **to ~ a complaint** porter plainte; **~r** n locataire m/f; **(with room and meals)** pensionnaire m/f.

lodgings ['lɔdʒɪŋz] n chambre f; meublé m.

loft [lɔft] n grenier m.

lofty ['lɔftɪ] a élevé(e); **(haughty)** hautain(e).

log [lɔg] n **(of wood)** bûche f; **(book)** = **logbook**.

logbook ['lɔgbuk] n **(NAUT)** livre m or journal m de bord; **(AVIAT)** carnet m de vol; **(of car)** = carte grise.

loggerheads ['lɔgəhɛdz] npl: **at ~ (with)** à couteaux tirés (avec).

logic ['lɔdʒɪk] n logique f; **~al** a logique.

loin [lɔɪn] n **(CULIN)** filet m, longe f.

loiter ['lɔɪtə*] vi s'attarder; **to ~ (about)** traîner, musarder; **(pej)** rôder.

loll [lɔl] vi **(also: ~ about)** se prélasser, fainéanter.

lollipop ['lɔlɪpɔp] n sucette f; **~ man/lady** n **(Brit)** contractuel/le qui fait traverser la rue aux enfants.

London ['lʌndən] n Londres m; **~er** n Londonien/ne.

lone [ləun] a solitaire.

loneliness ['ləunlɪnɪs] n solitude f, isolement m.

lonely ['ləunlɪ] a seul(e); solitaire, isolé(e).

long [lɔŋ] a long(longue) // ad longtemps // vi: **to ~ for sth** avoir très envie de qch; attendre qch avec impatience; **to ~ to do** avoir très envie de faire; attendre avec impatience de faire; **in the ~ run** à la longue; finalement; **so or as ~ as** pourvu que; **don't be ~** dépêchez-vous; **how ~ is this river/course?** quelle est la longueur de ce fleuve/la durée de ce cours?; **6 metres ~** (long) de 6 mètres; **6 months ~** qui dure 6 mois, de 6 mois; **all night ~** toute la nuit; **he no ~er comes** il ne vient plus; **~**

before longtemps avant; **before ~** (+ future) avant peu, dans peu de temps; (+ past) peu de temps après; **at ~ last** enfin; **~-distance** a **(race)** de fond; **(call)** interurbain(e); **~hand** n écriture normale or courante; **~ing** n désir m, envie f, nostalgie f.

longitude ['lɔŋgɪtjuːd] n longitude f.

long: ~ jump n saut m en longueur; **~-playing** a: **~-playing record (L.P.)** n (disque m) 33 tours m inv; **~-range** a à longue portée; **~-sighted** a presbyte; **(fig)** prévoyant(e); **~-standing** a de longue date; **~-suffering** a à la patience résignée; extrêmement patient(e); **~-term** a à long terme; **~ wave** n grandes ondes; **~-winded** a intarissable, interminable.

loo [luː] n **(Brit col)** w.-c. mpl, petit coin.

look [luk] vi regarder; **(seem)** sembler, paraître, avoir l'air; **(building etc)**: **to ~ south/on to the sea** donner au sud/sur la mer // n regard m; **(appearance)** air m, allure f, aspect m; **~s** npl mine f; physique m, beauté f; **to ~ after** vt fus s'occuper de, prendre soin de; garder, surveiller; **to ~ at** vt fus regarder; **to ~ back** vi se retourner pour regarder; **to ~ back on (event etc)** évoquer, repenser à; **to ~ down on** vt fus **(fig)** regarder de haut, dédaigner; **to ~ for** vt fus chercher; **to ~ forward to** vt fus attendre avec impatience; **we ~ forward to hearing from you** dans l'attente de vous lire; **to ~ into** vt fus examiner, étudier; **to ~ on** vi regarder (en spectateur); **to ~ out** vi **(beware)** prendre garde (à), faire attention (à); **to ~ out for** vt fus être à la recherche de; guetter; **to ~ round** vi regarder derrière soi, se retourner; **to ~ to** vt fus veiller à; **(rely on)** compter sur; **to ~ up** vi lever les yeux; **(im-**

prove) s'améliorer // *vt* (*word*) chercher; (*friend*) passer voir; **to ~ up** *vt* fus avoir du respect pour; **~out** *n* poste *m* de guet; guetteur *m*; **to be on the ~out (for)** guetter.

loom [lu:m] *n* métier *m* à tisser // *vi* surgir; (*fig*) menacer.

loony ['lu:nɪ] *n* (*col*) timbré/e, cinglé/e.

loop [lu:p] *n* boucle *f*; **~hole** *n* porte *f* de sortie (*fig*); échappatoire *f*.

loose [lu:s] *a* (*knot, screw*) desserré(e); (*stone*) branlant(e); (*clothes*) vague, ample, lâche; (*animal*) en liberté, échappé(e); (*life*) dissolu(e); (*morals, discipline*) relâché(e); (*thinking*) peu rigoureux(euse), vague; (*translation*) approximatif(ive); **~ change** *n* petite monnaie; **~ chippings** *npl* (*on road*) gravillons *mpl*; **to be at a ~ end** or (*US*) **at ~ ends** ne pas trop savoir quoi faire; **~ly** *ad* sans serrer; approximativement; **~n** *vt* desserrer, relâcher, défaire.

loot [lu:t] *n* butin *m* // *vt* piller.

lop [lɔp] **to ~ off** couper, trancher.

lop-sided ['lɔp'saɪdd] *a* de travers, asymétrique.

lord [lɔːd] *n* seigneur *m*; **L~ Smith** lord Smith; **the L~** le Seigneur; **the (House of) L~s** (*Brit*) la Chambre des Lords; **~ship** *n*: **your L~ship** Monsieur le comte (*or* le baron *or* le Juge).

lore [lɔː*] *n* tradition *f* (*pl*).

lorry ['lɔrɪ] *n* (*Brit*) camion *m*; **~ driver** *n* (*Brit*) camionneur *m*, routier *m*.

lose [lu:z], *pt, pp* **lost** *vt* perdre; (*opportunity*) manquer, perdre; (*pursuers*) distancer, semer // *vi* perdre; **to ~ (time)** (*clock*) retarder; **to get lost** *vi* se perdre; **~r** *n* perdant/e.

loss [lɔs] *n* perte *f*; **to be at a ~** être perplexe *or* embarrassé(e).

lost [lɔst] *pt, pp of* **lose** // *a* perdu(e); **~ property**, (*US*) **~ and found** *n* objets trouvés.

lot [lɔt] *n* (*at auctions*) lot *m*; (*destiny*) sort *m*, destinée *f*; **the ~** le tout; tous *mpl*, toutes *fpl*; **a ~** beaucoup; **a ~ of** beaucoup de; **~s of** des tas de; **to draw ~s (for sth)** tirer (qch) au sort.

lotion ['ləʊʃən] *n* lotion *f*.

lottery ['lɔtərɪ] *n* loterie *f*.

loud [laud] *a* bruyant(e), sonore, fort(e); (*gaudy*) voyant(e), tapageur(euse) // *ad* (*speak etc*) fort; **~hailer** *n* (*Brit*) porte-voix *m inv*; **~ly** *ad* fort, bruyamment; **~speaker** *n* haut-parleur *m*.

lounge [laundʒ] *n* salon *m* // *vi* se prélasser, paresser; **~ suit** *n* (*Brit*) complet *m*; (*woman's*) 'tenue de ville'.

louse [laus], *pl* **lice** *n* pou *m*.

lousy ['lauzɪ] *a* (*fig*) infect(e), moche.

lout [laut] *n* rustre *m*, butor *m*.

louvre, (*US*) **louver** ['lu:və*] *a* (*door, window*) à claire-voie.

lovable ['lʌvəbl] *a* très sympathique; adorable.

love [lʌv] *n* amour *m* // *vt* aimer; aimer beaucoup; **to be in ~ with** être amoureux(euse) de; **to make ~** faire l'amour; **'15 ~'** (*TENNIS*) '15 à rien *or* zéro'; **~ affair** *n* liaison (amoureuse); **~ life** *n* vie sentimentale.

lovely ['lʌvlɪ] *a* (*très*) joli(e); ravissant(e), charmant(e); agréable.

lover ['lʌvə*] *n* amant *m*; (*amateur*): **a ~ of** ami(e) de; un(e) amoureux(euse) de.

loving ['lʌvɪŋ] *a* affectueux(euse), tendre, aimant(e).

low [ləʊ] *a* bas(basse) // *ad* bas // *n* (*METEOROLOGY*) dépression *f* // *vi* (*cow*) mugir; **to feel ~** se sentir déprimé(e); **to turn (down)** *vt* baisser; **~cut** *a* (*dress*) décolleté(e); **~er** *vt* abaisser, baisser; **~fat** *a* maigre; **~lands** *npl* (*GEO*) plaines *fpl*; **~ly** *a* humble, modeste; **~lying** *a* à faible altitude.

loyal ['lɔɪəl] *a* loyal(e), fidèle; **~ty** *n* loyauté *f*, fidélité *f*.

lozenge ['lɔzɪndʒ] n (MED) pastille f; (GEOM) losange m.
L.P. n abbr of **long-playing record**.
L-plates ['elpleɪts] npl (Brit) plaques fpl d'apprenti conducteur.
Ltd abbr see **limited**.
lubricant ['lu:brɪkənt] n lubrifiant m.
lubricate ['lu:brɪkeɪt] vt lubrifier, graisser.
luck [lʌk] n chance f; **bad ~** malchance f, malheur m; **good ~!** bonne chance!; **~ily** ad heureusement, par bonheur; **~y a** (person) qui a de la chance; (coincidence) heureux(euse); (number etc) qui porte bonheur.
ludicrous ['lu:dɪkrəs] a ridicule, absurde.
lug [lʌg] vt traîner, tirer.
luggage ['lʌgɪdʒ] n bagages mpl; **~ rack** n (in train) porte-bagages m inv; (on car) galerie f.
lukewarm ['lu:kwɔ:m] a tiède.
lull [lʌl] n accalmie f // vt (child) bercer; (person, fear) apaiser, calmer.
lullaby ['lʌləbaɪ] n berceuse f.
lumbago [lʌm'beɪgəu] n lumbago m.
lumber ['lʌmbə*] n bric-à-brac m inv; **~jack** n bûcheron m.
luminous ['lu:mɪnəs] a lumineux(euse).
lump [lʌmp] n morceau m; (in sauce) grumeau m; (swelling) grosseur f // vt (also: **~ together**) réunir, mettre en tas; **~ sum** n somme globale ou forfaitaire.
lunacy ['lu:nəsɪ] n démence f, folie f.
lunar ['lu:nə*] a lunaire.
lunatic ['lu:nətɪk] a, n fou(folle), dément(e).
lunch [lʌntʃ] n déjeuner m.
luncheon ['lʌntʃən] n déjeuner m; **~ meat** n sorte de saucisson; **~ voucher** n chèque-repas m.
lung [lʌŋ] n poumon m.
lunge [lʌndʒ] vi (also: **~ forward**) faire un mouvement brusque en avant; **to ~ at** envoyer ou assener un coup à.
lurch [lə:tʃ] vi vaciller, tituber // n

écart m brusque, embardée f; **to leave sb in the ~** laisser qn se débrouiller or se dépêtrer tout(e) seul(e).
lure [luə*] n appât m, leurre m // vt attirer ou persuader par la ruse.
lurid ['luərɪd] a affreux(euse), atroce.
lurk [lə:k] vi se tapir, se cacher.
luscious ['lʌʃəs] a succulent(e); appétissant(e).
lush [lʌʃ] a luxuriant(e).
lust [lʌst] n luxure f; lubricité f; désir m; (fig) **~ for** soif f de; **to ~ after** vt fus convoiter, désirer.
lusty ['lʌstɪ] a vigoureux(euse), robuste.
Luxembourg ['lʌksəmbə:g] n Luxembourg m.
luxurious [lʌg'zjuərɪəs] a luxueux(euse).
luxury ['lʌkʃərɪ] n luxe m // cpd de luxe.
lying ['laɪɪŋ] n mensonge s m(pl).
lyric ['lɪrɪk] a lyrique; **~s** npl (of song) paroles fpl; **~al** a lyrique.

M

m. abbr of **metre, mile, million**.
M.A. abbr see **master**.
mac [mæk] n (Brit) imper(méable) m.
mace [meɪs] n masse f; (spice) macis m.
machine [mə'ʃi:n] n machine f // vt (dress etc) coudre à la machine; **~gun** n mitrailleuse f; **~ry** n machinerie f, machines fpl; (fig) mécanisme(s) m(pl).
mackerel ['mækrl] n (pl inv) maquereau m.
mackintosh ['mækɪntɔʃ] n (Brit) imperméable m.
mad [mæd] a fou(folle); (foolish) insensé(e); (angry) furieux(euse).
madam ['mædəm] n madame f.
madden ['mædn] vt exaspérer.
made [meɪd] pt, pp of **make**.
Madeira [mə'dɪərə] n (GEO) Madère

f; *(wine)* madère *m.*

made-to-measure ['meɪdtə'meʒə*]
a (Brit) fait(e) sur mesure.

madly ['mædlɪ] *ad* follement.

madman ['mædmən] *n* fou *m,* aliéné
m.

madness ['mædnɪs] *n* folie *f.*

magazine [mægə'zi:n] *n (PRESS)*
magazine *m,* revue *f; (MIL: store)*
dépôt *m,* arsenal *m; (of firearm)* magasin *m.*

maggot ['mægət] *n* ver *m,* asticot *m.*

magic ['mædʒɪk] *n* magie *f // a* magique; **~al** *a* magique; **~ian**
[mə'dʒɪʃən] *n* magicien/ne.

magistrate ['mædʒɪstreɪt] *n* magistrat *m;* juge *m.*

magnet ['mægnɪt] *n* aimant *m;* **~ic**
[-'nɛtɪk] *a* magnétique.

magnificent [mæg'nɪfɪsnt] *a* superbe, magnifique.

magnify ['mægnɪfaɪ] *vt* grossir;
(sound) amplifier; **~ing glass** *n*
loupe *f.*

magnitude ['mægnɪtju:d] *n* ampleur
f.

magpie ['mægpaɪ] *n* pie *f.*

mahogany [mə'hɔgənɪ] *n* acajou *m.*

maid [meɪd] *n* bonne *f; a ~ (pej)*
vieille fille.

maiden ['meɪdn] *n* jeune fille *f // a
(aunt etc)* non mariée; *(speech,
voyage)* inaugural(e); **~ name** *n*
nom *m* de jeune fille.

mail [meɪl] *n* poste *f; (letters)* courrier *m // vt* envoyer (par la poste);
~box *n (US)* boîte *f* aux lettres;
~ing list *n* liste *f* d'adresses;
~order *n* vente *f* or achat *m* par correspondance.

maim [meɪm] *vt* mutiler.

main [meɪn] *a* principal(e) *// n (pipe)*
conduite principale, canalisation *f;*
the **~s** *(ELEC)* le secteur; **in the ~**
dans l'ensemble; **~frame** *n
(COMPUT)* (gros) ordinateur, unité
centrale; **~land** *n* continent *m;* **~ly**
ad principalement, surtout; **~ road**
n grand-route *f;* **~stream** *n* courant
principal; **~stay** *n (fig)* pilier *m.*

maintain [meɪn'teɪn] *vt* entretenir;
(continue) maintenir, préserver;
(affirm) soutenir; **maintenance**
['meɪntənəns] *n* entretien *m; (alimony)* pension *f* alimentaire.

maize [meɪz] *n* maïs *m.*

majestic [mə'dʒɛstɪk] *a* majes-
tueux(euse).

majesty ['mædʒɪstɪ] *n* majesté *f.*

major ['meɪdʒə*] *n (MIL)* commandant *m // a* important(e), princi-
pal(e); *(MUS)* majeur(e).

Majorca [mə'jɔ:kə] *n* Majorque *f.*

majority [mə'dʒɔrɪtɪ] *n* majorité *f.*

make [meɪk] *vt (pt, pp* **made)** faire;
(manufacture) faire, fabriquer;
(cause to be): **to ~ sb sad** *etc* rendre qn triste *etc; (force):* **to ~ sb
do sth** obliger qn à faire qch, faire
faire qch à qn; *(equal):* **2 and 2 ~ 4**
2 et 2 font 4 *// n* fabrication *f;
(brand)* marque *f;* **to ~ a fool of sb**
(ridicule) ridiculiser qn; *(trick)* avoir
or duper qn; **to ~ a profit** faire un
or des bénéfice(s); **to ~ a loss** essuyer une perte; **to ~ it** *(arrive)* arriver; *(achieve sth)* parvenir à qch;
what time do you ~ it? quelle
heure avez-vous?; **to ~ do with** se
contenter de; se débrouiller avec;
to ~ for *vt fus (place)* se diriger vers;
to ~ out *vt (write out)* écrire;
(cheque) faire; *(understand)*
comprendre; *(see)* distinguer; **to ~
up** *vt (invent)* imaginer, inventer;
(parcel) faire *// vi* se réconcilier;
(with cosmetics) se farder; **to ~ up
for** *vt fus* compenser;
racheter; **~-believe** *n:* **a world of
~-believe** un pays de chimères; **it's
just ~-believe** c'est pour faire semblant; c'est de l'invention pure; **~r** *n*
fabricant *m;* **~shift** *a* provisoire,
improvisé(e); **~-up** *n* maquillage
m; **~-up remover** *n* démaquillant
m.

making ['meɪkɪŋ] *n (fig):* **in the ~**
en formation *or* gestation; **to have
the ~s of** *(actor, athlete etc)* avoir
l'étoffe de.

malaria [məˈlɛərɪə] n malaria f.

Malaya [məˈleɪə] n Malaisie f.

male [meɪl] n (BIOL, ELEC) mâle m // a (sex, attitude) masculin(e); mâle; (child etc) du sexe masculin.

malevolent [məˈlevələnt] a malveillant(e).

malfunction [mælˈfʌŋkʃən] n fonctionnement défectueux.

malice [ˈmælɪs] n méchanceté f, malveillance f; **malicious** [məˈlɪʃəs] a méchant(e), malveillant(e); (LAW) avec intention criminelle.

malign [məˈlaɪn] vt diffamer, calomnier.

malignant [məˈlɪgnənt] a (MED) malin(igne).

mall ¶mɔːl] n (also: **shopping ~**) centre commercial.

mallet [ˈmælɪt] n maillet m.

malpractice [mælˈpræktɪs] n faute professionnelle; négligence f.

malt [mɔːlt] n malt m // cpd (whisky) pur malt.

Malta [ˈmɔːltə] n Malte f.

mammal [ˈmæml] n mammifère m.

mammoth [ˈmæməθ] n mammouth m // a géant(e), monstre.

man [mæn], pl **men** n homme m; (CHESS) pièce f; (DRAUGHTS) pion m // vt garnir d'hommes; servir, assurer le fonctionnement de; être de service à; **an old ~** un vieillard; **~ and wife** mari et femme.

manage [ˈmænɪdʒ] vi se débrouiller // vt (be in charge of) s'occuper de; gérer; to ~ to se débrouiller pour faire; réussir à faire; **~able** a maniable; faisable; **~ment** n administration f, direction f; **~r** n directeur m; administrateur m; (of hotel etc) gérant m; (of artist) impresario m; **~ress** [-ˈɔ'rɛs] n directrice f; gérante f; **~rial** [-ɔ'dʒɪərɪəl] a directorial(e); **managing** a: **managing director** directeur général.

mandarin [ˈmændərɪn] n (also: ~ **orange**) mandarine f; (person) mandarin m.

mandatory [ˈmændətərɪ] a obliga-

toire; (powers etc) mandataire.

mane [meɪn] n crinière f.

maneuver etc [məˈnuːvə*] (US) = **manoeuvre** etc.

manfully [ˈmænfəlɪ] ad vaillamment.

mangle [ˈmæŋgl] vt déchiqueter; mutiler.

mango, **~es** [ˈmæŋgəu] n mangue f.

mangy [ˈmeɪndʒɪ] a galeux(euse).

manhandle [ˈmænhændl] vt malmener.

manhole [ˈmænhəul] n trou m d'homme.

manhood [ˈmænhud] n âge m d'homme; virilité f.

man-hour [ˈmænˈauə*] n heure f de main-d'œuvre.

mania [ˈmeɪnɪə] n manie f; **~c** [ˈmeɪnɪæk] n maniaque m/f.

manic [ˈmænɪk] a maniaque.

manicure [ˈmænɪkjuə*] n manucure f; **~ set** n trousse f à ongles.

manifest [ˈmænɪfɛst] vt manifester // a manifeste, évident(e).

manifesto [mænɪˈfɛstəu] n manifeste m.

manipulate [məˈnɪpjuleɪt] vt manipuler.

mankind [mænˈkaɪnd] n humanité f, genre humain.

manly [ˈmænlɪ] a viril(e); courageux(euse).

man-made [ˈmænˈmeɪd] a artificiel(le).

manner [ˈmænə*] n manière f, façon f; **~s** npl manières fpl; **~ism** n particularité f de langage (or de comportement), tic m.

manoeuvre, (US) **maneuver** [məˈnuːvə*] vt, vi manœuvrer // n manœuvre f.

manor [ˈmænə*] n (also: ~ **house**) manoir m.

manpower [ˈmænpauə*] n main-d'œuvre f.

mansion [ˈmænʃən] n château m, manoir m.

manslaughter [ˈmænslɔːtə*] n homicide m involontaire.

mantelpiece [ˈmæntlpiːs] n cheminée f.

manual ['mænjuəl] a manuel(le) // n manuel m.

manufacture [mænju'fæktʃə*] vt fabriquer // n fabrication f; **~r** n fabricant m.

manure [mə'njuə*] n fumier m; (artificial) engrais m.

manuscript ['mænjuskrɪpt] n manuscrit m.

many ['menɪ] a beaucoup de, de nombreux(euses) // pronoun beaucoup, un grand nombre; **a great ~** un grand nombre (de); **a ~ ...** bien des ..., plus d'un(e) ...

map [mæp] n carte f // vt dresser la carte de; **to ~ out** vt tracer.

maple ['meɪpl] n érable m.

mar [ma:*] vt gâcher, gâter.

marathon ['mærəθən] n marathon m.

marble ['ma:bl] n marbre m; (toy) bille f.

March [ma:tʃ] n mars m.

march [ma:tʃ] vi marcher au pas; défiler // n marche f; (demonstration) rallye m.

mare [mɛə*] n jument f.

margarine [ma:dʒə'ri:n] n margarine f.

margin ['ma:dʒɪn] n marge f; **~al** (seat) n (POL) siège disputé.

marigold ['mærɪgəuld] n souci m.

marijuana [mærɪ'wa:nə] n marijuana f.

marine [mə'ri:n] a marin(e) // n fusilier marin; (US) marine m.

marital ['mærɪtl] a matrimonial(e); **~ status** situation f de famille.

mark [ma:k] n marque f; (of skid etc) trace f; (Brit SCOL) note f; (SPORT) cible f; (currency) mark m // vt marquer; (stain) tacher; (Brit SCOL) noter; corriger; **to ~ time** marquer le pas; **to ~ out** vt désigner; **~er** n (sign) jalon m; (bookmark) signet m.

market ['ma:kɪt] n marché m // vt (COMM) commercialiser; **~ garden** n (Brit) jardin maraîcher; **~ing** n

marketing m; **~place** n place f de marché; (COMM) marché m; **~ research** n étude f de marché; **~ value** n valeur marchande; valeur du marché.

marksman ['ma:ksmən] n tireur m d'élite.

marmalade ['ma:məleɪd] n confiture f d'oranges.

maroon [mə'ru:n] vt (fig): **to be ~ed (in** or **at)** être bloqué(e) (à) // a bordeaux inv.

marquee [ma:'ki:] n chapiteau m.

marriage ['mærɪdʒ] n mariage m; **~ bureau** n agence matrimoniale; **~ certificate** n extrait m d'acte de mariage.

married ['mærɪd] a marié(e); (life, love) conjugal(e).

marrow ['mærəu] n moelle f; (vegetable) courge f.

marry ['mærɪ] vt épouser, se marier avec; (subj: father, priest etc) marier // vi (also: **get married**) se marier.

Mars [ma:z] n (planet) Mars f.

marsh [ma:ʃ] n marais m, marécage m.

marshal ['ma:ʃl] n maréchal m; (US: fire, police) ≈ capitaine m // vt rassembler.

martyr ['ma:tə*] n martyr/e // vt martyriser; **~dom** n martyre m.

marvel ['ma:vl] n merveille f // vi: **to ~ (at)** s'émerveiller (de); **~lous,** (US) **~ous** a merveilleux(euse).

Marxist ['ma:ksɪst] a, n marxiste (m/f).

marzipan ['ma:zɪpæn] n pâte f d'amandes.

mascara [mæs'ka:rə] n mascara m.

masculine ['mæskjulɪn] a masculin(e).

mashed [mæʃt] a: **~ potatoes** purée f de pommes de terre.

mask [ma:sk] n masque m // vt masquer.

mason ['meɪsn] n (also: **stone~**) maçon m; (also: **free~**) franc-maçon m; **~ry** n maçonnerie f.

masquerade [mæskə'reɪd] *n* bal masqué; (*fig*) mascarade *f* // *vi*: to ~ as se faire passer pour

mass [mæs] *n* multitude *f*, masse *f*; (*PHYSICS*) masse; (*REL*) messe *f* // *vi* se masser; **the ~es** les masses.

massacre ['mæsəkə*] *n* massacre *m*.

massage ['mæsɑːʒ] *n* massage *m* // *vt* masser.

massive ['mæsɪv] *a* énorme, massif(ive).

mass media ['mæs'miːdɪə] *npl* mass-media *mpl*.

mass-production ['mæsprə'dʌkʃən] *n* fabrication *f* en série.

mast [mɑːst] *n* mât *m*.

master ['mɑːstə*] *n* maître *m*; (*in secondary school*) professeur *m*; (*title for boys*): **M~ X** Monsieur X // *vt* maîtriser; (*learn*) apprendre à fond; (*understand*) posséder parfaitement *or* à fond; **~ key** passepartout *m inv*; **~ly** *a* magistral(e); **~mind** *n* esprit supérieur // *vt* diriger, être le cerveau de; **M~ of Arts/Science (M.A./M.Sc.)** *n* ≈ titulaire *m/f* d'une maîtrise (en lettres/sciences); **~piece** *n* chef-d'œuvre *m*; **~y** *n* maîtrise *f*, connaissance parfaite.

mat [mæt] *n* petit tapis; (*also: door*~) paillasson *m* // *a* = **matt**.

match [mætʃ] *n* allumette *f*; (*game*) match *m*, partie *f*; (*fig*) égal(e); mariage *m*; parti *m* // *vt* (*go well with*) aller bien avec, s'assortir à; (*equal*) égaler, valoir // *vi* être assorti(e); **to be a good ~** être bien assorti(e); **~box** *n* boîte *f* d'allumettes; **~ing** *a* assorti(e).

mate [meɪt] *n* camarade *m/f* de travail; (*col*) copain/copine; (*animal*) partenaire *m/f*, mâle/femelle; (*in merchant navy*) second *m* // *vi* s'accoupler // *vt* accoupler.

material [mə'tɪərɪəl] *n* (*substance*) matière *f*, matériau *m*; (*cloth*) tissu *m*, étoffe *f* // *a* matériel(le); (*important*) essentiel(le); **~s** *npl* matériaux *mpl*.

maternal [mə'tɜːnl] *a* maternel(le).

maternity [mə'tɜːnɪtɪ] *n* maternité *f*; **~ dress** *n* robe *f* de grossesse; **~ hospital** *n* maternité *f*.

math [mæθ] *n* (*US*) = **maths**.

mathematical [mæθə'mætɪkl] *a* mathématique.

mathematics [mæθə'mætɪks] *n* mathématiques *fpl*.

maths, (*US*) **math** [mæθs, mæθ] *n* math(s) *fpl*.

matinée ['mætɪneɪ] *n* matinée *f*.

mating ['meɪtɪŋ] *n* accouplement *m*.

matriculation [mətrɪkju'leɪʃən] *n* inscription *f*.

matrimonial [mætrɪ'məunɪəl] *a* matrimonial(e), conjugal(e).

matrimony ['mætrɪmənɪ] *n* mariage *m*.

matron ['meɪtrən] *n* (*in hospital*) infirmière-chef *f*; (*in school*) infirmière; **~ly** *a* de matrone; imposant(e).

matt [mæt] *a* mat(e).

matted ['mætɪd] *a* emmêlé(e).

matter ['mætə*] *n* question *f*; (*PHYSICS*) matière *f*, substance *f*; (*content*) contenu *m*, fond *m*; (*MED: pus*) pus *m* // *vi* importer; **it doesn't ~** cela n'a pas d'importance; (*I don't mind*) cela ne fait rien; **what's the ~?** qu'est-ce qu'il y a?, qu'est-ce qui ne va pas?; **no ~ what** quoiqu'il arrive; **as a ~ of course** tout naturellement; **as a ~ of fact** en fait; **~-of-fact** *a* terre à terre, neutre.

mattress ['mætrɪs] *n* matelas *m*.

mature [mə'tjuə*] *a* mûr(e); (*cheese*) fait(e) // *vi* mûrir; se faire.

maul [mɔːl] *vt* lacérer.

mauve [məuv] *a* mauve.

maximum ['mæksɪməm] *a* maximum // *n* (*pl* **maxima** ['mæksɪmə]) maximum *m*.

May [meɪ] *n* mai *m*.

may [meɪ] *vi* (*conditional*: **might**) (*indicating possibility*): **he ~ come** il se peut qu'il vienne; (*be allowed to*): **~ I smoke?** puis-je fumer?; (*wishes*): **~ God bless you!** (que)

Dieu vous bénisse!

maybe ['meɪbɪ] *ad* peut-être; ~ he'll ... peut-être qu'il ....

May Day *n* le Premier mai.

mayhem ['meɪhem] *n* grabuge *m*.

mayonnaise [meɪə'neɪz] *n* mayonnaise *f*.

mayor [mɛə*] *n* maire *m*; ~**ess** *n* maire *m*; épouse *f* du maire.

maze [meɪz] *n* labyrinthe *m*, dédale *m*.

M.D. *abbr* = *Doctor of Medicine*.

me [miː] *pronoun* me, m' + *vowel*; (*stressed, after prep*) moi; **he heard** ~ il m'a entendu(e); **give a book** donnez-moi un livre; **after** ~ après moi.

meadow ['mɛdəʊ] *n* prairie *f*, pré *m*.

meagre, (*US*) **meager** ['miːgə*] *a* maigre.

meal [miːl] *n* repas *m*; (*flour*) farine *f*; ~**time** *n* l'heure *f* du repas.

mean [miːn] *a* (*with money*) avare, radin(e); (*unkind*) mesquin(e), méchant(e); (*average*) moyen(ne) // *vt* (*pt, pp* **meant**) (*signify*) signifier, vouloir dire; (*intend*): **to** ~ **to do** avoir l'intention de faire // *n* moyenne *f*; ~**s** *npl* moyens *mpl*; **by** ~**s of** par l'intermédiaire de; au moyen de; **by all** ~**s** je vous en prie; **to be meant for sb/sth** être destiné(e) à qn/qch; **do you** ~ **it?** vous êtes sérieux?; **what do you** ~? que voulez-vous dire?

meander [mɪ'ændə*] *vi* faire des méandres; (*fig*) flâner.

meaning ['miːnɪŋ] *n* signification *f*, sens *m*; ~**ful** *a* significatif(ive); ~**less** *a* dénué(e) de sens.

meant [mɛnt] *pt, pp* of **mean**.

meantime ['miːntaɪm] *ad*, **meanwhile** ['miːnwaɪl] *ad* (*also*: **in the** ~) pendant ce temps.

measles ['miːzlz] *n* rougeole *f*.

measly ['miːzlɪ] *a* (*col*) minable.

measure ['mɛʒə*] *vt, vi* mesurer // *n* mesure *f*; (*ruler*) règle (graduée); ~**ments** *npl* mesures *fpl*; **chest/hip**

~**ment** tour *m* de poitrine/hanches.

meat [miːt] *n* viande *f*; ~**ball** *n* boulette *f* de viande; ~**y** *a* avec beaucoup de viande, plein(e) de viande; (*fig*) substantiel(le).

Mecca ['mɛkə] *n* la Mecque.

mechanic [mɪ'kænɪk] *n* mécanicien *m*; ~**s** *n* mécanique *f* // *npl* mécanisme *m*; ~**al** *a* mécanique.

mechanism ['mɛkənɪzəm] *n* mécanisme *m*.

medal ['mɛdl] *n* médaille *f*; ~**lion** [mɪ'dælɪən] *n* médaillon *m*.

meddle ['mɛdl] *vi*: **to** ~ **in** se mêler de, s'occuper de; **to** ~ **with** toucher à.

media ['miːdɪə] *npl* media *mpl*.

mediaeval [mɛdɪ'iːvl] *a* = **medieval**.

median ['miːdɪən] *n* (*US: also:* ~ **strip**) bande médiane.

mediate ['miːdɪeɪt] *vi* s'interposer; servir d'intermédiaire.

Medicaid ['mɛdɪkeɪd] *n* (*US*) *assistance médicale aux indigents*.

medical ['mɛdɪkl] *a* médical(e).

Medicare ['mɛdɪkɛə*] *n* (*US*) *assistance médicale aux personnes âgées*.

medicated ['mɛdɪkeɪtɪd] *a* traitant(e), médicamenteux(euse).

medicine ['mɛdsɪn] *n* médecine *f*; (*drug*) médicament *m*.

medieval [mɛdɪ'iːvl] *a* médiéval(e).

mediocre [miːdɪ'əʊkə*] *a* médiocre.

meditate ['mɛdɪteɪt] *vi* méditer.

Mediterranean [mɛdɪtə'reɪnɪən] *a* méditerranéen(ne); **the** ~ (**Sea**) la (mer) Méditerranée.

medium ['miːdɪəm] *a* moyen(ne) // *n* (*pl* **media**: *means*) moyen *m*; (*pl* **mediums**: *person*) médium *m*; **the happy** ~ le juste milieu; ~ **wave** *n* ondes moyennes.

medley ['mɛdlɪ] *n* mélange *m*.

meek [miːk] *a* doux(douce), humble.

meet [miːt] *pt, pp* **met** *vt* rencontrer; (*by arrangement*) retrouver, rejoindre; (*for the first time*) faire la connaissance de; (*go and fetch*): **I'll** ~ **you at the station** j'irai te chercher à la gare; (fig) faire face à; satisfaire à; se joindre à // vi se rencontrer; se retrouver; (join: objects) se réunir; (join: objects) se joindre; **to ~ with** vt fus rencontrer; **~ing** n rencontre f; (session: of club etc) réunion f; (interview) entrevue f; **she's at a ~ing** (COMM) elle est en conférence.

megabyte ['megəbait] n (COMPUT) méga-octet m.

megaphone ['megəfəun] n porte-voix m inv.

melancholy ['melənkəli] n mélancolie f // a mélancolique.

mellow ['meləu] a velouté(e), doux(douce); (colour) riche et profond(e); (fruit) mûr(e) // vi (person) s'adoucir.

melody ['melədi] n mélodie f.

melon ['melən] n melon m.

melt [melt] vi fondre; (become soft) s'amollir; (fig) s'attendrir // vt faire fondre; (person) attendrir; **to ~ away** vi fondre complètement; **to ~ down** vt fondre; **~down** n fusion f (du cœur d'un réacteur nucléaire); **~ing pot** n (fig) creuset m.

member ['membə*] n membre m; **M~ of Parliament (MP)** (Brit) député m; **M~ of the European Parliament (MEP)** (Brit) Eurodéputé m; **~ship** n adhésion f; statut m de membre; (nombre m de) membres mpl, adhérents mpl; **~ship card** n carte f de membre.

memento [mə'mentəu] n souvenir m.

memo ['meməu] n note f (de service).

memoirs ['memwɑ:z] npl mémoires mpl.

memorandum, pl **memoranda** [memə'rændəm, -də] n note f (de service); (DIPLOMACY) mémorandum m.

memorial [mi'mɔ:riəl] n mémorial m // a commémoratif(ive).

memorize ['meməraiz] vt apprendre par cœur; retenir.

memory ['meməri] n mémoire f; (recollection) souvenir m.

men [men] npl of **man**.

menace ['menəs] n menace f // vt menacer.

mend [mend] vt réparer; (darn) raccommoder, repriser // n reprise f; **on the ~** en voie de guérison.

menial ['mi:niəl] a de domestique, inférieur(e); subalterne.

meningitis [menin'dʒaitis] n méningite f.

menopause ['menəupɔ:z] n ménopause f.

menstruation [menstru'eiʃən] n menstruation f.

mental ['mentl] a mental(e).

mentality [men'tæliti] n mentalité f.

mention ['menʃən] n mention f // vt mentionner, faire mention de; **don't ~ it!** je vous en prie, il n'y a pas de quoi!

menu ['menju:] n (set ~, COMPUT) menu m; (printed) carte f.

MEP n abbr of **Member of the European Parliament**.

mercenary ['mə:sinəri] a mercantile // n mercenaire m.

merchandise ['mə:tʃəndaiz] n marchandises fpl.

merchant ['mə:tʃənt] n négociant m, marchand m; **~ bank** n (Brit) banque f d'affaires; **~ navy**, (US) **~ marine** n marine marchande.

merciful ['mə:siful] a miséricordieux(euse), clément(e).

merciless ['mə:silis] a impitoyable, sans pitié.

mercury ['mə:kjuri] n mercure m.

mercy ['mə:si] n pitié f, merci f; (REL) miséricorde f; **at the ~ of** à la merci de.

mere [miə*] a simple; **~ly** ad simplement, purement.

merge [mə:dʒ] vt unir // vi se fondre; (COMM) fusionner; **~r** n (COMM) fusion f.

meringue [mə'ræŋ] n meringue f.

merit ['merit] n mérite m, valeur f // vt mériter.

mermaid ['mə:meɪd] n sirène f.

merry ['mɛrɪ] a gai(e); M~ Christmas! Joyeux Noël!; **~-go-round** n manège m.

mesh [mɛʃ] n maille f; filet m.

mesmerize ['mɛzməraɪz] vt hypnotiser; fasciner.

mess [mɛs] n désordre m, fouillis m, pagaille f; (MIL) mess m, cantine f; **to ~ about or around** vi (col) perdre son temps; **to ~ about or around with** vt fus (col) chambarder, tripoter; **to ~ up** vt salir; chambarder; gâcher.

message ['mɛsɪdʒ] n message m.

messenger ['mɛsɪndʒə*] n messager m.

Messrs [mɛsrz] abbr (on letters) MM.

messy ['mɛsɪ] a sale; en désordre.

met [mɛt] pt, pp of **meet**.

metal ['mɛtl] n métal m; **~lic** [-'tælɪk] a métallique.

mete [mi:t]: **to ~ out** vt fus infliger.

meteorology [mi:tɪə'rɔlədʒɪ] n météorologie f.

meter ['mi:tə*] n (instrument) compteur m; (US: unit) = metre.

method ['mɛθəd] n méthode f; **~ical** [mɪ'θɔdɪkl] a méthodique.

Methodist ['mɛθədɪst] a, n méthodiste (m/f).

methylated spirit ['mɛθɪleɪtɪd-] n (Brit: also: **meths**) alcool m à brûler.

metre, (US) meter ['mi:tə*] n mètre m.

metric ['mɛtrɪk] a métrique.

metropolitan [mɛtrə'pɔlɪtən] a métropolitain(e); **the M~ Police** (Brit) la police londonienne.

mettle ['mɛtl] n courage m.

mew [mju:] vi (cat) miauler.

mews [mju:z] n: **~ cottage** (Brit) maisonnette aménagée dans une ancienne écurie ou remise.

Mexico ['mɛksɪkəu] n Mexique m.

miaow [mi:'au] vi miauler.

mice [maɪs] npl of **mouse**.

micro ['maɪkrəu] n (also: **~compu-**

ter) micro-ordinateur m.

microchip ['maɪkrəutʃɪp] n puce f.

microphone ['maɪkrəfəun] n microphone m.

microscope ['maɪkrəskəup] n microscope m.

microwave ['maɪkrəuweɪv] n (also: **~ oven**) four m à micro-ondes.

mid [mɪd] a: **~ May** la mi-mai; **~-afternoon** le milieu de l'après-midi; **in ~ air** en plein ciel; **~day** n midi m.

middle ['mɪdl] n milieu m; (waist) ceinture f, taille f // a du milieu; **in the ~ of the night** au milieu de la nuit; **~-aged** a d'un certain âge; **the M~ Ages** npl le moyen âge; **~-class** a ≈ bourgeois(e); **the ~ class(es)** n(pl) ≈ les classes moyennes; **M~ East** n Proche-Orient m, Moyen-Orient m; **~man** n intermédiaire m; **~ name** n deuxième nom m; **~weight** n (BOXING) poids moyen.

middling ['mɪdlɪŋ] a moyen(ne).

midge [mɪdʒ] n moucheron m.

midget ['mɪdʒɪt] n nain(e).

Midlands ['mɪdləndz] npl comtés du centre de l'Angleterre.

midnight ['mɪdnaɪt] n minuit m.

midriff ['mɪdrɪf] n estomac m, taille f.

midst [mɪdst] n: **in the ~ of** au milieu de.

midsummer [mɪd'sʌmə*] n milieu m de l'été.

midway [mɪd'weɪ] a, ad: **~ (between)** à mi-chemin (entre).

midweek [mɪd'wi:k] n milieu m de la semaine.

midwife ['mɪdwaɪf], pl **midwives** [-vz] n sage-femme f; **~ry** [-wɪfərɪ] n obstétrique f.

might [maɪt] vb see **may** // n puissance f, force f; **~y** a puissant(e).

migraine ['mi:greɪn] n migraine f.

migrant ['maɪgrənt] a (bird) migrateur(trice); (person) migrant(e); nomade; (worker) saisonnier(ère).

migrate [maɪ'greɪt] vi émigrer.

mike [maɪk] n abbr (= microphone) micro m.

mild [maɪld] a doux(douce); (reproach) léger(ère); (illness) bénin(igne).

mildew ['mɪldjuː] n mildiou m.

mildly ['maɪldlɪ] ad doucement; légèrement; **to put it ~** c'est le moins qu'on puisse dire.

mile [maɪl] n mil(l)e m (= 1609 m); **~age** n distance f en milles, ≈ kilométrage m; **~stone** n borne f; (fig) jalon m.

militant ['mɪlɪtnt] a, n militant(e).

military ['mɪlɪtərɪ] a militaire.

milk [mɪlk] n lait m // vt (cow) traire; (fig) dépouiller, plumer; **~ chocolate** n chocolat m au lait; **~man** n laitier m; **~ shake** n milk-shake m; **~y** a lacté(e); (colour) laiteux(euse); **M~y Way** n Voie lactée.

mill [mɪl] n moulin m; (factory) usine f, fabrique f; (spinning ~) filature f; (flour ~) minoterie f // vt moudre, broyer // vi (also: **~ about**) grouiller.

miller ['mɪlə*] n meunier m.

millet ['mɪlɪt] n millet m.

milli... ['mɪlɪ] prefix: **~gram(me)** n milligramme m; **~metre**, (US) **~meter** n millimètre m.

millinery ['mɪlɪnərɪ] n modes fpl.

million ['mɪljən] n million m; **~aire** n millionnaire m.

millstone ['mɪlstəun] n meule f.

milometer [maɪ'lɔmɪtə*] n ≈ compteur m kilométrique.

mime [maɪm] n mime m // vt, vi mimer.

mimic ['mɪmɪk] n imitateur/trice f // vt imiter, contrefaire; **~ry** n imitation f.

min. abbr of **minute(s)**, **minimum**.

mince [mɪns] vt hacher // vi (in walking) marcher à petits pas maniérés // n (Brit CULIN) viande hachée, hachis m; **~meat** n hachis de fruits secs utilisés en pâtisserie; **~ pie** n sorte de tarte aux fruits secs; **~r** n

hachoir m.

mind [maɪnd] n esprit m // vt (attend to, look after) s'occuper de; (be careful) faire attention à; (object to): I don't ~ the noise je ne crains pas le bruit, le bruit ne me dérange pas; **I don't ~** cela ne me dérange pas; it is on my ~ cela me préoccupe; to **my ~** à mon avis or sens; to be out of one's ~ ne plus avoir toute sa raison; to bear sth in ~ tenir compte de qch; to make up one's ~ se décider; ~ **you,** ~ remarquez ~; je vous assure ~; **never ~** ne vous en faites pas; **'~ the step'** attention à la marche'; **~er** n (child~er) gardienne f; (bodyguard) ange gardien (fig); **~ful** a: **~ful of** attentif(ive) à, soucieux(euse) de; **~less** a irréfléchi(e).

mine [maɪn] pronoun le(la) mien(ne), les miens(miennes) // a: this book is ~ ce livre est à moi // n mine f // vt (coal) extraire; (ship, beach) miner.

miner ['maɪnə*] n mineur m.

mineral ['mɪnərəl] a minéral(e) // n minéral m; **~s** npl (Brit: soft drinks) boissons gazeuses (sucrées); **~ water** n eau minérale.

minesweeper ['maɪnswiːpə*] n dragueur m de mines.

mingle ['mɪŋgl] vi: **to ~ with** se mêler à.

miniature ['mɪnətʃə*] a (en) miniature // n miniature f.

minibus ['mɪnɪbʌs] n minibus m.

minimum ['mɪnɪməm] a, n minimum (m).

mining ['maɪnɪŋ] n exploitation minière // a minier(ère); de mineurs.

miniskirt ['mɪnɪskəːt] n mini-jupe f.

minister ['mɪnɪstə*] n (Brit POL) ministre m; (REL) pasteur m // vi: **to ~ to** sb donner ses soins à qn; **to ~ to sb's needs** pourvoir aux besoins de qn; **~ial** [-'tɪərɪəl] a (Brit POL) ministériel(le).

ministry ['mɪnɪstrɪ] n (Brit POL) ministère m; (REL): **to go into the ~**

devenir pasteur.

mink [mɪŋk] n vison m.

minnow ['mɪnəu] n vairon m.

minor ['maɪnə*] a petit(e), de peu d'importance; (MUS) mineur(e) // n (LAW) mineur/e.

minority [maɪ'nɔrɪtɪ] n minorité f.

mint [mɪnt] n (plant) menthe f; (sweet) bonbon m à la menthe // vt (coins) battre; **the (Royal) M~**, (US) **the (US) M~** ≈ l'hôtel de la Monnaie; **in ~ condition** à l'état de neuf.

minus ['maɪnəs] n (also: ~ **sign**) signe m moins // prep moins.

minute a [maɪ'njuːt] minuscule; (detail) minutieux(euse) // n ['mɪnɪt] minute f; (official record) procès-verbal m, compte rendu; **~s** npl procès-verbal.

miracle ['mɪrəkl] n miracle m.

mirage ['mɪrɑːʒ] n mirage m.

mire ['maɪə*] n bourbe f, boue f.

mirror ['mɪrə*] n miroir m, glace f // vt refléter.

mirth [mə:θ] n gaieté f.

misadventure [mɪsəd'ventʃə*] n mésaventure f; **death by ~** décès accidentel.

misapprehension ['mɪsæprɪ'henʃən] n malentendu m, méprise f.

misbehave [mɪsbɪ'heɪv] vi se conduire mal.

miscarriage ['mɪskærɪdʒ] n (MED) fausse couche; **~ of justice** erreur f judiciaire.

miscellaneous [mɪsɪ'leɪnɪəs] a (items) divers(es); (selection) varié(e).

mischief ['mɪstʃɪf] n (naughtiness) sottises fpl; (harm) mal m, dommage m; (maliciousness) méchanceté f; **mischievous** a (naughty) coquin(e), espiègle; (harmful) méchant(e).

misconception ['mɪskən'sepʃən] n idée fausse.

misconduct [mɪs'kɔndʌkt] n inconduite f; **professional ~** faute professionnelle.

misconstrue [mɪskən'struː] vt mal interpréter.

misdeed [mɪs'diːd] n méfait m.

misdemeanour, (US) **misdemeanor** [mɪsdɪ'miːnə*] n écart m de conduite; infraction f.

miser ['maɪzə*] n avare m/f.

miserable ['mɪzərəbl] a malheureux(euse); (wretched) misérable.

miserly ['maɪzəlɪ] a avare.

misery ['mɪzərɪ] n (unhappiness) tristesse f; (pain) souffrances fpl; (wretchedness) misère f.

misfire [mɪs'faɪə*] vi rater; (car engine) avoir des ratés.

misfit ['mɪsfɪt] n (person) inadapté/e.

misfortune [mɪs'fɔːtʃən] n malchance f, malheur m.

misgiving(s) [mɪs'gɪvɪŋ(z)] n(pl) craintes fpl, soupçons mpl.

misguided [mɪs'gaɪdɪd] a malavisé(e).

mishandle [mɪs'hændl] vt (treat roughly) malmener; (mismanage) mal s'y prendre pour faire or résoudre etc.

mishap ['mɪshæp] n mésaventure f.

misinterpret [mɪsɪn'tə:prɪt] vt mal interpréter.

misjudge [mɪs'dʒʌdʒ] vt méjuger, se méprendre sur le compte de.

mislay [mɪs'leɪ] vt irg égarer.

mislead [mɪs'liːd] vt irg induire en erreur; **~ing** a trompeur(euse).

mismanage [mɪs'mænɪdʒ]

misnomer [mɪs'nəumə*] n terme or qualificatif trompeur or peu approprié.

misplace [mɪs'pleɪs] vt égarer.

misprint ['mɪsprɪnt] n faute f d'impression.

Miss [mɪs] n Mademoiselle.

miss [mɪs] vt (fail to get) manquer, rater; (regret the absence of): **I ~ him/it** il/cela me manque // vi manquer // n (shot) coup manqué; **to ~ out** vt (Brit) oublier.

misshapen [mɪs'ʃeɪpən] a difforme.

missile ['mɪsaɪl] n (AVIAT) missile m; (object thrown) projectile m.

missing ['mɪsɪŋ] a manquant(e); (af-

ter escape, disaster: person) dispa-
ru(e); **to go ~** disparaître.

mission ['mɪʃən] n mission f; **~ary**
n missionnaire m/f.

misspent ['mɪs'spent] a: **his ~**
youth sa folle jeunesse.

mist [mɪst] n brume f, brouillard m //
vi (also: **~ over, ~ up**) devenir bru-
meux(euse); (Brit: windows) s'em-
buer.

mistake [mɪs'teɪk] n erreur f, faute f
// vt (irg: like take) mal comprendre; se méprendre sur; **to make a**
~ se tromper, faire une erreur; **~**
by par erreur, par inadvertance; **to**
~ for prendre pour; **~n** a (idea etc)
erroné(e); **to be ~n** faire erreur, se
tromper.

mister ['mɪstə*] n (col) Monsieur m;
see **Mr.**

mistletoe ['mɪsltəu] n gui m.

mistook [mɪs'tuk] pt of **mistake**.

mistress ['mɪstrɪs] n maîtresse f;
(Brit: in primary school) institutrice
f; see **Mrs.**

mistrust [mɪs'trʌst] vt se méfier de.

misty ['mɪstɪ] a brumeux(euse).

misunderstand [mɪsʌndə'stænd] vt,
vi irg mal comprendre; **~ing** n méprise f, malentendu m.

misuse n [mɪs'juːs] mauvais emploi;
(of power) abus m // vt [mɪs'juːz] mal
employer; abuser de.

mitigate ['mɪtɪgeɪt] vt atténuer.

mitt(en) ['mɪt(n)] n mitaine f;
moufle f.

mix [mɪks] vt mélanger // n mélange m // vi mélange m; dosage m;
to ~ up mélanger; (confuse)
confondre; **~ed** a (assorted) assor-
tis(ies); (school etc) mixte; **~ed**
grill n assortiment m de grillades;
~ed-up a (confused) désorienté(e),
embrouillé(e); **~er** n (for food) batteur m, mixeur m; (person): **he is a**
good ~er il est très liant; **~ture** n
assortiment m, mélange m; (MED)
préparation f; **~-up** n confusion f.

moan [məun] n gémissement m // vi
gémir; (col: complain): **to ~**

(about) se plaindre (de).

moat [məut] n fossé m, douves fpl.

mob [mɔb] n foule f; (disorderly) cohue f; (pej): **the ~** la populace // vt
assaillir.

mobile ['məubaɪl] a mobile // n mobile m; **~ home** n caravane f.

mock [mɔk] vt ridiculiser, se moquer
de // a faux(fausse); **~ery** n moque-
rie f, raillerie f.

mod [mɔd] a see **convenience**.

mode [məud] n mode m.

model ['mɔdl] n modèle m; (person:
for fashion) mannequin m; (: for artist) modèle // vt modeler // vi travailler comme mannequin // a (railway:
toy) modèle réduit inv; (child, factory) modèle; **to ~ clothes** présenter
des vêtements.

modem ['məudɛm] n modem m.

moderate a n, ['mɔdərət] modé-
ré(e) // n (POL) modéré/e // vb
['mɔdəreɪt] vi se modérer, se calmer
// vt modérer.

modern ['mɔdən] a moderne; **~ize**
vt moderniser.

modest ['mɔdɪst] a modeste; **~y** n
modestie f.

modicum ['mɔdɪkəm] n: **a ~ of** un
minimum de.

modify ['mɔdɪfaɪ] vt modifier.

mogul ['məugl] n (fig) nabab m.

mohair ['məuhɛə*] n mohair m.

moist [mɔɪst] a humide, moite; **~en**
['mɔɪsn] vt humecter, mouiller légèrement; **~ure** ['mɔɪstʃə*] n humidité f; (on glass) buée f; **~urizer**
['mɔɪstʃəraɪzə*] n produit hydratant.

molar ['məulə*] n molaire f.

molasses [məu'læsɪz] n mélasse f.

mold [məuld] n, vt (US) = **mould**.

mole [məul] n (animal) taupe f;
(spot) grain m de beauté.

molest [məu'lest] vt tracasser; molester.

mollycoddle ['mɔlɪkɔdl] vt chou-
chouter, couver.

molt [məult] vi (US) = **moult**.

molten ['məultən] a fondu(e).

mom [mɔm] n (US) = **mum**.

moment ['məumənt] n moment m, instant m; importance f; **at the ~** à ce moment; **~ary** a momentané(e), passager(ère); **~ous** [-'mentəs] a important(e), capital(e).

momentum [məu'mentəm] n élan m, vitesse acquise; **to gather ~** prendre de la vitesse.

mommy ['mɔmɪ] n (US) = **mummy**.

Monaco ['mɔnəkəu] n Monaco m.

monarch ['mɔnək] n monarque m; **~y** n monarchie f.

monastery ['mɔnəstərɪ] n monastère m.

Monday ['mʌndɪ] n lundi m.

monetary ['mʌnɪtərɪ] a monétaire.

money ['mʌnɪ] n argent m; **to make ~** gagner de l'argent; faire des bénéfices; rapporter; **~lender** n prêteur/euse; **~ order** n mandat m; **~spinner** n (col) mine f d'or (fig).

mongrel ['mʌngrəl] n (dog) bâtard m.

monitor ['mɔnɪtə*] n (SCOL) chef de classe; (TV, COMPUT) moniteur m // vt contrôler.

monk [mʌŋk] n moine m.

monkey ['mʌŋkɪ] n singe m; **~ nut** n (Brit) cacahuète f; **~ wrench** n clé f à molette.

mono... ['mɔnəu] prefix: **~chrome** a monochrome.

monopoly [mə'nɔpəlɪ] n monopole m.

monotone ['mɔnətəun] n ton m (or voix f) monocorde.

monotonous [mə'nɔtənəs] a monotone.

monsoon [mɔn'suːn] n mousson f.

monster ['mɔnstə*] n monstre m.

monstrous ['mɔnstrəs] a (huge) gigantesque; (atrocious) monstrueux(euse), atroce.

month [mʌnθ] n mois m; **~ly** a mensuel(le) // ad mensuellement // n (magazine) mensuel m, publication mensuelle.

monument ['mɔnjumənt] n monument m.

moo [muː] vi meugler, beugler.

mood [muːd] n humeur f, disposition f; **to be in a good/bad ~** être de bonne/mauvaise humeur; **~y** a (variable) d'humeur changeante, lunatique; (sullen) morose, maussade.

moon [muːn] n lune f; **~light** n clair m de lune; **~lighting** n travail m au noir; **~lit** a éclairé(e) par la lune; (night) de lune.

moor [muə*] n lande f // vt (ship) amarrer // vi mouiller.

moorland ['muələnd] n lande f.

moose [muːs] n (pl inv) élan m.

mop [mɔp] n balai m à laver // vt éponger, essuyer; **to ~ up** vt éponger; **~ of hair** tignasse f.

mope [məup] vi avoir le cafard, se morfondre.

moped ['məuped] n cyclomoteur m.

moral ['mɔrl] a moral(e) // n morale f; **~s** npl moralité f.

morale [mɔ'rɑːl] n moral m.

morality [mə'rælɪtɪ] n moralité f.

morass [mə'ræs] n marais m, marécage m.

more [mɔː*] ♦ a 1 (greater in number etc) plus (de), davantage; **~ people/work (than)** plus de gens/de travail (que)

2 (additional) encore de; **do you want (some) ~ tea?** voulez-vous encore du thé?; **I have no or I don't have any ~ money** je n'ai plus d'argent; **it'll take a few ~ weeks** ça prendra encore quelques semaines

♦ pronoun plus, davantage; **~ than 10 plus de 10**; **it cost ~ than we expected** cela a coûté plus que prévu; **I want ~** j'en veux plus or davantage; **is there any ~?** est-ce qu'il en reste?; **there's no ~** il n'y en a plus; **a little ~** un peu plus; **many/much ~** beaucoup plus, bien davantage

♦ ad: **~ dangerous/easily (than)** plus dangereux/facilement (que);

and ~ expensive de plus en plus
cher; ~ or less plus ou moins; ~
than ever plus que jamais.

moreover [mɔː'rəʊvə*] ad de plus.

morning ['mɔːnɪŋ] n matin m; matinée f; **in the** ~ le matin; **7 o'clock in the** ~ 7 heures du matin.

Morocco [mə'rɒkəʊ] n Maroc m.

moron ['mɔːrɒn] n idiot(e), minus m/f.

Morse [mɔːs] n (also: ~ **code**) morse m.

morsel ['mɔːsl] n bouchée f.

mortal ['mɔːtl] a, n mortel(le); ~**ity** [-'tælɪt] n mortalité f.

mortar ['mɔːtə*] n mortier m.

mortgage ['mɔːgɪdʒ] n hypothèque f; (loan) prêt m (or crédit m) hypothécaire; ~ **company** n (US) société f de crédit immobilier.

mortuary ['mɔːtjʊərɪ] n morgue f.

mosaic [məʊ'zeɪɪk] n mosaïque f.

Moscow ['mɒskəʊ] n Moscou m.

Moslem ['mɒzləm] a, n = **Muslim**.

mosque [mɒsk] n mosquée f.

mosquito, ~**es** [mɒs'kiːtəʊ] n moustique m.

moss [mɒs] n mousse f.

most [məʊst] a la plupart de; le plus de // pronoun la plupart // ad le plus; (very) très, extrêmement; **the** ~ (also: + adjective) le plus; ~ **of** la plus grande partie de; ~ **of them** la plupart d'entre eux; **I saw the** (~) ~ j'en ai vu la plupart; c'est moi qui en ai vu le plus; **at the** (**very**) ~ au plus; **to make the** ~ **of** profiter au maximum de; ~**ly** ad surtout, principalement.

MOT n abbr (Brit: = Ministry of Transport): **the** ~ (**test**) la visite technique (annuelle) obligatoire des véhicules à moteur.

motel [məʊ'tɛl] n motel m.

moth [mɒθ] n papillon m de nuit; mite f; ~**ball** n boule f de naphtaline.

mother ['mʌðə*] n mère f // vt (care for) dorloter; ~**hood** n maternité f; ~**-in-law** n belle-mère f; ~**ly** a maternel(le); ~**-of-pearl** n nacre f; ~**-to-be** n future maman; ~**tongue** n langue maternelle.

motion ['məʊʃən] n mouvement m; (gesture) geste m; (at meeting) motion f // vt, vi: **to** ~ (**to**) **sb to do** faire signe à qn de faire; ~**less** a immobile, sans mouvement; ~ **picture** n film m.

motivated ['məʊtɪveɪtɪd] a motivé(e).

motive ['məʊtɪv] n motif m, mobile m.

motley ['mɒtlɪ] a hétéroclite; bigarré(e), bariolé(e).

motor ['məʊtə*] n moteur m; (Brit col: vehicle) auto f // a automoteur(trice); ~**bike** n moto f; ~**boat** n bateau m à moteur; ~**car** n (Brit) automobile f; ~**cycle** n vélomoteur m; ~**cyclist** n motocycliste m/f; ~**ing** n (Brit) tourisme m automobile; ~**ist** n automobiliste m/f; ~**racing** n (Brit) course f automobile; ~**way** n (Brit) autoroute f.

mottled ['mɒtld] a tacheté(e), marbré(e).

motto, ~**es** ['mɒtəʊ] n devise f.

mould, (US) **mold** [məʊld] n moule m; (mildew) moisissure f // vt mouler, modeler; (fig) façonner; ~**er** vi (decay) moisir; ~**y** a moisi(e).

moult, (US) **molt** [məʊlt] vi muer.

mound [maʊnd] n monticule m, tertre m.

mount [maʊnt] n mont m, montagne f; (horse) monture f; (for jewel etc) monture f // vt monter // vi (also: ~ **up**) s'élever, monter.

mountain ['maʊntɪn] n montagne f // cpd de (la) montagne; ~**eer** [-'nɪə*] n alpiniste m/f; ~**eering** [-'nɪərɪŋ] n alpinisme m; ~**ous** a montagneux(euse); ~**side** n flanc m or versant m de la montagne.

mourn [mɔːn] vt pleurer // vi: **to** ~ (**for**) se lamenter (sur); ~ **er** n parent(e) or ami(e) du défunt; personne f en deuil; ~**ful** a triste, lugubre; ~**ing** n deuil m // cpd (dress) de deuil; **in** ~**ing** en deuil.

mouse [maus], *pl* **mice** *n* (*also* COMPUT) souris *f*; ~**trap** *n* souricière *f*.

mousse [mu:s] *n* mousse *f*.

moustache [məsˈtɑːʃ] *n* moustache(s) *f(pl)*.

mousy [ˈmausɪ] *a* (*person*) effacé(e); (*hair*) d'un châtain terne.

mouth, ~**s** [mauθ, -ðz] *n* bouche *f*; (*of dog, cat*) gueule *f*; (*of river*) embouchure *f*; (*of bottle*) goulot *m*; (*opening*) orifice *m*; ~**ful** *n* bouchée *f*; ~ **organ** *n* harmonica *m*; ~**piece** *n* (*of musical instrument*) embouchure *f*; (*spokesman*) porteparole *m inv*; ~**wash** *n* eau de bouche; ~**watering** *a* qui met l'eau à la bouche.

movable [ˈmuːvəbl] *a* mobile.

move [muːv] *n* (*movement*) mouvement *m*; (*in game*) coup *m*; (*: turn to play*) tour *m*; (*change of house*) déménagement *m* // *vt* déplacer, bouger; (*emotionally*) émouvoir // *vi* (POL: *resolution etc*) proposer // *vi* (*gen*) bouger, remuer; (*traffic*) circuler; (*also*: ~ **house**) déménager; **to** ~ **towards** se diriger vers; **to** ~ **sb to do sth** pousser *or* inciter qn à faire qch; **to get a** ~ **on** se dépêcher, se remuer; **to** ~ **about** *or* **around** *vi* (*fidget*) remuer; (*travel*) voyager, se déplacer; **to** ~ **along** *vi* se pousser; **to** ~ **away** *vi* s'en aller, s'éloigner; **to** ~ **back** *vi* revenir, retourner; **to** ~ **forward** *vi* avancer // *vt* avancer; (*people*) faire avancer; **to** ~ **in** *vi* (*to a house*) emménager; **to** ~ **on** *vi* se remettre en route // *vt* (*on-lookers*) faire circuler; **to** ~ **out** *vi* (*of house*) déménager; **to** ~ **over** *vi* se pousser, se déplacer; **to** ~ **up** *vi* avancer; (*employee*) avoir de l'avancement.

movement [ˈmuːvmənt] *n* mouvement *m*.

movie [ˈmuːvɪ] *n* film *m*; **the** ~**s** le cinéma; ~ **camera** *n* caméra *f*.

moving [ˈmuːvɪŋ] *a* en mouvement;

émouvant(e).

mow, *pt* **mowed**, *pp* **mowed** *or* **mown** [məu, -n] *vt* faucher; (*lawn*) tondre; **to** ~ **down** *vt* faucher; ~**er** *n* (*also*: **lawnmower**) tondeuse *f* à gazon.

MP *n abbr of* **member of parliament.**

m.p.h. *abbr* = **miles per hour** (60 *m.p.h.* = 96 *km/h*).

Mr, Mr. [ˈmistəʳ] *n*: ~ **Smith** Monsieur Smith, M. Smith.

Mrs, Mr. [ˈmisiz] *n*: ~ **Smith** Madame Smith, Mme Smith.

Ms, Ms. [miz] *n* (= *Miss or Mrs*): ~ **Smith** ≈ Madame Smith, Mme Smith.

M.Sc. *abbr see* **master.**

much [mʌtʃ] *a* beaucoup de // *ad, pronoun* beaucoup; **how** ~ **is it?** combien est-ce que ça coûte?; **too** ~ trop (de); **as** ~ **as** autant de.

muck [mʌk] *n* (*mud*) boue *f*; (*dirt*) ordures *fpl*; **to** ~ **about** *or* **around** *vi* (*col*) faire l'imbécile; (*waste time*) traînasser; **to** ~ **up** *vt* (*col*: *ruin*) gâcher, esquinter.

mud [mʌd] *n* boue *f*.

muddle [ˈmʌdl] *n* pagaille *f*; désordre *m*, fouillis *m* // *vt* (*also*: ~ **up**) brouiller, embrouiller; **to be in a** ~ (*person*) ne plus savoir où l'on en est; **to** ~ **through** *vi* se débrouiller.

muddy [ˈmʌdɪ] *a* boueux(euse).

mud: ~**guard** *n* garde-boue *m inv*; ~**slinging** *n* médisance *f*, dénigrement *m*.

muff [mʌf] *n* manchon *m* // *vt* (*chance*) rater, louper.

muffin [ˈmʌfɪn] *n* petit pain rond et plat.

muffle [ˈmʌfl] *vt* (*sound*) assourdir, étouffer; (*against cold*) emmitoufler.

muffler [ˈmʌfləʳ] *n* (US AUT) silencieux *m*.

mug [mʌg] *n* (*cup*) grande tasse (*sans soucoupe*), chope *f*; (*: for beer*) chope; (*col*: *face*) bouille *f*; (*: fool*) poire *f* // *vt* (*assault*) agresser; ~**ging** *n* agression *f*.

muggy ['mʌgɪ] a lourd(e), moite.

mule [mju:l] n mule f.

mull [mʌl]: to ~ over vt réfléchir à.

mulled [mʌld] a: ~ wine vin chaud.

multi-level ['mʌltɪlevl] a (US) = **multistorey**.

multiple ['mʌltɪpl] a, n multiple (m); ~ **sclerosis** n sclérose f en plaques.

multiplication [mʌltɪplɪ'keɪʃən] n multiplication f.

multiply ['mʌltɪplaɪ] vt multiplier // vi se multiplier.

multistorey ['mʌltɪ'stɔ:rɪ] a (Brit: building) à étages; (: car park) à étages or niveaux multiples.

mum [mʌm] n (Brit) maman f // a: to keep ~ ne pas souffler mot.

mumble ['mʌmbl] vt, vi marmotter, marmonner.

mummy ['mʌmɪ] n (Brit: mother) maman f; (embalmed) momie f.

mumps [mʌmps] n oreillons mpl.

munch [mʌntʃ] vt, vi mâcher.

mundane [mʌn'deɪn] a banal(e), terre à terre inv.

municipal [mju:'nɪsɪpl] a municipal(e).

mural ['mjuərl] n peinture murale.

murder ['mə:də*] n meurtre m, assassinat m // vt assassiner; ~**er** n meurtrier m, assassin m; ~**ous** a meurtrier(ère).

murky ['mə:kɪ] a sombre, ténébreux(euse).

murmur ['mə:mə*] n murmure m // vt, vi murmurer.

muscle ['mʌsl] n muscle m; to ~ in vi s'imposer, s'immiscer.

muscular ['mʌskjulə*] a musculaire; (person, arm) musclé(e).

muse [mju:z] vi méditer, songer.

museum [mju:'zɪəm] n musée m.

mushroom ['mʌʃrum] n champignon m.

music ['mju:zɪk] n musique f; ~**al** a musical(e); (person) musicien(ne) // n (show) comédie musicale; ~**al instrument** n instrument m de musique; ~**ian** [-'zɪʃən] n musicien/ne.

Muslim ['mʌzlɪm] a, n musulman/e.

muslin ['mʌzlɪn] n mousseline f.

mussel ['mʌsl] n moule f.

must [mʌst] auxiliary vb (obligation): I ~ do it je dois le faire, il faut que je le fasse; (probability): he ~ be there by now il doit y être maintenant, il y est probablement maintenant; I ~ have made a mistake j'ai dû me tromper // n nécessité f, impératif m; it's a ~ c'est indispensable.

mustard ['mʌstəd] n moutarde f.

muster ['mʌstə*] vt rassembler.

mustn't ['mʌsnt] = must not.

musty ['mʌstɪ] a qui sent le moisi or le renfermé.

mute [mju:t] a, n muet(te).

muted ['mju:tɪd] a assourdi(e); voilé(e).

mutiny ['mju:tɪnɪ] n mutinerie f.

mutter ['mʌtə*] vt, vi marmonner, marmotter.

mutton ['mʌtn] n mouton m.

mutual ['mju:tʃuəl] a mutuel(le), réciproque.

muzzle ['mʌzl] n museau m; (protective device) muselière f; (of gun) gueule f.

my [maɪ] a mon(ma), mes pl; ~ **house/ car/gloves** ma maison/mon auto/mes gants; I've washed ~ **hair/cut** ~ **finger** je me suis lavé les cheveux/coupé le doigt.

myself [maɪ'self] pronoun (reflexive) me; (emphatic) moi-même; (after prep) moi; see also **oneself**.

mysterious [mɪs'tɪərɪəs] a mystérieux(euse).

mystery ['mɪstərɪ] n mystère m.

mystify ['mɪstɪfaɪ] vt mystifier; (puzzle) ébahir.

myth [mɪθ] n mythe m; ~**ology** [mɪ'θɔlədʒɪ] n mythologie f.

N

n/a *abbr = not applicable.*

nab [næb] *vt* pincer, attraper.

nag [næg] *vt* (*person*) être toujours après, reprendre sans arrêt; **~ging** *a* (*doubt, pain*) persistant(e).

nail [neɪl] *n* (*human*) ongle *m*; (*metal*) clou *m* // *vt* clouer; **to ~ sb down to a date/price** contraindre qn à accepter ou donner une date/un prix; **~brush** *n* brosse *f* à ongles; **~file** *n* lime *f* à ongles; **~ polish** *n* vernis *m* à ongles; **~ polish remover** *n* dissolvant *m*; **~ scissors** *npl* ciseaux *mpl* à ongles; **~ varnish** *n* (*Brit*) = **~ polish**.

naïve [naɪ'iːv] *a* naïf(ïve).

naked ['neɪkɪd] *a* nu(e).

name [neɪm] *n* nom *m*; réputation *f* // *vt* nommer; citer; (*price, date*) fixer, donner; **by ~** par son nom; **~less** *a* sans nom; (*witness, contributor*) anonyme; **~ly** *ad* à savoir; **~sake** *n* homonyme *m*.

nanny ['nænɪ] *n* bonne *f* d'enfants.

nap [næp] *n* (*sleep*) (petit) somme; **to be caught ~ping** être pris à l'improviste ou en défaut.

nape [neɪp] *n*: **~ of the neck** nuque *f*.

napkin ['næpkɪn] *n* serviette *f* (de table).

nappy ['næpɪ] *n* (*Brit*) couche *f* (*gen pl*); **~ rash** *n*: **to have ~** avoir les fesses rouges.

narcissus, *pl* **narcissi** [naː'sɪsəs, -saɪ] *n* narcisse *m*.

narcotic [naː'kɒtɪk] *n* (*drug*) stupéfiant *m*; (*MED*) narcotique *m* // *a* narcotique.

narrative ['nærətɪv] *n* récit *m* // *a* narratif(ive).

narrow ['nærəu] *a* étroit(e); (*fig*) restreint(e), limité(e) // *vi* devenir plus étroit, se rétrécir; **to have a ~ escape** l'échapper belle; **to ~ sth down to** réduire qch à; **~ly** *ad*: he

~ly missed injury/the tree il a failli se blesser/rentrer dans l'arbre; **~-minded** *a* à l'esprit étroit, borné(e).

nasty ['naːstɪ] *a* (*person*) méchant(e); très désagréable; (*smell*) dégoûtant(e); (*wound, situation*) mauvais(e).

nation ['neɪʃən] *n* nation *f*.

national ['næʃənl] *a* national(e) *n* (*abroad*) ressortissant(e); (*when home*) national(e); **~ dress** *n* costume national; **N~ Health Service (NHS)** *n* (*Brit*) service national de santé, ≈ Sécurité Sociale; **N~ Insurance** *n* (*Brit*) ≈ Sécurité Sociale; **~ism** *n* nationalisme *m*; **~ity** [-'nælɪtɪ] *n* nationalité *f*; **~ize** *vt* nationaliser; **~ly** *ad* du point de vue national; dans le pays entier.

nation-wide ['neɪʃənwaɪd] *a* s'étendant à l'ensemble du pays; (*problem*) à l'échelle du pays entier // *ad* à travers ou dans tout le pays.

native ['neɪtɪv] *n* habitant(e) du pays, autochtone *m/f*; (*in colonies*) indigène *m/f* // *a* du pays, indigène; (*country*) natal(e); (*ability*) inné(e); **a ~ of Russia** une personne originaire de Russie; **a ~ speaker of French** une personne de langue maternelle française; **~ language** *n* langue maternelle.

NATO ['neɪtəu] *n abbr* (= *North Atlantic Treaty Organization*) O.T.A.N. *f*.

natural ['nætʃrəl] *a* naturel(le); **~ gas** *n* gaz naturel; **~ize** *vt* naturaliser; (*plant*) acclimater; **to become ~ized** (*person*) se faire naturaliser; **~ly** *ad* naturellement.

nature ['neɪtʃə*] *n* nature *f*; **by ~** par tempérament, de nature.

naught [nɔːt] *n* = **nought**.

naughty ['nɔːtɪ] *a* (*child*) vilain(e), pas sage; (*story, film*) polisson(ne).

nausea ['nɔːsɪə] *n* nausée *f*; **nauseate** ['nɔːsɪeɪt] *vt* écœurer, donner la nausée à.

naval ['neɪvl] *a* naval(e); **~ officer** *n* officier *m* de marine.

nave [neɪv] n nef f.

navel ['neɪvl] n nombril m.

navigate ['nævɪgeɪt] vt diriger, piloter // vi naviguer; **navigation** [-'geɪʃən] n navigation f; **navigator** n navigateur m.

navvy ['nævɪ] n (Brit) terrassier m.

navy ['neɪvɪ] n marine f; ~(**-blue**) a bleu marine inv.

Nazi ['nɑːtsɪ] n Nazi/e.

NB abbr (= nota bene) NB.

near [nɪə*] a proche // ad près // prep (also: ~ **to**) près de // vt approcher de; ~**by** [nɪə'baɪ] a proche // ad tout près, à proximité; ~**ly** ad presque; **I** ~**ly fell** j'ai failli tomber; ~ **miss** n collision évitée de justesse; (when aiming) coup manqué de peu or de justesse; ~**side** n (AUT: right-hand drive) côté m gauche; ~**-sighted** a myope.

neat [niːt] a (person, work) soigné(e); (room etc) bien tenu(e) or rangé(e); (solution, plan) habile; (spirits) pur(e); ~**ly** ad avec soin or ordre; habilement.

necessarily ['nesɪsrɪlɪ] ad nécessairement.

necessary ['nesɪsərɪ] a nécessaire.

necessity [nɪ'sesɪtɪ] n nécessité f; chose nécessaire or essentielle.

neck [nek] n cou m; (of horse, garment) encolure f; (of bottle) goulot m // vi (col) se peloter; ~ **and** ~ à égalité.

necklace ['neklɪs] n collier m.

neckline ['neklaɪn] n encolure f.

necktie ['nektaɪ] n cravate f.

need [niːd] n besoin m // vt avoir besoin de; **to** ~ **to do** devoir faire; avoir besoin de faire; **you don't** ~ **to go** vous n'avez pas besoin or vous n'êtes pas obligé de partir.

needle ['niːdl] n aiguille f // vt asticoter, tourmenter.

needless ['niːdlɪs] a inutile.

needlework ['niːdlwəːk] n (activity) travaux mpl d'aiguille; (object) ouvrage m.

needn't ['niːdnt] = **need not**.

needy ['niːdɪ] a nécessiteux(euse).

negative ['negətɪv] n (PHOT, ELEC) négatif m; (LING) terme m de négation // a négatif(ive).

neglect [nɪ'glekt] vt négliger // n (of person, duty, garden) le fait de négliger; (state of) ~ abandon m.

negligee ['neglɪʒeɪ] n déshabillé m.

negligence ['neglɪdʒəns] n négligence f.

negotiate [nɪ'gəʊʃɪeɪt] vi, vt négocier; **negotiation** [-'eɪʃən] n négociation f, pourparlers mpl.

Negro ['niːgrəʊ] a (gen) noir(e); (music, arts) nègre, noir // n (pl: ~es) Noir/e.

neigh [neɪ] vi hennir.

neighbour, (US) **neighbor** ['neɪbə*] n voisin/e; ~**hood** n quartier m; voisinage m; ~**ing** a voisin(e), avoisinant(e); ~**ly** a obligeant(e); (relations) de bon voisinage.

neither ['naɪðə*] a, pronoun aucun(e) (des deux), ni l'un(e) ni l'autre // cj: **I didn't move and** ~ **did Claude** je n'ai pas bougé, (et) Claude non plus; ..., ~ **did I refuse** ..., (et or mais) je n'ai pas non plus refusé // ad: ~ **good nor bad** ni bon ni mauvais.

neon ['niːən] n néon m; ~ **light** n lampe f au néon.

nephew ['nevjuː] n neveu m.

nerve [nəːv] n nerf m; (fig) sangfroid m, courage m; aplomb m, toupet m; **to have a fit of** ~**s** avoir le trac; ~**-racking** a angoissant(e).

nervous ['nəːvəs] a nerveux(euse); inquiet(ète), plein(e) d'appréhension; ~ **breakdown** n dépression nerveuse.

nest [nest] n nid m // vi (se) nicher, faire son nid; ~ **egg** n (fig) bas m de laine, magot m.

nestle ['nesl] vi se blottir.

net [net] n filet m // a net(te) // vt (fish etc) prendre au filet; (profit) rapporter; ~**ball** n netball m; ~ **curtains** npl voilages mpl.

Netherlands ['neðələndz] *npl*: the ~ les Pays-Bas *mpl*.

nett [net] *a* = **net**.

netting ['netiŋ] *n (for fence etc)* treillis *m*, grillage *m*.

nettle ['netl] *n* ortie *f*.

network ['netwɜːk] *n* réseau *m*.

neurotic [njuə'rɒtik] *a, n* névrosé(e).

neuter ['njuːtə*] *a, n* neutre (*m*) // *vt (cat etc)* châtrer, couper.

neutral ['njuːtrəl] *a* neutre // *n (AUT)* point mort; ~**ize** *vt* neutraliser.

never ['nevə*] *ad* (ne ...) jamais; ~ **again** plus jamais; *see also* **mind**; ~-**ending** *a* interminable; ~**theless** [nevəðə'les] *ad* néanmoins, malgré tout.

new [njuː] *a* neuf(neuve); *(brand new)* neuf(neuve); ~-**born** *a* nouveau-né(e); ~-**comer** ['njuːkʌmə*] *n* nouveau venu/nouvelle venue; ~-**fangled** ['njuːfæŋgld] *a (pej)* ultra-moderne (et farfelu(e)); ~-**found** *a* de fraîche date; *(friend)* nouveau(nouvelle); ~**ly** *ad* nouvellement, récemment; ~**ly-weds** *npl* jeunes mariés *mpl*.

news [njuːz] *n* nouvelle(s) *f(pl)*; *(RADIO, TV)* informations *fpl*, actualités *fpl*; **a piece of** ~ une nouvelle; ~ **agency** *n* agence *f* de presse; ~-**agent** *n (Brit)* marchand *m* de journaux; ~**caster** *n* présentateur/trice; ~**dealer** *n (US)* = ~-**agent**; ~ **flash** *n* flash *m* d'information; ~**letter** *n* bulletin *m*; ~**paper** *n* journal *m*; ~**print** *n* papier *m* (de) journal; ~**reader** *n* = ~**caster**; ~**reel** *n* actualités (filmées) *fpl*; ~ **stand** *n* kiosque *m* à journaux.

newt [njuːt] *n* triton *m*.

New Year [njuː'jɪə*] *n* Nouvel An; ~'**s Day** *n* le jour de l'An; ~'**s Eve** *n* la Saint-Sylvestre.

New Zealand [njuː'ziːlənd] *n* la Nouvelle-Zélande; ~**er** *n* Néo-zélandais/e.

next [nekst] *a (seat, room)* voisin(e), d'à côté; *(meeting, bus stop)* sui-vant(e); *prochain(e)* // *ad* à la fois sui-vante; la prochaine fois; *(after-wards)* ensuite; the ~ **day** le lende-main, le jour suivant *or* d'après; ~ **year** l'année prochaine; **when do we meet** ~? quand nous revoyons-nous?; ~ **door** *ad* à côté; ~-**of-kin** *n* parent le plus proche; ~ **to** *prep* à côté de; ~ **to nothing** pres-que rien.

NHS *n abbr of* National Health Service.

nib [nib] *n (of pen)* (bec *m* de) plume *f*.

nibble ['nibl] *vt* grignoter.

nice [nais] *a (holiday, trip)* agréable; *(flat, picture)* joli(e); *(person)* gen-til(le); *(distinction, point)* subtil(e); ~-**looking** *a* joli(e); ~**ly** *ad* agréa-blement; joliment; gentiment; subti-lement.

niceties ['naisitiz] *npl* subtilités *fpl*.

nick [nik] *n* encoche *f* // *vt (col)* fau-cher, piquer; **in the** ~ **of time** juste à temps.

nickel ['nikl] *n* nickel *m*; *(US)* pièce de 5 cents.

nickname ['nikneim] *n* surnom *m* // *vt* surnommer.

niece [niːs] *n* nièce *f*.

Nigeria [nai'dʒiəriə] *n* Nigéria *m or f*.

nigger ['nigə*] *n (col!: highly offen-sive)* nègre *m*, négresse *f*.

niggling ['nigliŋ] *a* tatillon(ne).

night [nait] *n* nuit *f*; *(evening)* soir *m*; **at** ~ la nuit; **by** ~ de nuit; **the** ~ **before last** avant-hier soir; ~**cap** *n* boisson prise avant le coucher; ~ **club** *n* boîte *f* de nuit; ~**dress** *n* chemise *f* de nuit; ~**fall** *n* tombée *f* de la nuit; ~**gown** *n*, ~**ie** ['naiti] *n* chemise *f* de nuit.

nightingale ['naitiŋgeil] *n* rossignol *m*.

night life *n* vie *f* nocturne.

nightly ['naitli] *a* de chaque nuit *or* soir; *(by night)* nocturne // *ad* chaque nuit *or* soir; nuitamment.

nightmare ['naitmeə*] *n* cauchemar *m*.

night: ~ **porter** n gardien de nuit, concierge m de service la nuit; ~ **school** n cours mpl du soir; ~ **shift** n équipe f de nuit; ~**time** n nuit f.

nil [nɪl] n rien m; (Brit SPORT) zéro m.

Nile [naɪl] n: the ~ le Nil.

nimble ['nɪmbl] a agile.

nine [naɪn] num neuf; ~**teen** num dix-neuf; ~**ty** num quatre-vingt-dix.

ninth [naɪnθ] num neuvième.

nip [nɪp] vt pincer.

nipple ['nɪpl] n (ANAT) mamelon m, bout m du sein.

nitrogen ['naɪtrədʒən] n azote m.

no [nəu] ♦ ad (opposite of 'yes') non; **are you coming?** - ~ **(I'm not)** est-ce que vous venez? - non; **would you like some more?** - ~ **thank you** vous en voulez encore? - non merci
♦ a (not any) pas de, aucun(e) (used with 'ne'); **I have** ~ **money/books** je n'ai pas d'argent/de livres; ~ **student would have done it** aucun étudiant ne l'aurait fait; '~ **smoking**' 'défense de fumer'; '~ **dogs**' 'les chiens ne sont pas admis'
♦ n (pl ~**es**) non m.

nobility [nəu'bɪlɪtɪ] n noblesse f.

noble ['nəubl] a noble.

nobody ['nəubədɪ] pronoun personne (with negative).

nod [nɔd] vi faire un signe de la tête (affirmatif ou amical); (sleep) somnoler // vt: **to** ~ **one's head** faire un signe de la tête; (in agreement) faire signe que oui // n signe m de (la) tête; **to** ~ **off** vi s'assoupir.

noise [nɔɪz] n bruit m; **noisy** a bruyant(e).

nominal ['nɔmɪnl] a (rent, fee) symbolique; (value) nominal(e).

nominate ['nɔmɪneɪt] vt (propose) proposer; (elect) nommer.

nominee [nɔmɪ'ni:] n candidat agréé; personne nommée.

non... [nɔn] prefix non-; ~**alcoholic** a non-alcoolisé(e); ~**committal** ['nɔnkə'mɪtl] a évasif(ive).

nondescript ['nɔndɪskrɪpt] a quelconque, indéfinissable.

none [nʌn] pronoun aucun/e; ~ **of you** aucun d'entre vous, personne parmi vous; **I've** ~ **left** je n'en ai plus; **he's** ~ **the worse for it** il ne s'en porte pas plus mal.

nonentity [nɔ'nentɪtɪ] n personne insignifiante.

nonetheless [nʌnðə'les] ad néanmoins.

non: ~**existent** a inexistant(e); ~**fiction** n littérature f non-romanesque.

nonplussed [nɔn'plʌst] a perplexe.

nonsense ['nɔnsəns] n absurdités fpl, idioties fpl; ~! ne dites pas d'idioties!

non: ~**smoker** n non-fumeur m; ~**stick** qui n'attache pas; ~**stop** a direct(e), sans arrêt (or escale) // ad sans arrêt.

noodles ['nu:dlz] npl nouilles fpl.

nook [nuk] n: ~**s and crannies** recoins mpl.

noon [nu:n] n midi m.

no one ['nəuwʌn] pronoun = **nobody**.

noose [nu:s] n nœud coulant; (hangman's) corde f.

nor [nɔ:*] cj = **neither** // ad see **neither**.

norm [nɔ:m] n norme f.

normal ['nɔ:ml] a normal(e); ~**ly** ad normalement.

Normandy ['nɔ:məndɪ] n Normandie f.

north [nɔ:θ] n nord m // a du nord, nord inv // ad au or vers le nord; **N~ America** n Amérique f du Nord; ~**east** n nord-est m; ~**erly** ['nɔ:ðəlɪ] a du nord; ~**ern** ['nɔ:ðən] a du nord, septentrional(e); **N~ern Ireland** n Irlande f du Nord; **N~ Pole** n pôle m Nord; **N~ Sea** n mer f du Nord;

~ward(s) ['nɔːwəd(z)] *ad* vers le nord; **~-west** *n* nord-ouest *m*.

Norway ['nɔːweɪ] *n* Norvège *f*.

Norwegian [nɔː'wiːdʒən] *a* norvégien(ne) // *n* Norvégien/ne; (*LING*) norvégien *m*.

nose [nəuz] *n* nez *m*; (*fig*) flair *m* // *vi*: **to ~ about** fouiner or fureter (partout); **~-dive** *n* (descente *f* en) piqué *m*; **~y** *a* = **nosy**.

nostalgia [nɔs'tældʒɪə] *n* nostalgie *f*.

nostril ['nɔstrɪl] *n* narine *f*; (*of horse*) naseau *m*.

nosy ['nəuzɪ] *a* curieux(euse).

not [nɔt] *ad* (ne ...) pas; **he is ~ or isn't here** il n'est pas ici; **you must ~ or you mustn't do that** tu ne dois pas faire ça; **it's too late, isn't it ~** il est trop tard, n'est-ce pas?; **~ yet/now** pas encore/maintenant; **~ at all** pas du tout; *see also* **all**, **only**.

notably ['nəutəblɪ] *ad* en particulier; (*markedly*) spécialement.

notary ['nəutərɪ] *n* (*also*: **~ public**) notaire *m*.

notch [nɔtʃ] *n* encoche *f*.

note [nəut] *n* note *f*; (*letter*) mot *m*; (*banknote*) billet *m* // *vt* (*also*: **~ down**) noter; (*notice*) constater; **~book** *n* carnet *m*; **~d** [nəutɪd] *a* réputé(e); **~pad** *n* bloc-notes *m*; **~paper** *n* papier *m* à lettres.

nothing ['nʌθɪŋ] *n* rien *m*; **he does ~** il ne fait rien; **~ new** rien de nouveau; **for ~** (*free*) pour rien, gratuitement.

notice ['nəutɪs] *n* avis *m*; (*of leaving*) congé *m* // *vt* remarquer, s'apercevoir de; **to take ~ of** prêter attention à; **to bring sth to sb's ~** porter qch à la connaissance de qn; **at short ~** dans un délai très court; **until further ~** jusqu'à nouvel ordre; **to hand in one's ~** donner sa démission, démissionner; **~able** *a* visible; **~ board** *n* (*Brit*) panneau *m* d'affichage.

notify ['nəutɪfaɪ] *vt*: **to ~ sth to sb** notifier qch à qn; **to ~ sb of sth**

avertir qn de qch.

notion ['nəuʃən] *n* idée *f*; (*concept*) notion *f*.

notorious [nəu'tɔːrɪəs] *a* notoire (*souvent en mal*).

notwithstanding [nɔtwiθ'stændɪŋ] *ad* néanmoins // *prep* en dépit de.

nought [nɔːt] *n* zéro *m*.

noun [naun] *n* nom *m*.

nourish ['nʌrɪʃ] *vt* nourrir; **~ing** *a* nourrissant(e); **~ment** *n* nourriture *f*.

novel ['nɔvl] *n* roman *m* // *a* nouveau(nouvelle), original(e); **~ist** *n* romancier *m*; **~ty** *n* nouveauté *f*.

November [nəu'vembə*] *n* novembre *m*.

now [nau] *ad* maintenant // *cj*: **~ (that)** maintenant que; **right ~** tout de suite; **by ~** à l'heure qu'il est; **just ~:** **I saw her just ~** je viens de la voir, je l'ai vue à l'instant; **I'll read it just ~** je vais le lire à l'instant or dès maintenant; **~ and then, ~ and again** de temps en temps; **from ~ on** dorénavant; **~adays** ['nauədeɪz] *ad* de nos jours.

nowhere ['nəuwɛə*] *ad* nulle part.

nozzle ['nɔzl] *n* (*of hose*) jet *m*, lance *f*.

nuclear ['njuːklɪə*] *a* nucléaire.

nucleus, *pl* **nuclei** ['njuːklɪəs, 'njuːklɪaɪ] *n* noyau *m*.

nude [njuːd] *a* nu(e) // *n* (*ART*) nu *m*; **in the ~** (tout(e)) nu(e).

nudge [nʌdʒ] *vt* donner un (petit) coup de coude à.

nudist ['njuːdɪst] *n* nudiste *m/f*.

nuisance ['njuːsns] *n*: **it's a ~** c'est (très) ennuyeux or gênant; **he's a ~** il est assommant or casse-pieds; **what a ~!** quelle barbe!

null [nʌl] *a*: **~ and void** nul(le) et non avenu(e).

numb [nʌm] *a* engourdi(e).

number ['nʌmbə*] *n* nombre *m*; (*numeral*) chiffre *m*; (*of house, car, telephone, newspaper*) numéro *m* // *vt* numéroter; (*include*) compter; **a ~ of** un certain nombre de; **to be ~ed**

among compter parmi; **they were seven in** ~ ils étaient (au nombre de) sept; ~ **plate** n (Brit AUT) plaque f minéralogique or d'immatriculation.

numeral ['nju:mərəl] n chiffre m.

numerate ['nju:mərɪt] a: **to be** ~ avoir des notions d'arithmétique.

numerical [nju:'mɛrɪkl] a numérique.

numerous ['nju:mərəs] a nombreux(euse).

nun [nʌn] n religieuse f.

nurse [nə:s] n infirmière f // vt (patient, cold) soigner; (baby: Brit) bercer (dans ses bras); (: US) allaiter, nourrir.

nursery ['nə:sərɪ] n (room) nursery f; (institution) pouponnière f; (for plants) pépinière f; ~ **rhyme** n comptine f, chansonnette f pour enfants; ~ **school** n école maternelle; ~ **slope** n (Brit SKI) piste f pour débutants.

nursing ['nə:sɪŋ] n (profession) profession f d'infirmière; ~ **home** n clinique f; maison f de convalescence.

nurture ['nə:tʃə] vt élever.

nut [nʌt] n (of metal) écrou m; (fruit) noix f, noisette f, cacahuète f (terme générique en anglais); **he's** ~**s** (col) il est dingue; ~**crackers** npl casse-noix m inv, casse-noisette(s) m.

nutmeg ['nʌtmɛg] n (noix f) muscade f.

nutritious [nju:'trɪʃəs] a nutritif(ive), nourrissant(e).

nutshell ['nʌtʃɛl] n coquille f de noix; **in a** ~ en un mot.

nylon ['naɪlɔn] n nylon m // a de or en nylon.

O

oak [əuk] n chêne m // a de or en (bois de) chêne.

O.A.P. abbr of **old-age pensioner**.

oar [ɔ:*] n aviron m, rame f.

oasis, pl **oases** [əu'eɪsɪs] n oasis f.

oath [əuθ] n serment m; (swear word) juron m.

oatmeal ['əutmi:l] n flocons mpl d'avoine.

oats [əuts] n avoine f.

obedience [ə'bi:dɪəns] n obéissance f.

obedient [ə'bi:dɪənt] a obéissant(e).

obey [ə'beɪ] vt obéir à; (instructions) se conformer à // vi obéir.

obituary [ə'bɪtjuərɪ] n nécrologie f.

object n ['ɔbdʒɪkt] objet m; (purpose) but m, objet; (LING) complément m d'objet // vi [əb'dʒɛkt]: **to** ~ **to** (attitude) désapprouver; (proposal) protester contre; **expense is no** ~ l'argent n'est pas un problème; **I** ~! je proteste!; **he** ~**ed that ...** il a fait valoir or a objecté que ...; ~**ion** [əb'dʒɛkʃən] n objection f; (drawback) inconvénient m; ~**ionable** [əb'dʒɛkʃənəbl] a très désagréable; choquant(e); ~**ive** n objectif m // a objectif(ive).

obligation [ɔblɪ'geɪʃən] n obligation f, devoir m; (debt) dette f (de reconnaissance); **without** ~ sans engagement.

oblige [ə'blaɪdʒ] vt (force): **to** ~ **sb to do** obliger or forcer qn à faire; (do a favour) rendre service à, obliger; **to be** ~**d to sb for sth** être obligé(e) à qn de qch; **obliging** a obligeant(e), serviable.

oblique [ə'bli:k] a oblique; (allusion) indirect(e).

obliterate [ə'blɪtəreɪt] vt effacer.

oblivion [ə'blɪvɪən] n oubli m.

oblivious [ə'blɪvɪəs] a: ~ **of** oublieux(euse) de.

oblong ['ɔblɔŋ] a oblong(ue) // n rectangle m.

obnoxious [əb'nɔkʃəs] a odieux (euse); (smell) nauséabond(e).

oboe ['əubəu] n hautbois m.

obscene [əb'si:n] a obscène.

obscure [əb'skjuə*] a obscur(e) // vt obscurcir; (hide: sun) cacher.

observant [əb'zə:vnt] a observateur(trice).

observation [ɔbzə'veɪʃən] n observation f; (by police etc) surveillance f.

observatory [əb'zə:vətrɪ] n observatoire m.

observe [əb'zə:v] vt observer; (remark) faire observer ou remarquer; **~r** n observateur/trice.

obsess [əb'sɛs] vt obséder; **~ive** a obsédant(e).

obsolescence [ɔbsə'lɛsns] n vieillissement m.

obsolete ['ɔbsəli:t] a dépassé(e); démodé(e).

obstacle ['ɔbstəkl] n obstacle m.

obstinate ['ɔbstɪnɪt] a obstiné(e); (pain, cold) persistant(e).

obstruct [əb'strʌkt] vt (block) boucher, obstruer; (halt) arrêter; (hinder) entraver.

obtain [əb'teɪn] vt obtenir // vi avoir cours; **~able** a qu'on peut obtenir.

obtrusive [əb'tru:sɪv] a (person) importun(e); (smell) pénétrant(e); (building etc) trop en évidence.

obvious ['ɔbvɪəs] a évident(e), manifeste; **~ly** ad manifestement; bien sûr.

occasion [ə'keɪʒən] n occasion f; (event) événement m // vt occasionner, causer; **~al** a pris(e) or fait(e) etc de temps en temps; occasionnel(le); **~ally** ad de temps en temps, quelquefois.

occupation [ɔkju'peɪʃən] n occupation f; (job) métier m, profession f; **~al hazard** n risque m du métier.

occupier ['ɔkjupaɪə*] n occupant/e.

occupy ['ɔkjupaɪ] vt occuper; **to ~ o.s. with** or **by doing** s'occuper à faire.

occur [ə'kə:*] vi se produire; (difficulty, opportunity) se présenter; (phenomenon, error) se rencontrer; **to ~ to sb** venir à l'esprit de qn; **~rence** n présence f, existence f; cas m, fait m.

ocean ['əuʃən] n océan m; **~going** a de haute mer.

o'clock [ə'klɔk] ad: **it is 5 ~** il est 5 heures.

OCR n abbr of **optical character recognition/reader.**

October [ɔk'təubə*] n octobre m.

octopus ['ɔktəpəs] n pieuvre f.

odd [ɔd] a (strange) bizarre, curieux(euse); (number) impair(e); (left over) qui reste, en plus; (not of a set) dépareillé(e); 60 ~ 60 et quelques; **at ~ times** de temps en temps; **the ~ one out** l'exception f; **~s and ends** npl de petites choses; **~ity** n bizarrerie f; (person) excentrique m/f; **~ jobs** npl petits travaux divers; **~ly** ad bizarrement, curieusement; **~ments** npl (COMM) fins fpl de série; **~s** npl (in betting) cote f; **it makes no ~s** cela n'a pas d'importance; **at ~s** en désaccord.

odometer [ɔ'dɔmɪtə*] n odomètre m.

odour, (US) **odor** ['əudə*] n odeur f.

of [ɔv, əv] prep **1** (gen) de; **a friend ~ ours** un de nos amis; **a boy ~ 10** un garçon de 10 ans; **that was kind ~ you** c'était gentil de votre part

2 (expressing quantity, amount, dates etc) de; **a kilo ~ flour** un kilo de farine; **how much ~ this do you need?** combien vous en faut-il?; **there were 3 ~ them** (people) ils étaient 3; (objects) il y en avait 3; **3 ~ us went** 3 d'entre nous sont allé(e)s; **the 5th ~ July** le 5 juillet

3 (from, out of) en, de; **a statue ~ marble** une statue de or en marbre; **made ~ wood** (fait) en bois.

off [ɔf] a, ad (engine) coupé(e); (tap) fermé(e); (Brit: food: bad) mauvais(e), avancé(e); (: milk) tourné(e); (absent) absent(e); (cancelled) annulé(e) // prep: sur; **to be ~** (to leave) partir, s'en aller; **to be ~ sick** être absent pour cause de maladie; **a day ~** un jour de congé; **to have an ~ day** n'être pas en forme; **he had his coat ~** il avait enlevé son manteau; 10% ~ (COMM) 10% de rabais; ~ **the coast** au large de la côte; **I'm ~ meat** je ne mange plus de viande; je n'aime plus la viande; **on the ~** chance à tout hasard.

offal ['ɔfl] n (CULIN) abats mpl.

offbeat ['ɔfbi:t] a excentrique.

off-colour ['ɔf'kʌlə*] a (Brit: ill) malade, mal fichu/e.

offence, (US) offense ['ɔ'fɛns] n (crime) délit m, infraction f; **to take ~ at** se vexer de, s'offenser de.

offend [ə'fɛnd] vt (person) offenser, blesser; **~er** n délinquant/e; (against regulations) contrevenant/e.

offensive [ə'fɛnsɪv] a offensant(e), choquant(e); (smell etc) très déplaisant(e); (weapon) offensif(ive) // n (MIL) offensive f.

offer ['ɔfə*] n offre f, proposition f // vt offrir, proposer; **'on ~'** (COMM) 'en promotion'; **~ing** n offrande f.

offhand [ɔf'hænd] a désinvolte // ad spontanément.

office ['ɔfɪs] n (place) bureau m; (position) charge f, fonction f; **doctor's ~** (US) cabinet m (médical); **to take ~** entrer en fonctions; **~ automation** n bureautique f; **~ block, ~ building** n immeuble m de bureaux; **~ hours** npl heures fpl de bureau; (US MED) heures de consultation.

officer ['ɔfɪsə*] n (MIL etc) officier m; (of organization) membre m du bureau directeur; (also: **police ~**) agent m (de police).

office worker n employé/e de bureau.

official [ə'fɪʃl] a (authorized) officiel(le) // n officiel m; (civil servant) fonctionnaire m/f; employé/e; **~dom** n administration f, bureaucratie f.

officiate [ə'fɪʃɪeɪt] vi (REL) officier; **to ~ at a marriage** célébrer un mariage.

officious [ə'fɪʃəs] a trop empressé(e).

offing ['ɔfɪŋ] n: **in the ~** (fig) en

perspective.

off: ~-licence n (Brit: shop) débit m de vins et de spiritueux; **~-line** a, ad (COMPUT) (en mode) autonome; (: switched off) non connecté(e); **~-peak** a aux heures creuses; **~-putting** a (Brit) rébarbatif(ive); rebutant(e), peu engageant(e); **~-season** a, ad hors-saison inv.

offset ['ɔfsɛt] vt irg (counteract) contrebalancer, compenser.

offshoot ['ɔfʃu:t] n (fig) ramification f, antenne f; (: of discussion etc) conséquence f.

offshore ['ɔf'ʃɔ:*] a (breeze) de terre; (island) proche de littoral, (fishing) côtier(ère).

offside ['ɔf'saɪd] a (SPORT) hors jeu // n (AUT: with right-hand drive) côté droit.

offspring ['ɔfsprɪŋ] n progéniture f.

off: ~-stage ad dans les coulisses; **~-the-peg, (US) ~-the-rack** ad en prêt-à-porter; **~-white** a blanc cassé inv.

often ['ɔfn] ad souvent; **how ~ do you go?** vous y allez tous les combien?; **how ~ have you gone there?** vous y êtes allé combien de fois?

ogle ['əʊgl] vt lorgner.

oh [əʊ] excl ô!, oh!; ah!

oil [ɔɪl] n huile f; (petroleum) pétrole m; (for central heating) mazout m // vt (machine) graisser; **~can** n burette f de graissage; (for storing) bidon m à huile; **~field** n gisement m de pétrole; **~filter** n (AUT) filtre m à huile; **~fired** a au mazout; **~painting** n peinture f à l'huile; **~rig** n derrick m; (at sea) plate-forme pétrolière; **~skins** npl ciré m; **~tanker** n pétrolier m; **~well** n puits m de pétrole; **~y** a huileux(euse); (food) gras(se).

ointment ['ɔɪntmənt] n onguent m.

O.K., okay ['əʊ'keɪ] excl d'accord! // vt approuver, donner son accord à; **is it ~?, are you ~?** ça va?

old [əʊld] a vieux(vieille); (person)

vieux, âgé(e); *(former)* **ancien(ne), vieux; how ~ are you?** quel âge avez-vous?; **he's 10 years ~** il a 10 ans, il est âgé de 10 ans; **~er brother/sister** frère/sœur aîné(e); **~ age** *n* vieillesse *f*; **~-age pensioner (O.A.P.)** *(Brit)* retraité(e); **~-fashioned** *a* démodé(e); *(person)* vieux jeu *inv*.

olive ['ɒlɪv] *n (fruit)* olive *f*; *(tree)* olivier *m* // *a (also: ~-green)* (vert) olive *inv*; **~ oil** *n* huile *f* d'olive.

Olympic [əʊˈlɪmpɪk] *a* olympique; **the ~ Games,** **the ~s** les Jeux *mpl* olympiques.

omelet(te) ['ɒmlɪt] *n* omelette *f*.

omen ['əʊmən] *n* présage *m*.

ominous ['ɒmɪnəs] *a* menaçant(e), inquiétant(e); *(event)* de mauvais augure.

omit [əʊˈmɪt] *vt* omettre.

KEYWORD

on [ɒn] ♦ *prep* **1** *(indicating position)* sur; **~ the table** sur la table; **~ the wall** sur le *or* au mur; **~ the left** sur la gauche

2 *(indicating means, method, condition etc)*: **~ foot** à pied; **~ the train/plane** *(be)* dans le train/l'avion; *(go)* en train/avion; **~ the telephone/radio/television** au téléphone/à la radio/à la télévision; **to be ~ drugs** se droguer; **~ holiday** en vacances

3 *(referring to time)*: **~ Friday** vendredi; **~ Fridays** le vendredi; **~ June 20th** le 20 juin; **a week ~ Friday** vendredi en huit; **~ arrival** à l'arrivée; **~ seeing this** en voyant cela

4 *(about, concerning)* sur; de; **a book ~** Balzac/physics un livre sur Balzac/de physique

♦ *ad* **1** *(referring to dress, covering)*: **to have one's coat ~** avoir (mis) son manteau; **to put one's coat ~** mettre son manteau; **what's she got ~?** qu'est-ce qu'elle porte?; **screw the lid ~ tightly** vissez bien

le couvercle

2 *(further, continuously)*: **to walk etc ~** continuer à marcher *etc*; **~ and off** de temps à autre

♦ *a* **1** *(in operation: machine)* en marche; *(: radio, TV, light)* allumé(e); *(: tap, gas)* ouvert(e); *(: brakes)* mis(e); **is the meeting still ~?** *(not cancelled)* est-ce que la réunion a bien lieu?; *(in progress)* la réunion dure-t-elle encore?; **when is this film ~?** quand passe ce film?

2 *(col)*: **that's not ~!** *(not acceptable)* cela ne se fait pas!; *(not possible)* pas question!

once [wʌns] *ad* une fois; *(formerly)* autrefois // *cj* une fois que; **~ he had left/it was done** une fois qu'il fut parti/que ce fut terminé; **at ~** tout de suite, immédiatement; *(simultaneously)* à la fois; **~ more** encore une fois; **~ and for all** une fois pour toutes; **~ upon a time** il y avait une fois, il était une fois.

oncoming ['ɒnkʌmɪŋ] *a (traffic)* venant en sens inverse.

KEYWORD

one [wʌn] ♦ *num* un(e); **~ hundred and fifty** cent cinquante; **~ day** un jour

♦ *a* **1** *(sole)* seul(e), unique; **the ~ book which** l'unique *or* le seul livre qui; **the ~ man who** le seul (homme) qui

2 *(same)* même; **they came in the ~ car** ils sont venus dans la même voiture

♦ *pronoun* **1**: **this ~** celui-ci/celle-ci; **that ~** celui-là/celle-là; **I've already got ~/a red ~** j'en ai déjà un(e)/un(e) rouge; **~ by ~** un(e) à *or* par un(e)

2: **~ another** l'un(e) l'autre; **to look at ~ another** se regarder

3 *(impersonal)* on; **~ never knows** on ne sait jamais; **to cut ~'s finger** se couper le doigt.

one: ~**-armed bandit** *n* machine *f* à sous; ~**-day excursion** *n* (*US*) billet *m* d'aller-retour (valable pour la journée); ~**-man** *a* (*business*) dirigé(e) par un seul homme; ~**-man band** *n* homme-orchestre *m*; ~**-off** *n* (*Brit col*) exemplaire *m* unique.

oneself [wʌn'sɛlf] *pronoun* (*reflexive*) se; (*after prep*) soi(-même); (*emphatic*) soi-même; **to hurt** ~ se faire mal; **to keep sth for** ~ garder qch pour soi; **to talk to** ~ se parler à soi-même.

one: ~**-sided** *a* (*argument*) unilatéral(e); ~**-to**~ *a* (*relationship*) univoque; ~**-upmanship** [-'ʌpmənʃɪp] *n* l'art de faire mieux que les autres; ~**-way** *a* (*street, traffic*) à sens unique.

ongoing ['ɒngəʊɪŋ] *a* en cours; suivi(e).

onion ['ʌnjən] *n* oignon *m*.

on-line ['ɒn'laɪn] *a, ad* (*COMPUT*) en ligne; (: *switched on*) connecté(e).

onlooker ['ɒnlʊkə*] *n* spectateur/trice.

only ['əʊnlɪ] *ad* seulement // *a* seul(e), unique // *cj* seulement, mais; **an** ~ **child** un enfant unique; **not** ~ ... **but also** non seulement ... mais aussi; **I took** ~ **one** je n'en ai pris qu'un, j'en ai seulement pris un.

onset ['ɒnsɛt] *n* début *m*; (*of winter, old age*) approche *f*.

onshore ['ɒnʃɔ:*] *a* (*wind*) du large.

onslaught ['ɒnslɔ:t] *n* attaque *f*, assaut *m*.

onto ['ɒntu] *prep* = **on to**.

onus ['əʊnəs] *n* responsabilité *f*.

onward(s) ['ɒnwəd(z)] *ad* (*move*) en avant.

ooze [u:z] *vi* suinter.

opaque [əʊ'peɪk] *a* opaque.

OPEC ['əʊpɛk] *n abbr* (= *Organization of petroleum exporting countries*) O.P.E.P. *f* (= *Organisation des pays exportateurs de pétrole*).

open ['əʊpn] *a* ouvert(e); (*car*) découvert(e); (*road, view*) dégagé(e);

(*meeting*) public(ique); (*admiration*) manifeste; (*question*) non résolu(e): (*enemy*) déclaré(e) // *vt* ouvrir // *vi* (*flower, eyes, door, debate*) s'ouvrir; (*shop, bank, museum*) ouvrir; (*book etc: commence*) commencer, débuter; **in the** ~ (**air**) en plein air; **to** ~ **on to** *vt fus* (*subj: room, door*) donner sur; **to** ~ **up** *vt* ouvrir; (*blocked road*) dégager // *vi* s'ouvrir; ~**ing** *n* ouverture *f*; (*opportunity*) occasion *f*; débouché *m*; (*job*) poste vacant; ~**ly** *ad* ouvertement; ~**-minded** *a* à l'esprit ouvert; ~**-plan** *a* sans cloisons.

opera ['ɒpərə] *n* opéra *m*; ~ **house** *n* opéra *m*.

operate ['ɒpəreɪt] *vt* (*machine*) faire marcher, faire fonctionner; (*system*) pratiquer // *vi* fonctionner; (*drug*) faire effet; **to** ~ **on sb** (**for**) (*MED*) opérer qn (de).

operatic [ɒpə'rætɪk] *a* d'opéra.

operating ['ɒpəreɪtɪŋ] *a:* ~ **table/theatre** table *f*/salle *f* d'opération.

operation [ɒpə'reɪʃən] *n* opération *f*; (*of machine*) fonctionnement *m*; **to be in** ~ (*machine*) être en service; (*system*) être en vigueur; **to have an** ~ (*MED*) se faire opérer.

operative ['ɒpərətɪv] *a* (*measure*) en vigueur.

operator ['ɒpəreɪtə*] *n* (*of machine*) opérateur/trice; (*TEL*) téléphoniste *m/f*.

opinion [ə'pɪnɪən] *n* opinion *f*, avis *m*; **in my** ~ à mon avis; ~**ated** *a* aux idées bien arrêtées; ~ **poll** *n* sondage *m* (d'opinion).

opponent [ə'pəʊnənt] *n* adversaire *m/f*.

opportunist [ɒpə'tju:nɪst] *n* opportuniste *m/f*.

opportunity [ɒpə'tju:nɪtɪ] *n* occasion *f*; **to take the** ~ **of doing** profiter de l'occasion pour faire; en profiter pour faire.

oppose [ə'pəʊz] *vt* s'opposer à; ~**d to** *a* opposé(e) à; **as** ~**d to** par opposition à; **opposing** *a* (*side*) opposé(e).

opposite ['ɔpəzit] *a* opposé(e); *(house etc)* d'en face // *ad* en face // *prep* en face de // ~ opposé m, contraire m; *(of word)* contraire.

opposition [ɔpə'zɪʃən] *n* opposition *f*.

oppress [ə'prɛs] *vt* opprimer.

opt [ɔpt] *vi*: to ~ for opter pour; to ~ to do choisir de faire; to ~ out of choisir de ne pas participer à or de ne pas faire.

optical ['ɔptɪkl] *a* optique; *(instrument)* d'optique; ~ **character recognition/reader (OCR)** *n* lecture *f*/lecteur *m* optique.

optician [ɔp'tɪʃən] *n* opticien·ne.

optimist ['ɔptɪmɪst] *n* optimiste *m/f*; ~**ic** [-'mɪstɪk] *a* optimiste.

option ['ɔpʃən] *n* choix *m*, option *f*; *(SCOL)* matière *f* à option; *(COMM)* option; ~**al** *a* facultatif(ive); *(COMM)* en option.

or [ɔ:*] *cj* ou; *(with negative)*: he hasn't seen ~ heard anything il n'a rien vu ni entendu; ~ **else** sinon; ou bien.

oral ['ɔ:rəl] *a* oral(e) // *n* oral *m*.

orange ['ɔrɪndʒ] *n (fruit)* orange *f* // *a* orange *inv.*

orator ['ɔrətə*] *n* orateur/trice.

orbit ['ɔ:bɪt] *n* orbite *f*.

orchard ['ɔ:tʃəd] *n* verger *m*.

orchestra ['ɔ:kɪstrə] *n* orchestre *m*; *(US: seating)* (fauteuils mpl d')orchestre; **orchestral** [-'kɛstrəl] *a* orchestral(e); *(concert)* symphonique.

orchid ['ɔ:kɪd] *n* orchidée *f*.

ordain [ɔ:'deɪn] *vt (REL)* ordonner; *(decide)* décréter.

ordeal [ɔ:'di:l] *n* épreuve *f*.

order ['ɔ:də*] *n* ordre *m*; *(COMM)* commande *f* // *vt* ordonner; *(COMM)* commander; in ~ en ordre; *(of document)* en règle; in *(working)* ~ en état de marche; in ~ of size par ordre de grandeur; in ~ to do/that pour faire/que + *sub*; in ~ to/that pour faire/que + *sub*; in ~ to do/that pour faire/que + *sub*; in ~ en commande; to ~ sb to do ordon-

ner à qn de faire; ~ **form** *n* bon *m* de commande; ~**ly** *n (MIL)* ordonnance *f* // *a (room)* en ordre; *(mind)* méthodique; *(person)* qui a de l'ordre.

ordinary ['ɔ:dnrɪ] *a* ordinaire, normal(e); *(pej)* ordinaire, quelconque; **out of the** ~ exceptionnel(le).

ordnance ['ɔ:dnəns] *n (MIL: unit)* service *m* du matériel.

ore [ɔ:*] *n* minerai *m*.

organ ['ɔ:gən] *n* organe *m*; *(MUS)* orgue *m*, orgues *fpl*; ~**ic** [ɔ:'gænɪk] *a* organique.

organization [ɔ:gənaɪ'zeɪʃən] *n* organisation *f*.

organize ['ɔ:gənaɪz] *vt* organiser; ~**r** *n* organisateur/trice.

orgasm ['ɔ:gæzəm] *n* orgasme *m*.

orgy ['ɔ:dʒɪ] *n* orgie *f*.

Orient ['ɔ:rɪənt] *n*: the ~ l'Orient *m*; **oriental** [-'ɛntl] *a* oriental(e).

origin ['ɔrɪdʒɪn] *n* origine *f*.

original [ə'rɪdʒɪnl] *a* original(e); *(earliest)* originel(le) // *n* original *m*; ~**ly** *ad (at first)* à l'origine.

originate [ə'rɪdʒɪneɪt] *vi*: to ~ **from** être originaire de; *(suggestion)* provenir de; to ~ **in** prendre naissance dans; avoir son origine dans.

Orkneys ['ɔ:knɪz] *npl*: the ~ *(also: the Orkney Islands)* les Orcades *fpl*.

ornament ['ɔ:nəmənt] *n* ornement *m*; *(trinket)* bibelot *m*; ~**al** [-'mɛntl] *a* décoratif(ive); *(garden)* d'agrément.

ornate [ɔ:'neɪt] *a* très orné(e).

orphan ['ɔ:fn] *n* orphelin·e // *vt*: to be ~**ed** devenir orphelin; ~**age** *n* orphelinat *m*.

orthopaedic, *(US)* **orthopedic** [ɔ:θə'pi:dɪk] *a* orthopédique.

ostensibly [ɔs'tɛnsɪblɪ] *ad* en apparence.

ostentatious [ɔstɛn'teɪʃəs] *a* prétentieux(euse); ostentatoire.

ostracize ['ɔstrəsaɪz] *vt* frapper d'ostracisme.

ostrich ['ɔstrɪtʃ] *n* autruche *f*.

other ['ʌðə*] a autre // pronoun: the ~ (one) l'autre; ~s (~ people) d'autres; ~ than autrement que; à part; ~wise ad, cj autrement.

otter ['ɔtə*] n loutre f.

ouch [autʃ] excl aïe!

ought [ɔ:t] auxiliary vb: I ~ to do it je devrais le faire, il faudrait que je le fasse; this ~ to have been corrected cela aurait dû être corrigé; he ~ to win il devrait gagner.

ounce [auns] n once f (= 28.35g; 16 in a pound).

our ['auə*] a notre, nos pl; see my; ~s pronoun le(la) nôtre, les nôtres; see also mine; ~selves pronoun pl (reflexive, after preposition) nous; (emphatic) nous-mêmes; see also oneself.

oust [aust] vt évincer.

out [aut] ad dehors; (published, not at home etc) sorti(e); (light, fire) éteint(e); ~ here ici; ~ there là-bas; he's ~ (absent) il est sorti; (unconscious) il est sans connaissance; to be ~ in one's calculations s'être trompé dans ses calculs; to run/back etc ~ sortir en courant/en reculant etc; ~ loud ad à haute voix; ~ of (outside) en dehors de; (because of: anger etc) par; (from among): ~ of 10 sur 10; (without): ~ of petrol sans essence, à court d'essence; ~ of order (machine) en panne; (TEL: line) en dérangement; ~-and-~ a (liar, thief etc) véritable.

outback ['autbæk] n campagne isolée; (in Australia) intérieur m.

outboard ['autbɔ:d] n: ~ (motor) (moteur m) hors-bord m.

outbreak ['autbreik] n accès m; début m; éruption f.

outburst ['autbə:st] n explosion f, accès m.

outcast ['autkɑ:st] n exilé(e); (socially) paria m.

outcome ['autkʌm] n issue f, résultat m.

outcrop ['autkrɔp] n (of rock) affleurement m.

outcry ['autkrai] n tollé (général).

outdated [aut'deitid] a démodé(e).

outdo [aut'du:] vt irg surpasser.

outdoor [aut'dɔ:*] a de or en plein air; ~s ad dehors; au grand air.

outer ['autə*] a extérieur(e); ~ space n espace m cosmique.

outfit ['autfit] n équipement m; (clothes) tenue f; '~ter's' (Brit) 'confection pour hommes'.

outgoing ['autgəuiŋ] a (character) ouvert(e), extraverti(e); ~s npl (Brit: expenses) dépenses fpl.

outgrow [aut'grəu] vt irg (clothes) devenir trop grand(e) pour.

outhouse ['authaus] n appentis m, remise f.

outing ['autiŋ] n sortie f; excursion f.

outlandish [aut'lændiʃ] a étrange.

outlaw ['autlɔ:] n hors-la-loi m inv.

outlay ['autlei] n dépenses fpl; (investment) mise f de fonds.

outlet ['autlet] n (for liquid etc) issue f, sortie f; (US: ELEC) prise f de courant; (for emotion) exutoire m; (for goods) débouché m; (also: retail ~) point m de vente.

outline ['autlain] n (shape) contour m; (summary) esquisse f, grandes lignes.

outlive [aut'liv] vt survivre à.

outlook ['autluk] n perspective f.

outlying ['autlaiiŋ] a écarté(e).

outmoded [aut'məudid] a démodé(e); dépassé(e).

outnumber [aut'nʌmbə*] vt surpasser en nombre.

out-of-date [autəv'deit] a (passport) périmé(e); (theory etc) dépassé(e); (custom) désuet(ète); (clothes etc) démodé(e).

out-of-the-way [autəvðə'wei] a (place) loin de tout.

outpatient ['autpeiʃənt] n malade m/f en consultation externe.

outpost ['autpəust] n avant-poste m.

output ['autput] n rendement m, production f; (COMPUT) sortie f.

outrage ['autreidʒ] n atrocité f, acte m de violence; scandale m // vt outrager; **~ous** [-'reidʒəs] a atroce; scandaleux(euse).

outright ad [aut'rait] complètement; catégoriquement; carrément; sur le coup // a ['autrait] complet(ète); catégorique.

outset ['autset] n début m.

outside [aut'said] n extérieur m // a extérieur(e) // ad (au) dehors, à l'extérieur // prep hors de, à l'extérieur de; **at the ~** (fig) au plus ou maximum; **~ lane** n (AUT: in Britain) voie f de droite; **~-left/-right** n (FOOTBALL) ailier gauche/droit; **~ line** n (TEL) ligne extérieure; **~r** n (in race etc) outsider m; (stranger) étranger/ère.

outsize ['autsaiz] a énorme; (clothes) grande taille inv.

outskirts ['autskə:ts] npl faubourgs mpl.

outspoken [aut'spəukən] a très franc(franche).

outstanding [aut'stændiŋ] a remarquable, exceptionnel(le); (unfinished) en suspens; en souffrance; non réglé(e).

outstay [aut'stei] vt: **to ~ one's welcome** abuser de l'hospitalité de son hôte.

outstretched [aut'stretʃt] a (hand) tendu(e); (body) étendu(e).

outstrip [aut'strip] vt (competitors, demand) dépasser.

out-tray ['auttrei] n courrier m 'départ'.

outward ['autwəd] a (sign, appearances) extérieur(e); (journey) (d')aller; **~ly** ad extérieurement; en apparence.

outweigh [aut'wei] vt l'emporter sur.

outwit [aut'wit] vt se montrer plus malin que.

oval ['əuvl] a, n ovale (m).

ovary ['əuvəri] n ovaire m.

oven ['ʌvn] n four m; **~proof** a al-

lant au four.

over ['əuvə*] ad (par-)dessus // a (or ad) (finished) fini(e), terminé(e); (too much) en plus // prep sur; par-dessus; (above) au-dessus de; (on the other side of) de l'autre côté de; (more than) plus de; (during) pendant; **~ here** ici; **~ there** là-bas; **all ~** (everywhere) partout; (finished) fini(e); **~ and ~** (again) à plusieurs reprises; **~ and above** en plus de; **to ask sb ~** inviter qn (à passer).

overall a n, ['əuvərɔ:l] a (length) total(e); (study) d'ensemble // n (Brit) blouse f // ad [əuvər'ɔ:l] dans l'ensemble, en général; **~s** npl bleus mpl (de travail).

overawe [əuvər'ɔ:] vt impressionner.

overbalance [əuvə'bæləns] vi basculer.

overbearing [əuvə'bɛəriŋ] a impérieux(euse), autoritaire.

overboard ['əuvəbɔ:d] ad (NAUT) par-dessus bord.

overbook [əuvə'buk] vt faire du surbooking.

overcast ['əuvəka:st] a couvert(e).

overcharge [əuvə'tʃa:dʒ] vt: **to ~ sb for sth** faire payer qch trop cher à qn.

overcoat ['əuvəkəut] n pardessus m.

overcome [əuvə'kʌm] vt irg triompher de; surmonter; **~ with grief** accablé(e) de douleur.

overcrowded [əuvə'kraudid] a bondé(e).

overdo [əuvə'du:] vt irg exagérer; (overcook) trop cuire.

overdose ['əuvədəus] n dose excessive.

overdraft ['əuvədra:ft] n découvert m.

overdrawn [əuvə'drɔ:n] a (account) à découvert.

overdue [əuvə'dju:] a en retard; (recognition) tardif(ive).

overflow [əuvə'fləu] vi déborder // n ['əuvəfləu] trop-plein m; (also: **~pipe**) tuyau m d'écoulement, trop-plein m.

overgrown [əuvə'grəun] a (garden) envahi(e) par la végétation.

overhaul vt [əuvə'hɔ:l] réviser // n ['əuvəhɔ:l] révision f.

overhead ad [əuvə'hed] au-dessus // a, n ['əuvəhed] a aérien(ne); (lighting) vertical(e) // n (US) = ~s; ~s npl frais généraux.

overhear [əuvə'hɪə*] vt irg entendre (par hasard).

overheat [əuvə'hi:t] vi (engine) chauffer.

overjoyed [əuvə'dʒɔɪd] a ravi(e), enchanté(e).

overkill ['əuvəkɪl] n: that would be ~ ce serait trop.

overlap [əuvə'læp] vi se chevaucher.

overleaf [əuvə'li:f] ad au verso.

overload [əuvə'ləud] vt surcharger.

overlook [əuvə'luk] vt (have view of) donner sur; (miss) oublier, négliger; (forgive) fermer les yeux sur.

overnight ad [əuvə'naɪt] (happen) durant la nuit; (fig) soudain // a ['əuvənaɪt] d'une (or de) nuit; soudain(e); he stayed there ~ il y a passé la nuit.

overpower [əuvə'pauə*] vt vaincre; (fig) accabler; ~ing a irrésistible, (heat, stench) suffocant(e).

overrate [əuvə'reɪt] vt surestimer.

override [əuvə'raɪd] vt (irg: like ride) (order, objection) passer outre à; (decision) annuler; **overriding** a prépondérant(e).

overrule [əuvə'ru:l] vt (decision) annuler; (claim) rejeter.

overrun [əuvə'rʌn] vt (irg: like run) (country) occuper; (time limit) dépasser.

overseas [əuvə'si:z] ad outre-mer; (abroad) à l'étranger // a (trade) extérieur(e); (visitor) étranger(ère).

overseer ['əuvəsɪə*] n (in factory) contremaître m.

overshadow [əuvə'ʃædəu] vt (fig) éclipser.

overshoot [əuvə'ʃu:t] vt irg dépasser.

oversight ['əuvəsaɪt] n omission f, oubli m.

oversleep [əuvə'sli:p] vi irg se réveiller (trop) tard.

overstep [əuvə'step] vt: to ~ the mark dépasser la mesure.

overt [əu'və:t] a non dissimulé(e).

overtake [əuvə'teɪk] vt irg dépasser; (AUT) dépasser, doubler.

overthrow [əuvə'θrəu] vt irg (government) renverser.

overtime ['əuvətaɪm] n heures fpl supplémentaires.

overtone ['əuvətəun] n (also: ~s) note f, sous-entendus mpl.

overture ['əuvətʃuə*] n (MUS, fig) ouverture f.

overturn [əuvə'tə:n] vt renverser // vi se retourner.

overweight [əuvə'weɪt] a (person) trop gros(se); (luggage) trop lourd(e).

overwhelm [əuvə'welm] vt accabler; submerger; écraser; ~ing a (victory, defeat) écrasant(e); (desire) irrésistible.

overwork [əuvə'wə:k] n surmenage m.

overwrought [əuvə'rɔ:t] a excédé(e).

owe [əu] vt devoir; to ~ sb sth, to ~ sth to sb devoir qch à qn.

owing to ['əuɪŋtu:] prep à cause de, en raison de.

owl [aul] n hibou m.

own [əun] vt posséder // a propre; a room of my ~ une chambre à moi, ma propre chambre; to get one's ~ back prendre sa revanche; on one's ~ tout(e) seul(e); to ~ up vi avouer; ~er n propriétaire m/f; ~ership n possession f.

ox, pl oxen [ɔks, 'ɔksn] n bœuf m.

oxtail ['ɔksteɪl] n: ~ soup soupe f à la queue de bœuf.

oxygen ['ɔksɪdʒən] n oxygène m; ~ mask n masque m à oxygène.

oyster ['ɔɪstə*] n huître f.

oz. abbr of **ounce(s)**.

P

p [pi:] *abbr of* **penny, pence.**

pa [pɑ:] *n* (*col*) papa *m*.

P.A. *n abbr of* **personal assistant, public address system.**

p.a. *abbr of* **per annum.**

pace [peɪs] *n* pas *m*; (*speed*) allure *f*; vitesse *f* // *vi*: **to ~ up and down** faire les cent pas; **to keep ~ with** aller à la même vitesse que; (*events*) se tenir au courant de; **~maker** *n* (*MED*) stimulateur *m* cardiaque.

pacific [pə'sɪfɪk] *a* pacifique // *n*: **the P~ (Ocean)** le Pacifique, l'océan *m* Pacifique.

pack [pæk] *n* paquet *m*; ballot *m*; (*of hounds*) meute *f*; (*of thieves etc*) bande *f*; (*of cards*) jeu *m* // *vt* (*goods*) empaqueter, emballer; (*in suitcase etc*) emballer; (*box*) remplir; (*cram*) entasser; (*press down*) tasser; damer; **to ~ (one's bags)** faire ses bagages; **to ~ off** *vt* (*person*) envoyer (promener), expédier.

package [pækɪdʒ] *n* paquet *m*; ballot *m*; (*also: ~ deal*) marché global; forfait *m*; **~ tour** *n* voyage organisé.

packed lunch *n* repas froid.

packet [pækɪt] *n* paquet *m*.

packing [pækɪŋ] *n* emballage *m*; **~ case** *n* caisse *f* (d'emballage).

pact [pækt] *n* pacte *m*; traité *m*.

pad [pæd] *n* bloc(-notes) *m*; (*for inking*) tampon *m* encreur; (*col: flat*) piaule *f* // *vt* rembourrer; **~ding** *n* rembourrage *m*.

paddle [pædl] *n* (*oar*) pagaie *f*; (*US: for table tennis*) raquette *f* de ping-pong // *vi* barboter, faire trempette // *vt*: **to ~ a canoe** *etc* pagayer; **~ steamer** *n* bateau *m* à aubes; **paddling pool** *n* (*Brit*) petit bassin.

paddy [pædi] *n*: **~ field** *n* rizière *f*.

padlock [pædlɔk] *n* cadenas *m*.

paediatrics, (US) pediatrics

[pi:dɪ'ætrɪks] *n* pédiatrie *f*.

pagan [peɪgən] *a, n* païen(ne).

page [peɪdʒ] *n* (*of book*) page *f*; (*also: ~ boy*) groom *m*, chasseur *m*; (*at wedding*) garçon *m* d'honneur // *vt* (*in hotel etc*) (faire) appeler.

pageant [pædʒənt] *n* spectacle *m* historique; grande cérémonie; **~ry** *n* apparat *m*, pompe *f*.

paid [peɪd] *pt, pp of* **pay** // *a* (*work, official*) rémunéré(e); **to put ~ to** (*Brit*) mettre fin à, régler.

pail [peɪl] *n* seau *m*.

pain [peɪn] *n* douleur *f*; **to be in ~** souffrir, avoir mal; **to take ~s to do sth** se donner du mal pour faire; **~ed** *a* peiné(e), chagrin(e); **~ful** *a* douloureux(euse); difficile, pénible; **~fully** *ad* (*fig: very*) terriblement; **~killer** *n* calmant *m*; **~less** *a* indolore.

painstaking [peɪnzteɪkɪŋ] *a* (*person*) soigneux(euse); (*work*) soigné(e).

paint [peɪnt] *n* peinture *f* // *vt* peindre; (*fig*) dépeindre; **to ~ the door blue** peindre la porte en bleu; **~brush** *n* pinceau *m*; **~er** *n* peintre *m*; **~ing** *n* peinture *f*; (*picture*) tableau *m*; **~work** *n* peintures *fpl*; (*of car*) peinture *f*.

pair [peə*] *n* (*of shoes, gloves etc*) paire *f*; (*of people*) couple *m*; duo *m*; paire; **a ~ of scissors** (paire de) ciseaux *mpl*; **~ of trousers** pantalon *m*.

pajamas [pɪ'dʒɑ:məz] *npl* (*US*) pyjama(s) *m(pl)*.

Pakistan [pɑ:kɪ'stɑ:n] *n* Pakistan *m*; **~i** *a* pakistanais(e) // *n* Pakistanais/e.

pal [pæl] *n* (*col*) copain/copine.

palace [pæləs] *n* palais *m*.

palatable [pælɪtəbl] *a* bon(bonne), agréable au goût.

palate [pælɪt] *n* palais *m* (*ANAT*).

palatial [pə'leɪʃəl] *a* grandiose, magnifique.

palaver [pə'lɑ:və*] *n* palabres *fpl* or *mpl*; histoire(s) *f(pl)*.

pale [peɪl] *a* pâle; **to grow ~** pâlir // *n*: **beyond the ~** au ban de la société.

Palestine ['pælɪstaɪn] *n* Palestine *f*;

Palestinian [-'tɪnɪən] *a* palestinien(ne) // *n* Palestinien/ne.

palette ['pælɪt] *n* palette *f*.

paling ['peɪlɪŋ] *n* (*stake*) palis *m*; (*fence*) palissade *f*.

pall [pɔ:l] *n* (*of smoke*) voile *m* // *vi*: **to ~ (on)** devenir lassant (pour).

pallet ['pælɪt] *n* (*for goods*) palette *f*.

pallid ['pælɪd] *a* blême.

pallor ['pælə*] *n* pâleur *f*.

palm [pɑ:m] *n* (*ANAT*) paume *f*; (*also*: **~ tree**) palmier *m*; (*leaf, symbol*) palme *f* // *vt*: **to ~ sth off on sb** (*col*) refiler qch à qn; **P~ Sunday** *n* le dimanche des Rameaux.

palpable ['pælpəbl] *a* évident(e), manifeste.

paltry ['pɔ:ltrɪ] *a* dérisoire, piètre.

pamper ['pæmpə*] *vt* gâter, dorloter.

pamphlet ['pæmflət] *n* brochure *f*.

pan [pæn] *n* (*also*: **sauce~**) casserole *f*; (*also*: **frying ~**) poêle *f*; (*of lavatory*) cuvette *f* // *vi* (*CINEMA*) faire un panoramique.

pancake ['pænkeɪk] *n* crêpe *f*.

panda ['pændə] *n* panda *m*; **~ car** *n* (*Brit*) ≈ voiture *f* pie (fam).

pandemonium [pændɪ'məunɪəm] *n* tohu-bohu *m*.

pander ['pændə*] *vi*: **to ~ to** flatter bassement; obéir servilement à.

pane [peɪn] *n* carreau *m* (de fenêtre).

panel ['pænl] *n* (*of wood, cloth etc*) panneau *m*; (*RADIO, TV*) panel *m*, invités *mpl*, experts *mpl*; **~ling**, (*US*) **~ing** *n* boiseries *fpl*.

pang [pæŋ] *n*: **~s of remorse** pincements *mpl* de remords; **~s of hunger/ conscience** tiraillements *mpl* d'estomac/de la conscience.

panic ['pænɪk] *n* panique *f*, affolement *m* // *vi* s'affoler, paniquer; **~ky** *a* (*person*) qui panique or s'affole facilement; **~-stricken** *a* affo-

pansy ['pænzɪ] *n* (*BOT*) pensée *f*; (*col*) tapette *f*, pédé *m*.

pant [pænt] *vi* haleter.

panther ['pænθə*] *n* panthère *f*.

panties ['pæntɪz] *npl* slip *m*, culotte *f*.

pantihose ['pæntɪhəuz] *n* (*US*) collant *m*.

pantomime ['pæntəmaɪm] *n* (*Brit*) spectacle *m* de Noël.

pantry ['pæntrɪ] *n* garde-manger *m* *inv*; (*room*) office *f* or *m*.

pants [pænts] *n* (*Brit*: *woman's*) culotte *f*, slip *m*; (: *man's*) slip, caleçon *m*; (*US*: *trousers*) pantalon *m*.

paper ['peɪpə*] *n* papier *m*; (*also*: **wall~**) papier peint; (*also*: **news~**) journal *m*; (*study, article*) article *m*; (*exam*) épreuve écrite // *a* en *or* de papier // *vt* tapisser (de papier peint); **~s** *npl* (*also*: **identity ~s**) papiers (d'identité); **~back** *n* livre *m* de poche; livre broché *or* non relié; **~ clip** *n* trombone *m*; **~ hankie** *n* mouchoir *m* en papier; **~weight** *n* presse-papiers *m* *inv*; **~work** *n* paperasserie *f*.

par [pɑ:*] *n* pair *m*; (*GOLF*) normale *f* du parcours; **on a ~ with** à égalité avec, au même niveau que.

parable ['pærəbl] *n* parabole *f* (*REL*).

parachute [ˈpærəʃuːt] *n* parachute *m*.

parade [pə'reɪd] *n* défilé *m*; (*inspection*) revue *f*; (*street*) boulevard *m* // *vt* faire étalage de // *vi* défiler.

paradise ['pærədaɪs] *n* paradis *m*.

paradox ['pærədɔks] *n* paradoxe *m*; **~ically** [-'dɔksɪklɪ] *ad* paradoxalement.

paraffin ['pærəfɪn] *n* (*Brit*): **~ (oil)** pétrole (lampant).

paragraph ['pærəgrɑ:f] *n* paragraphe *m*.

parallel ['pærəlɛl] *a* parallèle; (*fig*) analogue // *n* (*line*) parallèle *f*; (*fig, GEO*) parallèle *m*.

paralysis [pə'rælɪsɪs] *n* paralysie *f*.

paralyze ['pærəlaɪz] *vt* paralyser.

paramount ['pærəmaunt] *a*: of importance de la plus haute *or* grande importance.

paranoid ['pærənɔɪd] *a* (PSYCH) paranoïaque; (neurotic) paranoïde.

paraphernalia [pærəfə'neɪlɪə] *n* attirail *m*, affaires *fpl*.

parasol ['pærə'sɔl] *n* ombrelle *f*; parasol *m*.

paratrooper ['pærətru:pə°] *n* parachutiste *m* (soldat).

parcel ['pɑ:sl] *n* paquet *m*, colis *m* // *vt* (also: ~ **up**) empaqueter.

parch [pɑ:tʃ] *vt* dessécher; **~ed** *a* (person) assoiffé(e).

parchment ['pɑ:tʃmənt] *n* parchemin *m*.

pardon ['pɑ:dn] *n* pardon *m*; grâce *f* // *vt* pardonner à; (LAW) gracier; ~ **me!** excusez-moi!; **I beg your ~!** pardon!, je suis désolé!; **(I beg your) ~?**, (US) ~ **me?** pardon?

parent ['pɛərənt] *n* père *m or* mère *f*; ~**s** *npl* parents *mpl*.

Paris ['pærɪs] *n* Paris.

parish ['pærɪʃ] *n* paroisse *f*; (civil) ≈ commune *f* // *a* paroissial(e).

Parisian [pə'rɪzɪən] *a* parisien(ne) // *n* Parisien/ne.

park [pɑ:k] *n* parc *m*, jardin public *m* // *vt* garer // *vi* se garer.

parking ['pɑ:kɪŋ] *n* stationnement *m*; **'no ~'** 'stationnement interdit'; ~ **lot** *n* (US) parking *m*, parc de stationnement; ~ **meter** *n* parcomètre *m*; ~ **ticket** *n* P.V. *m*.

parlance ['pɑ:ləns] *n* langage *m*.

parliament ['pɑ:ləmənt] *n* parlement *m*; ~**ary** [-'mɛntərɪ] *a* parlementaire.

parlour, (US) **parlor** ['pɑ:lə°] *n* salon *m*.

parochial [pə'rəukɪəl] *a* paroissial(e); (pej) à l'esprit de clocher.

parody ['pærədɪ] *n* parodie *f*.

parole [pə'rəul] *n*: **on** ~ en liberté conditionnelle.

parrot ['pærət] *n* perroquet *m*.

parry ['pærɪ] *vt* esquiver, parer à.

parsley ['pɑ:slɪ] *n* persil *m*.

parsnip ['pɑ:snɪp] *n* panais *m*.

parson ['pɑ:sn] *n* ecclésiastique *m*; (Church of England) pasteur *m*.

part [pɑ:t] *n* partie *f*; (of machine) pièce *f*; (THEATRE etc) rôle *m*; (MUS) voix *f*; (US: in hair) raie *f* // *a* partiel(le) // *ad*: = **partly** // *vt* séparer // *vi* (people) se séparer; (roads) se diviser; **to take** ~ **in** participer à, prendre part à; **for my** ~ en ce qui me concerne; **to take sth in good** ~ prendre qch du bon côté; **to take sb's** ~ prendre le parti de qn, prendre parti pour qn; **for the most** ~ en grande partie; dans la plupart des cas; **to ~ with** *vt fus* se séparer de; se défaire de; ~ **exchange** *n* (Brit): **in** ~ **exchange** en reprise.

partial ['pɑ:ʃl] *a* partiel(le); (unjust) partial(e); **to be** ~ **to** aimer, avoir un faible pour.

participate [pɑ:'tɪsɪpeɪt] *vi*: **to** ~ **(in)** participer (à), prendre part (à).

participation [-'peɪʃn] *n* participation *f*.

participle ['pɑ:tɪsɪpl] *n* participe *m*.

particle ['pɑ:tɪkl] *n* particule *f*.

particular [pə'tɪkjulə°] *a* particulier(ère); spécial(e); (detailed) détaillé(e); (fussy) difficile; méticuleux(euse); ~**s** *npl* détails *mpl*; (information) renseignements *mpl*; **in** ~ *ad* surtout, en particulier; ~**ly** *ad* particulièrement; en particulier.

parting ['pɑ:tɪŋ] *n* séparation *f*; (Brit: in hair) raie *f* // *a* d'adieu.

partisan [pɑ:tɪ'zæn] *n* partisan/e // *a* partisan(e); de parti.

partition [pɑ:'tɪʃn] *n* (POL) partition *f*, division *f*; (wall) cloison *f*.

partly ['pɑ:tlɪ] *ad* en partie, partiellement.

partner ['pɑ:tnə°] *n* (COMM) associé/e; (SPORT) partenaire *m/f*; (at dance) cavalier/ère; ~**ship** *n* association *f*.

partridge ['pɑ:trɪdʒ] *n* perdrix *f*.

part-time ['pɑ:t'taɪm] *a, ad* à mi-temps, à temps partiel.

party ['pɑ:tɪ] *n* (POL) parti *m*;

(team) équipe f; groupe m; (LAW) partie f; (celebration) réception f; soirée f; fête f // a (POL) de or du parti; de partis; ~ **dress** n robe habillée; ~ **line** n (TEL) ligne partagée.

pass [pɑːs] vt (time, object) passer; (place) passer devant; (car, friend) croiser; (exam) être reçu(e) à, réussir; (candidate) admettre; (overtake, surpass) dépasser; (approve) approuver, accepter // vi passer; (SCOL) être reçu(e) or admis(e), réussir // n (permit) laissez-passer m inv; carte f d'accès or d'abonnement; (in mountains) col m; (SPORT) passe f; (SCOL: also: ~ **mark**): **to get a ~** être reçu(e) (sans mention); **to ~ sth through a ring** etc (faire) passer qch dans un anneau etc; **to make a ~ at sb** (col) faire des avances à qn; **to ~ away** vi mourir; **to ~ by** vi passer // vt négliger; **to ~ on** vt (news, object) transmettre; (illness) passer; **to ~ out** vi s'évanouir; **to ~ up** vt (opportunity) laisser passer; ~**able** a (road) praticable; (work) acceptable.

passage ['pæsɪdʒ] n (also: ~**way**) couloir m; (gen, in book) passage m; (by boat) traversée f.

passbook ['pɑːsbʊk] n livret m.

passenger ['pæsɪndʒə*] n passager/ère.

passer-by ['pɑːsə'baɪ] n passant/e.

passing ['pɑːsɪŋ] a (fig) passager(ère); **in ~**, en passant; ~ **place** n (AUT) aire f de croisement.

passion ['pæʃən] n passion f; amour m; ~**ate** a passionné(e).

passive ['pæsɪv] a (also LING) passif(ive).

Passover ['pɑːsəʊvə*] n Pâque f (juive).

passport ['pɑːspɔːt] n passeport m; ~ **control** n contrôle m des passeports.

password ['pɑːswɜːd] n mot m de passe.

past [pɑːst] prep (further than) au

delà de, plus loin que; après; (later than) après // a passé(e); (president etc) ancien(ne) // n passé m; **he's ~ forty** il a dépassé la quarantaine, il a plus de or passé quarante ans; **for the ~ few/3 days** depuis quelques/3 jours; ces derniers/3 derniers jours; **he ran ~ me** il m'a dépassé en courant; il a passé devant moi en courant.

pasta ['pæstə] n pâtes fpl.

paste [peɪst] n (glue) colle f (de pâte); (jewellery) strass m; (CULIN) pâté m (à tartiner); pâte f // vt coller.

pasteurized ['pæstəraɪzd] a pasteurisé(e).

pastille ['pæstl] n pastille f.

pastime ['pɑːstaɪm] n passe-temps m inv, distraction f.

pastor ['pɑːstə*] n pasteur m.

pastry ['peɪstrɪ] n pâte f; (cake) pâtisserie f.

pasture ['pɑːstʃə*] n pâturage m.

pasty n ['pæstɪ] petit pâté en croûte // a ['peɪstɪ] pâteux(euse); (complexion) terreux(euse).

pat [pæt] vt donner une petite tape à.

patch [pætʃ] n (of material) pièce f; (spot) tache f; (of land) parcelle f // vt (clothes) rapiécer; **(to go through) a bad ~** (passer par) une période difficile; **to ~ up** vt réparer; ~**y** a inégal(e).

pâté ['pæteɪ] n pâté m, terrine f.

patent ['peɪtnt] n brevet m (d'invention) // vt faire breveter // a patent(e), manifeste; ~ **leather** n cuir verni.

paternal [pə'tɜːnl] a paternel(le).

path [pɑːθ] n chemin m, sentier m; allée f; (of planet) course f; (of missile) trajectoire f.

pathetic [pə'θetɪk] a (pitiful) pitoyable; (very bad) lamentable, minable; (moving) pathétique.

pathological [pæθə'lɒdʒɪkl] a pathologique.

pathos ['peɪθɒs] n pathétique m.

patience ['peɪʃns] n patience f;

(Brit: CARDS) réussite f.

patient ['peɪʃnt] n patient/e; malade m/f // a patient(e).

patriotic [pætrɪ'ɒtɪk] a patriotique; (person) patriote.

patrol [pə'trəʊl] n patrouille f // vt patrouiller dans; ~ **car** n voiture f de police; ~**man** n (US) agent m de police.

patron ['peɪtrən] n (in shop) client/e; (of charity) patron/ne; ~ **of the arts** mécène m; ~**ize** ['pætrənaɪz] vt être (un) client or un habitué de; (fig) traiter avec condescendance.

patter ['pætə*] n crépitement m, tapotement m; (sales talk) boniment m.

pattern ['pætən] n modèle m; (SEWING) patron m; (design) motif m; (sample) échantillon m.

paunch [pɔːntʃ] n gros ventre, bedaine f.

pauper ['pɔːpə*] n indigent/e.

pause [pɔːz] n pause f, arrêt m (MUS) silence m // vi faire une pause, s'arrêter.

pave [peɪv] vt paver, daller; **to ~ the way for** ouvrir la voie à.

pavement ['peɪvmənt] n (Brit) trottoir m.

pavilion [pə'vɪlɪən] n pavillon m, tente f.

paving ['peɪvɪŋ] n pavage m, dallage m; ~ **stone** n pavé m.

paw [pɔː] n patte f.

pawn [pɔːn] n gage m; (CHESS, also fig) pion m // vt mettre en gage; ~**broker** n prêteur m sur gages; ~**shop** n mont-de-piété m.

pay [peɪ] n salaire m; paie f // vb (pt, pp **paid**) vt payer // vi payer; (be profitable) être rentable; **to ~ attention (to)** prêter attention (à); **to ~ back** vt rembourser; **to ~ for** vt payer; **to ~ in** vt verser; **to ~ off** vt régler, acquitter; rembourser // vi (scheme, decision) se révéler payant(e); **to ~ up** vt régler; ~**able** a: ~**able to sb** à l'ordre de qn; ~**ee** n bénéficiaire m/f; ~ **en-**

velope n (US) = ~ **packet**; ~**ment** n paiement m; règlement m; versement m; **advance** ~**ment** acompte m; paiement anticipé; **monthly** ~**ment** mensualité f; ~ **packet** n (Brit) paie f; ~**phone** n cabine f téléphonique, téléphone public; ~**roll** n registre m du personnel; ~ **slip** n bulletin m de paie.

PC n abbr of **personal computer**.

p.c. abbr of **per cent.**

pea [piː] n (petit) pois.

peace [piːs] n paix f; (calm) calme m, tranquillité f; ~**able** a paisible; ~**ful** a paisible, calme.

peach [piːtʃ] n pêche f.

peacock ['piːkɒk] n paon m.

peak [piːk] n (mountain) pic m, cime f; (fig: highest level) maximum m; (: of career, fame) apogée m; ~ **hours** npl heures fpl d'affluence.

peal [piːl] n (of bells) carillon m; ~**s of laughter** éclats mpl de rire.

peanut ['piːnʌt] n arachide f, cacahuète f.

pear [pɛə*] n poire f.

pearl [pɜːl] n perle f.

peasant ['pɛznt] n paysan/ne.

peat [piːt] n tourbe f.

pebble ['pɛbl] n galet m, caillou m.

peck [pɛk] vt (also: ~ **at**) donner un coup de bec à; (food) picorer // n coup m de bec; (kiss) bécot m; ~**ing order** n ordre m des préséances; ~**ish** a (Brit col): **I feel** ~**ish** je mangerais bien quelque chose.

peculiar [pɪ'kjuːlɪə*] a étrange, bizarre, curieux(euse); particulier(ère); ~ **to** particulier à.

pedal ['pɛdl] n pédale f // vi pédaler.

pedantic [pɪ'dæntɪk] a pédant(e).

peddler ['pɛdlə*] n marchand ambulant.

pedestal ['pɛdəstl] n piédestal m.

pedestrian [pɪ'dɛstrɪən] n piéton m; ~ **crossing** n (Brit) passage clouté.

pediatrics [piːdɪ'ætrɪks] n (US) = **paediatrics**.

pedigree ['pɛdɪgriː] n ascendance f; (of animal) pedigree m // cpd (ani-

mal) de race.

pedlar ['pedlə*] *n* = **peddler**.

pee [pi:] *vi* (col) faire pipi, pisser.

peek [pi:k] *vi* jeter un coup d'œil (furtif).

peel [pi:l] *n* pelure *f*, épluchure *f*; (of orange, lemon) écorce *f* // *vt* (peler, éplucher // *vi* (paint etc) s'écailler; (wallpaper) se décoller.

peep [pi:p] *n* (Brit: look) coup d'œil furtif; (sound) pépiement *m*; // *vi* (Brit) jeter un coup d'œil (furtif); **to ~ out** *vi* se montrer (furtivement); **~hole** *n* judas *m*.

peer [pɪə*] *vi*: **to ~ at** regarder attentivement, scruter // *n* (noble) pair *m*; (equal) pair, égal/e; **~age** *n* pairie *f*.

peeved [pi:vd] *a* irrité(e), ennuyé(e).

peevish ['pi:vɪʃ] *a* grincheux(euse), maussade.

peg [peg] *n* cheville *f*; (for coat etc) patère *f*; (Brit: also: clothes ~) pince *f* à linge // *vt* (prices) contrôler, stabiliser.

Peking [pi:'kɪŋ] *n* Pékin.

pelican crossing ['pelɪkən-] *n* (Brit AUT) feu *m* à commande manuelle.

pellet ['pelɪt] *n* boulette *f*; (of lead) plomb *m*.

pelmet ['pelmɪt] *n* cantonnière *f*; lambrequin *m*.

pelt [pelt] *vt*: **to ~ sb (with)** bombarder qn (de) // *vi* (rain) tomber à seaux // *n* peau *f*.

pelvis ['pelvɪs] *n* bassin *m*.

pen [pen] *n* (for writing) stylo *m*; (for sheep) parc *m*.

penal ['pi:nl] *a* pénal(e); **~ize** *vt* pénaliser; (fig) désavantager.

penalty ['penltɪ] *n* pénalité *f*; sanction *f*; (fine) amende *f*; (SPORT) pénalisation *f*; **~ (kick)** *n* (FOOTBALL) penalty *m*.

penance ['penəns] *n* pénitence *f*.

pence [pens] *npl of* **penny**.

pencil ['pensl] *n* crayon *m*; **~ case** *n* trousse *f* (d'écolier); **~ sharpener** *n* taille-crayon(s) *m inv*.

pendant ['pendnt] *n* pendentif *m*.

pending ['pendɪŋ] *prep* en attendant // *a* en suspens.

pendulum ['pendjuləm] *n* pendule *m*; (of clock) balancier *m*.

penetrate ['penɪtreɪt] *vt* pénétrer dans; pénétrer.

penfriend ['penfrend] *n* (Brit) correspondant/e.

penguin ['pengwɪn] *n* pingouin *m*.

penicillin [penɪ'sɪlɪn] *n* pénicilline *f*.

peninsula [pə'nɪnsjulə] *n* péninsule *f*.

penis ['pi:nɪs] *n* pénis *m*, verge *f*.

penitent ['penɪtnt] *a* repentant(e).

penitentiary [penɪ'tenʃərɪ] *n* (US) prison *f*.

penknife ['pennaɪf] *n* canif *m*.

pen name *n* nom *m* de plume, pseudonyme *m*.

penniless ['penɪlɪs] *a* sans le sou.

penny, *pl* **pennies** *or* (Brit) **pence** ['penɪ, 'penɪz, pens] *n* penny *m* (*pl* pennies); (US) = cent.

penpal ['penpæl] *n* correspondant/e.

pension ['penʃən] *n* retraite *f*; (MIL) pension *f*; **~er** *n* (Brit) retraité/e.

penthouse ['penthaus] *n* appartement *m* (de luxe) en attique.

pent-up ['pentʌp] *a* (feelings) refoulé(e).

people ['pi:pl] *npl* gens *mpl*; personnes *fpl*; (citizens) peuple *m* // *n* (nation, race) peuple *m* // *vt* peupler; **several ~ came** plusieurs personnes sont venues; **the room was full of ~** la salle était pleine de monde or de gens.

pep [pep] *n* (col) entrain *m*, dynamisme *m*; **to ~ up** *vt* remonter.

pepper ['pepə*] *n* poivre *m*; (vegetable) poivron *m* // *vt* poivrer; **~mint** *n* (plant) menthe poivrée; (sweet) pastille *f* de menthe.

peptalk ['peptɔ:k] *n* (col) (petit) discours d'encouragement.

per [pə:*] *prep* par; **~ hour** (miles etc) à l'heure; (pay) de l'heure; **~ kilo** etc le kilo etc; **~ day/person** par jour/personne; **~ annum** ad par an; **~ capita** a, ad par personne, par habitant.

perceive [pəˈsiːv] vt percevoir; (*notice*) remarquer, s'apercevoir de.

per cent [pəˈsɛnt] ad pour cent.

percentage [pəˈsɛntɪdʒ] n pourcentage m.

perception [pəˈsɛpʃən] n perception f; sensibilité f; perspicacité f.

perceptive [pəˈsɛptɪv] a pénétrant(e); perspicace.

perch [pəːtʃ] n (*fish*) perche f; (*for bird*) perchoir m // vi (*se*) percher.

percolator [ˈpəːkəleɪtə*] n percolateur m; cafetière f électrique.

perennial [pəˈrɛnɪəl] a perpétuel(le); (*BOT*) vivace // n plante f vivace.

perfect a n, [ˈpəːfɪkt] a parfait(e) // n (*also:* ~ **tense**) parfait m // vt [pəˈfɛkt] parfaire; mettre au point; **~ly** ad parfaitement.

perforate [ˈpəːfəreɪt] vt perforer, percer; **perforation** [-ˈreɪʃən] n perforation f; (*line of holes*) pointillé m.

perform [pəˈfɔːm] vt (*carry out*) exécuter, remplir; (*concert etc*) jouer, donner // vi jouer; **~ance** n représentation f, spectacle m; (*of an artist*) interprétation f; (*of player etc*) prestation f; (*of car, engine*) performance f; **~er** n artiste m/f; **~ing** a (*animal*) savant(e).

perfume [ˈpəːfjuːm] n parfum m.

perfunctory [pəˈfʌŋktərɪ] a négligent(e), pour la forme.

perhaps [pəˈhæps] ad peut-être.

peril [ˈpɛrɪl] n péril m.

perimeter [pəˈrɪmɪtə*] n périmètre m; ~ **wall** n mur m d'enceinte.

period [ˈpɪərɪəd] n période f; (*HISTORY*) époque f; (*SCOL*) cours m; (*full stop*) point m; (*MED*) règles fpl // a (*costume, furniture*) d'époque; **~ic** [-ˈɔdɪk] a périodique; **~ical** [-ˈɔdɪk] a périodique // n périodique m.

peripheral [pəˈrɪfərəl] a périphérique // n (*COMPUT*) périphérique m.

perish [ˈpɛrɪʃ] vi périr, mourir; (*decay*) se détériorer; **~able** a périssable.

perjury [ˈpəːdʒərɪ] n (*LAW: in court*) faux témoignage; (*breach of oath*) parjure m.

perk [pəːk] n avantage m, à-côté m; **to ~ up** vi (*cheer up*) se ragaillardir; **~y** a (*cheerful*) guilleret(te), gai(e).

perm [pəːm] n (*for hair*) permanente f.

permanent [ˈpəːmənənt] a permanent(e).

permeate [ˈpəːmɪeɪt] vi s'infiltrer // vt s'infiltrer dans; pénétrer.

permissible [pəˈmɪsɪbl] a permis(e), acceptable.

permission [pəˈmɪʃən] n permission f, autorisation f.

permissive [pəˈmɪsɪv] a tolérant(e); **the ~ society** la société de tolérance.

permit n [ˈpəːmɪt] permis m // vt [pəˈmɪt] permettre; **to ~ sb to do** autoriser qn à faire, permettre à qn de faire.

perpendicular [pəːpənˈdɪkjulə*] a, n perpendiculaire (f).

perplex [pəˈplɛks] vt rendre perplexe; (*complicate*) embrouiller.

persecute [ˈpəːsɪkjuːt] vt persécuter.

persevere [pəːsɪˈvɪə*] vi persévérer.

Persian [ˈpəːʃən] a persan(e) // n (*LING*) persan m; **the (~) Gulf** le golfe Persique.

persist [pəˈsɪst] vi: **to ~ (in doing)** persister (à faire), s'obstiner (à faire); **~ent** a persistant(e), tenace.

person [ˈpəːsn] n personne f; **in ~** en personne; **~able** a de belle prestance, au physique attrayant; **~al** a personnel(le); individuel(le); (*PHYS*) en personne; **~al assistant (P.A.)** n secrétaire privé/e; **~al computer (PC)** n ordinateur individuel; **~ality** [-ˈnælɪtɪ] n personnalité f; **~ally** ad personnellement.

personnel [pəːsəˈnɛl] n personnel m.

perspective [pəˈspɛktɪv] n perspective f.

perspiration [pəːspɪˈreɪʃən] n transpiration f.

persuade [pəˈsweɪd] vt: **to ~ sb to**

do sth persuader qn de faire qch, amener or décider qn à faire qch.

pert [pə:t] a (bold) effronté(e), impertinent(e).

pertaining [pə'teɪnɪŋ]: ~ **to** prep relatif(ive) à.

peruse [pə'ru:z] vt lire (attentivement).

pervade [pə'veɪd] vt se répandre dans, envahir.

perverse [pə'və:s] a pervers(e); (stubborn) entêté(e), contrariant(e).

pervert n ['pə:və:t] perverti/e // vt [pə'və:t] pervertir.

pessimist ['pɛsɪmɪst] n pessimiste m/f; ~**ic** [-'mɪstɪk] a pessimiste.

pest [pɛst] n animal m (or insecte m) nuisible; (fig) fléau m.

pester ['pɛstə*] vt importuner, harceler.

pet [pɛt] n animal familier; (favourite) chouchou m // vt choyer // vi (col) se peloter.

petal ['pɛtl] n pétale m.

peter ['pi:tə*]: **to** ~ **out** vi s'épuiser; s'affaiblir.

petite [pə'ti:t] a menu(e).

petition [pə'tɪʃən] n pétition f.

petrified ['pɛtrɪfaɪd] a (fig) mort(e) de peur.

petrol ['pɛtrəl] n (Brit) essence f; **two-star** ~ essence f ordinaire; **four-star** ~ super m; ~ **can** n bidon m à essence.

petroleum [pə'trəʊlɪəm] n pétrole m.

petrol: ~ **pump** n (Brit) pompe f à essence; ~ **station** n (Brit) station-service f; ~ **tank** n (Brit) réservoir m d'essence.

petticoat ['pɛtɪkəʊt] n jupon m.

petty ['pɛtɪ] a (mean) mesquin(e); (unimportant) insignifiant(e), sans importance; ~ **cash** n menue monnaie; ~ **officer** n second-maître m.

petulant ['pɛtjulənt] a irritable.

pew [pju:] n banc m d'église).

pewter ['pju:tə*] n étain m.

phantom ['fæntəm] n fantôme m; (vision) fantasme m.

pharmacy ['fɑ:məsɪ] n pharmacie f.

phase [feɪz] n phase f, période f // vt: **to** ~ **in/out** introduire/supprimer qch progressivement.

Ph.D. abbr (= Doctor of Philosophy) title ≈ Docteur m en Droit or Lettres etc // n ≈ doctorat m; titulaire m d'un doctorat.

pheasant ['fɛznt] n faisan m.

phenomenon, pl **phenomena** [fə'nɔmɪnən, -nə] n phénomène m.

philosophical [fɪlə'sɔfɪkl] a philosophique.

philosophy [fɪ'lɔsəfɪ] n philosophie f.

phobia ['fəʊbjə] n phobie f.

phone [fəʊn] n téléphone m // vt téléphoner; **to be on the** ~ avoir le téléphone; (be calling) être au téléphone; **to** ~ **back** vt, vi rappeler; **to** ~ **up** vt téléphoner à // vi téléphoner; ~ **book** n annuaire m; ~ **box** or **booth** n cabine f téléphonique; ~ **call** n coup m de fil or de téléphone; ~**-in** n (Brit RADIO, TV) programme m à ligne ouverte.

phonetics [fə'nɛtɪks] n phonétique f.

phoney ['fəʊnɪ] a faux(fausse), factice.

phonograph ['fəʊnəgrɑ:f] n (US) électrophone m.

phony ['fəʊnɪ] a = **phoney**.

photo ['fəʊtəʊ] n photo f.

photo... ['fəʊtəʊ] prefix: ~**copier** n machine f à photocopier; ~**copy** n photocopie f // vt photocopier; ~**graph** n photographie f // vt photographier; ~**grapher** [fə'tɔgrəfə*] n photographe m/f; ~**graphy** [fə'tɔgrəfɪ] n photographie f.

phrase [freɪz] n expression f; (LING) locution f // vt exprimer; ~ **book** n recueil m d'expressions (pour touristes).

physical ['fɪzɪkl] a physique; ~ **education** n éducation f physique; ~**ly** ad physiquement.

physician [fɪ'zɪʃən] n médecin m.

physicist ['fɪzɪsɪst] n physicien/ne.

physics ['fɪzɪks] n physique f.

physiotherapy [fɪzɪəʊ'θerəpɪ] n kinésithérapie f.

physique [fɪ'ziːk] n physique m; constitution f.

pianist ['piːənɪst] n pianiste m/f.

piano ['pjɑːnəʊ] n piano m.

pick [pɪk] n (tool: also: ~axe) pic m, pioche f // vt choisir; (gather) cueillir; **take your ~** faites votre choix; **the ~ of** le(la) meilleur(e) de; **to ~ off** vt (kill) tuer soigneusement et) abattre; **to ~ on** vt fus (person) harceler; **to ~ out** vt choisir; (distinguish) distinguer; **to ~ up** vi (improve) remonter, s'améliorer // vt ramasser; (telephone) décrocher; (collect) passer prendre; (AUT: give lift to) prendre; (learn) apprendre; **to ~ up speed** prendre de la vitesse; **to ~ o.s. up** se relever.

picket ['pɪkɪt] n (in strike) gréviste m/f participant à un piquet de grève; piquet m de grève // vt mettre un piquet de grève devant.

pickle ['pɪkl] n (also: ~s: as condiment) pickles mpl // vt conserver dans du vinaigre ou dans de la saumure.

pickpocket ['pɪkpɒkɪt] n pickpocket m.

pickup ['pɪkʌp] n (Brit: on record player) bras m pick-up; (small truck) pick-up m inv.

picnic ['pɪknɪk] n pique-nique m.

pictorial [pɪk'tɔːrɪəl] a illustré(e).

picture ['pɪktʃə*] n image f; (painting) peinture f, tableau m; (photograph) photo(graphie) f; (drawing) dessin m; (film) film m // vt se représenter; (describe) dépeindre, représenter; **the ~s** (Brit) le cinéma; **~ book** n livre m d'images.

picturesque [pɪktʃə'resk] a pittoresque.

pie [paɪ] n tourte f; (of meat) pâté m en croûte.

piece [piːs] n morceau m; (of land) parcelle f; (item): **a ~ of furniture/advice** un meuble/conseil // vt: **to ~**

together rassembler; **to take to ~s** démonter; **~meal** ad par bouts; **~work** n travail m aux pièces.

pie chart n graphique m à secteurs, camembert m

pier [pɪə*] n jetée f; (of bridge etc) pile f.

pierce [pɪəs] vt percer, transpercer.

pig [pɪg] n cochon m, porc m.

pigeon ['pɪdʒən] n pigeon m; **~hole** n casier m.

piggy bank ['pɪgɪbæŋk] n tirelire f.

pigheaded ['pɪg'hedɪd] a entêté(e), têtu(e).

pigskin ['pɪgskɪn] n (peau m de) porc m.

pigsty ['pɪgstaɪ] n porcherie f.

pigtail ['pɪgteɪl] n natte f, tresse f.

pike [paɪk] n (spear) pique f; (fish) brochet m.

pilchard ['pɪltʃəd] n pilchard m (sorte de sardine).

pile [paɪl] n (pillar, of books) pile f; (heap) tas m; (of carpet) épaisseur f // vt (also: ~ up) vt empiler, entasser // vi s'entasser; **to ~ into** (car) s'entasser dans.

piles [paɪlz] npl hémorroïdes fpl.

pileup ['paɪlʌp] n (AUT) télescopage m, collision f en série.

pilfering ['pɪlfərɪŋ] n chapardage m.

pilgrim ['pɪlgrɪm] n pèlerin m.

pill [pɪl] n pilule f; **the ~** la pilule.

pillage ['pɪlɪdʒ] vt piller.

pillar ['pɪlə*] n pilier m; **~ box** n (Brit) boîte f aux lettres.

pillion ['pɪljən] n (of motor cycle) siège m arrière.

pillow ['pɪləʊ] n oreiller m; **~case** n taie f d'oreiller.

pilot ['paɪlət] n pilote m // cpd (scheme etc) pilote, expérimental(e) // vt piloter; **~ light** n veilleuse f.

pimp [pɪmp] n souteneur m, maquereau m.

pimple ['pɪmpl] n bouton m.

pin [pɪn] n épingle f; (TECH) cheville f // vt épingler; **~s and needles** fourmis fpl; **to ~ sb down** (fig) obliger qn à répondre; **to ~ sth on sb**

(fig) mettre qch sur le dos de qn.

pinafore ['pɪnəfɔː*] n tablier m.

pinball ['pɪnbɔ:l] n *(also:* ~ **machine)** flipper m.

pincers ['pɪnsəz] npl tenailles fpl.

pinch [pɪntʃ] n pincement m; *(of salt etc)* pincée f // vt pincer; *(col: steal)* piquer, chiper // vi *(shoe)* serrer; **at a** ~ à la rigueur.

pincushion ['pɪnkʊʃən] n pelote f à épingles.

pine [paɪn] n *(also:* ~ **tree)** pin m // vi: **to** ~ **for** aspirer à, désirer ardemment; **to** ~ **away** vi dépérir.

pineapple ['paɪnæpl] n ananas m.

ping [pɪŋ] n *(noise)* tintement m; ~-**pong** ® n ping-pong m ®.

pink [pɪŋk] a rose m; *(colour)* rose m; *(BOT)* œillet m, mignardise f.

pinpoint ['pɪnpɔɪnt] vt indiquer (avec précision).

pint [paɪnt] n pinte f *(Brit = 0.57 l; US = 0.47 l)*; *(Brit col)* ≈ demi m, ≈ pot m.

pioneer [paɪə'nɪə*] n explorateur/trice; *(early settler, fig)* pionnier m.

pious ['paɪəs] a pieux(euse).

pip [pɪp] n *(seed)* pépin m; *(Brit: time signal on radio)* top m.

pipe [paɪp] n tuyau m, conduite f; *(for smoking)* pipe f; *(MUS)* pipeau m // vt amener par tuyau; ~**s** npl *(also:* **bag**~**s)** cornemuse f; **to** ~ **down** vi *(col)* se taire; ~ **cleaner** n cure-pipe m; ~ **dream** n chimère f, utopie f; ~**line** n pipe-line m; ~ r n joueur/euse de pipeau *(or de cornemuse)*.

piping ['paɪpɪŋ] ad: ~ **hot** très chaud(e).

pique [pi:k] n dépit m.

pirate ['paɪərət] n pirate m.

Pisces ['paɪsi:z] n les Poissons mpl.

piss [pɪs] vi *(col)* pisser; ~**ed** a *(col: drunk)* bourré(e).

pistol ['pɪstl] n pistolet m.

piston ['pɪstən] n piston m.

pit [pɪt] n trou m, fosse f; *(also:* **coal** ~**)** puits m de mine; *(also:* **orchestra** ~**)** fosse f d'orchestre // vt: **to** ~

sb against sb opposer qn à qn; ~**s** npl *(AUT)* aire f de service.

pitch [pɪtʃ] n *(throw)* lancement m; *(MUS)* ton m; *(of voice)* hauteur f; *(Brit SPORT)* terrain m; *(NAUT)* tangage m; *(tar)* poix f // vt *(throw)* lancer // vi *(fall)* tomber; *(NAUT)* tanguer; **to** ~ **a tent** dresser une tente; ~**ed battle** n bataille rangée.

pitcher ['pɪtʃə*] n cruche f.

pitchfork ['pɪtʃfɔ:k] n fourche f.

piteous ['pɪtɪəs] a pitoyable.

pitfall ['pɪtfɔ:l] n trappe f, piège m.

pith [pɪθ] n *(of plant)* moelle f; *(of orange)* intérieur m de l'écorce; *(fig)* essence f, vigueur f.

pithy ['pɪθɪ] a piquant(e); vigoureux(euse).

pitiful ['pɪtɪful] a *(touching)* pitoyable; *(contemptible)* lamentable.

pitiless ['pɪtɪlɪs] a impitoyable.

pittance ['pɪtns] n salaire m de misère.

pity ['pɪtɪ] n pitié f // vt plaindre; **what a** ~! quel dommage!

pivot ['pɪvət] n pivot m.

pizza ['pi:tsə] n pizza f.

placard ['plækɑ:d] n affiche f.

placate [plə'keɪt] vt apaiser, calmer.

place [pleɪs] n endroit m, lieu m; *(proper position, rank, seat)* place f; *(house)* maison f, logement m; *(home)*: **at/to his** ~ chez lui // vt *(object)* placer, mettre; *(identify)* situer; reconnaître; **to take** ~ avoir lieu; se passer; **to change** ~ **s with sb** changer de place avec qn; **to** ~ **an order** passer une commande; **out of** ~ *(not suitable)* déplacé(e), inopportun(e); **in the first** ~ d'abord, en premier.

plague [pleɪg] n fléau m; *(MED)* peste f // vt *(fig)* tourmenter.

plaice [pleɪs] n *(pl inv)* carrelet m.

plaid [plæd] n tissu écossais.

plain [pleɪn] a *(clear)* clair(e), évident(e); *(simple)* simple, ordinaire; *(frank)* franc(franche); *(not handsome)* quelconque, ordinaire; *(cigarette)* sans filtre; *(without seasoning* *etc*) nature *inv*; (*in one colour*) uni(e) // *ad* franchement, carrément // *n* plaine *f*; ~ **chocolate** *n* chocolat *m* à croquer; ~ **clothes**: **in** ~ **clothes** (*police*) en civil; ~**ly** *ad* clairement; (*frankly*) carrément, sans détours.

plaintiff ['pleɪntɪf] *n* plaignant/e.

plait [plæt] *n* tresse *f*, natte *f*.

plan [plæn] *n* plan *m*; (*scheme*) projet *m* // *vt* (*think in advance*) projeter; (*prepare*) organiser // *vi* faire des projets.

plane [pleɪn] *n* (AVIAT) avion *m*; (*tree*) platane *m*; (*tool*) rabot *m*; (ART, MATH etc) plan *m* // *a* plan(e), plat(e) // *vt* (*with tool*) raboter.

planet ['plænɪt] *n* planète *f*.

plank [plæŋk] *n* planche *f*.

planning ['plænɪŋ] *n* planification *f*; **family** ~ planning familial; ~ **permission** *n* permis *m* de construire.

plant [plɑːnt] *n* plante *f*; (*machinery*) matériel *m*; (*factory*) usine *f* // *vt* planter; (*colony*) établir; (*bomb*) déposer, poser.

plaster ['plɑːstə*] *n* plâtre *m*; (*also*: ~ **of Paris**) plâtre à mouler; (Brit: *also*: **sticking** ~) pansement adhésif // *vt* plâtrer; (*cover*): **to** ~ **with** couvrir de; **in** ~ (*leg etc*) dans le plâtre; ~**ed** *a* (*col*) soûl(e).

plastic ['plæstɪk] *n* plastique *m* // *a* (*made of plastic*) en plastique; (*flexible*) plastique, malléable; (*art*) plastique; ~ **bag** *n* sac *m* en plastique.

plasticine ['plæstɪsi:n] *n* ® pâte *f* à modeler.

plastic surgery *n* chirurgie *f* esthétique.

plate [pleɪt] *n* (*dish*) assiette *f*; (*sheet of metal*, PHOT) plaque *f*; (*in book*) gravure *f*.

plateau, ~**s** *or* ~**x** ['plætəʊ, -z] *n* plateau *m*.

plate glass *n* verre *m* (de vitrine).

platform ['plætfɔːm] *n* (*at meeting*) tribune *f*; (Brit: *of bus*) plate-forme *f*; (*stage*) estrade *f*; (RAIL) quai *m*; ~ **ticket** *n* (Brit) billet *m* de quai.

platinum ['plætɪnəm] *n* platine *m*.

platoon [plə'tuːn] *n* peloton *m*.

platter ['plætə*] *n* plat *m*.

plausible ['plɔːzɪbl] *a* plausible; (*person*) convaincant(e).

play [pleɪ] *n* jeu *m*; (THEATRE) pièce *f* (de théâtre) // *vt* (*game*) jouer à; (*team, opponent*) jouer contre; (*instrument*) jouer de; (*play, part, piece of music, note*) jouer // *vi* jouer; **to** ~ **safe** ne prendre aucun risque; **to** ~ **down** *vt* minimiser; **to** ~ **up** *vi* (*cause trouble*) faire des siennes; ~**boy** *n* playboy *m*; ~**er** *n* joueur/euse; (THEATRE) acteur/trice; (MUS) musicien/ne; ~**ful** *a* enjoué(e); ~**ground** *n* cour *f* de récréation; ~**group** *n* garderie *f*; ~**ing card** *n* carte *f* à jouer; ~**ing field** *n* terrain *m* de sport; ~**mate** *n* camarade *m/f*, copain/copine; ~**off** *n* (SPORT) belle *f*; ~**pen** *n* parc *m* (pour bébé); ~**school** *n* = ~**group**; ~**thing** *n* jouet *m*; ~**wright** *n* dramaturge *m*.

plc *abbr* (= *public limited company*) SARL *f*.

plea [pli:] *n* (*request*) appel *m*; (*excuse*) excuse *f*; (LAW) défense *f*.

plead [pli:d] *vt* plaider; (*give as excuse*) invoquer // *vi* (LAW) plaider; (*beg*): **to** ~ **with sb** implorer qn.

pleasant ['plɛznt] *a* agréable; ~**ries** *npl* (*polite remarks*) civilités *fpl*.

please [pli:z] *vt* plaire à // *vi* (*think fit*): **do as you** ~ faites comme il vous plaira; ~! s'il te (*or* vous) plaît; ~ **yourself!** à ta (*or* votre) guise!; ~**d** *a*: ~**d (with)** content(e) (de); ~**d to meet you** enchanté (de faire votre connaissance); **pleasing** *a* plaisant(e), qui fait plaisir.

pleasure ['plɛʒə*] *n* plaisir *m*; '**it's a** ~' 'je vous en prie'.

pleat [pli:t] *n* pli *m*.

pledge [plɛdʒ] *n* gage *m*; (*promise*) promesse *f* // *vt* engager; promettre.

plentiful ['plɛntɪful] *a* abondant(e), copieux(euse).

plenty ['plɛntɪ] *n* abondance *f*; ~ **of**

beaucoup de; (bien) assez de.

pliable ['plaɪəbl] a flexible; (person) malléable.

pliers ['plaɪəz] npl pinces fpl.

plight [plaɪt] n situation f critique.

plimsolls ['plɪmsɔlz] npl (Brit) (chaussures fpl de) tennis fpl.

plinth [plɪnθ] n socle m.

plod [plɔd] vi avancer péniblement; (fig) peiner; **~der** n bûcheur/euse.

plonk [plɔŋk] (col) n (Brit: wine) pinard m, piquette f // vt: **to ~ down** poser brusquement qch.

plot [plɔt] n complot m, conspiration f; (of story, play) intrigue f; (of land) lot m de terrain, lopin m // vt (mark out) pointer; relever; (conspire) comploter // vi comploter; **~ter** n (instrument) table traçante, traceur m.

plough, (US) **plow** [plaʊ] n charrue f // vt (earth) labourer; **to ~ back** vt (COMM) réinvestir; **to ~ through** vt fus (snow etc) avancer péniblement dans.

ploy [plɔɪ] n stratagème m.

pluck [plʌk] vt (fruit) cueillir; (musical instrument) pincer; (bird) plumer // n courage m, cran m; **to ~ up courage** prendre son courage à deux mains; **~y** a courageux(euse).

plug [plʌg] n bouchon m, bonde f; (ELEC) prise f de courant; (AUT: also: **spark(ing) ~**) bougie f // vt (hole) boucher; (col: advertise) faire du battage pour, matraquer; **to ~ in** vt (ELEC) brancher.

plum [plʌm] n (fruit) prune f // a: **~ job** (col) travail m en or.

plumb [plʌm] a vertical(e) // n plomb m // ad (exactly) en plein // vt sonder.

plumber ['plʌmə*] n plombier m.

plumbing ['plʌmɪŋ] n (trade) plomberie f; (piping) tuyauterie f.

plummet ['plʌmɪt] vi plonger, dégringoler.

plump [plʌmp] a rondelet(te), dodu(e), bien en chair // vt: **to ~ sth (down) on** laisser tomber qch lour-

dement sur; **to ~ for** vt fus (col: choose) se décider pour.

plunder ['plʌndə*] n pillage m // vt piller.

plunge [plʌndʒ] n plongeon m // vt plonger // vi (fall) tomber, dégringoler; **to take the ~** se jeter à l'eau; **~r** n piston m; (débouchoir à ventouse f.

pluperfect [plu:'pə:fɪkt] n plus-que-parfait m.

plural ['plʊərl] a pluriel(le) // n pluriel m.

plus [plʌs] n (also: **~ sign**) signe m plus // prep plus; **ten/twenty ~** plus de dix/vingt.

plush [plʌʃ] a somptueux(euse).

ply [plaɪ] n (of wool) fil m; (of wood) feuille f, épaisseur f // vt (tool) manier; (a trade) exercer // vi (ship) faire la navette; **to ~ sb with drink** donner continuellement à boire à qn; **~wood** n contre-plaqué m.

P.M. abbr of **Prime Minister**.

p.m. ad abbr (= post meridiem) de l'après-midi.

pneumatic drill [nju:'mætɪk-] n marteau-piqueur m.

pneumonia [nju:'məʊnɪə] n pneumonie f.

poach [pəʊtʃ] vt (cook) pocher; (steal) pêcher (or chasser) sans permis // vi braconner; **~er** n braconnier m.

P.O. Box n abbr of **Post Office Box**.

pocket ['pɔkɪt] n poche f // vt empocher; **to be out of ~** (Brit) en être de sa poche; **~book** n (wallet) portefeuille m; (notebook) carnet m; **~knife** n canif m; **~ money** n argent m de poche.

pod [pɔd] n cosse f.

podgy ['pɔdʒɪ] a rondelet(te).

podiatrist [pɔ'di:ɪtrɪst] n (US) pédicure m/f, podologue m/f.

poem ['pəʊɪm] n poème m.

poet ['pəʊɪt] n poète m; **~ic** [-'etɪk] a poétique; **~ laureate** n poète lauréat (nommé et appointé par la Cour royale); **~ry** n poésie f.

poignant ['pɔɪnjənt] a poignant(e); (sharp) vif(vive).

point [pɔɪnt] n (tip) pointe f; (in time) moment m; (in space) endroit m; (GEOM, SCOL, SPORT, on scale) point m; (subject, idea) point, sujet m; (also: decimal ~): 2 ~ 3 (2.3) 2 virgule 3 (2,3) // vt (show) indiquer; (wall, window) jointoyer; (gun etc): **to ~ sth at** braquer or diriger qch sur // vi montrer du doigt; **~s** npl (AUT) vis platinées; (RAIL) aiguillage m; **to be on the ~ of doing sth** être sur le point de faire qch; **to make a ~** faire une remarque; **to get the ~** comprendre, saisir; **to come to the ~** en venir au fait; **there's no ~ (in doing)** cela ne sert à rien (de faire); **to ~ out** vt faire remarquer, souligner; **to ~ to** vt fus montrer du doigt; (fig) signaler; **~-blank** ad (also: **at ~-blank range**) à bout portant; (fig) catégorique; **~ed** a (shape) pointu(e); (remark) plein(e) de sous-entendus; **~edly** ad d'une manière significative; **~er** n (stick) baguette f; (needle) aiguille f; (dog) chien m d'arrêt; **~less** a inutile, vain(e); **~ of view** n point m de vue.

poise [pɔɪz] n (balance) équilibre m; (of head, body) port m; (calmness) calme m // vt placer en équilibre.

poison ['pɔɪzn] n poison m // vt empoisonner; **~ing** n empoisonnement m; **~ous** a (snake) venimeux(euse); (substance etc) vénéneux(euse).

poke [pəuk] vt (fire) tisonner; (jab with finger, stick etc) piquer; pousser du doigt; (put): **to ~ sth in(to)** fourrer or enfoncer qch dans; **to ~ about** vi fureter.

poker ['pəukə*] n tisonnier m; (CARDS) poker m; **~-faced** a au visage impassible.

poky ['pəukɪ] a exigu(ë).

Poland ['pəulənd] n Pologne f.

polar ['pəulə*] a polaire; **~ bear** n

ours blanc.

Pole [pəul] n Polonais/e.

pole [pəul] n (of wood) mât m, perche f; (ELEC) poteau m; (GEO) pôle m; **~ bean** n (US) haricot m (à rames); **~ vault** n saut m à la perche.

police [pə'liːs] npl police f // vt maintenir l'ordre dans; **~ car** n voiture f de police; **~man** n agent m de police, policier m; **~ station** n commissariat m de police; **~woman** n femme-agent f.

policy ['pɒlɪsɪ] n politique f; (also: **insurance ~**) police f (d'assurance).

polio ['pəulɪəu] n polio f.

Polish ['pəulɪʃ] a polonais(e) // n (LING) polonais m.

polish ['pɒlɪʃ] n (for shoes) cirage m; (for floor) cire f, encaustique f; (for nails) vernis m; (shine) éclat m, poli m; (fig: refinement) raffinement m // vt (put polish on shoes, wood) cirer; (make shiny) astiquer, faire briller; (fig: improve) perfectionner; **to ~ off** vt (work) expédier; (food) liquider; **~ed** a (fig) raffiné(e).

polite [pə'laɪt] a poli(e); **~ness** n politesse f.

politic ['pɒlɪtɪk] a diplomatique; **~al** [pə'lɪtɪkl] a politique; **~ally** ad politiquement; **~ian** [-'tɪʃən] n homme m politique, politicien m; **~s** npl politique f.

polka ['pɒlkə] n polka f; **~ dot** n pois m.

poll [pəul] n scrutin m, vote m; (also: **opinion ~**) sondage m (d'opinion) // vt obtenir.

pollen ['pɒlən] n pollen m.

polling ['pəulɪŋ] (Brit): **~ booth** n isoloir m; **~ day** n jour m des élections; **~ station** n bureau m de vote.

pollution [pə'luːʃən] n pollution f.

polo ['pəuləu] n polo m; **~-neck** a à col roulé.

polytechnic [pɒlɪ'teknɪk] n (college) I.U.T. m, Institut m Universitaire de Technologie.

polythene ['pɒlɪθiːn] n polyéthylène

m; ~ **bag** n sac m en plastique.

pomegranate ['pɔmɪgrænɪt] n grenade f.

pomp [pɔmp] n pompe f, faste f, apparat m.

pompous ['pɔmpəs] a pompeux(euse).

pond [pɔnd] n étang m; mare f.

ponder ['pɔndə*] vt considérer, peser; ~**ous** a pesant(e), lourd(e).

pong [pɔŋ] n (Brit col) puanteur f.

pony ['pəunɪ] n poney m; ~**tail** n queue f de cheval; ~ **trekking** n (Brit) randonnée f à cheval.

poodle ['pu:dl] n caniche m.

pool [pu:l] n (of rain) flaque f; (pond) mare f; (artificial) bassin m; (also: **swimming** ~) piscine f; (sth shared) fonds commun; (money at cards) cagnotte f; (billiards) poule f // vt mettre en commun; **typing** ~ pool m dactylographique; (football) ~**s** npl ≈ loto sportif.

poor [puə*] a pauvre; (mediocre) médiocre, faible, mauvais(e) // npl: **the** ~ les pauvres mpl; ~**ly** ad pauvrement; médiocrement // a souffrant(e), malade.

pop [pɔp] n (noise) bruit sec; (MUS) musique f pop; (US col: father) papa m // vt (put) fourrer, mettre (rapidement) // vi éclater; (cork) sauter; **to** ~ **in** vi entrer en passant; **to** ~ **out** vi sortir; **to** ~ **up** vi apparaître, surgir; ~ **concert** n concert m pop.

pope [pəup] n pape m.

poplar ['pɔplə*] n peuplier m.

poppy ['pɔpɪ] n coquelicot m; pavot m.

popsicle ['pɔpsɪkl] n (US) esquimau m.

popular ['pɔpjulə*] a populaire; (fashionable) à la mode; ~**ize** vt populariser; (science) vulgariser.

population [pɔpju'leɪʃən] n population f.

porcelain ['pɔ:slɪn] n porcelaine f.

porch [pɔ:tʃ] n porche m.

porcupine ['pɔ:kjupaɪn] n porc-épic

m.

pore [pɔ:*] n pore m // vi: **to** ~ **over** s'absorber dans, être plongé(e) dans.

pork [pɔ:k] n porc m.

pornography [pɔ:'nɔgrəfɪ] n pornographie f.

porpoise ['pɔ:pəs] n marsouin m.

porridge ['pɔrɪdʒ] n porridge m.

port [pɔ:t] n (harbour) port m; (opening in ship) sabord m; (NAUT: left side) bâbord m; (wine) porto m; ~ **of call** escale f.

portable ['pɔ:təbl] a portatif(ive).

portent ['pɔ:tɛnt] n présage m.

porter ['pɔ:tə*] n (for luggage) porteur m; (doorkeeper) gardien/ne; portier m.

portfolio [pɔ:t'fəuliəu] n portefeuille m; (of artist) portfolio m.

porthole ['pɔ:thəul] n hublot m.

portion ['pɔ:ʃən] n portion f, part f.

portly ['pɔ:tlɪ] a corpulent(e).

portrait ['pɔ:treɪt] n portrait m.

portray [pɔ:'treɪ] vt faire le portrait de; (in writing) dépeindre, représenter.

Portugal ['pɔ:tjugl] n Portugal m.

Portuguese [pɔ:tju'gi:z] a portugais(e) // n (pl inv) Portugais/e; (LING) portugais m.

pose [pəuz] n pose f; (pej) affectation f // vi poser; (pretend): **to** ~ **as** se poser en // vt poser, créer.

posh [pɔʃ] a (col) chic inv.

position [pə'zɪʃən] n position f; (job) situation f.

positive ['pɔzɪtɪv] a positif(ive); (certain) sûr(e), certain(e); (definite) formel(le), catégorique; indéniable, réel(le).

posse ['pɔsɪ] n (US) détachement m.

possess [pə'zɛs] vt posséder; ~**ion** [pə'zɛʃən] n possession f.

possibility [pɔsɪ'bɪlɪtɪ] n possibilité f; éventualité f.

possible ['pɔsɪbl] a possible; **as big as** ~ aussi gros que possible.

possibly ['pɔsɪblɪ] ad (perhaps) peut-être; **if you** ~ **can** si cela vous est possible; **I cannot** ~ **come** il m'est impossible de venir.

post [pəʊst] n poste f; (Brit: collection) levée f; (: letters, delivery) courrier m; (job, situation) poste m; (pole) poteau m // vt (Brit: send by post; MIL) poster; (Brit: appoint): **to ~** to affecter à; (notice) afficher; **~age** n affranchissement m; **~al order** n mandat-(poste) m; **~box** n (Brit) boîte f aux lettres; **~card** n carte postale; **~code** n (Brit) code postal.

poster ['pəʊstə*] n affiche f.

poste restante ['pəʊst'rɛstɑ̃:nt] n poste restante.

postgraduate ['pəʊst'grædjuət] n étudiant/e de troisième cycle.

posthumous ['pɒstjʊməs] a posthume.

postman ['pəʊstmən] n facteur m.

postmark ['pəʊstmɑ:k] n cachet m (de la poste).

postmaster ['pəʊstmɑ:stə*] n receveur m des postes.

post-mortem [pəʊst'mɔ:təm] n autopsie f.

post office ['pəʊstɒfɪs] n (building) poste f; (organization): the Post Office les Postes; **Post Office Box (P.O. Box)** n boîte postale (B.P.).

postpone [pəs'pəʊn] vt remettre (à plus tard), reculer.

posture ['pɒstʃə*] n posture f, attitude f.

postwar ['pəʊst'wɔ:*] a d'après-guerre.

posy ['pəʊzɪ] n petit bouquet.

pot [pɒt] n (for cooking) marmite f, casserole f; (for plants, jam) pot m; (col: marijuana) herbe f // vt (plant) mettre en pot; **to go to ~** (col: work, performance) aller à vau-l'eau.

potato, ~es [pə'teɪtəʊ] n pomme f de terre; **~ peeler** n éplucheur de légumes m.

potent ['pəʊtnt] a puissant(e); (drink) fort(e), très alcoolisé(e).

potential [pə'tɛnʃl] a potentiel(le) // n potentiel m; **~ly** ad en puissance.

pothole ['pɒthəʊl] n (in road) nid m de poule; (Brit: underground) gouffre m, caverne f; **potholing** n (Brit): **to go potholing** faire de la spéléologie.

potluck [pɒt'lʌk] n: **to take ~** tenter sa chance.

potshot ['pɒtʃɒt] n: **to take ~s** or **a ~ at** canarder.

potted ['pɒtɪd] a (food) en conserve; (plant) en pot.

potter ['pɒtə*] n potier m // vi: **to ~ around, ~ about** bricoler; **~y** n poterie f.

potty ['pɒtɪ] a (col: mad) dingue // n (child's) pot m.

pouch [paʊtʃ] n (ZOOL) poche f; (for tobacco) blague f.

poultry ['pəʊltrɪ] n volaille f.

pounce [paʊns] vi: **to ~ (on)** bondir (sur), fondre sur.

pound [paʊnd] n livre f (weight = 453g, 16 ounces; money = 100 pence); (for dogs, cars) fourrière f // vt (beat) bourrer de coups, marteler; (crush) piler, pulvériser // vi (beat) battre violemment, taper.

pour [pɔ:*] vt verser // vi couler à flots; (rain) pleuvoir à verse; **to ~ away** or **off** vt vider; **to ~ in** vi (people) affluer, se précipiter; **to ~ out** vi (people) sortir en masse // vt vider; déverser; (serve: a drink) verser; **~ing** a: **~ing rain** pluie torrentielle.

pout [paʊt] vi faire la moue.

poverty ['pɒvətɪ] n pauvreté f, misère f; **~-stricken** a pauvre, déshérité(e).

powder ['paʊdə*] n poudre f // vt poudrer; **to ~ one's face** or **nose** se poudrer; **~ compact** n poudrier m; **~ed milk** n lait m en poudre; **~ puff** n houppette f; **~ room** n toilettes fpl (pour dames).

power ['paʊə*] n (strength) puissance f, force f; (ability, POL: of party, leader) pouvoir m; (MATH) puissance; (of speech, thought) faculté f; (ELEC) courant m // vt marcher; **to be in ~** (POL etc) être au pouvoir; **~ cut** n (Brit) coupure f de courant; **~ failure** n panne f de courant; **~ful** a puissant(e); **~less** a impuissant(e); **~ point** n (Brit) prise f de courant; **~ station** n centrale f électrique.

p.p. abbr (= per procurationem): **~ J. Smith** pour M. J. Smith.

PR n abbr of **public relations**.

practicable ['præktɪkəbl] a (scheme) réalisable.

practical ['præktɪkl] a pratique; **~ity** [-'kælɪtɪ] n (no pl) (of situation etc) aspect m pratique; **~ joke** n farce f; **~ly** ad (almost) pratiquement.

practice ['præktɪs] n pratique f; (of profession) exercice m; (at football etc) entraînement m; (business) cabinet m; clientèle f // vi, vt (US = **practise**); **in ~** (in reality) en pratique; **out of ~** rouillé(e).

practise, (US) **practice** ['præktɪs] vt (work at: piano, one's backhand etc) s'exercer à, travailler; (train for: skiing, running etc) s'entraîner à; (a sport, religion, method) pratiquer; (profession) exercer // vi s'exercer, travailler; (train) s'entraîner; **practising** a (Christian etc) pratiquant(e); (lawyer) en exercice.

practitioner [præk'tɪʃənə*] n praticien/ne.

prairie ['prɛərɪ] n savane f; (US): **the ~s** la Prairie.

praise [preɪz] n éloge(s) m(pl), louange(s) f(pl) // vt louer, faire l'éloge de.

pram [præm] n (Brit) landau m, voiture f d'enfant.

prance [prɑːns] vi (horse) caracoler.

prank [præŋk] n farce f.

prawn [prɔːn] n crevette f (rose).

pray [preɪ] vi prier.

prayer [prɛə*] n prière f.

preach [priːtʃ] vi, vt prêcher.

precaution [prɪ'kɔːʃən] n précaution f.

precede [prɪ'siːd] vt, vi précéder.

precedence ['prɛsɪdəns] n préséance f.

precedent ['prɛsɪdənt] n précédent m.

precinct ['priːsɪŋkt] n (round cathedral) pourtour m, enceinte f; **~s** mpl (neighbourhood) alentours mpl, environs mpl; **pedestrian ~** (Brit) zone piétonnière.

precious ['prɛʃəs] a précieux(euse).

precipitate a [prɪ'sɪpɪtɪt] (hasty) précipité(e) // vt [prɪ'sɪpɪteɪt] précipiter.

precise [prɪ'saɪs] a précis(e); **~ly** ad précisément.

preclude [prɪ'kluːd] vt exclure.

precocious [prɪ'kəʊʃəs] a précoce.

precondition [priːkən'dɪʃən] n condition f nécessaire.

predecessor ['priːdɪsɛsə*] n prédécesseur m.

predicament [prɪ'dɪkəmənt] n situation f difficile.

predict [prɪ'dɪkt] vt prédire; **~able** a prévisible.

predominantly [prɪ'dɒmɪnəntlɪ] ad en majeure partie; surtout.

preen [priːn] vt: **to ~ itself** (bird) se lisser les plumes; **to ~ o.s.** s'admirer.

prefab ['priːfæb] n bâtiment préfabriqué.

preface ['prɛfəs] n préface f.

prefect ['priːfɛkt] n (Brit: in school) élève chargé(e) de certaines fonctions de discipline; (in France) préfet m.

prefer [prɪ'fɜː*] vt préférer; **~ably** ['prɛfrəblɪ] ad de préférence; **~ence** ['prɛfrəns] n préférence f; **~ential** [prɛfə'rɛnʃəl] a préférentiel(le); **~ential treatment** traitement m de faveur.

prefix ['priːfɪks] n préfixe m.

pregnancy ['prɛgnənsɪ] n grossesse f.

pregnant ['prɛgnənt] a enceinte af.

prehistoric ['priːhɪs'tɔrɪk] a préhistorique.

prejudice ['prɛdʒʊdɪs] n préjugé m;

(harm) tort *m*, préjudice *m* // *vt* porter préjudice à; **~d** *a (person)* plein(e) de préjugés; *(view)* préconçu(e), partial(e).

premarital ['pri:'mærɪtl] *a* avant le mariage.

premature ['prɛmətʃuə*] *a* prématuré(e).

premier ['prɛmɪə*] *a* premier(ère), capital(e), primordial(e) // *n (POL)* premier ministre.

première ['prɛmɪə*] *n* première *f*.

premise ['prɛmɪs] *n* prémisse *f*; **~s** *npl* locaux *mpl*; **on the ~s** sur les lieux; sur place.

premium ['pri:mɪəm] *n* prime *f*; **to be at a ~** faire prime; **~ bond** *n (Brit)* bon *m* à lot, obligation *f* à prime.

premonition [prɛmə'nɪʃən] *n* prémonition *f*.

preoccupied [pri:'ɔkjupaɪd] *a* préoccupé(e).

prep [prɛp] *n (SCOL: study)* étude *f*; **~ school** *n* = **preparatory school**.

prepaid [pri:'peɪd] *a* payé(e) d'avance.

preparation [prɛpə'reɪʃən] *n* préparation *f*; **~s** *npl (for trip, war)* préparatifs *mpl*.

preparatory [prɪ'pærətərɪ]: **~ school** *n* école primaire privée.

prepare [prɪ'pɛə*] *vt* préparer // *vi*: **to ~ for** se préparer à; **~d** *a* prêt(e) à.

preposition [prɛpə'zɪʃən] *n* préposition *f*.

preposterous [prɪ'pɔstərəs] *a* absurde.

prerequisite [pri:'rɛkwɪzɪt] *n* condition *f* préalable.

prescribe [prɪ'skraɪb] *vt* prescrire.

prescription [prɪ'skrɪpʃən] *n* prescription *f*; *(MED)* ordonnance *f*.

presence ['prɛzns] *n* présence *f*; **~ of mind** présence d'esprit.

present ['prɛznt] *a* présent(e) // *n* cadeau *m*; *(also: ~ tense)* présent *m* // ['prɪ'zɛnt] présenter; *(give)* **to**

~ sb with sth offrir qch à qn; **to give sb a ~** offrir un cadeau à qn; **at ~** au moment; **~ation** [-'teɪʃən] *n* présentation *f*; *(gift)* cadeau *m*, présent *m*; *(ceremony)* remise *f* du cadeau; **~-day** *a* contemporain(e), actuel(le); **~er** [-'zɛntə*] *n (RADIO, TV)* présentateur/trice; **~ly** *ad (soon)* tout à l'heure, bientôt; *(at present)* en ce moment.

preservative [prɪ'zə:vətɪv] *n* agent *m* de conservation.

preserve [prɪ'zə:v] *vt (keep safe)* préserver, protéger; *(maintain)* conserver, garder; *(food)* mettre en conserve // *n (for game, fish)* réserve *f*; *(often pl: jam)* confiture *f*; *(: fruit)* fruits *mpl* en conserve.

president ['prɛzɪdənt] *n* présidente/e; **~ial** [-'dɛnʃl] *a* présidentiel(le).

press [prɛs] *n (tool, machine, newspapers)* presse *f*; *(for wine)* pressoir *m*; *(crowd)* cohue *f*, foule *f* // *vt (push)* appuyer sur; *(squeeze)* presser, serrer; *(clothes: iron)* repasser; *(pursue)* talonner; *(insist)*: **to ~ sth on sb** presser qn d'accepter qch // *vi* appuyer, peser; se presser; **we are ~ed for time** le temps nous manque; **to ~ for sth** faire pression pour obtenir qch; **to ~ on** *vi* continuer; **~ conference** *n* conférence *f* de presse; **~ing** *a* urgent(e), pressant(e) // *n* repassage *m*; **~ stud** *n (Brit)* bouton-pression *m*; **~-up** *n (Brit)* traction *f*.

pressure ['prɛʃə*] *n* pression *f*; *(stress)* tension *f*; **~ cooker** *n* cocotte-minute *f*, autocuiseur *m*; **~ gauge** *n* manomètre *m*; **~ group** *n* groupe *m* de pression.

prestige [prɛs'ti:ʒ] *n* prestige *m*.

presumably [prɪ'zju:məblɪ] *ad* vraisemblablement.

presume [prɪ'zju:m] *vt* présumer, supposer; **to ~ to do** *(dare)* se permettre de faire.

presumption [prɪ'zʌmpʃən] *n* supposition *f*, présomption *f*; *(boldness)* audace *f*.

pretence, (US) **pretense** [prɪ'tɛns] n (claim) prétention f; **to make a ~ of doing** faire semblant de faire.

pretend [prɪ'tɛnd] vt (feign) feindre, simuler // vi (feign) faire semblant; (claim): **to ~ to sth** prétendre à qch; **to ~ to do** faire semblant de faire.

pretense [prɪ'tɛns] n (US) = **pretence.**

pretension [prɪ'tɛnʃən] n prétention f.

pretext ['priːtɛkst] n prétexte m.

pretty ['prɪtɪ] a joli(e) // ad assez.

prevail [prɪ'veɪl] vi (win) l'emporter, prévaloir; (be usual) avoir cours; (persuade): **to ~ (up)on sb to do** persuader qn de faire; **~ing** a dominant(e).

prevalent ['prɛvələnt] a répandu(e), courant(e); (fashion) en vogue.

prevent [prɪ'vɛnt] vt: **to ~ (from doing)** empêcher (de faire); **~ive** a préventif(ive).

preview ['priːvjuː] n (of film) avant-première f; (fig) aperçu m.

previous ['priːvɪəs] a précédent(e); antérieur(e); **~ly** ad précédemment, auparavant.

prewar ['priː'wɔː] a d'avant-guerre.

prey [preɪ] n proie f // vi: **to ~ on** s'attaquer à.

price [praɪs] n prix m // vt (goods) fixer le prix de; tarifer; **~less** a sans prix, inestimable; **~ list** n liste f des prix, tarif m.

prick [prɪk] n piqûre f // vt piquer; **to ~ up one's ears** dresser or tendre l'oreille.

prickle ['prɪkl] n (of plant) épine f; (sensation) picotement m.

prickly ['prɪklɪ] a piquant(e), épineux(euse); (fig: person) irritable; **~ heat** n fièvre f miliaire.

pride [praɪd] n orgueil m; fierté f // vt: **to ~ o.s. on** se flatter de; s'enorgueillir de.

priest [priːst] n prêtre m; **~hood** n prêtrise f, sacerdoce m.

prig [prɪg] n poseur/euse, fat m.

prim [prɪm] a collet monté inv, guindé(e).

primarily ['praɪmərɪlɪ] ad principalement, essentiellement.

primary ['praɪmərɪ] a primaire (e); (first in importance) premier(ère), primordial(e); **~ school** n (Brit) école primaire f.

prime [praɪm] a primordial(e), fondamental(e); (excellent) excellent(e) // vt (gun, pump) amorcer; (fig) mettre au courant; **in the ~ of life** dans la fleur de l'âge; **P~ Minister (P.M.)** n Premier ministre.

primer ['praɪmə*] n (book) manuel m élémentaire; (paint) apprêt m.

primeval [praɪ'miːvl] a primitif(ive); (forest) vierge.

primitive ['prɪmɪtɪv] a primitif(ive).

primrose ['prɪmrəʊz] n primevère f.

primus (stove) ['praɪməs(stəʊv)] n ® (Brit) réchaud m de camping.

prince [prɪns] n prince m.

princess [prɪn'sɛs] n princesse f.

principal ['prɪnsɪpl] a principal(e) // n (headmaster) directeur m, principal m.

principle ['prɪnsɪpl] n principe m; **in/on ~** en/par principe.

print [prɪnt] n (mark) empreinte f; (letters) caractères mpl; (fabric) imprimé m; (ART) gravure f, estampe f; (PHOT) épreuve f // vt imprimer; (publish) publier; (write in capitals) écrire en majuscules; **out of ~** épuisé(e); **~ed matter** n imprimés mpl; **~er** n imprimeur m; (machine) imprimante f; **~ing** n impression f; **~out** n listage m.

prior ['praɪə*] a antérieur(e), précédent(e) // n prieur m; **~ to doing** avant de faire.

priority [praɪ'ɒrɪtɪ] n priorité f.

prise [praɪz] vt: **to ~ open** forcer.

prison ['prɪzn] n prison f // cpd pénitentiaire; **~er** n prisonnier/ère.

pristine ['prɪstiːn] a virginal(e).

privacy ['prɪvəsɪ] n intimité f, solitude f.

private ['praɪvɪt] a privé(e); personnel(le); (house, car, lesson) particulier(ère) // n soldat m de deuxième classe; '~' (on envelope) 'personnelle'; **in ~** en privé; **~ enterprise** n l'entreprise privée; **~ eye** n détective privé; **~ly** ad en privé; (within oneself) intérieurement; **~ property** n propriété privée; **privatize** vt privatiser.

privet ['privit] n troène m.

privilege ['privilidʒ] n privilège m.

privy ['privi] a: **to be ~ to** être au courant de; **~ council** n conseil privé.

prize [praiz] n prix m // a (example, idiot) parfait(e); (bull, novel) gros(se); ~ vt priser, faire grand cas de; **~ giving** n distribution f des prix; **~winner** n gagnant/e.

pro [prəu] n (SPORT) professionnel/le; **the ~s and cons** le pour et le contre.

probability [prɔbə'biliti] n probabilité f.

probable ['prɔbəbl] a probable; **probably** ad probablement.

probation [prə'beiʃən] n (in employment) essai m; (LAW) liberté surveillée; **on ~** (employee) à l'essai; (LAW) en liberté surveillée.

probe [prəub] n (MED, SPACE) sonde f; (enquiry) enquête f, investigation f // vt sonder, explorer.

problem ['prɔbləm] n problème m.

procedure [prə'si:dʒə*] n (ADMIN, LAW) procédure f; (method) marche f à suivre, façon f de procéder.

proceed [prə'si:d] vi (go forward) avancer; (go about it) procéder; (continue): **to ~ (with)** continuer, poursuivre; **to ~** aller à; passer à; **to ~ to do** se mettre à faire; **~ings** npl mesures fpl; (LAW) poursuites fpl; (meeting) réunion f, séance f; (records) compte rendu; actes mpl; **~s** ['prəusi:dz] npl produit m, recette f.

process ['prəuses] n processus m; (method) procédé m // vt traiter; **~ing** n traitement m.

procession [prə'seʃən] n défilé m, cortège m; **funeral ~** cortège m funèbre; convoi m mortuaire.

proclaim [prə'kleim] vt déclarer, proclamer.

procrastinate [prəu'kræstineit] vi faire traîner les choses, vouloir tout remettre au lendemain.

prod [prɔd] vt pousser.

prodigal ['prɔdigl] a prodigue.

prodigy ['prɔdidʒi] n prodige m.

produce n ['prɔdju:s] (AGR) produits mpl // vt [prə'dju:s] produire; (to show) présenter; (cause) provoquer, causer; (THEATRE) monter, mettre en scène; **~r** n (THEATRE) metteur m en scène; (AGR, CINEMA) producteur m.

product ['prɔdʌkt] n produit m.

production [prə'dʌkʃən] n production f; (THEATRE) mise f en scène; **~ line** n chaîne f (de fabrication).

productivity [prɔdʌk'tiviti] n productivité f.

profane [prə'fein] a sacrilège; (lay) profane.

profession [prə'feʃən] n profession f; **~al** n (SPORT) professionnel/le // a professionnel(le); (work) de professionnel.

professor [prə'fesə*] n professeur m (titulaire d'une chaire).

proficiency [prə'fiʃənsi] n compétence f, aptitude f.

profile ['prəufail] n profil m.

profit ['prɔfit] n bénéfice m; profit m // vi: **to ~ (by** or **from)** profiter (de); **~able** a lucratif(ive), rentable.

profiteering [prɔfi'tiəriŋ] n (pej) mercantilisme m.

profound [prə'faund] a profond(e).

profusely [prə'fju:sli] ad abondamment; avec effusion.

progeny ['prɔdʒini] n progéniture f; descendants mpl.

programme, (US) **program** ['prəugræm] n programme m; (RADIO, TV) émission f // vt programmer; **~r**, (US) **programer** n programmeur/euse.

progress n ['prəʊgres] progrès m // vi [prə'gres] progresser, avancer; **in ~** en cours; **to make ~** progresser, faire des progrès, être en progrès; **~ive** ['gresɪv] a progressif(ive); (person) progressiste.

prohibit [prə'hɪbɪt] vt interdire, défendre.

project n ['prɒdʒekt] (plan) projet m, plan m; (venture) opération f, entreprise f; (gen, SCOL: research) étude f, dossier m // vb [prə'dʒekt] vt projeter // vi (stick out) faire saillie, s'avancer.

projection [prə'dʒekʃən] n projection f; saillie f.

projector [prə'dʒektə*] n projecteur m.

prolong [prə'lɒŋ] vt prolonger.

prom [prɒm] n abbr of promenade; (US: ball) bal m d'étudiants.

promenade [prɒmə'nɑːd] n (by sea) esplanade f, promenade f; **~ concert** n concert m (de musique classique).

prominent ['prɒmɪnənt] a (standing out) proéminent(e); (important) important(e).

promiscuous [prə'mɪskjuəs] a (sexually) de mœurs légères.

promise ['prɒmɪs] n promesse f // vi, vi promettre; **promising** a prometteur(euse).

promote [prə'məʊt] vt promouvoir; (venture, event) encourager, mettre sur pied; (new product) lancer; **~r** n (of sporting event) organisateur/trice; **promotion** [-'məʊʃən] n promotion f.

prompt [prɒmpt] a rapide // a (punctually) à l'heure // n (COMPUT) message m (de guidage) // vt inciter, provoquer; (THEATRE) souffler (son rôle or ses répliques) à; **~ly** ad rapidement, sans délai; ponctuellement.

prone [prəʊn] a (lying) couché(e) (face contre terre); **~ to** enclin(e) à.

prong [prɒŋ] n pointe f; (of fork)

dent f.

pronoun ['prəʊnaʊn] n pronom m.

pronounce [prə'naʊns] vt prononcer // vi: **to ~ (up)on** se prononcer sur.

pronunciation [prənʌnsɪ'eɪʃən] n prononciation f.

proof [pruːf] n épreuve f; (test, of book, PHOT) degré m // a: **~ against** à l'épreuve de.

prop [prɒp] n support m, étai m // vt (also: **~ up**) étayer, soutenir; (lean): **to ~ sth against** appuyer qch contre or à.

propaganda [prɒpə'gændə] n propagande f.

propel [prə'pel] vt propulser, faire avancer; **~ler** n hélice f; **~ling pencil** n (Brit) porte-mine m inv.

propensity [prə'pensɪtɪ] n propension f.

proper ['prɒpə*] a (suited, right) approprié(e), bon(bonne); (seemly) correct(e), convenable; (authentic) vrai(e), véritable; (col: real) n + fini(e), vrai(e); **~ly** ad correctement, convenablement; bel et bien; **he doesn't eat/study ~ly** il mange/étudie mal; **~ noun** n nom m propre.

property ['prɒpətɪ] n (things owned) biens mpl, propriété(s) f(pl); (land etc) immeuble m; terres fpl, domaine m; (CHEM etc: quality) propriété f; **~ owner** n propriétaire m.

prophecy ['prɒfɪsɪ] n prophétie f.

prophesy ['prɒfɪsaɪ] vt prédire.

prophet ['prɒfɪt] n prophète m.

proportion [prə'pɔːʃən] n proportion f; (share) part f; partie f; **~al**, **~ate** a proportionnel(le).

proposal [prə'pəʊzl] n proposition f, offre f; (plan) projet m; (of marriage) demande f en mariage.

propose [prə'pəʊz] vt proposer, suggérer // vi faire sa demande en mariage; **to ~ to do** avoir l'intention de faire.

proposition [prɒpə'zɪʃən] n proposition f.

propriety [prə'praɪətɪ] n (seemliness) bienséance f, convenance f.

prose [prəuz] n prose f; (SCOL: translation) thème m.

prosecute ['prɔsɪkjuːt] vt poursuivre; **prosecution** [-'kjuːʃən] n poursuites fpl judiciaires; (accusing side) accusation f; **prosecutor** n procureur m; (also: **public prosecutor**) ministère public.

prospect n ['prɔspekt] perspective f; (hope) espoir m, chances fpl // vt [prə'spekt] prospecter; **~s** npl (for work etc) possibilités fpl d'avenir, débouchés mpl; **prospective** [-'spektɪv] a (possible) éventuel(le); (future) futur(e).

prospectus [prə'spektəs] n prospectus m.

prosperity [prɔs'perɪtɪ] n prospérité f.

prostitute ['prɔstɪtjuːt] n prostituée f.

protect [prə'tekt] vt protéger; **~ion** n protection f; **~ive** a protecteur(trice).

protein ['prəutiːn] n protéine f.

protest n ['prəutest] protestation f // vb [prə'test] vi protester // vt protester de.

Protestant ['prɔtɪstənt] a, n protestant(e).

protester [prə'testə*] n manifestant/e.

protracted [prə'træktɪd] a prolongé(e).

protrude [prə'truːd] vi avancer, dépasser.

proud [praud] a fier(ère); (pej) orgueilleux(euse).

prove [pruːv] vt prouver, démontrer // vi: **to ~ correct** etc s'avérer juste etc; **to ~ o.s.** montrer ce dont on est capable.

proverb ['prɔvəːb] n proverbe m.

provide [prə'vaɪd] vt fournir; **to ~ sb with sth** fournir qch à qn; **to ~ for** vt fus (sb) subvenir aux besoins de; (emergency) prévoir; **~d (that)** cj à condition que + sub.

providing [prə'vaɪdɪŋ] cj à condition que + sub.

province ['prɔvɪns] n province f; **provincial** [prə'vɪnʃəl] a provincial(e).

provision [prə'vɪʒən] n (supply) provision f; (supplying) fourniture f; approvisionnement m; (stipulation) disposition f; **~s** npl (food) provisions fpl; **~al** a provisoire.

proviso [prə'vaɪzəu] n condition f.

provocative [prə'vɔkətɪv] a provocateur(trice), provocant(e).

provoke [prə'vəuk] vt provoquer; inciter.

prow [prau] n proue f.

prowess ['prauɪs] n prouesse f.

prowl [praul] vi (also: ~ about, ~ around) rôder // n: **on the ~** à l'affût; **~er** n rôdeur/euse.

proxy ['prɔksɪ] n procuration f.

prudent ['pruːdnt] a prudent(e).

prudish ['pruːdɪʃ] a prude, pudibond(e).

prune [pruːn] n pruneau m // vt élaguer.

pry [praɪ] vi: **to ~ into** fourrer son nez dans.

PS n abbr (= postscript) p.s.

psalm [sɑːm] n psaume m.

pseudo- ['sjuːdəu] prefix pseudo-; **pseudonym** n pseudonyme m.

psyche ['saɪkɪ] n psychisme m.

psychiatric [saɪkɪ'ætrɪk] a psychiatrique.

psychiatrist [saɪ'kaɪətrɪst] n psychiatre m/f.

psychic ['saɪkɪk] a (also: **~al**) (méta)psychique; (person) doué(e) de télépathie or d'un sixième sens.

psychoanalyst [saɪkəu'ænəlɪst] n psychanalyste m/f.

psychological [saɪkə'lɔdʒɪkl] a psychologique.

psychologist [saɪ'kɔlədʒɪst] n psychologue m/f.

psychology [saɪ'kɔlədʒɪ] n psychologie f.

P.T.O. abbr (= please turn over) T.S.V.P.

pub [pʌb] n abbr (= public house) pub m.

pubic ['pjuːbɪk] a pubien(ne), du pubis.

public ['pʌblɪk] a public(ique) // n public m; **in ~** en public; **~ address system (P.A.)** n (système m de) sonorisation f; haut-parleurs mpl.

publican ['pʌblɪkən] n patron de pub.

public: **~ company** n société f anonyme (cotée en bourse); **~ convenience** n (Brit) toilettes fpl; **~ holiday** n jour férié; **~ house** n (Brit) pub m.

publicity [pʌb'lɪsɪtɪ] n publicité f.

publicize ['pʌblɪsaɪz] vt faire connaître, rendre public(ique).

publicly ['pʌblɪklɪ] ad publiquement.

public: **~ opinion** n opinion publique; **~ relations (PR)** n relations publiques; **~ school** n (Brit) école privée; (US) école publique; **~-spirited** a qui fait preuve de civisme; **~ transport** n transports mpl en commun.

publish ['pʌblɪʃ] vt publier; **~er** n éditeur m; **~ing** n (industry) édition f.

puck [pʌk] n (ICE HOCKEY) palet m.

pucker ['pʌkə*] vt plisser.

pudding ['pʊdɪŋ] n (Brit: sweet) dessert m, entremets m; (sausage) boudin m; **black ~** boudin (noir).

puddle ['pʌdl] n flaque f d'eau.

puff [pʌf] n bouffée f // vt: **to ~ one's pipe** tirer sur sa pipe // vi sortir par bouffées; (pant) haleter; **to ~ out smoke** envoyer des bouffées de fumée; **~ed** a (col: out of breath) tout(e) essoufflé(e); **~ pastry** n pâte feuilletée; **~y** a bouffi(e), boursouflé(e).

pull [pʊl] n (tug) to give sth a ~ tirer sur qch; (fig) influence f // vt tirer; (muscle) se claquer // vi tirer; **to ~ to pieces** mettre en morceaux; **to ~ one's punches** ménager son adversaire; **to ~ one's weight** y mettre du sien; **to ~ o.s. together**

se ressaisir; **to ~ sb's leg** faire marcher qn; **to ~ apart** vt séparer; (break) mettre en pièces, démantibuler; **to ~ down** vt baisser, abaisser; (house) démolir; (tree) abattre; **to ~ in** vi (AUT) se ranger; (RAIL) entrer en gare; **to ~ off** vt enlever, ôter; (deal etc) conclure; **to ~ out** vi démarrer, partir; (withdraw) se retirer; (AUT: come out of line) déboîter // vt sortir; arracher; (withdraw) retirer; **to ~ over** vi (AUT) se ranger; **to ~ through** vi s'en sortir; (stop) s'arrêter // vt remonter; (uproot) déraciner, arracher; (stop) arrêter.

pulley ['pʊlɪ] n poulie f.

pullover ['pʊləʊvə*] n pull-over m, tricot m.

pulp [pʌlp] n (of fruit) pulpe f; (for paper) pâte f à papier.

pulpit ['pʊlpɪt] n chaire f.

pulsate [pʌl'seɪt] vi battre, palpiter; (music) vibrer.

pulse [pʌls] n (of blood) pouls m; (of heart) battement m; (of music, engine) vibrations fpl.

pummel ['pʌml] vt rouer de coups.

pump [pʌmp] n pompe f; (shoe) escarpin m // vt pomper; (fig: col) faire parler; **to ~ up** vt gonfler.

pumpkin ['pʌmpkɪn] n potiron m, citrouille f.

pun [pʌn] n jeu m de mots, calembour m.

punch [pʌntʃ] n (blow) coup m de poing; (fig: force) vivacité f, mordant m; (tool) poinçon m; (drink) punch m // vt (hit): **to ~ sb/sth** donner un coup de poing à qn/sur qch; (make a hole) poinçonner, perforer; **~-line** n (of joke) conclusion f; **~-up** n (Brit col) bagarre f.

punctual ['pʌŋktjuəl] a ponctuel(le).

punctuation [pʌŋktju'eɪʃən] n ponctuation f.

puncture ['pʌŋktʃə*] n crevaison f.

pundit ['pʌndɪt] n individu m qui pontifie, pontife m.

pungent ['pʌndʒənt] a piquant(e);

(fig) mordant(e), caustique.

punish ['pʌnɪʃ] vt punir; **~ment** n punition f, châtiment m.

punk [pʌŋk] n (also: **~ rocker**) punk m/f; (also: **~ rock**) le punk; (US col: hoodlum) voyou m.

punt [pʌnt] n (boat) bachot m.

punter ['pʌntə*] n (Brit: gambler) parieur/euse.

puny ['pju:nɪ] a chétif/ive.

pup [pʌp] n chiot m.

pupil ['pju:pl] n élève m/f.

puppet ['pʌpɪt] n marionnette f, pantin m.

puppy ['pʌpɪ] n chiot m, petit chien.

purchase ['pɜ:tʃɪs] n achat m // vt acheter; **~r** n acheteur/euse.

pure [pjuə*] a pur(e).

purely ['pjuəlɪ] ad purement.

purge [pɜ:dʒ] n (MED) purge f; (POL) épuration f, purge // vt purger.

purl [pɜ:l] n maille f à l'envers.

purple ['pɜ:pl] a violet(te); cramoisi(e).

purport [pɜ:'pɔ:t] vi: to **~** be/do prétendre être/faire.

purpose ['pɜ:pəs] n intention f, but m; on **~** exprès; **~ful** a déterminé(e), résolu(e).

purr [pɜ:*] vi ronronner.

purse [pɜ:s] n porte-monnaie m inv, bourse f // vt serrer, pincer.

purser ['pɜ:sə*] n (NAUT) commissaire m du bord.

pursue [pə'sju:] vt poursuivre.

pursuit [pə'sju:t] n poursuite f; (occupation) occupation f, activité f.

purveyor [pə'veɪə*] n fournisseur m.

push [puʃ] n poussée f; (effort) gros effort; (drive) énergie f // vt pousser; (button) appuyer sur; (thrust): to **~ sth (into)** enfoncer qch (dans); (fig) mettre en avant, faire de la publicité pour // vi pousser; appuyer; to **~ aside** vt écarter; to **~ off** vi (col) filer, ficher le camp; to **~ on** vi (continue) continuer; to **~ through** vt (measure) faire voter; to **~ up** vt (total, prices) faire monter; **~chair** n (Brit) poussette f; **~er** n

(drug **~er**) revendeur/euse (de drogue), ravitailleur/euse (en drogue); **~over** n (col): it's a **~over** c'est un jeu d'enfant; **~-up** n (US) traction f; **~y** a (pej) arriviste.

puss, pussy(-cat) [pus, 'pusɪ(kæt)] n minet m.

put, pt, pp **put** [put] vt mettre, poser, placer; (say) dire, exprimer; (a question) poser; (estimate) estimer; to **~ about** vi (NAUT) virer de bord // vt (rumour) faire courir; to **~ across** vt (ideas etc) communiquer; faire comprendre; to **~ away** vt (store) ranger; to **~ back** vt (replace) remettre, replacer; (postpone) remettre, (delay) retarder; to **~ by** vt (money) mettre de côté, économiser; to **~ down** vt (parcel etc) poser, déposer; (pay) verser; (in writing) mettre par écrit, inscrire; (suppress: revolt etc) réprimer, faire cesser; (attribute) attribuer; to **~ forward** vt (ideas) avancer, proposer; (date) avancer; to **~ in** vt (gas, electricity) installer; (application, complaint) soumettre; to **~ off** vt (light etc) éteindre; (postpone) remettre à plus tard, ajourner; (discourage) dissuader; to **~ on** vt (clothes, lipstick etc) mettre; (light etc) allumer; (play etc) monter; (food, meal) servir; (: cook) mettre à cuire ou à chauffer; (airs, weight) prendre; (brake) mettre; to **~ out** vt mettre dehors; (one's hand) tendre; (news, rumour) faire courir, répandre; (light etc) éteindre; (person: inconvenience) déranger, gêner; to **~ up** vt (raise) lever, relever, remonter; (pin up) afficher; (hang) accrocher; (build) construire, ériger; (a tent) monter; (increase) augmenter; (accommodate) loger; to **~ up with** vt fus supporter.

putt [pʌt] vt frôler (la balle) // n coup roulé; **~ing green** n green m.

putty ['pʌtɪ] n mastic m.

puzzle ['pʌzl] n énigme f, mystère m; (jigsaw) puzzle m; (also: crossword ~) problème *m* de mots croisés *// vt* intriguer, rendre perplexe *// vi* se creuser la tête.

pyjamas [pɪ'dʒɑːməz] *npl* (*Brit*) pyjama *m*.

pyramid ['pɪrəmɪd] *n* pyramide *f*.

Pyrenees [pɪrɪ'niːz] *npl*: the ~ les Pyrénées *fpl*.

Q

quack [kwæk] *n* (*of duck*) coin-coin *m inv*; (*pej*: *doctor*) charlatan *m*.

quad [kwɔd] *abbr of* **quadrangle, quadruplet**.

quadrangle ['kwɔdræŋgl] *n* (*MATH*) quadrilatère *m*; (*courtyard*: *abbr*: quad) cour *f*.

quadruple [kwɔ'druːpl] *vt, vi* quadrupler.

quadruplet [kwɔ'druːplɪt] *n* quadruplée.

quagmire ['kwægmaɪə*] *n* bourbier *m*.

quail [kweɪl] *n* (*ZOOL*) caille *f // vi* (*person*) perdre courage.

quaint [kweɪnt] *a* bizarre; (*old-fashioned*) désuet(ète); au charme vieillot, pittoresque.

quake [kweɪk] *vi* trembler *// n abbr of* **earthquake**.

qualification [kwɔlɪfɪ'keɪʃən] *n* (*degree etc*) diplôme *m*; (*ability*) compétence *f*, qualification *f*; (*limitation*) réserve *f*, restriction *f*.

qualified ['kwɔlɪfaɪd] *a* diplômé(e); (*able*) compétent(e), qualifié(e); (*limited*) conditionnel(le).

qualify ['kwɔlɪfaɪ] *vt* qualifier; (*limit*: *statement*) apporter des réserves à *// vi*: to ~ (as) obtenir son diplôme (de); to ~ (for) remplir les conditions requises (pour); (*SPORT*) se qualifier (pour).

quality ['kwɔlɪtɪ] *n* qualité *f*.

qualm [kwɑːm] *n* doute *m*; scrupule *m*.

quandary ['kwɔndrɪ] *n*: in a ~ devant un dilemme, dans l'embarras.

quantity ['kwɔntɪtɪ] *n* quantité *f*; ~ **surveyor** *n* métreur *m* vérificateur.

quarantine ['kwɔrəntiːn] *n* quarantaine *f*.

quarrel ['kwɔrl] *n* querelle *f*, dispute *f // vi* se disputer, se quereller; ~**some** *a* querelleur(euse).

quarry ['kwɔrɪ] *n* (*for stone*) carrière *f*; (*animal*) proie *f*, gibier *m // vt* (*marble etc*) extraire.

quart [kwɔːt] *n* ≈ litre *m*.

quarter ['kwɔːtə*] *n* quart *m*; (*of year*) trimestre *m*; (*district*) quartier *m // vt* partager en quartiers *ou* en quatre; (*MIL*) caserner, cantonner; ~**s** *npl* logement *m*; (*MIL*) quartiers *mpl*, cantonnement *m*; a ~ **of an** **hour** un quart d'heure; ~ **final** *n* quart *m* de finale; ~**ly** *a* trimestriel(le) *// ad* tous les trois mois; ~**master** *n* (*MIL*) intendant *m* militaire de troisième classe; (*NAUT*) maître *m* de manœuvre.

quartet(te) [kwɔː'tet] *n* quatuor *m*; (*jazz players*) quartette *m*.

quartz [kwɔːts] *n* quartz *m*.

quash [kwɔʃ] *vt* (*verdict*) annuler.

quaver ['kweɪvə*] *vi* trembler.

quay [kiː] *n* (*also*: ~**side**) quai *m*.

queasy ['kwiːzɪ] *a* (*stomach*) délicat(e); to feel ~ avoir mal au cœur.

queen [kwiːn] *n* (*gen*) reine *f*; (*CARDS etc*) dame *f*; ~ **mother** *n* reine mère *f*.

queer [kwɪə*] *a* étrange, curieux(euse); (*suspicious*) louche *// n* (*col*) homosexuel *m*.

quell [kwel] *vt* réprimer, étouffer.

quench [kwentʃ] *vt* (*flames*) éteindre; to ~ **one's thirst** se désaltérer.

querulous ['kwɛrʊləs] *a* (*person*) récriminateur(trice); (*voice*) plaintif(ive).

query ['kwɪərɪ] *n* question *f*; (*doubt*) doute *m*; (*question mark*) point *m* d'interrogation *// vt* mettre en question ou en doute.

quest [kwest] *n* recherche *f*, quête *f*.

question ['kwestʃən] *n* question *f // vt* (*person*) interroger; (*plan*, *idea*) mettre en question *or* en doute; **it's a ~ of doing** il s'agit de faire; **beyond ~** sans aucun doute; **out of the ~** hors de question; **~able** *a* discutable; **~ mark** *n* point *m* d'interrogation.

questionnaire [kwɛstʃə'nɛə*] *n* questionnaire *m*.

queue [kju:] *n* (*Brit*) queue *f*, file *f* // *vi* faire la queue.

quibble ['kwɪbl] *vi* ergoter, chicaner.

quick [kwɪk] *a* rapide; (*reply*) prompt(e), rapide; (*mind*) vif(vive) // *ad* vite, rapidement // *n*: **cut to the ~** (*fig*) touché(e) au vif; **be ~!** dépêche-toi!; **~en** *vt* accélérer, presser; (*rouse*) stimuler // *vi* s'accélérer, devenir plus rapide; **~ly** *ad* vite, rapidement; **~sand** *n* sables mouvants; **~-witted** *a* à l'esprit vif.

quid [kwɪd] *n* (*pl inv*) (*Brit col*) livre *f*.

quiet ['kwaɪət] *a* tranquille, calme; (*ceremony, colour*) discret(ète) // *n* tranquillité *f*, calme *m* // *vt, vi* (*US*) = **~en; ~en** *vt*: **keep ~!** tais-toi!; **~en** (*also*: **~en down**) *vi* se calmer, s'apaiser // *vt* calmer, apaiser; **~ly** *ad* tranquillement, calmement; discrètement.

quilt [kwɪlt] *n* édredon *m*; (*continental ~*) couette *f*.

quin [kwɪn] *n abbr of* **quintuplet**.

quintuplet [kwɪn'tju:plɪt] *n* quintuplé/e.

quip [kwɪp] *n* remarque piquante *or* spirituelle, pointe *f*.

quirk [kwə:k] *n* bizarrerie *f*.

quit, *pt, pp* **quit** *or* **quitted** [kwɪt] *vt* quitter // *vi* (*give up*) abandonner, renoncer; (*resign*) démissionner.

quite [kwaɪt] *ad* (*rather*) assez, plutôt; (*entirely*) complètement, tout à fait; **I ~ understand** je comprends très bien; **~ a few of them** un assez grand nombre d'entre eux; **~ (so)!** exactement!

quits [kwɪts] *a*: **~ (with)** quitte (envers); **let's call it ~** restons-en là.

quiver ['kwɪvə*] *vi* trembler, frémir.

quiz [kwɪz] *n* (*game*) jeu-concours *m*; test *m* de connaissances // *vt* interroger; **~zical** *a* narquois(e).

quota ['kwəʊtə] *n* quota *m*.

quotation [kwəʊ'teɪʃən] *n* citation *f*; (*of shares etc*) cote *f*, cours *m*; (*estimate*) devis *m*; **~ marks** *npl* guillemets *mpl*.

quote [kwəʊt] *n* citation *f* // *vt* (*sentence*) citer; (*price*) donner, fixer; (*shares*) coter // *vi*: **to ~ from** citer.

R

rabbi ['ræbaɪ] *n* rabbin *m*.

rabbit ['ræbɪt] *n* lapin *m*; **~ hutch** *n* clapier *m*.

rabble ['ræbl] *n* (*pej*) populace *f*.

rabies ['reɪbi:z] *n* rage *f*.

RAC *n abbr* (*Brit*) = *Royal Automobile Club*.

race [reɪs] *n* race *f*; (*competition, rush*) course *f* // *vt* (*person*) faire la course avec; (*horse*) faire courir; (*engine*) emballer // *vi* courir; (*engine*) s'emballer; **~ car** *n* (*US*) = **racing car**; **~ car driver** *n* (*US*) = **racing driver**; **~course** *n* champ *m* de courses; **~horse** *n* cheval *m* de course; **~track** *n* piste *f*.

racial ['reɪʃl] *a* racial(e); **~ist** *a, n* raciste (*m/f*).

racing ['reɪsɪŋ] *n* courses *fpl*; **~ car** *n* (*Brit*) voiture *f* de course; **~ driver** *n* (*Brit*) pilote *m* de course.

racism ['reɪsɪzəm] *n* racisme *m*; **racist** *a, n* raciste (*m/f*).

rack [ræk] *n* (*also*: **luggage ~**) filet *m* à bagages; (*also*: **roof ~**) galerie *f* // *vt* tourmenter; **to ~ one's brains** se creuser la cervelle.

racket ['rækɪt] *n* (*for tennis*) raquette *f*; (*noise*) tapage *m*; vacarme *m*; (*swindle*) escroquerie *f*; (*organized crime*) racket *m*.

racquet ['rækɪt] *n* raquette *f*.

racy ['reɪsɪ] *a* plein(e) de verve; osé(e).

radar ['reɪdə:*] n radar m.

radial ['reɪdɪəl] a (also: ~-ply) à carcasse radiale.

radiant ['reɪdɪənt] a rayonnant(e).

radiate ['reɪdɪeɪt] vt (heat) émettre, dégager // vi (lines) rayonner.

radiation [reɪdɪ'eɪʃən] n rayonnement m; (radioactive) radiation f.

radiator ['reɪdɪeɪtə*] n radiateur m.

radical ['rædɪkl] a radical(e).

radii ['reɪdɪaɪ] npl of radius.

radio ['reɪdɪəu] n radio f; on the ~ à la radio.

radioactive [reɪdɪəu'æktɪv] a radioactif(ive).

radio station n station f de radio.

radish ['rædɪʃ] n radis m.

radius ['reɪdɪəs], pl **radii** n rayon m.

RAF n abbr of Royal Air Force.

raffle ['ræfl] n tombola f.

raft [rɑ:ft] n (craft; also: life ~) radeau m.

rafter ['rɑ:ftə*] n chevron m.

rag [ræg] n chiffon m; (pej: newspaper) feuille f, torchon m; (for charity) attractions organisées par les étudiants au profit d'œuvres de charité // vt (Brit) chahuter, mettre en boîte; ~s npl haillons mpl; ~-and-bone man n (Brit) = ~man; ~ doll n poupée f de chiffon.

rage [reɪdʒ] n (fury) rage f, fureur f // vi (person) être furieux(euse) de rage; (storm) faire rage, être déchaîné(e); it's all the ~ cela fait fureur.

ragged ['rægɪd] a (edge) inégal(e), qui accroche; (cuff) effiloché(e); (appearance) déguenillé(e).

ragman ['rægmæn] n chiffonnier m.

raid [reɪd] n (MIL) raid m; (criminal) hold-up m, raid m; (by police) descente f, rafle f // vt faire un raid sur or un hold-up dans or une descente dans.

rail [reɪl] n (on stair) rampe f; (on bridge, balcony) balustrade f; (of ship) bastingage m; (for train) rail m; ~s npl rails mpl, voie ferrée; by ~ par chemin de fer; ~ing(s) n(pl) grille f; ~way, (US) ~road n che-

min m de fer; ~way line n ligne f de chemin de fer; ~wayman n cheminot m; ~way station n gare f.

rain [reɪn] n pluie f // vi pleuvoir; in the ~ sous la pluie; it's ~ing il pleut; ~bow n arc-en-ciel m; ~coat n imperméable m; ~drop n goutte f de pluie; ~fall n chute f de pluie; (measurement) hauteur f des précipitations; ~y a pluvieux(euse).

raise [reɪz] n augmentation f // vt (lift) lever; hausser; (build) ériger; (increase) augmenter; (a protest, doubt) provoquer, causer; (a question) soulever; (cattle, family) élever; (crop) faire pousser; (army, funds) rassembler; (loan) obtenir; to ~ one's voice élever la voix.

raisin ['reɪzn] n raisin sec.

rake [reɪk] n (tool) râteau m; (person) débauché m // vt (garden) ratisser; (with machine gun) balayer.

rally ['rælɪ] n (POL etc) meeting m, rassemblement m; (AUT) rallye m; (TENNIS) échange m // vt rassembler, rallier // vi se rallier; (sick person) aller mieux; (Stock Exchange) reprendre; to ~ round vt fus se rallier à; venir en aide à.

RAM [ræm] n abbr (= random access memory) mémoire vive.

ram [ræm] n bélier m // vt enfoncer; (soil) tasser; (crash into) emboutir, percuter; éperonner.

ramble ['ræmbl] n randonnée f // vi (pej: also: ~ on) discourir, pérorer; ~r n promeneur/euse, randonneur/euse; (BOT) rosier grimpant; **rambling** a (speech) décousu(e); (BOT) grimpant(e).

ramp [ræmp] n (incline) rampe f; (in garage) pont m; on ~, off ~ (US AUT) bretelle f d'accès.

rampage [ræm'peɪdʒ] n: to be on the ~ se déchaîner.

rampant ['ræmpənt] a (disease etc) qui sévit.

ramshackle ['ræmʃækl] a (house) délabré(e); (car etc) déglingué(e).

ran [ræn] pt of **run**.

ranch [rɑːntʃ] n ranch m; **~er** n propriétaire m de ranch; cowboy m.

rancid ['rænsɪd] a rance.

rancour, (US) **rancor** ['ræŋkə*] n rancune f.

random ['rændəm] a fait(e) or établi(e) au hasard; (COMPUT, MATH) aléatoire // n: **at ~** au hasard.

randy ['rændɪ] a (Brit col) excité(e); lubrique.

rang [ræŋ] pt of **ring**.

range [reɪndʒ] n (of mountains) chaîne f; (of missile, voice) portée f; (of products) choix m, gamme f; (MIL: also: **shooting ~**) champ m de tir; (indoor) stand m de tir; (also: **kitchen ~**) fourneau m (de cuisine) // vt (place) mettre en rang, placer; (roam) parcourir // vi: **to ~ over** couvrir; **to ~ from ... to** aller de ... à.

ranger ['reɪndʒə*] n garde forestier.

rank [ræŋk] n rang m; (MIL) grade m; (Brit: also: **taxi ~**) station f de taxis // vi: **to ~ among** compter or se classer parmi // a (qui sent) fort(e); extrême; **the ~s** (MIL) la troupe; **the ~ and file** (fig) la masse, la base.

rankle ['ræŋkl] vi (insult) rester sur le cœur.

ransack ['rænsæk] vt fouiller (à fond); (plunder) piller.

ransom ['rænsəm] n rançon f; **to hold sb to ~** (fig) exercer un chantage sur qn.

rant [rænt] vi fulminer.

rap [ræp] vt frapper sur or à; taper sur.

rape [reɪp] n viol m; (BOT) colza m // vt violer; **~(seed) oil** n huile f de colza.

rapid ['ræpɪd] a rapide; **~s** npl (GEO) rapides mpl; **~ly** ad rapidement.

rapist ['reɪpɪst] n auteur m d'un viol.

rapport [ræ'pɔː*] n entente f.

rapture ['ræptʃə*] n extase f, ravis-

sement m.

rare [rɛə*] a rare; (CULIN: steak) saignant(e).

rarely ['rɛəlɪ] ad rarement.

raring ['rɛərɪŋ] a: **to be ~ to go** (col) être très impatient(e) de commencer.

rascal ['rɑːskl] n vaurien m.

rash [ræʃ] a imprudent(e), irréfléchi(e) // n (MED) rougeur f, éruption f.

rasher ['ræʃə*] n fine tranche (de lard).

raspberry ['rɑːzbərɪ] n framboise f.

rasping ['rɑːspɪŋ] a: **~ noise** grincement m.

rat [ræt] n rat m.

rate [reɪt] n (ratio) taux m, pourcentage m; (speed) vitesse f, rythme m; (price) tarif m // vt classer; évaluer; **to ~ sb/sth as** considérer qn/qch comme; **~s** npl (Brit) impôts locaux; (fees) tarifs mpl; **~able value** n (Brit) valeur locative imposable; **~payer** n (Brit) contribuable m/f (payant les impôts locaux).

rather ['rɑːðə*] ad plutôt; **it's ~ expensive** c'est assez cher; (too much) c'est un peu cher; **there's ~ a lot** il y en a beaucoup; **I would** or **I'd ~ go** j'aimerais mieux or je préférerais partir.

rating ['reɪtɪŋ] n classement m, cote f; (NAUT: category) classe f; (: Brit : sailor) matelot m.

ratio ['reɪʃɪəu] n proportion f.

ration ['ræʃən] n (gen pl) ration(s) f(pl).

rational ['ræʃənl] a raisonnable, sensé(e); (solution, reasoning) logique; (MED) lucide; **~e** [-'nɑːl] n raisonnement m; justification f; **~ize** vt rationaliser; (conduct) essayer d'expliquer or de motiver.

rat race n foire f d'empoigne.

rattle ['rætl] n cliquetis m; (louder) bruit m de ferraille; (object: of baby) hochet m; (: of sports fan) crécelle f // vi cliqueter; faire un bruit de ferraille or du bruit // vt agiter (bruyamment); **~snake** n serpent m à sonnettes.

raucous ['rɔ:kəs] a rauque.

rave [reɪv] vi (in anger) s'emporter; (with enthusiasm) s'extasier; (MED) délirer.

raven ['reɪvn] n corbeau m.

ravenous ['rævənəs] a affamé(e).

ravine [rə'vi:n] n ravin m.

raving ['reɪvɪŋ] a: ~ **lunatic** n fou furieux/folle furieuse.

ravishing ['rævɪʃɪŋ] a enchanteur(eresse).

raw [rɔ:] a (uncooked) cru(e); (not processed) brut(e); (sore) à vif, irrité(e); (inexperienced) inexpérimenté(e); ~ **deal** n (col) sale coup m; ~ **material** n matière première.

ray [reɪ] n rayon m; ~ **of hope** n lueur f d'espoir.

raze [reɪz] vt raser, détruire.

razor ['reɪzə*] n rasoir m; ~ **blade** n lame f de rasoir.

Rd abbr of **road**.

re [ri:] prep concernant.

reach [ri:tʃ] n portée f, atteinte f; (of river etc) étendue f // vi s'étendre; parvenir à // vi s'étendre; **out of/ within** ~ hors de/à portée; **to ~ out** vi: **to ~ out for** allonger le bras pour prendre.

react [ri:'ækt] vi réagir; **~ion** [-'ækʃən] n réaction f.

reactor [ri:'æktə*] n réacteur m.

read, pt, pp **read** [ri:d, red] vi lire // vt lire; (understand) comprendre, interpréter; (study) étudier; (subj: instrument etc) indiquer, marquer; **to ~ out** vt lire à haute voix; **~able** a facile or agréable à lire; **~er** n lecteur/trice; (book) livre m de lecture; (Brit: at university) maître m de conférences; **~ership** n (of paper etc) (nombre m de) lecteurs mpl.

readily ['redɪlɪ] ad volontiers, avec empressement; (easily) facilement.

readiness ['redɪnɪs] n empressement m; **in** ~ (prepared) prêt(e).

reading ['ri:dɪŋ] n lecture f; (understanding) interprétation f; (on instru-

ment) indications fpl.

ready ['redɪ] a prêt(e); (willing) prêt, disposé(e); (quick) prompt(e); (available) disponible // ad: ~-**cooked** tout(e) cuit(e) (d'avance) // n: **at the** ~ (MIL) prêt à faire feu; (fig) tout(e) prêt(e); **to get** ~ vi se préparer // vt préparer; **~-made** a tout(e) fait(e); ~ **money** (argent m) liquide m; ~ **reckoner** n barème m; **~-to-wear** a en prêt-à-porter.

real [rɪəl] a réel(le); véritable; **in ~ terms** dans la réalité; ~ **estate** n biens fonciers or immobiliers; **~istic** [-'lɪstɪk] a réaliste.

reality [ri:'ælɪtɪ] n réalité f.

realization [rɪəlaɪ'zeɪʃən] n prise f de conscience; réalisation f.

realize ['rɪəlaɪz] vt (understand) se rendre compte de; (a project, COMM: asset) réaliser.

really ['rɪəlɪ] ad vraiment; **~?** c'est vrai?

realm [rɛlm] n royaume m.

realtor ['rɪəltə*] n (US) agent immobilier.

reap [ri:p] vt moissonner; (fig) récolter.

reappear [ri:ə'pɪə*] vi réapparaître, reparaître.

rear [rɪə*] a de derrière, arrière inv; (AUT: wheel etc) arrière // n arrière m, derrière m // vt (cattle, family) élever // vi (also: ~ **up**: animal) se cabrer.

rear-view ['rɪəvju:]: ~ **mirror** n (AUT) rétroviseur m.

reason ['ri:zn] n raison f // vi: **to ~ with sb** raisonner qn, faire entendre raison à qn; **to have** ~ **to think** avoir lieu de penser; **it stands to ~ that** il va sans dire que; **~able** a raisonnable; (not bad) acceptable; **~ably** ad raisonnablement; **~ing** n raisonnement m.

reassurance [ri:ə'ʃuərəns] n réconfort m; assurance f, garantie f.

reassure [ri:ə'ʃuə*] vt rassurer; **to ~ sb of** donner à qn l'assurance répétée de.

rebate ['ri:beɪt] n (on product) rabais m; (on tax etc) dégrèvement m; (re-payment) remboursement m.

rebel n ['rɛbl] rebelle m/f // vi [rɪ'bɛl] se rebeller, se révolter; ~**lious** a rebelle.

rebound vi [rɪ'baʊnd] (ball) rebondir // n ['ri:baʊnd] rebond m.

rebuff [rɪ'bʌf] n rebuffade f.

rebuke [rɪ'bju:k] vt réprimander.

rebut [rɪ'bʌt] vt réfuter.

recall [rɪ'kɔ:l] vt rappeler; (remember) se rappeler, se souvenir de // n rappel m.

recant [rɪ'kænt] vi se rétracter; (REL) abjurer.

recap ['ri:kæp] vt, vi récapituler.

recapitulate [ri:kə'pɪtjʊleɪt] vt, vi = recap.

rec'd abbr = received.

recede [rɪ'si:d] vi s'éloigner; reculer; redescendre; **receding** a (forehead, chin) fuyant(e); **receding hairline** front dégarni.

receipt [rɪ'si:t] n (document) reçu m; (for parcel etc) accusé m de réception; (act of receiving) réception f; ~**s** npl (COMM) recettes fpl.

receive [rɪ'si:v] vt recevoir.

receiver [rɪ'si:və*] n (TEL) récepteur m, combiné m; (of stolen goods) receleur m; (LAW) administrateur m judiciaire.

recent ['ri:snt] a récent(e); ~**ly** ad récemment.

receptacle [rɪ'sɛptɪkl] n récipient m.

reception [rɪ'sɛpʃən] n réception f; (welcome) accueil m; ~ **desk** n réception f; ~**ist** n réceptionniste m/f.

recess [rɪ'sɛs] n (in room) renfoncement m; (for bed) alcôve f; (secret place) recoin m; (POL etc: holiday) vacances fpl; ~**ion** [-'sɛʃən] n récession f.

recipe ['rɛsɪpɪ] n recette f.

recipient [rɪ'sɪpɪənt] n bénéficiaire m/f; (of letter) destinataire m/f.

recital [rɪ'saɪtl] n récital m.

recite [rɪ'saɪt] vt (poem) réciter.

reckless ['rɛkləs] a (driver etc) imprudent(e).

reckon ['rɛkən] vt (count) calculer, compter; (consider) considérer, estimer; (think): I ~ **that** ... je pense que ...; **to ~ on** vt fus compter sur, s'attendre à; ~**ing** n compte m, calcul m; estimation f.

reclaim [rɪ'kleɪm] vt (land) amender; (: from sea) assécher; (: from forest) défricher; (demand back) réclamer (le remboursement or la restitution de).

recline [rɪ'klaɪn] vi être allongé(e) or étendu(e); **reclining** a (seat) à dossier réglable.

recluse [rɪ'klu:s] n reclus/e, ermite m.

recognition [rɛkəg'nɪʃən] n reconnaissance f; **to gain** ~ être reconnu(e); **transformed beyond** ~ méconnaissable.

recognize ['rɛkəgnaɪz] vt: **to ~ (by/as)** reconnaître (à/comme étant).

recoil [rɪ'kɔɪl] vi (person): **to ~ (from)** reculer (devant) // n (of gun) recul m.

recollect [rɛkə'lɛkt] vt se rappeler, se souvenir de; ~**ion** [-'lɛkʃən] n souvenir m.

recommend [rɛkə'mɛnd] vt recommander.

reconcile ['rɛkənsaɪl] vt (two people) réconcilier; (two facts) concilier, accorder; **to ~ o.s. to** se résigner à.

recondition [ri:kən'dɪʃən] vt remettre à neuf; réviser entièrement.

reconnoitre, (US) **reconnoiter** [rɛkə'nɔɪtə*] (MIL) vt reconnaître // vi faire une reconnaissance.

reconstruct [ri:kən'strʌkt] vt (building) reconstruire; (crime) reconstituer.

record n ['rɛkɔ:d] rapport m, récit m; (of meeting etc) procès-verbal m; (register) registre m; (file) dossier m; (also: **police ~**) casier m judiciaire; (MUS: disc) disque m //

(SPORT) record m // vt [rɪ'kɔːd] (set down) noter; (relate) rapporter; (MUS: song etc) enregistrer; **in ~ time** dans un temps record inv; **to keep a ~ of** noter; **off the ~** a officieux(euse) // ad officieusement; **~ card** n (in file) fiche f; **~ed delivery** n (Brit POST): **~ed delivery letter** etc lettre etc recommandée; **~er** n (LAW) avocat nommé à la fonction de juge; (MUS) flûte f à bec; **~ holder** n (SPORT) détenteur/trice du record; **~ing** n (MUS) enregistrement m; **~ player** n électrophone m.

recount [rɪ'kaunt] vt raconter.

re-count n [rɪ'kaunt] (POL: of votes) pointage m // vt [rɪ'kaunt] recompter.

recoup [rɪ'kuːp] vt: **to ~ one's losses** récupérer ce qu'on a perdu, se refaire.

recourse [rɪ'kɔːs] n recours m; expédient m.

recover [rɪ'kʌvə*] vt récupérer // vi (from illness) se rétablir; (from shock) se remettre; (country) se redresser.

recovery [rɪ'kʌvərɪ] n récupération f; rétablissement m; redressement m.

recreation [rekrɪ'eɪʃən] n récréation f, détente f; **~al** a pour la détente, récréatif(ive).

recruit [rɪ'kruːt] n recrue f // vt recruter.

rectangle ['rektæŋgl] n rectangle m; **rectangular** [-'tæŋgjulə*] a rectangulaire.

rectify ['rektɪfaɪ] vt (error) rectifier, corriger; (omission) réparer.

rector ['rektə*] n (REL) pasteur m; **rectory** n presbytère m.

recuperate [rɪ'kjuːpəreɪt] vi récupérer; (from illness) se rétablir.

recur [rɪ'kəː*] vi se reproduire; (idea, opportunity) se retrouver; (symptoms) réapparaître; **~rent** a périodique, fréquent(e).

red [red] n rouge m; (POL: pej)

rouge m/f // a rouge; **in the ~** (account) à découvert; (business) en déficit; **~ carpet treatment** n réception f en grande pompe; **R~ Cross** n Croix-Rouge f; **~ currant** n groseille f; **~den** vt, vi rougir; **~dish** a rougeâtre; (hair) plutôt roux(rousse).

redeem [rɪ'diːm] vt (debt) rembourser; (sth in pawn) dégager; (fig, also REL) racheter; **~ing** (a feature) qui sauve, qui rachète (le reste).

redeploy [riːdɪ'plɔɪ] vt (resources) réorganiser.

red-haired [red'heəd] a roux (rousse).

red-handed [red'hændɪd] a: **to be caught ~** être pris(e) en flagrant délit or la main dans le sac.

redhead ['redhed] n roux/rousse.

red herring n (fig) diversion f, fausse piste.

red-hot [red'hɔt] a chauffé(e) au rouge, brûlant(e).

redirect [riːdaɪ'rekt] vt (mail) faire suivre.

red light n: **to go through a ~** (AUT) brûler un feu rouge; **red-light district** n quartier réservé.

redo [riː'duː] vt irg refaire.

redolent ['redələnt] a: **~ of** odeur sent; (fig) qui évoque.

redress [rɪ'dres] n réparation f // vt redresser.

Red Sea n: **the ~** la mer Rouge.

redskin ['redskɪn] n Peau-Rouge m/f.

red tape n (fig) paperasserie (administrative).

reduce [rɪ'djuːs] vt réduire; (lower) abaisser; **'~ speed now'** (AUT) 'ralentir'; **reduction** [rɪ'dʌkʃən] n réduction f; (of price) baisse f; (discount) rabais m; réduction.

redundancy [rɪ'dʌndənsɪ] n licenciement m, mise f au chômage.

redundant [rɪ'dʌndnt] a (worker) mis(e) au chômage, licencié(e); (detail, object) superflu(e); **to be made ~** être licencié(e), être mis(e) au chômage.

reed [ri:d] n (BOT) roseau m.

reef [ri:f] n (at sea) récif m, écueil m.

reek [ri:k] vi: **to ~ (of)** puer, empester.

reel [ri:l] n bobine f; (TECH) dévidoir m; (FISHING) moulinet m; (CINEMA) bande f // vt (TECH) bobiner; (also: **~ up**) enrouler // vi (sway) chanceler.

ref [rɛf] n abbr (col: = referee) arbitre m.

refectory [rɪˈfɛktərɪ] n réfectoire m.

refer [rɪˈfəː*] vt: **to ~ sth to** sb to (dispute, decision) soumettre qch à; **to ~ sb to** (inquirer: for information) adresser or envoyer qn à; (reader: to text) renvoyer qn à; (fig vt fus (allude to) parler de, faire allusion à; (apply to) s'appliquer à; (consult) se reporter à.

referee [rɛfəˈriː] n arbitre m; (Brit: for job application) répondant/e.

reference ['rɛfrəns] n référence f, renvoi m; (mention) allusion f, mention f; (for job application: letter) références; lettre f de recommandation; (: person) répondant/e; **with ~ to** en ce qui concerne; (COMM: in letter) me référant à; **~ book** n ouvrage m de référence.

refill vt [riːˈfɪl] remplir à nouveau; (pen, lighter etc) recharger // n ['riːfɪl] (for pen etc) recharge f.

refine [rɪˈfaɪn] vt (sugar, oil) raffiner; (taste) affiner; **~d** a (person, taste) raffiné(e).

reflect [rɪˈflɛkt] vt (light, image) réfléchir, refléter; (fig) refléter // vi (think) réfléchir, méditer; **to ~ on** vt fus (discredit) porter atteinte à, faire tort à; **~ion** [-ˈflɛkʃən] n réflexion f; (image) reflet m; (criticism): **~ion on** critique f de; atteinte f à; **on ~ion** réflexion faite.

reflex [ˈriːflɛks] a, n réflexe (m); **~ive** [rɪˈflɛksɪv] a (LING) réfléchi(e).

reform [rɪˈfɔːm] n réforme f // vt reformer; **the R~ation** [rɛfəˈmeɪʃən] n la Réforme; **~atory** n (US) ≈ centre m d'éducation surveillée.

refrain [rɪˈfreɪn] vi: **to ~ from doing** s'abstenir de faire // n refrain m.

refresh [rɪˈfrɛʃ] vt rafraîchir; (subj: food) redonner des forces à; (: sleep) reposer; **~er course** n (Brit) cours m de recyclage; **~ing** a (drink) rafraîchissant(e); (sleep) réparateur(trice); **~ments** npl rafraîchissements mpl.

refrigerator [rɪˈfrɪdʒəreɪtə*] n réfrigérateur m, frigidaire m.

refuel [riːˈfjuəl] vi se ravitailler en carburant.

refuge [ˈrɛfjuːdʒ] n refuge m; **to take ~ in** se réfugier dans.

refugee [rɛfjuˈdʒiː] n réfugié/e.

refund n [ˈriːfʌnd] remboursement m // vt [rɪˈfʌnd] rembourser.

refurbish [riːˈfəːbɪʃ] vt remettre à neuf.

refusal [rɪˈfjuːzəl] n refus m; **to have first ~** on avoir droit de préemption sur.

refuse n [ˈrɛfjuːs] ordures fpl, détritus mpl // vt, vi [rɪˈfjuːz] refuser; **~ collection** n ramassage m d'ordures.

regain [rɪˈgeɪn] vt regagner; retrouver.

regal [ˈriːgl] a royal(e); **~ia** [rɪˈgeɪlɪə] n insignes mpl de la royauté.

regard [rɪˈgɑːd] n respect m, estime f, considération f // vt considérer; **to give one's ~s to** faire ses amitiés à; **'with kindest ~s'** 'bien amicalement'; **~ing, as ~s, with ~ to** prep en ce qui concerne; **~less** ad quand même; **~less of** sans se soucier de.

régime [reɪˈʒiːm] n régime m.

regiment n [ˈrɛdʒɪmənt] n régiment m // vt [ˈrɛdʒɪmɛnt] imposer une discipline trop stricte à; **~al** [-ˈmɛntl] a d'un or du régiment.

region [ˈriːdʒən] n région f; **in the ~ of** (fig) aux alentours de; **~al** a régional(e).

register ['rɛdʒɪstə*] n registre m;
(also: **electoral ~**) liste électorale //
vt enregistrer, inscrire; (birth) déclarer; (vehicle) immatriculer; (luggage) enregistrer; (letter) envoyer
en recommandé; (subj: instrument)
marquer // vi se faire inscrire; (at
hotel) signer le registre; (make impression) être (bien) compris(e);
~ed a (design) déposé(e); (Brit:
letter) recommandé(e); **~ed trademark** n marque déposée.

registrar ['rɛdʒɪstrɑ:*] n officier m
de l'état civil; secrétaire (général).

registration [rɛdʒɪs'treɪʃən] n (act)
enregistrement m; inscription f;
(AUT: also: **~ number**) numéro m
d'immatriculation.

registry ['rɛdʒɪstrɪ] n bureau m de
l'enregistrement; **~ office** n (Brit)
bureau m de l'état civil; **to get married in a ~ office** ≈ se marier à la
mairie.

regret [rɪ'grɛt] n regret m // vt regretter; **~fully** ad à or avec regret.

regular ['rɛgjulə*] a régulier(ère);
(usual) habituel(le), normal(e); (soldier) de métier; (COMM: size) ordinaire // n (client etc) habitué/e; **~ly**
ad régulièrement.

regulate ['rɛgjuleɪt] vt régler; **regulation** [-'leɪʃən] n (rule) règlement
m; (adjustment) réglage m.

rehabilitation ['ri:həbɪlɪ'teɪʃən] n
(of offender) réhabilitation f; (of disabled) rééducation f, réadaptation f.

rehearsal [rɪ'hə:səl] n répétition f.

rehearse [rɪ'hə:s] vt répéter.

reign [reɪn] n règne m // vi régner.

reimburse [ri:ɪm'bə:s] vt rembourser.

rein [reɪn] n (for horse) rêne f.

reindeer ['reɪndɪə*] n (pl inv) renne
m.

reinforce [ri:ɪn'fɔ:s] vt renforcer;
~d concrete n béton armé;
~ments npl (MIL) renfort(s) m(pl).

reinstate [ri:ɪn'steɪt] vt rétablir, réintégrer.

reject n ['ri:dʒɛkt] (COMM) article m

de rebut // vt [rɪ'dʒɛkt] refuser;
(COMM: goods) mettre au rebut;
(idea) rejeter; **~ion** [rɪ'dʒɛkʃən] n
rejet m, refus m.

rejoice [rɪ'dʒɔɪs] vi: **to ~** (at or
over) se réjouir (de).

rejuvenate [rɪ'dʒu:vəneɪt] vt rajeunir.

relapse [rɪ'læps] n (MED) rechute f.

relate [rɪ'leɪt] vt (tell) raconter;
(connect) établir un rapport entre //
vi: **to ~ to** se rapporter à; **~d** a
parenté(e); **relating to** prep concernant.

relation [rɪ'leɪʃən] n (person)
parent/e; (link) rapport m, lien m;
~ship n rapport m, lien m; (personal ties) relations fpl, rapports;
(also: **family ~ship**) lien de parenté; (affair) liaison f.

relative ['rɛlətɪv] n parent/e // a rela-
tif(ive); (respective) respectif(ive);
all her ~s toute sa famille.

relax [rɪ'læks] vi se relâcher; (person: unwind) se détendre // vt relâcher; (mind, person) détendre;
~ation [ri:læk'seɪʃən] n relâchement
m; détente f; (entertainment) distraction f; **~ed** a relâché(e); déten-
du(e); **~ing** a délassant(e).

relay ['ri:leɪ] n (SPORT) course f de
relais // vt (message) retransmettre,
relayer.

release [rɪ'li:s] n (from prison, obligation) libération f; (of gas etc)
émission f; (of film etc) sortie f; (record) disque m; (device) déclencheur
m // vt (prisoner) libérer; (book,
film) sortir; (report, news) rendre
public, publier; (gas etc) émettre,
dégager; (free: from wreckage etc)
dégager; (TECH: catch, spring etc)
déclencher; (let go) relâcher; lâcher;
desserrer.

relegate ['rɛlɪgeɪt] vt reléguer;
(SPORT): **to be ~d** descendre dans
une division inférieure.

relent [rɪ'lɛnt] vi se laisser fléchir;
~less a implacable.

relevant ['rɛləvənt] a approprié(e);

(fact) significatif(ive); *(information)* utile, pertinent(e); **~ to** ayant rapport à, approprié à.

reliable [rɪ'laɪəbl] a *(person, firm)* sérieux(euse), fiable; *(method, machine)* fiable; **reliably** ad: **to be reliably informed** savoir de source sûre.

reliance [rɪ'laɪəns] n: **~ (on)** confiance f (en); besoin m (de), dépendance f (de).

relic ['rɛlɪk] n *(REL)* relique f; *(of the past)* vestige m.

relief [rɪ'li:f] n *(from pain, anxiety)* soulagement m; *(help, supplies)* secours m(pl); *(of guard)* relève f; *(ART, GEO)* relief m.

relieve [rɪ'li:v] vt *(pain, patient)* soulager; *(bring relief)* secourir; *(take over from: gen)* relayer; *(: guard)* relever; **to ~ sb of sth** débarrasser qn de qch; **to ~ o.s.** se soulager, faire ses besoins.

religion [rɪ'lɪdʒən] n religion f; **religious** a religieux(euse); *(book)* de piété.

relinquish [rɪ'lɪŋkwɪʃ] vt abandonner; *(plan, habit)* renoncer à.

relish ['rɛlɪʃ] n *(CULIN)* condiment m; *(enjoyment)* délectation f // vt *(food etc)* savourer; **to ~ doing** se délecter à faire.

relocate [ri:ləu'keɪt] vt installer ailleurs // vi déménager, s'installer ailleurs.

reluctance [rɪ'lʌktəns] n répugnance f.

reluctant [rɪ'lʌktənt] a peu disposé(e), qui hésite; **~ly** ad à contrecœur, sans enthousiasme.

rely [rɪ'laɪ]: **to ~ on** vt fus compter sur; *(be dependent)* dépendre de.

remain [rɪ'meɪn] vi rester; **~der** n reste m; *(COMM)* fin f de série; **~ing** a qui reste; **~s** npl restes mpl.

remand [rɪ'mɑ:nd] n: **on ~** en détention préventive // vt: **to ~ in custody** écrouer; renvoyer en détention provisoire; **~ home** *(Brit)* maison f d'arrêt.

remark [rɪ'mɑ:k] n remarque f, observation f // vt *(say)* (faire) remarquer, dire; *(notice)* remarquer; **~able** a remarquable.

remedial [rɪ'mi:dɪəl] a *(tuition, classes)* de rattrapage.

remedy ['rɛmɪdɪ] n: **~ (for)** remède m (contre or à) // vt remédier à.

remember [rɪ'mɛmbə*] vt se rappeler, se souvenir de; **remembrance** n souvenir m; mémoire f.

remind [rɪ'maɪnd] vt: **to ~ sb of sth** rappeler qch à qn; **to ~ sb to do** faire penser à qn à faire, rappeler à qn qu'il doit faire; **~er** n rappel m; *(note etc)* pense-bête m.

reminisce [rɛmɪ'nɪs] vi: **to ~ (about)** évoquer ses souvenirs (de).

reminiscent [rɛmɪ'nɪsnt] a: **~ of** qui rappelle, qui fait penser à.

remiss [rɪ'mɪs] a négligent(e).

remission [rɪ'mɪʃən] n rémission f; *(of debt, sentence)* remise f; *(of fee)* exemption f.

remit [rɪ'mɪt] vt *(send: money)* envoyer; **~tance** n envoi m, paiement m.

remnant ['rɛmnənt] n reste m, restant m; **~s** npl *(COMM)* coupons mpl, fins fpl de série.

remorse [rɪ'mɔ:s] n remords m; **~ful** a plein(e) de remords; **~less** a *(fig)* impitoyable.

remote [rɪ'məut] a éloigné(e), lointain(e); *(person)* distant(e); **~ control** n télécommande f; **~ly** ad au loin; *(slightly)* très vaguement.

remould ['ri:məuld] n *(Brit: tyre)* pneu rechapé.

removable [rɪ'mu:vəbl] a *(detachable)* amovible.

removal [rɪ'mu:vəl] n *(taking away)* enlèvement m; suppression f; *(Brit: from house)* déménagement m; *(from office: dismissal)* renvoi m; *(MED)* ablation f; **~ van** n *(Brit)* camion m de déménagement.

remove [rɪ'mu:v] vt enlever, retirer; *(employee)* renvoyer; *(stain)* faire partir; (doubt, abuse) supprimer; **~rs** npl (Brit: company) entreprise f de déménagement.

render ['rɛndə*] vt rendre; **~ing** n (MUS etc) interprétation f.

rendez-vous ['rɔndɪvuː] n rendez-vous m inv // vi opérer une jonction, se rejoindre.

renew [rɪ'njuː] vt renouveler; (negotiations) reprendre; (acquaintance) renouer; **~al** n renouvellement m; reprise f.

renounce [rɪ'naʊns] vt renoncer à; (disown) renier.

renovate ['rɛnəveɪt] vt rénover; (art work) restaurer.

renown [rɪ'naʊn] n renommée f; **~ed** a renommé(e).

rent [rɛnt] n loyer m // vt louer; **~al** n (for television, car) prix m de location f.

rep [rɛp] n abbr (COMM: = representative) représentant m (de commerce); (THEATRE: = repertory) théâtre m de répertoire.

repair [rɪ'pɛə*] n réparation f // vt réparer; **in good/bad** ~ en bon/mauvais état; **~ kit** n trousse f de réparations.

repartee [rɛpɑː'tiː] n repartie f.

repatriate [riː'pætrɪeɪt] vt rapatrier.

repay [riː'peɪ] vt irg (money, creditor) rembourser; (sb's efforts) récompenser; **~ment** n remboursement m; récompense f.

repeal [rɪ'piːl] n (of law) abrogation f; (of sentence) annulation f // vt abroger; annuler.

repeat [rɪ'piːt] n (RADIO, TV) reprise f // vt répéter; (pattern) reproduire; (promise, attack, also COMM: order) renouveler; (SCOL: a class) redoubler // vi répéter; **~edly** ad souvent, à plusieurs reprises.

repel [rɪ'pɛl] vt (lit, fig) repousser; **~lent** a repoussant(e) // n: insect **~lent** insectifuge m.

repent [rɪ'pɛnt] vi: to ~ (of) se repentir (de); **~ance** n repentir m.

repertory ['rɛpətərɪ] n (also: ~

theatre) théâtre m de répertoire.

repetition [rɛpɪ'tɪʃən] n répétition f.

repetitive [rɪ'pɛtɪtɪv] a (movement, work) répétitif(ive); (speech) plein(e) de répétitions.

replace [rɪ'pleɪs] vt (put back) remettre, replacer; (take the place of) remplacer; **~ment** n replacement m; remplacement m; (person) remplaçant/e.

replay [riː'pleɪ] n (of match) match rejoué; (of tape, film) répétition f.

replenish [rɪ'plɛnɪʃ] vt (glass) remplir (de nouveau); (stock etc) réapprovisionner.

replete [rɪ'pliːt] a rempli(e); (well-fed) rassasié(e).

replica ['rɛplɪkə] n réplique f, copie exacte.

reply [rɪ'plaɪ] n réponse f // vi répondre; ~ **coupon** n coupon-réponse m.

report [rɪ'pɔːt] n rapport m; (PRESS etc) reportage m; (Brit: also: school ~) bulletin m (scolaire); (of gun) détonation f // vt rapporter, faire un compte rendu de; (PRESS etc) faire un reportage sur; (bring to notice: occurrence; : person) signaler // vi (make a report) faire un rapport (or un reportage); (present o.s.): to ~ (to sb) se présenter (chez qn); ~ **card** n (US, Scottish) bulletin m scolaire; **~edly** ad: she is ~edly living in ... elle habiterait ...; he ~edly told them to ... il leur aurait ordonné de ...; ~er n reporter m.

repose [rɪ'pəʊz] n: in ~ en or au repos.

represent [rɛprɪ'zɛnt] vt représenter; **~ation** [-'teɪʃən] n représentation f; **~ations** npl (protest) démarche f; **~ative** n représentant/e; (US POL) député m // a représentatif(ive), caractéristique.

repress [rɪ'prɛs] vt réprimer; **~ion** [-'prɛʃən] n répression f.

reprieve [rɪ'priːv] n (LAW) grâce f; (fig) sursis m, délai m.

reprisal [rɪ'praɪzl] n représailles fpl.

reproach [rɪ'prəutʃ] vt: to ~ sb with sth reprocher qch à qn; **~ful** a de reproche.

reproduce [ri:prə'dju:s] vt reproduire // vi se reproduire; **reproduction** [-'dʌkʃən] n reproduction f.

reproof [rɪ'pru:f] n reproche m.

reptile ['reptaɪl] n reptile m.

republic [rɪ'pʌblɪk] n république f; **~an** a, n républicain(e).

repulsive [rɪ'pʌlsɪv] a repoussant(e), répulsif(ive).

reputable ['repjutəbl] a de bonne réputation; (occupation) honorable.

reputation [repju'teɪʃən] n réputation f.

repute [rɪ'pju:t] n (bonne) réputation; **~d** a réputé(e); **~dly** ad d'après ce qu'on dit.

request [rɪ'kwest] n demande f; (formal) requête f // vt: to ~ (of or from sb) demander (à qn); ~ **stop** n (Brit: for bus) arrêt m facultatif.

require [rɪ'kwaɪə*] vt (need: subj: person) avoir besoin de; (: thing, situation) demander; (want) vouloir; exiger; (order) obliger; **~ment** n exigence f; besoin m; condition requise.

requisite ['rekwɪzɪt] n chose f nécessaire // a nécessaire.

requisition [rekwɪ'zɪʃən] n: ~ (for) demande f (de) // vt (MIL) réquisitionner.

rescue ['reskju:] n sauvetage m; (help) secours mpl // vt sauver; ~ **party** n équipe f de sauvetage; **~r** n sauveteur m.

research [rɪ'sə:tʃ] n recherche(s) f(pl) // vt faire des recherches sur.

resemblance [rɪ'zembləns] n ressemblance f.

resemble [rɪ'zembl] vt ressembler à.

resent [rɪ'zent] vt éprouver du ressentiment de, être contrarié par; **~ful** a irrité(e), plein(e) de ressentiment; **~ment** n ressentiment m.

reservation [rezə'veɪʃən] n (booking) réservation f; (doubt) réserve f; (protected area) réserve f; (Brit: on

road: also: **central** ~) bande f médiane; **to make a** ~ (in an hotel/a restaurant/on a plane) réserver or retenir une chambre/une table/une place.

reserve [rɪ'zə:v] n réserve f; (SPORT) remplaçant/e // vt (seats etc) réserver, retenir; **~s** npl (MIL) réservistes mpl; **in** ~ en réserve; **~d** a réservé(e).

reshuffle [ri:'ʃʌfl] n: Cabinet ~ (POL) remaniement ministériel.

residence ['rezɪdəns] n résidence f; ~ **permit** n (Brit) permis m de séjour.

resident ['rezɪdənt] n résident/e // a résidant(e); **~ial** [-'denʃəl] a de résidence; (area) résidentiel(le).

residue ['rezɪdju:] n reste m; (CHEM, PHYSICS) résidu m.

resign [rɪ'zaɪn] vt (one's post) se démettre de // vi démissionner; **to o.s.** to (endure) se résigner à; **~ation** [rezɪg'neɪʃən] n démission f; résignation f; **~ed** a résigné(e).

resilience [rɪ'zɪlɪəns] n (of material) élasticité f; (of person) ressort m.

resilient [rɪ'zɪlɪənt] a (person) qui réagit, qui a du ressort.

resist [rɪ'zɪst] vt résister à; **~ance** n résistance f.

resolution [rezə'lu:ʃən] n résolution f.

resolve [rɪ'zɔlv] n résolution f // vi (decide): **to** ~ **to do** résoudre or décider de faire // vt (problem) résoudre.

resort [rɪ'zɔ:t] n (town) station f; (recourse) recours m // vi: **to** ~ **to** avoir recours à; **in the last** ~ en dernier ressort.

resounding [rɪ'zaundɪŋ] a retentissant(e).

resource [rɪ'sɔ:s] n ressource f; **~s** npl ressources.

respect [rɪs'pekt] n respect m // vt respecter; **~s** npl respects, hommages mpl; **with** ~ **to** en ce qui concerne; **in this** ~ sous ce rapport, à cet égard; **~able** a respectable;

~ful *a* respectueux(euse).

respite ['respait] *n* répit *m*.

resplendent [ris'plendənt] *a* resplendissant(e).

respond [ris'pɔnd] *vi* répondre; *(to treatment)* réagir.

response [ris'pɔns] *n* réponse *f*; *(to treatment)* réaction *f*.

responsibility [rispɔnsi'biliti] *n* responsabilité *f*.

responsible [ris'pɔnsibl] *a* *(liable)*: ~ **(for)** responsable (de); *(person)* digne de confiance; *(job)* qui comporte des responsabilités; **responsibly** *ad* avec sérieux.

responsive [ris'pɔnsiv] *a* qui n'est pas réservé(e) *or* indifférent(e).

rest [rest] *n* repos *m*; *(stop)* arrêt *m*, pause *f*; *(MUS)* silence *m*; *(support)* support *m*, appui *m*; *(remainder)* reste *m*, restant *m* // *vi* se reposer; *(be supported)*: **to** ~ **on** appuyer *or* reposer sur; *(remain)* rester // *vt* *(lean)*: **to** ~ **sth on/against** appuyer qch sur/contre; **the** ~ **of them** les autres; **it** ~**s with him to** c'est à lui de.

restaurant ['restərɔŋ] *n* restaurant *m*; ~ **car** *n* *(Brit)* wagon-restaurant *m*.

restful ['restful] *a* reposant(e).

restitution [resti'tju:ʃən] *n* *(act)* restitution *f*; *(reparation)* réparation *f*.

restive ['restiv] *a* agité(e), impatient(e); *(horse)* rétif(ive).

restless ['restlis] *a* agité(e).

restoration [restə'reiʃən] *n* restauration *f*; restitution *f*.

restore [ri'stɔ:*] *vt* *(building)* restaurer; *(sth stolen)* restituer; *(peace, health)* rétablir.

restrain [ris'trein] *vt* *(feeling)* contenir; *(person)*: **to** ~ **(from doing)** retenir (de faire); ~**ed** *a* *(style)* sobre; *(manner)* mesuré(e); ~**t** *n* *(restriction)* contrainte *f*; *(moderation)* retenue *f*.

restrict [ris'trikt] *vt* restreindre, limiter; ~**ion** [-kʃən] *n* restriction *f*, limitation *f*.

rest room *n* *(US)* toilettes *fpl*.

result [ri'zʌlt] *n* résultat *m* // *vi*: **to** ~ **in** aboutir à, se terminer par; **as a** ~ **of** à la suite de.

resume [ri'zju:m] *vt, vi* *(work, journey)* reprendre.

résumé ['reizjumei] *n* résumé *m*; *(US)* curriculum vitae *m*.

resumption [ri'zʌmpʃən] *n* reprise *f*.

resurgence [ri'sə:dʒəns] *n* réapparition *f*.

resurrection [rezə'rekʃən] *n* résurrection *f*.

resuscitate [ri'sʌsiteit] *vt* *(MED)* réanimer.

retail ['ri:teil] *n* *(vente *f* au)* détail *m* // *cpd* de *or* au détail // *vt* vendre au détail; **to** ~ **at** détaillant/e; ~ **price** *n* prix *m* de détail.

retain [ri'tein] *vt* *(keep)* garder, conserver; *(employ)* engager; ~**er** *n* *(servant)* serviteur *m*; *(fee)* acompte *m*, provision *f*.

retaliate [ri'tælieit] *vi*: **to** ~ **(against)** se venger (de); **retaliation** [-'eiʃən] *n* représailles *fpl*, vengeance *f*.

retarded [ri'tɑ:did] *a* retardé(e).

retch [retʃ] *vi* avoir des haut-le-cœur.

retentive [ri'tentiv] *a*: ~ **memory** excellente mémoire.

retina ['retinə] *n* rétine *f*.

retinue ['retinju:] *n* suite *f*, cortège *m*.

retire [ri'taiə*] *vi* *(give up work)* prendre sa retraite; *(withdraw)* se retirer, partir; *(go to bed)* (aller) se coucher; ~**d** *a* *(person)* retraité(e); ~**ment** *n* retraite *f*; **retiring** *a* *(person)* réservé(e).

retort [ri'tɔ:t] *vi* riposter.

retrace [ri:'treis] *vt* reconstituer; **to** ~ **one's steps** revenir sur ses pas.

retract [ri'trækt] *vt* *(statement, claws)* rétracter; *(undercarriage, aerial)* rentrer, escamoter // *vi* se rétracter; rentrer.

retrain [ri:'trein] *vt* *(worker)* recycler.

retread ['riːtred] n (tyre) pneu rechapé.

retreat [rɪ'triːt] n retraite f // vi battre en retraite; (flood) reculer.

retribution [retrɪ'bjuːʃən] n châtiment m.

retrieval [rɪ'triːvəl] n (see vb) récupération f; réparation f; recherche f et extraction f.

retrieve [rɪ'triːv] vt (sth lost) récupérer; (situation, honour) sauver; (error, loss) réparer; (COMPUT) rechercher; ~r n chien m d'arrêt.

retrospect ['retrəspekt] n: **in** ~ rétrospectivement, après coup; ~**ive** [-'spektɪv] a (law) rétroactif(ive).

return [rɪ'təːn] n (going or coming back) retour m; (of sth stolen etc) restitution f; (recompense) récompense f; (FINANCE: from land, shares) rapport m; (report) relevé m, rapport // cpd (journey) de retour; (Brit: ticket) aller et retour; (match) retour // vi (person etc: come back) revenir; (: go back) retourner // vt rendre; (bring back) rapporter; (send back) renvoyer; (put back) remettre; (POL: candidate) élire; ~**s** npl (COMM) recettes fpl; bénéfices mpl; **in** ~ (**for**) en échange (de); **by** ~ (**of post**) par retour (du courrier); **many happy** ~**s (of the day)!** bon anniversaire!

reunion [riː'juːnɪən] n réunion f.

reunite [riːju'naɪt] vt réunir.

rev [rev] n abbr (= revolution: AUT) tour m // vb (also: ~ **up**) vt emballer // vi s'emballer.

revamp ['riːvæmp] vt (house) retaper; (firm) réorganiser.

reveal [rɪ'viːl] vt (make known) révéler; (display) laisser voir; ~**ing** a révélateur(trice); (dress) au décolleté généreux or suggestif.

revel ['revl] vi: **to** ~ **in sth/in doing** se délecter de qch/à faire.

revelry ['revlrɪ] n festivités fpl.

revenge [rɪ'vendʒ] n vengeance f; (in game etc) revanche f // vt venger; **to take** ~ se venger.

revenue ['revənjuː] n revenu m.

reverberate [rɪ'vəːbəreɪt] vi (sound) retentir, se répercuter; (light) se réverbérer.

reverence ['revərəns] n vénération f, révérence f.

Reverend ['revərənd] a (in titles): **the** ~ **John Smith** (Anglican) le révérend John Smith; (Catholic) l'abbé (John) Smith; (Protestant) le pasteur (John) Smith.

reversal [rɪ'vəːsl] n (of opinion) revirement m.

reverse [rɪ'vəːs] n contraire m, opposé m; (back) dos m, envers m; (AUT: also: ~ **gear**) marche f arrière // a (order, direction) opposé(e), inverse // vt (turn) renverser, retourner; (change) renverser, changer complètement; (LAW: judgment) réformer // vi (Brit AUT) faire marche arrière; ~**d charge call** n (Brit TEL) communication f en PCV; ~**versing lights** npl (Brit AUT) feux mpl de marche arrière or de recul.

revert [rɪ'vəːt] vi: **to** ~ **to** revenir à, retourner à.

review [rɪ'vjuː] n revue f; (of book, film) critique f // vt passer en revue; faire la critique de; ~**er** n critique m.

revile [rɪ'vaɪl] vt injurier.

revise [rɪ'vaɪz] vt (manuscript) revoir, corriger; (opinion) réviser, modifier; (study: subject, notes) réviser; **revision** [rɪ'vɪʒən] n révision f.

revival [rɪ'vaɪvl] n reprise f; (rétablissement m; (of faith) renouveau m.

revive [rɪ'vaɪv] vt (person) ranimer; (custom) rétablir; (hope, courage) redonner; (play, fashion) reprendre // vi (person) reprendre connaissance; (hope) renaître; (activity) reprendre.

revolt [rɪ'vəult] n révolte f // vi se révolter, se rebeller // vt révolter, dégoûter; ~**ing** a dégoûtant(e).

revolution [revə'luːʃən] n révolution f; (of wheel etc) tour m, révolution f; ~**ary** a, n révolutionnaire (m/f).

revolve [rɪ'vɔlv] *vi* tourner.
revolver [rɪ'vɔlvə*] *n* revolver *m*.
revolving [rɪ'vɔlvɪŋ] *a*: ~ *chair* pivotant(e); (*light*) tournant(e); ~ **door** *n* (porte *f* à) tambour *m*.
revulsion [rɪ'vʌlʃən] *n* dégoût *m*, répugnance *f*.
reward [rɪ'wɔːd] *n* récompense *f* // *vt*: to ~ (*for*) récompenser (de); ~**ing** *a* (*fig*) qui (en) vaut la peine, gratifiant(e).
rewire [riː'waɪə*] *vt* (*house*) refaire l'installation électrique de.
reword [riː'wɜːd] *vt* formuler *or* exprimer différemment.
rheumatism ['ruːmətɪzəm] *n* rhumatisme *m*.
Rhine [raɪn] *n*: the ~ le Rhin.
rhinoceros [raɪ'nɔsərəs] *n* rhinocéros *m*.
Rhone [rəun] *n*: the ~ le Rhône.
rhubarb ['ruːbɑːb] *n* rhubarbe *f*.
rhyme [raɪm] *n* rime *f*; (*verse*) vers *mpl*.
rhythm ['rɪðm] *n* rythme *m*.
rib [rɪb] *n* (*ANAT*) côte *f* // *vt* (*mock*) taquiner.
ribald ['rɪbəld] *a* paillard(e).
ribbon ['rɪbən] *n* ruban *m*; **in ~s** (*torn*) en lambeaux.
rice [raɪs] *n* riz *m*.
rich [rɪtʃ] *a* riche; (*gift, clothes*) somptueux(euse); the ~ *npl* les riches *mpl*; ~**es** *npl* richesses *fpl*; ~**ly** *ad* richement; (*deserved, earned*) largement, grandement; ~**ness** *n* richesse *f*.
rickets ['rɪkɪts] *n* rachitisme *m*.
rickety ['rɪkɪtɪ] *a* branlant(e).
rickshaw ['rɪkʃɔː] *n* pousse(-pousse) *m*.
rid, *pt*, *pp* **rid** [rɪd] *vt*: to ~ sb of débarrasser qn de; to get ~ of se débarrasser de.
ridden ['rɪdn] *pp* of **ride**.
riddle ['rɪdl] *n* (*puzzle*) énigme *f* // *vt*: to be ~**d with** être criblé(e) de.
ride [raɪd] *n* promenade *f*, tour *m*; (*distance covered*) trajet *m* // *vb* (*pt* **rode**, *pp* **ridden** [rəud, 'rɪdn]) *vi* (as

sport) monter (à cheval), faire du cheval; (*go somewhere: on horse, bicycle*) aller (à cheval *or* bicyclette etc); (*journey: on bicycle, motorcycle, bus*) rouler // *vt* (a certain *horse*) monter; (*distance*) parcourir, faire; to ~ **a horse/bicycle/camel** monter à cheval/à bicyclette/à dos de chameau; to ~ **at anchor** (*NAUT*) être à l'ancre; **to take sb for a ~** (*fig*) faire marcher qn; rouler qn; ~**r** *n* cavalier/ère; (*in race*) jockey *m*; (*on bicycle*) cycliste *m/f*; (*on motorcycle*) motocycliste *m/f*; (*in document*) annexe *f*, clause additionnelle.
ridge [rɪdʒ] *n* (*of hill*) faîte *m*; (*of roof, mountain*) arête *f*; (*on object*) strie *f*.
ridicule ['rɪdɪkjuːl] *n* ridicule *m*; dérision *f*.
ridiculous [rɪ'dɪkjuləs] *a* ridicule.
riding ['raɪdɪŋ] *n* équitation *f*; ~ **school** *n* manège *m*, école *f* d'équitation.
rife [raɪf] *a* répandu(e); ~ **with** abondant(e) en.
riffraff ['rɪfræf] *n* racaille *f*.
rifle ['raɪfl] *n* fusil *m* (à canon rayé) // *vt* vider, dévaliser; ~ **range** *n* champ *m* de tir; (*indoor*) stand *m* de tir.
rift [rɪft] *n* fente *f*, fissure *f*; (*fig: disagreement*) désaccord *m*.
rig [rɪg] *n* (*also: oil* ~: *on land*) derrick *m*; (*: at sea*) plate-forme pétrolière // *vt* (*election etc*) truquer; to ~ **out** *vt* (*Brit*) habiller; (*: pej*) fringuer, attifer; to ~ **up** *vt* arranger, faire avec des moyens de fortune; ~**ging** *n* (*NAUT*) gréement *m*.
right [raɪt] *a* (*true*) juste, exact(e); (*correctly chosen: answer, road etc*) bon(bonne); (*suitable*) approprié(e), convenable; (*just*) juste, équitable; (*morally good*) bien *inv*; (*not left*) droit(e) // *n* (*title, claim*) droit *m*; (*not left*) droite *f* // *ad* (*answer*) correctement; (*not on the left*) à droite // *vt* redresser // *excl* bon!; **to be ~** (*person*) avoir raison; (*answer*) être

juste or correct(e); **by ~s** en toute justice; **on the ~** à droite; **to be in the ~** avoir raison; **~ now** en ce moment même; tout de suite; **~ against the wall** tout contre le mur; **~ ahead** tout droit; droit devant; **in the middle** en plein milieu; **~ away** immédiatement; **~ angle** n angle droit; **~eous** ['raɪtʃəs] a droit(e), vertueux(euse); (anger) justifié(e); **~ful** a (heir) légitime; **~handed** a (person) droitier(ère); **~-hand man** n bras droit (fig); **~hand side** n côté droit; **~ly** ad bien, correctement; (with reason) à juste titre; **~ of way** n droit m de passage; (AUT) priorité f; **~-wing** a (POL) de droite.

rigid ['rɪdʒɪd] a rigide; (principle) strict(e).

rigmarole ['rɪgmərəul] n galimatias m, comédie f.

rigorous ['rɪgərəs] a rigoureux(euse).

rile [raɪl] vt agacer.

rim [rɪm] n bord m; (of spectacles) monture f; (of wheel) jante f.

rind [raɪnd] n (of bacon) couenne f; (of lemon etc) écorce f.

ring [rɪŋ] n anneau m; (on finger) bague f; (also: **wedding ~**) alliance f; (for napkin) rond m; (of people, objects) cercle m; (of spies) réseau m; (of smoke etc) rond; (arena) piste f, arène f; (for boxing) ring m; (sound of bell) sonnerie f; (telephone call) coup m de téléphone // vb (pt **rang**, pp **rung**) vi (person, bell) sonner; (also: **~ out**: voice, words) retentir; (TEL) téléphoner // vt (Brit TEL: also: **~ up**) téléphoner à; **to ~ the bell** sonner; **to ~ back** vt, vi (TEL) rappeler; **to ~ off** vi (Brit TEL) raccrocher; **~ing** n tintement m; sonnerie f; (in ears) bourdonnement m; **~ing tone** n (Brit TEL) sonnerie f; **~leader** n (of gang) chef m, meneur m.

ringlets ['rɪŋlɪts] npl anglaises fpl.

ring road n (Brit) route f de ceinture.

rink [rɪŋk] n (also: **ice ~**) patinoire f.

rinse [rɪns] vt rincer.

riot ['raɪət] n émeute f, bagarres fpl // vi faire une émeute, manifester avec violence; **to run ~** se déchaîner; **~ous** a tapageur(euse); tordant(e).

rip [rɪp] n déchirure f // vt déchirer // vi se déchirer; **~cord** n poignée f d'ouverture.

ripe [raɪp] a (fruit) mûr(e); (cheese) fait(e); **~n** vt mûrir // vi mûrir; se faire.

rip-off ['rɪpɔf] n (col): **it's a ~!** c'est du vol manifeste!

ripple ['rɪpl] n ride f, ondulation f; égrènement m, cascade f // vi se rider, onduler // vt rider, faire onduler.

rise [raɪz] n (slope) côte f, pente f; (hill) élévation f; (increase: in wages: Brit) augmentation f; (: in prices, temperature) hausse f, augmentation; (fig: to power etc) essor m, ascension f // vi (pt **rose**, pp **risen** [rauz, rɪzn]) s'élever, monter; (prices) augmenter, monter; (waters, river) monter; (sun, wind, person: from chair, bed) se lever; (sun: ~ up: rebel) se révolter; se rebeller; **to give ~ to** donner lieu à; **to ~ to the occasion** se montrer à la hauteur; **rising** a (increasing: number, prices) en hausse; (tide) montant(e); (sun, moon) levant(e) // n (uprising) soulèvement m, insurrection f.

risk [rɪsk] n risque m; danger m // vt risquer; (venture) hasarder; **at ~** en danger; **at one's own ~** à ses risques et périls; **~y** a risqué(e).

rissole ['rɪsəul] n croquette f.

rite [raɪt] n rite m; **last ~s** derniers sacrements.

ritual ['rɪtjuəl] a rituel(le) // n rituel m.

rival ['raɪvl] n rival/e; (in business) concurrent/e // a rival(e); qui fait concurrence // vt être en concurrence avec; **to ~ sb/sth** in rivaliser avec qn/qch qn; **~ry** n rivalité f, concurrence f.

river ['rɪvə*] n rivière f; (major, also fig) fleuve m // cpd (port, traffic) fluvial(e); **~up/down** = en amont/aval; **~bank** n rive f, berge f.

rivet ['rɪvɪt] n rivet m // vt riveter; (fig) river, fixer.

Riviera [rɪvɪ'eərə] n: the (French) ~ la Côte d'Azur; the Italian ~ la Riviera (italienne).

road [rəud] n route f; (small) chemin m; (in town) rue f; (fig) chemin, voie f; **major/minor** ~ route principale or à priorité/voie secondaire; **~block** n barrage routier; **~hog** n chauffard m; **~map** n carte routière; **~safety** n sécurité routière; **~side** n bord m de la route, bas-côté m; **~sign** n panneau m de signalisation; **~way** n chaussée f; **~works** npl travaux mpl (de réfection des routes); **~worthy** a en bon état de marche.

roam [rəum] vi errer, vagabonder // vt parcourir, errer par.

roar [rɔ:*] n rugissement m; (of crowd) hurlements mpl; (of vehicle, thunder, storm) grondement m // vi rugir; hurler; gronder; to ~ with laughter éclater de rire; to do a ~ing trade faire des affaires d'or.

roast [rəust] n rôti m // vt (meat) (faire) rôtir; **~beef** n rôti m de bœuf, rosbif m.

rob [rɔb] vt (person) voler; (bank) dévaliser; to ~ sb of sth voler or dérober qch à qn; (fig: deprive) priver qn de qch; **~ber** n bandit m, voleur m; **~bery** n vol m.

robe [rəub] n (for ceremony etc) robe f; (also: bath ~) peignoir m; (US) couverture f // vt revêtir (d'une robe).

robin ['rɔbɪn] n rouge-gorge m.

robot ['rəubɔt] n robot m.

robust [rəu'bʌst] a robuste; (material, appetite) solide.

rock [rɔk] n (substance) roche f, roc m; (boulder) rocher m; roche; (Brit: sweet) ≈ sucre m d'orge // vt (swing

gently: cradle) balancer; (: child) bercer; (shake) ébranler, secouer // vi se balancer; être ébranlé(e) or secoué(e); **on the ~s** (drink) avec des glaçons; (ship) sur les écueils; (marriage etc) en train de craquer; **~and roll** n rock and roll m, rock'n'roll m; **~bottom** n (fig) niveau le plus bas // a (fig: prices) sacrifié(e); **~ery** n (jardin m de) rocaille f.

rocket ['rɔkɪt] n fusée f; (MIL) fusée, roquette f.

rocking ['rɔkɪŋ]: **~chair** n fauteuil m à bascule; **~horse** n cheval m à bascule.

rocky ['rɔkɪ] a (hill) rocheux(euse); (path) rocailleux(euse); (unsteady: table) branlant(e).

rod [rɔd] n (metallic) tringle f; (TECH) tige f; (wooden) baguette f; (also: fishing ~) canne f à pêche.

rode [rəud] pt of ride.

rodent ['rəudnt] n rongeur m.

rodeo ['rəudɪəu] n rodéo m.

roe [rəu] n (species: also: ~ deer) chevreuil m; (of fish, also: hard ~) œufs mpl de poisson; **soft** ~ laitance f.

rogue [rəug] n coquin/e.

role [rəul] n rôle m.

roll [rəul] n rouleau m; (of banknotes) liasse f; (also: bread ~) petit pain; (register) liste f; (sound: of drums etc) roulement m; (movement: of ship) roulis m // vt rouler; (also: ~ up: string) enrouler; (also: ~ out: pastry) étendre au rouleau // vi rouler; (wheel) tourner; to ~ about or around vi rouler ça et là; (person) se rouler par terre; to ~ by (time) s'écouler, passer; to ~ in vi (mail, cash) affluer; to ~ over vi se retourner; to ~ up vi (col: arrive) arriver, s'amener // vt (carpet) rouler; **~call** n appel m; **~er** n rouleau m; (wheel) roulette f; **~er coaster** n montagnes fpl russes; **~er skates** npl patins mpl à roulettes.

rolling ['rəʊlɪŋ] a (landscape) onduleux(euse); ~ **pin** n rouleau m à pâtisserie; ~ **stock** n (RAIL) matériel roulant.

ROM [rɔm] n abbr (= read only memory) mémoire morte.

Roman ['rəʊmən] a romain(e) // n Romain/e; ~ **Catholic** a, n catholique (m/f).

romance [rə'mæns] n histoire f ou film m ou aventure f romanesque; (charm) poésie f; (love affair) idylle f.

Romania [rəʊ'meɪnɪə] n = **Rumania.**

Roman numeral n chiffre romain.

romantic [rə'mæntɪk] a romantique; sentimental(e).

Rome [rəʊm] n Rome.

romp [rɔmp] n jeux bruyants // vi (also: ~ **about**) s'ébattre, jouer bruyamment.

rompers ['rɔmpəz] npl barboteuse f.

roof, pl ~**s** [ru:f] n toit m; (of tunnel, cave) plafond m // vt couvrir (d'un toit); **the ~ of the mouth** la voûte du palais; ~**ing** n toiture f; ~ **rack** n (AUT) galerie f.

rook [ruk] n (bird) freux m; (CHESS) tour f.

room [ru:m] n (in house) pièce f; (also: bed~) chambre f (à coucher); (in school etc) salle f; (space) place f; ~**s** npl (lodging) meublé m; '~**s to let'**, (US) '~**s for rent'** 'chambres à louer'; ~**ing house** n (US) maison f ou immeuble m de rapport; ~**mate** n camarade m/f de chambre; ~ **service** n service m des chambres (dans un hôtel); ~**y** a spacieux(euse); (garment) ample.

roost [ru:st] n juchoir m // vi se jucher.

rooster ['ru:stə*] n coq m.

root [ru:t] n (BOT, MATH) racine f; (fig: of problem) origine f, fond m // vi (plant) s'enraciner; to ~ **about** vi (fig) fouiller; to ~ **for** vt fus applaudir; to ~ **out** vt extirper.

rope [rəʊp] n corde f; (NAUT) cor-

dage m // vt (box) corder; (climbers) encorder; to ~ **sb in** (fig) embringuer qn; to **know the ~s** (fig) être au courant, connaître les ficelles.

rosary ['rəʊzərɪ] n chapelet m.

rose [rəʊz] pt of **rise** // n rose f; (also: ~**bush**) rosier m; (on watering can) pomme f à rose.

rosé ['rəʊzeɪ] n rosé m.

rose: ~**bud** n bouton m de rose; ~**bush** n rosier m.

rosemary ['rəʊzmərɪ] n romarin m.

roster ['rɔstə*] n: **duty** ~ tableau m de service.

rostrum ['rɔstrəm] n tribune f (pour un orateur etc).

rosy ['rəʊzɪ] a rose; **a** ~ **future** un bel avenir.

rot [rɔt] n (decay) pourriture f; (fig: pej) idioties fpl, balivernes fpl // vt, vi pourrir.

rota ['rəʊtə] n liste f, tableau m de service; **on a** ~ **basis** par roulement.

rotary ['rəʊtərɪ] a rotatif(ive).

rotate [rəʊ'teɪt] vt (revolve) faire tourner; (change round: crops) alterner; (: jobs) faire à tour de rôle // vi (revolve) tourner; **rotating** a (movement) tournant(e).

rote [rəʊt] n: **by** ~ machinalement, par cœur.

rotten ['rɔtn] a (decayed) pourri(e); (dishonest) corrompu(e); (col: bad) mauvais(e), moche; to **feel** ~ (ill) être mal fichu(e).

rough [rʌf] a (cloth, skin) rêche, rugueux(euse); (terrain) accidenté(e); (path) rocailleux(euse); (voice) rauque, rude; (person, manner: coarse) rude, fruste; (: violent) brutal(e); (district, weather) mauvais(e); (plan) ébauché(e); (guess) approximatif(ive) // n (GOLF) rough m; to ~ **it** vivre à la dure; to **sleep** ~ (Brit) coucher à la dure; ~**age** n fibres fpl diététiques; ~**and-ready** a rudimentaire; ~**cast** n crépi m; ~ **copy**, ~ **draft** n brouillon m; ~**ly** ad (handle) rudement, brutalement;

(make) grossièrement; *(approximately)* à peu près, en gros.

roulette [ru:'let] *n* roulette *f*.

Roumania [ru:'meɪnɪə] *n* = **Rumania**.

round [raund] *a* rond(e) // *n* rond *m*, cercle *m*; *(Brit: of toast)* tranche *f*; *(duty: of policeman, milkman etc)* tournée *f*; *(: of doctor)* visites *fpl*; *(game: of cards, in competition)* partie *f*; *(BOXING)* round *m*; *(of talks)* série *f* // *vt (corner)* tourner; *(bend)* prendre; *(cape)* doubler // *prep* autour de // *ad*: **all ~** tout autour; **the long way ~** (par) le chemin le plus long; **all the year ~** toute l'année; **it's just ~ the corner** c'est juste après le coin; *(fig)* c'est tout près; **the clock** 24 heures sur 24; **to go ~** faire le tour ou un détour; **to go to sb's (house)** aller chez qn; **to go the back** passez par derrière; **to go ~ a house** visiter une maison, faire le tour d'une maison; **enough to go ~** assez pour tout le monde; **to go the ~s** *(disease, story)* circuler; **~ of ammunition** *n* cartouche *f*; **~ of applause** *n* ban *m*, applaudissements *mpl*; **~ of drinks** *n* tournée *f*; **~ of sandwiches** *n* sandwich *m*; **to ~ off** *vt (speech etc)* terminer; **to ~ up** *vt* rassembler; *(criminals)* effectuer une rafle de; *(prices)* arrondir (au chiffre supérieur); **~about** *n (Brit AUT)* rond-point *m* (à sens giratoire); *(: at fair)* manège *m* (de chevaux de bois) // *a (route, means)* détourné(e); **~ers** *npl (game)* ~ balle *f* au camp; **~ly** *ad (fig)* tout net, carrément; **~-shouldered** *a* au dos rond; **~ trip** *n (voyage m)* aller et retour *m*; **~up** *n* rassemblement *m*; *(of criminals)* rafle *f*.

rouse [rauz] *vt (wake up)* réveiller; *(stir up)* susciter; provoquer; éveiller; **rousing** *a (welcome)* enthousiaste.

rout [raut] *n (MIL)* déroute *f*.

route [ru:t] *n* itinéraire *m*; *(of bus)* parcours *m*; *(of trade, shipping)* route *f*; **~ map** *n (Brit: for journey)* croquis *m* d'itinéraire.

routine [ru:'ti:n] *a (work)* ordinaire, courant(e); *(procedure)* d'usage // *n (pej)* routine *f*; *(THEATRE)* numéro *m*; **daily ~** occupations journalières.

roving ['rəuvɪŋ] *a (life)* vagabond(e).

row [rəu] *n (line)* rangée *f*; *(of people, seats, KNITTING)* rang *m*; *(behind one another: of cars, people)* file *f*; [rau] *(noise)* vacarme *m*; *(dispute)* dispute *f*, querelle *f*; *(scolding)* réprimande *f*, savon *m* // *vi (in boat)* ramer; *(as sport)* faire de l'aviron; [rau] se disputer, se quereller // *vt (boat)* faire aller à la rame ou à l'aviron; **in a ~** *(fig)* d'affilée; **~boat** *n (US)* canot *m* (à rames).

rowdy ['raudɪ] *a* chahuteur(euse); bagarreur(euse) // *n* voyou *m*.

rowing ['rəuɪŋ] *n* canotage *m*; *(as sport)* aviron *m*; **~ boat** *n (Brit)* canot *m* (à rames).

royal ['rɔɪəl] *a* royal(e); **R~ Air Force (RAF)** *n* armée de l'air britannique.

royalty ['rɔɪəltɪ] *n (royal persons)* (membres *mpl* de la) famille royale; *(payment: to author)* droits *mpl* d'auteur; *(: to inventor)* royalties *fpl*.

r.p.m. *abbr (AUT:* = *revs per minute)* tr/mn *(= tours/minute).*

R.S.V.P. *abbr (= répondez s'il vous plaît)* R.S.V.P.

Rt Hon. *abbr (Brit:* = Right Honourable) titre donné aux députés de la Chambre des communes.

rub [rʌb] *n (with cloth)* coup *m* de chiffon ou de torchon; *(on person)* friction *f* // *vt* frictionner; **to ~ sb up** ou *(US)* **~ sb the wrong way** prendre qn à rebrousse-poil; **to ~ off** *vi* partir; **to ~ off on** *vt fus* déteindre sur; **to ~ out** *vt* effacer.

rubber ['rʌbə*] *n* caoutchouc *m*; *(Brit: eraser)* gomme *f* (à effacer); **~ band** *n* élastique *m*; **~ plant** *n* caoutchouc *m* (plante verte).

rubbish ['rʌbɪʃ] *n (from household)* ordures *fpl*; *(fig: pej)* choses *fpl* sans valeur; camelote f; bêtises fpl, idioties fpl; ~ **bin** n (Brit) boîte f à ordures, poubelle f; ~ **dump** n (in town) décharge publique, dépotoir m.

rubble ['rʌbl] n décombres mpl; (smaller) gravats mpl.

ruby ['ru:bɪ] n rubis m.

rucksack ['rʌksæk] n sac m à dos.

ructions ['rʌkʃənz] npl grabuge m.

rudder ['rʌdə*] n gouvernail m.

ruddy ['rʌdɪ] a (face) coloré(e); (col: damned) sacré(e), fichu(e).

rude [ru:d] a (impolite: person) impoli(e); (: word, manners) grossier(ère); (shocking) indécent(e), inconvenant(e).

rueful ['ru:ful] a triste.

ruffian ['rʌfɪən] n brute f, voyou m.

ruffle ['rʌfl] vt (hair) ébouriffer; (clothes) chiffonner; (water) agiter; (fig: person) émouvoir, faire perdre son flegme à.

rug [rʌg] n petit tapis; (Brit: for knees) couverture f.

rugby ['rʌgbɪ] n (also: ~ football) rugby m.

rugged ['rʌgɪd] a (landscape) accidenté(e); (features, kindness, character) rude; (determination) farouche.

rugger ['rʌgə*] n (Brit col) rugby m.

ruin [ruɪn] n ruine f // vt ruiner; (spoil: clothes) abîmer; ~s npl ruine(s).

rule [ru:l] n règle f; (regulation) règlement m; (government) autorité f, gouvernement m // vt (country) gouverner; (person) dominer; (decide) décider // vi commander; décider; (LAW) statuer; **as a** ~ normalement, en règle générale; **to** ~ **out** vt exclure; ~**d** a (paper) réglé(e); ~**r** n (sovereign) souverain(e); (leader) chef m (d'État); (for measuring) règle f; **ruling** a (party) au pouvoir; (class) dirigeant(e) // n (LAW) décision f.

rum [rʌm] n rhum m // a (col) bizarre.

Rumania [ru:ˈmeɪnɪə] n Roumanie f.

rumble ['rʌmbl] vi gronder; (stomach, pipe) gargouiller.

rummage ['rʌmɪdʒ] vi fouiller.

rumour, (US) **rumor** ['ru:mə*] n rumeur f, bruit m (qui court) // vt: **it is** ~**ed that** he bruit court que.

rump [rʌmp] n (of animal) croupe f; ~ **steak** n rumsteck m.

rumpus ['rʌmpəs] n (col) tapage m, chahut m; (quarrel) prise f de bec.

run [rʌn] n (pas m de) course f; (outing) tour m ou promenade f (en voiture); parcours m, trajet m; (series) suite f, série f; (THEATRE) série de représentations; (SKI) piste f; (in tights, stockings) maille filée, échelle f // vb (pt ran, pp run) vt (operate: business) diriger; (: hotel, house) tenir; (COMPUT) exécuter; (force through: rope, pipe): **to** ~ **sth through** faire passer qch à travers; (to pass: hand, finger): **to** ~ **sth over** promener or passer qch sur; (water, bath) faire couler // vi courir; (pass: road etc) passer; (work: machine, factory) marcher; (bus, train: operate) être en service; (: travel) circuler; (continue: play) se jouer; (: contract) être valide; (slide: drawer etc) glisser; (flow: river, bath) couler; (colours, washing) déteindre; (in election) être candidat, se présenter; **there was a** ~ **on** (meat, tickets) les gens se sont rués sur; **in the long** ~ à longue échéance; à la longue; en fin de compte; **on the** ~ en fuite; **I'll** ~ **you to the station** je vais vous emmener or conduire à la gare; **to** ~ **a risk** courir un risque; **to** ~ **about** or **around** vi (children) courir çà et là; **to** ~ **across** vt fus (find) trouver par hasard; **to** ~ **away** vi s'enfuir; **to** ~ **down** vt (production) réduire progressivement; (factory) réduire progressivement la production m; (AUT) renverser; (criticize) critiquer, dénigrer; **to be** ~ **down** (person: tired) être fatigué(e) or à plat; **to** ~ **in** vt (Brit: car) roder; **to** ~

into vt fus (meet: person) rencontrer par hasard; (: trouble) se heurter à; (collide with) heurter; **to ~ off** vi s'enfuir // vt (water) laisser s'écouler; **to ~ out** vi (person) sortir en courant; (liquid) couler; (lease) expirer; (money) être épuisé(e); **to ~ out of** vt fus se trouver à court de; **to ~ over** vt (AUT) écraser // vt fus (revise) revoir, reprendre; **to ~ through** vt fus (instructions) reprendre, revoir; **to ~ up** vt (debt) laisser accumuler; **to ~ up against** (difficulties) se heurter à; **~away** a (horse) emballé(e); (truck) fou(folle); (inflation) galopant(e).

rung [rʌŋ] pp of **ring** // n (of ladder) barreau m.

runner ['rʌnə*] n (in race: person) coureur/euse; (: horse) partant m; (on sledge) patin m; (for drawer etc) coulisseau m; (carpet: in hall etc) chemin m; **~ bean** n (Brit) haricot m (à rames); **~up** n second/e.

running ['rʌnɪŋ] n course f; direction f; organisation f; marche f, fonctionnement m // a (water) courant(e); (costs) de gestion; (commentary) suivi(e); **to be in/out of the ~** for sth être/ne pas être sur les rangs pour qch; **6 days ~** 6 jours de suite.

runny ['rʌnɪ] a qui coule.

run-of-the-mill ['rʌnəvðə'mɪl] a ordinaire, banal(e).

runt [rʌnt] n (also pej) avorton m.

run-up ['rʌnʌp] n: **~ to sth** (election etc) période f précédant qch.

runway ['rʌnweɪ] n (AVIAT) piste f (d'envol or d'atterrissage).

rupee [ru:'pi:] n roupie f.

rupture ['rʌptʃə*] n (MED) hernie f.

rural ['ruərl] a rural(e).

rush [rʌʃ] n course précipitée; (of crowd) ruée f, bousculade f; (hurry) hâte f, bousculade; (current) flot m; (BOT) jonc m // vt transporter or envoyer d'urgence; (attack: town etc) prendre d'assaut // vi se précipiter; **~ hour** n heures fpl de pointe or d'affluence.

rusk [rʌsk] n biscotte f.

Russia ['rʌʃə] n Russie f; **~n** a russe // n Russe m/f; (LING) russe m.

rust [rʌst] n rouille f // vi rouiller.

rustic ['rʌstɪk] a rustique.

rustle ['rʌsl] vi bruire, produire un bruissement // vt (paper) froisser; (US: cattle) voler.

rustproof ['rʌstpru:f] a inoxydable.

rusty ['rʌstɪ] a rouillé(e).

rut [rʌt] n ornière f; (ZOOL) rut m; **to be in a ~** suivre l'ornière, s'encroûter.

ruthless ['ru:θlɪs] a sans pitié, impitoyable.

rye [raɪ] n seigle m.

S

Sabbath ['sæbəθ] n (Jewish) sabbat m; (Christian) dimanche m.

sabotage ['sæbətɑ:ʒ] n sabotage m // vt saboter.

saccharin(e) ['sækərɪn] n saccharine f.

sachet ['sæʃeɪ] n sachet m.

sack [sæk] n (bag) sac m // vt (dismiss) renvoyer, mettre à la porte; (plunder) piller, mettre à sac; **to get the ~** être renvoyé(e) or mis à la porte; **~ing** n toile f à sac; renvoi m.

sacrament ['sækrəmənt] n sacrement m.

sacred ['seɪkrɪd] a sacré(e).

sacrifice ['sækrɪfaɪs] n sacrifice m // vt sacrifier.

sad [sæd] a (unhappy) triste; (deplorable) triste, fâcheux(euse).

saddle ['sædl] n selle f // vt (horse) seller; **to be ~d with sth** (col) avoir qch sur les bras; **~bag** n sacoche f.

sadistic [sə'dɪstɪk] a sadique.

sadness ['sædnɪs] n tristesse f.

s.a.e. n abbr = stamped addressed envelope.

safe [seɪf] a (out of danger) hors de

danger, en sécurité; (*not dangerous*) sans danger; (*cautious*) prudent(e); (*sure: bet etc*) assuré(e) // n coffre-fort m; ~ **from** à l'abri de; ~ **and sound** sain(e) et sauf(sauve); (*just*) **to be on the ~ side** pour plus de sûreté, par précaution; ~**conduct** n sauf-conduit m; ~**deposit** n (*vault*) dépôt m de coffres-forts; (*box*) coffre-fort m; ~**guard** n sauvegarde f, protection f // vt sauvegarder, protéger; ~**keeping** n bonne garde; ~**ly** ad sans danger, sans risque; (*without mishap*) sans accident.

safety ['seɪftɪ] n sécurité f; ~ **belt** n ceinture f de sécurité; ~ **pin** n épingle f de sûreté or de nourrice; ~ **valve** n soupape f de sûreté.

sag [sæg] vi s'affaisser, fléchir; pendre.

sage [seɪdʒ] n (*herb*) sauge f; (*man*) sage m.

Sagittarius [sædʒɪ'tɛərɪəs] n le Sagittaire.

Sahara [sə'hɑːrə] n: **the ~** (**Desert**) le (désert du) Sahara.

said [sɛd] pt, pp of **say**.

sail [seɪl] n (*on boat*) voile f; (*trip*): **to go for a ~** faire un tour en bateau // vt (*boat*) manœuvrer, piloter // vi (*travel: ship*) avancer, naviguer; (: *passenger*) aller or se rendre (en bateau); (*set off*) partir, prendre la mer; (*SPORT*) faire de la voile; **they ~ed into Le Havre** ils sont entrés dans le port du Havre; **to ~ through** vi, vt fus (*fig*) réussir haut la main; ~**boat** n (*US*) bateau m à voiles, voilier m; ~**ing** n (*SPORT*) voile f; **to go ~ing** faire de la voile; ~**ing ship** n grand voilier m; ~**or** n marin m, matelot m.

saint [seɪnt] n saint/e.

sake [seɪk] n: **for the ~ of** pour (l'amour de), dans l'intérêt de; par égard pour.

salad ['sæləd] n salade f; ~ **bowl** n saladier m; ~ **cream** n (*Brit*) (sorte f de) mayonnaise f; ~ **dressing** n vinaigrette f.

salary ['sælərɪ] n salaire m, traitement m.

sale [seɪl] n vente f; (*at reduced prices*) soldes mpl; '**for ~**' 'à vendre'; **on ~** en vente; **on ~ or return** vendu(e) avec faculté de retour; ~**room** n salle f des ventes; ~**s assistant**, (*US*) ~**s clerk** n vendeur/euse; ~**sman** n vendeur m; (*representative*) représentant m de commerce; ~**swoman** n vendeuse f.

salient ['seɪlɪənt] a saillant(e).

sallow ['sæləʊ] a cireux(euse).

salmon ['sæmən] n (*pl inv*) saumon m.

saloon [sə'luːn] n (*US*) bar m; (*Brit AUT*) berline f; (*ship's lounge*) salon m.

salt [sɔːlt] n sel m // vt saler // cpd de sel; (*CULIN*) salé(e); **to ~ away** vt (*col: money*) mettre de côté; ~ **cellar** n salière f; ~**water** a (d'eau) de mer; ~**y** a salé(e).

salute [sə'luːt] n salut m // vt saluer.

salvage ['sælvɪdʒ] n (*saving*) sauvetage m; (*things saved*) biens sauvés or récupérés // vt sauver, récupérer.

salvation [sæl'veɪʃən] n salut m; **S~ Army** n Armée f du Salut.

same [seɪm] a même // pronoun: **the ~** le (la) même, les mêmes; **the ~ book as** le même livre que; **at the ~ time** en même temps; **all** or **just the ~** tout de même, quand même; **to do the ~** faire de même, en faire autant; **to do the ~ as sb** faire comme qn; **the ~ to you!** et à vous de même!; (*after insult*) toi-même!

sample ['sɑːmpl] n échantillon m; (*MED*) prélèvement m // vt (*food, wine*) goûter.

sanctimonious [sæŋktɪ'məʊnɪəs] a moralisateur(trice).

sanction ['sæŋkʃən] n sanction f.

sanctity ['sæŋktɪtɪ] n sainteté f, caractère sacré.

sanctuary ['sæŋktjʊərɪ] n (*holy place*) sanctuaire m; (*refuge*) asile m; (*for wild life*) réserve f.

sand [sænd] *n* sable *m* // *vt* sabler.

sandal ['sændl] *n* sandale *f*.

sandbox ['sændbɒks] *n* (US) = **sandpit.**

sandcastle ['sændkɑ:sl] *n* château *m* de sable.

sandpaper ['sændpeipə*] *n* papier *m* de verre.

sandpit ['sændpit] *n* (for children) tas *m* de sable.

sandstone ['sændstəun] *n* grès *m*.

sandwich ['sændwitʃ] *n* sandwich *m* // *vt* (also: ~ **in**) intercaler; **cheese/ham** ~ sandwich au fromage/jambon; ~ **board** *n* panneau publicitaire (porté par un homme-sandwich); ~ **course** *n* (Brit) cours *m* de formation professionnelle.

sandy ['sændi] *a* sablonneux(euse); couvert(e) de sable; (colour) sable *inv*, blond roux *inv*.

sane [sein] *a* sain(e) d'esprit; (outlook) sensé(e), sain(e).

sang [sæŋ] *pt of* **sing.**

sanitary ['sænitəri] *a* (system, arrangements) sanitaire; (clean) hygiénique; ~ **towel**, (US) ~ **napkin** *n* serviette *f* hygiénique.

sanitation [sæni'teiʃən] *n* (in house) installations *fpl* sanitaires; (in town) système *m* sanitaire; ~ **department** *n* (US) service *m* de voirie.

sanity ['sæniti] *n* santé mentale; (common sense) bon sens.

sank [sæŋk] *pt of* **sink.**

Santa Claus [sæntə'klɔ:z] *n* le Père Noël.

sap [sæp] *n* (of plants) sève *f* // *vt* (strength) saper, miner.

sapling ['sæpliŋ] *n* jeune arbre *m*.

sapphire ['sæfaiə*] *n* saphir *m*.

sarcasm ['sɑ:kæzm] *n* sarcasme *m*, raillerie *f*.

sardine [sɑ:'di:n] *n* sardine *f*.

Sardinia [sɑ:'diniə] *n* Sardaigne *f*.

sash [sæʃ] *n* écharpe *f*.

sat [sæt] *pt, pp of* **sit.**

satchel ['sætʃl] *n* cartable *m*.

sated ['seitid] *a* repu(e); blasé(e).

satellite ['sætəlait] *a, n* satellite (*m*).

satin ['sætin] *n* satin *m* // *a* en or de satin, satiné(e).

satire ['sætaiə*] *n* satire *f*.

satisfaction [sætis'fækʃən] *n* satisfaction *f*.

satisfactory [sætis'fæktəri] *a* satisfaisant(e).

satisfy ['sætisfai] *vt* satisfaire, contenter; (convince) convaincre, persuader; ~**ing** *a* satisfaisant(e).

Saturday ['sætədi] *n* samedi *m*.

sauce [sɔ:s] *n* sauce *f*; ~**pan** *n* casserole *f*.

saucer ['sɔ:sə*] *n* soucoupe *f*.

saucy ['sɔ:si] *a* impertinent(e).

Saudi: ['saudi]: ~ **Arabia** *n* Arabie Saoudite; ~ **(Arabian)** *a* saoudien(ne) // *n* Saoudien/ne.

sauna ['sɔ:nə] *n* sauna *m*.

saunter ['sɔ:ntə*] *vi*: **to** ~ **to** aller en flânant or se balader jusqu'à.

sausage ['sɔsidʒ] *n* saucisse *f*; ~ **roll** *n* friand *m*.

savage ['sævidʒ] *a* (cruel, fierce) brutal(e), féroce; (primitive) primitif(ive), sauvage // *n* sauvage *m/f* // *vt* attaquer férocement.

save [seiv] *vt* (person, belongings) sauver; (money) mettre de côté, économiser; (time) (faire) gagner; (food) garder; (COMPUT) sauvegarder; (avoid: trouble) éviter // *vi* (also: ~ **up**) mettre de l'argent de côté // *n* (SPORT) arrêt *m* (du ballon) // *prep* sauf, à l'exception de.

saving ['seiviŋ] *n* économie *f* // *a*: **the** ~ **grace of** ce qui rachète; ~**s** *npl* économies *fpl*; ~**s bank** *n* caisse *f* d'épargne.

saviour, (US) **savior** ['seivjə*] *n* sauveur *m*.

savour, (US) **savor** ['seivə*] *vt* savourer; ~**y** *a* (dish: not sweet) salé(e).

saw [sɔ:] *pt of* **see** *n* (tool) scie *f* // *vt* (pt **sawed**, pp **sawed** or **sawn** [sɔ:n]) scier; ~**dust** *n* sciure *f*; ~**mill** *n* scierie *f*; ~**n-off shotgun** *n* carabine *f* à canon scié.

saxophone ['sæksəfəun] *n* saxophone m.

say [seɪ] n: **to have one's ~** dire ce qu'on a à dire; **to have a** or **some ~ in sth** avoir son mot à dire dans qch // vt (pt, pp **said**) dire; could you ~ **that again?**: pourriez-vous répéter ceci?; **that goes without ~ing** cela va sans dire, cela va de soi; **~ing** n dicton m, proverbe m.

scab [skæb] n croûte f; (pej) jaune m.

scaffold ['skæfəuld] n échafaud m; **~ing** n échafaudage m.

scald [skɔːld] n brûlure f // vt ébouillanter.

scale [skeɪl] n (of fish) écaille f; (MUS) gamme f; (of ruler, thermometer etc) graduation f, échelle (graduée); (of salaries, fees etc) barème m; (of map, also size, extent) échelle // vt (mountain) escalader; **~s** npl balance f; (larger) bascule f; **on a large ~** sur une grande échelle, en grand; **~ of charges** tableau m des tarifs; (ECON) barème m des redevances; **to ~ down** réduire; **~ model** n modèle m à l'échelle.

scallop ['skɔləp] n coquille f Saint-Jacques.

scalp [skælp] n cuir chevelu // vt scalper.

scamper ['skæmpə*] vi: **to ~ away**, **~ off** détaler.

scampi ['skæmpɪ] npl langoustines (frites), scampi fmpl.

scan [skæn] vt scruter, examiner; (glance at quickly) parcourir; (TV, RADAR) balayer.

scandal ['skændl] n scandale m; (gossip) ragots mpl.

Scandinavia [skændɪ'neɪvɪə] n Scandinavie f; **~n** a scandinave // n Scandinave m/f.

scant [skænt] a insuffisant(e); **~y** a peu abondant(e), insuffisant(e), maigre.

scapegoat ['skeɪpɡəut] n bouc m émissaire.

scar [skɑː] n cicatrice f.

scarce [skɛəs] a rare, peu abon-

dant(e); **~ly** ad à peine, presque pas; **scarcity** n rareté f, manque m, pénurie f.

scare [skɛə*] n peur f, panique f // vt effrayer, faire peur à; **to ~ sb stiff** faire une peur bleue à qn; **bomb ~** alerte f à la bombe; **~crow** n épouvantail m; **~d: to be ~d** avoir peur.

scarf, pl **scarves** [skɑːf, skɑːvz] n (long) écharpe f; (square) foulard m.

scarlet ['skɑːlɪt] a écarlate.

scathing ['skeɪðɪŋ] a cinglant(e), acerbe.

scatter ['skætə*] vt éparpiller, répandre; (crowd) disperser // vi se disperser; **~brained** a écervelé(e), étourdi(e).

scavenger ['skævəndʒə*] n éboueur m.

scene [siːn] n (THEATRE, fig etc) scène f; (of crime, accident) lieu(x) m(pl), endroit m; (sight, view) spectacle m, vue f; **~ry** n (THEATRE) décor(s) m(pl); (landscape) paysage m; **scenic** a scénique; offrant de beaux paysages or panoramas.

scent [sɛnt] n parfum m, odeur f; (fig: track) piste f; (sense of smell) odorat m.

sceptical ['skɛptɪkəl] a sceptique.

schedule ['ʃɛdjuːl, (US) 'skɛdjuːl] n programme m, plan m; (of trains) horaire m; (of prices etc) barème m, tarif m // vt prévoir; **on ~** à l'heure (prévue); à la date prévue; **to be ahead of/behind ~** avoir de l'avance/du retard; **~d flight** n vol régulier.

scheme [skiːm] n plan m, projet m; (method) procédé m; (dishonest plan, plot) complot m, combine f; (arrangement) arrangement m, classification f; (pension – etc) régime m // vt, vi comploter, manigancer; **scheming** a rusé(e), intrigant(e) // n manigances fpl, intrigues fpl.

scholar ['skɔlə*] n érudit/e; **~ly** a érudit(e), savant(e); **~ship** n érudition f; (grant) bourse f (d'études).

school [skuːl] n (gen) école f; (in university) faculté f; (secondary school) collège m, lycée m // cpd scolaire // vt (animal) dresser; ~**book** n livre m scolaire or de classe; ~**boy** n écolier m; collégien m, lycéen m; ~**children** npl écoliers mpl; collégiens mpl; lycéens mpl; ~**days** npl années fpl de scolarité; ~**girl** n écolière f; collégienne f, lycéenne f; ~**ing** n instruction f, études fpl; ~**master** n (primary) instituteur m; (secondary) professeur m; ~**mistress** n institutrice f; professeur m; ~**teacher** n instituteur/trice; professeur m.

sciatica [saɪˈætɪkə] n sciatique f.

science [ˈsaɪəns] n science f; ~ **fiction** n science-fiction f; **scientific** [-ˈtɪfɪk] a scientifique; **scientist** n scientifique m/f; (eminent) savant m.

scissors [ˈsɪzəz] npl ciseaux mpl.

scoff [skɔf] vt (Brit col: eat) avaler, bouffer // vi: to ~ (at) (mock) se moquer (de).

scold [skəuld] vt gronder, attraper.

scone [skɔn] n sorte de petit pain rond au lait.

scoop [skuːp] n pelle f (à main); (for ice cream) boule f à glace; (PRESS) reportage exclusif or à sensation; to ~ **out** vt évider, creuser; to ~ **up** vt ramasser.

scooter [ˈskuːtə*] n (motor cycle) scooter m; (toy) trottinette f.

scope [skəup] n (capacity: of plan, undertaking) portée f, envergure f; (: of person) compétence f, capacités fpl; (opportunity) possibilités fpl; **within the** ~ **of** dans les limites de.

scorch [skɔːtʃ] vt (clothes) brûler (légèrement), roussir; (earth, grass) dessécher, brûler.

score [skɔː*] n score m, décompte m des points; (MUS) partition f; (twenty) vingt // vt (goal, point) marquer; (success) remporter // vi (FOOTBALL) marquer un but; (keep score) compter les points; **on that** ~ sur ce chapitre, à cet

égard; to ~ 6 **out of 10** obtenir 6 sur 10; to ~ **out** vt rayer, barrer, biffer; ~**board** n tableau m.

scorn [skɔːn] n mépris m, dédain m.

Scorpio [ˈskɔːpɪəu] n le Scorpion.

Scot [skɔt] n Écossais/e.

scotch [skɔtʃ] vt faire échouer; enrayer; étouffer; **S**~ n whisky m, scotch m.

scot-free [ˈskɔtˈfriː] ad: **to get off** ~ (unpunished) s'en tirer sans être puni.

Scotland [ˈskɔtlənd] n Écosse f.

Scots [skɔts] a écossais(e); ~**man/woman** n Écossais/e.

Scottish [ˈskɔtɪʃ] a écossais(e).

scoundrel [ˈskaundrl] n vaurien m.

scour [ˈskauə*] vt (clean) récurer; frotter; décaper; (search) battre, parcourir.

scourge [skɜːdʒ] n fléau m.

scout [skaut] n (MIL) éclaireur m; (also: boy ~) scout m; to ~ **around** vi explorer, chercher.

scowl [skaul] vi se renfrogner, avoir l'air maussade; to ~ **at** regarder de travers.

scrabble [ˈskræbl] vi (claw): to ~ (at) gratter; (also: ~ **around**: search) chercher à tâtons // n ® Scrabble m ®.

scraggy [ˈskrægɪ] a décharné(e).

scram [skræm] vi (col) ficher le camp.

scramble [ˈskræmbl] n bousculade f, ruée f // vi avancer tant bien que mal (à quatre pattes or en grimpant); to ~ **out** sortir or descendre à toute vitesse; to ~ **for** se bousculer or se disputer pour (avoir); ~**d eggs** npl œufs brouillés.

scrap [skræp] n bout m, morceau m; (fight) bagarre f; (also: ~ **iron**) ferraille f // vt jeter, mettre au rebut; (fig) abandonner, laisser tomber // vi (fight) se bagarrer; ~**s** npl (waste) déchets mpl; ~**book** n album m; ~ **dealer** n marchand m de ferraille.

scrape [skreɪp] vt, vi gratter, racler // n: **to get into a** ~ s'attirer des ennuis; **to ~ through** réussir de justesse; **~r** n grattoir m, racloir m.

scrap: **~ heap** n (fig): **on the ~ heap** au rancart or rebut; **~ merchant** n (Brit) marchand m de ferraille; **~ paper** n papier m brouillon.

scratch [skrætʃ] n égratignure f, rayure f, éraflure f; (from claw) coup m de griffe // a: **~ team** équipe de fortune or improvisée // vt (record) rayer; (paint etc) érafler; (with claw, nail) griffer // vt (se) gratter; **to start from ~** partir de zéro; **to be up to ~** être à la hauteur.

scrawl [skrɔ:l] vi gribouiller.

scrawny ['skrɔ:nɪ] a décharné(e).

scream [skri:m] n cri perçant, hurlement m // vi crier, hurler.

scree [skri:] n éboulis m.

screech [skri:tʃ] vi hurler; (tyres, brakes) crisser, grincer.

screen [skri:n] n écran m, paravent m; (CINEMA, TV) écran m; (fig) écran, rideau m // vt masquer, cacher; (from the wind etc) abriter, protéger; (film) projeter; (candidates etc) filtrer; **~ing** n (MED) test m or tests de dépistage; **~play** n scénario m.

screw [skru:] n vis f; (propeller) hélice f // vt visser; **to ~ up** (paper etc) froisser; (col: ruin) bousiller; **~driver** n tournevis m.

scribble ['skrɪbl] vt gribouiller, griffonner.

script [skrɪpt] n (CINEMA etc) scénario m, texte m; (in exam) copie f.

Scripture ['skrɪptʃə*] n Ecriture Sainte.

scroll [skrəul] n rouleau m.

scrounge [skraundʒ] vt (col): **to ~ sth (off or from sb)** se faire payer qch (par qn), emprunter qch (à qn) // vi: **to ~ on sb** vivre aux crochets de qn.

scrub [skrʌb] n (clean) nettoyage m (à la brosse); (land) broussailles fpl // vt (floor) nettoyer à la brosse;

(pan) récurer; (washing) frotter; (reject) annuler.

scruff [skrʌf] n: **by the ~ of the neck** par la peau du cou.

scruffy ['skrʌfɪ] a débraillé(e).

scrum(mage) ['skrʌm(ɪdʒ)] n (RUGBY) mêlée f.

scruple ['skru:pl] n scrupule m.

scrutiny ['skru:tɪnɪ] n examen minutieux.

scuff [skʌf] vt érafler.

scuffle ['skʌfl] n échauffourée f, rixe f.

scullery ['skʌlərɪ] n arrière-cuisine f.

sculptor ['skʌlptə*] n sculpteur m.

sculpture ['skʌlptʃə*] n sculpture f.

scum [skʌm] n écume f, mousse f; (pej: people) rebut m, lie f.

scupper ['skʌpə*] vt saborder.

scurrilous ['skʌrɪləs] a haineux(euse), virulent(e); calomnieux(euse).

scurry ['skʌrɪ] vi filer à toute allure; **to ~ off** détaler, se sauver.

scuttle ['skʌtl] n (NAUT) écoutille f; (also: **coal ~**) seau m (à charbon) // vt (ship) saborder // vi (scamper): **to ~ away, ~ off** détaler.

scythe [saɪð] n faux f.

SDP n abbr (Brit) = Social Democratic Party.

sea [si:] n mer f // cpd marin(e), de (la) mer; maritime; (fig) (travel) par mer, en bateau; **on the ~** (boat) en mer; (town) au bord de la mer; **to be all at ~** (fig) nager complètement; **out to ~** au large; (out) at **~** en mer; **~board** n côte f; **~food** n fruits mpl de mer; **~ front** n bord m de mer; **~gull** n mouette f.

seal [si:l] n (animal) phoque m; (stamp) sceau m, cachet m; (impression) cachet, estampille f // vt sceller; (envelope) coller; (: with seal) cacheter; **to ~ off** (close) condamner; (forbid entry to) interdire l'accès de.

sea level n niveau m de la mer.

seam [si:m] n couture f; (of coal)

veine f, filon m.

seaman ['si:mən] n marin m.

seamy ['si:mɪ] a louche, mal famé(e).

seance ['seɪɒns] n séance f de spiritisme.

seaplane ['si:pleɪn] n hydravion m.

search [sə:tʃ] n (for person, thing) recherche(s) f(pl); (of drawer, pockets) fouille f; (LAW: at sb's home) perquisition f // vt fouiller; (examine) examiner minutieusement; scruter // vi: to ~ for chercher; to ~ through vt fus fouiller; in ~ of à la recherche de; ~ing a pénétrant(e); minutieux(euse); ~light n projecteur m; ~ party n expédition f de secours; ~ warrant n mandat m de perquisition.

seashore ['si:ʃɔ:*] n rivage m, plage f, bord m de (la) mer.

seasick ['si:sɪk] a qui a le mal de mer.

seaside ['si:saɪd] n bord m de la mer; ~ resort n station f balnéaire.

season ['si:zn] n saison f // vt assaisonner, relever; ~al a saisonnier(ère); ~ed a (fig) expérimenté(e); ~ ticket n carte f d'abonnement.

seat [si:t] n siège m; (in bus, train: place) place f; (PARLIAMENT) siège; (buttocks) postérieur m; (of trousers) fond m // vt faire asseoir, placer; (have room for) avoir des places assises pour, pouvoir accueillir; ~ belt n ceinture f de sécurité.

sea water n eau f de mer.

seaweed ['si:wi:d] n algues fpl.

seaworthy ['si:wə:ðɪ] a en état de naviguer.

sec. abbr of **second(s)**.

secluded [sɪ'klu:dɪd] a retiré(e), à l'écart.

seclusion [sɪ'klu:ʒən] n solitude f.

second ['sɛkənd] num deuxième, second(e) // ad (in race etc) en seconde position // n (unit of time) seconde f; (in series, position) deuxième m/f, second/e; (AUT: also: ~

gear) seconde f; (COMM: imperfect) article m de second choix // vt (motion) appuyer; ~ary a secondaire; ~ary school n collège m, lycée m; ~class n de deuxième classe // ad (RAIL) en seconde; ~hand a d'occasion; de seconde main; ~ hand n (on clock) trotteuse f; ~ly ad deuxièmement; ~ment [sɪ'kɔndmənt] n (Brit) détachement m; ~rate a de deuxième ordre, de qualité inférieure; ~ thoughts npl doutes mpl; on ~ thoughts or (US) thought à la réflexion.

secrecy ['si:krəsɪ] n secret m.

secret ['si:krɪt] a secret(ète) // n secret m; in ~ en secret, secrètement, en cachette.

secretary ['sɛkrətərɪ] n secrétaire m/f; (COMM) secrétaire général; S~ of State (for) (Brit POL) ministre m (de).

secretive ['si:krətɪv] a réservé(e); (pej) cachottier(ère), dissimulé(e).

sectarian [sɛk'tɛərɪən] a sectaire.

section ['sɛkʃən] n coupe f, section f; (department) section; (COMM) rayon m; (of document) section, article m, paragraphe m.

sector ['sɛktə*] n secteur m.

secular ['sɛkjulə*] a profane; laïque; séculier(ère).

secure [sɪ'kjuə*] a (free from anxiety) sans inquiétude, sécurisé(e); (firmly fixed) solide, bien attaché(e) (or fermé(e) etc); (in safe place) en lieu sûr, en sûreté // vt (fix) fixer, attacher; (get) obtenir, se procurer.

security [sɪ'kjuərɪtɪ] n sécurité f, mesures fpl de sécurité; (for loan) caution f, garantie f.

sedan [sɪ'dæn] n (US AUT) berline f.

sedate [sɪ'deɪt] a calme; posé(e) // vt donner des sédatifs à.

sedative ['sɛdɪtɪv] n calmant m, sédatif m.

seduce [sɪ'dju:s] vt (gen) séduire; **seduction** [-'dʌkʃən] n séduction f; **seductive** [-'dʌktɪv] a séduisant(e), séducteur(trice).

see [si:] *vb* (*pt* **saw**, *pp* **seen**) *vt* (*gen*) voir; (*accompany*): **to ~ sb to the door** reconduire *or* raccompagner qn jusqu'à la porte // *vi* voir // *vt* évêche *m*; **to ~ that** (*ensure*) veiller à ce que + *sub*, faire en sorte que + *sub*, s'assurer que; **~ you soon!** à bientôt!; **to ~ about** *vt fus* s'occuper de; **to ~ off** *vt* accompagner (à la gare *or* à l'aéroport *etc*); **to ~ through** *vt* mener à bonne fin // *vt fus* voir clair dans; **to ~ to** *vt fus* s'occuper de, se charger de.

seed [si:d] *n* graine *f*, (*fig*) germe *m*; (*TENNIS*) tête *f* de série; **to go to ~** monter en graine; (*fig*) se laisser aller; **~ling** *n* jeune plant *m*, semis *m*; **~y** *a* (*shabby*) minable, miteux(euse).

seeing ['si:ɪŋ] *cj*: **~ (that)** vu que, étant donné que.

seek [si:k], *pt*, *pp* **sought** *vt* chercher, rechercher.

seem [si:m] *vi* sembler, paraître; **there ~s to be** ... il semble qu'il y a ...; on dirait qu'il y a ...; **~ingly** *ad* apparemment.

seen [si:n] *pp* of **see**.

seep [si:p] *vi* suinter, filtrer.

seesaw ['si:sɔ:] *n* (jeu *m* de) bascule *f*.

seethe [si:ð] *vi* être en effervescence; **to ~ with anger** bouillir de colère.

see-through ['si:θru:] *a* transparent(e).

segregate ['segrɪgeɪt] *vt* séparer, isoler.

seize [si:z] *vt* (*grasp*) saisir, attraper; (*take possession of*) s'emparer de; (*LAW*) saisir; **to ~ (up)on** *vt fus* saisir, sauter sur; **to ~ up** *vi* (*TECH*) se gripper.

seizure ['si:ʒə*] *n* (*MED*) crise *f*, attaque *f*; (*LAW*) saisie *f*.

seldom ['seldəm] *ad* rarement.

select [sɪ'lekt] *a* choisi(e), d'élite; *vt* sélect *inv* // *vt* sélectionner, choisir; **~ion** [-'lekʃən] *n* sélection *f*, choix *m*.

self [self] *n* (*pl* **selves**): **the ~** le moi *inv* // *prefix* auto-; **~-catering** *a* (*Brit*) avec cuisine, où l'on peut faire sa cuisine; **~-centred**, (*US*) **-centered** *a* égocentrique; **~-coloured**, (*US*) **-colored** *a* uni(e); **~-confidence** *n* confiance *f* en soi; **~-conscious** *a* timide, qui manque d'assurance; **~-contained** *a* (*Brit: flat*) avec entrée particulière, indépendant(e); **~-control** *n* maîtrise *f* de soi; **~-defence**, (*US*) **-defense** *n* légitime défense *f*; **~-discipline** *n* discipline personnelle; **~-employed** *a* qui travaille à son compte; **~-evident** *a* évident(e), qui va de soi; **~-governing** *a* autonome; **~-indulgent** *a* qui ne se refuse rien; **~-interest** *n* intérêt personnel; **~-ish** *a* égoïste; **~-ishness** *n* égoïsme *m*; **~-less** *a* désintéressé(e); **~-pity** *n* apitoiement *m* sur soi-même; **~-possessed** *a* assuré(e); **~-preservation** *n* instinct *m* de conservation; **~-respect** *n* respect *m* de soi, amour-propre *m*; **~-righteous** *a* satisfait(e) de soi, pharisaïque; **~-sacrifice** *n* abnégation *f*; **~-satisfied** *a* content(e) de soi, suffisant(e); **~-service** *a*, *n* libre-service (*m*), self-service (*m*); **~-sufficient** *a* indépendant(e); **~-taught** *a* autodidacte.

sell [sel], *pt*, *pp* **sold** *vt* vendre // *vi* se vendre; **to ~ at** *or* **for 10 F** se vendre 10 F; **to ~ off** *vt* liquider; **to ~ out** *vi*: **to ~ out (to sb/sth)** (*COMM*) vendre son fonds *or* son affaire (à qn/qch) // *vt* vendre tout son stock de; **the tickets are all sold out** il ne reste plus de billets; **~-by date** *n* date *f* limite de vente; **~er** *n* vendeur/euse, marchand/e; **~ing price** *n* prix *m* de vente.

sellotape ['seləuteɪp] *n* ® (*Brit*) papier collant, scotch *m* ®.

sellout ['selaut] *n* trahison *f*, capitulation *f*; (*of tickets*): **it was a ~** tous les billets ont été vendus.

selves [selvz] *npl* of **self**.

semblance ['sembləns] n semblant m.

semen ['si:mən] n sperme m.

semester [sɪ'mestə*] n (US) semestre m.

semi ['semɪ] prefix semi-, demi-; à demi, à moitié; ~**circle** n demi-cercle m; ~**colon** n point-virgule m; ~**detached (house)** n (Brit) maison jumelée or jumelle; ~**final** n demi-finale f.

seminar ['semɪnɑ:*] n séminaire m.

seminary ['semɪnərɪ] n (REL: for priests) séminaire m.

semiskilled ['semɪ'skɪld] a: ~ **worker** n ouvrier/ère spécialisé(e).

senate ['senɪt] n sénat m; **senator** n sénateur m.

send [send], pt, pp **sent** vt envoyer; **to** ~ **away** vt (letter, goods) envoyer, expédier; **to** ~ **away for** vt fus commander par correspondance, se faire envoyer; **to** ~ **back** vt renvoyer; **to** ~ **for** vt fus envoyer chercher; faire venir; **to** ~ **off** vt (goods) envoyer, expédier; (Brit SPORT: player) expulser or renvoyer du terrain; **to** ~ **out** vt (invitation) envoyer (par la poste); **to** ~ **up** vt (person, price) faire monter; (Brit: parody) mettre en boîte, parodier; ~**er** n expéditeur/trice; ~**off** n: a **good** ~**off** des adieux chaleureux.

senior ['si:nɪə*] a (older) aîné(e), plus âgé(e); (of higher rank) supérieur(e) // n aîné(e); (in service) personne f qui a plus d'ancienneté; ~ **citizen** n personne âgée; ~**ity** [-'ɒrɪtɪ] n priorité f d'âge, ancienneté f.

sensation [sen'seɪʃən] n sensation f; ~**al** a qui fait sensation; (marvellous) sensationnel(le).

sense [sens] n sens m; (feeling) sentiment m; (meaning) signification f; (wisdom) bon sens // vt sentir, pressentir; **it makes** ~ c'est logique; ~**s** npl raison f; ~**less** a insensé(e), stupide; (unconscious) sans connaissance.

sensibility [sensɪ'bɪlɪtɪ] n sensibilité f; **sensibilities** npl susceptibilité f.

sensible ['sensɪbl] a sensé(e), raisonnable; sage; pratique.

sensitive ['sensɪtɪv] a sensible.

sensual ['sensjuəl] a sensuel(le).

sensuous ['sensjuəs] a voluptueux(euse), sensuel(le).

sent [sent] pt, pp of **send**.

sentence ['sentns] n (LING) phrase f; (LAW: judgment) condamnation f, sentence f; (: punishment) peine f // vt: **to** ~ **sb to death/to 5 years** condamner qn à mort/à 5 ans.

sentiment ['sentɪmənt] n sentiment m; (opinion) opinion f, avis m; ~**al** [-'mentl] a sentimental(e).

sentry ['sentrɪ] n sentinelle f, factionnaire m.

separate a ['seprɪt] séparé(e), indépendant(e), différent(e) // vb ['sepəreɪt] vt séparer // vi se séparer; ~**s** npl (clothes) coordonnés mpl; ~**ly** ad séparément; **separation** [-'reɪʃən] n séparation f.

September [sep'tembə*] n septembre m.

septic ['septɪk] a septique; (wound) infecté(e); ~ **tank** n fosse f septique.

sequel ['si:kwl] n conséquence f; séquelles fpl; (of story) suite f.

sequence ['si:kwəns] n ordre m, suite f.

sequin ['si:kwɪn] n paillette f.

serene [sɪ'ri:n] a serein(e), calme, paisible.

sergeant ['sɑ:dʒənt] n sergent m; (POLICE) brigadier m.

serial ['sɪərɪəl] n feuilleton m; ~ **number** n numéro m de série.

series ['sɪərɪs] n (pl inv) série f; (PUBLISHING) collection f.

serious ['sɪərɪəs] a sérieux(euse), réfléchi(e); grave; ~**ly** ad sérieusement, gravement.

sermon ['sə:mən] n sermon m.

serrated [sɪ'reɪtɪd] a en dents de scie.

servant ['sə:vənt] n domestique m/f;

(fig) serviteur/servante.

serve [səːv] vt (employer etc) servir, être au service de; (purpose) servir à; (customer, food, meal) servir; (apprenticeship) faire, accomplir; (prison term) faire; purger // vi (also TENNIS) servir; (be useful): to ~ as/for/ to do servir de/à/à faire // n (TENNIS) service m; it ~s him right c'est bien fait pour lui; to ~ out, ~ up vt (food) servir.

service [ˈsəːvis] n (gen) service m; (AUT: maintenance) révision f // vt (car, washing machine) réviser; the S~s les forces armées; to be of ~ to sb rendre service à qn; dinner ~ service m de table; ~able a pratique, commode; ~ charge n (Brit) service m; ~man n militaire m; ~ station n station-service.

serviette [səːviˈɛt] n (Brit) serviette f (de table).

session [ˈsɛʃən] n (sitting) séance f; (SCOL) année f scolaire (or universitaire).

set [sɛt] n série f, assortiment m; (of tools etc) jeu m; (RADIO, TV) poste m; (TENNIS) set m; (group of people) cercle m, milieu m; (CINEMA) plateau m; (THEATRE: stage) scène f; (: scenery) décor m; (MATH) ensemble m; (HAIRDRESSING) mise f en plis // a (fixed) fixe, déterminé(e); (ready) prêt(e) // vb (pt, pp set) vt (place) mettre, poser, placer; (fix, establish) fixer; (: record) établir; (adjust) régler; (decide: rules etc) fixer, choisir; (TYP) composer // vi (sun) se coucher; (jam, jelly, concrete) prendre; to be ~ on doing être résolu à faire; to ~ to (music) mettre en musique; to ~ on fire mettre le feu à; to ~ free libérer; to ~ sth going déclencher qch; to ~ sail partir, prendre la mer; to ~ about vt fus (task) entreprendre, se mettre à; to ~ aside vt mettre de côté; to ~ back vt (in time): to ~ back (by) retarder (de); to ~ off

(bomb) faire exploser; (cause to start) déclencher; (show up well) mettre en valeur, faire valoir; to ~ out vi: to ~ out to do entreprendre de faire; avoir pour but or intention de faire // vt (arrange) disposer; (state) présenter, exposer; to ~ up vt (organization) fonder, constituer; ~back n (hitch) revers m, contretemps m; ~ menu n menu m.

settee [sɛˈtiː] n canapé m.

setting [ˈsɛtiŋ] n cadre m; (of jewel) monture f.

settle [ˈsɛtl] vt (argument, matter) régler; (problem) résoudre; (MED: calm) calmer // vi (bird, dust etc) se poser; (sediment) se déposer; (also: ~ down) s'installer, se fixer; se caler; se ranger; to ~ for sth accepter qch, se contenter de qch; to ~ in vi s'installer; to ~ on sth opter or se décider pour qch; to ~ up with sb régler (ce que l'on doit à) qn; ~ment n (payment) règlement m; (agreement) accord m; (colony) colonie f; (village etc) établissement m; hameau m; ~r n colon m.

setup [ˈsɛtʌp] n (arrangement) manière f dont les choses sont organisées; (situation) situation f, allure f des choses.

seven [ˈsɛvn] num sept; ~teen num dix-sept; ~th num septième; ~ty num soixante-dix.

sever [ˈsɛvəˈ] vt couper, trancher; (relations) rompre.

several [ˈsɛvərl] a, pronoun plusieurs m/pl; ~ of us plusieurs d'entre nous.

severance [ˈsɛvərəns] n (of relations) rupture f; ~ pay n indemnité f de licenciement.

severe [siˈviəˈ] a sévère, strict(e); (serious) grave, sérieux(euse); (hard) rigoureux(euse), dur(e); (plain) sévère, austère; **severity** [siˈvɛriti] n sévérité f; gravité f; rigueur f.

sew [səu], pt sewed, pp sewn vt, vi coudre; to ~ up vt (re)coudre.

sewage ['su:ɪdʒ] n vidange(s) f(pl).

sewer ['su:ə*] n égout m.

sewing ['səʊɪŋ] n couture f; ~ **machine** n machine f à coudre.

sewn [səʊn] pp of **sew**.

sex [sɛks] n sexe m; to have ~ **with** avoir des rapports (sexuels) avec; ~**ist** a, n sexiste (m/f).

sexual ['sɛksjʊəl] a sexuel(le).

sexy ['sɛksɪ] a sexy inv.

shabby ['ʃæbɪ] a miteux(euse); (behaviour) mesquin(e), méprisable.

shack [ʃæk] n cabane f, hutte f.

shackles ['ʃæklz] npl chaînes fpl, entraves fpl.

shade [ʃeɪd] n ombre f; (for lamp) abat-jour m inv; (of colour) nuance f, ton m; (small quantity): a ~ of a smaller tout en tout petit peu plus petit.

shadow ['ʃædəʊ] n ombre f // vt (follow) filer; ~ **cabinet** n (Brit POL) cabinet parallèle formé par le parti qui n'est pas au pouvoir; ~**y** a ombragé(e); (dim) vague, indistinct(e).

shady ['ʃeɪdɪ] a ombragé(e); (fig: dishonest) louche, véreux(euse).

shaft [ʃɑːft] n (of arrow, spear) hampe f; (AUT, TECH) arbre m; (of mine) puits m; (of lift) cage f; (of light) rayon m, trait m.

shaggy ['ʃægɪ] a hirsute; en broussaille.

shake [ʃeɪk] vb (pt shook, pp shaken [ʃuk, 'ʃeɪkn]) vt secouer; (bottle, cocktail) agiter; (house, confidence) ébranler // vi trembler // n secousse f; to ~ one's head (in refusal) dire ou faire non de la tête; (in dismay) secouer la tête; to ~ hands with sb serrer la main à qn; to ~ off vt secouer; (fig) se débarrasser de; to ~ up vt secouer; **shaky** a (hand, voice) tremblant(e); (building) branlant(e), peu solide.

shall [ʃæl] auxiliary vb: I ~ go j'irai; ~ I open the door? j'ouvre la porte?; I'll get the coffee, ~ I? je vais chercher le café, d'accord?

shallow ['ʃæləʊ] a peu profond(e); (fig) superficiel(le).

sham [ʃæm] n frime f; (jewellery, furniture) imitation f.

shambles ['ʃæmblz] n confusion f, pagaïe f, fouillis m.

shame [ʃeɪm] n honte f // vt faire honte à; it is a ~ (that/to do) c'est dommage (que + sub/de faire); what a ~! quel dommage!; ~**faced** a honteux(euse), penaud(e); ~**ful** a honteux(euse), scandaleux(euse); ~**less** a éhonté(e), effronté(e); (immodest) impudique.

shampoo [ʃæm'puː] n shampooing m // vt faire un shampooing à; ~ **and set** n shampooing m et mise f en plis.

shamrock ['ʃæmrɔk] n trèfle m (emblème national de l'Irlande).

shandy ['ʃændɪ] n bière panachée.

shan't [ʃɑːnt] = **shall not**.

shanty town ['ʃæntɪ-] n bidonville m.

shape [ʃeɪp] n forme f // vt façonner, modeler; (statement) formuler; (sb's ideas) former; (sb's life) déterminer // vi (also: ~ up: events) prendre tournure; (: person) faire des progrès, s'en sortir; to take ~ prendre forme ou tournure; ~**-shaped** suffix: heart-shaped en forme de cœur; ~**less** a informe, sans forme; ~**ly** a bien proportionné(e), beau(belle).

share [ʃɛə*] n (thing received, contribution) part f; (COMM) action f // vt partager; (have in common) avoir en commun; to ~ out (among or between) partager (entre); ~**holder** n actionnaire m/f.

shark [ʃɑːk] n requin m.

sharp [ʃɑːp] a (razor, knife) tranchant(e), bien aiguisé(e); (point) aigu(guë); (nose, chin) pointu(e); (outline) net(te); (cold, pain) vif(vive); (MUS) dièse; (voice) coupant(e); (person: quick-witted) malin(igne), éveillé(e); (: unscrupulous) malhonnête // n (MUS) dièse m // ad: at 2 o'clock ~ à 2 heures pile or tapantes; **~en** vt aiguiser; (pencil) tailler; (fig) aviver; **~er** n (also: **pencil ~er**) taille-crayon(s) m inv; **~eyed** a à qui rien n'échappe; **~ly** ad (turn, stop) brusquement; (stand out) nettement; (criticize, retort) sèchement, vertement.

shatter ['ʃætə*] vt briser; (fig: upset) bouleverser; (: ruin) briser, ruiner // vi voler en éclats, se briser.

shave [ʃeɪv] vt raser // vi se raser // n: to have a **~** se raser; **~r** n (also: **electric ~r**) rasoir m électrique.

shaving ['ʃeɪvɪŋ] n (action) rasage m; **~s** npl (of wood etc) copeaux mpl; **~ brush** n blaireau m; **~ cream** n crème f à raser.

shawl [ʃɔːl] n châle m.

she [ʃiː] pronoun elle; **~cat** n chatte f; **~elephant** n éléphant m femelle; NB: for ships, countries follow the gender of your translation.

sheaf [ʃiːf], pl **sheaves** n gerbe f.

shear [ʃɪə*] vt (pt **~ed**, pp **~ed** or **shorn**) (sheep) tondre; **to ~ off** vi (branch) partir, se détacher; **~s** npl (for hedge) cisaille(s) f(pl).

sheath [ʃiːθ] n gaine f, fourreau m, étui m; (contraceptive) préservatif m.

sheaves [ʃiːvz] npl of **sheaf**.

shed [ʃed] n remise f; hangar m // vt (pt, pp **shed**) (leaves, fur etc) perdre; (tears) verser, répandre.

she'd [ʃiːd] = **she had**; **she would**.

sheen [ʃiːn] n lustre m.

sheep [ʃiːp] n (pl inv) mouton m; **~dog** n chien de berger; **~ish** a penaud(e), timide; **~skin** n peau f de mouton.

sheer [ʃɪə*] a (utter) pur(e), pur et simple; (steep) à pic, abrupt(e); (almost transparent) extrêmement fin(e) // ad à pic, abruptement.

sheet [ʃiːt] n (on bed) drap m; (of paper) feuille f; (of glass, metal) feuille f, plaque f.

sheik(h) [ʃeɪk] n cheik m.

shelf [ʃelf], pl **shelves** n étagère f, rayon m.

shell [ʃel] n (on beach) coquillage m; (of egg, nut etc) coquille f; (explosive) obus m; (of building) carcasse f // vt (crab, prawn etc) décortiquer; (peas) écosser; (MIL) bombarder (d'obus).

she'll [ʃiːl] = **she will, she shall**.

shellfish ['ʃelfɪʃ] n (pl inv) (crab etc) crustacé m; (scallop etc) coquillage m; (pl: as food) crustacés m; coquillages.

shelter ['ʃeltə*] n abri m, refuge m // vt abriter, protéger; (give lodging to) donner asile à // vi s'abriter, se mettre à l'abri.

shelve [ʃelv] vt (fig) mettre en suspens or en sommeil; **~s** npl of **shelf**.

shepherd ['ʃepəd] n berger m // vt (guide) guider, escorter; **~'s pie** n ≈ hachis m Parmentier.

sheriff ['ʃerɪf] n shérif m.

sherry ['ʃerɪ] n xérès m, sherry m.

she's [ʃiːz] = **she is, she has**.

Shetland ['ʃetlənd] n (also: **the ~s, the ~ Isles**) les îles fpl Shetland.

shield [ʃiːld] n bouclier m // vt: **to ~ (from)** protéger (de or contre).

shift [ʃɪft] n (change) changement m; (of workers) équipe f, poste m // vt déplacer, changer de place; (remove) enlever // vi changer de place, bouger; **~less** a (person) fainéant(e); sans énergie; **~ work** n travail m en équipe or par relais // par roulement; **~y** a sournois(e); (eyes) fuyant(e).

shilling ['ʃɪlɪŋ] n (Brit) shilling m (= 12 old pence; 20 in a pound).

shilly-shally ['ʃɪlɪʃælɪ] vi tergiverser, atermoyer.

shimmer ['ʃɪmə*] vi miroiter, chatoyer.

shin [ʃɪn] n tibia m.

shine [ʃaɪn] n éclat m, brillant m // vb (pt, pp **shone**) vi briller // vt faire briller or reluire; (torch): **to ~ on** braquer sur.

shingle ['ʃɪŋgl] n (on beach) galets mpl; (on roof) bardeau m; ~s n (MED) zona m.

shiny ['ʃaɪnɪ] a brillant(e).

ship [ʃɪp] n bateau m; (large) navire m // vt transporter (par mer); (send) expédier (par mer); (load) charger, embarquer; ~**building** n construction navale; ~**ment** n cargaison f, chargement m; ~**ping** n (ships) navires mpl; (traffic) navigation f; ~**shape** a en ordre impeccable; ~**wreck** n épave f; (event) naufrage m // vt: to be ~**wrecked** faire naufrage; ~**yard** n chantier naval.

shire ['ʃaɪə*] n (Brit) comté m.

shirk [ʃəːk] vt esquiver, se dérober à.

shirt [ʃəːt] n (man's) chemise f; in ~sleeves en bras de chemise.

shit [ʃɪt] excl (col!) merde! (!).

shiver ['ʃɪvə*] vi frissonner.

shoal [ʃəʊl] n (of fish) banc m.

shock [ʃɔk] n (impact) choc m, heurt m; (ELEC) secousse f; (emotional) choc, secousse; (MED) commotion f, choc // vt choquer, scandaliser; bouleverser; ~ **absorber** n amortisseur m; ~**ing** a choquant(e), scandaleux(euse); épouvantable, révoltant(e).

shod [ʃɔd] pt, pp of shoe.

shoddy ['ʃɔdɪ] a de mauvaise qualité, mal fait(e).

shoe [ʃuː] n chaussure f, soulier m; (also: horse~) fer m à cheval // vt (pt, pp shod) (horse) ferrer; ~**horn** n chausse-pied m; ~**lace** n lacet m (de soulier); ~ **polish** n cirage m; ~**shop** n magasin m de chaussures; ~**string** n (fig): on a ~**string** avec un budget dérisoire.

shone [ʃɔn] pt, pp of shine.

shoo [ʃuː] excl (allez,) ouste!

shook [ʃuk] pt of shake.

shoot [ʃuːt] n (on branch, seedling) pousse f // vb (pt, pp shot) vt (game) chasser; tirer; abattre; (person) blesser (or tuer) d'un coup de fusil (or de revolver); (execute) fusiller; (film) tourner // vi (with gun, bow):

to ~ (at) tirer (sur); (FOOTBALL) shooter, tirer; to ~ **down** vt (plane) abattre; to ~ **in/out** vi entrer/sortir comme une flèche; to ~ **up** vi (fig) monter en flèche; ~**ing** n (shots) coups mpl de feu, fusillade f; (HUNTING) chasse f; ~**ing star** n étoile filante.

shop [ʃɔp] n magasin m; (workshop) atelier m // vi (also: go ~**ping**) faire ses courses ou ses achats; ~ **assistant** n (Brit) vendeur/euse; ~ **floor** n (Brit: fig) ouvriers mpl; ~**keeper** n marchand/e, commerçant/e; ~**lifting** n vol m à l'étalage; ~**per** n personne f qui fait ses courses, acheteur/euse; ~**ping** n (goods) achats mpl, provisions fpl; ~**ping bag** n sac m (à provisions); ~**ping centre**, (US) ~**ping center** n centre commercial; ~-**soiled** a défraîchi(e), qui a fait la vitrine; ~ **steward** n (Brit INDUSTRY) délégué/e syndical(e); ~ **window** n vitrine f.

shore [ʃɔː*] n (of sea, lake) rivage m, rive f // vt: to ~ (**up**) étayer.

shorn [ʃɔːn] pp of shear.

short [ʃɔːt] a (not long) court(e); (soon finished) court, bref(brève); (person, step) petit(e); (curt) brusque, sec(sèche); (insufficient) insuffisant(e) // n (also: ~ **film**) court métrage; (a pair of) ~s un short; to be ~ **of sth** être à court de ou manquer de qch; in ~ bref; en bref; ~ **of doing** à moins de faire; everything ~ of tout sauf; it is ~ **for** c'est l'abréviation de ou le diminutif de; to **cut** ~ (speech, visit) abréger; to **fall** ~ **of** ne pas être à la hauteur de; to **stop** ~ s'arrêter net; to **stop** ~ **of** ne pas aller jusqu'à; ~**age** n manque m, pénurie f; ~**bread** n petit(e) sablé m; ~**change** vt ne pas rendre assez à; ~**circuit** n court-circuit m // vt court-circuiter; ~**coming** n défaut m; ~**(crust) pastry** n (Brit) pâte brisée; ~**cut** n raccourci m; ~**en** vt raccourcir; (text, visit) abréger; ~**fall** n déficit m; ~**hand** n (Brit) sténo(graphie) f; ~**hand typist** n (Brit) sténodactylo m/f; ~ **list** n (Brit: for job) liste f des candidats sélectionnés; ~**ly** ad étroit, sous peu; ~**sighted** a (Brit) myope; (fig) qui manque de clairvoyance; ~**staffed** a à court de personnel; ~ **story** n nouvelle f; ~**tempered** a qui s'emporte facilement; ~**term** a (effect) à court terme; ~**wave** n (RADIO) ondes courtes.

shot [ʃɔt] pt, pp of **shoot** // n coup m (de feu); (person) tireur m; (try) coup, essai m; (injection) piqûre f; (PHOT) photo f; **like a** ~ comme une flèche; (very readily) sans hésiter; ~**gun** n fusil m de chasse.

should [ʃud] auxiliary vb: **I** ~ **go now** je devrais partir maintenant; **he** ~ **be there now** il devrait être arrivé maintenant; **I** ~ **go if I were you** si j'étais vous j'irais; **I** ~ **like to** j'aimerais bien, volontiers.

shoulder ['ʃəuldə*] n épaule f; (Brit: of road): **hard** ~ accotement m // vt (fig) endosser, se charger de; ~ **bag** n sac m à bandoulière; ~**blade** n omoplate f; ~ **strap** n bretelle f.

shouldn't ['ʃudnt] = **should not**.

shout [ʃaut] n cri m // vt crier // vi crier, pousser des cris; **to** ~ **down** vt huer; ~**ing** n cris mpl.

shove [ʃʌv] vt pousser; (col: put): **to** ~ **sth in** fourrer ou ficher qch dans; **to** ~ **off** vi (NAUT) pousser au large; (fig: col) ficher le camp.

shovel ['ʃʌvl] n pelle f.

show [ʃəu] n (of emotion) manifestation f, démonstration f; (semblance) semblant m, apparence f; (exhibition) exposition f, salon m; (THEATRE) spectacle m, représentation f; (CINEMA) séance f // vb (pt ~**ed**, pp **shown**) vt montrer; (courage etc) faire preuve de, manifester; (exhibit) exposer // vi se voir, être visible; **on** ~ (exhibits etc) exposé(e); **to** ~ **in**

vt (person) faire entrer; **to** ~ **off** vi (pej) crâner // vt (display) faire valoir; (pej) faire étalage de; **to** ~ **out** vt (person) reconduire (jusqu'à la porte); **to** ~ **up** vi (stand out) ressortir; (col: turn up) se montrer // vt démontrer; (unmask) démasquer, dénoncer; ~ **business** n le monde du spectacle; ~**down** n épreuve f de force.

shower ['ʃauə*] n (rain) averse f; (of stones etc) pluie f, grêle f; (also: ~**bath**) douche f // vi prendre une douche, se doucher // vt: **to** ~ **sb with** (gifts etc) combler qn de; (abuse) accabler qn de; (missiles) bombarder qn de; ~**proof** a imperméable.

showing ['ʃəuiŋ] n (of film) projection f.

show jumping n concours m hippique.

shown [ʃəun] pp of **show**.

show-off ['ʃəuɔf] n (col: person) crâneur/euse, m'as-tu-vu/e.

showroom ['ʃəurum] n magasin m ou salle f d'exposition.

shrank [ʃræŋk] pt of **shrink**.

shrapnel ['ʃræpnl] n éclats mpl d'obus.

shred [ʃred] n (gen pl) lambeau m, petit morceau // vt mettre en lambeaux, déchirer; (CULIN) râper; couper en lanières; ~**der** n (for vegetables) râpeur m; (for documents) destructeur m de documents.

shrewd [ʃru:d] a astucieux(euse), perspicace.

shriek [ʃri:k] vt, vi hurler, crier.

shrill [ʃril] a perçant(e), aigu(guë), strident(e).

shrimp [ʃrimp] n crevette grise.

shrine [ʃrain] n châsse f; (place) lieu m de pèlerinage.

shrink [ʃriŋk], pt **shrank**, pp **shrunk** vi rétrécir; (fig) se réduire; se contracter // vt (wool) (faire) rétrécir // n (col: pej) psychanalyste m/f; **to** ~ **from** (doing) sth reculer devant (la pensée de faire) qch;

~**age** n rétrécissement m; ~**wrap** vt emballer sous film plastique.

shrivel ['ʃrɪvl] (also: ~ up) vt ratatiner, flétrir // vi se ratatiner, flétrir.

shroud [ʃraud] n linceul m // vt: ~**ed in mystery** enveloppé de mystère.

Shrove Tuesday ['ʃrəʊv-] n (le) Mardi gras.

shrub [ʃrʌb] n arbuste m; ~**bery** n massif m d'arbustes.

shrug [ʃrʌg] vt, vi: to ~ (one's shoulders) hausser les épaules; to ~ off vt faire fi de.

shrunk [ʃrʌŋk] pp of **shrink**.

shudder ['ʃʌdə*] n frisson(ne)ment m, frémir.

shuffle ['ʃʌfl] vt (cards) battre; to ~ (one's feet) traîner les pieds.

shun [ʃʌn] vt éviter, fuir.

shunt [ʃʌnt] vt (RAIL: direct) aiguiller; (: divert) détourner.

shut, pt, pp **shut** [ʃʌt] vt fermer // vi se fermer; to ~ **down** vt, vi fermer définitivement; to ~ **off** vt couper, arrêter; to ~ **up** vi (col: keep quiet) se taire // vt (close) fermer; (silence) faire taire; ~**ter** n volet m; (PHOT) obturateur m.

shuttle ['ʃʌtl] n navette f; (also: ~ service) (service m de) navette f.

shuttlecock ['ʃʌtlkɔk] n volant m (de badminton).

shy [ʃaɪ] a timide.

siblings ['sɪblɪŋz] npl enfants mpl d'un même couple.

Sicily ['sɪsɪlɪ] n Sicile f.

sick [sɪk] a (ill) malade; (vomiting): **to be** ~ vomir; (humour) noir(e), macabre; **to feel** ~ avoir envie de vomir, avoir mal au cœur; **to be** ~ **of** (fig) en avoir assez de; ~**bay** n infirmerie f; ~**en** vt écœurer // vi: **to be** ~**ening for sth** (cold etc) couver qch.

sickle ['sɪkl] n faucille f.

sick: ~ **leave** n congé m de maladie; ~**ly** a maladif(ive), souffreteux(euse); (causing nausea) écœurant(e); ~**ness** n maladie f; (vomiting) vomissement(s) m(pl); ~ **pay** n indemnité f de maladie.

side [saɪd] n côté m; (of lake, road) bord m // (of door, entrance) latéral(e) // vi: **to** ~ **with sb** prendre le parti de qn, se ranger du côté de qn; **by the** ~ **of** à côté de; ~ **by** ~ côte à côte; **to take** ~**s** (with) prendre parti (pour); ~**board** n buffet m; ~**boards** (Brit), ~**burns** (whiskers) pattes fpl; ~ **effect** n (MED) effet m secondaire; ~**light** n (AUT) veilleuse f; ~**line** n (SPORT) (ligne f de) touche f; (fig) activité f secondaire; ~**long** a oblique, de coin; ~**saddle** ad en amazone; ~**show** n attraction f; ~**step** vt (fig) éluder; éviter; ~**street** n rue transversale; ~**track** n (fig) faire dévier de son sujet; ~**walk** n (US) trottoir m; ~**ways** ad de côté.

siding ['saɪdɪŋ] n (RAIL) voie f de garage.

sidle ['saɪdl] vi: **to** ~ **up** (**to**) s'approcher furtivement (de).

siege [siːdʒ] n siège m.

sieve [sɪv] n tamis m, passoire f.

sift [sɪft] vt passer au tamis or au crible; (fig) passer au crible.

sigh [saɪ] n soupir m // vi soupirer, pousser un soupir.

sight [saɪt] n (faculty) vue f (spectacle) spectacle m; (on gun) mire f // vt apercevoir; **in** ~ visible; (fig) en vue; **out of** ~ hors de vue; ~**seeing** n tourisme m; **to go** ~**seeing** faire du tourisme.

sign [saɪn] n (gen) signe m; (with hand etc) signe, geste m; (notice) panneau m, écriteau m // vt signer; **to** ~ **on** (MIL) s'engager; (as unemployed) s'inscrire au chômage // vt (MIL) engager; (employee) embaucher; **to** ~ **over** vt: **to** ~ **sth over to sb** céder qch par écrit à qn; **to** ~ **up** (MIL) vt engager // vi s'engager.

signal ['sɪgnl] n signal m // vi (AUT) mettre son clignotant // vt (person) faire signe à; (message) communiquer par signaux; ~**man** n (RAIL) aiguilleur m.

signature ['signətʃə] n signature f; ~ **tune** n indicatif musical.

signet ring ['signət-] n chevalière f.

significance [sig'nifikəns] n signification f; importance f.

significant [sig'nifikənt] a significatif(ive); (important) important(e), considérable.

signpost ['sainpəust] n poteau indicateur.

silence ['sailns] n silence m // vt faire taire, réduire au silence; ~**r** n (on gun, Brit AUT) silencieux m.

silent ['sailnt] a silencieux(euse); (film) muet(te); **to remain** ~ garder le silence, ne rien dire; ~ **partner** n (COMM) bailleur m de fonds, commanditaire m.

silhouette [silu:'et] n silhouette f.

silicon chip ['silikən-] n puce f électronique.

silk [silk] n soie f // cpd de or en soie; ~**y** a soyeux(euse).

silly ['sili] a stupide, sot(te), bête.

silt [silt] n vase f; limon m.

silver ['silvə*] n argent m; (money) monnaie f (en pièces d'argent); (also: ~ware) argenterie f // cpd d'argent, en argent; ~ **paper** n (Brit) papier m d'argent or d'étain; ~**plated** a plaqué(e) argent; ~**smith** n orfèvre m/f; ~**y** a argenté(e).

similar ['similə*] a: ~ (**to**) semblable (à); ~**ly** ad de la même façon, de même.

simile ['simili] n comparaison f.

simmer ['simə*] vi cuire à feu doux, mijoter.

simpering ['simpəriŋ] a minaudier(ère), nunuche.

simple ['simpl] a simple; **simplicity** [-'plisiti] n simplicité f.

simultaneous [siməl'teiniəs] a simultané(e).

sin [sin] n péché m // vi pécher.

since [sins] ad, prep depuis // cj (time) depuis que; (because) puis-

que, étant donné que, comme; ~ **then** depuis ce moment-là.

sincere [sin'siə*] a sincère; **sincerity** [-'seriti] n sincérité f.

sinew ['sinju:] n tendon m; ~**s** npl muscles mpl.

sinful ['sinful] a coupable.

sing [siŋ], pt **sang**, pp **sung** vt, vi chanter.

singe [sindʒ] vt brûler légèrement; (clothes) roussir.

singer ['siŋə*] n chanteur/euse.

singing ['siŋiŋ] n chant m.

single ['siŋgl] a seul(e), unique; (unmarried) célibataire; (not double) simple // n (Brit: also: ~ **ticket**) aller m (simple); (record) 45 tours m; ~**s** npl (TENNIS) simple m; **to ~ out** vt choisir; distinguer; ~ **bed** n lit m à une place or d'une personne; ~**breasted** a droit(e); ~ **file** n: **in ~ file** en file indienne; ~**handed** ad tout(e) seul(e), sans (aucune) aide; ~**minded** a résolu(e), tenace; ~ **room** n chambre f à un lit or pour une personne.

singlet ['siŋglit] n tricot m de corps.

singly ['siŋgli] ad séparément.

singular ['siŋgjulə*] a singulier(ère), étrange; (LING) (au) singulier, du singulier // n (LING) singulier m.

sinister ['sinistə*] a sinistre.

sink [siŋk] n évier m // vb (pt **sank**, pp **sunk**) vt (ship) (faire) couler, faire sombrer; (foundations) creuser; (piles etc): **to ~ sth into** enfoncer qch dans // vi couler, sombrer; (ground etc) s'affaisser; **to ~ in** vi s'enfoncer, pénétrer.

sinner ['sinə*] n pécheur/eresse.

sinus ['sainəs] n (ANAT) sinus m inv.

sip [sip] vt boire à petites gorgées.

siphon ['saifən] n siphon m; **to ~ off** vt siphonner.

sir [sə:*] n monsieur m; S~ **John Smith** sir John Smith; **yes** ~ oui Monsieur.

siren ['saiərn] n sirène f.

sirloin ['sə:lɔin] n aloyau m.

sissy ['sisi] n (col: coward) poule

mouillée.

sister ['sɪstə*] n sœur f; (nun) religieuse f, (bonne) sœur; (Brit: nurse) infirmière f en chef; **~-in-law** n belle-sœur f.

sit [sɪt], pt, pp **sat** vi s'asseoir; (assembly) être en séance, siéger; (for painter) poser // vt (exam) passer, se présenter à; **to ~ down** vi s'asseoir; **to ~ in on** vi fus assister à; **to ~ up** vi s'asseoir; (not go to bed) rester debout, ne pas se coucher.

sitcom ['sɪtkɔm] n abbr (= situation comedy) comédie f de situation.

site [saɪt] n emplacement m, site m; (also: building ~) chantier m.

sit-in ['sɪtɪn] n (demonstration) sit-in m inv, occupation f de locaux.

sitting ['sɪtɪŋ] n (of assembly etc) séance f; (in canteen) service m; **~ room** n salon m.

situated ['sɪtjueɪtɪd] a situé(e).

situation [sɪtju'eɪʃən] n situation f; **'~s vacant/wanted'** (Brit) 'offres/demandes d'emploi'.

six [sɪks] num six; **~teen** num seize; **~th** a sixième; **~ty** num soixante.

size [saɪz] n taille f; dimensions fpl; (of clothing) taille f; (of shoes) pointure f; (glue) colle f; **to ~ up** vt juger, jauger; **~able** a assez grand(e) or gros(se); assez important(e).

sizzle ['sɪzl] vi grésiller.

skate [skeɪt] n patin m; (fish: pl inv) raie f // vi patiner; **~board** n skateboard m, planche f à roulettes; **~r** n patineur/euse; **skating** n patinage m; **skating rink** n patinoire f.

skeleton ['skɛlɪtn] n squelette m; (outline) schéma m; **~ key** n passepartout m; **~ staff** n effectifs réduits.

skeptical ['skɛptɪkl] a (US) = **sceptical.**

sketch [skɛtʃ] n (drawing) croquis m, esquisse f; (THEATRE) sketch m, saynète f // vt esquisser, faire un croquis or une esquisse de; **~ book** n carnet m à dessin; **~y** a incomplet(ète), fragmentaire.

skewer ['skju:ə*] n brochette f.

ski [ski:] n ski m // vi skier, faire du ski; **~ boot** n chaussure f de ski.

skid [skɪd] vi déraper.

skier ['ski:ə*] n skieur/euse.

skiing ['ski:ɪŋ] n ski m.

ski jump n saut m à skis.

skilful ['skɪlful] a habile, adroit(e).

ski lift n remonte-pente m inv.

skill [skɪl] n habileté f, adresse f, talent m; **~ed** a habile, adroit(e); (worker) qualifié(e).

skim [skɪm] vt (milk) écrémer; (soup) écumer; (glide over) raser, effleurer // vi: **to ~ through** (fig) parcourir; **~med milk** n lait écrémé.

skimp [skɪmp] vt (work) bâcler, faire à la va-vite; (cloth etc) lésiner sur; **~y** a étriqué(e); maigre.

skin [skɪn] n peau f // vt (fruit etc) éplucher; (animal) écorcher; **~-deep** a superficiel(le); **~-diving** n plongée sous-marine; **~ny** a maigre, maigrichon(ne); **~tight** a (dress etc) collant(e), ajusté(e).

skip [skɪp] n petit bond or saut; (container) benne f // vi gambader, sautiller; (with rope) sauter à la corde // vt (pass over) sauter.

ski: **~ pants** npl fuseau m (de ski); **~ pole** n bâton m de ski.

skipper ['skɪpə*] n (NAUT, SPORT) capitaine m.

skipping rope ['skɪpɪŋ-] n (Brit) corde f à sauter.

skirmish ['skə:mɪʃ] n escarmouche f, accrochage m.

skirt [skə:t] n jupe f // vt longer, contourner.

ski suit n combinaison f de ski.

skit [skɪt] n sketch m satirique.

skittle ['skɪtl] n quille f; **~s** n (game) (jeu m de) quilles fpl.

skive [skaɪv] vi (Brit col) tirer au flanc.

skulk [skʌlk] vi rôder furtivement.

skull [skʌl] n crâne m.

skunk [skʌŋk] n mouffette f.

sky [skaɪ] n ciel m; **~light** n lucarne f; **~scraper** n gratte-ciel m inv.

slab [slæb] n plaque f; dalle f.

slack [slæk] a (loose) lâche, desserré(e); (slow) stagnant(e); (careless) négligent(e), peu sérieux(euse) or consciencieux(euse) // n (in rope etc) mou m; **~s** npl pantalon m; **~en** (also: **~en off**) vi ralentir, diminuer // vt relâcher.

slag [slæg] n scories fpl; **~ heap** n crassier m.

slain [sleɪn] pp of **slay**.

slam [slæm] vt (door) (faire) claquer; (throw) jeter violemment, flanquer; (criticize) éreinter, démolir // vi claquer.

slander ['slɑːndə*] n calomnie f; diffamation f.

slang [slæŋ] n argot m.

slant [slɑːnt] n inclinaison f; (fig) angle m, point m de vue; **~ed** a tendancieux(euse); **~ing** a en pente, incliné(e); couché(e).

slap [slæp] n claque f, gifle f; tape f // vt donner une claque ou une gifle ou une tape à // ad (directly) tout droit, en plein; **~dash** a fait(e) sans soin or à la va-vite; (person) insouciant(e), négligent(e); **~stick** n (comedy) grosse farce, style m tarte à la crème; **~-up** a: a **~-up meal** (Brit) un repas plein or fameux.

slash [slæʃ] vt entailler, taillader; (fig: prices) casser.

slat [slæt] n latte f, lame f.

slate [sleɪt] n ardoise f // vt (fig: criticize) éreinter, démolir.

slaughter ['slɔːtə*] n carnage m, massacre m // vt (animal) abattre; (people) massacrer.

slave [sleɪv] n esclave m/f // vi (also: **~ away**) trimer, travailler comme un forçat; **~ry** n esclavage m.

slay [sleɪ], pt **slew**, pp **slain** vt (formal) tuer.

sleazy ['sliːzɪ] a miteux(euse), minable.

sledge [slɛdʒ] n luge f; **~hammer** n marteau m de forgeron.

sleek [sliːk] a (hair, fur) brillant(e), luisant(e); (car, boat) aux lignes pures or élégantes.

sleep [sliːp] n sommeil m // vi (pt, pp **slept**) dormir; (spend night) dormir, coucher; **to go to ~** s'endormir; **to ~ in** vi (lie late) faire la grasse matinée; (oversleep) se réveiller trop tard; **~er** n (person) dormeur/euse; (Brit RAIL: on track) traverse f; (: train) train m de voitures-lits; **~ing bag** n sac m de couchage; **~ing car** n wagon-lits m, voiture-lits f; **~ing pill** n somnifère m; **~less** a: a **~less night** une nuit blanche; **~walker** n somnambule m/f; **~y** a qui a envie de dormir; (fig) endormi(e).

sleet [sliːt] n neige fondue.

sleeve [sliːv] n manche f.

sleigh [sleɪ] n traîneau m.

sleight [slaɪt] n: **~ of hand** tour m de passe-passe.

slender ['slɛndə*] a svelte, mince; faible, ténu(e).

slept [slɛpt] pt, pp of **sleep**.

slew [sluː] vi virer, pivoter // pt of **slay**.

slice [slaɪs] n tranche f; (round) rondelle f // vt couper en tranches (or en rondelles).

slick [slɪk] a brillant(e) en apparence; mielleux(euse) // n (also: **oil ~**) nappe f de pétrole, marée noire.

slide [slaɪd] n (in playground) toboggan m; (PHOT) diapositive f; (Brit: also: **hair ~**) barrette f; (in prices) chute f, baisse f // vb (pt, pp **slid** [slɪd]) vt (faire) glisser // vi glisser; **~ rule** n règle f à calcul; **sliding** a (door) coulissant(e); **sliding scale** n échelle f mobile.

slight [slaɪt] a (slim) mince, menu(e); (frail) frêle; (trivial) faible, insignifiant(e); (small) petit(e), léger(ère) (before it) n offense f, affront m // vt (offend) blesser, offenser; **not in the ~est** pas le moins du monde, pas du tout; **~ly** ad légèrement, un peu.

slim [slɪm] *a* mince // *vi* maigrir, suivre un régime amaigrissant.

slime [slaɪm] *n* vase *f*; substance visqueuse.

slimming ['slɪmɪŋ] *n* amaigrissement *m*.

sling [slɪŋ] *n* (*MED*) écharpe *f* // *vt* (*pt*, *pp* slung) lancer, jeter.

slip [slɪp] *n* faux pas; (*mistake*) erreur *f*; étourderie *f*; bévue *f*; (*underskirt*) combinaison *f*; (*of paper*) petite feuille, fiche *f* // *vt* (*slide*) glisser // *vi* (*slide*) glisser; (*move smoothly*): to ~ into/out of se glisser or se faufiler dans/hors de; (*decline*) baisser; to ~ sth on/off enfiler/enlever qch; to give sb the ~ fausser compagnie à qn; a ~ of the tongue un lapsus; to ~ away *vi* s'esquiver; ~ped disc *n* déplacement *m* de vertèbres.

slipper ['slɪpə*] *n* pantoufle *f*.

slippery ['slɪpərɪ] *a* glissant(e); insaisissable.

slip road *n* (*Brit*: to motorway) bretelle *f* d'accès.

slipshod ['slɪpʃɔd] *a* négligé(e), peu soigné(e).

slip-up ['slɪpʌp] *n* bévue *f*.

slipway ['slɪpweɪ] *n* cale *f* (de construction or de lancement).

slit [slɪt] *n* fente *f*; (*cut*) incision *f*; (*tear*) déchirure *f* // *vt* (*pt*, *pp* slit) fendre; couper; inciser; déchirer.

slither ['slɪðə*] *vi* glisser, déraper.

sliver ['slɪvə*] *n* (*of glass, wood*) éclat *m*; (*of cheese etc*) petit morceau, fine tranche.

slob [slɔb] *n* (*col*) rustaud(e).

slog [slɔg] (*Brit*) *n* gros effort; tâche fastidieuse // *vi* travailler très dur.

slogan ['slaugan] *n* slogan *m*.

slop [slɔp] *vi* (*also*: ~ over) renverser; déborder // *vt* répandre; renverser.

slope [sləup] *n* pente *f*, côte *f*; (*side of mountain*) versant *m*; (*slant*) inclinaison *f* // *vi*: to ~ down être *or* descendre en pente; to ~ up monter.

sloppy ['slɔpɪ] *a* (*work*) peu soi-

gné(e), bâclé(e); (*appearance*) négligé(e), débraillé(e); (*film etc*) sentimental(e).

slot [slɔt] *n* fente *f* // *vt*: to ~ sth into encastrer *or* insérer qch dans // *vi*: to ~ into s'encastrer *or* s'insérer dans; ~ machine *n* (*Brit*: *vending machine*) distributeur *m* (automatique), machine *f* à sous; (*for gambling*) appareil *m* *or* machine *f* à sous.

sloth [sləuθ] *n* (*laziness*) paresse *f*.

slouch [slautʃ] *vi* avoir le dos rond, être voûté(e); to ~ about *vi* (*laze*) traîner à ne rien faire.

slovenly ['slʌvənlɪ] *a* sale, débraillé(e).

slow [sləu] *a* lent(e); (*watch*): to be ~ retarder // *ad* lentement // *vt*, *vi* (*also*: ~ down, ~ up) ralentir; ' ~ ' (*road sign*) 'ralentir'; ~ly *ad* lentement; ~ motion *n*: in ~ motion au ralenti.

sludge [slʌdʒ] *n* boue *f*.

slug [slʌg] *n* limace *f*; (*bullet*) balle *f*; ~gish *a* mou(molle), lent(e).

sluice [slu:s] *n* vanne *f*; écluse *f*.

slum [slʌm] *n* taudis *m*.

slumber ['slʌmbə*] *n* sommeil *m*.

slump [slʌmp] *n* baisse soudaine, effondrement *m*; crise *f* // *vi* s'effondrer, s'affaisser.

slung [slʌŋ] *pt*, *pp* *of* **sling**.

slur [slə:*] *n* bredouillement *m*; (*smear*): ~ (on) atteinte *f* (à); insinuation *f* (contre) // *vt* mal articuler.

slush [slʌʃ] *n* neige fondue; ~ fund *n* caisse noire, fonds secrets.

slut [slʌt] *n* souillon *f*.

sly [slaɪ] *a* rusé(e); sournois(e).

smack [smæk] *n* (*slap*) tape *f*; (*on face*) gifle *f* // *vt* donner une tape à; gifler; (*child*) donner la fessée à // *vi*: to ~ of avoir des relents de, sentir.

small [smɔ:l] *a* petit(e); ~ ads *npl* (*Brit*) petites annonces; ~ change *n* petite *or* menue monnaie; ~holder *n* (*Brit*) petit cultivateur; ~ hours *npl*: in the ~ hours au petit matin; ~pox *n* variole *f*; ~ talk *n* menus propos.

smart [smɑːt] *a* élégant(e), chic *inv*; (*clever*) intelligent(e), astucieux(euse), futé(e); (*quick*) rapide, vif(vive), prompt(e) // *vi* faire mal, brûler; **to ~en up** *vi* devenir plus élégant(e), se faire beau(belle) // *vt* rendre plus élégant(e).

smash [smæʃ] *n* (*also*: **~-up**) collision *f*, accident *m* // *vt* casser, briser, fracasser; (*opponent*) écraser; (*hopes*) ruiner, détruire; (*SPORT: record*) pulvériser // *vi* se briser, se fracasser; s'écraser; **~ing** *a* (*col*) formidable.

smattering ['smætərɪŋ] *n*: **a ~ of** quelques notions de.

smear [smɪə*] *n* tache *f*, salissure *f*; trace *f*; (*MED*) frottis *m* // *vt* enduire; (*fig*) porter atteinte à.

smell [smɛl] *n* odeur *f*; (*sense*) odorat *m* // *vb* (*pt, pp* smelt *or* smelled [smɛlt, smɛld]) *vt* sentir // *vi* (*food etc*): **to ~ (of)** sentir; (*pej*) sentir mauvais; **it ~s good/~s of garlic** ça sent bon/sent l'ail; **~y** *a* qui sent mauvais, malodorant(e).

smile [smaɪl] *n* sourire *m* // *vi* sourire.

smirk [smɔːk] *n* petit sourire suffisant *or* affecté.

smith [smɪθ] *n* maréchal-ferrant *m*; forgeron *m*; **~y** ['smɪðɪ] *n* forge *f*.

smock [smɔk] *n* blouse *f*, sarrau *m*.

smog [smɔg] *n* brouillard mêlé de fumée.

smoke [smɔuk] *n* fumée *f* // *vt, vi* fumer; **~d** *a* (*bacon, glass*) fumé(e); **~r** *n* (*person*) fumeur/euse; (*RAIL*) wagon *m* fumeurs; **~ screen** *n* rideau *m* or écran *m* de fumée; (*fig*) paravent *m*; **smoking** *n*: '**no smoking**' (*sign*) 'défense de fumer'; **smoky** *a* enfumé(e).

smolder ['smɔuldə*] *vi* (*US*) = **smoulder**.

smooth [smuːð] *a* lisse; (*sauce*) onctueux(euse); (*flavour, whisky*) moelleux(euse), sans âpreté; (*movement*) régulier(ère), sans à-coups *or* heurts; (*person*) doucereux(euse), miel-leux(euse) // *vt* lisser, défroisser; (*also*: **~ out**: *creases, difficulties*) faire disparaître.

smother ['smʌðə*] *vt* étouffer.

smoulder, (*US*) **smolder** ['smɔuldə*] *vi* couver.

smudge [smʌdʒ] *n* tache *f*, bavure *f* // *vt* salir, maculer.

smug [smʌg] *a* suffisant(e), content(e) de soi.

smuggle ['smʌgl] *vt* passer en contrebande *or* en fraude; **~r** *n* contrebandier/ère; **smuggling** *n* contrebande *f*.

smutty ['smʌtɪ] *a* (*fig*) grossier(ère), obscène.

snack [snæk] *n* casse-croûte *m inv*; **~ bar** *n* snack(-bar) *m*.

snag [snæg] *n* inconvénient *m*, difficulté *f*.

snail [sneɪl] *n* escargot *m*.

snake [sneɪk] *n* serpent *m*.

snap [snæp] *n* (*sound*) claquement *m*, bruit sec; (*photograph*) photo *f*, instantané *m*; (*game*) sorte de jeu de bataille // *a* subit(e); fait(e) sans réfléchir // *vt* faire claquer; (*break*) casser net; (*photograph*) prendre un instantané de // *vi* se casser net *or* avec un bruit sec; **to ~ open/shut** s'ouvrir/se refermer brusquement; **to ~ at** *vt fus* (*subj: dog*) essayer de mordre; **to ~ off** *vt* (*break*) casser net; **to ~ up** *vt* sauter sur, saisir; **~py** *a* prompt(e); (*slogan*) qui a du punch; **~shot** *n* photo *f*, instantané *m*.

snare [snɛə*] *n* piège *m*.

snarl [snɑːl] *vi* gronder.

snatch [snætʃ] *n* (*fig*) vol *m*; (*small amount*): **~es of** des fragments *mpl* or bribes *fpl* de // *vt* saisir (d'un geste vif); (*steal*) voler.

sneak [sniːk] *vi*: **to ~ in/out** entrer/sortir furtivement or à la dérobée; **~ers** *npl* chaussures *fpl* de tennis or basket; **~y** a sournois(e).

sneer [snɪə*] *vi* ricaner, sourire d'un air sarcastique.

sneeze [sniːz] *vi* éternuer.

sniff [snɪf] vi renifler // vt renifler, flairer.

snigger ['snɪgə*] vi ricaner; pouffer de rire.

snip [snɪp] n petit bout; (bargain) (bonne) occasion or affaire // vt couper.

sniper ['snaɪpə*] n (marksman) tireur embusqué.

snippet ['snɪpɪt] n bribes fpl.

snivelling ['snɪvlɪŋ] a (whimpering) larmoyant(e), pleurnicheur(euse).

snob [snɔb] n snob m/f; ~**bish** a snob inv.

snooker ['snu:kə*] n sorte de jeu de billard.

snoop ['snu:p] vi: to ~ on sb espionner qn; to ~ about somewhere fourrer son nez quelque part.

snooty ['snu:tɪ] a snob inv, prétentieux(euse).

snooze [snu:z] n petit somme // vi faire un petit somme.

snore [snɔ:*] vi ronfler; **snoring** n ronflement(s) m(pl).

snorkel ['snɔ:kl] n (of swimmer) tuba m.

snort [snɔ:t] vi grogner; (horse) renâcler.

snotty ['snɔtɪ] a morveux(euse).

snout [snaut] n museau m.

snow [snəu] n neige f // vi neiger; ~**ball** n boule f de neige; ~**bound** a enneigé(e), bloqué(e) par la neige; ~**drift** n congère f; ~**drop** n perce-neige m; ~**fall** n chute f de neige; ~**flake** n flocon m de neige; ~**man** n bonhomme m de neige; ~**plough**, (US) ~**plow** n chasseneige m inv; ~**shoe** n raquette f (pour la neige); ~**storm** n tempête f de neige.

snub [snʌb] vt repousser, snober // n rebuffade f; ~-**nosed** a au nez retroussé.

snuff [snʌf] n tabac m à priser.

snug [snʌg] a douillet(te), confortable.

snuggle ['snʌgl] vi: to ~ up to sb se serrer or se blottir contre qn.

---

so [səu] ◆ ad 1 (thus, likewise) ainsi; if ~ si oui; I hope/think ~ je l'espère/le crois; **do/have I** moi aussi; it's 5 o'clock - ~ it is! il est 5 heures - en effet! or c'est vrai!; I hope/think ~ je l'espère/le crois; ~ **far** jusqu'ici, jusqu'à maintenant; (in past) jusque-là

2 (in comparisons etc: to such a degree) si, tellement; ~ **big (that)** si or tellement grand (que); she's not ~ **clever as her brother** elle n'est pas aussi intelligente que son frère

3: ~ **much** a, ad tant (de); **I've got** ~ **much work** j'ai tant de travail; I love you ~ **much** je vous aime tant; ~ **many** tant (de)

4 (phrases): 10 or ~ à peu près or environ 10; ~ **long!** (col: goodbye) au revoir!, à un de ces jours!

◆ cj 1 (expressing purpose): ~ **as to** do pour or afin de faire; ~ **(that)** pour que or afin que + sub

2 (expressing result) donc, par conséquent; ~ **that** si bien que, de (telle) sorte que.

---

soak [səuk] vt faire tremper // vi tremper; to ~ **in** il être absorbé(e); to ~ **up** vt absorber.

so-and-so ['səuəndsəu] n (somebody) un tel(une telle).

soap [səup] n savon m; ~-**flakes** npl paillettes fpl de savon; ~ **opera** n feuilleton télévisé; ~-**powder** n lessive f; ~**y** a savonneux(euse).

soar [sɔ:*] vi monter (en flèche), s'élancer.

sob [sɔb] n sanglot m // vi sangloter.

sober ['səubə*] a qui n'est pas (or plus) ivre; (sedate) sérieux(euse), sensé(e); (moderate) mesuré(e); (colour, style) sobre, discret(ète); to ~ **up** vt dégriser // vi se dégriser.

so-called ['səu'kɔ:ld] a soi-disant inv.

soccer ['sɔkə*] n football m.

social ['səuʃl] a social(e) // n (petite) fête; ~ **club** n amicale f, foyer m; ~**ism** n socialisme m; ~**ist** a, n socialiste *(m/f)*; ~**ize** *vi*: **to** ~**ize (with)** lier connaissance (avec); parler (avec); ~ **security** n aide sociale; ~ **work** n assistance sociale; ~ **worker** n assistant/e social(e).

society [sə'saɪətɪ] n société *f*; (*club*) société, association *f*; (*also*: **high** ~) (haute) société, grand monde.

sociology [səʊsɪ'ɒlədʒɪ] n sociologie *f*.

sock [sɔk] n chaussette *f* // *vt* (*col*: *hit*) flanquer un coup à.

socket ['sɔkɪt] n cavité *f*; (*ELEC*: *also*: **wall** ~) prise *f* de courant; (: *for light bulb*) douille *f*.

sod [sɔd] n (*of earth*) motte *f*; (*Brit col!*) con m (!); salaud m (!).

soda ['səʊdə] n (*CHEM*) soude *f*; (*also*: ~ **water**) eau *f* de Seltz; (*US*: *also*: ~ **pop**) soda m.

sodden ['sɔdn] a trempé(e); détrempé(e).

sofa ['səʊfə] n sofa m, canapé m.

soft [sɔft] a (*not rough*) doux(douce); (*not hard*) doux; mou(molle); (*not loud*) doux, léger(ère); (*kind*) gentil(le); (*weak*) indulgent(e); (*stupid*) stupide, débile; ~ **drink** n boisson non alcoolisée; ~**en** ['sɔfn] *vt* (r)amollir; (*fig*) atténuer // *vi* se ramollir; s'adoucir; s'atténuer; ~**ly** *ad* doucement; gentiment; ~**ness** n douceur *f*.

software ['sɔftwɛə*] n (*COMPUT*) logiciel m, software m.

soggy ['sɔgɪ] a trempé(e); détrempé(e).

soil [sɔɪl] n (*earth*) sol m, terre *f* // *vt* salir; (*fig*) souiller.

solace ['sɔlɪs] n consolation *f*.

solar ['səʊlə*] a solaire.

sold [səʊld] *pt, pp of* sell; ~ **out** a (*COMM*) épuisé(e).

solder ['səʊldə*] *vt* souder (*au fil à souder*) // n soudure *f*.

soldier ['səʊldʒə*] n soldat m, militaire m.

sole [səʊl] n (*of foot*) plante *f*; (*of shoe*) semelle *f*; (*fish*: *pl inv*) sole *f* // a seul(e), unique.

solemn ['sɔləm] a solennel(le); sérieux(euse), grave.

sole trader n (*COMM*) chef m d'entreprise individuelle.

solicit [sə'lɪsɪt] *vt* (*request*) solliciter // *vi* (*prostitute*) racoler.

solicitor [sə'lɪsɪtə*] n (*Brit*: *for wills etc*) ≈ notaire m; (: *in court*) ≈ avocat m.

solid ['sɔlɪd] a (*not hollow*) plein(e), compact(e); massif(ive); (*strong, sound, reliable, not liquid*) solide; (*meal*) consistant(e), substantiel(le) // n solide m.

solidarity [sɔlɪ'dærɪtɪ] n solidarité *f*.

solitary ['sɔlɪtərɪ] a solitaire; ~ **confinement** n (*LAW*) isolement m.

solo ['səʊləʊ] n solo m; ~**ist** n soliste *m/f*.

soluble ['sɔljubl] a soluble.

solution [sə'luːʃən] n solution *f*.

solve [sɔlv] *vt* résoudre.

solvent ['sɔlvənt] a (*COMM*) solvable // n (*CHEM*) (dis)solvant m.

KEYWORD

some [sʌm] ♦ a **1** (*a certain amount or number of*): ~ **tea/water/ice cream** du thé/de l'eau/de la glace; ~ **children/apples** des enfants/pommes

2 (*certain: in contrasts*): ~ **people say that** ... il y a des gens qui disent que ...; ~ **films were excellent, but most were mediocre** certains films étaient excellents, mais la plupart étaient médiocres

3 (*unspecified*): ~ **woman was asking for you** il y avait un dame qui vous demandait; **he was asking for** ~ **book (or other)** il demandait un livre quelconque; ~ **day** un de ces jours; ~ **day next week** un jour la semaine prochaine

♦ *pronoun* **1** (*a certain number*) quelques-uns/fs, certain(e)s; **I've got** ~ (*books etc*) j'en ai (quelques-uns); ~ (*of them*) **have been sold** certains ont été vendus

2 (*a certain amount*) un peu; **I've**

got ~ (*money, milk*) j'en ai un peu
◆ *ad*: ~ **10 people** quelque 10 personnes, 10 personnes environ.

somebody [sʌmbədɪ] *pronoun* =
someone.
somehow ['sʌmhau] *ad* d'une façon
ou d'une autre; (*for some reason*)
pour une raison ou une autre.
someone ['sʌmwʌn] *pronoun* quelqu'un.
someplace ['sʌmpleɪs] *ad* (*US*) =
somewhere.
somersault ['sʌməsɔːlt] *n* culbute *f*,
saut périlleux // *vi* faire la culbute *or*
un saut périlleux; (*car*) faire un tonneau.
something ['sʌmθɪŋ] *pronoun* quelque chose *m*; ~ **interesting** quelque
chose d'intéressant.
sometime ['sʌmtaɪm] *ad* (*in future*)
un de ces jours, un jour ou l'autre;
(*in past*): ~ **last month** au cours du
mois dernier.
sometimes ['sʌmtaɪmz] *ad* quelquefois, parfois.
somewhat ['sʌmwɔt] *ad* quelque
peu, un peu.
somewhere ['sʌmwɛə*] *ad* quelque
part.
son [sʌn] *n* fils *m*.
song [sɔŋ] *n* chanson *f*.
sonic ['sɔnɪk] *a* (*boom*) supersonique.
son-in-law ['sʌnɪnlɔː] *n* gendre *m*,
beau-fils *m*.
sonny ['sʌnɪ] *n* (*col*) fiston *m*.
soon [suːn] *ad* bientôt; (*early*) tôt; ~
afterwards peu après; *see also*:
~**er** *ad* (*time*) plus tôt; (*preference*): **I would** ~**er do** j'aimerais
autant *or* je préférerais faire; ~**er
or later** tôt ou tard.
soot [sut] *n* suie *f*.
soothe [suːð] *vt* calmer, apaiser.
sophisticated [sə'fɪstɪkeɪtɪd] *a* raffiné(e); sophistiqué(e); hautement
perfectionné(e), très complexe.
sophomore ['sɔfəmɔː*] *n* (*US*)
étudiant/e de seconde année.
sopping ['sɔpɪŋ] *a* (*also*: ~ **wet**)

tout(e) trempé(e).
soppy ['sɔpɪ] *a* (*pej*) sentimental(e).
soprano [sə'prɑːnəu] *n* (*voice*) soprano *m*; (*singer*) soprano *m/f*.
sorcerer ['sɔːsərə*] *n* sorcier *m*.
sore [sɔː*] *a* (*painful*) douloureux(euse), sensible; (*offended*)
contrarié(e), vexé(e) // *n* plaie *f*; ~**ly**
ad (*tempted*) fortement.
sorrow ['sɔrəu] *n* peine *f*, chagrin *m*.
sorry ['sɔrɪ] *a* (*condition,
excuse*) triste, déplorable; ~! pardon!, excusez-moi!; **to feel** ~ **for sb**
plaindre qn.
sort [sɔːt] *n* genre *m*, espèce *f*, sorte *f*
// *vt* (*also*: ~ **out**: *papers*) trier;
classer; ranger; (: *letters etc*) trier;
(: *problems*) résoudre, régler; ~**ing
office** *n* bureau *m* de tri.
SOS *n abbr* (= *save our souls*) S.O.S.
m.
so-so ['səusəu] *ad* comme ci comme
ça.
sought [sɔːt] *pt, pp of* **seek**.
soul [səul] *n* âme *f*; ~**-destroying** *a*
démoralisant(e); ~**ful** *a* plein(e) de
sentiment.
sound [saund] *a* (*healthy*) en bonne
santé, sain(e); (*safe, not damaged*)
solide, en bon état; (*reliable, not
superficial*) sérieux(euse), solide;
(*sensible*) sensé(e) // *ad*: ~ **asleep**
dormant d'un profond sommeil // *n*
(*noise*) son *m*; bruit *m*; (*GEO*) détroit *m*, bras *m* de mer // *vt* (*alarm*)
sonner; (*also*: ~ **out**: *opinions*) sonder // *vi* sonner, retentir; (*fig: seem*)
sembler (être); **to** ~ **like** ressembler
à; ~ **barrier** *n* mur *m* du son; ~
effects *npl* bruitage *m*; ~**ly** *ad*
(*sleep*) profondément; (*beat*) complètement, à plate couture; ~**proof** *a*
insonorisé(e); ~**track** *n* (*of film*)
bande *f* sonore.
soup [suːp] *n* soupe *f*, potage *m*; **in
the** ~ (*fig*) dans le pétrin; ~ **plate**
n assiette creuse *or* à soupe; ~**spoon** *n* cuiller *f* à soupe.
sour ['sauə*] *a* aigre; **it's** ~ **grapes**
(*fig*) c'est du dépit.

source [sɔːs] n source f.

south [sauθ] n sud m // a sud inv, du sud // ad au sud, vers le sud; **S~ Africa** n Afrique f du Sud; **S~ African** a sud-africain(e) // n Sud-Africain/e; **S~ America** n Amérique f du Sud; **S~ American** a sud-américain(e) // n Sud-Américain(e); **~-east** n sud-est m; **~erly** ['sʌðəli] a du sud; au sud; **~ern** ['sʌðən] a (du) sud; méridional(e); exposé(e) au sud; **S~ Pole** n Pôle m Sud; **~ward(s)** ad vers le sud; **~-west** n sud-ouest m.

souvenir [suːvə'nɪə*] n souvenir m (objet).

sovereign ['sɔvrɪn] a, n souverain(e).

soviet ['səuvɪət] a soviétique; **the S~ Union** l'Union f soviétique.

sow n [sau] truie f // vt [səu] (pt ~ed, pp sown [səun]) semer.

soya ['sɔɪə], (US) **soy** [sɔɪ] n: **~ bean** n graine f de soja; **~ sauce** n sauce f de soja.

spa [spɑː] n (town) station thermale; (US: also: **health ~**) établissement m de cure de rajeunissement etc.

space [speɪs] n (gen) espace m; (room) place f; espace; (length of time) laps m de temps // cpd spatial(e) // vt (also: **~ out**) espacer; **~craft** n engin spatial; **~man/woman** n astronaute m/f, cosmonaute m/f; **~ship** n = **~craft**; **spacing** n espacement m.

spade [speɪd] n (tool) bêche f, pelle f; (child's) pelle f; **~s** npl (CARDS) pique m.

Spain [speɪn] n Espagne f.

span [spæn] pt of **spin** // n (of bird, plane) envergure f; (of arch) portée f; (in time) espace m de temps, durée f // vt enjamber, franchir; (fig) couvrir, embrasser.

Spaniard ['spænjəd] n Espagnol/e.

spaniel ['spænjəl] n épagneul m.

Spanish ['spænɪʃ] a espagnol(e), d'Espagne // n (LING) espagnol m; **the ~** npl les Espagnols mpl.

spank [spæŋk] vt donner une fessée à.

spanner ['spænə*] n (Brit) clé f (de mécanicien).

spar [spɑː] n espar m // vi (BOXING) s'entraîner.

spare [spɛə*] a de réserve, de rechange; (surplus) en or en trop, de reste // n (part) pièce f de rechange, pièce détachée // vt (do without) se passer de; (afford to give) donner, accorder, passer; (refrain from hurting) épargner; (refrain from using) ménager; **to ~** (surplus) en surplus, de trop; **~ part** n pièce f de rechange, pièce détachée; **~ time** n moments mpl de loisir; **~ wheel** n (AUT) roue f de secours.

sparing ['spɛərɪŋ] a: **to be ~ with** ménager; **~ly** ad avec modération.

spark [spɑːk] n étincelle f; **~(ing) plug** n bougie f.

sparkle ['spɑːkl] n scintillement m, étincellement m, éclat m // vi étinceler, scintiller; (bubble) pétiller; **sparkling** a étincelant(e), scintillant(e); (wine) mousseux(euse), pétillant(e).

sparrow ['spærəu] n moineau m.

sparse [spɑːs] a clairsemé(e).

spartan ['spɑːtən] a (fig) spartiate.

spasm ['spæzəm] n (MED) spasme m; (fig) accès m; **~odic** [-'mɔdɪk] a (fig) intermittent(e).

spastic ['spæstɪk] n handicapé/e moteur.

spat [spæt] pt, pp of **spit**.

spate [speɪt] n (fig): **~ of** avalanche f or torrent m de; **in ~** (river) en crue.

spatter ['spætə*] vt éclabousser // vi gicler.

spawn [spɔːn] vi frayer // n frai m.

speak [spiːk], pt **spoke**, pp **spoken** vt (language) parler; (truth) dire // vi parler; (make a speech) prendre la parole; **to ~ to sb/of or about sth** parler à qn/de qch; **~ up!** parle plus fort!; **~er** n (in public) orateur m; (also: **loud~er**) haut-parleur m;

(POL): **the S~er** le président de la chambre des Communes (Brit) des Représentants (US).

spear [spɪə*] n lance f; **~head** vt (attack etc) mener.

spec [spɛk] n (col): **on ~** à tout hasard.

special ['spɛʃl] a spécial(e); **~ist** n spécialiste m/f; **~ity** [spɛʃɪ'ælɪtɪ] n spécialité f; **~ize** vi: **to ~ize (in)** se spécialiser (dans); **~ly** ad spécialement, particulièrement.

species ['spi:ʃiːz] n espèce f.

specific [spə'sɪfɪk] a précis(e); particulier(ère); (BOT, CHEM etc) spécifique; **~ally** ad expressément, explicitement.

specimen ['spɛsɪmən] n spécimen m, échantillon m; (MED) prélèvement m.

speck [spɛk] n petite tache, petit point; (particle) grain m.

speckled ['spɛkld] a tacheté(e), moucheté(e).

specs [spɛks] npl (col) lunettes fpl.

spectacle ['spɛktəkl] n spectacle m; **~s** npl lunettes fpl; **spectacular** [-'tækjulə*] a spectaculaire // n (CINEMA etc) superproduction f.

spectator [spɛk'teɪtə*] n spectateur/trice.

spectrum, pl **spectra** ['spɛktrəm, -rə] n spectre m; (fig) gamme f.

speculation [spɛkju'leɪʃən] n spéculation f; conjectures fpl.

speech [spi:tʃ] n (faculty) parole f; (talk) discours m; allocution f; (manner of speaking) façon f de parler, langage m; (enunciation) élocution f; **~less** a muet(te).

speed [spi:d] n vitesse f; (promptness) rapidité f; **at full** or **top ~** à toute vitesse or allure; **to ~ up** vi aller plus vite, accélérer // vt accélérer; **~boat** n vedette f, hors-bord m inv; **~ily** ad rapidement, promptement; **~ing** n (AUT) excès m de vitesse; **~ limit** n limitation f de vitesse, vitesse maximale permise; **~ometer** [spɪ'dɔmɪtə*] n compteur

m (de vitesse); **~way** n (SPORT) piste f de vitesse pour motos; (also: **~way racing**) épreuve(s) f(pl) de vitesse de motos; **~y** a rapide, prompt(e).

spell [spɛl] n (also: **magic ~**) sortilège m, charme m; (period of time) (courte) période f // vt (pt, pp **spelt** (Brit) or **~ed** [spɛlt, spɛld]) (in writing) écrire, orthographier; (aloud) épeler; (fig) signifier; **to cast a ~ on sb** jeter un sort à qn; **he can't ~** il fait des fautes d'orthographe; **~bound** a envoûté(e), subjugué(e); **~ing** n orthographe f.

spend, pt, pp **spent** [spɛnd, spɛnt] vt (money) dépenser; (time, life) passer; consacrer; **~thrift** n dépensier/ère.

sperm [spə:m] n spermatozoïde m; (semen) sperme m.

spew [spju:] vt vomir.

sphere [sfɪə*] n sphère f.

spice [spaɪs] n épice f.

spick-and-span ['spɪkən'spæn] a impeccable.

spicy ['spaɪsɪ] a épicé(e), relevé(e); (fig) piquant(e).

spider ['spaɪdə*] n araignée f.

spike [spaɪk] n pointe f.

spill, pt, pp **spilt** or **~ed** [spɪl, -t, -d] vt renverser; répandre // vi se répandre; **to ~ over** vi déborder.

spin [spɪn] n (revolution of wheel) tour m; (AVIAT) (chute f en) vrille f; (trip in car) petit tour, balade f // vb (pt spun, span, pp spun) vt (wool etc) filer; (wheel) faire tourner // vi tourner, tournoyer; **to ~ out** vt faire durer.

spinach ['spɪnɪtʃ] n épinard m; (as food) épinards.

spinal ['spaɪnl] a vertébral(e), spinal(e); **~ cord** n moelle épinière.

spindly ['spɪndlɪ] a grêle, filiforme.

spin-dryer [spɪn'draɪə*] n (Brit) essoreuse f.

spine [spaɪn] n colonne vertébrale; (thorn) épine f, piquant m.

spinning ['spɪnɪŋ] n (of thread)

filage m; (by machine) filature f; ~ **top** n toupie f; ~ **wheel** n rouet m.

spin-off ['spɪnɔf] n avantage inattendu; sous-produit m.

spinster ['spɪnstə*] n célibataire f; vieille fille.

spiral ['spaɪərl] n spirale f // à en spirale // vi (fig) monter en flèche; ~ **staircase** n escalier m en colimaçon.

spire ['spaɪə*] n flèche f, aiguille f.

spirit ['spɪrɪt] n (soul) esprit m, âme f; (ghost) esprit, revenant m; (mood) esprit, âme t d'esprit; (courage) courage m, énergie f; ~s npl (drink) spiritueux mpl, alcool m; in good ~s de bonne humeur; ~ed a vif(vive), fougueux(euse), plein(e) d'allant; ~ level n niveau m à bulle.

spiritual ['spɪrɪtjuəl] a spirituel(le); religieux(euse).

spit [spɪt] n (for roasting) broche f // vi (pt, pp **spat**) cracher; (sound) crépiter.

spite [spaɪt] n rancune f, dépit m // vt contrarier, vexer; in ~ of en dépit de, malgré; ~**ful** a malveillant(e), rancunier(ère).

spittle ['spɪtl] n salive f; bave f; crachat m.

splash [splæʃ] n éclaboussement m; (of colour) tache f // excl (sound) plouf // vt éclabousser // vi (also: ~ about) barboter, patauger.

spleen [spli:n] n (ANAT) rate f.

splendid ['splendɪd] a splendide, superbe, magnifique.

splint [splɪnt] n attelle f, éclisse f.

splinter ['splɪntə*] n (wood) écharde f; (metal) éclat m // vi se fragmenter.

split [splɪt] n fente f, déchirure f; (fig: POL) scission f // vb (pt, pp **split**) vt fendre, déchirer; (party) diviser; (work, profits) partager, répartir // vi (divide) se diviser; to ~ **up** vi (couple) se séparer, rompre; (meeting) se disperser.

splutter ['splʌtə*] vi bafouiller; postillonner.

spoil, pt, pp **spoilt** or ~**ed** [spɔɪl, -t, -d] vt (damage) abîmer; (mar) gâcher; (child) gâter; ~**s** npl butin m; ~**sport** n trouble-fête m, rabat-joie m inv.

spoke [spəuk] pt of **speak** // n rayon m.

spoken ['spəukn] pp of **speak**.

spokesman ['spəuksmən], **spokeswoman** ['-wumən] n porte-parole m inv.

sponge [spʌndʒ] n éponge f // vt éponger // vi: to ~ **off** or **on** vivre aux crochets de; ~ **bag** n (Brit) trousse f de toilette; ~ **cake** n ≈ biscuit m de Savoie.

sponsor ['spɔnsə*] n (RADIO, TV) personne f (or organisme m) qui assure le patronage // vt patronner; parrainer; ~**ship** n patronage m; parrainage m.

spontaneous [spɔn'teɪnɪəs] a spontané(e).

spooky ['spu:kɪ] a qui donne la chair de poule.

spool [spu:l] n bobine f.

spoon [spu:n] n cuiller f; ~**feed** vt nourrir à la cuiller; (fig) mâcher le travail à; ~**ful** n cuillerée f.

sport [spɔ:t] n sport m; (person) chic type/chic fille // vt arborer; ~**ing** a sportif(ive); to give sb a ~**ing chance** donner sa chance à qn; ~ **jacket** n (US) = ~s **jacket**; ~s **car** n voiture f de sport; ~s **jacket** n veste f de sport; ~**sman** n sportif m; ~**smanship** n esprit sportif, sportivité f; ~**swear** n vêtements mpl de sport; ~**swoman** n sportive f; ~**y** a sportif(ive).

spot [spɔt] n tache f; (dot: on pattern) pois m; (pimple) bouton m; (place) endroit m, coin m; (small amount): a ~ of un peu de // vt (notice) apercevoir, repérer; on the ~ sur place, sur les lieux; ~ **check** n sondage m, vérification ponctuelle; ~**less** a immaculé(e); ~**light** n projecteur m; (AUT) phare m auxiliaire; ~**ted** a tacheté(e), moucheté(e); à pois; **~ty** a (face) boutonneux(euse).

spouse [spauz] n époux/épouse.

spout [spaut] n (of jug) bec m; (of liquid) jet m // vi jaillir.

sprain [sprein] n entorse f, foulure f // vt: **to ~ one's ankle** se fouler or se tordre la cheville.

sprang [spræŋ] pt of **spring**.

sprawl [sprɔːl] vi s'étaler.

spray [sprei] n jet m (en fines gouttelettes); (container) vaporisateur m, bombe f; (of flowers) petit bouquet // vt vaporiser, pulvériser; (crops) traiter.

spread [spred] n propagation f; (distribution) répartition f; (CULIN) pâte f à tartiner // vt (pt, pp **spread**) vt étendre, étaler; répandre; propager // vi s'étendre; se répandre; se propager; **~-eagled** ['spred:iːgld] a étendu(e) bras et jambes écartés; **~sheet** n (COMPUT) tableur m.

spree [spriː] n: **to go on a ~** faire la fête.

sprightly ['spraitli] a alerte.

spring [sprɪŋ] n (leap) bond m, saut m; (coiled metal) ressort m; (season) printemps m; (of water) source f // vi (pt **sprang**, pp **sprung**) bondir, sauter; **to ~ from** provenir de; **to ~ up** vi (problem) se présenter, surgir; **~board** n tremplin m; **~-clean** n (also: **~-cleaning**) grand nettoyage de printemps; **~-time** n printemps m; **~y** a élastique, souple.

sprinkle ['sprɪŋkl] vt (pour) répandre; verser; **to ~ water etc on, ~ with water etc** asperger d'eau etc; **to ~ sugar etc on, ~ with sugar etc** saupoudrer de sucre etc; **~r** n (for lawn) arroseur m; (to put out fire) diffuseur m d'extincteur automatique d'incendie.

sprint [sprint] n sprint m // vi sprinter.

sprout [spraut] vi germer, pousser; **~s** npl (also: **Brussels ~s**) choux mpl de Bruxelles.

spruce [spruːs] n épicéa m // a

net(te), pimpant(e).

sprung [sprʌŋ] pp of **spring**.

spry [sprai] a alerte, vif(vive).

spun [spʌn] pt, pp of **spin**.

spur [spəː*] n éperon m; (fig) aiguillon m // vt (also: **~ on**) éperonner; aiguillonner; **on the ~ of the moment** sous l'impulsion du moment.

spurious ['spjuəriəs] a faux(fausse).

spurn [spəːn] vt repousser avec mépris.

spurt [spəːt] vi jaillir, gicler.

spy [spai] n espion/ne // vi: **to ~ on** espionner, épier // vt (see) apercevoir; **~ing** n espionnage m.

sq. (MATH) **Sq.**, (in address) abbr of **square**.

squabble ['skwɔbl] vi se chamailler.

squad [skwɔd] n (MIL, POLICE) escouade f, groupe m; (FOOTBALL) contingent m.

squadron ['skwɔdrn] n (MIL) escadron m; (AVIAT, NAUT) escadrille f.

squalid ['skwɔlid] a sordide, ignoble.

squall [skwɔːl] n rafale f, bourrasque f.

squalor ['skwɔlə*] n conditions fpl sordides.

squander ['skwɔndə*] vt gaspiller, dilapider.

square [skwɛə*] n carré m; (in town) place f; (instrument) équerre f // a carré(e); (honest) honnête, régulier(ère); (col: ideas, tastes) vieux jeu inv; qui retarde // vt (arrange) régler; arranger; (MATH) élever au carré // vt (agree) cadrer, s'accorder; **all ~** quitte; à égalité; **a ~ meal** un repas convenable; **2 metres ~** de 2 mètres sur 2; **1 metre** 1 mètre carré.

squash [skwɔʃ] n (Brit: drink): **lemon/orange ~** citronnade f/ orangeade f; (SPORT) squash m // vt écraser.

squat [skwɔt] a petit(e) et épais(se), ramassé(e) // vi s'accroupir; **~ter** n squatter m.

squawk [skwɔːk] vi pousser un or des gloussement(s).

squeak [skwiːk] *vi* grincer, crier.

squeal [skwiːl] *vi* pousser un ou des cri(s) aigu(s) ou perçant(s).

squeamish ['skwiːmɪʃ] *a* facilement dégoûté(e); facilement scandalisé(e).

squeeze [skwiːz] *n* pression *f*; restrictions *fpl* de crédit // *vt* presser; (hand, arm) serrer; **to ~ out** *vt* exprimer; (fig) soutirer.

squelch [skweltʃ] *vi* faire un bruit de succion; patauger.

squib [skwɪb] *n* pétard *m*.

squid [skwɪd] *n* calmar *m*.

squiggle ['skwɪgl] *n* gribouillis *m*.

squint [skwɪnt] *vi* loucher // *n*: **he has a ~** il louche, il louche d'un strabisme; **to ~ at sth** regarder qch du coin de l'œil; (quickly) jeter un coup d'œil à qch.

squire ['skwaɪə*] *n* (Brit) propriétaire terrien.

squirm [skwəːm] *vi* se tortiller.

squirrel ['skwɪrəl] *n* écureuil *m*.

squirt [skwəːt] *vi* jaillir, gicler.

Sr *abbr* de **senior**.

St *abbr* de **saint, street**.

stab [stæb] *n* (with knife etc) coup *m* (de couteau etc); (col: try): **to have a ~ at (doing) sth** s'essayer à (faire) qch // *vt* poignarder.

stable ['steɪbl] *n* écurie *f* // *a* stable.

stack [stæk] *n* tas *m*, pile *f* // *vt* empiler, entasser.

stadium ['steɪdɪəm] *n* stade *m*.

staff [staːf] *n* (work force) personnel *m*; (: Brit SCOL) professeurs *mpl*; (: servants) domestiques *mpl*; (MIL) état-major *m*; (stick) perche *f*, bâton *m* // *vt* pourvoir en personnel.

stag [stæg] *n* cerf *m*.

stage [steɪdʒ] *n* scène *f*; (profession): **the ~** le théâtre; (point) étape *f*, stade *m*; (platform) estrade *f* // *vt* (play) monter, mettre en scène; (demonstration) organiser; (fig: perform: recovery etc) effectuer; **in ~s** par étapes, par degrés; **~coach** *n* diligence *f*; **~ door** *n* entrée *f* des artistes; **~ manager** *n* régisseur *m*.

stagger ['stægə*] *vi* chanceler, titu-

ber // *vt* (person) stupéfier; bouleverser; (hours, holidays) étaler, échelonner.

stagnate [stæg'neɪt] *vi* stagner, croupir.

stag party *n* enterrement *m* de vie de garçon.

staid [steɪd] *a* posé(e), rassis(e).

stain [steɪn] *n* tache *f*; (colouring) colorant *m* // *vt* tacher; (wood) teindre; **~ed glass window** *n* vitrail *m*; **~less** *a* (steel) inoxydable; **~ remover** *n* détachant *m*.

stair [steə*] *n* (step) marche *f*; **~s** *npl* escalier *m*; **on the ~s** dans l'escalier; **~case, ~way** *n* escalier *m*.

stake [steɪk] *n* pieu *m*, poteau *m*; (BETTING) enjeu *m* // *vt* risquer, jouer; **to be at ~** être en jeu.

stale [steɪl] *a* (bread) rassis(e); (beer) éventé(e); (smell) de renfermé.

stalemate ['steɪlmeɪt] *n* pat *m*; (fig) impasse *f*.

stalk [stɔːk] *n* tige *f* // *vt* traquer // *vi* marcher avec raideur.

stall [stɔːl] *n* éventaire *m*, étal *m*; (in stable) stalle *f* // *vt* (AUT) caler // *vi* (AUT) caler; (fig) essayer de gagner du temps; **~s** *npl* (Brit: in cinema, theatre) orchestre *m*.

stallion ['stælɪən] *n* étalon *m* (cheval).

stalwart ['stɔːlwət] *n* partisan *m* fidèle.

stamina ['stæmɪnə] *n* vigueur *f*, endurance *f*.

stammer ['stæmə*] *n* bégaiement *m* // *vi* bégayer.

stamp [stæmp] *n* timbre *m*; (mark, also fig) empreinte *f*; (on document) cachet *m* // *vi* (also: **~ one's foot**) taper du pied // *vt* tamponner, estamper; (letter) timbrer; **~ album** *n* album *m* de timbres(-poste); **~ collecting** *n* philatélie *f*.

stampede [stæm'piːd] *n* ruée *f*.

stance [stæns] *n* position *f*.

stand [stænd] *n* (position) position *f*; (MIL) résistance *f*; (structure) guéridon *m*; support *m*; (*COMM*) étalage *m*, stand *m*; (*SPORT*) tribune *f* // *vb* (*pt, pp* **stood**) *vi* être ou se tenir (debout); (*rise*) se lever, se mettre debout; (*be placed*) se trouver // *vt* (*place*) mettre, poser; (*tolerate, withstand*) supporter; **to make a ~** prendre position; **to ~ for parliament** (*Brit*) se présenter aux élections (*comme candidat à la députation*); **to ~ by** *vi* (*be ready*) se tenir prêt(e) // *vt fus* (*opinion*) s'en tenir à; **to ~ down** (*withdraw*) se retirer; **to ~ for** *vt fus* (*signify*) signifier; (*tolerate*) supporter, tolérer; **to ~ in for** *vt fus* remplacer; **to ~ out** *vi* (*be prominent*) ressortir; **to ~ up** *vi* (*rise*) se lever, se mettre debout; **to ~ up for** *vt fus* défendre; **to ~ up to** *vt fus* tenir tête à, résister à.

standard ['stændəd] *n* niveau voulu; (*flag*) étendard *m* // *a* (*size etc*) ordinaire, normal(e); courant(e); **~s** *npl* (*morals*) morale *f*, principes *mpl*; **~ lamp** *n* (*Brit*) lampadaire *m*; **~ of living** *n* niveau de vie.

stand-by ['stændbaɪ] *n* remplaçant *m*; **to be on ~** se tenir prêt(e) (à intervenir); être de garde; **~ ticket** *n* (*AVIAT*) billet *m* sans garantie.

stand-in ['stændɪn] *n* remplaçant *m*; (*CINEMA*) doublure *f*.

standing ['stændɪŋ] *a* debout *inv* // *n* réputation *f*, rang *m*, standing *m*; **of many years'** ~ qui dure ou existe depuis longtemps; **~ order** *n* (*Brit*: *at bank*) virement *m* automatique, prélèvement *m* bancaire; **~ orders** *npl* (*MIL*) règlement *m*; **~ room** *n* places *fpl* debout.

stand-offish [stænd'ɔfɪʃ] *a* distant(e), froid(e).

standpoint ['stændpɔɪnt] *n* point de vue.

standstill ['stændstɪl] *n*: **at a ~** à l'arrêt; (*fig*) au point mort; **to come to a ~** s'immobiliser, s'arrêter.

stank [stæŋk] *pt of* **stink**.

staple ['steɪpl] *n* (*for papers*) agrafe

f // *a* (*food etc*) de base, principal(e) // *vt* agrafer; **~r** *n* agrafeuse *f*.

star [stɑ:*] *n* étoile *f*; (*celebrity*) vedette *f* // *vi*: **to ~ (in)** être la vedette (de) // *vt* (*CINEMA*) avoir pour vedette.

starboard ['stɑ:bəd] *n* tribord *m*.

starch [stɑ:tʃ] *n* amidon *m*.

stardom ['stɑ:dəm] *n* célébrité *f*.

stare [stɛə*] *n* regard *m* fixe // *vi*: **to ~ at** regarder fixement.

starfish ['stɑ:fɪʃ] *n* étoile *f* de mer.

stark [stɑ:k] *a* (*bleak*) désolé(e), morne *f* // *ad*: **~ naked** complètement nu(e).

starling ['stɑ:lɪŋ] *n* étourneau *m*.

starry ['stɑ:rɪ] *a* étoilé(e); **~-eyed** *a* (*innocent*) ingénu(e).

start [stɑ:t] *n* commencement *m*, début *m*; (*of race*) départ *m*; (*sudden movement*) sursaut *m* // *vt* commencer // *vi* partir, se mettre en route; (*jump*) sursauter; **to ~ doing or to do sth** se mettre à faire qch; **to ~ off** *vi* commencer; (*leave*) partir; **to ~ up** *vi* commencer; (*car*) démarrer // *vt* déclencher; (*car*) mettre en marche; **~er** *n* (*AUT*) démarreur *m*; (*SPORT*: *official*) starter *m*; (: *runner, horse*) partant *m*; (*Brit CULIN*) entrée *f*; **~ing point** *n* point *m* de départ.

startle ['stɑ:tl] *vt* faire sursauter; donner un choc à.

starvation [stɑ:'veɪʃən] *n* faim *f*, famine *f*.

starve [stɑ:v] *vi* mourir de faim; être affamé(e) // *vt* affamer.

state [steɪt] *n* état *m* // *vt* déclarer, affirmer; formuler; **the S~s** les États-Unis *mpl*; **to be in a ~** être dans tous ses états; **~ly** *a* majestueux(euse), imposant(e); **~ment** *n* déclaration *f*, (*LAW*) déposition *f*; **~sman** *n* homme *m* d'État.

static ['stætɪk] *n* (*RADIO*) parasites *mpl* // *a* statique.

station ['steɪʃən] *n* gare *f*; poste *m* (*militaire ou de police etc*); (*rank*) condition *f*, rang *m* // *vt* placer, poster.

stationary ['steɪʃnərɪ] *a* à l'arrêt, immobile.

stationer ['steɪʃənə*] *n* papetier/ère; **~s (shop)** *n* papeterie *f*; **~y** *n* papier *m* à lettres, petit matériel de bureau.

station master *n* (RAIL) chef *m* de gare.

station wagon *n* (US) break *m*.

statistic [stə'tɪstɪk] *n* statistique *f*; **~s** (*science*) statistique *f*.

statue ['stætju:] *n* statue *f*.

status ['steɪtəs] *n* position *f*, situation *f*; prestige *m*; statut *m*; **~ symbol** *n* marque *f* de standing.

statute ['stætju:t] *n* loi *f*; **~s** *npl* (*of club etc*) statuts *mpl*; **statutory** *a* statutaire, prévu(e) par un article de loi.

staunch [stɔ:ntʃ] *a* sûr(e), loyal(e).

stave [steɪv] *n* (MUS) portée *f* // *vt*: **to ~ off** (*attack*) parer; (*threat*) conjurer.

stay [steɪ] *n* (*period of time*) séjour *m* // *vi* rester; (*reside*) loger; (*spend some time*) séjourner; **to ~ put** ne pas bouger; **to ~ with friends** loger chez des amis; **to ~ the night** passer la nuit; **to ~ behind** *vi* rester en arrière; **to ~ in** *vi* (*at home*) rester à la maison; **to ~ on** *vi* rester; **to ~ out** *vi* (*of house*) ne pas rentrer; **to ~ up** *vi* (*at night*) ne pas se coucher; **~ing power** *n* endurance *f*.

stead [stɛd] *n*: **in sb's ~** à la place de qn; **to stand sb in good ~** être très utile ou servir beaucoup à qn.

steadfast ['stɛdfɑ:st] *a* ferme, résolu(e).

steadily ['stɛdɪlɪ] *ad* progressivement; sans arrêt; (*walk*) d'un pas ferme.

steady ['stɛdɪ] *a* stable, solide, ferme; (*regular*) constant(e), régulier(ère); (*person*) calme, pondéré(e) // *vt* stabiliser; assujettir; calmer; **to ~ o.s.** reprendre son aplomb.

steak [steɪk] *n* (*meat*) bifteck *m*,

steak *m*; (*fish*) tranche *f*.

steal [sti:l], *pt* **stole**, *pp* **stolen** *vt*, *vi* voler.

stealth [stɛlθ] *n*: **by ~** furtivement; **~y** *a* furtif(ive).

steam [sti:m] *n* vapeur *f* // *vt* passer à la vapeur; (CULIN) cuire à la vapeur // *vi* fumer; (*ship*): **to ~ along** filer; **~ engine** *n* locomotive *f* à vapeur; **~er** *n* (bateau *m* à) vapeur *m*; **~roller** *n* rouleau compresseur; **~ship** *n* = **~er**; **~y** *a* embué(e), humide.

steel [sti:l] *n* acier *m* // *cpd* d'acier; **~works** *n* aciérie *f*.

steep [sti:p] *a* raide, escarpé(e); (*price*) très élevé(e), excessif(ive) // *vt* (faire) tremper.

steeple ['sti:pl] *n* clocher *m*.

steer [stɪə*] *n* bœuf *m* // *vt* diriger, gouverner; guider // *vi* tenir le gouvernail; **~ing** *n* (AUT) conduite *f*; **~ing wheel** *n* volant *m*.

stem [stɛm] *n* (*of plant*) tige *f*; (*of leaf, fruit*) queue *f*; (*of glass*) pied *m* // *vt* contenir, endiguer, juguler; **to ~ from** *vt fus* provenir de, découler de.

stench [stɛntʃ] *n* puanteur *f*.

stencil ['stɛnsl] *n* stencil *m*; pochoir *m* // *vt* polycopier.

stenographer [stɛ'nɔgrəfə*] *n* (US) sténographe *m/f*.

step [stɛp] *n* pas *m*; (*stair*) marche *f*; (*action*) mesure *f*, disposition *f* // *vi*: **to ~ forward** faire un pas en avant, avancer; **~s** *npl* (*Brit*) = **stepladder**; **to be in/out of ~ (with)** (*fig*) aller dans le sens (de)/ être déphasé(e) (par rapport à); **to ~ down** *vi* (*fig*) se retirer, se désister; **to ~ off** *vt fus* descendre de; **to ~ up** *vt* augmenter; intensifier; **~brother** *n* demi-frère *m*; **~daughter** *n* belle-fille *f*; **~father** *n* beau-père *m*; **~ladder** *n* escabeau *m*; **~mother** *n* belle-mère *f*; **~ping stone** *n* pierre *f* de gué; (*fig*) tremplin *m*; **~sister** *n* demi-sœur *f*; **~son** *n* beau-fils *m*.

stereo ['steriəu] n (system) stéréo f; (record player) chaîne f stéréo // a (also: ~phonic) stéréophonique.

sterile ['sterail] a stérile; **sterilize** ['sterilaiz] vt stériliser.

sterling ['stə:lıŋ] a (silver) de bon aloi, fin(e); (fig) à toute épreuve, excellent(e) // n (ECON) livres fpl sterling inv; a **pound** ~ une livre sterling.

stern [stə:n] a sévère // n (NAUT) arrière m, poupe f.

stew [stju:] n ragoût m // vt, vi cuire à la casserole.

steward ['stju:əd] n (AVIAT, NAUT, RAIL) steward m; (in club etc) intendant m; ~**ess** n hôtesse f.

stick [stık] n bâton m; morceau m // vb (pt, pp **stuck**) vt (glue) coller; (thrust): **to** ~ **sth into** piquer or planter or enfoncer qch dans; (col: put) mettre, fourrer; (col: tolerate) supporter // vi se planter; tenir; (remain) rester; **to** ~ **out, to** ~ **up** vi dépasser, sortir; **to** ~ **up for** vt fus défendre; ~**er** n auto-collant m; ~**ing plaster** n sparadrap m, pansement adhésif.

stickler ['stıklə*] n: **to be a** ~ **for** être pointilleux(euse) sur.

stick-up ['stıkʌp] n braquage m, hold-up m.

sticky ['stıkı] a poisseux(euse); (label) adhésif(ive).

stiff [stıf] a raide; rigide; dur(e); (difficult) difficile, ardu(e); (cold) froid(e), distant(e); (strong, high) fort(e), élevé(e); ~**en** vt raidir, renforcer // vi se raidir; se durcir; ~**neck** n torticolis m.

stifle ['staıfl] vt étouffer, réprimer.

stigma, pl (BOT, MED, REL) ~**ta,** (fig) ~**s** ['stıgmə, stıg'ma:tə] n stigmate m.

stile [staıl] n échalier m.

stiletto [stı'letəu] n (Brit: also: ~ **heel**) talon m aiguille.

still [stıl] a immobile; calme, tranquille // ad (up to this time) encore, toujours; (even) encore; (nonethe-

less) quand même, tout de même; ~**born** a mort-né(e); ~ **life** n nature morte.

stilt [stılt] n échasse f; (pile) pilotis m.

stilted ['stıltıd] a guindé(e), emprunté(e).

stimulate ['stımjuleıt] vt stimuler.

stimulus, pl **stimuli** ['stımjuləs, 'stımjulaı] n stimulant m; (BIOL, PSYCH) stimulus m.

sting [stıŋ] n piqûre f; (organ) dard m // vt, vi (pt, pp **stung**) piquer.

stingy ['stındʒı] a avare, pingre.

stink [stıŋk] n puanteur f // vi (pt **stank,** pp **stunk**) puer, empester; ~**ing** a (fig: col) infect(e), vache; a ~**ing** ... un(e) foutu(e) ....

stint [stınt] n part f de travail // vi: **to** ~ **on** lésiner sur, être chiche de.

stir [stə:*] n agitation f, sensation f // vt remuer // vi remuer, bouger; **to** ~ **up** vt exciter.

stirrup ['stırəp] n étrier m.

stitch [stıtʃ] n (SEWING) point m; (KNITTING) maille f; (MED) point de suture; (pain) point de côté m // vt coudre, piquer; suturer.

stoat [stəut] n hermine f (avec son pelage d'été).

stock [stɔk] n réserve f, provision f; (COMM) stock m; (AGR) cheptel m, bétail m; (CULIN) bouillon m; (FINANCE) valeurs fpl, titres mpl // a (fig: reply etc) courant(e); classique // vt (have in stock) avoir, vendre; **in/out of** ~ en stock or en magasin/épuisé(e); **to take** ~ (fig) faire le point; ~**s and shares** valeurs (mobilières), titres; **to** ~ **up** vi: **to** ~ **up (with)** s'approvisionner (en).

stockbroker ['stɔkbrəukə*] n agent m de change.

stock cube n bouillon-cube m.

stock exchange n Bourse f (des valeurs).

stocking ['stɔkıŋ] n bas m.

stock: ~ **market** n Bourse f, marché financier; ~ **phrase** n cliché m; ~**pile** n stock m, réserve f // vt stocker, accumuler; ~**taking** n (Brit COMM) inventaire m.

stocky ['stɒkɪ] a trapu(e), râblé(e).

stodgy ['stɒdʒɪ] a bourratif(ive), lourd(e).

stoke [stəuk] vt garnir, entretenir; chauffer.

stole [stəul] pt of **steal** // n étole f.

stolen ['stəuln] pp of **steal**.

stolid ['stɒlɪd] a impassible, flegmatique.

stomach ['stʌmək] n estomac m; (abdomen) ventre m // vt supporter, digérer; ~ **ache** n mal m à l'estomac or au ventre.

stone [stəun] n pierre f; (pebble) caillou m, galet m; (in fruit) noyau m; (MED) calcul m; (Brit: weight) = 6.348 kg; 14 pounds // cpd de or en pierre // vt dénoyauter; ~**cold** a complètement froid(e); ~**deaf** a sourd(e) comme un pot; ~**work** n maçonnerie f.

stood [stud] pt, pp of **stand**.

stool [stuːl] n tabouret m.

stoop [stuːp] vi (also: **have a** ~) être voûté(e); (bend) se baisser.

stop [stɒp] n arrêt m; halte f; (in punctuation) point m // vt arrêter; (break off) interrompre; (also: put a ~ to) mettre fin à // vi s'arrêter; (rain, noise etc) cesser, s'arrêter; to ~ **doing sth** cesser or arrêter de faire qch; to ~ **dead** vi s'arrêter net; to ~ **off** vi faire une courte halte; to ~ **up** vt (hole) boucher; ~**gap** n (person) bouche-trou m; (measure) mesure f intérimaire; ~**lights** npl (AUT) signaux mpl de stop, feux mpl arrière; ~**over** n halte f; (AVIAT) escale f.

stoppage ['stɒpɪdʒ] n arrêt m; (of pay) retenue f; (strike) arrêt de travail.

stopper ['stɒpə*] n bouchon m.

stop press n nouvelles fpl de dernière heure.

stopwatch ['stɒpwɒtʃ] n chronomètre m.

storage ['stɔːrɪdʒ] n emmagasinage

m; (COMPUT) mise f en mémoire or réserve; ~ **heater** n radiateur m électrique par accumulation.

store [stɔː*] n provision f, réserve f; (depot) entrepôt m; (Brit: large shop) grand magasin; (US) magasin m // vt emmagasiner; ~**s** npl provisions; to ~ **up** vt mettre en réserve, emmagasiner; ~**room** n réserve f, magasin m.

storey, (US) **story** ['stɔːrɪ] n étage m.

stork [stɔːk] n cigogne f.

storm [stɔːm] n orage m, tempête f; ouragan m // vi (fig) fulminer // vt prendre d'assaut; ~**y** a orageux(euse).

story ['stɔːrɪ] n histoire f; récit m; (US) = **storey**; ~**book** n livre m d'histoires or de contes.

stout [staut] a solide; (brave) intrépide; (fat) gros(se), corpulent(e) // n bière brune.

stove [stəuv] n (for cooking) fourneau m; (: small) réchaud m; (for heating) poêle m.

stow [stəu] vt ranger; cacher; ~**away** n passager(ère) clandestin(e).

straddle ['strædl] vt enjamber, être à cheval sur.

straggle ['strægl] vi être (or marcher) en désordre; ~**r** n traînard(e).

straight [streɪt] a droit(e); (frank) honnête, franc(franche) // ad (tout) droit; (drink) sec, sans eau; to put or get ~ mettre en ordre, mettre de l'ordre dans; ~ **away**, ~ **off** (at once) tout de suite; ~**en** vt (also: ~**en out**) redresser; ~**faced** a impassible; ~**forward** a simple; honnête, direct(e).

strain [streɪn] n (TECH) tension f; pression f; (physical) effort m; (mental) tension (nerveuse); (MED) entorse f; (streak, trace) tendance f; élément m // vt tendre fortement; mettre à l'épreuve; (filter) passer, filtrer // vi peiner, fournir un gros effort; ~**s** npl (MUS) accords mpl, ac-

cents *mpl*; **~ed** *a* (*laugh etc*) for-
cé(e), contraint(e); (*relations*) ten-
du(e); **~er** *n* passoire *f*.

strait [streɪt] *n* (GEO) détroit *m*;
~jacket *n* camisole *f* de force; **~
laced** *a* collet monté *inv*.

strand [strænd] *n* (*of thread*) fil *m*,
brin *m*; **~ed** *a* en rade, en plan.

strange [streɪndʒ] *a* (*not known*) in-
connu(e); (*odd*) étrange, bizarre; **~**
n inconnu/e; étranger/ère.

strangle ['stræŋgl] *vt* étrangler; **~
hold** *n* (*fig*) emprise totale, mainmise *f*.

strap [stræp] *n* lanière *f*, courroie *f*,
sangle *f*; (*of slip, dress*) bretelle *f* //
vt attacher (avec une courroie *etc*).

strategic [strə'tiːdʒɪk] *a* stratégique.

strategy ['strætɪdʒɪ] *n* stratégie *f*.

straw [strɔː] *n* paille *f*; **that's the
last ~!** ça c'est le comble!

strawberry ['strɔːbərɪ] *n* fraise *f*.

stray [streɪ] *a* (*animal*) perdu(e), er-
rant(e) // *vi* s'égarer; **~ bullet** *n*
balle perdue.

streak [striːk] *n* raie *f*, bande *f*, filet
m; (*fig: of madness etc*): **a ~ of** une
or des tendance(s) à // *vt* zébrer,
strier // *vi*: **to ~ past** passer à toute
allure.

stream [striːm] *n* ruisseau *m*; courant *m*, flot *m*; (*of people*) défilé in-
interrompu, flot *m* // *vt* (SCOL) répartir
par niveau // *vi* ruisseler; **to ~ in/out**
entrer/sortir à flots.

streamer ['striːmə*] *n* serpentin *m*,
banderole *f*.

streamlined ['striːmlaɪnd] *a*
(AVIAT) fuselé(e), profilé(e); (AUT)
aérodynamique; (*fig*) rationalisé(e).

street [striːt] *n* rue *f* // *cpd* de la rue;
des rues; **~car** *n* (US) tramway *m*;
~ lamp *n* réverbère *m*; **~ plan** *n*
plan *m* des rues; **~wise** *a* (*col*) fu-
té(e), réaliste.

strength [streŋθ] *n* force *f*; (*of girder, knot etc*) solidité *f*; **~en** *vt* fortifier; renforcer; tremper.

strenuous ['strenjuəs] *a* vigou-
reux(euse), énergique; (*tiring*)

ardu(e), fatigant(e).

stress [stres] *n* (*force, pressure*)
pression *f*; (*mental strain*) tension
(nerveuse); (*accent*) accent *m* // *vt*
insister sur, souligner.

stretch [stretʃ] *n* (*of sand etc*) étendue *f* // *vi* s'étirer; (*extend*): **to ~ to**
or as far as s'étendre jusqu'à // *vt*
tendre, étirer; (*spread*) étendre; (*fig*)
pousser (au maximum); **to ~ out**
vi s'étendre // *vt* (*arm etc*) allonger,
tendre; (*to spread*) étendre.

stretcher ['stretʃə*] *n* brancard *m*,
civière *f*.

strewn [struːn] *a*: **~ with** jonché(e)
de.

stricken ['strɪkən] *a* (*person*) très
éprouvé(e); (*city, industry etc*) dé-
vasté(e); **~ with** (*disease etc*) frap-
pé(e) or atteint(e) de.

strict [strɪkt] *a* strict(e).

stride [straɪd] *n* grand pas, enjambée
f // *vi* (*pt* **strode**, *pp* **stridden**
[strəʊd, 'strɪdn]) marcher à grands
pas.

strife [straɪf] *n* conflit *m*, dissensions
fpl.

strike [straɪk] *n* grève *f* (*of oil etc*)
découverte *f*; (*attack*) raid *m* // *vb*
(*pt, pp* **struck**) *vt* frapper; (*oil etc*)
trouver, découvrir // *vi* faire grève;
(*attack*) attaquer; (*clock*) sonner; **to
~** (*workers*) en grève; **to ~ a
match** frotter une allumette; **to ~
down** *vt* (*fig*) terrasser; **to ~ out**
vt rayer; **to ~ up** *vi* (MUS) se mettre à jouer; **to ~ up a friendship
with** se lier d'amitié avec; **~r** *n* gréviste *m/f*; (SPORT) buteur *m*; **striking** *a* frappant(e), saisissant(e).

string [strɪŋ] *n* ficelle *f*, fil *m*; (*row*)
rang *m*; chapelet *m*; filet *m*; (MUS)
corde *f* // *vt* (*pt, pp* **strung**): **to ~
out** échelonner; **to ~ together** enchaîner; **the ~s** *npl* (MUS) les ins-
truments *mpl* à cordes; **to pull ~s**
(*fig*) faire jouer le piston; **~ bean** *n*
haricot vert; **~(ed) instrument** *n*
(MUS) instrument *m* à cordes.

stringent ['strɪndʒənt] *a* rigoureux(euse); (*need*) impérieux(euse).

strip [strɪp] n bande f // vt déshabiller; dégarnir, dépouiller; (*also:* ~ **down**: *machine*) démonter // vi se déshabiller; ~ **cartoon** n bande dessinée.

stripe [straɪp] n raie f, rayure f; ~d a rayé(e), à rayures.

strip lighting n éclairage m au néon or fluorescent.

stripper ['strɪpə*] n strip-teaseuse f.

strive, pt **strove**, pp **striven** [straɪv, strəuv, 'strɪvn] vi: **to** ~ **to do** s'efforcer de faire.

strode [strəud] pt of **stride**.

stroke [strəuk] n coup m; (*MED*) attaque f; (*caress*) caresse f // vt caresser; **at a** ~ d'un (seul) coup.

stroll [strəul] n petite promenade // vi flâner, se promener nonchalamment; ~**er** n (*US*) poussette f.

strong [strɔŋ] a fort(e); vigoureux(euse); solide; vif(vive); **they are 50** ~ ils sont au nombre de 50; ~**box** n coffre-fort m; ~**hold** n bastion m; ~**ly** ad fortement, avec force; vigoureusement; solidement; ~**room** n chambre forte.

strove [strəuv] pt, pp of **strive**.

struck [strʌk] pt, pp of **strike**.

structural ['strʌktʃərəl] a structural(e); (*CONSTR*) de construction; affectant les parties portantes.

structure ['strʌktʃə*] n structure f; (*building*) construction f; édifice m.

struggle ['strʌgl] n lutte f // vi lutter, se battre.

strum [strʌm] vt (*guitar*) gratter de.

strung [strʌŋ] pt, pp of **string**.

strut [strʌt] n étai m, support m // vi se pavaner.

stub [stʌb] n bout m; (*of ticket etc*) talon m // vt: **to** ~ **one's toe** se heurter le doigt de pied; **to** ~ **out** vt écraser.

stubble ['stʌbl] n chaume m; (*on chin*) barbe f de plusieurs jours.

stubborn ['stʌbən] a têtu(e), obstiné(e); opiniâtre.

stucco ['stʌkəu] n stuc m.

stuck [stʌk] pt, pp of **stick** // a (*jammed*) bloqué(e), coincé(e); ~**up** a prétentieux(euse).

stud [stʌd] n clou m (à grosse tête); bouton m de col; (*of horses*) écurie f, haras m; (*also:* ~ **horse**) étalon m // vt (*fig*): ~**ded with** parsemé(e) or criblé(e) de.

student ['stju:dənt] n étudiant/e // cpd estudiantin(e); universitaire; d'étudiant; ~ **driver** n (*US*) (conducteur/trice) débutant(e).

studio ['stju:dɪəu] n studio m, atelier m.

studious ['stju:dɪəs] a studieux(euse), appliqué(e); (*studied*) étudié(e); ~**ly** ad (*carefully*) soigneusement.

study ['stʌdɪ] n étude f; (*room*) bureau m // vt étudier; examiner // vi étudier, faire ses études.

stuff [stʌf] n chose(s) f(pl), truc m; affaires fpl, trucs; (*substance*) substance f // vt rembourrer; (*CULIN*) farcir; ~**ing** n bourre f, rembourrage m; (*CULIN*) farce f; ~**y** a (*room*) mal ventilé(e) or aéré(e); (*ideas*) vieux jeu inv.

stumble ['stʌmbl] vi trébucher; **to** ~ **across** (*fig*) tomber sur; **stumbling block** n pierre f d'achoppement.

stump [stʌmp] n souche f; (*of limb*) moignon m // vt: **to be** ~**ed** sécher, ne pas savoir que répondre.

stun [stʌn] vt étourdir; abasourdir.

stung [stʌŋ] pt, pp of **sting**.

stunk [stʌŋk] pp of **stink**.

stunt [stʌnt] n tour m de force; truc m publicitaire; (*AVIAT*) acrobatie f // vt retarder, arrêter; ~**ed** a rabougri(e); ~**man** n cascadeur m.

stupendous [stju:'pɛndəs] a prodigieux(euse), fantastique.

stupid ['stju:pɪd] a stupide, bête; ~**ity** [-'pɪdɪtɪ] n stupidité f, bêtise f.

sturdy ['stɜ:dɪ] a robuste, vigoureux(euse); solide.

stutter ['stʌtə*] vi bégayer.

sty [staɪ] n (*of pigs*) porcherie f.

stye [staɪ] n (MED) orgelet m.

style [staɪl] n style m; (distinction) allure f, cachet m, style; **stylish** a élégant(e), chic inv; **stylist** n (hair stylist) coiffeur/euse.

stylus ['staɪləs] n (of record player) pointe f de lecture.

suave [swɑːv] a doucereux(euse), onctueux(euse).

sub... [sʌb] préfix sub..., sous-; **~conscious** a subconscient(e) // n subconscient m; **~contract** vt sous-traiter.

subdue [səb'djuː] vt subjuguer, soumettre; **~d** a contenu(e), atténué(e); (light) tamisé(e); (person) qui a perdu de son entrain.

subject n ['sʌbdʒɪkt] sujet m; (SCOL) matière f // vt [səb'dʒɛkt]: **to ~ to** soumettre à; exposer à; **to be ~ to** (law) être soumis(e) à; (disease) être sujet(te) à; **~ive** [səb'dʒɛktɪv] a subjectif(ive); **~ matter** n sujet m; contenu m.

subjunctive [səb'dʒʌŋktɪv] n subjonctif m.

sublet [sʌb'lɛt] vt sous-louer.

submachine gun [sʌbmə'ʃiːn-] n fusil-mitrailleur m.

submarine [sʌbmə'riːn] n sous-marin m.

submerge [səb'mɜːdʒ] vt submerger; immerger // vi plonger.

submission [səb'mɪʃən] n soumission f.

submissive [səb'mɪsɪv] a soumis(e).

submit [səb'mɪt] vt soumettre // vi se soumettre.

subnormal [sʌb'nɔːməl] a au-dessous de la normale; (backward) arriéré(e).

subordinate [sə'bɔːdɪnət] a, n subordonné(e).

subpoena [səb'piːnə] n (LAW) citation f, assignation f.

subscribe [səb'skraɪb] vi cotiser; **to ~ to** (opinion, fund) souscrire à; (newspaper) s'abonner à; être abonné(e) à; **~r** n (to periodical, telephone) abonné/e.

subscription [səb'skrɪpʃən] n souscription f; abonnement m.

subsequent ['sʌbsɪkwənt] a ultérieur(e), suivant(e); consécutif(ive); **~ly** ad par la suite.

subside [səb'saɪd] vi s'affaisser; (flood) baisser; (wind) tomber; **~nce** ['saɪdns] n affaissement m.

subsidiary [səb'sɪdɪərɪ] a subsidiaire; accessoire // n filiale f.

subsidize ['sʌbsɪdaɪz] vt subventionner.

subsidy ['sʌbsɪdɪ] n subvention f.

substance ['sʌbstəns] n substance f; (fig) essentiel m.

substantial [səb'stænʃl] a substantiel(le); (fig) important(e).

substantiate [səb'stænʃɪeɪt] vt étayer, fournir des preuves à l'appui de.

substitute ['sʌbstɪtjuːt] n (person) remplaçant(e); (thing) succédané m // vt: **to ~ sth/sb for** substituer qch/qn à, remplacer par qch/qn.

subterranean [sʌbtə'reɪnɪən] a souterrain(e).

subtitle ['sʌbtaɪtl] n (CINEMA) sous-titre m.

subtle ['sʌtl] a subtil(e).

subtotal [sʌb'təʊtl] n total partiel.

subtract [səb'trækt] vt soustraire, retrancher; **~ion** [-'trækʃən] n soustraction f.

suburb ['sʌbɜːb] n faubourg m; **the ~s** la banlieue; **~an** [sə'bɜːbən] a de banlieue, suburbain(e); **~ia** [sə'bɜːbɪə] n la banlieue.

subway ['sʌbweɪ] n (US) métro m; (Brit) passage souterrain.

succeed [sək'siːd] vi réussir; avoir du succès // vt succéder à; **to ~ in doing** réussir à faire; **~ing** a (following) suivant(e).

success [sək'sɛs] n succès m; réussite f; **~ful** (venture) couronné(e) de succès; **to be ~ful** (in doing) réussir (à faire); **~fully** ad avec succès.

succession [sək'sɛʃən] n succession f.

successive [sək'sɛsɪv] *a* successif(ive); consécutif(ive).

such [sʌtʃ] *a* tel(telle); *(of that kind)*: ~ **a book** un livre de ce genre or pareil, un tel livre; ~ **books** des livres de ce genre or pareils, de tels livres; *(so much)*: ~ **courage** un tel courage // *ad* si; ~ **a long trip** un si long voyage; ~ **good books** de si bons livres; ~ **a lot of** tellement or tant de; ~ **as** *(like)* tel(telle) que, comme; ~ **a noise** ~ **as** to un bruit de nature à; **as** ~ *ad* en tant que tel(telle), à proprement parler; ~-**and**-~ *a* tel(telle) ou tel(telle).

suck [sʌk] *vt* sucer; *(breast, bottle)* téter; ~**er** *n* (BOT, ZOOL, TECH) ventouse *f*; *(col)* naïf/ïve, poire *f*.

suction ['sʌkʃən] *n* succion *f*.

sudden ['sʌdn] *a* soudain(e), subit(e); **all of a** ~ soudain, tout à coup; ~**ly** *ad* brusquement, tout à coup, soudain.

suds [sʌdz] *npl* eau savonneuse.

sue [su:] *vt* poursuivre en justice, intenter un procès à.

suede [sweɪd] *n* daim *m*, cuir suédé // *cpd* de daim.

suet ['sʊɪt] *n* graisse *f* de rognon or de bœuf.

suffer ['sʌfə*] *vt* souffrir, subir; *(bear)* tolérer, supporter // *vi* souffrir; ~**er** *n* malade *m/f*; victime *m/f*; ~**ing** *n* souffrance(s) *f(pl)*.

sufficient [sə'fɪʃənt] *a* suffisant(e); ~ **money** suffisamment d'argent; ~**ly** *ad* suffisamment, assez.

suffocate ['sʌfəkeɪt] *vi* suffoquer; étouffer.

suffused [sə'fju:zd] *a*: **to be** ~ **with** baigner dans, être imprégné(e) de.

sugar ['ʃʊgə*] *n* sucre *m* // *vt* sucrer; ~ **beet** *n* betterave sucrière; ~ **cane** *n* canne *f* à sucre; ~**y** *a* sucré(e).

suggest [sə'dʒɛst] *vt* suggérer, proposer; dénoter; ~**ion** *n* [-'dʒɛstʃən] *n* suggestion *f*.

suicide ['sʊɪsaɪd] *n* suicide *m*.

suit [su:t] *n* *(man's)* costume *m*,

complet *m*; *(woman's)* tailleur *m*, ensemble *m*; *(CARDS)* couleur *f* // *vt* aller à; convenir à; *(adapt)*: **to** ~ **sth to** adapter or approprier qch à; ~**able** *a* qui convient; approprié(e); ~**ably** *ad* comme il se doit (or se devait etc), convenablement.

suitcase [su:tkeɪs] *n* valise *f*.

suite [swi:t] *n* *(of rooms, also MUS)* suite *f*; *(furniture)*: **bedroom/dining room** ~ (ensemble *m* de) chambre *f* à coucher/salle *f* à manger.

suitor ['su:tə*] *n* soupirant *m*, prétendant *m*.

sulfur ['sʌlfə*] *n* *(US)* = **sulphur**.

sulk [sʌlk] *vi* bouder; ~**y** *a* boudeur(euse), maussade.

sullen ['sʌlən] *a* renfrogné(e), maussade; morne.

sulphur, *(US)* **sulfur** ['sʌlfə*] *n* soufre *m*.

sultan ['sʌltən] *n* sultan *m*.

sultana [sʌl'tɑ:nə] *n* *(fruit)* raisin (sec) de Smyrne.

sultry ['sʌltrɪ] *a* étouffant(e).

sum [sʌm] *n* somme *f*; *(SCOL etc)* calcul *m*; **to** ~ **up** *vt, vi* résumer.

summarize ['sʌməraɪz] *vt* résumer.

summary ['sʌmərɪ] *n* résumé *m* // *a* *(justice)* sommaire.

summer ['sʌmə*] *n* été *m* // *cpd* d'été, estival(e); ~**house** *n* *(in garden)* pavillon *m*; ~**time** *n* *(season)* été *m*; ~ **time** *n* *(by clock)* heure *f* d'été.

summit ['sʌmɪt] *n* sommet *m*.

summon ['sʌmən] *vt* appeler, convoquer; **to** ~ **up** *vt* rassembler, faire appel à; ~**s** *n* citation *f*, assignation *f*.

sump [sʌmp] *n* *(Brit AUT)* carter *m*.

sun [sʌn] *n* soleil *m*; **in the** ~ au soleil; ~**bathe** *vi* prendre un bain de soleil; ~**burn** *n* coup *m* de soleil; *(tan)* bronzage *m*.

Sunday ['sʌndɪ] *n* dimanche *m*; ~ **school** *n* ≈ catéchisme *m*.

sundial ['sʌndaɪəl] *n* cadran *m* solaire.

sundown ['sʌndaʊn] *n* coucher *m* du soleil.

sundry ['sʌndrɪ] a divers(e), différent(e); **all and ~** tout le monde, n'importe qui; **sundries** npl articles divers.

sunflower ['sʌnflauə*] n tournesol m.

sung [sʌŋ] pp of **sing**.

sunglasses ['sʌnɡlɑːsɪz] npl lunettes fpl de soleil.

sunk [sʌŋk] pp of **sink**.

sun: **~light** n (lumière f du) soleil m; **~ny** a ensoleillé(e); (fig) épanoui(e), radieux(euse); **~rise** n lever m du soleil; **~roof** n (AUT) toit ouvrant; **~set** n coucher m du soleil; **~shade** n (over table) parasol m; **~shine** n (lumière f du) soleil m; **~stroke** n insolation f, coup m de soleil; **~tan** n bronzage m; **~tan oil** n huile f solaire.

super ['suːpə*] a (col) formidable.

superannuation [suːpərænjuˈeɪʃən] n cotisations fpl pour la pension.

superb [suːˈpəːb] a superbe, magnifique.

supercilious [suːpəˈsɪlɪəs] a hautain(e), dédaigneux(euse).

superficial [suːpəˈfɪʃəl] a superficiel(le).

superintendent [suːpərɪnˈtendənt] n directeur/trice; (POLICE) ≈ commissaire m.

superior [suˈpɪərɪə*] a, n supérieur(e); **~ity** [-ˈɔrɪtɪ] n supériorité f.

superlative [suˈpəːlətɪv] a sans pareil(le), suprême // n (LING) superlatif m.

superman ['suːpəmæn] n surhomme m.

supermarket ['suːpəmɑːkɪt] n supermarché m.

supernatural [suːpəˈnætʃərəl] a surnaturel(le).

superpower ['suːpəpauə*] n (POL) superpuissance f.

supersede [suːpəˈsiːd] vt remplacer, supplanter.

superstitious [suːpəˈstɪʃəs] a superstitieux(euse).

supervise ['suːpəvaɪz] vt surveiller; diriger; **supervision** [-ˈvɪʒən] n surveillance f; contrôle m; **supervisor** n surveillant/e; (in shop) chef m de rayon.

supine ['suːpaɪn] a couché(e) or étendu(e) sur le dos.

supper ['sʌpə*] n dîner m; (late) souper m.

supple ['sʌpl] a souple.

supplement n ['sʌplɪmənt] supplément m // vt [sʌplɪˈment] ajouter à, compléter; **~ary** [-ˈmentərɪ] a supplémentaire.

supplier [səˈplaɪə*] n fournisseur m.

supply [səˈplaɪ] vt (provide) fournir; (equip): **to ~ (with)** approvisionner or ravitailler (en); fournir (en); alimenter (en) // n provision f, réserve f; (supplying) approvisionnement m; (TECH) alimentation f // cpd (teacher etc) suppléant(e); **supplies** npl (food) vivres mpl; (MIL) subsistances fpl.

support [səˈpɔːt] n (moral, financial etc) soutien m, appui m; (TECH) support m, soutien m // vt soutenir, supporter; (financially) subvenir aux besoins de; (uphold) être pour, être partisan de, appuyer; **~er** n (POL etc) partisan/e; (SPORT) supporter m.

suppose [səˈpauz] vt, vi supposer; imaginer; **to be ~d to do** être censé(e) faire; **~dly** [səˈpauzɪdlɪ] ad soi-disant; **supposing** cj si, à supposer que + sub.

suppress [səˈpres] vt réprimer; supprimer; étouffer; refouler.

supreme [suˈpriːm] a suprême.

surcharge ['səːtʃɑːdʒ] n surcharge f; (extra tax) surtaxe f.

sure [ʃuə*] a (gen) sûr(e); (definite, convinced) sûr, certain(e); **~!** (of course) bien sûr!; **~ enough** effectivement; **to make ~ of sth** s'assurer de or vérifier qch; **to make ~ that** s'assurer or vérifier que; **~ly** ad sûrement; certainement.

surety ['ʃuərətɪ] n caution f.

surf [sə:f] n ressac m.

surface ['sə:fis] n surface f // vt (road) poser le revêtement de // vi remonter à la surface; faire surface; **~ mail** n courrier m par voie de terre (or maritime).

surfboard ['sə:fbɔ:d] n planche f de surf.

surfeit ['sə:fit] n: **a ~ of** un excès de; une indigestion de.

surfing ['sə:fiŋ] n surf m.

surge [sə:dʒ] n vague f, montée f // vi déferler.

surgeon ['sə:dʒən] n chirurgien m.

surgery ['sə:dʒəri] n chirurgie f; (Brit: room) cabinet m (de consultation); **to undergo ~** être opéré(e); **~ hours** npl (Brit) heures fpl de consultation.

surgical ['sə:dʒikl] a chirurgical(e); **~ spirit** n (Brit) alcool m à 90°.

surly ['sə:li] a revêche, maussade.

surname ['sə:neim] n nom m de famille.

surplus ['sə:pləs] n surplus m, excédent m // a en surplus, de trop.

surprise [sə'praiz] n (gen) surprise f; (astonishment) étonnement m // vt surprendre; étonner; **surprising** a surprenant(e), étonnant(e); **surprisingly** ad (easy, helpful) étonnamment, étrangement.

surrender [sə'rendə*] n reddition f, capitulation f // vi se rendre, capituler.

surreptitious [sʌrəp'tiʃəs] a subreptice, furtif(ive).

surrogate ['sʌrəgit] n substitut m; **~ mother** n mère porteuse or de substitution.

surround [sə'raund] vt entourer; (MIL etc) encercler; **~ing** a environnant(e); **~ings** npl environs mpl, alentours mpl.

surveillance [sə:'veiləns] n surveillance f.

survey ['sə:vei] n enquête f, étude f; (in housebuying etc) inspection f, (rapport m d')expertise f; (of land) levé m // vt [sə:'vei] passer en revue;

enquêter sur; inspecter; **~or** n expert m; (arpenteur m) géomètre m.

survival [sə'vaivl] n survie f; (relic) vestige m.

survive [sə'vaiv] vi survivre; (custom etc) subsister // vt survivre à; **survivor** n survivant/e.

susceptible [sə'septəbl] a: **~ (to)** sensible (à); (disease) prédisposé(e) (à).

suspect a, n ['sʌspekt] suspect(e) // vt [səs'pekt] soupçonner, suspecter.

suspend [səs'pend] vt suspendre; **~ed sentence** n condamnation f avec sursis; **~er belt** n porte-jarretelles m inv; **~ers** npl (Brit) jarretelles fpl; (US) bretelles fpl.

suspense [səs'pens] n attente f; (in film etc) suspense m.

suspension [səs'penʃən] n (gen, AUT) suspension f; (of driving licence) retrait m provisoire; **~ bridge** n pont suspendu.

suspicion [səs'piʃən] n soupçon(s) m(pl).

suspicious [səs'piʃəs] a (suspecting) soupçonneux(euse), méfiant(e); (causing suspicion) suspect(e).

sustain [səs'tein] vt supporter; soutenir; corroborer; (suffer) subir; recevoir; **~ed** a (effort) soutenu(e), prolongé(e).

sustenance ['sʌstinəns] n nourriture f; moyens mpl de subsistance.

swab [swɔb] n (MED) tampon m; prélèvement m.

swagger ['swægə*] vi plastronner.

swallow ['swɔləu] n (bird) hirondelle f // vt avaler; (fig) gober; **to ~ up** vt engloutir.

swam [swæm] pt of **swim**.

swamp [swɔmp] n marais m, marécage m // vt submerger.

swan [swɔn] n cygne m.

swap [swɔp] vt: **to ~ (for)** échanger (contre), troquer (contre).

swarm [swɔ:m] n essaim m // vi fourmiller, grouiller.

swarthy ['swɔ:ði] a basané(e), bistré(e).

swastika ['swɔstɪkə] *n* croix gammée.

swat [swɔt] *vt* écraser.

sway [sweɪ] *vi* se balancer, osciller; tanguer // *vt* (*influence*) influencer.

swear [sweə*], *pt* **swore**, *pp* **sworn** *vi* jurer; **to ~ to** sth jurer de qch; **~word** *n* gros mot, juron *m*.

sweat [swet] *n* sueur *f*, transpiration *f* // *vi* suer.

sweater ['swetə*] *n* tricot *m*, pull *m*.

sweaty ['swetɪ] *a* en sueur, moite *or* mouillé(e) de sueur.

Swede [swiːd] *n* Suédois/e.

swede [swiːd] *n* (*Brit*) rutabaga *m*.

Sweden ['swiːdn] *n* Suède *f*.

Swedish ['swiːdɪʃ] *a* suédois(e) // *n* (*LING*) suédois *m*.

sweep [swiːp] *n* coup *m* de balai; (*curve*) grande courbe; (*range*) champ *m*; (*also*: **chimney ~**) ramoneur *m* // *vb* (*pt, pp* **swept**) *vt* balayer // *vi* avancer majestueusement *or* rapidement; s'élancer; s'étendre; **to ~ away** *vt* balayer; entraîner; emporter; **to ~ past** *vi* passer majestueusement *or* rapidement; **to ~ up** *vt, vi* balayer; **~ing** *a* (*gesture*) large; circulaire; **a ~ing statement** une généralisation hâtive.

sweet [swiːt] *n* (*Brit*: *pudding*) dessert *m*; (*candy*) bonbon *m* // *a* doux(douce); (*not savoury*) sucré(e); (*fresh*) frais(fraîche), pur(e); (*fig*) agréable, doux, gentil(le); mignon(ne); **~corn** *n* maïs doux; **~en** *vt* sucrer; adoucir; **~heart** *n* amoureux/euse; **~ness** *n* goût sucré; douceur *f*; **~ pea** *n* pois *m* de senteur.

swell [swel] *n* (*of sea*) houle *f* // *a* (*col*: *excellent*) chouette // *vb* (*pt* **~ed**, *pp* **swollen** *or* **~ed**) *vt* augmenter; grossir // *vi* grossir, augmenter; (*sound*) s'enfler; (*MED*) enfler; **~ing** *n* (*MED*) enflure *f*; grosseur *f*.

sweltering ['sweltərɪŋ] *a* étouffant(e), oppressant(e).

swept [swept] *pt, pp* of **sweep**.

swerve [swəːv] *vi* faire une embardée *or* un écart; dévier.

swift [swɪft] *n* (*bird*) martinet *m* // *a* rapide, prompt(e).

swig [swɪg] *n* (*col*: *drink*) lampée *f*.

swill [swɪl] *n* pâtée *f* // *vt* (*also*: **~ out, ~ down**) laver à grande eau.

swim [swɪm] *n*: **to go for a ~** aller nager *or* se baigner // *vb* (*pt* **swam**, *pp* **swum**) *vi* nager; (*SPORT*) faire de la natation; (*head, room*) tourner // *vt* traverser (à la nage); faire (à la nage); **~mer** *n* nageur/euse; **~ming** *n* nage *f*, natation *f*; **~ming cap** *n* bonnet *m* de bain; **~ming costume** *n* (*Brit*) maillot *m* de bain; **~ming pool** *n* piscine *f*; **~suit** *n* maillot *m* (de bain).

swindle ['swɪndl] *n* escroquerie *f*.

swine [swaɪn] *n* (*pl inv*) pourceau *m*, porc *m*; (*col!*) salaud *m* (!).

swing [swɪŋ] *n* balançoire *f*; (*movement*) balancement *m*, oscillations *fpl*; (*MUS*) swing *m*; rythme *m* // *vb* (*pt, pp* **swung**) *vt* balancer, faire osciller; (*also*: **~ round**) tourner, faire virer // *vi* se balancer, osciller; (*also*: **~ round**) virer, tourner; **to be in full ~** battre son plein; **~ door**, (*US*) **~ing door** *n* porte battante.

swingeing ['swɪndʒɪŋ] *a* (*Brit*) écrasant(e); considérable.

swipe [swaɪp] *vt* (*hit*) frapper à toute volée; gifler; (*col*: *steal*) piquer.

swirl [swəːl] *vi* tourbillonner, tournoyer.

swish [swɪʃ] *a* (*col*: *smart*) rupin(e) // *vi* siffler.

Swiss [swɪs] *a* suisse // *n* (*pl inv*) Suisse/esse.

switch [swɪtʃ] *n* (*for light, radio etc*) bouton *m*; (*change*) changement *m*, revirement *m* // *vt* (*change*) changer; intervertir; **to ~ off** *vt* éteindre; (*engine*) arrêter; **to ~ on** *vt* allumer; (*engine, machine*) mettre en marche; **~board** *n* (*TEL*) standard *m*.

Switzerland ['swɪtsələnd] *n* Suisse *f*.

swivel ['swɪvl] *vi* (*also*: **~ round**) pivoter, tourner.

swollen ['swəʊlən] *pp* of **swell**.
swoon [swu:n] *vi* se pâmer.
swoop [swu:p] *vi* (*also*: ~ **down**) descendre en piqué, piquer.
swop [swɒp] *vt* = **swap**.
sword [sɔ:d] *n* épée *f*; ~**fish** *n* espadon *m*.
swore [swɔ:*] *pt* of **swear**.
sworn [swɔ:n] *pp* of **swear**.
swot [swɒt] *vt, vi* bûcher, potasser.
swum [swʌm] *pp* of **swim**.
swung [swʌŋ] *pt, pp* of **swing**.
syllable ['sɪləbl] *n* syllabe *f*.
syllabus ['sɪləbəs] *n* programme *m*.
symbol ['sɪmbl] *n* symbole *m*.
symmetry ['sɪmɪtrɪ] *n* symétrie *f*.
sympathetic [sɪmpə'θetɪk] *a* compatissant(e); bienveillant(e), compréhensif(ive); ~ **towards** bien disposé(e) envers.
sympathize ['sɪmpəθaɪz] *vi*: to ~ **with** sb plaindre qn; s'associer à la douleur de qn; ~**r** *n* (*POL*) sympathisant*e.
sympathy ['sɪmpəθɪ] *n* compassion *f*; **in** ~ **with** en accord avec; (*strike*) en ou par solidarité avec; **with our deepest** ~ en vous priant d'accepter nos sincères condoléances.
symphony ['sɪmfənɪ] *n* symphonie *f*.
symptom ['sɪmptəm] *n* symptôme *m*; indice *m*.
synagogue ['sɪnəgɒg] *n* synagogue *f*.
syndicate ['sɪndɪkɪt] *n* syndicat *m*, coopérative *f*.
synonym ['sɪnənɪm] *n* synonyme *m*.
syntax ['sɪntæks] *n* syntaxe *f*.
synthetic [sɪn'θetɪk] *a* synthétique.
syphon ['saɪfən] *n, vb* = **siphon**.
Syria ['sɪrɪə] *n* Syrie *f*.
syringe [sɪ'rɪndʒ] *n* seringue *f*.
syrup ['sɪrəp] *n* sirop *m*; (*also*: golden ~) mélasse raffinée.
system ['sɪstəm] *n* système *m*; (*order*) méthode *f*; (*ANAT*) organisme *m*; ~**atic** [-'mætɪk] *a* systématique; méthodique; ~ **disk** *n* (*COMPUT*) disque *m* système; ~**s analyst** *n* analyste-programmeur *m/f*.

T

ta [tɑ:] *excl* (*Brit col*) merci!
tab [tæb] *n* (*loop on coat etc*) attache *f*; (*label*) étiquette *f*; **to keep** ~**s on** (*fig*) surveiller.
tabby ['tæbɪ] *n* (*also*: ~ **cat**) chat/te tigré(e).
table ['teɪbl] *n* table *f* // *vt* (*Brit: motion etc*) présenter; **to lay or set the** ~ mettre le couvert ou la table; ~ **of contents** *n* table *f* des matières; ~**cloth** *n* nappe *f*; ~ **d'hôte** [tɑ:bl'dəʊt] *a* (*meal*) à prix fixe; ~ **lamp** *n* lampe décorative; ~**mat** *n* (*for plate*) napperon *m*, set *m*; (*for hot dish*) dessous-de-plat *m inv*; ~**spoon** *n* cuiller *f* de service; (*also*: ~**spoonful**: *as measurement*) cuillerée *f* à soupe.
tablet ['tæblɪt] *n* (*MED*) comprimé *m*; (*: for sucking*) pastille *f*; (*for writing*) bloc *m*; (*of stone*) plaque *f*.
table: ~ tennis *n* ping-pong *m*, tennis *m* de table; ~ **wine** *n* vin *m* de table.
tabulate ['tæbjuleɪt] *vt* (*data, figures*) mettre sous forme de table(s).
tacit ['tæsɪt] *a* tacite.
tack [tæk] *n* (*nail*) petit clou; (*stitch*) point *m* de bâti; (*NAUT*) bord *m*, bordée *f* // *vt* clouer; bâtir // *vi* tirer un or des bord(s).
tackle ['tækl] *n* matériel *m*, équipement *m*; (*for lifting*) appareil *m* de levage; (*RUGBY*) plaquage *m* // *vt* (*difficulty*) s'attaquer à; (*RUGBY*) plaquer.
tacky ['tækɪ] *a* collant(e); pas sec(sèche).
tact [tækt] *n* tact *m*; ~**ful** *a* plein(e) de tact.
tactical ['tæktɪkl] *a* tactique.
tactics ['tæktɪks] *n, npl* tactique *f*.
tactless ['tæktlɪs] *a* qui manque de tact.
tadpole ['tædpəʊl] *n* têtard *m*.
taffy ['tæfɪ] *n* (*US*) (bonbon *m* au) ca-

ramel m.

tag [tæg] n étiquette f; **to ~ along** vi suivre.

tail [teɪl] n queue f; (of shirt) pan m // vt (follow) suivre, filer; **to ~ away, ~ off** vi (in size, quality etc) baisser peu à peu; **~back** n (Brit AUT) bouchon m; **~ coat** n habit m; **~ end** n bout m, fin f; **~gate** n (AUT) hayon m arrière.

tailor ['teɪlə*] n tailleur m (artisan); **~ing** n (cut) coupe f; **~-made** a fait(e) sur mesure; (fig) conçu(e) spécialement.

tailwind ['teɪlwɪnd] n vent m arrière inv.

tainted ['teɪntɪd] a (food) gâté(e); (water, air) infecté(e); (fig) souillé(e).

take, pt **took**, pp **taken** [teɪk, tuk, 'teɪkn] vt prendre; (gain: prize) remporter; (require: effort, courage) demander; (tolerate) accepter, supporter; (hold: passengers etc) contenir; (accompany) emmener, accompagner; (bring, carry) apporter, emporter; (exam) passer, se présenter à; **to ~ sth from** (drawer etc) prendre qch dans; (person) prendre qch à; **I ~ it that** je suppose que; **to ~ for a walk** (child, dog) emmener promener; **to ~ after** vt fus ressembler à; **to ~ apart** vt démonter; **to ~ away** vt emporter; enlever; **to ~ back** vt (return) rendre, rapporter; (one's words) retirer; **to ~ down** vt (building) démolir; (letter etc) prendre, écrire; **to ~ in** vt (deceive) tromper, rouler; (understand) comprendre, saisir; (include) couvrir, inclure; (lodger) prendre; **to ~ off** vi (AVIAT) décoller // vt (remove) enlever; (imitate) imiter, pasticher; **to ~ on** vt (work) accepter, se charger de; (employee) prendre, embaucher; (opponent) accepter de se battre contre; **to ~ out** vt sortir; (remove) enlever; (licence) prendre, se procurer; **to ~ sth out of sth** enlever qch de; (drawer, pocket etc)

prendre qch dans qch; **to ~ over** vt (business) reprendre // vi: **to ~ over from sb** prendre la relève de qn; **to ~ to** vt fus (person) se prendre d'amitié pour; (activity) prendre goût à; **to ~ up** vt (one's story, a dress) reprendre; (occupy: time, space) prendre, occuper; (engage in: hobby etc) se mettre à; **~away** a (food) à emporter; **~home pay** n salaire net; **~off** n (AVIAT) décollage m; **~out** a (US) = **~away**; **~over** n (COMM) rachat m.

takings ['teɪkɪŋz] npl (COMM) recette f.

talc [tælk] n (also: **~um powder**) talc m.

tale [teɪl] n (story) conte m, histoire f; (account) récit m; (pej) histoire f; **to tell ~s** (fig) rapporter.

talent ['tælnt] n talent m, don m; **~ed** a doué(e), plein(e) de talent.

talk [tɔːk] n propos mpl; (gossip) racontars mpl (pej); (conversation) discussion f; (interview) entretien m; (a speech) causerie f, exposé m // vi (chatter) bavarder; **~s** npl (POL etc) entretiens mpl; conférence f; **to ~ about** parler de; (converse) s'entretenir or parler de; **to ~ sb out of/into doing** persuader qn de ne pas faire/de faire; **to ~ shop** parler métier or affaires; **to ~ over** vt discuter (de); **~ative** a bavard(e); **~ show** n causerie (télévisée or radiodiffusée).

tall [tɔːl] a (person) grand(e); (building, tree) haut(e); **to be 6 feet ~** mesurer 1 mètre 80; **~boy** n (Brit) grande commode; **~ story** n histoire f invraisemblable.

tally ['tælɪ] n compte m // vi: **to ~ (with)** correspondre (à).

talon ['tælən] n griffe f; (eagle) serre f.

tame [teɪm] a apprivoisé(e); (fig: story, style) insipide.

tamper ['tæmpə*] vi: **to ~ with** toucher à (en cachette ou sans permission).

tampon ['tæmpən] n tampon m hygiénique or périodique.

tan [tæn] n (also: **sun~**) bronzage m // vt, vi bronzer, brunir // a (colour) brun roux inv.

tang [tæŋ] n odeur (or saveur) piquante.

tangent ['tændʒənt] n (MATH) tangente f; **to go off at a ~** (fig) changer complètement de direction.

tangerine [tændʒə'ri:n] n mandarine f.

tangle ['tæŋgl] n enchevêtrement m // vt enchevêtrer.

tank [tæŋk] n réservoir m; (for processing) cuve f; (for fish) aquarium m; (MIL) char m d'assaut, tank m.

tanker ['tæŋkə*] n (ship) pétrolier m, tanker m; (truck) camion-citerne m.

tantalizing ['tæntəlaɪzɪŋ] a (smell) extrêmement appétissant(e); (offer) terriblement tentant(e).

tantamount ['tæntəmaunt] a: **~ to** qui équivaut à.

tantrum ['tæntrəm] n accès m de colère.

tap [tæp] n (on sink etc) robinet m; (gentle blow) petite tape f; (resources) exploiter, utiliser; (telephone) mettre sur écoute; **on ~** (fig: resources) disponible; **~-dancing** n claquettes fpl.

tape [teɪp] n ruban m; (also: **magnetic ~**) bande f (magnétique) // vt (record) enregistrer (sur bande); **~ measure** n mètre m à ruban.

taper ['teɪpə*] n cierge m // vi s'effiler.

tape recorder n magnétophone m.

tapestry ['tæpɪstrɪ] n tapisserie f.

tar [tɑ:] n goudron m.

target ['tɑ:gɪt] n cible f; (fig: objective) objectif m.

tariff ['tærɪf] n (COMM) tarif m; (taxes) tarif douanier.

tarmac ['tɑ:mæk] n (Brit: on road) macadam m; (AVIAT) aire f d'envol.

tarnish ['tɑ:nɪʃ] vt ternir.

tarpaulin [tɑ:'pɔ:lɪn] n bâche goudronnée.

tarragon ['tærəgən] n estragon m.

tart [tɑ:t] n (CULIN) tarte f; (Brit col: pej: woman) poule f // a (flavour) aigre, acide(tte); **to ~ o.s. up** (col) se faire beau(belle); (: pej) s'attifer.

tartan ['tɑ:tn] n tartan m // a écossais(e).

tartar ['tɑ:tə*] n (on teeth) tartre m; **~ sauce** n sauce f tartare.

task [tɑ:sk] n tâche f; **to take to ~** prendre à partie; **~ force** n (MIL, POLICE) détachement spécial.

tassel ['tæsl] n gland m; pompon m.

taste [teɪst] n goût m; (fig: glimpse, idea) aperçu m // vt goûter // vi: **to ~ of** (fish etc) avoir le or un goût de; **it ~s like fish** ça a un or le goût de poisson, on dirait du poisson; **you can ~ the garlic (in it)** on sent bien l'ail; **can I have a ~ of this wine?** puis-je goûter un peu de ce vin?; **to have a ~ for sth** aimer qch, avoir un penchant pour qch; **in good/bad ~** de bon/mauvais goût; **~ful** a de bon goût; **~less** a (food) qui n'a aucun goût; (remark) de mauvais goût; **tasty** a savoureux(euse), délicieux(euse).

tatters ['tætəz] npl: **in ~** (also: **tattered**) en lambeaux.

tattoo [tə'tu:] n tatouage m; (spectacle) parade f militaire // vt tatouer.

taught [tɔ:t] pt, pp of **teach**.

taunt [tɔ:nt] n raillerie f // vt railler.

Taurus ['tɔ:rəs] n le Taureau.

taut [tɔ:t] a tendu(e).

tawdry ['tɔ:drɪ] a (d'un mauvais goût) criard.

tax [tæks] n (on goods etc) taxe f; (on income) impôts mpl, contributions fpl // vt taxer; imposer; (fig: strain: patience etc) mettre à l'épreuve; **~able** a (income) imposable; **~ation** [-'seɪʃən] n taxation f; impôts mpl, contributions fpl; **~ avoidance** n évasion fiscale; **~ collector** n percepteur m; **~ disc** n (Brit AUT) vignette f (automobile); **~ evasion** n fraude fiscale; **~-free**

a exempt(e) d'impôts.

taxi ['tæksɪ] *n* taxi *m* // *vi* (*AVIAT*) rouler (lentement) au sol; ~ **driver** *n* chauffeur *m* de taxi; ~ **rank** (*Brit*), ~ **stand** *n* station *f* de taxis.

tax: ~ **payer** *n* contribuable *m/f*; ~ **relief** *n* dégrèvement *or* allègement fiscal; ~ **return** *n* déclaration *f* d'impôts *or* de revenus.

TB *n abbr* = tuberculosis.

tea [tiː] *n* thé *m*; (*Brit: snack: for children*) goûter *m*; **high** ~ (*Brit*) collation combinant goûter et dîner; ~ **bag** *n* sachet *m* de thé; ~ **break** *n* (*Brit*) pause-thé *f*.

teach [tiːtʃ] , *pt, pp* **taught** *vt*: to ~ sb sth, ~ sth to sb apprendre qch à qn; (*in school etc*) enseigner qch à qn // *vi* enseigner; ~**er** *n* (*in secondary school*) professeur *m*; (*in primary school*) instituteur/trice; ~**ing** *n* enseignement *m*.

tea cosy *n* couvre-théière *m*.

teacup ['tiːkʌp] *n* tasse *f* à thé.

teak [tiːk] *n* teck *m*.

team [tiːm] *n* équipe *f*; (*of animals*) attelage *m*; ~**work** *n* travail *m* d'équipe.

teapot ['tiːpɔt] *n* théière *f*.

tear [tɛə*] déchirure *f*; [tɪə*] larme *f* // *vb* [tɛə*] (*pt* **tore**, *pp* **torn**) *vt* déchirer // *vi* se déchirer; **in** ~**s** en larmes; **to** ~ **along** *vi* (*rush*) aller à toute vitesse; **to** ~ **up** *vi* (*sheet of paper etc*) déchirer, mettre en morceaux *or* pièces; ~**ful** *a* larmoyant(e); ~ **gas** *n* gaz *m* lacrymogène.

tearoom ['tiːruːm] *n* salon *m* de thé.

tease [tiːz] *vt* taquiner; (*unkindly*) tourmenter.

tea set *n* service *m* à thé.

teaspoon ['tiːspuːn] *n* petite cuiller; (*also:* ~**ful:** *as measurement*) = cuillerée *f* à café.

teat [tiːt] *n* tétine *f*.

teatime ['tiːtaɪm] *n* l'heure *f* du thé.

tea towel *n* (*Brit*) torchon *m* (à vaisselle).

technical ['tɛknɪkl] *a* technique;

~**ity** [-'kælɪt] *n* technicité *f*; (*detail*) détail *m* technique.

technician [tɛk'nɪʃən] *n* technicien/ne.

technique [tɛk'niːk] *n* technique *f*.

technological [tɛknə'lɔdʒɪkl] *a* technologique.

technology [tɛk'nɔlədʒɪ] *n* technologie *f*.

teddy (bear) ['tɛdɪ(bɛə*)] *n* ours *m* (en peluche).

tedious ['tiːdɪəs] *a* fastidieux(euse).

tee [tiː] *n* (*GOLF*) tee *m*.

teem [tiːm] *vi*: to ~ (**with**) grouiller (de); **it is** ~**ing (with rain)** il pleut à torrents.

teenage ['tiːneɪdʒ] *a* (*fashions etc*) pour jeunes, pour adolescents; ~**r** *n* jeune *m/f*, adolescent/e.

teens [tiːnz] *npl*: **to be in one's** ~ être adolescent(e).

tee-shirt ['tiːʃəːt] *n* = T-shirt.

teeter ['tiːtə*] *vi* chanceler, vaciller.

teeth [tiːθ] *npl of* **tooth**.

teethe [tiːð] *vi* percer ses dents.

teething ['tiːðɪŋ]: ~ **ring** *n* anneau *m* (*pour bébé qui perce ses dents*); ~ **troubles** *npl* (*fig*) difficultés initiales.

teetotal ['tiː'təutl] *a* (*person*) qui ne boit jamais d'alcool.

telegram ['tɛlɪɡræm] *n* télégramme *m*.

telegraph ['tɛlɪɡrɑːf] *n* télégraphe *m*.

telephone ['tɛlɪfəun] *n* téléphone *m* // *vt* (*person*) téléphoner à; (*message*) téléphoner; ~ **booth**, (*Brit*) ~ **box** *n* cabine *f* téléphonique; ~ **call** *n* coup *m* de téléphone, appel *m* téléphonique, communication *f* téléphonique; ~ **directory** *n* annuaire *m* (du téléphone); ~ **number** *n* numéro *m* de téléphone; ~ **operator** téléphoniste *m/f*, standardiste *m/f*.

telephonist [tə'lɛfənɪst] *n* (*Brit*) téléphoniste *m/f*.

telephoto ['tɛlɪ'fəutəu] *a*: ~ **lens** *n* téléobjectif *m*.

telescope ['tɛlɪskəup] *n* télescope *m*.

televise ['tɛlɪvaɪz] vt téléviser.

television ['tɛlɪvɪʒən] n télévision f; **~ set** n poste m de télévision.

telex ['tɛlɛks] n télex m.

tell [tɛl], pt, pp **told** vt dire; (relate: story) raconter; (distinguish): to ~ sth from distinguer qch de // vi (talk): to ~ (of) parler (de); (have effect) se faire sentir, se voir; to ~ sb to do sth dire à qn de faire; to ~ off vt réprimander, gronder; **~er** n (in bank) caissier/ère; **~ing** a (remark, detail) révélateur(trice); **~tale** a (sign) éloquent(e), révélateur(trice).

telly ['tɛlɪ] n abbr (Brit col: = television) télé f.

temp [tɛmp] n abbr (= temporary) (secrétaire f) intérimaire f.

temper ['tɛmpə*] n (nature) caractère m; (mood) humeur f; (fit of anger) colère f // vt (moderate) tempérer, adoucir; **to be in a ~** être en colère; **to lose one's ~** se mettre en colère.

temperament ['tɛmprəmənt] n (nature) tempérament m; **~al** [-'mɛntl] a capricieux(euse).

temperate ['tɛmprət] a modéré(e); (climate) tempéré(e).

temperature ['tɛmprətʃə*] n température f; **to have** ou **run a ~** avoir de la fièvre.

tempest ['tɛmpɪst] n tempête f.

template ['tɛmplɪt] n patron m.

temple ['tɛmpl] n (building) temple m; (ANAT) tempe f.

temporary ['tɛmpərərɪ] a temporaire, provisoire; (job, worker) temporaire; **~ secretary** n (secrétaire f) intérimaire f.

tempt [tɛmpt] vt tenter; **to ~ sb into doing** induire qn à faire; **~ation** [-'teɪʃən] n tentation f.

ten [tɛn] num dix.

tenable ['tɛnəbl] a défendable.

tenacity [tə'næsɪtɪ] n ténacité f.

tenancy ['tɛnənsɪ] n location f; état m de locataire.

tenant ['tɛnənt] n locataire m/f.

tend [tɛnd] vt s'occuper de // vi: to ~ to do sth avoir tendance à faire.

tendency ['tɛndənsɪ] n tendance f.

tender ['tɛndə*] a tendre; (delicate) délicat(e); (sore) sensible; (affectionate) tendre, doux(douce) // n (COMM: offer) soumission f // vt offrir.

tenement ['tɛnəmənt] n immeuble m (de rapport).

tenet ['tɛnət] n principe m.

tennis ['tɛnɪs] n tennis m; **~ ball** n balle f de tennis; **~ court** n (court m de) tennis; **~ player** n joueur/euse de tennis; **~ racket** n raquette f de tennis; **~ shoes** npl (chaussures fpl de) tennis mpl.

tenor ['tɛnə*] n (MUS) ténor m; (of speech etc) sens général.

tense [tɛns] a tendu(e) // n (LING) temps m.

tension ['tɛnʃən] n tension f.

tent [tɛnt] n tente f.

tentative ['tɛntətɪv] a timide, hésitant(e); (conclusion) provisoire.

tenterhooks ['tɛntəhuks] npl: **on ~** sur des charbons ardents.

tenth [tɛnθ] num dixième.

tent peg n piquet m de tente; **~ pole** n montant m de tente.

tenuous ['tɛnjuəs] a ténu(e).

tenure ['tɛnjuə*] n (of property) bail m; (of job) période f de jouissance; statut m de titulaire.

tepid ['tɛpɪd] a tiède.

term [tə:m] n (limit) terme m; (word) terme, mot m; (SCOL) trimestre m; (LAW) session f // vt appeler; **~s** npl (conditions) conditions fpl; (COMM) tarif m; **~ of imprisonment** peine f de prison; **in the short/long ~** à court/long terme; **to come to ~s with** (problem) faire face à.

terminal ['tə:mɪnl] a terminal(e); (disease) dans sa phase terminale // n (ELEC) borne f; (for oil, ore etc, COMPUT) terminal m; (also: **air ~**) aérogare f; (Brit: also: **coach ~**) gare routière.

terminate ['tɜːmɪneɪt] vt mettre fin
à // vi: **to ~ in** finir en ou par.
terminus, pl **termini** ['tɜːmɪnəs,
'tɜːmɪnaɪ] n terminus m inv.
terrace ['terəs] n terrasse f; (Brit:
row of houses) rangée f de maisons
(attenantes les unes aux autres); **the
~s** (Brit SPORT) les gradins mpl;
~d a (garden) en terrasses.
terracotta ['terə'kɒtə] n terre cuite.
terrain [tɛ'reɪn] n terrain m (sol).
terrible ['terɪbl] a terrible, atroce;
(weather, work) affreux(euse), épouvantable; **terribly** ad terriblement;
(very badly) affreusement mal.
terrier ['terɪə*] n terrier m (chien).
terrific [tə'rɪfɪk] a fantastique, incroyable, terrible; (wonderful) formidable, sensationnel(le).
terrify ['terɪfaɪ] vt terrifier.
territory ['terɪtərɪ] n territoire m.
terror ['terə*] n terreur f; **~ism** n
terrorisme m; **~ist** n terroriste m/f.
terse [tɜːs] a (style) concis(e); (reply) laconique.
Terylene ['terɪliːn] n ® tergal m ®.
test [test] n (trial, check) essai m; (:
of goods in factory) contrôle m; (of
courage etc) épreuve f; (MED) examens mpl; (CHEM) analyses fpl;
(exam: of intelligence etc) test m
(d'aptitude); (: in school) interrogation f de contrôle; (also: **driving ~**)
(examen du) permis de conduire //
vt essayer; contrôler; mettre à
l'épreuve; examiner; analyser; tester; faire subir une interrogation (de
contrôle) à.
testament ['testəmənt] n testament
m; **the Old/New T~** l'Ancien/le Nouveau Testament.
testicle ['testɪkl] n testicule m.
testify ['testɪfaɪ] vi (LAW) témoigner,
déposer; **to ~ to sth** (LAW) attester
qch; (gen) témoigner de qch.
testimony ['testɪmənɪ] n (LAW) témoignage m, déposition f.
test: **~ match** n (CRICKET, RUG-
BY) match international; **~ pilot** n
pilote m d'essai; **~ tube** n éprou-

vette f.
tetanus ['tetənəs] n tétanos m.
tether ['teðə*] vt attacher // n: **at
the end of one's ~** à bout (de patience).
text [tekst] n texte m; **~book** n manuel m.
textile ['tekstaɪl] n textile m.
texture ['tekstʃə*] n texture f; (of
skin, paper etc) grain m.
Thames [temz] n: **the ~** la Tamise.
than [ðæn, ðən] cj que; (with numerals): **more ~ 10/once** plus de 10/
d'une fois; **I have more/less ~** you
j'en ai plus/moins que toi; **she has
more apples ~ pears** elle a plus de
pommes que de poires.
thank [θæŋk] vt remercier, dire merci
à; **~ you (very much)** merci
(beaucoup); **~s** npl remerciements
mpl // excl merci!; **~s to** prep grâce
à; **~ful** a: **~ful (for)** reconnais-
sant(e) (de); **~less** a ingrat(e);
T~sgiving (Day) n jour m d'action
de grâce.

KEYWORD

that [ðæt] ♦ a (demonstrative: pl
those) ce, cet + vowel or h mute, f
cette; ~ **man/woman/book** cet
homme/cette femme/ce livre; (not
'this') cet homme-là/cette femme-là/
ce livre-là; ~ **one** celui-là/celle-là)
♦ pronoun 1 (demonstrative: pl
those) ce; (not 'this one') cela, ça;
who's ~? qui est-ce?; **what's ~?**
qu'est-ce que c'est?; **is ~ you?**
c'est toi?; **I prefer this to ~** je préfère ceci à cela ou ça; **~'s what he
said** c'est ce voilà ce qu'il a dit; **~ is
(to say)** c'est-à-dire, à savoir
2 (relative: subject) qui; (: object)
que; (: indirect) lequel(laquelle), pl
lesquels(lesquelles); **the book ~ I
read** le livre que j'ai lu; **the books
~ are in the library** les livres qui
sont dans la bibliothèque; **all ~ I
have** tout ce que j'ai; **the box ~ I
put it in** la boîte dans laquelle je l'ai
mis; **the people ~ I spoke to** les

gens auxquels *or* à qui j'ai parlé
3 *(relative: of time)* où; the day ~ he came le jour où il est venu
◆ *cj* que; he thought ~ I was ill il pensait que j'étais malade
◆ *ad (demonstrative):* I can't work ~ **much** je ne peux pas travailler autant que cela; I didn't know it was ~ **bad** je ne savais pas que c'était si *or* aussi mauvais; it's ~ **about ~ high** c'est à peu près de cette hauteur.

thatched [θætʃt] *a (roof)* de chaume; ~ **cottage** chaumière *f.*

thaw [θɔ:] *n* dégel *m // vi (ice)* fondre; *(food)* dégeler *// vt (food)* (faire) dégeler *//* it's ~ing *(weather)* il dégèle.

KEYWORD

the [ði:, ðə] *definite article* **1** *(gen)* le, *f* la, l' *vowel or h mute,* pl les (NB: à + le(s) = au(x); de + le = du; de + les = des); ~ **boy/girl/ink** le garçon/la fille/l'encre; ~ **children** les enfants; ~ **history of ~ world** l'histoire du monde; **give it to ~ postman** donne-le au facteur; **to play ~ piano/flute** jouer du piano/de la flûte; ~ **rich and ~ poor** les riches et les pauvres
2 *(in titles):* **Elizabeth ~ First** Élisabeth première; **Peter ~ Great** Pierre le Grand
3 *(in comparisons):* ~ **more he works,** ~ **more he earns** plus il travaille, plus il gagne de l'argent.

theatre, *(US)* **theater** ['θɪətə*] *n* théâtre *m;* ~**-goer** *n* habitué du théâtre.

theatrical [θɪ'ætrɪkl] *a* théâtral(e).

theft [θeft] *n* vol *m (larcin).*

their [ðɛə*] *a* leur, pl leurs; ~**s** *pronoun* le(la) leur, les leurs; *see also* my, mine.

them [ðɛm, ðəm] *pronoun (direct)* les; *(indirect)* leur; *(stressed, after prep)* eux(elles); *see also* me.

theme [θi:m] *n* thème *m;* ~ **song** *n* chanson principale.

themselves [ðəm'sɛlvz] *pl pronoun (reflexive)* se; *(emphatic)* eux-mêmes(elles-mêmes); *see also* oneself.

then [ðɛn] *ad (at that time)* alors, à ce moment-là; *(next)* puis, ensuite; *(and also)* et puis *// cj (therefore)* alors, dans ce cas *// a:* the ~ president le président d'alors or de l'époque; **by** ~ *(past)* à ce moment-là; *(future)* d'ici là; **from** ~ **on** dès lors.

theology [θɪ'ɔlədʒɪ] *n* théologie *f.*

theoretical [θɪə'rɛtɪkl] *a* théorique.

theory ['θɪərɪ] *n* théorie *f.*

therapy ['θɛrəpɪ] *n* thérapie *f.*

KEYWORD

there ['ðɛə*] *ad* **1:** ~ **is,** ~ **are** il y a; ~ **are 3 of them** *(people, things)* il y en a 3; ~ **has been an accident** il y a eu un accident
2 *(referring to place)* là, là-bas; it's ~ c'est là(-bas); **in/on/up/down** ~ là-dedans/là-dessus/là-haut/en bas; he **went** ~ **on Friday** il y est allé vendredi; **I want that book** ~ je veux ce livre-là; ~ **he is!** le voilà!
3: ~ ~, *(esp to child)* allons, allons!

thereabouts [ðɛərə'bauts] *ad (place)* par là, près de là; *(amount)* environ, à peu près.

thereafter [ðɛər'ɑ:ftə*] *ad* par la suite.

thereby [ðɛə'baɪ] *ad* ainsi.

therefore ['ðɛəfɔ:*] *ad* donc, par conséquent.

there's [ðɛəz] = **there is, there has.**

thermal ['θə:ml] *a* thermique.

thermometer [θə'mɔmɪtə*] *n* thermomètre *m.*

Thermos ['θə:məs] *n* ® *(also:* ~ **flask)** thermos *m* or *f inv* ®.

thermostat ['θə:məustæt] *n* thermostat *m.*

thesaurus [θɪ'sɔ:rəs] *n* dictionnaire

m synonymique.

these [ðiːz] *pl pronoun* ceux-ci(celles-ci) // *pl a* ces; (*not 'those'*): ~ books ces livres-ci.

thesis, *pl* **theses** ['θiːsɪs, 'θiːsiːz] *n* thèse *f*.

they [ðeɪ] *pl pronoun* ils(elles), (*stressed*) eux(elles); ~ say that ... (*it is said that*) on dit que ...; ~'**d** = **they had, they would;** ~'**ll** = **they shall, they will;** ~'**re** = **they are;** ~'**ve** = **they have.**

thick [θɪk] *a* épais(se); (*crowd*) dense; (*stupid*) bête, borné(e) // *n*: in the ~ of au beau milieu de, en plein cœur de; it's 20 cm ~ ça a 20 cm d'épaisseur; ~**en** *vi* s'épaissir // *vt* (*sauce etc*) épaissir; ~**ness** *n* épaisseur *f*; ~**set** *a* trapu(e), costaud(e); ~**skinned** *a* (*fig*) peu sensible.

thief, *pl* **thieves** [θiːf, θiːvz] *n* voleur/euse.

thigh [θaɪ] *n* cuisse *f*.

thimble ['θɪmbl] *n de m* (à coudre).

thin [θɪn] *a* mince; (*person*) maigre; (*soup*) peu épais(se); (*hair, crowd*) clairsemé(e); (*fog*) léger(ère) // *vt* (*hair*) éclaircir; **to** ~ (**down**) (*sauce, paint*) délayer.

thing [θɪŋ] *n* chose *f*; (*object*) objet *m*; (*contraption*) truc *m*; ~**s** *npl* (*belongings*) affaires *fpl*; **the best** ~ **would be to** le mieux serait de; **how are** ~**s?** comment ça va?

think [θɪŋk] , *pt, pp* **thought** *vi* penser, réfléchir // *vt* penser, croire; (*imagine*) s'imaginer; **to** ~ **of** penser à; **what did you** ~ **of them?** qu'avez-vous pensé d'eux?; **I'll** ~ **about it** je vais y réfléchir; **to** ~ **of doing** avoir l'idée de faire; **I** ~ **so/not** je crois ou pense que oui/non; **to** ~ **well of** avoir une haute opinion de; **to** ~ **over** *vt* bien réfléchir à; **to** ~ **up** *vt* inventer, trouver; ~ **tank** *n* groupe *m* de réflexion.

third [θəːd] *num* troisième // *n* troisième *m/f*; (*fraction*) tiers *m*; (*Brit SCOL: degree*) ≈ licence *f* avec men-

tion passable; ~**ly** *ad* troisièmement; ~ **party insurance** *n* (*Brit*) assurance *f* au tiers; ~-**rate** *a* de qualité médiocre; **the T~ World** *n* le Tiers-Monde *m*.

thirst [θəːst] *n* soif *f*; ~**y** *a* (*person*) qui a soif, assoiffé(e).

thirteen ['θəː'tiːn] *num* treize.

thirty ['θəːtɪ] *num* trente.

this [ðɪs] ♦ *a* (*demonstrative*: *pl* **these**) ce, cet + *vowel or h mute*, cette; ~ **man/woman/book** cet homme/cette femme/ce livre; (*not 'that'*) cet homme-ci/cette femme-ci/ce livre-ci; ~ **one** celui-ci(celle-ci) ♦ *pronoun* (*demonstrative*: *pl* **these**) ce; (*not 'that one'*) celui-ci(celle-ci), ceci; **who is** ~? qui est-ce?; **what's** ~? qu'est-ce que c'est?; **I prefer** ~ **to that** je préfère ceci à cela; ~ **is what he said** voici ce qu'il a dit; ~ **is Mr Brown** (*in introductions*) je vous présente Mr Brown; (*in photo*) c'est Mr Brown; (*on telephone*) ici Mr Brown ♦ *ad* (*demonstrative*): **it was about** ~ **big** c'était à peu près de cette grandeur *ou* grand comme ça; **I didn't know it was** ~ **bad** je ne savais pas que c'était si *ou* aussi mauvais.

thistle ['θɪsl] *n* chardon *m*.

thong [θɒŋ] *n* lanière *f*.

thorn [θɔːn] *n* épine *f*.

thorough ['θʌrə] *a* (*search*) minutieux(euse); (*knowledge, research*) approfondi(e); (*work*) consciencieux(euse); (*cleaning*) à fond; ~**bred** *n* (*horse*) pur-sang *m inv*; ~**fare** *n* rue *f*; '**no** '~**fare**' 'passage interdit'; ~**ly** *ad* minutieusement; en profondeur; à fond; **he** ~**ly agreed** il était tout à fait d'accord.

those [ðəʊz] *pl pronoun* ceux-là(celles-là) // *pl a* ces; (*not 'these'*): ~ **books** ces livres-là.

though [ðəʊ] *cj* bien que + *sub*,

quoique + sub // ad pourtant.

thought [θɔːt] pt, pp of think // n pensée f; (opinion) avis m; (intention) intention f; **~ful** a pensif(ive); réfléchi(e); (considerate) prévenant(e); **~less** a étourdi(e); qui manque de considération.

thousand ['θauzənd] num mille; **one ~** mille; **~s of** des milliers de; **~th** num millième.

thrash [θræʃ] vt rouer de coups; donner une correction à; (defeat) battre à plate couture; **to ~ about** vi se débattre; **to ~ out** vi débattre de.

thread [θrɛd] n fil m; (of screw) pas m, filetage m // vt (needle) enfiler; **~bare** a râpé(e), élimé(e).

threat [θrɛt] n menace f; **~en** vi (storm) menacer // vt: **to ~en sb with sth/to do** menacer qn de qch/de faire.

three [θriː] num trois; **~-dimensional** a à trois dimensions; (film) en relief; **~-piece suit** n complet m (avec gilet); **~-piece suite** n salon m comprenant un canapé et deux fauteuils assortis; **~-ply** a (wood) à trois épaisseurs; (wool) trois fils inv.

thresh [θrɛʃ] vt (AGR) battre.

threshold ['θrɛʃhould] n seuil m.

threw [θruː] pt of throw.

thrifty ['θrɪftɪ] a économe.

thrill [θrɪl] n frisson m, émotion f // vi tressaillir, frissonner // vt (audience) électriser; **to be ~ed** (with gift etc) être ravi; **~er** n film m (or roman m or pièce f) à suspense; **~ing** a saisissant(e), excitant(e).

thrive, pt **thrived**, **throve**, pp **thrived**, [θraɪv, θrəuv, 'θrɪvn] vi pousser or se développer bien; (business) prospérer; **he ~s on it** cela lui réussit; **thriving** a vigoureux(euse); prospère.

throat [θrəut] n gorge f; **to have a sore ~** avoir mal à la gorge.

throb [θrɔb] vi (heart) palpiter; (engine) vibrer; (with pain) lanciner; (wound) causer des élancements.

throes [θrəuz] npl: **in the ~ of** au beau milieu de; en proie à.

throne [θrəun] n trône m.

throng [θrɔŋ] n foule f // vt se presser dans.

throttle [θrɔtl] n (AUT) accélérateur m // vt étrangler.

through [θruː] prep à travers; (time) pendant, durant; (by means of) par, par l'intermédiaire de; (owing to) à cause de // a (ticket, train, passage) direct(e) // ad à travers; **to put sb ~ to** (TEL) passer qn à qn; **to be ~** (TEL) avoir la communication; (have finished) avoir fini; **'no ~ way'** 'impasse'; **~out** prep (place) partout dans; (time) durant // ad (place) partout; (time) tout le (la) // ad partout.

throve [θrəuv] pt of thrive.

throw [θrəu] n jet m; (SPORT) lancer m // vt (pt threw, pp thrown [θruː, θrəun]) lancer, jeter; (SPORT) lancer; (rider) désarçonner; (fig) décontenancer; (pottery) tourner; **to ~ a party** donner une réception; **to ~ away** vt jeter; **to ~ off** vt se débarrasser de; **to ~ out** vt jeter dehors; (reject) rejeter; **to ~ up** vt vomir; **~away** a à jeter; **~-in** n (SPORT) remise f en jeu.

thru [θruː] prep, a, ad (US) = through.

thrush [θrʌʃ] n grive f.

thrust [θrʌst] n (TECH) poussée f // vt (pt, pp thrust) pousser brusquement; (push in) enfoncer.

thug [θʌg] n voyou m.

thumb [θʌm] n (ANAT) pouce m // vt (book) feuilleter; **to ~ a lift** faire de l'auto-stop, arrêter une voiture; **~tack** n (US) punaise f (clou).

thump [θʌmp] n grand coup; (sound) bruit sourd // vt cogner sur // vi cogner, frapper.

thunder ['θʌndə*] n tonnerre m // vi tonner; (train etc): **to ~ past** passer dans un grondement or un bruit de tonnerre; **~bolt** n foudre f; **~clap** n coup m de tonnerre; **~storm**

orage m; ~**y** a orageux(euse).

Thursday ['θə:zdɪ] n jeudi m.

thus [ðʌs] ad ainsi.

thwart [θwɔ:t] vt contrecarrer.

thyme [taɪm] n thym m.

tiara [tɪ'ɑ:rə] n (woman's) diadème m.

tick [tɪk] n (sound: of clock) tic-tac m; (mark) coche f; (ZOOL) tique f; (Brit col): **in a** ~ dans un instant // vi faire tic-tac // vt cocher; **to** ~ **off** vt cocher; (person) réprimander, attraper; **to** ~ **over** vi (engine) tourner au ralenti; (fig) aller ou marcher doucettement.

ticket ['tɪkɪt] n billet m; (for bus, tube) ticket m; (in shop: on goods) étiquette f; (: from cash register) reçu m, ticket; (for library) carte f; ~ **collector** n contrôleur/euse; ~ **office** n guichet m, bureau m de vente des billets.

tickle ['tɪkl] n chatouillement m // vt chatouiller; (fig) plaire à; faire rire.

tidal ['taɪdl] a à marée; ~ **wave** n raz-de-marée m inv.

tidbit ['tɪdbɪt] n (US) = **titbit**.

tiddlywinks ['tɪdlɪwɪŋks] n jeu m de puce.

tide [taɪd] n marée f; (fig: of events) cours m // vt: **to** ~ **sb over** dépanner qn; **high/low** ~ marée haute/basse.

tidy ['taɪdɪ] a (room) bien rangé(e); (dress, work) net(nette), soigné(e); (person) ordonné(e), qui a de l'ordre // vt (also: ~ **up**) ranger; **to** ~ **o.s. up** s'arranger.

tie [taɪ] n (string etc) cordon m; (Brit: also: **neck**~) cravate f; (fig: link) lien m; (SPORT: draw) égalité f de points; match nul // vt (parcel) attacher; (ribbon) nouer // vi (SPORT) faire match nul; finir à égalité de points; **to** ~ **sth in a bow** faire un nœud à ou avec qch; **to** ~ **a knot in sth** faire un nœud à qch; **to** ~ **down** vt attacher; (fig): **to** ~ **sb down to** contraindre qn à accepter; **to** ~ **up** vt (parcel) ficeler; (dog,

boat) attacher; (arrangements) conclure; **to be** ~**d up** (busy) être pris ou occupé.

tier [tɪə*] n gradin m; (of cake) étage m.

tiff [tɪf] n petite querelle.

tiger ['taɪgə*] n tigre m.

tight [taɪt] a (rope) tendu(e), raide; (clothes) étroit(e), très juste; (budget, programme, bend) serré(e); (control) strict(e), sévère; (col: drunk) ivre, rond(e) // ad (squeeze) très fort; (shut) à bloc, hermétiquement; ~**s** npl (Brit) collant m; ~**en** vt (rope) tendre; (screw) resserrer; (control) renforcer // vi se tendre, se resserrer; ~**-fisted** a avare; ~**ly** ad (grasp) bien, très fort; ~**rope** n corde f raide.

tile [taɪl] n (on roof) tuile f; (on wall or floor) carreau m.

till [tɪl] n caisse (enregistreuse) // vt (land) cultiver // prep, cj = **until**.

tiller ['tɪlə*] n (NAUT) barre f (du gouvernail).

tilt [tɪlt] vt pencher, incliner // vi pencher, être incliné(e).

timber ['tɪmbə*] n (material) bois m de construction; (trees) arbres mpl.

time [taɪm] n temps m; (epoch: often pl) époque f, temps; (by clock) heure f; (moment) moment m; (occasion, also MATH) fois f; (MUS) mesure f // vt (race) chronométrer; (programme) minuter; (remark etc) choisir le moment de; **a long** ~ un long moment, longtemps; **for the** ~ **being** pour le moment; **4 at a** ~ 4 à la fois; **from** ~ **to** ~ de temps en temps; **in** ~ (soon enough) à temps; (after some time) avec le temps, à la longue; (MUS) en mesure; **in a week's** ~ dans une semaine; **in no** ~ en un rien de temps; **any** ~ n'importe quand; **on** ~ à l'heure; **5** ~ **5** 5 fois 5; **what** ~ **is it?** quelle heure est-il?; **to have a good** ~ bien s'amuser; ~'**s up!** c'est l'heure!; ~ **bomb** n bombe f à retardement; ~ **lag** n décalage m; (in travel) décalage horaire; ~**less** a éternel(le); ~**ly** a opportun(e); ~ **off** n temps m libre; ~**r** n (~ **switch**) minuteur m; (in kitchen) compte-minutes m inv; ~ **scale** n délais mpl; ~ **switch** n (Brit) minuteur m; (for lighting) minuterie f; ~**table** n (RAIL) (indicateur m) horaire m; (SCOL) emploi m du temps; ~ **zone** n fuseau m horaire.

timid ['tɪmɪd] a timide; (easily scared) peureux(euse).

timing ['taɪmɪŋ] n minutage m; chronométrage m; **the ~ of his resignation** le moment choisi pour sa démission.

timpani ['tɪmpənɪ] npl timbales fpl.

tin [tɪn] n étain m; (also: ~ **plate**) fer-blanc m; (Brit: can) boîte f (de conserve); (for baking) moule m (à gâteau); ~**foil** n papier m d'étain.

tinge [tɪndʒ] n nuance f // vt: ~**d with** teinté(e) de.

tingle ['tɪŋgl] vi picoter.

tinker ['tɪŋkə*] n rétameur ambulant; (gipsy) romanichel m; **to ~ with** vt fus bricoler, rafistoler.

tinkle ['tɪŋkl] vi tinter.

tinned [tɪnd] a (Brit: food) en boîte, en conserve.

tin opener ['-əupnə*] n (Brit) ouvre-boîte(s) m.

tinsel ['tɪnsl] n guirlandes fpl de Noël (argentées).

tint [tɪnt] n teinte f; (for hair) shampooing colorant; ~**ed** a (hair) teinté(e); (spectacles, glass) teinté(e).

tiny ['taɪnɪ] a minuscule.

tip [tɪp] n (end) bout m; (protective: on umbrella etc) embout m; (gratuity) pourboire m; (for coal) terril m; (Brit: for rubbish) décharge f; (advice) tuyau m // vt (waiter) donner un pourboire à; (tilt) incliner; (overturn: also: ~ **over**) renverser; (empty: also: ~ **out**) déverser; ~-**off** n (hint) tuyau m; ~**ped** a (Brit: cigarette) (à bout) filtre inv.

tipsy ['tɪpsɪ] a un peu ivre, éméché(e).

tiptoe ['tɪptəu] n: **on ~** sur la pointe des pieds.

tiptop ['tɪp'tɔp] a: **in ~ condition** en excellent état.

tire ['taɪə*] n (US) = **tyre** // vt fatiguer // vi se fatiguer; ~**d** a fatigué(e); **to be ~d of** en avoir assez de, être las(lasse) de; ~**some** a ennuyeux(euse); **tiring** a fatigant(e).

tissue ['tɪʃu:] n tissu m; (paper handkerchief) mouchoir m en papier, kleenex m ®; ~ **paper** n papier m de soie.

tit [tɪt] n (bird) mésange f; **to give ~ for tat** rendre coup pour coup.

titbit ['tɪtbɪt] , (US) **tidbit** ['tɪdbɪt] n (food) friandise f; (news) potin m.

titivate ['tɪtɪveɪt] vt pomponner.

title ['taɪtl] n titre m; ~ **deed** n (LAW) titre (constitutif) de propriété; ~ **role** n rôle principal.

titter ['tɪtə*] vi rire (bêtement).

titular ['tɪtjulə*] a (in name only) nominal(e).

TM abbr of **trademark**.

<hr>

KEYWORD

to [tu:, tə] ◆ prep **1** (direction) à; **to go ~ France/Portugal/London/ school** aller en France/au Portugal/à Londres/à l'école; **to go ~ Claude's/the doctor's** aller chez Claude/le docteur; **the road ~ Edinburgh** la route d'Édimbourg **2** (as far as) (jusqu')à; **to count ~ 10** compter jusqu'à 10; **from 40 ~ 50 people** de 40 à 50 personnes **3** (expressions of time): **a quarter ~ 5** 5 heures moins le quart; **it's twenty ~ 3** il est 3 heures moins vingt **4** (for, of) de; **the key ~ the front door** la clé de la porte d'entrée; **a letter ~ his wife** une lettre (adressée) à sa femme **5** (expressing indirect object) à; **to give sth ~ sb** donner qch à qn; **to talk ~ sb** parler à qn **6** (in relation to) à; **3 goals ~ 2** 3 (buts) à 2; **30 miles ~ the gallon**

≈9,4 litres aux cent (km)

7 (purpose, result): to come ~ sb's aid venir au secours de qn, porter secours à qn; to sentence sb ~ death condamner qn à mort; ~ my surprise à ma grande surprise

◆ with vb **1** (simple infinitive): ~ go/eat aller/manger

2 (following another vb): to want/ try/ start ~ do vouloir/essayer de/commencer à faire; see also relevant verb

3 (with vb omitted): I don't want ~ je ne veux pas

4 (purpose, result) pour; I did it ~ help you je l'ai fait pour vous aider

5 (equivalent to relative clause): I have things ~ do j'ai des choses à faire; the main thing is ~ try l'important est d'essayer

6 (after adjective etc): ready ~ go prêt(e) à partir; too old/young ~ ... trop vieux/jeune pour ...; see also relevant adjective etc

◆ ad: push/pull the door ~ tirez/poussez la porte.

toad [təud] n crapaud m; ~**stool** n champignon (vénéneux).

toast [təust] n (CULIN) pain grillé, toast m; (drink, speech) toast m // vt (CULIN) faire griller; (drink to) porter un toast à; a piece or slice of ~ un toast; ~**er** n grille-pain m inv.

tobacco [tə'bækəu] n tabac m; ~**nist** n marchand/e de tabac; ~**nist's (shop)** n (bureau m de) tabac m.

toboggan [tə'bɔgən] n toboggan m; (child's) luge f.

today [tə'dei] ad, n (also fig) aujourd'hui (m).

toddler ['tɔdlə*] n enfant m/f qui commence à marcher, bambin m.

toddy ['tɔdi] n grog m.

to-do [tə'du:] n (fuss) histoire f, affaire f.

toe [təu] n doigt m de pied, orteil m; (of shoe) bout m; to ~ the line (fig) obéir, se conformer.

toffee ['tɔfi] n caramel m.

toga ['təugə] n toge f.

together [tə'geðə*] ad ensemble; (at same time) en même temps; ~ with prep avec.

toil [tɔil] n dur travail, labeur m.

toilet ['tɔilət] n (Brit: lavatory) toilettes fpl, cabinets mpl // cpd (bag, soap etc) de toilette; ~ **bowl** n cuvette f des w.-c.; ~ **paper** n papier m hygiénique; ~**ries** npl articles mpl de toilette; ~ **roll** n rouleau m de papier hygiénique; ~ **water** n eau f de toilette.

token ['təukən] n (sign) marque f, témoignage m; (voucher) bon m, coupon m; **book/record** ~ n (Brit) chèque-livre/disque m.

told [təuld] pt, pp of **tell**.

tolerable ['tɔlərəbl] a (bearable) tolérable; (fairly good) passable.

tolerant ['tɔlərnt] a: ~ (of) tolérant(e) (à l'égard de).

tolerate ['tɔləreit] vt supporter; (MED, TECH) tolérer.

toll [təul] n (tax, charge) péage m // vi (bell) sonner; the accident ~ on the roads le nombre des victimes de la route.

tomato, ~**es** [tə'mɑ:təu] n tomate f.

tomb [tu:m] n tombe f.

tomboy ['tɔmbɔi] n garçon manqué.

tombstone ['tu:mstəun] n pierre tombale.

tomcat ['tɔmkæt] n matou m.

tomorrow [tə'mɔrəu] ad, n (also fig) demain (m); the day after ~ après-demain; a week ~ demain en huit; ~ **morning** demain matin.

ton [tʌn] n tonne f (Brit = 1016 kg; US = 907 kg; metric = 1000 kg); (NAUT: also: **register** ~) tonneau m (= 2.83 cu.m); ~**s of** (col) des tas de.

tone [təun] n ton m; (of radio) tonalité f // vi s'harmoniser; **to** ~ **down** vt (colour, criticism) adoucir; (sound) baisser; **to** ~ **up** vt (muscles) tonifier; ~-**deaf** a qui n'a pas d'oreille.

tongs [tɒŋz] npl pinces fpl; (for coal) pincettes fpl; (for hair) fer m à friser.

tongue [tʌŋ] n langue f; ~ **in cheek** ad ironiquement; ~**tied** a (fig) muet(te); ~**twister** n phrase f très difficile à prononcer.

tonic ['tɒnɪk] n (MED) tonique m; (also: ~ **water**) tonic m.

tonight [tə'naɪt] ad, n cette nuit; (this evening) ce soir.

tonsil ['tɒnsl] n amygdale f; ~**litis** ['laɪtɪs] n amygdalite f.

too [tu:] ad (excessively) trop; (also) aussi; ~ **much** ad trop // a trop de; ~ **many** a trop de; ~ **bad**! tant pis!

took [tuk] pt of **take**.

tool [tu:l] n outil m // vt travailler, ouvrager; ~ **box** n boîte f à outils.

toot [tu:t] vi siffler; (with car-horn) klaxonner.

tooth [tu:θ], pl **teeth** [ti:θ] (ANAT TECH), dent f; ~**ache** n mal m de dents; ~**brush** n brosse f à dents; ~**paste** n (pâte f) dentifrice m; ~**pick** n cure-dent m.

top [tɒp] n (of mountain, head) sommet m; (of page, ladder) haut m; (of box, cupboard, table) dessus m; (lid: of box, jar) couvercle m; (: of bottle) bouchon m; (toy) toupie f // a du haut; (in rank) premier(ère); (best) meilleur(e) // vt (exceed) dépasser; (be first in) être en tête de; **on** ~ **of** sur; (in addition to) en plus de; **from** ~ **to bottom** de fond en comble; **to** ~ **up**, (US) **to** ~ **off** vt remplir; ~ **floor** n dernier étage; ~ **hat** n haut-de-forme m; ~**heavy** a (object) trop lourd(e) du haut.

topic ['tɒpɪk] n sujet m, thème m; ~**al** a d'actualité.

top: ~**less** a (bather etc) aux seins nus; ~**level** a (talks) à l'échelon le plus élevé.

topple ['tɒpl] vt renverser, faire tomber // vi basculer; tomber.

top-secret ['tɒp'si:krɪt] a ultra-secret(ète).

topsy-turvy ['tɒpsɪ'tɜ:vɪ] a, ad sens dessus-dessous.

torch [tɔ:tʃ] n torche f; (Brit: electric) lampe f de poche.

tore [tɔ:*] pt of **tear**.

torment [tɔ:ment] tourment m // vt [tɔ:'ment] tourmenter; (fig: annoy) agacer.

torn [tɔ:n] pp of **tear**.

tornado, ~es [tɔ:'neɪdəu] n tornade f.

torpedo, ~es [tɔ:'pi:dəu] n torpille f.

torrent ['tɒrnt] n torrent m.

tortoise ['tɔ:təs] n tortue f; ~**shell** ['tɔ:təʃel] a en écaille.

torture ['tɔ:tʃə*] n torture f // vt torturer.

Tory ['tɔ:rɪ] (Brit POL) a tory (pl tories), conservateur(trice) // n tory m/f, conservateur/trice.

toss [tɒs] vt lancer, jeter; (pancake) faire sauter; (head) rejeter en arrière; **to** ~ **a coin** jouer à pile ou face; **to** ~ **up for sth** jouer qch à pile ou face; **to** ~ **and turn** (in bed) se tourner et se retourner.

tot [tɒt] n (Brit: drink) petit verre; (child) bambin m.

total ['təutl] a total(e) // n total m // vt (add up) faire le total de, totaliser; (amount to) s'élever à.

totally ['təutəlɪ] ad totalement.

totter ['tɒtə*] vi chanceler.

touch [tʌtʃ] n contact m, toucher m; (sense, also skill: of pianist etc) toucher; (fig: note, also FOOTBALL) touche f // vi (gen) toucher; (tamper with) toucher à; **a** ~ **of** (fig) un petit peu de; une touche de; **in** ~ **with** en contact ou rapport avec; **to get in** ~ **with** prendre contact avec; **to lose** ~ (friends) se perdre de vue; **to** **on** vt fus (topic) effleurer, toucher; **to** ~ **up** vt (paint) retoucher; ~**and-go** a incertain(e); ~**down** n atterrissage m; (on sea) amerrissage m; (US FOOTBALL) but m; ~**ed** a touché(e); (col) cinglé(e); ~**ing** a touchant(e), attendrissant(e); ~**line** n (SPORT) (ligne f de) touche f; ~**y**

a (person) susceptible.

tough [tʌf] *a* dur(e); *(resistant)* résistant(e), solide; *(meat)* dur, coriace.

toupee ['tu:peɪ] *n* postiche *m*.

tour ['tuə*] *n* voyage *m*; *(also:* **package** ~) voyage organisé; *(of town, museum)* tour *m*, visite *f*; *(by artist)* tournée *f // vt* visiter; **~ing** *n* voyages *mpl* touristiques, tourisme *m*.

tourism ['tuərɪzm] *n* tourisme *m*.

tourist ['tuərɪst] *n* touriste *m/f // ad (travel)* en classe touriste *// cpd* touristique; ~ **office** *n* syndicat *m* d'initiative.

tournament ['tuənəmənt] *n* tournoi *m*.

tousled ['tauzld] *a (hair)* ébouriffé(e).

tout [taut] *vi*: **to ~ for** essayer de raccrocher, racoler *// n (also:* **ticket** ~) revendeur *m* de billets.

tow [tau] *vt* remorquer; **'on** ~', *(US)* **'in** ~' *(AUT)* 'véhicule en remorque'.

toward(s) [tə'wɔːd(z)] *prep* vers; *(of attitude)* envers, à l'égard de; *(of purpose)* pour.

towel ['tauəl] *n* serviette *f (de toilette)*; *(also:* **tea** ~) torchon *m*; **~ling** *n (fabric)* tissu-éponge *m*; ~ **rail**, *(US)* ~ **rack** *n* porte-serviettes *m inv*.

tower ['tauə*] *n* tour *f*; ~ **block** *n (Brit)* tour *f* (d'habitation); **~ing** *a* très haut(e), imposant(e).

town [taun] *n* ville *f*; **to go to** ~ aller en ville; *(fig)* mettre le paquet; ~ **centre** *n* centre *m* de la ville, centre-ville *m*; ~ **clerk** *n* ≈ secrétaire *m/f* de mairie; ~ **council** *n* conseil municipal; ~ **hall** *n* ≈ mairie *f*; ~ **plan** *n* plan *m* de ville; ~ **planning** *n* urbanisme *m*.

towrope ['təurəup] *n (câble *m* de) remorque *f*.

tow truck *n (US)* dépanneuse *f*.

toy [tɔɪ] *n* jouet *m*; **to ~ with** *vt fus* jouer avec; *(idea)* caresser.

trace [treɪs] *n* trace *f // vt (draw)* tracer, dessiner; *(follow)* suivre la trace

de; *(locate)* retrouver; **tracing paper** *n* papier-calque *m*.

track [træk] *n (mark)* trace *f*; *(path: gen)* chemin *m*, piste *f*; *(: of bullet etc)* trajectoire *f*; *(: of suspect, animal)* piste *f*; *(RAIL)* voie ferrée, rails *mpl*; *(on tape, SPORT)* piste *f*; *(on record)* plage *f // vt* suivre la trace ou la piste de; **to keep ~ of** suivre; **to ~ down** *vt (prey)* trouver et capturer; *(sth lost)* finir par retrouver; **~suit** *n* survêtement *m*.

tract [trækt] *n (GEO)* étendue *f*, zone *f*; *(pamphlet)* tract *m*.

tractor ['træktə*] *n* tracteur *m*.

trade [treɪd] *n* commerce *m*; *(skill, job)* métier *m // vi* faire du commerce; **to ~ with/in** faire du commerce avec/le commerce de; **to ~ in** *vt (old car etc)* faire reprendre; ~ **fair** *n* foire(-exposition) commerciale; **~-in price** *n* prix *m* à la reprise; **~mark** *n* marque *f* de fabrique; **~name** *n* marque déposée; **~r** *n* commerçant/e, négociant/e; **~sman** *n (shopkeeper)* commerçant; ~ **union** *n* syndicat *m*; ~ **unionist** *n* syndicaliste *m/f*; **trading** *n* affaires *fpl*, commerce *m*; **trading estate** *n (Brit)* zone industrielle.

tradition [trə'dɪʃən] *n* tradition *f*; **~al** *a* traditionnel(le).

traffic ['træfɪk] *n* trafic *m*; *(cars)* circulation *f // vi*: **to ~ in** *(pej: liquor, drugs)* faire le trafic de; ~ **circle** *n (US)* rond-point *m*; ~ **jam** *n* embouteillage *m*; ~ **lights** *npl* feux *mpl* (de signalisation); ~ **warden** *n* contractuel/le.

tragedy ['trædʒədɪ] *n* tragédie *f*.

tragic ['trædʒɪk] *a* tragique.

trail [treɪl] *n (tracks)* trace *f*, piste *f*; *(path)* chemin *m*, piste; *(of smoke etc)* traînée *f // vt* traîner; tirer; *(follow)* suivre *// vi* traîner; **to ~ behind** *vi* traîner, être à la traîne; **~er** *n (AUT)* remorque *f*; *(US)* caravane *f*; *(CINEMA)* court film de lancement; **~er truck** *n (US)* (camion *m*) semi-remorque *m*.

train [treɪn] n train m; (in underground) rame f; (of dress) traîne f // vt (apprentice, doctor etc) former; (sportsman) entraîner; (dog) dresser; (memory) exercer; (point: gun etc): **to ~ sth on** braquer qch sur // vi recevoir sa formation; s'entraîner; **one's ~ of thought** le fil de sa pensée; **~ed** a qualifié(e), qui a reçu une formation; dressé(e); **~ee** [treɪ'niː] n stagiaire m/f; (in trade) apprenti/e; **~er** n (SPORT) entraîneur/euse; (of dogs etc) dresseur/euse; **~ing** n formation f; entraînement m; dressage m; **in ~ing** (SPORT) à l'entraînement; (fit) en forme; **~ing college** n école professionnelle; (for teachers) ≈ école normale; **~ing shoes** npl chaussures fpl de sport.

traipse [treɪps] vi (se) traîner, déambuler.

trait [treɪt] n trait m (de caractère).

traitor ['treɪtə*] n traître m.

tram [træm] n (Brit: also: **~car**) tram(way) m.

tramp [træmp] n (person) vagabond/e, clochard(e); (col: pej: woman): **to be a ~** être coureuse // vt (walk through: town, streets) parcourir à pied.

trample ['træmpl] vt: **to ~ (underfoot)** piétiner; (fig) bafouer.

trampoline ['træmpəliːn] n trampolino m.

tranquil ['træŋkwɪl] a tranquille; **~lizer** n (MED) tranquillisant m.

transact [træn'zækt] vt (business) traiter; **~ion** [-'zækʃən] n transaction f; **~ions** npl (minutes) actes mpl.

transatlantic ['trænzət'læntɪk] a transatlantique.

transfer n ['trænsfə*] (gen, also SPORT) transfert m; (POL: of power) passation f; (picture, design) décalcomanie f; (: stick-on) autocollant m // vt [træns'fə:*] transférer; passer; décalquer.

transform [træns'fɔ:m] vt transfor-

mer.

transfusion [træns'fju:ʒən] n transfusion f.

transient ['trænzɪənt] a transitoire, éphémère.

transistor [træn'zɪstə*] n (ELEC; also: **~ radio**) transistor m.

transit ['trænzɪt] n: **in ~** en transit.

transitive ['trænzɪtɪv] a (LING) transitif(ive).

translate [trænz'leɪt] vt traduire; **translation** [-'leɪʃən] n traduction f; (SCOL: as opposed to prose) version f; **translator** n traducteur/trice.

transmission [trænz'mɪʃən] n transmission f.

transmit [trænz'mɪt] vt transmettre; (RADIO, TV) émettre; **~ter** n émetteur m.

transparency [træns'pɛərnsɪ] n (Brit PHOT) diapositive f.

transparent [træns'pærnt] a transparent(e).

transpire [træn'spaɪə*] vi (turn out): **it ~d that ...** on a appris que ...; (happen) arriver.

transplant vt [træns'plɑ:nt] (plante) planter; (seedlings) repiquer // n ['trænsplɑ:nt] (MED) transplantation f.

transport n ['trænspɔ:t] transport m // vt [træns'pɔ:t] transporter; **~ation** [-'teɪʃən] n (moyen m de) transport m; (of prisoners) transportation f; **~ café** n (Brit) ≈ restaurant m de routiers.

trap [træp] n (snare, trick) piège m; (carriage) cabriolet m // vt prendre au piège; (immobilize) bloquer; (jam) coincer; **~ door** n trappe f.

trapeze [trə'pi:z] n trapèze m.

trappings ['træpɪŋz] npl ornements mpl; attributs mpl.

trash [træʃ] n (pej: goods) camelote f; (: nonsense) sottises fpl; **~ can** n (US) boîte f à ordures.

trauma ['trɔ:mə] n traumatisme m; **~tic** [-'mætɪk] a traumatisant(e).

travel ['trævl] n voyage(s) m(pl) // vi voyager; (move) aller, se déplacer //

vt (*distance*) parcourir; ~ **agency** *n* agence *f* de voyages; ~ **agent** *n* agent *m* de voyages; ~**ler,** (*US*) ~**er** *n* voyageur/euse; ~**ler's cheque** *n* chèque *m* de voyage; ~**ling,** (*US*) ~**ing** *n* voyage(s) *m*(*pl*) // *cpd* (*bag, clock*) de voyage; (*expenses*) de déplacement; ~ **sickness** *n* mal *m* de la route (*or* de mer *or* de l'air).

travesty ['trævəstɪ] *n* parodie *f*.

trawler ['trɔːlə*] *n* chalutier *m*.

tray [treɪ] *n* (*for carrying*) plateau *m*; (*on desk*) corbeille *f*.

treachery ['tretʃərɪ] *n* traîtrise *f*.

treacle ['triːkl] *n* mélasse *f*.

tread [trɛd] *n* pas *m*; (*sound*) bruit *m* de pas; (*of tyre*) chape *f*, bande *f* de roulement // *vi* (*pt* trod, *pp* trodden) marcher; **to ~ on** *vt fus* marcher sur.

treason ['triːzn] *n* trahison *f*.

treasure ['trɛʒə*] *n* trésor *m* // *vt* (*value*) tenir beaucoup à; (*store*) conserver précieusement.

treasurer ['trɛʒərə*] *n* trésorier/ère.

treasury ['trɛʒərɪ] *n* trésorerie *f*; the T~, (*US*) the T~ Department *le* ministère des Finances.

treat [triːt] *n* petit cadeau, petite surprise // *vt* traiter; **to ~ sb to sth** offrir qch à qn.

treatise ['triːtɪz] *n* traité *m* (*ouvrage*).

treatment ['triːtmənt] *n* traitement *m*.

treaty ['triːtɪ] *n* traité *m*.

treble ['trɛbl] *a* triple // *vt, vi* tripler; ~ **clef** *n* clé *f* de sol.

tree [triː] *n* arbre *m*.

trek [trɛk] *n* voyage *m*; randonnée *f*; (*tiring walk*) tirée *f* // *vi* (*as holiday*) faire de la randonnée.

tremble ['trɛmbl] *vi* trembler.

tremendous [trɪ'mɛndəs] *a* (*enormous*) énorme, fantastique; (*excellent*) formidable.

tremor ['trɛmə*] *n* tremblement *m*; (*also*: **earth ~**) secousse *f* sismique.

trench [trɛntʃ] *n* tranchée *f*.

trend [trɛnd] *n* (*tendency*) tendance

f; (*of events*) cours *m*; (*fashion*) mode *f*; ~**y a** (*idea*) dans le vent; (*clothes*) dernier cri *inv*.

trepidation [trɛpɪ'deɪʃən] *n* vive agitation.

trespass ['trɛspəs] *vi*: **to ~ on** s'introduire sans permission dans; (*fig*) empiéter sur; '**no ~ing**' 'propriété privée', 'défense d'entrer'.

tress [trɛs] *n* boucle *f* de cheveux.

trestle ['trɛsl] *n* tréteau *m*; ~ **table** *n* table *f* à tréteaux.

trial ['traɪəl] *n* (*LAW*) procès *m*, jugement *m*; (*test: of machine etc*) essai *m*; (*hardship*) épreuve *f*; (*worry*) souci *m*; **by ~ and error** par tâtonnements.

triangle ['traɪæŋgl] *n* (*MATH, MUS*) triangle *m*.

tribe [traɪb] *n* tribu *f*.

tribunal [traɪ'bjuːnl] *n* tribunal *m*.

tributary ['trɪbjutərɪ] *n* (*river*) affluent *m*.

tribute ['trɪbjuːt] *n* tribut *m*, hommage *m*; **to pay ~ to** rendre hommage à.

trice [traɪs] *n*: **in a ~** en un clin d'œil.

trick [trɪk] *n* ruse *f*; (*clever act*) astuce *f*; (*joke*) tour *m*; (*CARDS*) levée *f* // *vt* attraper, rouler; **to play a ~ on sb** jouer un tour à qn; **that should do the ~** ça devrait faire l'affaire; ~**ery** *n* ruse *f*.

trickle ['trɪkl] *n* (*of water etc*) filet *m* // *vi* couler en un filet *ou* goutte à goutte.

tricky ['trɪkɪ] *a* difficile, délicat(e).

tricycle ['traɪsɪkl] *n* tricycle *m*.

trifle ['traɪfl] *n* bagatelle *f*; (*CULIN*) ~ diplomate *m* // *ad*: **a ~ long** un peu long; **trifling** *a* insignifiant(e).

trigger ['trɪgə*] *n* (*of gun*) gâchette *f*; **to ~ off** *vt* déclencher.

trim [trɪm] *a* net(te); (*house, garden*) bien tenu(e); (*figure*) svelte // *n* (*haircut etc*) légère coupe; (*embellishment*) finitions *fpl*; (*on car*) garnitures *fpl* // *vt* couper légèrement; (*decorate*): **to ~ (with)** décorer

(de); (NAUT: a sail) gréer;
~mings npl décorations fpl; (extras: gen CULIN) garniture f.

trinket ['trɪŋkɪt] n bibelot m; (piece
of jewellery) colifichet m.

trip [trɪp] n voyage m; (excursion)
excursion f; (stumble) faux pas // vi
(stumble) faire un faux pas, trébucher; (go lightly) marcher d'un pas
léger; on a ~ en voyage; to ~ up
vi trébucher // vt faire un croc-en-
jambe à.

tripe [traɪp] n (CULIN) tripes fpl;
(pej: rubbish) idioties fpl.

triple ['trɪpl] a triple.

triplets ['trɪplɪts] npl triplés/ées.

tripod ['traɪpɔd] n trépied m.

trite [traɪt] a banal(e).

triumph ['traɪəmf] n triomphe m //
vi: to ~ (over) triompher (de).

trivia ['trɪvɪə] npl futilités fpl.

trivial ['trɪvɪəl] a insignifiant(e);
(commonplace) banal(e).

trod [trɔd] pt of tread; ~den pp of
tread.

trolley ['trɔlɪ] n chariot m.

trombone [trɔm'bəun] n trombone
m.

troop [truːp] n bande f, groupe m;
~s npl (MIL) troupes fpl; (: men)
hommes mpl, soldats mpl; to ~ in/
out vi entrer/sortir en groupe; ~er
n (MIL) soldat m de cavalerie; ~ing
the colour n (ceremony) le salut au
drapeau.

trophy ['trəufɪ] n trophée m.

tropic ['trɔpɪk] n tropique m; ~al a
tropical(e).

trot [trɔt] n trot m // vi trotter; on
the ~ (Brit fig) d'affilée.

trouble ['trʌbl] n difficulté(s) f(pl),
problème(s) m(pl); (worry) ennuis
mpl, soucis mpl; (bother, effort)
peine f; (POL) conflits mpl, troubles
mpl; (MED): stomach etc ~ troubles gastriques etc // vt déranger, gêner; (worry) inquiéter // vi: to ~ to
do prendre la peine de faire; ~s npl
(POL etc) troubles mpl; to be in ~
avoir des ennuis; (ship, climber etc)

être en difficulté; it's no ~! je vous
en prie!; what's the ~? qu'est-ce
qui ne va pas?; ~d a (person) in-
quiet(ète); (epoch, life) agité(e);
~maker n élément perturbateur,
fauteur m de troubles; ~shooter n
(in conflict) conciliateur m; ~some
a ennuyeux(euse), gênant(e).

trough [trɔf] n (also: drinking ~)
abreuvoir m; (also: feeding ~) auge
f; (channel) chenal m.

trousers ['trauzəz] npl pantalon m;
short ~ culottes courtes.

trout [traut] n (pl inv) truite f.

trowel ['trauəl] n truelle f.

truant ['truənt] n: to play ~ (Brit)
faire l'école buissonnière.

truce [truːs] n trêve f.

truck [trʌk] n camion m; (RAIL) wagon m à plate-forme; (for luggage)
chariot m (à bagages); ~ driver n
camionneur m; ~ farm n (US) jardin maraîcher.

truculent ['trʌkjulənt] a agres-
sif(ive).

trudge [trʌdʒ] vi marcher lourdement, se traîner.

true [truː] a vrai(e); (accurate)
exact(e); (genuine) vrai, véritable;
(faithful) fidèle.

truffle ['trʌfl] n truffe f.

truly ['truːlɪ] ad vraiment, réellement; (truthfully) sans mentir;
(faithfully) fidèlement.

trump [trʌmp] n atout m; ~ed-up a
inventé(e) (de toutes pièces).

trumpet ['trʌmpɪt] n trompette f.

truncheon ['trʌntʃən] n bâton m
(d'agent de police); matraque f.

trundle ['trʌndl] vt, vi: to ~ along
rouler bruyamment.

trunk [trʌŋk] n (of tree, person)
tronc m; (of elephant) trompe f;
(case) malle f; (US AUT) coffre m;
~s npl (also: swimming ~s) maillot m ou slip m de bain.

truss [trʌs] n (MED) bandage m her-
niaire; to ~ (up) n (CULIN) brider.

trust [trʌst] n confiance f; (LAW)
fidéicommis m; (COMM) trust m // vt

(rely on) avoir confiance en; *(entrust)*: **to ~ sth to sb** confier qch à qn; **~ed** a en qui l'on a confiance; **~ee** [trʌs'tiː] n *(LAW)* fidéicommissaire m/f; *(of school etc)* administrateur/trice; **~ful, ~ing** a confiant(e); **~worthy** a digne de confiance.

truth, ~s [truːθ, truːðz] n vérité f; **~ful** a *(person)* qui dit la vérité; *(description)* exact(e), vrai(e).

try [traɪ] n essai m, tentative f; *(RUGBY)* essai m // vt *(LAW)* juger; *(test: sth new)* essayer, tester; *(strain)* éprouver // vi essayer; **to ~ to do sth** essayer de faire; *(seek)* chercher à faire; **to ~ on** vt *(clothes)* essayer; **to ~ out** vt essayer, mettre à l'essai; **~ing** a pénible.

T-shirt ['tiːʃəːt] n tee-shirt m.

T-square ['tiːskwɛə*] n équerre f en T.

tub [tʌb] n cuve f; baquet m; *(bath)* baignoire f.

tuba ['tjuːbə] n tuba m.

tubby ['tʌbɪ] a rondelet(te).

tube [tjuːb] n tube m; *(Brit: underground)* métro m; *(for tyre)* chambre f à air.

tubing ['tjuːbɪŋ] n tubes mpl; **a piece of ~** un tube.

TUC n abbr *(Brit: = Trades Union Congress)* confédération f des syndicats britanniques.

tuck [tʌk] n *(SEWING)* pli m, rempli m // vt *(put)* mettre; **to ~ away** vt cacher, ranger; **to ~ in** vt rentrer; *(child)* border // vi *(eat)* manger de bon appétit; attaquer le repas; **to ~ up** vt *(child)* border; **~ shop** n boutique f à provisions *(dans une école)*.

Tuesday ['tjuːzdɪ] n mardi m.

tuft [tʌft] n touffe f.

tug [tʌg] n *(ship)* remorqueur m // vt tirer (sur); **~-of-war** n lutte f à la corde.

tuition [tjuː'ɪʃən] n *(Brit)* leçons fpl; *(: private ~)* cours particuliers; *(US: school fees)* frais mpl de scolarité.

tulip ['tjuːlɪp] n tulipe f.

tumble ['tʌmbl] n *(fall)* chute f, culbute f // vi tomber, dégringoler; *(with somersault)* faire une *ou* des culbute(s); **to ~ to sth** *(col)* réaliser qch; **~down** a délabré(e); **~ dryer** n *(Brit)* séchoir m (à linge) à air chaud.

tumbler ['tʌmblə*] n verre (droit), gobelet m.

tummy ['tʌmɪ] n *(col)* ventre m.

tumour, *(US)* **tumor** ['tjuːmə*] n tumeur f.

tuna ['tjuːnə] n *(pl inv)* *(also: ~ fish)* thon m.

tune [tjuːn] n *(melody)* air m // vt *(MUS)* accorder; *(RADIO, TV, AUT)* régler, mettre au point; **to be in/out of ~** *(instrument)* être accordé/désaccordé; *(singer)* chanter juste/faux; **to ~ in (to)** *(RADIO, TV)* se mettre à l'écoute (de); **to ~ up** vi *(musician)* accorder son instrument; **~ful** a mélodieux(euse).

tunic ['tjuːnɪk] n tunique f.

tuning ['tjuːnɪŋ] n réglage m; **~ fork** n diapason m.

Tunisia [tjuː'nɪzɪə] n Tunisie f.

tunnel ['tʌnl] n tunnel m; *(in mine)* galerie f.

turbulence ['tə:bjuləns] n *(AVIAT)* turbulence f.

tureen [tə'riːn] n soupière f.

turf [tə:f] n gazon m; *(clod)* motte f (de gazon) // vt gazonner; **to ~ out** vt *(col)* jeter; jeter dehors.

turgid ['tə:dʒɪd] a *(speech)* pompeux(euse).

Turkey ['tə:kɪ] n Turquie f.

turkey ['tə:kɪ] n dindon m, dinde f.

Turkish ['tə:kɪʃ] a turc(turque) // n *(LING)* turc m.

turmoil ['tə:mɔɪl] n trouble m, bouleversement m.

turn [tə:n] n tour m; *(in road)* tournant m; *(tendency: of mind, events)* tournure f; *(performance)* numéro m; *(MED)* crise f, attaque f // vt tourner; *(collar, steak)* retourner;

(milk) faire tourner; (change): to ~ sth into changer qch en // vi tourner; (person: look back) se (re)tourner; (reverse direction) faire demi-tour; (change) changer; (become) devenir; to ~ into se changer en; a good ~ un service; it gave me quite a ~ ça m'a fait un coup; 'no left ~' (AUT) 'défense de tourner à gauche'; it's your ~ c'est à votre tour; in ~ à son tour; à tour de rôle; to take ~s se relayer; to take ~s at faire à tour de rôle; to ~ away vi se détourner, tourner la tête; to ~ back vi revenir, faire demi-tour; to ~ down vt (refuse) rejeter, refuser; (reduce) baisser; (fold) rabattre; to ~ in vi (col: go to bed) aller se coucher // vt (fold) rentrer; to ~ off vi (from road) tourner // vt (light, radio etc) éteindre; (engine) arrêter; to ~ on vt (light, radio etc) allumer; (engine) mettre en marche; to ~ out vt (light, gas) éteindre // vi: to ~ out to be ... s'avérer ..., se révéler ...; to ~ over vi (person) se retourner // vt (object) retourner; (page) tourner; to ~ round vi faire demi-tour; (rotate) tourner; to ~ up (person) arriver, se pointer; (lost object) être retrouvé(e) // vt (collar) remonter; (increase: sound, volume etc) mettre plus fort; ~ing n (in road) tournant m; ~ing point n (fig) tournant m, moment décisif.

turnip ['tə:nɪp] n navet m.

turnout ['tə:naut] n (nombre m de personnes dans l') assistance f.

turnover ['tə:nəuvə*] n (COMM: amount of money) chiffre m d'affaires; (: of goods) roulement m; (CULIN) sorte de chausson.

turnpike ['tə:npaɪk] n (US) autoroute f à péage.

turnstile ['tə:nstaɪl] n tourniquet m (d'entrée).

turntable ['tə:nteɪbl] n (on record player) platine f.

turn-up ['tə:nʌp] n (Brit: on trou-

sers) revers m.

turpentine ['tə:pəntaɪn] n (also: turps) (essence f de) térébenthine f.

turquoise ['tə:kwɔɪz] n (stone) turquoise f // a turquoise inv.

turret ['tʌrɪt] n tourelle f.

turtle ['tə:tl] n tortue marine; ~neck (sweater) n pullover m à col montant.

tusk [tʌsk] n défense f.

tussle ['tʌsl] n bagarre f, mêlée f.

tutor ['tju:tə*] n (in college) directeur/trice d'études; (private teacher) précepteur/trice; ~ial [-'tɔ:rɪəl] n (SCOL) (séance f de) travaux mpl pratiques.

tuxedo [tʌk'si:dəu] n (US) smoking m.

TV [ti:'vi:] n abbr (= television) télé f.

twang [twæŋ] n (of instrument) son vibrant; (of voice) ton nasillard.

tweed [twi:d] n tweed m.

tweezers ['twi:zəz] npl pince f à épiler.

twelfth [twelfθ] num douzième.

twelve [twelv] num douze; at ~ (o'clock) à midi; (midnight) à minuit.

twentieth ['twentɪɪθ] num vingtième.

twenty ['twentɪ] num vingt.

twice [twaɪs] ad deux fois; ~ as much deux fois plus.

twiddle ['twɪdl] vt, vi: to ~ (with) sth tripoter qch; to ~ one's thumbs (fig) se tourner les pouces.

twig [twɪg] n brindille f // vt, vi (col) piger.

twilight ['twaɪlaɪt] n crépuscule m.

twin [twɪn] a, n jumeau(elle) // vt jumeler; ~(-bedded) room n chambre f à deux lits.

twine [twaɪn] n ficelle f // vi (plant) s'enrouler.

twinge [twɪndʒ] n (of pain) élancement m; (of conscience) remords m.

twinkle ['twɪŋkl] vi scintiller; (eyes) pétiller.

twirl [twə:l] vt faire tournoyer // vi

tournoyer.

twist [twist] n torsion f, tour m; (in wire, flex) tortillon m; (in story) coup m de théâtre // vt tordre; (weave) entortiller; (roll around) enrouler; (fig) déformer // vi s'entortiller; s'enrouler; (road) serpenter.

twit [twit] n (col) crétin(e).

twitch [twitʃ] vi se convulser; avoir un tic.

two [tu:] num deux; to put ~ and ~ together (fig) faire le rapport; ~door a (AUT) à deux portes; ~faced a (pej: person) faux(fausse); ~fold ad: to increase ~fold doubler; ~piece (suit) n (costume m) deux-pièces m inv; ~piece (swimsuit) n (maillot m de bain) deux-pièces m inv; ~seater n (plane) (avion m) biplace m; (car) voiture f à deux places; ~some n (people) couple m; ~way a (traffic) dans les deux sens.

tycoon [taɪˈkuːn] n: (business) ~ gros homme d'affaires.

type [taɪp] n (category) genre m, espèce f; (model) modèle m; (example) type m; (TYP) type, caractère m // vt (letter etc) taper (à la machine); ~cast a (actor) condamné(e) à toujours jouer le même rôle; ~face n (TYP) œil m (de caractères); ~script n texte dactylographié; ~writer n machine f à écrire; ~written a dactylographié(e).

typhoid ['taɪfɔɪd] n typhoïde f.

typical ['tɪpɪkl] a typique, caractéristique.

typing ['taɪpɪŋ] n dactylo(graphie) f.

typist ['taɪpɪst] n dactylo m/f.

tyrant ['taɪərnt] n tyran m.

tyre, (US) **tire** [taɪə*] n pneu m; ~ **pressure** n pression f (de gonflage).

U

U-bend ['juːˈbɛnd] n (AUT, in pipe) coude m.

udder ['ʌdə*] n pis m, mamelle f.

UFO ['juːfəu] n abbr (= unidentified flying object) ovni m.

Uganda [juːˈɡændə] n Ouganda m.

ugh [əːh] excl pouah!

ugly ['ʌɡlɪ] a laid(e), vilain(e); (fig) répugnant(e).

UK n abbr see **united**.

ulcer ['ʌlsə*] n ulcère m; (also: mouth ~) aphte f.

Ulster ['ʌlstə*] n Ulster m.

ulterior [ʌlˈtɪərɪə*] a ultérieur(e); ~ **motive** n arrière-pensée f.

ultimate ['ʌltɪmət] a ultime, final(e); (authority) suprême; ~ly ad en fin de compte; finalement; par l'ultime.

ultrasound ['ʌltrəsaund] n (MED) ultrason m.

umbilical cord [ʌmbɪˈlaɪkl-] n cordon ombilical.

umbrella [ʌmˈbrɛlə] n parapluie m.

umpire ['ʌmpaɪə*] n arbitre m.

umpteen [ʌmpˈtiːn] a je ne sais combien de; for the ~th time pour la nième fois.

UN, UNO n abbr of United Nations (Organization).

unable [ʌnˈeɪbl] a: to be ~ to ne (pas) pouvoir, être dans l'impossibilité de; être incapable de.

unaccompanied [ʌnəˈkʌmpənɪd] a (child, lady) non accompagné(e).

unaccountably [ʌnəˈkauntəblɪ] ad inexplicablement.

unaccustomed [ʌnəˈkʌstəmd] a inaccoutumé(e), inhabituel(le); to be ~ to sth ne pas avoir l'habitude de qch.

unanimous [juːˈnænɪməs] a unanime; ~ly ad à l'unanimité.

unarmed [ʌnˈɑːmd] a (without a weapon) non armé(e); (combat) sans armes.

unassuming [ʌnəˈsjuːmɪŋ] a modeste, sans prétentions.

unattached [ʌnə'tætʃt] a libre, sans attaches.

unattended [ʌnə'tɛndɪd] a (car, child, luggage) sans surveillance.

unauthorized [ʌn'ɔːθəraɪzd] a non autorisé(e), sans autorisation.

unavoidable [ʌnə'vɔɪdəbl] a inévitable.

unaware [ʌnə'wɛə*] a: to be ~ of ignorer, ne pas savoir, être inconscient(e) de; ~s ad à l'improviste, au dépourvu.

unbalanced [ʌn'bælənst] a déséquilibré(e).

unbearable [ʌn'bɛərəbl] a insupportable.

unbeknown(st) [ʌnbɪ'nəʊn(st)] ad: ~ to à l'insu de.

unbelievable [ʌnbɪ'liːvəbl] a incroyable.

unbend [ʌn'bɛnd] vb (irg) vi se détendre // vt (wire) redresser, détordre.

unbias(s)ed [ʌn'baɪəst] a impartial(e).

unborn [ʌn'bɔːn] a à naître.

unbreakable [ʌn'breɪkəbl] a incassable.

unbroken [ʌn'brəʊkən] a intact(e), continu(e).

unbutton [ʌn'bʌtn] vt déboutonner.

uncalled-for [ʌn'kɔːldfɔː*] a déplacé(e), injustifié(e).

uncanny [ʌn'kænɪ] a étrange, troublant(e).

unceasing [ʌn'siːsɪŋ] a incessant(e), continu(e).

unceremonious [ʌnserɪ'məʊnɪəs] a (abrupt, rude) brusque.

uncertain [ʌn'sɜːtn] a incertain(e); mal assuré(e); ~ty n incertitude f, doutes mpl.

unchecked [ʌn'tʃɛkt] a non réprimé(e).

uncivilized [ʌn'sɪvɪlaɪzd] a (gen) non civilisé(e); (fig: behaviour etc) barbare.

uncle ['ʌŋkl] n oncle m.

uncomfortable [ʌn'kʌmfətəbl] a inconfortable; (uneasy) mal à l'aise, gêné(e); désagréable.

uncommon [ʌn'kɔmən] a rare, singulier(ère), peu commun(e).

uncompromising [ʌn'kɔmprəmaɪzɪŋ] a intransigeant(e), inflexible.

unconcerned [ʌnkən'sɜːnd] a: to be ~ (about) ne pas s'inquiéter (de).

unconditional [ʌnkən'dɪʃənl] a sans conditions.

unconscious [ʌn'kɔnʃəs] a sans connaissance, évanoui(e); (unaware) inconscient(e) // n: the ~ l'inconscient m; ~ly ad inconsciemment, sans s'en rendre compte.

uncontrollable [ʌnkən'trəʊləbl] a irrépressible; indiscipliné(e).

unconventional [ʌnkən'vɛnʃənl] a non conventionnel(le).

uncouth [ʌn'kuːθ] a grossier(ère), fruste.

uncover [ʌn'kʌvə*] vt découvrir.

undecided [ʌndɪ'saɪdɪd] a indécis(e), irrésolu(e).

under ['ʌndə*] prep sous; (less than) (de) moins de; au-dessous de; (according to) selon, en vertu de // ad au-dessous, en dessous; from ~ sth de dessous or de sous qch; ~ there là-dessous; ~ repair en (cours de) réparation.

under... ['ʌndə*] prefix sous-; ~age a qui n'a pas l'âge réglementaire; ~carriage n (Brit AVIAT) train m d'atterrissage; ~charge vt ne pas faire payer assez à; ~coat n (paint) couche f de fond; ~cover a secret(ète), clandestin(e); ~current n courant sous-jacent; ~cut vt irg vendre moins cher que; ~developed a sous-développé(e); ~dog n opprimé m; ~done a (CULIN) saignant(e); (pej) pas assez cuit(e); ~estimate vt sous-estimer, mésestimer; ~fed a sous-alimenté(e); ~foot ad sous les pieds; ~go vt irg subir; (treatment) suivre; ~graduate n étudiant/e (qui prépare la licence); ~ground n (Brit: railway) métro m; (POL) clandestinité f // a souterrain(e); (fig) clandestin(e); **~growth** n broussailles fpl, sousbois m; **~hand(ed)** a (fig) sournois(e), en dessous; **~lie** vt irg être à la base de; **~line** vt souligner; **~ling** ['ʌndəlɪŋ] n (pej) sous-fifre m, subalterne m; **~mine** vt saper, miner; **~neath** [ʌndə'ni:θ] ad (en) dessous // prep sous, au-dessous de; **~paid** a sous-payé(e); **~pants** npl caleçon m, slip m; **~pass** n (Brit) passage souterrain; (: on motorway) passage inférieur; **~privileged** a défavorisé(e), économiquement faible; **~rate** vt sous-estimer, mésestimer; **~shirt** n (US) tricot m de corps; **~shorts** npl (US) caleçon m, slip m; **~side** n dessous m; **~skirt** n (Brit) jupon m.

understand [ʌndə'stænd] vb (irg: like stand) vt, vi comprendre; **I ~ that ...** je me suis laissé dire que ...; je crois comprendre que ...; **~able** a compréhensible; **~ing** a compréhensif(ive) // n compréhension f; (agreement) accord m.

understatement ['ʌndəsteɪtmənt] n: that's an ~ c'est (bien) peu dire, le terme est faible.

understood [ʌndə'stud] pt, pp of **understand** // a entendu(e); (implied) sous-entendu(e).

understudy ['ʌndəstʌdɪ] n doublure f.

undertake [ʌndə'teɪk] vt irg entreprendre; se charger de; **to ~ to do sth** s'engager à faire qch.

undertaker ['ʌndəteɪkə*] n entrepreneur m des pompes funèbres, croque-mort m.

undertaking ['ʌndəteɪkɪŋ] n entreprise f; (promise) promesse f.

undertone ['ʌndətəun] n: **in an ~** à mi-voix.

underwater [ʌndə'wɔ:tə*] ad sous l'eau // a sous-marin(e).

underwear ['ʌndəwɛə*] n sous-vêtements mpl; (women's only) dessous mpl.

underworld [ʌndəwə:ld] n (of crime) milieu m, pègre f.

underwriter ['ʌndəraɪtə*] n (INSURANCE) souscripteur m.

undies ['ʌndɪz] npl (col) dessous mpl, lingerie f.

undo [ʌn'du:] vt irg défaire; **~ing** n ruine f, perte f.

undoubted [ʌn'dautɪd] a indubitable, certain(e); **~ly** ad sans aucun doute.

undress [ʌn'drɛs] vi se déshabiller.

undue [ʌn'dju:] a indu(e), excessif(ive).

undulating ['ʌndjuleɪtɪŋ] a ondoyant(e), onduleux(euse).

unduly [ʌn'dju:lɪ] ad trop, excessivement.

unearth [ʌn'ə:θ] vt déterrer; (fig) dénicher.

unearthly [ʌn'ə:θlɪ] a surnaturel(le); (hour) indu(e), impossible.

uneasy [ʌn'i:zɪ] a mal à l'aise, gêné(e); (worried) inquiet(ète).

unemployed [ʌnɪm'plɔɪd] a sans travail, au chômage // n: **the ~** les chômeurs mpl.

unemployment [ʌnɪm'plɔɪmənt] n chômage m.

unending [ʌn'ɛndɪŋ] a interminable.

unerring [ʌn'ə:rɪŋ] a infaillible, sûr(e).

uneven [ʌn'i:vn] a inégal(e); irrégulier(ère).

unexpected [ʌnɪk'spɛktɪd] a inattendu(e), imprévu(e); **~ly** ad à l'improviste.

unfailing [ʌn'feɪlɪŋ] a inépuisable; infaillible.

unfair [ʌn'fɛə*] a: **~ (to)** injuste (envers).

unfaithful [ʌn'feɪθful] a infidèle.

unfamiliar [ʌnfə'mɪlɪə*] a étrange, inconnu(e).

unfashionable [ʌn'fæʃnəbl] a (clothes) démodé(e); (district) déshérité(e), pas à la mode.

unfasten [ʌn'fɑ:sn] vt défaire; détacher.

unfavourable, (US) unfavorable

[ʌn'feɪvərəbl] a défavorable.

unfeeling [ʌn'fi:lɪŋ] a insensible, dur(e).

unfit [ʌn'fɪt] a en mauvaise santé; pas en forme; (incompetent): ~ (for) impropre (à); (work, service) inapte (à).

unfold [ʌn'fəʊld] vt déplier; (fig) révéler, exposer // vi se dérouler.

unforeseen ['ʌnfɔ:'si:n] a imprévu(e).

unforgettable [ʌnfə'getəbl] a inoubliable.

unfortunate [ʌn'fɔ:tʃnət] a malheureux(euse); (event, remark) malencontreux(euse); **~ly** ad malheureusement.

unfounded [ʌn'faʊndɪd] a sans fondement.

unfriendly [ʌn'frendlɪ] a froid(e), inamical(e).

ungainly [ʌn'geɪnlɪ] a gauche, dégingandé(e).

ungodly [ʌn'gɒdlɪ] a: at an ~ hour à une heure indue.

ungrateful [ʌn'greɪtful] a ingrat(e).

unhappiness [ʌn'hæpɪnɪs] n tristesse f, peine f.

unhappy [ʌn'hæpɪ] a triste, malheureux(euse); **~ with** (arrangements etc) mécontent(e) de, peu satisfait(e) de.

unharmed [ʌn'hɑ:md] a indemne, sain et sauf(sauve).

unhealthy [ʌn'helθɪ] a (gen) malsain(e); (person) maladif(ive).

unheard-of [ʌn'hɜ:dɔv] a inouï(e), sans précédent.

uniform ['ju:nɪfɔ:m] n uniforme m // a uniforme.

uninhabited [ʌnɪn'hæbɪtɪd] a inhabité(e).

union ['ju:njən] n union f; (also: trade ~) syndicat m // cpd du syndicat, syndical(e); **U~ Jack** n drapeau du Royaume-Uni.

unique [ju:'ni:k] a unique.

unit ['ju:nɪt] n unité f; (section: of furniture etc) élément m, bloc m; (team, squad) groupe m, service m.

unite [ju:'naɪt] vt unir // vi s'unir; **~d** a uni(e); unifié(e); (efforts) conjugué(e); **U~d Kingdom** (UK) n Royaume-Uni m; **U~d Nations (Organization) (UN, UNO)** n (Organisation f des) Nations Unies (O.N.U.); **U~d States (of America) (US, USA)** n États-Unis mpl.

unit trust n (Brit) société f d'investissement, ≈ SICAV f.

unity ['ju:nɪtɪ] n unité f.

universal [ju:nɪ'vɜ:sl] a universel(le).

universe ['ju:nɪvɜ:s] n univers m.

university [ju:nɪ'vɜ:sɪtɪ] n université f.

unjust [ʌn'dʒʌst] a injuste.

unkempt [ʌn'kempt] a mal tenu(e), débraillé(e); mal peigné(e).

unkind [ʌn'kaɪnd] a peu gentil(le), méchant(e).

unknown [ʌn'nəʊn] a inconnu(e).

unlawful [ʌn'lɔ:ful] a illégal(e).

unleash [ʌn'li:ʃ] vt détacher; (fig) déchaîner, déclencher.

unless [ʌn'les] cj: ~ he leaves à moins qu'il ne parte; ~ we leave à moins que nous ne (ne) partions, à moins de partir; ~ otherwise stated sauf indication contraire.

unlike [ʌn'laɪk] a dissemblable, différent(e) // prep à la différence de, contrairement à.

unlikely [ʌn'laɪklɪ] a improbable; invraisemblable.

unlisted [ʌn'lɪstɪd] a (US TEL) sur la liste rouge.

unload [ʌn'ləʊd] vt décharger.

unlock [ʌn'lɒk] vt ouvrir.

unlucky [ʌn'lʌkɪ] a malchanceux(euse); (object, number) qui porte malheur; **to be** ~ ne pas avoir de chance.

unmarried [ʌn'mærɪd] a célibataire.

unmistakable [ʌnmɪs'teɪkəbl] a indubitable; qu'on ne peut pas ne pas reconnaître.

unmitigated [ʌn'mɪtɪgeɪtɪd] a non mitigé(e), absolu(e), pur(e).

unnatural [ʌn'nætʃrəl] a non naturel(le); contre nature.

unnecessary [ʌnˈnɛsəsəri] a inutile, superflu(e).

unnoticed [ʌnˈnəʊtɪst] a: (to go) ~ (passer) inaperçu(e).

UNO [ˈjuːnəʊ] n abbr of **United Nations Organization**.

unobtainable [ʌnəbˈteɪnəbl] a (TEL) impossible à obtenir.

unobtrusive [ʌnəbˈtruːsɪv] a discret(ète).

unofficial [ʌnəˈfɪʃl] a non officiel(le); (strike) ≈ non sanctionné(e) par la centrale.

unpack [ʌnˈpæk] vi défaire sa valise.

unpalatable [ʌnˈpælətəbl] a (truth) désagréable (à entendre).

unparalleled [ʌnˈpærəleld] a incomparable, sans égal.

unpleasant [ʌnˈpleznt] a déplaisant(e), désagréable.

unplug [ʌnˈplʌg] vt débrancher.

unpopular [ʌnˈpɒpjʊlə•] a impopulaire.

unprecedented [ʌnˈprɛsɪdəntɪd] a sans précédent.

unpredictable [ʌnprɪˈdɪktəbl] a imprévisible.

unprofessional [ʌnprəˈfɛʃnl] a (conduct) contraire à la déontologie.

unqualified [ʌnˈkwɒlɪfaɪd] a (teacher) non diplômé(e), sans titres; (success) sans réserve, total(e).

unquestionably [ʌnˈkwɛstʃənəblɪ] ad incontestablement.

unravel [ʌnˈrævl] vt démêler.

unreal [ʌnˈrɪəl] a irréel(le).

unrealistic [ʌnrɪəˈlɪstɪk] a irréaliste; peu réaliste.

unreasonable [ʌnˈriːznəbl] a qui n'est pas raisonnable.

unrelated [ʌnrɪˈleɪtɪd] a sans rapport; sans lien de parenté.

unreliable [ʌnrɪˈlaɪəbl] a sur qui (ou quoi) on ne peut pas compter, peu fiable.

unremitting [ʌnrɪˈmɪtɪŋ] a inlassable, infatigable, acharné(e).

unreservedly [ʌnrɪˈzɜːvɪdlɪ] ad sans réserve.

unrest [ʌnˈrɛst] n agitation f, troubles mpl.

unroll [ʌnˈrəʊl] vt dérouler.

unruly [ʌnˈruːlɪ] a indiscipliné(e).

unsafe [ʌnˈseɪf] a dangereux(euse), hasardeux(euse).

unsaid [ʌnˈsɛd] a: to leave sth ~ passer qch sous silence.

unsatisfactory [ˈʌnsætɪsˈfæktərɪ] a qui laisse à désirer.

unsavoury,   **(US)**   **unsavory** [ʌnˈseɪvərɪ] a (fig) peu recommandable, répugnant(e).

unscathed [ʌnˈskeɪðd] a indemne.

unscrew [ʌnˈskruː] vt dévisser.

unscrupulous [ʌnˈskruːpjʊləs] a sans scrupules.

unsettled [ʌnˈsɛtld] a perturbé(e); instable; incertain(e).

unshaven [ʌnˈʃeɪvn] a non or mal rasé(e).

unsightly [ʌnˈsaɪtlɪ] a disgracieux(euse), laid(e).

unskilled [ʌnˈskɪld] a: ~ worker manœuvre m.

unspeakable [ʌnˈspiːkəbl] a indicible; (awful) innommable.

unstable [ʌnˈsteɪbl] a instable.

unsteady [ʌnˈstɛdɪ] a mal assuré(e), chancelant(e), instable.

unstuck [ʌnˈstʌk] a: to come ~ se décoller; (fig) faire fiasco.

unsuccessful [ʌnsəkˈsɛsfʊl] a (attempt) infructueux(euse); (writer, proposal) qui n'a pas de succès; (marriage) malheureux(euse), qui ne réussit pas; to be ~ (in attempting sth) ne pas réussir; ne pas avoir de succès; (application) ne pas être retenu(e).

unsuitable [ʌnˈsuːtəbl] a qui ne convient pas, peu approprié(e); inopportun(e).

unsure [ʌnˈʃʊə•] a pas sûr(e); to be ~ of o.s. manquer de confiance en soi.

unsympathetic [ˈʌnsɪmpəˈθɛtɪk] a (person) antipathique; (altitude) hostile.

untapped [ʌnˈtæpt] a (resources) inexploité(e).

unthinkable [ʌn'θɪŋkəbl] *a* impensable, inconcevable.

untidy [ʌn'taɪdɪ] *a* (*room*) en désordre; (*appearance*) désordonné(e), débraillé(e); (*person*) sans ordre, désordonné; débraillé; (*work*) peu soigné(e).

untie [ʌn'taɪ] *vt* (*knot, parcel*) défaire; (*prisoner, dog*) détacher.

until [ən'tɪl] *prep* jusqu'à; (*after negative*) avant // *cj* jusqu'à ce que + *sub*, en attendant que + *sub*; (*in past, after negative*) avant que + *sub*; ~ **now** jusqu'à présent, jusqu'ici; ~ **then** jusque-là.

untimely [ʌn'taɪmlɪ] *a* inopportun(e); (*death*) prématuré(e).

untold [ʌn'təʊld] *a* incalculable; indescriptible.

untoward [ʌntə'wɔːd] *a* fâcheux(euse), malencontreux(euse).

untranslatable [ʌntrænz'leɪtəbl] *a* intraduisible.

unused [ʌn'juːzd] *a* neuf(neuve).

unusual [ʌn'juːʒuəl] *a* insolite, exceptionnel(le), rare.

unveil [ʌn'veɪl] *vt* dévoiler.

unwavering [ʌn'weɪvərɪŋ] *a* inébranlable.

unwelcome [ʌn'wɛlkəm] *a* importun(e); de trop.

unwell [ʌn'wɛl] *a* indisposé(e), souffrant(e); **to feel** ~ ne pas se sentir bien.

unwieldy [ʌn'wiːldɪ] *a* difficile à manier.

unwilling [ʌn'wɪlɪŋ] *a*: **to be** ~ **to do** ne pas vouloir faire; ~**ly** *ad* à contrecœur, contre son gré.

unwind [ʌn'waɪnd] *vb* (*irg*) *vt* dérouler // *vi* (*relax*) se détendre.

unwise [ʌn'waɪz] *a* déraisonnable.

unwitting [ʌn'wɪtɪŋ] *a* involontaire.

unworkable [ʌn'wɜːkəbl] *a* (*plan*) inexploitable.

unworthy [ʌn'wɜːðɪ] *a* indigne.

unwrap [ʌn'ræp] *vt* défaire; ouvrir.

unwritten [ʌn'rɪtn] *a* (*agreement*) tacite.

---

up [ʌp] ◆ *prep*: **he went** ~ **the stairs/the hill** il a monté l'escalier/la colline; **the cat was** ~ **a tree** le chat était dans un arbre; **they live further** ~ **the street** ils habitent plus haut dans la rue

◆ *ad* **1** (*upwards, higher*): ~ **in the sky/the mountains** (là-haut) dans le ciel/les montagnes; **put it a bit higher** mettez-le un peu plus haut; ~ **there** là-haut; ~ **above** au-dessus **2**: **to be** ~ (*out of bed*) être levé(e) (*prices*) avoir augmenté ou monté **3**: ~ **to** (*as far as*) jusqu'à; ~ **to now** jusqu'à présent **4**: **to be** ~ **to** (*depending on*): **it's** ~ **to you** c'est à vous de décider; (*equal to*): **he's not** ~ **to it** (*job, task etc*) il n'est pas à la hauteur; (*col: be doing*): **what is he** ~ **to?** qu'est-ce qu'il peut bien faire?

◆ *n*: ~**s and downs** hauts et bas *mpl*.

---

up-and-coming [ʌpənd'kʌmɪŋ] *a* plein(e) d'avenir *ou* de promesses.

upbringing ['ʌpbrɪŋɪŋ] *n* éducation *f*.

update [ʌp'deɪt] *vt* mettre à jour.

upheaval [ʌp'hiːvl] *n* bouleversement *m*; branle-bas *m*; crise *f*.

uphill [ʌp'hɪl] *a* qui monte; (*fig: task*) difficile, pénible // *ad*: **to go** ~ monter.

uphold [ʌp'həʊld] *vt irg* maintenir; soutenir.

upholstery [ʌp'həʊlstərɪ] *n* rembourrage *m*; (*of car*) garniture *f*.

upkeep ['ʌpkiːp] *n* entretien *m*.

upon [ə'pɒn] *prep* sur.

upper ['ʌpə*] *a* supérieur(e); du dessus // *n* (*of shoe*) empeigne *f*; ~-**class** *a* ≈ bourgeois(e); ~ **hand** *n*: **to have the** ~ **hand** avoir le dessus; ~**most** *a* (le) plus haut(e).

upright ['ʌpraɪt] *a* droit(e); vertical(e); (*fig*) droit, honnête // *n* montant *m*.

uprising ['ʌpraɪzɪŋ] n soulèvement m, insurrection f.

uproar ['ʌprɔ:'] n tumulte m, vacarme m.

uproot [ʌp'ru:t] vt déraciner.

upset n ['ʌpset] dérangement m // vt [ʌp'set] (irg: like set) (glass etc) renverser; (plan) déranger; (person: offend) contrarier; (: grieve) faire de la peine à; bouleverser // a [ʌp'set] contrarié(e); peiné(e); (stomach) détraqué(e), dérangé(e).

upshot ['ʌpʃɔt] n résultat m.

upside-down ['ʌpsaɪd'daun] ad à l'envers.

upstairs [ʌp'stɛəz] ad en haut // a (room) du dessus, d'en haut.

upstart ['ʌpstɑ:t] n parvenu/e.

upstream [ʌp'stri:m] ad en amont.

uptake ['ʌpteɪk] n: he is quick/slow on the ~ il comprend vite/est lent à comprendre.

uptight [ʌp'taɪt] a (col) très tendu(e), crispé(e).

up-to-date ['ʌptə'deɪt] a moderne; très récent(e).

upturn ['ʌptə:n] n (in luck) retournement m; (COMM: in market) hausse f.

upward ['ʌpwəd] a ascendant(e); vers le haut; ~(s) ad vers le haut.

urban ['ə:bən] a urbain(e).

urbane [ə:'beɪn] a urbain(e), courtois(e).

urchin ['ə:tʃɪn] n gosse m, garnement m.

urge [ə:dʒ] n besoin m; envie f; forte envie, désir m // vt: to ~ sb to do exhorter qn à faire, pousser qn à faire; recommander vivement à qn de faire.

urgency ['ə:dʒənsɪ] n urgence f; (of tone) insistance f.

urgent ['ə:dʒənt] a urgent(e).

urine ['juərɪn] n urine f.

urn [ə:n] n urne f; (also: tea ~) fontaine f à thé.

US, USA n abbr of **United States (of America)**.

us [ʌs] pronoun nous; see also **me**.

use n [ju:s] emploi m, utilisation f; usage m // vt [ju:z] se servir de, utiliser, employer; she ~d to do it le faisait (autrefois), elle avait coutume de le faire; **in** ~ en usage; **out of** ~ hors d'usage; **to be of** ~ servir, être utile; **it's no** ~ ça ne sert à rien; **to be ~d to** avoir l'habitude de, être habitué(e) à; **to ~ up** vt finir, épuiser; consommer; ~**d a** (car) d'occasion; ~**ful a** utile; ~**fulness** n utilité f; ~**less a** inutile; ~**r** n utilisateur/trice, usager m; ~**r-friendly** a (computer) convivial(e), facile d'emploi.

usher ['ʌʃə'] n placeur m; ~**ette** [-'ret] n (in cinema) ouvreuse f.

USSR n: **the** ~ l'URSS f.

usual ['ju:ʒuəl] a habituel(le); **as** ~ comme d'habitude; ~**ly** ad d'habitude, d'ordinaire.

utensil [ju:'tensl] n ustensile m; **kitchen** ~**s** batterie f de cuisine.

uterus ['ju:tərəs] n utérus m.

utility [ju:'tɪlɪtɪ] n utilité f; (also: **public** ~) service public; ~ **room** n buanderie f.

utmost ['ʌtməust] a extrême, le(la) plus grand(e) // n: **to do one's** ~ faire tout son possible.

utter ['ʌtə'] a total(e), complet(ète) // vt prononcer, proférer; émettre; ~**ance** n paroles fpl; ~**ly** ad complètement, totalement.

U-turn ['ju:'tə:n] n demi-tour m.

V

v. abbr of **verse, versus, volt**; (= **vide**) voir.

vacancy ['veɪkənsɪ] n (Brit: job) poste vacant; (room) chambre f disponible.

vacant ['veɪkənt] a (post) vacant(e); (seat etc) libre, disponible; (expression) distrait(e); ~ **lot** n (US) terrain inoccupé, (for sale) terrain à vendre.

vacate [və'keɪt] vt quitter.

vacation [vəˈkeɪʃən] *n* vacances *fpl*.

vaccinate [ˈvæksɪneɪt] *vt* vacciner.

vacuum [ˈvækjum] *n* vide *m*; ~ **bottle** *n* (*US*) = ~ **flask**; ~ **cleaner** *n* aspirateur *m*; ~ **flask** *n* (*Brit*) bouteille *f* thermos ®; ~**-packed** *a* emballé(e) sous vide.

vagina [vəˈdʒaɪnə] *n* vagin *m*.

vagrant [ˈveɪɡrnt] *n* vagabond/e, mendiant/e.

vague [veɪɡ] *a* vague, imprécis(e); (*blurred*: *photo*, *memory*) flou(e); ~**ly** *ad* vaguement.

vain [veɪn] *a* (*useless*) vain(e); (*conceited*) vaniteux(euse); **in** ~ en vain.

valentine [ˈvælntaɪn] *n* (*also*: ~ *card*) carte *f* de la Saint-Valentin.

valiant [ˈvælɪənt] *a* vaillant(e).

valid [ˈvælɪd] *a* valide, valable; (*excuse*) valable.

valley [ˈvælɪ] *n* vallée *f*.

valour, (*US*) **valor** [ˈvælə*] *n* courage *m*.

valuable [ˈvæljuəbl] *a* (*jewel*) de grande valeur; (*time*) précieux(euse); ~**s** *npl* objets *mpl* de valeur.

valuation [væljuˈeɪʃən] *n* évaluation *f*, expertise *f*.

value [ˈvælju:] *n* valeur *f* // *vt* (*fix price*) évaluer, expertiser; (*cherish*) tenir à; ~ **added tax (VAT)** *n* (*Brit*) taxe *f* à la valeur ajoutée (T.V.A.); ~**d** *a* (*appreciated*) estimé(e).

valve [vælv] *n* (*in machine*) soupape *f*; (*on tyre*) valve *f*; (*in radio*) lampe *f*.

van [væn] *n* (*AUT*) camionnette *f*; (*Brit RAIL*) fourgon *m*.

vandal [ˈvændl] *n* vandale *m/f*; ~**ism** *n* vandalisme *m*; ~**ize** *vt* saccager.

vanilla [vəˈnɪlə] *n* vanille *f*.

vanish [ˈvænɪʃ] *vi* disparaître.

vanity [ˈvænɪtɪ] *n* vanité *f*; ~ **case** *n* sac *m* de toilette.

vantage [ˈvɑːntɪdʒ] *n*: ~ **point** bonne position.

vapour, (*US*) **vapor** [ˈveɪpə*] *n* vapeur *f*; (*on window*) buée *f*.

variable [ˈvɛərɪəbl] *a* variable; (*mood*) changeant(e).

variance [ˈvɛərɪəns] *n*: **to be at** ~ (**with**) être en désaccord (avec); (*facts*) être en contradiction (avec).

varicose [ˈværɪkəus] *a*: ~ **veins** varices *fpl*.

varied [ˈvɛərɪd] *a* varié(e), divers(e).

variety [vəˈraɪətɪ] *n* variété *f*; (*quantity*) nombre *m*, quantité *f*; ~ **show** *n* (*spectacle m de*) variétés *fpl*.

various [ˈvɛərɪəs] *a* divers(e), différent(e); (*several*) divers, plusieurs.

varnish [ˈvɑːnɪʃ] *n* vernis *m* // *vt* vernir.

vary [ˈvɛərɪ] *vt*, *vi* varier, changer.

vase [vɑːz] *n* vase *m*.

vaseline [ˈvæsɪliːn] *n* ® vaseline *f*.

vast [vɑːst] *a* vaste, immense; (*amount*, *success*) énorme; ~**ly** *ad* infiniment, extrêmement.

VAT [væt] *n abbr of* **value added tax**.

vat [væt] *n* cuve *f*.

vault [vɔːlt] *n* (*of roof*) voûte *f*; (*tomb*) caveau *m*; (*in bank*) salle *f* des coffres; chambre forte; (*jump*) saut *m* // *vt* (*also*: ~ **over**) sauter (d'un bond).

vaunted [ˈvɔːntɪd] *a*: **much-**~ tant célébré(e).

VCR *n abbr of* **video cassette recorder**.

VD *n abbr of* **venereal disease**.

VDU *n abbr of* **visual display unit**.

veal [viːl] *n* veau *m*.

veer [vɪə*] *vi* tourner, virer.

vegetable [ˈvedʒtəbl] *n* légume *m* // *a* végétal(e).

vegetarian [vedʒɪˈtɛərɪən] *a*, *n* végétarien(ne).

vehement [ˈviːɪmənt] *a* violent(e), impétueux(euse); (*impassioned*) ardent(e).

vehicle [ˈviːɪkl] *n* véhicule *m*.

veil [veɪl] *n* voile *m* // *vt* voiler.

vein [veɪn] *n* veine *f*; (*on leaf*) nervure *f*; (*fig*: *mood*) esprit *m*.

velvet ['vɛlvɪt] *n* velours *m*.

vending machine ['vɛndɪŋ-] *n* distributeur *m* automatique.

veneer [və'nɪə*] *n* placage *m* de bois; (*fig*) vernis *m*.

venereal [vɪ'nɪərɪəl] *a*: ~ **disease** (VD) *n* maladie vénérienne.

Venetian [vɪ'ni:ʃən] *a*: ~ **blind** store vénitien.

vengeance ['vɛndʒəns] *n* vengeance *f*; **with a** ~ (*fig*) vraiment, pour de bon.

venison ['vɛnɪsn] *n* venaison *f*.

venom ['vɛnəm] *n* venin *m*.

vent [vɛnt] *n* conduit *m* d'aération; (*in dress, jacket*) fente *f* // *vt* (*fig: one's feelings*) donner libre cours à.

ventilate ['vɛntɪleɪt] *vt* (*room*) ventiler, aérer; **ventilator** *n* ventilateur *m*.

ventriloquist [vɛn'trɪləkwɪst] *n* ventriloque *m/f*.

venture ['vɛntʃə*] *n* entreprise *f* // *vt* risquer, hasarder // *vi* s'aventurer.

venue ['vɛnju:] *n* lieu *m* de rendez-vous or rencontre.

verb [və:b] *n* verbe *m*; ~**al** *a* verbal(e); (*translation*) littéral(e).

verbatim [və:'beɪtɪm] *a, ad* mot pour mot.

verdict ['və:dɪkt] *n* verdict *m*.

verge [və:dʒ] *n* (*Brit*) bord *m*; **on the** ~ **of** doing sur le point de faire; **to** ~ **on** *vt fus* approcher de.

vermin ['və:mɪn] *npl* animaux *mpl* nuisibles; (*insects*) vermine *f*.

vermouth ['və:məθ] *n* vermouth *m*.

versatile ['və:sətaɪl] *a* polyvalent(e).

verse [və:s] *n* vers *mpl*; (*stanza*) strophe *f*; (*in bible*) verset *m*.

version ['və:ʃən] *n* version *f*.

versus ['və:səs] *prep* contre.

vertical ['və:tɪkl] *a* vertical(e) // *n* verticale *f*; ~**ly** *ad* verticalement.

vertigo ['və:tɪgəu] *n* vertige *m*.

verve [və:v] *n* brio *m*; enthousiasme *m*.

very ['vɛrɪ] *ad* très // *a*: **the** ~ **book which** le livre même que; **at the** ~

end tout à la fin; **the** ~ **last** le tout dernier; **at the** ~ **least** au moins; ~ **much** beaucoup.

vessel ['vɛsl] *n* (*ANAT, NAUT*) vaisseau *m*; (*container*) récipient *m*.

vest [vɛst] *n* (*Brit*) tricot de corps; (*US: waistcoat*) gilet *m*; ~**ed interests** *npl* (*COMM*) droits acquis.

vestry ['vɛstrɪ] *n* sacristie *f*.

vet [vɛt] *n abbr* (= *veterinary surgeon*) vétérinaire *m/f* // *vt* examiner minutieusement; (*text*) revoir.

veteran ['vɛtərn] *n* vétéran *m*; (*also*: ~ **war**) ancien combattant.

veterinary ['vɛtrɪnərɪ] *a* vétérinaire; ~ **surgeon**, (*US*) **veterinarian** [vɛtrə'nɛərɪən] *n* vétérinaire *m/f*.

veto ['vi:təu] *n* (*pl* ~**es**) veto *m* // *vt* opposer son veto à.

vex [vɛks] *vt* fâcher, contrarier; ~**ed** *a* (*question*) controversée(e).

VHF *abbr* (= *very high frequency*) VHF *f*.

via ['vaɪə] *prep* par, via.

viable ['vaɪəbl] *a* viable.

vibrate [vaɪ'breɪt] *vi*: **to** ~ (**with**) vibrer (de); (*resound*) retentir (de).

vicar ['vɪkə*] *n* pasteur *m* (*de l'Église anglicane*); ~**age** *n* presbytère *m*.

vicarious [vɪ'kɛərɪəs] *a* indirect(e).

vice [vaɪs] *n* (*evil*) vice *m*; (*TECH*) étau *m*.

vice- ['vaɪs] *prefix* vice-.

vice squad *n* ≈ brigade mondaine.

vice versa ['vaɪsɪ'və:sə] *ad* vice versa.

vicinity [vɪ'sɪnɪtɪ] *n* environs *mpl*, alentours *mpl*.

vicious ['vɪʃəs] *a* (*remark*) cruel(le), méchant(e); (*blow*) brutal(e); ~ **circle** *n* cercle vicieux.

victim ['vɪktɪm] *n* victime *f*.

victor ['vɪktə*] *n* vainqueur *m*.

Victorian [vɪk'tɔ:rɪən] *a* victorien(ne).

victory ['vɪktərɪ] *n* victoire *f*.

video ['vɪdɪəu] *cpd* vidéo *inv* // *n* (~-**film**) vidéo *f*; (*also*: ~ **cassette**) vidéocassette *f*; (*also*: ~ **cassette re-**

corder) magnétoscope *m*; ~ **tape** *n* bande *f* vidéo *inv*; (*cassette*) vidéo-cassette *f*.

vie [vaɪ] *vi*: **to** ~ **with** rivaliser avec.

Vienna [vɪˈɛnə] *n* Vienne.

Vietnam [ˈvjɛtˈnæm] *n* Viet-Nam *m*, Vietnam *m*; ~**ese** [-nəˈmiːz] *a* viet-namien(ne) // *n* (*pl inv*) Vietnamien/ne.

view [vjuː] *n* vue *f*; (*opinion*) avis *m*, vue *f*; (*situation*) considérer; (*house*) visiter; **on** ~ (*in museum etc*) exposé(e); **in full** ~ **of** sous les yeux de; (*building etc*) devant; **in** ~ **of the fact that** étant donné que; ~**er** *n* (*viewfinder*) viseur *m*; (*small projector*) visionneuse *f*; (*TV*) téléspectateur/trice; ~**finder** *n* viseur *m*; ~**point** *n* point *m* de vue.

vigil [ˈvɪdʒɪl] *n* veille *f*.

vigorous [ˈvɪɡərəs] *a* vigou-reux(euse).

vile [vaɪl] *a* (*action*) vil(e); (*smell*) abominable; (*temper*) massa-crant(e).

villa [ˈvɪlə] *n* villa *f*.

village [ˈvɪlɪdʒ] *n* village *m*; ~**r** *n* villageois/e.

villain [ˈvɪlən] *n* (*scoundrel*) scélérat *m*; (*criminal*) bandit *m*; (*in novel etc*) traître *m*.

vindicate [ˈvɪndɪkeɪt] *vt* défendre avec succès; justifier.

vindictive [vɪnˈdɪktɪv] *a* vindica-tif(ive), rancunier(ère).

vine [vaɪn] *n* vigne *f*; (*climbing plant*) plante grimpante.

vinegar [ˈvɪnɪɡə*] *n* vinaigre *m*.

vineyard [ˈvɪnjɑːd] *n* vignoble *m*.

vintage [ˈvɪntɪdʒ] *n* (*year*) année *f*, millésime *m*; ~ **wine** *n* vin *m* de grand cru.

violate [ˈvaɪəleɪt] *vt* violer.

violence [ˈvaɪələns] *n* violence *f*; (*POL etc*) incidents violents.

violent [ˈvaɪələnt] *a* violent(e).

violet [ˈvaɪələt] *a* (*colour*) violet(te) // *n* (*plant*) violette *f*.

violin [vaɪəˈlɪn] *n* violon *m*; ~**ist** *n* violoniste *m/f*.

VIP *n* *abbr* (= *very important person*) V.I.P. *m*.

virgin [ˈvəːdʒɪn] *n* vierge *f* // *a* vierge.

Virgo [ˈvəːɡəu] *n* la Vierge.

virile [ˈvɪraɪl] *a* viril(e).

virtually [ˈvəːtjuəlɪ] *ad* (*almost*) pra-tiquement.

virtue [ˈvəːtjuː] *n* vertu *f*; (*advan-tage*) mérite *m*, avantage *m*; **by** ~ **of** par le fait de.

virtuous [ˈvəːtjuəs] *a* vertueux(euse).

virus [ˈvaɪərəs] *n* virus *m*.

visa [ˈviːzə] *n* visa *m*.

visibility [vɪzɪˈbɪlɪtɪ] *n* visibilité *f*.

visible [ˈvɪzəbl] *a* visible.

vision [ˈvɪʒən] *n* (*sight*) vue *f*, vision *f*; (*foresight, in dream*) vision.

visit [ˈvɪzɪt] *n* visite *f*; (*stay*) séjour *m* // *vt* (*person*) rendre visite à; (*place*) visiter; ~**ing hours** *npl* (*in hospital etc*) heures *fpl* de visite; ~**or** *n* visiteur/euse; (*in hotel*) client/e; ~**ors' book** *n* livre *m* d'or; (*in hotel*) registre *m*.

visor [ˈvaɪzə*] *n* visière *f*.

vista [ˈvɪstə] *n* vue *f*, perspective *f*.

visual [ˈvɪzjuəl] *a* visuel(le); ~ **aid** *n* support visuel (pour l'enseignement); ~ **display unit (VDU)** *n* console *f* de visualisation, visuel *m*.

visualize [ˈvɪzjuəlaɪz] *vt* se représen-ter; (*foresee*) prévoir.

vital [ˈvaɪtl] *a* vital(e); ~**ly** *ad* extrê-mement; ~ **statistics** *npl* (*fig*) men-surations *fpl*.

vitamin [ˈvɪtəmɪn] *n* vitamine *f*.

vivacious [vɪˈveɪʃəs] *a* animé(e), qui a de la vivacité.

vivid [ˈvɪvɪd] *a* (*account*) frap-pant(e); (*light, imagination*) vif(vive); ~**ly** *ad* (*describe*) d'une manière vivante; (*remember*) de fa-çon précise.

V-neck [ˈviːnɛk] *n* décolleté *m* en V.

vocabulary [vəuˈkæbjulərɪ] *n* voca-bulaire *m*.

vocal [ˈvəukl] *a* vocal(e); (*articulate*) qui sait s'exprimer; ~ **chords** *npl* cordes vocales.

vocation [vəuˈkeɪʃən] *n* vocation *f*;

~**al** a professionnel(le).
vociferous [vəˈsɪfərəs] a bruyant(e).
vodka [ˈvɒdkə] n vodka f.
vogue [vəʊg] n mode f; (popularity) vogue f.
voice [vɔɪs] n voix f; (opinion) avis m // vt (opinion) exprimer, formuler.
void [vɔɪd] n vide m // a nul(le); ~ **of** vide de, dépourvu(e) de.
volatile [ˈvɒlətaɪl] a volatil(e); (fig) versatile.
volcano, ~**es** [vɒlˈkeɪnəʊ] n volcan m.
volition [vəˈlɪʃən] n: **of one's own** ~ de son propre gré.
volley [ˈvɒlɪ] n (of gunfire) salve f; (of stones etc) pluie f, volée f; (TENNIS etc) volée f; ~**ball** n volley(-ball) m.
volt [vəʊlt] n volt m; ~**age** n tension f, voltage m.
volume [ˈvɒljuːm] n volume m.
voluntarily [ˈvɒləntrɪlɪ] ad volontairement; bénévolement.
voluntary [ˈvɒləntərɪ] a volontaire; (unpaid) bénévole.
volunteer [vɒlənˈtɪə*] n volontaire m/f // vi (MIL) s'engager comme volontaire; **to** ~ **to do** se proposer pour faire.
vomit [ˈvɒmɪt] vt, vi vomir.
vote [vəʊt] n vote m, suffrage m; (cast) voix f, vote; (franchise) droit m de vote // vt (chairman) élire // vi voter; ~ **of censure** motion f de censure; ~ **of thanks** discours m de remerciement; ~**r** n électeur/trice; **voting** n scrutin m.
vouch [vaʊtʃ]: **to** ~ **for** vt fus se porter garant de.
voucher [ˈvaʊtʃə*] n (for meal, petrol) bon m; (receipt) reçu m.
vow [vaʊ] n vœu m, serment m // vi jurer.
vowel [ˈvaʊəl] n voyelle f.
voyage [ˈvɔɪɪdʒ] n voyage m par mer, traversée f.
vulgar [ˈvʌlgə*] a vulgaire.
vulnerable [ˈvʌlnərəbl] a vulnérable.
vulture [ˈvʌltʃə*] n vautour m.

W

wad [wɒd] n (of cotton wool, paper) tampon m; (of banknotes etc) liasse f.
waddle [ˈwɒdl] vi se dandiner.
wade [weɪd] vi: **to** ~ **through** marcher dans, patauger dans // vt passer à gué.
wafer [ˈweɪfə*] n (CULIN) gaufrette f.
waffle [ˈwɒfl] n (CULIN) gaufre f; (col) rabâchage m; remplissage m.
waft [wɒft] vt porter // vi flotter.
wag [wæg] vt agiter, remuer // vi remuer.
wage [weɪdʒ] n (also: ~s) salaire m, paye f // vt: **to** ~ **war** faire la guerre; ~ **packet** n (enveloppe f de) paye f.
wager [ˈweɪdʒə*] n pari m.
waggle [ˈwægl] vt, vi remuer.
wag(g)on [ˈwægən] n (horse-drawn) chariot m; (Brit RAIL) wagon m (de marchandises).
wail [weɪl] n gémir; (siren) hurler.
waist [weɪst] n taille f, ceinture f; ~**coat** n (Brit) gilet m; ~**line** n (tour m de) taille f.
wait [weɪt] n attente f // vt attendre; **to lie in** ~ **for** guetter; **to** ~ **for** attendre; **I can't** ~ **to** (fig) je meurs d'envie de; **to** ~ **behind** vi rester (à attendre); **to** ~ **on** vt fus servir; ~**er** n garçon m (de café), serveur m; ~**ing** n: **'no** ~**ing'** (Brit AUT) 'stationnement interdit'; ~**ing list** n liste f d'attente; ~**ing room** n salle f d'attente; ~**ress** n serveuse f.
waive [weɪv] vt renoncer à, abandonner.
wake [weɪk] vb (pt woke, ~**d**, pp woken, ~**d**) vt (also: ~ **up**) réveiller // vi (also: ~ **up**) se réveiller // n (for dead person) veillée f mortuaire; (NAUT) sillage m; ~**n** vt, vi = **wake**.
Wales [weɪlz] n pays m de Galles.

walk [wɔ:k] n promenade f; (short) petit tour; (gait) démarche f; (path) chemin m; (in park etc) allée f // vi marcher; (for pleasure, exercise) se promener // vt (distance) faire à pied; (dog) promener; **10 minutes' ~ from** à 10 minutes de marche de; **from all ~s of life** de toutes conditions sociales; **to ~ out on** vt fus (col) quitter, plaquer; **~er** n (person) marcheur/euse; **~ie-talkie** [wɔ:kɪ'tɔ:kɪ] n talkie-walkie m; **~ing** n marche f à pied; **~ing stick** n canne f; **~out** n (of workers) grève-surprise f; **~over** n (col) victoire f or examen m etc facile; **~way** n promenade f.

wall [wɔ:l] n mur m; (of tunnel, cave) paroi f; **~ed** a (city) fortifié(e).

wallet [wɔlɪt] n portefeuille m.

wallflower [wɔ:lflauə*] n giroflée f; **to be a ~** (fig) faire tapisserie.

wallop [wɔləp] vt (col) taper sur.

wallow [wɔləu] vi se vautrer.

wallpaper [wɔ:lpeɪpə*] n papier peint.

wally [wɔlɪ] n (col) imbécile m/f.

walnut [wɔ:lnʌt] n noix f; (tree) noyer m.

walrus, pl **~** or **~es** [wɔ:lrəs] n morse m.

waltz [wɔ:lts] n valse f // vi valser.

wan [wɔn] a pâle; triste.

wand [wɔnd] n (also: **magic ~**) baguette f (magique).

wander [wɔndə*] vi (person) errer, aller sans but; (thoughts) vagabonder; (river) serpenter // vt errer dans.

wane [weɪn] vi (moon) décroître; (reputation) décliner.

wangle [wæŋgl] vt (Brit col) se débrouiller pour avoir; carotter.

want [wɔnt] vt vouloir; (need) avoir besoin de; (lack) manquer de // n: **~ for** ~ of par manque de, faute de; **~s** npl (needs) besoins mpl; **to ~ to do** vouloir faire; **to ~ sb to do** vouloir que qn fasse; **~ing** a: **to be**

found ~ing ne pas être à la hauteur.

wanton [wɔntn] a capricieux(euse); dévergondé(e).

war [wɔ:*] n guerre f; **to make ~ (on)** faire la guerre (à).

ward [wɔ:d] n (in hospital) salle f; (POL) section électorale; (LAW: child) pupille m/f; **to ~ off** vt parer, éviter.

warden [wɔ:dn] n (Brit: of institution) directeur/trice; (of park, game reserve) gardien/ne; (Brit: also: **traffic ~**) contractuel/le.

warder [wɔ:də*] n (Brit) gardien m de prison.

wardrobe [wɔ:drəub] n (cupboard) armoire f; (clothes) garde-robe f; (THEATRE) costumes mpl.

warehouse [wɛəhaus] n entrepôt m.

wares [wɛəz] npl marchandises fpl.

warfare [wɔ:fɛə*] n guerre f.

warhead [wɔ:hɛd] n (MIL) ogive f.

warily [wɛərɪlɪ] ad avec prudence.

warm [wɔ:m] a chaud(e); (thanks, welcome, applause) chaleureux(euse); **it's ~** il fait chaud; **I'm ~** j'ai chaud; **to ~ up** vi (person, room) se réchauffer; (water) chauffer; (athlete, discussion) s'échauffer // vt réchauffer; chauffer; (engine) faire chauffer; **~-hearted** a affectueux(euse); **~ly** ad chaudement; vivement; chaleureusement; **~th** n chaleur f.

warn [wɔ:n] vt avertir, prévenir; **~ing** n avertissement m; (notice) avis m; **~ing light** n avertisseur lumineux; **~ing triangle** n (AUT) triangle m de présignalisation.

warp [wɔ:p] vi travailler, se voiler // vt violer; (fig) pervertir.

warrant [wɔrnt] n (guarantee) garantie f; (LAW: to arrest) mandat m d'arrêt; (: to search) mandat de perquisition.

warranty [wɔrəntɪ] n garantie f.

warren [wɔrən] n (of rabbits) terriers mpl, garenne f.

warrior [wɔrɪə*] n guerrier/ère.

Warsaw [wɔ:sɔ:] n Varsovie.

warship ['wɔːʃɪp] n navire m de guerre.

wart [wɔːt] n verrue f.

wartime ['wɔːtaɪm] n: **in ~** en temps de guerre.

wary ['wɛərɪ] a prudent(e).

was [wɒz] pt of **be**.

wash [wɒʃ] vt laver // vi se laver // n (paint) badigeon m; (washing programme) lavage m; (of ship) sillage m; **to have a ~** se laver, faire sa toilette; **to ~ away** vt (stain) enlever au lavage; (subj: river etc) emporter; **to ~ off** vi partir au lavage; **to ~ up** vi (Brit) faire la vaisselle; (US) se débarbouiller; **~able** a lavable; **~basin**, (US) **~bowl** n lavabo m; **~cloth** n (US) gant m de toilette; **~er** n (TECH) rondelle f, joint m; **~ing** n (linen etc) lessive f; **~ing machine** n machine f à laver; **~ing powder** n (Brit) lessive f (en poudre); **~ing-up** n vaisselle f; **~ing-up liquid** n produit m pour la vaisselle; **~out** n (col) désastre m; **~room** n toilettes fpl.

wasn't ['wɒznt] = **was not**.

wasp [wɒsp] n guêpe f.

wastage ['weɪstɪdʒ] n gaspillage m; (in manufacturing, transport etc) déchet m; **natural ~** départs naturels.

waste [weɪst] n gaspillage m; (of time) perte f; (rubbish) déchets mpl; (also: household **~**) ordures fpl // a (material) de rebut; (land) inculte // vt gaspiller; (time, opportunity) perdre; **~s** npl étendue f désertique; **to ~ away** vi dépérir; **~ disposal unit** n (Brit) broyeur m d'ordures; **~ful** a gaspilleur(euse); (process) peu économique; **~ ground** n (Brit) terrain m vague; **~paper basket** n corbeille f à papier; **~ pipe** n (tuyau m de) vidange f.

watch [wɒtʃ] n montre f; (act of watching) surveillance f; guet m; (guard: MIL) sentinelle f; (NAUT) homme m de quart; (NAUT: spell of duty) quart m // vt (look at) observer; (: match, programme) regarder; (spy on, guard) surveiller; (be careful to) faire attention à // vi regarder; (keep guard) monter la garde; **to ~ out** vi faire attention; **~dog** n chien m de garde; (fig) gardien(ne), vigilant(e); **~maker** n horloger/ère; **~man** n gardien m; (also: night **~man**) veilleur m de nuit; **~ strap** n bracelet m de montre.

water ['wɔːtə*] n eau f // vt (plant) arroser // vi (eyes) larmoyer; **in British ~s** dans les eaux territoriales Britanniques; **to ~ down** vt (milk) couper d'eau; (fig: story) édulcorer; **~colour** n aquarelle f; **~colours** npl couleurs fpl pour aquarelle; **~cress** n cresson m (de fontaine); **~fall** n chute f d'eau; **~ heater** n chauffe-eau m; **~ ice** n sorbet m; **~ing can** n arrosoir m; **~ lily** n nénuphar m; **~logged** a détrempé(e); imbibé(e) d'eau; **~line** n (NAUT) ligne f de flottaison; **~ main** n canalisation f d'eau; **~mark** n (on paper) filigrane m; **~melon** n pastèque f; **~proof** a imperméable; **~shed** n (GEO) ligne f de partage des eaux; (fig) moment m critique, point décisif; **~skiing** n ski m nautique; **~tight** a étanche; **~way** n cours m d'eau navigable; **~works** npl station f hydraulique; **~y** a (colour) délavé(e); (coffee) trop faible.

watt [wɒt] n watt m.

wave [weɪv] n vague f; (of hand) geste m, signe m; (RADIO) onde f; (in hair) ondulation f // vi faire signe de la main; (flag) flotter au vent // vt (handkerchief) agiter; (stick) brandir; **~length** n longueur f d'ondes.

waver ['weɪvə*] vi vaciller; (voice) trembler; (person) hésiter.

wavy ['weɪvɪ] a ondulé(e); (hair) ondu-leux(euse).

wax [wæks] n cire f; (for skis) fart m // vt cirer; (car) lustrer // vi (moon) croître; **~works** npl personnages mpl de cire; musée m de cire.

way [weɪ] n chemin m, voie f; (path, access) passage m; (distance) distance f; (direction) chemin, direction f; (manner) façon f, manière f; (habit) habitude f, façon; (condition) état m; **which** ~? — par où or de quel côté? — par ici; **on the** ~ (en route) en route; **to be in the** ~ être en route; **to be in the** ~ bloquer le passage; (fig) gêner; **to go out of one's** ~ **to do** (fig) se donner du mal pour faire; **to lose one's** ~ perdre son chemin; **in a** ~ d'un côté; **in some** ~s à certains égards; d'un côté; **by the** ~ ... à propos ...; '~ **in**' (Brit) 'entrée'; '~ **out**' (Brit) 'sortie'.

waylay [weɪˈleɪ] vt irg attaquer; (fig): **I got waylaid** quelqu'un m'a accroché.

wayward [ˈweɪwəd] a capricieux(euse), entêté(e).

W.C. [ˈdʌbljuˈsiː] n (Brit) w.-c. mpl, waters mpl.

we [wiː] pl pronoun nous.

weak [wiːk] a faible; (health) fragile; (beam etc) peu solide; **~en** vi faiblir // vt affaiblir; **~ling** n gringalet m; faible m/f; **~ness** n faiblesse f; (fault) point m faible.

wealth [welθ] n (money, resources) richesse(s) f(pl); (of details) profusion f; **~y** a riche.

wean [wiːn] vt sevrer.

weapon [ˈwɛpən] n arme f.

wear [wɛə*] n (use) usage m; (deterioration through use) usure f; (clothing): **sports/baby** ~ vêtements mpl de sport/pour bébés // vb (pt **wore**, pp **worn**) vt (clothes) porter; mettre; (damage: through use) user // vi (last) faire de l'usage; (rub etc through) s'user; **evening** ~ tenue f de soirée; **to** ~ **away** vt user, ronger // vi s'user, être rongé(e); **to** ~ **down** vt user; (strength) épuiser; **to** ~ **off** vi disparaître; **to** ~ **on** vi se poursuivre; passer; **to** ~ **out** vt user; (person, strength) épuiser; ~

and tear n usure f.

weary [ˈwɪərɪ] a (tired) épuisé(e); (dispirited) las(lasse) // vt lasser; abattu(e).

weasel [ˈwiːzl] n (ZOOL) belette f.

weather [ˈwɛðə*] n temps m // vt (wood) faire mûrir; (tempest, crisis) essuyer, être pris(e) dans; survivre à, tenir le coup durant; **under the** ~ (fig: ill) mal fichu(e); **~-beaten** a (person) hâlé(e); (building) dégradé(e) par les intempéries; **~cock** n girouette f; ~ **forecast** n prévisions fpl météorologiques, météo f; ~ **vane** n =**cock**.

weave [wiːv] pt **wove**, pp **woven** [wiːv, wəʊv, ˈwəʊvən] vt (cloth) tisser; (basket) tresser; ~ r n tisserand/e.

web [web] n (of spider) toile f; (on foot) palmure f; (fabric, also fig) tissu m.

wed [wed], pt, pp **wedded** vt épouser // vi se marier.

we'd [wiːd] = **we had**, **we would**.

wedding [ˈwedɪŋ] n mariage m; **silver/ golden** ~ **anniversary** noces fpl d'argent/d'or; ~ **day** n jour m du mariage; ~ **dress** n robe f de mariage; ~ **ring** n alliance f.

wedge [wedʒ] n (of wood etc) coin m; (under door etc) cale f; (of cake) part f // vt (fix) caler; (push) enfoncer, coincer.

wedlock [ˈwedlɒk] n (union f du) mariage m.

Wednesday [ˈwednzdɪ] n mercredi m.

wee [wiː] a (Scottish) petit(e); tout(e) petit(e).

weed [wiːd] n mauvaise herbe // vt désherber; **~killer** n désherbant m; **~y** a (man) gringalet.

week [wiːk] n semaine f; **a** ~ **today/on Friday** aujourd'hui/ vendredi en huit; **~day** n jour m de semaine; (COMM) jour ouvrable; **~end** n week-end m; **~ly** ad une fois par semaine, chaque semaine // a, n hebdomadaire (m).

weep [wiːp], pt, pp **wept** vi (person) pleurer; **~ing willow** n saule pleureur.

weigh [weɪ] *vt, vi* peser; **to ~** **down** *vt* (*branch*) faire plier; (*fig: with worry*) accabler; **to ~ up** *vt* examiner.

weight [weɪt] *n* poids *m*; **to lose/put on ~** maigrir/grossir; **~ing** *n* (*allowance*) indemnité *f*, allocation *f*; **~ lifter** *n* haltérophile *m*; **~y** *a* lourd(e).

weir [wɪə*] *n* barrage *m*.

weird [wɪəd] *a* bizarre; (*eerie*) surnaturel(le).

welcome ['wɛlkəm] *a* bienvenu(e) // *n* accueil *m* // *vt* accueillir; (*also:* **bid ~**) souhaiter la bienvenue à; (*be glad of*) se réjouir de; **to be ~** être le(la) bienvenu(e); **thank you ~ you're ~!** merci — de rien *or* il n'y a pas de quoi.

weld [wɛld] *n* soudure *f* // *vt* souder.

welfare ['wɛlfɛə*] *n* bien-être *m*; **~ state** *n* État-providence *m*.

well [wɛl] *n* puits *m* // *ad* bien // *a*: **to be ~** aller bien // *excl* eh bien!; bon!; enfin!; **as ~** aussi, également; **as ~ as** aussi bien que; en plus de; **~ done!** bravo!; **get ~ soon** remets-toi vite!; **to do ~** in sth bien réussir en *or* dans qch; **to ~ up** *vi* monter.

we'll [wiːl] = **we will**, **we shall**.

well: **~-behaved** *a* sage obéissant(e);. **~-being** *n* être *m*; **~-built** *a* (*person*) bien bâti(e); **~-dressed** *a* bien habillé(e), bien vêtu(e); **~-heeled** *a* (*col: wealthy*) fortuné(e), riche.

wellingtons ['wɛlɪŋtənz] *npl* (*also:* **wellington boots**) bottes *fpl* de caoutchouc.

well: **~-known** *a* (*person*) bien connu(e); **~-mannered** *a* bien élevé(e); **~-meaning** *a* bien intentionné(e); **~-off** *a* aisé(e), assez riche; **~-read** *a* cultivé(e); **~-to-do** *a* aisé(e), assez riche; **~-wisher** *n*: scores of **~-wishers** had gathered de nombreux amis et admirateurs s'étaient rassemblés.

Welsh [wɛlʃ] *a* gallois(e) // *n* (*LING*) gallois *m*; **the ~** *npl* les Gallois *mpl*; **~man/woman** *n* Gallois/e; **~ rarebit** *n* croûte *f* au fromage.

went [wɛnt] *pt of* **go**.

wept [wɛpt] *pt, pp of* **weep**.

were [wəː*] *pt of* **be**.

we're [wɪə*] = **we are**.

weren't [wəːnt] = **were not**.

west [wɛst] *n* ouest *m* // *a* ouest *inv*, de *or* à l'ouest // *ad* à *or* vers l'ouest; **the W~** l'Occident *m*, l'Ouest; **the W~ Country** *n* (*Brit*) le sud-ouest de l'Angleterre; **~erly** *a* (*wind*) d'ouest; **~ern** *a* occidental(e), de *or* à l'ouest // *n* (*CINEMA*) western *m*; **W~ Germany** *n* Allemagne *f* de l'Ouest; **W~ Indian** *a* antillais(e) // *n* Antillais/e; **W~ Indies** *npl* Antilles *fpl*; **~ward(s)** *ad* vers l'ouest.

wet [wɛt] *a* mouillé(e); (*damp*) humide; (*soaked*) trempé(e); (*rainy*) pluvieux,euse; **to get ~** se mouiller; '**~ paint**' 'attention peinture fraîche'; **~ blanket** *n* (*fig*) rabat-joie *m inv*; **~ suit** *n* combinaison *f* de plongée.

we've [wiːv] = **we have**.

whack [wæk] *vt* donner un grand coup à.

whale [weɪl] *n* (*ZOOL*) baleine *f*.

wharf, *pl* **wharves** [woːf, woːvz] *n* quai *m*.

KEYWORD

---

what [wɔt] ◆ *a* quel(le), *pl* quels(quelles); **~ size is he?** quelle taille fait-il?; **~ colour is it?** de quelle couleur est-ce?; **~ books do you need?** quels livres vous faut-il?; **~ a mess!** quel désordre!

◆ *pronoun* **1** (*interrogative*) que, *prep* + quoi; **~ are you doing?** que faites-vous?, qu'est-ce que vous faites?; **~ is happening?** qu'est-ce qui se passe?, que se passe-t-il?; **~ are you talking about?** de quoi parlez-vous?; **~ is it called?** comment est-ce que ça s'appelle?; **~ about me?**

et moi?; ~ **about doing ...?** et si on faisait ...?

2 (*relative: subject*) ce qui; (: *direct object*) ce que; (: *indirect object*) ce + *prep* + quoi, ce dont; **I saw** ~ **you did/was on the table** j'ai vu ce que vous avez fait/ce qui était sur la table; **tell me** ~ **you remember** dites-moi ce dont vous vous souvenez

◆ *excl* (*disbelieving*) quoi!, comment!

whatever [wɔt'ɛvə*] *a*: ~ **book** quel que soit le livre que (*or* qui) + *sub*; n'importe quel livre // *pronoun*: **do** ~ **is necessary** faites (tout) ce qui est nécessaire; ~ **happens** quoi qu'il arrive; **no reason** ~ *or* **whatsoever** pas la moindre raison; **nothing** ~ rien du tout.

wheat [wi:t] *n* blé *m*, froment *m*.

wheedle [wi:dl] *vt*: **to** ~ **sb into doing sth** cajoler *or* enjôler qn pour qu'il fasse qch; **to** ~ **sth out of sb** obtenir qch de qn par des cajoleries.

wheel [wi:l] *n* roue *f*; (*AUT: also: steering* ~) volant *m*; (*NAUT*) gouvernail *m* // *vt* pousser, rouler // *vi* (*also:* ~ **round**) tourner; ~**barrow** *n* brouette *f*; ~**chair** *n* fauteuil roulant; ~ **clamp** *n* (*AUT*) sabot *m* (de Denver).

wheeze [wi:z] *vi* respirer bruyamment.

───────

KEYWORD

when [wɛn] ◆ *ad* quand; ~ **did it happen?** quand est ce que c'est arrivé?

◆ *cj* **1** (*at, during, after the time that*) quand, lorsque; **she was reading** ~ **I came in** elle lisait quand *or* lorsque je suis entré

2 (*on, at which*): **on the day** ~ **I met him** le jour où je l'ai rencontré

3 (*whereas*) alors que; **you said I was wrong** ~ **in fact I was right** vous avez dit que j'avais tort alors qu'en fait j'avais raison.

───────

whenever [wɛn'ɛvə*] *ad* quand // *cj* quand; (*every time that*) chaque fois que; **you may leave** ~ **you like** vous pouvez partir quand vous voulez.

where [wɛə*] *ad, cj* où; **this is** ~ c'est là que; ~**abouts** *ad* où donc // *n*: **sb's ~abouts** l'endroit où se trouve qn; ~**as** *cj* alors que; ~**by** *pronoun* par lequel (*or* laquelle *etc*); ~**upon** *cj* sur quoi, et sur ce; ~**ver** [-'ɛvə*] *ad* où donc // *cj* où que + *sub*; ~**withal** *n* moyens *mpl*.

whet [wɛt] *vt* aiguiser.

whether [wɛðə*] *cj* si; **I don't know** ~ **to accept or not** je ne sais pas si je dois accepter ou non; **it's doubtful** ~ il est peu probable que; ~ **you go or not** que vous y alliez ou non.

───────

KEYWORD

which [wɪtʃ] ◆ *a* **1** (*interrogative: direct, indirect*) quel(le), *pl* quels(quelles); ~ **picture do you want?** quel tableau voulez-vous?; ~ **one?** lequel(laquelle)?

2: in ~ **case** auquel cas

◆ *pronoun* **1** (*interrogative*) lequel(laquelle), *pl* lesquels-(lesquelles); **I don't mind** ~ (*of these*) **are yours?** lesquels sont à vous?; **here are the books** — **tell me** ~ **you want** voici les livres — dites-moi lesquels *or* ceux que vous voulez

2 (*relative: subject*) qui; (: *object*) que, *prep* + lequel(laquelle) (NB: à + *lequel* = auquel; de + *lequel* = duquel); **the apple** ~ **you ate/**~ **is on the table** la pomme que vous avez mangée/qui est sur la table; **the chair on** ~ **you are sitting** la chaise sur laquelle vous êtes assis; **the book of** ~ **you spoke** le livre dont vous avez parlé; **he said he knew,** ~ **is true/I feared** il a dit qu'il le savait, ce qui est vrai/ce que je craignais; **after** ~ après quoi.

whichever [wɪtʃ'evə*] a: take ~ book you prefer prenez le livre que vous préférez, peu importe lequel; ~ way you do something de quelque façon que vous + sub.

whiff [wɪf] n bouffée f.

while [waɪl] n moment m // cj pendant que; (as long as) tant que; (whereas) alors que; bien que + sub; for a ~ pendant quelque temps; to ~ away vt (time) (faire) passer.

whim [wɪm] n caprice m.

whimper ['wɪmpə*] vi geindre.

whimsical ['wɪmzɪkl] a (person) capricieux(euse); (look) étrange.

whine [waɪn] vi gémir, geindre, pleurnicher.

whip [wɪp] n fouet m; (for riding) cravache f; (POL: person) chef m de file (assurant la discipline dans son groupe parlementaire) // vt fouetter; (snatch) enlever (or sortir) brusquement; **~ped cream** n crème fouettée; **~-round** n (Brit) collecte f.

whirl [wə:l] vt faire tourbillonner; faire tournoyer // vi tourbillonner; **~pool** n tourbillon m; **~wind** n tornade f.

whirr [wə:*] vi bruire; ronronner; vrombir.

whisk [wɪsk] n (CULIN) fouet m // vt fouetter, battre; to ~ sb away or off emmener qn rapidement.

whisker ['wɪskə*] n: ~s (of animal) moustaches fpl; (of man) favoris mpl.

whisky, (Irish, US) **whiskey** ['wɪskɪ] n whisky m.

whisper ['wɪspə*] vt, vi chuchoter.

whistle ['wɪsl] n (sound) sifflement m; (object) sifflet m // vi siffler.

white [waɪt] a blanc(blanche); (with fear) blême // n blanc m; (person) blanc/blanche; ~ **coffee** n (Brit) café m au lait, (café) crème m; **~-collar worker** n employé-e de bureau; ~ **elephant** n (fig) objet dispendieux et superflu; ~ **lie** n pieux mensonge; ~ **paper** n (POL) livre blanc; **~wash** vt blanchir à la

chaux; (fig) blanchir.

whiting ['waɪtɪŋ] n (pl inv) (fish) merlan m.

Whitsun ['wɪtsn] n la Pentecôte.

whittle ['wɪtl] vt: to ~ away, ~ down (costs) réduire, rogner.

whizz [wɪz] vi aller (or passer) à toute vitesse; ~ **kid** n (col) petit prodige.

who [hu:] pronoun qui.

whodunit [hu:'dʌnɪt] n (col) roman policier.

whoever [hu:'evə*] pronoun: ~ finds it celui(celle) qui le trouve, (qui que ce soit), quiconque le trouve; **ask ~ you like** demandez à qui vous voulez; ~ **he marries** qui que ce soit or quelle que soit la personne qu'il épouse; ~ **told you that?** qui a bien pu vous dire ça?

whole [həʊl] a (complete) entier(ère), tout(e); (not broken) intact(e), complet(ète) // n (total) totalité f; (sth not broken) tout m; the ~ **of the town** la ville tout entière; **on the ~, as a ~** dans l'ensemble; **~hearted** a sans réserve(s), sincère; **~meal** a (bread, flour) complet(ète); **~sale** n (vente f en) gros m // a de gros; (destruction) systématique; **~saler** n grossiste m/f; **~some** a sain(e); (advice) salutaire; **~wheat** a = **~meal;**

wholly ad entièrement, tout à fait.

KEYWORD

whom [hu:m] pronoun **1** (interrogative) qui; ~ **did you see?** qui avez-vous vu? **to ~ did you give it?** à qui l'avez-vous donné?
2 (relative, gen, prep + qui) (check syntax of French used): **the man ~ I saw/to ~ I spoke** l'homme que j'ai vu/à qui j'ai parlé.

---

whooping cough ['hu:pɪŋkɒf] n coqueluche f.

whore [hɔ:*] n (col: pej) putain f.

whose [huːz] ◆ a 1 (possessive: interrogative): ~ book is this? à qui est ce livre?; ~ pencil have you taken? à qui est le crayon que vous avez pris?, c'est le crayon de qui que vous avez pris?; ~ daughter are you? de qui êtes-vous la fille?
2 (possessive: relative): the man ~ son you rescued l'homme dont or de qui vous avez sauvé le fils; the girl ~ sister you were speaking to la fille à la sœur de qui or de laquelle vous parliez; the woman ~ car was stolen la femme dont la voiture a été volée
◆ pronoun à qui; ~ is this? à qui est ceci?; I know ~ it is je sais à qui c'est.

why [waɪ] ad pourquoi // excl eh bien!, tiens!; the reason ~ la raison pour laquelle; tell me ~ dites-moi pourquoi; ~ not? pourquoi pas?; ~ever ad pourquoi donc, mais pourquoi.

wick [wɪk] n mèche f (de bougie).

wicked ['wɪkɪd] a mauvais(e), méchant(e); inique; cruel(le); (mischievous) malicieux(euse).

wicker ['wɪkə*] n osier m; (also: ~work) vannerie f.

wicket ['wɪkɪt] n (CRICKET) guichet m; espace compris entre les deux guichets.

wide [waɪd] a large; (area, knowledge) vaste, étendu(e); (choice) grand(e) // ad: to open ~ ouvrir tout grand; to shoot ~ tirer à côté; ~angle lens n objectif m grandangulaire; ~-awake a bien éveillé(e); ~ly ad (differing) radicalement; (spaced) sur une grande étendue; (believed) généralement; ~n vt or élargir; ~ open a grand(e) ouvert(e); ~spread a (belief etc) très répandu(e).

widow ['wɪdəu] n veuve f; ~er n veuf m.

width [wɪdθ] n largeur f.

wield [wiːld] vt (sword) manier; (power) exercer.

wife, wives [waɪf, waɪvz] n femme (mariée), épouse f.

wig [wɪg] n perruque f.

wiggle ['wɪgl] vt agiter, remuer.

wild [waɪld] a sauvage; (sea) déchaîné(e); (idea, life) fou(folle); extravagant(e); ~s npl régions fpl sauvages; ~erness ['wɪldənɪs] n désert m, région f sauvage; ~-goose chase n (fig) fausse piste; ~life n faune f (et flore f) sauvage(s); ~ly ad (applaud) frénétiquement; (hit, guess) au hasard; (happy) follement.

wilful ['wɪlful] a (person) obstiné(e); (action) délibéré(e); (crime) prémédité(e).

will [wɪl] ◆ auxiliary vb 1 (forming future tense): I ~ finish it tomorrow je le finirai demain; I ~ have finished it by tomorrow je l'aurai fini d'ici demain; ~ you do it? — yes I ~/no I won't le ferez-vous? — oui/non
2 (in conjectures, predictions): he ~ or he'll be there by now il doit être arrivé à l'heure qu'il est; that ~ be the postman ça doit être le facteur
3 (in commands, requests, offers): ~ you be quiet! voulez-vous bien vous taire!; ~ you help me? est-ce que vous pouvez m'aider?; ~ you have a cup of tea? voulez-vous une tasse de thé?; I won't put up with it! je ne le tolérerai pas!
◆ vt (pt, pp ~ed): to ~ sb to do souhaiter ardemment que qn fasse; he ~ed himself to go on par un suprême effort de volonté, il continua
◆ n volonté f; testament m.

willing ['wɪlɪŋ] a de bonne volonté, serviable; he's ~ to do it il est disposé à le faire, il veut bien le faire; ~ly ad volontiers; ~ness a bonne volonté.

willow ['wɪləu] n saule m.

will power n volonté f.

willy-nilly ['wɪlɪ'nɪlɪ] ad bon gré mal gré.

wilt [wɪlt] vi dépérir.

wily ['waɪlɪ] a rusé(e).

win [wɪn] n (in sports etc) victoire f // vb (pt, pp **won** [wʌn]) vt (battle, money) gagner; (prize) remporter; (popularity) acquérir // vi gagner; **to ~ over**, (Brit) **~ round** vt gagner, se concilier.

wince [wɪns] vi tressaillir.

winch [wɪntʃ] n treuil m.

wind n [wɪnd] (also MED) vent m // vb [waɪnd] (pt, pp **wound** [waund]) vt enrouler; (wrap) envelopper; (clock, toy) remonter; (take breath away: [wɪnd]) couper le souffle à // vi (road, river) serpenter; **to ~ up** vt (clock) remonter; (debate) terminer, clôturer; **~fall** n coup m de chance; **~ing** a (road) sinueux(euse); (staircase) tournant(e); **~ instrument** n (MUS) instrument m à vent; **~mill** n moulin m à vent.

window ['wɪndəu] n fenêtre f; (in car, train, also: **~pane**) vitre f; (in shop etc) vitrine f; **~ box** n jardinière f; **~ cleaner** n (person) laveur/euse de vitres; **~ ledge** n rebord m de la fenêtre; **~ pane** n vitre f, carreau m; **~sill** n (inside) appui m de la fenêtre; (outside) rebord m de la fenêtre.

windpipe ['wɪndpaɪp] n gosier m.

windscreen, (US) **windshield** ['wɪndskriːn, 'wɪndʃiːld] n pare-brise m inv; **~ washer** n lave-glace m inv; **~ wiper** n essuie-glace m inv.

windswept ['wɪndswept] a balayé(e) par le vent.

windy ['wɪndɪ] a venté(e), venteux(euse); **it's ~** il y a du vent.

wine [waɪn] n vin m; **~ cellar** n cave f à vins; **~ glass** n verre m à vin; **~ list** n carte f des vins; **~ tasting** n dégustation f (de vins); **~**

waiter n sommelier m.

wing [wɪŋ] n aile f; **~s** npl (THEATRE) coulisses fpl; **~er** n (SPORT) ailier m.

wink [wɪŋk] n clin m d'œil // vi faire un clin d'œil; (blink) cligner des yeux.

winner ['wɪnə*] n gagnant/e.

winning ['wɪnɪŋ] a (team) gagnant(e); (goal) décisif(ive); **~s** npl gains mpl; **~ post** n poteau m d'arrivée.

winter ['wɪntə*] n hiver m // vi hiverner; **~ sports** npl sports mpl d'hiver.

wintry ['wɪntrɪ] a hivernal(e).

wipe [waɪp] n coup m de torchon (or de chiffon or d'éponge) // vt essuyer; **to ~ off** vt essuyer; **to ~ out** vt (debt) régler; (memory) oublier; (destroy) anéantir; **to ~ up** vt essuyer.

wire ['waɪə*] n fil m (de fer); (ELEC) fil électrique; (TEL) télégramme m // vt (house) faire l'installation électrique de; (also: **~ up**) brancher.

wireless ['waɪəlɪs] n (Brit) télégraphie f sans fil; (set) T.S.F. f.

wiring ['waɪərɪŋ] n installation f électrique.

wiry ['waɪərɪ] a noueux(euse), nerveux(euse).

wisdom ['wɪzdəm] n sagesse f; (of action) prudence f; **~ tooth** n dent f de sagesse.

wise [waɪz] a sage, prudent(e), judicieux(euse).

...wise [waɪz] suffix: time~ en ce qui concerne le temps, question temps.

wish [wɪʃ] n (desire) désir m; (specific desire) souhait m, vœu m // vt souhaiter, désirer, vouloir; best **~es** (on birthday etc) meilleurs vœux; **with best ~es** (in letter) bien amicalement; **to ~ sb goodbye** dire au revoir à qn; **he ~ed me well** il me souhaitait de réussir; **to ~ to do/sb to do** désirer or vouloir faire/que qn fasse; **to ~ for** souhaiter; **it's ~ful thinking** c'est prendre ses désirs pour des réalités.

wishy-washy [ˈwɪʃɪˈwɒʃɪ] a (col: colour) délavé(e); (: ideas, argument) faiblard(e).

wisp [wɪsp] n fine mèche (de cheveux); (of smoke) mince volute f.

wistful [ˈwɪstful] a mélancolique.

wit [wɪt] n (gen pl) intelligence f, esprit m; présence f d'esprit; (wittiness) esprit; (person) homme/femme d'esprit.

witch [wɪtʃ] n sorcière f.

KEYWORD

with [wɪð, wɪθ] prep **1** (in the company of) avec; (at the home of) chez; **we stayed ~ friends** nous avons logé chez des amis; **I'll be ~ you in a minute** je suis à vous dans un instant
2 (descriptive): **a room ~ a view** une chambre avec vue; **the man ~ the grey hat/blue eyes** l'homme au chapeau gris/aux yeux bleus
3 (indicating manner, means, cause): **~ tears in her eyes** les larmes aux yeux; **to walk ~ a stick** marcher avec une canne; **red ~ anger** rouge de colère; **to shake ~ fear** trembler de peur; **to fill sth ~ water** remplir qch d'eau
4: I'm ~ you (I understand) je vous suis; **to be ~ it** (col: up-to-date) être dans le vent.

---

withdraw [wɪθˈdrɔ:] vb (irg) vt retirer // vi se retirer; (go back on promise) se rétracter; **~al** n retrait m; (MED) état m de manque; **~n** a (person) renfermé(e).

wither [ˈwɪðə*] vi se faner.

withhold [wɪθˈhəuld] vt irg (money) retenir; (decision) remettre; (permission): **to ~ (from)** refuser (à); (information): **to ~ (from)** cacher (à).

within [wɪðˈɪn] prep à l'intérieur de // ad à l'intérieur; **~ sight of** en vue

de; **~ a mile of** à moins d'un mille de; **~ the week** avant la fin de la semaine.

without [wɪðˈaut] prep sans.

withstand [wɪθˈstænd] vt irg résister à.

witness [ˈwɪtnɪs] n (person) témoin m; (evidence) témoignage m // vt (event) être témoin de; (document) attester l'authenticité de; **~ box**, (US) **~ stand** n barre f des témoins.

witticism [ˈwɪtɪsɪzm] n mot m d'esprit.

witty [ˈwɪtɪ] a spirituel(le), plein(e) d'esprit.

wives [waɪvz] npl of **wife**.

wizard [ˈwɪzəd] n magicien m.

wk abbr of **week**.

wobble [ˈwɒbl] vi trembler; (chair) branler.

woe [wəu] n malheur m.

woke [wəuk] pt of **wake**; **~n** pp of **wake**.

wolf, pl **wolves** [wulf, wulvz] n loup m.

woman, pl **women** [ˈwumən, ˈwɪmɪn] n femme f; **~ doctor** n femme f médecin; **women's lib** n (col) MLF m.

womb [wu:m] n (ANAT) utérus m.

women [ˈwɪmɪn] npl of **woman**.

won [wʌn] pt, pp of **win**.

wonder [ˈwʌndə*] n merveille f, miracle m; (feeling) émerveillement m // vi: **to ~ whether** se demander si; **to ~ at** s'étonner de; s'émerveiller de; **to ~ about** songer à; **it's no wonder that** il n'est pas étonnant que + sub; **~ful** a merveilleux(euse).

won't [wəunt] = **will not**.

woo [wu:] vt (woman) faire la cour à.

wood [wud] n (timber, forest) bois m; **~ carving** n sculpture f en or sur bois; **~ed** a boisé(e); **~en** a en bois; (fig) raide; inexpressif(ive); **~pecker** n pic m (oiseau); **~wind** n (MUS) bois m; **the ~wind** (MUS) les bois; **~work** n menuiserie f; **~worm** n ver m du bois.

wool [wul] n laine f; **to pull the ~
over sb's eyes** (fig) en faire ac-
croire à qn; **~len**, (US) **~en** a de
laine; (industry) lainier(ère); **~lens**
npl lainages mpl; **~ly**, (US) **~y** a
laineux(euse); (fig: ideas) confus(e).

word [wə:d] n mot m; (spoken) mot,
parole f; (promise) parole; (news)
nouvelles fpl // vt rédiger, formuler;
in other ~s en d'autres termes; **to
break/ keep one's ~** manquer à/
tenir sa parole; **~ing** n termes mpl,
langage m; libellé m; **~ processing** n traitement m de texte; **~ processor** n machine f de traitement de
texte.

wore [wɔ:*] pt of wear.

work [wə:k] n travail m; (ART, LIT-
ERATURE) œuvre f // vi travailler;
(mechanism) marcher, fonctionner;
(plan etc) marcher; (medicine) agir
// vt (clay, wood etc) travailler;
(mine etc) exploiter; (machine) faire
marcher ou fonctionner; **to be out of
~** être au chômage; **~s** n (Brit: factory) usine f // npl (of clock, machine) mécanisme m; **to ~ loose** vi
se défaire, se desserrer; **to ~ on** vt
fus travailler à; (principle) se baser
sur; **to ~ out** vi (plans etc) marcher // vt (problem) résoudre; (plan)
élaborer; **it ~s out at £100** ça fait
100 livres; **to get ~ed up** se mettre
dans tous ses états; **~able** a (solution) réalisable; **~aholic** n bourreau
m de travail; **~er** n travailleur/euse,
ouvrier/ère; **~force** n main-d'œuvre
f; **~ing class** n classe ouvrière;
~ing-class a ouvrière(ère); **~ing
man** n travailleur m; **~ing order**
n: **in ~ing order** en état de marche;
~man n ouvrier m; **~manship** n
métier m, habileté f; facture f;
~sheet n feuille f de programmation; **~shop** n atelier m; **~ station**
n poste m de travail; **~-to-rule** n
(Brit) grève f du zèle.

world [wə:ld] n monde m // cpd
(champion) du monde; (power, war)
mondial(e); **to think the ~ of sb**

(fig) ne jurer que par qn; **~ly** a de
ce monde; **~wide** a universel(le).

worm [wə:m] n ver m.

worn [wɔ:n] pp of wear // a usé(e);
~-out a (object) complètement
usé(e); (person) épuisé(e).

worried [ˈwʌrɪd] a inquiet(ète).

worry [ˈwʌrɪ] n souci m // vt inquiéter // vi s'inquiéter, se faire du souci.

worse [wə:s] a pire, plus mauvais(e)
// ad plus mal // n pire m; **a change
for the ~** une détérioration; **~n** vt, vi
empirer; **~ off** a moins à l'aise
financièrement; (fig): **you'll be
~ off this way** ça ira moins bien de
cette façon.

worship [ˈwə:ʃɪp] n culte m // vt
(God) rendre un culte à; (person)
adorer; **Your W~** (Brit: to mayor)
Monsieur le Maire; (: to judge) Monsieur le Juge.

worst [wə:st] a (le) pire, (le)la)
plus mauvais(e) // ad le plus mal // n
pire m; **at ~** au pis aller.

worsted [ˈwustɪd] n: **(wool)** ~ laine
peignée.

worth [wə:θ] n valeur f // a: **to be
~** valoir; **it's ~ it** cela en vaut la
peine; **it is ~ one's while (to do)**
on gagne (à faire); **~less** a qui ne
vaut rien; **~while** a (activity) qui
en vaut la peine; (cause) louable.

worthy [ˈwə:ðɪ] a (person) digne;
(motive) louable; **~ of** digne de.

KEYWORD

---

would [wud] auxiliary vb **1** (conditional tense): **if you asked him he
~ do it** si vous le lui demandiez, il le
ferait; **if you had asked him he ~
have done it** si vous le lui aviez demandé, il l'aurait fait

2 (in offers, invitations, requests):
~ you like a biscuit? voulez-vous ou
voudriez-vous un biscuit?; **~ you
close the door please?** voulez-vous
fermer la porte, s'il vous plaît

3 (in indirect speech): **I said I ~** do
it j'ai dit que je le ferais

4 (emphatic): **it WOULD have to**

snow today! naturellement il neige *or* il fallait qu'il neige aujourd'hui!
5 (*insistence*): she ~n't do it elle n'a pas voulu *or* elle a refusé de le faire
6 (*conjecture*): it ~ have been midnight il devait être minuit
7 (*indicating habit*): he ~ go there on Mondays il y allait le lundi.

would-be ['wudbi:] *a* (*pej*) soidisant.

wouldn't ['wudnt] = **would not**.

wound *vb* [waund] *pt, pp of* **wind** // *n, vt* [wu:nd] *n* blessure *f* // *vt* blesser.

wove [wəuv] *pt of* **weave**; ~**n** *pp of* **weave**.

wrangle ['ræŋgl] *n* dispute *f*.

wrap [ræp] *n* (*stole*) écharpe *f*; (*cape*) pèlerine *f* // *vt* (*also*: ~ up) envelopper; ~**per** *n* (*Brit*: *of book*) couverture *f*; ~**ping paper** *n* papier *m* d'emballage; (*for gift*) papier cadeau.

wrath [rɔθ] *n* courroux *m*.

wreak [ri:k] *vt*: to ~ havoc on avoir un effet désastreux sur; to ~ vengeance (on) se venger (de).

wreath, ~**s** [ri:θ, ri:ðz] *n* couronne *f*.

wreck [rɛk] *n* (*sea disaster*) naufrage *m*; (*ship*) épave *f*; (*pej*: *person*) loque humaine // *vt* démolir; (*ship*) provoquer le naufrage de; (*fig*) briser, ruiner; ~**age** *n* débris *mpl*; (*of building*) décombres *mpl*; (*of ship*) épave *f*.

wren [rɛn] *n* (*ZOOL*) roitelet *m*.

wrench [rɛntʃ] *n* (*TECH*) clé *f* (à écrous); (*tug*) violent mouvement de torsion; (*fig*) arrachement *m* // *vt* tirer violemment sur, tordre; to ~ **sth from** arracher qch (violemment) à *or* de.

wrestle ['rɛsl] *vi*: to ~ (with sb) lutter (avec qn); to ~ **with** (*fig*) se débattre avec, lutter contre; ~**r** *n* lutteur/euse; **wrestling** *n* lutte *f*; (*also*: **all-in wrestling**) catch *m*.

wretched ['rɛtʃɪd] *a* misérable; (*col*) maudit(e).

wriggle ['rɪgl] *vi* se tortiller.

wring [rɪŋ], *pt, pp* **wrung** *vt* tordre; (*wet clothes*) essorer; (*fig*): to ~ **sth out of** arracher qch à.

wrinkle ['rɪŋkl] *n* (*on skin*) ride *f*; (*on paper etc*) pli *m* // *vt* rider, plisser // *vi* se plisser.

wrist [rɪst] *n* poignet *m*; ~**watch** *n* montre-bracelet *f*.

writ [rɪt] *n* acte *m* judiciaire.

write [raɪt], *pt* **wrote**, *pp* **written** *vt, vi* écrire; to ~ **down** *vt* noter; (*put in writing*) mettre par écrit; to ~ **off** *vt* (*debt*) passer aux profits et pertes; (*depreciate*) amortir; to ~ **out** *vt* écrire; (*copy*) recopier; to ~ **up** *vt* rédiger; ~**-off** *n* perte totale; ~**r** *n* auteur *m*, écrivain *m*.

writhe [raɪð] *vi* se tordre.

writing ['raɪtɪŋ] *n* écriture *f*; (*of author*) œuvres *fpl*; **in** ~ par écrit; ~ **paper** *n* papier *m* à lettres.

written ['rɪtn] *pp of* **write**.

wrong [rɔŋ] *n* faux(fausse); (*incorrectly chosen*: *number, road etc*) mauvais(e); (*not suitable*) qui ne convient pas; (*wicked*) mal; (*unfair*) injuste // *ad* faux // *n* tort *m* // *vt* faire du tort à, léser; you are ~ **to do it** tu as tort de le faire; you are ~ **about that,** you've got it ~ tu te trompes; to be in the ~ avoir tort; what's ~? qu'est-ce qui ne va pas? to go ~ (*person*) se tromper; (*plan*) mal tourner; (*machine*) tomber en panne; ~**ful** *a* injustifié(e); ~**ly** *ad* à tort.

wrote [rəut] *pt of* **write**.

wrought [rɔ:t] *a*: ~ **iron** fer forgé.

wrung [rʌŋ] *pt, pp of* **wring**.

wry [raɪ] *a* désabusé(e).

wt. *abbr of* **weight**.

X Y Z

Xmas ['eksməs] *n abbr of* **Christmas.**

X-ray [eks'reɪ] *n* rayon *m* X; *(photograph)* radio(graphie) *f*.

xylophone ['zaɪləfəʊn] *n* xylophone *m*.

yacht [jɒt] *n* yacht *m*; voilier *m*; ~**ing** *n* yachting *m*, navigation *f* de plaisance.

Yank [jæŋk], **Yankee** ['jæŋkɪ] *n (pej)* Ameriloque *m/f*.

yap [jæp] *vi (dog)* japper.

yard [jɑːd] *n (of house etc)* cour *f*; *(measure)* yard *m* (= 914 *mm*; 3 *feet)*; ~**stick** *n (fig)* mesure *f*, critère *m*.

yarn [jɑːn] *n* fil *m*; *(tale)* longue histoire.

yawn [jɔːn] *n* bâillement *m* // *vi* bâiller; ~**ing** *a (gap)* béant(e).

yd. *abbr of* **yard(s)**.

yeah [jɛə] *ad (col)* ouais.

year [jɪə*] *n* an *m*, année *f*; **to be** 8 ~**s old** avoir 8 ans; **an eight-~-old child** un enfant de huit ans; ~**ly** *a* annuel(le) // *ad* annuellement.

yearn [jəːn] *vi*: **to ~ for sth** aspirer à qch, languir après qch; **to ~ to do** aspirer à faire; ~**ing** *n* désir ardent, envie *f*.

yeast [jiːst] *n* levure *f*.

yell [jɛl] *vi* hurler.

yellow ['jɛləʊ] *a*, *n* jaune *(m)*.

yelp [jɛlp] *vi* japper, glapir.

yeoman ['jəʊmən] *n*: **Y~ of the Guard** hallebardier *m* de la garde royale.

yes [jɛs] *ad* oui; *(answering negative question)* si // *n* oui *m*; **to say/answer ~** dire/répondre oui.

yesterday ['jɛstədɪ] *ad*, *n* hier *(m)*; ~ **morning/evening** hier matin/soir; **all day ~** toute la journée d'hier.

yet [jɛt] *ad* encore; déjà // *cj* pourtant, néanmoins; **it is not finished** ~ ce n'est pas encore fini *or* toujours pas fini; **the best** ~ le meilleur jusqu'ici *or* jusque-là; **as** ~ jusqu'ici, encore.

yew [juː] *n* if *m*.

yield [jiːld] *n* production *f*, rendement *m*; rapport *m* // *vt* produire, rendre, rapporter; *(surrender)* céder // *vi* céder; *(US AUT)* céder la priorité.

YMCA *n abbr (= Young Men's Christian Association)* YMCA *m*.

yoga ['jəʊgə] *n* yoga *m*.

yog(h)ourt, yog(h)urt ['jəʊgət] *n* yaourt *m*.

yoke [jəʊk] *n* joug *m*.

yolk [jəʊk] *n* jaune *m* (d'œuf).

yonder ['jɒndə*] *ad* là(-bas).

KEYWORD

you [juː] *pronoun* **1** *(subject)* tu; *(polite form)* vous; *(pl)* vous; **French enjoy your food** vous autres Français, vous aimez bien manger; ~ **and I will go** toi et moi *or* vous et moi, nous irons

2 *(object: direct, indirect)* te, t' + *vowel*; vous; **I know** ~ je te *or* vous connais; **I gave it to** ~ je te l'ai donné, je vous l'ai donné

3 *(stressed)* toi; vous; **I told YOU to do it** c'est à toi *or* vous que j'ai dit de le faire

4 *(after prep, in comparisons)* toi; vous; **it's for** ~ c'est pour toi *or* vous; **she's younger than** ~ elle est plus jeune que toi *or* vous

5 *(impersonal: one)* on; **fresh air does** ~ **good** l'air frais fait du bien; ~ **never know** on ne sait jamais.

you'd [juːd] = **you had**; **you would**.

you'll [juːl] = **you will, you shall**.

young [jʌŋ] *a* jeune // *npl (of animal)* petits *mpl*; *(people):* **the** ~ les jeunes, la jeunesse; ~**er** *a (brother etc)* cadet(te); ~**ster** *n* jeune *m (garçon m); (child)* enfant *m/f*.

your [jɔː*] *a* ton(ta), tes *pl*; *(polite form, pl)* votre, vos *pl; see also* **my.**

you're [jʊə*] = **you are**.

yours [jɔ:z] *pronoun* le(la) tien(ne), les tiens(tiennes); *(polite form, pl)* le(la) vôtre, les vôtres; **yours sincerely/faithfully** je vous prie d'agréer l'expression de mes sentiments les meilleurs/mes sentiments respectueux *or* dévoués; *see also* **mine**.

yourself [jɔ:'sɛlf] *pronoun (reflexive)* te; *(: polite form)* vous; *(after prep)* toi; vous; *(emphatic)* toi-même; vous-même; **yourselves** *pl pronoun* vous; *(emphatic)* vous-mêmes; *see also* **oneself**.

youth [ju:θ] *n* jeunesse *f*; *(young man) (pl* ~s [ju:ðz]) jeune homme *m*; ~ **club** *n* centre *m* de jeunes; ~**ful** *a* jeune; de jeunesse; juvénile; ~ **hostel** *n* auberge *f* de jeunesse.

you've [ju:v] = **you have**.

YTS *n abbr (Brit:* = *Youth Training Scheme)* ≈ TUC *m*.

Yugoslav ['ju:gəuslɑ:v] *a* yougoslave // *n* Yougoslave *m/f*.

Yugoslavia ['ju:gəu'slɑ:vɪə] *n* Yougoslavie *f*.

yuppie ['jʌpɪ] *n* yuppie *m/f*.

YWCA *n abbr* (= ᵛoung Women's Christian Association) YWCA *m*.

zany ['zeɪnɪ] *a* farfelu(e), loufoque.

zap [zæp] *vt (COMPUT)* effacer.

zeal [zi:l] *n* zèle *m*, ferveur *f*; empressement *m*.

zebra ['zi:brə] *n* zèbre *m*; ~ **crossing** *n (Brit)* passage *m* pour piétons.

zero ['zɪərəu] *n* zéro *m*.

zest [zɛst] *n* entrain *m*, élan *m*; zeste *m*.

zigzag ['zɪgzæg] *n* zigzag *m*.

Zimbabwe [zɪm'bɑ:bwɪ] *n* Zimbabwe *m*.

zinc [zɪŋk] *n* zinc *m*.

zip [zɪp] *n* (*also:* ~ **fastener**, *(US)* ~**per**) fermeture *f* éclair ® // *vt (also:* ~ **up**) fermer avec une fermeture éclair ®; ~ **code** *n (US)* code postal.

zodiac ['zəudɪæk] *n* zodiaque *m*.

zone [zəun] *n* zone *f*; *(subdivision of town)* secteur *m*.

zoo [zu:] *n* zoo *m*.

zoology [zu:'ɔlədʒɪ] *n* zoologie *f*.

zoom [zu:m] *vi:* to ~ **past** passer en trombe; ~ **lens** *n* zoom *m*.

zucchini [tsu:'ki:nɪ] *n(pl) (US)* courgette(s) *f(pl)*.

VERB TABLES

1 Participe présent *2* Participe passé *3* Présent *4* Imparfait *5* Futur *6* Conditionnel *7* Subjonctif présent

acquérir *1* acquérant *2* acquis *3* acquiers, acquérons, acquièrent *4* acquérais *5* acquerrai *7* acquière

ALLER *1* allant *2* allé *3* vais, vas, va, allons, allez, vont *4* allais *5* irai *6* irais *7* aille

asseoir *1* asseyant *2* assis *3* assieds, asseyons, asseyez, asseyent *4* asseyais *5* assiérai *7* asseye

atteindre *1* atteignant *2* atteint *3* atteins, atteignons *4* atteignais *7* atteigne

AVOIR *1* ayant *2* eu *3* ai, as, a, avons, avez, ont *4* avais *5* aurai *6* aurais *7* aie, aies, ait, ayons, ayez, aient

battre *1* battant *2* battu *3* bats, bat, battons *4* battais *7* batte

boire *1* buvant *2* bu *3* bois, buvons, boivent *4* buvais *7* boive

bouillir *1* bouillant *2* bouilli *3* bous, bouillons *4* bouillais *7* bouille

conclure *1* concluant *2* conclu *3* conclus, concluons *4* concluais *7* conclue

conduire *1* conduisant *2* conduit *3* conduis, conduisons *4* conduisais *7* conduise

connaître *1* connaissant *2* connu *3* connais, connaît, connaissons *4* connaissais *7* connaisse

coudre *1* cousant *2* cousu *3* couds, cousons, cousez, cousent *4* cousais *7* couse

courir *1* courant *2* couru *3* cours, courons *4* courais *5* courrai *7* coure

couvrir *1* couvrant *2* couvert *3* couvre, couvrons *4* couvrais *7* couvre

craindre *1* craignant *2* craint *3* crains, craignons *4* craignais *7* craigne

croire *1* croyant *2* cru *3* crois, croyons, croient *4* croyais *7* croie

croître *1* croissant *2* crû, crue, crus, crues *3* crois, croissons *4* croissais *7* croisse

cueillir *1* cueillant *2* cueilli *3* cueille, cueillons *4* cueillais *5* cueillerai *7* cueille

devoir *1* devant *2* dû, due, dus, dues *3* dois, devons, doivent *4* devais *5* devrai *7* doive

dire *1* disant *2* dit *3* dis, disons, dites, disent *4* disais *7* dise

dormir *1* dormant *2* dormi *3* dors, dormons *4* dormais *7* dorme

écrire *1* écrivant *2* écrit *3* écris, écrivons *4* écrivais *7* écrive

ÊTRE *1* étant *2* été *3* suis, es, est, sommes, êtes, sont *4* étais *5* serai *6* serais *7* sois, sois, soit, soyons, soyez, soient

FAIRE *1* faisant *2* fait *3* fais, fais, fait, faisons, faites, font *4* faisais *5* ferai *6* ferais *7* fasse

falloir *2* fallu *3* faut *4* fallait *5* faudra *7* faille

FINIR *1* finissant *2* fini *3* finis, finis, finit, finissons, finissez, finissent *4* finissais *5* finirai *6* finirais *7* finisse

fuir *1* fuyant *2* fui *3* fuis, fuyons, fuient *4* fuyais *7* fuie

joindre *1* joignant *2* joint *3* joins, joignons *4* joignais *7* joigne

lire *1* lisant *2* lu *3* lis, lisons *4* lisais *7* lise

luire *1* luisant *2* lui *3* luis, luisons *4* luisais *7* luise

maudire *1* maudissant *2* maudit *3* maudis, maudissons *4* maudissais *7* maudisse

mentir *1* mentant *2* menti *3* mens, mentons *4* mentais *7* mente

mettre *1* mettant *2* mis *3* mets, mettons *4* mettais *7* mette

mourir *1* mourant *2* mort *3* meurs, mourons, meurent *4* mourais *5* mourrai *7* meure

naitre *1* naissant *2* né *3* nais, naît, naissons *4* naissais *7* naisse

offrir *1* offrant *2* offert *3* offre, offrons *4* offrais *7* offre

PARLER *1* parlant *2* parlé *3* parle, parles, parle, parlons, parlez, parlent *4* parlais, parlais, parlait, parlions, parliez, parlaient *5* parlerai, parleras, parlera, parlerons, parlerez, parleront *6* parlerais, parlerais, parlerait, parlerions, parleriez, parleraient *7* parle, parles, parle, parlions, parliez, parlent *impératif* parle! parlez!

partir *1* partant *2* parti *3* pars, partons *4* partais *7* parte

plaire *1* plaisant *2* plu *3* plais, plaît, plaisons *4* plaisais *7* plaise

pleuvoir *1* pleuvant *2* plu *3* pleut, pleuvent *4* pleuvait *5* pleuvra *7* pleuve

pourvoir *1* pourvoyant *2* pourvu *3* pourvois, pourvoyons, pourvoient *4* pourvoyais *7* pourvoie

pouvoir *1* pouvant *2* pu *3* peux, peut, pouvons, peuvent *4* pouvais *5* pourrai *7* puisse

prendre *1* prenant *2* pris *3* prends, prenons, prennent *4* prenais *7* prenne

prévoir *like voir 5* prévoirai

RECEVOIR *1* recevant *2* reçu *3* reçois, reçois, reçoit, recevons, recevez, reçoivent *4* recevais *5* recevrai *6* recevrais *7* reçoive

RENDRE *1* rendant *2* rendu *3* rends, rends, rend, rendons, rendez, rendent *4* rendais *5* rendrai *6* rendrais *7* rende

résoudre *1* résolvant *2* résolu *3* résous, résolvons *4* résolvais *7* résolve

rire *1* riant *2* ri *3* ris, rions *4* riais *7* rie

savoir *1* sachant *2* su *3* sais, savons, savent *4* savais *5* saurai *7* sache *impératif* sache, sachons, sachez

servir *1* servant *2* servi *3* sers, servons *4* servais *7* serve

sortir *1* sortant *2* sorti *3* sors, sortons *4* sortais *7* sorte

souffrir *1* souffrant *2* souffert *3* souffre, souffrons *4* souffrais *7* souffre

suffire *1* suffisant *2* suffi *3* suffis, suffisons *4* suffisais *7* suffise

suivre *1* suivant *2* suivi *3* suis, suivons *4* suivais *7* suive

taire *1* taisant *2* tu *3* tais, taisons *4* taisais *7* taise

tenir *1* tenant *2* tenu *3* tiens, tenons, tiennent *4* tenais *5* tiendrai *7* tienne

vaincre *1* vainquant *2* vaincu *3* vaincs, vainc, vainquons *4* vainquais *7* vainque

valoir *1* valant *2* valu *3* vaux, vaut, valons *4* valais *5* vaudrai *7* vaille

venir *1* venant *2* venu *3* viens, venons, viennent *4* venais *5* viendrai *7* vienne

vivre *1* vivant *2* vécu *3* vis, vivons *4* vivais *7* vive

voir *1* voyant *2* vu *3* vois, voyons, voient *4* voyais *5* verrai *7* voie

vouloir *1* voulant *2* voulu *3* veux, veut, voulons, veulent *4* voulais *5* voudrai *7* veuille *impératif* veuillez

VERBES IRRÉGULIERS

present	pt	pp	present	pt	pp
arise	arose	arisen	deal	dealt	dealt
awake	awoke	awaked	dig	dug	dug
be (am,	was,	been	do (3rd	did	done
is, are;	were		person;		
being)			he/she/		
			it/does)		
bear	bore	born(e)	draw	drew	drawn
beat	beat	beaten	dream	dreamed,	dreamed,
become	became	become		dreamt	dreamt
befall	befell	befallen	drink	drank	drunk
begin	began	begun	drive	drove	driven
behold	beheld	beheld	dwell	dwelt	dwelt
bend	bent	bent	eat	ate	eaten
beseech	besought	besought	fall	fell	fallen
beset	beset	beset	feed	fed	fed
bet	bet,	bet,	feel	felt	felt
	betted	betted	fight	fought	fought
bid	bid	bid	find	found	found
bind	bound	bound	flee	fled	fled
bite	bit	bitten	fling	flung	flung
bleed	bled	bled	fly	flew	flown
blow	blew	blown	forbid	forbade	forbidden
break	broke	broken	forego	forewent	foregone
breed	bred	bred	foresee	foresaw	foreseen
bring	brought	brought	foretell	foretold	foretold
build	built	built	forget	forgot	forgotten
burn	burnt,	burnt,	forgive	forgave	forgiven
	burned	burned	forsake	forsook	forsaken
burst	burst	burst	freeze	froze	frozen
buy	bought	bought	get	got	got, (US)
can	could	(been			gotten
		able)	give	gave	given
cast	cast	cast	go	went	gone
catch	caught	caught	(goes)		
choose	chose	chosen	grind	ground	ground
cling	clung	clung	grow	grew	grown
come	came	come	hang	hung,	hung,
cost	cost	cost		hanged	hanged
creep	crept	crept	have	had	had
cut	cut	cut			

313

present	pt	pp	present	pt	pp
hear	heard	heard	rise	rose	risen
hide	hid	hidden	run	ran	run
hit	hit	hit	saw	sawed	sawn
hold	held	held	say	said	said
hurt	hurt	hurt	see	saw	seen
keep	kept	kept	seek	sought	sought
kneel	knelt,	knelt,	sell	sold	sold
	kneeled	kneeled	send	sent	sent
know	knew	known	set	set	set
lay	laid	laid	shake	shook	shaken
lead	led	led	shall	should	—
lean	leant,	leant,	shear	sheared	shorn,
	leaned	leaned			sheared
leap	leapt,	leapt,	shed	shed	shed
	leaped	leaped	shine	shone	shone
learn	learnt,	learnt,	shoot	shot	shot
	learned	learned	show	showed	shown
leave	left	left	shrink	shrank	shrunk
lend	lent	lent	shut	shut	shut
let	let	let	sing	sang	sung
lie	lay	lain	sink	sank	sunk
(lying)			sit	sat	sat
light	lit,	lit,	slay	slew	slain
	lighted	lighted	sleep	slept	slept
lose	lost	lost	slide	slid	slid
make	made	made	sling	slung	slung
may	might	—	slit	slit	slit
mean	meant	meant	smell	smelt,	smelt,
meet	met	met		smelled	smelled
mistake	mistook	mistaken	sow	sowed	sown,
mow	mowed	mown			sowed
		mowed	speak	spoke	spoken
must	(had to)	(had to)	speed	sped,	sped,
pay	paid	paid		speeded	speeded
put	put	put	spell	spelt,	spelt,
quit	quit,	quit,		spelled	spelled
	quitted	quitted	spend	spent	spent
read	read	read	spill	spilt,	spilt,
rend	rent	rent		spilled	spilled
rid	rid	rid	spin	spun	spun
ride	rode	ridden	spit	spat	spat
ring	rang	rung	split	split	split

present	pt	pp	present	pt	pp
spoil	spoiled, spoilt	spoiled, spoilt	teach	taught	taught
			tear	tore	torn
spread	spread	spread	tell	told	told
spring	sprang	sprung	think	thought	thought
stand	stood	stood	throw	threw	thrown
steal	stole	stolen	thrust	thrust	thrust
stick	stuck	stuck	tread	trod	trodden
sting	stung	stung	wake	woke, waked	woken, waked
stink	stank	stunk			
stride	strode	strode	waylay	waylaid	waylaid
stroke	struck	struck, stricken	wear	wore	worn
			weave	wove, weaved	woven, weaved
strive	strove	striven			
swear	swore	sworn	wed	wedded, wed	wedded, wed
sweep	swept	swept			
swell	swelled	swollen, swelled	weep	wept	wept
			win	won	won
swim	swam	swum	wind	wound	wound
swing	swung	swung	wring	wrung	wrung
take	took	taken	write	wrote	written

LES NOMBRES

NUMBERS

un (une)	1	one
deux	2	two
trois	3	three
quatre	4	four
cinq	5	five
six	6	six
sept	7	seven
huit	8	eight
neuf	9	nine
dix	10	ten
onze	11	eleven
douze	12	twelve
treize	13	thirteen
quatorze	14	fourteen
quinze	15	fifteen
seize	16	sixteen
dix-sept	17	seventeen
dix-huit	18	eighteen
dix-neuf	19	nineteen
vingt	20	twenty
vingt et un (une)	21	twenty-one
vingt-deux	22	twenty-two
trente	30	thirty
quarante	40	forty
cinquante	50	fifty
soixante	60	sixty
soixante-dix	70	seventy
soixante et onze	71	seventy-one
soixante-douze	72	seventy-two
quatre-vingts	80	eighty
quatre-vingt-un (-une)	81	eighty-one
quatre-vingt-dix	90	ninety
quatre-vingt-onze	91	ninety-one
cent	100	a hundred
cent un (une)	101	a hundred and one
trois cents	300	three hundred
trois cent un (une)	301	three hundred and one
mille	1 000	a thousand
un million	1 000 000	a million

premier (première), 1er	first, 1st
deuxième, 2e or 2ème	second, 2nd
troisième, 3e or 3ème	third, 3rd
quatrième	fourth, 4th
cinquième	fifth, 5th
sixième	sixth, 6th

LES NOMBRES

septième
huitième
neuvième
dixième
onzième
douzième
treizième
quatorzième
quinzième
seizième
dix-septième
dix-huitième
dix-neuvième
vingtième
vingt-et-unième
vingt-deuxième
trentième
centième
cent-unième
millième

NUMBERS

seventh
eighth
ninth
tenth
eleventh
twelfth
thirteenth
fourteenth
fifteenth
sixteenth
seventeenth
eighteenth
nineteenth
twentieth
twenty-first
twenty-second
thirtieth
hundredth
hundred-and-first
thousandth

Les Fractions etc

un demi
un tiers
deux tiers
un quart
un cinquième
zéro virgule cinq, 0,5
trois virgule quatre, 3,4
dix pour cent
cent pour cent

Fractions etc

a half
a third
two thirds
a quarter
a fifth
(nought) point five, 0.5
three point four, 3.4
ten per cent
a hundred per cent

Exemples

il habite au dix
c'est au chapitre sept
à la page sept
il habite au septième (étage)
il est arrivé (le) septième
une part d'un septième
échelle au vingt-cinq millième

Examples

he lives at number 10
it's in chapter 7
on page 7
he lives on the 7th floor
he came in 7th
a share of one seventh
scale one to twenty-five thousand

L'HEURE

quelle heure est-il?

il est ...

minuit	midnight, twelve p.m.
une heure (du matin)	one o'clock (in the morning), one (a.m.)
une heure cinq	five past one
une heure dix	ten past one
une heure et quart	a quarter past one, one fifteen
une heure vingt-cinq	twenty-five past one, one twenty-five
une heure et demie, une heure trente	half past one, one thirty
une heure trente-cinq, deux heures moins vingt-cinq	twenty-five to two, one thirty-five
deux heures moins vingt, une heure quarante	twenty to two, one forty
deux heures moins le quart, une heure quarante-cinq	a quarter to two, one forty-five
deux heures moins dix, une heure cinquante	ten to two, one fifty
midi	twelve o'clock, midday, noon
deux heures (de l'après-midi)	two o'clock (in the afternoon), two (p.m.)
sept heures (du soir)	seven o'clock (in the evening), seven (p.m.)

à quelle heure?

à minuit	at midnight
à sept heures	at seven o'clock
dans vingt minutes	in twenty minutes
il y a quinze minutes	fifteen minutes ago

THE TIME

what time is it?

it's ...

at what time?